The Longman Anthology of Drama and Theater

COMPACT EDITION

The Longman Anthology
of Drama and Theater

COMPACT EDITION

The Longman Anthology of Drama and Theater

A GLOBAL PERSPECTIVE

COMPACT EDITION

Michael L. Greenwald
Texas A&M University

Roger Schultz
Texas A&M University

Roberto D. Pomo
California State University at Sacramento

Longman

New York   Boston   San Francisco
London   Toronto   Sydney   Tokyo   Singapore   Madrid
Mexico City   Munich   Paris   Cape Town   Hong Kong   Montreal

Vice President and Editor-in-Chief: Joseph Terry
Acquisitions Editor: Erika Berg
Marketing Manager: Melanie Craig
Full Service Production Manager: Mark Naccarelli
Project Coordination, Text Design, and Electronic Page Makeup: Nesbitt Graphics, Inc.
Cover Design Manager: Wendy Ann Fredericks
Cover Designer: Joan O'Connor
Cover Photo: © Roderick Chen/Superstock
Art Studio: Mapping Specialists, Inc.
Photo Researcher: Photosearch, Inc.
Manufacturing Buyer: Roy Pickering
Printer and Binder: Courier/Westford
Cover Printer: Lehigh Press, Inc.

For permission to use copyrighted material, grateful acknowledgment is made to the copyright
holders on pp. 835–837, which are hereby made part of this copyright page.

Library of Congress Cataloging-in-Publication Data

Greenwald, Michael L., 1945–
    The Longman anthology of drama and theater : a global perspective / Michael L.
  Greenwald, Roger Schultz, Roberto D. Pomo.—Compact ed.
       p.   cm.
    Includes bibliographical references and index.
    ISBN 0-321-08898-0
     1. Theater—History.   2. Drama—History and criticism.   3. Drama—Collections.   I.
  Schultz, Roger.   II. Darío Pomo, Roberto.   III. Longman (Firm)   IV. Title.

PN1655 .G74 2001b
792'.09—dc21

                                                                      2001050437

Please visit our website at http://www.ablongman.com

ISBN 0-321-08898-0

1 2 3 4 5 6 7 8 9 10—CRW—04 03 02 01

CONTENTS

Preface   xi

PART I: The Theoretical and Practical Foundations of Theater   1

CHAPTER 1: Stories, Rituals, and Theater: *A Foundation for the Theatrical Arts*   3

The Theatrical Impulse   3
The Storyteller   3
The Barong or Trance Dance of Bali   4
    FORUM: "THE THEATRE AS IT WAS AND AS IT IS" BY ROBERT EDMUND JONES   5
A Broadway Musical   6
Rituals Versus Theater   6
An Autumnal Ritual in America   8
The Origins of Theater   8
Common Ground for Uncommon Cultures   9
    CENTER STAGE: THE *ABYDOS PASSION PLAY*   10
Reading a Play   14
Susan Glaspell, TRIFLES   15
    SPOTLIGHT: THE MOTHER OF THE MODERN AMERICAN THEATER:
        SUSAN GLASPELL (1882–1948)   21

CHAPTER 2: From Theater to Drama   23

The Dramatic Impulse   23
The Poetics of Aristotle   24
The Elements of Drama   24
    FORUM: "FROM *THE POETICS*" BY ARISTOTLE   26
The Principal Genres of Drama   35
    SPOTLIGHT: MELODRAMA AND FARCE   44
Styles and Conventions   46

PART II: An Anthology of Western Drama   51

CHAPTER 3: The Theater of Greece and Rome   53
    GREECE   54

Contents

The Origins of the Theater in Greece   56

    SPOTLIGHT: The Hellenistic Theater   57

The Greek Mind   58

    SPOTLIGHT: The Conventions of Greek Theater   60

Playwrights and Acting   62

Sophocles, *OEDIPUS THE KING*   63✓

    SPOTLIGHT: The Curse on the House of Thebes   64

    CENTER STAGE: The First Performance of *Oedipus the King*   88

    CENTER STAGE: *Oedipus the King* at the Teatro Olympico, 1585   90

    FORUMS: "Ode to *Oedipus*" by Tyrone Guthrie   91

        "Guthrie Directs 'Ritual' Performance of *Oedipus Rex* at Edinburgh Fête" by Patrick Gibbs   92

    SPOTLIGHT: Greek Old Comedy and *Lysistrata* Synopsis   93

ROME   94

The Development of Roman Theater   96

Playwrights and Popular Entertainments   96

Theaters and Acting   97

The Fall of Rome   98

CHAPTER 4:   The Early Modern Theater   101

THE MIDDLE AGES   102

Rites and Folk Drama   104

Religious Drama   104

Performance Conventions   105

Anonymous, *THE BROME PLAY OF ABRAHAM AND ISAAC*   109

Anonymous, *EVERYMAN*   117✓

THE EUROPEAN RENAISSANCE   132

The Renaissance Mind   134

The Need for Order   135

    CENTER STAGE: Commedia dell'Arte   136

    CENTER STAGE: The Masque   138

Hierarchies Onstage and Off   140

The Role of Tragedy   140

Playhouses and Scenery   141

Acting   141

Playwriting: The Neoclassicists Versus the Romantics   142

  ■ **England   144**

William Shakespeare, *HAMLET, PRINCE OF DENMARK*   146

    SPOTLIGHT: Making Shakespeare's Language User-Friendly   148

    SPOTLIGHT: Shakespeare's Two Theaters   210

CENTER STAGE: HAMLET AT THE GLOBE THEATER, 1601   212

FORUMS [HAMLET IN PRODUCTION]:

"HAMLET: PICTURESQUE AND REFINED" BY LUCIA GILBERT CALHOUN   214

"RICHARD BURTON AS HAMLET—GIELGUD'S PRODUCTION AT THE LUNT–FONTANNE" BY HOWARD TAUBMAN   215

"SHAKESPEARE Á LA RUSSE: KOZINTSEV'S HAMLET" BY ARTHUR KNIGHT   216

■ Spain   218

SPOTLIGHT: THEATER AND DRAMA IN THE SPANISH SIGLO D'ORO: CALDERÓN'S LIFE'S A DREAM   220

SPOTLIGHT: THE SPANISH THEATER: THE CORRALES   223

■ France   224

Molière, TARTUFFE   226 ✓

SPOTLIGHT: THE FRENCH THEATER   258

CENTER STAGE: THE (THIRD) OPENING NIGHT OF TARTUFFE   258

CENTER STAGE: TARTUFFE AT THE THÉÂTRE DU SOLEIL, 1995   260

SPOTLIGHT: THE SECRET LIFE OF A CON MAN: ANTONY SHER ON PLAYING TARTUFFE (AN INTERVIEW BY FRANCESCA SIMON)   262

THE LATE SEVENTEENTH AND EIGHTEENTH CENTURIES   264

SPOTLIGHT: THE COMEDY OF MANNERS   266

SPOTLIGHT: THE CONVENTIONS OF THE RESTORATION THEATER   268

Sentimental Comedy   268
Laughing Comedy   270
Bourgeois Tragedy   270

CHAPTER 5:   The Modern Theater   273

ROMANTICISM   274

SPOTLIGHT: AMERICA'S GREATEST HIT: UNCLE TOM'S CABIN   276

The Melodrama   279

SPOTLIGHT: THE MINSTREL SHOW   280

The Romantic Revolution and Hernani   281

REALISM AND NATURALISM   282

The Well-Made Play   284
Influences on Realism   284
The Problem Play   286
The Rise of the Director   286
Naturalism   287
The Fathers of Realism: Ibsen, Strindberg, and Chekhov   288
Intimate Theaters   289
The Second Generation of Realists   290

Henrik Ibsen, A DOLL'S HOUSE   292

CENTER STAGE: THE TARANTELLA AND OTHER HEALING DANCES   323

Contents

Anton Chekhov, *THE CHERRY ORCHARD*   324 ✓

EXPRESSIONISM AND THE EPIC THEATER   **348**

Expressionism   350
The Epic Theater   350
   SPOTLIGHT: THEATER IN THE INDUSTRIAL AGE   353

Bertolt Brecht, *THE GOOD WOMAN OF SETZUAN*   354

Arthur Miller, *DEATH OF A SALESMAN: Certain Private Conversations in Two Acts and a Requiem*   388
   FORUMS:
      "TRAGEDY AND THE COMMON MAN" BY ARTHUR MILLER   429
      "*DEATH OF A SALESMAN:* POWERFUL TRAGEDY" BY WILLIAM HAWKINS   430
      "EVEN AS YOU AND I" BY JOHN MASON BROWN   431
      "WILLY LOMAN GETS CHINA TERRITORY" BY CHRISTOPHER S. WREN   433

ABSURDISM   **436**
   SPOTLIGHT: *WAITING FOR GODOT:* THE MODERN MASTERPIECE   438

Edward Albee, *THE AMERICAN DREAM: A Play in One Scene   (1959–1960)*   441

CHAPTER 6:   The Contemporary Theater   461

CONTEMPORARY WESTERN WORLD   **462**

Influences on Contemporary Thought   464
Postmodernism and the Theater   465
Artaud and the Theater of Cruelty   467
Theater Collectives and Alternative Theater   468
Contemporary Playwriting   469
Acting in Contemporary Plays   470
Contemporary Dramatic Criticism: Deconstructionism and Others   471

Caryl Churchill, *TOP GIRLS*   473

Tony Kushner, *ANGELS IN AMERICA, PART ONE: MILLENNIUM APPROACHES*   504 ✓
   FORUMS:
      "EMBRACING ALL POSSIBILITIES IN ART AND LIFE" BY FRANK RICH   540
      "TONY KUSHNER CONSIDERS THE LONG-STANDING PROBLEMS OF VIRTUE AND HAPPINESS" BY DAVID SAVRAN   541

PART III: An Anthology of Non-Western Drama   545

CHAPTER 7:   The Theater of Asia   547

   INDIA   **550**

The Origins of Indian Drama   552
The Types of Indian Drama   553
The Conventions of Classical Indian Theater   553
    SPOTLIGHT: THE SANSKRIT MASTERPIECE OF INDIA: *THE RECOGNITION OF ŚAKUNTALĀ*
       (ABHIJĀNAŚĀKUNTĀLAM)   554
Dance and Folk Drama in India   557
The Modern Theater of India   557

CHINA   558

The History of Chinese Theater   560
    CENTER STAGE: SPRING FESTIVAL IN CHINA   562
The Conventions of Chinese Theater   564
    CENTER STAGE: A NIGHT AT THE CHINESE OPERA: THE *HUA-GU* OPERA OF
       HUNAN   566
Anonymous, *THE QING DING PEARL (THE LUCKY PEARL)*   571

JAPAN   580

The Noh Theater   582
The Kabuki Theater   585
    CENTER STAGE: THE TANABATA FESTIVAL OF JAPAN   590
The Contemporary Japanese Theater: Shingeki   591
Namiki Gohei III, *KANJINCHŌ (THE SUBSCRIPTION LIST)*   593

CHAPTER 8:   The Theater of Africa and the African Diaspora   607

AFRICA   608

The Roots of African Theater   610
Postcolonial Drama in Africa   611
    CENTER STAGE: SOUTH AFRICAN TOWNSHIP THEATER   612
The Conventions of African Theater   615
Athol Fugard, "MASTER HAROLD" . . . *AND THE BOYS*   616
    SPOTLIGHT: SOUTH AFRICA'S MARKET THEATRE AND THE
       INDEPENDENT THEATER PHENOMENON   638
Wole Soyinka, *DEATH AND THE KING'S HORSEMAN*   639
    CENTER STAGE: YORUBAN OBATALA FESTIVAL IN EDE, NIGERIA, WEST AFRICA   668

AFRICAN AMERICAN THEATER   670

The Development of African American Theater   672
    SPOTLIGHT: *A RAISIN IN THE SUN*: PORTRAIT OF AMERICA IN TRANSITION   674
August Wilson, *FENCES*   676 ✓

THE CARIBBEAN   708

Cuba   711
Puerto Rico   711

Contents

Haiti and Jamaica   712
Trinidad-Tobago   712
Derek Walcott, *TI-JEAN AND HIS BROTHERS*   714
   CENTER STAGE: THE TRINIDAD CARNIVAL   738

CHAPTER 9:   The Theater of Latin America   741

The Development of Latin American Theater   741
LATIN AMERICA   744
   SPOTLIGHT: POPULAR THEATER IN LATIN AMERICA   746
   CENTER STAGE: THEATER IN MESOAMERICA   748
**Sor Juana Inés de la Cruz, *THE DIVINE NARCISSUS (EL DIVINO
   NARCISSO)*   750** ✓
   CENTER STAGE: THE YAQUI EASTER OF THE SOUTHWEST UNITED STATES   760
**Luis Valdez, *NO SACO NADA DE LA ESCUELA (I DON'T GET NOTHIN
   FROM SCHOOL)*   761**
Elena Garro, *A SOLID HOME (UN HOGAR SOLIDO)*   773
   CENTER STAGE: DÍA DE LOS MUERTOS IN MEXICO   782
**Egon Wolff, *PAPER FLOWERS (FLORES DE PAPEL): A Play in Six
   Scenes*   783**

APPENDIX A: The Student as Critic   809

The Production Review   809
Critical Essays   811
A Few Technical Notes   813
General Questions About a Play and Its Performance   814
A Sample Outline for a Critical Essay on *Ti-Jean and His Brothers*   814

APPENDIX B: Glossary of Terms   816

APPENDIX C: Bibliography   829

Acknowledgments   835
Photo Credits   837
Index   838

PREFACE

The Longman Anthology of Drama and Theater: A Global Perspective, Compact Edition, offers students of theater and dramatic literature a truly global collection of plays designed for Introduction to Drama and Theater courses. While we acknowledge the presence of other fine drama anthologies, none offers such a richly varied selection from the traditional Western canon, Asia, Africa, Latin America, and the Caribbean.

Twenty-three Indispensable Plays from the Western and Non-Western Traditions

Our selection of 23 significant plays from both the Western and non-Western canon offers teachers and students maximum flexibility, whether they are pursuing a primarily traditional course of study, an emphasis on the diverse voices in the world's theater, or a combination of the two. We have included nine short plays (e.g., Elena Garro's *A Solid Home* and Edward Albee's *The American Dream*) that can be accommodated in a single class period.

In addition to 14 indispensable plays from the West's traditional classical and modern canon, we present a broad range of drama (nine plays) from around the globe, including:

Kanjinchō (The Subscription List), a Kabuki play;
"MASTER HAROLD" . . . *and the boys*, by Athol Fugard, and *Death and the King's Horseman*, by Wole Soyinka, two plays by Africa's preeminent playwrights;
The Divine Narcissus, the first truly Mexican colonial drama, by Sor Juana Inés de la Cruz, and *A Solid Home*, by Elena Garro, a modern play employing the magic realism of Mexico;
Paper Flowers, by Egon Wolff, a surrealistic drama from Chile that won the prestigious Casa de Las Americas award (1970) as the best play from Latin America;
Ti-Jean and His Brothers, a political folktale by Nobel laureate Derek Walcott.

We have puposefully chosen some Western plays that are indebted to other cultures for both their thematic material and their performance style:

Bertolt Brecht's *The Good Woman of Setzuan* reflects Chinese theater techniques;
August Wilson's *Fences* addresses the African diaspora within the context of contemporary American social drama.

Other indispensable Western plays are included as well:

Sophocles' *Oedipus the King*, widely acknowledged as the most important of the Greek tragedies;
Examples of two liturgical dramas from the Middle Ages (*The Brome Play of Abraham and Isaac* and *Everyman*);
Significant works from the European Renaissance (Shakespeare's *Hamlet*) and the Enlightenment (Molière's *Tartuffe*);

Plays by the pioneers of social realism (Ibsen, Chekhov, Miller), the epic theater (Brecht), and absurdist theater (Albee).

Important voices, heretofore underrepresented, are heard:

Minority playwright Luis Valdez (*No saco nada de la escuela*) and feminist playwright Caryl Churchill (*Top Girls*);

The most innovative drama of the 1990s (Tony Kushner's *Angels in America, Part One: Millennium Approaches*) addresses current issues as the world redefines itself.

A Special Note on Part Three

In the past twenty years there has been a remarkable growth in the study of non-Western theater and drama in university curricula throughout the West. In the 1960s and 1970s courses in non-Western drama were virtually nonexistent, but fortunately that is rapidly changing as we now appreciate the wealth of possibilities an understanding of non-Western theater can bring to artists and audiences alike.

To that end we offer here an admittedly brief introduction to these non-Western theaters:

- Asia (India, China, and Japan);
- Africa (particularly South Africa and Nigeria) and the African diaspora (African American and Caribbean theater);
- Latin America (Mesoamerica, Mexico, Mexican American, and South America)

To keep the anthology compact we also include summaries and discussions of significant plays that represent important material that the instructor may not have time to cover in a semester course (e.g., Aristophanes' *Lysistrata*, Kālidāsa's *The Recognition of Śakuntalā*, Calderón's *Life's a Dream*, Hansberry's *A Raisin in the Sun*, and Beckett's *Waiting for Godot*, for which publication rights are not available).

Rituals, Ceremonies, and Folk Customs

In addition to the remarkable offering of international plays, the text contains many examples of rituals, ceremonies, and folk customs that illuminate the human need to create theater. Descriptions of many cultural rituals enhance our understanding of specific plays:

The Yoruban Obatala helps us understand Soyinka's *Death and the King's Horseman*;
Elena Garro's *A Solid Home* laughs at death, as does Mexico's festive Día de los Muertos;
A Yaqui Indian Easter ritual complements ancient Aztec rites described in Sor Juana Inéz' *The Divine Narcissus*;
A discussion of the history of the Italian *tarentella* illuminates a key dramatic moment in Ibsen's *A Doll House*.

Furthermore, the ritual origins of theater are addressed by looking in some detail at the birth of theater in Greece, Mesoamerica, Africa, and Asia. The role of the storyteller (bard, *griot*, *cha*, or *cancionero*) is also examined to provide a better understanding of the impulses that prompted humans to create theater.

Flexible Organization

While *the Longman Anthology of Drama and Theater, Compact Edition*, provides the most comprehensive coverage of theater conventions and history available in such a text, it is carefully organized to allow a broad variety of teaching and learning approaches. The two chapters that compose *Part I: The Theoretical and Practical Foundations of Theater* examine the roots of theater and the theoretical and critical foundations of theater and drama. The four chapters of *Part II: An Anthology of Western Drama* and the three chapters of *Part III: An Anthology of Non-West-*

ern Drama are divided into historical and geographical sections, each preceded by a brief overview of the cultural and historical context that shaped the plays. A map and timeline of key historical, cultural, and artistic events precedes each section in Parts II and III. The plays can be taught by themselves or with as much supporting material as time and inclination allow.

Preceding each section of plays we offer a brief overview of the history of the theater from its origins in Europe, Asia, Africa, and the Americas to the present. We consider the ideas that inspired the dramas as well as the particulars of performance. Of necessity, the survey is limited, and you should consult one of the many fine theater history texts to explore a topic in more depth. We have divided this survey of plays into seven areas within Western and non-Western sections:

The Classical Theater (c. 535 B.C.E. to c. 600 C.E.)
- Greece
- Rome

Early Europe (c. 1000 C.E. to 1700 C.E.)
- The Medieval Theater
- The Theater of the European Renaissance and Enlightenment
  - England
  - Spain
  - France
- The Late Seventeenth and Eighteenth Centuries

The Modern Theater (1800–1970)
- Romanticism
- Realism
- Expressionism and the Epic Theater
- The Theater of the Absurd

The Contemporary Theater (1970 to the Present)

Asian Theater (c. 600 B.C.E. to the Present)
- India: Classical Sanskrit Drama
- China: Classical Yuan Drama and the Peking Opera
- Japan: The Noh Theater and the Kabuki Theater

The Theater of Africa and the African Diaspora
- Africa
- African American Theater
- The Caribbean

The Theater of Latin America
- Mesoamerica
- Mexico and Mexican American Theater
- South America

In light of many complex issues and overlapping thought and style, it is difficult to categorize events with such apparent precision. However, this framework provides a useful starting point for an exploration of the theater.

Pedagogical Support

Headnotes
Each play is introduced by the most thorough headnote available; each includes biographical information about the playwright and the historical context of the play. Because the text has been written by practicing theater artists who have acted in or directed many of the plays, the discussions of all plays acknowledge the performance dimension that is crucial to student understanding of the theater.

Center Stage Essays

Throughout the text, we have provided brief boxed essays that supplement the play or commentary with which they appear. **Center Stage** boxed essays present dramatic descriptions of special performances, in many cases the first performance of a well-known play. For instance, students can read about *Oedipus the King* as it was performed at the Theatre of Dionysus in ancient Athens, at the Teatro Olympico in 1585 Italy, and by Tyrone Guthrie's company in 1955. Productions of *Hamlet, Tartuffe, Death of a Salesman* and *Angels in America; Part One: Millennium Approaches* are similarly featured. A photograph, inviting students to experience the event with their visual imagination, in the theatrical tradition, accompanies most Center Stage essays.

Spotlight Essays

Spotlight boxed essays identify and discuss the staging conventions of particular theaters; students may read about the conventions of the Hellenistic theater, Greek Old Comedy, Shakespeare's two theaters, popular theater in Latin America, South African township theater, and many others.

Forum Essays

Thirteen essays and extracts in the form of important critical documents, reviews, and interviews by critics, theoreticians, and theater artists illuminate plays and discussions throughout the text. These appear under the general heading **Forum,** and include the writings of such masters as Aristotle and Arthur Miller. Students can learn directly from theater artists such as Tony Kushner.

Appendixes

To supplement the text, we offer:

- A two-part primer on critical writing for students, the first dealing with production reviews, the second on critical analysis of a play script;
- A glossary of principal terms used in the text;
- A bibliography of essential works for each chapter and section of the text.

Supplements

Instructor's Manual. An outline summary of each section and questions for discussion and writing, as well as a comprehensive list of films and videotapes that illustrate ideas in the textbook, are included in the *Instructor's Manual.*

Website. *The Longman Anthology of Drama and Theater, Compact Edition,* is supported by a lavish website at *www.ablongman.com/greenwald.* Featuring additional information on playwrights, plays, and related works, as well as an abundance of links, the site extends and enhances the text and brings its contents to life in real-world contexts.

Evaluating a Performance. Complete with worksheets, *Evaluating a Performance* leads students through the process of writing a lively, thoughtful review. Students' critical thinking skills are developed as they evaluate a play, the director, the acting, and the set designs. This workbook is FREE when bundled with the text. Please contact your local Longman representative for details about how to order a Value Pack.

Acknowledgments

We are indebted to many people who have contributed their expertise to the completion of this volume. To them we offer Shakespeare's words from *Twelfth Night:*

> [We] can no other answer make but thanks,
> And thanks; and ever oft good turns
> Are shuffled off with such uncurrent pay.

We begin with our editor at Longman, Erika Berg, and thank her for steering the final manuscript to press. For editing the manuscript, we thank Viqi Wagner. Lois Lombardo provided both expertise and patience as she helped organize the manuscript in its many forms and oversee the production stages.

Our thanks also to the many reviewers whose comments and particular suggestions have helped make this a better and more accurate text: Bonnie Anderson, San Diego State University; Cathy Brookshire, James Madison University; Kristin Bryant, Portland Community College; Kathleen Campbell, Austin College; Joshua Fisher, West Virginia University; Tom Isbell, University of Minnesota at Duluth; Walter Johnson, Cumberland Community College; Margaret Kelso, Humboldt University; Owen Smith, California State University, Northridge; and Eula Thompson, Jefferson State Community College. As is often the case, we learned and benefited most from our severest critics, and we trust they will see their input in the completed project.

Others contributed their scholarship to this project, and to them we offer our deepest gratitude. Contributors: Allen Alford of Temple Community College; Lisajo Epstein; Bernardine Banning of Radford University; Ayumi Kazama and Sayaka Sudo. Secretarial and office help: Amanda Watkins, Pat Nies; Judy Wade; and student workers: Amber Bel'chere; Tricia Hale; Abby Johnson; Amanda Mitchell; Allisia Montalvo; Eric Montalvo; Doug Sandlin; Leslie Spieks; and Kelly Zayas. And special thanks to Ann Marie Welsh, theater critic at the *San Diego Union-Tribune*, for her provocative observations and enthusiasm; and Peter Schwab, the math guru at the Bishop's School, whose computer savvy helped enormously.

Finally, and most importantly, we thank our families for their saintly patience and support: our wives, Demetra, Kristi, and Ruthie and our children, Sean, Jennifer, Eric, Peter, Elizabeth, Anna, and Will—to whom we dedicate this book with our love. And we further dedicate this book to our dear friend and mentor, Professor Robert A. Egan, who died in October 2000.

Michael L. Greenwald
Roger Schultz
Roberto D. Pomo

PART I

The Theoretical and Practical Foundations of Theater

All the world's a stage,
And all the men and women
merely players . . .

WILLIAM SHAKESPEARE

Masked Sandaran warriors guard the Barong as part of a sacred trance rite in Bali. The costumes and masks attest to a universal impulse to invest special events with theatrical artifice.

CHAPTER 1

STORIES, RITUALS, AND THEATER

A Foundation for the Theatrical Arts

The Theatrical Impulse

Of all the arts, the theater is among the oldest and the most instinctive. Though you may have never read or attended a play, you demonstrate an innate theatricality when you embellish your activities with symbolic words and gestures, or with such visual symbols as costumes and decorations. You choose the perfect attire for a date or an interview because it will help establish the image (or character) you wish your audience to perceive. A teacher slings a sheet about the shoulders to play Socrates for an audience of students. Children play games to learn about their emerging roles in the world, as well as for their amusement. Flowers are ordered, musicians are hired, and a white gown is designed for a magnificent ritual performed before an audience to signify the union of two people in love. Flowers are ordered, musicians are hired, a casket is draped in black, and an audience returns to mourn the passing of one of its own.

Our daily English vocabulary is filled with the language of the theater. We talk about "acting" properly in a given situation. Headlines proclaim the "tragedy" of a plane crash, the "drama" of a trial, or a "comedy of errors" involving the local athletic team. CEOs think in terms of best- or worst-case *scenarios*. Parents command their children not to make "a scene." We accuse a two-faced person of being a hypocrite (a word actually derived from the Greek word *hypokrites*, or "actor," i.e., someone who pretends to be something he is not).

Little wonder, then, that we should devise theater as one of our principal means of communication. Though we live in a high-tech age with many electronic diversions to instruct and entertain us, live theater remains an integral part of people's lives throughout the world. Before beginning a formal study of the theater as an art, consider some of the creative impulses that prefigure it. Because theater depends on the power of the imagination, transport yourself back in time as you imagine yourself in each of the following situations.

The Storyteller

As shadows dance against the wall of a cliff in West Africa, an old *griot* entrances the Dogon people with a heroic tale about a blacksmith who stole a piece of the sun from the gods so that the Dogon might live more fruitfully. The storyteller suddenly rises and transforms himself, almost magically, from mere man into the mighty blacksmith. His voice deepens and his body seems to grow as he defiantly shakes his fist at the gods. The Dogon shout as one to encourage his bravery and their voices echo through the night.

Thousands of miles to the east, a Brahman *sūtradhara* retells the much-loved story of Gautama, the sacred Buddha, who sacrifices himself to a hungry tigress so that she might feed her seven starving cubs. For his noble act, Gautama is rewarded in his next life as he returns to a life of luxury as Prince Siddhartha. To illustrate how a beautiful girl enchants the prince, the priest sways rhythmically to the accompaniment of drums and a stringed instrument. His audience no longer sees him as a man, but as a dancer radiant in the glow of the smiling Buddha.

Among the Pueblo of North America, a *shaman*—part healer, part prophet, and conjurer of many stories—hunches to show his young disciples how Coyote, the mischief maker in Amerindian lore, stalks its prey. The boys admire the shaman's mime, for they have often seen Coyote's offspring on the mesas. Entranced by the magic of the moment, the boys also imitate Coyote as they become a chorus of cavorting dancers. The shaman, wearing the pelt of an actual coyote, laughs at the boys, satisfied that they have surrendered themselves to the power of Coyote this night.

In the agora, the marketplace of a Greek village, a blind poet-singer describes the deadly battle between Achilles, warrior-hero of the Argive army, and Hector, prince of Troy. As Hector suffers a deathblow from Achilles, the storyteller falls to the ground to show the agony of the dying prince. The Greek villagers are at once entertained and instructed by this man they call a *rhapsode*—literally, a "song-stitcher." Over the centuries other rhapsodes add to his story, and they, too, enliven their stories by imitating the actions of the epic heroes.

In Africa, Asia, the Americas, and Europe, we see the roots of an art we call theater in the tales of the griot and rhapsode. In China, Ireland, and Chile, they were called the *wu*, the bard, and the *cancionero*; they too invented stories and myths to help people understand their place in the world. At some point *mimesis*—the art of imitation—was introduced to physically and vocally re-create the characters of the story. And would they not likely have added costumes and perhaps a mask? And may we not imagine that at some point others in the audience rose to help tell the story through mime, voice, and costumes? Robert Edmund Jones, the admired American scene designer, has written an imaginative account of this process (see Forum, "The Theatre As It Was and As It Is").

You, too, are a storyteller—and an actor. You have embellished a story while telling a friend about an event as you gestured broadly, changed your voice, and—if only for an instant—became the person in your story. If you have not done so recently, you surely did so as a child. In a very real sense you were acting, and you were creating theater just as the griot or the rhapsode did centuries ago.

Over 2,200 years ago the Greek philosopher Plato suggested that the Greek rhapsodes were as much actors as poets. In the *Ion*—a dialogue between Socrates and General Ion—Plato noted that "rhapsodes and actors are wise" because they are inspired by the gods themselves to instruct people even as they entertain them.

Storytelling and the instinct to act out the story are but two of the cornerstones of the theatrical arts. Among others are rituals, ceremonies, pageantry, and carnivals—we have many words for activities that use theatrical elements. Coincidentally, Plato's student, Aristotle, suggested that theater in Greece might have grown from religious rites in honor of the god Dionysus; *The Nātyaśātra*, the sacred book of Hindu dramaturgy, begins with an account of a ritual performed by the gods themselves in the celestial theater of the goddess Indra. Such matters are dealt with elsewhere, but first consider the link between storytelling, rituals, and modern theater. As a starting point, consider the annual retelling of an ancient story about a terrifying witch from the island of Bali in the western Pacific.

The Barong or Trance Dance of Bali

Behind the sacred temple of Poera Panataran on Bali, a rice farmer named Ida Njoman puts on a huge mask to become the principal actor in a cosmic drama that has been performed for centuries. The dragonlike mask represents Rangda, an evil witch (perhaps derived from the Hindu goddess Durga) who opposes the Barong, a life-giving lion who defends the village against her destructive powers. In this universal battle between good and evil, between creation and destruction, local farmers, dressed in the traditional plaid sarong, carry short swords (kris) to dispel Rangda's evil powers. The entire village gathers under an enormous banyan tree in front of the temple honoring Banaspati Radja, king of the benevolent spirits. This ritual drama is un-

F O R U M

"The Theatre As It Was and As It Is"

ROBERT EDMUND JONES

Robert Edmund Jones, one of the United States' preeminent scene designers, imagines one of the first theatrical performances in human history.

I am going to ask you to do the most difficult thing in the world—to imagine. Let us imagine ourselves back in the Stone Age, in the days of the cave man and the mammoth and the Altamira frescoes. It is night. We are all sitting together around a fire—Ook and Pow and Pung and Glup and Little Zowie and all the rest of us. We sit close together. We like to be together. It is safer that way, if wild beasts attack us. And besides, we are happier when we are together. We are afraid to be alone. Over on that side of the fire the leaders of the tribe are sitting together—the strongest men, the men who can run fastest and fight hardest and endure longest. They have killed a lion today. We are excited about this thrilling event. We are all talking about it. We are always afraid of silence. We feel safer when somebody is talking. There is something strange about silence, strange like the black night around us, something we can never understand.

The lion's skin lies close by, near the fire. Suddenly the leader jumps to his feet. "I killed the lion! I did it! I followed him! He sprang at me! I struck at him with my spear! He fell down! He lay still!"

He is telling us. We listen. But all at once an idea comes to his dim brain. "I know a better way to tell you. See! It was like this! *Let me show you!*"

In that instant drama is born.

The leader goes on. "Sit around me in a circle—you, and you, and you—right here, where I can reach out and touch you all." And so with one inclusive gesture he makes—a theatre . . .

The leader continues: "You, Ook, over there—you stand up and be the lion. Here is the lion's skin. You put it on and be the lion and I'll kill you and we'll show them how it was." Ook gets up. He hangs the skin over his shoulders. He drops on his hands and knees and growls. How terrible he is! Of course, he isn't the real lion. We know that. The real lion is dead. We killed him today. Of course, Ook isn't a lion. Of course not. He doesn't even look like a lion. "You needn't try to scare us, Ook. We know you. We aren't afraid of you!" And yet, in some mysterious way, Ook *is* the lion. He isn't like the rest of us any longer. He is Ook all right, but he is a lion, too.

And now these two men—the world's first actors—begin to show us what the hunt was like. They do not tell us. They *show* us. They *act* it for us. The hunter lies in ambush. The lion growls. The hunter poises his spear. The lion leaps. We all join in with yells and howls of excitement and terror. The first community chorus! The spear is thrown. The lion falls and lies still.

The drama is finished.

Now Ook takes off the lion's skin and sits beside us and is himself again. Just like you. Just like me. Good old Ook. No, not quite like you or me. Ook will be, as long as he lives, the man who can be a lion when he wants to. Pshaw! A man can't be a lion! How can a man be a lion? But Ook can make us believe it, just the same. Something strange happens to that man Ook sometimes. The lion's spirit gets into him. And we shall always look up to him and admire him and perhaps be secretly a little afraid of him. Ook is an actor. He will always be different from the rest of us, a little apart from us. For he can summon spirits.

Many thousands of years have passed since that first moment of inspiration when the theatre sprang into being. But we still like to get together, we still dread to be alone, we are still a little awed by silence, we still like to make believe, . . . we are still lost in wonder before this magical art of the theatre. It is really a kind of magic, this art. We call it glamour or poetry or romance, but that doesn't explain it. In some mysterious way these old, simple, ancestral moods still survive in us, and an actor can make them live again for a while. We become children once more. We believe.

derscored by the hypnotic beat of drums and bamboo xylophones played by the gamelan, the sacred musicians.

The climax of this drama is riveting: Rangda casts a spell on the attacking dancers, whose swords are turned violently toward their chests. However, those who believe in the goodness of the Barong are not harmed, and the sharp swords bend grotesquely against the men's breastbones. The dancers fall into a deep trance and eventually awaken, exhausted from their encounter with the Evil One. Ida Njoman remains entranced hours after this performance in which he willingly sacrifices himself by portraying Rangda for the good of his neighbors. The village celebrates its liberation from evil as girls, each named after a flower, dance the *sang hyang* to celebrate life. An old priest pours a libation on the ground to purify it, while smoke from a sacred brazier is wafted into the faces of the congregation as they return to their homes, purified by their experience at the Barong (or "trance") dance.

A Broadway Musical

Meanwhile, in New York City a spectacular musical, *The Lion King,* plays nightly at the venerable New Amsterdam Theater on Broadway, as it has since September 1997. An audience pays $80 a ticket to watch a company of professional actor-dancers portray an assortment of animal characters to the accompaniment of musicians seated near the stage. The director, Julie Taymor, has significantly adapted theater techniques she learned in Southeast Asia to this tale about Africa. The performers who transform themselves into lions and other creatures of the African veldt entrance the audience. True, the costuming, the makeup, and Taymor's inventive puppetry aid this illusion, but it is still the performers' mime and dance that charm the audience into accepting this "magical lie." The play reaches its climax when the Lion Prince defeats his murderous uncle in a battle every bit as thrilling as that between Rangda and the Barong. (More than a few stories in the theater involve princes who defeat murderous uncles: see *Hamlet.*) The spectators cheer enthusiastically and return to their homes, refreshed by the "magic" of the evening. They feel that they, too, have participated in the triumph of the good in this entertaining diversion.

Rituals Versus Theater

Though the dance of the Barong and *The Lion King* share common traits such as music, costumes, and storytelling, there are significant differences between the two. The Balinese drama is a *ritual.* Rituals are:

Director Julie Taymor used puppetry and theatrical techniques she learned in Indonesia as she staged The Lion King *on Broadway.*

- symbolic actions developed by and performed for a community, usually to satisfy its spiritual or cultural needs;
- arranged in patterns that eventually—often over many generations—become precise in their execution;
- believed to have originally been performed to achieve "magical" effects, such as controlling the weather or the success of a hunt.

Note that "ritual" and "ceremony" are not necessarily synonymous terms. Ceremonies are formalized actions meant to sanction a political, social, or religious concept. A graduation is a social ceremony, whereas the inauguration of a president is a political ceremony. In many cultures, rituals and ceremonies are often sources of formal theater and drama, which are deliberate artistic mediums.

While it employs elements we identify with ritual (chanting, the rite in which Rafiki anoints Simba), *The Lion King* is an entertainment that melds a variety of arts: theater, dance, music, literature, and the visual arts. Theater as an art form can be distinguished from rituals in several ways:

- It is deliberately created by (usually) professional writers, directors, musicians, performers, and designers, and it is meticulously planned and rehearsed.
- Most contemporary commercial theater is created primarily to entertain, though *The Lion King* has an instructive value in the lessons it teaches and the culture it portrays.
- Modern theatrical art depends on commercial success to sustain itself.
- Contemporary theater addresses various sociological, political, psychological, and aesthetic needs of its audience.
- Theater depends upon an audience that chooses to attend the play.

Rituals and ceremonies often contribute to the theater. Appended to selected plays throughout this text you will find descriptions of rituals, ceremonies, and folk customs around the world that may help us understand the plays. Though the particulars of these events differ from place to place because of cultural influences, the impulses to use theatrical means to engage both participants and audiences are universal:

- The Yoruban Obatala Festival (Nigeria, West Africa) is a two-week reenactment of a cosmic battle between a Yoruban hero-god and his captor. Wole Soyinka's *Death and the King's Horseman* uses elements of Yoruban ritual (see Chapter 8).
- Día de los Muertos (Mexico) is an autumnal festival in which people dressed as skeletons mock death even as they recognize it as an essential part of life's experience. Elena Garro's *A Solid Home* is a short play that also laughs at death (see Chapter 9).
- The Yaqui Easter (Southwestern United States) is a fascinating rite that combines pre-Columbian rituals with those of the Christian tradition as a young man performs a mysterious deer dance on Easter morning. Sor Juana Inés de la Cruz's *The Divine Narcissus* also merges the rituals of indigenous people in Mesoamerica with Christian theology (see Chapter 9).
- The Italian *tarantella*, a vigorous dance intended to counter the poison of a spider bite, is but one of many healing dances performed by people throughout the world. Ibsen employs the *tarantella* in his exposé of the poison infecting Norwegian society in *A Doll's House* (see Chapter 5).
- The Tanabata Festival (Japan) commemorates the fate of mythical lovers as young people tie love poems to bamboo shoots as pledges of fidelity (see Chapter 7).
- Carnival (Trinidad), like Mardi Gras, is a pre-Lenten Caribbean street festival in which thousands of performers wear colorful costumes to liberate themselves from the doldrums of daily life. Carnival originated in 1830 to celebrate the liberation of slaves. Derek Walcott's *Ti-Jean and His Brothers* also addresses some of the political issues that spawned the Trinidad Carnival (see Chapter 8).

An Autumnal Ritual in America

Some may dismiss such rituals, ceremonies, and folk customs as remnants of bygone days that were developed by superstitious peoples and maintained by tradition-loving moderns. Imagine cultural anthropologists in the year 2500 examining the communal activities of an American town in the late twentieth century. They might note that thousands gather on an autumn afternoon in a huge amphitheater to watch a battle between young warriors with names like Wildcats and Golden Bears. The combatants, esteemed for their strength, speed, and bravery, wear colorful headpieces bearing icons of the animals they emulate. Ecstatic followers also appear in gaudy dress, and some even paint their faces or chests in colors sacred to the community. Many gather at midnight to chant before a towering bonfire to insure success in battle.

Musicians dressed in matching livery parade around the arena as maidens dance vigorously. The observers of this autumnal rite chant strange incantations: "Hold 'em Tigers, Hold 'em Tigers!" Some are known only to the initiated: "Hullabaloo, Kanek, Kanek. . . ." One tribe, the Eli, chant from an ancient Athenian comedy by Aristophanes: "Brekekkekex, Co-ax. Co-ax, Co-ax, Co-ax." The warriors enter the arena by running a ceremonial phalanx formed by the musicians and maidens. A masked being dressed as the animal or other totem with which the community identifies leads them. The sage elders who maintain order in this contest emerge from a dark tunnel, dressed in identical zebralike clothing to manifest their authority. An elder produces a sacred talon (often a coin of the realm) to determine the order of the proceedings. Symbolic gestures inform the spectators that one group of warriors will take possession of the contested object—made from the skin of a pig—while the other will "defend the north goal."

As the battle unfolds, the faithful have an appropriate supplication for every situation: "First and ten, do it again! We like it, we like it!" Eventually one tribe advances the sacred pigskin into its antagonist's territory and a great celebration ensues. The hero who has penetrated the forbidden land improvises a triumphant dance as he hurls the pigskin into the earth while his worshippers chant ecstatically.

Halfway through the contest—as the warriors rest in the dark recesses of the stadium— the audience is treated to a spectacle as the musicians create huge artworks on the amphitheater floor. Festive floats—vestiges of medieval theatricals—are paraded about while beautiful maidens, wearing jeweled headdresses and carrying greenery, salute the audience.

The battle continues into the fading light during this, "the dying time" of year. At the conclusion of the contest, the opposing forces sing their most sacred hymns: "When the twilight shadows gather out upon the campus green. . . ." The winners exit chanting mantras to celebrate their victory ("We're Number One!"), while the vanquished meditate on their failure, chins buried in their chests. As night settles on the land, the spectators head for meeting-houses where quantities of food and drink are consumed to celebrate and console.

This description of the modern American football game suggests that, for all our technology, we are not unlike our ancestors. The game has elements common to rituals, though the football game is not a ritual, per se. Its audience lacks "ritual expectancy" because football fans are not consciously aware of the ritual purpose of the event, which for them is primarily an entertainment. Nonetheless, it reflects the core values of the competitive, commercial society that supports it, while also addressing such essential needs of humans who seek order, spectacle, and communal celebration.

The Origins of Theater

Exactly when rituals passed into the realm of theater varies from culture to culture. But there are some striking similarities when we consider examples of the evolution of theater throughout the world, each of which is covered in greater depth in Parts II and III:

- Aristotle tells us that Greek theater grew from springtime rituals honoring Dionysus, the god of wine, fertility, and both the creative and irrational forces in humans. Other scholars suggest that Greek theater grew from rites in honor of the dead, sacred mysteries, or harvest dances.

- The theater of India is said to have originated from the Hindu gods Brahma, Vishnu, and Siva ("the lord of the dance"), who inspired the priest Bharata to write and perform plays. An entire book in the sacred Vedas is dedicated to theatrical presentation.
- The first professional actors in China were monks hired by farmers to perform sacred rites during the planting and harvest seasons.
- The Yoruba of Africa believe that Ogun—the Creative Essence in the universe—created theater to bridge the gap between humans and the cosmos. Ogun himself is said to have been the first actor when he assumed human form to save humans from their exile.
- The Noh theater of Japan began in religious and agricultural festivals sponsored by Buddhist monks. Specifically, the *surugaku* ("monkey dance") and the *dengaku* ("field dance") are cited as sources of the Noh.
- In medieval Europe, a major strain of theater was born in the great cathedrals as church ministers reenacted the mystery of Christ's resurrection on Easter morning.
- Among the Maya of Mesoamerica, professional entertainers called *tlaquetzque* performed cosmic dramas in spectacular costumes to honor sun gods. These provide us with one of the great myths of creation (*The Popol Vuh*) and the only extant play (*The Rabinal Achi*) from the pre-Columbian Americas.

In most instances, theater seems to have evolved from seasonal and agricultural rites acknowledging the power of some metaphysical force. Consequently, the first "actors" were often priests or shamans responsible for the well-being of the community. Many of the impulses that generated theater around the world may be found in the *Abydos Passion Play*, which was performed in Egypt for almost two thousand years. (See Center Stage box, The *Abydos Passion Play*.)

Common Ground for Uncommon Cultures

Though specific cultural forces such as power, ideology, economic status, race, gender, and historical circumstances shape particular rituals, ceremonies, and theatrical events, shared factors suggest why we, whatever our culture, often rely on—or invent—theatrical means to communicate:

1. ***We are mimetic beings.*** Aristotle began his famous treatise on theater with the observation that "the instinct for imitation is implanted in man from childhood." On its simplest level we learn by imitating how others walk, talk, dress, behave, and so on. This is *nonperformative* imitation because we are not imitating for the benefit of others. More consciously, we also frequently embellish our conversations by imitating the words, vocal patterns, and gestures of others, though we never relinquish our own personality while doing so. Though this is *performative*, it is not theater, as such, but it typifies our predisposition to imitate those about us. Actors begin with this instinct and elevate it to art. In 1402 Zeami, who (with his father, Kan-ami) founded Noh theater in Japan, wrote "Role playing involves imitation, in every particular, with nothing left out."

2. ***We seek order.*** Whether an ancient Hindu rite, a modern wedding ceremony, or a collegiate bonfire, rituals exist to give order to an often chaotic world. By carefully structuring a ritual, by controlling the elements that define it (e.g., words, dress, gestures, and visual elements), and by performing it in the presence of the community, there evolves a sense that we can—or would like to—control our destinies. Tragedy, discussed in Chapter 2, reminds us that this is not always possible. The preparation for a ritual can itself become a means of diminishing anxieties. For example, people in Europe, New Orleans, and even tropical Trinidad prepare for Carnival and Mardi Gras as a means of overcoming the midwinter "blahs." The repetition of the event fosters a familiarity that also calms. Passing the lore of the ritual from generation to generation establishes traditions while it promotes communal unity.

CENTER STAGE   THE *ABYDOS PASSION PLAY*

That Egypt, among the first great Mediterranean civilizations, should develop a sophisticated theatricalized ritual is not surprising. It had a complex mythology, a ruling class viewed as powerful deities (the pharaohs), and a strong dependence on the cycle of the seasons to sustain life in the arid Nile valley. What we know about actual theatrical practice, as well as a more formal drama, in ancient Egypt is severely limited to hieroglyphs collectively known as the Pyramid Texts. These artifacts date to about 2500 B.C.E. and are the source of considerable scholarly debate about their meaning and the extent to which drama actually existed in Egypt. Some argue that priests enacted events from the lives of the pharaohs as a means of keeping their spirits (and therefore their power) alive, while others suggest that the glyphs merely illustrate poems and other literary forms.

The *Memphite Drama* and especially the *Abydos Passion Play* are generally regarded as the two most representative forms of Egyptian theater. Keep in mind that both titles were coined by archaeologists who discovered the fragmentary texts upon which our limited knowledge rests. The *Memphite Drama* was likely performed on the first day of spring and recounts the resurrection of Osiris, son of the earth and the sky, who was killed, dismembered, and buried by his jealous brother, Set. Osiris was resurrected by his sister and wife, Isis. Where his body had been buried, the land was especially fertile and produced rich crops. Horus, the son of Osiris, eventually destroyed Set in a cosmic battle. Again we see the traditional themes of death and resurrection, good confronting evil, and the need for plentitude to sustain the tribe providing rich

The Abydos Passion Play *was performed in honor of the Egyptian sun god, Osiris, for 2,000 years; note the sunburst on the headdress in this bronze statue from the Ptolemaic Period.*

material for early dramas. The *Memphite Drama* celebrates not only the resurrection of Osiris, the slain god-king, but the coronation of Horus. It is possible that the pharaoh himself played Horus in this yearly drama to associate himself with the god.

The *Abydos Passion Play* is regarded as the most important of the Egyptian drama-rituals. Abydos, the most sacred

spot in Egypt, was associated with Osiris, and each spring the faithful gathered to reenact his story of resurrection and redemption. We know little about the particulars of this dramatization (which might have been performed over a number of weeks), but we do possess fragments written by Ikernofret about 1860 B.C.E. They suggest that the *Abydos Passion Play* was a spectacle that included battles, magnificent river barges, burial ceremonies, and coronations. According to Ikernofret's account (perhaps the first piece of recorded "performance criticism" in the world), mime and dance, music and song, recitations of great speeches, and even audience participation were ingredients in this ritual. Ikernofret, himself a participant, tells us that he reenacted "the Feast of the Going Forth" of Upwawet by repelling

. . . *the foe from the sacred barque. I overthrew the enemies of Osiris.*

I celebrated the "Great Going-Forth," following the god at his gong. . . .

I led the way of the god to his tomb before Peker, I championed Wennofer at "That Day of the Great Conflict;" I slew all the enemies of Nedyt.

The *Abydos Passion Play* might have been performed annually (or at least regularly) from about 2500 B.C.E. until about 550 B.C.E. (very close to the time when, most scholars agree, formal theater began in Greece), which would make it the longest-running drama in world history. However fragmented the information we possess about it, this Nile River drama provides more evidence about the theatrical impulses of our ancestors.

We know that many rituals, ceremonies, and even the theater itself evolved from either the agricultural calendar or spiritual-religious impulses—or both, since nature and gods were often one to early peoples. Literary critics such as Northrop Frye and Suzanne Langer (a biologist who became an art theorist) have written about plays in terms of their seasonal elements. Tragedies are autumnal plays about dying, while comedies are springtime plays about new life. Recall that the most memorable song in *The Lion King* celebrates this "circle of life."

Because it is an art form, formal theater also gives order. To make art is to select, to plan, to control, to determine an outcome. Our ancestors were, it has been argued, trying to become godlike in their early rituals; their masks often suggested spirit-world beings such as gods and ancestors. Even the modern artist is a creator-god, as Daniel Boorstin writes in *The Creators* (1992), a history of the artistic achievements of humans throughout the world:

> Mystified by the power to create, it is no wonder that man should imagine the artist to be god-like. . . . Across the world, the urge to create needed no express reason and conquered all obstacles. Man's power to make the new was the power to outlive himself in his creations. . . . He dared to make images of himself and of the life around him. He made his words into worlds, to relive his past and reshape his future.

3. We are communal beings. Tadashi Suzuki, a contemporary theater artist from Japan, defines a primary appeal of the theater when he writes that

> the works of novelists, painters, and composers are provided their essence by their sole creators. Such is not the case with theater. The theater is what it is because various performers occupy the same space, living at that precise moment in a collaborative creation.

Suzuki's observation is even more significant when we add that the audience also occupies the same space and is as much a part of the "collaborative creation" as are the performers.

Most of us crave social alliances for our well-being, and social interaction is inherent in the theatrical act. In the modern world of commerce, going to the theater is often an expensive activity that requires planning, dressing up, travel, and other special preparations. Why then do we still attend the theater in large numbers? Why aren't we simply content to go to a movie or, less expensively, rent a video? Why leave the comfort of our homes, and their readily accessible refrigerator and bathroom, to pay $10 to $100 to go to a play? The answers are complex because art and theater are complex subjects; however, two reasons merit consideration.

First, part of theater's lasting appeal has to do with the live contact between actor and audience. Movies can give audiences vicarious thrills and stunning action, but they cannot give us a live being taking the risks that are central to the theater experience. Actors walk a tightrope as they work their way through a script each night, however many times they've performed it. Such elements of "danger" are important to live theater, and those who watch also share that danger. Actors and audiences undertake a collective journey.

More importantly, theater depends very much on the contributions of the audience. A painting by Michelangelo is frozen for eternity; once a film goes into "the can" it is fixed forever and an audience cannot affect the film. Every performance in theater, however, is a new event, even a musical, such as *Cats*, which ran for over 7,000 performances in New York. Because actors are human, they can adjust their performance to fit the responses of the audience. "How's the house tonight?" is the universal actor's question. In a very real sense, the audience contributes to the event as much as the performers, and together actors and audience create theater.

4. We use "masks" throughout our lives. Given their importance to life-sustaining rituals, it is not surprising that masks have been found in virtually every culture throughout human history. Masks are, of course, the quintessential symbol of the theater. "Mask" here is used in both its specific and literal sense (i.e., a face covering) and in its most general and figurative senses (any form of disguise, such as costume, makeup, or hairpieces). In our evolution, we

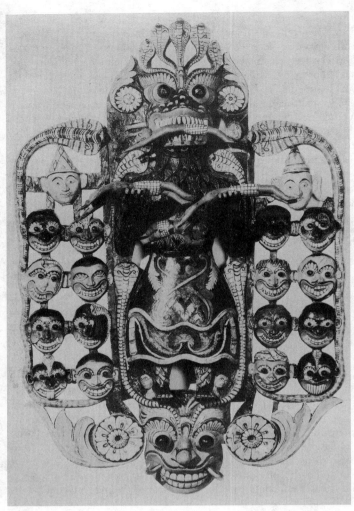

The face of evil may be found in an ancient mask of Mvaha-kola, a demon in the mythology of Ceylon, and more recently in the mask of Darth Vader, the dark spirit of the universe in George Lucas's 1983 film The Empire Strikes Back *(see photo opposite).*

have passed from "spiritual masks," rooted in religion, to "psychological masks," as defined in T. S. Eliot's poem "The Love Song of J. Alfred Prufrock," which asks, "Shall I prepare a face to meet the faces that I meet?"

Consider the ways in which masks serve many functions:

- *Masks transform*, that is, they make individuals into something more than they are in their ordinary world. They take on a magical quality that can make a mere mortal superhuman, even godlike. The Chinese theater scholar Tao-Ching Hsu argues that "a mask may fail to terrify or to amuse but it never fails to mystify. We are instinctively afraid of the unknown, hence even the most absurd mask can inspire religious awe." In a similar vein, anthropologists describe the positive flow of energy between the spiritual and material worlds that is generated by masks.
- *Masks liberate* because they embolden us and permit us to do things we might not ordinarily do. A mugger wears a mask both to protect his identity and to abet his courage. People

The mask of Darth Vader.

often wear masks at festivals, such as that in Trinidad, because masks allow them to behave more boldly—even break social taboos—without censure.

- *Masks encourage imagination.* Samuel Taylor Coleridge, the nineteenth-century critic and poet, wrote eloquently about the "willing suspension of disbelief"—that is, the audience's ability to accept the "lie" that is central to an act of theater. Coleridge's observation manifests itself most readily in masked drama. Few styles of theater are as imaginative as that of China and Japan, both of which make liberal use of masks or painted faces in their performances.
- *Masks are metaphors* because they symbolize something else. A play is not life itself, but a metaphor for life from which we may derive understanding and enjoyment. Masks enhance the metaphorical aspect of the dramatic experience. In many forms of theater (e.g., the Italian *commedia dell'arte* and the Javanese *Wayang Topeng*) masks immediately establish the symbolic nature of a character.
- *Masks are aesthetic.* That masks are collected as objets d'art attests to their appeal as both art and as a source of fascination. It is worth noting that much "modern art" (e.g., that of Picasso, Henry Moore, the Cubists, and other avant-garde artists) was inspired by masks from Africa.

5. *We enjoy and need entertainment.* Because rituals, and later the theater, confront life's most elemental issues—creation and destruction, birth and death, decay and resurrection—one might assume that the only worthwhile plays are profound or mystic. We must also acknowledge that at heart we retain a childlike fascination with storytelling, imaginative games, and fantasy. It is no accident that so much of the vocabulary of the theater is shared with children's activities: "play," "pretend," and "make believe." Like children's games, plays are learning events that provide a safe, entertaining means of experiencing life's challenges without actually suffering the discomfort of the real thing. We may cry in the theater; we may experience great fear and suspense; and we may be shocked by outrageous acts. Like a good roller-coaster ride, in the theater we experience the thrills and even the dangers of our journey, all the while knowing we cannot really be hurt. That's part of the entertainment.

Reading a Play

Now entertain yourself by reading a short play that helped lay the foundation of modern American theater: *Trifles* by Susan Glaspell (the first woman to win the Pulitzer Prize in drama). Although it was written in 1916, its theme of spousal abuse is quite contemporary. You may recognize some of the play's issues in the headlines of your daily paper, a reminder that theater and drama are tools that help us confront and understand our most horrible problems.

On one level *Trifles* is an example of that most popular of mystery genres, the whodunit (Sophocles' *Oedipus the King,* which you will read in Chapter 3, is the prototype of this kind of play). A farmer has been murdered and the townsmen, led by the sheriff, gather to sort through evidence that may lead them to the killer. Because of their status in this male-dominated world, the neighbor women are relegated to the kitchen. As the men traipse about the house searching for clues and chuckling at the women's conversations about "trifles," they are oblivious to crucial clues to the murder. These they dismiss as merely sloppy housekeeping, though the women—Mrs. Peters and Mrs. Hale—know that the unseen Minnie Foster Wright was in fact a meticulous housekeeper. Bit by bit, the women—and you—will realize the identity of the murderer and, more importantly, the reason for the murder.

On another level, *Trifles* is a "rebellion" play (not unlike Ibsen's *A Doll's House,* Chapter 5) that promotes change in society. The two neighbor women quietly rebel by withholding their knowledge about the murder from the men who have patronized them. As a historical footnote, it is worth mentioning that Glaspell converted her play into a short story, which she retitled "A Jury of Her Peers." Just as the play title is ironic (the "trifles" within the Wright house hold significant truths), the short story title was especially ironic in 1917 because women, in most states, were not allowed to serve on juries, nor were they allowed to vote until 1920. Yet Mrs. Peters and Mrs. Hale prove to be the shrewdest of jurors in their analysis of the "crime," and they cast a resounding vote against abuse and disrespect in their conspiracy of silence.

For all its sociology and its status as an important step in the development of modern realistic drama, *Trifles* reflects many of the impulses that have caused people to create theater. We have seen that early rituals often grew out of life-and-death struggles; so, too, does *Trifles* portray people at their most destructive (there is even a bizarre animal sacrifice in the play). We believe Minnie's workaday routines—e.g., quilting—are in fact personal rituals that help her cope with the harshness of her existence.

Read this short drama carefully (and with an active imagination: see the house and hear the conversations). In the next chapter we will frequently refer to *Trifles* to illustrate those elements that make theater "drama." Our analysis of Glaspell's play appears in the "boxed" portions of Chapter 2.

A photograph of the Provincetown Players' original production of Trifles *appeared in a 1917 edition of* Theatre Magazine, *a sign that the Greenwich Village artists had become a force in the American theater.*

TRIFLES

S U S A N   G L A S P E L L

SCENE: *The kitchen in the now abandoned farmhouse of John Wright, a gloomy kitchen, and left without having been put in order—unwashed pans under the sink, a loaf of bread outside the breadbox, a dish towel on the table— other signs of incompleted work. At the rear the outer door opens, and the Sheriff comes in, followed by the County Attorney and Hale. The Sheriff and Hale are men in middle life, the County Attorney is a young man; all are much bundled up and go at once to the stove. They are followed by the two women—the Sheriff's Wife first; she is a slight wiry woman, a thin nervous face. Mrs. Hale is larger and would ordinarily be called more comfortable looking, but she is disturbed now and looks fearfully about as she enters. The women have come in slowly and stand close together near the door.*

COUNTY ATTORNEY (*rubbing his hands*). This feels good. Come up to the fire, ladies.

MRS. PETERS (*after taking a step forward*). I'm not—cold.

SHERIFF (*unbuttoning his overcoat and stepping away from the stove as if to the beginning of official business*). Now, Mr. Hale, before we move things about, you explain to Mr. Henderson just what you saw when you came here yesterday morning.

COUNTY ATTORNEY. By the way, has anything been moved? Are things just as you left them yesterday?

SHERIFF (*looking about*). It's just the same. When it dropped below zero last night, I thought I'd better send Frank out this morning to make a fire for us—no use getting pneumonia with a big case on; but I told him not to touch anything except the stove—and you know Frank.

COUNTY ATTORNEY. Somebody should have been left here yesterday.

SHERIFF. Oh—yesterday. When I had to send Frank to Morris Center for that man who went crazy—I want you to know I had my hands full yesterday. I knew you could get back from Omaha by today, and as long as I went over everything here myself—

COUNTY ATTORNEY. Well, Mr. Hale, tell just what happened when you came here yesterday morning.

HALE. Harry and I had started to town with a load of potatoes. We came along the road from my place; and as I got here, I said, "I'm going to see if I can't get John Wright to go in with me on a party telephone." I spoke to Wright about it once before, and he put me off, saying folks talked too much anyway, and all he asked was peace and quiet—I guess you know about how much he talked himself; but I thought maybe if I went to the house and talked about it before his wife, though I said to Harry that I didn't know as what his wife wanted made much difference to John—

COUNTY ATTORNEY. Let's talk about that later, Mr. Hale. I do want to talk about that, but tell now just what happened when you got to the house.

HALE. I didn't hear or see anything; I knocked at the door, and still it was all quiet inside. I knew they must be up, it was past eight o'clock. So I knocked again, and I thought I heard somebody say, "Come in." I wasn't sure, I'm not sure yet, but I opened the door—this door (indicating the door by which the two women are still standing), and there in that rocker—(pointing to it) sat Mrs. Wright. (They all look at the rocker.)

COUNTY ATTORNEY. What—was she doing?

HALE. She was rockin' back and forth. She had her apron in her hand and was kind of—pleating it.

COUNTY ATTORNEY. And how did she—look?

HALE. Well, she looked queer.

COUNTY ATTORNEY. How do you mean—queer?

HALE. Well, as if she didn't know what she was going to do next. And kind of done up.

COUNTY ATTORNEY. How did she seem to feel about your coming?

HALE. Why, I don't think she minded—one way or other. She didn't pay much attention. I said, "How do, Mrs. Wright, it's cold, ain't it?" And she said, "Is it?"—and went on kind of pleating at her apron. Well, I was surprised; she didn't ask me to come up to the stove, or to set down, but just sat there, not even looking at me, so I said, "I want to see John." And then she—laughed. I guess you would call it a laugh. I thought of Harry and the team outside, so I said a little sharp: "Can't I see John?" "No," she says, kind o' dull like. "Ain't he home?" says I. "Yes," says she, "he's home." "Then why can't I see him?" I asked her, out of patience. "'Cause he's dead," says she. "Dead?" says I. She just nodded her head, not getting a bit excited, but rockin' back and forth. "Why—where is he?" says I, not knowing what to say. She just pointed upstairs—like that (himself pointing to the room above). I got up, with the idea of going up there. I walked from there to here—then I says, "Why, what did he die of?" "He died of a rope around his neck," says she, and just went on pleatin' at her apron. Well, I went out and called Harry. I thought I might—need help. We went upstairs, and there he was lyin'—

COUNTY ATTORNEY. I think I'd rather have you go into that upstairs, where you can point it all out. Just go on now with the rest of the story.

HALE. Well, my first thought was to get that rope off. I looked ... (Stops, his face twitches.) ... but Harry, he went up to him, and he said, "No, he's dead all right, and we'd better not touch anything." So we went back downstairs. She was still sitting that same way. "Has anybody been notified?" I asked. "No," says she, unconcerned. "Who did this, Mrs. Wright?" said Harry. He said it businesslike—and she stopped pleatin' of her apron. "I don't know," she says. "You don't know?" says Harry. "No," says she, "Weren't you sleepin' in the bed with him?" says Harry. "Yes," says she, "but I was on the inside." "Somebody slipped a rope round his neck and strangled him, and you didn't wake up?" says Harry. "I didn't wake up," she said after him. We must 'a looked as if we didn't see how that could be, for after a minute she said, "I sleep sound." Harry was going to ask her more questions, but I said maybe we ought to let her tell her story first to the coroner, or the sheriff, so Harry went fast as he could to Rivers' place, where there's a telephone.

COUNTY ATTORNEY. And what did Mrs. Wright do when she knew that you had gone for the coroner?

HALE. She moved from that chair to this over here ... (Pointing to a small chair in the corner.) ... and just sat there with her hands held together and looking down. I got a feeling that I ought to make some conversation, so I said I had come in to see if John wanted to put in a telephone, and at that she started to laugh, and then she stopped and looked at me—scared. (The County Attorney, who has had his notebook out, makes a note.) I dunno, maybe it wasn't scared. I wouldn't like to say it was. Soon Harry got back, and then Dr. Lloyd came, and you, Mr. Peters, and so I guess that's all I know that you don't.

COUNTY ATTORNEY (looking around). I guess we'll go upstairs first—and then out to the barn and around there. (To the Sheriff.) You're convinced that there was nothing important here—nothing that would point to any motive?

SHERIFF. Nothing here but kitchen things.

(The County Attorney, after again looking around the kitchen, opens the door of a cupboard closet. He gets up on a chair and looks on a shelf. Pulls his hand away, sticky.)

COUNTY ATTORNEY. Here's a nice mess.

(The women draw nearer.)

MRS. PETERS (to the other woman). Oh, her fruit; it did freeze. (To the Lawyer.) She worried about that when it turned so cold. She said the fir'd go out and her jars would break.

SHERIFF. Well, can you beat the women! Held for murder and worryin' about her preserves.

COUNTY ATTORNEY. I guess before we're through she may have something more serious than preserves to worry about.

HALE. Well, women are used to worrying over trifles.

(*The two women move a little closer together.*)

COUNTY ATTORNEY (*with the gallantry of a young politician*). And yet, for all their worries, what would we do without the ladies? (*The women do not unbend. He goes to the sink, takes a dipperful of water from the pail and, pouring it into a basin, washes his hands. Starts to wipe them on the roller towel, turns it for a cleaner place.*) Dirty towels! (*Kicks his foot against the pans under the sink.*) Not much of a housekeeper, would you say, ladies?

MRS. HALE (*stiffly*). There's a great deal of work to be done on a farm.

COUNTY ATTORNEY. To be sure. And yet . . . (*With a little bow to her.*) . . . I know there are some Dickson county farmhouses which do not have such roller towels. (*He gives it a pull to expose its full length again.*)

MRS. HALE. Those towels get dirty awful quick. Men's hands aren't always as clean as they might be.

COUNTY ATTORNEY. Ah, loyal to your sex, I see. But you and Mrs. Wright were neighbors. I suppose you were friends, too.

MRS. HALE (*shaking her head*). I've not seen much of her of late years. I've not been in this house—it's more than a year.

COUNTY ATTORNEY. And why was that? You didn't like her?

MRS. HALE. I liked her all well enough. Farmers' wives have their hands full, Mr. Henderson. And then—

COUNTY ATTORNEY. Yes—?

MRS. HALE (*looking about*). It never seemed a very cheerful place.

COUNTY ATTORNEY. No—it's not cheerful. I shouldn't say she had the homemaking instinct.

MRS. HALE. Well, I don't know as Wright had, either.

COUNTY ATTORNEY. You mean that they didn't get on very well?

MRS. HALE. No, I don't mean anything. But I don't think a place'd be any cheerfuler for John Wright's being in it.

COUNTY ATTORNEY. I'd like to talk more of that a little later. I want to get the lay of things upstairs now. (*He goes to the left, where three steps lead to a stair door.*)

SHERIFF. I suppose anything Mrs. Peters does'll be all right. She was to take in some clothes for her, you know, and a few little things. We left in such a hurry yesterday.

COUNTY ATTORNEY. Yes, but I would like to see what you take, Mrs. Peters, and keep an eye out for anything that might be of use to us.

MRS. PETERS. Yes, Mr. Henderson.

(*The women listen to the men's steps on the stairs, then look about the kitchen.*)

MRS. HALE. I'd hate to have men coming into my kitchen, snooping around and criticizing. (*She arranges the pans under sink which the Lawyer had shoved out of place.*)

MRS. PETERS. Of course it's no more than their duty.

MRS. HALE. Duty's all right, but I guess that deputy sheriff that came out to make the fire might have got a little of this on. (*Gives the roller towel a pull.*) Wish I'd thought of that sooner. Seems mean to talk about her for not having things slicked up when she had to come away in such a hurry.

MRS. PETERS (*who has gone to a small table in the left rear corner of the room, and lifted one end of a towel that covers a pan*). She had bread set. (*Stands still.*)

MRS. HALE (*eyes fixed on a loaf of bread beside the breadbox, which is on a low shelf at the other side of the room. Moves slowly toward it*). She was going to put this in there. (*Picks up loaf, then abruptly drops it. In a manner of returning to familiar things.*) It's a shame about her fruit. I wonder if it's all gone. (*Gets up on the chair and looks.*) I think there's some here that's all right, Mrs. Peters. Yes—here; (*Holding it toward the window.*) this is cherries, too. (*Looking again.*) I declare I believe that's the only one. (*Gets down, bottle in her hand. Goes to the sink and wipes it off on the outside.*) She'll feel awful bad after all her hard work in the hot weather. I remember the afternoon I put up my cherries last summer. (*She puts the bottle on the big kitchen table, center of the room, front table. With a sigh, is about to sit down in the rocking chair. Before she is seated realizes what chair it is; with a slow look at it, steps back. The chair, which she has touched, rocks back and forth.*)

MRS. PETERS. Well, I must get those things from the front room closet. (*She goes to the door at the right, but after looking into the other room steps back.*) You coming with me, Mrs. Hale? You could help me carry them. (*They go into the other room; reappear, Mrs. Peters carrying a dress and skirt, Mrs. Hale following with a pair of shoes.*)

MRS. PETERS. My, it's cold in there. (*She puts the cloth on the big table, and hurries to the stove.*)

MRS. HALE (*examining the skirt*). Wright was close. I think maybe that's why she kept so much to herself. She didn't even belong to the Ladies' Aid. I suppose she felt she couldn't do her part, and then you don't enjoy things when you feel shabby. She used to wear pretty clothes and be lively, when she was Minnie Foster, one of the town girls singing in the choir. But that—oh, that was thirty years ago. This all you was to take in?

MRS. PETERS. She said she wanted an apron. Funny thing to want, for there isn't much to get you dirty in jail, goodness knows. But I suppose just to make her feel more natural. She said they was in the top drawer in this cupboard. Yes, here. And then her little shawl that always hung behind the door. (*Opens stair door and looks.*) Yes, here it is. (*Quickly shuts door leading upstairs.*)

MRS. HALE (*abruptly moving toward her*). Mrs. Peters?

MRS. PETERS. Yes, Mrs. Hale?

MRS. HALE. Do you think she did it?

MRS. PETERS (*in a frightened voice*). Oh, I don't know.

MRS. HALE. Well, I don't think she did. Asking for an apron and her little shawl. Worrying about her fruit.

MRS. PETERS (*starts to speak, glances up, where footsteps are heard in the room above. In a low voice*). Mr. Peters says it looks bad for her. Mr. Henderson is awful sarcastic in speech, and he'll make fun of her sayin' she didn't wake up.

MRS. HALE. Well, I guess John Wright didn't wake when they was slipping that rope under his neck.

MRS. PETERS. No, it's strange. It must have been done awful crafty and still. They say it was such a—funny way to kill a man, rigging it all up like that.

MRS. HALE. That's just what Mr. Hale said. There was a gun in the house. He says that's what he can't understand.

MRS. PETERS. Mr. Henderson said coming out that what was needed for the case was a motive; something to show anger, or—sudden feeling.

MRS. HALE (*who is standing by the table*). Well, I don't see any signs of anger around here. (*She puts her hand on the dish towel which lies on the table, stands looking down at the table, one half of which is clean, the other half messy.*) It's wiped here. (*Makes a move as if to finish work, then turns and looks at loaf of bread outside the breadbox. Drops towel. In that voice of coming back to familiar things.*) Wonder how they are finding things upstairs? I hope she had it a little more red-up there. You know, it seems kind of *sneaking*. Locking her up in town and then coming out here and trying to get her own house to turn against her!

MRS. PETERS. But, Mrs. Hale, the law is the law.

MRS. HALE. I s'pose 'tis. (*Unbuttoning her coat.*) Better loosen up your things, Mrs. Peters. You won't feel them when you go out.

(*Mrs. Peters takes off her fur tippet, goes to hang it on hook at the back of room, stands looking at the under part of the small corner table.*)

MRS. PETERS. She was piecing a quilt. (*She brings the large sewing basket, and they look at the bright pieces.*)

MRS. HALE. It's log cabin pattern. Pretty, isn't it? I wonder if she was goin' to quilt or just knot it?

(*Footsteps have been heard coming down the stairs. The Sheriff enters, followed by Hale and the County Attorney.*)

SHERIFF. They wonder if she was going to quilt it or just knot it. (*The men laugh, the women look abashed.*)

COUNTY ATTORNEY (*rubbing his hands over the stove*). Frank's fire didn't do much up there, did it? Well, let's go out to the barn and get that cleared up.

(*The men go outside.*)

MRS. HALE (*resentfully*). I don't know as there's anything so strange, our takin' up our time with little things while we're waiting for them to get the evidence. (*She sits down at the big table, smoothing out a block with decision.*) I don't see as it's anything to laugh about.

MRS. PETERS (*apologetically*). Of course they've got awful important things on their minds. (*Pulls up a chair and joins Mrs. Hale at the table.*)

MRS. HALE (*examining another block*). Mrs. Peters, look at this one. Here, this is the one she was working on, and look at the sewing! All the rest of it has been so nice and even. And look at this! It's all over the place! Why, it looks as if she didn't know what she was about! (*After she has said this, they look at each other, then started to glance back at the door. After an instant Mrs. Hale has pulled at a knot and ripped the sewing.*)

MRS. PETERS. Oh, what are you doing, Mrs. Hale?

MRS. HALE (*mildly*). Just pulling out a stitch or two that's not sewed very good. (*Threading a needle.*) Bad sewing always made me fidgety.

MRS. PETERS (*nervously*). I don't think we ought to touch things.

MRS. HALE. I'll just finish up this end. (*Suddenly stopping and leaning forward.*) Mrs. Peters?

MRS. PETERS. Yes, Mrs. Hale?

MRS. HALE. What do you suppose she was so nervous about?

MRS. PETERS. Oh—I don't know. I don't know as she was nervous. I sometimes sew awful queer when I'm just tired. (*Mrs. Hale starts to say something, looks at Mrs. Peters, then goes on sewing.*) Well, I must get these things wrapped up. They may be through sooner than we think. (*Putting apron and other things together.*) I wonder where I can find a piece of paper, and string.

MRS. HALE. In that cupboard, maybe.

MRS. PETERS (*looking in cupboard*). Why, here's a birdcage. (*Holds it up.*) Did she have a bird, Mrs. Hale?

MRS. HALE. Why, I don't know whether she did or not—I've not been here for so long. There was a man around last year selling canaries cheap, but I don't know as she took one; maybe she did. She used to sing real pretty herself.

MRS. PETERS (*glancing around*). Seems funny to think of a bird here. But she must have had one, or why should she have a cage? I wonder what happened to it?

MRS. HALE. I s'pose maybe the cat got it.

MRS. PETERS. No, she didn't have a cat. She's got that feeling some people have about cats—being afraid of them. My cat got in her room, and she was real upset and asked me to take it out.

MRS. HALE. My sister Bessie was like that. Queer, ain't it?

MRS. PETERS (*examining the cage*). Why, look at this door. It's broke. One hinge is pulled apart.

MRS. HALE (*looking, too*). Looks as if someone must have been rough with it.

MRS. PETERS. Why, yes. (*She brings the cage forward and puts it on the table.*)

MRS. HALE. I wish if they're going to find any evidence they'd be about it. I don't like this place.

MRS. PETERS. But I'm awful glad you came with me, Mrs. Hale. It would be lonesome for me sitting here alone.

MRS. HALE. It would, wouldn't it? (*Dropping her sewing.*) But I tell you what I do wish, Mrs. Peters. I wish I had come over sometimes when *she* was here. I—(*Looking around the room.*)—wish I had.

MRS. PETERS. But of course you were awful busy, Mrs. Hale—your house and your children.

MRS. HALE. I could've come. I stayed away because it weren't cheerful—and that's why I ought to have come. I—I've never liked this place. Maybe because it's down in a hollow, and you don't see the road. I dunno what it is, but it's a lonesome place and always was. I wish I had come over to see Minnie Foster sometimes. I can see now—(*Shakes her head.*)

MRS. PETERS. Well, you mustn't reproach yourself, Mrs. Hale. Somehow we just don't see how it is with other folks until—something comes up.

MRS. HALE. Not having children makes less work—but it makes a quiet house, and Wright out to work all day, and no company when he did come in. Did you know John Wright, Mrs. Peters?

MRS. PETERS. Not to know him; I've seen him in town. They say he was a good man.

MRS. HALE. Yes—good; he didn't drink, and kept his word as well as most, I guess, and paid his debts. But he was a hard man, Mrs. Peters. Just to pass the time of day with him. (*Shivers.*) Like a raw wind that gets to the bone. (*Pauses, her eye falling on the cage.*) I should think she would 'a wanted a bird. But what do you suppose went with it?

MRS. PETERS. I don't know, unless it got sick and died. (*She reaches over and swings the broken door, swings it again; both women watch it.*)

MRS. HALE. You weren't raised round here, were you? (*Mrs. Peters shakes her head.*) You didn't know—her?

MRS. PETERS. Not till they brought her yesterday.

MRS. HALE. She—come to think of it, she was kind of like a bird herself—real sweet and pretty, but kind of timid and—fluttery. How—she—did—change. (*Silence; then as if struck by a happy thought and relieved to get back to everyday things.*) Tell you what, Mrs. Peters, why don't you take the quilt in with you? It might take up her mind.

MRS. PETERS. Why, I think that's a real nice idea, Mrs. Hale. There couldn't possibly be any objection to it, could there? Now, just what would I take? I wonder if her patches are in here—and her things. (*They look in the sewing basket.*)

MRS. HALE. Here's some red. I expect this has got sewing things in it (*Brings out a fancy box.*) What a pretty box. Looks like something somebody would give you. Maybe her scissors are in here. (*Opens box. Suddenly puts her hand to her nose.*) Why—(*Mrs. Peters bends nearer, then turns her face away.*) There's something wrapped up in this piece of silk.

MRS. PETERS. Why, this isn't her scissors.

MRS. HALE (*lifting the silk*). Oh, Mrs. Peters—it's—(*Mrs. Peters bends closer.*)

MRS. PETERS. It's the bird.

MRS. HALE (*jumping up*). But, Mrs. Peters—look at it. Its neck! Look at its neck! It's all—other side *to.*

MRS. PETERS. Somebody—wrung—its neck.

(*Their eyes meet. A look of growing comprehension of horror. Steps are heard outside. Mrs. Hale slips box under quilt pieces, and sinks into her chair. Enter Sheriff and County Attorney. Mrs. Peters rises.*)

COUNTY ATTORNEY (*as one turning from serious things to little pleasantries*). Well, ladies, have you decided whether she was going to quilt it or knot it?

MRS. PETERS. We think she was going to—knot it.

COUNTY ATTORNEY. Well, that's interesting, I'm sure. (*Seeing the birdcage.*) Has the bird flown?

MRS. HALE (*putting more quilt pieces over the box*). We think the—cat got it.

COUNTY ATTORNEY (*preoccupied*). Is there a cat?

(*Mrs. Hale glances in a quick covert way at Mrs. Peters.*)

MRS. PETERS. Well, not now. They're superstitious, you know. They leave.

COUNTY ATTORNEY (*to Sheriff Peters, continuing an interrupted conversation*). No sign at all of anyone having come from the outside. Their own rope. Now let's go up again and go over it piece by piece. (*They start upstairs.*) It would have to have been someone who knew just the—

(*Mrs. Peters sits down. The two women sit there not looking at one another, but as if peering into something and at the same time holding back. When they talk now, it is the manner of feeling their way over strange ground, as if afraid of what they are saying, but as if they cannot help saying it.*)

MRS. HALE. She liked the bird. She was going to bury it in that pretty box.

MRS. PETERS (*in a whisper*). When I was a girl—my kitten—there was a boy took a hatchet, and before my eyes—and before I could get there—(*Covers her face an instant.*) If they hadn't held me back, I would have—(*Catches herself, looks upstairs where steps are heard, falters weakly.*)—hurt him.

MRS. HALE (*with a slow look around her*). I wonder how it would seem never to have had any children around. (*Pause.*) No, Wright wouldn't like the bird—a thing that sang. She used to sing. He killed that, too.

MRS. PETERS (*moving uneasily*). We don't know who killed the bird.

MRS. HALE. I knew John Wright.

MRS. PETERS. It was an awful thing was done in this house that night, Mrs. Hale. Killing a man while he slept, slipping a rope around his neck that choked the life out of him.

MRS. HALE. His neck. Choked the life out of him.

(Her hand goes out and rests on the birdcage.)

MRS. PETERS (with a rising voice). We don't know who killed him. We don't know.

MRS. HALE (her own feeling not interrupted). If there'd been years and years of nothing, then a bird to sing to you, it would be awful—still, after the bird was still.

MRS. PETERS (something within her speaking). I know what stillness is. When we homesteaded in Dakota, and my first baby died—after he was two years old, and me with no other then—

MRS. HALE (moving). How soon do you suppose they'll be through, looking for evidence?

MRS. PETERS. I know what stillness is. (Pulling herself back.) The law has got to punish crime, Mrs. Hale.

MRS. HALE (not as if answering that). I wish you'd seen Minnie Foster when she wore a white dress with blue ribbons and stood up there in the choir and sang. (A look around the room.) Oh, I wish I'd come over here once in a while! That was a crime! That was a crime! Who's going to punish that?

MRS. PETERS (looking upstairs). We mustn't—take on.

MRS. HALE. I might have known she needed help! I know how things can be—for women. I tell you, it's queer, Mrs. Peters. We live close together and we live far apart. We all go through the same things—it's all just a different kind of the same thing. (Brushes her eyes, noticing the bottle of fruit, reaches out for it.) If I was you, I wouldn't tell her her fruit was gone. Tell her it ain't. Tell her it's all right. Take this in to prove it to her. She—she may never know whether it was broke or not.

MRS. PETERS (takes the bottle, looks about for something to wrap it in; takes petticoat from the clothes brought from the other room, very nervously begins winding this around the bottle. In a false voice). My, it's a good thing the men couldn't hear us. Wouldn't they just laugh! Getting all stirred up over a little thing like a—dead canary. As if that could have anything to do with—with—wouldn't they laugh!

(The men are heard coming downstairs.)

MRS. HALE (under her breath). Maybe they would—maybe they wouldn't.

COUNTY ATTORNEY. No, Peters, it's all perfectly clear except a reason for doing it. But you know juries when it comes to women. If there was some definite thing. Some-

thing to show—something to make a story about—a thing that would connect up with this strange way of doing it.

(The women's eyes meet for an instant. Enter Hale from outer door.)

HALE. Well, I've got the team around. Pretty cold out there.

COUNTY ATTORNEY. I'm going to stay here awhile by myself. (To the Sheriff.) You can send Frank out for me, can't you? I want to go over everything. I'm not satisfied that we can't do better.

SHERIFF. Do you want to see what Mrs. Peters is going to take in?

(The Lawyer goes to the table, picks up the apron, laughs.)

COUNTY ATTORNEY. Oh I guess they're not very dangerous things the ladies have picked up. (Moves a few things about, disturbing the quilt pieces which cover the box. Steps back.) No, Mrs. Peters doesn't need supervising. For that matter, a sheriff's wife is married to the law. Ever think of it that way, Mrs. Peters?

MRS. PETERS. Not—just that way.

SHERIFF (chuckling). Married to the law. (Moves toward the other room.) I just want you to come in here a minute, George. We ought to take a look at these windows.

COUNTY ATTORNEY (scoffingly). Oh, windows!

SHERIFF. We'll be right out, Mr. Hale.

(Hale goes outside. The Sheriff follows the County Attorney into the other room. Then Mrs. Hale rises, hands tight together, looking intensely at Mrs. Peters, whose eyes take a slow turn, finally meeting, Mrs. Hale's. A moment Mrs. Hale holds her, then her own eyes point the way to where the box is concealed. Suddenly Mrs. Peters throws back quilt pieces and tries to put the box in the bag she is wearing. It is too big. She opens box, starts to take the bird out, cannot touch it, goes to pieces, stands there helpless. Sound of a knob turning in the other room. Mrs. Hale snatches the box and puts it in the pocket of her big coat. Enter County Attorney and Sheriff.)

COUNTY ATTORNEY (facetiously). Well, Henry, at least we found out that she was not going to quilt it. She was going to—what is it you call it, ladies?

MRS. HALE (her hand against her pocket). We call it—knot it, Mr. Henderson.

CURTAIN

SPOTLIGHT

THE MOTHER OF THE MODERN AMERICAN THEATER: SUSAN GLASPELL (1882–1948)

If Eugene O'Neill is regarded as "the father of the modern American theater," it is no less fitting to remember Susan Glaspell as its "mother." Though not as well known as O'Neill, Glaspell was an integral part of the movement that brought American drama to maturity in the early years of the twentieth century. In 1931 she became the first woman to win a Pulitzer Prize in drama (for *Alison's House,* a drama based loosely on the life of poet Emily Dickinson), an award that helped mark the acceptance of women in the American theater.

The Iowa-born Glaspell attended Drake University in Des Moines, where she studied literature and journalism. While working as a journalist in 1908, she met George Cram Cook, a professor at Iowa University, whom she married in 1913 (after his first marriage ended in divorce and after she had been exposed to the avant-garde artistic movements of Paris). The couple gravitated to Provincetown, a resort town on Cape Cod, where they joined other artists, in-cluding O'Neill, to produce short plays modeled on the new European drama. The first play produced at Province-town was *Suppressed Desires*—co-authored by Glaspell and Cook—a still amusing satire on Freudian psychology. The Cook-led troupe attempted to duplicate their Provincetown successes at an old stable on MacDougall Street in New York's Greenwich Village. It was there, at the Provincetown Playhouse, that the plays of Glaspell, O'Neill, e. e. cummings, Sherwood Anderson, and Edna Ferber caught the attention of New York theater patrons who were intrigued by the realism, expressionism, and other experimental styles in this noncommercial setting. In 1925 Glaspell and Cook distanced themselves from the Provincetown Players when O'Neill assumed the leadership of the theater while the couple was in Greece (where Cook died).

Throughout her literary career Glaspell maintained the spirit of innovation and the contemporary that marked the Provincetown enterprise. In her full-length play, *The Inheritors* (1921), she challenged jingoistic Americanism in World War I while calling for greater individual freedom (especially for women) and tolerance of unpopular viewpoints. Her Pulitzer Prize was tainted by controversy, largely because she held such liberal ideas. Also in 1921 she wrote her most experimental work, *The Verge,* an expressionistic drama that portrayed the inner workings of the mind of the so-called new woman. In both her short and longer pieces, Glaspell presented strong central female characters who sought autonomy in a male-dominated society. *Trifles* (1916) remains the best-known, most frequently produced of these plays.

From 1936 to 1938 Glaspell was chief administrator of the government-sponsored Federal Theater Project's Midwest Bureau, a position that acknowledged her importance as a founder of the community and regional theater movement in America and as one of the standard-bearers for women's issues in art.

Arthur Miller, among the modern era's finest playwrights, sits in an ancient Greek theater at Epidaurus.

CHAPTER 2

FROM THEATER TO DRAMA

The Dramatic Impulse

Although rituals and ceremonies involve theatrical artistry, theater, in its fullest sense, becomes one of the arts when it is fused with drama. Although the two terms are often used interchangeably, there is a crucial distinction between *theater* and *drama*. Theater derives from the ancient Greek word for the space in which plays were performed, *theatron,* or "seeing place." Drama also derives from a Greek word, *drao,* which means "to do" or "to act." Drama depicts human actions, conveyed in story form, which are performed by actors, singers, dancers, or mimes. Those things that are seen—scenery, costumes, lighting, gestures, movement—enhance the story by giving it a concrete reality, though not always realistically. This is theater.

While the telling of epic tales to ancient peoples provided material for dramas such as *Oedipus the King* or *The Recognition of Śakuntalā,* the stories in themselves are not "dramatic," though they surely contain dramatic elements. What separates a play from an epic story like that of Ulysses, a ritualized enactment such as the Yoruban Obatala, or a novel? Because a play is usually bound by restrictions not normally confronting the storyteller, dramatists must be selective in the events they portray. Homer may devote lengthy passages to a minute description of Achilles' shield; the Yoruba may take two weeks to commemorate the battles of their ancestors; and Steinbeck may write an entire chapter about a turtle crossing a road in *The Grapes of Wrath.* But the playwright must, in most cases, create a script that can be told—as Shakespeare puts it—in "two hours traffic" on the stage. There are, of course, exceptions; it is not uncommon for plays in Asia, especially in Japan and India, to take many hours to perform. And the performance of Tony Kushner's two-part *Angels in America* requires about seven hours.

Furthermore, a play is written in the present tense—it takes place now. Playwright Thornton Wilder provides a helpful distinction between drama and other forms of narrative writing: "A novel [narrative form] is what one person tells us *took* place; a play [dramatic form] is what *takes* place" (emphases ours).

Thus, a play is a specialized, concise, and calculated form of storytelling that makes unusual demands on the writer. Look carefully at the spelling of *playwright.* The word is not spelled "playwrite," that is, one who writes plays. *Playwright* stems from an ancient Saxon word, *wyrhta,* meaning a worker or craftsman, such as a "boatwright" or "wheelwright." Surely a playwright is one who crafts, shapes, and purposefully constructs the story for maximum effect. In *The Poetics,* Aristotle makes a crucial distinction between the *mythos* (or story) and the *praxis* (or action, i.e., the careful arrangement of the events of the story).

Perhaps the most notable means by which the playwright focuses a story is through *conflict,* the clash of opposing forces. The Greeks often referred to a play as an *agon* ("contest" or "debate"). Its central character was the *protagonist* or "first contestant," and the *antagonist* was the opposing character. In Western drama we still use these terms to identify the primary characters in a play. Virtually all stories are based on conflict because it gets an audience involved in the action: we want to know how the conflict will be resolved. Every scene in a play is propelled by conflict, either by external or internal forces. The finest dramas are about people who ultimately must resolve inner conflicts that have been exacerbated by external forces. For instance, Oedipus may be in conflict with Creon or Teiresias, but he ultimately struggles with himself to learn who he truly is. *Kanjinchō*, one of the eighteen great Kabuki plays (see Chapter 7), depicts the warrior Benkei's dilemma. Benkei must choose between his need to respect Prince Yamamoto, whom he must protect (an interior conflict), and his duty to beat the prince before an enemy, whom he must trick so that the prince may escape (exterior conflict).

Film and television are generally much better equipped to portray external conflicts such as wars, "shoot-'em-ups," high-speed chases, and natural catastrophes. Despite the advantage of the close-up in film, the older, stately stage is actually better suited to the careful exploration of an intense personal dilemma because it is presented live and close to a living audience.

While rituals and ceremonies influence our lives and give order in an uncertain world, drama further organizes our experience into a manageable, perceptible form that instructs us, preserves our values, enhances our sense of community, and gives us pleasure. That is a function of all art. Let us consider how drama performs these functions.

The Poetics of Aristotle

In the West we customarily turn to Aristotle's *The Poetics*, written about 335 B.C.E., as a guide to our understanding of drama, just as the Japanese look to Zeami's *Kadensho* or the Indians seek the wisdom of Bharata's *Nātyaśātra*. Aristotle wrote *The Poetics* because his mentor, Plato, disparaged the theatrical arts. At the risk of oversimplifying the argument, Plato believed that a play was essentially a "lie" that portrayed humanity's basest actions. Furthermore, Plato felt that summoning up powerful emotions impeded clear thought. Aristotle countered Plato's arguments by systematically analyzing a number of plays, most written in the century before he lived, to illustrate:

- why the theater could be an effective teaching tool;
- what made plays effective works of art.

Importantly, Aristotle's comments were never meant to be rules about how plays must be written or performed. Rather, they were thoughtful observations that suggested, "All things being equal, *this* will make a play work more effectively, *that* will not." Unfortunately, Aristotle's comments were raised to dogma in Renaissance Italy and France, and a disservice was done to *The Poetics* (see Forum that follows).

Because it remains the standard tool for the discussion of drama in our Western culture, we use Aristotle's tract as a starting point for our exploration of the dramatic arts, but with two caveats:

- Much contemporary Western drama has significantly deviated from the ideas espoused in *The Poetics*. We shall identify important examples throughout this text.
- Because it derived from other cultures and their belief systems, legitimate variations of and additions to dramatic methodology are found in non-Western drama. Again, we shall note these where appropriate.

The Elements of Drama

Applying a scientist's analytical skills to Greek drama, Aristotle identified six elements that enhance not only the storytelling, but also the instructive and aesthetic values of a play. Though he was specifically discussing Greek tragedy, his comments are useful for analyzing the makeup of most dramatic works, including those written as alternatives to Aristotelian drama. The first four elements—plot, character, thought, and diction—relate to drama, the remaining two—music and spectacle—to theater. Combined they constitute the essence of the theatrical arts and provide us with a useful starting point in our exploration of world drama. As you have now read *Trifles*, we will refer to it (as well as some plays that you may read) to illustrate key points about the elements of drama. The *Trifles* sections have been highlighted for easy reference.

Plot

Aristotle refers to plot as the "soul" of dramatic poetry. While we tend to think of plot as the story line, it actually refers to the arrangement of the incidents—the calculated structure that achieves maximum intellectual, emotional, and aesthetic effect.

There are essentially three types of plot:

1. The climactic plot: The most traditional form of plotting, the climactic (or linear) plot begins with the exposition of a problem, builds on a series of minor crises to a major climax and its resolution. Causality is paramount in climactic plotting; that is, one event precipitates another. *Oedipus the King* is the prototype of the climactic plot, and most plays written prior to the late nineteenth century use such plots. It is possible to have several linear plots (or *subplots*) existing simultaneously; usually they interconnect in the final act. Shakespeare is especially adept at subplotting in such plays as *Hamlet*, which has three plots, each about a son who must avenge his father's death.

> *Trifles* is a climactic plot because it deals with a single story that builds to its conclusion as the two women discover the terrible secret of the Wright household. However, it does not contain overt action; rather, it is structured around a series of conversations that gradually reveal the truth about the murder.

2. The episodic plot: Many Asian plays, Shakespeare's history plays, South African township plays, and particularly works by the modern dramatist Bertolt Brecht (such as *The Good Woman of Setzuan*) employ an episodic plot. They consist of numerous events that are related thematically if not always by a single dramatic action. Most novels and the great myths such as *The Iliad* and *The Mahabharata* of India are episodic.

3. The cyclic plot: Plot structures usually reflect the values and philosophy of the societies that produce them. As an outgrowth of a modern philosophy that suggests that there seem to be no answers for life's dilemmas and that our problems cannot be neatly resolved, some dramas employ the cyclic plot. They are intentionally unresolved; instead, they end much the way they began, suggesting the futility of life. Modern writers of the theater of the absurd, such as Samuel Beckett and Eugene Ionesco, employ cyclic plots in such works as *The Bald Soprano*, the last line of which is exactly the same as its first.

Is it possible to have a "plotless" play? Because they are often meditations on life, many Noh plays seem to have little plot, as Western audiences understand the term. Many recent Western plays adhere to the theory that conventional artistic forms—for example, the traditional plot—no longer reflect the reality of human experience. Beckett's *Waiting for Godot*, for instance, has no discernible plot. One critic even argued that it is a play in which nothing happens—twice! In Tom Stoppard's witty retelling of the Hamlet myth, *Rosencrantz and Guildenstern Are Dead* (1967), one of the characters exclaims, "Incidents! All we get are incidents. Is it too much to ask for a little sustained action?" Stoppard's line reflects the trend toward incidental plotting in much contemporary drama, which often portrays people living multiple realities that may not be comprehensibly connected.

FORUM

"From *The Poetics*"

ARISTOTLE

The following excerpts from The Poetics *contain Aristotle's essential analysis of the tragic impulse and the elements of drama. The classic definition of Western tragedy may be found in part 2. Parts 4–10 contain an analysis of plot, character is discussed at the end of part 10, and the role of the Chorus is addressed in part 11.*

1. Epic poetry and Tragedy, Comedy also and Dithyrambic poetry, and the music of the flute and of the lyre in their forms, are all in their general conception modes of imitation.

2. Tragedy, then, is an imitation of an action that is serious, complete, and of a certain magnitude; in language embellished with each kind of artistic ornament, the several kinds being found in separate parts of the play; in the form of action, not of narrative; through pity and fear affecting the proper purgation of these emotions.

3. Every Tragedy, therefore, must have six parts, which parts determine its quality—namely, Plot, Character, Diction, Thought, Spectacle, Song.

4. The Plot, then, is the first principle, and as it were, the soul of a tragedy: Character holds the second place. A similar fact is seen in painting. The most beautiful colours, laid on confusedly, will not give as much pleasure as the chalk outline of a portrait. Thus Tragedy is the imitation of an action, and of the agents mainly with a view of the action.

5. Unity of plot does not, as some persons think, consist in the unity of the hero. For infinitely various are the incidents in one man's life which cannot be reduced to unity; and so, too, there are many actions of one man out of which we cannot make one action, hence the error, as it appears, of all poets who have composed a Heracleid, Theseid, or other poems of the kind. They imagine that as Heracles was one man, the story of Heracles must also be a unity. But Homer, as in all

From *Aristotle's Theory of Poetry and Fine Art*, translated by Samuel Henry Butcher. New York: MacMillan, 1895.

else he is of surpassing merit, here too—whether from art or natural genius—seems to have happily discerned the truth. In composing *The Odyssey* he did not include all the adventures of Odysseus—such as his wound on Parnassus, or his feigned madness at the mustering or the host—incidents between which there was no necessary or probable connexion: but he made *The Odyssey*, and likewise *The Iliad*, to centre round an action that in our sense of the word is one. As therefore, in the other imitative arts, the imitation is one when the object action and that a whole, the structural union of the parts being such that, if any one of them is displaced or removed, the whole will be disjointed and disturbed. For a thing whose presence or absence makes no visible difference, is not an organic part of the whole.

6. It is, moreover, evident from what has been said, that it is not the function of the poet to relate what has happened, but what may happen—what is possible according to the law of probability or necessity. The poet and the historian differ not by writing in verse or in prose. The work of Herodotus might be put into verse, and it would still be a species of history, with metre no less than without it. The true difference is that one relates what has happened, the other what may happen. Poetry, therefore, is a more philosophical and a higher thing than history: for poetry tends to express the universal, history the particular. By the universal I mean how a person of a certain type will on occasion speak or act, according to the law of probability or necessity; and it is this universality at which poetry aims in the names she attaches to the personages. The particular is—for example—what Alcibiades did or suffered.

7. Plots are either Simple or Complex, for the actions in real life, of which the plots are an imitation, obviously show a similar distinction. An action which is one and continuous in the sense above defined, I call Simple, when the change of fortune takes place without Reversal of the Situation and without Recognition. A Complex action is one in which the change is accompanied by such Reversal, or by Recogni-

Regardless of how we classify their plots, plays do have structures that organize experience, and even contemporary scripts retain elemental devices you should know as you read or watch plays. Technically, the elements noted in the following discussion compose the "well-made play," a form that was especially popular in the nineteenth century. Still, these elements may be found, however subtly, in most plays, Western and Eastern, classical and modern:

- The *exposition* provides the necessary background of time, place, plot, character, and social context for understanding the play and its issues. Necessarily, there is considerable exposition early in a play, but playwrights also distribute the exposition throughout.

tion, or by both. These last should arise from the internal structure of the plot, so that what follows should be the necessary or probable result of the preceding action. It makes all the difference whether any given event is a case of propter hoc or post hoc. Reversal of the Situation is a change by which the action veers round to its opposite, subject always to our rule of probability or necessity. Thus in the Oedipus, the messenger comes to cheer Oedipus and free him from his alarms about his mother, but by revealing who he is, he produces the opposite effect.

8. Recognition, as the name indicates, is a change from ignorance to knowledge, producing love or hate between the persons destined by the poet for good or bad fortune. The best form of recognition is coincident with a Reversal of the Situation, as in the Oedipus.

9. A perfect tragedy would, as we have seen, be arranged not on the simple but on the complex plan. It should, moreover, imitate actions which excite pity and fear, this being the distinctive mark of tragic imitation. It follows plainly, in the first place, that the change of fortune presented must not be the spectacle of a virtuous man brought from prosperity to adversity: for this moves neither pity nor fear: it merely shocks us. Nor, again, that of a bad man passing adversity to prosperity: for nothing can be more alien to the spirit of Tragedy: it possesses no single tragic quality; it neither satisfies the moral sense nor calls forth pity and fear. Nor, again, should the downfall of the utter villain be exhibited. A plot of this kind would, doubtless, satisfy the moral sense, but it would inspire pity nor fear; for pity is aroused by unmerited misfortune, fear by the misfortune of a man like ourselves. Such an event, therefore, will neither be pitiful nor terrible. There remains, then, the character between these two extremes—that of a man who is not eminently good and just, yet whose misfortune is brought about not by vice or depravity, but by some error of frailty. He must be one who is highly renowned and prosperous—a personage like Oedipus, Thyestes, or other illustrious men of such families. A well-constructed plot should therefore be single in its issue, rather than double as some maintain. The change of fortune should not be from bad to good, but reversely, from good to bad. It should come about as the result not of vice, but of some error of frailty, in a character either such as we have described, or better rather than worse.

10. Fear and pity may be aroused by spectacular means; but they may also result from the inner structure of the piece, which is the better way, and indicates a superior poet. For the plot ought to be so constructed that, even without aid of the eye, he who hears the tale told will thrill with horror and melt to pity at what takes place. This is the impression we should receive from hearing the story Oedipus. But to produce this effect by the mere spectacle is a less artistic method, and dependent on extraneous aids. Those who employ spectacular means to create a sense not of terrible but only of the monstrous, are strangers to the purpose of tragedy; for we must not only demand of tragedy any and every kind of pleasure, but only that which is proper to it. And since the pleasure which the poet should afford is that which comes through pity and fear through imitation, it is evident that this quality must be impressed upon the incidents.

In respect of Character there are four things to be aimed at. First, and most important, it must be good. Now any speech or action that manifests moral purpose of any kind will be expressive of character: the character will be good if the purpose is good. This rule is relative to each class. Even a woman may be good, and also a slave; though the woman may be said to be an inferior being, and the slave quite worthless. The second thing to aim at is propriety. There is a type of manly valor; but valor in a woman, or unscrupulous cleverness, is inappropriate. Thirdly, character must be true to life: for this is a distinct thing from goodness and propriety, as here described. The fourth point is consistency; for though the subject of the imitation, who suggested the type, be inconsistent, still he must be consistently inconsistent.

11. The Chorus too should be regarded as one of the actors: it should be an integral part of the whole, and share in the action, in the manner not of *Euripides* but of *Sophocles*. As for the later poets, their choral songs pertain little to the subject of the piece as to that of any other tragedy. They are, therefore, sung as mere interludes—a practice first begun by Agathon. Yet what difference is there between introducing such choral interludes, and transferring a speech, of even a whole act, from one play to another?

It may be accurately said the whole play is expository because we are constantly learning about the events in the Wright house; even the final line provides a key piece of exposition. Mr. Hale's first speech is a traditional "exposition speech" because it summarizes the events of the previous day; the subsequent conversation between Hale and the County Attorney provides considerable exposition.

- The *point of attack* (or the *inciting incident*) clearly marks the moment at which the play's principal conflict begins. Think of it as a "point of no return" at which the protagonist and the antagonist begin the battle that constitutes the majority of the play's action.

> The point of attack may be found in Hale's long speech in which he recounts his conversation with Mrs. Wright. Specifically, it occurs when Minnie tells Hale that Mr. Wright is "dead." Note that Glaspell reinforces this moment by having Hale repeat the word "dead," which is italicized. The subsequent action of the play involves finding out why Wright was killed—and, of course, who killed him.

- The *complication* (or *rising action*) depicts the struggle between the opposing forces through a series of crises, which move the action forward. In a multiact play, each scene usually mirrors the construction of the entire play. It has its own exposition, point of attack, and complication.

> Obviously a short play such as *Trifles* cannot have a lengthy series of complications (or 'rising action'). Still, there is an upward movement in the action, marked by each succeeding conversation:
> - The interrogation of Mrs. Peters by the Attorney and the Sheriff;
> - The lengthy exchange between Mrs. Hale and Mrs. Peters in which the women raise questions about the murder and Minnie's life with John Wright (which is contrasted with recollections of her life before the marriage);
> - The discovery of the dead bird.

- The *climax* usually occurs late in the play and marks the moment in which the protagonist's imminent triumph or defeat is clearly decided. This moment is sometimes referred to as the *obligatory scene* because we expect a final confrontation between the protagonist and the antagonist and its resolution. Most climactic scenes offer the protagonist a moment of discovery (or recognition) to enhance the instructive power of the drama.

> The climax of *Trifles* occurs when the two women realize that Minnie killed her husband because he silenced the songbird.

- The *denouement* (or *falling action*) "ties up" the loose ends of the plot. The fate of the characters is revealed, harmony is restored, and the future is determined. Modern playwrights often avoid denouements to maintain ambiguity and mystery.

> The denouement is quite subtle in *Trifles:* the women engage in a conspiracy of silence to protect Minnie's "story." Mrs. Hale's last line ("We call it—knot it") is, ironically, a veiled threat in which the women assert their independence from the men.

Character

As pleasurable as it may be to hear a good tale well told, it is ultimately the human element that engages us at the highest level in the theater. Though plays are about ideas, we respond to a play emotionally because it portrays human beings for which we have some feeling. In 1839 the German writer Friedrich Hebbel cautioned that "bad playwrights with good heads give us their scheme instead of characters and their system instead of passions." Aristotle reminds us that character is "that which reveals moral purpose." Even notorious villains such as Tartuffe or Shakespeare's Richard III intrigue us because we see in them the darker side of human nature.

There may be a finite number of plots, but there are infinite possibilities in the creation of character. Given our modern fascination with psychology, character has in many ways supplanted plot as drama's primary element, particularly in Western drama, which characteristically emphasizes the individual. Eastern drama, by contrast, tends to focus on the more general aspects of human behavior. *The Nātyaśātra*, in fact, counsels Indian dramatists to portray the generality of humanity, while the actor-dancers in the theater of China, Japan, and India train arduously to learn the gestures and movements of particular kinds of characters such as the warrior, the maiden, or the beggar.

While classical writers have rendered fascinating portraits of the human mind under duress (e.g., in the Kabuki play *Kanjinchō*, Benkei is deeply troubled that he must beat his master even though the act saves the Prince's life), in the West the "psychological drama" is primarily a product of the modern age, though *Hamlet* surely qualifies as a psychological drama. Anton Chekhov's Russian dramas did much to advance the way we perceive dramatic character. His plays are a particular challenge because there is little overt action in them; as we listen to their seemingly mundane conversations, we realize that his characters *are* the drama.

Two particular categories of characters have served the theater well for thousands of years:

- *Stock characters* are instantly recognizable types, such as the bragging soldier, the sassy servant, the conniving trickster, the wise elder, the ingenue (or youth), and the grumpy old man. Such types are frequently servants to the plot; that is, they exist to advance the story efficiently because they do not need great psychological depth. They are often secondary to the principal characters, though many plays are entirely devoted to stock characters alone. For instance, the ancient Greek comic playwright Menander wrote a play about the grumpy old man (*The Grouch*) that serves as the prototype of the character we associate with Walter Matthau in such films as *Grumpy Old Men*. Molière favored sassy serving maids (a role the Chinese would refer to as a *hua tan*); Dorine in *Tartuffe* is the epitome of such a character. Serious plays, even tragedies, also rely on stock characters. Teiresias, the blind prophet who could "see" what others could not, was a staple of many Greek tragedies. Prior to the twentieth century, plays were often written for specific acting troupes, called "stock companies," comprising performers who had perfected certain types. You will have little trouble recognizing stock characters, as much television fare depends on them.

> Because *Trifles* is a modern realistic drama, it does not rely on overtly stock characters. Still, you recognize several traditional "types" necessary for a small-town drama: the sheriff, the talkative neighbor (Mr. Hale), the "prim" old women (Mrs. Peters and Mrs. Hale) who, ostensibly, are only extensions of their husbands. The best-drawn character in the play, however, is the one we never see: Minnie Foster Wright. The women's conversation gradually reveals a fully drawn character, capable of singing beautifully or murdering violently. Minnie is the archetype of the abused woman, who—like Medea—seeks revenge.

- *Archetypal characters* are recurring figures that speak to all peoples of all times. They reside in our "collective unconscious," according to Swiss psychologist Carl Jung, who calls them "primordial images." Archetypal characters transcend the particulars of a given story and its culture to become universal symbols of virtues, vices, and human dilemmas. For instance, Prometheus is the archetype of the individual who sacrifices himself for the benefit of a greater good; that we often refer to such figures as Promethean suggests their archetypal nature. Hamlet, Sigismund in *Life's a Dream*, Olunde in *Death and the King's*

Horseman, and even Simba in *The Lion King* are similar in many ways: Each is a young prince struggling to mature while at odds with his elders, his society, and particularly himself. Oedipus is the archetype of the sighted man who cannot see the truth until he loses his sight. Throughout this anthology you will read about many characters who are blind to truths about themselves and others when they are most prosperous: Orgon, King Dushyanta, Nora Helmer, and Willy Loman.

In most plays we look for growth and change in principal characters. Characters usually change because something profound happens to them. Aristotle referred to this moment of change as a *reversal* of fortune, which usually precipitates or results from a *recognition* (or, to put it in archetypal terms, a moment when the blindness is lifted).

Trifles actually contains two sets of recognition and reversal:
- Within the play itself the two women recognize the truth about Minnie's abusive husband and why she had to kill him; then they form a conspiracy of silence to protect their friend. This is a reversal because they choose to no longer be submissive women and defy the men with their conspiracy of silence.
- In the "offstage" story, Minnie finally "recognizes" that her husband is an abusive lout (when she "discovers" the dead bird); she "reverses" her situation by killing Wright.

As you read these plays, be alert for those characters who change most dramatically in the course of the play (invariably it is the protagonist), and the precise moment that prompts the change. In the contemporary theater, characters often change little because playwrights depict people trapped by their own inertia. Their plight is that they cannot change. Chekhov, Beckett, and Tennessee Williams provide significant examples of such characters.

Today playwrights often explore the manner in which we live multifaceted lives defined by those with whom we come in contact. To our lover we may be one thing, to a neighbor another, and to an employer yet another. Accordingly, playwrights now frequently portray characters as fragmented beings, the many parts of which suggest the whole. Thus several actors may portray a single character or, conversely, a single actor may portray several characters within the same play. In *Angels in America, Part One: Millennium Approaches*, Tony Kushner demands that the same actor play multiple roles for thematic purpose (see Chapter 6).

One must also consider the phenomenon of the "anticharacter," another contemporary device meant to illustrate that the industrial world has stripped humans of their identity and individualism. Characters may now appear as generic ciphers, often bearing such nondescript names as "He" or "the Woman," or even worse, "A" or "B." As with plot and the other elements of drama, characterization can be an indicator of the way a society sees itself. Edward Albee's bitter satire on contemporary life in the United States, *The American Dream*, typifies absurdist characterization—people are reduced to generic types—as it is rendered by many contemporary writers.

Thought

For Aristotle, thought (sometimes referred to as "idea" or "theme") was a means of testing the idea the play posited through "proof and refutation," a reminder that plays were contests of conflicting ideas. Today, of course, most plays use words to argue their ideas. The German playwright Bertolt Brecht is especially noted for the lively debates in his plays, such as *The Good Woman of Setzuan*, which ends with various characters pleading their case to the gods (see Chapter 5).

Thought, beliefs, values—there are many terms to be used here—vary from culture to culture and are subject to change and reevaluation. Because most of us are products of Western culture, there is a tendency to evaluate the "thoughts" raised by plays from other cultures in terms of our own experience. This is certainly one of the issues raised in Wole Soyinka's Nigerian drama, *Death and the King's Horseman*, as British colonialists attempt to impose their value system on a Yoruban tribal leader. The introductions to the plays in this collection attempt to provide some historical and cultural contexts that help you understand non-Western dramatists—and, of course, those from the West whose culture we may not readily understand.

The Roman orator and artist Horace advised a would-be dramatist that it was the function of the poet-dramatist to "instruct and delight" (*docere et dulcere*). At the heart of his argument was the very issue under consideration here: theater exists to provide learning experiences while entertaining us. In earliest times, instruction most often centered on religion or the life cycle. Today plays from both the East and the West often attempt to influence audiences concerning political and social issues; indeed, a play can serve as an instrument of social criticism. Tony Kushner's *Angels in America, Part One: Millennium Approaches* addresses the AIDS crisis and American politics, while Anton Chekhov's *The Cherry Orchard* examines the problems of Russian society as it underwent radical changes in its lifestyles at the turn of the twentieth century. As a general rule we can say plays that only teach are usually heavy-handed, and plays that only entertain are ultimately less satisfying than those that achieve a balance between thought and diversion. Plays that lack profundity can still be good, even great, theater. The slapstick farce, for instance, has little time for philosophy and only the most elemental moralizing. Yet the very nature of farce has much to say about our place in the world, random accidents of chance, and our ability to triumph over chaos.

Despite its brevity and simple plot, *Trifles* is a complex play that explores a number of ideas such as spousal abuse, the status of women, and justifiable homicide. And like many modern realistic plays, it raises questions rather than providing answers:
- Is it justifiable for a woman to resort to killing an abusive spouse?
- Are Mrs. Peters and Mrs. Hale culpable for concealing evidence, however "trifling," to protect Minnie?

One of the healthiest aspects of the contemporary theater is the rich diversity of human thought. Never has drama been so truly global in both its content (thought) and expression. Notice, for instance, the mix of Western and non-Western thought and performance techniques as you read *The Good Woman of Setzuan*—or see *The Lion King*.

Diction

By "diction" Aristotle meant language, and although theater in its literal sense is about "seeing," the verbal dimension is central to the dramatic arts. Hamlet tells us that "tonight we'll hear a play," an expression that was in common usage well into the nineteenth century. Ironically, as we enter a new millennium, we are a much more visually oriented society than almost any other since the invention of the printing press. We are constantly bombarded with visual stimuli, most commonly in film and on television. In the era of MTV the image reigns, and thus "hearing" or reading a play, especially a classic, may be a challenge to those accustomed to quick cuts, wipes, and montages. Well-crafted writing still retains the power to spark an audience's imagination. A Prakrit verse from ancient India celebrates the power of diction in the theater:

> *Glory to speech!*
> *For she sits in the mouth of poets*
> *And creates whole worlds anew,*
> *Laughing at the ancient creator!*

In most cultures plays were first written in verse, for several reasons. First, music was an integral part of the theatrical experience, and so it remains in most non-Western drama. Thus, playwrights wrote plays in verse because it best suited the musical dimension of the theater. Furthermore, most early plays dealt with larger-than-life characters that required heightened language. Audiences, then as now, enjoyed the sound of a well-crafted, majestic line, as in Shakespeare's *Hamlet*:

> What a piece of work is a man, how noble in reason, how infinite in faculties, in form and moving how express and admirable, in action how like an angel, in apprehension how like a god: the beauty of the world, the paragon of animals . . .

In the early twentieth century, Bernard Shaw captivated audiences with witty, well-written lines, such as these from *Man and Superman*:

> Are we agreed that Life is a force which was made of innumerable experiments in organizing itself; that the mammoth and the man, the mouse and the megatherium, the flies and the fleas and the Fathers of the Church, are more or less successful attempts to build that raw force into higher and higher individuals, the ideal individual being omnipotent, omniscient, infallible, and withal completely, unilludedly self-conscious: in short, a god?

Modern realistic drama, on the other hand, often attempts to replicate the rhythms, cadences, and especially the vocabulary of everyday speech, as seen in this passage from David Mamet's *American Buffalo*, an award-winning play of the 1970s:

> We're talking about money for chrissake, huh? We're talking about cards. Friendship is friendship, and a wonderful thing, and I am all for it. I have never said different, and you know me on this point. Okay. But let's just keep it separate huh, let's just keep the two apart, and maybe we can deal with each other like some human beings.

The point here is not to disparage modern drama, but to illustrate that it is a function of drama to show, in Shakespeare's words, "the age and body of the time his form and pressure," an elegant way of saying that the theater reflects the manners, mores, and speech of the audience for whom the plays are written.

In the late twentieth century some brilliantly innovative writers have transformed the language of the street into a theatrical vocabulary that is as poetic as that of the great writers of the past. Read Sam Shepard's inventive, richly poetical use of the "hip" language of rock 'n' roll in *Tooth of Crime* (1972) as two rock stars "slug it out" with words:

> You could use a little cow flop on yer shoes, boy. Yo' music's in yo' head. You a blind minstrel with a phony shuffle. You got a wound gapin' 'tween the chords and the pickin.' Chuck Berry can't even mend you up. You doin' a pantomime in the eye of a hurricane. Ain't even got the sense to signal for help. You lost the barrelhouse, you lost the honkey-tonk. You lost your feelings in a suburban country club the first time they ask you to play "Risin' River Blues" for the debutante ball. You ripped your own self off and now all you got is yo' poison to call yo' gift. You a punk chump with a sequin nose and you'll need more'n a Les Paul Gibson to bring you home.

More recently, Suzan-Lori Parks draws on the colloquial speech of African Americans to extraordinary effect in such plays as *The Death of the Last Black Man in the Whole Entire World* (1990):

> I kin tell whats mines by whets gots my looks. Ssmymethod. Try it by testin it and it turns out true. Every time. Fool proofly. Look down at my foot and wonder if its mine. Foot mine? I kin

ask it and foot answers back with uh "yes Sir"—not like you and me Say "yes Sir" but us "yes Sir" peculiar tuh thuh foot.

As you read or see a play, keep in mind the purpose of the language employed by the playwright. Whether the language is lofty and poetic, colloquial or mundane, there is invariably a dramatic reason for it. Even the natural speech of contemporary drama is as calculated and painstakingly written as the most florid poetry in classical drama because language reflects character. Successful playwrights find a "voice" for each character in the play. Beware the play in which everyone speaks alike.

Trifles uses the language of everyday speech, its rhythms and cadences. People onstage talk very much as the people who attended the play might talk, often in incomplete sentences and phrases. Note that Glaspell attempts to replicate colloquial speech in such expressions as "dunno" (i.e. "don't know") and "ain't it." Though it is written in (then) contemporary prose, Glaspell's language has a rustic, poetic quality in such lines as: "We live close together and we live far apart. We all go through the same things—it's all just a different kind of the same thing." Also, be aware that silences are important throughout the play. At times, the absence of language communicates the play's meaning.

Plays are not usually written for reading audiences, but for professional actors, sometimes for particular actors. A playwright knows that an intelligent, talented actor can wrench extraordinary meaning out of a word. Thus, when you read a play it is crucial that you try to hear the lines in your mind's ear, or try reading it aloud. There are actually three "texts" that you must confront. You will be reading a *text*—words on a page. From that you will derive the *context*—the social situation, the character relationships, the ideas being contested. Out of this grows the *subtext* of the play—the underlying meaning of the words the characters choose to use. In classical plays subtext is less subtle: these are people who wear their hearts on their sleeves and we can often take what they say at face value. In the modern theater, where characters often hide (or are unsure of) their true feelings and thoughts, subtext becomes far more important.

Dramatic speech takes many forms. Our earliest plays, contain long, poetic passages, a reminder that much drama may have developed from hymns to the gods or songs to mark an event central to the life of a community. Eventually *dialogue*—the exchange of lines between two or more characters—dominated the play script, though *monologues* (in which a character speaks a lengthy passage to other characters) and *soliloquies* (in which a character, usually alone onstage, speaks to the audience) are still a part of the theater. The monologue and soliloquy became less prominent in early modern plays that attempted to portray life realistically. Yet playwrights, realists and otherwise, have always appreciated that the monologue (like the soliloquy) is a conduit to an individual's consciousness. Beckett's short play *Rockaby* (1981) perhaps best captures this phenomenon: a single character sits in a rocking chair listening to her own monologue about impending death. Many playwrights specialize in the dramatic monologue: Jane Martin, Eric Bogosian, and John Leguizamo are among the best known. Anna Deavere Smith's *Twilight: Los Angeles, 1992* comprises more than 60 monologues. In many ways, the resurgence of the monologic drama brings the theater full cycle; we have again entered the domain of the ancient storyteller.

While play scripts consist almost exclusively of dialogues and monologues, *stage direction* has become an integral part of the playwright's diction (although Aristotle never read a stage direction). The ancient Greek playwrights, like Shakespeare and Molière, like Kālidāsa in the courts of India and Zeami in feudal Japan, had no need for stage directions, as they worked directly with the actors when their plays were first staged. Stage directions today are important pieces of exposition that can describe setting, costume, appearance, psychological states, and other things that enable you to imagine the play in your mind's eye.

Stage directions that have become commonplace in the modern theater are *pause* and *silence*. Judiciously used, silence can be a powerful means of communication in the theater, and therefore it is an important element of a play's diction. Harold Pinter, the much-imitated

British playwright, has said, "It is in the silence that my characters are most evident to me." Be sure to "listen" for the silences as you read such scripts as Chekhov's *The Cherry Orchard*.

Music

Aristotle included music among his six elements largely because the only plays he knew employed music, song, and dance. He recognized that music also manifests the human desire for harmony in the world, and thus it held "chief place among the embellishments" of a drama. In the West music became less prominent in the realistic theater and, in many cases, disappeared completely. It remains among the most characteristic elements of Asian drama. The Peking opera, the Japanese Noh and Kabuki theaters, and much Indian theater can rightfully be classified as forms of musical theater. South African township theater invariably uses popular *mbaquanga* music to underscore its action.

Actually, actors, directors, and designers constantly use musical terminology as they prepare even the most realistic plays. They talk of "tempo" and "rhythm" in speeches and scenes, and they cite the "orchestration" of voices as they work. Mamet's monosyllabic dialogue establishes mesmerizing rhythms that are as central to the experience of his plays as iambic pentameter was to Shakespeare's. Actors, especially comedians, are obsessed with getting their "timing" down, as are lighting designers who use "fade counts" to dim the lights. Directors cast shows for the musicality of the actors' voices and the harmonious (or perhaps dissonant) blend of their vocal qualities. The "music" of a play is perhaps the most difficult of drama's six elements to appreciate while reading, but it is there, and an awareness of a play's music enriches our experience.

> Although Glaspell did not script music into the play, *Trifles* (like most dramas) benefits from the blend of contrasting voices. This is especially important here because the "bass" tones of the Sheriff and the other men are countered by the lighter, hushed tones of the two women. The aural dialectic is crucial to the meaning of the play as the men speak in loud, authoritative voices (which adds to the play's irony), while the women (who know the truth) speak in soft (pianissimo) tones. The director of the play needs to pay special attention to the sound of the voices when casting *Trifles*.

Spectacle

Spectacle refers to those elements of a production that appeal to the eye. While scenery, costume, makeup, masks, and lighting are the principal elements of spectacle, the presence of the actors, their movements, and their body language also contribute to the visual appeal of a play. Aristotle actually dismissed spectacle as the "least artistic" of the six elements of drama because it depends "more on the art of the stage machinist than the poet." However, he also recognized that spectacle has "an emotional attraction of its own." You are no doubt aware of the importance of costume, scenery, and lighting in a play, but also consider gesture, movement, and the physical relationship of the actors to each other and to the audience. The very size, shape, and configuration of the theater space affect the way we react to a play. As you read the plays in this collection, try to picture the scenery and costumes, consider where lighting might enhance a dramatic moment, and imagine the movements and gestures of the characters.

> Although the play does not use spectacular scenery, the many objects that dominate the simple setting create the atmosphere of the play and provide clues about the murder. Simply, this is a play that cannot be produced without careful attention to visual objects. Glaspell's detailed description of Minnie's kitchen is more than an attempt to create a realistic ambience; the opening stage direction is rife with clues about the mysteries of the Wright household. Also, there is "spectacle" in the women's furtive glances as the men clumsily traipse about the house searching for evidence.

Is it possible to have effective theater without spectacle? Yes. It can also exist without playwrights, directors, designers, and others. In reality, there are only four things necessary to create theater:

- An *idea* to be communicated, though it need not be scripted; there is a rich history of improvised theater.
- A *performer* such as an actor, a singer, a dancer, a mime, or a storyteller.
- An *audience;* the audience may consist of one person, without whom there cannot truly be a theater event. That is how important you are to the making of theater.
- A *space* in which the previous three elements come together. (See the diagram on the essential elements of theater.)

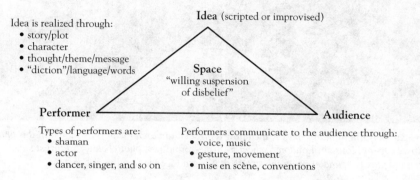

The space need not be a formal theater or a stage. Peter Brook has said, "I can take any space, an empty space, and create theater." And he has—on the deserts of Iran, in the market square of an African village, and in an abandoned railway depot in Paris. A cliché reminds us that all an actor needs to create theater are "two boards and a passion."

The Principal Genres of Drama

Genre is a Western literary term that classifies a work into a distinctive type according to the treatment of the subject matter and the perspective of the writer. Like Polonius, the counselor to King Claudius in *Hamlet*, one can overclassify plays into "tragedy, comedy, history, pastoral, pastoral-comical, historical-pastoral, tragical-historical, tragical-comical-historical-pastoral. . . ." For expediency, let us limit the major kinds of Western plays to three primary genres—tragedy, comedy, and tragicomedy. Subgenres such as the comedy of manners and satire will be discussed with specific plays. And it bears noting that in the late twentieth century, playwrights frequently subvert traditional genres by parodying them, melding them for shock effect, or otherwise negating standard principles to extend the boundaries of drama. We shall, however, begin with the orthodox before proceeding to some striking alternatives.

Non-Western drama, especially in Asia, which was (until recently) less influenced by Western drama, has distinctive genres based largely on traditional modes of performance, as opposed to the West's classification of genres according to the serious or comic treatment of the themes. In India, for instance, plays are divided into ten major types, according to subject matter. The *nataka*, the most important, is a play in four to ten acts that portrays mythological beings (such as Śakuntalā and King Dushyanta), and that appeals primarily to the erotic and/or heroic sentiments (*rasas*) in the audience. Given our cultural experience, most of us in the West would likely classify *Śakuntalā* as a romance (a subset of tragicomedy), and one can make the case that it is indeed a romance. However, we ought to be open to the aesthetics of other cultures as we learn about and discuss their theater and drama. Specific non-Western genres will be discussed in conjunction with particular plays.

Actors can perform in many spaces, including a proscenium arch theater, as shown in this photo of the Royal Opera House in London, a theater-in-the-round (see photo below), a thrust stage (see photo on next page), and even on the streets of Nigeria (see photo on next page).

A theater-in-the-round: Krasnaya Presnya Theater, Moscow.

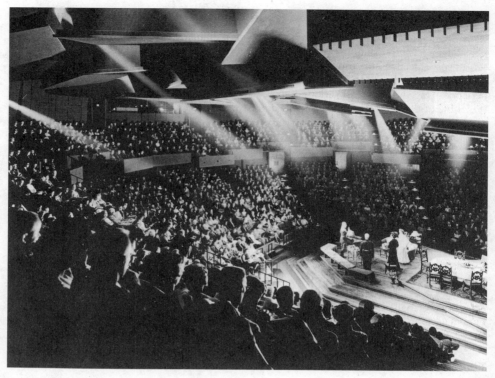

A thrust stage: Guthrie Theater, Minneapolis.

Street theater: Oshogbo Center for the Arts, Nigeria.

Tragedy Versus Comedy

Tragedy and comedy, the oldest and most elemental dramatic genres, reflect the way in which playwrights wish to examine human endeavors. Horace Walpole, the British philosopher, observed that tragedy is for "those who feel," while comedy is "for those who think," a distinction that suggests the degree to which the audience is involved in or detached from the theater experience. Tragedy, or at least serious drama, asks us to engage ourselves more fully in the emotional life of the central character, while comedy asks us to stand back and judge the folly of a play's characters.

Paradoxically, tragedy, for all its gravity and depiction of suffering and death, begins with an optimistic premise: as human beings, we possess nearly unlimited potential. Tragedy cautions, however, that we are only "godlike" and not gods ourselves. Comedy, for all the laughter and pleasure it brings, stems from the darker notion that we are fallible and foible-ridden. The mischievous Puck best invokes this comic premise in *A Midsummer Night's Dream* when he exclaims, "Lord, what fools these mortals be!"

Whatever their views of humanity, both genres share two common premises: things do go wrong and we are accountable for our actions. Causality, the recognition that actions lead to other actions, is central to the telling of a story, be it serious or comic. In tragedy actions have serious consequences that lead to suffering and death; in comedy, though there may be momentary threats of dire consequences, transgressions are ultimately forgiven and misfortune gives way to celebration. In some modern dramas, on the other hand, traditional notions of causality are challenged; the theater of the absurd (see Chapter 5), for instance, suggests that human actions—and misery—cannot necessarily be ascribed to the cause-and-effect principle. In the absurdist world, randomness reigns.

Tragedy

We offer here an essentially Western theory of tragedy. Because tragedy (and much comedy) is grounded in a culture's belief systems, it may be perceived differently in other cultures. Wole Soyinka, the Nigerian playwright and dramatic theorist, writes that

> the artist labors from an in-built, intuitive responsibility not only to himself but his roots. The test of the narrowness or the breadth of his vision however is whether it is his accidental situations which he tries to stretch to embrace his race and society or the fundamental truths of his community which inform his vision and enable him to acquire even a prophetic insight into the evolution of that society.

Soyinka's insight extends to readers and audiences as well: an audience's appreciation of a work is tempered by its roots. However, a knowledge of other cultures and the art they produce increases an appreciation of their work.

Again Aristotle's *Poetics* is the traditional starting point for an understanding of Western tragedy. Even those, such as Bertolt Brecht and Agusto Boal, who have refuted Aristotle's precepts, have had to acknowledge that he provided the foundation on which Western dramatic theory is built. Aristotle defined *tragedy* as "an imitation of an action that is serious, complete, and of a certain magnitude; in language embellished with each kind of artistic ornament, the several kinds being found in separate parts of the play; in the form of action, not of narration; through pity and fear effecting the proper purgation of these emotions." Consider two key components of this definition, the first and last phrases:

". . . an imitation of an action . . ."
Noting that we are innately mimetic, Aristotle argued that the "imitation" (i.e., the play) is not life itself but only a metaphor for life in which an actor plays another being. Though "action" (*praxis*) refers to a play's narrative line, Aristotle observed that the artistic and selective arrangement of the events (*mythos*) affect an audience's intellectual and emotional responses. Tragic action traces the "fall" of an individual from prosperity to misery, usually through an

Although the traditional Greek masks of comedy and tragedy are well known in the West, a comic mask from India (above) and a tragic mask from Japan (next page) symbolize the universality of drama's two major genres.

error in judgment. The tragic impulse may be seen in King Dushyanta's lament in the Sanskrit drama *The Recognition of Śakuntalā*:

> *Each day of our own life we slip and fall into error*
> *Through negligence that we are unaware of;*
> *How then can we fully know what paths*
> *The life of each one of our subjects takes?*

Even as tragic heroes fall, there is a corresponding counterthrust in which they move from ignorance to knowledge. This schematic portrays the tragic action:

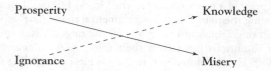

Prosperity → **Knowledge**

Ignorance → **Misery**

Two major principles are at work in this diagram: *reversal* and *recognition*. The downward (falling) movement from prosperity to misery is, in effect, a reversal (*peripeteia*) as things turn out differently and more disastrously for the tragic protagonist than anticipated. At the same time there is a recognition in the upward movement from ignorance to knowledge that brings understanding to both the protagonist and to the audience that watches the calamitous fall. Aristotle was careful to note that "the fall" must not happen to a thoroughly "virtuous man"

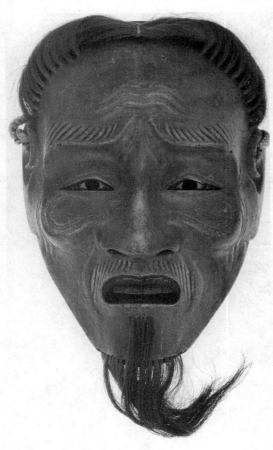

Tragic mask from Japan.

because this would "merely shock us." In life we know that good people are often the victims of terrible accidents, but tragedy as an art form does not deal with random accidents. It makes misfortune probable, even necessary. Nor does tragedy deal with the demise of "the utter villain." Though this satisfies our sense of morality and justice, it does not inspire pity and fear. The tragic hero, Aristotle says, ought to be one who is "not eminently good and just," yet one whose "misfortune is brought about not by vice and depravity, but by some error or frailty." In short the hero is one like ourselves and one in whom we can invest sympathy. Aristotle's observation that tragic heroes ought to be "highborn" may be attributed to the hierarchical society in which he lived. Arthur Miller's essay "Tragedy and the Common Man" (See Chapter 5) makes an eloquent case for democratizing the genre.

Whether highborn or common, the tragic hero makes a fateful "error in judgment." The term "tragic flaw" is often used to denote the protagonist's error, but flaw may be too strong a term. To describe the error of a tragic character, the Greeks borrowed an archer's term, *hamartia*, which means "missing the mark." It is less judgmental than "flaw" as it merely implies the tragic figure attempted to do something and was off the target. Often tragic heroes are motivated by the best of intentions but fail in their mission. As nineteenth-century German philosopher Georg W. F. Hegel pointed out, tragedy is most compelling when it involves the opposition of conflicting goods. In *Death and the King's Horseman*, for example, Pilkington's need to preserve the law of the state is pitted against Elesin's desire to observe Yoruban sacred law by accompanying the dead king in death.

Still, tragic heroes are human and thus susceptible to failure. *Hubris* (*hybris*) is most often applied to this defect of character, and it is frequently defined as "excessive pride," though this phrase is used too narrowly. To the Greeks hubris was applied to any form of excess, as it meant "swollen"; it was most often used to describe nature run amok (as in a swollen or flooded river). A popular Greek motto was "*medan agan*," or "nothing in excess," a reminder that excessive behaviors often lead to catastrophe. Pride is the most common form of excess displayed by tragic characters. It is often synonymous with the attempt to be godlike, to transcend one's mortal limitations. The idea is not exclusively Greek, of course; one finds it in myriad cultures, most famously in the biblical warning that "pride goeth before a fall." Though it is a melodrama, the Chinese opera *The Qing Ding Pearl* depicts the fall of a haughty tax collector. Tragic characters are by their very nature excessive, a mark of both their greatness and their humanity. Timid people are not likely to be tragic; heroes and heroines must be big enough to shake the universe. Like Prometheus, they must be bold enough to steal the fire of the gods, and like Oedipus they must pursue the truth whatever the price.

Ultimately, tragedy occurs not because the tragic protagonist is defeated or dies. Death is a natural part of the life process. As Hamlet says,

> If it [death] be now, 'tis not to come; if it be not to come, it will be now; if it be not now, yet it will come; the readiness is all. Since no man has aught of what he leaves, what is't to leave betimes? Let be.

The tragedy is that the heroes are defeated or die precisely at the moment when they are most "alive," that is, when they have an absolute knowledge of the great design of life. Imagine what a king an Oedipus or a Hamlet would be if he could rule with the certain knowledge of his strength and limitations. The action imitated in a tragedy brings heroes from that ignorance about themselves and their world to a profound knowledge, but only at an enormous price.

". . . through pity and fear effecting the proper purgation of these emotions."

This move from ignorance to knowledge inspires *catharsis*, and it is central to the tragic experience. (Scholars have debated this term for centuries: prior to 1931 there were over 1,400 different interpretations of catharsis, and, of course, many have been added since then.) Catharsis invariably accompanies the hero's recognition that is central to the tragic action. Much of the dignity we award tragic heroes stems from the nobility with which they accept responsibility for their actions. When Oedipus says "To this guilt I bore witness against myself" we are hearing a moment of catharsis.

Can true tragedy happen without recognition and its attendant catharsis? This is a debated point; contemporary tragicomedy involves characters who cannot (or will not) recognize their shortcomings and continue to live in ignorance. American critic Robert Brustein argues that modern "tragic heroes" are victims of psychology and sociology. Their plight may be pitiable, or more accurately pathetic. There is not the same ennobling uplift we experience in the presence of bona fide tragic heroes who face the worst life has to offer.

This passage concerning pity and fear may well be among Aristotle's most useful observations about the persuasive power of theater. He observes that in a tragedy two primary emotions are summoned. Pity implies an attraction to one (like ourselves) who is suffering, while fear suggests a retreat from an impending evil or doom. These polar feelings complement one another to form a holistic response in which:

- we are moved by the suffering of tragic heroes;
- we are sufficiently distanced so that we may judge their actions.

This dual response thus cleanses—or purges—us, and thus the audience achieves its catharsis. Aristotle, a practitioner of the healing arts, knew that a cathartic agent cleansed the body of its impurities. A tragedy was, for Aristotle, a purging device for our spirits. Gerald Else argues that purgation enhances our ability to pity the tragic "doer" rather than condemning him. Catharsis "issues a license, so to speak, which says, 'you may pity this man for he is . . . like us, a good man rather than a bad and he is free of pollution.'"

Are pity, fear, and catharsis present in plays that are not tragedies? Absolutely. In fact, the melodrama, especially in films such as *Titanic*, thrives on summoning up powerful emotions, pity and fear in particular. They then provide a cathartic ending in which the good are (usually) rewarded while the villainous are soundly and spectacularly punished. In contrast to tragedy, however, melodramas most often deal with moral issues that can be too simply reduced to "good" versus "evil." Such melodramas are invariably driven by a villainous force, rarely by the protagonist's character. In truth, the vast majority of serious plays, especially those written after the Renaissance, are not tragedies in the classical sense, even though many end with the defeat or death of the protagonist. (See Spotlight box, Melodrama and Farce.)

In many Asian countries, people believe that catastrophe in this life provides enlightenment to prepare one for a future life. (E.g., Śakuntalā believes that her misfortunes are "the consequences of some wrongdoing on my part in a former birth.") In the East, death is often viewed as a passageway to a new life and that the "fallen heroes" will enter their next lives better prepared to confront life's challenges. And in some Eastern cultures, notably India and China, tragedy—as we understand it in the West—does not exist because playwrights are expected (under the codes of Hindu and Confucian thought) to render "just" endings in which the good are rewarded and the wicked punished. Transgressors in Japanese Noh and Kabuki dramas frequently become monks who wander the earth doing good works in reparation for their misdeeds.

Comedy

According to eighteenth-century literary critic Samuel Johnson, "comedy has been unpropitious to definers" because scholars and theorists have reached little accord on the topic of what makes people laugh. Comedy, even more so than tragedy, is dependent on the mores and customs of a particular culture. This is why we can refer to "British humor" and "French farce" as identifiable entities. To further complicate the issue, there are numerous subsets of comedy (the comedy of manners, slapstick, bawdry, the grotesque, the absurd, benign comedy, sentimental comedy, and so on), often appealing to particular people at a given time in history.

The classical definition of Western comedy derives from an anonymous work, the *Tractatus Coislinianus*, composed about the second century B.C.E. It neatly parallels Aristotle's description of tragedy and may be a remnant of his teachings. If tragedy deals with actions that are "serious" and of "a certain magnitude," comedy deals with those that are "ludicrous" and "imperfect." While tragedy provokes "pity" and "fear," comedy induces "laughter" and "pleasure" (notoriously ambiguous phrases) that also "purge" the emotions of the spectators. If tragedy deals with individuals at odds with the cosmos, comedy depends on a social world in which the comic hero (or buffoon) is at odds with the norms of society.

Comedy is very much about the here and now, and as such does not always translate well for subsequent generations. In some comedies the norms of society are strictly upheld, while in others they may be exposed and overthrown as an anarchic younger generation forges a new society. The women of *Lysistrata* challenge the destructive norms espoused by the men, while the young lovers in Molière's *Tartuffe* rebel against the tyranny of their elders as they attempt to build a new society free from hypocrisy. Many classical comedies end with a marriage (or two or three), a dance, or a banquet. The Greeks referred to this as a *komos* ("joyful union") that marks a new beginning for those who have survived the chaos of the play's action. Invariably, the *komos* suggests fertility (marriages), long life (banquets), and the restoration of the community's social order (dances). Such endings likely evolved from ancient agricultural festivals, and we find variations on the *komos* in virtually all cultures. The "wine dance" that concludes the Kabuki drama *Kanjinchō* reminds us that theater in Japan might have derived from such festivals.

Whereas only a select few have the nobility of spirit to achieve tragic heroism, comedy is fundamentally democratic in that virtually all people, by nature of their folly, are candidates for comedy. As Thornton Wilder wrote in *Our Town*, "Whenever you come near the human race, there's layers and layers of nonsense." The television show *America's Funniest Home Videos* illustrates that even the most dignified person can be, under the right circumstances, wonderfully, howlingly comic.

So what is the difference between comedy and tragedy if both spring from human ignorance? On its simplest level, tragic heroes seek knowledge and play for much higher stakes to obtain it; they take on nothing less than the gods themselves on their journey of discovery. The stakes are rarely as high in comedy. In *Tartuffe* Orgon threatens his daughter with death, but the conventions of romantic comedies are such that we know that death is improbable. Comedy is indeed "much ado about nothing," although the characters involved may feel hopelessly trapped and threatened by the proceedings. But we—on our thrones outside the action—have a greater perspective and know intuitively, like Puck, that by the final act "Naught shall go ill . . . and all shall be well."

Comic characters are frequently inflexible beings whose dilemmas are brought on by their unwillingness to accept change or the predictability with which they react to a situation. In 1900 Henri Bergson, a French philosopher, observed that laughter is induced by "mechanical inelasticity," which means that the more humans behave like machines, the funnier they are. Recall Charlie Chaplin's famous walk, especially as he rounded corners, for a classic example of physical mannerisms reduced to mechanisms. Chinese folk opera features a popular character called "the hobbler" with a similarly funny, mechanical walk. Tragic figures, such as Oedipus, can also be rigid and inflexible but there is nobility in their resoluteness as they confront momentous issues. The comic hero's rigidity is out of proportion to the seriousness of the situation and is thereby laughable. Some comic characters, Orgon in *Tartuffe,* for instance, are reformed through the process of reversal and recognition, while others staunchly refuse to change, even as the society about them goes merrily on its way to a better world.

The principles of reversal and recognition are also applicable to comedy, but often in quite different ways. Comedy thrives on reversals (though not catastrophic ones) to move its intricate plots along at a brisk pace. As a general rule, comedy demands rapid pacing, both in its plotting and in its playing. A cardinal rule of the comedian is "Don't give the audience too much time to think about the improbabilities." Serious drama invites a more deliberate pace as we, like the tragic figures, reflect on the significance of the action.

Recognition is often a more nebulous element in comedy, as some characters never recognize their folly. Often recognition is imposed on the characters by an external force—a long-lost uncle, a timely letter, the disclosure of a secret, even the gods themselves stepping into the action to sort out the bumblings of the characters. To illustrate this point, consider speeches from two of Shakespeare's plays, likely written within a year of each other. Early in *Twelfth Night* the heroine, Viola, becomes aware of her dilemma: while dressed as a young man (cross-dressing is a popular convention of comedy) she has fallen in love with a duke who loves another young woman, Olivia, who—alas—has fallen in love with Viola's male countenance. At the end of act 2, scene 1 she expresses her dismay:

> *Time, thou must untangle this—not I;*
>
> *It is too hard a knot for me t'untie.*

In contrast, when Hamlet learns at the end of act 1 that his father has been murdered by his uncle and that he, alone, must right this wrong, he cries out:

> *The Time is out of joint, O cursed spite*
>
> *That ever I was born to set it right.*

These speeches epitomize a fundamental difference between comedy and tragedy. In comedy there is the implicit notion that humans may be incapable of resolving their dilemmas, that an external agent—Time or Fortune—must intervene to set things straight. Only Hamlet himself, however, can "set it right" because tragic figures must embrace their fates without flinching. Fate is not the product of peevish gods who "kill us for their sport," as Shakespeare says in *King Lear.* Oliver Taplin argues in *Greek Tragedy in Action* (1988) that Fate is a combination of the will of the gods and the will of the tragic figure. To summarize, benevolent Fortune hovers over the world of comedy waiting to restore harmony, while Fate looms large in the tragic world as it follows the hero's quest for certainty.

Tragicomedy

The German novelist Thomas Mann remarked that the great triumph of modern art is that "it has ceased to recognize the categories of tragic and comic . . . and views life as tragicomedy." Though the term is attributed to the Roman playwright Plautus in the second century B.C.E., and though we can find examples of it in the works of Euripides, Kālidāsa, Shakespeare, and

---

SPOTLIGHT   **MELODRAMA AND FARCE**

While we can usually place a particular play within one of the three primary genres of drama, there are significant subsets of each, such as high comedy, satiric comedy, the romance, and sentimental dramas. Examples of the most common types and their particular characteristics are covered in the discussion of the specific plays. Melodrama and farce, in particular, complement our understanding of tragedy and comedy.

Melodrama

Melodrama often carries a negative connotation and suggests tawdry dramas in which mustache-twirling villains tie damsels-in-distress to the railroad tracks while square-jawed heroes ride to the rescue. This is "meller-dramer," a nineteenth-century variant on the much older, more respected melodrama. In truth many plays, including some of our most esteemed tragedies, have melodramatic elements. Stripped of its cosmic implications, *Hamlet* is a pretty lurid melodrama filled with ghosts skulking about castles, cloak-and-dagger espionage, and shocking, violent deaths.

Originally, a *melo drame* was a serious play accompanied by music to heighten its emotional impact. The Chinese refer to their operas by the generic term *melodrama*, which is quite fitting given the ubiquitous use of music that underscores every action in a Chinese play. In 1775 the French political philosopher Jean-Jacques Rousseau coined the term to describe his short play *Pygmalion* (a monologue set to music). Eventually, *melodrama* was applied to a sensational play in which:

- ingenious plots produce moments of danger for the protagonists;
- characters are thinly drawn symbols of singular virtues and vices pitted against one another;
- morality is reduced to its most simple elements;
- the emotional appeal surpasses any intellectual pretensions;
- poetic justice triumphs by the final curtain.

Like tragedy, the melodrama asks us to feel for the protagonists, to experience pity and fear, and to come away from the experience cleansed. But in melodrama the conflicts are almost always external, and the protagonists are frequently victims of villains. Tragedy demands that the hero's own personality contains the seeds of his or her downfall and that the hero ultimately recognizes this truth. While melodrama may flirt with tragedy by putting its heroes in life-threatening situations, its reliance on purely external circumstances diminishes the possibility of tragedy.

Uncle Tom's Cabin, the most popular stage play in America in the nineteenth century, typifies melodrama at both its best and at its most excessive. Many social dramas, especially those with an undercurrent of propaganda, are steeped in melodramatic techniques because they rely on oppressive villains (bankers, landowners, and bosses) to stir their audiences to action. *A Raisin in the Sun*, an outstanding play by any criterion, is—at heart—a melodrama. The term need not be pejorative, as there are numerous respected plays that are properly classified as melodramas.

---

other pre-twentieth-century dramatists, tragicomedy is associated most with the modern era. Bernard Shaw credits Henrik Ibsen as being "the dramatic poet who firmly established tragicomedy as a much deeper and grimmer entertainment than tragedy."

Tragicomedy is more than a mere fusion of tragic events that threaten the lives of characters and the comic resolution that saves them. Melodrama often thrives on such plotting. Contemporary tragicomedy is born of a philosophy that denies a discernible order in the cosmos. Neither Fate nor Fortune plays a hand in human activity, which dramatists often judge to be futile and inconsequential. This pessimistic view was born of the chaos of the century's great wars, the Great Depression, and the threat of nuclear annihilation. The result is tragicomedy, which paradoxically arouses pity and fear through laughter. Modern dramatists such as Beckett, Pinter, Albee, and Kushner have made a specialty of grimly comic plays in which laughter is an antidote for the conundrums of life.

Reversal and recognition are not always present in tragicomedy, at least overtly. Characters are often too shackled by their own inertia to allow for a reversal of fortune. Chekhov's characters, trapped physically on isolated Russian estates and mentally by their inability to adjust to changes, are the prototypes of this phenomenon. Beckett, who wrote that "habit is the great deadener," has invented an apt metaphor, however disturbing, for the malaise of contemporary life. In his play *Happy Days*, the central character, Winnie, is buried to her neck in a waste heap throughout the play. In *Rockaby* Beckett's heroine is as chained to her rocking chair as Prometheus was to his mountain, though for quite different reasons. Beckett's character sits

Farce

Farce is the comedic equivalent of the melodrama. It also depends on an ingenious plot, a series of sticky situations in which broadly drawn characters must extricate themselves (usually by bounding at breakneck speed through any one of the doors that traditionally dominate farce's landscape!). Traditionally, there is a manipulated ending that resolves the confusion. Comedy has long been used as a social corrective as aberrant behaviors are laughed out of existence. There is an implied moral foundation to comedy. But farce is amoral. The audience does not laugh at immoral behavior (such as adultery) but rather at the situations in which the miscreants find themselves. Farce does not ask us to judge human behaviors; it is satisfied only that we laugh at the ingenious situations and the dexterity of the farceurs.

Farce is derived from a medieval French word, *farcir*, which means "to stuff." Like their Italian and ancient Roman counterparts, early French comedies relied on physical humor to "stuff" or fill out the plots. Thus farce is occasionally confused with *slapstick comedy*, which is grounded in the physical humor of pratfalls, beatings, and variations on pie-in-the-face routines. While farce may employ much physical humor, it transcends mere slapstick in the cleverness of its plotting and in its spirit of anarchy. Eric Bentley, whose analysis of the psychological appeal of farce is among the finest essays on the genre, argues that farce is ultimately about fulfilling repressed desires. It allows us to punch our boss in the nose or tread our way through the adventures of an adulterous love affair vicariously. We laugh from the safety of our theater seat. Though farce may lack profundity, it remains among the most difficult forms for actors to play, as reflected in the story of the old vaudevillian on his deathbed who is asked if dying is difficult. "Dying is easy," he wheezes, "it's comedy that's hard." He no doubt had played in a farce or two!

One means of achieving the tragicomic effect in the late twentieth century has been to fuse elements of farce with serious intent. The Europeans have a glorious history of clowning in their circuses and popular entertainments such as mime and puppetry. They have produced a number of playwrights (Romania's Eugene Ionesco, Belgium's Michel de Ghelderode, Switzerland's Friedrich Duerrenmatt, England's Joe Orton and Tom Stoppard, and Italy's Dario Fo) who have successfully blended farce and existential philosophy. The Middle Europeans have used the laughter of farce to distance more serious political messages in their struggle against totalitarian regimes. The Poles, long the victims of subjugation, have been especially effective in this realm. Slawomir Mrozek (1930–), contemporary Poland's leading dramatist, even wrote a play he billed as a "melo-farce" (*The Turkey*, 1960). Tewfik al-Hakim, Egypt's most notable playwright in the twentieth century, is also remembered for his fusion of farce and social commentary in such plays as *The Donkey Market* and *Fate of a Cockroach*.

there solely because she sat there yesterday, as she will sit there tomorrow. Amusing? Perhaps. Pathetic? Certainly. In tragicomedy we often invest much the same emotional energy in the dilemma of the character as we do in tragedy, yet there is no corresponding purgation derived from our encounter with one "better than we are." Too often our laughter in a tragicomedy stems from the realization that the characters are too much like we are.

In much modern tragicomedy the traditional elements of drama have been reshaped. Causality—and thereby plotting—has been replaced by "the action of inaction." Characters are less prone to act and more inclined to discuss dilemmas rather than confront them. "There are no brave causes anymore," laments Jimmy Porter in *Look Back in Anger* (1956), John Osborne's assault on modern life.

Just as there exists ambiguity in a world without certainty, there is a corresponding ambiguity in characterization. Aristotle's argument that characters must be "consistent even in their inconsistency" has found new meaning in tragicomedy. Contradictions are now the norm rather than the exception. In his essay *L'Umorismo* (1920), Luigi Pirandello notes that the concept of humor in Italy is far different from England's, where humor is a species of wit. For Pirandello, a pioneer of tragicomic drama, humor is a darker enterprise in which the artist is acutely aware of the contraries of life, the suffering and the comedy. "The humorist," says Pirandello, whose comments are particularly appropriate to the tragicomedian, "pays attention to the body and the shadow, sometimes more to the shadow than the body." Coincidentally, Pirandello's ideas are not uniquely Western; similar beliefs about the simultaneity of the serious and the comic are found in many Eastern philosophies, which embrace the dualities of life. The drama of Mexico (e.g., Elena Garro's *A Solid Home*) and Latin America (Egon Wolff's *Paper Flowers*) is especially notable for its fusion of these seemingly disparate moods.

The playwright invites the audience to see life's many ironies. But modern characters are unable, often unwilling, to recognize their complicity in their dilemmas. And, if they do have a glimmer of insight, they are unable, perhaps unwilling, to act on it. This may be illustrated by the final moment of Beckett's *Waiting for Godot* (1953). The two tramps who have waited futilely for someone called "Godot" agree that they cannot continue their hopeless vigil. The play ends with an apparent resolution:

> VLADIMIR. *Well? Shall we go?*
> ESTRAGON. *Yes, let's go.*

But the final stage direction captures simultaneously the tragedy and comedy of their lives: "*They do not move. Curtain.*" We laugh at the incongruity between aspiration and realization, yet we are shaken by the futility of it all because it is a disturbingly true imitation of human nature.

Ultimately, tragicomedy is darker, less hopeful than tragedy or comedy. Although tragedy begins with the premise of potential greatness in humanity and ends with defeat, there is nevertheless a sense of triumph in the tragic protagonist's willingness to confront human shortcomings. Although comedy begins with the premise that we are folly-bound, it concludes with the promise of a better society as seen in its reconciliations, dances, feasts, and weddings. But in tragicomedy there is rarely the release of spirit observed in the other genres. There are only two tramps who "do not move" in a cosmos where inertia reigns.

Styles and Conventions

Whereas genre is indicative of a distinctive type of drama according to the treatment of the subject matter and the perspective of the writer, *style* is indicative of the manner of presentation. Tragedies, comedies, tragicomedies—and the myriad other subgenres—can be performed in a variety of styles.

Among the most appealing aspects of going to the theater on a regular basis is seeing the many ways in which a play can be written, performed, staged, and designed. You might visit ten different Shakespeare festivals in a summer, see a production of *Hamlet* at each, and come away from your ten experiences viewing the play and the productions quite differently. A familiarity with styles and conventions will help you further appreciate live theater.

Styles

Style is the manner in which a play is written, directed, designed, and performed. Because it implies the degree of artificiality involved in the performance, perhaps it is easier to see style in nonrealistic works. Both the classical Greek style and Kabuki, for instance, use masks, padded costumes, and elevated shoes. And in both, the writing employs heightened language, much of it sung and danced. By contrast, the style demanded by American realists such as David Mamet and Marsha Norman is as far removed from a Greek or Kabuki performance as one can imagine. The actors wear clothing that seems "everyday." They talk in conversational, intimate tones, while movement, gestures, and body attitudes seem entirely natural, even antitheatrical. Some critics propose that modern realism is "antistyle," though realism does have a definable style.

Theater productions in all cultures can be divided into two principal performance styles: *presentational* and *representational*. The latter, with which Western audiences may be more familiar, asks the audience to accept as "real" that which they see onstage. It is most closely associated with modern Western theater. Presentational theater acknowledges the presence of spectators who know they are watching a theatrical event. Thus it uses such conventions as direct address to the audience through asides, soliloquies, and songs. The actors are as apt to

The classic lines of a Greek temple (the Hephaisteion [Theseion] shown here) contrast with the more complex architecture of the Brighton Pavilion, which opened in England during the Romantic era.

The Brighton Pavilion.

play to the audience as to each other. Shakespeare opens his history play *Henry V* with an actor stepping forward to address the audience in a speech that is a prescription for presentational theater:

> *Piece out our imperfections with your thoughts;*
>
> *Into a thousand parts divide one man*
>
> *And make imaginary puissance.*
>
> *Think, when we talk of horses, that you see them*
>
> *Printing their proud hoofs i' th' receiving earth;*
>
> *For 'tis your thoughts that now must deck our kings . . .*

In presentational theater, the design elements are overtly theatrical—or, at the other extreme, nonexistent—with little pretense of realism. In fact, this style is often referred to as *theatrical* because it reminds us that what we see onstage is an imaginative "lie" that is only a metaphor for life, not life itself.

With the representational style, the "lie" exists in the auditorium because it suggests that the audience is not really in a theater, but that it is eavesdropping upon actual life through an invisible "fourth wall" into a private room. In *A Doll's House*, Henrik Ibsen describes the realistic detail of the Helmer household in his opening stage direction: *A comfortably and tastefully, but not expensively furnished room. . . . Engravings on the wall. A what-not with china and other bric-a-brac; a small bookcase with leather-bound books. A carpet on the floor; a fire in the stove.* In the representational theater there is often less call for the audience's "imaginary forces" to work.

Furthermore, the actors do not openly acknowledge the presence of the audience, though they are always carefully gauging its response. They play to one another onstage, though they usually "cheat out" so that they remain more visible to the audience. The design elements attempt to convince the audience that everything it sees and hears is "the real thing."

Is it possible to blend the presentational and representational styles in one production? It happens frequently. *Death of a Salesman,* an essentially realistic play, is overlaid with a theatrical style. Willy's "visions" are nonrealistic conventions that allow the audience to see inside his troubled mind. Bertolt Brecht frequently achieves his "alienation effect" by changing styles abruptly to provoke the audience into thinking about the play's issues. Some Latino theater artists favor a style known as *magical realism*, which allows a play to shift between realism and the fantastical in a heartbeat. Chilean playwright Egon Wolff's *Paper Flowers* employs this style for both thematic and theatrical purposes.

Directors may tell their designers that they want to do a "stylized" version of a play, and the designers understand that they are being asked for a nonrealistic approach. For instance, Giles Havergill "stylized" Chekhov's *The Seagull* for the Glasgow Citizens' Theater by having each actor sit facing the audience as he or she recited the lines of the first act as a poem. Conversely, John Barton's 1979 production of *The Merchant of Venice* for the Royal Shakespeare Company was both acted and designed as if it were a modern realistic play.

Styles often reflect the time or philosophy of the society that produces them. The deliberate movement and chanting of the Noh theater has its roots in Buddhist meditation, while the classic theater of India uses dance because drama was shaped by Siva, the Lord of the Dance. In contrast, Western realism is largely a synthesis of nineteenth-century scientific empiricism and the democratic revolution that swept Europe and America. Hence, its style mirrors the daily activities of ordinary people who are observed in a laboratory-like setting that meticulously re-creates their environment. One can more fully appreciate a theater piece, printed or performed, by knowing some of the cultural contexts of both the age that produced it and the age in which it is currently performed.

The "Isms" are another way of categorizing various theatrical styles. "Ism" is a much-used suffix that denotes both a distinctive doctrine and the characteristic features associated with it. For instance, the Greeks believed in the ideal of a harmonious, well-ordered cosmos; therefore, they placed a premium on simplicity, balance, proportion, and symmetry—characteristics we associate with Classicism. Conversely, Romanticism embraces extremes, contrast, freedom of form and experimentation, all an outgrowth of the Romantic belief that humans should be free from restraint and rules. Compare the Greek temple with the picture of the Pavilion at Brighton, England, which was built at the height of the Romantic era. Specific Isms, such as Expressionism or Theatricalism, will be examined within the context of particular plays and in the discussion of historical contexts preceding each group of plays.

In addition to the so-called Isms, many movements within the theater have characteristic styles. They include the theater of the absurd, the epic theater, and the theater of cruelty. Many of these movements freely combine other forms. Brecht's epic theater, for instance, grew out of German Expressionism during World War I, yet it also employs Theatricalism, Realism, and Romanticism to achieve its ends.

Conventions

Conventions are theater's rules of the game. Think of a deck of playing cards, its various suits, face cards, number cards, and possibly jokers. Many kinds of games can be played with those same 52 cards. So, too, with theater. It begins with the same "cards": an idea (usually scripted), performers, a space, and an audience. The performers may or may not wear formal costumes, makeup, or masks. They may act in front of spectacular scenery or on a bare floor. They may address the audience directly or they may ignore the audience altogether. They may speak in prose or poetry, or they may not speak at all, choosing instead to sing, dance, or mime the idea. The performance space may be a multi-million-dollar theater or it may be a "black box" in a church basement. Curiously, the audience will accept the performers and the story they present no matter which of these options is exercised, if the performers are good at what they do and if the idea engages the audience. Recall that Coleridge defined the "willing suspension of disbelief" as the audience's ability to accept the illusion inherent in the theater event. It is the first convention of the theater and all others stem from it.

A convention is the agreement between the performers and the audience to accept whatever happens in the theater space as "believable"—though not necessarily realistic—for the duration of the play. Although he writes about the Chinese theater, Tao-Ching Hsu aptly summarizes the purpose and appeal of conventions in theaters throughout the world: "Conventions, once accepted, are no longer felt as such; they appear natural and do not distract the mind from other matters of the play."

Often we do not think about conventions as they happen: a brightly lit auditorium suddenly dims to blackness, a curtain rises, and we forget we are in a theater. We accept that we are suddenly in the court of the Chinese emperor Han, in a market in Nigeria, or in the world of the dead in Mexico. A play ends, the lights fade to black and suddenly Dustin Hoffman, not Willy Loman, is standing before us to receive our applause. At other times, the conventions are so startling that they force us to stop and consider their import. Many theater companies throughout Latin America encourage actors to engage their audiences in discussion of social issues within the context of a play; audiences are challenged to provide resolutions to problems.

The Japanese theater is especially rich in its use of nonrealistic conventions. For instance, in Kabuki an actor enters through the audience via a long runway (the *hanimichi*); he suddenly stops, elevates himself on one leg, and strikes an exaggerated pose (*mie*) for several seconds to allow the audience to reflect on his character and costume. (The use of the male pronoun here is deliberate: a convention of the Kabuki theater is that only men act, though there is now a women's Kabuki in Tokyo). To Westerners steeped in the conventions of realism, Kabuki's conventions might seem "hammy." Similarly, while experiencing their first realistic Western play, Japanese playgoers—accustomed to singing and a persistent musical accompaniment in their theater—might find it disconcerting that the actors speak only to each other in rather hushed tones. To study theater and its rich history throughout the world is to study its many conventions. As virtually every period we will consider has its own set of conventions, be it the Greek chorus or Indian *mudras* (hand gestures), we will include a brief summary of the most important "ground rules" for each.

Biff confronts Willy and his "woman in Boston" in the Bejing production of Death of a Salesman, *directed by Arthur Miller in 1982. Read a review of this production in Chapter 5.*

Much of the most interesting experimental work undertaken in this century has applied the conventions of one culture to the theater works of another. Bertolt Brecht's work in the German theater in the 1930s borrowed techniques from the Chinese theater. Arianne Mnouchkine and her Paris-based *Théâtre du Soleil* often adopts conventions of Asian theater in its production of European classics; for example, Aeschylus's *The Oresteia* featured conventions from India's Kathakali dance theater. Conversely, Chinese actors, influenced by Miller's production of *Death of a Salesman* in Beijing in 1982, now avidly study American "method" acting and its realistic conventions.

Not all acts of theater are created alike, and a few trips to the theater will quickly acquaint you with the many performance styles available to theater artists. They are as rich and diverse as the people creating and viewing them are.

PART II

An Anthology of Western Drama

> "I'm going to have a copy of this play put in that cornerstone, so that people a thousand—two thousand—years from now will know a few simple facts about us. . . . This is the way we were, in our growing up, in our marrying, in our living, and in our dying."
>
> Thornton Wilder, *Our Town*

*Sir Peter Hall merged classical and modern sensibilities in his production of
Aeschylus's* The Oresteia *at the National Theater of Great Britain (1981).
Orestes is pursued by the chorus of Furies in the trilogy's final play.*

CHAPTER 3

THE THEATER OF GREECE AND ROME

It is fitting we begin our survey of Western theater by returning to Greece and Rome, the civilizations that laid the foundation for Western civilization and its arts. Without minimizing the significant artistic contributions made by various Mediterranean cultures—notably the Egyptians, whose drama was discussed in Chapter 1—it was first the Greeks, then the Romans, who built the foundation for the development of drama in the West.

From the Greeks and Romans, we have inherited a rich legacy of democracy, laws, and social organization. And as importantly, these two civilizations—which dominated the Western world for over a thousand years—provided us with models for architecture, sculpture, poetry, painting, and, of course, theater and drama. The latter group—the Arts—was intended to ensure an order sought by the former. Socrates, the venerable philosopher, declared that "the unexamined life is not worth living," and the theater, the great meeting place of the Greeks (and, admittedly, to a lesser degree the Romans), emerged as a locus for the collective examination of humanity's place and purpose in this world. Significantly, the examination was conducted against the backdrop of the cosmos itself in the great outdoor theatrons of the Hellenic world.

Today we commonly use words bequeathed us by Greek and Roman theater artists: tragedy, drama, hypocrite, prologue, catharsis, histrionic, and ludicrous (from the Roman word for "play"). These remind us that life and art were not things set apart from one another; rather, they were interdependent. Perhaps the greatest legacy, however, of the Greco-Roman theaters was the focus on the individual who is brought to a moment of self-examination and self-awareness. Subsequent Western literature has continued this emphasis on the individual caught in moments of crisis.

We commonly refer to the Greco-Roman age as "classical" because their arts often achieved a perfection we still use as a standard by which we judge the worthiness of a work. Furthermore, they created models for future generations of artists to emulate or reject, but not to ignore. As we discuss the evolution of drama from the fifth century B.C.E. through the twentieth century C.E., you may be surprised at how often we must return to Greece and Rome as points of reference. So let us return to Greece, where it all began.

GREECE

Artistic and Cultural Events

534:
First tragic competitions at City Dionysia

c. 550:
Thespis introduces "the first speaker"

c. 650:
Records of dithyrambic choruses

c. 800–700:
Homeric Age: the great epics

471:
Aeschylus adds second actor to tragedy

c. 468:
Sophocles adds third actor to tragedy

c. 500–404: Old Comedy

c. 430:
Sophocles' *Oedipus the King*

c. 411:
Aristophanes' *Lysistrata*

400–c. 320:
Middle Comedy

336–300:
New Comedy

c. 335:
Aristotle's *The Poetics*

c. 320:
Menander's *The Grouch*

800 B.C.E.	700 B.C.E.	600 B.C.E.	500 B.C.E.	400 B.C.E.	300 B.C.E.

Historical and Political Events

600–300:
Classical Age

509–265:
The Republic

560–510:
Peisistratus rules Athens

462–429:
Age of Pericles, Athen's Golden Age

431–404:
Peloponnesian War

399:
Socrates executed

404:
Athens falls to Sparta

336–146:
Hellenistic Age

The Origins of the Theater in Greece

There is considerable debate about the precise beginnings of theater in the Western world, largely because the evidence is incomplete and often contradictory. Many historians, however, cite the Dionysian *dithyramb* as the origin of European theater and its subsequent drama. No less a figure than Aristotle supports this theory in his *The Poetics* (c. 335 B.C.E.), although in recent years Aristotle's commentary has been challenged. In 1964 Gerald Else theorized that drama (specifically tragedy) originated in the fertile minds of two Athenian playwrights, Thespis and Aeschylus, about whom more will be said. Aristotle's account of the dithyrambic origins of theater and Else's theory on the origins of tragedy are not necessarily incompatible. The traditional account is presented here with the caveat that scholars have not reached accord on the issue. Else rightly points out that his argument (like that of Aristotle's) is "a theory. With the evidence that we have available, no one can honestly claim to offer anything more." It should be noted that the Greek word for "ritual" was *dromenon*, meaning "something performed" or "to perform rites"; it was often used with the phrase *ta hiera*, "holy sacrifice." By the fifth century *dromenon* was applied to the performance of plays ("a thing done or performed"), which suggests that the early Greeks understood the evolutionary relationship between ritual and drama.

Early in his treatise Aristotle refers to *dithyrambs*, which were originally improvised hymns and dances performed in honor of Dionysus, a lesser agrarian deity associated with fertility and wine, and by extension with the passionate, irrational forces that wine induces. Dionysus, a patron of the creative force in humans, also could be fiercely destructive, as we see in *The Bacchae*, the only extant tragedy about him. Dionysus was the offspring of an illicit union between Zeus and a mortal, Semele. Each year he was buried in the earth at harvest time to protect him from jealous gods who resented his power. In the spring he came to life again (his name means "twice born") and blessed the land where he slept for the winter with plenty. The guardians of Dionysus were *satyrs*, a race of half-men, half-goats (with the tails of horses). The word *tragedy*—denoting a particular form of drama that developed much later—derives from *tragodia* ("song of the goats"), perhaps a reference to the dithyrambic worshippers who dressed in goatskins. There is evidence that winners of the dithyrambic contests were given goats as prizes, and goats may have been sacrificed at the sacred altar (*thymele*) during these rites.

To ensure that Dionysus would bless the land, animals, and humans with healthy offspring, a public celebration in the god's honor was held each spring (about the time Christians celebrate the Resurrection of Christ, their god-king, at Easter). This cult of Dionysus can be traced as far back as the fifteenth century B.C.E., roughly a thousand years before formal theater developed in Greece. Much wine was consumed, as it was believed to be the blood of the god himself. Dithyrambs were performed in his honor, as were ecstatic dances, vestiges of the older agrarian matriarchy. This excerpt from Euripides' *The Bacchae* echoes the ancient dithyrambs sung to Dionysus (or Bacchus, as the Romans referred to him):

> Hither, O fragrant of Timolus the Golden,
>> Come with the voice of the timbrel and drum;
> Let the cry of your joyance uplift and embolden
>> The God of the joy-cry; O Bacchanals, come!

Aristotle says that processions in honor of Dionysus were held throughout Greece and the Mediterranean, notably in the Peloponnese and Megara. But the cult of Dionysus is most closely associated with Athens, where the ruler (*tyrannos*) Peisistratus declared Dionysus his particular deity. Men dressed as satyrs led the procession, while the nuns of Dionysus (*maenads*, the "mad ones") carried the bough of an evergreen (*thrysus*) to remind the people of Dionysus's return to life. The priests of Dionysus officiated at these *City Dionysia*, which eventually became more social and political than religious events. The 10 (later 15) tribes that ruled Athens each provided a dithyrambic chorus for the Dionysia, thereby adding a political dimension to what was originally purely religious. John Winkler and Froma Zeitlin provide a useful analogue to the experience of these ancient Dionysia for modern audiences:

> Even to come close to the authentic experience [of the Dionysia], and hence in some part to the meaning, of attending a "play" in ancient Athens, we would have to imagine that Arthur Miller, Tennessee Williams, and Sam Shepard had each written three serious plays and a farce for a one-time performance on a national holiday—say, the Fourth of July—in honor of an ancient god-hero, perhaps a cross between George Washington and Johnny Appleseed, and that these were preceded by a parade of congressional representatives and cabinet secretaries and federal judges and governors and mayors, that the plays were performed after ceremonies honoring the war dead and our national allies, that bishops and generals and mothers superior had prominent places in the front rows, and that the choruses who sang and danced were composed . . . of West Point cadets, dressed sometimes as old veterans, sometimes as servants or refugees or prisoners of war, occasionally (but only rarely) as young men.
>
> John Winkler and Froma Zeitlin, *Nothing to Do with Dionysus?* (1990, p. 5)

To improve the quality of the dithyrambs, and because humans enjoy competition (remember, the Greeks gave us the Olympic Games), contests became integral to the Dionysia. Both the composers of the best dithyrambs and the choruses that sang and danced them were rewarded. Dithyrambic competitions continued well into the fourth century, though the songs themselves carried a much weaker association with the cult of Dionysus.

We surmise that eventually someone was inspired to call for one member of the chorus to step aside and assume the role of Dionysus. This actor, known as a *hypokrites* ("the answerer," or literally "from under the mask"), engaged the dithyrambic chorus in dialogue. Later, the chorus questioned other gods and heroes of mythology; eventually, the great mythic tales so loved by the Greeks were "acted out" and "plays" evolved. Tradition suggests a young dithyrambic performer, Thespis, emerged from the chorus of 50 at the City Dionysia in Athens about the middle of the sixth century to become the first solo actor. Thespis ("inspired by god") covered his face with white paint and hung flowers about his face, thus giving us the first known "mask" in the Greek theater. Else believes that it was Thespis who reshaped the old Homeric myths into "action," as opposed to a "telling," as an early attempt at tragedy. Whatever his contributions, Thespis is revered as the first Western actor and his followers are known as thespians. Aeschylus, often called the father of tragedy because his genius raised the genre to an art form distinct from other kinds of plays, created the second actor and thus made true dialogue and conflict possible. Sophocles, whose dramas epitomize the greatness of Greece's golden age, used a third speaking role to provide greater contrast among characters. Euripides emphasized individual characters by diminishing the role of the chorus. These three tragedians produced the greatest drama of the fifth century, and established standards by which subsequent playwrights in the West would be judged.

Those who question the dithyrambic origins of theater in ancient Greece have suggested other possibilities based on some form of ritualistic or ceremonial activity:

- ecstatic rites of passage involving the seasons or puberty (e.g., Gilbert Murray and Jane Harrison)
- tomb and hero-cult worship (William Ridgeway)
- shamanistic practices by Dionysian priests (E. T. Kirby)
- dances performed by women while threshing grain

It is not our purpose here to offer a complete history of the evolution of theater in ancient Greece. For now, you need only be aware that Western theater apparently developed about 2,500 years ago from rites similar in impulse to those described in Chapter 1. At its roots are a recognition of forces superior to us, communal celebrations of triumphs, lamentations about death, and the ritualization of common beliefs through the use of storytelling, music, dance, gesture, masks, and costumes. (See Spotlight box, The Hellenistic Theater.)

SPOTLIGHT THE HELLENISTIC THEATER

Because the Dionysia were communal events in which the free male populace of the city-state (*polis*) was expected to participate, it became necessary to build permanent spaces for the performance of the dithyrambs and, much later, plays. The architecture of the classical Greek theater, which evolved over many years, reminds us of the spiritual roots of theater. Significantly, the theaters were outdoor affairs; thus dramas about mythic heroes and their gods were played against the natural backdrop of the universe itself. Because the chorus was always central to the Dionysia, the place where it sang and danced became the premiere architectural feature of the early Greek theaters. A sacred circle, measuring between 60 to 90 feet in diameter, was the focal point for the singing and dancing chorus. Appropriately, it was named the *orchestra*, or "the dancing place." At its center was the *thymele* (or altar; there were two in some theaters) at which sacrifices were offered, a remnant of the spiritual beginnings of the Greek theater. To improve both visibility and acoustics, the individual actors may have performed on a platform, or *logeion*. (You can still purchase orchestra or loge seats in large theaters today.) The actors donned padded costumes and masks to make them more readily visible to the enormous audiences, which may have numbered 15,000. A small dressing hut or tent, which the Greeks called a *skene*, originally stood some distance from the playing area, but eventually was moved directly behind the *logeion* to mask entrances and to provide both scenic backdrops and acoustical support. One of the theater's most frequently used terms, "scene," comes from this architectural feature of the early Greek theaters. To improve sight lines, the audience was elevated above the playing area by sculpting seats into hillsides. Special seats for the

The ruins of the ancient theater at Delphi, the holy site where oracles foretold the fate of Greek heroes such as Oedipus. The picture reminds us that the tragedies were played against a backdrop of the cosmos itself.

priests of Dionysus were placed closest to the orchestra; as the Dionysia became more civic than religious affairs, seating for public officials became more prominent. The audience area was known as the *theatron*, or "seeing place." Today we customarily refer to the audience area as "the auditorium," or "hearing place," which suggests that the spoken word gradually supplanted dancing and choral singing as the primary means of communication. Still, *theatron* provides us with the terms *theatre* (the art of making spectacle and drama) and *theater* (most often used to denote the architectural space in which the plays are performed). We now use the generic term "theater" (and this Americanized spelling) to denote a wide variety of activities in which spectacle (e.g., costumes, masks, scenery) and physical action is integral to the event.

The Greek Mind

Whether its origins were in ancient dithyrambic rites, ceremonies such as burials and agricultural fetes, or even the genius of Thespis and Aeschylus, three elements of the Greek mind inform Greek drama. First, the Greeks were humanists who believed that human beings are "the measure of all things." To the Greeks humans were godlike in their unlimited potential for greatness. Indeed, tragedy was devised to remind the Greeks that they were only god*like* and not gods themselves.

Second, the Greeks understood that even exceptional beings were accountable to the natural order of things. *Dikē* represented a universal justice that insured that everything in creation behaved according to a master plan that humans might not understand. When *dikē* was upset—either through human or divine error—*anankē* ("necessity") demanded that the resultant chaos be harnessed to restore harmony and order; often this could only be accomplished through the death of the perpetrator. The *Erinyes*—sometimes called the Furies—acted as a type of cosmic police force deployed to restore *dikē*. Aeschylus's magnificent trilogy, *The Oresteia*, illustrates how the *Erinyes* were transformed into the *Eumenides* ("the kindly ones"), a more benevolent force that maintained harmony through reconciliation rather than retribution. The Greeks believed their vast pantheon of gods cooperated with humans to maintain *dikē*. That, at least, was the theory. The plays were written to depict the consequences of a mutual inability to adhere to *dikē*'s plan.

Third, the Greeks appreciated the complexity of life, as the dichotomy between the ideal of the perfect human and the reality of human error suggests. They enjoyed debate (*agon*) and in most Greek communities one could find an area of the agora (marketplace) set aside for discussions of social, political, and philosophical issues. The great Socratic questions—"What is man?" and "What is the highest good?"—were central to these lively discussions. Furthermore, debate fostered Greece's greatest legacy to subsequent generations: democracy and the free exchange of ideas. Greek dramas, which may have begun as religious affairs, became political events that promoted the general good. Predictably, they are filled with debates such as those between Oedipus and Teiresias or Lysistrata and the Athenian commissioner. The words we use to identify the principal characters in a play—protagonist and antagonist—derive from debate. A protagonist was the "first contestant," and the one who opposed her or him was the antagonist.

Because the dramatic festivals glorified the *polis* (city-state) and its ideals, the theaters were built to house the entire free, male population of the *polis*. The Theater of Dionysus in Athens held perhaps 14,000, while the great theaters at Epidaurus and Ephesus seated 17,000 and 25,000, respectively. Women and slaves could attend the theater, but all free men were expected to attend. Such male-centered attitudes raise questions about the role of women in classical Greek drama. Women held a curious, even contradictory, place in Greek society that is reflected in the plays. They were not considered citizens of the *polis*. Solon, Greece's most famous lawgiver, relegated them to the home, while Aristotle argued in *The Poetics* that as a class women were "inferior" (though he allowed that "a woman can be good"). Women were treated as chattel to be owned by men who valued them primarily as incubators for healthy offspring. For example, in *The Oresteia* Apollo argues that Agamemnon is the true parent of Orestes and that Clytemnestra was merely the carrier of his seed. Thus Orestes had every right—even a sacred duty under the patriarchal system—to kill his "mother." While men certainly could love women (a common theme in many myths), it was generally accepted that an ideal love could take place only between equals—that is, men. Thus some Greeks practiced homosexuality (an issue in the Achilles-Patroclus relationship in the *Iliad*). Though society relegated women to second-class status, in the plays they were frequently portrayed as wellsprings of common sense and civility. Antigone becomes the defender of divine law in Sophocles' play, while Aristophanes' heroine Lysistrata devises the plan to save Greece from the devastating effects of the Peloponnesian War. This paradoxical view of women may be explained in various ways: first, the propensity to debate encouraged the Greeks to accept both sides of an issue, even when presented by a female character. Sue Ellen Case and other feminist critics, however, argue that the depiction of women in Athenian theater was actually a product of a male-dominated social system and that women were portrayed, both as written and as performed by men, as men wished them to act.

SPOTLIGHT   THE CONVENTIONS OF GREEK THEATER

The Greek ideal promoted a worldview that was ordered, harmonious, and beautiful. In fact, the Greek word for "universe," which included the totality of their experience, was *cosmos*, a synonym for beauty (as in "cosmetics"). To the Greeks, the universe was indeed a beautiful place, and their tragedies were reminders of the consequences when human arrogance upset the natural order of things, which they called *dikē*. The virtues of order, harmony, unity, and beauty became signatures of what we now call *Classicism*; in the Renaissance, an era that imitated Greco-Roman ideals, a rebirth of Classicism (*Neoclassicism*) had a profound effect on theater and drama.

Because playwriting, theater architecture, and performance methods reflect the current culture, the style and conventions of Greek theater and drama are founded on the classical ideal. To enhance your reading of Greek drama, familiarize yourself with the play structure, the theater space, and the acting style. Keep in mind that these conventions developed to complement the subject matter of the plays themselves. Marshall McLuhan's observation that "the medium *is* the message" is as applicable to Greek theater in the fifth century B.C.E. as it is to contemporary television.

The Structure of a Greek Play

Because Greek drama descended from ancient rituals, the plays retain a structure that is as carefully ordered as a church service. The principal parts of a Greek play (both tragedy and comedy), in the order in which they appear, are:

The *prologue*: Like the preface to this book, the prologue prepares the audience for what follows. The prologue customarily consists of a dialogue between two or three characters who provide us with exposition about the conflict that the play must resolve. Euripides, who experimented with the forms of drama, often used a single character to present his prologues. In *Oedipus the King*, Oedi-

pus is confronted by a priest who begs the monarch to liberate the Thebans from the terrible plague.

The *parados*: Because the chorus existed long before the emergence of formal, scripted dramas, it retained its prominence and was accorded a ceremonial entrance. The *parados* usually introduced the thematic concerns of the play, as well as creating its emotional atmosphere. Like the choric odes, it was sung and danced, much like the older *dithyrambs* that preceded formal drama.

Episodes are the "acts" of a Greek play. Here, the actual story of Oedipus, for example, is told through a series of scenes, usually about five. The episodes focus on what happens in a play. Here are found the structural units described in Chapter 2: complication, rising action, crisis, climax, reversal, recognition, and resolution. Some episodes were dedicated to particular conventions of Greek drama. Because the Greeks enjoyed debate, there was invariably an *agon*, or contest, in which conflicting characters argued their positions; see the heated discussion between Oedipus and Teiresias. Coinciding with the recognition and its attendant reversal was the *komos*, which—in tragedy—was a great outpouring of emotion, usually grief. In comedy, the *komos* was a joyful celebration, the culmination of the action of the play. One episode, usually occurring quite late in the action, often was allotted to the appearance of a "messenger" whose sole purpose was to describe offstage action, usually the violent death or mutilation of a character; *Oedipus the King* provides a notable example of such a speech. Greek tragedies, with very few exceptions (e.g., Sophocles' *Ajax*), do not show violent acts onstage, although they are about calamitous violence. Exhibiting violence violated the Greek sense of decorum and diminished the role of the audience's imagination.

Stasima (Odes): Throughout the middle section of the play, episodes alternate with the choric odes. After

each episode the chorus commented on the action and heightened the mood. This was accomplished by a lengthy song, complemented by a dance. The *stasima* were usually divided into *strophes* and *antistrophes*, or "turns" and "counterturns," which suggests something about the dance movements of the chorus. Just as the episodes tell us what is happening in a play, the *stasima* frequently tell us why something happens. The chorus customarily speaks for the community and reflects on the consequences of human action. Furthermore, the *stasima* often link the present action with the mythic past and thus bolster the cosmic implications of the plays. Though the *stasima* may seem strange to us because apparently nothing is "happening," they are invaluable guides to the thematic purpose and emotional pitch of the play. They function very much like song-and-dance numbers in the modern musical (which actually derived from Greek drama when Renaissance scholars attempted to re-create Greek drama—opera, then operetta, and eventually musical comedy were born of this effort).

The *exodos*: After the final episode, in which the fate of the protagonist is made known, the principal characters leave the stage. The chorus exits with a final hymn in which the lesson of the tragedy is stated, much the way a fairy tale or Aesop's fable ends with "and the moral of the story is. . . ." Compared with the *parados* and other *stasima*, the *exodos* is quite short because a prolonged speech would be anticlimactic.

Greek comedy also employed two particular features, the *agon* and the *parabisis*, which are discussed in conjunction with Greek Old Comedy.

The Physical Theater and Scenery

As the shape of the Greek theater suggests, everything about its design reflects the Greek preoccupation with order and harmony. Note the graceful rings that form the *theatron* where the audience sat (see p. 58), as well as the great circle of the *orchestra* where the chorus sang and danced. To the right and left of the orchestra were the *paradoi*—pathways or ramps which provided the chorus and spectators access to the orchestra and theatron. The raised *logeion*, on which the principal characters may have stood, was backed by a *skene*, itself a model of harmony and balance with its three perfectly spaced doors. The doors traditionally signified locale to the audience: the center door was invariably "the palace" door, while the side doors usually suggested a way to the seaport or to a rural area (depending on the geographical orientation of the theater); thus when the Shepherd enters from the right door, they assumed he had arrived from the countryside.

Because of their enormous size and the construction problems they presented, the theaters were built outdoors, usually at the base of a hillside to facilitate the construction of the *theatron*. The stories the Greeks told, the characters that enacted them, and the cosmic themes they illustrated were all larger than life, and could be performed in the Greek mind only against the backdrop of the universe itself. Just as so much of contemporary drama needs small, intimate spaces to examine the interior lives of the ordinary people who cross its stages, the Greeks needed vast, open spaces large enough to contain characters who could, in H. D. F. Kitto's words, "shake their fists at the gods."

The Greeks used little scenery and thus relied on the evocative power of language to create time and place. Because their stories were universal, the particulars of place were insignificant. Three visual elements invite discussion, however. *Periaktoi* were triangular prisms on which suggestions of locale—forest, seacoast, or palace—were painted. Sophocles is reputed to have invented these ingenious devices, which could be rotated to suggest a change in locale. Although violence was rarely shown on Greek stages, the *ekkyklema*, a small platform mounted on wheels, was apparently used to display the bodies of the dead. In Aeschylus's *Agamemnon*, the bodies of Agamemnon and his concubine, Cassandra, were wheeled onstage through the center door via the *ekkyklema*. On those very rare occasions when interior scenes were necessary, the *ekkyklema* may have been used to suggest the "indoors." Perhaps the most famous piece of Greek stage technology was the *mēchane*, an elaborate rope-and-pulley device that allowed supernatural beings to be lowered from the roof of the *skene* to suggest that heavenly intervention was necessary in human affairs. Euripides used the *mēchane* in a rather cynical fashion to intimate that gods were capricious and entirely fallible as interlopers in human affairs. Aristophanes employed the device to great effect in many of his comedies. As a literary term, a *deus ex machina* (a Latin phrase for "god from a machine") is an external agent who appears suddenly (and often mysteriously) to help resolve the plot. The King's Officer in Molière's *Tartuffe* is an example of the *deus ex machina*, a term directly ascribable to one of the more spectacular conventions of Greek theater.

Acting Styles

Acting styles throughout the history of the theater have been dictated by several factors, including the language of the script, the playing space, and other accoutrements, such as costume, masks, and makeup, with which an actor must deal. This is especially true of the Greeks, who necessarily developed some of the most distinctive conventions of Western theater. Little wonder that the emblem of Western theater today is a Greek mask! Because the tragic plays depicted heroic characters whose passions and deeds exceeded those of ordinary mortals, the actors necessarily had to project themselves physically and vocally. Furthermore, the enormous size of the theaters promoted an acting style, almost operatic by our standards, that depended on large gestures and declamatory speech when song was not used. The costumes helped the actors in their quest to measure up to the characters they portrayed. The actors wore a large headpiece (*onkos*) that increased their stature. To this was affixed a mask made of thin cloth, cork, and light wood; the mask suggested the dominant passion that enveloped a character, though characters could switch masks to indicate a change of personality. The masks also made it possible for an actor to play more than one character, as the traditional Greek acting company usually consisted of 3 actors, the chorus leader (the *koryphaios*), and the chorus, which numbered from 12 to 15. To insure proportion, the body was enlarged by padded robes and thick-soled footwear (*kothornoi*), though some argue that these boots were actually a Roman addition. The principal characters wore masks and robes that distinguished them by sex, social rank, and personality; the chorus was dressed alike and wore simpler robes and footwear that would not interfere with their lively dances. There is evidence that the Greeks used a more realistic acting style than we might surmise. Psychological detail, genuine human emotions, and true-to-life situations abound in the plays (especially in those of Euripides, whom Sophocles referred to as a "realist"). And there is the story of the actor Polus of Aegina. When he played Electra, Polus used an urn containing the ashes of his own son to motivate him in the scene in which Electra weeps over Orestes' remains— the world's first "Method actor"! Psychological truths and motivational techniques aside, Greek acting demanded much physical and vocal skill, especially when we consider that the actors had to perform four plays, a *tetralogy* of three tragedies and a satyr comedy, in a single day at the Dionysia.

Playwrights and Acting

Three playwrights are largely responsible for the greatest of the Greek tragedies. Though many men wrote plays, we have only the works of Aeschylus (525–456 B.C.E.), Sophocles (c. 496–406 B.C.E.), and Euripides (c. 480–406 B.C.E.). Because he wrote as tragedy was being created, Aeschylus's plays are most concerned with issues of theology and the shaping of a moral order in Greek society. *The Oresteia*, the only extant trilogy, traces the evolution of justice among gods and humans as it shows how we "must suffer, suffer into truth." Sophocles, by contrast, focused on the dilemma of the individual at a moment of intense crisis (see the introduction to *Oedipus the King*, later in this chapter). Sophoclean drama elevated tragedy in its depiction of the hero's journey to self-knowledge after a catastrophic reversal of fortune. Euripides is said to have diminished Greek tragedy with cynical works that challenged the power of the gods themselves. Such assessments of Euripides' purpose—as represented in the writings of the comic playwright Aristophanes (448–380 B.C.E.) and by the German philosopher Friedrich Nietzsche (1844–1900)—fail to account for the complexity of the last of the great Greek tragedians, whose works are perhaps the most accessible to late-twentieth-century audiences.

Greek acting was also a product of the cultural and social influences that shaped the dramas. Because their drama evolved from choric song and subsequently became political and moral debates, Greek actors relied on declamation. Furthermore, because of the vast size of Greek theaters, they were obligated to use sweeping gestures, a resonant voice, and stylized movement to make themselves heard and seen. They wore a large headpiece (*onkos*) and masks, padded robes, and (possibly) elevated shoes (*kothornoi*), which also necessitated stylized performance. Given the larger-than-life quality of the characters they played, as well as their unbridled passions, the style was appropriate. Actors customarily played more than one role in a play (including those of women) which further precluded naturalistic acting. (See Spotlight box, The Conventions of Greek Theater.)

After nearly a century-long Golden Age, Greek idealism was severely challenged by the Peloponnesian War (431–404 B.C.E.), which pitted Athens and Sparta in a destructive civil war. By the end of the fifth century, a bankrupt, decimated, and cynical Athens severely curtailed debate and freedom of expression. The new cynicism is reflected in the tragedies of Euripides and the comedies of Aristophanes. (See Spotlight box, Greek Old Comedy and *Lysistrata* Synopsis.) By the fourth century, tragedy had deteriorated into melodrama, and comedy shifted from the satires of Aristophanes to the safer comedy of Menander (c. 342–c. 291 B.C.E.), which depicted common people in everyday situations, speaking more lifelike dialogue. Though we would never mistake his plays as realistic, they were an important step in the evolution of this distinctly Western style of performance. Moreover, Menander created a variety of stock characters—the giddy young lover, the conniving manservant—who would become staples of Western comedy to this day. Menander's sole surviving comedy, *Dyskalos* (*The Grouch*, 320 B.C.E.), is about the "grumpy old man" we associate with Walter Matthau's screen persona. It was Menander who, in effect, developed the prototype for television sitcoms.

OEDIPUS THE KING

SOPHOCLES

SOPHOCLES (C. 496–406 B.C.E.)

The second of the great Greek tragedians, Sophocles authored some 120 dramas, including *Oedipus the King, Antigone,* and *Oedipus at Colonus,* and won at least 18 first prizes for playwriting in the City Dionysia. Born in Colonus, Sophocles received an excellent education and at age 16 led the boys' chorus in a celebration of the victory over Persia. In his maturity he was a model Greek citizen, serving as imperial treasurer and state commissioner; he was twice elected to the office of general and was a priest of Asclepias. Among his contributions to the development of theater are the introduction of the third actor, the invention of painted scenery, and the introduction of a new style of music. He is also credited with reducing the role of the chorus, thereby placing greater emphasis on individual characters. Unlike Aeschylus, he rarely acted in his own plays, reputedly because of his weak voice. As a playwright, he was a master craftsman who carefully planned exposition and intricately developed complications to create moving recognition scenes and heartrending, often ironic, reversals. Both Sophocles' diction and his use of irony are unmatched by his contemporaries. His characters are unique. Unlike those of Aeschylus, who are often characterized as "superhuman" or "godlike," and those of Euripides, who are described as "realistic," Sophocles' idealized characters are drawn neither as gods nor as they are, but, in his own words, "as they ought to be." Invariably they face choices and make decisions that lead them through suffering to self-realization. They represent the most noble achievements of the human spirit. The presence of the strong hand of fate and the undeniable existence and power of the gods is often present in Sophocles' plays.

OEDIPUS THE KING (428 B.C.E.)

Not only is *Oedipus the King* the most well known Greek tragedy, it is, according to Aristotle, the best of the canon. On no less than ten occasions in *The Poetics,* Aristotle uses *Oedipus the King* as an illustration when referring to "the perfect tragedy" or the "best means" of creating the tragic effect. For example, he cites *Oedipus the King* when he prescribes the preferred form of recognition as one that is coincident with *peripeteia* (the reversal). Likewise, when he identifies the qualities of a tragic hero, describes the type of action that arouses the pity and fear that lead to catharsis, and illustrates the need for probable and necessary action, *Oedipus the King* is his model. Given his admiration for the play, it is indeed easy to understand how many critics have ascribed to Aristotle the description of *Oedipus the King* as "the perfect tragedy."

What is it about the play that has captured and held the attention of playgoers for over 2000 years? To begin with, it is based on a fascinating story. The Greeks who saw the original production may have known the story as well as we know the stories of George Washington and Abe Lincoln, but familiarity with the story facilitates understanding of the play. *Oedipus the King* gives us one chapter in the story of the house of Thebes, an elaborate and intricately involved tale about the ancient Greek city and its leaders and the struggle for an understand-

SPOTLIGHT THE CURSE ON THE HOUSE OF THEBES

Long before the play begins, the young Cadmus (son of Agenor, king of Tyre and father of Semele, Dionysus's mother) searched the world for his sister, Europa, who had been seduced and carried off by Zeus. While on his quest, Cadmus founded the city of Thebes, populating it with warriors who sprang from the planted teeth of a monster he had slain. Cadmus ruled Thebes until his death and was succeeded by his son Polydoros, who was succeeded by his son, Labdacos. When Labdacos died, his brother Lycos served as regent for the infant Laius and ruled Thebes until he was overthrown by Amphion.

When Amphion died, the Thebans invited the exiled Laius, who had found refuge in Pisa, to reclaim his throne. Laius's joyful return soon soured as his marriage to Jocasta deteriorated. The marriage had been one of political convenience, for Jocasta was a daughter of one of the "sown men." To make matters worse, she appeared to be sterile. While secretly visiting the oracle of Apollo at Delphi, Laius learned of the curse that was placed upon him—any child of his born to Jocasta would be his murderer. The lack of an heir and the secret curse on the house of Thebes, coupled with his preference for the bed of Chrysippus, a young man from the court of Pelops in Pisa, motivated Laius to divorce Jocasta. Before that happened, however, Jocasta, feigning acquiescence, succeeded in enticing Laius one last time to her bed, where the seeds of Oedipus and the eventual destruction of Thebes were sown. In time Jocasta bore a son and, thinking that she had succeeded in tying Laius to her,

she presented her husband with the child, Oedipus. Outraged, Laius revealed the curse to her and gave the child, its ankles riveted together, to a trusted servant who was told to abandon it on the slopes of Mount Kithaeron. Fearing that any child born to Jocasta might fulfill the curse, Laius put Jocasta away and, to her great shame, spent his time dallying with Chrysippus.

True to their nature, the gods, especially Ares, Apollo, and Hera, were not pleased with the course of events in Thebes. Ares, the god of war, was still angered by the death of his sacred dragon at the hands of Cadmus; Apollo, the god of light, truth, and order, was displeased by the irrationality of the humans; and Hera, goddess of married women, already twice wounded by Zeus's assignations with Europa and Semele, was offended by Laius's banishment of Jocasta. With the support of Ares and Apollo, she sent the Sphinx to plague the city, devouring all who failed to answer her riddle.

In the meantime, Oedipus (which means "swollen foot"), supposedly abandoned on the slopes of Kithaeron, had been passed on to a shepherd who in turn gave the boy to the childless Polybus and Merope, the king and queen of Corinth. The young Oedipus grew to manhood as their royal heir. Then, after having been taunted and called a bastard by a drunken acquaintance, Oedipus began to question his origins and, dissatisfied with his parents' affirmation of his lineage, he journeyed to Apollo's shrine at Delphi, where he queried the oracle regarding his origins. In place of an answer, he

was confronted with the prophecy that he would one day kill his father and marry his mother. Appalled, Oedipus left Delphi and headed not back "home" but in the opposite direction, hoping to foil the prophecy. As he fled Delphi he encountered Laius and, in a fit of rage at being forced off the road by the king, killed Laius and his entourage. He continued toward Thebes and was confronted by the Sphinx, whose riddle he successfully answered.[1] Bested by Oedipus, the Sphinx threw herself off the cliff; unimpeded, Oedipus entered Thebes, where he was welcomed as a hero and, not unlike his father before him, given the hand of Jocasta in marriage as he ascended the Theban throne.

After years of successful reign and a happy marriage, which was blessed with four children—sons Etiocles and Polynices and daughters Antigone and Ismene—it appeared that the prophecy regarding Oedipus and the house of Thebes might prove to be inaccurate. However, a blight fell on the land and neither plant nor animal nor human being was well; in fact, all were sterile. Apparently the power of the gods was still a force with which to be reckoned. It is at this point that Sophocles begins his play.

---

[1]"What goes on four legs in the morning, two legs in the afternoon, three legs at night; is of one voice, and is the strongest when it has the least?" Man! He crawls on all fours as a baby, walks upright as an adult, and needs the help of a staff in old age; he has always the one voice and is most powerful when he uses the fewest legs.

---

ing of life and the roles of the gods and fate in the lives of its citizens. Specifically this play portrays the results of the curse that declares that Oedipus is destined to kill his father and marry his mother. (See Spotlight box, The Curse on the House of Thebes.)

Intriguing as this story may be, the key to Sophocles' brilliance is not his subject matter but his superb skill as a playwright. He takes an age-old story and carefully arranges the incidents to cleverly, but subtly, motivate the action of the agents. Through a strong sense of character, he imbues this action with the eternal human quest for cosmic knowledge and self-realization.

In plotting the play, Sophocles carefully rearranges the incidents of the myth to hold our interest and build suspense. By beginning the play at the end of the story, he allows Oedipus to live his final day in Thebes and simultaneously relive the major events of his life. As he moves slowly and painfully toward the end of his day of destiny, Oedipus also moves backward, swiftly but equally painfully, through the various crises of his life until the play's climax, when the mysteries of his own birth and his father's death are revealed. As each forward step leads him closer to identifying the slayer of Laius, a backward leap leads him closer to his own identity. Each new discovery about the present reveals more information about the past, and, conversely, each new scrap of evidence concerning the past sheds light on the present.

Sophocles carefully creates characters as individuals of depth and understanding whose behavior is logical and believable, whose actions are probable and necessary responses to the actions that precede them. In each scene, Sophocles presents Oedipus locked in conflict with both himself and another character. Throughout he displays great hubris—excessive pride—which had been the motivating force throughout Oedipus's life; it led him to question the legitimacy of his birth, drove him to consult the oracle at Delphi, and ultimately prompted the attack on his father. From his earliest comments, when he blatantly identifies himself as "Oedipus whom all men call the great," through the final scene, in which in his anguish he sees himself as "the greatly miserable, / the most accursed, whom God too hates / above all men on earth," it is apparent that Oedipus's *hamartia* (tragic flaw) is his pride. Tragically, it leads to errors in judgement and his precipitous fall from kingship.

However, it is also clear in each scene that, despite his pride, Oedipus is also motivated by his great concern for Thebes. From his early lamentation that his "spirit groans / for the city" to his final pleas to "drive me from [Thebes] with all the speed you can," he is committed to doing what is right for the city. Thus, he becomes that "intermediate kind of personage," neither all good nor all bad, identified by Aristotle as the ideal tragic hero. Perhaps more intriguing than this dialectic in his character is the sense of personal responsibility Sophocles instills in Oedipus. How easy it might have been for him to claim innocence by way of ignorance. After all, he did not know Laius was his father or that Jocasta was his mother or that Thebes was his birthplace. How easy it might have been for him to plead for mercy upon discovering the truth. This he does not do. Instead, he takes responsibility for each of his actions and stands ready to accept the consequences. It is from this sense of character that Sophocles depicts the human quest for cosmic knowledge and self-realization.

Our initial reaction to Oedipus might easily be a clichéd view—that he was caught between the proverbial rock and a hard place, that he was damned if he did and damned if he didn't, that he was a victim of circumstances, that he was not responsible for his actions. After all, it was preordained that he would kill his father and marry his mother—"the gods had spoken." Such a reaction, however, is based on our modern-day understanding of the deity and religion. We are children of the modern Western world and, as such, we perceive god in a monotheistic sense. We picture a single god who is omnipotent, omniscient, and omnipresent. It is from such a perspective that we hear the oracle's curse and assume that it is preordained. However, Sophocles and his audience had a different theology. As children of the ancient Greek world, they perceived their gods in a polytheistic sense; they pictured many gods, none omnipotent, omniscient, or omnipresent. Their sense of the gods was that of superhuman beings who were subject to the same passions and desires as humans. They believed that no god was in complete control and that, in fact, they often warred among themselves for the control of humans. To the Greeks all life, including that of the gods, was controlled by *anankē* ("necessity" or "what has to be") or *moira* ("the sharer-out" or "fate"). Therefore, it was not possible for any one god to preordain or predetermine the life of a human being. Thus, Sophocles created not a picture of predetermined life but a picture of an individual with a great sense of character who, though indeed caught between the rock and the hard place, understood that he was damned if he did and damned if he didn't. He saw himself, not as a victim of circumstances but as an independent agent who, in spite of the consequences, was willing to accept responsibility for his actions. By the end of the play, Oedipus has come to an understanding not only of himself but of human nature and our place in the world. Thus the play transcends the particulars of Greek mythology and stands forever as a parable of the relationship each of us must make with the metaphysical world.

This production at Stratford, Ontario in 1955 attempted to capture the ritualistic spirit of Oedipus the King; *Douglas Campbell, wearing an onkos, played the tragic king and appeared here with members of the Stratford Festival Acting Company. Directed by Sir Tyrone Guthrie and designed by Tanya Moiseiwitsch, this production was called* Oedipus Rex.

OEDIPUS THE KING

S O P H O C L E S

Translated by David Grene

CHARACTERS
OEDIPUS, *King of Thebes*
JOCASTA, *His Wife*
CREON, *His Brother-in-Law*
TEIRESIAS, *an Old Blind Prophet*
A PRIEST
FIRST MESSENGER
SECOND MESSENGER
A HERDSMAN
A CHORUS OF OLD MEN OF THEBES

SCENE: *In front of the palace of Oedipus at Thebes. To the right of the stage near the altar stands the Priest with a crowd of children. Oedipus emerges from the central door.*

OEDIPUS.
    Children, young sons and daughters of old Cadmus,
    why do you sit here with your suppliant crowns?
    The town is heavy with a mingled burden
    of sounds and smells, of groans and hymns and incense;

    I did not think it fit that I should hear   5
    of this from messengers but came myself,—
    I Oedipus whom all men call the Great.
                    (*He turns to the Priest.*)
    You're old and they are young; come, speak for them.
    What do you fear or want, that you sit here
    suppliant? Indeed I'm willing to give all   10
    that you may need; I would be very hard
    should I not pity suppliants like these.

PRIEST.
    O ruler of my country, Oedipus,
    you see our company around the altar;
    you see our ages; some of us, like these,   15
    who cannot yet fly far, and some of us
    heavy with age; these children are the chosen
    among the young, and I the priest of Zeus.
    Within the market place sit others crowned
    with suppliant garlands, at the double shrine   20
    of Pallas and the temple where Ismenus
    gives oracles by fire. King, you yourself
    have seen our city reeling like a wreck

already; it can scarcely lift its prow
25   out of the depths, out of the bloody surf.
A blight is on the fruitful plants of the earth,
A blight is on the cattle in the fields,
a blight is on our women that no children
are born to them; a God that carries fire,
30   a deadly pestilence, is on our town,
strikes us and spares not, and the house of Cadmus
is emptied of its people while black Death
grows rich in groaning and in lamentation.
We have not come as suppliants to this altar
35   because we thought of you as of a God,
but rather judging you the first of men
in all the chances of this life and when
we mortals have to do with more than man.
You came and by your coming saved our city,
40   freed us from tribute which we paid of old
to the Sphinx, cruel singer. This you did
in virtue of no knowledge we could give you,
in virtue of no teaching; it was God
that aided you, men say, and you are held
45   with God's assistance to have saved our lives.
Now Oedipus, Greatest in all men's eyes,
here falling at your feet we all entreat you,
find us some strength for rescue.
Perhaps you'll hear a wise word from some God,
50   perhaps you will learn something from a man
(for I have seen that for the skilled of practice
the outcome of their counsels live the most).
Noblest of men, go, and raise up our city,
go,—and give heed. For now this land of ours
55   calls you its savior since you saved it once.
So, let us never speak about your reign
as of a time when first our feet were set
secure on high, but later fell to ruin.
Raise up our city, save it and raise it up.
60   Once you have brought us luck with happy omen;
be no less now in fortune.
If you will rule this land, as now you rule it,
better to rule it full of men than empty.
For neither tower nor ship is anything
65   when empty, and none live in it together.
OEDIPUS.
I pity you, children. You have come full of longing,
but I have known the story before you told it
only too well. I know you are all sick,
yet there is not one of you, sick though you are,
70   that is as sick as I myself.
Your several sorrows each have single scope
and touch but one of you. My spirit groans
for city and myself and you at once.
You have not roused me like a man from sleep;
75   know that I have given many tears to this,
gone many ways wandering in thought,
but as I thought I found only one remedy

and that I took. I sent Menoeceus' son
Creon, Jocasta's brother, to Apollo,
to his Pythian temple,   80
that he might learn there by what act or word
I could save this city. As I count the days,
it vexes me what ails him; he is gone
far longer than he needed for the journey.
But when he comes, then, may I prove a villain,   85
if I shall not do all the God commands.
PRIEST.
Thanks for your gracious words. Your servants here
signal that Creon is this moment coming.
OEDIPUS.
His face is bright. O holy Lord Apollo,
grant that his news too may be bright for us   90
and bring us safety.
PRIEST.
It is happy news,
I think, for else his head would not be crowned
with sprigs of fruitful laurel.
OEDIPUS.
                                        We will know soon,
he's within hail. Lord Creon, my good brother,   95
what is the word you bring from the God?

                                        (Creon enters.)
CREON.
A good word,—for things hard to bear themselves
if in the final issue all is well
I count complete good fortune.
OEDIPUS.
                                        What do you mean?
What you have said so far   100
leaves me uncertain whether to trust or fear.
CREON.
If you will hear my news before these others
I am ready to speak, or else to go within.
OEDIPUS.
Speak it to all;
the grief I bear, I bear it more for these   105
than for my own heart.
CREON.
                                        I will tell you, then,
what I heard from the God.
King Phoebus in plain words commanded us
to drive out a pollution from our land,
pollution grown ingrained within the land;   110
drive it out, said the God, not cherish it,
till it's past cure.
OEDIPUS.
                                        What is the rite
of purification? How shall it be done?
CREON.
By banishing a man, or expiation
of blood by blood, since it is murder guilt   115
which holds our city in this destroying storm.

OEDIPUS.
    Who is this man whose fate the God pronounces?
CREON.
    My lord, before you piloted the state
    we had a king called Laius.
OEDIPUS.
120   I know of him by hearsay. I have not seen him.
CREON.
    The God commanded clearly: let some one
    punish with force this dead man's murderers.
OEDIPUS.
    Where are they in the world? Where would a trace
    of this old crime be found? It would be hard
    to guess where.
CREON.
125   The clue is in this land;
    that which is sought is found;
    the unheeded thing escapes:
    so said the God.
OEDIPUS.
            Was it at home,
    or in the country that death came upon him,
130   or in another country travelling?
CREON.
    He went, he said himself, upon an embassy,
    but never returned when he set out from home.
OEDIPUS.
    Was there no messenger, no fellow traveller
    who knew what happened? Such a one might tell
135   something of use.
CREON.
    They were all killed save one. He fled in terror
    and he could tell us nothing in clear terms
    of what he knew, nothing, but one thing only.
OEDIPUS.
    What was it?
140   If we could even find a slim beginning
    in which to hope, we might discover much.
CREON.
    This man said that the robbers they encountered
    were many and the hands that did the murder
    were many; it was no man's single power.
OEDIPUS.
145   How could a robber dare a deed like this
    were he not helped with money from the city,
    money and treachery?
CREON.
            That indeed was thought.
    But Laius was dead and in our trouble
    there was none to help.
OEDIPUS.
150   What trouble was so great to hinder you
    inquiring out the murder of your king?
CREON.
    The riddling Sphinx induced us to neglect

mysterious crimes and rather seek solution
of troubles at our feet.
OEDIPUS.
    I will bring this to light again. King Phoebus   155
fittingly took this care about the dead,
and you too fittingly.
And justly you will see in me an ally,
a champion of my country and the God.
For when I drive pollution from the land   160
I will not serve a distant friend's advantage,
but act in my own interest. Whoever
he was that killed the king may readily
wish to dispatch me with the murderous hand;
so helping the dead king I help myself.   165
Come, children, take your suppliant boughs and go;
up from the altars now. Call the assembly
and let it meet upon the understanding
that I'll do everything. God will decide
whether we prosper or remain in sorrow.   170
PRIEST.
    Rise, children—it was this we came to seek,
which of himself the king now offers us.
May Phoebus who gave us the oracle
come to our rescue and stay the plague.

(Exeunt all but the Chorus.)

CHORUS.

STROPHE

What is the sweet spoken word of God from the shrine
    of Pytho rich in gold   175
that has come to glorious Thebes?
I am stretched on the rack of doubt, and terror and trem-
    bling hold
my heart, O Delian Healer, and I worship full of fears
for what doom you will bring to pass, new or renewed in
    the revolving years.
Speak to me, immortal voice,   180
child of golden Hope.

ANTISTROPHE

First I call on you, Athene, deathless daughter of Zeus,
and Artemis, Earth Upholder,
who sits in the midst of the market place in the throne
    which men call Fame,
and Phoebus, the Far Shooter, three averters of Fate,   185
come to us now, if ever before, when ruin rushed upon
    the state,
you drove destruction's flame away
out of our land.

STROPHE

Our sorrows defy number;
all the ship's timbers are rotten;   190
taking of thought is no spear for the driving away of the
    plague.

There are no growing children in this famous land;
there are no women bearing the pangs of childbirth.
You may see them one with another, like birds swift on
the wing,
195 quicker than fire unmastered,
speeding away to the coast of the Western God.

ANTISTROPHE

In the unnumbered deaths
of its people the city dies;
those children that are born lie dead on the naked earth
unpitied, spreading contagion of death; and gray haired
200 mothers and wives
everywhere stand at the altar's edge, suppliant, moaning;
the hymn to the healing God rings out but with it the
wailing voices are blended.
From these our sufferings grant us, O golden Daughter of
Zeus,
glad-faced deliverance.

STROPHE

There is no clash of brazen shields but our fight is with
205 the War God,
a War God ringed with the cries of men, a savage God
who burns us;
grant that he turn in racing course backwards out of our
country's bounds
to the great palace of Amphitrite or where the waves of
the Thracian sea
deny the stranger safe anchorage.
210 Whatsoever escapes the night
at last the light of day revisits;
so smite the War God, Father Zeus,
beneath your thunderbolt,
for you are the Lord of the lightning, the lightning that
carries fire.

ANTISTROPHE

And your unconquered arrow shafts, winged by the
golden corded bow,
215 Lycean King, I beg to be at our side for help;
and the gleaming torches of Artemis with which she
scours the Lycean hills,
and I call on the God with the turban of gold, who gave
his name to this country of ours,
the Bacchic God with the wind flushed face,
220 Evian One, who travel
with the Maenad company,
combat the God that burns us
with your torch of pine;
for the God that is our enemy is a God unhonoured
among the Gods.

(Oedipus returns.)

OEDIPUS.
For what you ask me—if you will hear my words,   225
and hearing welcome them and fight the plague,
you will find strength and lightening of your load.

Hark to me; what I say to you, I say
as one that is a stranger to the story
as stranger to the deed. For I would not   230
be far upon the track if I alone
were tracing it without a clue. But now,
since after all was finished, I became
a citizen among you, citizens—
now I proclaim to all the men of Thebes: 235
who so among you knows the murderer
by whose hand Laius, son of Labdacus,
died—I command him to tell everything
to me,—yes, though he fears himself to take the blame
on his own head; for bitter punishment   240
he shall have none, but leave this land unharmed.
Or if he knows the murderer, another,
a foreigner, still let him speak the truth.
For I will pay him and be grateful, too.
But if you shall keep silence, if perhaps   245
some one of you, to shield a guilty friend,
or for his own sake shall reject my words—
hear what I shall do then:
I forbid that man, whoever he be, my land,
my land where I hold sovereignty and throne;   250
and I forbid any to welcome him
or cry him greeting or make him a sharer
in sacrifice or offering to the Gods,
or give him water for his hands to wash.
I command all to drive him from their homes,   255
since he is our pollution, as the oracle
of Pytho's God proclaimed him now to me.
So I stand forth a champion of the God
and of the man who died.
Upon the murderer I invoke this curse—   260
whether he is one man and all unknown,
or one of many—may he wear out his life
in misery to miserable doom!
If with my knowledge he lives at my hearth
I pray that I myself may feel my curse.   265
On you I lay my charge to fulfill all this
for me, for the God, and for this land of ours
destroyed and blighted, by the God forsaken.

Even were this no matter of God's ordinance
it would not fit you so to leave it lie,   270
unpurified, since a good man is dead
and one that was a king. Search it out.
Since I am now the holder of his office,
and have his bed and wife that once was his,
and had his line not been unfortunate   275
we would have common children—(fortune leaped

69

upon his head)—because of all these things,
I fight in his defence as for my father,
and I shall try all means to take the murderer
280 of Laius the son of Labdacus
the son of Polydorus and before him
of Cadmus and before him of Agenor.
Those who do not obey me, may the Gods
grant no crops springing from the ground they plough
285 nor children to their women! May a fate
like this, or one still worse than this consume them!
For you whom these words please, the other Thebans,
may Justice as your ally and all the gods
live with you, blessing you now and for ever!

CHORUS.
290 As you have held me to my oath, I speak:
I neither killed the king nor can declare
the killer; but since Phoebus set the quest
it is his part to tell who the man is.

OEDIPUS.
Right; but to put compulsion on the Gods
295 against their will—no man can do that.

CHORUS.
May I then say what I think second best?

OEDIPUS.
If there's a third best, too, spare not to tell it.

CHORUS.
I know that what the Lord Teiresias
sees, is most often what the Lord Apollo
300 sees. If you should inquire of this from him
you might find out most clearly.

OEDIPUS.
Even in this my actions have not been sluggard.
On Creon's word I have sent two messengers
and why the prophet is not here already
I have been wondering.

CHORUS.
305   His skill apart
there is besides only an old faint story.

OEDIPUS.
What is it?
I look at every story.

CHORUS.
                    It was said
that he was killed by certain wayfarers.

OEDIPUS.
310 I heard that, too, but no one saw the killer.

CHORUS.
Yet if he has a share of fear at all,
his courage will not stand firm, hearing your curse.

OEDIPUS.
The man who in the doing did not shrink
will fear no word.

CHORUS.
                    Here comes his prosecutor:
315 led by your men the godly prophet comes
in whom alone of mankind truth is native.

(Enter Teiresias, led by a little boy.)

OEDIPUS.
Teiresias, you are versed in everything,
things teachable and things not to be spoken,
things of the heaven and earth-creeping things.
320 You have no eyes but in your mind you know
with what a plague our city is afflicted.
My lord, in you alone we find a champion,
in you alone one that can rescue us.
Perhaps you have not heard the messengers,
325 but Phoebus sent in answer to our sending
an oracle declaring that our freedom
from this disease would only come when we
should learn the names of those who killed King
    Laius,
and kill them or expel from our country.
330 Do not begrudge us oracles from birds,
or any other way of prophecy
within your skill; save yourself and the city,
save me; redeem the debt of our pollution
that lies on us because of this dead man.
335 We are in your hands; pains are most nobly taken
to help another when you have means and power.

TEIRESIAS.
Alas, how terrible is wisdom when
it brings no profit to the man that's wise!
This I knew well, but had forgotten it,
else I would not have come here.

OEDIPUS.
340   What is this?
How sad you are now you have come!

TEIRESIAS.
                              Let me
go home. It will be easiest for us both
to bear our several destinies to the end
if you will follow my advice.

OEDIPUS.
                    You'd rob us
345 of this your gift of prophecy? You talk
as one who had no care for law nor love
for Thebes who reared you.

TEIRESIAS.
Yes, but I see that even your own words
miss the mark; therefore I must fear for mine.

OEDIPUS.
350 For God's sake if you know of anything,
do not turn from us; all of us kneel to you,
all of us here, your suppliants.

TEIRESIAS.
All of you here know nothing. I will not
bring to the light of day my troubles, mine—
rather than call them yours.

OEDIPUS.
355   What do you mean?
You know of something but refuse to speak.
Would you betray us and destroy the city?

TEIRESIAS.
    I will not bring this pain upon us both,
    neither on you nor on myself. Why is it
360   you question me and waste your labour? I
    will tell you nothing.
OEDIPUS.
    You would provoke a stone! Tell us, you villain,
    tell us, and do not stand there quietly
    unmoved and balking at the issue.
TEIRESIAS.
365   You blame my temper but you do not see
    your own that lives within you; it is me
    you chide.
OEDIPUS.
    Who would not feel his temper rise
    at words like these with which you shame our city?
TEIRESIAS.
    Of themselves things will come, although I hide them
    and breathe no word of them.
OEDIPUS.
370   Since they will come
    tell them to me.
TEIRESIAS.
            I will say nothing further.
    Against this answer let your temper rage
    as wildly as you will.
OEDIPUS.
             Indeed I am
    so angry I shall not hold back a jot
375   of what I think. For I would have you know
    I think you were complotter of the deed
    and doer of the deed save in so far
    as for the actual killing. Had you had eyes
    I would have said alone you murdered him.
TEIRESIAS.
380   Yes? Then I warn you faithfully to keep
    the letter of your proclamation and
    from this day forth to speak no word of greeting
    to these nor me; you are the land's pollution.
OEDIPUS.
    How shamelessly you started up this taunt!
    How do you think you will escape?
TEIRESIAS.
385   I have.
    I have escaped; the truth is what I cherish
    and that's my strength.
OEDIPUS.
            And who has taught you truth?
    Not your profession surely!
TEIRESIAS.
            You have taught me,
    for you have made me speak against my will.
OEDIPUS.
390   Speak what? Tell me again that I may learn it better.
TEIRESIAS.
    Did you not understand before or would you

provoke me into speaking?
OEDIPUS.
                 I did not grasp it,
    not so to call it known. Say it again.
TEIRESIAS.
    I say you are the murderer of the king
    whose murderer you seek.
OEDIPUS.
                Not twice you shall   395
    say calumnies like this and stay unpunished.
TEIRESIAS.
    Shall I say more to tempt your anger more?
OEDIPUS.
    As much as you desire; it will be said
    in vain.
TEIRESIAS.
        I say that with those you love best
    you live in foulest shame unconsciously   400
    and do not see where you are in calamity.
OEDIPUS.
    Do you imagine you can always talk
    like this, and live to laugh at it hereafter?
TEIRESIAS.
    Yes, if the truth has anything of strength.
OEDIPUS.
    It has, but not for you; it has no strength   405
    for you because you are blind in mind and ears
    as well as in your eyes.
TEIRESIAS.
             You are a poor wretch
    to taunt me with the very insults which
    every one soon will heap upon yourself.
OEDIPUS.
    Your life is one long night so that you cannot   410
    hurt me or any other who sees the light.
TEIRESIAS.
    It is not fate that I should be your ruin,
    Apollo is enough; it is his care
    to work this out.
OEDIPUS.
            Was this your design
    or Creon's?
TEIRESIAS.
           Creon is no hurt to you,   415
    but you are to yourself.
OEDIPUS.
    Wealth, sovereignty and skill outmatching skill
    for the contrivance of an envied life!
    Great store of jealousy fill your treasury chests,
    if my friend Creon, friend from the first and loyal,   420
    thus secretly attacks me, secretly
    desires to drive me out and secretly
    suborns this juggling, trick devising quack,
    this wily beggar who has only eyes
    for his own gains, but blindness in his skill.   425
    For, tell me, where have you seen clear, Teiresias,

with your prophetic eyes? When the dark singer,
the sphinx, was in your country, did you speak
word of deliverance to its citizens?
430 And yet the riddle's answer was not the province
of a chance comer. It was a prophet's task
and plainly you had no such gift of prophecy
from birds nor otherwise from any God
to glean a word of knowledge. But I came,
435 Oedipus, who knew nothing, and I stopped her.
I solved the riddle by my wit alone.
Mine was no knowledge got from birds. And now
you would expel me,
because you think that you will find a place
440 by Creon's throne. I think you will be sorry,
both you and your accomplice, for your plot
to drive me out. And did I not regard you
as an old man, some suffering would have taught you
that what was in your heart was treason.

CHORUS.
445 We look at this man's words and yours, my king,
and we find both have spoken them in anger.
We need no angry words but only thought
how we may best hit the God's meaning for us.

TEIRESIAS.
If you are king, at least I have the right
450 no less to speak in my defence against you.
Of that much I am master. I am no slave
of yours, but Loxias', and so I shall not
enroll myself with Creon for my patron.
Since you have taunted me with being blind,
455 here is my word for you.
You have your eyes but see not where you are
in sin, nor where you live, nor whom you live with.
Do you know who your parents are? Unknowing
you are an enemy to kith and kin
460 in death, beneath the earth, and in this life.
A deadly footed, double striking curse,
from father and mother both, shall drive you forth
out of this land, with darkness on your eyes,
that now have such straight vision. Shall there be
465 a place will not be harbour to your cries,
a corner of Cithaeron will not ring
in echo to your cries, soon, soon,—
when you shall learn the secret of your marriage,
which steered you to a haven in this house,—
470 haven no haven, after lucky voyage?
And of the multitude of other evils
establishing a grim equality
between you and your children, you know nothing.
So, muddy with contempt my words and Creon's!
475 Misery shall grind no man as it will you.

OEDIPUS.
Is it endurable that I should hear
such words from him? Go and a curse go with you!
Quick, home with you! Out of my house at once!

TEIRESIAS.
I would not have come either had you not called me.

OEDIPUS.
I did not know then you would talk like a fool—   480
or it would have been long before I called you.

TEIRESIAS.
I am a fool then, as it seems to you—
but to the parents who have bred you, wise.

OEDIPUS.
What parents? Stop! Who are they of all the world?

TEIRESIAS.
This day will show your birth and will destroy you.   485

OEDIPUS.
How needlessly your riddles darken everything.

TEIRESIAS.
But it's in riddle answering you are strongest.

OEDIPUS.
Yes, Taunt me where you will find me great.

TEIRESIAS.
It is this very luck that has destroyed you.

OEDIPUS.
I do not care, if it has saved this city.   490

TEIRESIAS.
Well, I will go. Come, boy, lead me away.

OEDIPUS.
Yes, lead him off. So long as you are here,
you'll be a stumbling block and a vexation;
once gone, you will not trouble me again.

TEIRESIAS.
                                        I have said
what I came here to say not fearing your   495
countenance: there is no way you can hurt me.
I tell you, king, this man, this murderer
(whom you have long declared you are in search of,
indicting him in threatening proclamation
as murderer of Laius)—he is here.   500
In name he is a stranger among citizens
but soon he will be shown to be a citizen
true native Theban, and he'll have no joy
of the discovery: blindness for sight
and beggary for riches his exchange,   505
he shall go journeying to a foreign country
tapping his way before him with a stick,
He shall be proved father and brother both
to his own children in his house; to her
that gave him birth, a son and husband both;   510
a fellow sower in his father's bed
with that same father that he murdered.
Go within, reckon that out, and if you find me
mistaken, say I have no skill in prophecy.
            (*Exeunt separately Teiresias and Oedipus.*)

CHORUS.

STROPHE

Who is the man proclaimed   515

by Delphi's prophetic rock
as the bloody handed murderer,
the doer of deeds that none dare name?
Now is the time for him to run
520   with a stronger foot
than Pegasus
for the child of Zeus leaps in arms upon him
with fire and the lightning bolt,
and terribly close on his heels
525   are the Fates that never miss.

ANTISTROPHE

Lately from snowy Parnassus
clearly the voice flashed forth,
bidding each Theban track him down,
the unknown murderer.
530   In the savage forests he lurks and in
the caverns like
the mountain bull.
He is sad and lonely, and lonely his feet
that carry him far from the navel of earth;
535   but its prophecies, ever living,
flutter around his head.

STROPHE

The augur has spread confusion,
terrible confusion;
I do not approve what was said
540   nor can I deny it.
I do not know what to say;
I am in a flutter of foreboding;
I never heard in the present
nor past of a quarrel between
545   the sons of Labdacus and Polybus,
that I might bring as proof
in attacking the popular fame
of Oedipus, seeking
to take vengeance for undiscovered
550   death in the line of Labdacus.

ANTISTROPHE

Truly Zeus and Apollo are wise
and in human things all knowing;
but amongst men there is no
distinct judgment, between the prophet
555   and me—which of us is right.
One man may pass another in wisdom
but I would never agree
with those that find fault with the king
till I should see the word
560   proved right beyond doubt. For once
in visible from the Sphinx
came on him and all of us

saw his wisdom and in that test
he saved the city. So he will not be condemned by my
    mind.

(Enter Creon.)

CREON.
Citizens, I have come because I heard   565
deadly words spread about me, that the king
accuses me. I cannot take that from him.
If he believes that in these present troubles
he has been wronged by me in word or deed
I do not want to live on with the burden   570
of such a scandal on me. The report
injures me doubly and most vitally—
for I'll be called a traitor to my city
and traitor also to my friends and you.
CHORUS.
Perhaps it was a sudden gust of anger   575
that forced that insult from him, and no judgment.
CREON.
But did he say that it was in compliance
with schemes of mine that the seer told him lies?
CHORUS.
Yes, he said that, but why, I do not know.
CREON.
Were his eyes straight in his head? Was his mind right   580
when he accused me in this fashion?
CHORUS.
I do not know; I have no eyes to see
what princes do. Here comes the king himself.

(Enter Oedipus.)

OEDIPUS.
You, sir, how is it you come here? Have you so much
brazen-faced daring that you venture in   585
my house although you are proved manifestly
the murderer of that man, and though you tried,
openly, highway robbery of my crown?
For God's sake, tell me what you saw in me,
what cowardice or what stupidity,   590
that made you lay a plot like this against me?
Did you imagine I should not observe
the crafty scheme that stole upon me or
seeing it, take no means to counter it?
Was it not stupid of you to make the attempt,   595
to try to hunt down royal power without
the people at your back or friends? For only
with the people at your back or money can
the hunt end in the capture of a crown.
CREON.
Do you know what you're doing? Will you listen   600
to words to answer yours, and then pass judgment?
OEDIPUS.
You're quick to speak, but I am slow to grasp you,
for I have found you dangerous,—and my foe.
CREON.
First of all hear what I shall say to that.

OEDIPUS.
605　At least don't tell me that you are not guilty.
CREON.
　　If you think obstinacy without wisdom
　　a valuable possession, you are wrong.
OEDIPUS.
　　And you are wrong if you believe that one,
　　a criminal, will not be punished only
　　because he is my kinsman.
CREON.
　　　　　　　　　　This is but just—
610　but tell me, then, of what offense I'm guilty?
OEDIPUS.
　　Did you or did you not urge me to send
　　to this prophetic mumbler?
CREON.
　　　　　　　　　　I did indeed,
　　and I shall stand by what I told you.
OEDIPUS.
615　How long ago is it since Laius. . .
CREON.
　　What about Laius? I don't understand.
OEDIPUS.
　　Vanished—died—was murdered?
CREON.
　　　　　　　　　　It is long,
　　a long, long time to reckon.
OEDIPUS.
　　　　　　　　　　Was this prophet
　　in the profession then?
CREON.
　　　　　　　　　　He was, and honoured
620　as highly as he is today.
OEDIPUS.
　　At that time did he say a word about me?
CREON.
　　Never, at least when I was near him.
OEDIPUS.
　　You never made a search for the dead man?
CREON.
　　We searched, indeed, but never learned of anything.
OEDIPUS.
625　Why did our wise old friend not say this then?
CREON.
　　I don't know; and when I know nothing, I
　　usually hold my tongue.
OEDIPUS.
　　　　　　　　　　You know this much,
　　and can declare this much if you are loyal.
CREON.
　　What is it? If I know, I'll not deny it.
OEDIPUS.
630　That he would not have said that I killed Laius
　　had he not met you first.
CREON.
　　　　　　　　　　You know yourself

whether he said this, but I demand that I
should hear as much from you as you from me.
OEDIPUS.
　　Then hear,—I'll not be proved a murderer.
CREON.
　　Well, then. You're married to my sister.
OEDIPUS.
　　　　　　　　　　Yes,　　　　635
　　that I am not disposed to deny.
CREON.
　　　　　　　　　　You rule
　　this country giving her an equal share
　　in the government?
OEDIPUS.
　　　　　　　　　　Yes, everything she wants
　　she has from me.
CREON.
　　　　　　　　　　And I, as thirdsman to you,
　　am rated as the equal of you two?　　　　640
OEDIPUS.
　　Yes, and it's there you've proved yourself false friend.
CREON.
　　Not if you will reflect on it as I do.
　　Consider, first, if you think any one
　　would choose to rule and fear rather than rule
　　and sleep untroubled by a fear if power　　　　645
　　were equal in both cases. I, at least,
　　I was not born with such a frantic yearning
　　to be a king—but to do what kings do.
　　And so it is with every one who has learned
　　wisdom and self-control. As it stands now,　　　　650
　　the prizes are all mine—and without fear.
　　But if I were the king myself, I must
　　do much that went against the grain.
　　How should despotic rule seem sweeter to me
　　than painless power and an assured authority?　　　　655
　　I am not so besotted yet that I
　　want other honours than those that come with profit.
　　Now every man's my pleasure; every man greets me;
　　now those who are your suitors fawn on me,—
　　success for them depends upon my favour.　　　　660
　　Why should I let all this go to win that?
　　My mind would not be traitor if it's wise;
　　I am no treason lover, of my nature,
　　nor would I ever dare to join a plot.
　　Prove what I say. Go to the oracle　　　　665
　　at Pytho and inquire about the answers,
　　if they are as I told you. For the rest,
　　if you discover I laid any plot
　　together with the seer, kill me, I say,
　　not only by your vote but by my own.　　　　670
　　But do not charge me on obscure opinion
　　without some proof to back it. It's not just
　　lightly to count your knaves as honest men,
　　nor honest men as knaves. To throw away
　　an honest friend is, as it were, to throw　　　　675

your life away, which a man loves the best.
In time you will know all with certainty;
time is the only test of honest men,
one day is space enough to know a rogue.

CHORUS.

680   His words are wise, king, if one fears to fall.
Those who are quick of temper are not safe.

OEDIPUS.

When he that plots against me secretly
moves quickly, I must quickly counterplot.
If I wait taking no decisive measure

685   his business will be done, and mine be spoiled.

CREON.

What do you want to do then? Banish me?

OEDIPUS.

No, certainly; kill you, not banish you[1]

CREON.

I do not think that you've your wits about you.

OEDIPUS.

For my own interests, yes.

CREON.

                But for mine, too,
you should think equally.

OEDIPUS.

690   You are a rogue.

CREON.

Suppose you do not understand?

OEDIPUS.

                But yet
I must be ruler.

CREON.

          Not if you rule badly.

OEDIPUS.

O, city, city!

CREON.

        I too have some share
in the city; it is not yours alone.

CHORUS.

695   Stop, my lords! Here—and in the nick of time
I see Jocasta coming from the house;
with her help lay the quarrel that now stirs you.

                      (*Enter Jocasta.*)

JOCASTA.

For shame! Why have you raised this foolish
    squabbling
brawl? Are you not ashamed to air your private
700   griefs when the country's sick? Go in, you, Oedipus,
and you, too, Creon, into the house. Don't magnify
your nothing troubles.

---

1. Two lines omitted here owing to the confusion in the dialogue
consequent on the loss of a third line. The lines as they stand in
Jebb's edition (1902) are:
OED.: That you may show what manner of thing is envy.
CREON: You speak as one that will not yield or trust.
[OED. lost line.]

CREON.

            Sister, Oedipus,
your husband, thinks he has the right to do
terrible wrongs—he has but to choose between
two terrors: banishing or killing me.   705

OEDIPUS.

He's right, Jocasta; for I find him plotting
with knavish tricks against my person.

CREON.

That God may never bless me! May I die
accursed, if I have been guilty of
one tittle of the charge you bring against me!   710

JOCASTA.

I beg you, Oedipus, trust him in this,
spare him for the sake of this his oath to God,
for my sake, and the sake of those who stand here.

CHORUS.

Be gracious, be merciful,
we beg of you   715

OEDIPUS.

In what would you have me yield?

CHORUS.

He has been no silly child in the past.
He is strong in his oath now.
Spare him.

OEDIPUS.

Do you know what you ask?   720

CHORUS.

Yes.

OEDIPUS.

Tell me then.

CHORUS.

He has been your friend before all men's eyes; do not cast
him away dishonoured on an obscure conjecture.

OEDIPUS.

I would have you know that this request of yours   725
really requests my death or banishment.

CHORUS.

May the Sun God, king of Gods, forbid! May I die
without God's blessing, without friends' help, if I had any
such thought. But my spirit is broken by my unhappiness
for my wasting country; and this would but add troubles   730
amongst ourselves to the other troubles.

OEDIPUS.

Well, let him go then—if I must die ten times for it,
or be sent out dishonoured into exile.
It is your lips that prayed for him I pitied,
not his; wherever he is, I shall hate him.   735

CREON.

I see you sulk in yielding and you're dangerous
when you are out of temper; natures like yours
are justly heaviest for themselves to bear.

OEDIPUS.

Leave me alone! Take yourself off, I tell you.

CREON.

I'll go, you have not known me, but they have,   740

and they have known my innocence.

(*Exit.*)

CHORUS.
Won't you take him inside, lady?

JOCASTA.
Yes, when I've found out what was the matter.

CHORUS.
There was some misconceived suspicion of a story, and
    on the other side the sting of injustice.

JOCASTA.
745 So, on both sides?

CHORUS.
Yes.

JOCASTA.
What was the story?

CHORUS.
I think it best, in the interests of the country, to leave it
where it ended.

OEDIPUS.
750 You see where you have ended, straight of judgment
although you are, by softening my anger.

CHORUS.
Sir, I have said before and I say again—be sure that I would
have been proved a madman, bankrupt in sane council, if I
should put you away, you who steered the country I love
755 safely when she was crazed with troubles. God grant that
now, too, you may prove a fortunate guide for us.

JOCASTA.
Tell me, my lord, I beg of you, what was it
that roused your anger so?

OEDIPUS.
                Yes, I will tell you.
I honour you more than I honour them.
760 It was Creon and the plots he laid against me.

JOCASTA.
Tell me—if you can clearly tell the quarrel—

OEDIPUS.
                        Creon says
that I'm the murderer of Laius.

JOCASTA.
Of his own knowledge or on information?

OEDIPUS.
He sent this rascal prophet to me, since
765 he keeps his own mouth clean of any guilt.

JOCASTA.
Do not concern yourself about this matter;
listen to me and learn that human beings
have no part in the craft of prophecy.
Of that I'll show you a short proof.
770 There was an oracle once that came to Laius,—
I will not say that it was Phoebus' own,
but it was from his servants—and it told him
that it was fate that he should die a victim
at the hands of his own son, a son to be born
775 of Laius and me. But, see now, he,
the king, was killed by foreign highway robbers

at a place where three roads meet—so goes the story;
and for the son—before three days were out
after his birth King Laius pierced his ankles
and by the hands of others cast him forth   780
upon a pathless hillside. So Apollo
failed to fulfill his oracle to the son,
that he should kill his father, and to Laius
also proved false in that the thing he feared,
death at his son's hands, never came to pass.   785
So clear in this case were the oracles,
so clear and false. Give them no heed, I say;
what God discovers need of, easily
he shows to us himself.

OEDIPUS.
               O dear Jocasta,
as I hear this from you, there comes upon me   790
a wandering of the soul—I could run mad.

JOCASTA.
What trouble is it, that you turn again
and speak like this?

OEDIPUS.
           I thought I heard you say
that Laius was killed at a crossroads.

JOCASTA.
Yes, that was how the story went and still   795
that word goes round.

OEDIPUS.
          Where is this place, Jocasta,
where he was murdered?

JOCASTA.
          Phocis is the country
and the road splits there, one of the two roads from Delphi,
another comes from Daulia.

OEDIPUS.
          How long ago is this?

JOCASTA.
The news came to the city just before   800
you became king and all men's eyes looked to you.
What is it, Oedipus, that's in your mind?

OEDIPUS.
What have you designed, O Zeus, to do with me?

JOCASTA.
What is the thought that troubles your heart?

OEDIPUS.
Don't ask me yet—tell me of Laius—   805
How did he look? How old or young was he?

JOCASTA.
He was a tall man and his hair was grizzled
already—nearly white—and in his form
not unlike you.

OEDIPUS.
       O God, I think I have
called curses on myself in ignorance.   810

JOCASTA.
What do you mean? I am terrified
when I look at you.

OEDIPUS.
                              I have a deadly fear
  that the old seer had eyes. You'll show me more
  if you can tell me one more thing.
JOCASTA.
                                        I will.
815 I'm frightened—but if I can understand,
  I'll tell you all you ask.
OEDIPUS.
                          How was his company?
  Had he few with him when he went this journey,
  or many servants, as would suit a prince?
JOCASTA.
  In all there were but five, and among them
820 a herald; and one carriage for the king.
OEDIPUS.
  It's plain—it's plain—who was it told you this?
JOCASTA.
  The only servant that escaped safe home.
OEDIPUS.
  Is he at home now?
JOCASTA.
                        No, when he came home again
  and saw you king and Laius was dead,
825 he came to me and touched my hand and begged
  that I should send him to the fields to be
  my shepherd and so he might see the city
  as far off as he might. So I
  sent him away. He was an honest man,
830 as slaves go, and was worthy of far more
  than what he asked of me.
OEDIPUS.
  O, how I wish that he could come back quickly!
JOCASTA.
  He can. Why is your heart so set on this?
OEDIPUS.
  O dear Jocasta, I am full of fears
835 that I have spoken far too much; and therefore
  I wish to see this shepherd.
JOCASTA.
                                He will come;
  but, Oedipus, I think I'm worthy too
  to know what it is that disquiets you.
OEDIPUS.
  It shall not be kept from you, since my mind
840 has gone so far with its forebodings. Whom
  should I confide in rather than you, who is there
  of more importance to me who have passed
  through such a fortune?
  Polybus was my father, king of Corinth,
845 and Merope, the Dorian, my mother.
  I was held greatest of the citizens
  in Corinth till a curious chance befell me
  as I shall tell you—curious, indeed,
  but hardly worth the store I set upon it.
850 There was a dinner and at it a man,

a drunken man, accused me in his drink
of being bastard. I was furious
but held my temper under for that day.
Next day I went and taxed my parents with it;
they took the insult very ill from him,   855
the drunken fellow who had uttered it.
So I was comforted for their part, but
still this thing rankled always, for the story
crept about widely. And I went at last
to Pytho, though my parents did not know.   860
But Phoebus sent me home again unhonoured
in what I came to learn, but he foretold
other and desperate horrors to befall me,
that I was fated to lie with my mother,
and show to daylight an accursed breed   865
which men would not endure, and I was doomed
to be murderer of the father that begot me.
When I heard this I fled, and in the days
that followed I would measure from the stars
the whereabouts of Corinth—yes, I fled   870
to somewhere where I should not see fulfilled
the infamies told in that dreadful oracle.
And as I journeyed I came to the place
where, as you say, this king met with his death.
Jocasta, I will tell you the whole truth.   875
When I was near the branching of the crossroads,
going on foot, I was encountered by
a herald and a carriage with a man in it,
just as you tell me. He that led the way
and the old man himself wanted to thrust me   880
out of the road by force. I became angry
and struck the coachman who was pushing me.
When the old man saw this he watched his moment,
and as I passed he struck me from his carriage,
full on the head with his two pointed goad.   885
But he was paid in full and presently
my stick had struck him backwards from the car
and he rolled out of it. And then I killed them
all. If it happened there was any tie
of kinship twixt this man and Laius,   890
who is then now more miserable than I,
what man on earth so hated by the Gods,
since neither citizen nor foreigner
may welcome me at home or even greet me,
but drive me out of doors? And it is I,   895
I and no other have so cursed myself.
And I pollute the bed of him I killed
by the hands that killed him. Was I not born evil?
Am I not utterly unclean? I had to fly
and in my banishment not even see   900
my kindred nor set foot in my own country,
or otherwise my fate was to be yoked
in marriage with my mother and kill my father,
Polybus who begot me and had reared me.
Would not one rightly judge and say that on me   905
these things were sent by some malignant God?

O no, no, no—O holy majesty
of God on high, may I not see that day!
May I be gone out of men's sight before
910   I see the deadly taint of this disaster
come upon me.

CHORUS.

Sir, we too fear these things. But until you see this man
face to face and hear his story, hope.

OEDIPUS.

Yes, I have just this much of hope—to wait until the
915   herdsman comes.

JOCASTA.

And when he comes, what do you want with him?

OEDIPUS.

I'll tell you; if I find that his story is the same as yours, I at
least will be clear of this guilt.

JOCASTA.

Why what so particularly did you learn from my story?

OEDIPUS.

920   You said that he spoke of highway *robbers* who killed
Laius. Now if he uses the same number, it was not I who
killed him. One man cannot be the same as many. But if
he speaks of a man travelling alone, then clearly the burden of the guilt inclines towards me.

JOCASTA.

925   Be sure, at least, that this was how he told the story. He
cannot unsay it now, for every one in the city heard it—
not I alone. But, Oedipus, even if he diverges from what
he said then, he shall never prove that the murder of
Laius squares rightly with the prophecy—for Loxias de-
930   clared that the king should be killed by his own son. And
that poor creature did not kill him surely,—for he died
himself first. So as far as prophecy goes, henceforward I
shall not look to the right hand or the left.

OEDIPUS.

Right. But yet, send some one for the peasant to bring
935   him here; do not neglect it.

JOCASTA.

I will send quickly. Now let me go indoors. I will do nothing except what pleases you.

(*Exeunt.*)

CHORUS.

STROPHE

May destiny ever find me
pious in word and deed
940   prescribed by the laws that live on high:
laws begotten in the clear air of heaven,
whose only father is Olympus;
no mortal nature brought them to birth,
no forgetfulness shall lull them to sleep;
945   for God is great in them and grows not old.

ANTISTROPHE

Insolence breeds the tyrant, insolence
if it is glutted with a surfeit, unseasonable, unprofitable,

climbs to the roof-top and plunges
sheer down to the ruin that must be,
and there its feet are no service.   950
But I pray that the God may never
abolish the eager ambition that profits the state.
For I shall never cease to hold the God as our protector.

STROPHE

If a man walks with haughtiness
of hand or word and gives no heed   955
to Justice and the shrines of Gods
despises—may an evil doom
smite him for his ill-starred pride of heart!—
if he reaps gains without justice
and will not hold from impiety   960
and his fingers itch for untouchable things.
When such things are done, what man shall contrive
to shield his soul from the shafts of the God?
When such deeds are held in honour,
why should I honour the Gods in the dance?   965

ANTISTROPHE

No longer to the holy place,
to the navel of earth I'll go
to worship, nor to Abae
nor to Olympia,
unless the oracles are proved to fit,   970
for all men's hands to point at.
O Zeus, if you are rightly called
the sovereign lord, all-mastering,
let this not escape you nor your ever-living power!
The oracles concerning Laius   975
are old and dim and men regard them not.
Apollo is nowhere clear in honour; God's service per-
  ishes.

(*Enter Jocasta, carrying garlands.*)

JOCASTA.

Princes of the land, I have had the thought to go
to the Gods' temples, bringing in my hand
garlands and gifts of incense, as you see.   980
For Oedipus excites himself too much
at every sort of trouble, not conjecturing,
like a man of sense, what will be from what was,
but he is always at the speaker's mercy,
when he speaks terrors. I can do no good   985
by my advice, and so I came as suppliant
to you, Lycaean Apollo, who are nearest.
These are the symbols of my prayer and this
my prayer: grant us escape free of the curse.
Now when we look to him we are all afraid;   990
he's pilot of our ship and he is frightened.

(*Enter Messenger.*)

MESSENGER.

Might I learn from you, sirs, where is the house of Oedipus? Or best of all, if you know, where is the king himself?

CHORUS.

995 This is his house and he is within doors. This lady is his wife and mother of his children.

MESSENGER.

God bless you, lady, and God bless your household! God bless Oedipus' noble wife!

JOCASTA.

God bless you, sir, for your kind greeting! What do you want of us that you have come here? What have you to tell us?

1000

MESSENGER.

Good news, lady. Good for your house and for your husband.

JOCASTA.

What is your news? Who sent you to us?

MESSENGER.

1005 I come from Corinth and the news I bring will give you pleasure. Perhaps a little pain too.

JOCASTA.

What is this news of double meaning?

MESSENGER.

The people of the Isthmus will choose Oedipus to be their king. That is the rumour there.

JOCASTA.

But isn't their king still old Polybus?

MESSENGER.

1010 No. He is in his grave. Death has got him.

JOCASTA.

Is that the truth? Is Oedipus' father dead?

MESSENGER.

May I die myself if it be otherwise!

JOCASTA.

(to a servant.)

Be quick and run to the king with the news! O oracles of the Gods, where are you now? It was from this man Oedipus fled, lest he should be his murderer! And now he is dead, in the course of nature, and not killed by Oedipus.

1015

(Enter Oedipus.)

OEDIPUS.

Dearest Jocasta, why have you sent for me?

JOCASTA.

Listen to this man and when you hear reflect what is the outcome of the holy oracles of the Gods.

OEDIPUS.

1020 Who is he? What is his message for me?

JOCASTA.

He is from Corinth and he tells us that your father Polybus is dead and gone.

OEDIPUS.

What's this you say, sir? Tell me yourself.

MESSENGER.

Since this is the first matter you want clearly told: Polybus has gone down to death. You may be sure of it.

1025

OEDIPUS.

By treachery or sickness?

MESSENGER.

A small thing will put old bodies asleep.

OEDIPUS.

So he died of sickness, it seems,—poor old man!

MESSENGER.

Yes, and of age—the long years he had measured.

OEDIPUS.

Ha! Ha! O dear Jocasta, why should one look to the Pythian hearth? Why should one look to the birds screaming overhead? They prophesied that I should kill my father! But he's dead, and hidden deep in earth, and I stand here who never laid a hand on spear against him,— unless perhaps he died of longing for me, and thus I am his murderer. But they, the oracles, as they stand—he's taken them away with him, they're dead as he himself is, and worthless.

1030

1035

JOCASTA.

That I told you before now.

1040

OEDIPUS.

You did, but I was misled by my fear.

JOCASTA.

Then lay no more of them to heart, not one.

OEDIPUS.

But surely I must fear my mother's bed?

JOCASTA.

Why should man fear since chance is all in all for him, and he can clearly foreknow nothing? Best to live lightly, as one can, unthinkingly. As to your mother's marriage bed,—don't fear it. Before this, in dreams too, as well as oracles, many a man has lain with his own mother. But he to whom such things are nothing bears his life most easily.

1045

1050

OEDIPUS.

All that you say would be said perfectly if she were dead; but since she lives I must still fear, although you talk so well, Jocasta.

JOCASTA.

Still in your father's death there's light of comfort?

1055

OEDIPUS.

Great light of comfort; but I fear the living.

MESSENGER.

Who is the woman that makes you afraid?

OEDIPUS.

Merope, old man, Polybus' wife.

MESSENGER.

What about her frightens the queen and you?

OEDIPUS.

A terrible oracle, stranger, from the Gods.

1060

MESSENGER.

Can it be told? Or does the sacred law forbid another to have knowledge of it?

OEDIPUS.

    O no! Once on a time Loxias said
that I should lie with my own mother and
1065   take on my hands the blood of my own father.
And so for these long years I've lived away
from Corinth; it has been to my great happiness;
but yet it's sweet to see the face of parents.

MESSENGER.

    This was the fear which drove you out of Corinth?

OEDIPUS.

1070   Old man, I did not wish to kill my father.

MESSENGER.

    Why should I not free you from this fear, sir,
since I have come to you in all goodwill?

OEDIPUS.

    You would not find me thankless if you did.

MESSENGER.

    Why, it was just for this I brought the news,—
1075   to earn your thanks when you had come safe home.

OEDIPUS.

    No, I will never come near my parents.

MESSENGER.

                  Son,
it's very plain you don't know what you're doing.

OEDIPUS.

    What do you mean, old man? For God's sake, tell me.

MESSENGER.

    If your homecoming is checked by fears like these.

OEDIPUS.

1080   Yes, I'm afraid that Phoebus may prove right.

MESSENGER.

    The murder and the incest?

OEDIPUS.

              Yes, old man;
that is my constant terror.

MESSENGER.

            Do you know
that all your fears are empty?

OEDIPUS.

             How is that,
if they are father and mother and I their son?

MESSENGER.

1085   Because Polybus was no kin to you in blood.

OEDIPUS.

    What, was not Polybus my father?

MESSENGER.

    No more than I but just so much.

OEDIPUS.

           How can
my father be my father as much as one
that's nothing to me?

MESSENGER.

         Neither he nor I
begat you.

OEDIPUS.

        Why then did he call me son?   1090

MESSENGER.

    A gift he took you from these hands of mine.

OEDIPUS.

    Did he love so much what he took from another's
        hand?

MESSENGER.

    His childlessness before persuaded him.

OEDIPUS.

    Was I a child you bought or found when I
was given to him?

MESSENGER.

          On Cithaeron's slopes   1095
in the twisting thickets you were found.

OEDIPUS.

             And why
were you a traveller in those parts?

MESSENGER.

            I was
in charge of mountain flocks.

OEDIPUS.

          You were a shepherd?
A hireling vagrant?

MESSENGER.

          Yes, but at least at that time
the man that saved your life, son.   1100

OEDIPUS.

    What ailed me when you took me in your arms?

MESSENGER.

    In that your ankles should be witnesses.

OEDIPUS.

    Why do you speak of that old pain?

MESSENGER.

          I loosed you;
the tendons of your feet were pierced and fettered,—

OEDIPUS.

    My swaddling clothes brought me a rare disgrace.   1105

MESSENGER.

    So that from this you're called your present name.

OEDIPUS.

    Was this my father's doing or my mother's?
For God's sake, tell me.

MESSENGER.

          I don't know, but he
who gave you to me has more knowledge than I.   1110

OEDIPUS.

    You yourself did not find me then? You took me
from someone else?

MESSENGER.

         Yes, from another shepherd.

OEDIPUS.

    Who was he? Do you know him well enough
to tell?

MESSENGER.

      He was called Laius' man.

OEDIPUS.

1115   You mean the king who reigned here in the old days?

MESSENGER.

    Yes, he was that man's shepherd.

OEDIPUS.

                 Is he alive

still, so that I could see him?

MESSENGER.

              You who live here

would know that best.

OEDIPUS.

          Do any of you here

know of this shepherd whom he speaks about

1120   in town or in the fields? Tell me. It's time

that this was found out once for all.

CHORUS.

I think he is none other than the peasant

whom you have sought to see already; but

Jocasta here can tell us best of that.

OEDIPUS.

1125   Jocasta, do you know about this man

whom we have sent for? Is he the man he mentions?

JOCASTA.

Why ask of whom he spoke? Don't give it heed;

nor try to keep in mind what has been said.

It will be wasted labour.

OEDIPUS.

         With such clues

1130   I could not fail to bring my birth to light.

JOCASTA.

I beg you—do not hunt this out—I beg you,

if you have any care for your own life.

What I am suffering is enough.

OEDIPUS.

         Keep up

your heart, Jocasta. Though I'm proved a slave,

1135   thrice slave, and though my mother is thrice slave,

you'll not be shown to be of lowly lineage.

JOCASTA.

O be persuaded by me, I entreat you;

do not do this.

OEDIPUS.

I will not be persuaded to let be

1140   the chance of finding out the whole thing clearly.

JOCASTA.

It is because I wish you well that I

give you this counsel—and it's the best counsel.

OEDIPUS.

Then the best counsel vexes me, and has

for some while since.

JOCASTA.

         O Oedipus, God help you!

God keep you from the knowledge of who you are!   1145

OEDIPUS.

Here, some one, go and fetch the shepherd for me;

and let her find her joy in her rich family!

JOCASTA.

O Oedipus, unhappy Oedipus!

that is all I can call you, and the last thing

that I shall ever call you.   1150

               (*Exit.*)

CHORUS.

Why has the queen gone, Oedipus, in wild

grief rushing from us? I am afraid that trouble

will break out of this silence.

OEDIPUS.

Break out what will! I at least shall be

willing to see my ancestry, though humble.   1155

Perhaps she is ashamed of my low birth,

for she has all a woman's high-flown pride.

But I account myself a child of Fortune,

beneficent Fortune, and I shall not be

dishonoured. She's the mother from whom I spring;   1160

the months, my brothers, marked me, now as small,

and now again as mighty. Such is my breeding,

and I shall never prove so false to it,

as not to find the secret of my birth.

CHORUS.

STROPHE

If I am a prophet and wise of heart   1165

you shall not fail, Cithaeron,

by the limitless sky, you shall not!—

to know at tomorrow's full moon

that Oedipus honours you,

as native to him and mother and nurse at once;   1170

and that you are honoured in dancing by us, as finding

    favour in sight of our king.

Apollo, to whom we cry, find these things pleasing!

ANTISTROPHE

Who was it bore you, child? One of

the long-lived nymphs who lay with Pan—

the father who treads the hills?   1175

Or was she a bride of Loxias, your mother? The grassy

    slopes

are all of them dear to him. Or perhaps Cyllene's king

or the Bacchants' God that lives on the tops

of the hills received you a gift from some

one of the Helicon Nymphs, with whom he mostly

    plays?   1180

        (*Enter an old man, led by Oedipus' servants.*)

OEDIPUS.

If someone like myself who never met him

Sophocles

may make a guess,—I think this is the herdsman,
whom we were seeking. His old age is consonant
with the other. And besides, the men who bring him
1185   I recognize as my own servants. You
perhaps may better me in knowledge since
you've seen the man before.

CHORUS.
                              You can be sure
I recognize him. For if Laius
had ever an honest shepherd, this was he.

OEDIPUS.
1190   You, sir, from Corinth, I must ask you first,
is this the man you spoke of?

MESSENGER.
                                    This is he
before your eyes.

OEDIPUS.
                Old man, look here at me
and tell me what I ask you. Were you ever
a servant of King Laius?

HERDSMAN.
                            I was,—
1195   no slave he bought but reared in his own house.

OEDIPUS.
What did you do as work? How did you live?

HERDSMAN.
Most of my life was spent among the flocks.

OEDIPUS.
In what part of the country did you live?

HERDSMAN.
Cithaeron and the places near to it.

OEDIPUS.
1200   And somewhere there perhaps you knew this man?

HERDSMAN.
What was his occupation? Who?

OEDIPUS.
                                This man here,
have you had any dealings with him?

HERDSMAN.
                                        No—
not such that I can quickly call to mind.

MESSENGER.
That is no wonder, master. But I'll make him remember
1205   what he does not know. For I know, that he well knows
the country of Cithaeron, how he with two flocks, I with
one kept company for three years—each year half a year
—from spring till autumn time and then when winter
came I drove my flocks to our fold home again and he to
1210   Laius' steadings. Well—am I right or not in what I said
we did?

HERDSMAN.
You're right—although it's a long time ago.

MESSENGER.
Do you remember giving me a child

to bring up as my foster child?

HERDSMAN.
                            What's this?
Why do you ask this question?

MESSENGER.
                            Look old man,   1215
here he is—here's the man who was that child!

HERDSMAN.
Death take you! Won't you hold your tongue?

OEDIPUS.
                                        No, no,
do no find fault with him, old man. Your words
are more at fault than his.

HERDSMAN.
                        O best of masters,
how do I give offense?

OEDIPUS.
                    When you refuse   1220
to speak about the child of whom he asks you.

HERDSMAN.
He speaks out of his ignorance, without meaning.

OEDIPUS.
If you'll not talk to gratify me, you
will talk with pain to urge you.

HERDSMAN.
                            O, please, sir,
don't hurt an old man, sir.

OEDIPUS.
                                    (to the servants.)
                        Here, one of you,   1225
twist his hands behind him.

HERDSMAN.
                        Why, God help me, why?
What do you want to know?

OEDIPUS.
                        You gave a child
to him,—the child he asked you of?

HERDSMAN.
                                    I did.
I wish I'd died the day I did.

OEDIPUS.
                            You will
unless you tell me truly.

HERDSMAN.
                            And I'll die   1230
far worse if I should tell you.

OEDIPUS.
                            This fellow
is bent on more delays, as it would seem.

HERDSMAN.
O no, no! I have told you that I gave it.

OEDIPUS.
Where did you get this child from? Was it your own or
did you get it from another?

82

HERDSMAN.

1235   Not
my own at all; I had it from some one.
OEDIPUS.
     One of these citizens? or from what house?
HERDSMAN.
     O master, please—I beg you, master, please
don't ask me more.
OEDIPUS.
                You're a dead man if I
ask you again.
HERDSMAN.
1240   It was one of the children
of Laius.
OEDIPUS.
     A slave? Or born in wedlock?
HERDSMAN.
     O God, I am on the brink of frightful speech.
OEDIPUS.
     And I of frightful hearing. But I must hear.
HERDSMAN.
     The child was called his child; but she within,
1245   your wife would tell you best how all this was.
OEDIPUS.
     She gave it to you?
HERDSMAN.
                Yes, she did, my lord.
OEDIPUS.
     To do what with it?
HERDSMAN.
                Make away with it.
OEDIPUS.
     She was so hard—its mother?
HERDSMAN.
                     Aye, through fear
of evil oracles.
OEDIPUS.
          Which?
HERDSMAN.
                They said that he
should kill his parents.
OEDIPUS.
1250   How was it that you
gave it away to this old man?
HERDSMAN.
                O master,
I pitied it, and thought that I could send it
off to another country and this man
was from another country. But he saved it
1255   for the most terrible troubles. If you are
the man he says you are, you're bred to misery.
OEDIPUS.
     O, O, O, they will all come,
all come out clearly! Light of the sun, let me

look upon you no more after today!
I who first saw the light bred of a match   1260
accursed, and accursed in my living
with them I lived with, cursed in my killing.
                    (*Exeunt all but the Chorus.*)
CHORUS.

STROPHE

O generations of men, how I
count you as equal with those who live
not at all!
What man, what man on earth wins more   1265
of happiness than a seeming
and after that turning away?
Oedipus, you are my pattern of this,
Oedipus, you and your fate!
Luckless Oedipus, whom of all men   1270
I envy not at all.

ANTISTROPHE

In as much as he shot his bolt
beyond the others and won the prize
of happiness complete—   1275
O Zeus—and killed and reduced to nought
the hooked taloned maid of the riddling speech,
standing a tower against death for my land:
hence he was called my king and hence
was honoured the highest of all   1280
honours; and hence he ruled
in the great city of Thebes.

STROPHE

But now whose tale is more miserable?
Who is there lives with a savager fate?
Whose troubles so reverse his life as his?   1285

O Oedipus, the famous prince
for whom a great haven
the same both as father and son
sufficed for generation,
how, O how, have the furrows ploughed   1290
by your father endured to bear you, poor wretch,
and hold their peace so long?

ANTISTROPHE

Time who sees all has found you out
against your will; judges your marriage accursed,
begetter and begot at one in it.   1295

O child of Laius,
would I had never seen you.
I weep for you and cry

a dirge of lamentation.
1300　To speak directly, I drew my breath
from you at the first and so now I lull
my mouth to sleep with your name.

(Enter a second Messenger.)

SECOND MESSENGER.
O Princes always honoured by our country,
what deeds you'll hear of and what horrors see,
1305　what grief you'll feel, if you as true born Thebans
care for the house of Labdacus's sons.
Phasis nor Ister cannot purge this house,
I think, with all their streams, such things
it hides, such evils shortly will bring forth
1310　into the light, whether they will or not;
and troubles hurt the most
when they prove self-inflicted.

CHORUS.
What we had known before did not fall short
of bitter groaning's worth; what's more to tell?

SECOND MESSENGER.
1315　Shortest to hear and tell—our glorious queen
Jocasta's dead.

CHORUS.
Unhappy woman! How?

SECOND MESSENGER.
By her own hand. The worst of what was done
you cannot know. You did not see the sight.
Yet in so far as I remember it
1320　you'll hear the end of our unlucky queen.
When she came raging into the house she went
straight to her marriage bed, tearing her hair
with both her hands, and crying upon Laius
long dead—Do you remember, Laius,
1325　that night long past which bred a child for us
to send you to your death and leave
a mother making children with her son?
And then she groaned and cursed the bed in which
she brought forth husband by her husband, children
1330　by her own child, an infamous double bond.
How after that she died I do not know,—
for Oedipus distracted us from seeing.
He burst upon us shouting and we looked
to him as he paced frantically around,
1335　begging us always: Give me a sword, I say,
to find this wife no wife, this mother's womb,
this field of double sowing whence I sprang
and where I sowed my children! As he raved
some god showed him the way—none of us there.
1340　Bellowing terribly and led by some
invisible guide he rushed on the two doors,—
wrenching the hollow bolts out of their sockets,
he charged inside. There, there, we saw his wife
hanging, the twisted rope around her neck.
1345　When he saw her, he cried out fearfully
and cut the dangling noose. Then, as she lay,

poor woman, on the ground, what happened after,
was terrible to see. He tore the brooches—
the gold chased brooches fastening her robe—
1350　away from her and lifting them up high
dashed them on his own eyeballs, shrieking out
such things as: they will never see the crime
I have committed or had done upon me!
Dark eyes, now in the days to come look on
1355　forbidden faces, do not recognize
those whom you long for—with such imprecations
he struck his eyes again and yet again
with the brooches. And the bleeding eyeballs gushed
and stained his beard—no sluggish oozing drops
1360　but a black rain and bloody hail poured down.

So it has broken—and not on one head
but troubles mixed for husband and for wife.
The fortune of the days gone by was true
good fortune—but today groans and destruction
1365　and death and shame—of all ills can be named
not one is missing.

CHORUS.
Is he now in any ease from pain?

SECOND MESSENGER.
He shouts
for some one to unbar the doors and show him
to all the men of Thebes, his father's killer,
1370　his mother's—no I cannot say the word,
it is unholy—for he'll cast himself,
out of the land, he says, and not remain
to bring a curse upon his house, the curse
he called upon it in his proclamation. But
1375　he wants for strength, aye, and someone to guide him;
his sickness is too great to bear. You, too,
will be shown that. The bolts are opening.
Soon you will see a sight to waken pity
even in the horror of it.

(Enter the blinded Oedipus.)

CHORUS.
1380　This is a terrible sight for men to see!
I never found a worse!
Poor wretch, what madness came upon you!
What evil spirit leaped upon your life
to your ill-luck—a leap beyond man's strength!
1385　Indeed I pity you, but I cannot
look at you, though there's much I want to ask
and much to learn and much to see.
I shudder at the sight of you.

OEDIPUS.
O, O,
1390　where am I going? Where is my voice
borne on the wind to and fro?
Spirit, how far have you sprung?

CHORUS.
To a terrible place whereof men's ears

may not hear, nor their eyes behold it.

OEDIPUS.

1395   Darkness!

Horror of darkness enfolding, resistless, unspeakable
   visitant sped by an ill wind in haste!
madness and stabbing pain and memory
of evil deeds I have done!

CHORUS.

In such misfortunes it's no wonder
1400   if double weighs the burden of your grief.

OEDIPUS.

My friend,
you are the only one steadfast, the only one that attends
   on me;
you still stay nursing the blind man.
Your care is not unnoticed. I can know
1405   your voice, although this darkness is my world.

CHORUS.

Doer of dreadful deeds, how did you dare
so far to do despite to your own eyes?
what spirit urged you to it?

OEDIPUS.

It was Apollo, friends, Apollo,
that brought this bitter bitterness, my sorrows to comple-
1410   tion.
But the hand that struck me
was none but my own.
Why should I see
whose vision showed me nothing sweet to see?

CHORUS.

1415   These things are as you say.

OEDIPUS.

What can I see to love?
What greeting can touch my ears with joy?
Take me away, and haste—to a place out of the way!
Take me away, my friends, the greatly miserable,
1420   the most accursed, whom God too hates
above all men on earth!

CHORUS.

Unhappy in your mind and your misfortune,
would I had never known you!

OEDIPUS.

Curse on the man who took
1425   the cruel bonds from off my legs, as I lay in the field.
He stole me from death and saved me,
no kindly service.
Had I died then
I would not be so burdensome to friends.

CHORUS.

1430   I, too, could have wished it had been so.

OEDIPUS.

Then I would not have come
to kill my father and marry my mother infamously.
Now I am godless and child of impurity,
begetter in the same seed that created my wretched self.

If there is any ill worse than ill,
   that is the lot of Oedipus.   1435

CHORUS.

I cannot say your remedy was good;
you would be better dead than blind and living.

OEDIPUS.

What I have done here was best done—don't tell me
otherwise, do not give me further counsel.   1440
I do not know with what eyes I could look
upon my father when I die and go
under the earth, nor yet my wretched mother—
those two to whom I have done things deserving
worse punishment than hanging. Would the sight   1445
of children, bred as mine are, gladden me?
No, not these eyes, never. And my city,
its towers and sacred places of the Gods,
of these I robbed my miserable self
when I commanded all to drive *him* out,   1450
the criminal since proved by God impure
and of the race of Laius.
To this guilt I bore witness against myself—
with what eyes shall I look upon my people?
No. If there were a means to choke the fountain   1455
of hearing I would not have stayed my hand
from locking up my miserable carcase,
seeing and hearing nothing; it is sweet
to keep our thoughts out of the range of hurt.
Cithaeron, why did you receive me? why   1460
having received me did you not kill me straight?
And so I had not shown to men my birth.

O Polybus and Corinth and the house,
the old house that I used to call my father's—
what fairness you were nurse to, and what foulness   1465
festered beneath! Now I am found to be
a sinner and a son of sinners. Crossroads,
and hidden glade, oak and the narrow way
at the crossroads, that drank my father's blood
offered you by my hands, do you remember   1470
still what I did as you looked on, and what
I did when I came here? O marriage, marriage!
you bred me and again when you had bred
bred children of your child and showed to men
brides, wives and mothers and the foulest deeds   1475
that can be in this world of ours.

Come—it's unfit to say what is unfit
to do.—I beg of you in God's name hide me
somewhere outside your country, yes, or kill me,
or throw me into the sea, to be forever   1480
out of your sight. Approach and deign to touch me
for all my wretchedness, and do not fear.
No man but I can bear my evil doom.

CHORUS.

Here Creon comes in fit time to perform

or give advice in what you ask of us.
Creon is left sole ruler in your stead.

OEDIPUS.

Creon! Creon! What shall I say to him?
How can I justly hope that he will trust me?
In what is past I have been proved towards him
an utter liar.

(Enter Creon.)

CREON.

Oedipus, I've come
not so that I might laugh at you nor taunt you
with evil of the past. But if you still
are without shame before the face of men
reverence at least the flame that gives all life,
our Lord the Sun, and do not show unveiled
to him pollution such that neither land
nor holy rain nor light of day can welcome.

(To a servant.)

Be quick and take him in. It is most decent
that only kin should see and hear the troubles
of kin.

OEDIPUS.

I beg you, since you've torn me from
my dreadful expectations and have come
in a most noble spirit to a man
that has used you vilely—do a thing for me.
I shall speak for your own good, not for my own.

CREON.

What do you need that you would ask of me?

OEDIPUS.

Drive me from here with all the speed you can
to where I may not hear a human voice.

CREON.

Be sure, I would have done this had not I
wished first of all to learn from the God the course
of action I should follow.

OEDIPUS.

But his word
has been quite clear to let the parricide,
the sinner, die.

CREON.

Yes, that indeed was said.
But in the present need we had best discover
what we should do.

OEDIPUS.

And will you ask about
a man so wretched?

CREON.

Now even you will trust
the God.

OEDIPUS.

So. I command you—
and will beseech you—
to her that lies inside that house give burial
as you would have it; she is yours and rightly
you will perform the rites for her. For me—

never let this my father's city have me
living a dweller in it. Leave me live
in the mountains where Cithaeron is, that's called
my mountain, which my mother and my father
while they were living would have made my tomb.
So I may die by their decree who sought
indeed to kill me. Yet I know this much:
no sickness and no other thing will kill me.
I would not have been saved from death if not
for some strange evil fate. Well, let my fate
go where it will.

Creon, you need not care
about my sons; they're men and so wherever
they are, they will not lack a livelihood.
But my two girls—so sad and pitiful—
whose table never stood apart from mine,
and everything I touched they always shared—
O Creon, have a thought for them! And most
I wish that you might suffer me to touch them
and sorrow with them.

(Enter Antigone and Ismene,
Oedipus' two daughters.)

O my lord! O true noble Creon! Can I
really be touching them, as when I saw?
What shall I say?
Yes, I can hear them sobbing—my two darlings!
and Creon has had pity and has sent me
what I loved most?
Am I right?

CREON.

You're right: it was I gave you this
because I knew from old days how you loved them
as I see now.

OEDIPUS.

God bless you for it, Creon,
and may God guard you better on your road
than he did me!

O children,
where are you? Come here, come to my hands,
a brother's hands which turned your father's eyes,
those bright eyes you knew once, to what you see,
a father seeing nothing, knowing nothing,
begetting you from his own source of life.
I weep for you—I cannot see your faces—
I weep when I think of the bitterness
there will be in your lives, how you must live
before the world. At what assemblages
of citizens will you make one? to what
gay company will you go and not come home
in tears instead of sharing in the holiday?
And when you're ripe for marriage, who will he be,
the man who'll risk to take such infamy
as shall cling to my children, to bring hurt
on them and those that marry with them? What
curse is not there? "Your father killed his father
and sowed the seed where he had sprung himself

and begot you out of the womb that held him."
1570 These insults you will hear. Then who will marry you?
No one, my children; clearly you are doomed
to waste away in barrenness unmarried.
Son of Menoeceus, since you are all the father
left these two girls, and we, their parents, both
1575 are dead to them—do not allow them wander
like beggars, poor and husbandless.
They are of your own blood.
And do not make them equal with myself
in wretchedness; for you can see them now
1580 so young, so utterly alone, save for you only.
Touch my hand, noble Creon, and say yes.
If you were older, children, and were wiser,
there's much advice I'd give you. But as it is,
let this be what you pray: give me a life
1585 wherever there is opportunity
to live, and better life than was my father's.

CREON.
Your tears have had enough of scope; now go within the
    house.

OEDIPUS.
I must obey, though bitter of heart.

CREON.
In season, all is good.

OEDIPUS.
Do you know on what conditions I obey?

CREON.
1590   You tell me them,
and I shall know them when I hear.

OEDIPUS.
             That you shall send me out
to live away from Thebes.

CREON.
                That gift you must ask of the Gods.

OEDIPUS.
But I'm now hated by the Gods.

CREON.
             So quickly you'll obtain your prayer.

OEDIPUS.
You consent then?

CREON.
          What I do not mean, I do not use to say.

OEDIPUS.
Now lead me away from here.

CREON.
          Let go the children, then, and come. 1595

OEDIPUS.
Do not take them from me.

CREON.
        Do not seek to be master in everything,
for the things you mastered did not follow you through-
    out your life.

             (As Creon and Oedipus go out.)

CHORUS.
You that live in my ancestral Thebes, behold this
    Oedipus,—
him who knew the famous riddles and was a man most
    masterful;
not a citizen who did not look with envy on his lot— 1600
see him now and see the breakers of misfortune swallow
    him!
Look upon that last day always. Count no mortal happy
    till
he has passed the final limit of his life secure from pain.

CENTER STAGE   THE FIRST PERFORMANCE OF *OEDIPUS THE KING*

Not unlike our own religious festivals such as Christmas, Easter, Hanukkah, and Ramadan, the City Dionysia was a time of great celebration in Athens. Since Peisistratus moved the rural Dionysian Festival of the Fruits of the Earth to Athens in 534 B.C.E., this springtime festival was one of the highlights of the Athenian year.

On a beautiful March morning in 428 B.C.E., Athenians prepared to celebrate the City Dionysia, among the most exciting events of their year. For the moment, the burdens of everyday life and the transactions of civic and legal affairs were put aside as they gathered to celebrate and worship Dionysus.

The first two days of the City Dionysia were richly ceremonial, much like the opening of the Olympic Games. There was a huge parade, numerous religious and civic ceremonies, sacrifices to the gods, and much singing and dancing. On the first day Athenian audiences watched the *proagon* (or "previews") of the dramas that they would witness over the next six days. Next, they were introduced to the three honored playwrights, each of whom presented his cast and said something about his plays. On the second day they heard the sacred dithyrambs, and on the following day they viewed the performances of five comedies. However, their real joy sprang from the anticipation of yet another entry by a favorite playwright, Sophocles. The people of Athens eagerly anticipated the awards ceremony on the final day of the festival when the winning plays would be announced. They had heard that Philocles, the nephew of Aeschylus, had entered an excellent tetralogy.

Four new plays by Sophocles, including *Oedipus the King*, would be performed that day. Although Athenians were familiar with the story of Oedipus—it was among the best known in their mythology—they were eager to know how Sophocles would retell the story and what new insights he might provide. After packing a lunch of cheese, olives, and bread and filling their wineskins with the blood of Dionysus himself, thousands of spectators made the long trek on the Eleusian Way, which led through the center of the city to the southern slope of the Acropolis to the Theater of Dionysus.

As they entered the *theatron* through the *parados*, they saw the small *skene* directly in front of them. This scene building served as a changing room for the principal actors who usually played several roles in a single play. As they looked up into the *theatron*, they saw wooden benches that held about 15,000 spectators, with a section designated for each of the Attic tribes. In the years to come the city fathers would build permanent stone seating and a more ornate marble *skene*, which would last for centuries. Across the *orchestra*, where the chorus sang and danced throughout the day, stood a large throne reserved for the priest of Dionysus, who presided over the performances. On either side of this throne were five smaller seats for the leaders of each of the ten Attic tribes. The elected city officials and important civic leaders sat in the rows immediately behind the priest and the tribal leaders.

Though the performance of Sophocles' plays was anticipated with great interest, an important ceremony—the selection of the judges—must be completed before they commenced. Prior to the Dionysia, the many nominations from each tribe were placed in urns. The *archon*—the wealthy citizen who sponsored the festival—selected one name from each tribal urn and the ten judges, fairly chosen, were installed after promising to deliver an impartial judgement. After the three tetralogies were performed, each judge placed the name of the winning playwright in a large urn. To allow the gods to have their vote, the archon drew only five ballots and the winning playwright was determined by a majority of those five fated votes.

The priests of Dionysus lit a sacred fire in the *thymele*, the sacred altar at the center of the orchestra; the Athenians rose to sing prayers of supplication to Dionysus, asking him to bless their soil and the seeds they have planted, their herds, and themselves—that they may enjoy good crops and healthy offspring. As the first of Sophocles' plays began, the audience sat quietly, even as the sacred smoke from the *thymele* drifted over the theater. As the prologue unfolded, the people of Thebes themselves were burning offerings to the gods as they begged for an end to the terrible plague that has ravaged their city. The *skene* door opened ominously and Tlepolemus, who played Oedipus, entered to address the Priest, played by Nicostratus, an especially versatile actor who would also portray Jocasta, the Second Messenger, and the Old Herdsman. A third actor, Cleidemides, played Creon, as well as the First Messenger and Teiresias. While these actors may have been well known to the Athenian audience, it was impossible to recognize them because of the masks and *onkoi* (large headpieces) they wore. To assume a new character, they simply changed costumes, headpieces, and masks, which told audiences the age, gender, social status, and especially the emotional state of each character they portrayed.

Because the actors wore large, padded costumes, including large, thick-soled boots called *kothornoi*, and because of the majestic dialogue, they performed in a grand and rhetorical acting style. Sometimes they used declamation to approximate everyday speech; at other times they employed recitative, a type of chanting. Of course, they also sang many passages. Their movements were sweeping and exaggerated so that even those who sat in the farthest reaches of the *theatron* missed neither a word nor a gesture. The actors and chorus spoke directly to the spectators to make them feel as though they were in the midst of the action.

After the initial exchange of dialogue among Oedipus and the Priest, the *orchestra* was vacated and the Chorus of Theban Elders entered through

Oedipus confronts the Sphinx in this drawing taken from an ancient Athenian vessel: It is one of the few contemporary graphic representations of Greece's most famous tragic hero.

the *paradoi*. They sang and danced their first *stasimon*, a translation that does not begin to suggest the lively spectacle it produced. During this first choral ode, 15 actors, all male, were divided into two groups to dance in *strophes* and *antistrophes*. Their intricate dance steps, which Sophocles himself taught the chorus, were as important to the enjoyment of the play as the drama itself.

After the song, the next *episode* began, and the audience listened intently, as did the chorus, which stood quietly about the *orchestra*, as Cleidemides reentered as Teiresias to engage Oedipus in the first *agon* of the play. The pace of the dialogue quickened to suggest the intensity of the debate. Per-

ceptive Athenians smiled wryly as they watched Oedipus—he who defeated the dreadful Sphinx by answering her riddle—refuse to answer Teiresias's riddle. "By Zeus," they thought, "doesn't he know that Teiresias speaks for the gods themselves?" As the play unfolded the 15,000 Athenians found themselves caught up in Sophocles' bold plotting and the gradual intertwining of Oedipus's search for both the slayer of Laius and for his own identity. As each *episode* concluded, they were enlightened by the chorus's *stasima,* which not only entertained them with songs and dances, but also provided the communal standards against which Oedipus's actions were judged. Sophocles cleverly used

this chorus of elders as participants in the action and as common people—like those sitting in the *theatron*—who stood outside the action to observe Oedipus's struggle. They spoke for all present when they sang "Count no mortal happy till he has passed the final limit of his life secure from pain."

After Oedipus discovered that he was indeed the killer of Laius in the scene with the Old Herdsman, he disappeared into the *skene*. He returned moments later—his royal robes spattered with blood—wearing another *onkos* and mask. Two gaping, black holes, each oozing blood, symbolized the terror of Oedipus's dreadful act. Although the audience was prepared for this pitiful sight by the Messenger's horrifying description of Jocasta's suicide and Oedipus's blinding, the image of this lonely and once-proud king terrified them. Creon reentered, leading Oedipus's two infant daughters, and the silent crowd was moved to tears when the blinded, disgraced monarch embraced them for the last time. These two sights—the bloody mask and a father clinging to his innocent girls—were Sophocles' triumph as a playwright.

The audience sat in the *theatron* emotionally drained. They felt pity and fear as they suffered with Oedipus; but through that experience they learned—like Oedipus himself—about themselves, their lives, and their gods. They discussed this quietly as they awaited the two tragedies yet to be performed that morning. And they thanked their gods that the day would end with the satyr play and an opportunity for laughter.

CENTER STAGE — OEDIPUS THE KING AT THE TEATRO OLYMPICO, 1585

Vicenza, a small town near Venice, gave the theater world perhaps its most elaborate production of Sophocles' *Oedipus the King* on March 3, 1585. It was, in the words of Filippo Pigafetta, an aristocrat in attendance, a spectacle of "theatrical pomp and magnificence." *Oedipus*—"the noblest tragedy ever written," in Pigafetta's estimation—was chosen to open the new Teatro Olympico, which had been designed by one of Italy's greatest architects, Andrea Palladio (1518–1580). The new theater, which stands today as the oldest surviving Renaissance theater, was the centerpiece of the Olympic Academy, founded by aristocrats in 1556 as a center for the study of Greek theater.

However, the theater Palladio and his assistant, Vincenzo Scamozzi (1552–1616), designed was actually patterned after a Roman theater. It held about 3,000 spectators who, although they sat indoors, were treated to the illusion that they were in an ancient outdoor theater. The semielliptical auditorium (as opposed to the Roman semicircle) was adorned with almost 80 statues of the academicians, friezes, and frescoes. A small orchestra pit fronted the wide (88 feet) yet shallow (22 feet) playing area. The stage was backed by a richly ornamented permanent facade, which remains the prototype of the proscenium arch. Five doors were cut into this facade, behind which Scamozzi added perspective vistas of a Roman street scene. The effect suggested the narrow walks and alleyways of an ancient city, and all audience members could look down at least one of these streets from seats in the auditorium. Actors could not, of course, venture up one of these curious roadways without destroying the illusion created by the perspective; speeches were delivered strictly from the stage in front of the facade. Still, the new theater was unparalleled in the world and richly clothed Italians gathered at the Teatro Olympico early in the afternoon to see this marvel. The sense of occasion was heightened by the presence of Empress Maria of Austria, a guest of academy president Leonardo Valmarana. The French ambassador and his family were also in the audience that evening.

At 7:30 *Oedipus the King* began with a resounding fanfare of trumpets and drums; fireworks erupted as the great curtain of the Teatro Olympico was lowered into a slot in the forestage to reveal Scamozzi's spectacular vista. Perfume wafted through the auditorium, as Pigafetta tells us, "to indicate that in the city in Thebes, according to the ancient legend, incense was burned to placate the wrath of the gods." The prologue began, and the actors spoke Sophocles' text in an Italian translation by the scholarly Orsato Giustiniani. Music and songs were composed for the

The Teatro Olympico opened at Vicenza, Italy, in 1585 with Angelo Ingegneri's elaborate production of Oedipus the King.

production by the organist at St. Mark's, the great cathedral of Venice. Scamozzi's settings were complemented by the costumes of Alesandro Maganza, who dressed Oedipus's guards in Turkish attire. All was lit to suggest bright sunlight in Thebes, an effect created by placing bottles of colored water in front of banks of candles.

The three-and-a-half-hour production was performed by "actors of the best sort . . . dressed neatly and lavishly according to each one's station." Actually, we know little about the quality or style of the acting, save for Pigafetta's general comments quoted here. Of the size and spectacle of the production, however, there can be little doubt. Over 80 actors filled the Olympico's stage. Oedipus had a retinue of 32 (24 archers alone!), Jocasta was surrounded by "matrons, ladies in waiting, and pages," and Creon enjoyed a similar entourage. The chorus consisted of 15, much like Sophocles', seven on each side of the stage with the leader in the center; the chorus spoke, rather than sang, "in pleasing unison." Remember that Sophocles wrote the play for 3 actors who played 9 speaking roles and a chorus of 15. Though the academy was dedicated to preserving the work of the Greeks, its production of *Oedipus* at the Olympico transformed Sophocles' design into something far more elaborate. To be fair, the Italians were motivated by Aristotle's comments about the "magnitude" of tragedy, attributes best realized in the Renaissance mind through the sheer size of the spectacle. Though this production of *Oedipus the King* might have fallen short of its goal of re-creating the power of Greek tragedy, it succeeded in making visual splendor an integral part of theater. It also prepared theater audiences for that theatrical diversion we now call "grand opera."

FORUMS

"Ode to Oedipus"

Tyrone Guthrie

Tyrone Guthrie directed Oedipus Rex *at the Stratford, Ontario Festival in 1956. Because of its acclaim, it was subsequently filmed. In conjunction with the opening of the film in January 1957, Guthrie was asked to write about his treatment of the play for both stage and film. He wrote the following article for the* New York Times.

Oedipus Rex was written more than two thousand years ago. Since then it has been revived thousands and thousands of times in many languages and in every part of the world.

Its persistent appeal to audiences is the more remarkable when you remember how differently people have regarded the theatre in different epochs and different parts of the world; how not merely the architecture of theatres and techniques of theatrical presentation have varied, but how the ideas and intentions both of producers and playgoers change.

In this connection it would be nice to feel that our own attitude is more intelligent, sophisticated and wise than that of the Athenian public two thousand years ago. But such a feeling can hardly be justified.

We regard the theatre as an entertainment. It may occasionally be serious; but to justify its seriousness it has to give evidence of compensating qualities. Light entertainment bears no such burden of proof. To admit to being serious in the theatre is almost—not quite, but almost—to admit to being a bore. The quality of a modern play is judged in terms of "success"; and success is judged in terms of the number of people who pay for admission.

Those of us who regard ourselves as professionals—and it is significant that this term now connotes that we draw our living out of the theatre rather than devoting our lives to it—have to be extremely careful how we talk about our professional aims and ideals. It is legitimate to talk in technical terms about conventions or styles of acting, direction, design and so on; it is certainly legitimate to talk in economic terms about the profits and the losses, successes and failures, how, and how not, to "promote" theatrical works.

When people start to talk about moral purposes, when they suggest that the purpose of art in general, and the theatre in particular, might possibly be to make mankind a little bit wiser or happier, or even just better adapted to his environment . . . they seem to be getting too big for their boots.

In Athens in 400 B.C.E. there was no "professional" theatre. Every year the spring festival, in celebration of the return of warmth and fertility to mother earth, was the occasion for the performance of—I will not say plays, because that word already implies decadence—dramas. The word signifies no more than actions, or doings or goings-on, which recapitulated in poetic form (which signifies no more than that the goings-on were carefully planned) certain myths or stories which seemed to the Greeks then, and have seemed so since to anybody who thought about them carefully, to have some important bearing on man's past, present, and future.

(continued)

These dramas were "religious" in the sense that they were truly serious. But they certainly did not take the Party Line as regards Olympus. Sophocles in *Oedipus Rex* was, in my opinion, offering a calculated and dangerous criticism of Apollo in a manner infinitely more undermining to faith than anything to which a prince of any church might now object—in, for instance, *Baby Doll* [a film script by Tennessee Williams].

In Athens the festival plays were "produced," most sumptuously, by wealthy members of the community as an act of piety and of public service. In the time of Sophocles the actors did not get paid. Later they did; but history does not record whether the performances were on that account more, or less, efficient; more, or less, devout; more, or less, interesting.

In filming *Oedipus Rex* we have used the translation of the great Irish poet, William Butler Yeats. We have not attempted to fiddle with the text and turn it into a screen play. We assumed that one of the reasons for the play's survival was because, as well as being about something interesting, the material was well presented; its form, as well as its content, was important. Therefore we based the film on a stage production, made for the Shakespeare Festival at Stratford, Ontario, which had proved itself able to grip and to move an audience.

The film is not, of course, just a photographic record of that performance. It makes some attempt to use the advantages of the mechanical eye and ear; some attempts to obviate their drawbacks. It makes no attempt to persuade the audience that what is seen and heard is "really" happening. Throughout emphasis is placed on the ritual character of the drama: the actors commemorate and comment upon the sacrifice of Oedipus—one man whose destruction was expedient that his people might live—in a manner analogous to Christian priests' commemoration and comment on Christ's sacrifice.

This may sound pretentious; and, if to be serious is pretentious, then it is so—very. But while all of us connected with this film did take our work seriously, we have not so lost our heads as to doubt that, if our effort is any good at all, it is only because we tried hard to interpret a good script.

"Guthrie Directs 'Ritual' Performance of *Oedipus Rex* at Edinburgh Fête"

PATRICK GIBBS

The following review of Oedipus Rex, *as directed by Tyrone Guthrie for the Stratford, Ontario Festival appeared in the* New York Times *on September 4, 1956. It was based on a performance at the Edinburgh Festival, one of Europe's premiere theater events. The review suggests the liabilities of using Greek theater conventions in a modern theater.*

"We endeavor to present the tragedy as a Ritual," writes Tyrone Guthrie, in a program note to *Oedipus Rex* given tonight by the Stratford, Ontario Festival Company at the Assembly Hall.

To this end the actors are masked as in ancient Greek times. They also wore the buskin or elevated boots, adding a few inches to their height. Even so, their masks, which are elaborate affairs leaving only the mouth uncovered, are so large that the characters, otherwise conventionally attired, seem dwarfed rather than superhuman.

As for the chorus, its masks are grotesque, coming near to caricature with the exaggerated features. Wearing monkish cowls in drab colors, the chorus recalled giant slugs as they draped themselves over the steps of the apron stage.

Visually, therefore, it was not exactly the impression of an Attic ritual that Mr. Guthrie achieved. The declamatory methods of his actors recalled the chanting of responses in a Church of England service or the pulpit manner of some old-fashioned preacher.

The performance indeed is stylized throughout and makes a purely formal approach to the intellect alone. At the play's greater moments—Oedipus' realization of his guilt, his appearance with his eyes out, or the farewell to his little daughters—one's feelings were completely disengaged.

This might well be an effective production in an open-air theater seating 20,000 persons—the conditions of performance in ancient Greece. In the confines of this little hall, it had little more than the interest of a fresh and thoughtful approach.

Douglas Campbell's Oedipus, with his measured and mannered delivery, his stylized shrieks and groans, and his symbolic gestures, fitted well into the production.

The translation based on the works of Sophocles was by William Butler Yeats; it can seldom have sounded quite so bleak. All being considered, the reception was remarkably warm.

Comedy in the Greco-Roman world evolved in three stages: Old, Middle, and New Comedy. Old Comedy, typified by the plays of Aristophanes, flourished in Athens until the end of the Peloponnesian War (404 B.C.E.) when freedom of speech was severely curtailed. A safer, more neutral comedy focusing on common life and devoid of political humor seems to have thrived until about 336 B.C.E.; *Plutus*, among Aristophanes' last plays, is one of the few extant Middle Comedies. Menander (342–299 B.C.E.) is credited with developing New Comedy, which was subsequently perfected by the twin giants of Roman comic drama, Plautus and Terence. New Comedy, with its emphasis on middle-class people in domestic situations, remains with us today, largely in the guise of television "sitcoms." Neil Simon is the master of New Comedy in the contemporary theater; his first play, *Come Blow Your Horn* (1960) resembles Terence's *Brothers*.

Aristophanes' *Lysistrata* remains the best known of the Old Comedies, largely because its antiwar message and its sexy story line transcend the particulars of the Peloponnesian War and Athenian politics. It is frequently performed, often in updated contexts to comment on current issues. A brief synopsis of the plot is useful here so that you may better understand the conventions of Old Comedy described below:

Tired of the ongoing war between Athens and Sparta, the women of these city states band together under Lysistrata's leadership (her name means "stop the armies"). They agree to end the war by refusing to make love with their men until hostilities cease. The women take over the Acropolis and the state treasury, which prompts the Athenian Commissioner to demand an end to their rebellion. He and Lysistrata debate the merits of the women's actions, and Lysistrata effectively argues that women are the ultimate victims of war and that their daily work makes them better judges of "the natural order of things" than the barbarous men. There are a series of amusing scenes—most notably a comic romp

in which the sweet young Myhrrine tantalizes her husband, Kinesias, only to leave him unfulfilled. The play ends when the beautiful goddess Peace (a.k.a. Harmony) intervenes and helps restore a tenuous peace. The men and women of Athens and Sparta celebrate the end of the war (alas, only a futile dream) with songs, dances, and lovemaking.

Although Old Comedy was characteristically topical and satiric, it retained vestiges of the various fertility and agricultural festivals that preceded the evolution of formal drama in Greece. In addition to political barbs, there is considerable sexual humor, both verbal and physical. Actors frequently wore the *phallus*, a grotesque reproduction of the male sex organ, about their waists, the legacy of ancient fertility rituals. Men played all roles, including female characters, and much of the hilarity stemmed from the "drag show" aspect of the performances. In the spirit of comedy, which exaggerates human folly, the actors also wore heavily padded costumes and relied on broad, physical playing.

Like the tragedies, Old Comedy had a precise structure. The plays began with a *prologue* that not only provided the exposition but also established a *happy idea* (i.e., the play's thesis) to be tested. Lysistrata, for instance, suggests that the women of Athens and Sparta unite in a sex strike to curtail the war. The entrance of the chorus, or *parados*, was a spectacular event as they were traditionally dressed in extravagant costumes to suggest clouds, frogs, or birds; their ensuing song and dance was as colorful and pleasing to the ear as anything the Broadway stage can offer. Like tragedy, the plot was developed through a series of alternating *episodes* and *stasima*. Customarily, the episodes were a loosely connected series of thematically related sketches that tested the happy idea and satirized the issues of the play. It may help to think of Old Comedy as an American musical comedy or vaudeville show in which plot was secondary. (*Lysistrata* is, however, more tightly structured than most Old Comedies.) The middle episode traditionally presented the *agon* ("debate")

about the merits of the happy idea; the debate between Lysistrata and the Athenian Commissioner is among the most profound *agons* in Greek comedy. Playwrights were obligated to write *agons* according to a rigid set of rules concerning the number, length, and meter of the lines, the order of speeches, the role of the *koryphaios* (chorus leader), the climactic moment, and so on. For instance, the first speaker in the *agon* always lost the debate. In spirit and function the *strophes* were much like production numbers in the modern musical: elaborate song and dances intended to create mood, comment on the issues of the play, and provide spectacle. One *strophe* was dedicated to the *parabisis* ("harangue"), in which the playwright stopped the action to address topical issues of concern to him and the audiences. In the most famous parabisis, Aristophanes inserted a speech into a revival of *The Clouds* that lambasted the judges and his audience for not awarding him a coveted prize for his efforts! Like the *agon*, the *parabisis* was bound by rigid guidelines; it had to be a hundred lines long and was carefully divided into sections that observed particular moods and meters. Such policies challenged the creativity of the playwrights and insured that all entrants were playing by the same rules.

Old Comedy ended with an *exodos*, or, more particularly, a *komos* ("joyful celebration") in which the conflicting parties celebrated their newfound unity and the resolution of the "happy idea" (which, in some plays like *The Clouds*, was rejected). The *komos* in *Lysistrata* bears special mention: technically, it is a *gamos*, or "union of the sexes," yet another reminder of the fertility rites from which the plays evolved. The exuberant dance to Aphrodite performed by the women and their newly reformed men represents one of the finest *gamos* in all dramatic literature. In subsequent ages, the spirit of the *komos* and *gamos* manifest themselves in banquets (*The Taming of the Shrew*), weddings (*A Midsummer Night's Dream*), and, of course, more dances. The extraordinary finale of Kenneth Branagh's film version of *Much Ado About Nothing* captures the spirit of Old Comedy's *gamos*.

ROME

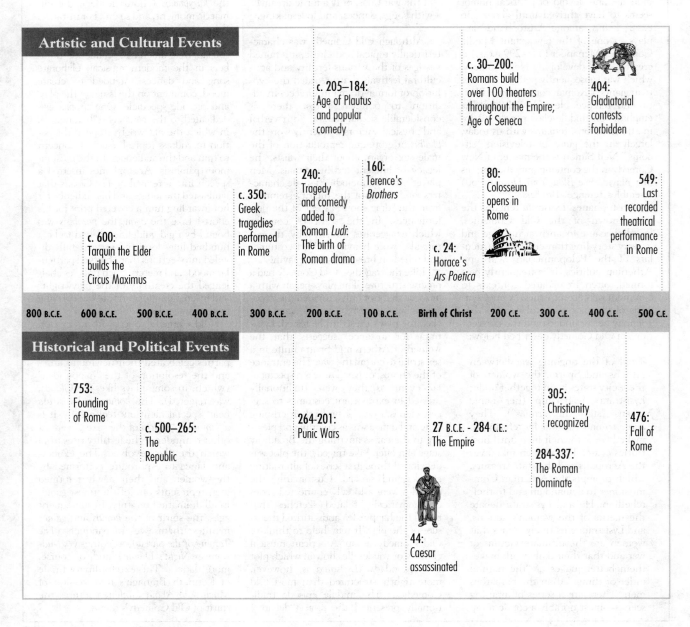

Artistic and Cultural Events

c. 600:
Tarquin the Elder
builds the
Circus Maximus

c. 350:
Greek
tragedies
performed
in Rome

240:
Tragedy
and comedy
added to
Roman *Ludi*:
The birth of
Roman drama

c. 205–184:
Age of Plautus
and popular
comedy

160:
Terence's
Brothers

c. 30–200:
Romans build
over 100 theaters
throughout the Empire;
Age of Seneca

c. 24:
Horace's
Ars Poetica

80:
Colosseum
opens in
Rome

404:
Gladiatorial
contests
forbidden

549:
Last
recorded
theatrical
performance
in Rome

800 B.C.E.	600 B.C.E.	500 B.C.E.	400 B.C.E.	300 B.C.E.	200 B.C.E.	100 B.C.E.	Birth of Christ	200 C.E.	300 C.E.	400 C.E.	500 C.E.

Historical and Political Events

753:
Founding
of Rome

c. 500–265:
The
Republic

264-201:
Punic Wars

27 B.C.E. - 284 C.E.:
The Empire

44:
Caesar
assassinated

305:
Christianity
recognized

284-337:
The Roman
Dominate

476:
Fall of
Rome

The Development of Roman Theater

Even as Greece was in decline, Rome was ascending as the supreme Western power. As they conquered the Mediterranean world, Romans assimilated the best features in architecture, literature, and the arts of other cultures. From the Greeks, the Romans borrowed the essential design of the theater space, the tragedies of Euripides, and the comedies of Menander, adding distinctively Roman touches to each.

Prior to their conquest of the Hellenic world, Roman theater had developed from ancient rites (*ludi*) honoring various gods associated with fertility, the planting season, and the harvest. However, Rome did not develop a formal drama until about 240 B.C.E., when the performance of plays was added to the *ludi Romani*, a popular festival that included athletic contests as well as singing, dancing, and clowning. Early Roman actors were called *histriones* ("storytellers"), and we still use the word *histrionic* to describe behavior that is showy or theatrical.

Although the Romans also worshipped a pantheon, neither the early *ludi* nor the subsequent drama evidenced a religious purpose similar to that of the Greeks. Roman religion was less communal, largely because individual families chose particular gods to whom they offered obeisance. The Romans actually referred to their theaters as temples and adorned them with statuary in honor of gods. However, Roman drama never addressed the cosmic and spiritual issues so central to Greek tragedy. For Romans, theater was primarily a diversion.

Playwrights and Popular Entertainments

Though the Romans imitated the Greek tragedians—particularly Euripides, who was closest to them in time and temperament—Roman tragedy was decidedly inferior. However, it was the Romans—specifically Seneca (4 B.C.E.–65 C.E.)—who most influenced Renaissance tragedians, particularly in England. The Spanish-born Seneca wrote a number of tragedies, none of which we can be sure was actually performed. His tragedies were probably closet dramas, that is, plays written to be read by aristocratic citizens. Seneca's tragedies are noted for their violent and sensational action, their fascination with villainous characters, and their depiction of ghosts, witches, and the occult. These elements resurfaced in Elizabethan England as *Macbeth*'s spirits, as the many dead bodies that cover *Hamlet*'s stage, and as the diabolical Iago. As Shakespeare and his contemporaries learned their Latin, they read the plays of Seneca and incorporated many of his characteristics into their plays, which are referred to as "Senecan tragedies."

Seneca was the most eloquent spokesman for Stoicism, one of Rome's dominant philosophies. Despite the wealth generated by their vast empire, Romans saw life as hard and subject to misfortune. Some turned to Hedonism or Epicureanism, with their credos *Carpe diem* ("Seize the day") and "Eat, drink, and be merry, for tomorrow we die." The Stoics resigned themselves to suffer life's tribulations by maintaining a "holy calm" in the face of adversity. Giving in to one's emotions only compounded the problem because passion was an enemy of reason. Stoicism has two implications for drama. First, its philosophy of resignation diminished the possibility of tragedy: tragic heroes do not merely accept adversity, they rise to meet it. Second, the battle between passion and reason became a central concern of Renaissance dramatists who knew Seneca's work.

Roman comedy is more memorable than Roman tragedy, and also had a far more profound influence on Renaissance drama than its Greek counterpart. Roman comedy developed from two strains: folk comedies performed in the provinces of Italy and literate dramas written largely in imitation of the Greek Menander. Indeed, Horace (65–8 B.C.E.), the Roman orator, poet, and literary critic, advised young playwrights to imitate Greek models in his *Ars Poetica,* a document that stands beside Aristotle's *The Poetics* as one of the monuments of classical dramatic theory. In the province of Atella, masked and grotesquely padded actors performed short farces about middle-class life. Such comedies produced many of the stock characters we associate with Roman comedy: the braggart warrior, the trickster servant, the Senex (Old Man), and the country bumpkin. Such types became staples of the literate drama and of the Italian *commedia dell'arte* in the Late Middle Ages and Renaissance.

Rome's finest literary comedies were written by Plautus and Terence, each of whom represents a significantly different approach to the genre. Plautus (254–184 B.C.E.) was the world's first professional playwright because he wrote (and performed) plays as a commercial venture. Such plays as *Amphitryon* and *The Rope* are slight in content yet superbly structured for comic effect. They rely on stock characters to move their improbable, yet entertaining, plots to a satisfying conclusion. A typical Plautine comedy portrays a young man seeking the love of a seemingly unreachable woman. The youth, who often challenges his own father for her affections, is aided by a wise servant who creates mischief and ultimately helps the lad win her. There is little moral purpose to Plautus's plays, as they existed solely to entertain the working-class audiences who filled Rome's public theaters. *The Comedy of Errors*, among Shakespeare's first comedies, was adapted from Plautus's *The Menaechmi*, and the popular Broadway musical *A Funny Thing Happened on the Way to the Forum* (1962, revived 1996) is based on several Plautine scripts.

In contrast to Plautus's comedies are those of Terence (185–159 B.C.E.), a Carthaginian slave (and perhaps Africa's first notable dramatist) who was brought to Rome and educated by Greek teachers. Terence borrowed both techniques and subject matter from the New Comedy of Menander. His comedies, such as *Brothers*, were written for Roman aristocrats and are more literate and instructive than those of Plautus. A moral strain runs through his works that cannot be found in Plautus; consequently, it was Terence who became the model for medieval and Renaissance playwrights. His comedies were performed in the learning academies of Europe and contributed to the evolution of the *commedia erudita* ("learned comedy") of the Italian Renaissance.

Perhaps Rome's ultimate contribution to world theater was popular entertainment. In addition to the commercially successful works of Plautus, Romans could attend a variety of spectacles catering to the masses. As early as 600 B.C.E., the emperor Tarquin erected the enormous Circus Maximus, the prototype of the modern sports arena, where Romans witnessed chariot races, gladiatorial contests, equestrian events, animal exhibitions and fights (*venationes*), and other entertainments we associate with the modern circus. Romans also produced *naumachiae*, spectacular sea battles staged in flooded arenas; in 46 B.C.E. Julius Caesar constructed a lake for a *naumachia* that featured almost 20,000 combatants. As people were actually killed and wounded in these battles, we might say that Roman spectacles represented some of the most "realistic" theatricals in the history of world theater. When Christian rulers came to power in the fourth century, they pointed to the barbarism of such spectacles and banned theatrical activity.

Theaters and Acting

As the ancient world's supreme architects, the Romans built magnificent theaters to accommodate their entertainments. Using the Greek model of the *theatron*, the *orchestra,* and the *skene*, the Romans built theaters that were noticeably different in one aspect. The typical Roman theater formed a single edifice with no separation of the auditorium (or *cavea*), the orchestra (now a half-circle reflecting the diminished role of the chorus in Roman drama), and the playing space (*pulpitum*), which was backed by the *scaenae*. The *frons scaenae* (facade) contained many alcoves for statues of gods and emperors, and traditionally featured three doors facing the audience. This three-door arrangement is a trademark of Roman comedy, and a large number of Renaissance comedies require "three houses" for their plots. The Romans appear to have used little scenery in their plays, but they did invent the act curtain (*auleum*), which was raised and lowered by telescoping poles from a trough on the forestage. The Roman theater was more intimate than the Greek, allowing for such playwriting devices as the aside (a speech directed to the audience that apparently is not heard by other characters). Asides, especially popular in comedies of intrigue, became one of the most distinctive features of Renaissance comedy. Roman theaters became the models for the great Italian Renaissance theaters such as the Teatro Olympico (1585) and Teatro Farnese (1616).

Tile frescoes found on the walls of Roman ruins tell us much about Roman actors. They wore masks and wigs that were apparently more lifelike than the highly exaggerated masks the Greeks wore in their vast amphitheaters. Unlike Greece, which revered the best actors in the City Dionysia, Rome afforded actors little status. Actors were drawn from the lower classes, even among slaves imported to perform the basest tasks. The lead actor in a Roman company was called the *dominus gregis* ("leader of the sheep"), and his company was the *grex* ("herd"), an indication of the low esteem given actors in Rome. Roscius (c. 126 B.C.E.–62 C.E.) was Rome's best-known actor and perhaps the world's first "star." He is remembered by subsequent generations: Shakespeare refers to him several times in his plays, and the great nineteenth-century American tragedian Edwin Forrest was billed as "the young Roscius."

The Fall of Rome

As Rome fell into decline, its theater also degenerated. Bawdy spectacles and blasphemous parodies of Christian ceremonies offended church fathers who were gaining power in Rome. In 200 C.E., Tertulian wrote "On the Spectacles," in which he attacked actors as a corrupting influence ("The polluted things pollute us"). A hundred years later Constantine became Rome's first Christian emperor, and by the end of the fourth century Christians were forbidden by church edict to attend theater events. The last recorded performance of a theatrical event in Rome occurred in 549 C.E. The long-standing antipathy between some Christian sects and the theater remains another legacy of the late Roman theater.

A 1772 oil painting by Marco Marcola captures the energy and color of a
street performance by a commedia dell'arte company; it also suggests that
the middle class has emerged as a powerful force in theater.

CHAPTER 4

THE EARLY MODERN THEATER

It may seem strange to note that the "modern" theater began in the Middle Ages, but the designation exists for two reasons:

- Modern, as it is used here, merely distinguishes those plays written after the ancient—or classical—ages of Greece and Rome. After the fall of Rome, little formal drama existed until the Middle Ages, although considerable theatrical activity took place in the guise of rituals, folk customs, and especially in the work of itinerant actors, troubadours, minstrels, and others who kept the art of performance alive.
- We can actually trace the evolution of the modern theater to the plays of medieval writers as well as those of the Renaissance and subsequent eras. Collectively they portrayed the dilemmas of individuals faced with the challenges of living in this world and thus increased the secularization of a drama that culminates in the great social dramas of the modern era. Though Greek and Roman plays also focused on individuals within a social setting, the modern theater has been more influenced by—and developed in an unbroken line from—the drama of the Middle Ages.

THE MIDDLE AGES

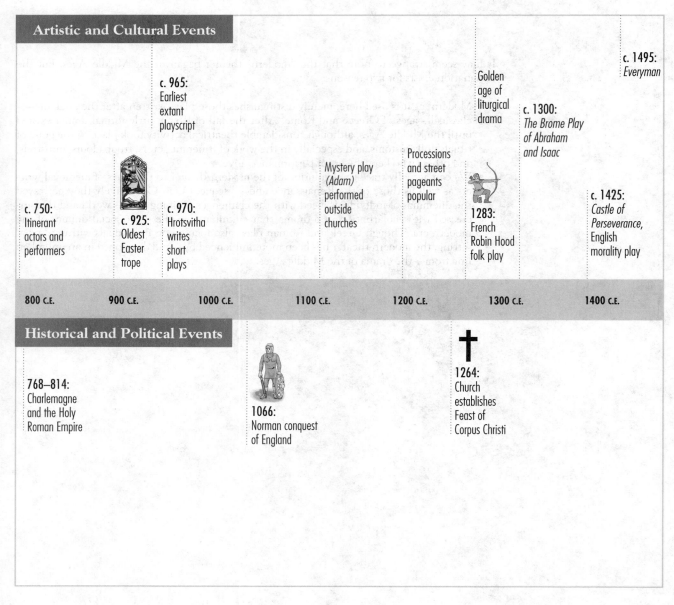

Artistic and Cultural Events

c. 750:
Itinerant
actors and
performers

c. 925:
Oldest
Easter
trope

c. 965:
Earliest
extant
playscript

c. 970:
Hrotsvitha
writes
short
plays

Mystery play
(*Adam*)
performed
outside
churches

Processions
and street
pageants
popular

1283:
French
Robin Hood
folk play

Golden
age of
liturgical
drama

c. 1300:
*The Brome Play
of Abraham
and Isaac*

c. 1425:
*Castle of
Perseverance,*
English
morality play

c. 1495:
Everyman

| 800 C.E. | 900 C.E. | 1000 C.E. | 1100 C.E. | 1200 C.E. | 1300 C.E. | 1400 C.E. |

Historical and Political Events

768–814:
Charlemagne
and the Holy
Roman Empire

1066:
Norman conquest
of England

1264:
Church
establishes
Feast of
Corpus Christi

Rites and Folk Drama

Though there was little written drama after the fall of Rome, the spirit of theater was kept alive in pagan rites, many of which were subsumed into Christian ceremonies and holy days. Ironically, the Christians, who had curtailed theater in Roman times, used many attributes we associate with the theater: costumes (vestments), antiphonal song, storytelling, the re-creation of past events, and instruction. Folk celebrations, such as the mummers' plays of northwestern Europe, also flourished. The songs and stories of troubadours sustained an oral tradition that inspired subsequent literate drama. Clearly there was fertile soil in which the seeds of formal theater and drama could germinate.

Two strains of nonreligious theatricals could be found in feudal Europe. Minstrels and traveling actors, variously called *mimi, scurrae, joculatores, jongleurs,* or *histriones,* kept alive the storytelling tradition as well as theatrical performances. These were largely remnants of the antique mimes of Roman times, who specialized in clowning, parodying church and political figures, and even mocking death itself. The Germanic emperor Theodoric the Great extended his royal patronage to such performers in the sixth century. In France medieval audiences enjoyed *sotties,* short farces that burlesqued church customs, and *sermons joyeaux,* parodies of liturgical homilies. (*Tartuffe* is perhaps a sophisticated offshoot of the *sottie.*) By the thirteenth century mature urban secular drama could be found in many medieval villages.

A rich body of folk drama and agrarian rituals also furthered secular theater. There are many varieties of such innovative theatricals, the most famous of which may be *mummery* and the *Robin Hood* plays. "Mumming"—which derives from a German word (*mumme*) for silence or "closed lips"—grew from gift-giving rituals in feudal Europe. People of lesser social rank disguised with masks and colorful costumes arrived at the home or manor of a superior, such as a king or lord, bearing gifts. The mummers treated their host to a vigorous dance before departing as silently as they came. Over a long period of time, these festivities evolved into lively plays with a discernible structure. In the nineteenth century, there was a colorful mummers' play in which a doctor with magical powers restored a dead person to life. A young boy dressed as a woman (the "Betsy") and a spirited trickster were often major characters in mummers' plays. *Robin Hood* plays evolved from May Day celebrations marking the advent of spring. Young men and women, bedecked with flowers and greenery, sang and danced around a large pole (its phallic nature derived from ancient fertility rites) in a rite reminiscent of the ancient Dionysian revels in Greece. In the fifteenth century one such reveler dressed himself as the heroic outlaw Robin Hood to preside as "the Lord of May." As might be expected, short plays based on folktales and ballads were created to commemorate the good-hearted outlaw's exploits. Though we think of Robin Hood as an English figure, examples of *Robin Hood* plays exist in many countries (see *The Qing Ding Pearl* from China). Such folk festivals and dramas contributed to the lore of plays in the Renaissance. Shakespeare's *Twelfth Night* and *A Midsummer Night's Dream* are often-cited examples.

Religious Drama

The most memorable drama (if only because we have better records) and that which first reflected uniquely medieval values was created in the great churches that dominated the medieval landscape. Whereas the Greeks sang dithyrambs honoring Dionysus, medieval Christians sang *tropes,* short biblical passages set to music, as part of their liturgy. The most famous of these is the *Quem Quaeritis* trope, a reenactment of the visit of the three Marys to the tomb of Christ on Easter morning. About 925 C.E. this trope was performed when a deacon played the attending angel who asked the women, "Whom do you seek (i.e., *Quem quaeritis?*) in the tomb, O Christian women?" Three subalterns answered, "We seek Jesus who has died," to which the deacon-angel responded: "He is not here, he has risen." This short exchange is generally recognized as among the first formal dramas in the post-Roman Western world. Like its Greek antecedent, it derived from communal celebrations observing the resurrection of a slain god-king. It was held in the early spring, and it too used mimicry, costumes (or priestly vestments), simple spectacle, and storytelling to impart sacred tenets to the congregation. Other stories from the Bible were enacted in various locations (*sedes*) throughout the church.

Other forms of biblically inspired drama soon emerged as a complement to such simple church dramas as the *Quem Quaeritis* trope. These were vernacular plays—as opposed to the Latin plays in the church—that were performed in town squares or open fields, usually in conjunction with the Feast of Corpus Christi, which Pope Urban VI established in 1264. In fact, they are often referred to as the Corpus Christi cycles because they portrayed the cycle of biblical events from the Creation to the Day of Judgement. As the plays grew in size and scope, trade and craft guilds were given the responsibility of performing individual stories from the great biblical epic. The individual plays are often called mystery plays because they were performed by the *maestri* (skilled) guilds. Individual towns, such as York, England, soon became known for their great cycle dramas, which included as many as 42 individual mystery plays. The cycles thrived between 1350 and 1550, though records also document much later performances. Though the cycles were similar in many respects, significant and often colorful differences indicate the contributions of various towns and guilds. *Abraham and Isaac* suggests the kind of play performed in the great cycles, though there are several variants on this famous story.

In addition to the biblical epics, anonymous Christian dramatists also portrayed the dilemmas of ordinary men and women tempted by the world, the flesh, and, of course, the devil. These allegorical works, called *morality plays*, instructed the faithful in correct behavior and featured allegorical characters symbolizing virtues (Strength, Beauty, Goodness) and vices (Greed, Lust, Rumor). *Everyman* is the best-known of the medieval morality plays.

These liturgical dramas, however sacred their stories and messages, were also significant social and political events in medieval towns. Indeed a curious mixture of the heavenly and the earthly became a hallmark of medieval religious plays. In one famous example, *The Second Shepherd's Play*, a medieval version of the "trickster" steals a sheep on Christmas Eve. When angry shepherds invade his home to reclaim the lost lamb, the thief and his wife wrap it in swaddling clothes and lay it in a manger to pass it off as their newborn child. This parody of Christ's birth was not intended to be sacrilegious; rather, it was a reminder to medieval audiences that Christ entered the world to redeem sinners like the sheep thief.

The actual presentation of the plays enhanced this humanization of the great religious tales. The plays were customarily performed by common laborers; not until the fifteenth century did professional actors take over the presentation of the cycle plays, and then only in some areas of Europe. Actors wore contemporary clothing, used colloquial speech, and performed workaday tasks instantly recognized by the audiences who gathered in squares or fields. To the medieval mind, history was cyclical, and all humans, whatever their place in time, were subject to the same errors and tribulations while on their pilgrimage to heaven. This notion of *historification* had two implications for the drama. First, the plays themselves were prefigurations of subsequent events, that is, a story from the Old Testament foreshadowed one from the New (see the discussion of *Abraham and Isaac* preceding the play). Both the Old and New Testament stories had immediate implications for a contemporary audience. Second, because one's place in history was relative, there was no need for historical accuracy in costuming, stage business, or even storytelling. Noah was properly dressed in a medieval leather apron and jerkin, and it was entirely natural that he should use medieval tools to build his ark. One might say that the medieval performers invented "modern dress" theater, but not in ignorance; rather, it was a forthright attempt to make the stories of the Bible immediate and accessible to the people who watched them. Well-educated writers in the Renaissance, including Shakespeare, retained such anachronisms in their plays.

Performance Conventions

Medieval artists relied heavily on visual stimuli because few people could read or write. Thus *illuminations* were cultivated to make concrete—in purely visual terms—those things that seemed abstract. Prominent examples of illuminations can still be found in the enormous

A mansion (or "little house") was one of the primary scenic backdrops for medieval liturgical plays; from the 1547 Valenciennes Passion Play.

cathedrals that dominated medieval towns. Their walls were adorned with brilliant stained-glass illustrations of the events of the Bible, while the great rosette windows at either end of the church were visual metaphors of "God's eye" watching human deeds. Manuscripts were illustrated with vividly colored pictures to illuminate the texts. The mystery and morality plays themselves were, in essence, living illuminations that made Christian lore and doctrine concrete and accessible.

Consequently, medieval plays were presented with an extraordinary attention to the visual. In addition to the simple stages (*mansions*) found in the churches, the outdoor dramas were performed on several types of stages that varied from town to town, century to century. The *booth stage* was a raised platform (*platea*) on trestles (or perhaps ale kegs) backed by a colorful curtain. *Pageant wagons*, perhaps the most famous of the medieval stages, were ambulatory stages using carts or farm wagons, the beds of which served as the stage. The *simultaneous stage*, such as that employed in Valenciennes, France, was actually a single enormous stage containing a number of *mansions* representing locales such as Jerusalem, the Temple, God's throne, and, of course, hell. *Rounds* were found largely in southwestern England, where Caesar's legions had encampments. They consisted of a large circle (based on the ancient orchestra?) that contained seating for the audience and, at perhaps a half-dozen places on the perimeter, mansions representing heaven, Abraham's house, and hell itself.

Skilled craftsmen, who spent much of the year in preparation for the cycle, presented the plays. Accordingly, the ingenuity and complexity of the scenery was remarkable. We know there were imaginative flying devices and other technical wizardry, called *secrets* because they created an aura of mystery. An especially noteworthy scenic device was the Hellmouth, a huge

Pageant wagons, the forerunners of parade floats, were perhaps the most versatile scenic devices used in the Middle Ages; they are also referred to as "ambulatory stages."

structure representing the grotesque face of a devil. Sinners were dragged through the jaws of the Hellmouth by cavorting devils; often smoke and ashes billowed from the jaws to suggest the horrors of hell. One French Hellmouth was so elaborate that it required 17 men to operate its various pulleys, winches, and bellows.

Devils were among the most carefully costumed characters in the medieval plays; animal skins and grotesque masks were intended to frighten medieval audiences. Yet the devils were comedic as well as frightening, and often provided much of the comic relief with their tricks and jests. The devils were yet another variation on the trickster found in entertainments around the world. Arlecchino in the *commedia dell'arte* is akin to the medieval devil; he usually wore a black, grotesque mask. Devils, by the way, often "passed the hat" among audiences to collect money to underwrite the performance of the plays.

The medieval cycle plays, then, were as much a celebration of medieval life and community as they were a religious experience. Virtually all members of society participated in the plays as audience, craftsman, or performer. They were sources of civic pride, and they instilled in the people an appetite for theater. As Europe became more secularized, its drama become more human-centered. The medieval religious and secular plays—simultaneously simple and sophisticated, sublime and grotesque—provided a solid foundation on which the great humanist dramas of the Renaissance were built.

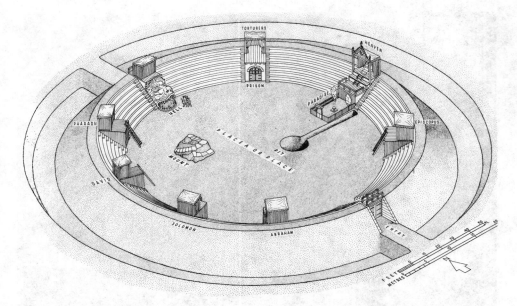

"Rounds" may have derived from ancient Roman theaters, especially those found near Cornwall in southwestern England.

The booth stage, a raised platform backed by a curtain, may have been the model for the stage in Elizabethan theaters such as Shakespeare's Globe.

THE BROME PLAY OF ABRAHAM AND ISAAC

ANONYMOUS

ABRAHAM AND ISAAC (C. 1300–1400)

Abraham and Isaac is an anonymous medieval play of the genre commonly known as mystery plays, short dramas based on events from the Bible. While the subject matter may well concern the "mysteries" of the Judeo-Christian heritage, the term actually derives from a Middle English term, *maestri*, which referred to the trade and craft guilds—or "masters"—who were assigned the performance of various plays within the lengthy, multiplay cycles. This text of *Abraham and Isaac* has not been attributed to a particular cycle (although each had its version) but was preserved in a fifteenth-century manuscript at Brome Manor in England. It is a superb example of the universality of the mystery plays; though it is based on Jewish characters and told through Christian eyes, it is ultimately about human feelings.

Despite its doggerel verse—the pronounced meter and rhyme were memory aids for illiterate actors—the play is emotionally powerful because of the humanity rendered by the unknown playwright (or playwrights—these plays were frequently developed over a number of years). The biblical account (Gen. 22:1–19) of the testing of Abraham's fidelity to God is, frankly, rather sterile, matter-of-fact, and undramatic. There is no conflict between God and Abraham. Nowhere is there a sense of the patriarch's agony (" . . . this child's words wound my heart"); unlike Prometheus, he does not "dare" challenge his Lord. In particular, there is no hint of Isaac's heart-wrenching reactions, which are simultaneously human and heroic. The two requests that he makes of his father in the play—first, that Abraham spare Sarah any anguish over the ordeal ("tell not my mother of God's request, say that I am gone to a far country") and second, that the sacrifice happen quickly and painlessly—are so profoundly touching that they eclipse the original biblical passage.

The common denominator among the many surviving mystery plays is their extraordinary humanity. Consider two examples from other plays. There were several versions of the Great Flood that destroyed the world; while the particulars may vary, virtually all include comic portraits of Noah and his wife. Noah is pictured as a harried, somewhat henpecked husband weary of his shrewish wife's nagging. In some of the plays she is rendered as a drunkard who has to be forcibly carried onto the ark by her sons. Noah's news that the Lord has commanded him to make an ark in preparation for a great deluge provokes a raucous argument which disintegrates into a Punch-and-Judy show, as the following lines suggest:

> WIFE. But in a little while,
> What with game and guile,
> I shall smite and smile
> And pay him [Noah] back instead.
> NOAH. Hush! hold thy tongue, ramshit, or I shall thee still.
> Wife. As I thrive, if thou smite, I shall pay thee back with skill.

And the fight is on. Certainly the medieval playwrights intended no disrespect for their subject matter; these were, after all, church-sanctioned events. Rather, the comic portraiture, the colloquial language, and the physical humor were intended to entertain the commoners for whom the plays were intended. Having engaged the audience on one level, the lessons of the Bible stories could be more successfully imparted. Also, the actor playing Noah was most likely a common workingman, perhaps a shipwright (who better to perform the story of the Flood?). Suppose the week before the play, given in conjunction with the Corpus Christi holy days in spring, the townspeople overheard that shipwright arguing with his wife; imagine the effect when he plays the biblical character and fights with his stage wife. Life meets Art, and the reality of the biblical message is comically and truthfully manifested.

More seriously, in a play from the York cycle called *The Crucifixion*, Christ is a relatively minor character. The focus is on the executioners who fall into petty arguments about the most efficient manner to fulfill their gory task. They argue about measurements, body weights, how tight the ropes should be stretched, and the like. Each soldier becomes more petty and sadistic than the others, and in the process, the audience appreciates both the agony of Christ's death and the reasons why he returned to die for sinners. The play chillingly exposes human cruelty and self-centeredness in the realistic characterizations of the executioners.

In each of the plays described here the actors would have dressed in contemporary clothing, that is, the apparel of the workingman. In many ways, both the texts and performance of medieval plays contributed to the growth of realism in Western theater. The actor playing God in *Noah* and the angel who liberates Isaac may have worn clerical robes because biblical patriarchs and other elevated figures often wore the clothes of church officials to reinforce the stature of clerics in the Christian community. Contemporary, rather than biblical, dress was purposeful rather than a result of ignorance. To the medieval mind, all people were pilgrims on a journey to eternity. It mattered little where a person was placed on the great continuum of existence, so it was plausible for a medieval audience to accept Noah dressed as a shipwright or Isaac in the jerkin and hose worn by young men in medieval England. Such anachronisms continue into the secular dramas of the Renaissance, which is why we find clocks chiming in Shakespeare's *Julius Caesar*.

Anachronisms actually provide an understanding of biblical literature in whatever form it was rendered. *Prefiguration*—that is, one incident in the Bible foreshadowing another—was a central tenet of Christian teaching. The story of Abraham and Isaac prefigures that of Christ and the Father, who allowed his son to be slain for a greater good. The story of the flood prefigures the Day of Judgment, when the world will be destroyed and humans will be judged worthy or unworthy of salvation. Thus the theatrical anachronisms were reminders that the events of the Bible were relevant to contemporary life because they would likely happen again. This spirit of the past informing the present shaped the great history plays, or chronicles, of Elizabethan England. In our time, Brecht "historicizes" contemporary social problems by setting them in parallel situations of the past. Indeed, it is a function of drama to depict human stories, regardless of the particulars of time and place, so that others may apply them to their own needs.

A medieval illumination from a Jewish manuscript depicts the sacrifice of Isaac by his father, Abraham; the biblical tale inspired many artists and dramatists.

THE BROME PLAY OF ABRAHAM AND ISAAC

ANONYMOUS

CHARACTERS
ABRAHAM
ISAAC, *his son*
DEUS
THE ANGEL
THE DOCTOR

[*Enter Abraham and Isaac.*]

ABRAHAM [*Kneeling*]. Father of Heaven, omnipotent,
   With all my heart to thee I call.
   Thou hast given me both land and rent;

And my livelihood thou hast me sent;
I thank thee highly evermore of all.
First of the earth thou madest Adam,
And Eve also to be his wife;
All other creatures of them two came.
And now thou hast granted to me, Abraham,
Here in this land to lead my life.

In my age thou hast granted me this,
That this young child with me shall wone.
I love nothing so much, ywis,
Except thine own self, dear Father of bliss,

111

As Isaac here, my own sweet son.

I have divers children mo,
The which I love not half so well.
This fair sweet child, he cheers me so
In every place where that I go,
That no disease may me befall.

And therefore, Father of Heaven, I thee pray
For his health and also for his grace.
Now, Lord, keep him both night and day,
That never disease nor terror may
Come to my child in no place.

[*Rises.*]

Now come on, Isaac, my own sweet child;
Go we home and take our rest.
ISAAC. Abraham, mine own father so mild,
To follow you I am full pressed,
Both early and late.
ABRAHAM. Come on, sweet child; I love thee best
Of all the children that ever I begot.
DEUS [*Speaks from above*]. Mine angel, fast hie thee thy way,
And on to middle-earth anon thou go;
Abraham's heart now will I assay,
Whether that he be steadfast or no.

Say I commanded him for to take
Isaac, his young son, that he loves so well,
And with his blood sacrifice he make,
If any of my friendship he will fell.

Show him the way on to the hill
Where that his sacrifice shall be.
I shall assay now his good will,
Whether he loveth better his child or me.
All men shall take example by him
My commandments how they shall keep.
ABRAHAM [*Kneeling*]. Now, Father of Heaven, that formed
all thing,
My prayers to thee I make again,
For this day my tender-offering
Here must I give to thee, certain.
Ah! Lord God, Almighty King,
What manner best will make thee most fain?
If I had thereof true knowing,
It should be done with all my main,
Full soon anon.
To do thy pleasing on a hill,
Verily, it is my will,
Dear Father, God in Trinity.

THE ANGEL. Abraham! Abraham! will thou rest!
Our Lord commandeth thee for to take
Isaac, thy young son, that thou loveth best,
And with his blood sacrifice that thou make.

Into the Land of Vision thou go,

And offer thy child unto thy Lord;
I shall thee lead and show also.
Unto God's behest, Abraham, accord,
And follow me upon this green.

ABRAHAM. Welcome to me be my Lord's command,
And his behest I will not withstand.
Yet Isaac, my young son in land,
A full dear child to me hath been.

I had rather, if God had been pleased,
For to a for-bore all the goods that I have,
Than Isaac my son should be diseased,
So God in Heaven my soul may save!

I loved no thing so much on earth,
And now I must the child go kill.
Ah, Lord God, my conscience is strongly stirred!
And yet, my dear Lord, I am sore afraid
To begrudge anything against your will.
I love my child as my life,
But yet I love my God much more.
For though my heart would make any strife,
Yet will I not spare for child nor wife,
But do after my Lord's lore.

Though I love my son never so well,
Yet smite off his head soon I shall.
Ah! Father of Heaven, to thee I kneel;
A hard death my son shall feel,
For to honor thee, Lord, withal!

THE ANGEL. Abraham! Abraham! This is well said,
And all these commandments look that thou keep.
But in my heart be nothing dismayed.
ABRAHAM. Nay, nay, forsooth, I hold me well paid
To please my God the best that I have.

For though my heart be heavily set
To see the blood of my own dear son,
Yet for all this I will not let,
But Isaac, my son, I will go get,
And come as fast as ever we can.

Now, Isaac, my own son dear,
Where art thou, child? Speak to me.
ISAAC. My father, sweet father, I am here,
And make my prayers to the Trinity.

ABRAHAM. Rise up, my child, and fast come hither,
My gentle bairn that art so wise,
For we two, child, must go together
And unto my Lord make sacrifice.

ISAAC. I am full ready, my father. Lo!
Given at your hands, I stand right here,
And whatsoever ye bid me do,
It shall be done with glad cheer,

Full well and fine.

ABRAHAM. Ah! Isaac, my own son so dear,
God's blessing I give thee, and mine.

Hold this faggot upon thy back,
And here myself fire shall bring.
ISAAC. Father, all this here will I pack,
I am full fain to do your bidding.
ABRAHAM [*Aside*]. Ah! Lord of Heaven, my hands I wring,
This child's words all do wound my heart.

Now, Isaac, son, go we our way
Unto yon mount with all our main.
ISAAC. Go we, my dear father, as fast as I may;
To follow you I am full fain,
Although I be slender.
ABRAHAM [*Aside*]. Ah! Lord, my heart breaketh in twain,
This child's words, they be so tender.

[*They arrive at the Mount.*]

Ah, Isaac, son, anon lay it down,
No longer upon thy back it hold,
For I must make ready full soon
To honor my Lord God as I should.

ISAAC. Lo, my dear father, where it is.

To cheer you always I draw me near.
But, father, I marvel sore of this,
Why that ye make this heavy cheer;

And also, father, evermore dread I:
Where is your quick beast that ye should kill?
Both fire and wood we have ready,
But quick beast have we none on this hill.

A quick beast, I wot well, must be dead
Your sacrifice for to make.
ABRAHAM. Dread thee naught, my child, I thee red,
Our Lord will send me one to this stead
Some manner of beast for to take
Through his sweet sond.
ISAAC. Yea, father, but my heart beginneth to quake
To see that sharp sword in your hand.

Why bear ye your sword drawn so?
Of your countenance I have much wonder.
ABRAHAM. Ah! Father of Heaven, so I am woe!
This child here breaks my heart asunder.

ISAAC. Tell me, my dear father, ere that ye cease,
Bear ye your sword drawn for me?
ABRAHAM. Ah, Isaac, sweet son, peace, peace!
For ywis thou breakest my heart in three.
ISAAC. Now truly, somewhat, father, ye think,
That ye mourn thus more and more.
ABRAHAM [*Aside*]. Ah! Lord of Heaven, thy grace let sink,
For my heart was never half so sore.

ISAAC. I pray you, father, that ye will let me that wit,
Whether shall I have any harm or no.
ABRAHAM. Ywis, sweet son, I may not tell thee yet,
My heart is now so full of woe.

ISAAC. Dear father, I pray you, hide it not from me,
But some of your thought that ye tell me.
ABRAHAM. Ah! Isaac, Isaac, I must kill thee!
ISAAC. Kill me, father? Alas! what have I done?
If I have trespassed against you ought,
With a rod ye may make me full mild;
And with your sharp sword kill me nought,
For ywis, father, I am but a child.

ABRAHAM. I am full sorry, son, thy blood for to spill,
But truly, my child, I may not choose.
ISAAC. Now I would to God my mother were here on this
hill!
She would kneel for me on both her knees
To save my life.
And since that my mother is not here,
I pray you, father, change your cheer,
And kill me not with your knife.

ABRAHAM. Forsooth, son, unless I thee kill,
I should grieve God right sore, I dread.
It is his commandment and also his will,
That I should do this same deed.

He commanded me, son, for certain,
To make my sacrifice with thy blood.
ISAAC. And is it God's will that I should be slain?
ABRAHAM. Yea, truly, Isaac, my son so good,
And therefore my hands I wring.

ISAAC. Now, father, against my Lord's will
I will never grudge, loud nor still.
He might have sent me a better destiny
If it had been his pleasure.

ABRAHAM. Forsooth, son, but if I did this deed,
Grievously displeased our Lord will be.
ISAAC. Nay, nay, father, God forbid
That ever ye should grieve him for me.
Ye have other children, one or two,
The which ye should love well by kind.
I pray you, father, make ye no woe;
For, be I once dead, and from you go,
I shall be soon out of your mind.
Therefore do our Lord's bidding,
And when I am dead, then pray for me.
But, good father, tell ye my mother nothing;
Say that I am in another country dwelling.
ABRAHAM. Ah, Isaac, Isaac, blessèd may thou be!

My heart beginneth strongly to rise,
To see the blood of thy blessèd body.

ISAAC. Father, since it may be no other wise,
    Let it pass over, as well as I.
    But, father, ere I go unto my death,
    I pray you bless me with your hand.
ABRAHAM. Now, Isaac, with all my breath
    My blessing I give thee upon this land,
    And God's also thereto, ywis.
    Isaac, Isaac, son, up thou stand,
    Thy fair sweet mouth that I may kiss.

ISAAC. Now farewell, my own father so fine;
    And greet well my mother on earth.
    But I pray you, father, to hide my eyne,
    That I see not the stroke of your sharp sword,
    That my flesh shall defile.
ABRAHAM. Son, thy words make me to weep full sore;
    Now, my dear son Isaac, speak no more.

ISAAC. Ah! my own dear father, wherefore?
    We shall speak together here but a while.

    And since that I must needs be dead,
    Yet, my dear father, to you I pray,
    Smite but few strokes at my head,
    And make an end as soon as ye may,
    And tarry not too long.
ABRAHAM. Thy meek words, child, make me afraid;
    So "Welaway!" may be my song,
    Except alone God's will.
    Ah! Isaac, my own sweet child,
    Yet kiss me again upon this hill!
    In all this world is none so mild.
ISAAC. Now truly, father, all this tarrying
    It doth my heart but harm;
    I pray you, father, make an ending.
ABRAHAM. Come up, sweet son, into my arm.
    I must bind thy hands two,
    Although thou be never so mild.
ISAAC. Ah! mercy, father! Why should ye do so?
ABRAHAM. That thou should'st not hinder me, my child.

ISAAC. Nay, ywis, father, I will not hinder you.
    Do on, for me, your will;
    And on the purpose that ye have set you,
    For God's love, keep it for thee still.

    I am full sorry this day to die,
    But yet I want not my God to grieve.
    Do on your list for me hardily;
    My fair sweet father, I give you leave.

    But father, I pray you evermore,
    Tell my mother never a bit;
    If she wist it, she would weep full sore,
    For ywis, father, she loveth me full well.
    God's blessing may she have!

    Now farewell, my mother so sweet!
    We two be like no more to meet.
ABRAHAM. Ah, Isaac, Isaac, son, thou makest me weep,
    And with thy words thou distemperest me.

ISAAC. Ywis, sweet father, I am sorry to grieve you.
    I cry you mercy of that I have done.
    And of all tresspass that ever I did move you;
    Now, dear father, forgive me that I have done.
    God of Heaven be with me!

ABRAHAM. Ah! dear child, leave off thy moans;
    In all thy life thou grieved me never once.
    Now blessèd be thou, body and bones,
    that ever thou wert bred and born!
    Thou hast been to me child full good.
    But ywis, child, though I mourn never so fast,
    Yet must I needs here at the last
    In this place shed all thy blood.
    Therefore, my dear son, here shall thou lie.
    Unto my work I must me stead.
    I wish, I had as lief myself to die,
    If God will be pleased with my deed,
    And mine own body for to offer.
ISAAC. Ah, mercy, father, mourn ye no more!
    Your weeping maketh my heart sore,
    As my own death that I shall suffer.

    Your kerchief, father, about my eyes ye wind.
ABRAHAM. So I shall, my sweetest child on earth.
ISAAC. Now yet, good father, have this in mind,
    And smite me not often with your sharp sword,
    But hastily that it be sped.

Here Abraham laid a cloth on Isaac's face, thus saying:

ABRAHAM. Now farewell, my child so full of grace.
ISAAC. Ah!! father, father, turn downward my face,
    For of your sharp sword I am ever adread.
ABRAHAM [*Aside*]. To do this deed I am full sorry,
    But, Lord, thy behest I will not withstand.
ISAAC. Ah! Father of Heaven, to thee I cry;
    Lord, receive me into thy hand.

ABRAHAM. Lo! now is the time come, certain,
    That my sword in his neck shall bite.
    Ah, Lord, my heart resisteth thee again;
    I may not find it in my heart to smite;
    My heart will not now thereto.
    Yet fain I would work my Lord's will,
    But this young innocent lieth so still,
    I may not find it in my heart him to kill.
    Oh! Father of heaven, what shall I do?

ISAAC. Ah, mercy, father, why tarry ye so,
    And let me lie thus long on this heath?
    Now I would to God the stroke were do!

Father, I pray you heartily, shorten me of my woe,
And let me not look thus after my death.

ABRAHAM. Now, heart, why would'st not thou break in three?
Yet shall thou not make me to my God unmild.
I will no longer hold back for thee,
For that my God aggrieved would be.
Now hold the stroke, my own dear child.

Here Abraham drew his stroke, and the Angel took the sword in his hand suddenly.

THE ANGEL. I am an angel, thou mayest see blithe,
That from heaven to thee is sent.
Our Lord thanks thee an hundred sythe
For the keeping of his commandment.
He knoweth thy will, and also thy heart,
That thou dreadest him above all things;
And some of thy heaviness for to depart
A fair ram yonder I did bring.

He standeth tied, lo, among the briars.
Now, Abraham, amend thy mood,
For Isaac, they young son that here is,
This day shall not shed his blood.

Go, make thy sacrifice with yonder ram.
Now farewell, blesséd Abraham,
For unto heaven I go now home;
The way is full straight.
Take up thy son so free.

ABRAHAM. Ah! Lord, I thank thee of thy great grace,
Now am I eased in divers wise.
Arise up, Isaac, my dear son, arise;
Arise up, sweet child, and come to me.

ISAAC. Ah! mercy, father, why smite ye not?
Ah! smite on, father, once with your knife.
ABRAHAM. Peace, my sweet son, and take no thought,
For our Lord of Heaven hath granted thy life
By his angel now,

That thou shalt not die this day, son, truly.
ISAAC. Ah, father, full glad then were I;
I wish—father—I say—I wish
If this tale were true!
ABRAHAM. An hundred times, my son fair of hue,
For joy thy mouth now will I kiss.

ISAAC. Ah! my dear father, Abraham,
Will not God be wroth that we do thus?
ABRAHAM. No, no, hardily, my sweet son,
For yon same ram he hath us sent
Hither down to us.

Yon beast shall die here in thy stead,
In the worship of our Lord alone.

Go, fetch him hither, my child, indeed.
ISAAC. Father, I will go seize him by the head,
And bring yon beast with me anon.
Ah, sheep, sheep, blesséd may thou be,
That ever thou were sent down hither!
Thou shall this day die for me
In the worship of the Holy Trinity.
Now come fast and go we together
To my Father of Heaven.
Though thou be never so gentle and good,
Yet had I liefer thou sheddest thy blood
I wish, sheep, than I.
Lo, father, I have brought here full smart
This gentle sheep, and him to you I give.
But, Lord God, I thank thee with all my heart,
For I am glad that I shall live,
And kiss once my dear mother.
ABRAHAM. Now be right merry, my sweet child,
For this quick beast, that is so mild,
Here I shall present before all other.

ISAAC. And I will fast begin to blow;
This fire shall burn a full good speed.
But father, while I stoop down low,
Ye will not kill me with your sword, I trow?
ABRAHAM. No, hardily, sweet son; have no dread;
My mourning is past.
ISAAC. Yea! but I would that sword were in a gled,
For, ywis, father, it makes me full ill aghast.

Here Abraham made his offering, kneeling and saying thus:

ABRAHAM. Now, Lord God of Heaven in Trinity,
Almight God omnipotent,
My offering I make in the worship of thee,
And with this quick beast I thee present.
Lord, receive thou mine intent,
As [thou] art God and ground of our grace.

DEUS. Abraham, Abraham, well may thou speed,
And Isaac, thy young son, thee by!
Truly, Abraham, for this deed
I shall multiply both your seed,
As thick as stars be in the sky,
Both more and less.
And as thick as gravel in the sea,
So thick multiplied your seed shall be.
This grant I you for your goodness.

Of you shall come fruits great [won],
And ever be in bliss without end,
For ye dread me as God alone
And keep my commandments every one;
My blessing I give, wheresoever ye wend.
ABRAHAM. Lo Isaac, my son, how think ye

Of this work that we have wrought?
Full glad and blithe we may be,
Against the will of God that we grudged naught,
Upon this fair heath.

ISAAC. Ah! father, I thank our Lord in every deal,
That my wit served me so well
For to dread God more than my death.

ABRAHAM. Why, dear worthy son, wert thou adread?
Heartily, child, tell me thy lore.

ISAAC. Yea, by my faith, father, now have I red,
I was never so afraid before
As I have been on yon hill.
But, by my faith, father, I swear
I will nevermore come there
But it be against my will.

ABRAHAM. Yea! come on with me, my own sweet son,
And homeward fast now let us go.

ISAAC. By my faith, father, thereto I grant;
I had never so good will to go home,
And to speak with my dear mother.

ABRAHAM. Ah! Lord of Heaven, I thank thee.
For now may I lead home with me
Isaac, my young son so free,
The gentlest child above all other,
This may I well avow.

Now go we forth, my blesséd son.

ISAAC. I grant, father, and let us go;
For, by my troth, were I at home,
I would never go out again so.
I pray God give us grace evermore,
And all those that we be beholden to.

[*Exeunt.*]

[*Enter Doctor.*]

DOCTOR. Lo, sovereigns and sirs, now have we showed
This solemn story to great and small.
It is a good lesson to be learnéd and lewd
And to the wisest of us all,
Without any barring.
For this story showeth you [here]
How we should keep, to our power,
God's commandments without grudging.

Think ye, sirs, and God sent an angel
And commanded you your child be slain,
By your troth, is there any of you
That either would grudge or strive there again?
How think ye now, sirs, thereby?

I think there be three or four or more.
And these women, that weep so sorrowfully
When that their children die them fro,
As nature will and kind,
It is but folly, I may well avow,
To grudge against God or to grieve you;
For ye shall never see him mischiefed, well I know,
By land nor water, bear this in mind.

And grudge not against our Lord God
In wealth or woe, whether that he you send,
Though ye be never so hard bestead;
For when he will, he may it amend,
His commandments truly if ye keep with good heart,
As this story hath now showed you before;
And faithfully serve him while ye be quart,
That ye may please God both even and morn.
Now Jesu, that wore the crown of thorn,
Bring us all to heaven's bliss!

FINIS.

EVERYMAN

ANONYMOUS

EVERYMAN (C. 1495)

In addition to mystery plays, two other forms of Christian drama developed in the Middle Ages: the *miracle play* and the *morality play*. The former dealt with the saints and martyrs of the Roman Catholic Church and are thus referred to as *saints plays*. We may think of these venerated souls as the equivalents of Greek heroes for they, too, were admired for their courage and virtue. But in the Christian schema, classical tragedy was impossible. The tragedy in Christendom was to lose one's soul in the next life. In this world the Christian was expected to bear "the slings and arrows of outrageous fortune" silently. Though serene acceptance of misfortune may bolster one's chances for eternal salvation, it is decidedly undramatic. The most memorable saints plays were those that fused popular legend and folk works to create a hybrid drama. For instance, the English *St. George Play* mixed sword dancing, popular folk plays, and Christian lore to create a popular entertainment that has lasted a thousand years.

It is the morality play, however, that retains the most lasting influence on subsequent Western drama. Whereas mystery and miracle plays dealt with specific biblical or historical figures, the moralities were about common people and as such helped lay a foundation for subsequent secular drama.

The most famous morality play was simply called *Everyman*, a work that might have been derived from a fifteenth-century Dutch drama called *Elkerlyc*. The title indicates that the play's protagonist represented each person who watched it. Moralities dramatized the battle between good and evil for the soul of an ordinary person on life's pilgrimage towards eternity. Abstractions of virtues and vices were personified as allegorical characters such as Beauty, Strength, Wantonness, Rumor, or Greed. Because he was omnipresent in medieval life in the form of wars and plagues, the character of Death (*Mors*) hovered over the action, grim and indifferent to the battle between good angels and those three great tempters of humans, "the World, the Flesh, and the Devil." Death tells Everyman:

> . . . *the tide abideth no man,*
>
> *And in the world each living creature*
>
> *For Adam's sin must die of nature.*

"Adam's sin" is a reference to the Fall in the Garden of Eden, the Christian version of the tragic paradigm. In Christian plays, the Fall becomes the equivalent of Fate in the ancient world because it accounts for human weaknesses and their consequences. Although the protagonist is usually saved by the heavenly virtues, in some moralities he is lost and a horde of devils, alternately frightening and comical, drags the soul of the unrepentant sinner into eternal hell fire, often depicted as a Hellmouth. Thus we see an attempt to induce pity and fear in medieval audiences. Though there may be little subtlety in the message of these didactic plays, we do find remarkably well drawn characters and truthful insights into the human personality in many of the allegorical characters. This emphasis on the plight of the individual establishes a foundation for the human-centered dramas of the Renaissance and thereafter. Martin Stevens, in fact, argues that medieval drama "can be seen as the birth of bourgeois literature—the beginning, not the ending, of something important—as an expression of a time of transition."

Many of the most highly regarded Renaissance plays show discernible elements of the morality play, Christopher Marlowe's *Doctor Faustus* (1588) being the most prominent example. A malcontented scholar sells his soul to Mephistopheles in exchange for 24 years of worldly delights. In one memorable scene Faustus is actually confronted by a "good" and a "bad" angel; elsewhere he is entertained by visions of the Seven Deadly Sins in a dazzling theatrical coup. Alvin Kernan has argued that Shakespeare's chronicle plays are political moralities in which England is an "every-country" tempted by good and evil forces (represented by rebels). Sir John Falstaff is referred to as an "old reverend Vice," an unmistakable allusion to a prominent morality character. Later, Restoration and Georgian comedies, such as *The School for Scandal*, presented characters such as Sir Benjamin Backbite and Lady Sneerwell, descendants of Rumor and Gossip, two of the most vicious characters in the moralities. In the twentieth century, the plays of Bernard Shaw and Bertolt Brecht, often characterized as didactic, contain elements drawn from the morality play tradition.

Medievals saw Death, who might appear at any moment, as a very real presence in their lives; thus he was a leading actor in their serious and comic morality plays, as well as in their art.

EVERYMAN

——— A N O N Y M O U S ———

CHARACTERS
GOD
MESSENGER
DEATH
EVERYMAN
FELLOWSHIP
KINDRED
COUSIN
GOODS
GOOD DEEDS
KNOWLEDGE
CONFESSION
BEAUTY

STRENGTH
DISCRETION
FIVE WITS
ANGEL
DOCTOR

Here Beginneth a Treatise how the High Father of Heaven Sendeth Death to Summon Every Creature to Come and Give Account of their Lives in this World, and is in Manner of a Moral Play.

[Enter Messenger as a Prologue.]

Anonymous

MESSENGER.
    I pray you all give your audience,
    And hear this matter with reverence,
    By figure° a moral play.
    The *Summoning of Everyman* called it is,
5   That of our lives and ending shows
    How transitory we be all day.
    This matter is wondrous precious,
    But the intent° of it is more gracious,
    And sweet to bear away.
10   The story saith: Man, in the beginning
    Look well, and take good heed to the ending,
    Be you never so gay!
    Ye think sin in the beginning full sweet,
    Which in the end causeth the soul to weep,
15   When the body lieth in clay.
    Here shall you see how Fellowship and Jollity,
    Both Strength, Pleasure, and Beauty,
    Will fade from thee as flower in May;
    For ye shall hear how our Heaven King
20   Calleth Everyman to a general reckoning.
    Give audience, and hear what he doth say.

                                   [Exit.]

    God speaketh.

GOD.
    I perceive, here in my majesty,
    How that all creatures be to me unkind,°
    Living without dread in worldly prosperity.
25   Of ghostly sight° the people be so blind,
    Drowned in sin, they know me not for their God.
    In worldly riches is all their mind;
    They fear not my rightwiseness,° the sharp rod.
    My law that I showed, when I for them died,
30   They forget clean, and shedding of my blood red;
    I hanged between two, it cannot be denied;
    To get them life I suffered° to be dead;
    I healed their feet, with thorns hurt was my head.
    I could do no more than I did, truly;
35   And now I see the people do clean forsake me.
    They use the seven deadly sins° damnable,
    As pride, covetise, wrath, and lechery
    Now in the world be made commendable;
    And thus they leave of angels, the heavenly company.
40   Every man liveth so after his own pleasure,
    And yet of their life they be nothing sure.
    I see the more that I them forbear
    The worse they be from year to year.

    All that liveth appaireth° fast;
    Therefore I will, in all the haste,   45
    Have a reckoning of every man's person;
    For, and° I leave the people thus alone
    In their life and wicked tempests,
    Verily they will become much worse than beasts;
    For now one would by envy another up eat;   50
    Charity° they do all clean forget.
    I hoped well that every man
    In my glory should make his mansion,
    And thereto I had them all elect.
    But now I see, like traitors deject,   55
    They thank me not for the pleasure that I to them meant,
    Nor yet for their being that I them have lent.
    I proffered the people great multitude of mercy,
    And few there be that asketh it heartily.
    They be so cumbered with worldly riches   60
    That needs on them I must do justice,
    On every man living, without fear.
    Where art thou, Death, thou mighty messenger?

                              [Enter Death.]

DEATH.
    Almighty God, I am here at your will,
    Your commandment to fulfill.

GOD.   65
    Go thou to Everyman,
    And show him, in my name,
    A pilgrimage he must on him take,
    Which he in no wise may escape;
    And that he bring with him a sure reckoning
    Without delay or any tarrying.   70

                              [Exit God]

DEATH.
    Lord, I will in the world go run overall,°
    And cruelly outsearch both great and small.
    Every man will I beset that liveth beastly
    Out of God's laws, and dreadeth not folly.
    He that loveth riches I will strike with my dart,   75
    His sight to blind, and from heaven to depart°—
    Except that alms be his good friend—
    In hell for to dwell, world without end.
    Lo, yonder I see Everyman walking.
    Full little he thinketh on my coming;   80
    His mind is on fleshly lusts and his treasure,
    And great pain it shall cause him to endure
    Before the Lord, Heaven King.

    [Enter Everyman.]

2–3 **matter . . . figure** the *matter* is the story and the moral doctrine; the *figure* is the literary form, in this case a play **8 intent** meaning **22 unkind** (1) unnatural (2) ungrateful **25 ghostly sight** spiritual insight **28 rightwiseness** righteousness **32 suffered** allowed **36 seven deadly sins** four are named in the next line; the other three are envy, gluttony, and sloth

44 appaireth becomes worse **47 and** if **51 Charity** love (of God and of one's fellows) **72 overall** everywhere **77 depart** sunder

85   Everyman, stand still! Whither art thou going
    Thus gaily? Hast thou thy Maker forgot?
EVERYMAN.
    Why askest thou?
    Wouldest thou wit?°
DEATH.
    Yea, sir; I will show you:
90   In great haste I am sent to thee
    From God out of his majesty.
EVERYMAN.
    What, sent to me?
DEATH.
    Yea, certainly.
    Though thou have forget him here,
95   He thinketh on thee in the heavenly sphere,
    As, ere we depart, thou shalt know.
EVERYMAN.
    What desireth God of me?
DEATH.
    That shall I show thee:
    A reckoning he will needs have
100   Without any longer respite.
EVERYMAN.
    To give a reckoning longer leisure I crave;
    This blind° matter troubleth my wit.
DEATH.
    On thee thou must take a long journey;
    Therefore thy book of count° with thee thou bring,
105   For turn again° thou cannot by no way.
    And look thou be sure of thy reckoning,
    For before God thou shalt answer, and show
    Thy many bad deeds, and good but a few;
    How thou hast spent thy life, and in what wise,
110   Before the chief Lord of paradise.
    Have ado that we were in that way,°
    For, wit thou well, thou shalt make none attorney.°
EVERYMAN.
    Full unready I am such reckoning to give.
    I know thee not. What messenger art thou?
DEATH.
115   I am Death, that no man dreadeth,°
    For every man I rest,° and no man spareth;
    For it is God's commandment
    That all to me shall be obedient.
EVERYMAN.
    O Death, thou comest when I had thee least in mind!
120   In thy power it lieth me to save;
    Yet of my good° will I give thee, if thou will be kind;
    Yea, a thousand pound shalt thou have,
    And defer this matter till another day.

DEATH.
    Everyman, it may not be, by no way.
    I set not by gold, silver, nor riches,
125   Ne° by pope, emperor, king, duke, ne princes;
    For, and I would receive gifts great,
    All the world I might get;
    But my custom is clean contrary.
    I give thee no respite. Come hence, and not tarry. 130
EVERYMAN.
    Alas, shall I have no longer respite?
    I may say Death giveth no warning!
    To think on thee, it maketh my heart sick,
    For all unready is my book of reckoning.
    But twelve year and I might have abiding, 135
    My counting-book I would make so clear
    That my reckoning I should not need to fear.
    Wherefore, Death, I pray thee, for God's mercy,
    Spare me till I be provided of remedy.
DEATH.
    Thee availeth not to cry, weep, and pray; 140
    But haste thee lightly° that thou were gone that journey,
    And prove thy friends, if thou can;
    For, wit thou well, the tide° abideth no man,
    And in the world each living creature
    For Adam's sin must die of nature.° 145
EVERYMAN.
    Death, if I should this pilgrimage take,
    And my reckoning surely make,
    Show me, for° Saint Charity,
    Should I not come again shortly?
DEATH.
    No, Everyman; and thou be once there, 150
    Thou mayst never more come here,
    Trust me verily.
EVERYMAN.
    O gracious God in the high seat celestial,
    Have mercy on me in this most need!
    Shall I have no company from this vale terrestrial 155
    Of mine acquaintance, that way me to lead?
DEATH.
    Yea, if any be so hardy
    That would go with thee and bear thee company.
    Hie° thee that thou were gone to God's magnificence,
    Thy reckoning to give before his presence. 160
    What, weenest° thou thy life is given thee,
    And thy worldly goods also?
EVERYMAN.
    I had wend° so, verily.
DEATH.
    Nay, nay; it was but lent thee;
    For as soon as thou art go, 165

88 wit know   **102 blind** obscure   **104 book of count** account book
105 turn again return   **111 Have . . . way** Get ready that we may
be on that road   **112 make none attorney** have no attorney   **115
no man dreadeth** dreads no man   **116 rest** arrest   **121 good** wealth

126 Ne Nor   **141 lightly** quickly   **143 tide** time   **145 of nature**
as a natural thing   **148 for** in the name of   **159 Hie** Hurry   **161
weenest** think   **163 wend** thought

Another a while shall have it, and then go therefro,°
Even as thou hast done.
Everyman, thou art mad! Thou hast thy wits five,
And here on earth will not amend thy life;
170 For suddenly I do come.
EVERYMAN.
O wretched caitiff,° whither shall I flee,
That I might scape this endless sorrow?
Now, gentle Death, spare me till tomorrow,
That I may amend me
175 With good advisement.°
DEATH.
Nay, thereto I will not consent,
Nor no man will I respite;
But to the heart suddenly I shall smite
Without any advisement.
180 And now out of thy sight I will me hie.
See thou make thee ready shortly,
For thou mayst say this is the day
That no man living may scape away.

[Exit Death.]

EVERYMAN.
Alas, I may well weep with sighs deep!
185 Now have I no manner of company
To help me in my journey, and me to keep;
And also my writing is full unready.
How shall I do now for to excuse me?
I would to God I had never be get!°
190 To my soul a full great profit it had be;
For now I fear pains huge and great.
The time passeth. Lord, help, that all wrought!
For though I mourn it availeth nought.
The day passeth, and is almost ago.°
195 I wot° not well what for to do.
To whom were I best my complaint to make?
What and I to Fellowship thereof spake,
And showed him of this sudden chance?
For in him is all mine affiance;°
200 We have in the world so many a day
Be good friends in sport and play.
I see him yonder certainly.
I trust that he will bear me company;
Therefore to him will I speak to ease my sorrow.
205 Well met, good Fellowship, and good morrow!

Fellowship speaketh.

FELLOWSHIP.
Everyman, good morrow, by this day!
Sir, why lookest thou so piteously?
If any thing be amiss, I pray thee me say,
That I may help to remedy.

EVERYMAN.
Yea, good Fellowship, yea;   210
I am in great jeopardy.
FELLOWSHIP.
My true friend, show to me your mind;
I will not forsake thee to my life's end
In the way of good company.
EVERYMAN.
That was well spoken, and lovingly.   215
FELLOWSHIP.
Sir, I must needs know your heaviness;°
I have pity to see you in any distress.
If any have you wronged, ye shall revenged be,
Though I on the ground be slain for thee,
Though that I know before that I should die.   220
EVERYMAN.
Verily, Fellowship, gramercy.°
FELLOWSHIP.
Tush! by thy thanks I set not a straw.
Show me your grief, and say no more.
EVERYMAN.
If I my heart should to you break,°
And then you to turn your mind from me,   225
And would not me comfort when ye hear me speak,
Then should I ten times sorrier be.
FELLOWSHIP.
Sir, I say as I will do, indeed.
EVERYMAN.
Then be you a good friend at need!
I have found you true here before.   230
FELLOWSHIP.
And so ye shall evermore;
For, in faith, and thou go to hell,
I will not forsake thee by the way.
EVERYMAN.
Ye speak like a good friend; I believe you well.
I shall deserve it, and I may.   235
FELLOWSHIP.
I speak of no deserving, by this day!
For he that will say, and nothing do,
Is not worthy with good company to go;
Therefore show me the grief of your mind,
As to your friend most loving and kind.   240
EVERYMAN.
I shall show you how it is:
Commanded I am to go a journey—
A long way, hard and dangerous—
And give a strait count, without delay,
Before the high Judge, Adonai.°   245
Wherefore, I pray you, bear me company,
As ye have promised, in this journey.

---

166 therefro from it   **171 wretched caitiff** captive wretch   **175 good advisement** proper reflection   **189 be get** been born   **194 ago** gone by   **195 wot** know   **199 affiance** trust

216 heaviness sorrow   **221 gramercy** thanks   **224 break** open
245 Adonai a Hebrew name for God; in Christian liturgy, Christ

FELLOWSHIP.
    That is matter indeed. Promise is duty;
    But, and I should take such a voyage on me,
250   I know it well, it should be to my pain.
    Also it maketh me afeard, certain.
    But let us take counsel here as well as we can,
    For your words would fear° a strong man.
EVERYMAN.
    Why, ye said if I had need
255   Ye would me never forsake, quick° ne dead,
    Though it were to hell, truly.
FELLOWSHIP.
    So I said, certainly,
    But such pleasures be set aside, the sooth° to say.
    And also, if we took such a journey,
260   When should we come again?
EVERYMAN.
    Nay, never again, till the day of doom.
FELLOWSHIP.
    In faith, then will not I come there!
    Who hath you these tidings brought?
EVERYMAN.
    Indeed, Death was with me here.
FELLOWSHIP.
265   Now, by God that all hath bought,°
    If Death were the messenger,
    For no man that is living today
    I will not go that loath journey—
    Not for the father that begat me!
EVERYMAN.
270   Ye promised otherwise, pardie.°
FELLOWSHIP.
    I wot well I said so, truly.
    And yet if thou wilt eat, and drink, and make good
      cheer,
    Or haunt to women the lusty company,°
    I would not forsake you while the day is clear,
275   Trust me verily.
EVERYMAN.
    Yea, thereto ye would be ready!
    To go to mirth, solace, and play,
    Your mind will sooner apply,
    Than to bear me company in my long journey.
FELLOWSHIP.
280   Now, in good faith, I will not that way.
    But and thou will murder, or any man kill,
    In that I will help thee with a good will.
EVERYMAN.
    O, that is a simple advice, indeed.
    Gentle fellow, help me in my necessity!

We have loved long, and now I need;   285
    And now, gentle Fellowship, remember me.
FELLOWSHIP.
    Whether ye have loved me or no,
    By Saint John, I will not with thee go.
EVERYMAN.
    Yet, I pray thee, take the labor, and do so much for me
    To bring me forward,° for Saint Charity,   290
    And comfort me till I come without the town.
FELLOWSHIP.
    Nay, and thou would give me a new gown,
    I will not a foot with thee go;
    But, and thou had tarried, I would not have left thee so.
    And as now God speed thee in thy journey,   295
    For from thee I will depart as fast as I may.
EVERYMAN.
    Whither away, Fellowship? Will you forsake me?
FELLOWSHIP.
    Yea, by my fay!° To God I betake° thee.
EVERYMAN.
    Farewell, good Fellowship; for thee my heart is sore.
    Adieu for ever! I shall see thee no more.   300
FELLOWSHIP.
    In faith, Everyman, farewell now at the end,
    For you I will remember that parting is mourning.
                  [*Exit Fellowship.*]
EVERYMAN.
    Alack! shall we thus depart° indeed—
    Ah, Lady, help!—without any more comfort?
    Lo, Fellowship forsaketh me in my most need.   305
    For help in this world whither shall I resort?
    Fellowship here before with me would merry make,
    And now little sorrow for me doth he take.
    It is said, "In prosperity men friends may find,
    Which in adversity be full unkind."   310
    Now whither for succor shall I flee,
    Sith that° Fellowship hath forsaken me?
    To my kinsmen I will, truly,
    Praying them to help me in my necessity.
    I believe that they will do so,   315
    For kind° will creep where it may not go.
    I will go say,° for yonder I see them go.
    Where be ye now, my friends and kinsmen?

[*Enter Kindred and Cousin.*]

KINDRED.
    Here be we now at your commandment.
    Cousin, I pray you show us your intent   320
    In any wise, and do not spare.°

---

253 **fear** frighten   255 **quick** alive 258 **sooth** truth   265 **bought** redeemed   270 **pardie** by God   273 **haunt . . . company** frequent the delightful company of women

290 **bring me forward** accompany me   298 **fay** faith **betake** commend   303 **depart** separate   312 **Sith that** Since   316 **kind** kinship, family (the idea is that blood ties will find a way)   317 **say** try, essay   321 **spare** hold back

Anonymous

COUSIN.
Yea, Everyman, and to us declare
If ye be disposed to go any whither;
For, wit you well, we will live and die together.
KINDRED.
325   In wealth and woe we will with you hold,
For over his kin a man may be bold.°
EVERYMAN.
Gramercy, my friends and kinsmen kind.
Now shall I show you the grief of my mind:
I was commanded by a messenger,
330   That is a high king's chief officer;
He bade me go a pilgrimage, to my pain,
And I know well I shall never come again;
Also I must give a reckoning strait,
For I have a great enemy° that hath me in wait,
335   Which intendeth me for to hinder.
KINDRED.
What account is that which ye must render?
That would I know.
EVERYMAN.
Of all my works I must show
How I have lived and my days spent;
340   Also of ill deeds that I have used°
In my time sith life was me lent;
And of all virtues that I have refused.
Therefore, I pray you, go thither with me
To help to make mine account, for Saint Charity.
COUSIN.
345   What, to go thither? Is that the matter?
Nay, Everyman, I had leifer fast° bread and water
All this five year and more.
EVERYMAN.
Alas, that ever I was bore!°
For now shall I never be merry,
350   If that you forsake me.
KINDRED.
Ah, sir, what, ye be a merry man!
Take good heart to you, and make no moan.
But one thing I warn you, by Saint Anne—
As for me, ye shall go alone.
EVERYMAN.
355   My Cousin, will you not with me go?
COUSIN.
No, by Our Lady! I have the cramp in my toe.
Trust not to me, for, so God me speed.°
I will deceive you in your most need.

KINDRED.
It availeth not us to tice.°
Ye shall have my maid with all my heart;   360
She loveth to go to feasts, there to be nice,°
And to dance, and abroad to start.°
I will give her leave to help you in that journey,
If that you and she may agree.
EVERYMAN.
Now show me the very effect of your mind: 365
Will you go with me, or abide behind?
KINDRED.
Abide behind? Yea, that will I, and I may!
Therefore farewell till another day.

                                        [Exit Kindred.]
EVERYMAN.
How should I be merry or glad?
For fair promises men to me make,   370
But when I have most need they me forsake.
I am deceived; that maketh me sad.
COUSIN.
Cousin Everyman, farewell now,
For verily I will not go with you.
Also of mine own an unready reckoning   375
I have to account; therefore I make tarrying.
Now God keep thee, for now I go.   *[Exit Cousin.]*
EVERYMAN.
Ah, Jesus, is all come hereto?°
Lo, fair words maketh fools fain;°
They promise, and nothing will do certain.   380
My kinsmen promised me faithfully
For to abide with me steadfastly;
And now fast away do they flee.
Even so Fellowship promised me.
What friend were best me of to provide?°   385
I lose my time here longer to abide.
Yet in my mind a thing there is;
All my life I have loved riches;
If that my Good° now help me might,
He would make my heart full light.   390
I will speak to him in this distress.
Where art thou, my Goods and riches?
GOODS.
[Within.] Who calleth me? Everyman? What! hast thou
haste?
I lie here in corners, trussed and piled so high,
And in chests I am locked so fast,   395
Also sacked in bags. Thou mayst see with thine eye
I cannot stir; in packs low I lie.
What would ye have? Lightly me say.

---

326 over his kin . . . bold a man may command his kinsmen **334 enemy** that is, the Devil **340 used** practiced **346 leifer fast** would rather have nothing but **348 bore** born **357 so God me speed** so may God cause me to prosper

359 tice entice **361 nice** wanton **362 abroad to start** go gadding about **378 hereto** to this **379 fain** glad **385 of me to provide** to provide me with **389 Good** wealth

124

EVERYMAN.
>Come hither, Good, in all the haste thou may,
400   For of counsel I must desire thee.

[*Enter Goods.*]

GOODS.
>Sir, and ye in the world have sorrow or adversity,
>That can I help you to remedy shortly.

EVERYMAN.
>It is another disease that grieveth me;
>In this world it is not, I tell thee so.
405   I am sent for another way to go,
>To give a strait count general
>Before the highest Jupiter of all;
>And all my life I have had joy and pleasure in thee,
>Therefore, I pray thee, go with me;
410   For, peradventure, thou mayst before God Almighty
>My reckoning help to clean and purify;
>For it is said ever among°
>That "money maketh all right that is wrong."

GOODS.
>Nay, Everyman, I sing another song.
415   I follow no man in such voyages;
>For, and I went with thee,
>Thou shouldst fare much the worse for me;
>For because on me thou did set thy mind,
>Thy reckoning I have made blotted and blind,
420   That thine account thou cannot make truly—
>And that hast thou for the love of me.

EVERYMAN.
>That would grieve me full sore,
>When I should come to that fearful answer.
>Up, let us go thither together.

GOODS.
425   Nay, not so! I am too brittle, I may not endure.
>I will follow no man one foot, be ye sure.

EVERYMAN.
>Alas, I have thee loved, and had great pleasure
>All my life-days on good and treasure.

GOODS.
>That is to thy damnation, without lesing,°
430   For my love is contrary to the love everlasting.
>But if thou had me loved moderately during,
>As to the poor to give part of me,
>Then shouldst thou not in this dolor be,
>Nor in this great sorrow and care.

EVERYMAN.
435   Lo, now was I deceived ere I was ware,
>And all I may wite° misspending of time.

GOODS.
>What, weenest thou that I am thine?

EVERYMAN.
>I had wend so.

GOODS.
>Nay, Everyman, I say no.
>As for a while I was lent thee;
440   A season thou hast had me in prosperity.
>My condition is man's soul to kill;
>If I save one, a thousand I do spill.°
>Weenest thou that I will follow thee?
>Nay, not from this world, verily.
445

EVERYMAN.
>I had wend otherwise.

GOODS.
>Therefore to thy soul Good is a thief;
>For when thou art dead, this is my guise°—
>Another to deceive in this same wise
>As I have done thee, and all to his soul's reprief.°
450

EVERYMAN.
>O false Good, cursed may thou be,
>Thou traitor to God, that hast deceived me
>And caught me in thy snare!

GOODS.
>Mary!° thou brought thyself in care,
>Whereof I am right glad;
455
>I must needs laugh, I cannot be sad.

EVERYMAN.
>Ah, Good, thou hast had long my heartly° love;
>I gave thee that which should be the Lord's above.
>But wilt thou not go with me indeed?
>I pray thee truth to say.
460

GOODS.
>No, so God me speed!
>Therefore farewell, and have good day.   [*Exit Goods.*]

EVERYMAN.
>O, to whom shall I make my moan
>For to go with me in that heavy journey?
>First Fellowship said he would with me gone—
465
>His words were very pleasant and gay,
>But afterward he left me alone.
>Then spake I to my kinsmen, all in despair,
>And also they gave me words fair—
>They lacked no fair speaking,
470
>But all forsook me in the ending.
>Then went I to my Goods, that I loved best,
>In hope to have comfort, but there had I least;
>For my Goods sharply did me tell
>That he bringeth many into hell.
475
>Then of myself I was ashamed,
>And so I am worthy to be blamed.
>Thus may I well myself hate.
>Of whom shall I now counsel take?
>I think that I shall never speed
480
>Till that I go to my Good Deed.

---

412 ever among every now and then   **429 lesing** lying   **436 wite** blame on

443 spill destroy   **448 guise** custom, practice   **450 reprief** reproof   **454 Mary** By Mary (an expletive)   **457 heartly** hearty

But, alas, she is so weak
That she can neither go° nor speak.
Yet will I venture on her now.
485   My Good Deeds, where be you?

[*Good Deeds speaks from the ground.*]

GOOD DEEDS.
Here I lie, cold in the ground.
Thy sins hath me sore bound,
That I cannot stir.
EVERYMAN.
O Good Deeds, I stand in fear!
490   I must you pray of counsel,
For help now should come right well.
GOOD DEEDS.
Everyman, I have understanding
That ye be summoned account to make
Before Messias, of Jerusalem King;
495   And you do by me,° that journey with you will I take.
EVERYMAN.
Therefore I come to you, my moan to make.
I pray you that ye will go with me.
GOOD DEEDS.
I would full fain, but I cannot stand, verily.
EVERYMAN.
Why, is there anything on you fall?
GOOD DEEDS.
500   Yea, sir, I may thank you of° all;
If ye had perfectly cheered me,
Your book of count full ready had be.
Look, the books of your works and deeds eke!°
Behold how they lie under the feet
505   To your soul's heaviness.
EVERYMAN.
Our Lord Jesus help me!
For one letter here I cannot see.
GOOD DEEDS.
There is a blind reckoning in time of distress.
EVERYMAN.
Good Deeds, I pray you help me in this need,
510   Or else I am for ever damned indeed;
Therefore help me to make reckoning
Before the Redeemer of all thing,
That King is, and was, and ever shall.
GOOD DEEDS.
Everyman, I am sorry of your fall,
515   And fain would I help you, and I were able.
EVERYMAN.
Good Deeds, your counsel I pray you give me.
GOOD DEEDS.
That shall I do verily;

Though that on my feet I may not go,
I have a sister that shall with you also,
Called Knowledge,° which shall with you abide,   520
To help you to make that dreadful reckoning.

[*Enter Knowledge.*]

KNOWLEDGE.
Everyman, I will go with thee, and be thy guide,
In thy most need to go by thy side.
EVERYMAN.
In good condition I am now in every thing,
And am wholly content with this good thing,   525
Thanked be God my creator.
GOOD DEEDS.
And when she hath brought you there
Where thou shalt heal thee of thy smart,°
Then go you with your reckoning and your Good Deeds
together,
For to make you joyful at heart   530
Before the Blessed Trinity.
EVERYMAN.
My Good Deeds, gramercy!
I am well content, certainly,
With your words sweet.
KNOWLEDGE.
Now go we together lovingly   535
To Confession, that cleansing river.
EVERYMAN.
For joy I weep; I would we were there!
But, I pray you give me cognition
Where dwelleth that holy man, Confession?
KNOWLEDGE.
In the House of Salvation: 540
We shall find him in that place,
That shall us comfort, by God's grace.

[*Knowledge leads Everyman to Confession.*]

Lo, this is Confession. Kneel down and ask mercy,
For he is in good conceit° with God Almighty.
EVERYMAN.
O glorious fountain, that all uncleanness doth clarify,   545
Wash from me the spots of vice unclean,
That on me no sin may be seen.
I come with Knowledge for my redemption,
Redempt with heart and full contrition;
For I am commanded a pilgrimage to take,   550
And great accounts before God to make.
Now I pray you, Shrift,° mother of Salvation,
Help my Good Deeds for my piteous exclamation.

---

483 **go** walk   495 **And you do by me** If you do as I advise   500 **of**
for   503 **eke** also

520 **Knowledge** acknowledgement of sin, the first step to contrition (*Knowledge* is not scientific knowledge, but is knowledge of
Christianity—the knowledge that tells us we are dependent on
God's grace)   528 **smart** pain   544 **good conceit** high esteem
552 **Shrift** Confession

CONFESSION.
     I know your sorrow well, Everyman.
555 Because with Knowledge ye come to me,
     I will you comfort as well as I can,
     And a precious jewel I will give thee,
     Called penance, voider of adversity;
     Therewith shall your body chastised be,
560 With abstinence and perseverance in God's service.
     Here shall you receive that scourge of me,
     Which is penance strong that ye must endure,
     To remember thy Savior was scourged for thee
     With sharp scourges, and suffered it patiently;
565 So must thou, ere thou scape that painful pilgrimage.
     Knowledge, keep him in this voyage,
     And by that time Good Deeds will be with thee.
     But in any wise be siker° of mercy,
     For your time draweth fast; and° ye will saved be,
570 Ask God mercy, and he will grant truly.
     When with the scourge of penance man doth him° bind,
     The oil of forgiveness then shall he find.
EVERYMAN.
     Thanked be God for his gracious work!
     For now I will my penance begin;
575 This hath rejoiced and lighted my heart,
     Though the knots be painful and hard within.
KNOWLEDGE.
     Everyman, look your penance that ye fulfill,
     What pain that ever it to you be;
     And Knowledge shall give you counsel at will
580 How your account ye shall make clearly.
EVERYMAN.
     O eternal God, O heavenly figure,
     O way of rightwiseness, O goodly vision,
     Which descended down in a virgin pure
     Because he would every man redeem,
585 Which Adam forfeited by his disobedience,
     O blessed Godhead, elect and high divine,
     Forgive my grievous offense;
     Here I cry thee mercy in this presence.
     O ghostly treasure, O ransomer and redeemer,
590 Of all the world hope and conductor,°
     Mirror of joy, and founder of mercy,
     Which enlumineth heaven and earth thereby,
     Hear my clamorous complaint, though it late be;
     Receive my prayers, unworthy of thy benignity.
595 Though I be a sinner most abominable,
     Yet let my name be written in Moses' table.
     O Mary, pray to the Maker of all thing,
     Me for to help at my ending,
     And save me from the power of my enemy,
600 For Death assaileth me strongly.

     And, Lady, that I may by mean of thy prayer
     Of your Son's glory to be partner,
     By the means of his passion, I it crave.
     I beseech you help my soul to save.
     Knowledge, give me the scourge of penance;   605
     My flesh therewith shall give acquittance.°
     I will now begin, if God give me grace.
KNOWLEDGE.
     Everyman, God give you time and space!
     Thus I bequeath you in the hands of our Savior.
     Now may you make your reckoning sure.   610
EVERYMAN.
     In the name of the Holy Trinity,
     My body sore punished shall be.
     Take this, body, for the sin of the flesh! [Scourges himself.]
     Also thou delightest to go gay and fresh,
     And in the way of damnation thou did me bring;   615
     Therefore suffer now strokes of punishing.
     Now of penance I will wade the water clear,
     To save me from purgatory, that sharp fire.

     [Good Deeds rises from the floor.]

GOOD DEEDS.
     I thank God, now I can walk and go,
     And am delivered of my sickness and woe.   620
     Therefore with Everyman I will go, and not spare;
     His good works I will help him to declare.
KNOWLEDGE.
     Now, Everyman, be merry and glad!
     Your Good Deeds cometh now; ye may not be sad.
     Now is your Good Deeds whole and sound,   625
     Going upright upon the ground.
EVERYMAN.
     My heart is light, and shall be evermore;
     Now will I smite faster than I did before.
GOOD DEEDS.
     Everyman, pilgrim, my special friend,
     Blessed be thou without end;   630
     For thee is preparate° the eternal glory.
     Ye have me made whole and sound,
     Therefore I will bide by thee in every stound.°
EVERYMAN.
     Welcome, my Good Deeds! Now I hear thy voice,
     I weep for very sweetness of love.   635
KNOWLEDGE.
     Be no more sad, but ever rejoice;
     God seeth thy living in his throne above.
     Put on this garment to thy behove,°
     Which is wet with your tears,
     Or else before God you may it miss,   640
     When ye to your journey's end come shall.

568 siker certain   **569 and** if   **571 him** himself   **590 conductor**
guide

606 acquittance atonement   **631 preparate** prepared   **633
stound** moment (i.e., in every fierce attack)   **638 behove** benefit

EVERYMAN.
Gentle Knowledge, what do ye it call?

KNOWLEDGE.
It is a garment of sorrow;
From pain it will you borrow;°
645   Contrition it is,
That getteth forgiveness;
It pleaseth God passing well.

GOOD DEEDS.
Everyman, will you wear it for your heal?

EVERYMAN.
Now blessed be Jesu, Mary's Son,
650   For now have I on true contrition.
And let us go now without tarrying.
Good Deeds, have we clear our reckoning?

GOOD DEEDS.
Yea, indeed, I have here.

EVERYMAN.
Then I trust we need not fear.
655   Now, friends, let us not part in twain.

KNOWLEDGE.
Nay, Everyman, that will we not, certain.

GOOD DEEDS.
Yet must thou lead with thee
Three persons of great might.

EVERYMAN.
Who should they be?

GOOD DEEDS.
660   Discretion and Strength they hight,°
And thy Beauty may not abide behind.

EVERYMAN.
Also ye must call to mind
Your Five Wits° as for your counselors.

GOOD DEEDS.
You must have them ready at all hours.

EVERYMAN.
665   How shall I get them hither?

KNOWLEDGE.
You must call them all together,
And they will hear you incontinent.°

EVERYMAN.
My friends, come hither and be present,
Discretion, Strength, my Five Wits, and Beauty.

[Enter Beauty, Strength, Discretion, and Five Wits.]

BEAUTY.
670   Here at your will we be all ready.
What will ye that we should do?

GOOD DEEDS.
That ye would with Everyman go,
And help him in his pilgrimage.
Advise you, will ye with him or not in that voyage?

STRENGTH.
We will bring him all thither,   675
To his help and comfort, ye may believe me.

DISCRETION.
So will we go with him all together.

EVERYMAN.
Almighty God, loved may thou be!
I give thee laud that I have hither brought
Strength, Discretion, Beauty, and Five Wits. Lack I
nought.   680
And my Good Deeds, with Knowledge clear,
All be in my company at my will here.
I desire no more to° my business.

STRENGTH.
And I, Strength, will by you stand in distress,
Though thou would in battle fight on the ground.   685

FIVE WITS.
And though it were through the world round,
We will not depart for sweet ne sour.

BEAUTY
No more will I unto death's hour,
Whatsoever thereof befall.

DISCRETION.
Everyman, advise you° first of all;   690
Go with a good advisement and deliberation.
We all give you virtuous monition°
That all shall be well.

EVERYMAN.
My friends, harken what I will tell:
I pray God reward you in his heavenly sphere.   695
Now harken, all that be here,
For I will make my testament
Here before you all present:
In alms half my good I will give with my hands twain
In the way of charity with good intent,   700
And the other half still shall remain
In queth,° to be returned there° it ought to be.
This I do in despite of the fiend of hell,
To go quite out of his peril
Ever after and this day.   705

KNOWLEDGE.
Everyman, harken what I say:
Go to Priesthood, I you advise,
And receive of him in any wise
The holy sacrament and ointment together.
Then shortly see ye turn again hither;   710
We will all abide you here.

---

644 borrow redeem   **660 hight** are called   **663 Five Wits** five
physical senses (they are Everyman's "counselors" because they provide him with sensory data on which Discretion, that is, reason, op-
erates)   **667 incontinent** immediately

683 to for   **690 advise you** consider the matter   **692 monition**
admonition   **702 queth** bequest **there** where

FIVE WITS.

Yea, Everyman, hie you that ye ready were.
There is no emperor, king, duke, ne baron,
That of God hath commission
715   As hath the least priest in the world being;°
For of the blessed sacraments pure and benign
He bareth the keys, and thereof hath the cure°
For man's redemption—it is ever sure—
Which God for our soul's medicine
720   Gave us out of his heart with great pain
Here in this transitory life, for thee and me.
The blessed sacraments seven there be:
Baptism, confirmation, with priesthood good,
And the sacrament of God's precious flesh and blood,
725   Marriage, the holy extreme unction, and penance.
These seven be good to have in remembrance,
Gracious sacraments of high divinity.

EVERYMAN.

Fain would I receive that holy body,
And meekly to my ghostly° father I will go.

FIVE WITS.

730   Everyman, that is the best that ye can do.
God will you to salvation bring,
For priesthood exceedeth all other thing:
To us Holy Scripture they do teach,
And converteth man from sin heaven to reach;
735   God hath to them more power given
Than to any angel that is in heaven.
With five words° he may consecrate,
God's body in flesh and blood to make,
And handleth his Maker between his hands.
740   The priest bindeth and unbindeth all bands,
Both in earth and in heaven.
Thou ministers° all the sacraments seven;
Though we kissed thy feet, thou were worthy;
Thou art surgeon that cureth sin deadly;
745   No remedy we find under God
But all only° priesthood.
Everyman, God gave priests that dignity,
And setteth them in his stead among us to be.
Thus be they above angels in degree.

        [*Exit Everyman to receive the last sacraments from the priest.*]

KNOWLEDGE.

750   If priests be good, it is so,° surely.
But when Jesus hanged on the cross with great smart,
There he gave out of his blessed heart
The same sacrament in great torment.

He sold them not to us, that Lord omnipotent.
Therefore Saint Peter the apostle doth say   755
That Jesu's curse hath all they
Which God their Savior do buy or sell,
Or they for any money do take or tell.°
Sinful priests giveth the sinners example bad;
Their children sitteth by other men's fires, I have heard; 760
And some haunteth women's company
With unclean life, as lusts of lechery:
These be with sin made blind.

FIVE WITS.

I trust to God no such may we find.
Therefore let us priesthood honor,   765
And follow their doctrine for our souls' succor.
We be their sheep, and they shepherds be,
By whom we all be kept in surety.
Peace, for yonder I see Everyman come,
Which hath made true satisfaction.   770

GOOD DEEDS.

Methink it is he indeed.

[*Re-enter Everyman.*]

EVERYMAN.

Now Jesu be your alder speed!°
I have received the sacrament for my redemption,
And then mine extreme unction.°
Blessed be all they that counseled me to take it!   775
And now, friends, let us go without longer respite;
I thank God that ye have tarried so long.
Now set each of you on this rod° your hand,
And shortly follow me.
I go before there° I would be; God be our guide!   780

STRENGTH.

Everyman, we will not from you go
Till ye have done this voyage long.

DISCRETION.

I, Discretion, will bide by you also.

EVERYMAN.

And though this pilgrimage be never so strong,°
I will never part you fro.   785

STRENGTH.

Everyman, I will be as sure by thee
As ever I did by Judas Maccabee.°

[*They go together to the grave.*]

EVERYMAN.

Alas, I am so faint I may not stand;
My limbs under me doth fold.
Friends, let us not turn again to this land,   790

---

715 **being** living   717 **cure** charge, spiritual responsibility (with a pun on medical healing, indicated in 719)   729 **ghostly** spiritual   737 **five words** *Hoc est enim corpus meum* (For this is my body), from the sacrament of the Eucharist   742 **ministers** administers   746 **only** except   750 **it is so** that is, "above angels in degree"

758 **tell** count   772 **Now Jesu . . . speed** Now may Jesus let you all prosper   774 **unction** the last rites of the Catholic Church given to the sick and dying   778 **rod** cross   780 **there** where   784 **strong** hard   787 **Judas Maccabee** Judas Maccabeus, ancient Jewish leader noted for his military exploits

Not for all the world's gold;
For into this cave must I creep
And turn to earth, and there to sleep.

BEAUTY.
What, into this grave? Alas!

EVERYMAN.
795   Yea, there shall ye consume, more and less.°

BEAUTY.
And what, should I smother here?

EVERYMAN.
Yea, by my faith, and never more appear.
In this world live no more we shall,
But in heaven before the highest Lord of all.

BEAUTY.
800   I cross out all this! Adieu, by Saint John!
I take my cap in my lap, and am gone.

EVERYMAN.
What, Beauty, whither will ye?

BEAUTY.
Peace, I am deaf; I look not behind me,
Not and thou wouldest give me all the gold in thy chest.
                               [*Exit Beauty.*]

EVERYMAN.
805   Alas, whereto may I trust?
Beauty goeth fast away from me;
She promised with me to live and die.

STRENGTH.
Everyman, I will thee also forsake and deny;
Thy game liketh° me not at all.

EVERYMAN.
810   Why, then, ye will forsake me all?
Sweet Strength, tarry a little space.

STRENGTH.
Nay, sir, by the rood of grace!
I will hie me from thee fast,
Though thou weep till they heart to-brast.°

EVERYMAN.
815   Ye would ever bide by me, ye said.

STRENGTH.
Yea, I have you far enough conveyed.
Ye be old enough, I understand,
Your pilgrimage to take on hand;
I repent me that I hither came.

EVERYMAN.
820   Strength, you to displease I am to blame;
Yet promise is debt, this ye well wot.

STRENGTH.
In faith, I care not.
Thou are but a fool to complain;
You spend your speech and waste your brain.
825   Go, thrust thee into the ground!
                               [*Exit Strength.*]

795 more and less high and low, that is, people of all ranks   **809 liketh** pleases   **814 to-brast** burst to pieces

EVERYMAN.
I had wend surer I should you have found.
He that trusteth in his Strength
She him deceiveth at the length.
Both Strength and Beauty forsaketh me;
Yet they promised me fair and lovingly.   830

DISCRETION.
Everyman, I will after Strength be gone;
As for me, I will leave you alone.

EVERYMAN.
Why, Discretion, will ye forsake me?

DISCRETION.
Yea, in faith, I will go from thee,
For when Strength goeth before   835
I follow after evermore.

EVERYMAN.
Yet, I pray thee, for the love of the Trinity,
Look in my grave once piteously.

DISCRETION.
Nay, so nigh will I not come;
Farewell, everyone!   840
                               [*Exit Discretion.*]

EVERYMAN.
O, all thing faileth, save God alone—
Beauty, Strength, and Discretion;
For when Death bloweth his blast,
They all run from me full fast.

FIVE WITS.
Everyman, my leave now of thee I take;   845
I will follow the other, for here I thee forsake.

EVERYMAN.
Alas, then may I wail and weep,
For I took you for my best friend.

FIVE WITS.
I will no longer thee keep;
Now farewell, and there an end.   850
                               [*Exit Five Wits.*]

EVERYMAN.
O Jesu, help! All hath forsaken me.

GOOD DEEDS.
Nay, Everyman; I will bide with thee.
I will not forsake thee indeed;
Thou shalt find me a good friend at need.

EVERYMAN.
Gramercy, Good Deeds! Now may I true friends see.   855
They have forsaken me, every one;
I loved them better than my Good Deeds alone.
Knowledge, will ye forsake me also?

KNOWLEDGE.
Yea, Everyman, when ye to Death shall go;
But not yet, for no manner of danger.   860

EVERYMAN.
Gramercy, Knowledge, with all my heart.

KNOWLEDGE.
Nay, yet I will not from hence depart

Till I see where ye shall be come.

EVERYMAN.

Methink, alas, that I must be gone
865　To make my reckoning and my debts pay,
For I see my time is nigh spent away.
Take example, all ye that this do hear or see,
How they that I loved best do forsake me,
Except my Good Deeds that bideth truly.

GOOD DEEDS.

870　All earthly things is but vanity:
Beauty, Strength, and Discretion do man forsake,
Foolish friends, and kinsmen, that fair spake—
All fleeth save Good Deeds, and that am I.

EVERYMAN.

Have mercy on me, God most mighty;
875　And stand by me, thou mother and maid, Holy Mary.

GOOD DEEDS.

Fear not; I will speak for thee.

EVERYMAN.

Here I cry God mercy.

GOOD DEEDS.

Short° our end, and minish° our pain;
Let us go and never come again.

EVERYMAN.

880　Into thy hands, Lord, my soul I commend;
Receive it, Lord, that it be not lost.
As thou me boughtest, so me defend,
And save me from the fiend's boast,
That I may appear with that blessed host
885　That shall be saved at the day of doom.
In manus tuas, of might's most
For ever, *commendo spiritum meum.*°

　　　　[Everyman and Good Deeds descend into the grave.]

KNOWLEDGE.

Now hath he suffered that we all shall endure;
The Good Deeds shall make all sure.
890　Now hath he made ending.
Methinketh that I hear angels sing,
And make great joy and melody
Where Everyman's soul received shall be.

[Enter Angel.]

ANGEL.

Come, excellent elect spouse, to Jesu!
Here above thou shalt go　　　　　　　　　　895
Because of thy singular virtue.
Now the soul is taken the body fro,
Thy reckoning is crystal clear.
Now shalt thou in to the heavenly sphere,
Unto the which all ye shall come　　　　　　900
That liveth well before the day of doom.

　　　　　　　　　　　　　[Exit Knowledge.]

Enter Doctor [of Theology]

DOCTOR.

This moral men may have in mind.
Ye hearers, take it of worth,° old and young,
And forsake Pride, for he deceiveth you in the end;
And remember Beauty, Five Wits, Strength, and Discretion,　　　　　　　　　　905
They all at the last do every man forsake,
Save° his Good Deeds there doth he take.
But beware, and they be small
Before God, he hath no help at all;
None excuse may be there for every man.　　910
Alas, how shall he do then?
For after death amends may no man make,
For then mercy and pity doth him forsake.
If his reckoning be not clear when he doth come,
God will say: *"Ite, maledicti, in ignem eternum."*°　915
And he that hath his account whole and sound,
High in heaven he shall be crowned;
Unto which place God bring us all thither,
That we may live body and soul together.
Thereto help the Trinity!　　　　　　　　920
Amen, say ye, for Saint Charity.

　　　　　　　　　　　　　[Exit Doctor.]

THUS ENDETH THIS MORAL PLAY OF EVERYMAN.

---

878 Short Shorten **minish** diminish　**886–87 In manus . . . meum** "Into thy hands I commit my spirit"; Christ's last words, according to Luke 23.46

903 take it of worth value it　**907 Save** Only　**915 Ite . . . eternum** "Depart from me, ye cursed, into everlasting fire" (Christ's words in Matthew 25.41)

THE EUROPEAN RENAISSANCE

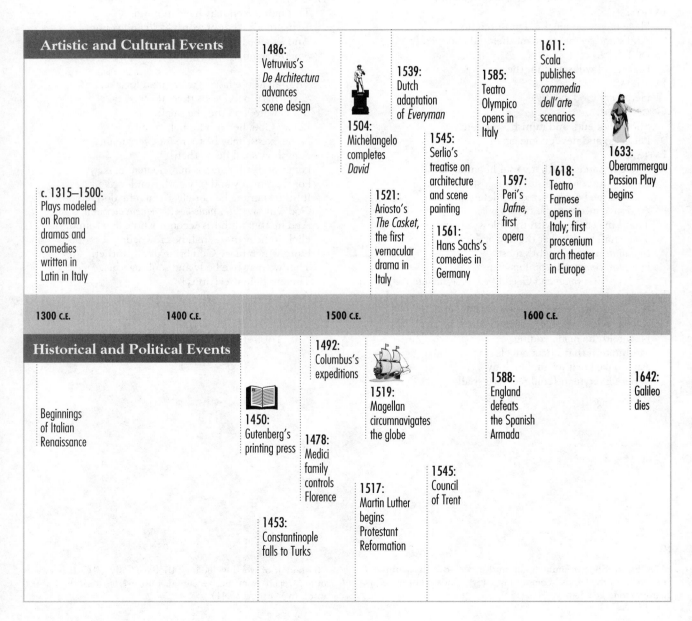

Artistic and Cultural Events

c. 1315–1500:
Plays modeled on Roman dramas and comedies written in Latin in Italy

1486:
Vetruvius's *De Architectura* advances scene design

1504:
Michelangelo completes *David*

1521:
Ariosto's *The Casket*, the first vernacular drama in Italy

1539:
Dutch adaptation of *Everyman*

1545:
Serlio's treatise on architecture and scene painting

1561:
Hans Sachs's comedies in Germany

1585:
Teatro Olympico opens in Italy

1597:
Peri's *Dafne*, first opera

1611:
Scala publishes *commedia dell'arte* scenarios

1618:
Teatro Farnese opens in Italy; first proscenium arch theater in Europe

1633:
Oberammergau Passion Play begins

1300 C.E. **1400 C.E.** **1500 C.E.** **1600 C.E.**

Historical and Political Events

Beginnings of Italian Renaissance

1450:
Gutenberg's printing press

1453:
Constantinople falls to Turks

1478:
Medici family controls Florence

1492:
Columbus's expeditions

1517:
Martin Luther begins Protestant Reformation

1519:
Magellan circumnavigates the globe

1545:
Council of Trent

1588:
England defeats the Spanish Armada

1642:
Galileo dies

In a roughly hundred-year span—from 1576, when the first public theater was erected in England, to 1675, when France and Spain were enjoying their finest dramas—Western theater achieved perhaps its greatest artistry on all levels. This was the age of exceptional playwrights, as well as the heyday of the Italian street comedy (see Center Stage box, *Commedia dell'arte*). Scenic splendor and stage machinery emerged as a principal reason to attend the theater as drama moved indoors, housed in majestic buildings. Spanish drama reveled in its *Siglo d'Oro* (Golden Century), as did French drama of the *Gran Siècle* (Great Century). After a half-century of unparalleled brilliance, the English theaters were closed amid civil war, only to reopen eighteen years later in a new burst of energy in the Restoration.

European drama found fresh voices in newly discovered lands as colonists used the theater to remind them of home. Spain sent its first professional acting companies to Peru as early as the 1520s, and soon Spanish *comedias* and *autos* were performed from Lima to Mexico City, the birthplace of the first significant playwright of the Americas, Sor Juana Inés de la Cruz (See Chapter 9). In 1598 Spanish conquistadors celebrated their trek across the Chihuahua Desert by acting a short *comedia*, written for the occasion by Farfan de los Gobos, near what is now El Paso, Texas—among the first instances of European drama in what would become the United States. In 1604 a French-language play was performed in the Louisiana territories, and in 1665 *Ye Bare and Ye Cubbe*, by William Darby, became the first English-language play to be presented in the American colonies. These are examples of the first European drama in the colonies, although Native Americans had, of course, been performing a variety of rituals, ceremonies, and dances for thousands of years.

The Renaissance Mind

Though many factors explain the extraordinary output of quality drama and spectacular production from 1576 to 1675, two merit attention here. First, this was an age of humanism, a time when artists glorified human potential. The Protestant Reformation contributed to the humanist revival by weakening Catholicism's monopoly on thought. A renewed interest in Greco-Roman culture encouraged artists to look to older, pre-Christian models for subject matter and style. The result was an increased secularization of the theater and a corresponding emphasis on life in *this* world.

Second, theater thrived under the patronage of monarchs and the nobility. Granted, self-aggrandizement was not the least of the motivations for royal largesse. Yet the fact remains that Shakespeare and Molière each wrote—and flourished in—companies called "the King's Men." Sebastiano Serlio, Inigo Jones, and Giacomo Torelli designed for the Medicis, James I, and Louis XIV, respectively, while Spanish drama peaked under King Felipe IV, himself an amateur actor. To glorify themselves and to protect their power bases, the rulers of Europe enhanced the quality of the arts in general, theater in particular. What better way to display one's munificence than to invite hundreds of people to one's own court theater to witness a play performed by the country's finest actors amid the grandest spectacle one could imagine? In the ducal palaces of Italy, at Whitehall in London, at Louis XIV's retreat at Versailles, and at Felipe IV's Palacio Buen Retiro in Madrid, theater flourished (see Center Stage box, The Masque).

Although the powerful contributed to the growth of the theater, we must also remember that this was the age in which capitalism and the free market system were born. Shakespeare's company might indeed have been the King's Men, but it had to compete with other companies vying for audiences on the South Bank of London. Much of the dynamic in Renaissance drama was generated by a need to serve two masters simultaneously—royalty and the emerging middle-class theater patron.

Like the society it mirrored, Renaissance theater represented a synthesis of religion, the new humanism, royal politics, and changing economic structures. The worldview—one of several competing philosophies that shaped Renaissance thought—is perhaps best understood within the context of the *Great Chain of Being*. Originally a medieval concept, it was adapted for more secular uses during the Renaissance to sustain political hierarchies. The Chain of Being depicted the totality of creation as an interlinked chain with the Divinity at the highest end and nonliving matter (i.e., a grain of sand) at the other. Below God on this vertical chain were angels, below them humanity, followed by the animal kingdom, plants, and so on. Smaller chains extended horizontally from each link: ranked categories of angels, for example, formed hierarchies. The chain called *humanitas* had its series of links, with the king or queen in superior positions, followed by other nobles, an upper class, a middle class, common laborers, and ultimately beggars at the lower extreme. Shakespeare had some fun with this precept in *Hamlet* (4.2): The prince tells Claudius that "a man may fish with the worm that hath eat of a king, and eat of the fish that hath fed of that worm," all of which shows "how a king may go a progress through the guts of a beggar." Hamlet, like so many Renaissance artists, was keenly aware that Death was the sole being truly indifferent to one's place on the chain.

King Lear speaks of the "little world of man" (3.1.10), yet another reference to an integral aspect of Renaissance thought. Each person, king or beggar, was a microcosm of the larger world, and thus all people were monarchs unto themselves and thus charged with the responsibility of ruling wisely. Just as a hierarchy existed in the greater cosmos, so, too, one's body had a hierarchical structure. The intellect, which elevated humans above beasts, was preeminent, with the passions and biological drives subservient to the mind. Thus when passion rules—as it does for Sigismund in *Life's a Dream*—chaos follows.

The Need for Order

Renaissance artists were acutely aware of the presence of chaos in their ostensibly ideal world. The Chain of Being suggested order and harmony for all of creation, and thus it was used to validate the so-called divine right of kings. But human greed, jealousy, and ambition often provoked lesser beings to climb upward. The majority of the era's plays explore the turmoil that results from "vaulting ambition." In one of Shakespeare's lesser-known plays, *Troilus and Cressida* (1607), Ulysses, commander of the Greek army, argues that the Trojan War has thrown the Mediterranean world into disarray. He cites an example from nature to illustrate his point; the phrase that is not italicized is a variant on the Chain-of-Being metaphor:

> *The heavens themselves, the planets, and this centre*
> *Observe degree, priority, and place*
>
> . . . .
>
> *. . . But when the planets*
> *In evil mixture to disorder wander,*
> *What plagues, and what portents, what mutiny,*
> *What raging of the sea, shaking of the earth,*
> *Commotion of the winds, frights, changes, horrors,*
> *Divert and crack, rend and deracinate*
> *The unity and married calm of states*
> *Quite from their future? O, when degree is shaked,*
> Which is *the ladder of all high designs,*
> *The enterprise is sick. . . .*
> *Take but degree away, untune the string,*
> *And hark what discord follows.*
>
> (1.3.75 ff.)

CENTER STAGE   COMMEDIA DELL'ARTE

Although the *commedia dell'arte* cannot be counted among the great literary movements in the history of theater, it is among the most influential and colorful. From Watteau to Picasso, *commedia* actors have long been among the favorite subjects of artists; no prephotographic period in Western theater history is as well documented in artwork as is the *commedia*. (The Kabuki theater enjoys a similar status in Japan.) The improvised antics of wandering street players of Renaissance Italy have given us many words that are commonplace in our daily lives: *harlequin*, *domino*, *zany*, and, most notably, *slapstick*. The writings of Molière, Lope de Vega, and Shakespeare show the discernible influence of the Italian comedians. Modern actors and directors such as Stanislavsky, Chaplin, Reinhardt, and Brook admit indebtedness to the improvisational style of the *commedia*.

The various names associated with Italian street theater suggest its salient features:

- *commedia dell'arte* ("comedy of the guild or by professionals in the art"; art here means not only "artistry" but "savoir faire")
- *commedia improvisa* ("improvised comedy")
- *commedia non scrita* ("unscripted comedy")
- *commedia a mascera* ("masked comedy")
- *commedia dell'arte all'improviso* ("professional improvised comedy")

Commedia may thus be defined as a form of comedy which, unlike the formal, scripted, aristocratic comedies of the Italian courts and learning academies, was performed by professional comedians in the streets of Renaissance Italy. Such artists were professionals in that they depended on the generosity of their audiences for their livelihood. But textbook definitions cannot begin to capture the essence of these street performances, which remain among the West's most significant examples of populist theater.

Despite scholarly debate as to its origins, the resemblance between the street comedy of sixteenth-century Italy and that of the ancient world are undeniable. Roving bands of comedians entertained ancient Greeks with improvised performances, and even Thespis—the so-called first tragic actor—traveled from town to town, like Sustarion before him, with a wagonload of white-faced vagabonds who performed comedy with music. The *hilarodi* of ancient Greece were famed for their ability to improvise farcical bits of comedy from loosely constructed scenarios, as were the Roman *lenones* (or "flatfeet," so named because they did not wear the tragic buskins). The Italian province of Atella was renowned for its farces, frequently performed at harvest time, which bear a resemblance to the subsequent *commedia* plays. Two centuries before Christ, Plautus, the father of popular entertainment in the West, wrote comedies for Roman workingmen containing situations and character types found throughout the *commedia*. The *commedia* as we know it took root in late-fifteenth-century Italy, and blossomed in the sixteenth and seventeenth centuries (Molière shared a

Pantalone's Serenade depicts old Pantalone attempting to impress an attractive young inamorata while Arlecchino—in his traditional diamond suit—laughs at his folly.

theater with an Italian company in Paris in the mid–seventeenth century), and slowly decayed into little more than obscene, predictable street performances when Carlo Goldoni (1707–1792) and Carlo Gozzi (1720–1806) attempted to rescue it by the mid–eighteenth century.

A typical *commedia* company consisted of some twelve to fifteen *maschere* ("maskers"), each of whom played well-honed roles befitting their age, talent, and physical type. Two elderly men (the lecherous, greedy Pantalone and the pedantic Doctor), two servants (the witty Arlecchino, or Harlequin, and the wicked Brighella), a sassy maidservant (Columbina or Smeraldina), a bragging military man (the Capitano), and at least two pair of *inamorati* (lovers) formed the nucleus of the company. These were augmented by various *zanni* (clowns, musicians, acrobats) who played minor roles and occasionally took center stage when the imaginations of the traditional characters flagged.

The company arrived in a town square towing their properties in wooden carts; they announced their presence with song, dances, and comical physical feats to attract crowds. The players set up a makeshift theater on a mountebank stage: a raised platform with a curtained backdrop. The properties of these itinerant companies were necessarily few and purely functional: a bench, a chair, a trunk, musical instruments, perhaps a monkey, and a chest of brightly colored drapes.

The artistic success of the company—not to mention its livelihood—depended almost entirely on the acting rather than the scenarios or stage effects. The Italian comedians developed a unique spirit of camaraderie in their playing, not unlike a vaudeville act like Abbott and Costello, which produced an impressive ensemble. *Commedia* actors had to meet demands rarely encountered in more conventional theater forms. They were obliged to be acrobats, dancers, orators—men and women of extraordinary imagination grounded in a thorough knowledge of human nature.

Their stage movement was spirited, often violent, and acrobatic; their verbal ingenuity was uncanny.

Though they relied on their imaginations to improvise a witty speech, the comedians were guided by a *scenario*, a brief outline of each scene and of what each actor was expected to do in it. Gozzi tells us that such *scenari* were "written entirely on a small slip of paper and posted under a little light in the wings for greater convenience of the troupe." Prior to the performance, the company manager (*il guido maestro*), who usually composed the scenario, read the outline to the company. The plots were familiar to actors and audiences alike: young lovers, frustrated by imposing parents or guardians, are aided in their love quest by conniving servants.

Each actor kept a *zibbaldoni*, or "commonplace book," which contained hundreds of phrases, jokes, and set speeches that could be readily adapted to virtually any comic situation. These comic speeches, collectively known as *concetti*, were described by a seventeenth-century actor, Niccolo Barbieri, who noted that each actor was "stored with phrases, declarations of love, reproaches, deliriums, and despairs." According to the type of role he played, an actor's *zibbaldoni* also contained boasts, obscene jokes, angry tirades, streams of wild oaths, and occasionally gibberish. For instance, the Doctor specialized in riddling couplets, gnomic aphorisms, and burlesque prescriptions, all punctuated by nonsensical Latin. The young lovers excelled in mythological tirades and classical quotations.

Of all the trappings of the *commedia dell'arte*, perhaps the *lazzi*—physical stage business—are the most intriguing. These hilarious stage antics have been preserved in the performances of circus clowns, vaudevillians, and silent film comedians. Because it depended on visual humor, *lazzi* became the foundation of a *commedia* performance. According to tradition, the word *lazzi* was derived from a Lombard pronunciation of the Tuscan "*lacci*," which meant "ribbon" or "laces." It may

also mean "knots" because the stage business "tied" the plot strands together. In addition to producing laughter, *lazzi* fulfilled several functions in the telling of a *commedia* tale: an actor would resort to *lazzi* whenever a scene began to lag or his eloquence gave out. *Zanni* kept the audience amused with their *lazzi* as the ever-active troupe caught its collective breath.

Other cultures have also produced *commedia*-like theatrics, a testimony to the universality of clowning and comic theater. The Cherokee of North America, for instance, developed the Booger Dance, an example of clowning that predates European contact. Later, it was altered to make the European invaders the objects of satire. Masked "boogers," or non–Native Americans, invaded an all-night dance party, playfully hitting spectators, grabbing women, breaking wind, acting deranged. Asked their identity, they broke wind and gave nonsensical, obscene answers. Hopi clowns were especially noted for their parodies of fertility rites in the pueblos, as were the Chapayekas described in the Yaqui Easter ceremony. The skeleton dancers of Mexico's Día de los Muertos attempt to laugh death away with their improvised clowning in the cemeteries (see Chapter 9). Devil figures in the medieval cycle plays were more often comic than fearsome. The Chinese folk play *Picking Turnips* (described in the Center Stage box, A Night at the Chinese Opera), features a traditional clown, known as a *ch'ou*, whom sixteenth-century Italians would instantly recognize as Arlecchino's Asian cousin. Most cultures, in fact, offer a variant on this wily underling, or trickster. The Germans call him Hanswurst or Peter Pickleherring; the French know him as Scapin; and to the British he is Punch. He is also prevalent in folktales from myriad cultures: the Coyote stories of Native Americans, the Monkey King of the Far East, and B'rer Rabbit in the American South. The Italian *commedia dell'arte*, however, remains as the theater's most noteworthy example of improvised clowning and comic chaos.

CENTER STAGE   THE MASQUE

If one of its key elements is spectacle, then the theater certainly reached its height in purely visual terms during the Renaissance, with the Italian *intermezzi* and the English court masques. No expense was spared to ensure that the masquers and their audiences reveled in opulent splendor. In addition to their entertainment value, masques became a primary means by which monarchs and nobles displayed their wealth and power through the politics of conspicuous consumption. The court masque contributed in no small way to the English civil war: it was cited by commoners and Puritans as examples of royal decadence and fiscal irresponsibility.

On the evening of January 6, 1512, Henry VIII and nine courtly companions celebrated Twelfth Night, the official end of the Christmas season, by dressing themselves in elaborate costumes to "invade" the English court, where they shocked the ladies by asking them to dance. The women demurely refused the masked gentlemen's requests because they had heard scandalous stories about licentious wit at the Italian courts, where courtiers participated in spectacular entertainments (*intermezzi*) performed between courses of a banquet. Historian Edward Hall, who described the events in Henry's court, wrote that this "maske"

was "a thyne not seen afore in England." Actually, masquelike activities appeared in England as early as 1377, when 130 Londoners donned the costumes of devils, knights, and clerical figures such as priests, bishops, and even the pope himself. These maskers gamboled to Prince Richard's retreat at Kennington, where they entertained the future king, who was so charmed by their merrymaking that he joined their revelry. In 1501 Prince Arthur's marriage to Catherine of Aragon was celebrated with dances and pageants, and the great hall at Westminster was adorned with spectacular scenery, including a castle housing eight maidens and a sailing ship carrying eight knights. Whether the English masque can be dated from Kennington, Westminster, or Henry's court is of less importance than recognizing that royal entertainments played an integral part in shaping the history of English theater.

Originally, interludes (England), *intermezzi* (Italy), *entreméses* (Spain), and *entremets* (France) were brief skits or dialogues, often allegorical, devised to entertain royalty and the wealthy between courses at lengthy banquets (which might last eight to ten hours). Songs and dances, frequently derived from rustic agricultural festivals, were added to the

playlets. In fifteenth-century Italian courts *intermezzi* were performed as part of pastoral plays about shepherds and woodland nymphs. Eventually these expanded into extravaganzas portraying classical themes with lavish scenery, costumes, and lighting effects. The country's finest composers and musicians were hired to orchestrate these spectacles, and poets, actors, and dancers added their artistry. Thus *intermezzi* evolved into a full-blown theater genre unto itself.

Consider a famous example of an *intermezzo*. To celebrate the marriage of Lucrezia Borgia to the son of the duke of Ferrara, the pope himself hosted a banquet at which an allegorical drama about the alliance between Ferrara and Rome was presented. Royal couples participated in masked dancing, led by no less than the powerful Cesare Borgia. The duke returned the pope's favor (to best him?) by arranging an entertainment for the newlyweds in Ferrara. It included a dance of savages around the figure of a beautiful woman who was saved by the triumphant arrival of the god of love, accompanied by a full orchestra of musicians. As Eros set the maiden free, a large model of the globe split in half to reveal twelve Swiss guards performing a military dance with full weaponry.

Bernardo Buontalenti's design for The Harmony of the Spheres *(1589) illustrates the grand spectacle that epitomized the* intermezzi *and masques at Renaissance courts.*

Word of such extravaganzas soon reached England, where the vainglorious Henry determined to dazzle his court with comparable entertainments. When Hall described the masque at Henry's court, he dutifully noted that all was done "after the manner of Italie." Masques—to use the French spelling, which did not come into vogue until the early seventeenth century—continued throughout the reigns of Henry VIII and his daughter, Elizabeth I, who enjoyed expensive court entertainments despite her reputation for frugality. In particular, Elizabeth enjoyed masques that portrayed various trades such as fishmongers, farmers, and mariners. In 1591 the gentlemen of Gray's Inn presented a masque at Elizabeth's court entitled *Proteus and the Adamantine Rock*, which became the prototype of subsequent court entertainments.

One might compare the unfolding of a masque to the unwrapping of an exotic gift in which many layers are exposed one at a time, each more colorful and elaborate than the previous one. Masques were customarily "one-shot" affairs, often consuming a full year's resources of time, money, and labor; hence, there was a sense of a ritual unfolding in these meticulously planned spectacles. They traditionally began with an introductory song and, beginning with Elizabeth's reign, a "presenter" (or master of ceremonies), whose poetic speech set the tone and theme of the events to follow. This was followed by the entry of the masquers, a magnificent procession in resplendent costumes. A series of dances, derived from popular social dances of the day, alternated with stories drawn from classical mythology. Not surprisingly, they emphasized the restorative powers of the reigning monarchs, who were compared to the deities of antiquity. After a final song, dance, and perhaps a bit of dialogue, the masquers were carried away, often via cloud machines that hoisted them into the heavens. Professional actors were hired to recite the dialogue, but the dances and nonspeaking roles were usually played by courtiers and, on occasion, by

the royalty. Queen Anne, wife of James I, was a frequent participant, as were Charles I, his wife Henrietta Maria, and their children. There is evidence that the actor who played Ariel in Shakespeare's last play, *The Tempest* (1612), wore a costume designed specifically for James's son, the duke of York, who had appeared in a masque at Whitehall.

The masque was elevated as an artistic enterprise when poet-playwright Ben Jonson assumed the status of royal masquer for James in 1603. The scholarly Jonson believed the masque should be a dramatic poem based on classical learning. He devised a unified piece in which poet, designer, and musicians collaborated to achieve a single vision. Jonson's intentions were undermined, however, when he feuded with Inigo Jones, who designed scenery and costumes for the Stuart court. Jones, who argued for the supremacy of the visual elements, turned Charles and Henrietta Maria against Jonson, who lost his position as court poet, a development that marked the beginning of the decline of the masque in England.

In addition to his unparalleled poetry, perhaps Jonson's greatest contribution to the masque was the development of the so-called antimasque. In 1609, at Queen Anne's request, Jonson wrote *The Masque of Queens Celebrated from the House of Fame*, in which he sought to bring novelty to the performance by inserting a grotesque parody of the traditional masque. Every manner of fiendish character (witches, monsters, and devils) cavorted to the delight of the audience in this antimasque, which became a staple of future court revels.

Under Charles and Henrietta Maria the masques degenerated into flimsy excuses for ingenious displays of scenography and a variety of dances that had little relationship to one another. For those outside the palace walls, the masques became a loathed symbol of court decadence. Ironically, the final masque at the court of Charles I, *Salmacida Spolia* (1640), depicted a violent storm in which a Fury challenged evil spirits to "bring discord throughout England."

At their height, the masques were a powerful tool for reinforcing the authority of the monarchy. They asserted the divine right of kings by equating royalty with the gods themselves. The god-kings were invariably idealized as beneficent, protective beings who brought prosperity and harmony to their subjects. As people became more critical of the monarchy, the masques only enforced the notion that kingship was about artifice and false shows of power and glory.

Masques are more than a curiosity from the royal theater of the Renaissance. They influenced much of the high-quality literature of the era. Many romances, such as Beaumont and Fletcher's *The Faithful Shepardess*, and Shakespeare's later plays, *The Winter's Tale* and *The Tempest*, contain masques within their dramatic construction. In *The Tempest*, Prospero calls up the goddesses of fertility (Juno, Iris, Ceres) to bless the wedding of Miranda and Ferdinand; elsewhere the miscreants who would overthrow Prospero are tormented and chased by strange, frightening beings in what Shakespeare intended to be an antimasque. A number of the Jacobean tragedies used antimasques, most notably Webster's *The Duchess of Malfi*, which features a horrific scene in which the Duchess is tormented by the criminally insane.

Not only did the masque affect the structure of late Renaissance drama, but to some degree grand opera, the operetta, and even the modern musical theater retain an element of the Renaissance masques in their scenic splendor. For example, *Cats* has an essentially masquelike construction: it is a series of colorful dances performed by mythological cats against spectacular scenery. It even ends with Deuteronomy, King of Cats, escorting Grizabella into the heavens atop a floating tire—a modern variant on the cloud machine. Charity balls, presidential inaugurals, coronations, and other major civic events often use theatrical embellishments we associate with masques. Though monarchs may not preside over them (beauty queens aside), they give us some sense of the spirit of the Renaissance masque.

Hierarchies Onstage and Off

As might be expected, Renaissance-era plays feature protagonists who are royalty (Hamlet), who are of high birth (the Duchess of Malfi), or who have acquired power (Othello). Even the comedies—which traditionally center on middle-class life—feature the specter of royalty controlling events. Note that it is the King's Officer who intervenes to save Orgon and his family in *Tartuffe*, less a contrived ending than a nod to the beneficence of Louis XIV. Playwrights portrayed the dilemmas of the royal and upper classes because they were (as they remain today) a source of fascination for audiences and because the fall of the mighty served as a powerful lesson for lesser mortals. Witnessing the catastrophes of kings and queens reinforced the belief that each man and woman was a "little kingdom" that must be ruled with wisdom and temperance. As Sigismund says at the conclusion of *Life's a Dream*, a play about the proper uses of public and personal kingship:

> Since I would be a conqueror
>
> I see I must first
>
> Make a conquest of myself.

Quickly scan the Cast of Characters prefacing most Renaissance plays, especially the tragedies. You will note that the characters are listed not in order of dramatic importance, nor in order of appearance. In this age, playwrights customarily listed characters in a strict hierarchical order that reflected the society in which they lived. Women are listed separately from—and only after—the male roles, a reflection of the patriarchal societies depicted in the plays.

Another manifestation of the hierarchical nature of the drama can be found in the final speech of each play. Note that invariably it is the highest-ranking person onstage who, quite literally, gets the last word. In Shakespeare's tragedies, it is the new sovereign who speaks, a symbol of the new order that will emerge from the chaos. Hence, Fortinbras speaks last in *Hamlet*. Such formality carries into comedy as well. In *A Midsummer Night's Dream* Shakespeare gives each of the reigning powers—Duke Theseus and the Fairy King Oberon—a final speech. We can, however, note a subtle shift in *Tartuffe*, in which a member of the middle class delivers the final speech. Commoners, enriched by world exploration and new economic opportunities, were clearly emerging as a power in society and in the theater, onstage and off.

The Role of Tragedy

The exploration of the Americas and the Far East was an important by-product of the strong monarchies that dominated Europe. Royalty, who sought to enrich their coffers, kingdoms, and egos, financed the expeditions of Columbus and those who followed him. Whatever deleterious effects these conquerors may have had on indigenous cultures, their exploits fueled the imaginations of their nations. Correspondingly, the dramas of the age reflect this same sense of discovery and optimism. The great paradox of the Renaissance rests on this simultaneous recognition of humanity's dual nature: superhuman accomplishments in art, exploration, and statecraft were offset by human weakness, folly, and—of course—death. A. C. Bradley's assessment of the Shakespearean tragic hero is no less applicable to those created by Marlowe, Corneille, Racine, Lope de Vega, or Calderón:

> The center of the tragic impression . . . is the impression of waste. "What a piece of work is man!" we cry, "so much more terrible than we knew! Why should he be so if this beauty and greatness only tortures itself and throws itself away?" . . . Everywhere from the crushed rocks beneath our feet to the soul of man, we see power, intelligence, life and glory, which astound us and seem to call for our worship. And everywhere we see them perishing, devouring one another and destroying themselves, often with dreadful pain, as though they came into being for no other end.

A. C. Bradley, SHAKESPEAREAN TRAGEDY, 1904

As we saw with the Greek dramas, the characters, all "overreachers," speak in a language that transcends the ordinary. With few exceptions, Renaissance plays were written in verse, or "heightened language." There are no small issues nor ordinary men and women here, and they require extraordinary language—"the mighty line" of English verse and the lofty Alexandrines of the French—to express themselves.

Playhouses and Scenery

The very playhouses in which Renaissance dramas (and others into the eighteenth century) were performed reinforced social stratification. Then, as now, people with more power, prestige, and money sat in preferred seats, while the middle class sat in the next best seats and the commoners, when they were permitted to attend the theater, stood or sat in the farthest reaches of the auditorium. In Elizabethan England, however, "groundlings" stood in front of the great thrust stage.

Interestingly, it was a major development in scenic design that affected the architecture and seating practices of this era. In 1545 Sebastiano Serlio, a painter and historian, published a treatise on perspective, the technique of rendering three-dimensional space on flat surfaces by making objects in the distance seem smaller than those in the foreground. Perspective was actually an outgrowth of science, especially geometry and its study of planes and a "vanishing point." Serlio applied his theories of scenic design at the court theaters in Italy, rendering examples of comical, tragic, and pastoral scenes. As marvelous, even lifelike, as these perspective drawings were, there were two liabilities. Actors could not venture upstage and act amid the drawings without grossly distorting the illusion. And the perspective was perfectly accurate from but a single seat in the auditorium—the so-called duke's seat placed on a straight line directly in front of the vanishing point. The farther one sat to the right or left of this point, the more distorted the perspective. When permanent theater spaces were built, as they were in Vicenza and Versailles, they retained the royal box and the elongated auditorium from which royal retinues could better view the scenic spectacle.

Though Elizabethan public theaters were more democratic, they too reflected the society that attended them. There were clearly defined areas for the working class (the "pit" or yard where they stood), the middle class (any one of three galleries), and the gentry ("the lords' room"). After the Puritans seized power in 1642, courtiers fled to France and Italy, where they attended plays in newly designed playhouses. When drama returned to the English stage in 1660, new theaters were built in imitation of the Continental playhouses, right down to the "king's box" where Charles II and his consorts sat. More thorough accounts of the structures and conventions of the English, French, and Spanish theaters are appended to representative plays from these countries.

Acting

European theaters might have been smaller and more intimate than the enormous Greek spaces, but actors still had to measure up to their characters and the language of the plays. The acting style of the period demanded size and stature, particularly in France and Italy, where actors portrayed an idealized version of their heroes. Consequently, they employed formal gestures and poses to manifest their characters. Again, reigning monarchs may have contributed to this stylization. King Louis XIV prided himself on his balletic skills. Eager to please their king, French courtiers quickly adopted the formal, self-conscious poses of ballet dancers, and soon actors mirrored these customs in their performances. The English theater seems to have undergone a transition from the blustering style of an Edward Alleyn in the 1580s to a more moderate technique, typified by Richard Burbage, as the theater moved into the new century. Unfortunately, little is known about the acting style of the Spanish, though Lope de Vega wrote about the need for a more naturalistic performance mode. We must remember that his advice to the players, like Shakespeare's in act 3 of *Hamlet*, must be taken within the context of his time.

Playwriting: The Neoclassicists Versus the Romantics

Renaissance plays may be divided into two general categories:

- Those that followed the strict rules of Neoclassicism; patterned after Greek and Roman dramas, these plays respected the rules of time, place, and action; used few characters; and did not mix comic with serious material.
- Those that disregarded the unities of time, place, and action; freely mixed genres, plots, and subplots; and incorporated the full spectrum of society in their tales.

The former were found largely in Italy and France, the bastions of Neoclassicism, while the latter flourished in England and Spain, whose drama later inspired the Romantics.

Despite its beginnings in Italy in the mid–sixteenth century, by 1630 Neoclassicism found its true home in France, where it remained firmly entrenched until Victor Hugo led an artistic revolution with the production of *Hernani* in 1830. Because France became the artistic and cultural center of Europe by the late seventeenth century, Neoclassic drama influenced the development of drama throughout Europe and America.

In 1561 the Italian theorist Julius Caesar Scaliger's "Seven Books of the Poetics" was published in Paris, and soon the French offered their observations on Aristotle's "rules." In particular, Jean de La Taille (c. 1540–1608) insisted on observing the unities of time, place, and action in his "On the Art of Tragedy," published in 1572. The dictates of Scaliger, La Taille, and others provided Neoclassic drama with its most distinctive characteristic: a nearly idolatrous adherence to the rules.

Neoclassicism embraced more than the laws of the unities, the segregation of the tragic and comic impulses, and the simplicity of form and language. It sought *vraisemblance* ("appearance of Truth"), which was an idealized truth, that is, the way the world *ought* to be. Dramas had to be plausible and could not offend anyone's sense of day-to-day reality. The doctrine rested on the impulse, equal parts Christian dogma and classical humanism, to use the theater to teach moral lessons through three critical elements:

- *Morality* assumed that the universe is organized and just. Playwrights were duty bound to show that the good were rewarded and the wicked punished—which is, of course, the doctrine of "poetic justice," on which melodrama thrived.
- *Generality* dictated that what was shown on the stage must be applicable to all humanity.
- *Decorum* divided humanity into well-defined categories according to social status, sex, age, and so on. Playwrights—and actors—were compelled to show individual behavior that was in accordance with society's expectations. A king must speak with the dignity of a king and servants must provide wise counsel to their betters.

The Neoclassic rules were severely tested in 1637 in one of the most famous controversies in theater history. Pierre Corneille (1606–1684) wrote *Le Cid*, an undeniably entertaining play based on a Spanish mythic hero. Conscious of Neoclassic dictates, Corneille compressed the events of many years and locales into a five-act play, dutifully observing the unity of time by limiting the action to a single day. Despite the play's popularity, critics complained that the play violated a number of principles. Cardinal Richelieu, chief counselor to Louis XIV and an avid theater patron himself, submitted the play to the French Academy, which he founded to promote French arts and sciences. The merits and weaknesses of the play were passionately debated. Its sternest critics cited a number of irregularities that violated the principles of *vraisemblance*:

- It contained too many events for a single day.
- The play's heroine failed to mourn properly the death of her father.

- She received her lover in her private chambers, an unthinkable breach of decorum in the eyes of French Christians who expected much more of a noblewoman.
- It provided a happy resolution to an otherwise serious play.

The playwright argued that audiences enjoyed the play despite these lapses. He pointed to the ancients, who themselves violated virtue and poetic justice in plays such as Euripides' *Medea*. Ultimately, Corneille was mildly censured for his "irregularities"—and he indignantly retired from the stage for three years. Significantly, the controversy established the inviolability of the Neoclassic rules. Thus "living classicism"—sought by a public that wanted pleasure from its drama—suffered at the hands of "theoretical classicism"—which dictated codes of writing in the name of reason and morality. The Academy's proclamation that "any pleasure outside the rules cannot bring quality" influenced French writing for almost two hundred years. Of the subsequent French tragedians, only Jean Racine had the genius to use the rules to his advantage.

Such controversies did not affect English or Spanish playwriting. Shakespeare and Calderón, and their talented peers, wrote sprawling dramas with multiple plots that contained both comic and serious elements. They portrayed kings and commoners with equal enthusiasm; and they conjured locales that defied the unities of time and place. The most memorable and lasting drama of the Renaissance (save Molière's work) was produced in the Elizabethan public theaters and the Spanish *corrales*. The English theater, in particular, became a more commercial enterprise that could not afford to be bound by rules and tradition. The middle class, which sought entertainment, became the arbiter of taste. As the commercial theater expanded elsewhere, English plays provided a model for the theatrical free market. Middle-class tastes influenced the drama as much, perhaps more, than did monarchs and wealthy patrons.

ENGLAND

Artistic and Cultural Events

1550:
Ralph Roister-Doister, Nicholas Udall advances popular theater

1572:
Acting profession legalized

1599:
Globe theater opens

1613:
Globe theater burns

1520:
The Four PP, farce by John Heywood, first major secular drama

1564:
Shakespeare born in Stratford-upon-Avon

1576:
James Burbage builds the Theater, first public theater in London

1588:
Doctor Faustus, Christopher Marlowe; bridges medieval and Renaissance tragedy

1611:
King James Bible

1623:
Shakespeare's actors publish Folio edition of his plays

1400 C.E.	1500 C.E.		1600 C.E.

Historical and Political Events

1601:
Earl of Essex disgraced; England disillusioned

1625–1642:
Charles I

1558–1603:
Elizabeth I

1642–1660:
Civil War; Puritans close public theaters

1507–1558:
Henry VIII

1592–1594:
Plague years in London

1487:
War of the Roses ends and Tudor line established

1588:
England defeats the Spanish Armada

1603–1625:
James I

1605:
Gunpowder plot against monarchy

HAMLET, PRINCE OF DENMARK
WILLIAM SHAKESPEARE

WILLIAM SHAKESPEARE (1564–1616)

Shakespeare, the most quoted, most produced playwright in the world, left us few facts concerning his life. Baptismal records from Holy Trinity Church in Stratford-upon-Avon, located in the rich farming and sheep country of central England, indicate that he was likely born on April 23, 1564, to Mary Arden and John Shakespeare, a glover and civic leader. He received a classically based education at the Stratford Grammar School, where he first encountered the works of Plautus, Terence, and Seneca, the Roman playwrights who show a traceable influence on his plays, particularly such early efforts as *The Comedy of Errors* (based on Plautus's *The Menaechmi*) and *Titus Andronicus*. Unlike Marlowe and other of his contemporaries, Shakespeare did not have a university education. In 1582 he married a woman eight years his senior, Anne Hathaway, a union which produced three children, only one of whom had a child, Lady Elizabeth Bernard, who had no heirs; thus Shakespeare has no known direct descendants.

We do not know when Shakespeare left Stratford and journeyed to London, though it is likely that he was working in the city by the late 1580s. Certainly by 1592 he was prominent enough that playwright Robert Greene attacked him as "an upstart crow." About 1590 his *Henry VI* plays had appeared and quickly established him as a potent voice in the newly thriving public theaters of London. While the theaters were closed because of a devastating plague in late 1592, Shakespeare wrote his great poems, *Venus and Adonis* and *Lucrece*, which he dedicated to the earl of Southampton, his benefactor. When the theaters reopened in 1594, Shakespeare, with Richard Burbage and Will Kempe, became a "star" of the Lord Chamberlain's Men, a newly formed professional company in London. Shakespeare was the company's resident playwright (although it also acted plays by Jonson and others), Burbage its principal tragic actor, and Kempe its premiere comedian. This trio led the Lord Chamberlain's Men to both artistic and financial success; by 1599 the company built the Globe theater on the south bank of the Thames River. As playwright and actor, Shakespeare was given one-tenth ownership in the Globe. When James I became king in 1603, the Chamberlain's Men were given the title of the King's Men, a testimony to their prestige in England's cultural life. Shakespeare, however, retired from the theater and London life in 1612 to return to Stratford, where he lived at New Place, the stately home he had purchased in 1597. He died on April 23 (his traditional birthday) in 1616 and was buried in the sanctuary of Holy Trinity Church. A plaque celebrating his artistry was erected over the grave, but his most enduring monument was the collection of his plays, the so-called First Folio, published in 1623 by the actors for whom he wrote. His colleague and rival Ben Jonson wrote his epitaph, proclaiming that Shakespeare wrote "not for an age, but for all time."

Shakespeare is credited with 37 plays and had a hand in several others, as joint authorship was a common practice of the age. The canon embraces virtually all of the genres popular in the English Renaissance, and he employs a remarkable variety of literary styles in his work. From vulgar prose to exquisite verse, from rhetorical bombast to lyrical poetry, from patriotic speeches to intensely personal soliloquies, Shakespeare created the fullest spectrum of human discourse ever written by a single person. (See Spotlight box, Making Shakespeare's Language User-Friendly).

After some initial experimentation with style and form, Shakespeare wrote sequences of plays that generally can be grouped by period and genre. "The chronicle plays" were based on medieval English history and served as a warning to his countrymen that rebellion is ruinous; although the plays are about such monarchs as Richard II, Henry IV (two parts), Henry V, Henry VI (three parts), and Richard III, England herself is the protagonist of the chronicles as her very soul is warred over by Vices (rebel factions) and Virtues (the Tudor kings). These plays were Shakespeare's primary endeavor until the mid-1590s, when he turned his attention to romantic comedies (*Two Gentlemen of Verona, The Merchant of Venice, A Midsummer Night's Dream, As You Like It, The Merry Wives of Windsor, Much Ado About Nothing,* and *Twelfth Night*) and the tragic *Romeo and Juliet*; the plays are bound by an exploration of the various facets of love and are marked by a benevolent treatment of human folly. From 1600 to about 1607 Shakespeare produced his great tragedies (*Julius Caesar, Hamlet, Othello, Macbeth, King Lear, Coriolanus,* and *Antony and Cleopatra*), in which he explored deeper questions of mortality and human failure. At this time he also wrote a group of plays, neither fully comedic nor tragic, known as "the problem plays" (*Measure for Measure, All's Well That Ends Well, Troilus and Cressida,* and *Timon of Athens*), which reflect the uncertainty and cynicism of the first years of the reign of James I (1603–1625). Shakespeare spent the last four years of his playwriting career writing the great romances (*Pericles, Cymbeline, The Winter's Tale,* and *The Tempest*), which fuse the sweep of the chronicles, the mystery of the tragedies, and the optimistic resolution of the comedies. These plays portray the fullest range of human types and behaviors, explore the broadest range of public and private issues, and embrace the most complete emotional palette created by the mind of a single artist in human history.

Shakespeare is truly the world's playwright. Today more than 250 theater companies throughout the world are dedicated to the production of his plays (over 120 in the United States alone). In 1988 China held a Shakespeare festival in which 22 plays were performed in an 18-day span in Beijing and Shanghai. The Japanese publish more Shakespearean articles and books than are generated in many English-speaking countries. More is written about Shakespeare and his works than about any other nonreligious being, and only the Judeo-Christian Bible is more frequently quoted than Shakespeare's lines, a fact that more than validates the prophecy of the opening of his Sonnet 55:

> Not marble, nor the gilded monuments
> Of princes shall outlive this pow'rful rhyme.

HAMLET, PRINCE OF DENMARK (C.1601)

No play in the history of the theater has generated more commentary than *Hamlet*. In 1964 the Polish critic Jan Kott observed that a *bibliography* of the books and essays written about the play would equal the size of the Warsaw telephone directory—imagine how that volume has grown since then! And with the possible exceptions of *A Midsummer Night's Dream* and *Richard III*, no play has been produced more often than Shakespeare's tragedy of the prince of Denmark. The greatest actors in Western theater have played the role, from Richard Burbage (who created the role) to Kenneth Branagh (whose four-hour-and-twenty-minute 1996 film presented the text in its entirety). For four centuries actors have been judged by how well they play Hamlet. There are at least a score of film versions of the play, including one starring Mel Gibson, who portrayed the "delicate and tender prince" as a "lethal weapon." The role has also attracted actors throughout Asia, Africa, and Latin America. Many women have played the role, including the great French actor Sarah Bernhardt and Dame Judith Anderson (who was 72 when she played Hamlet). And in Denver an enterprising gambler actually won a hundred-dollar bet in 1874 when he memorized the complete text in three days!

What, then, may be said of *Hamlet* that has not already been said, either in essays or in performance? Not much, though we frequently use *Hamlet* throughout this text to illustrate points about dramaturgy, performance, and tragedy. The more pertinent question may be

Shakespeare's language need not be a source of anxiety if you understand a few simple precepts. First of all, it is not "Old English" but is among the first uses of Modern English. The history of the English language can be divided into three phases. Old English derived from various Germanic tribes and lasted until the Norman Conquest (1066 C.E.); *Beowulf* is the best-known literary work composed in Old English, which is very much a foreign language. After the French conquered Britain, there was an infusion of Latin-based language, mostly in the form of French, which became the official language of the English court. This blend of Old English and French produced Middle English, which flourished from about 1200 to 1500. Chaucer's famous *Canterbury Tales* is a masterpiece of Middle English. After the Wars of the Roses and the establishment of the Tudor line under King Henry VII, there was a move to purge English of its French influence. Though this attempt largely failed, the linguistic phenomenon known as "the great vowel shift" in the late fifteenth and early sixteenth centuries precipitated an essentially new language: Modern English. Shakespeare was among its pioneers and is estimated to have contributed over 8,000 words to our vocabulary. If there is anything foreign about Shakespeare's language, it is the exceptional ingenuity with which he used it. Shakespeare and his contemporaries were experimenting with the possibilities of their new language to discover its potential. You, too,

should read the plays in that same spirit of discovery and playfulness.

You are probably aware that most of Shakespeare's plays are written in *iambic pentameter*, a term that indicates the number of stressed syllables—or beats—in a line. The typical line of Shakespearean blank (unrhymed) verse does indeed consist of 10 syllables, half of them stressed, the other half unstressed, in a pattern like this:

u [unstressed] / [stressed] **u / u / u / u /**

Or to borrow a line from Sonnet 29, you might say:

that THEN i SCORN to CHANGE my STATE with KINGS.

Shakespeare used this metric form to approximate natural speech in English drama, which had inherited the verse forms of the medievals who relied heavily on the symmetrical four-beat line:

And now I wax old,
Sick, sorry, and cold;
As muck upon cold
I wither away.

(from "Noah and His Sons," *The Wakefield Pageant*, modern version by John Gassner)

Some early Tudor tragedies used the unwieldy "fourteener," a 14-syllable, 7-beat line:

Do well or ill, I do dare avouch, some evil on me will speak.

No, truly, yet I do not mean the King's precepts to break;
To place I mean for to return my duty to fulfill.

(Thomas Preston, *Cambises*, 1569)

Read each set of lines aloud and you quickly hear the artificiality of the lines; imagine listening to this for a couple of hours! By using the five-beat line, Shakespeare and his contemporaries approximated the normal rhythms of English speech. The iambic pattern—puh-POM, puh-POM, puh-POM—has been likened to the sound of the heartbeat. We can say that iambic pentameter, then, is as natural as life itself.

If Shakespeare wrote every line in strict iambic pentameter, the verse would become monotonous and predictable. Shakespeare breaks the pattern to achieve variety and, more importantly, to provide his actors with subtle stage directions about how to interpret a line. Shakespeare did not, like so many modern playwrights, write detailed stage directions, but they are there in the lines. A basic understanding of his "code" can make reading his plays easier—and more enjoyable.

Shakespeare gets his effects by setting up iambic pentameter as the norm for dramatic speech, and then—significantly—he breaks the pattern to highlight key moments. Look at this short passage from act 2, scene 2 of *Macbeth*,

"Why has this play proven irresistible to actors, audiences, and critics since Shakespeare wrote it in (probably) 1601?" We might add psychologists to this list of *Hamlet* devotees. Numerous case studies have been written about the prince—all for a man whom Shakespeare would call "a fiction, a dream of passion" (2.2.552).

This is precisely Hamlet's attraction: He seems genuinely real to us, partly because he is among the most essential archetypes created by humanity, partly because he is so recognizably human in his many contradictions. As he is a part of the "collective unconscious" described by Jung, he is the universal portrait of the essentially decent person confronted by an onerous task. At the same time he emerges as a particular individual, who—like each of us—is a mass of contradictions defying categorization.

Shakespeare did not "invent" Hamlet. His roots may be found as far back as Aeschylus's Orestes, the prince of Argos who was compelled to avenge the death of his father, Agamem-

in which Macbeth has just returned from killing King Duncan:

MACBETH. I have done the deed.
    Didst thou not hear a noise?
LADY MACBETH. I heard the owl
    scream and the crickets cry.
    Did not you speak?
MACBETH.   When?
LADY MACBETH.   Now.
MACBETH.   As
                        I descended?
LADY MACBETH. Ay.
MACBETH. Hark!
    Who lies i'the second chamber?
LADY MACBETH.   Don-
                        albain.
MACBETH. This is a sorry sight.
LADY MACBETH. A foolish thought
    to say a sorry sight.

Don't be dismayed by the way the words are written on the page; it is all part of the code and there is nothing terribly mysterious about it. Here the language, and the way it is constructed, *is* the dramatic action.

Macbeth's first line contains an abnormal number of stresses to show that his mind is troubled by the horrible murder he has just committed: "I have DONE the DEED. DIDST thou NOT HEAR a NOISE?" Note also that the repeated "d" and "t" sounds echo Macbeth's own heartbeat, which surely must be pounding frantically. Lady Macbeth responds with a more regular line: "I HEARD the OWL SCREAM and the

CRICKets CRY." It is a five-beat line, but just irregular enough to suggest Lady Macbeth's anxiety. Nature is rebelling at the act ("owl scream") and she, too, is a bit unnerved. Notice that Shakespeare plants a couple of interesting sound effects to heighten the scene. The phrases "owl scream" and "crickets cry" are onomatopoetic; that is, they imitate the very sounds they describe to create atmosphere.

The next four lines are "shared lines"—combined they make up a single line of blank verse. Shakespeare is telling his actors to "pick up the pace," to speak quickly without pausing between lines. The Macbeths are jumping at shadows and their hurried speech reflects this. The dialogue here is as naturalistic and clipped as any modern passage. Lady Macbeth's response ("Ay") is a line unto itself; in contrast to the quickly paced lines before it, Shakespeare is scripting a lengthy pause as the Macbeths pause to regain their composure. Macbeth's "Hark!" also denotes a long pause. "Hark," of course, means "Listen!" and the pause is there to allow time for them to listen.

After another shared line to establish that King Duncan's son (and potential heir) sleeps in the adjoining chamber, Shakespeare concludes this sequence with two very telling lines. Macbeth's line ("THIS is a SORry SIGHT") is short and irregular in its rhythm to reflect his anxiety. The pause implied by the short line suggests that Lady Macbeth takes a moment to com-

pose herself (and to assess Macbeth's panic?). She then responds with a line of perfect iambic pentameter: "a FOOLish THOUGHT to SAY a SORry SIGHT." She is in complete control (or wishes to suggest she is), and her line has a calming effect on Macbeth. Note the dominance of the "s" (or sibilant) sounds in Lady Macbeth's line; they, too, are a stage direction to the actor to "Shhhh" Macbeth. As the play progresses, by the way, Lady Macbeth's speech becomes more irregular to reflect her growing madness; by contrast, Macbeth's speech becomes more composed as he adjusts to his status as murderer-king. Shakespeare's language invariably mirrors its character's personality, or as actor Ben Kingsley says: "In Shakespeare, language *is* the character."

Did Shakespeare sit down and consciously plan each line for these effects? Perhaps a couple, but most of it came instinctively. It was his genius, just as Beethoven's genius was to hear music in his head.

Shakespeare and his contemporaries used other forms of writing in their plays: rhymed verse, couplets, occasionally doggerel verse, and prose. For now, remember that Shakespeare's language, in addition to its vivid word pictures and emotional power, is an integral part of the dramatic action. Not only does it define character and situation, its very structure helps actors—and you—read the plays.

non. To accomplish this he had to kill his mother (Clytemnestra) and his morally reprehensible stepfather (Aegisthus). In contrast to Hamlet, Orestes goes mad *after* he murders them. Furthermore, psychologist Ernest Jones, among others, has argued that Hamlet may also be aligned with Oedipus, partly because he too must discover who he is, largely because of his preoccupation with his mother's sex life. The Oedipal implications of the Hamlet-Gertrude relationship were prominent in both the 1948 Laurence Olivier film and in Franco Zeffirelli's 1992 version with Gibson and Glenn Close.

Though Shakespeare never mentions the Greek legends of either Orestes or Oedipus in his writings, we cannot conclude that he was unaware of them. In any case, the story of "the put-upon prince" is so ingrained in the human psyche that he found in it the Norse myth of Amlothi. This Viking warrior, whose name means "desperate in battle," feigned madness to conquer his enemies. The story worked its way into the Elizabethan world through Saxo Grammaticus's thirteenth-century *History of the Danish People* and in a 1576 French text by Belleforêst, with significant changes, just as Shakespeare made alterations for his needs. Also, the anonymous *Ur-Hamlet* may have preceded Shakespeare's play or been influenced by it; some respected Shakespearean scholars (e.g., Peter Alexander and Harold Bloom) contend that the *Ur-Hamlet* may have been a first draft of the play written by the young playwright about 1589. Both contain the Ghost, the play-within-the-play, and the climactic duel between the prince and his young rival. Clearly Shakespeare saw material for a rich theater tale in these early sources.

Actually, the playwright need have looked no further for inspiration than his rival theaters on London's South Bank. A bloody melodrama called *The Spanish Tragedy* was among the most popular plays in the 1590s. It was written by Thomas Kyd, a mediocre playwright who might be forgotten had not *Hamlet* made him the most famous footnote to Elizabethan drama. (To be fair, Kyd's play is still performed with some regularity, though largely as a curiosity.) *The Spanish Tragedy* heightened the vogue for the revenge tragedy in England; though the British did not invent the genre (the Roman Seneca is often credited with this feat), they made it a mainstay of their dramatic tradition. Contrary to the Shakespearean *Hamlet*, Kyd's play portrays a crazed father (Hieronimo) who avenges the death of his son (Horatio) by performing in a play that reconstructs the son's death. However, in this "play within the play" two guilty individuals are actually killed by Hieronimo, who, to avoid confessing, bites out his own tongue before killing himself. Such gory goings-on packed them in at the Rose and other theaters, where it was revived regularly. Shakespeare the theater owner no doubt urged Shakespeare the playwright to devise a script that would make Londoners forget Kyd. Shakespeare the actor is believed to have played Old Hamlet's Ghost at the Globe and later at the Blackfriars. (See Spotlight box, Shakespeare's Two Theaters, following the text of *Hamlet*.)

As he did throughout his career, Shakespeare took these several well-known tales and fashioned a fresh work that surpasses the originals as a story, as a portrait of people in action (or even inaction), and as a statement about the human condition. First, he added a subplot in which two other sons (Fortinbras and Laertes) must also avenge the murder of their fathers. Each follows a different path to revenge. Laertes is the man of passion who comes "hot-blooded" from France and will not be deterred from his mission. He dies "a victim of mine own treachery." Hamlet, in his own words, thinks "too precisely on th'event," and is (seemingly) paralyzed into inaction. He is the new Renaissance man who weighs things carefully before acting. He also dies. It is the third son, Fortinbras, the Norwegian prince, who achieves his end and—significantly to Shakespeare's audience—gains the crown. Fortinbras balances reason and passion, and thereby triumphs in this morality about the right uses of our intellects and emotions. (It is worth noting that the Fortinbras subplot is often cut because of the play's length, which unfortunately diminishes the multiple perspectives inherent in Shakespeare's design.)

But if *Hamlet* were merely a cautionary tale about the battle between our reason and our emotions, it would not enjoy its status as the world's most scrutinized play. Rather, the play's fascination comes from the ambiguity of its central character. Even if you have neither read nor seen the play, you probably have heard that Hamlet's problem is that he procrastinates, that he is the man of inaction in a world demanding action. But does a procrastinator follow the "most horrible" spirit of his father despite the warnings of his friends, whom he threatens to kill if they stop him? Can a man of inaction ruthlessly kill the counselor to the king without a moment's hesitation? Can he concoct a scheme to get some traveling actors to play "something like the murder of his father," and even compose with lightning speed "some dozen or sixteen lines" to insert in their play? Does a paralyzed man leap into the grave of his dead lover to fight her brother to prove that "forty thousand brothers / Could not with their quantity equal his love?" This was, by the way, the same woman to whom he said, "I loved you not."

Consider also other common perceptions of Hamlet:

- He has been called the consummate rationalist, yet throughout much of the play we can never be sure if he is feigning madness or if he has indeed slipped into madness.
- He is "a delicate and tender prince" who is repulsed by the thought of having to murder, yet he coldly dispatches his schoolmates (Rosencrantz and Guildenstern) to brutal deaths. They are, he says, "not near my conscience."

- He is, we are told, consumed by melancholy and spends much of the play meditating on death, yet he emerges as Shakespeare's only tragic hero with an enviable sense of humor. He speaks some of Shakespeare's most comical lines as he mocks both those around him and himself.
- Ophelia tells us he is "the scholar's eye, the expectancy and rose of the fair state" (i.e., the ideal gentleman), yet he abuses her and his mother with some of the most vile language uttered by any Shakespearean character.
- He will not kill himself because he fears that "the Almighty hath set his canon 'gainst self-slaughter," yet he has no qualms about playing god himself. In 3.4, he deliberately refuses to kill his uncle, who, he knows with certainty, is the murderer of his father. He chooses to wait until he is certain that death will dispatch Claudius to eternal damnation. This is his fatal "error in judgment"; it precipitates his tragic ending as well as those of Polonius, Ophelia, Laertes, Rosencrantz, Guildenstern, Gertrude, and—only finally—Claudius.

Hamlet himself is awed by his contradictory nature. His many soliloquies—no Shakespearean character is alone onstage more than Hamlet—are his attempts to resolve his many ambiguities. That he entrusts the audience with the privilege of sharing his innermost doubts and fears further endears him to us.

In the final analysis, Hamlet seems not the creation of a playwright—yet he assuredly is. This playwright has created a human portrait of such complexity and contradiction that we cannot help but think of him as one of us. Or, as Coleridge said, "I have a smack of Hamlet." Surely each of us has a smack of Hamlet as we, too, stand before a world that makes impossible demands on us, armed only with the myriad contradictions that make us human.

Hamlet *is perhaps the world's best-known play: Roger Rees (left) played the prince at Stratford-upon-Avon in 1984, and the Korean Drama Center (right) produced the tragedy in Seoul in 1977.*

HAMLET, PRINCE OF DENMARK

WILLIAM SHAKESPEARE

[DRAMATIS PERSONAE
GHOST *of Hamlet, the former King of Denmark*
CLAUDIUS, *King of Denmark, the former King's brother*
GERTRUDE, *Queen of Denmark, widow of the former King and now wife of Claudius*
HAMLET, *Prince of Denmark, son of the late King and of Gertrude*
POLONIUS, *councillor to the King*
LAERTES, *his son*
OPHELIA, *his daughter*
REYNALDO, *his servant*
HORATIO, *Hamlet's friend and fellow student*
VOLTIMAND,
CORNELIUS,
ROSENCRANTZ,
GUILDENSTERN, } *members of the Danish court*
OSRIC,
A GENTLEMAN,
A LORD,
BERNARDO,
FRANCISCO, } *officers and soldiers on watch*
MARCELLUS,
FORTINBRAS, *Prince of Norway*

CAPTAIN *in his army*
Three or Four Players, *taking the roles of* PROLOGUE, PLAYER KING, PLAYER QUEEN, *and* LUCIANUS
Two MESSENGERS
FIRST SAILOR
Two CLOWNS, *a gravedigger and his companion*
PRIEST
FIRST AMBASSADOR *from England*
Lords, Soldiers, Attendants, Guards, other Players, Followers of Laertes, other Sailors, another Ambassador or Ambassadors from England
SCENE: *Denmark*]

1.1° *Enter Bernardo and Francisco, two sentinels,* [*meeting*].

BERNARDO. Who's there?
FRANCISCO.
    Nay, answer me.° Stand and unfold yourself.°
BERNARDO. Long live the King!

1.1. Location: Elsinore castle. A guard platform.
2 me (Francisco emphasizes that *he* is the sentry currently on watch.) **unfold yourself** reveal your identity

FRANCISCO. Bernardo?

5   BERNARDO. He.

FRANCISCO.
    You come most carefully upon your hour.

BERNARDO.
    'Tis now struck twelve. Get thee to bed, Francisco.

FRANCISCO.
    For this relief much thanks. 'Tis bitter cold,
    And I am sick at heart.

10 BERNARDO. Have you had quiet guard?

FRANCISCO. Not a mouse stirring.

BERNARDO. Well, good night.
    If you do meet Horatio and Marcellus,
    The rivals° of my watch, bid them make haste.

    Enter Horatio and Marcellus.

FRANCISCO.
15 I think I hear them.—Stand, ho! Who is there?

HORATIO. Friends to this ground.°

MARCELLUS. And liegemen to the Dane.°

FRANCISCO. Give° you good night.

MARCELLUS.
    O, farewell, honest soldier. Who hath relieved you?

FRANCISCO.
20 Bernardo hath my place. Give you good night.
                                                Exit Francisco.

MARCELLUS. Holla! Bernardo!

BERNARDO. Say, what, is Horatio there?

HORATIO. A piece of him.

BERNARDO.
    Welcome, Horatio. Welcome, good Marcellus.

HORATIO.
25 What, has this thing appeared again tonight?

BERNARDO. I have seen nothing.

MARCELLUS.
    Horatio says 'tis but our fantasy,°
    And will not let belief take hold of him
    Touching this dreaded sight twice seen of us.
30 Therefore I have entreated him along°
    With us to watch° the minutes of this night,
    That if again this apparition come
    He may approve° our eyes and speak to it.

HORATIO.
    Tush, tush, 'twill not appear.

BERNARDO.
                                    Sit down awhile,
35 And let us once again assail your ears,
    That are so fortified against our story,
    What° we have two nights seen.

HORATIO.   Well, sit we down,
    And let us hear Bernardo speak of this.

BERNARDO. Last night of all,°
    When yond same star that's westward from the pole°   40
    Had made his° course t' illume° that part of heaven
    Where now it burns, Marcellus and myself,
    The bell then beating one—

    Enter Ghost.

MARCELLUS.
    Peace, break thee off! Look where it comes again!

BERNARDO.
    In the same figure like the King that's dead.   45

MARCELLUS.
    Thou art a scholar.° Speak to it, Horatio.

BERNARDO.
    Looks 'a° not like the King? Mark it, Horatio.

HORATIO.
    Most like. It harrows me with fear and wonder.

BERNARDO.
    It would be spoke to.°

MARCELLUS.   Speak to it, Horatio.

HORATIO.
    What art thou that usurp'st° this time of night,   50
    Together with that fair and warlike form
    In which the majesty of buried Denmark°
    Did sometime march?° By heaven, I charge thee,
        speak!

MARCELLUS.
    It is offended.

BERNARDO.   See, it stalks away.

HORATIO.
    Stay! Speak, speak! I charge thee, speak!   55
                                            Exit Ghost.

MARCELLUS. 'Tis gone and will not answer.

BERNARDO.
    How now, Horatio? You tremble an look pale.
    Is not this something more than fantasy?
    What think you on 't?°

HORATIO.
    Before my God, I might not this believe   60
    Without the sensible° and true avouch°
    Of mine own eyes.

MARCELLUS.   Is it not like the King?

HORATIO. As thou art to thyself.
    Such was the very armor he had on

---

14 rivals partners   **16 ground** country, land   **17 liegemen to the Dane** men sworn to serve the Danish king   **18 Give** i.e., may God give   **27 fantasy** imagination   **30 along** to come along   **31 watch** keep watch during   **33 approve** corroborate   **37 What** with what

39 Last . . . all i.e., this very last night. (Emphatic.)   **40 pole** polestar, north star   **41 his** its. **illume** illuminate   **46 scholar** one learned enough to know how to question a ghost properly   **47 'a** he   **49 It . . . to** (It was commonly believed that a ghost could not speak until spoken to.)   **50 usurp'st** wrongfully takes over   **52 buried Denmark** the buried King of Denmark   **53 sometime** formerly   **59 on 't** of it   **61 sensible** confirmed by the senses. **avouch** warrant, evidence

65 When he had the ambitious Norway° combated.
    So frowned he once when, in an angry parle,°
    He smote the sledded° Polacks° on the ice.
    'Tis strange.
MARCELLUS.
    Thus twice before, and jump° at this dead hour,
70 With martial stalk° hath he gone by our watch.
HORATIO.
    In what particular thought to work° I know not,
    But in the gross and scope° of mine opinion
    This bodes some strange eruption to our state.
MARCELLUS.
    Good now,° sit down, and tell me, he that knows,
75 Why this same strict and most observant watch
    So nightly toils° the subject° of the land,
    And why such daily cast° of brazen cannon
    And foreign mart° for implements of war,
    Why such impress° of shipwrights, whose sore task
80 Does not divide the Sunday from the week.
    What might be toward,° that this sweaty haste
    Doth make the night joint-laborer with the day?
    Who is 't that can inform me?
HORATIO.   That can I;
    At least, the whisper goes so. Our last king,
85 Whose image even but now appeared to us,
    Was, as you know, by Fortinbras of Norway,
    Thereto pricked on° by a most emulate° pride,°
    Dared to the combat; in which our valiant Hamlet—
    For so this side of our known world° esteemed him—
90 Did slay this Fortinbras; who by a sealed° compact
    Well ratified by law an heraldry
    Did forfeit, with his life, all those his lands
    Which he stood seized° of, to the conqueror;
    Against the° which a moiety competent°
95 Was gagèd° by our king, which had returned°
    To the inheritance° of Fortinbras
    Had he been vanquisher, as, by the same cov'nant°
    And carriage of the article designed,°
    His fell to Hamlet. Now, sir, young Fortinbras,

Of unimprovèd mettle° hot and full,   100
Hath in the skirts° of Norway here and there
Sharked up° a list° of lawless resolutes°
For food and diet° to some enterprise
That hath a stomach° in 't, which is no other—
As it doth well appear unto our state—   105
But to recover of us, by strong hand
And terms compulsatory, those foresaid lands
So by his father lost. And this, I take it,
Is the main motive of our preparations,
The source of this our watch, and the chief head°   110
Of this posthaste and rummage° in the land.
BERNARDO.
I think it be no other but e'en so.
Well may it sort° that this portentous figure
Comes armèd through our watch so like the King
That was and is the question° of these wars.   115
HORATIO.
A mote° it is to trouble the mind's eye.
In the most high and palmy° state of Rome,
A little ere the mightiest Julius fell,
The graves stood tenantless, and the sheeted° dead
Did squeak and gibber in the Roman streets;   120
As° stars with trains° of fire and dews of blood,
Disasters° in the sun; and the moist star°
Upon whose influence Neptune's° empire stands°
Was sick almost to doomsday° with eclipse.
And even the like precurse° of feared events,   125
As harbingers° preceding still° the fates
And prologue to the omen° coming on,
Have heaven and earth together demonstrated
Unto our climatures° and countrymen.

      Enter Ghost.

But soft,° behold! Lo, where it comes again!   130
I'll cross° it, though it blast° me. (*It spread his° arms.*)
      Stay, illusion!

65 **Norway** King of Norway   66 **parle** parley   67 **sledded** traveling on sleds. **Polacks** Poles   69 **jump** exactly   70 **stalk** stride   71 **to work** i.e., to collect my thoughts and try to understand this   72 **gross and scope** general drift   74 **Good now** (An expression denoting entreaty or expostulation.)   76 **toils** causes to toil. **subject** subjects   77 **cast** casting   78 **mart** buying and selling   79 **impress** impressment, conscription   81 **toward** in preparation   87 **Thereto . . . pride** (Refers to old Fortinbras, not the Danish King.) **pricked on** incited. **emulate** emulous, ambitious   89 **this . . . world** i.e., all Europe, the Western world   90 **sealed** certified, confirmed   93 **seized** possessed   94 **Against the** in return for. **moiety competent** corresponding portion   95 **gagèd** engaged, pledged. **had returned** would have passed   96 **inheritance** possession   97 **cov'nant** i.e., the *sealed compact* of line 90   98 **carriage . . . designed** carrying out of the article or clause drawn up to cover the point

100 **unimprovèd mettle** untried, undisciplined spirits   101 **skirts** outlying regions, outskirts   102 **Sharked up** gathered up, as a shark takes fish. **list** i.e., troop. **resolutes** desperadoes   103 **For food and diet** i.e., they are to serve as *food,* or "means," *to some enterprise*; also they serve in return for the rations they get   104 **stomach** (1) a spirit of daring (2) an appetite that is fed by the *lawless resolutes*   110 **head** source   111 **rummage** bustle, commotion   113 **sort** suit   115 **question** focus of contention   116 **mote** speck of dust   117 **palmy** flourishing   119 **sheeted** shrouded   121 **As** (This abrupt transition suggests that matter is possibly omitted between lines 120 and 121.) **trains** trails   122 **Disasters** unfavorable signs or aspects. **moist star** i.e., moon, governing tides   123 **Neptune** god of the sea. **stands** depends   124 **sick . . . doomsday** (See Matthew 24:29 and Revelation 6:12.)   125 **precurse** heralding, foreshadowing   126 **harbingers** forerunners. **still** continually   127 **omen** calamitous event   129 **climatures** regions   130 **soft** i.e., enough, break off   131 **cross** stand in its path, confront. **blast** wither, strike with a curse. **s.d. his** its

154

If thou hast any sound or use of voice,
Speak to me!
If there be any good thing to be done

135 That may to thee do ease and grace to me,
Speak to me!
If thou art privy to° thy country's fate,
Which, happily,° foreknowing may avoid,
O, speak!

140 Or if thou hast uphoarded in thy life
Extorted treasure in the womb of earth,
For which, they say, you spirits oft walk in death,
Speak of it! (*The cock crows.*) Stay and speak!—
Stop it, Marcellus.
MARCELLUS.
Shall I strike at it with my partisan?°

145 HORATIO. Do, if it will not stand.   [*They strike at it.*]
BERNARDO. 'Tis here!
HORATIO. 'Tis here!   [*Exit Ghost.*]
MARCELLUS. 'Tis gone.
We do it wrong, being so majestical,

150 To offer it the show of violence,
For it is as the air invulnerable,
And our vain blows malicious mockery.
BERNARDO.
It was about to speak when the cock crew.
HORATIO.
And then it started like a guilty thing

155 Upon a fearful summons. I have heard
The cock, that is the trumpet° to the morn,
Doth with his lofty and shrill-sounding throat
Awake the god of day, and at his warning,
Whether in sea or fire, in earth or air,

160 Th' extravagant and erring° spirit hies°
To his confine; and of the truth herein
This present object made probation.°
MARCELLUS.
It faded on the crowing of the cock.
Some say that ever 'gainst° that season comes

165 Wherein our Savior's birth is celebrated,
This bird of dawning singeth all night long,
And then, they say, no spirit dare stir abroad;
The nights are wholesome, then no planets strike,°
No fairy takes,° nor witch hath power to charm,

170 So hallowed and so gracious° is that time.
HORATIO.
So have I heard and do in part believe it.
But, look, the morn in russet mantle clad

Walks o'er the dew of yon high eastward hill.
Break we our watch up, and by my advice
Let us impart what we have seen tonight   175
Unto young Hamlet; for upon my life,
This spirit, dumb to us, will speak to him.
Do you consent we shall acquaint him with it,
As needful in our loves, fitting our duty?
MARCELLUS.
Let's do 't, I pray, and I this morning know   180
Where we shall find him most conveniently.

                                        Exeunt.

1.2 °   *Flourish. Enter Claudius, King of Denmark,*
        Gertrude the Queen, [the] Council, as° Polonius
        and his son Laertes, Hamlet, cum aliis° [including
        Voltimand and Cornelius].

KING.
Though yet of Hamlet our° dear brother's death
The memory be green, and that it us befitted
To bear our hearts in grief and our whole kingdom
To be contracted in one brow of woe,
Yet so far hath discretion fought with nature   5
That we with wisest sorrow think on him
Together with remembrance of ourselves.
Therefore our sometime° sister, now our queen,
Th' imperial jointress° to this warlike state,
Have we, as 'twere with a defeated joy—   10
With an auspicious and a dropping eye,°
With mirth in funeral and with dirge in marriage,
In equal scale weighing delight and dole°—
Taken to wife. Nor have we herein barred
Your better wisdoms, which have freely gone   15
With this affair along. For all, our thanks.
Now follows that you know° young Fortinbras,
Holding a weak supposal° of our worth,
Or thinking by our late dear brother's death
Our state to be disjoint and out of frame,   20
Co-leaguèd with° this dream of his advantage,°
He hath not failed to pester us with message
Importing° the surrender of those lands
Lost by his father, with all bonds° of law,
To our most valiant brother. So much for him.   25

1.2. Location: The castle.
s.d. as i.e., such as including. **cum aliis** with others   **1 our** my.
(The royal "we"; also in the following lines.)   **8 sometime** former
9 jointress woman possessing property with her husband   **11 With
. . . eye** with one eye smiling and the other weeping   **13 dole** grief
17 that you know what you know already, that; or, that you be informed as follows   **18 weak supposal** low estimate   **21 Co-
leaguèd with** jointed to, allied with. **dream . . . advantage** illusory
hope of having the advantage. (His only ally is this hope.)   **23 importing** pertaining to   **24 bonds** contracts

137 privy to in on the secret of   **138 happily** haply, perchance
144 partisan long-handled spear   **156 trumpet** trumpeter   **160
extravagant and erring** wandering beyond bounds. (The words
have similar meaning.) **hies** hastens   **162 probation** proof   **164
'gainst** just before   **168 strike** destroy by evil influence   **169
takes** bewitches   **170 gracious** full of grace

Now for ourself and for this time of meeting.
Thus much the business is: we have here writ
To Norway, uncle of young Fortinbras—
Who, impotent° and bed-rid, scarcely hears
30 Of this his nephew's purpose—to suppress
His° further gait° herein, in that the levies,
The lists, and full proportions are all made
Out of his subject;° and we here dispatch
You, good Cornelius, and you, Voltimand,
35 For bearers of this greeting to old Norway,
Giving to you no further personal power
To business with the King more than the scope
Of these dilated° articles allow.   [*He gives a paper.*]
Farewell, and let your haste command your duty.°

CORNELIUS, VOLTIMAND.
40 In that, and all things, will we show our duty.

KING.
We doubt it nothing.° Heartily farewell.
                    [*Exeunt Voltimand and Cornelius.*]
And now, Laertes, what's the news with you?
You told us of some suit; what is 't, Laertes?
You cannot speak of reason to the Dane°
And lose your voice.° What wouldst thou beg,
45   Laertes,
That shall not be my offer, not thy asking?
The head is not more native° to the heart,
The hand more instrumental° to the mouth,
Than is the throne of Denmark to thy father.
Why wouldst thou have, Laertes?

50 LAERTES.   My dread lord,
Your leave and favor° to return to France,
From whence though willingly I came to Denmark
To show my duty in your coronation,
Yet now I must confess, that duty done,
55 My thoughts and wishes bend again toward France
And bow them to your gracious leave and pardon.°

KING.
Have you your father's leave? What says Polonius?

POLONIUS.
H'ath,° my lord, wrung from me my slow leave
By laborsome petition, and at last
60 Upon his will I sealed° my hard° consent.
I do beseech you, give him leave to go.

KING.
Take thy fair hour,° Laertes. Time be thine,
And thy best graces spend it at thy will!°
But now, my cousin° Hamlet, and my son—

HAMLET.
A little more than kin, and less than kind.°   65

KING.
How is it that the clouds still hang on you?

HAMLET.
Not so, my lord. I am too much in the sun.°

QUEEN.
Good Hamlet, cast thy nighted color° off,
And let thine eye look like a friend on Denmark.°
Do not forever with thy vailèd lids°   70
Seek for thy noble father in the dust.
Thou know'st 'tis common,° all that lives must die,
Passing through nature to eternity.

HAMLET.
Ay, madam, it is common.

QUEEN.   If it be,
Why seems it so particular° with thee?   75

HAMLET.
Seems, madam? Nay, it is. I know not "seems."
'Tis not alone my inky cloak, good Mother,
Nor customary° suits of solemn black,
Nor windy suspiration° of forced breath,
No, nor the fruitful° river in the eye,   80
Nor the dejected havior° of the visage,
Together with all forms, moods,° shapes of grief,
That can denote me truly. These indeed seem,
For they are actions that a man might play.
But I have that within which passes show;   85
These but the trappings and the suits of woe.

KING.
'Tis sweet and commendable in your nature, Hamlet,
To give these mourning duties to your father.
But you must know your father lost a father,
That father lost, lost his, and the survivor bound   90

62 **Take thy fair hour** enjoy your time of youth   63 **And . . . will**
and may your finest qualities guide the way you choose to spend
your time   64 **cousin** any kin not of the immediate family   65 **A
little . . . kind** i.e., closer than an ordinary nephew (since I am stepson), and yet more separated in natural feeling (with pun on *kind*
meaning "affectionate" and "natural," "lawful." This line is often
read as an aside, but it need not be. The King chooses perhaps not
to respond to Hamlet's cryptic and bitter remark.)   67 **the sun** i.e.,
the sunshine of the King's royal favor (with pun on *son*)   68
nighted color (1) mourning garments of black (2) dark melancholy
69 **Denmark** the King of Denmark   70 **vailèd lids** lowered eyes
72 **common** of universal occurrence. (But Hamlet plays on the
sense of "vulgar" in line 74.)   75 **particular** personal   78 **customary** (1) socially conventional (2) habitual with me   79 **suspi-
ration** sighing   80 **fruitful** abundant   81 **havior** expression   82
moods outward expression of feeling

29 **impotent** helpless   31 **His** i.e., Fortinbras'. **gait** proceeding
31–33 in that . . . subject since the levying of troops and supplies is
drawn entirely from the King of Norway's own subjects   38 **dilated**
set out at length   39 **let . . . duty** let your swift obeying of orders,
rather than mere words, express your dutifulness   41 **nothing** not
at all   44 **the Dane** the Danish king   45 **lose your voice** waste
your speech   47 **native** closely connected, related   48 **instrumental** serviceable   51 **leave and favor** kind permission   56 **bow
. . . pardon** entreatingly make a deep bow, asking your permission to
depart   58 **H'ath** he has   60 **sealed** (as if sealing a legal document). **hard** reluctant

In filial obligation for some term
To do obsequious° sorrow. But to persever°
In obstinate condolement° is a course
Of impious stubbornness. 'Tis unmanly grief.
95 It shows a will more incorrect to heaven,
A heart unfortified,° a mind impatient,
An understanding simple° and unschooled.
For what we know must be and is as common
As any the most vulgar thing to sense,°
100 Why should we in our peevish opposition
Take it to heart? Fie, 'tis a fault to heaven,
A fault against the dead, a fault to nature,
To reason most absurd, whose common theme
Is death of fathers, and who still° hath cried,
105 From the first corpse° till he that died today,
"This must be so." We pray you, throw to earth
This unprevailing° woe and think of us,
As of a father; for let the world take note,
You are the most immediate° to our throne,
110 And with no less nobility of love
Than that which dearest fathers bears his son
Do I impart toward° you. For° your intent
In going back to school° in Wittenberg,°
It is most retrograde° to our desire,
115 And we beseech you bend you° to remain
Here in the cheer and comfort of our eye,
Our chiefest courtier, cousin, and our son.

QUEEN.
Let not thy mother lose her prayers, Hamlet.
I pray thee, stay with us, go not to Wittenberg.

HAMLET.
120 I shall in all my best° obey you, madam.

KING.
Why, 'tis a loving and a fair reply.
Be as ourself in Denmark. Madam, come.
This gentle and unforced accord of Hamlet
Sits smiling to° my heart, in grace° whereof
125 No jocund° health that Denmark drinks today
But the great cannon to the clouds shall tell,
And the King's rouse° the heaven shall bruit again,°
Respeaking earthly thunder°. Come away.

Flourish. Exeunt all but Hamlet.

HAMLET.
O, that this too too sullied° flesh would melt,
Thaw, and resolve itself into a dew!   130
Or that the Everlasting had not fixed
His canon° 'gainst self-slaughter! O God, God,
How weary, stale, flat, and unprofitable
Seem to me all the uses° of this world!
Fie on 't, ah fie! 'Tis an unweeded garden   135
That grows to seed. Things rank and gross in nature
Possess it merely°. That it should come to this!
But two months dead—nay, not so much, not two.
So excellent a king, that was to° this
Hyperion° to a satyr°, so loving to my mother   140
That he might not beteem° the winds of heaven
Visit her face too roughly. Heaven and earth,
Must I remember? Why, she would hang on him
As if increase of appetite had grown
By what it fed on, and yet within a month—   145
Let me not think on 't; frailty, thy name is
    woman!—
A little month, or ere° those shoes were old
With which she followed my poor father's body,
Like Niobe°, all tears, why she, even she—
O God, a beast, that wants discourse of reason,°   150
Would have mourned long—married with my
    uncle,
My father's brother, but no more like my father
Than I to Hercules. Within a month,
Ere yet the salt of most unrighteous tears
Had left the flushing in her gallèd° eyes,   155
She married. O, most wicked speed, to post°
With such dexterity to incestuous° sheets!
It is not, nor it cannot come to good.
But break, my heart, for I must hold my tongue.

Enter Horatio, Marcellus, and Bernardo.

HORATIO.
Hail to your lordship!

HAMLET.   I am glad to see you well.   160
Horatio!—or I do forget myself.

---

92 obsequious suited to obsequies or funerals. **persever** persevere
93 condolement sorrowing **96 unfortified** i.e., against adversity
97 simple ignorant **99 As . . . sense** as the most ordinary experience **104 still** always **105 the first corpse** (Abel's) **107 unprevailing** unavailing, useless **109 most immediate** next in succession **112 impart toward** i.e., bestow my affection on. **For** as for
113 to school i.e., to your studies. **Wittenberg** famous German university founded in 1502 **114 retrograde** contrary **115 bend you** incline yourself **120 in all my best** to the best of my ability **124 to** i.e., at. **grace** thanksgiving **125 jocund** merry **127 rouse** drinking of a draft of liquor. **bruit again** loudly echo **128 thunder** i.e., of trumpet and kettledrum, sounded when the King drinks; see 1.4.8–12

129 sullied defiled. (The early quartos read *sallied*; the Folio, *solid*.)
132 canon law **134 all the uses** the whole routine **137 merely** completely **139 to** in comparison to **140 Hyperion** Titan sungod, father of Helios. **satyr** a lecherous creature of classical mythology, half-human but with a goat's legs, tail, ears, and horns **141 beteem** allow **147 or ere** even before **149 Niobe** Tantalus' daughter, Queen of Thebes, who boasted that she had more sons and daughters than Leto; for this, Apollo and Artemis, children of Leto, slew her fourteen children. She was turned by Zeus into a stone that continually dropped tears. **150 wants . . . reason** lacks the faculty of reason **155 gallèd** irritated, inflamed **156 post** hasten **157 incestuous** (In Shakespeare's days, the marriage of a man like Claudius to his deceased brother's wife was considered incestuous.)

HORATIO.
 The same, my lord, and your poor servant ever.
HAMLET.
 Sir, my good friend; I'll change that name° with you.
 And what make you from° Wittenberg, Horatio?
165 Marcellus.
MARCELLUS. My good lord.
HAMLET.
 I am very glad to see you. [*To Bernardo*.] Good even,
  sir.—
 But what in faith make you from Wittenberg?
HORATIO.
 A truant disposition, good my lord.
HAMLET.
170 I would not hear your enemy say so,
 Nor shall you do my ear that violence
 To make it truster of your own report
 Against yourself. I know you are no truant.
 But what is your affair in Elsinore?
175 We'll teach you to drink deep ere you depart.
HORATIO.
 My lord, I came to see your father's funeral.
HAMLET.
 I prithee, do not mock me, fellow student;
 I think it was to see my mother's wedding.
HORATIO.
 Indeed, my lord, it followed hard° upon.
HAMLET.
180 Thrift, thrift, Horatio! The funeral baked meats°
 Did coldly° furnish forth the marriage tables.
 Would I had met my dearest° foe in heaven
 Or ever° I had seen that day, Horatio!
 My father!—Methinks I see my father.
HORATIO.
 Where, my lord?
185 HAMLET.   In my mind's eye, Horatio.
HORATIO.
 I saw him once. 'A° was a goodly king.
HAMLET.
 'A was a man. Take him for all in all,
 I shall not look upon his like again.
HORATIO.
 My lord, I think I saw him yesternight.
190 HAMLET. Saw? Who?
HORATIO. My lord, the King your father.
HAMLET. The King my father?
HORATIO.
 Season your admiration° for a while

With an attent° ear till I may deliver,
Upon the witness of these gentlemen,   195
This marvel to you.
HAMLET.   For God's love, let me hear!
HORATIO.
Two nights together had these gentlemen,
Marcellus and Bernardo, on their watch,
In the dead waste° and middle of the night,
Been thus encountered. A figure like your father, 200
Armèd at point° exactly, cap-à-pie,°
Appears before them, and with solemn march
Goes slow and stately by them. Thrice he walked
By their oppressed and fear-surprisèd eyes
Within his truncheon's° length, whilst they, distilled° 205
Almost to jelly with the act° of fear,
Stand dumb and speak not to him. This to me
In dreadful° secrecy impart they did,
And I with them the third night kept the watch,
Where, as they had delivered, both in time, 210
Form of the thing, each word made true and good,
The apparition comes. I knew your father;
These hands are not more like.
HAMLET.   But where was this?
MARCELLUS.
My lord, upon the platform where we watch.
HAMLET.
Did you speak to it?
HORATIO.   My lord, I did, 215
But answer made it none. Yet once methought
It lifted up its head and did address
Itself to motion, like as it would speak;°
But even then° the morning cock crew loud,
And at the sound it shrunk in haste away 220
And vanished from our sight.
HAMLET.   'Tis very strange.
HORATIO.
As I do live, my nonored lord, 'tis true,
And we did think it writ down in our duty
To let you know of it.
HAMLET.
Indeed, indeed, sirs. But this troubles me. 225
Hold you the watch tonight?
ALL.   We do, my lord.
HAMLET. Armed, say you?
ALL. Armed, my lord.
HAMLET. From top to toe?
ALL. My lord, from head to foot. 230

HAMLET. Then saw you not his face?
HORATIO.
      O, yes, my lord, he wore his beaver° up.
HAMLET. What° looked he, frowningly?
HORATIO.
      A countenance more in sorrow than in anger.
235   HAMLET. Pale or red?
HORATIO. Nay, very pale.
HAMLET. And fixed his eyes upon you?
HORATIO. Most constantly.
HAMLET. I would I had been there.
240   HORATIO. It would have much amazed you.
HAMLET. Very like, very like. Stayed it long?
HORATIO.
      While one with moderate haste might tell° a hundred.
MARCELLUS, BERNARDO. Longer, longer.
HORATIO. Not when I saw 't.
245   HAMLET. His beard was grizzled°—no?
HORATIO.
      It was, as I have seen it in his life,
      A sable silvered.°
HAMLET.   I will watch tonight.
      Perchance 'twill walk again.
HORATIO.   I warrant° it will.
HAMLET.
      If it assume my noble father's person,
250   I'll speak to it though hell itself should gape
      And bid me hold my peace. I pray you all,
      If you have hitherto concealed this sight,
      Let it be tenable° in your silence still,
      And whatsoever else shall hap tonight,
255   Give it an understanding but no tongue.
      I will requite your loves. So, fare you well.
      Upon the platform twixt eleven and twelve
      I'll visit you.
ALL.   Our duty to your honor.
HAMLET.
      Your loves, as mine to you. Farewell.
                              Exeunt [all but Hamlet].
260   My father's spirit in arms! All is not well.
      I doubt° some foul play. Would the night were come!
      Till then sit still, my soul. Foul deeds will rise,
      Though all the earth o'erwhelm them, to men's eyes.
                                                      Exit.

1.3°   Enter Laertes and Ophelia, his sister.

LAERTES.
      My necessaries are embarked. Farewell.

232 beaver visor on the helmet   233 What how   242 tell count
245 grizzled gray   247 sable silvered black mixed with white
248 warrant assure you   253 tenable held   261 doubt suspect
1.3. Location: Polonius' chambers.

And, sister, as the winds give benefit
And convoy is assistant,° do not sleep
But let me hear from you.
OPHELIA.   Do you doubt that?
LAERTES.
      For Hamlet, and the trifling of his favor,   5
      Hold it a fashion and a toy in blood,°
      A violet in the youth of primy° nature,
      Forward,° not permanent, sweet, not lasting,
      The perfume and suppliance° of a minute—
      No more.
OPHELIA.   No more but so?
LAERTES.   Think it no more.   10
      For nature crescent° does not grow alone
      In thews° and bulk, but as this temple° waxes
      The inward service of the mind and soul
      Grows wide withal.° Perhaps he loves you now,
      And now no soil° nor cautel° doth besmirch   15
      The virtue of his will;° but you must fear,
      His greatness weighed,° his will is not his own.
      For he himself is subject to his birth.
      He may not, as unvalued persons do,
      Carve° for himself, for on his choice depends   20
      The safety and health of this whole state,
      And therefore must his choice be circumscribed
      Unto the voice and yielding° of that body
      Whereof he is the head. Then if he says he
         loves you,
      It fits your wisdom so far to believe it   25
      As he in his particular act and place°
      May give his saying deed, which is no further
      Than the main voice° of Denmark goes withal.°
      Then weigh what loss your honor may sustain
      If with too credent° ear you list° his songs,   30
      Or lose your heart, or your chaste treasure open
      To his unmastered importunity.
      Fear it, Ophelia, fear it, my dear sister,
      And keep you in the rear or your affection,°
      Out of the shot and danger of desire.   35
      The chariest° maid is prodigal enough
      If she unmask° her beauty to the moon.°

3 convey is assistant means of conveyance are available   6 toy in
blood passing amorous fancy   7 primy in its prime, springtime
8 Forward precocious   9 suppliance supply, filler   11 crescent
growing, waxing   12 thews bodily strength. temple i.e., body
14 Grows wide withal grows along with it   15 soil blemish. cau-
tel deceit   16 will desire   17 His greatness weighed if you take
into account his high position   20 Carve i.e., choose   23 voice
and yielding assent, approval   26 in . . . place in his particular restricted circumstances   28 main voice general assent. withal along
with   30 credent credulous. list listen to   34 keep . . . affection
don't advance as far as your affection might lead you. (A military
metaphor.)   36 chariest most scrupulously modest   37 If she unmask if she does no more than show her beauty. moon (Symbol of
chastity.)

Virtue itself scapes not calumnious strokes.
The canker galls° the infants of the spring
40 Too oft before their buttons° be disclosed,°
And in the morn and liquid dew° of youth
Contagious blastments° are most imminent.
Be wary then; best safety lies in fear.
Youth to itself rebels,° though none else near.
OPHELIA.
45 I shall the effect of this good lesson keep
As watchman to my heart. But, good my brother,
Do not, as some ungracious° pastors do,
Show me the steep and thorny way to heaven,
Whiles like a puffed° and reckless libertine
50 Himself the primrose path of dalliance treads,
And recks° not his own rede.°

        Enter Polonius.

LAERTES.   O, fear me not.°
I stay too long. But here my father comes.
A double blessing is a double° grace;
Occasion smiles upon a second leave.°
POLONIUS.
55 Yet here, Laertes? Aboard, aboard, for shame!
The wind sits in the shoulder of your sail,
And you are stayed for. There—my blessing with
        thee!
And these few precepts in thy memory
Look° thou character.° Give thy thoughts no tongue,
60 Nor any unproportioned° thought his° act.
Be thou familiar,° but by no means vulgar.°
Those friends thou hast, and their adoption tried,°
Grapple them unto thy soul with hoops of steel,
But do not dull thy palm° with entertainment
65 Of each new-hatched, unfledged courage.° Beware
Of entrance to a quarrel, but being in,
Bear 't that° th' opposèd may beware of thee.
Give every man thy ear, but few thy voice;
Take each man's censure,° but reserve thy judgment.

Costly thy habit° as thy purse can buy,   70
But not expressed in fancy°; rich, not gaudy,
For the apparel oft proclaims the man,
And they in France of the best rank and station
Are of a most select and generous chief in that.°
Neither a borrower nor a lender be,   75
For loan oft loses both itself and friend,
And borrowing dulleth edge of husbandry.°
This above all: to thine own self be true,
And it must follow, as the night the day,
Thou canst not then be false to any man.   80
Farewell. My blessing season° this in thee!
LAERTES.
Most humbly do I take my leave, my lord.
POLONIUS.
The time invests° you. Go, your servants tend.°
LAERTES.
Farewell, Ophelia, and remember well
What I have said to you.   85
OPHELIA.   'Tis in my memory locked,
And you yourself shall keep the key of it.
LAERTES Farewell.   *Exit Laertes.*
POLONIUS.
What is 't, Ophelia, he hath said to you?
OPHELIA.
So please you, something touching the Lord Hamlet.   90
POLONIUS. Marry,° well bethought.
'Tis told me he hath very oft of late
Given private time to you, and you yourself
Have of your audience been most free and bounteous.
If it be so—as so 'tis put on° me,   95
And that in way of caution—I must tell you
You do not understand yourself so clearly
As it behooves° my daughter and your honor.
What is between you? Give me up the truth.
OPHELIA.
He hath, my lord, of late made many tenders°   100
Of his affection to me.
POLONIUS.
Affection? Pooh! You speak like a green girl,
Unsifted° in such perilous circumstance.
Do you believe his tenders, as you call them?
OPHELIA.
I do not know, my lord, what I should think.   105
POLONIUS.
Marry, I will teach you. Think yourself a baby
That you have ta'en these tenders for true pay

---

39 canker galls cankerworm destroys   **40 buttons** buds. **disclosed** opened   **41 liquid dew** i.e., time when dew is fresh and bright   **42 blastments** blights   **44 Youth . . . rebels** youth is inherently rebellious   **47 ungracious** ungodly   **49 puffed** bloated, or swollen with pride   **51 recks** heeds. **rede** counsel. **fear me not** don't worry on my account   **53 double** (Laertes has already bid his father good-bye.)   **54 Occasion . . . leave** happy is the circumstance that provides a second leave-taking. (The goddess Occasion, or Opportunity, smiles.)   **59 Look** be sure that. **character** inscribe   **60 unproportioned** badly calculated, intemperate. **his** its   **61 familiar** sociable. **vulgar** common   **62 and their adoption tried** and also their suitability for adoption as friends having been tested   **64 dull thy palm** i.e., shake hands so often as to make the gesture meaningless   **65 courage** young man of spirit   **67 Bear 't that** manage it so that   **69 censure** opinion, judgment

---

70 habit clothing   **71 fancy** excessive ornament, decadent fashion   **74 Are . . . that** are of a most refined and well-bred preeminence in choosing what to wear   **77 husbandry** thrift   **81 season** mature   **83 invests** besieges, presses upon. **tend** attend, wait   **91 Marry** i.e., by the Virgin Mary. (A mild oath.)   **95 put on** impressed on, told to   **98 behooves** befits   **100 tenders** offers   **103 Unsifted** i.e., untried

Which are not sterling.° Tender° yourself more dearly,
Or—not to crack the wind° of the poor phrase,
110 Running it thus—you'll tender me a fool.°
OPHELIA.
My lord, he hath importuned me with love
In honorable fashion.
POLONIUS.
Ay, fashion° you may call it. Go to,° go to.
OPHELIA.
And hath given countenance° to his speech, my lord,
115 With almost all the holy vows of heaven.
POLONIUS.
Ay, springes° to catch woodcocks.° I do know,
When the blood burns, how prodigal° the soul
Lends the tongue vows. These blazes, daughter,
Giving more light than heat, extinct in both
120 Even in their promise as it° is a-making,
You must not take for fire. From this time
Be something° scanter of your maiden presence.
Set your entreatments° at a higher rate
Than a command to parle.° For Lord Hamlet,
125 Believe so much in him° that he is young,
And with a larger tether may he walk
Than may be given you. In few,° Ophelia,
Do not believe his vows, for they are brokers°,
Not of that dye° which their investments° show,
130 But mere implorators° of unholy suits,
Breathing° like sanctified and pious bawds,
The better to beguile. This is for all:°
I would not, in plain terms, from this time forth
Have you so slander° any moment° leisure
135 As to give words or talk with the Lord Hamlet.
Look to 't, I charge you. Come your ways.°
OPHELIA.
I shall obey, my lord.   Exeunt.

---

108 **sterling** legal currency. **Tender** hold, look after, offer 109
crack the wind i.e., run it until it is broken-winded 110 **tender
me a fool** (1) show yourself to me as a fool (2) show me up as a fool
(3) present me with a grandchild. (*Fool* was a term of endearment
for a child.) 113 **fashion** mere form, pretense. **Go to** (An expression of impatience.) 114 **countenance** credit, confirmation
116 **springes** snares. **woodcocks** birds easily caught; here used to
connote gullibility 117 **prodigal** prodigally 120 **it** i.e., the
promise 122 **something** somewhat 123 **entreatments** negotia-
tions for surrender. (A military term.) 124 **parle** discuss terms
with the enemy. (Polonius urges his daughter, in the metaphor of
military language, not to meet with Hamlet and consider giving in
to him merely because he requests an interview.) 125 **so . . . him**
this much concerning him 127 **in few** briefly 128 **brokers** go-
betweens, procurers 129 **dye** color or sort. **investments** clothes.
(The vows are not what they seem.) 130 **mere implorators** out
and out solicitors 131 **Breathing** speaking 132 **for all** once for
all, in sum 134 **slander** abuse, misuse. **moment** moment's 136
Come your ways come along

1.4°   *Enter Hamlet, Horatio, and Marcellus.*

HAMLET.
The air bites shrewdly;° it is very cold.
HORATIO.
It is a nipping and an eager° air.
HAMLET.
What hour now?
HORATIO.   I think it lacks of° twelve.
MARCELLUS.
No, it is struck.
HORATIO.   Indeed? I heard it not.
It then draws near the season°   5
Wherein the spirit held his wont° to walk.
  A flourish of trumpets, and two pieces° go off
  [*within*].
What does this mean, my lord?
HAMLET.
The King doth wake° tonight and takes his rouse°,
Keeps wassail,° and the swaggering upspring° reels;°
And as he drains his drafts of Rhenish° down,   10
The kettledrum and trumpet thus bray out
The triumph of his pledge.°
HORATIO.   Is it a custom?
HAMLET. Ay, marry, is 't,
But to my mind, though I am native here
And to the manner° born, it is a custom   15
More honored in the breach than the observance.°
This heavy-headed revel east and west°
Makes us traduced and taxed of° other nations.
They clepe° us drunkards, and with swinish phrase°
Soil our addition;° and indeed it takes   20
From our achievements, though performed at height,°
The pith and marrow of our attribute.°
So, oft it chances in particular men,
That for° some vicious mole of nature° in them,
As in their birth—wherein they are not guilty,   25
Since nature cannot choose his° origin—
By their o'ergrowth of some complexion,°

1.4. Location: The guard platform.
1 **shrewdly** keenly, sharply 2 **eager** biting 3 **lacks of** is just
short of 5 **season** time 6 **held his wont** was accustomed. **s.d.
pieces** i.e., of ordnance, cannon 8 **wake** stay awake and hold
revel. **takes his rouse** carouses 9 **wassail** carousal. **upspring** wild
German dance. **reels** dances 10 **Rhenish** Rhine wine 12 **The
triumph . . . pledge** i.e., his feat in draining the wine in a single
draft 15 **manner** custom (of drinking) 16 **More . . . obser-
vances** better neglected than followed 17 **east and west** i.e.,
everywhere 18 **taxed of** censured by 19 **clepe** call. **with swinish phrase** i.e., by calling us swine 20 **addition** reputation 21 **at
height** outstandingly 22 **The pith . . . attribute** the essence of
the reputation that others attribute to us 24 **for** on account of.
mole of nature natural blemish in one's constitution 26 **his** its
27 **their o'ergrowth . . . complexion** the excessive growth in individuals of some natural trait

Oft breaking down the pales° and forts of reason,
Or by some habit that too much o'erleavens°
30 The form of plausive° manners, that these men,
Carrying, I say, the stamp of one defect,
Being nature's livery° or fortune's star,°
His virtues else,° be they as pure as grace,
As infinite as man may undergo,°
35 Shall in the general censure° take corruption
From that particular fault. The dram of evil
Doth all the noble substance often dout
To his own scandal.°

Enter Ghost.

HORATIO.   Look, my lord, it comes!
HAMLET.
Angels and ministers of grace° defend us!
40 Be thou° a spirit of health° or goblin damned,
Bring° with thee airs from heaven or blasts from hell,
Be thy intents° wicked or charitable,
Thou com'st in such a questionable° shape
That I will speak to thee. I'll call thee Hamlet,
45 King, father, royal Dane. O, answer me!
Let me not burst in ignorance, but tell
Why thy canonized° bones, hearsèd° in death,
Have burst their cerements;° why the sepulcher
Wherein we saw thee quietly inurned°
50 Hath oped his ponderous and marble jaws
To cast thee up again. What may this mean,
That thou, dead corpse, again in complete steel,°
Revisits thus the glimpses of the moon,°
Making night hideous, and we fools of nature°
55 So horridly to shake our disposition°
With thoughts beyond the reaches of our souls?
Say, why is this? Wherefore? What should we do?
                    [*The Ghost*] *beckons* [*Hamlet*].

HORATIO.
It beckons you to go away with it,
As if it some impartment° did desire
To you alone.
MARCELLUS.   Look with what courteous action   60
It wafts you to a more removèd ground.
But do not go with it.
HORATIO.   No, by no means.
HAMLET.
It will not speak. Then I will follow it.
HORATIO.
Do not, my lord!
HAMLET.   Why, what should be the fear?
I do not set my life at a pin's fee,°   65
And for my soul, what can it do to that,
Being a thing immortal as itself?
It waves me forth again. I'll follow it.
HORATIO.
What if it tempt you toward the flood,° my lord,
Or to the dreadful summit of the cliff   70
That beetles o'er° his° base into the sea,
And there assume some other horrible form
Which might deprive your sovereignty of reason°
And draw you into madness? Think of it.
The very place puts toys of desperation,°   75
Without more motive, into every brain
That looks so many fathoms to the sea
And hears it roar beneath.
HAMLET.
It wafts me still.—Go on, I'll follow thee.
MARCELLUS.
You shall not go, my lord.   [*They try to stop him.*]
HAMLET.   Hold off your hands!   80
HORATIO.
Be ruled. You shall not go.
HAMLET.   My fate cries out,°
And makes each petty° artery° in this body
As hardy as the Nemean lion's° nerve.°
Still am I called. Unhand me, gentlemen.
By heaven, I'll make a ghost of him that lets° me!   85
I say, away!—Go on, I'll follow thee.
                    Exeunt Ghost and Hamlet.

HORATIO.
He waxes desperate with imagination.

---

28 pales palings, fences (as of a fortification)   **29 o'erleavens** induces a change throughout (as yeast works in dough)   **30 plausive** pleasing   **32 nature's livery** sign of one's servitude to nature. **fortune's star** the destiny that chance brings   **33 His virtues else** i.e., the other qualities of *these men* (line 30)   **34 may undergo** can sustain   **35 general censure** general opinion that people have of him   **36–38 The dram . . . scandal** i.e., the small drop of evil blots out or works against the noble substance of the whole and brings it into disrepute. To *dout* is to blot out. (A famous crux.)   **39 ministers of grace** messengers of God   **40 Be thou** whether you are. **spirit of health** good angel   **41 Bring** whether you bring   **42 Be thy intents** whether your intentions are   **43 questionable** inviting question   **47 canonized** buried according to the canons of the church. **hearsèd** coffined   **48 cerements** grave clothes   **49 inurned** entombed   **52 complete steel** full armor   **53 glimpses of the moon** pale and uncertain moonlight   **54 fools of nature** mere men, limited to natural knowledge and subject to nature   **55 So . . . disposition** to distress our mental composure so violently

59 impartment communication   **65 fee** value   **69 flood** sea   **71 beetles o'er** overhangs threateningly (like bushy eyebrows). **his** its   **73 deprive . . . reason** take away the rule of reason over your mind   **75 toys of desperation** fancies of desperate acts, i.e., suicide   **81 My fate cries out** my destiny summons me   **82 petty** weak. **artery** (through which the vital spirits were thought to have been conveyed)   **83 Nemean lion** one of the monsters slain by Hercules in his twelve labors. **nerve** sinew   **85 lets** hinders

MARCELLUS.
　　Let's follow. 'Tis not fit thus to obey him.
HORATIO.
　　Have after.° To what issue° will this come?
MARCELLUS.
90　　Something is rotten in the state of Denmark.
HORATIO.
　　Heaven will direct it.°
MARCELLUS.　　　　　　　　　Nay, let's follow him.

　　　　　　　　　　　　　　　　　　　Exeunt.

1.5°　　*Enter Ghost and Hamlet.*

HAMLET.
　　Whither will thou lead me? Speak. I'll go no further.
GHOST.
　　Mark me.
HAMLET.　　I will.
GHOST.　　　　　　My hour is almost come,
　　When I to sulfurous and tormenting flames
　　Must render up myself.
HAMLET.　　　　　　　　Alas, poor ghost!
GHOST.
5　　Pity me not, but lend thy serious hearing
　　To what I shall unfold.
HAMLET.　Speak. I am bound° to hear.
GHOST.
　　So art thou to revenge, when thou shalt hear.
HAMLET.　What?
GHOST.
10　　I am thy father's spirit,
　　Doomed for a certain term to walk the night,
　　And for the day confined to fast° in fires,
　　Till the foul crimes° done in my days of nature°
　　Are burnt and purged away. But that° I am forbid
15　　To tell the secrets of my prison house,
　　I could a tale unfold whose lightest word
　　Would harrow up° thy soul, freeze thy young blood,
　　Make thy two eyes like stars start from their spheres,°
　　Thy knotted and combinèd locks° to part,
20　　And each particular hair to stand on end
　　Like quills upon the fretful porcupine.

But this eternal blazon° must not be
To ears of flesh and blood. List, list, O, list!
If thou didst ever thy dear father love—
HAMLET.　O God!   25
GHOST.
　　Revenge his foul and most unnatural murder.
HAMLET.　Murder?
GHOST.
　　Murder most foul, as in the best° it is,
　　But this most foul, strange, and unnatural.
HAMLET.
　　Haste me to know 't, that I, with wings as swift   30
　　As meditation or the thoughts of love,
　　May sweep to my revenge.
GHOST.　　　　　　　　　　　I find thee apt;
　　And duller shouldst thou be° than the fat° weed
　　That roots itself in ease on Lethe° wharf,
　　Wouldst thou not stir in this. Now, Hamlet, hear.   35
　　'Tis given out that, sleeping in my orchard,°
　　A serpent stung me. So the whole ear of Denmark
　　Is by a forgèd process° of my death
　　Rankly abused.° But know, thou noble youth,
　　The serpent that did sting thy father's life   40
　　Now wears his crown.
HAMLET.　O, my prophetic soul! My uncle!
GHOST.
　　Ay, that incestuous, that adulterate° beast,
　　With witchcraft of his wit, with traitorous gifts°—
　　O wicked wit and gifts, that have the power   45
　　So to seduce!—won to his shameful lust
　　The will of my most seeming-virtuous queen.
　　O Hamlet, what a falling off was there!
　　From me, whose love was of that dignity
　　That it went hand in hand even with the vow°   50
　　I made to her in marriage, and to decline
　　Upon a wretch whose natural gifts were poor
　　To° those of mine!
　　But virtue,° as it never will be moved,
　　Though lewdness court it in a shape of heaven,°   55
　　So lust, though to a radiant angel linked,
　　Will sate itself in a celestial bed°
　　And prey on garbage.
　　But soft, methinks I scent the morning air.
　　Brief let me be. Sleeping within my orchard,   60

---

89 Have after let's go after him. **issue** outcome　**91 it** i.e., the outcome
1.5. Location: The battlements of the castle.
7 bound (1) ready (2) obligated by duty and fate. (The Ghost, in
line 8, answers in the second sense.)　**12 fast** do penance by fasting　**13 crimes** sins. **of nature** as a mortal　**14 But that** were it
not that　**17 harrow up** lacerate, tear　**18 spheres** i.e., eye-sock-
ets, here compared to the orbits or transparent revolving spheres in
which, according to Ptolemaic astronomy, the heavenly bodies were
fixed　**19 knotted . . . locks** hair neatly arranged and confined

22 eternal blazon revelation of the secrets of eternity　**28 in the
best** even at best　**33 shouldst thou be** you would have to be. **fat**
torpid, lethargic　**34 Lethe** the river of forgetfulness in Hades
36 orchard garden　**38 forgèd process** falsified account　**39
abused** deceived　**43 adulterate** adulterous　**44 gifts** (1) talents
(2) presents　**50 even with the vow** with the very vow　**53 To**
compared to　**54 virtue, as it** as virtue　**55 shape of heaven**
heavenly form　**57 sate . . . bed** cease to find sexual pleasure in a
virtuously lawful marriage

My custom always of the afternoon,
Upon my secure° hour thy uncle stole,
With juice of cursèd hebona° in a vial,
And in the porches of my ears° did pour
65 The leprous distillment,° whose effect
Holds such an enmity with blood of man
That swift as quicksilver it courses through
The natural gates and alleys of the body,
And with a sudden vigor it doth posset°
70 And curd, like eager° droppings into milk,
The thin and wholesome blood. So did it mine,
And a most instant tetter° barked° about,
Most lazar-like°, with vile and loathsome crust,
All my smooth body.
75 Thus was I, sleeping, by a brother's hand
Of life, of crown, of queen at once dispatched,°
Cut off even in the blossoms of my sin,
Unhouseled,° disappointed,° unaneled,°
No reckoning° made, but sent to my account
80 With all the imperfections on my head.
O, horrible! O, horrible, most horrible!
If thou hast nature° in thee, bear it not.
Let not the royal bed of Denmark be
A couch for luxury° and damnèd incest.
85 But, howsoever thou pursues this act,
Taint not thy mind nor let thy soul contrive
Against thy mother aught. Leave her to heaven
And to those thorns that in her bosom lodge,
To prick and sting her. Fare thee well at once.
90 The glowworm shows the matin° to be near,
And 'gins to pale his° uneffectual fire.
Adieu, adieu, adieu! Remember me.   [Exit.]
HAMLET.
O all you host of heaven! O earth! What else?
And shall I couple° hell? O, fie! Hold, hold,° my heart,
95 And you, my sinews, grow not instant° old,
But bear me stiffly up. Remember thee?
Ay, thou poor ghost, whiles memory holds a seat
In this distracted globe.° Remember thee?
Yea, from the table° of my memory

I'll wipe away all trivial fond° records,   100
All saws° of books, all forms,° all pressures° past
That youth and observation copied there,
And thy commandment all alone shall live
Within the book and volume of my brain,
Unmixed with baser matter. Yes, by heaven!   105
O most pernicious woman!
O villain, villain, smiling, damnèd villain!
My tables°—meet it is° I set it down
That one may smile, and smile, and be a villain.
At least I am sure it may be so in Denmark.   110
                         [Writing.]

So, uncle, there you are.° Now to my word:
It is "Adieu, adieu! Remember me."
I have sworn 't.

      Enter Horatio and Marcellus.

HORATIO. My lord, my lord!
MARCELLUS. Lord Hamlet!   115
HORATIO. Heavens secure him!°
HAMLET. So be it.
MARCELLUS. Hillo, ho, ho, my lord!
HAMLET. Hillo, ho, ho, boy! Come, bird, come.°
MARCELLUS. How is 't, my noble lord?   120
HORATIO. What news, my lord?
HAMLET. O, wonderful!
HORATIO. Good my lord, tell it.
HAMLET. No, you will reveal it.
HORATIO. Not I, my lord, by heaven.   125
MARCELLUS. Nor I, my lord.
HAMLET.
How say you, then, would heart of man once° think
   it?
But you'll be secret?
HORATIO, MARCELLUS. Ay, by heaven, my lord.
HAMLET.
There's never a villain dwelling in all Denmark
But he's an arrant° knave.   130
HORATIO.
There needs no ghost, my lord, come from the grave
To tell us this.
HAMLET.   Why, right, you are in the right.
And so, without more circumstance° at all,
O hold it fit that we shake hands and part,
You as your business and desire shall point you—   135
For every man hath business and desire,

62 **secure** confident, unsuspicious   63 **hebona** a poison. (The word seems to be a form of *ebony*, though it is thought perhaps to be related to *henbane*, a poison, or to *ebenus*, "yew.")   64 **porches of my ears** ears as a porch or entrance of the body   65 **leprous distillment** distillation causing leprosylike disfigurement   69 **posset** coagulate, curdle   70 **eager** sour, acid   72 **tetter** eruption of scabs. **barked** covered with a rough covering, like bark on a tree   73 **lazar-like** leperlike   76 **dispatched** suddenly deprived   78 **Unhouseled** without having received the Sacrament. **disappointed** unready (spiritually) for the last journey. **unaneled** without having received extreme unction   79 **reckoning** settling of accounts   82 **nature** i.e., the promptings of a son   84 **luxury** lechery   90 **matin** morning   91 **his** its   94 **couple** add. **Hold** hold together   95 **instant** instantly   98 **globe** (1) head (2) world   99 **table** tablet, slate

100 **fond** foolish   101 **saws** wise sayings. **forms** shapes or images copied onto the slate; general ideas. **pressures** impressions stamped   108 **tables** writing tablets. **meet it is** it is fitting   111 **there you are** i.e., there, I've written that down against you   116 **secure him** keep him safe   119 **Hillo . . . come** (A falconer's call to a hawk in air. Hamlet mocks the hallooing as though it were a part of hawking.)   127 **once** ever   130 **arrant** thoroughgoing   133 **circumstance** ceremony, elaboration

Such as it is—and for my own poor part,
Look you, I'll go pray.
HORATIO.
These are but wild and whirling words, my lord.
HAMLET.
140 I am sorry they offend you, heartily;
Yes, faith, heartily.
HORATIO.   There's no offense, my lord.
HAMLET.
Yes, by Saint Patrick,° but there is, Horatio,
And much offense° too. Touching this vision here,
It is an honest ghost,° that let me tell you.
145 For your desire to know what is between us,
O'ermaster 't as you may. And now, good friends,
As you are friends, scholars, and soldiers,
Give me one poor request.
HORATIO. What is 't, my lord? We will.
HAMLET.
150 Never make known what you have seen tonight.
HORATIO, MARCELLUS. My lord, we will not.
HAMLET. Nay, but swear 't.
HORATIO. In faith, my lord, not I.°
MARCELLUS. Nor I, my lord, in faith.
155 HAMLET. Upon my sword.°   [He holds out his sword.]
MARCELLUS. We have sworn, my lord, already.°
HAMLET. Indeed, upon my sword, indeed.
GHOST (cries under the stage). Swear.
HAMLET.
Ha, ha, boy, sayst thou so? Are thou there,
truepenny?°
160 Come on, you hear this fellow in the cellarage.
Consent to swear.
HORATIO.   Propose the oath, my lord.
HAMLET.
Never to speak of this that you have seen,
Swear by my sword.
GHOST [beneath]. Swear.   [They swear.]°
HAMLET.
165 Hic et ubique° Then we'll shift our ground.
[He moves to another spot.]
Come hither, gentlemen,

And lay your hands again upon my sword.
Swear by my sword
Never to speak of this that you have heard.
GHOST [beneath]. Swear by his sword.   [They swear.] 170
HAMLET.
Well said, old mole. Canst work i' th' earth so fast?
A worthy pioner!°—Once more remove, good friends.
[He moves again.]
HORATIO.
O day and night, but this is wondrous strange!
HAMLET.
And therefore as a stranger° give it welcome,
There are more things in heaven and earth, Horatio,   175
Than are dreamt of in your philosophy.°
But come;
Here, as before, never, so help you mercy,°
How strange or odd soe'er I bear myself—
As I perchance hereafter shall think meet   180
To put an antic° disposition on—
That you, at such times seeing me, never shall,
With arms encumbered° thus, or this headshake,
Or by pronouncing of some doubtful phrase
As "Well, we know," or "We could, an if° we
would,"   185
Or "If we list° to speak," or "There be, an if they
might,"°
Or such ambiguous giving out,° to note°
That you know aught° of me—this do swear,
So grace and mercy at your most need help you
GHOST [beneath]. Swear.   [They swear.] 190
HAMLET.
Rest, rest, perturbèd spirit! So, gentlemen,
With all my love I do° commend me to you;
And what so poor a man as Hamlet is
May do t' express his love and friending° to you,
God willing, shall not lack.° Let us go in together,   195
And still° your fingers on your lips, I pray.
The time° is out of joint. O cursèd spite°
That ever I was born to set it right!
[They wait for him to leave first.]
Nay, come, let's go together.°   Exeunt.

---

142 **Saint Patrick** (The keeper of Purgatory and patron saint of all blunders and confusion.) 143 **offense** (Hamlet deliberately changes Horatio's "no offense taken" to "an offense against all decency.") 144 **an honest ghost** i.e., a real ghost and not an evil spirit 153 **In faith . . . I** i.e., I swear not to tell what I have seen. (Horatio is not refusing to swear.) 155 **sword** i.e., the hilt in the form of a cross 156 **We . . . already** i.e., we swore *in faith* 159 **truepenny** honest old fellow 164 **s.d. They swear** (Seemingly they swear here, and at lines 170 and 190, as they lay their hands on Hamlet's sword. Triple oaths would have particular force; these three oaths deal with what they have seen, what they have heard, and what they promise about Hamlet's *antic disposition*.) 165 **Hic et ubique** here and everywhere. (Latin.)

172 **pioner** foot soldier assigned to dig tunnels and excavations 174 **as a stranger** i.e., needing your hospitality 176 **your philosophy** this subject called "natural philosophy" or "science" that people talk about 178 **so help you mercy** as you hope for God's mercy when you are judged 181 **antic** fantastic 183 **encumbered** folded 185 **an if** if 186 **list** wished. **There . . . might** i.e., there are people here (we, in fact) who could tell news if we were at liberty to do so 187 **giving out** intimation. **note** draw attention to the fact 188 **aught** i.e., something secret 192 **do . . . you** entrust myself to you 194 **friending** friendliness 195 **lack** be lacking 196 **still** always 197 **The time** the state of affairs. **spite** i.e., the spite of Fortune 199 **let's go together** (Probably they wait for him to leave first, but he refuses this ceremoniousness.)

2 . 1 °   *Enter old Polonius with his man [Reynaldo].*

POLONIUS.
  Give him this money and these notes, Reynaldo.
                    [*He gives money and papers.*]
REYNALDO. I will, my lord.
POLONIUS.
  You shall do marvelous° wisely, good Reynaldo,
  Before you visit him, to make inquire°
  Of his behavior.
5 REYNALDO.   My lord, I did intend it.
POLONIUS.
  Marry, well said, very well said. Look you, sir,
  Inquire me first what Danskers° are in Paris,
  And how, and who, what means,° and where they
      keep°,
  What company, at what expense; and finding
10 By this encompassment° and drift° of question
  That they do know my son, come you more nearer
  Than your particular demands will touch it.°
  Take you,° as 'twere, some distant knowledge of him,
  As thus, "I know his father and his friends,
15 And in part him." Do you mark this, Reynaldo?
REYNALDO. Ay, ver well, my lord.
POLONIUS.
  "And in part him, but," you may say, "not well.
  But if 't be he I mean, he's very wild.
  Addicted so and so," and there put on° him
20 What forgeries° you please—marry, none so rank°
  As may dishonor him, take heed of that,
  But, sir, such wanton,° wild, and usual slips
  As are companions noted and most known
  To youth and liberty.
25 REYNALDO. As gaming, my lord.
POLONIUS. Ay, or drinking, fencing, swearing,
    Quarreling, drabbing°—you may go so far.
REYNALDO. My lord, that would dishonor him.
POLONIUS.
  Faith, no, as you may season° it in the charge.
30 You must not put another scandal on him
  That he is open to incontinency;°
  That's not my meaning. But breathe his faults so quaintly°
  That they may seem the taints of liberty,°
  The flash and outbreak of a fiery mind,

  A savageness in unreclaimèd blood,   35
  Of general assault.°
REYNALDO. But, my good lord—
POLONIUS.
  Wherefore should you do this?
REYNALDO. Ay, my lord, I would know that.
POLONIUS. Marry, sir, here's my drift,   40
  And I believe it is a fetch of warrant.°
  You laying these slight sullies on my son,
  As 'twere a thing a little soiled wi' the working,°
  Mark you,
  Your party in converse,° him you would sound,°   45
  Having ever° seen in the prenominate crimes°
  The youth you breathe° of guilty, be assured
  He closes with you in this consequence:°
  "Good sir," or so, or "friend," or "gentleman,"
  According to the phrase or the addition°   50
  Of man and country.
REYNALDO.   Very good, my lord.
POLONIUS. And then, sir, does 'a this—'a does—what was
  I about to say? By the Mass, I was about to say
  something. Where did I leave?
REYNALDO. At "closes in the consequence."   55
POLONIUS.
  At "closes in the consequence," ay, marry.
  He closes thus: "I know the gentleman,
  I saw him yesterday," or "th' other day,"
  Or then, or then, with such or such, "and as you
      say,
  There was 'a gaming," "there o'ertook in 's rouse,"° 60
  "There falling out° at tennis," or perchance
  "I saw him enter such a house of sale,"
  Videlicet° a brothel, or so forth. See you now,
  Your bait of falsehood takes this carp° of truth;
  And thus do we of wisdom and of reach,°   65
  With windlasses° and with assays of bias,°
  By indirections find directions° out.
  So by my former lecture and advice
  Shall you my son. You have me, have° you not?

2.1. Location: Polonius' chambers.
3 marvelous marvelously 4 inquire inquiry 7 Danskers Danes
8 what means what wealth (they have). keep dwell 10 encompass-
ment roundabout talking. drift gradual approach or course 11–12
come . . . it you will find out more this way than by asking pointed
questions (*particular demands*) 13 Take you assume, pretend 19
put on impute to 20 forgeries invented tales. rank gross 22 wanton sportive, unrestrained 27 drabbing whoring 29 season temper, soften 31 incontinency habitual sexual excess 32 quaintly
artfully, subtly 33 taints of liberty faults resulting from free living

35–36 A savageness . . . assault a wildness in untamed youth that
assails all indiscriminately 41 fetch of warrant legitimate trick
43 soiled wi' the working soiled by handling while it is being
made, i.e., by involvement in the ways of the world. 45 converse
conversation. sound i.e., sound out 46 Having ever if he has ever.
prenominate crimes before-mentioned offenses 47 breathe speak
48 closes . . . consequence takes you into his confidence in some
fashion, as follows 50 addition title 60 o'ertook in 's rouse
overcome by drink 61 falling out quarreling 63 Videlicet
namely 64 carp a fish 65 reach capacity, ability 66 wind-
lasses i.e., circuitous paths. (Literally, circuits made to head off the
game in hunting.) assays of bias attempts through indirection (like
the curving path of the bowling ball, which is biased or weighted to
one side) 67 directions i.e., the way things really are 69 have
understand

REYNALDO.
  My lord, I have.
70 POLONIUS.   God b'wi'° ye; fare ye well.
REYNALDO. Good my lord.
POLONIUS.
  Observe his inclination in yourself.°
REYNALDO. I shall, my lord.
POLONIUS. And let him ply his music.
75 REYNALDO. Well, my lord.
POLONIUS.
  Farewell.   *Exit Reynaldo.*

    Enter Ophelia.

      How now, Ophelia, what's the matter?
OPHELIA.
  O my lord, my lord, I have been so affrighted!
POLONIUS. With what, i' the name of God?
OPHELIA.
  My lord, as I was sewing in my closet,°
80   Lord Hamlet, with his doublet° all unbraced,°
  No hat upon his head, his stockings fouled,
  Ungartered, and down-gyvèd° to his ankle,
  Pale as his shirt, his knees knocking each other,
  And with a look so piteous in purport°
85   As if he had been loosèd out of hell
  To speak of horrors—he comes before me.
POLONIUS.
  Mad for thy love?
OPHELIA.   My lord, I do not know,
  But truly I do fear it.
POLONIUS.   What said he?
OPHELIA.
  He took me by the wrist and held me hard.
90   Then goes he to the length of all his arm.
  And, with his other hand thus o'er his brow
  He falls to such perusal of my face
  As° 'a would draw it. Long stayed he so.
  At last, a little shaking of mine arm
95   And thrice his head thus waving up and down,
  He raised a sigh so piteous and profound
  As it did seem to shatter all his bulk°
  And end his being. That done, he lets me go,
  And with his head over his shoulder turned
100   He seemed to find his way without his eyes,
  For out o' doors he went without their helps,
  And to the last bended their light on me.
POLONIUS.
  Come, go with me. I will go seek the King.

This is the very ecstasy° of love,
Whose violent property° fordoes° itself   105
And leads the will to desperate undertakings
As oft as any passion under heaven
That does afflict our natures. I am sorry.
What, have you given him any hard words of late?
OPHELIA.
  No, my good lord, but as you did command   110
  I did repel his letters and denied
  His access to me.
POLONIUS.   That hath made him mad.
  I am sorry that with better heed and judgment
  I had not quoted° him. I feared he did but trifle
  And meant to wrack° thee. But beshrew° my jealousy! 115
  By heaven, it is as proper to our age°
  To cast beyond° ourselves in our opinions
  As it is common for the younger sort
  To lack discretion. Come, go we to the King.
  This must be known,° which, being kept close,° might
    move   120
  More grief to hide than hate to utter love.°
  Come.   *Exeunt.*

2.2°   *Flourish. Enter King and Queen, Rosencrantz, and*
       Guildenstern [with others].

KING.
  Welcome dear Rosencrantz and Guildenstern.
  Moreover that° we much did long to see you,
  The need we have to use you did provoke
  Our hasty sending. Something have you heard
  Of Hamlet's transformation—so call it,   5
  Sith nor° th' exterior nor the inward man
  Resembles that° it was. What it should be,
  More than his father's death, that thus hath put him
  So much from th' understanding of himself,
  I cannot dream of. I entreat you both   10
  That, being of so young days° brought up with him,
  And sith so neighbored to° his youth and havior,°

---

104 **ecstasy** madness   105 **property** nature. **fordoes** destroys   114 **quoted** observed   115 **wrack** ruin, seduce. **beshrew my jealousy** a plague upon my suspicious nature   116 **proper . . . age** charateristic of us (old) men   117 **cast beyond** overshoot, miscalculate. (A metaphor from hunting.)   120 **known** made known (to the King). **close** secret   120–121 **might . . . love** i.e., might cause more grief (because of what Hamlet might do) by hiding the knowledge of Hamlet's strange behavior to Ophelia than unpleasantness by telling it

2.2. Location: The castle.
2 Moreover that besides the fact that   **6 Sith nor** since neither
7 that what   **11 of . . . days** from such early youth   **12 And sith so neighbored to** and since you are (or, and since that time you are) intimately acquainted with. **havior** demeanor

That you vouchsafe your rest° here in our court
Some little time, so by your companies
15   To draw him on to pleasures, and to gather
So much as from occasion° you may glean,
Whether aught to us unknown afflicts him thus
That, opened,° lies within our remedy.

QUEEN.
Good gentlemen, he hath much talked of you,
20   And sure I am two men there is not living
To whom he more adheres. If it will please you
To show us so much gentry° and good will
As to expend your time with us awhile
For the supply and profit of our hope,°
25   Your visitation shall receive such thanks
As fits a king's remembrance.°

ROSENCRANTZ.   Both Your Majesties
Might, by the sovereign power you have of° us,
Put your dread° pleasures more into command
Than to entreaty.

GUILDENSTERN.   But we both obey,
30   And here give up ourselves in the full bent°
To lay our service freely at your feet,
To be commanded.

KING.
Thanks, Rosencrantz and gentle Guildenstern.

QUEEN.
Thanks, Guildenstern and gentle Rosencrantz.
35   And I beseech you instantly to visit
My too much changèd son. Go, some of you,
And bring these gentlemen where Hamlet is.

GUILDENSTERN.
Heavens make our presence and our practices°
Pleasant and helpful to him!

QUEEN.   Ay, amen!
Exeunt Rosencrantz and Guildenstern [with some
attendants].

Enter Polonius.

POLONIUS.
40   Th' ambassadors from Norway, my good lord,
Are joyfully returned.

KING.
Thou still° hast been the father of good news.

POLONIUS.
Have I, my lord? I assure my good liege
I hold my duty, as I hold° my soul,

Both to my God and to my gracious king;   45
And I do think, or else this brain of mine
Hunts not the trail of policy° so sure
As it hath used to do, that I have found
The very cause of Hamlet's lunacy.

KING.
O, speak of that! That do I long to hear.   50

POLONIUS.
Give first admittance to th' ambassadors.
My news shall be the fruit° to that great feast.

KING.
Thyself do grace° to them and bring them in.
                                          [Exit Polonius.]
He tells me, my dear Gertrude, he hath found
The head and source of all your son's distemper.   55

QUEEN.
I doubt it is no other but the main,°
His father's death and our o'erhasty marriage.

                Enter Ambassadors [Voltimand and Cornelius, with
                Polonius].

KING.
Well, we shall sift him.°—Welcome, my good
   friends!
Say, Voltimand, what from our brother° Norway?

VOLTIMAND.
Most fair return of greetings and desires.°   60
Upon our first°, he sent out to suppress
His nephew's levies, which to him appeared
To be a preparation 'gainst the Polack,
But, better looked into, he truly found
It was against Your Highness. Whereat grieved   65
That so his sickness, age, and impotence°
Was falsely borne in hand,° sends out arrests°
On Fortinbras, which he, in brief, obeys,
Receives rebuke from Norway, and in fine°
Makes vow before his uncle never more   70
To give th' assay° of arms against Your Majesty.
Whereon old Norway, overcome with joy,
Gives him three thousand crowns in annual fee
And his commission to employ those soldiers,
So levied as before, against the Polack,   75
With an entreaty, herein further shown,
                                          [giving a paper]
That it might please you to give quiet pass
Through your dominions for this enterprise

---

13 vouchsafe your rest please to stay   **16 occasion** opportunity
18 opened being revealed   **22 gentry** courtesy   **24 supply . . .
hope** aid and furtherance of what we hope for   **26 As fits . . . remembrance** as would be a fitting gift of a king who rewards true service   **27 of** over   **28 dread** inspiring awe   **30 in . . . bent** to the
utmost degree of our capacity. (An archery metaphor.)   **38 practices** doings   **42 still** always   **44 hold** maintain. **as** as firmly as

47 policy sagacity   **52 fruit** dessert   **53 grace** honor (punning on
grace said before a *feast*, line 52)   **56 doubt** fear, suspect. **main**
chief point, principal concern   **58 sift him** question Polonius
closely   **59 brother** fellow king   **60 desires** good wishes   **61
Upon our first** at our first words on the business   **66 impotence**
helplessness   **67 borne in hand** deluded, taken advantage of. **ar-
rests** orders to desist   **69 in fine** in conclusion   **71 give th' assay**
make trial of strength, challenge

On such regards of safety and allowance°
As therein are set down.

80 KING.   It likes° us well,
And at our more considered° time we'll read,
Answer, and think upon this business.
Meantime we thank you for your well-took labor.
Go to your rest; at night we'll feast together.
Most welcome home!   *Exeunt Ambassadors.*

85 POLONIUS.   This business is well ended.
My liege, and madam, to expostulate°
What majesty should be, what duty is,
Why day is day, night night, and time is time,
Were nothing but to waste night, day, and time.
90 Therefore, since brevity is the soul of wit,°
And tediousness the limbs and outward flourishes,
I will be brief. Your noble son is mad.
Mad call I it, for, to define true madness,
What is 't but to be nothing else but mad?
But let that go.
95 QUEEN.   More matter, with less art.
POLONIUS.
Madame, I swear I use no art at all.
That he's mad, 'tis true; 'tis true 'tis pity,
And pity 'tis 'tis true—a foolish figure,°
But farewell it, for I will use no art.
100 Mad let us grant him, then, and now remains
That we find out the cause of this effect,
Or rather say, the cause of this defect,
For this effect defective comes by cause.°
Thus it remains, and the remainder thus.
105 Perpend.°
I have a daughter—have while she is mine—
Who, in her duty and obedience, mark,
Hath given me this. Now gather and surmise.°
[*He reads the letter.*] "To the celestial and my soul's
110   idol, the most beautified Ophelia"—
That's an ill phrase, a vile phrase; "beautified" is a
vile phrase. But you shall hear. Thus: [*He reads.*]
"In her excellent white bosom,° these,° etc."
QUEEN. Came this from Hamlet to her?
POLONIUS.
115 Good madam, stay° awhile, I will be faithful.°

                                         [*He reads.*]

    "Doubt thou the stars are fire,
        Doubt that the sun doth move,

Doubt° truth to be a liar,
    But never doubt I love.
O dear Ophilia, I am ill at these numbers.° I have not art 120
to reckon° my groans. But that I love thee best, O most
best, believe it. Adieu.
            Thine evermore, most dear lady, whilst this
                machine° is to him, Hamlet."
This in obedience hath my daughter shown me,   125
And, more above,° hath his solicitings,
As they fell out° by time, by° means, and place,
All given to mine ear.°
KING.   But how hath she
Received his love?
POLONIUS.   What do you think of me?
KING.
As a man faithful and honorable.   130
POLONIUS.
I would fain° prove so. But what might you think,
When I had seen this hot love on the wing—
As I perceived it, I must tell you that,
Before my daughter told me—what might you,
Or my dear Majesty your queen here, think,   135
If I had played the desk or table book,°
Or given my heart a winking,° mute and dumb,
Or looked upon this love with idle° sight?
What might you think? No, I went round° to work,
And my young mistress thus I did bespeak:°   140
"Lord Hamlet is a prince out of thy star;°
This must not be." And then I prescripts° gave her,
That she should lock herself from his resort,°
Admit no messengers, receive no tokens.
Which done, she took the fruits of my advice;   145
And he, repellèd—a short tale to make—
Fell into a sadness, then into a fast,
Thence to a watch,° thence into a weakness,
Thence to a lightness,° and by this declension°
Into the madness wherein now he raves,   150
And all we mourn for.°
KING [*to the Queen*].   Do you think 'tis this?
QUEEN. It may be, very like.

---

118 Doubt suspect   **120 ill . . . numbers** unskilled at writing
verses   **121 reckon** (1) count (2) number metrically, scan   **124
machine** i.e., body   **126 more above** moreover   **127 fell out** occurred. **by** according to   **128 given . . . ear** i.e., told me about
131 fain gladly   **136 played . . . table book** i.e., remained shut up,
concealing the information   **137 given . . . winking** closed the
eyes of my heart to this   **138 with idle sight** complacently or in-
comprehendingly   **139 round** roundly, plainly   **140 bespeak** address   **141 out of thy star** above your sphere, position   **142 pre-
scripts** orders   **143 his resort** his visits   **148 watch** state of
sleeplessness   **149 lightness** lightheadedness. **declension** decline,
deterioration (with a pun on the grammatical sense)   **151 all we**
all of us, or, into everything that we

79 On . . . allowance i.e., with such considerations for the safety of
Denmark and permission for Fortinbras   **80 likes** pleases   **81
considered** suitable for deliberation   **86 expostulate** expound, inquire into   **90 wit** sense or judgment   **98 figure** figure of speech
103 For . . . cause i.e., for this defective behavior, this madness, has
a cause   **105 Perpend** consider   **108 gather and surmise** draw
your own conclusions   **113 In . . . bosom** (The letter is poetically
addressed to her heart.) **these** i.e., the letter   **115 stay** wait. **faithful** i.e., in reading the letter accurately

POLONIUS.
  Hath there been such a time—I would fain know
    that—
  That I have positively said "'Tis so,"
  When it proved otherwise?
155 KING.   Not that I know.
POLONIUS.
  Take this from this,° if this be otherwise.
  If circumstances lead me, I will find
  Where truth is hid, though it were hid indeed
  Within the center.°
KING.   How may we try° it further?
POLONIUS.
160 You know sometimes he walks four hours together
  Here in the lobby.
QUEEN.   So he does indeed.
POLONIUS.
  At such a time I'll loose° my daughter to him.
  Be you and I behind an arras° then.
  Mark the encounter. If he love her not
165 And be not from his reason fall'n thereon,°
  Le me be no assistant for a state,
  But keep a farm and carters.°
KING.   We will try it.

        Enter Hamlet [reading on a book.]

QUEEN.
  But look where sadly° the poor wretch comes reading.
POLONIUS.
  Away, I do beseech you both, away.
170 I'll board° him presently.° O, give me leave.°
                Exeunt King and Queen [with attendants].
  How does my good Lord Hamlet?
HAMLET. Well, God-a-mercy.°
POLONIUS. Do you know me, my lord?
HAMLET. Excellent well. You are a fishmonger.°
175 POLONIUS. Not I, my lord.
HAMLET. Then I would you were so honest a man.
POLONIUS. Honest, my lord?
HAMLET. Ay, sir. To be honest, as this world goes, is to be
  one picked out of ten thousand.
180 POLONIUS. That's very true, my lord.

HAMLET. For if the sun breed maggots in a dead dog, being a
  good kissing carrion°—Have you a daughter?
POLONIUS. I have, my lord.
HAMLET. Let her not walk i' the sun.° Conception° is a
  blessing, but as your daughter may conceive, friend, look   185
  to 't.
POLONIUS [*aside*]. How say you by that? Still harping on my
  daughter. Yet he knew me not at first; 'a° said I was a fishmonger. 'A is far gone. And truly in my youth I suffered
  much extremity for love, very near this. I'll speak to him   190
  again—What do you read, my lord?
HAMLET. Words, words, words.
POLONIUS. What is the matter,° my lord?
HAMLET. Between who?
POLONIUS. I mean, the matter that you read, my lord.   195
HAMLET. Slanders, sir; for the satirical rogue says here that
  old men have gray beards, that their faces are wrinkled,
  their eyes purging° thick amber° and plum-tree gum, and
  that they have a plentiful lack of wit,° together with most
  weak hams. All which, sir, though I most powerfully and   200
  potently believe, yet I hold it not honesty° to have it thus
  set down, for yourself, sir, shall grow old° as I am, if like a
  crab you could go backward.
POLONIUS [*aside*]. Thou this be madness, yet there is method
  in 't.—Will you walk out of the air,° my lord?   205
HAMLET. Into my grave.
POLONIUS. Indeed, that's out of the air. [*Aside.*] How preg-
  nant° sometimes his replies are! A happiness° that often
  madness hits on, which reason and sanity could not so
  prosperously° be delivered of. I will leave him and sud-   210
  denly° contrive the means of meeting between him and
  my daughter.—My honorable lord, I will most humbly
  take my leave of you.
HAMLET. You cannot, sir, take from me anything that I will
  more willing part withal°—except my life, except my life,   215
  except my life.

        Enter Guildenstern and Rosencrantz.

POLONIUS. Fare you well, my lord.
HAMLET. These tedious old fools!°
POLONIUS. You go to seek the Lord Hamlet. There he is.

---

156 **Take this from this** (The actor probably gestures, indicating that he means his head from his shoulders, or his staff of office or chain from his hands or neck, or something similar.) 159 **center** middle point of the earth (which is also the center of the Ptolemaic universe). **try** test, judge 162 **loose** (as one might release an animal that is being mated) 163 **arras** hanging, tapestry 165 **thereon** on that account 167 **carters** wagon drivers 168 **sadly** seriously 170 **board** accost. **presently** at once. **give me leave** i.e., excuse me, leave me alone. (Said to those he hurries offstage, including the King and Queen.) 172 **God-a-mercy** God have mercy, i.e., thank you 174 **fishmonger** fish merchant

182 **a good kissing carrion** i.e., a good piece of flesh for kissing, or for the sun to kiss 184 **i' the sun** in public (with additional implication of the sunshine of princely favors). **Conception** (1) understanding (2) pregnancy 188 **'a** he 193 **matter** substance. (But Hamlet plays on the sense of "basis for a dispute.") 198 **purging** discharging. **amber** i.e., resin, like the resinous *plum-tree gum* 199 **wit** understanding 201 **honesty** decency, decorum 202 **old** as old 205 **out of the air** (The open air was considered dangerous for sick people.) 208 **pregnant** quick-witted, full of meaning. **happiness** felicity of expression 210 **prosperously** successfully 211 **suddenly** immediately 215 **withal** with 218 **old fools** i.e., old men like Polonius

220 ROSENCRANTZ [*to Polonius*]. God save you, sir!

[*Exit Polonius.*]

GUILDENSTERN. My honored lord!

ROSENCRANTZ. My most dear lord!

HAMLET. My excellent good friends! How dost thou, Guildenstern? Ah, Rosencrantz! Good lads, how do you 225 both?

ROSENCRANTZ. As the indifferent° children of the earth.

GUILDENSTERN.
Happy in that we are not overhappy.
On Fortune's cap we are not the very button.

HAMLET. Nor the soles of her shoe?

230 ROSENCRANTZ. Neither, my lord.

HAMLET. Then you live about her waist, or in the middle of her favors?°

GUILDENSTERN. Faith, her privates we.°

HAMLET. In the secret parts of Fortune? O, most true, she is 235 a strumpet.° What news?

ROSENCRANTZ. None, my lord, but the world's grown honest.

HAMLET. Then is doomsday near. But your news is not true. Let me question more in particular. What have you, my 240 good friends, deserved at the hands of Fortune that she sends you to prison hither?

GUILDENSTERN. Prison, my lord?

HAMLET. Denmark's a prison.

ROSENCRANTZ. Then is the world one.

245 HAMLET. A goodly one, in which there are many confines,° wards,° and dungeons, Denmark being one o' the worst.

ROSENCRANTZ. We think not so, my lord.

HAMLET. Why then 'tis none to you, for there is nothing ei-250 ther good or bad but thinking makes it so. To me it is a prison.

ROSENCRANTZ. Why then, your ambition makes it one. 'Tis too narrow for your mind.

HAMLET. O God, I could be bounded in an nutshell and 255 count myself a king of infinite space, were it not that I have bad dreams.

GUILDENSTERN. Which dreams indeed are ambition, for the very substance of the ambitious° is merely the shadow of a dream.

260 HAMLET. A dream itself is but a shadow.

ROSENCRANTZ. Truly, and I hold ambition of so airy and light a quality that it is but a shadow's shadow.

HAMLET. Then are our beggars bodies,° and our monarchs

and outstretched° heroes the beggars' shadows. Shall we to the court? For, by my fay,° I cannot reason. 265

ROSENCRANTZ, GUILDENSTERN. We'll wait upon° you.

HAMLET. No such matter. I will not sort° with you with the rest of my servants, for, to speak to you like an honest man, I am most dreadfully attended.° But, in the beaten way° of friendship, what make° you at Elsinore? 270

ROSENCRANTZ. To visit you, my lord, no other occasion.

HAMLET. Beggar that I am, I am even poor in thanks; but I thank you, and sure, dear friends, my thanks are too dear a halfpenny.° Were you not sent for? Is it your own inclining? Is it a free° visitation? Come, come, deal justly 275 with me. Come, come. Nay, speak.

GUILDENSTERN. What should we say, my lord?

HAMLET. Anything but to the purpose.° You were sent for, and there is a kind of confession in your looks which your modesties° have not craft enough to color. I know the 280 good King and Queen have sent for you.

ROSENCRANTZ. To what end, my lord?

HAMLET. That you must teach me. But let me conjure° you, by the rights of our fellowship, by the consonancy of our youth,° by the obligation of our ever-preserved love, and 285 by what more dear a better° proposer could charge° you withal, be even° and direct with me whether you were sent for or no.

ROSENCRANTZ [*aside to Guildenstern*]. What say you?

HAMLET [*aside*]. Nay, then, I have an eye of° you.—If you 290 love me, hold not off.°

GUILDENSTERN. My lord, we were sent for.

HAMLET. I will tell you why; so shall my anticipation prevent your discovery,° and your secrecy to the King and Queen molt no feather.° I have of late—but wherefore I 295 know not—lost all my mirth, forgone all custom of exercises; and indeed it goes so heavily with my disposition that this goodly frame, the earth, seems to me a sterile promontory; this most excellent canopy, the air, look you, this brave° o'erhanging firmament, this majestical roof 300 fretted° with golden fire, why, it appeareth nothing to me

226 **indifferent** ordinary, at neither extreme of fortune or misfortune   232 **favors** i.e., sexual favors   233 **her privates we** i.e., (1) we are sexually intimate with Fortune, the fickle goddess who bestows her favors indiscriminately (2) we are her private citizens   235 **strumpet** prostitute. (A common epithet for indiscriminate Fortune; see line 491.)   246 **confines** places of confinement. **wards** cells   258 **the very . . . ambitious** that seemingly very substantial thing that the ambitious pursue   263 **bodies** i.e., solid substances rather than shadows (since beggars are not ambitious)

264 **outstretched** (1) far-reaching in their ambition (2) elongated as shadows   265 **fay** faith   266 **wait upon** accompany, attend. (But Hamlet uses the phrase in the sense of providing menial service.)   267 **sort** class, categorize   269 **dreadfully attended** waited upon in slovenly fashion   270 **beaten way** familiar path, tried-and-true course. **make** do   274 **too dear a halfpenny** (1) too expensive at even a halfpenny, i.e., of little worth (2) too expensive *by* a halfpenny in return for worthless kindness   275 **free** voluntary   278 **Anything but to the purpose** anything except a straightforward answer. (Said ironically.)   280 **modesties** sense of shame. **color** disguise   283 **conjure** adjure, entreat   284–285 **the consonancy of our youth** our closeness in our younger days   286 **better** more skillful   286–287 **charge** urge. **even** straight, honest   290 **of** on   291 **hold not off** don't hold back   293–294 **so . . . discovery** in that way my saying it first will spare you from revealing the truth   295 **molt no feather** i.e., not diminish in the least   300 **brave** splendid   301 **fretted** adorned (with fretwork, as in a vaulted ceiling)

but a foul and pestilent congregation° of vapors. What a piece of work° is a man! How noble in reason, how infinite in faculties, in form and moving how express° and admirable, in action how like an angel, in apprehension° how like a god! The beauty of the world, the paragon of animals! And yet, to me, what is this quintessence° of dust? Man delights not me—no, nor woman neither, though by your smiling you seem to say so.

ROSENCRANTZ. My lord, there was no such stuff in my thoughts.

HAMLET. Why did you laugh, then, when I said man delights not me?

ROSENCRANTZ. To think, my lord, if you delight not in man, what Lenten entertainment° the players shall receive from you. We coted° them on the way, and higher are they coming to offer you service.

HAMLET. He that plays the king shall be welcome; His Majesty shall have tribute° of° me. The adventurous knight shall use his foil and target,° the lover shall not sign gratis,° the humorous man° shall end his part in peace,° the clown shall make those laugh whose lungs are tickle o' the sear,° and the lady shall say her mind freely, or the blank verse shall halt° for 't. What players are they?

ROSENCRANTZ. Even those you were wont to take such delight in, the tragedians° of the city.

HAMLET. How chances it they travel? Their residence,° both in reputation and profit, was better both ways.

ROSENCRANTZ. I think their inhibition° comes by the means of the late° innovation.°

HAMLET. Do they hold the same estimation they did when I was in the city? Are they so followed?

ROSENCRANTZ. No, indeed are they not.

HAMLET. How comes it? Do they grow rusty?

ROSENCRANTZ. Nay, their endeavor keeps° in the wonted° pace. But there is, sir, an aerie° of children, little eyases,° that cry out on the top of question° and are most tyrannically° clapped for 't. These are now the fashion, and so berattle° the common stages°—so they call them—that many wearing rapiers° are afraid of goose quills° and dare scarce come thither.

HAMLET. What, are they children? Who maintains 'em? How are they escoted?° Will they pursue the quality° no longer than they can sing?° Will they not say afterwards, if they should grow themselves to common° players—as it is most like,° if their means are no better°—their writers do them wrong to make them exclaim against their own succession?°

ROSENCRANTZ. Faith, there has been much to-do° on both sides, and the nation holds it no sin to tar° them to controversy. There was for a while no money bid for argument unless the poet and the player went to cuffs in the question.°

HAMLET. Is 't possible?

GUILDENSTERN. O, there has been much throwing about of brains.

HAMLET. Do the boys carry it away?°

ROSENCRANTZ. Ay, that they do, my lord—Hercules and his load° too.

HAMLET. It is not very strange; for my uncle is King of Denmark, and those that would make mouths° at him while my father lived give twenty, forty, fifty, a hundred ducats° apiece for his picture in little.° 'Sblood,° there is something in this more than natural, if philosophy° could find it out.

A flourish [*of trumpets within*].

GUILDENSTERN. There are the players.

HAMLET. Gentlemen, you are welcome to Elsinore. Your

302–303 **congregation** mass. **piece of work** masterpiece   304 **express** well-framed, exact, expressive   305 **apprehension** power of comprehending   307 **quintessence** the fifth essence of ancient philosophy, beyond earth, water, air, and fire, supposed to be the substance of the heavenly bodies and to be latent in all things   315 **Lenten entertainment** meager reception (appropriate to Lent)   316 **coted** overtook and passed by   319 **tribute** (1) applause (2) homage paid in money. **of** from   320 **foil and target** sword and shield   321 **gratis** for nothing. **humorous man** eccentric character, dominated by one trait or "humor"   321–322 **in peace** i.e., with full license   323 **tickle o' the sear** easy on the trigger, ready to laugh easily. (A *sear* is part of a gunlock.)   324 **halt** limp   327 **tragedians** actors   328 **residence** remaining in their usual place, i.e., in the city   330 **inhibition** formal prohibition (from acting plays in the city)   331 **late** recent. **innovation** i.e., the new fashion in satirical plays performed by boy actors in the "private" theaters; or possibly a political uprising; or the strict limitations set on the theaters in London in 1600   335–360 **How . . . load too** (The passage, omitted from the early quartos, alludes to the so-called War of the Theaters, 1599–1602, the rivalry between the children's companies and the adult actors.)

336 **keeps** continues. **wonted** usual   337 **aerie** nest. **eyases** young hawks   338 **cry . . . question** speak shrilly, dominating the controversy (in decrying the public theaters)   338–339 **tyrannically** outrageously   340 **berattle** berate, clamor against. **common stages** public theaters   341 **many wearing rapiers** i.e., many men of fashion, afraid to patronize the common players for fear of being satirized by the poets writing for the boy actors. **goose quills** i.e., pens of satirists   344 **escoted** maintained. **quality** (acting) profession   344–345 **no longer . . . sing** i.e., only until their voices change   346 **common** regular, adult   347 **like** likely. **if . . . better** if they find no better way to support themselves   349 **succession** i.e., future careers   350 **to-do** ado   351 **tar** set on (as dogs)   352–354 **There . . . question** i.e., for a while, no money was offered by the acting companies to playwrights for the plot to a play unless the satirical poets who wrote for the boys and the adult actors came to blows in the play itself   358 **carry it away** i.e., win the day   359–360 **Hercules . . . load** (Thought to be an allusion to the sign of the Globe Theatre, which was Hercules bearing the world on his shoulders.)   362 **mouths** faces   363 **ducats** gold coins   364 **in little** in miniature. **'Sblood** by God's (Christ's) blood   365 **philosophy** i.e., scientific inquiry

370 hands, come then. Th' appurtenance° of welcome is
fashion and ceremony. Let me comply° with you in this
garb,° lest my extent° to the players, which, I tell you,
must show fairly outwards,° should more appear like
entertainment° than yours. You are welcome. But my
uncle-father and aunt-mother are deceived.

375 GUILDENSTERN. In what, my dear lord?

HAMLET. I am but mad north-north-west.° When the wind
is southerly I know a hawk from a handsaw.°

Enter Polonius.

POLONIUS. Well be with you, gentlemen!

HAMLET. Hark you, Guildenstern, and you too; at each ear a
380 hearer. That great baby you see there is not yet out of his
swaddling clouts.°

ROSENCRANTZ. Haply° he is the second time come to them,
for they say an old man is twice a child.

HAMLET. I will prophesy he comes to tell me of the players.
385 Mark it.—You say right, sir, o' Monday morning, 'twas
then indeed.

POLONIUS. My lord, I have news to tell you.

HAMLET. My lord, have news to tell you. When Roscius°
was an actor in Rome—

390 POLONIUS. The actors are come hither, my lord.

HAMLET. Buzz, buzz!°

POLONIUS. Upon my honor—

HAMLET. Then came each actor on his ass.

POLONIUS. The best actors in the world, either for tragedy,
395 comedy, history, pastoral, pastoral-comical, historical-
pastoral, tragical-historical, tragical-comical-historical-
pastoral, scene individable,° or poem unlimited.°
Seneca° cannot be too heavy, nor Plautus° too light.
For the law of writ and the liberty,° these are the only
400 men.

HAMLET. O Jephthah, judge of Israel,° what a treasure hadst
thou!

POLONIUS. What a treasure had he, my lord?

HAMLET. Why,
"One fair daughter, and no more,   405
The which he lovèd passing° well."

POLINIUS [*aside*]. Still on my daughter.

HAMLET. Am I not i' the right, old Jephthah?

POLONIUS. If you call me Jephthah, my lord, I have a daughter that I love passing well.   410

HAMLET. Nay, that follows not.

POLONIUS. What follows then, my lord?

HAMLET. Why,
"As by lot,° God wot,"°
and then, you know,   415
"It came to pass, as most like° it was"—
the first row° of the pious chanson° will show you
more,
for look where my abridgement° comes.

Enter the Players.

You are welcome, masters; welcome, all. I am glad to see 420
thee well. Welcome, good friends. O, old friend! Why,
thy face is valanced° since I saw thee last. Com'st thou
to beard° me in Denmark? What, my young lady° and
mistress! By 'r Lady,° your ladyship is nearer to heaven
than when I saw you last, by the altitude of a chopine.° 425
Pray God your voice, like a piece of uncurrent° gold, be
not cracked within the ring.° Masters, you are all
welcome. We'll e'en to 't° like French falconers, fly at
anything we see. We'll have a speech straight.° Come,
give us a taste of your quality.° Come, a passionate 430
speech.

FIRST PLAYER. What speech, my good lord?

HAMLET. I heard thee speak me a speech once, but it was
never acted, or if it was, not above once, for the play, I remember, pleased not the million; 'twas caviar to the gen- 435
eral.° But it was—as I received it, and others, whose judgments in such matters cried in the top of° mine—an
excellent play, well digested° in the scenes, set down with
as much modesty° as cunning°. I remember one said there

369 **appurtenance** proper accompaniment   370 **comply** observe
the formalities of courtesy   371 **garb** i.e., manner. **my extent** that
which I extend, i.e., my polite behavior   372 **show fairly outwards** show every evidence of cordiality   373 **entertainment** a
(warm) reception   376 **north-north-west** just off true north, only
partly   377 **hawk, handsaw** i.e., two very different things, though
also perhaps meaning a mattock (or *hack*) and a carpenter's cutting
tool, respectively; also birds, with a play on *hernshaw*, or heron
381 **swaddling clouts** cloths in which to wrap a newborn baby
382 **Haply** perhaps   388 **Roscius** a famous Roman actor who died
in 62 B.C.E.   391 **Buzz** (An interjection used to denote stale
news.)   397 **scene individable** a play observing the unity of place;
or perhaps one that is unclassifiable, or performed without intermission   397–398 **poem unlimited** a play disregarding the unities of
time and place; one that is all-inclusive   398 **Seneca** writer of
Latin tragedies. **Plautus** writer of Latin comedy   399 **law . . . liberty** dramatic composition both according to the rules and disregarding the rules. **these** i.e., the actors   401 **Jephthah . . . Israel**
(Jephthah had to sacrifice his daughter; see Judges 11. Hamlet goes
on to quote from a ballad on the theme.)

406 **passing** surpassingly   414 **lot** chance. **wot** knows   416 **like**
likely, probable   417 **row** stanza. **chanson** ballad, song   419 **my
abridgment** something that cuts short my conversation; also, a diversion   422 **valanced** fringed (with a beard)   423 **beard** confront, challenge (with obvious pun). **young lady** i.e., boy playing
women's parts   424 **By 'r Lady** by Our Lady   426 **chopine** thick-
soled shoe of Italian fashion   426–427 **uncurrent** not passable as
lawful coinage   427 **cracked . . . ring** i.e., changed from adolescent to male voice, no longer suitable for women's roles. (Coins featured rings enclosing the sovereign's head; if the coin was cracked
within this ring, it was unfit for currency.)   428 **e'en to 't** go at it
429 **straight** at once   430 **quality** professional skill   435–436
caviar to the general caviar to the multitude, i.e., a choice dish too
elegant for coarse tastes   437–438 **cried in the top of** i.e., spoke
with greater authority than   438 **digested** arranged, ordered
439 **modesty** moderation, restraint. **cunning** skill

440 were no sallets° in the lines to make the matter savory,
nor no matter in the phrase that might indict° the author
of affectation, but called it an honest method, as wholesome as sweet, and by very much more handsome° than
fine.° One speech in 't I chiefly loved: 'twas Aeneas' tale
445 to Dido, and thereabout of it especially when he speaks of
Priam's slaughter.° If it live in your memory, begin at this
line: let me see, let me see—
          "The rugged Pyrrhus,° like th' Hyrcanian beast"°—
'Tis not so. It begins with Pyrrhus:
450   "The rugged° Pyrrhus, he whose sable° arms,
          Black as his purpose, did the night resemble
          When he lay couchèd° in the ominous horse,°
          Hath now this dread and black complexion
          smeared
455   With heraldry more dismal.° Head to foot
          Now is he total gules,° horridly tricked°
          With blood of fathers, mothers, daughters, sons,
          Baked and impasted° with the parching streets,°
          That lend a tyrannous° and a damnèd light
460   To their lord's° murder. Roasted in wrath and fire,
          And thus o'ersizèd° with coagulate gore,
          With eyes like carbuncles,° the hellish Pyrrhus
          Old grandsire Priam seeks."
     So proceed you.
465 POLONIUS. 'Fore God, my lord, well spoken, with good ac-
     cent and good discretion.
     FIRST PLAYER.   "Anon he finds him
          Striking too short at Greeks. His antique° sword,
          Rebellious to his arm, lies where it falls,
          Repugnant° to command. Unequal matched,
470   Pyrrhus at Priam drives, in rage strikes wide,
          But with the whiff and wind of his fell° sword

Th' unnervèd° father falls. Then senseless Ilium,°
Seeming to feel this blow, with flaming top
Stoops to his° base, and with a hideous crash
Takes prisoner Pyrrhus' ear. For, lo! His sword,   475
Which was declining° on the milky° head
Of reverend Priam, seemed i' th' air to stick.
So as a painted° tyrant Pyrrhus stood,
And, like a neutral to his will and matter,°
Did nothing.   480
But as we often see against° some storm
A silence in the heavens, the rack° stand still,
The bold winds speechless, and the orb° below
As hush as death, anon the dreadful thunder
Doth rend the region,° so, after Pyrrhus' pause,   485
A rousèd vengeance sets him new a-work,
And never did the Cyclops'° hammers fall
On Mars's armor forged for proof eterne°
With less remorse° than Pyrrhus' bleeding sword
Now falls on Priam.   490
Out, out, thou strumpet Fortune! All you gods
In general synod° take away her power!
Break all the spokes and fellies° from her wheel,
And bowl the round nave° down the hill of heaven°
As low as to the fiends!"   495
POLONIUS. This is too long.
HAMLET. It shall to the barber's with your beard.—Prithee,
     say on. He's for a jig° or a tale of bawdry, or he sleeps. Say
     on; come to Hecuba.°
FIRST PLAYER. "But who, ah woe! had° seen the moblèd°   500
     queen"—
HAMLET. "The moblèd queen?"
POLONIUS. That's good. "Moblèd queen" is good.
FIRST PLAYER.
     "Run barefoot up and down, threat'ning the flames°
     With bisson rheum,° a clout° upon that head.   505
     Where late° the diadem stood, and, for a robe,
     About her lank and all o'erteemèd° loins
     A blanket, in the alarm of fear caught up—
     Who this had seen, with tongue in venom steeped,

440 **sallets** i.e., something savory, spicy improprieties   441 **indict**
convict   443 **handsome** well-proportioned   444 **fine** elaborately
ornamented, showy   446 **Priam's slaughter** the slaying of the rule
of Troy, when the Greeks finally took the city   448 **Pyrrhus** a
Greek hero in the Trojan War, also known as Neoptolemus, son of
Achilles—another avenging son. **Hyrcanian beast** i.e., tiger. (On
the death of Priam, see Virgil, *Aeneid*, 2.506 ff.; compare the whole
speech with Marlow's *Dido Queen of Carthage*, 2.1.214 ff. On the
Hyrcanian tiger, see *Aeneid*, 4.366–367. Hyrcania is on the Caspian
Sea.)   450 **rugged** shaggy, savage. **sable** black (for reasons of camouflage during the episode of he Trojan horse)   452 **couchèd** concealed. **ominous horse** fateful Trojan horse, by which the Greeks
gained access to Troy   455 **dismal** ill-omened   456 **total gules**
entirely red. (A heraldic term.) **tricked** spotted and smeared.
(Heraldic.)   458 **impasted** crusted, like a thick paste. **with . . .**
streets by the parching heat of the streets (because of the fires
everywehre)   459 **tyrannous** cruel   460 **their lord's** i.e., Priam's
461 **o'ersizèd** covered as with size or glue   462 **carbuncles** large
fiery-red precious stones thought to emit their own light   467 **an-**
tique ancient, long-used   469 **Repugnant** disobedient, resistant
471 **fell** cruel

472 **unnervèd** strengthless. **senseless Ilium** inanimate citadel of
Troy   474 **his** its   476 **declining** descending. **milky** white-haired
478 **painted** i.e., painted in a picture   479 **like . . . matter** i.e., as
though suspended between his intention and its fulfillment   481
against just before   482 **rack** mass of clouds   483 **orb** globe,
earth   485 **region** sky   487 **Cyclops** giant armor makers in the
smithy of Vulcan   488 **proof eterne** eternal resistance to assault
489 **remorse** pity   492 **synod** assembly   493 **fellies** pieces of
wood forming the rim of a wheel   494 **nave** hub. **hill of heaven**
Mount Olympus   498 **jig** comic song and dance often given at the
end of a play   499 **Hecuba** wife of Priam   500 **who . . . had** anyone who had (also in line 509). **moblèd** muffled   504 **threat'ning**
the flames i.e., weeping hard enough to dampen the flames   505
bisson rheum blinding tears. **clout** cloth   506 **late** lately   507
all o'erteemèd utterly worn out with bearing children

'Gainst Fortune's state° would treason have
    pronounced.°   510
But if the gods themselves did see her then
When she saw Pyrrhus make malicious sport
In mincing with his sword her husband's limbs,
The instant burst of clamor that she made,
Unless things mortal move them not at all,   515
Would have made milch° the burning eyes of heaven,°
And passion° in the gods."

POLONIUS. Look whe'er° he has not turned his color and has
    tears in 's eyes. Prithee, no more.

HAMLET. 'Tis well; I'll have thee speak out the rest of this   520
    soon.—Good my lord, will you see the players well be-
    stowed?° Do you hear, let them be well used, for they are
    the abstract° and brief chronicles of the time. After your
    death you were better have a bad epitaph than their ill
    report while you live.   525

POLONIUS. My lord, I will use them according to their
    desert.

HAMLET. God's bodikin,° man, much better. Use every man
    after° his desert, and who shall scape whipping? Use them
    after your own honor and dignity. The less they deserve,   530
    the more merit is in your bounty. Take them in.

POLONIUS. Come, sirs.   *[Exit.]*

HAMLET. Follow him, friends. We'll hear a play tomorrow.
    [As they start to leave, Hamlet detains the First Player.] Dost
    thou hear me, old friend? Can you play *The Murder of*   535
    Gonzago?

FIRST PLAYER. Ay, my lord.

HAMLET. We'll ha 't° tomorrow night. You could, for a need,
    study° a speech of some dozen or sixteen lines which I
    would set down and insert in 't, could you not?   540

FIRST PLAYER. Ay, my lord.

HAMLET. Very well. Follow that lord, and look you mock
    him not. (*Exeunt Players.*) My good friends, I'll leave you
    till night. You are welcome to Elsinore.

ROSENCRANTZ. Good my lord!   545
                Exeunt [Rosencrantz and Guildenstern].

HAMLET.
    Ay, so, goodbye to you.—Now I am alone.
    O, what a rogue and peasant slave am I!
    Is it not monstrous that this player here,
    But° in a fiction, in a dream of passion,
    Could force his soul so to his own conceit°   550

That from her working° all his visage wanned,°
Tears in his eyes, distraction in his aspect,°
A broken voice, and his whole function suiting
With forms to his conceit? °And all for nothing!
For Hecuba!   555
What's Hecuba to him, or he to Hecuba,
That he should weep for her? What would he do
Had he the motive and the cue for passion
That I have? He would drown the stage with tears
And cleave the general ear° with horrid° speech,   560
Make mad the guilty and appall° the free,°
Confound the ignorant,° and amaze° indeed
The very faculties of eyes and ears. Yet I,
A dull and muddy-mettled° rascal, peak
Like John-a-dreams°, unpregnant of° my cause,   565
And can say nothing—no, not for a king
Upon whose property° and most dear life
A damned defeat° was made. Am I a coward?
Who calls me villain? Breaks my pate° across?
Plucks off my beard and blows it in my face?   570
Tweaks me by the nose? Gives me the lie i' the throat°
As deep as to the lungs? Who does me this?
Ha, 'swounds,° I should take it; for it cannot be
But I am pigeon-livered° and lack gall
To make oppression bitter,° or ere this   575
I should ha' fatted all the region kites°
With this slave's offal.° Blood, bawdy villain!
Remorseless,° treacherous, lecherous, kindless° villain!
O, vengeance!
Why, what an ass am I! This is most brave,°   580
That I, the son of a dear father murdered,
Prompted to my revenge by heaven and hell,
Must like a whore unpack my heart with words
And fall a-cursing, like a very drab,°
A scullion!° Fie upon 't, foh! About,° my brains!   585
Hum, I have heard

---

551 from her working as a result of, or in response to, his soul's activity. **wanned** grew pale   **552 aspect** look, glance   **553–554 his whole . . . conceit** all his bodily powers responding with actions to suit his thought   **560 the general ear** everyone's ear. **horrid** horrible   **561 appall** (Literally, make pale.) **free** innocent   **562 Confound the ignorant** i.e., dumbfound those who know nothing of the crime that has been committed. **amaze** stun   **564 muddy-mettled** dull-spirited. **peak** mope, pine   **565 John-a-dreams** a sleepy, dreaming idler. **unpregnant of** not quickened by   **567 property** i.e., the crown; also character, quality   **568 damned defeat** damnable act of destruction   **569 pate** head   **571 Gives . . . throat** calls me an out-and-out liar   **573 'swounds** by his (Christ's) wounds   **574 pigeon-livered** (The pigeon or dove was popularly supposed to be mild because it secreted no gall.)   **575 bitter** i.e., bitter to me   **576 region kites** kites (birds of prey) of the air   **577 offal** entrails   **578 Remorseless** pitiless. **kindless** unnatural   **580 brave** fine, admirable. (Said ironically.)   **584 drab** whore   **585 scullion** menial kitchen servant (apt to be foulmouthed). **About** about it, to work

---

510 state rule, managing. **pronounced** proclaimed   **516 milch** milky, moist with tears. **burning eyes of heaven** i.e., heavenly bodies   **517 passion** overpowering emotion   **518 whe'er** whether   **522 bestowed** lodged   **523 abstract** summary account   **528 God's bodikin** by God's (Christ's) little body, *bodykin*. (Not to be confused with *bodkin*, "dagger.")   **529 after** according to   **538 ha 't** have it   **539 study** memorize   **549 But** merely   **550 force . . . conceit** bring his innermost being so entirely into accord with his conception (of the role)

That guilty creatures sitting at a play
Have by the very cunning° of the scene°
Been struck so to the soul that presently°
590 They have proclaimed their malefactions;
For murder, though it have no tongue, will speak
With most miraculous organ. I'll have these players
Play something like the murder of my father
Before mine uncle. I'll observe his looks;
595 I'll tent° him to the quick.° If 'a do blench,°
I know my course. The spirit that I have seen
May be the devil, and the devil hath power
T' assume a pleasing shape; yea, and perhaps,
Out of my weakness and my melancholy,
600 As he is very potent with such spirits,°
Abuses° me to damn me. I'll have grounds
More relative° than this. The play's the thing
Wherein I'll catch the conscience of the King.   *Exit.*

3.1°   *Enter King, Queen, Polonius, Ophelia,*
       Rosencrantz, Guildenstern, lords.

KING.
   And can you by no drift of conference°
   Get from him why he puts on this confusion,
   Grating so harshly all his days of quiet
   With turbulent and dangerous lunacy?
ROSENCRANTZ.
5   He does confess he feels himself distracted,
   But from what cause 'a will by no means speak.
GUILDENSTERN.
   Nor do we find him forward° to be sounded,°
   But with a crafty madness keeps aloof
   When we would bring him on to some confession
   Of his true state.
10 QUEEN.   Did he receive you well?
ROSENCRANTZ.   Most like a gentleman.
GUILDENSTERN.
   But with much forcing of his disposition.°
ROSENCRANTZ.
   Niggard° of question,° but of our demands
   Most free in his reply.
QUEEN.   Did you assay° him
15   To any pastime?
ROSENCRANTZ.
   Madam, it so fell out that certain players

We o'erraught° on the way. Of these we told him,
And there did seem in him a kind of joy
To hear of it. They are here about the court.
And, as I think, they have already order   20
This night to play before him.
POLONIUS.   'Tis most true,
   And he beseeched me to entreat Your Majesties
   To hear and see the matter.
KING.
   With all my heart, and it doth much content me
   To hear him so inclined.   25
   Good gentlemen, give him a further edge°
   And drive his purpose into these delights.
ROSENCRANTZ.
   We shall, my lord.
                     Exeunt Rosencrantz and Guildenstern.
KING.   Sweet Gertrude, leave us too,
   For we have closely° sent for Hamlet hither,
   That he, as 'twere by accident, may here   30
   Affront° Ophelia.
   Her father and myself, lawful espials,°
   Will so bestow ourselves that seeing, unseen,
   We may of their encounter frankly judge,
   And gather by him, as he is behaved,   35
   If 't be th' affliction of his love or no
   That thus he suffers for.
QUEEN.   I shall obey you.
   And for your part, Ophelia, I do wish
   That your good beauties be the happy cause
   Of Hamlet's wildness. So shall I hope your virtues 40
   Will bring him to his wonted° way again,
   To both your honors.
OPHELIA.   Madam, I wish it may.
                                            [Exit Queen.]
POLONIUS.
   Ophelia, walk you here.—Gracious,° so please you,
   We will bestow° ourselves. *[To Ophelia.]* Read on this
      book,   *[giving her a book]*
   That show of such an exercise° may color°   45
   Your loneliness.° We are oft to blame in this—
   'Tis too much proved°—that with devotion's visage
   And pious action we do sugar o'er
   The devil himself.
KING *[aside].* O, 'tis too true!   50
   How smart a lash that speech doth give my conscience!
   The harlot's cheek, beautied with plastering art,

---

588 cunning art, skill. **scene** dramatic presentation   **589 presently**
at once   **595 tent** probe. **the quick** the tender part of a wound, the
core. **blench** quail, flinch   **600 spirits** humors (of melancholy)
601 Abuses deludes   **602 relative** cogent, pertinent
3.1. Location: The castle.
1 drift of conference directing of conversation   **7 forward** willing.
sounded questioned   **12 disposition** inclination   **13 Niggard**
stingy. **question** conversation   **14 assay** try to win

17 o'erraught overtook   **26 edge** incitement   **29 closely** privately   **31 Affront** confront, meet   **32 espials** spies   **41 wonted**
accustomed   **43 Gracious** Your Grace (i.e., the king)   **44 bestow**
conceal   **45 exercise** religious exercise. (The book she reads is one
of devotion.) **color** give a plausible appearance to   **46 loneliness**
being alone   **47 too much proved** too often shown to be true, too
often practiced

Is not more ugly to° the thing° that helps it
Than is my deed to my most painted word.
55   O heavy burden!
POLONIUS.
    I hear him coming. Let's withdraw, my lord.
                        [*The King and Polonius withdraw.*]°

    Enter Hamlet. [*Ophelia pretends to read a book.*]

HAMLET.
    To be, or not to be, that is the question:
    Whether 'tis nobler in the mind to suffer
    The slings° and arrows of outrageous fortune,
60   Or to take arms against a sea of troubles
    And by opposing end them. To die, to sleep—
    No more—and by a sleep to say we end
    The heartache and the thousand natural shocks
    That flesh is heir to. 'Tis a consummation
65   Devoutly to be wished. To die, to sleep;
    To sleep, perchance to dream. Ay, there's the rub,°
    For in that sleep of death what dreams may come,
    When we have shuffled° off this mortal coil,°
    Must give us pause. There's the respect°
70   That makes calamity of so long life.°
    For who would bear the whips and scorns of time,
    Th' oppressor's wrong, the proud man's contumely,°
    The pangs of disprized° love, the law's delay,
    The insolence of office,° and the spurns°
75   That patient merit of th' unworthy takes,°
    When he himself might his quietus° make
    With a bare bodkin?° Who would fardels° bear,
    To grunt and sweat under a weary life,
    But that the dread of something after death,
80   The undiscovered country from whose bourn°
    No traveler returns, puzzles the will,
    And makes us rather bear those ills we have
    Than fly to others that we know not of?
    Thus conscience does make cowards of us all;
85   And thus the native hue° of resolution
    Is sicklied o'er with the pale cast° of thought,
    And enterprises of great pitch° and moment°

With this regard° their currents° turn awry
And lose the name of action.—Soft you° now,
The fair Ophelia. Nymph, in thy orisons°   90
Be all my sins remembered.
OPHELIA   Good my lord,
    How does your honor for this many a day?
HAMLET.
    I humbly thank you; well, well, well.
OPHELIA.
    My lord, I have remembrances of yours,
    That I have longèd long to redeliver.   95
    I pray you, now receive them.   [*She offers tokens.*]
HAMLET.
    No, not I, I never gave you aught.
OPHELIA.
    My honored lord, you know right well you did,
    And with them words of so sweet breath composed
    As made the things more rich. Their perfume lost, 100
    Take these again, for to the noble mind
    Rich gifts wax poor when givers prove unkind.
    There, my lord.   [*She gives tokens.*]
HAMLET. Ha, ha! Are you honest?°
OPHELIA. My lord?   105
HAMLET. Are you fair?°
OPHELIA. What means your lordship?
HAMLET. That if you be honest and fair, your honesty°
    should admit no discourse to° your beauty.
OPHELIA. Could beauty, my lord, have better commerce° 110
    than with honesty?
HAMLET. Ay, truly, for the power of beauty will sooner trans-
    form honesty from what it is to a bawd than the force of
    honesty can translate beauty into his° likeness. This was
    sometime° a paradox,° but now the time° gives it proof. I 115
    did love you once.
OPHELIA. Indeed, my lord, you made me believe so.
HAMLET. You should not have believed me, for virtue can-
    not so inoculate° our old stock but we shall relish of it.° I
    loved you not.   120
OPHELIA. I was the more deceived.
HAMLET. Get thee to a nunnery.° Why wouldst thou be a
    breeder of sinners? I am myself indifferent honest,° but
    yet I could accuse me of such things that it were better my
    mother had not borne me: I am very proud, revengeful, 125

---

53 **to** compared to. **the thing** i.e., the cosmetic   56 s.d. **withdraw**
(The King and Polonius may retire behind an arras. The stage directions specify that they "enter" again near the end of the scene.)
59 **slings** missiles   66 **rub** (Literally, an obstacle in the game of
bowls.)   68 **shuffled** sloughed, cast. **coil** turmoil   69 **respect**
consideration   70 **of . . . life** so long-lived, something we willingly
endure for so long (also suggesting that long life is itself a calamity).
72 **contumely** insolent abuse   73 **disprized** unvalued   74 **office**
officialdom. **spurns** insults   75 **of . . . takes** receives from unworthy persons   76 **quietus** acquaintance; here, death   77 **a bare
bodkin** a mere dagger, unsheathed. **fardels** burdens   80 **bourn**
frontier, boundary   85 **native hue** natural color, complexion   86
cast tinge, shade of color   87 **pitch** height (as of a falcon's flight).
moment importance

88 **regard** respect, consideration. **currents** courses   89 **Soft you** i.e.,
wait a minute, gently   90 **orisons** prayers   104 **honest** (1) truthful
(2) chaste   106 **fair** (1) beautiful (2) just, honorable   108 **your
honesty** your chastity   109 **discourse to** familiar dealings with
110–111 **commerce** dealings, intercourse   114 **his** its   115 **sometime** formerly. **a paradox** a view opposite to commonly held opinion.
the time the present age   119 **inoculate** graft, be engrafted to
119–120 **but . . . it** that we do not still have about us a taste of the
old stock, i.e., retain our sinfulness   122 **nunnery** convent (with
possibly an awareness that the word was also used derisively to denote
a brothel)   123 **indifferent honest** reasonably virtuous

ambitious, with more offenses at my beck° than I have
thoughts to put them in, imagination of give them shape,
or time to act them in. What should such fellows as I do
crawling between earth and heaven? We are arrant
130 knaves all; believe none of us. Go thy ways to a nunnery.
Where's your father?

OPHELIA. At home, my lord.

HAMLET. Let the doors be shut upon him, that he may play
the fool nowhere but in 's own house. Farewell.

135 OPHELIA. O, help him, you sweet heavens!

HAMLET. If thou dost marry, I'll give thee this plague for thy
dowry: be thou as chaste as ice, as pure as snow, thou shalt
not escape calumny. Get thee to a nunnery, farewell. Or,
if thou wilt needs marry, marry a fool, for wise men know
140 well enough what monsters° you° make of them. To a
nunnery, go, and quickly too. Farewell.

OPHELIA. Heavenly powers, restore him!

HAMLET. I have heard of your paintings too, well enough.
God hath given you one face, and you make yourselves
145 another. You jig,° you amble,° and you lisp, you nickname
God's creatures,° and make your wantonness your ignorance.° Go to, I'll no more on 't°; it hath made me mad. I
say we will have no more marriage. Those that are married already—all but one—shall live. The rest shall keep
150 as they are. To a nunnery, go.   *Exit.*

OPHELIA.
O, what a noble mind is here o'erthrown!
The courtier's, soldier's, scholar's, eye, tongue, sword,
Th' expectancy° and rose° of the fair state,
The glass of fashion and the mold of form,°
155 Th' observed of all observers,° quite, quite down!
And I, of ladies most deject and wretched,
That sucked the honey of his music° vows,
Now see that noble and most sovereign reason
Like sweet bells jangled out of tune and harsh,
160 That unmatched form and feature of blown° youth
Blasted° with ecstasy.° O, woe is me,
T' have seen what I have seen, see what I see!

Enter King and Polonius.

KING.
Love? His affections° do not that way tend;

Nor what he spake, though it lacked form a little,
Was not like madness. There's something in his soul   165
O'er which his melancholy sits on brood,°
And I no doubt° the hatch and the disclose°
Will be some danger; which for to prevent,
I have in quick determination
Thus set it down:° he shall with speed to England   170
For the demand of° our neglected tribute.
Haply the seas and countries different
With variable objects° shall expel
This something-settled matter in his heart,°
Whereon his brains still° beating puts him thus   175
From fashion of himself.° What think you on 't?

POLONIUS.
It shall do well. But yet do I believe
The origin and commencement of his grief
Sprung from neglected love.—How now, Ophelia?
You need not tell us what Lord Hamlet said;   180
We heard it all.—My lord, do as you please,
But, if you hold it fit, after the play
Let his queen-mother° all alone entreat him
To show his grief. Let her be round° with him;
And I'll be placed, so please you, in the ear   185
Of all their conference. If she find him not,°
To England send him, or confine him where
Your wisdom best shall think.

KING.   It shall be so.
Madness in great ones must not unwatched go.

                                                    Exeunt.

3.2°   *Enter Hamlet and three of the Players.*

HAMLET. Speak the speech, I pray you, as I pronounced it to
you, trippingly on the tongue. But if you mouth it, as
many of our players° do, I had as lief° the town crier
spoke my lines. Nor do not saw the air too much with
your hand, thus, but use all gently; for in the very torrent,   5
tempest, and, as I may say, whirlwind of your passion, you
must acquire and beget a temperance that may give it
smoothness. O, it offends me to the soul to hear a robus-
tious° periwig-pated° fellow tear a passion to tatters, to

126 **beck** command   140 **monsters** (An illusion to the horns of a
cuckold.) **you** i.e., you women   145 **jig** dance. **amble** move coyly
145–146 **you nickname . . . creatures** i.e., you give trendy names
to things in place of their God-given names   146–147 **make . . .
ignorance** i.e., excuse your affectation on the grounds of pretended
ignorance   147 **on 't** of it   153 **expectancy** hope. **rose** ornament
154 **The glass . . . form** the mirror of true self-fashioning and the
pattern of courtly behavior   155 **Th' observed . . . observers** i.e.,
the center of attention and honor in the court   157 **music** musical, sweetly uttered   160 **blown** blooming   161 **Blasted** withered. **ecstasy** madness   163 **affections** emotions, feelings

166 **sits on brood** sits like a bird on a nest, about to *hatch* mischief
(line 167)   167 **doubt** fear. **disclose** disclosure, hatching   170 **set
it down** resolved   171 **For . . . of** to demand   173 **variable objects** various sights and surroundings to divert him   174 **This
something . . . heart** the strange matter settled in his heart   175
still continually   176 **From . . . himself** out of his natural manner
183 **queen-mother** queen and mother   184 **round** blunt   186
find him not fails to discover what is troubling him
3.2. Location: The castle.
3 **our players** players nowadays. **I had as lief** I would just as soon
8–9 **robustious** violent, boisterous. **periwig-pated** wearing a wig

10 very rags, to split the ears of the groundlings°, who for the
most part are capable of° nothing but inexplicable dumb
shows° and noise. I would have such a fellow whipped for
o'erdoing Termagant.° It out-Herods Herod.° Pray you,
avoid it.

15 FIRST PLAYER. I warrant your honor.

HAMLET. Be not too tame neither, but let our own discretion
be your tutor. Suit the action to the word, the word to the
action, with this special observance, that you o'erstep not
the modesty° of nature. For anything so o'erdone is from°
20 the purpose of playing, whose end, both at the first and
now, was and is to hold as 't were the mirror up to nature,
to show virtue her feature, scorn° her own image, and the
very age and body of the time° his° form and pressure.°
Now this overdone or come tardy off,° though it makes
25 the unskillful° laugh, cannot but make the judicious
grieve, the censure of the which one° must in your al-
lowance° o'erweigh a whole theater of others. O, there be
players that I have seen play, and heard others praise, and
that highly, not to speak it profanely,° that, neither hav-
30 ing th' accent of Christians° nor the gait of Christian,
pagan, nor man,° have so strutted and bellowed that I
have thought some of nature's journeymen° had made
men and not made them well, they imitated humanity so
abominably.°

35 FIRST PLAYER. I hope we have reformed that indifferently°
with us, sir.

HAMLET. O, reform it altogether. And let those that play
your clowns speak no more than is set down for them; for
there be of them° that will themselves laugh, to set on
40 some quantity of barren° spectators to laugh too, though
in the meantime some necessary question of the play be
then to be considered. That's villainous, and shows a

most pitiful ambition in the fool that uses it. Go make
you ready.

[Exeunt Players.]

Enter Polonius, Guildenstern, and Rosencrantz.

How now, my lord, will the King hear this piece of work? 45

POLONIUS. And the Queen too, and that presently.°

HAMLET. Bid the players make haste. *[Exit Polonius.]*
Will you two help to hasten them?

ROSENCRANTZ.
Ay, my lord. *Exeunt they two.*

HAMLET. What ho, Horatio!

Enter Horatio.

HORATIO. Here, sweet lord, at your service. 50

HAMLET.
Horatio, thou art e'en as just a man
As e'er my conversation coped withal.°

HORATIO.
O, my dear lord—

HAMLET. Nay, do not think I flatter,
For what advancement may I hope from thee
That no revenue hast but thy good spirits 55
To feed and clothe thee? Why should the poor be
flattered?
No, let the candied° tongue lick absurd pomp,
And crook the pregnant° hinges of the knee
Where thrift° may follow fawning. Dost thou hear?
Since my dear soul was mistress of her choice 60
And could of men distinguish her election,°
Sh' hath sealed thee° for herself, for thou hast been
As one, in suffering all, that suffers nothing,
A man that Fortune's buffets and rewards
Hast ta'en with equal thanks; and blest are those 65
Whose blood° and judgment are so well commeddled°
That they are not a pipe for Fortune's finger
To sound what stop° she please. Give me that man
That is not passion's slave, and I will wear him
In my heart's core, ay, in my heart of heart, 70
As I do thee.—Something too much of this.—
There is a play tonight before the King.
One scene of it comes near the circumstance
Which I have told thee of my father's death.
I prithee, when thou seest that act afoot, 75
Even with the very comment of thy soul°

---

10 groundlings spectators who paid least and stood in the yard of
the theater   **11 capable of** able to understand   **11–12 dumb
shows** mimed performances, often used before Shakespeare's time
to precede a play or each act   **13 Termagant** a supposed deity of
the Mohammedans, not found in any English mediaval play but
elsewhere portrayed as violent and blustering. **Herod** Herod of
Jewry. (A character in *The Slaughter of the Innocents* and other cycle
plays. The part was played with great noise and fury.)   **19 modesty**
restraint, moderation. **from** contrary to   **22 scorn** i.e., something
foolish and deserving of scorn   **22–23 the very . . . time** i.e., the
present state of affairs   **23 his** its. **pressure** stamp, impressed character   **24 come tardy off** inadequately done   **25 the unskillful**
those lacking in judgment   **26 the censure . . . one** the judgment
of even one of whom   **26–27 your allowance** your scale of values
29 not . . . profanely (Hamlet anticipates his idea in lines 33–34
that some men were not made by God at all.)   **30 Christians** i.e.,
ordinary decent folk   **31 nor man** i.e., nor any human being at all
32 journeymen laborers who are not yet masters in their trade   **34
abominably** (Shakespeare's usual spelling, *abhominably*, suggests a
literal though etymologically incorrect meaning, "removed from
human nature.")   **35 indifferently** tolerably   **39 of them** some
among them   **40 barren** i.e., of wit

46 presently at once   **52 my . . . withal** my dealings encountered
57 candied sugared, flattering   **58 pregnant** compliant   **59 thrift**
profit   **61 could . . . election** could make distinguishing choices
among persons   **62 sealed thee** (Literally, as one would seal a legal
document to mark possession.)   **66 blood** passion. **commeddled**
commingled   **68 stop** hole in a wind instrument for controlling
the sound   **76 very . . . soul** your most penetrating observation
and consideration

Observe my uncle. If his occulted° guilt
Do not itself unkennel° in one speech,
It is a damnèd° ghost that we have seen,
80   And my imaginations are as foul
As Vulcan's stithy.° Give him heedful note,
For I mine eyes will rivet to his face,
And after we will both our judgments join
In censure of his seeming.°
HORATIO.   Well, my lord.
85   If 'a steal aught° the whilst this play is playing
And scape detecting, I will pay the theft.

> [*Flourish.*] *Enter trumpets and kettledrums, King,*
> *Queen, Polonius, Ophelia,* [*Rosencrantz, Guilden-*
> *stern, and other lords, with guards carrying torches*].

HAMLET. They are coming to the play. I must be idle.°
Get you a place. [*The King, Queen, and courtiers sit.*]
KING. How fares our cousin° Hamlet?
90   HAMLET. Excellent, i' faith, of the chameleon's dish:° I eat
the air, promise-crammed. You cannot feed capons° so.
KING. I have nothing with° this answer, Hamlet. These
words are not mine.°
HAMLET. No, nor mine now.° [*To Polonius.*] My lord, you
95   played once i' th' university, you say?
POLONIUS. That did I, my lord, and was accounted a good
actor.
HAMLET. What did you enact?
POLONIUS. I did enact Julius Caesar. I was killed i' the Capi-
100   tol; Brutus killed me.
HAMLET. It was a brute° part° of him to kill so capital a
calf° there.—Be the players ready?
ROSENCRANTZ. Ay, my lord. They stay upon° your
patience.
105   QUEEN. Come hither, my dear Hamlet, sit by me.
HAMLET. No, good Mother, here's metal° more attractive.
POLONIUS [*to the King*]. O, ho, do you mark that?
HAMLET. Lady, shall I lie in your lap?

> [*Lying down at Ophelia's feet.*]

OPHELIA. No, my lord.
HAMLET. I mean, my head upon your lap?   110
OPHELIA. Ay, my lord.
HAMLET. Do you think I meant country matters?°
OPHELIA. I think nothing, my lord.
HAMLET. That's a fair thought to lie between maids'
legs.   115
OPHELIA. What is, my lord?
HAMLET. Nothing.°
OPHELIA. You are merry, my lord.
HAMLET. Who, I?
OPHELIA. Ay, my lord.   120
HAMLET. O God, your only jig maker.° What should a man
do but be merry? For look you how cheerfully my mother
looks, and my father died within 's° two hours.
OPHELIA. Nay, 'tis twice two months, my lord.
HAMLET. So long? Nay then, let the devil wear black, for I'll   125
have a suit of sables.° O heavens! Die two months ago,
and not forgotten yet? Then there's hope a great man's
memory may outlive his life half a year. But, by 'r Lady, 'a
must build churches, then, or else shall 'a suffer not
thinking on,° with the hobbyhorse, whose epitaph is "For   130
O, for O, the hobbyhorse is forgot."°

The trumpets sound. Dumb show follows.

> *Enter a King and a Queen* [*very lovingly*]; *the*
> *Queen embracing him, and he her.* [*She kneels,*
> *and makes show of protestation unto him.*] *He*
> *takes her up, and declines his head upon her neck.*
> *He lies him down upon a bank of flowers. She,*
> *seeing him asleep, leaves him. Anon comes in*
> *another man, takes off his crown, kisses it, pours*
> *poison in the sleeper's ears, and leaves him. The*
> *Queen returns, finds the King dead, makes*
> *passionate action. The Poisoner with some three or*
> *four come in again, seem to condole with her. The*
> *dead body is carried away. The Poisoner woos the*
> *Queen with gifts; she seems harsh awhile, but in*
> *the end accepts love.*

---

77 occulted hidden   **78 unkennel** (As one would say of a fox driven from its lair.)   **79 damnèd** in league with Satan   **81 stithy**
smithy, place of stiths (anvils)   **84 censure of his seeming** judgment of his appearance or behavior   **85 If 'a steal aught** if he gets
away with anything   **87 idle** (1) unoccupied (2) mad   **89 cousin**
i.e., close relative   **90 chameleon's dish** (Chameleons were supposed to feed on air. Hamlet deliberately misinterprets the King's
fares as "feeds." By his phrase *eat the air* he also plays on the idea of
feeding himself with the promise of succession, of being the *heir*.)
91 capons roosters castrated and *crammed* with feed to make them
succulent   **92 have . . . with** make nothing of, or gain nothing
from   **93 are not mine** do not respond to what I asked   **94 nor
mine now** (Once spoken, words are proverbially no longer the
speaker's own—and hence should be uttered warily.)   **101 brute**
(The Latin meaning of *brutus*, "stupid," was often used punningly
with the name Brutus.)   **part** (1) deed (2) role   **102 calf** fool   **103
stay upon** await   **106 metal** substance that is *attractive*, i.e., mag-
netic, but with suggestion also of *mettle*, "disposition"

112 country matters sexual intercourse (making a bawdy pun on
the first syllable of *country*)   **117 Nothing** the figure zero or
naught, suggesting the female sexual anatomy. (*Thing* not infre-
quently has a bawdy connotation of male or female anatomy, and
the reference here could be male.)   **121 only jig maker** very best
composer of jigs, i.e., pointless merriment. (Hamlet replies sardon-
ically to Ophelia's observation that he is merry by saying, "If you're
looking for someone who is really merry, you've come to the right
person.")   **123 within 's** within this (i.e., these)   **126 suit of
sables** garments trimmed with the fur of the sable and hence suited
for a wealthy person, not a mourner (but with a pun on *sable*,
"black," ironically suggesting mourning once again)   **130 suffer
. . . on** undergo oblivion   **131 For . . . forgot** (Verse of a song occurring also in *Love's Labor's Lost*, 3.1.27–28. The hobbyhorse was a
character made up to resemble a horse and rider, appearing in the
morris dance and such May-game sports. This song laments the disappearance of such customs under pressure from the Puritans.)

[*Exeunt players.*]

OPHELIA. What means this, my lord?

HAMLET. Marry, this' miching mallico;° it means mischief.

135 OPHELIA. Belike° this show imports the argument° of the play.

      Enter Prologue.

HAMLET. We shall know by this fellow. The players cannot keep counsel;° they'll tell all.

OPHELIA. Will 'a tell us what this show meant?

140 HAMLET. Ay, or any show that you will show him. Be not you° ashamed to show, he'll not shame to tell you what it means.

OPHELIA. You are naught, you are naught.° I'll mark the play.

PROLOGUE.

145   For us, and for our tragedy,
    Here stooping° to your clemency,
    We beg your hearing patiently.   [*Exit.*]

HAMLET. Is this a prologue, or the posy of a ring?°

OPHELIA. 'Tis brief, my lord.

150 HAMLET. As woman's love.

    Enter [two Players as] King and Queen.

PLAYER KING.
    Full thirty times hath Phoebus' cart° gone round
    Neptune's salt wash° and Tellus'° orbèd ground,
    And thirty dozen moons with borrowed° sheen
    About the world have times twelve thirties been,
155   Since love our hearts and Hymen° did our hands
    Unite commutual° in most sacred bands.°

PLAYER QUEEN.
    So many journeys may the sun and moon
    Make us again count o'er ere love be done!
    But, woe is me, you are so sick of late,
160   So far from cheer and from your former state,
    That I distrust you. Yet, though I distrust,°
    Discomfort° you, my lord, it nothing° must.
    For women's fear and love hold quantity;°
    In neither aught, or in extremity.°

    Now, what my love is, proof° hath made you know, 165
    And as my love is sized,° my fear is so.
    Where love is great, the littlest doubts are fear;
    Where little fears grow great, great loves grows there.

PLAYER KING.
    Faith, I must leave thee, love, and shortly too;
    My operant powers° their functions leave to do.° 170
    And thou shalt live in this fair world behind,°
    Honored, beloved; and haply one as kind
    For husband shalt thou—

PLAYER QUEEN.   O, confound the rest!
    Such love must needs be treason in my breast.
    In second husband let me be accurst! 175
    None° wed the second but who° killed the first.

HAMLET. Wormwood, wormwood.°

PLAYER QUEEN.
    The instances° that second marriage move°
    Are base respects of thrift,° but none of love.
    A second time I kill my husband dead 180
    When second husband kisses me in bed.

PLAYER KING.
    I do believe you think what now you speak,
    But what we do determine oft we break.
    Purpose is but the slave to memory,°
    Of violent birth, but poor validity,° 185
    Which° now, like fruit unripe, sticks on the tree,
    But fall unshaken when they mellow be.
    Most necessary 'tis that we forget
    To pay ourselves what to ourselves is debt.°
    What to ourselves in passion we propose, 190
    The passion ending, doth the purpose lose.
    The violence of either grief or joy
    Their own enactures° with themselves destroy.
    Where joy most revels, grief doth most lament;
    Grief joys, joy grieves, on slender accident.° 195
    This world is not for aye,° nor 'tis not strange
    That even our loves should with our fortunes change;
    For 'tis a question left us yet to prove,
    Whether love lead fortune, or else fortune love.
    The great man down,° you mark his favorite flies; 200

---

133 **this' miching mallico** this is sneaking mischeif   135 **Belike** probably. **argument** plot   138 **counsel** secret   140–141 **Be not you** provided you are not   143 **naught** indecent. (Ophelia is reacting to Hamlet's pointed remarks about not being ashamed to show all.)   146 **stooping** bowing   148 **posy . . . ring** brief motto in verse inscribed in a ring   151 **Phoebus' cart** the sun-god's chariot, making its yearly cycle   152 **salt wash** the sea. **Tellus** goddes of the earth, of the *orbèd ground*   153 **borrowed** i.e., reflected   155 **Hymen** god of matrimony   156 **commutual** mutually. **bands** bonds   161 **distrust** am anxious about   162 **Discomfort** distress. **nothing** not at all   163 **hold quantity** keep proportion with one another   164 **In . . . extremity** i.e., women fear and love either too little or too much, but the two, fear and love, are equal in either case

165 **proof** experience   166 **sized** in size   170 **operant powers** vital functions. **leave to do** cease to perform   171 **behind** after I have gone   176 **None** i.e., let no woman. **but who** except the one who   177 **Wormwood** i.e., how bitter. (Literally, a bitter-tasting plant.)   178 **instances** motives. **move** motivate   179 **base . . . thrift** ignoble considerations of material prosperity   184 **Purpose . . . memory** our good intentions are subject to forgetfulness   185 **validity** strength, durability   186 **Which** i.e., purpose   188–189 **Most . . . debt** it's inevitable that in time we forget the obligations we have imposed on ourselves   193 **enactures** fulfillments   194–195 **Where . . . accident** the capacity for extreme joy and grief go together, and often one extreme is instantly changed into its opposite on the slightest provocation   196 **aye** ever   200 **down** fallen in fortune

The poor advanced makes friends of enemies.°
And hitherto° doth love on fortune tend;°
For who not needs° shall never lack a friend,
And who in want° a hollow friend doth try°
205 Directly seasons him° his enemy.
But, orderly to end where I begun,
Our wills and fates do so contrary run°
That our devices still° are overthrown;
Our thoughts are ours, their ends° none of our own.
210 So think thou wilt no second husband wed,
But die thy thoughts when thy first lord is dead.
PLAYER QUEEN.
Nor° earth to me give food, nor heaven light,
Sport and repose lock from me day and night,°
To desperation turn my trust and hope,
215 An anchor's cheer° in prison be my scope!°
Each opposite that blanks° the face of joy
Meet what I would have well and it destroy!°
Both here and hence° pursue me lasting strife
If, once a widow, ever I be wife!
220 HAMLET. If she should break it now!
PLAYER KING.
'Tis deeply sworn. Sweet, leave me here awhile;
My spirits° grow dull, and fain I would beguile
The tedious day with sleep.
PLAYER QUEEN.   Sleep rock thy brain,
And never come mischance between us twain!
          [He sleeps.] Exit [Player Queen].
225 HAMLET. Madam, how like you this play?
QUEEN. The lady doth protest too much,° methinks.
HAMLET. O, but she'll keep her word.
KING. Have you heard the argument?° Is there no offense°
in 't?
230 HAMLET. No, no, they do but jest, poison in jest.° No of-
fense° i' the world.
KING. What do you call the play?
HAMLET. *The Mousetrap.* Marry, how? Tropically.° This

play is the image of a murder done in Vienna. Gonzago
is the Duke's° name, his wife, Baptista. You shall   235
see anon. 'Tis a knavish piece of work, but what of
that? Your Majesty, and we that free° souls, it touches
us not. Let the galled jade° wince, our withers° are
unwrung.°

     Enter Lucianus.

This is one Lucianus, nephew to the King.   240
OPHELIA. You are as good as a chorus,° my lord.
HAMLET. I could interpret° between you and your love, if I
could see the puppets dallying.°
OPHELIA. You are keen, my lord, you are keen.°
HAMLET. It would cost you a groaning to take off mine   245
edge.
OPHELIA. Still better, and worse.°
HAMLET. So° you mis-take° your husbands. Begin, murderer;
leave thy damnable faces and begin. Come, the croaking
raven doth bellow for revenge.   250
LUCIANUS.
Thoughts black, hands apt, drugs fit, and time agree-
ing,
Confederate season,° else° no creature seeing,°
Thou mixture rank, of midnight weeds collected,
With Hecate's ban° thrice blasted, thrice infected,
Thy natural magic and dire property°   255
On wholesome life usurp immediately.
          [He pours the poison into the sleeper's ear.]
HAMLET. 'A poisons him i' the garden for his estate.° His°
name's Gonzago. The story is extant, and written in very
choice Italian. You shall see anon how the murderer gets
the love of Gonzago's wife.   260
          [Claudius rises.]
OPHELIA. The King rises.
HAMLET. What, frighted with false fire?°

201 The poor . . . enemies when one of humble station is promoted,
you see his enemies suddenly becoming his friends   202 hitherto up
to this point in the argument, or, to this extent. tend attend   203
who not needs he who is not in need (of wealth)   204 who in want
he who, being in need. try test (his generosity)   205 seasons him
ripens him into   207 Our . . . run what we want and what we get
go so contrary   208 devices still intentions continually   209
ends results   212 Nor let neither   213 Sport . . . night may day
deny me its pastimes and night its repose   215 anchor's cheer an-
chorite's or hermit's fate. my scope the extent of my happiness
216–217 Each . . . destroy may every adverse thing that causes the
face of joy to turn pale meet and destroy everything that I desire to
see prosper. blanks causes to blanch or grow pale   218 hence in the
life hereafter   222 spirits vital spirits   226 doth . . . much makes
too many promises and protestations   228 argument plot
228–231 offense . . . offense cause for objections . . . actual injury,
crime   230 jest make belief   233 Tropically figuratively. (The
First Quarto reading, *trapically,* suggests a pun on *trap* in *Mousetrap.*)

235 Duke's i.e., King's. (A slip that may be due to Shakespeare's
possible source, the alleged murder of the Duke of Urbino by Luigi
Gonzaga in 1538.)   237 free guiltless   238 galled jade horse
whose hide is rubbed by saddle or harness. withers the part between
the horse's shoulder blades   239 unwrung not rubbed sore   241
chorus (In many Elizabethan plays, the forthcoming action was explained by an actor known as the "chorus"; at a puppet show, the
actor who spoke the dialogue was known as an "interpreter," as indicated by the lines following.)   242 interpret (1) ventriloquize
the dialogue, as in pupet show (2) act as pander   243 puppets dallying (With suggestions of sexual play, continued in *keen,* "sexually
aroused," *groaning,* "moaning in pregnancy" and *edge,* "sexual desire" or "impetuosity.")   244 keen sharp, bitter   247 Still . . .
worse more keen, always *bettering* what other people say with witty
wordplay, but at the same time more offensive   248 So even thus
(in marriage). mis-take take falseheartedly and cheat on. (The marriage vows say "for better, for worse.")   252 Confederate season
the time and occasion conspiring (to assist the murderer). else otherwise. seeing seeing me   254 Hecate's ban the curse of Hecate,
the goddess of withcraft   255 dire property baleful quality   257
estate i.e., the kingship. His i.e., the King's   262 false fire the
blank discharge of a gun loaded with powder but no shot

QUEEN. How fares my lord?

POLONIUS. Give o'er the play.

265 KING. Give me some light. Away!

POLONIUS. Lights, lights, lights!

Exeunt all but Hamlet and Horatio.

HAMLET.

"Why, let the strucken deer go weep,
    The hart ungallèd° play.
For some must watch°, while some must sleep;
270   Thus runs the world away."°
Would not this,° sir, and a forest of feathers°—if the rest
of my fortunes turn Turk with° me—with two Provincial
roses° on my razed° shoes, get me a fellowship in a cry° of
players?°

275 HORATIO. Half a share.

HAMLET. A whole one, I.

"For thou dost know, O Damon° dear,
    This realm dismantled° was
Of Jove himself, and now reigns here
280   A very very—pajock."°

HORATIO. You might have rhymed.

HAMLET. O good Horatio, I'll take the ghost's word for a
thousand pound. Didst perceive?

HORATIO. Very well, my lord.

285 HAMLET. Upon the talk of the poisoning?

HORATIO. I did very well note him.

Enter Rosencrantz and Guildenstern.

HAMLET. Aha! Come, some music! Come, the recorders.°

"For if the King like not the comedy,
290   Why then, belike, he likes it not, perdy."°
    Come, some music.

GUILDENSTERN. Good my lord, vouchsafe me a word with
you.

HAMLET. Sir, a whole history.

295 GUILDENSTERN. The King, sir—

HAMLET. Ay, sir, what of him?

GUILDENSTGERN. Is in his retirement° marvelous distem-
pered.°

HAMLET. With drink, sir?

GUILDENSTERN. No, my lord, with choler.°   300

HAMLET. Your wisdom should show itself more richer to
signify this to the doctor, for for me to put him to his
purgation° would perhaps plunge him into more
choler.

GUILDENSTERN. Good my lord, put our discourse into some 305
frame° and start° not so wildly from my affair.

HAMLET. I am tame, sir. Pronounce.

GUILDENSTERN. The Queen, your mother, in most great affliction of spirit, hath sent me to you.

HAMLET. You are welcome.   310

GUILDENSTERN. Nay, good my lord, this courtesy is not of
the right breed.° If it shall please you to make me a
wholesome answer, I will do your mother's commandment; if not, your pardon° and my return shall be the end
of my business.   315

HAMLET. Sir, I cannot.

ROSENCRANTZ. What, my lord?

HAMLET. Make you a wholesome answer; my wit's diseased.
But, sir, such answer as I can make, you shall command,
or rather, as you say, my mother. Therefore no more, but 320
to the matter. My mother, you say—

ROSENCRANTZ. Then thus she says: your behavior hath
struck her into amazement and admiration.°

HAMLET. O wonderful son, that can so stonish a mother!
But is there no sequel at the heels of this mother's admi- 325
ration? Impart.

ROSENCRANTZ. She desires to speak with you in her closet°
ere you go to bed.

HAMLET. We shall obey, were she ten times our mother.
Have you any further trade with us?   330

ROSENCRANTZ. My lord, you once did love me.

HAMLET. And do still, by these pickers and stealers.°

ROSENCRANTZ. Good my lord, what is your cause of distemper? You do surely bar the door upon your own liberty° if
you deny° your griefs to your friend.   335

HAMLET. Sir, I lack advancement.

267–270 **Why . . . away** (Probably from an old ballad, with allusion to the popular belief that a wounded deer retires to weep and
die; compare with *As You Like It*, 2.1.33–66.)   268 **ungallèd** unaf-
flicted   269 **watch** remain awake   270 **Thus . . . away** thus the
world goes   271 **this** i.e., the play. **feathers** (Allusion to the
plumes that Elizabethan actors were fond of wearing.)   272 **turn
Turk with** turn renegade against, go back on   273 **Provincial
roses** rosettes of ribbon, named for roses grown in a part of France.
razed with ornamental slashing   273–274 **fellowship . . . players**
partnership in a theatrical company   274 **cry** pack (of hounds)
277 **Damon** the friend of Pythias, as Horatio is friend of Hamlet; or,
a traditional pastoral name   279–280 **This realm . . . pajock** i.e.,
Jove, representing divine authority and justice, has abandoned this
realm to its own devices, leaving in his stead only a peacock or vain
pretender to virtue (though the rhyme-word expected in place of
pajock or "peacock" suggests that the realm is now ruled over by an
"ass").   278 **dismantled** stripped, divested   287–288 **recorders**
wind instruments of the flute kind   290 **perdy** (A corruption of
the French *par dieu*, "by God.")

297 **retirement** withdrawal to his chambers   297–298 **distem-
pered** out of humor. (But Hamlet deliberately plays on the wider application to any illness of mind or body, as in lines 333–334, especially to drunkenness.)   300 **choler** anger. (But Hamlet takes the
word in its more basic humoral sense of "bilious disorder.")
302–303 **purgation** (Hamlet hints at something going beyond
medical treatment to blood-letting and the extraction of confession.)   306 **frame** order. **start** shy or jump away (like a horse; the
opposite of *tame* in line 307)   312 **breed** (1) kind (2) breeding,
manners   314 **pardon** permission to depart   323 **admiration** bewilderment   327 **closet** private chamber   332 **pickers and stealers** i.e., hands. (So called from the catechism, "to keep my hands
from picking and stealing.")   334 **liberty** i.e., being freed from *distemper*, line 334; but perhaps with a veiled threat as well. **335 deny**
refuse to share

ROSENCRANTZ. How can that be, when you have the voice
    of the King himself for our succession in Denmark?
HAMLET. Ay, sir, but "While the grass grows"°—the proverb
340   is something° musty.

        Enter the Players° with recorders.

    O, the recorders. Let me see one. [*He takes a recorder.*]
    To withdraw° with you: why do you go about to recover
    the wind° of me, as if you would drive me into a toil?°
GUILDENSTERN. O, my lord, if my duty be too bold, my love
345   is too unmannerly.°
HAMLET. I do not well understand that.° Will you play upon
    this pipe?
GUILDENSTERN. My lord, I cannot.
HAMLET. I pray you.
350 GUILDENSTERN. Believe me, I cannot.
HAMLET. I do beseech you.
GUILDENSTERN. I know no touch of it, my lord.
HAMLET. It is as easy as lying. Govern these ventages° with
    your fingers and thumb, give it breath with your mouth,
355   and it will discourse most eloquent music. Look you,
    these are the stops.
GUILDENSTERN. But these cannot I command to any utter-
    ance of harmony. I have not the skill.
HAMLET. Why, look you now, how unworthy a thing you
360   make of me! You would play upon me, you would seem to
    know my stops, you would pluck out the heart of my mys-
    tery, you would sound° me from my lowest note to the top
    of my compass,° and there is much music, excellent
    voice, in this little organ,° yet cannot you make it speak.
365   'Sblood, do you think I am easier to be played on than a
    pipe? Call me what instrument you will, though you can
    fret° me, you cannot play upon me.

        Enter Polonius.

    God bless you, sir!
POLONIUS. My lord, the Queen would speak with you, and
370   presently.°
HAMLET. Do you see yonder cloud that's almost in shape of a
    camel?
POLONIUS. By the Mass and 'tis, like a camel indeed.

HAMLET. Methinks it is like a weasel.
POLONIUS. It is backed like a weasel. 375
HAMLET. Or like a whale.
POLONIUS. Very like a whale.
HAMLET. Then I will come to my mother by and by.°
    [*Aside.*] They fool me° to the top of my bent.°—I will
    come by and by. 380
POLONIUS. I will say so. [*Exit.*]
HAMLET. "By and by" is easily said. Leave me, friends.
        [*Exeunt all but Hamlet.*]
    'Tis now the very witching time° of night,
    When churchyards yawn and hell itself breathes out
    Contagion to this world. Now could I drink hot blood 385
    And do such bitter business as the day
    Would quake to look on. Soft, now to my mother.
    O heart, lose not thy nature!° Let not ever
    The soul of Nero° enter this firm bosom.
    Let me be cruel, not unnatural; 390
    I will speak daggers to her, but use none.
    My tongue and soul in this be hypocrites:
    How in my words soever° she be shent,°
    To give them seals° never my soul consent! *Exit.*

3.3°   *Enter King, Rosencrantz, and Guildenstern.*
KING.
    I like him° not, nor stands it safe with us
    To let his madness range. Therefore prepare you.
    I your commission will forthwith dispatch,°
    And he to England shall along with you.
    The terms of our estate° may not endure 5
    Hazard so near 's as doth hourly grow
    Out of his brows.°
GUILDENSTERN.   We will ourselves provide.
    Most holy and religious fear° it is
    To keep those many many bodies safe
    That live and feed upon Your Majesty. 10
ROSENCRANTZ.
    The single and peculiar° life is bound
    With all the strength and armor of the mind
    To keep itself from noyance,° but much more

---

339 While . . . grows (The rest of the proverb is "the silly horse
starves"; Hamlet may not live long enough to succeed to the kingdom.) **340 something** somewhat. **s.d. Players** actors **342 withdrawn** speak privately **342–343 recover the wind** get to the
windward side (thus driving the game into the *toil*, or "net") **344
toil** snare **344–345 if . . . unmannerly** if I am using an unmannerly boldness, it is my love that occasions it **346 I . . . that** i.e., I
don't understand how genuine love can be unmannerly **353 ven-
tages** finger-holes or *stops* (line 357) of the recorder **362 sound**
(1) fathom (2) produce sound in **363 compass** range (of voice)
364 organ musical instrument **367 fret** irritate (with a quibble
on *fret*, meaning the piece of wood, gut, or metal that regulates the
fingering on an instrument) **370 presently** at once

378 by and by quite soon **379 fool me** trifle with me, humor my
fooling. **top of my bent** limit of my ability or endurance. (Literally,
the extent to which a bow may be bent.) **383 witching time** time
when spells are cast and evil is abroad **388 nature** natural feeling
389 Nero murderer of his mother, Agrippina **393 How . . . so-
ever** however much by my words. **shent** rebuked **394 give them
seals** i.e., confirm them with deeds
3.3. Location: The castle.
1 him i.e., his behavior **3 dispatch** prepare, cause to be drawn up
5 terms of our estate circumstances of my royal position **7 Out of
his brows** i.e., from his brain, in the form of plots and threats **8
religious fear** sacred concern **11 single and peculiar** individual
and private **13 noyance** harm

That sprit upon whose weal depends and rests
15 The lives of many. The cess° of majesty
Dies not alone, but like a gulf° doth draw
What's near it with it; or it is a massy° wheel
Fixed on the summit of the highest mount,
To whose huge spokes ten thousand lesser things
20 Are mortised° and adjoined, which, when it falls,°
Each small annexment, petty consequence,°
Attends° the boisterous ruin. Never alone
Did the King sigh, but with a general groan.

KING.
Arm° you, I pray you, to this speedy voyage,
25 For we will fetters put about this fear,
Which now goes too free-footed.

ROSENCRANTZ.   We will haste us.

Exeunt gentlemen [Rosencrantz and Guildenstern].

Enter Polonius.

POLONIUS.
My lord, he's going to his mother's closet.
Behind the arras° I'll convey myself
To hear the process.° I'll warrant she'll tax him home,°
30 And, as you said—and wisely was it said—
'Tis meet° that some more audience than a mother,
Since nature makes them partial, should o'erhear
The speech, of vantage.° Fare you well, my liege.
I'll call upon you ere you go to bed.
And tell you what I know.
35 KING.   Thanks, dear my lord.

Exit [Polonius]

O, my offense is rank! It smells to heaven.
It hath the primal eldest curse° upon 't,
A brother's murder. Pray can I not,
Though inclination be as sharp as will;°
40 My stronger guilt defeats my strong intent,
And like a man to double business bound°
I stand in pause where I shall first begin,
And both neglect. What if this cursèd hand
Were thicker than itself with brother's blood,
45 Is there not rain enough in the sweet heavens

To wash it white as snow? Whereto serves mercy
But to confront the visage of offense?°
And what's in prayer but this twofold force,
To be forestallèd° ere we come to fall,
Or pardoned being down? Then I'll look up. 50
My fault is past. But O, what form of prayer
Can serve my turn? "Forgive me my foul murder"?
That cannot be, since I am still possessed
Of those effects for which I did the murder:
My crown, mine own ambition, and my queen. 55
May one be pardoned and retain th' offense?°
In the corrupted currents° of this world
Offense's gilded hand° may shove by° justice,
And oft 'tis seen the wicked prize° itself
Buys out the law. But 'tis not so above. 60
There° is no shuffling,° there the action lies°
In his° true nature, and we ourselves compelled,
Even to the teeth and forehead° of our faults,
To give in° evidence. What then? What rests?°
Try what repentance can. What can it not? 65
Yet what can it, when one cannot repent?
O wretched state, O bosom black as death,
O limèd °soul that, struggling to be free,
Art more engaged!° Help, angels! Make assay.°
Bow, stubborn knees, and heart with strings of steel, 70
Be soft as sinews of the newborn babe!
All may be well.   [*He kneels.*]

Enter Hamlet.

HAMLET.
Now might I do it pat,° now 'a is a-praying;
And now I'll do 't. [*He draws his sword.*] And so 'a goes
to heaven,
And so am I revenged. That would be scanned:° 75
A villain kills my father, and for that,
I, his sole son, do this same villain send
To heaven.
Why, this is hire and salary, not revenge.
'A took my father grossly, full of bread,° 80
With all his crimes broad blown,° as flush° as May;

---

15 **cess** decease, cessation   16 **gulf** whirlpool   17 **massy** massive
20 **mortised** fastened (as with a fitted joint). **when it falls** i.e.,
when it descends, like the wheel of Fortune, bringing a king down
with it   21 **Each . . . consequence** i.e., every hanger-on and unim-
portant person or thing connected with the King   22 **Attends** par-
ticipates in   24 **Arm** prepare   28 **arras** screen of tapestry placed
around the walls of household apartments. (On the Elizabethan
stage, the arras was presumably over a door or discovery space in the
tiring-house facade.)   29 **process** proceedings. **tax him home** reprove him severely   31 **meet** fitting   33 **of vantage** from an ad-
vantageous place, or, in addition   37 **the primal eldest curse** the
curse of Cain, the first murderer; he killed his brother Abel   39
Though . . . will though my desire is as strong as my determination
41 **bound** (1) destined (2) obliged. (The King wants to repent and
still enjoy what he has gained.)

46–47 **Whereto . . . offense** what function does mercy serve other
than to meet sin face to face?   49 **forestallèd** prevented (from sin-
ning)   56 **th' offense** the thing for which one offended   57 **currents** courses   58 **gilded hand** hand offering gold as a bribe. **shove
by** thrust aside   59 **wicked prize** prize won by wickedness   61
There i.e., in heaven. **shuffling** escape by trickery. **the action lies**
the accusation is made manifest. (A legal metaphor.)   62 **his** its
63 **to the teeth and forehead** face to face, concealing nothing   64
give in provide. **rests** remains   68 **limèd** caught as with birdlime, a
sticky substance used to ensnare birds   69 **engaged** entangled.
assay trial. (Said to himself.)   73 **pat** opportunely   75 **would be
scanned** needs to be looked into, or, would be interpreted as follows
80 **grossly, full of bread** i.e., enjoying his worldly pleasures rather
than fasting. (See Ezekiel 16:49.)   81 **crimes broad blown** sins in
full bloom. **flush** vigorous

And how his audit° stands who knows save° heaven?
But in our circumstance and course of thought°
'Tis heavy with him. And am I then revenged,
85 To take him in the purging of his soul,
When he is fit and seasoned° for his passage?
No!
Up, sword, and know thou a more horrid hent.°

                             [He puts up his sword.]

When he is drunk asleep, or in his rage°
90 Or in th' incestuous pleasure of his bed,
At game,° a-swearing, or about some act
That has no relish° of salvation in 't —
Then trip him, that his heels may kick at heaven,
And that his soul may be as damned and black
95 As hell, whereto it goes. My mother stays.°
This physic° but prolongs thy sickly days.   *Exit.*
KING.
My words fly up, my thoughts remain below.
Words without thoughts never to heaven go.   *Exit.*

3 . 4 °   *Enter [Queen] Gertrude and Polonius.*
POLONIUS.
'A will come straight. Look you lay home° to him.
Tell him his pranks have been too broad° to bear with,
And that Your Grace screened and stood between
Much heat° and him. I'll shroud° me even here.
5 Pray you, be round° with him.
HAMLET (*within*). Mother, Mother, Mother!
QUEEN. I'll warrant you, fear me not.
Withdraw, I hear him coming.

                [Polonius hides behind the arras.]

    Enter Hamlet.

HAMLET. Now, Mother, what's the matter?
QUEEN.
10 Hamlet, thou hast thy father° much offended.
HAMLET.
Mother, you have my father much offended.
QUEEN.
Come, come, you answer with an idle° tongue.

HAMLET.
Go, go, you question with a wicked tongue.
QUEEN.
Why, how now, Hamlet?
HAMLET.   What's the matter now?
QUEEN.
Have you forgot me?°
HAMLET.   No, by the rood,° not so: 15
You are the Queen, your husband's brother's wife,
And—would it were not so!—you are my mother.
QUEEN.
Nay, then, I'll set those to you that can speak.°
HAMLET.
Come, come, and sit you down; you shall not budge.
You go not till I set you up a glass   20
Where you may see the inmost part of you.
QUEEN.
What will thou do? Thou wilt not murder me?
Help, ho!
POLONIUS [*behind the arras*]. What ho! Help!
HAMLET [*drawing*].
How now? A rat? Dead for a ducat, dead!°   25

    [He thrusts his rapier through the arras.]

POLONIUS [*behind the arras*].
O, I am slain!   *[He falls and dies.]*
QUEEN.   O me, what hast thou done?
HAMLET. Nay, I know not. Is it the King?
QUEEN.
O, what a rash and bloody deed is this!
HAMLET.
A bloody deed—almost as bad, good Mother,
As kill a king, and marry with his brother.   30
QUEEN.
As kill a king!
HAMLET.   Ay, lady, it was my word.
        [He parts the arras and discovers Polonius.]
Thou wretched, rash, intruding fool, farewell!
I took thee for thy better. Take thy fortune.
Thou find'st to be too busy° is some danger.—
Leave wringing of your hands. Peace, sit you down,   35
And let me wring your heart, for so I shall,
If it be made of penetrable stuff,
If damnèd custom° have not brazed° it so
That it be proof° and bulwark against sense.°
QUEEN.
What have I done, that thou dar'st wag thy tongue   40
In noise so rude against me?
HAMLET.   Such an act

---

82 audit account. **save** except for **83 in . . . thought** as we see it from our mortal perspective **86 seasoned** matured, readied **88 know . . . hent** await to be grasped by me on a more horrid occasion. **hent** act of seizing **89 drunk . . . rage** dead drunk, or in a fit of sexual passion **91 game** gambling **92 relish** trace, savor **95 stays** awaits (me) **96 physic** purging (by prayer), or, Hamlet's postponement of the killing
3.4. Location: The Queen's private chamber.
1 lay home thrust to the heart, reprove him soundly **2 broad** unrestrained **4 Much heat** i.e., the King's anger. **shroud** conceal (with ironic fitness to Polonius' imminent death. The word is only in the First Quarto; the Second Quarto and the Folio read "silence.") **5 round** blunt **10 thy father** i.e., your stepfather, Claudius **12 idle** foolish

15 forgot me i.e., forgotten that I am your mother. **rood** cross of Christ **18 speak** i.e., to someone so rude **25 Dead for a ducat** i.e., I bet a ducat he's dead; or, a ducat is his life's fee **34 busy** nosey **38 damnèd custom** habitual wickedness. **brazed** brazened, hardened **39 proof** armor. **sense** feeling

That blurs the grace and blush of modesty,
Calls virtue hypocrite, takes off the rose
From the fair forehead of an innocent love
45 And sets a blister° there, makes marriage vows
As false as dicers' oaths. O, such a deed
As from the body of contraction° plucks
The very soul, and sweet religion makes°
A rhapsody° of words. Heaven's face does glow
50 O'er this solidity and compound mass
With tristful visage, as against the doom,
Is thought-sick at the act.°
QUEEN.   Ay me, what act,
That roars so loud and thunders in the index?°
HAMLET [*showing her two likenesses*].
Look here upon this picture, and on this,
55 The counterfeit presentment° of two brothers.
See what a grace was seated on this brow:
Hyperion's° curls, the front° of Jove himself,
An eye like Mars° to threaten and command,
A station° like the herald Mercury°
60 New-lighted° on a heaven-kissing hill—
A combination and a form indeed
Where every god did seem to set his seal°
To give the world assurance of a man.
This was your husband. Look you now what follows:
65 Here is your husband, like a mildewed ear,°
Blasting° his wholesome brother. Have you eyes?
Could you on this fair mountain leave° to feed
And batten° on this moor?° Ha, have you eyes?
You cannot call it love, for at your age
70 The heyday° in the blood° is tame, it's humble,
And waits upon the judgment, and what judgment
Would step from this to this? Sense,° sure, you have
Else could you not have motion, but sure that sense
Is apoplexed,° for madness would not err,°

Nor sense to ecstasy was ne'er so thralled,   75
But° it reserved some quantity of choice
To serve in such a difference.° What devil was 't
That thus hath cozened° you at hoodman-blind?°
Eyes without feeling, feeling without sight,
Ears without hands or eyes, smelling sans° all,   80
Or but a sickly part of one true sense
Could not so mope.° O shame, where is thy blush?
Rebellious hell,
If thou canst mutine° in a matron's bones,
To flaming youth let virtue be as wax   85
And melt in her own fire.° Proclaim no shame
When the compulsive ardor gives the charge,
Since frost itself as actively doth burn,
And reason panders will.°
QUEEN. O Hamlet, speak no more!   90
Thou turn'st mine eyes into my very soul,
And there I see such black and grainèd° spots
As will not leave their tinct.°
HAMLET.   Nay, but to live
In the rank sweat of an enseamèd° bed,
Stewed° in corruption, honeying and making love   95
Over the nasty sty!
QUEEN. O, speak to me no more!
These words like daggers enter in my ears.
No more, sweet Hamlet!
HAMLET.   A murderer and a villain,
A slave that is not twentieth part the tithe°   100
Of your precedent lord,° a vice of kings,
A cutpurse of the empire and the rule,
That from a shelf the precious diadem stole
And put it in his pocket!
QUEEN. No more!   105

Enter Ghost [*in his nightgown*].

HAMLET. A king of shreds and patches°—
Save me, and hover o'er me with your wings,

---

45 sets a blister i.e., brands as a harlot   **47 contraction** the marriage contract   **48 sweet religion makes** i.e., makes marriage vows   **49 rhapsody** senseless string   **49–52 Heaven's . . . act** heaven's face blushes at this solid world compounded of the various elements, with sorrowful face as though the day of doom were near, and is sick with horror at the deed (i.e., Gertrude's marriage)   **53 index** table of contents, prelude or preface   **55 counterfeit presentment** portrayed representation   **57 Hyperion's** the sun-god's. **front** brow   **58 Mars** god of war   **59 station** manner of standing. **Mercury** winged messenger of the gods   **60 New-lighted** newly alighted   **62 set his seal** i.e., affix his approval   **65 ear** i.e., of grain   **66 Blasting** blighting   **67 leave** cease   **68 batten** gorge. **moor** barren or marshy ground (suggesting also "dark-skinned") **70 heyday** state of excitement. **blood** passion   **72 Sense** perception through the five senses (the function of the middle or sensible soul)   **74 apoplexed** paralyzed. (Hamlet goes on to explain that, without such a paralysis of will, mere madness would not so err, nor would the five senses so enthrall themselves to *ecstacy* or lunacy; even such deranged states of mind would be able to make the obvious choice between Hamlet Senior and Claudius.) **err** so err

76 But but that   **77 To . . . difference** to help in making a choice between two such men   **78 cozened** cheated. **hoodman-blind** blindman's buff. (In this game, says Hamlet, the devil must have pushed Claudius toward Gertrude while she was blindfolded.)   **80 sans** without   **82 mope** be dazed, act aimlessly   **84 mutine** incite mutiny   **85–86 be as wax . . . fire** melt like a candle or stick of sealing wax held over the candle flame   **86–89 Proclaim . . . will** call it no shameful business when the compelling ardor of youth delivers the attack, i.e., commits lechery, since the *frost* of advanced age burns with as active a fire of lust and reason perverts itself by fomenting lust rather than restraining it.   **92 grainèd** dyed in grain, indelible   **93 leave their tinct** surrender their color   **94 enseamèd** saturated in the grease and filth of passionate lovemaking   **95 Stewed** soaked, bathed (with a suggestion of "stew," brothel)   **100 tithe** tenth part   **101 precedent lord** former husband. **vice** buffoon. (A reference to the Vice of the morality plays.)   **106 shreds and patches** i.e., motley, the traditional costume of the clown or fool

You heavenly guards! What would your gracious figure?
QUEEN. Alas, he's mad!
HAMLET.
110 Do you not come your tardy son to chide,
That, lapsed° in time and passion, lets go by
Th' important° acting of your dread command?
O, say!
GHOST.
Do not forget. This visitation
115 Is but to whet thy almost blunted purpose.
But look, amazement° on thy mother sits.
O, step between her and her fighting soul!
Conceit° in weakest bodies strongest works.
Speak to her, Hamlet.
HAMLET.   How is it with you, lady?
120 QUEEN. Alas, how is 't with you,
That you do bend your eye on vacancy,
And with th' incorporal° air do hold discourse?
Forth at your eyes your spirits wildly peep,
And, as the sleeping soldiers in th' alarm,°
125 Your bedded° hair, like life in excrements,°
Start up and stand on end. O gentle son,
Upon the heat and flame of thy distemper°
Sprinkle cool patience. Whereon do you look?
HAMLET.
On him, on him! Look you how pale he glares!
130 His form and cause conjoined,° preaching to stones,
Would make them capable.°—Do not look upon me,
Lest with this piteous action you convert
My stern effects.° Then what I have to do
Will want true color—tears perchance for blood.°
135 QUEEN. To whom do you speak this?
HAMLET. Do you see nothing there?
QUEEN.
Nothing at all, yet all that is I see.
HAMLET. Nor did you nothing hear?
QUEEN. No, nothing but ourselves.
HAMLET.
140 Why, look you there, look how it steals away!
My father, in his habit° as° he lived!
Look where he goes even now out at the portal!

Exit Ghost.

QUEEN.
This is the very° coinage of your brain.
This bodiless creation ecstasy
Is very cunning in.°   145
HAMLET. Ecstasy?
My pulse as yours doth temperately keep time,
And makes as healthful music. It is not madness
That I have uttered. Bring me to the test,
And I the matter will reword,° which madness   150
Would gambol° from. Mother, for love of grace,
Lay not that flattering unction° to your soul
That not your trespass but my madness speaks.
It will but skin° and film the ulcerous place,
Whiles rank corruption, mining° all within,   155
Infects unseen. Confess yourself to heaven,
Repent what's past, avoid what is to come,
And do not spread the compost° on the weeds
To make them ranker. Forgive me this my virtue;°
For in the fatness° of these pursy° times   160
Virtue itself of vice must pardon beg,
Yea, curb° and woo for leave° to do him good.
QUEEN.
O Hamlet, thou hast cleft my heart in twain.
HAMLET.
O, throw away the worser part of it,
And live the purer with the other half.   165
Good night. But go not to my uncle's bed;
Assume a virtue, if you have it not.
That monster, custom, who will sense doth eat,°
Of habits devil,° is angel yet in this,
That to the use of actions fair and good   170
He likewise gives a frock or livery°
That aptly° is put on. Refrain tonight,
And that shall lend a kind of easiness
To the next abstinence; the next more easy;
For use° almost can change the stamp of nature,° 175
And either° . . . the devil, or throw him out
With wondrous potency. Once more, good night;
And when you are desirous to be blest,

---

111 lapsed delaying **112 important** importunate, urgent **116 amazement** distraction **118 Conceit** imagination **122 incorporal** immaterial **124 as . . . alarm** like soldiers called out of sleep by an alarum **125 bedded** laid flat. **like life in excrements** i.e., as though hair, an outgrowth of the body, had a life of its own. (Hair was thought to be lifeless because it lacks sensation, and so its standing on end would be unnatural and ominous.) **127 distemper** disorder **130 His . . . conjoined** his appearance joined to his cause for speaking **131 capable** receptive **132–133 convert . . . effects** divert me from my stern duty **134 want . . . blood** lack plausibility so that (with a play on the normal sense of *color*) I shall shed colorless tears instead of blood **141 habit** clothes. **as** as when

143 very mere **144–145 This . . . in** madness is skillful in creating this kind of hallucination **150 reword** repeat word for word **151 gambol** skip away **152 unction** ointment **154 skin** grow a skin for **155 mining** working under the surface **158 compost** manure **159 this my virtue** my virtuous talk in reproving you **160 fatness** grossness. **pursy** flabby, out of shape **162 curb** bow, bend the knee. **leave** permission **168 who . . . eat** which consumes all proper or natural feeling, all sensibility **169 Of habits devil** devil-like in prompting evil habits **171 livery** an outer appearance, a customary garb (and hence a predisposition easily assumed in time of stress) **172 aptly** readily **175 use** habit. **the stamps of nature** our inborn traits **176 And either** (A defective line, usually emended by inserting the word *master* after *either*, following the Fourth Quarto and early editors.)

I'll blessing beg of you.° For this same lord,

[*pointing to Polonius*]

180 I do repent; but heaven hath pleased it so
To punish me with this, and this with me,
That I must be their scourge and minister.°
I will bestow° him, and will answer° well
The death I gave him. So, again, good night.
185 I must be cruel only to be kind.
This° bad begins, and worse remains behind.°
One word more, good lady.

QUEEN.   What shall I do?

HAMLET.
Not this by no means that I bid you do:
Let the bloat° king tempt you again to bed,
190 Pinch wanton° on your cheek, call you his mouse,
And let him, for a pair of reechy kisses,
Or paddling° in your neck with his damned fingers,
Make you to ravel all this matter out°
That I essentially am not in madness,
195 But mad in craft.° 'Twere good° you let him know,
For who that's but a queen, fair, sober, wise,
Would from a paddock,° from a bat, a gib,°
Such dear concernings° hide? Who would do so?
No, in despite of sense and secrecy,°
200 Unpeg the basket° on the house's top,
Let the birds fly, and like the famous ape,°
To try conclusions,° in the basket creep
And break your own neck down.°

QUEEN.
Be thou assured, if words be made of breath,
205 And breath of life, I have no life to breathe
What thou hast said to me.

HAMLET.
I must to England. You know that?

QUEEN.   Alack,
I had forgot. 'Tis so concluded on.

HAMLET.
There's letters sealed, and my two schoolfellows,
Who I will trust as I will adders fanged,   210
They bear the mandate; they must sweep my way
And marshall me to knavery.° Let it work.°
For 'tis the sport to have the enginer°
Hoist with° his own petard,° and 't shall go hard
But I will° delve one yard below their mines°   215
And blow them at the moon. O, 'tis most sweet
When in one line° two crafts° directly meet.
This man shall set me packing.°
I'll lug the guts into the neighbor room.
Mother, good night indeed. This counselor   220
Is now most still, most secret, and most grave,
Who was in life a foolish prating knave.—
Come, sir, to draw toward an end° with you.—
Good night, Mother.

Exeunt [separately, Hamlet dragging in Polonius].

4.1°   *Enter King and Queen,° with Rosencrantz and*
Guildenstern.

KING.
There's matter° in these sighs, these profound heaves.°
You must translate; 'tis fit we understand them.
Where is your son?

QUEEN.
Bestow this place on us a little while.

[*Exeunt Rosencrantz and Guildenstern.*]
Ah, mine own lord, what have I seen tonight!   5

KING.
What, Gertrude? How does Hamlet?

QUEEN.
Mad as the sea and wind when both contend
Which is the mightier. In his lawless fit,

178–179 when . . . you i.e., when you are ready to be penitent and seek God's blessing, I will ask your blessing as a dutiful son should **182 their scourge and minister** i.e., agent of heavenly retribution. (By *scourge*, Hamlet also suggests that he himself will eventually suffer punishment in the process of fulfilling heaven's will.) **183 bestow** stow, dispose of. **answer** account or pay for. **186 This** i.e., the killing of Polonius. **behind** to come **189 bloat** bloated **190 Pinch wanton** i.e., leave his love pinches on your cheeks, branding you as wanton **191 reechy** dirty, filthy **192 paddling** fingering amorously **193 ravel . . . out** unravel, disclose **195 in craft** by cunning. **good** (Said sarcastically; also the following eight lines.) **197 paddock** toad. **gib** tomcat **198 dear concernings** important affairs **199 sense and secrecy** secrecy that common sense requires **200 Unpeg the basket** open the cage, i.e., let out the secret **201 famous ape** (In a story now lost.) **202 try conclusions** test the outcome (in which the ape apparently enters a cage from which birds have been released and then tries to fly out of the cage as they have done, falling to its death) **203 down** in the fall; utterly

211–212 sweep . . . knavery sweep a path before me and conduct me to some *knavery* or treachery prepared for me **212 work** proceed **213 enginer** maker of military contrivances **214 Hoist with** blown up by. **petard** an explosive used to blow in a door or make a breach **214–215 't shal . . . will** unless luck is against me, I will **215 mines** tunnels used in warfare to undermine the enemy's emplacements; Hamlet will countermine by going under their mines **217 in one line** i.e., mines and countermines on a collision course, or the countermines directly below the mines. **crafts** acts of guile, plots **218 set me packing** set me to making schemes, and set me to lugging (him), and, also, send me off in a hurry **223 draw . . . end** finish up (with a pun on *draw*, "pull") **4.1. Location:** The castle.
s.d. Enter . . . Queen (Some editors argue that Gertrude never exits in 3.4 and that the scene is continuous here, as suggested in the Folio, but the Second Quarto marks an entrance for her and at line 35 Claudius speaks of Gertrude's *closet* as though it were elsewhere. A short time has elapsed, during which the King has become aware of her highly wrought emotional state.) **1 matter** significance. **heaves** heavy sighs

Behind the arras hearing something stir,
10 Whips out his rapier, cries, "A rat, a rat!"
And in this brainish apprehension° kills
The unseen good old man.

KING.
                              O heavy° deed!
It had been so with us,° had we been there.
His liberty is full of threats to all—
15 To you yourself, to us, to everyone.
Alas, how shall this bloody deed be answered?°
It will be laid to us, whose providence°
Should have kept short,° restrained, and out of haunt°
This mad young man. But so much was our love,
20 We would not understand what was most fit,
But, like the owner of a foul disease,
To keep it from divulging,° let it feed
Even on the pith of life. Where is he gone?

QUEEN.
To draw apart the body he hath killed,
25 O'er whom his very madness, like some ore°
Among a mineral° of metals base,
Shows itself pure: 'a weeps for what is done.

KING. O Gertrude, come away!
The sun no sooner shall the mountains touch
30 But we will ship him hence, and this vile deed
We must with all our majesty and skill
Both countenance° and excuse.—Ho, Guildenstern!

Enter Rosencrantz and Guildenstern.

Friends both, go join you with some further aid.
Hamlet in madness hath Polonius slain,
35 And from his mother's closet hath he dragged him.
Go seek him out, speak fair, and bring the body
Into the chapel. I pray you, haste in this.
                    [*Exeunt Rosencrantz and Guildenstern.*]
Come, Gertrude, we'll call up our wisest friends
And let them know both what we mean to do
40 And what's ultimately done° . . . .
Whose whisper o'er the world's diameter,°
As level° as the cannon to his blank,°
Transports his poisoned shot, may miss our name
And hit the woundless° air. O, come away!
45 My soul is full of discord and dismay.   *Exeunt.*

---

11 **brainish apprehension** headstrong conception 12 **heavy** grievous 13 **us** i.e., me. (The royal "we"; also in line 15.) 16 **answered** explained 17 **providence** foresight 18 **short** i.e., on a short tether. **out of haunt** secluded 22 **divulging** becoming evident 25 **ore** vein of gold 26 **mineral** mine 32 **countenance** put the best face on 40 **And . . . done** (A defective line; conjectures as to the missing words include *So, haply, slander* [Capell and others]; *For, haply, slander* [Theobald and others]; and *So envious slander* [Jenkins].) 41 **diameter** extent from side to side. 42 **As level** with as direct aim. **his blank** its target at point-blank range. 44 **woundless** invulnerable

---

4 . 2 °   *Enter Hamlet.*

HAMLET. Safely stowed.
ROSENCRANTZ, GUILDENSTERN (*within*). Hamlet! Lord
    Hamlet!
HAMLET. But soft, what noise? Who calls on Hamlet? O,
    here they come.   5

        Enter Rosencrantz and Guildenstern.

ROSENCRANTZ.
    What have you done, my lord, with the dead body?
HAMLET.
    Compounded it with dust, whereto 'tis kin.
ROSENCRANTZ.
    Tell us where 'tis, that we may take it thence
    And bear it to the chapel.
HAMLET. Do not believe it.   10
ROSENCRANTZ. Believe what?
HAMLET. That I can keep your counsel and not mine own.°
    Besides, to be demanded of° a sponge, what replication°
    should be made by the son of a king?
ROSENCRANTZ. Take you me for a sponge, my lord?   15
HAMLET. Ay, sir, that soaks up the King's countenance,° his
    rewards, his authorities.° But such officers do the King
    best service in the end. He keeps them, like an ape, an
    apple, in the corner of his jaw, first mouthed to be last
    swallowed. When he needs what you have gleaned, it is   20
    but squeezing you, and, sponge, you shall be dry again.
ROSENCRANTZ. I understand you not, my lord.
HAMLET. I am glad of it. A knavish speech sleeps° in a fool-
    ish ear.
ROSENCRANTZ. My lord, you must tell us where the body is 25
    and go with us to the King.
HAMLET. The body is with the King, but the King is not
    with the body.° The King is a thing—
GUILDENSTERN. A thing, my lord?
HAMLET. Of nothing.° Bring me to him. Hide fox, and all   30
    after!°   *Exeunt* [*running*].

4.2. Location: The castle.
12 That . . . own i.e., that I can follow your advice (by telling where the body is) and still keep my own secret **13 demanded of** questioned by. **replication** reply **16 countenance** favor **17 authorities** delegated power, influence **23 sleeps in** has no meaning to **27–28 The . . . body** (Perhaps alludes to the legal commonplace of "the king's two bodies," which drew a distinction between the sacred office of kingship and the particular mortal who possessed it at any given time. Hence, although Claudius' body is necessarily a part of him, true kingship is not contained in it. Similarly, Claudius will have Polonius' body when it is found, but there is no kingship in this business either.) **30 Of nothing** (1) of no account (2) lacking the essence of kingship, as in lines 28–29 and note **30–31 Hide . . . after** (An old signal cry in the game of hide-and-seek, suggesting that Hamlet now runs away from them.)

4 . 3 °   *Enter King, and two or three.*

KING.

I have sent to seek him, and to find the body.
How dangerous is it that this man goes loose!
Yet must not we put the strong law on him.
He's loved of° the distracted° multitude,
5   Who like not in their judgment, but their eyes,°
And where 'tis so, th' offender's scourge is weighed,°
But never the offense. To bear all smooth and even,°
This sudden sending him away must seem
Deliberate pause.° Diseases desperate grown
10   By desperate appliance° are relieved,
Or not at all.

> *Enter Rosencrantz, [Guildenstern,]*
> *and all the rest.*

                    How now, what hath befall'n?

ROSENCRANTZ.

Where the dead body is bestowed, my lord,
We cannot get from him.

KING.   But where is he?

ROSENCRANTZ.

Without, my lord; guarded, to know your pleasure.

KING.

Bring him before us.

15   ROSENCRANTZ.   Ho! Bring in the lord.

They enter [with Hamlet].

KING. Now, Hamlet, where's Polonius?

HAMLET. At supper.

KING. At supper? Where?

HAMLET. Not where he eats, but where 'a is eaten. A certain
20   convocation of politic worms° are e'en° at him. Your
worm° is your only emperor for diet.° We fat all creatures
else to fat us, and we fat ourselves for maggots. Your fat
king and your lean beggar is but variable service°—two
dishes, but to one table. That's the end.

25   KING. Alas, alas!

HAMLET. A man may fish with the worm that hath eat° of a
king, and eat of the fish that hath fed of that worm.

KING. What dost thou mean by this?

HAMLET. Nothing but to show you how a king may go a
progress° through the guts of a beggar.   30

KING. Where is Polonius?

HAMLET. In heaven. Send thither to see. If your messenger
find him not there, seek him i' th' other place yourself.
But if indeed you find him not within this month, you
shall nose him as you go up the stairs into the lobby.   35

KING [*to some attendants*]. Go seek him there.

HAMLET. 'A will stay till you come.   [*Exeunt attendants.*]

KING.

Hamlet this deed, for thine especial safety—
Which we do tender,° as we dearly° grieve
For that which thou has done—must send thee hence   40
With fiery quickness. Therefore prepare thyself.
The bark° is ready, and the wind at help,
Th' associates tend,° and everything is bent°
For England.

HAMLET. For England!   45

KING. Ay, Hamlet.

HAMLET. Good.

KING.

So is it, if thou knew'st our purposes.

HAMLET. I see a cherub° that sees them. But come, for England! Farewell, dear mother.   50

KING. Thy loving father, Hamlet.

HAMLET. My mother. Father and mother is man and wife,
man and wife is one flesh, and so, my mother. Come, for
England.   *Exit.*

KING. Follow him at foot;° tempt him with speed abroad.   55
Delay it not. I'll have him hence tonight.
Away! For everything is sealed and done
That else leans on° th' affair. Pray you, make haste.
                                            [*Exeunt all but the King.*]
And, England,° if my love thou hold'st at aught°—
As my great power thereof may give thee sense,°   60
Since yet thy cicatrice° looks raw and red
After the Danish sword, and thy free awe°
Pays homage to us—thou mayst not coldly set°
Our sovereign process,° which imports at full,°
By letters congruing° to that effect,   65
The present° death of Hamlet. Do it, England,
For like the hectic° in my blood he rages,

4.3. Location: The castle.
4 of by. **distracted** fickle, unstable   **5 Who . . . eyes** who choose
not by judgment but by appearance   **6 scourge** punishment. (Literally, blow with a whip.) **weighed** sympathetically considered   **7
To . . . even** to manage the business in an unprovocative way   **9
Deliberate pause** carefully considered action   **10 appliance** remedies   **20 politic worms** crafty worms (suited to a master spy like
Polonius). **e'en** even now   **21 Your worm** your average worm.
Compare *your fat king and your lean beggar* in line 23.) **diet** food, eating (with a punning reference to the Diet of Worms, a famous *convocation* held in 1521)   **23 variable service** different courses of a
single meal   **26 eat** eaten. (pronounced *et.*)

30 progress royal journey of state   **39 tender** regard, hold dear.
dearly intensely   **42 bark** sailing vessel   **43 tend** wait. **bent** in
readiness   **49 cherub** (Cherubim are angles of knowledge. Hamlet
hints that both he and heaven are onto Claudius' tricks.)   **55 at
foot** close behind, at heel   **58 leans on** bears upon, is related to
59 England i.e., King of England. **at aught** at any value   **60 As
. . . sense** for so my great power may give you a just appreciation of
the importance of valuing my love   **61 cicatrice** scar   **62 free
awe** voluntary show of respect   **63 coldly set** regard with indifference   **64 process** command. **imports at full** conveys specific directions for   **65 congruing** agreeing   **66 present** immediate   **67
hectic** persistent fever

And thou must cure me. Till I know 'tis done,
Howe'er my haps,° my joys were ne'er begun.   *Exit.*

4.4°   *Enter Fortinbras with his army over the stage.*

FORTINBRAS.
    Go, Captain, from me greet the Danish king.
    Tell him that by his license° Fortinbras
    Craves the conveyance of° a promised march
    Over his kingdom. You know the rendezvous.
5   If that His Majesty would aught with us,
    We shall express our duty° in his eye;°
    And let him know so.
CAPTAIN. I will do 't, my lord.
FORTINBRAS. Go softly° on.   [*Exeunt all but the Captain.*]

    Enter Hamlet, Rosencrantz, [Guildenstern,] etc.

10 HAMLET. Good sir, whose powers° are these?
CAPTAIN. They are of Norway, sir.
HAMLET. How purposed, sir, I pray you?
CAPTAIN. Against some part of Poland.
HAMLET. Who commands them, sir?
CAPTAIN.
15   The nephew to old Norway, Fortinbras.
HAMLET.
    Goes it against the main° of Poland, sir,
    Or for some frontier?
CAPTAIN.
    Truly to speak, and with no addition,°
    We go to gain a little patch of ground
20 That hath in it no profit but the name.
    To pay° five ducats, five, I would not farm it;°
    Nor will it yield to Norway or the Pole
    A ranker° rate, should it be sold in fee.°
HAMLET.
    Why, then the Polack never will defend it.
CAPTAIN.
25   Yes, it is already garrisoned.
HAMLET.
    Two thousand souls and twenty thousand ducats
    Will not debate the question of this straw.°
    This is th' impostume° of much wealth and peace,
    That inward breaks, and shows no cause without
30 Why the man dies. I humbly thank you, sir.
CAPTAIN.
    God b' wi' you, sir.   [*Exit.*]

ROSENCRANTZ.
        Will 't please you go, my lord?
HAMLET.
    I'll be with you straight. Go a little before.
                [*Exeunt all except Hamlet.*]
    How all occasions do inform against° me
    And spur my dull revenge! What is a man,
    If his chief good and market of° his time   35
    Be but to sleep and feed? A beast, no more.
    Sure he that made us with such large discourse,°
    Looking before and after°, gave us not
    That capability and godlike reason
    To fust° in us unused. Now, whether it be   40
    Bestial oblivion,° or some craven° scruple
    Of thinking too precisely° on th' event°—
    A thought which, quartered, hath but one part wisdom
    And ever three parts coward—I do not know
    Why yet I live to say "This thing's to do,"   45
    Sith° I have cause, and will, and strength, and means
    To do 't. Examples gross° as earth exhort me:
    Witness this army of such mass and charge,°
    Led by a delicate and tender° prince,
    Whose spirit with divine ambition puffed   50
    Makes mouths° at the invisible event,°
    Exposing what is mortal and unsure
    To all that fortune, death, and danger dare,°
    Even for an eggshell. Rightly to be great
    Is not to stir without great argument   55
    But greatly to find quarrel in a straw
    When honor's at the stake.° How stand I, then,
    That have a father killed, a mother stained,
    Excitements of° my reason and my blood,
    And let all sleep, while to my shame I see   60
    The imminent death of twenty thousand men
    That for a fantasy° and trick° of fame
    Go to their graves like beds, fight for a plot°
    Whereon the numbers cannot try the cause,°
    Which is not tomb enough and continent°   65

33 **inform against** denounce, betray; take shape against   35 **market of** profit of, compensation for   37 **discourse** power of reasoning   38 **looking before and after** able to review past events and anticipate the future   40 **fust** grow moldy   41 **oblivion** forgetfulness. **craven** cowardly   42 **precisely** scrupulously. **event** outcome   46 **Sith** since   47 **gross** obvious   48 **charge** expense   49 **delicate and tender** of fine and youthful qualities   51 **Makes mouths** makes scornful faces. **invisible event** unforeseeable outcome   53 **dare** could do (to him)   54–57 **Rightly . . . stake** true greatness does not normally consist of rushing into action over some trivial provocation; however, when one's honor is involved, even a trifling insult requires that one respond greatly (?) **at the stake** (A metaphor from gambling or bear-baiting.)   59 **Excitements of** promptings by   62 **fantasy** fanciful caprice, illusion. **trick** trifle, deceit   63 **plot** plot of ground   64 **Whereon . . . cause** on which there is insufficient room for the soldiers needed to engage in a military contest   65 **continent** receptacle, container

69 **haps** fortunes
4.4. Location: The coast of Denmark.
2 **license** permission   3 **the conveyance of** escort during   6 **duty** respect. **eye** presence   9 **softly** slowly, circumspectly   10 **powers** forces   16 **main** main part   18 **addition** exaggeration   21 **To pay** i.e., for a yearly rental of. **farm it** take a lease of it   23 **ranker** higher. **in fee** fee simple, outright   27 **debate . . . straw** settle this trifling matter   28 **impostume** abscess

To hide the slain? O, from this time forth
My thoughts be bloody or be nothing worth!   *Exit.*

4 . 5 °   *Enter Horatio, [Queen] Gertrude, and a
            Gentleman.*

QUEEN.
    I will not speak with her.
GENTLEMAN.   She is importunate,
    Indeed distract.° Her mood will needs be pitied.
QUEEN. What would she have?
GENTLEMAN.
    She speaks much of her father, says she hears
    There's tricks° i' the world, and hems,° and beats her
            heart,°
5   Spurns enviously at straws,° speaks things in doubt°
    That carry but half sense. Her speech is nothing,
    Yet the unshapèd use° of it doth move
    The hearers to collection;° they yawn° at it,
10 And botch° the words up fit to their own thoughts,
    Which,° as her winks and nods and gestures yield°
            them,
    Indeed would make one think there might be thought,°
    Though nothing sure, yet much unhappily.°
HORATIO.
    'Twere good she were spoken with, for she may strew
15 Dangerous conjectures in ill-breeding° minds.
QUEEN. Let her come in.   [*Exit Gentleman.*]
    [*Aside.*] To my sick soul, as sin's true nature is,
    Each toy° seems prologue to some great amiss.°
    So full of artless jealousy is guilt,
20 It spills itself in fearing to be spilt.°

            Enter Ophelia° [distracted].

OPHELIA.
    Where is the beauteous majesty of Denmark?
QUEEN. How now, Ophelia?
OPHELIA (*she sings*).
    "How should I your true love know
            From another one?

By his cockle hat° and staff,   25
    And his sandal shoon."°
QUEEN. Alas, sweet lady, what imports this song?
OPHELIA. Say you? Nay, pray you, mark.
    "He is dead and gone, Lady,   (*Song.*)
        He is dead and gone;   30
    At his head a grass-green turf,
        At his heels a stone."
    O, ho!
QUEEN. Nay, but Ophelia—
OPHELIA. Pray you, mark.   35
    [*Sings.*] "White his shroud as the mountain snow"—

            Enter King.

QUEEN. Alas, look here, my lord.
OPHELIA.
    "Larded° with sweet flowers;   (*Song.*)
    Which bewept to the ground did not go
        With true-love showers."°   40
KING. How do you, pretty lady?
OPHELIA. Well, God 'ild° you! They say the owl° was a
    baker's daughter. Lord, we know what we are, but know
    not what we may be. God be at your table!
KING. Conceit° upon her father.   45
OPHELIA. Pray let's have no words of this; but when they
    ask you what it means, say you this:
    "Tomorrow is Saint Valentine's day,   (*Song.*)
        All in the morning betime,°
    And I a maid at your window,   50
        To be your Valentine.
    Then up he rose, and donned his clothes,
        And dupped° the chamber door,
    Let in the maid, that out a maid
        Never departed more."   55
KING. Pretty Ophelia—
OPHELIA. Indeed, la, without an oath, I'll make an end
    on 't:
    [*Sings.*] "By Gis° and by Saint Charity,
        Alack, and fie for shame!   60
    Young men will do 't, if they come to 't;
        By Cock,° they are to blame.
    Quoth she, 'Before you tumbled me,
        You promised me to wed.' "
He answers: 65
    " 'So would I ha' done, by yonder sun,
        An° thou hadst not come to my bed.' "

4.5. **Location: The castle.**
2 **distract** distracted   5 **tricks** deceptions. **hems** makes "hmm"
sounds. **heart** i.e., breast   6 **Spurns . . . straws** kicks spitefully,
takes offense at trifles. **in doubt** obscurely   8 **unshapèd use** incoherent manner   9 **collection** inference, a guess at some sort of
meaning. **yawn** gape, wonder; grasp. (The Folio reading, *aim*, is possible.)   10 **botch** patch   11 **Which** which words. **yield** deliver,
represent   12 **thought** intended   13 **unhappily** unpleasantly
near the truth, shrewdly   15 **ill-breeding** prone to suspect the worst
and to make mischief   18 **toy** trifle. **amiss** calamity   19–20 **So
. . . spilt** guilt is so full of suspicion that it unskillfully betrays itself
in fearing betrayal   20 **s.d. Enter Ophelia** (In the First Quarto,
Ophelia enters "playing on a lute, and her hair down, singing.")

25 **cockle hat** hat with cockleshell stuck in it as a sign that the
wearer had been a pilgrim to the shrine of Saint James of Com-
postella in Spain.   26 **shoon** shoes   38 **Larded** decorated   40
showers i.e., tears   42 **God 'ild** God yield or reward. **owl** (Refers
to a legend about a baker's daughter who was turned into an owl for
being ungenerous when Jesus begged a loaf of bread.)   45 **Conceit**
brooding   49 **betime** early   53 **dupped** did up, opened   59 **Gis**
Jesus   62 **Cock** (A perversion of "God" in oaths; here also with a
quibble on the slang word for penis.)   67 **An** if

KING. How long hath she been thus?

OPHELIA. I hope all will be well. We must be patient, but I
70   cannot choose but weep to think they would lay him i'
     the cold ground. My brother shall know of it. And so I
     thank you for your good counsel. Come, my coach! Good
     night, ladies, good night, sweet ladies, good night, good
     night.   [Exit.]

KING [to Horatio].
75 Follow her close. Give her good watch, I pray you.
                                      [Exit Horatio.]

O, this is the poison of deep grief; it springs
All from her father's death—and now behold!
O Gertrude, Gertrude,
When sorrows come, they come not single spies,°
80 But in battalions. First, her father slain;
Next, your son gone, and he most violent author
Of his own just remove;° the people muddied,°
Thick and unwholesome in their thoughts and whispers
For good Polonius' death—and we have done but
     greenly,°
85 In hugger-mugger° to inter him; poor Ophelia
Divided from herself and her fair judgment.
Without the which we are pictures or mere beasts;
Last, and as much containing° as all these,
Her brother is in secret come from France,
90 Feeds on this wonder, keeps himself in clouds,°
And wants° not buzzers° to infect his ear
With pestilent speeches of his father's death,
Wherein necessity,° of matter beggared,°
Will nothing stick our person to arraign
95 In ear and ear.° O my dear Gertrude, this,
Like to a murdering piece,° in many places
Gives me superfluous death.°   A noise within.

QUEEN. Alack, what noise is this?

KING. Attend!°
100 Where is my Switzers?° Let them guard the door.

         Enter a Messenger.

What is the matter?

MESSENGER.   Save yourself, my lord!
The ocean, overpeering of his list,°

Eats not the flats° with more impetuous haste
Than young Laertes, in a riotous head,°
O'erbears your officers. The rabble call him lord,   105
And, as° the world were now but to begin,
Antiquity forgot, custom not known,
The ratifiers and props of every word,°
They cry, "Choose we! Laertes shall be king!"
Caps,° hands, and tongues applaud it to the clouds,   110
"Laertes shall be king, Laertes king!"

QUEEN.
How cheerfully on the false trail they cry! A noise within.
O, this is counter,° you false Danish dogs!

         Enter Laertes with others.

KING. The doors are broke.

LAERTES.
Where is this King?—Sirs, stand you all without.   115

ALL. No, let's come in.

LAERTES. I pray you, give me leave.

ALL. We will, we will.

LAERTES.
I thank you. Keep the door. [Exeunt followers.] O thou
     vile king,
Give me my father!

QUEEN [restraining him]. Calmly, good Laertes.   120

LAERTES.
That drop of blood that's calm proclaims me bastard,
Cries cuckold to my father, brands the harlot
Even here, between° the chaste unsmirchèd brow
Of my true mother.

KING.   What is the cause, Laertes,
That thy rebellion looks so giantlike?   125
Let him go, Gertrude. Do not fear our° person.
There's such divinity doth hedge° a king
That treason can but peep to what it would,°
Acts little of his will°. Tell me, Laertes,
Why thou art thus incensed. Let him go, Gertrude.   130
Speak, man.

LAERTES.   Where is my father?

KING.   Dead.

QUEEN.
But not by him.

KING.   Let him demand his fill.

---

79 **spies** scouts sent in advance of the main force   82 **remove** removal. **muddied** stirred up, confused   84 **greenly** in an inexperienced way, foolishly   85 **hugger-mugger** secret haste   88 **as much containing** as full of serious matter   90 **Feeds . . . clouds** feeds his resentment or shocked grievance, holds himself inscrutable and aloof amid all this rumor   91 **wants** lacks. **buzzers** gossipers, informers   93 **necessity** i.e., the need to invent some plausible explanation. **of matter beggared** unprovided with facts   94–95 **Will . . . ear** will not hesitate to accuse my (royal) person in everybody's ears   96 **murdering piece** cannon loaded so as to scatter its shot   97 **Gives . . . death** kills me over and over   99 **Attend** i.e., guard me   100 **Switzers** Swiss guards, mercenaries   102 **overpeering of his list** overflowing its shore, boundary

103 **flats** i.e., flatlands near shore. **impetuous** violent (perhaps also with the meaning of *impiteous* [*impitious*, Q2], "pitiless")   104 **head** insurrection   106 **as** as if   108 **The ratifiers . . . word** i.e., *antiquity* (or tradition) and *custom* ought to confirm (*ratify*) and underprop our every word or promise   110 **Caps** (The caps are thrown in the air.)   113 **counter** (A hunting term, meaning to follow the trail in a direction opposite to that which the game has taken.)   123 **between** in the middle of   126 **fear our** fear for my   127 **hedge** protect, as with a surrounding barrier   128 **can . . . would** can only peep furtively, as through a barrier, at what it would intend   129 **Acts . . . will** (but) performs little of what it intends

LAERTES.
    How came he dead? I'll not be juggled with.°
    To hell, allegiance! Vows, to the blackest devil!
135 Conscience and grace, to the profoundest pit!
    I dare damnation. To this point I stand,°
    That both the worlds I give to negligence,°
    Let come what comes, only I'll be revenged
    Most throughly° for my father.
140 KING. Who shall stay you?
LAERTES. My will, not all the world's.°
    And for° my means, I'll husband them so well
    They shall go far with little.
KING.   Good Laertes,
    If you desire to know the certainty
145 Of your dear father, is 't writ in your revenge
    That, swoopstake,° you will draw both friend and foe,
    Winner and loser?
LAERTES. None but his enemies.
KING. Will you know them, then?
LAERTES.
150 To his good friends thus wide I'll ope my arms,
    And like the kind life-rendering pelican°
    Repast° them with my blood.
KING.
                                    Why, now you speak
    Like a good child and a true gentleman.
    That I am guiltless of your father's death,
155 And am most sensibly° in grief for it,
    It shall as level° to your judgment 'pear
    As day does to your eye.   A noise within.
LAERTES.
    How now, what noise is that?

            Enter Ophelia.

KING.   Let her come in.
LAERTES.
    O heat, dry up my brains! Tears seven times salt
160 Burn out the sense and virtue° of mine eye!
    By heaven, thy madness shall be paid with weight°
    Till our scale turn the beam.° O rose of May!
    Dear maid, kind sister, sweet Ophelia!
    O heavens, is 't possible a young maid's wits

    Should be as mortal as an old man's life?   165
    Nature is fine in° love, and where 'tis fine
    It sends some precious instance° of itself
    After the thing it loves.°
OPHELIA.
    "They bore him barefaced on the bier,   (Song.)
        Hey non nonny, nonny, hey nonny,   170
        And in his grave rained many a tear—"
    Fare you well, my dove!
LAERTES.
    Hadst thou thy wits and didst persuade° revenge,
    It could not move thus.
OPHELIA. You must sing "A-down a-down," and you "call   175
    him a-down-a.°" O, how the wheel° becomes it! It is the
    false steward° that stole his master's daughter.
LAERTES. This nothing's more than matter.°
OPHELIA. There's rosemary,° that's for remembrance; pray
    you, love, remember. And there is pansies;° that's for   180
    thoughts.
LAERTES. A document° in madness, thoughts and remem-
    brance fitted.
OPHELIA. There's fennel° for you, and columbines.° There's
    rue° for you, and here's some for me; we may call it herb   185
    of grace o' Sundays. You must wear your rue with a differ-
    ence.° There's a daisy°. I would give you some violets,°
    but they withered all when my father died. They say 'a
    made a good end—
    [Sings.] "For bonny sweet Robin is all my joy."   190
LAERTES.
    Thought° and affliction, passion,° hell itself,
    She turns to favor° and to prettiness.
OPHELIA.
    "And will 'a not come again?   (Song.)
    And will 'a not come again?

---

133 **juggled with** cheated, deceived   136 **To . . . stand** I am resolved in this   137 **both . . . negligence** i.e., both this world and
the next are of no consequence to me   139 **throughly** thoroughly
141 **My will . . . world's** I'll stop (stay) when my will is accomplished, not for anyone else's.   142 **for** as for   146 **swoopstake**
i.e., indiscriminately. (Literally, taking all stakes on the gambling
table at once. *Draw* is also a gambling term, meaning "take from.")
151 **pelican** (Refers to the belief that the female pelican fed its
young with its own blood.)   152 **Repast** feed   155 **sensibly** feelingly   156 **level** plain   160 **virtue** faculty, power   161 **paid
with weight** repaid, avenged equally or more   162 **beam** crossbar
of a balance

166 **fine in** refined by   167 **instance** token   168 **After . . . loves**
i.e., into the grave, along with Polonius   173 **persuade** argue co-
gently for   175–176 **You . . . a-down-a** (Ophelia assigns the
singing of refrains, like her own "Hey non nonny," to others present.)   176 **wheel** spinning wheel as accompaniment to the song,
or refrain   177 **false steward** (The story is unknown.)   178 **This
. . . matter** this seeming nonsense is more eloquent than sane utterance   179 **rosemary** (Used as a symbol of remembrance both at
weddings and at funerals.)   180 **pansies** (Emblem of love and
courtship; perhaps from French *pensées*, "thoughts.")   182 **document** instruction, lesson   184 **fennel** (Emblem of flattery.)
columbines (Emblems of unchastity or ingratitude.)   185 **rue**
(Emblem of repentance—a signification that is evident in its popular name, *herb of grace*.)   187 **with a difference** (A device used in
heraldry to distinguish one family from another on the coat of arms,
here suggesting that Ophelia and the others have different causes of
sorrow and repentance, perhaps with a play on *rue* in the sense of
"ruth," "pity.")   **daisy** (Emblem of dissembling, faithlessness.)   **violets**
(Emblems of faithfulness.)   191 **Thought** melancholy.   **passion**
suffering   192 **favor** grace, beauty

195   No, no, he is dead.
         Go to thy deathbed,
         He never will come again.

         "His beard was as white as snow,
         All flaxen was his poll.°
200   He is gone, he is gone,
             And we cast away moan.
         God ha' mercy on his soul!"
         And of all Christian souls, I pray God. God b' wi' you.
                                   [*Exit, followed by Gertrude.*]
         LAERTES. Do you see this, O God?
         KING.
205   Laertes, I must commune with your grief,
         Or you deny me right. Go but apart,
         Make choice of whom° your wisest friends you will,
         And they shall hear and judge twixt you and me.
         If by direct or by collateral hand°
210   They find us touched,° we will our kingdom give,
         Our crown, our life, and all that we call ours
         To you in satisfaction; but if not,
         Be you content to lend your patience to us,
         And we shall jointly labor with your soul
         To give it due content.
215   LAERTES.   Let this be so.
         His means of death, his obscure funeral—
         No trophy,° sword, nor hatchment° o'er his bones,
         No noble rite, nor formal ostentation°—
         Cry to be heard, as 'twere from heaven to earth,
         That° I must call 't in question.°
220   KING.   So you shall,
         And where th' offense is, let the great ax fall.
         I pray you, go with me.   *Exeunt.*

4 . 6 °   *Enter Horatio and others.*

HORATIO. What are they that would speak with me?
GENTLEMAN Seafaring men, sir. They say they have letters
    for you.
HORATIO. Let them come in.   [*Exit Gentleman.*]
5   I do not know from what part of the world
     I should be greeted, if not from Lord Hamlet.

         Enter Sailors.

FIRST SAILOR. God bless you, sir.
HORATIO. Let him bless thee too.
FIRST SAILOR. 'A shall, sir, an 't° please him. There's a letter

for you, sir—it came from th' ambassador° that was bound   10
for England—if your name be Horatio, as I am let to
know it is.   [*He gives a letter.*]
HORATIO [*reads*]. "Horatio, when thou shalt have overlooked this, give these fellows some means° to the King;
they have letters for him. Ere we were two days old at sea,   15
a pirate of very warlike appointment° gave us chase. Finding ourselves too slow of sail, we put on a compelled
valor, and in the grapple I boarded them. On the instant
they got clear of our ship, so I alone became their prisoner. They have dealt with me like thieves of mercy,° but   20
they knew what they did: I am to do a good turn for them.
Let the King have the letters I have sent, and repair° thou
to me with as much speed as thou wouldest fly death. I
have words to speak in thine ear will make thee dumb,
yet are they much too light for the bore° of the matter.   25
These good fellows will bring thee where I am. Rosencrantz and Guildenstern hold their course for England. Of
them I have much to tell thee. Farewell.
                      He that thou knowest thine, Hamlet."
Come, I will give you way° for these your letters,   30
And do 't the speedier that you may direct me
To him from whom you brought them.   *Exeunt.*

4 . 7 °   *Enter King and Laertes.*

KING.
Now must your conscience my acquittance seal,°
And you must put me in your heart for friend,
Sith° you have heard, and with a knowing ear,
That he which hath your noble father slain
Pursued my life.
LAERTES.   It well appears. But tell me   5
Why you proceeded not against these feats°
So crimeful and so capital° in nature,
As by your safety, greatness, wisdom, all things else,
You mainly° were stirred up.
KING. O, for two special reasons,   10
Which may to you perhaps seem much unsinewed,°
But yet to me they're strong. The Queen his mother
Lives almost by his looks, and for myself—
My virtue or my plague, be it either which—
She is so conjunctive° to my life and soul   15

---

199 **poll** head   207 **whom** whichever of   209 **collateral hand**
indirect agency   210 **us touched** me implicated   217 **trophy**
memorial. **hatchment** tablet displaying the armorial bearings of a
deceased person   218 **ostentation** ceremony   220 **That** so that.
call 't in question demand an explanation
4.6. Location: The castle.
9 **an 't** if it

10 **th' ambassador** (Evidently Hamlet. The sailor is being circum-
spect.)   13–14 **overlooked** looked over   14 **means** means of access   16 **appointment** equipage   20 **thieves of mercy** merciful
thieves   22 **repair** come   25 **bore** caliber, i.e., importance   30
way means of access
4.7. Location: The castle.
1 **my acquittance seal** confirm or acknowledge my innocence
3 **Sith** since   6 **feats** acts   7 **capital** punishable by death
9 **mainly** greatly   11 **unsinewed** weak   15 **conjunctive** closely
united. (An astronomical metaphor.)

That, as the star moves not but in his° sphere,°
I could not but by her. The other motive
Why to a public count° I might not go
Is the great love the general gender° bear him,
20 Who, dipping all his faults in their affection,
Work° like the spring° that turneth wood to stone,
Convert his gyves° to graces, so that my arrows,
Too slightly timbered° for so loud° a wind,
Would have reverted° to my bow again
25 But not where I had aimed them.

LAERTES.
    And so I have a noble father lost,
A sister driven into desperate terms,°
Whose worth, if praises may go back° again,
Stood challenger on mount° of all the age
30 For her perfections. But my revenge will come.

KING.
    Break not your sleeps for that. You must not think
That we are made of stuff so flat and dull
That we can let our beard be shook with danger
And think it pastime. You shortly shall hear more.
35 I loved your father, and we love ourself;
And that, I hope, will teach you to imagine—

        Enter a Messenger with letters.

How now? What news?

MESSENGER.   Letters, my lord, from Hamlet:
This is Your Majesty, this to the Queen.
                                    [*He gives letters.*]

KING. From Hamlet? Who brought them?

MESSENGER.
40 Sailors, my lord, they say. I saw them not.
They were given me by Claudio. He received them
Of him that brought them.

KING.   Laertes, you shall hear them.—
Leave us.   [*Exit Messenger.*]
[*He reads.*] "High and might, you shall know I am set
45 naked° on your kingdom. Tomorrow shall I beg leave to
see your kingly eyes, when I shall, first asking your pardon,° thereunto recount the occasion of my sudden and
more strange return.   Hamlet."
What should this mean? Are all the rest come back?
50 Or is it some abuse,° and no such thing?°

LAERTES.
    Know you the hand?

KING.   'Tis Hamlet's character.° "Naked!"
And in a postscript here he says "alone."
Can you devise° me?

LAERTES.
    I am lost in it, my lord. But let him come.
It warms the very sickness in my heart   55
That I shall live and tell him to this teeth,
"Thus didst thou."°

KING.   If it be so, Laertes—
As how should it be so? How otherwise?°—
Will you be ruled by me?

LAERTES.   Ay, my lord,
So° you will not o'errule me to a peace.   60

KING.
    To thine own peace. If he be now returned,
As checking° at his voyage, and that° he means
No more to undertake it, I will work him
To an exploit, now ripe in my device,°
Under the which he shall not choose but fall;   65
And for his death no wind of blame shall breathe,
But even his mother shall uncharge the practice°
And call it accident.

LAERTES.   My lord, I will be ruled,
The rather if you could devise it so
That I might be the organ.°

KING.   It falls right.   70
You have been talked of since your travel much,
And that in Hamlet's hearing, for a quality
Wherein they say you shine. Your sum of parts°
Did not together pluck such envy from him
As did that one, and that, in my regard,   75
Of the unworthiest siege.°

LAERTES. What part is that, my lord?

KING.
    A very ribbon in the cap of youth,
Yet needful too, for youth no less becomes°
The light and careless livery that it wears   80
Than settled age his sables° and his weeds°
Importing health and graveness.° Two months since
Here was a gentleman of Normandy.

---

16 his its. **sphere** one of the hollow spheres in which, according to
Ptolemaic astronomy, the planets were supposed to move **18
count** account, reckoning, indictment **19 general gender** common people **21 Work** operate, act. **spring** i.e., a spring with such
a concentration of lime that it coats a piece of wood with limestone,
in effect, gilding and petrifying it **22 gyves** fetters (which, gilded
by the people's praise, would look like badges of honor) **23
slightly timbered** light. **loud** (suggesting public outcry on Hamlet's
behalf) **24 reverted** returned **27 terms** state, condition **28
go back** i.e., recall what she was **29 on mount** set up on high
45 naked destitute, unarmed, without following **46–47 pardon**
permission **50 abuse** deceit. **no such thing** not what it appears

51 character handwriting **53 devise** explain to **57 Thus didst
thou** i.e., here's for what you did to my father **58 As . . . otherwise** how can this (Hamlet's return) be true? Yet how otherwise
than true (since we have the evidence of his letter)? **60 So** provided that **62 checking at** i.e., turning aside from (like a falcon
leaving the quarry to fly at a chance bird). **that** if **64 device** devising, invention **67 uncharge the practice** acquit the strategem
of being a plot **70 organ** agent, instrument **73 Your . . . parts**
i.e., all your other virtues **76 unworthiest siege** least important
rank **79 no less becomes** is no less suited by **81 his sables** its
rich robes furred with sable. **weeds** garments **82 Importing . . .
graveness** signifying a concern for health and dignified prosperity;
also, giving an impression of comfortable prosperity

I have seen myself, and served against, the French,
85   And they can well° on horseback, but this gallant
Had witchchraft in 't; he grew unto his seat,
And to such wondrous doing brought his horse
As had he been incorpsed and demi-natured°
With the brave beast. So far he topped° my thought
90   That I in forgery° of shapes and tricks
Come short of what he did.
LAERTES.   A Norman was 't?
KING. A Norman.
LAERTES.
Upon my life, Lamord.
KING.   The very same.
LAERTES.
I know him well. He is the brooch° indeed
95   And gem of all the nation.
KING. He made confession° of you,
And gave you such a masterly report
For art and exercise in your defense,°
And for your rapier most especial,
100   That he cried out 'twould be a sight indeed
If one could match you. Th' escrimers° of their nation,
He swore, had neither motion, guard, nor eye
If you opposed them. Sir, this report of his
Did Hamlet so envenom with his envy
105   That he could nothing do but wish and beg
Your sudden° coming o'er, to play° with you.
Now, out of this—
LAERTES.   What out of this, my lord?
KING.
Laertes, was your father dear to you?
Or are you like the painting of a sorrow,
A face without a heart?
110   LAERTES.   Why ask you this?
KING.
Not that I think you did not love your father,
But that I know love is begun by time,°
And that I see, in passages of proof,°
Time qualifies° the spark and fire of it.
115   There lives within the very flame of love
A kind of wick or snuff° that will abate it,
And nothing is at a like goodness still,°

For goodness, growing to a pleurisy,°
Dies in his own too much.° That° we would do,
We should do when we would; for this "would" changes
120   And hath abatements° and delays as many
As there are tongues, are hands, are accidents,°
And then this "should" is like a spendthrift sigh,°
That hurts by easing.° But, to the quick o' th' ulcer:°
Hamlet comes back. What would you undertake
125   To show yourself in deed your father's son
More than in words?
LAERTES.   To cut his throat i' the church.
KING.
No place, indeed, should murder sanctuarize;°
Revenge should have no bounds. But good Laertes,
Will you do this,° keep close within your chamber.
130   Hamlet returned shall know you are come home.
We'll put on those shall° praise your excellence
And set a double varnish on the fame
The Frenchman gave you, bring you in fine° together,
And wager on your heads. He, being remiss,°
135   Most generous°, and free from all contriving,
Will not peruse the foils, so that with ease,
Or with a little shuffling, you may choose
A sword unbated,° and in a pass of practice°
Requite him for your father.
LAERTES.   I will do 't,
140   And for that purpose I'll anoint my sword.
I bought an unction° of a mountebank°
So mortal that, but dip a knife in it,
Where it draws blood no cataplasm° so rare,
Collected from all simples° that have virtue°
145   Under the moon,° can save the thing from death
That is but scratched withal. I'll touch my point
With this contagion, that if I gall° him slightly,
It may be death.

---

118 pleurisy excess, plethora. (Literally, a chest inflammation.)
119 in . . . much of its own excess. **That** that which   **121 abatements** diminutions   **122 As . . . accidents** as there are tongues to dissuade, hands to prevent, and chance events to intervene   **123 spendthrift sigh** (An allusion to the belief that sighs draw blood from heart.)   **124 hurts by easing** i.e., costs the heart blood and wastes precious opportunity even while it affords emotional relief. **quick o' th' ulcer** i.e., heart of the matter   **128 sanctuarize** protect from punishment. (Alludes to the right of sanctuary with which certain religious places were invested.)   **130 Will you do this** if you wish to do this   **132 put on those shall** arrange for some to   **134 in fine** finally   **135 remiss** negligently unsuspicious   **136 generous** noble-minded   **139 unbated** not blunted, having no button. **pass of practice** treacherous thrust   **142 unction** ointment. **mountebank** quack doctor   **144 cataplasm** plaster or poultice   **145 simples** herbs. **virtue** potency   **146 Under the moon** i.e., anywhere (with reference perhaps to the belief that herbs gathered at night had a special power)   **148 gall** graze, wound

85 can well are skilled   **88 As . . . demi-natured** as if he had been of one body and nearly of one nature (like the centaur)   **89 topped** surpassed   **90 forgery** imagining   **94 brooch** ornament   **96 confession** testimonial, admission of superiority   **98 For . . . defense** with respect to your skill and practice with your weapon   **101 escrimers** fencers   **106 sudden** immediate. **play** fence   **112 begun by time** i.e., created by the right circumstance and hence subject to change   **113 passages of proof** actual instances that prove it   **114 qualifies** weakens, moderates   **116 snuff** the charred part of a candlewick   **117 nothing . . . still** nothing remains at a constant level of perfection

KING.   Let's further think of this,
150   Weigh what convenience both of time and means
    May fit us to our shape.° If this should fail,
    And that our drift look through our bad performance,°
    'Twere better not assayed. Therefore this project
    Should have a back or second, that might hold
155   If this did blast in proof.° Soft, let me see.
    We'll make a solemn wager on your cunnings°—
    I ha 't!
    When in your motion you are hot and dry—
    As° make your bouts more violent to that end—
160   And that he calls for drink, I'll have prepared him
    A chalice for the nonce,° whereon but sipping,
    If he by chance escape your venomed stuck,°
    Our purpose may hold there. [A cry within.] But stay,
        what noise?

        Enter Queen.

QUEEN.
    One woe doth tread upon another's heel,
165   So fast they follow. Your sister's drowned, Laertes.
LAERTES. Drowned! O, where?
QUEEN.
    There is a willow grows askant° the brook,
    That shows his hoar leaves° in the glassy stream;
    Therewith fantastic garlands did she make
170   Of crowflowers, nettles, daisies, and long purples,°
    That liberal° shepherds give a grosser name,°
    But our cold° maids do dead men's fingers call them.
    There on the pendent° boughs her crownet° weeds
    Clamb'ring to hang, an envious sliver° broke,
175   When down her weedy° trophies and herself
    Fell in the weeping brook. Her clothes spread wide,
    And mermaidlike awhile they bore her up,
    Which time she chanted snatches of old lauds,°
    As one incapable of° her own distress,
180   Or like a creature native and endued°
    Unto that element. But long it could not be
    Till that her garments, heavy with their drink,
    Pulled the poor wretch from her melodious lay

To muddy death.
LAERTES.   Alas, then she is drowned?
QUEEN. Drowned, drowned.   185
LAERTES.
    Too much of water hast thou, poor Ophelia,
    And therefore I forbid my tears. But yet
    It is our trick;° nature her custom holds,
    Let shame say what it will. [He weeps.] When these
        are gone,
    The woman will be out.° Adieu, my lord.   190
    I have a speech of fire that fain would blaze,
    But that this folly douts° it.   Exit.
KING.   Let's follow, Gertrude.
    How much I had to do to calm his rage!
    Now fear I this will give it start again;
    Therefore let's follow.   Exeunt.

5.1°   Enter two Clowns° [with spades and mattocks].

FIRST CLOWN. Is she to be buried in Christian burial, when
    she willfully seeks her own salvation?°
SECOND CLOWN. I tell thee she is; therefore make her grave
    straight.° The crowner° hath sat on her,° and finds it°
    Christian burial.   5
FIRST CLOWN. How can that be, unless she drowned herself
    in her own defense?
SECOND CLOWN. Why, 'tis found so.°
FIRST CLOWN. It must be se offendendo,° it cannot be else.
    For here lies the point: if I drown myself wittingly, it ar-   10
    gues an act, and an act hath three branches—it is to act,
    to do, and to perform. Argal,° she drowned herself wit-
    tingly.
SECOND CLOWN. Nay, but hear you, goodman° delver—
FIRST CLOWN. Give me leave. Here lies the water; good.   15
    Here stands the man; good. If the man go to this water
    and drown himself, it is, will he, nill he,° he goes, mark

you that. But if the water come to him and drown him, he
drowns not himself. Argal, he that is not guilty of his own
20 death shortens not his own life.

SECOND CLOWN. But is this law?

FIRST CLOWN. Ay, marry, is 't —crowner's quest° law.

SECOND CLOWN. Will you ha' the truth on 't? If this had not
been a gentlewoman, she should have been buried out o'
25 Christian burial.

FIRST CLOWN. Why, there thou sayst.° And the more pity
that great folk should have countenance° in this world to
drown or hang themselves, more than their even-Christian.° Come, my spade. There is no ancient° gentleman
30 but gardeners, ditchers, and grave makers. They hold up°
Adam's profession.

SECOND CLOWN. Was he a gentleman?

FIRST CLOWN. 'A was the first that ever bore arms.°

SECOND CLOWN. Why, he had none.

35 FIRST CLOWN. What, art a heathen? How dost thou understand the Scripture? The Scripture says Adam digged.
Could he dig without arms?° I'll put another question to
thee. If thou answerest me not to the purpose, confess
thyself°—

40 SECOND CLOWN. Go to.

FIRST CLOWN. What is he that builds stronger than either
the mason, the shipwright, or the carpenter?

SECOND CLOWN. The gallows maker, for that frame° out-
lives a thousand tenants.

45 FIRST CLOWN. I like thy wit well, in good faith. The gallows
does well. But how does it well? It does well° to those that
do ill. Now thou dost ill to say the gallows is built
stronger than the church. Argal, the gallows may do well
to thee. To 't again, come.

50 SECOND CLOWN. "Who builds stronger than a mason, a
shipwright, or a carpenter?"

FIRST CLOWN. Ay, tell me that, and unyoke.°

SECOND CLOWN. Marry, now I can tell.

FIRST CLOWN. To 't.

55 SECOND CLOWN. Mass,° I cannot tell.

Enter Hamlet and Horatio [at a distance].

FIRST CLOWN. Cudgel thy brains no more about it, for your
dull ass will not mend his pace with beating; and when
you are asked this question next, say "a grave maker." The

houses he makes last till doomsday. Go get thee in and
fetch me a stoup° of liquor.   60

[Exit Second Clown. First Clown digs.]

Song.

"In youth, when I did love, did love,°
    Methought it was very sweet,
To contract—O—the time for—a—my behove,°
    O, methought there—a—was nothing—a—
    meet."°

HAMLET. Has this fellow no feeling of his business, 'a° sings 65
in grave-making?

HORATIO. Custom hath made it in him a property of easiness.°

HAMLET. 'Tis e'en so. The hand of little employment hath
the daintier sense.°   70

FIRST CLOWN.

Song.

"But age with his stealing steps
    Hath clawed me in his clutch,
And hath shipped me into the land,°
    As if I had never been such."

[He throws up a skull.]

HAMLET. That skull had a tongue in it and could sing once. 75
How the knave jowls° it to the ground, as if 'twere Cain's
jawbone, that did the first murder! This might be the pate
of a politician,° which this ass now o'erreaches,° one that
would circumvent God, might it not?

HORATIO. It might, my lord.   80

HAMLET. Or of a courtier, which could say, "Good morrow, sweet lord! How dost thou, sweet lord?" This
might be my Lord Such-a-one, that praised my Lord
Such-a-one's horse when 'a meant to beg it, might it
not?   85

HORATIO. Ay, my lord.

HAMLET. Why, e'en so, and now my Lady Worm's, chapless,° and knocked about the mazard° with a sexton's
spade. Here's fine revolution,° an° we had the trick to
see° 't. Did these bones cost no more the breeding but° to 90

22 **quest** inquest   26 **there thou sayst** i.e., that's right   27 **countenance** privilege   28–29 **even-Christian** fellow Christians. **ancient** going back to ancient times   30 **hold up** maintain   33 **bore
arms** (To be entitled to bear a coat of arms would make Adam a gentleman, but as one who bore a spade, our common ancestor was an
ordinary delver in the earth.)   37 **arms** i.e., the arms of the body
38–39 **confess thyself** (The saying continues, "and be hanged.")
43 **frame** (1) gallows (2) structure   46 **does well** (1) is an apt answer (2) does a good turn   52 **unyoke** i.e., after this great effort, you
may unharness the team of your wits   55 **Mass** by the Mass

60 **stoup** two-quart measure   61 **In . . . love** (This and the two following stanzas with nonsensical variations, are from a poem attributed to Lord Vaux and printed in *Tottel's Miscellany*, 1557. The O
and *a* [for "ah"] seemingly are the grunts of the digger.)   63 **To contract . . . behove** i.e., to shorten the time for my own advantage.
(Perhaps he means to *prolong* it.)   64 **meet** suitable, i.e., more suitable   65 **'a** that he   67–68 **property of easiness** something he
can do easily and indifferently   70 **daintier sense** more delicate
sense of feeling   73 **into the land** i.e., toward my grave (?) (But
note the lack of rhyme in *steps, land*.)   76 **jowls** dashes (with a pun
on *jowl*, "jawbone")   78 **politician** schemer, plotter. **o'erreaches**
circumvents, gets the better of (with a quibble on the literal sense)
87–88 **chapless** having no lower jaw. **mazard** i.e., head. (Literally, a
drinking vessel.)   89 **revolution** turn of Fortune's wheel, change.
an if   89–90 **trick to see** knack of seeing. **cost . . . but** involve so
little expense and care in upbringing that we may

play at loggets° with them? Mine ache to think on 't.

FIRST CLOWN.   *Song.*

    "A picksax and a spade, a spade,
        For and° a shrouding sheet;
    O, a pit of clay for to be made

95   For such a guest is meet."

                     [He throws up another skull.]

HAMLET. There's another. Why may not that be the skull of a lawyer? Where be his quiddities° now, his quillities,° his cases, his tenures,° and his tricks? Why does he suffer this mad knave now to knock him about the sconce° with a

100 dirty shovel, and will not tell him of his action of battery?° Hum, this fellow might be in 's time a great buyer of land, with his statutes, his recognizances,° his fines, his double° vouchers,° his recoveries.° Is this the fine of his fines and the recovery of his recoveries, to have his fine

105 pate full of fine dirt?° Will his vouchers vouch him no more of his purchases, and double ones too, than the length and breadth of a pair of indentures?° The very conveyances° of his lands will scarcely lie in this box,° and must th' inheritor° himself have no more, ha?

110 HORATIO. Not a jot more, my lord.

HAMLET. Is not parchment made of sheepskins?

HORATIO. Ay, my lord, and of calves' skins too.

HAMLET. They are sheep and calves which seek out assurance in that.° I will speak to this fellow.—Whose grave's

115   this, sirrah?°

FIRST CLOWN. Mine, sir.

    [Sings.] "O, pit of clay for to be made
        For such a guest is meet."

HAMLET. I think it be thine, indeed, for thou liest in 't.

120 FIRST CLOWN. You lie out on 't, sir, and therefore 'tis not yours. For my part, I do not lie in t', yet it is mine.

HAMLET. Thou dost lie in 't, to be in 't and say it is thine. 'Tis for the dead, not for the quick;° therefore thou liest.

FIRST CLOWN. 'Tis a quick lie, sir; 'twill away again from me to you.   125

HAMLET. What man dost thou dig it for?

FIRST CLOWN. For no man, sir.

HAMLET. What woman, then?

FIRST CLOWN. For none, neither.

HAMLET. Who is to be buried in 't?   130

FIRST CLOWN. One that was a woman, sir, but, rest her soul, she's dead.

HAMLET. How absolute° the knave is! We must speak by the card°, or equivocation° will undo us. By the Lord, Horatio, this three years I have took° note of it: the age is 135 grown so picked° that the toe of the peasant comes so near the heel of the courtier, he galls his kibe.°—How long hast thou been grave maker?

FIRST CLOWN. Of all the days i' the year, I came to 't that day that our last king Hamlet overcame Fortinbras.   140

HAMLET. How long is that since?

FIRST CLOWN. Cannot you tell that? Every fool can tell that. It was that very day that young Hamlet was born—he that is mad and sent into England.

HAMLET. Ay, marry, why was he sent into England?   145

FIRST CLOWN. Why, because 'a was mad. 'A shall recover his wits there, or if 'a do not, 'tis no great matter there.

HAMLET. Why?

FIRST CLOWN. 'Twill not be seen in him there. There the men are as mad as he.   150

HAMLET. How came he mad?

FIRST CLOWN. Very strangely, they say.

HAMLET. How strangely?

FIRST CLOWN. Faith, e'en with losing his wits.

HAMLET. Upon what ground?°   155

FIRST CLOWN. Why, here in Denmark. I have been sexton here, man and boy, thirty years.

HAMLET. How long will a man lie i' th' earth ere he rot?

FIRST CLOWN. Faith, if 'a be not rotten before 'a die—as we have many pocky° corpses nowadays, that will scarce 160 hold the laying in°—'a will last you° some eight year or nine year. A tanner will last you nine year.

HAMLET. Why he more than another?

FIRST CLOWN. Why, sir, his hide is so tanned with his trade that 'a will keep out water a great while, and your water is a 165 sore° decayer of your whoreson° dead body. *[He picks up a*

---

91 loggets a game in which pieces of hard wood shaped like Indian clubs or bowling pins are thrown to lie as near as possible to a stake **93 For and** and moreover **97 quiddities** subtleties, quibbles. (From Latin *quid*, "a thing.") **quillities** verbal niceties, subtle distinctions. (Variation of *quiddities*.) **98 tenures** the holding of a piece of property or office, or the conditions or period of such holding **99 sconce** head **100–101 action of battery** lawsuit about physical assault **102 statutes, recognizances** legal documents guaranteeing a debt by attaching land and property **103 fines, recoveries** ways of converting entailed estates into "fee simple" or freehold. **double** signed by two signatories. **vouchers** guarantees of the legality of a title to real estate **104–105 fine of his fines . . . fine pate . . . fine dirt** end of his legal maneuvers . . . elegant head . . . minutely sifted dirt **107 pair of indentures** legal document drawn up in duplicate on a single sheet and then cut apart on a zigzag line so that each pair was uniquely matched. (Hamlet may refer to two rows of teeth or dentures.) **108 conveyances** deeds. **box** (1) deed box (2) coffin. ("Skull" has been suggested.) **109 inheritor** possessor, owner **113–114 assurance in that** safety in legal parchments **115 sirrah** (A term of address to inferiors.) **123 quick** living

133 absolute strict, precise **133–134 by the card** i.e., with precision. (Literally, by the mariner's compass-card, on which the points of the compass were marked.) **equivocation** ambiguity in the use of terms **135 took** taken **136 picked** refined, fastidious **137 galls his kibe** chafes the courtier's chilblain **155 ground** cause. (But, in the next line, the gravedigger takes the word in the sense of "land," "country.") **160 pocky** rotten, diseased. (Literally, with the pox, or syphilis.) **161 hold the laying in** hold together long enough to be interred. **last you** last. (*You* is used colloquially here and in the following lines.) **166 sore** i.e., terrible, great. **whoreson** i.e., vile, scurvy

skull.] Here's a skull now hath lien you° i' th' earth three-
and-twenty years.

HAMLET. Whose was it?

170 FIRST CLOWN. A whoreson mad fellow's it was. Whose do
you think it was?

HAMLET. Nay, I know not.

FIRST CLOWN. A pestilence on him for a mad rogue! 'A
poured a flagon of Rhenish° on my head once. This same
175 skull, sir, was, sir, Yorick's skull, the King's jester.

HAMLET. This?

FIRST CLOWN. E'en that.

HAMLET. Let me see. [*He takes the skull.*] Alas, poor Yorick! I
knew him, Horatio, a fellow of infinite jest, of most ex-
180 cellent fancy. He hath bore° me on his back a thousand
times, and now how abhorred in my imagination it is! My
gorge rises° at it. Here hung those lips that I have kissed I
know not how oft. Where be your gibes now? Your gam-
bols, your songs, your flashes of merriment that were
185 wont° to set the table on a roar? Not one now, to mock
your own grinning?° Quite chopfallen?° Now get you to
my lady's chamber and tell her, let her paint an inch
thick, to this favor° she must come. Make her laugh at
that. Prithee, Horatio, tell me one thing.

190 HORATIO. What's that, my lord?

HAMLET. Dost thou think Alexander looked o' this fashion
i' th' earth?

HORATIO. E'en so.

HAMLET. And smelt so? Pah! [*He throws down the skull.*]

195 HORATIO. E'en so, my lord.

HAMLET. To what bases uses we may return, Horatio! Why
may not imagination trace the noble dust of Alexander
till 'a find it stopping a bunghole?°

HORATIO. 'Twere to consider too curiously° to consider so.

200 HAMLET. No, faith, not a jot, but to follow him thither with
modesty° enough, and likelihood to lead it. As thus:
Alexander died, Alexander was buried, Alexander retur-
neth to dust, the dust is earth, of earth we make loam,°
and why of that loam whereto he was converted might
205 they not stop a beer barrel?

Imperious° Caesar, dead and turned to clay,
Might stop a hole to keep the wind away.
O, that that earth which kept the world in awe
Should patch a wall t' expel the winter's flaw!°

Enter King, Queen, Laertes, and the corpse [*of
Ophelia, in procession, with Priest, lords, etc.*].

But soft, but soft° awhile! Here comes the King,   210
The Queen, the courtiers. Who is this they follow?
And with such maimèd° rites? This doth betoken
The corpse they follow did with desperate hand
Fordo° its own life. 'Twas of some estate.°
Couch we° awhile and mark.   215
       [*He and Horatio conceal themselves.
       Ophelia's body is taken to the grave.*]

LAERTES. What ceremony else?

HAMLET [*to Horatio*].
That is Laertes, a very noble youth. Mark.

LAERTES. What ceremony else?

PRIEST.
Her obsequies have been as far enlarged
As we have warranty.° Here death was doubtful,   220
And but that great command o'ersways the order°
She should in ground unsanctified been lodged°
Till the last trumpet. For° charitable prayers,
Shards,° flints, and pebbles should be thrown on her.
Yet here she is allowed her virgin crants,°   225
Her maiden strewments,° and the bringing home
Of bell and burial.°

LAERTES.
Must there no more be done?

PRIEST.   No more be done.
We should profane the service of the dead
To sing a requiem and such rest° to her   230
As to peace-parted souls.°

LAERTES.   Lay her i' th' earth,
And from her fair and unpolluted flesh
May violets° spring! I tell thee, churlish priest,
A ministering angel shall my sister be
When thou liest howling.°

HAMLET [*to Horatio*].   What, the fair Ophelia!   235

QUEEN [*scattering flowers*]. Sweets to the sweet! Farewell.
I hoped thou shouldst have been my Hamlet's wife.
I thought thy bride-bed to have decked, sweet maid,
And not t' have strewed thy grave.

LAERTES.   O, treble woe

---

167 **lien you** lain. (See the note at line 163.)   174 **Rhenish** Rhine
wine   180 **bore** borne   182 **My gorge rises** i.e., I feel nauseated
184–185 **were wont** used   185–186 **mock your own grinning**
mock at the way your skull seems to be grinning (just as you used to
mock at yourself and those who grinned at you)   186 **chopfallen**
(1) lacking the lower jaw (2) dejected   188 **favor** aspect, appearance   198 **bunghole** hole for filling or emptying a cask   199 **curiously** minutely   201 **modesty** plausible moderation   203 **loam**
mortar consisting chiefly of moistened clay and straw   206 **Impe-
rious** imperial   209 **flaw** gust of wind

210 **soft** i.e., wait, be careful   212 **maimèd** mutilated, incomplete
214 **Fordo** destroy. **estate** rank   215 **Couch we** let's hide, lie low
220 **warranty** i.e., ecclesiastical authority   221 **great . . . order**
orders from on high overrule the prescribed procedures   222 **She
should . . . lodged** she should have been buried in unsanctified
ground   223 **For** in place of   224 **Shards** broken bits of pottery
225 **crants** garlands betokening maidenhood   226 **strewments**
flowers strewn on a coffin   226–227 **bringing . . . burial** laying
the body to rest, to the sound of the bell   230 **such rest** i.e., to
pray for such rest   231 **peace-parted souls** those who have died at
peace with God   232 **violets** (See 4.5.187 and note.)   235 **howling** i.e., in hell

240 Fall ten times treble on that cursèd head
Whose wicked deed thy most ingenious sense°
Deprived thee of! Hold off the earth awhile,
Till I have caught her once more in mine arms.
                    [*He leaps into the grave and embraces Ophelia.*]
Now pile your dust upon the quick and dead,
245 Till of this flat a mountain you have made
T' o'ertop old Pelion or the skyish head
Of blue Olympus.°
HAMLET [*coming forward*]. What is he whose grief
Bears such an emphasis,° whose phrase of sorrow
Conjures the wandering stars° and makes them stand
250 Like wonder-wounded° hearers? This is I,
Hamlet the Dane.°
LAERTES [*grappling with him*].° The devil take thy soul!
HAMLET. Thou pray'st not well.
I prithee, take thy fingers from my throat,
For though I am not splenitive° and rash,
255 Yet have I in me something dangerous,
Which let thy wisdom fear. Hold off thy hand.
KING. Pluck them asunder.
QUEEN. Hamlet, Hamlet!
ALL. Gentlemen!
260 HORATIO. Good my lord, be quiet.
                    [*Hamlet and Laertes are parted.*]
HAMLET.
Why, I will fight with him upon this theme
Until my eyelids will no longer wag.°
QUEEN. O my son, what theme?
HAMLET.
I loved Ophelia. Forty thousand brothers
265 Could not with all their quantity of love
Make up my sum. What wilt thou do for her?
KING. O, he is mad, Laertes.
QUEEN. For love of God, forbear him.°
HAMLET.
'Swounds°, show me what thou'lt do.

270 Woo't° weep? Woo't fight? Woo't fast? Woo't tear thyself?
Woo't drink up° eisel?° Eat a crocodile?°
I'll do 't. Dost come here to whine?
To outface me with leaping in her grave?
Be buried quick° with her, and so will I.
275 And if thou prate of mountains, let them throw
Millions of acres on us, till our ground,
Singeing his pate° against the burning zone,°
Make Ossa° like a wart! Nay, an° thou'lt mouth,°
I'll rant as well as thou.
QUEEN.   This is mere° madness,
280 And thus awhile the fit will work on him;
Anon, as patient as the female dove
When that her golden couplets° are disclosed,°
His silence wills sit drooping.
HAMLET.   Hear you, sir.
What is the reason that you use me thus?
285 I loved you ever. But it is no matter.
Let Hercules himself do what he may,
The cat will mew, and dog will have his day.°
                                        Exit Hamlet.
KING.
I pray thee, good Horatio, wait upon him.
                                        [*Exit*] *Horatio.*
[*To Laertes.*] Strengthen your patience in° our last night's
    speech;
290 We'll put the matter to the present push.°—
Good Gertrude, set some watch over your son.—
This grave shall have a living° monument.
An hour of quiet° shortly shall we see;
Till then, in patience our proceeding be.   *Exeunt.* 295

5 . 2 °   *Enter Hamlet and Horatio.*

HAMLET.
So much for this, sir; now shall you see the other.°

---

241 **ingenious sense** a mind that is quick, alert, of fine qualities
246–247 **Pelion, Olympus** sacred mountains in the north of Thessaly; see also *Ossa*, below, at line 281   248 **emphasis** i.e., rhetorical and florid emphasis. (*Phrase* has a similar rhetorical connotation.)   249 **wandering stars** planets   250 **wonder-wounded** struck with amazement   251 **the Dane** (This title normally signifies the King; see 1.1.17 and note.)   **s.d. grappling with him** The testimony of the First Quarto that "*Hamlet leaps in after Laertes*" and the "Elegy on Burbage" ("Oft have I seen him leap into the grave") seem to indicate one way in which this fight was staged; however, the difficulty of fitting two contenders and Ophelia's body into a confined space (probably the trapdoor) suggests to many editors the alternative, that Laertes jumps out of the grave to attack Hamlet.)   254 **splenitive** quick-tempered   262 **wag** move. (A fluttering eyelid is a conventional sign that life has not yet gone.)   268 **forbear him** leave him alone   269 **'Swounds** by His (Christ's) wounds

270 **Woo't** wilt thou   271 **drink up** drink deeply. **eisel** vinegar. **crocodile** (Crocodiles were tough and dangerous, and were supposed to shed hypocritical tears.)   274 **quick** alive   277 **his pate** its head, i.e., top. **burning zone** zone in the celestial sphere containing the sun's orbit, between the tropics of Cancer and Capricorn   278 **Ossa** another mountain in Thessaly. (In their war against the Olympian gods, the giants attempted to heap Ossa on Pelion to scale Olympus.) **an** if. **mouth** i.e., rant   279 **mere** utter   282 **golden couplets** two baby pigeons, covered with yellow down. **disclosed** hatched   286–287 **Let . . . day** i.e., (1) even Hercules couldn't stop Laertes' theatrical rant (2) I, too, will have my turn; i.e., despite any blustering attempts at interference, every person will sooner or later do what he or she must do   289 **in** i.e., by recalling   291 **present push** immediate test   293 **living** lasting. (For Laertes' private understanding, Claudius also hints that Hamlet's death will serve as such a monument.)   294 **hour of quiet** time free of conflict
5.2. Location. The castle.
1 **see the other** hear the other news

You do remember all the circumstance?
HORATIO. Remember it, my lord!
HAMLET.
　　Sir, in my heart there was a kind of fighting
5　　That would not let me sleep. Methought I lay
　　Worse than the mutines° in the bilboes.° Rashly,°
　　And praised be rashness for it—let us know°
　　Our indiscretion °sometimes serves as well
　　When our deep plots do pall,° and that should
　　　　learn° us
10　There's a divinity that shapes our ends,
　　Rough-hew° them how we will—
HORATIO.　　　　　　　　　　That is most certain.
HAMLET. Up from my cabin,
　　My sea-gown° scarfed° about me, in the dark
　　Groped I to find out them,° had my desire,
15　Fingered° their packet, and in fine° withdrew
　　To mine own room again, making so bold,
　　My fears forgetting manners, to unseal
　　Their grand commission; where I found, Horatio—
　　Ah, royal knavery!—an exact command,
20　Larded° with many several° sorts of reasons
　　Importing° Denmark's health and England's too,
　　With, ho! such bugs° and goblins in my life,°
　　That on the supervise,° no leisure bated,°
　　No, not to stay° the grinding of the ax,
　　My head should be struck off.
25 HORATIO.　　　　　　　　　Is 't possible?
HAMLET [giving a document].
　　Here's the commission. Read it at more leisure.
　　But will thou hear now how I did proceed?
HORATIO. I beseech you.
HAMLET.
　　Being thus benetted round with villainies—
30　Ere I could make a prologue to my brains,
　　They had begun the play°—I sat me down,
　　Devised a new commission, wrote it fair.°
　　I once did hold it, as our statists° do,
　　A baseness° to write fair, and labored much
35　How to forget that learning, but, sir, now

It did me yeoman's° service. Wilt thou know
　　Th' effect° of what I wrote?
HORATIO.　　　　　　　　　Ay, good my lord.
HAMLET.
　　An earnest conjuration° from the King,
　　As England was his faithful tributary,
　　As love between them like the palm° might flourish,　40
　　As peace should still° her wheaten garland° wear
　　And stand a comma° 'tween their amities,
　　And many suchlike "as"es° of great charge,°
　　That on the view and knowing of these contents,
　　Without debatement further more or less,　45
　　He should those bearers put to sudden death,
　　Not shriving time° allowed.
HORATIO.　　　　　　　　　How was this sealed?
HAMLET.
　　Why, even in that was heaven ordinant.°
　　I had my father's signet° in my purse,
　　Which was the model° of that Danish seal;　50
　　Folded the writ° up in the form of th' other,
　　Subscribed° it, gave 't th' impression,° placed it safely,
　　The changeling° never known. Now, the next day
　　Was our sea fight, and what to this was sequent°
　　Thou knowest already.　55
HORATIO.
　　So Guildenstern and Rosencrantz go to 't.
HAMLET.
　　Why, man, they did make love to this employment.
　　They are not near my conscience. Their defeat°
　　Does by their own insinuation° grow.
　　'Tis dangerous when the baser° nature comes　60
　　Between the pass° and fell° incensèd points
　　Of mighty opposites.°
HORATIO.　　　　　　　　Why, what a king is this!
HAMLET.
　　Does it not, think thee, stand me now upon°—
　　He that hath killed my king and whored my mother,
　　Popped in between th' election° and my hopes,　65

6 **mutines** mutineers. **bilboes** shackles. **Rashly** on impulse. (This adverb goes with lines 12 ff.)　7 **know** acknowledge　8 **indiscretion** lack of foresight and judgment (not an indiscreet act)　9 **pall** fail, falter, go stale. **learn** teach　11 **Rough-hew** shape roughly　13 **sea-gown** seaman's coat. **scarfed** loosely wrapped　14 **them** i.e., Rosencrantz and Guildenstern　15 **Fingered** pilfered, pinched. **in fine** finally, in conclusion　20 **Larded** garnished. **several** different　21 **Importing** relating to　22 **bugs** bugbears, hobgloblins. **in my life** i.e., to be feared if I were allowed to live　23 **supervise** reading. **leisure bated** delay allowed　24 **stay** await　30–31 **Ere . . . play** before I could consciously turn my brain to the matter, it had started working on a plan　32 **fair** in a clear hand　33 **statists** statesmen　34 **baseness** i.e., lower-class trait

36 **yeoman's** i.e., substantial, faithful, loyal　37 **effect** purport　38 **conjuration** entreaty　40 **palm** (An image of health; see Psalm 92:12.)　41 **still** always. **wheaten garland** (Symbolic of fruitful agriculture, of peace and plenty.)　42 **comma** (Indicating continuity, link.)　43 **"as"es** (1) the "where-ases" of a formal document (2) asses. **charge** (1) important (2) burden (appropriate to asses)　47 **shriving time** time for confession and absolution　48 **ordinant** directing　49 **signet** small seal　50 **model** replica　51 **writ** writing　52 **Subscribed** signed (with forged signature). **impression** i.e., with a wax seal　53 **changeling** i.e., substituted letter. (Literally, a fairy child substituted for a human one.)　54 **was sequent** followed　58 **defeat** destruction　59 **insinuation** intrusive intervention, sticking their noses in my business　60 **baser** of lower social station　61 **pass** thrust. **fell** fierce　62 **opposites** antagonists　63 **stand me now upon** become incumbent on me now　65 **election** (The Danish monarch was "elected" by a small number of high-ranking electors.)

Thrown out his angle° for my proper° life,
And with such cozenage°—is 't not perfect conscience
To quit° him with this arm? And is 't not to be damned
To let this canker° of our nature come
70　In° further evil?

HORATIO.
It must be shortly known to him from England
What is the issue of the business there.

HAMLET.
It will be short. The interim is mine,
And a man's life's no more than to say "one."°
75　But I am very sorry, good Horatio,
That to Laertes I forgot myself,
For by the image of my cause I see
The portraiture of his. I'll court his favors.
But, sure, the bravery° of his grief did put me
Into a tow'ring passion.

80　HORATIO.　　　　　　　　　　Peace, who comes here?

Enter a Courtier [Osric].

OSRIC.　Your lordship is right welcome back to Denmark.
HAMLET.　I humbly thank you, sir. [*To Horatio.*] Dost know
this water fly?
HORATIO.　No, my good lord.
85　HAMLET.　Thy state is the more gracious, for 'tis a vice to
know him. He hath much land, and fertile. Let a beast be
lord of beasts, and his crib° shall stand at the King's
mess.° 'Tis a chuff,° but, as I say, spacious in the possession of dirt.
90　OSRIC.　Sweet lord, if your lordship were at leisure, I should
impart a thing to you from His Majesty.
HAMLET.　I will receive it, sir, with all diligence of spirit. Put
your bonnet° to his° right use; 'tis for the head.
OSRIC.　I thank your lordship, it is very hot.
95　HAMLET.　No, believe me, 'tis very cold. The wind is
northerly.
OSRIC.　It is indifferent° cold, my lord, indeed.
HAMLET.　But yet methinks it is very sultry and hot for my
complexion.°
100　OSRIC.　Exceedingly, my lord. It is very sultry as 'twere—I
cannot tell how. My lord, His Majesty bade me signify to
you that 'a has laid a great wager on your head. Sir, this is
the matter—
HAMLET.　I beseech you, remember.

　　　　　　　[*Hamlet moves him to put on his hat.*]

OSRIC.　Nay, good my lord; for my ease,° in good faith. Sir, 105
here is newly come to court Laertes—believe me, an ab-
solute° gentleman, full of most excellent differences,° of
very soft society° and great showing.° Indeed, to speak
feelingly° of him, he is the card° or calendar° of gentry,°
for you shall find in him the continent of what part a gen- 110
tleman would see.°
HAMLET.　Sir, his definement° suffers no perdition° in
you,° though I know to divide him inventorially°
would dozy° th' arithmetic of memory, and yet but yaw°
neither° in respect of° his quick sail. But, in the verity 115
of extolment,° I take him to be a soul of great article,°
and his infusion° of such dearth and rareness° as, to
make true diction° of him, his semblable° is his mirror
and who else would trace° him his umbrage,° nothing
more.　　　　　　　　　　　　　　　　　　　　　　120
OSRIC.　Your lordship speaks most infallibly of him.
HAMLET.　The concernancy,° sir? Why do we wrap the gentleman in our more rawer breath?°
OSRIC.　Sir?
HORATIO.　Is 't not possible to understand in another 125
tongue?° You will do 't,° sir, really.
HAMLET.　What imports the nomination° of this gentle-
man?
OSRIC.　Of Laertes?
HORATIO. [*to Hamlet*].　His purse is empty already; all 's 130
golden words are spent.
HAMLET.　Of him, sir.
OSRIC.　I know you are not ignorant—
HAMLET.　I would you did, sir. Yet in faith if you did, it would
not much approve° me. Well, sir?　　　　　　　　135

66 angle fishhook. **proper** very　**67 cozenage** trickery　**68 quit**
requite, pay back　**69 canker** ulcer　**69–70 come in** grow into
74 a man's . . . "one" one's whole life occupies such a short time,
only as long as it takes to count to 1　**79 bravery** bravado　**86–88
Let . . . mess** i.e., if a man, no matter how beastlike, is as rich in
livestock and possessions as Osric, he may eat at the King's table
87 crib manger　**88 chuff** boor, churl. (The Second Quarto
spelling, *chough*, is a variant spelling that also suggests the meaning
here of "chattering jackdaw.")　**93 bonnet** any kind of cap or hat.
his its　**97 indifferent** somewhat　**99 complexion** temperament

105 for my ease (A conventional reply declining the invitation to
put his hat back on.)　**106–107 absolute** perfect　**107 differences** special qualities　**108 soft society** agreeable manners. **great
showing** distinguished appearance　**109 feelingly** with just perception. **card** chart, map. **calendar** guide. **gentry** good breeding
110–111 the continent . . . see one who contains in him all the
qualities a gentleman would like to see. (A *continent* is that which
contains.)　**112 definement** definition. (Hamlet proceeds to mock
Osric by throwing his lofty diction back at him.) **perdition** loss,
diminution　**113 you** your description. **divide him inventorially**
enumerate his graces　**114 dozy** dizzy. **yaw** swing unsteadily off
course. (Said of a ship.)　**115 neither** for all that. **in respect of** in
comparison with　**115–116 in . . . extolment** in true praise (of
him)　**116 of great article** one with many articles in his inventory
117 infusion essence, character infused into him by nature. **dearth
and rareness** rarity　**118 make true diction** speak truly　**118
semblable** only true likeness　**119 who . . . trace** any other person
who would wish to follow. **umbrage** shadow　**122 concernancy**
import, relevance　**123 rawer breath** unrefined speech that can
only come short in praising him　**125–126 to understand . . .
tongue** i.e., for you, Osric, to understand when someone else speaks
your language. (Horatio twits Osric for not being able to understand
the kind of flowery speech he himself uses, when Hamlet speaks in
such a vein. Alternatively, all this could be said to Hamlet.)　**126
You will do 't** i.e., you can if you try, or, you may well have to try (to
speak plainly)　**127 nomination** naming　**135 approve** commend

OSRIC. You are not ignorant of what excellence Laertes is—

HAMLET. I dare not confess that, lest I should compare with him in excellence. But to know a man well were to know himself.°

140

OSRIC. I mean, sir, for° his weapon; but in the imputation laid on him by them,° in his meed° he's unfellowed.°

HAMLET. What's his weapon?

OSRIC. Rapier and dagger.

145 HAMLET. That's two of his weapons—but well.°

OSRIC. The King, sir, hath wagered with him six Barbary horses, against the which he° has impawned,° as I take it, six French rapiers and poniards,° with their assigns,° as girdle, hangers,° and so.° Three of the carriages,° in

150 faith, are very dear to fancy,° very responsive° to the hilts, most delicate° carriages, and of very liberal conceit.°

HAMLET. What call you the carriages?

HORATIO [to Hamlet]. I knew you must be edified by the

155 margent° ere you had done.

OSRIC. The carriages, sir, are the hangers.

HAMLET. The phrase would be more germane to the matter if we could carry a cannon by our sides; I would it might be hangers till then. But, on: six Barbary horses against

160 six French swords, their assigns, and three liberal-conceited carriages; that's the French bet against the Danish. Why is this impawned, as you call it?

OSRIC. The King, sir, hath laid,° sir, that in a dozen passes° between yourself and him, he shall not exceed you three

165 hits. He hath laid on twelve for nine, and it would come to immediate trial, if your lordship would vouchsafe the answer.°

HAMLET. How if I answer no?

OSRIC. I mean, my lord, the opposition of your person in

170 trial.

HAMLET. Sir, I will walk here in the hall. If it please His Majesty, it is the breathing time° of day with me. Let° the foils be brought, the gentlemen willing, and the King hold his purpose, I will win for him an I can; if not, I will gain nothing but my shame and the odd hits.

175

OSRIC. Shall I deliver you° so?

HAMLET. To this effect, sir—after what flourish your nature will.

OSRIC. I commend° my duty to your lordship.

HAMLET. Yours, yours. [Exit Osric.] 'A does well to commend it himself; there are no tongues else for 's turn.°

180

HORATIO. This lapwing° runs away with the shell on his head.

HAMLET. 'A did comply with his dug° before 'a sucked it. Thus has he—and many more of the same breed that I know the drossy° age dotes on—only got the tune° of the time and, out of an habit of encounter,° a kind of yeasty° collection,° which carries them through and through the most fanned and winnowed opinions;° and do° but blow them to their trial, the bubbles are out.°

185

190

Enter a Lord.

LORD. My lord, His Majesty commended him to you by young Osric, who brings back to him that you attend him in the hall. He sends to know if your pleasure hold to play with Laertes, or that° you will take longer time.

HAMLET. I am constant to my purposes; they follow the King's pleasure. If his fitness speaks, mine is ready;° now or whensoever, provided I be so able as now.

195

LORD. The King and Queen and all are coming down.

HAMLET. In happy time.°

138–140 I dare . . . himself I dare not boast of knowing Laertes' excellence lest I seem to imply a comparable excellence in myself. Certainly, to know another person well, one must know oneself. 141 for i.e., with 141–142 imputation . . . them reputation given him by others 142 meed merit. unfellowed unmatched 145 but well but never mind 147 he i.e., Laertes. impawned staked, wagered 148 poniards daggers. assigns appurtenances 149 hangers straps on the sword belt (*girdle*), from which the sword hung. and so and so on. carriages (An affected way of saying *hangers*; literally, gun carriages.) 150 dear to fancy delightful to the fancy. responsive corresponding closely, matching or well adjusted 151 delicate (i.e., in workmanship) 151–152 liberal conceit elaborate design 155 margent margin of a book, place for explanatory notes 163 laid wagered. passes bouts. (The odds of the betting are hard to explain. Possibly the King bets that Hamlet will win at least five out of twelve, at which point Laertes raises the odds against himself by betting he will nine.) 166–167 vouchsafe the answer be so good as to accept the challenge. (Hamlet deliberately takes the phase in its literal sense of replying.)

172 breathing time exercise period. Let i.e., if 176 deliver you report what you say 179 commend commit to your favor. (A conventional salutation, but Hamlet wryly uses a more literal meaning, "recommend," "praise," in line 180.) 181 for 's turn for his purposes, i.e., to do it for him 182 lapwing (A proverbial type of youthful forwardness. Also, a bird that draws intruders away from its nest and was thought to run about with its head in the shell when newly hatched; a seeming reference to Osric's hat.) 184 comply . . . dug observe ceremonious formality toward his nurse's or mother's teat 186 drossy laden with scum and impurities, frivolous. tune temper, mood, manner of speech 187 an habit of encounter a demeanor in conversing (with courtiers of his own kind) yeasty frothy 188 collection i.e., of current phrases 188–189 carries . . . opinions sustains them right through the scrutiny of persons whose opinions are select and refined. (Literally, like grain separated from its chaff. Osric is both the chaff and the bubbly froth on the surface of the liquor that is soon blown away.) 189 and do yet do 189–190 blow . . . out test them by merely blowing on them, and their bubbles burst 194 that if 196 If . . . ready if he declares his readiness, my convenience waits on his 199 In happy time (A phrase of courtesy indicating that the time is convenient.)

200 LORD. The Queen desires you to use some gentle entertain-
ment° to Laertes before you fall to play.

HAMLET. She well instructs me.   *[Exit Lord.]*

HORATIO. You will lose, my lord.

HAMLET. I do not think so. Since he went into France, I
205   have been in continual practice; I shall win at the odds.
But thou wouldst not think how ill all's here about my
heart; but it is no matter.

HORATIO. Nay, good my lord—

HAMLET. It is but foolery, but it is such a kind of gaingiving°
210   as would perhaps trouble a woman.

HORATIO. If your mind dislike anything, obey it. I will forestall their repair° hither and say you are not fit.

HAMLET. Not a whit, we defy augury. There is special providence in the fall of a sparrow. If it be now, 'tis not to
215   come; if it be not to come, it will be now; if it be not now;
yet it will come. The readiness is all. Since no man of
aught he leaves knows, what is 't to leave betimes? Let
be.°

      A table prepared. [Enter] trumpets, drums, and offi-
      cers with cushions; King, Queen, [Osric,] and all the
      state; foils, daggers, [and wine borne in;] and
      Laertes.

KING.
    Come, Hamlet, come and take this hand from me.
               [The King puts Laertes' hand into Hamlet's.]

HAMLET *[to Laertes]*
220   Give me your pardon, sir. I have done you wrong,
But pardon 't as you are a gentleman.
This presence° knows,
And you must needs have heard, how I am punished°
With a sore distraction. What I have done
225   That might your nature, honor, and exception°
Roughly awake, I here proclaim was madness.
Was 't Hamlet wronged Laertes? Never Hamlet.
If Hamlet from himself be ta'en away,
And when he's not himself does wrong Laertes,
230   Then Hamlet does it not, Hamlet denies it.
Who does it, then? His madness. If 't be so,
Hamlet is of the faction° that is wronged;
His madness is poor Hamlet's enemy.
Sir, in this audience
235   Let my disclaiming from a purposed evil

Free me so far in your most generous thoughts
That I have° shot my arrow o'er the house
And hurt my brother.

LAERTES.   I am satisfied in nature,°
Whose motive° in this case should stir me most
To my revenge. But in my terms of honor   240
I stand aloof, and will no reconcilement
Till by some elder masters of known honor
I have a voice° and precedent of peace°
To keep my name ungored.° But till that time
I do receive your offered love like love,   245
And will not wrong it.

HAMLET.   I embrace it freely,
And will this brothers' wager frankly° play.—
Give us the foils. Come on.

LAERTES.   Come, one for me.

HAMLET.
    I'll be your foil,° Laertes. In mine ignorance
Your skill shall, like a star i' in the darkest night,   250
Stick fiery off° indeed.

LAERTES.   You mock me, sir.

HAMLET. No, by this hand.

KING.
    Give them the foils, young Osric. Cousin Hamlet,
You know the wager?

HAMLET.   Very well, my lord.
Your Grace has laid the odds o'° the weaker side.   255

KING.
    I do not fear it; I have seen you both.
But since he is bettered,° we have therefore odds.

LAERTES.
    This is too heavy. Let me see another.
            [He exchanges his foil for another.]

HAMLET.
    This likes me° well. These foils have all a length?
               [They prepare to play.]

OSRIC. Ay, my good lord.   260

KING.
    Set me the stoups of wine upon that table.
If Hamlet give the first or second hit,
Or quit in answer of the third exchange,°

---

237 **That I have** as if I had   238 **in nature** i.e., as to my personal
feelings   239 **motive** prompting   243 **voice** authoritative pro-
nouncement. **of peace** for reconciliation   244 **name ungored** reputation unwounded   247 **frankly** without ill feeling or the burden
of rancor   249 **foil** thin metal background which sets a jewel off
(with pun on the blunted rapier for fencing)   251 **Stick fiery off**
stand out brilliantly   255 **laid the odds o'** bet on, backed   257 **is
bettered** has improved; is the odds-on favorite. (Laertes' handicap is
the "three hits" specified in line 164.)   259 **likes me** pleases me
263 **Or . . . exchange** i.e., or requites Laertes in the third bout for
having won the first two

200–201 **entertainment** greeting 209 **gaingiving** misgiving
212 **repair** coming 216–218 **Since . . . Let be** since no one has
knowledge of what he is leaving behind, what does an early death
matter after all? Enough; don't struggle against it. 222 **presence**
royal assembly 223 **punished** afflicted 225 **exception** disapproval 232 **faction** party

Let all the battlements their ordnance fire.
265 The King shall drink to Hamlet's better breath,°
And in the cup an union° shall he throw
Richer than that which four successive kings
In Denmark's crown have worn. Give me the cups,
And let the kettle° to the trumpet speak,
270 The trumpet to the cannoneer without,
The cannons to the heavens, the heaven to earth,
"Now the King drinks to Hamlet." Come, begin.

                    Trumpets the while.

And you, the judges, bear a wary eye.
HAMLET. Come on, sir.
275 LAERTES. Come, my lord. [*The play. Hamlet scores a hit.*]
HAMLET. One.
LAERTES. No.
HAMLET. Judgment.
OSRIC.   A hit, a very palpable hit.

           Drum, trumpets, and shot. Flourish.
                    A piece goes off.

LAERTES. Well, again.
KING.
280   Stay, give me drink. Hamlet, this pearl is thine.

                [*He drinks, and throws a pearl in*
                          Hamlet's cup.]

Here's to thy health. Give him the cup.
HAMLET.
  I'll play this bout first. Set it by awhile.
  Come. [*They play.*] Another hit; what say you?
LAERTES. A touch, a touch, I do confess 't.
KING.
  Our son shall win.
285 QUEEN.   He's fat° and scant of breath.
  Here, Hamlet, take my napkin,° rub thy brows.
  The Queen carouses° to thy fortune, Hamlet.
HAMLET. Good madam!
KING. Gertrude, do not drink.
QUEEN.
290   I will, my lord, I pray you pardon me.   [*She drinks.*]
KING [*aside*].
  It is the poisoned cup. It is too late.
HAMLET.
  I dare not drink yet, madam; by and by.
QUEEN. Come, let me wipe thy face.
LAERTES [*to King*].
  My lord, I'll hit him now.
KING.   I do not think 't.

LAERTES [*aside*].
  And yet it is almost against my conscience.   295
HAMLET.
  Come, for the third, Laertes. You do but dally.
  I pray you, pass° with your best violence;
  I am afeard you make a wanton of me.°
LAERTES. Say you so? Come on.   [*They play.*]
OSRIC. Nothing neither way.   300
LAERTES.
  Have at you now!

    [*Laertes wounds Hamlet; then, in scuffling, they change*
             rapiers°, and Hamlet wounds Laertes.]

KING.   Part them! They are incensed.
HAMLET.
  Nay, come, again.   [*The Queen falls.*]
OSRIC.   Look to the Queen there, ho!
HORATIO.
  They bleed on both sides. How is it, my lord?
OSRIC. How is 't, Laertes?
LAERTES.
  Why, as a woodcock° to mine own springs,° Osric;   305
  I am justly killed with mine own treachery.
HAMLET.
  How does the Queen?
KING.   She swoons to see them bleed.
QUEEN.
  No, no, the drink, the drink—O my dear Hamlet—
  The drink, the drink! I am poisoned.   [*She dies.*]
HAMLET.
  O villainy! Ho, let the door be locked!   310
  Treachery! Seek it out.   [*Laertes falls. Exit Osric.*]
LAERTES.
  It is here, Hamlet. Hamlet, thou art slain.
  No med'cine in the world can do thee good;
  In thee there is not half an hour's life.
  The treacherous instruments is in thy hand,   315
  Unbated° and envenomed. The foul practice°
  Hath turned itself on me. Lo, here I lie,
  Never to rise again. Thy mother's poisoned.
  I can no more. The King, the King's to blame.
HAMLET.
  The point envenomed too? Then, venom, to thy work.   320

                    [*He stabs the King.*]

---

297 **pass** thrust   298 **make . . . me** i.e., treat me like a spoiled child, trifle with me   301 **s.d. in scuffling, they change rapiers** (This stage direction occurs in the Folio. According to a widespread stage tradition, Hamlet receives a scratch, realizes that Laertes' sword is unbated, and accordingly forces an exchange.)   305 **woodcock** a bird, a type of stupidity or as a decoy. **springes** trap, snare   316 **Unbated** not blunted with a button. **practice** plot

---

265 **better breath** improved vigor   266 **union** pearl. (So called, according to Pliny's *Natural History*, 9, because pearls are *unique*, never identical.)   269 **kettle** kettledrum   285 **fat** not physically fit, out of training   286 **napkin** handkerchief   287 **carouses** drinks a toast

ALL. Treason! Treason!
KING.
  O, yet defend me, friends! I am but hurt.
HAMLET [*forcing the King to drink*]. Here, thou incestuous,
  murderous, damnèd Dane,
325   Drink off this potion. Is thy union° here?
  Follow my mother.   [*The King dies.*]
LAERTES.   He is justly served.
  It is a poison tempered° by himself.
  Exchange forgiveness with me, noble Hamlet.
  Mine and my father's death come not upon thee,
330   Nor thine on me!   [*He dies.*]
HAMLET.
  Heaven make thee free of it! I follow thee.
  I am dead, Horatio. Wretched Queen, adieu!
  You that look pale and tremble at this chance,°
  That are but mutes° or audience to this act,
335   Had I but time—as this fell° sergeant,° Death,
  Is strict° in his arrest°—O, I could tell you—
  But let it be. Horatio, I am dead;
  Thou livest. Report me and my cause aright
  To the unsatisfied.
HORATIO.   Never believe it.
340   I am more an antique Roman° than a Dane.
  Here's yet some liquor left.
          [*He attempts to drink from the poisoned cup.*
                  Hamlet prevents him.]
HAMLET.   As thou'rt a man.
  Give me the cup! Let go! By heaven, I'll ha 't.
  O God, Horatio, what a wounded name,
  Things standing thus unknown, shall I leave
    behind me!
345   If thou didst ever hold me in thy heart,
  Absent thee from felicity awhile,
  And in this harsh world draw thy breath in pain
  To tell my story.   *A march afar off* [*and a volley within*].
  What warlike noise is this?

       Enter Osric.

OSRIC.
350   Young Fortinbras, with conquest come from Poland,
  To th' ambassadors of England gives
  This warlike volley.
HAMLET.   O, I die, Horatio!

  The potent poison quite o'ercrows° my spirit.
  I cannot live to hear the news from England,
  But I do prophesy th' election lights   355
  On Fortinbras. He has my dying voice.°
  So tell him, with th' occurrents° more and less
  Which have solicited°—the rest is silence.   [*He dies.*]
HORATIO.
  Now cracks a noble heart. Good night, sweet prince,
  And flights of angels sing thee to thy rest!   360
          [*March within.*]
  Why does the drum come hither?

     Enter Fortinbras, with the [*English*] *Ambassadors*
     [*with drum, colors, and attendants*].

FORTINBRAS.
  Where is this sight?
HORATIO.   What is it you would see?
  If aught of woe or wonder, cease your search.
FORTINBRAS.
  This quarry° cries on havoc.° O proud Death,
  What feast° is toward° in thine eternal cell,   365
  That thou so many princes at a shot
  So bloodily hast struck?
FIRST AMBASSADOR.   The sight is dismal,
  And our affairs from England come too late.
  The ears are senseless that should give us hearing,
  To tell him his commandment is fulfilled,   370
  That Rosencrantz and Guildenstern are dead.
  Where should we have our thanks?
HORATIO.   Not from his° mouth,
  Had it th' ability of life to thank you.
  He never gave commandment for their death.
  But since, so jump° upon this bloody question,°   375
  You from the Polack wars, and you from England,
  Are here arrived, give order that these bodies
  High on a stage° be placèd to the view,
  And let me speak to th' yet unknowing world
  How these things came about. So shall you hear   380
  Of carnal, bloody, and unnatural acts,
  Of accidental judgments,° casual° slaughters,
  Of deaths put on° by cunning and forced cause,°

---

325 **union** pearl. (See line 266; with grim puns on the word's other
meanings: marriage, shared death.)   **327 tempered** mixed   **333
chance** mischance   **334 mutes** silent observers. (Literally, actors
with nonspeaking parts.)   **335 fell** cruel. **sergeant** sheriff's officer
336 strict (1) severely just (2) unavoidable. **arrest** (1) taking into
custody (2) stopping my speech   **340 Roman** (Suicide was an
honorable choice for many Romans as an alternative to a dishonorable life.)

353 **o'ercrows** triumphs over (like the winner in a cockfight)
356 voice vote   **357 occurrents** events, incidents   **358 solicited**
moved, urged. (Hamlet doesn't finish saying what the events have
prompted—presumably, his acts of vengeance, or his reporting of
those events to Fortinbras.)   **364 quarry** heap of dead. **cries on
havoc** proclaims a general slaughter   **365 feast** i.e., Death feasting
on those who have fallen. **toward** in preparation   **372 his** i.e.,
Claudius'   **375 jump** precisely, immediately. **question** dispute, affair   **378 stage** platform   **382 judgments** retributions. **casual** occurring by chance.   **383 put on** instigated. **forced cause** contrivance

And, in this upshot, purposes mistook
385   Fall'n on th' inventors' heads. All this can I
Truly deliver.
FORTINBRAS.   Let us haste to hear it,
And call the noblest to the audience.
For me, with sorrow I embrace my fortune.
I have some rights of memory° in this kingdom,
390   Which now to claim my vantage° doth invite me.
HORATIO.
Of that I shall have also cause to speak,
And from his mouth whose voice will draw on more.°
But let this same be presently° performed,
Even while men's minds are wild, lest more mischance

On° plots and errors happen.
FORTINBRAS.   Let four captains   395
Bear Hamlet, like a soldier, to the stage,
For he was likely, had he been put on,°
To have proved most royal; and for his passage,°
The soldiers' music and the rite of war
Speak° loudly for him.   400
Take up the bodies. Such a sight as this
Becomes the field,° but here shows much amiss.
Go bid the soldiers shoot.
Exeunt [marching, bearing off the dead bodies;
a peal of ordnance is shot off].

---

389 of memory traditional, remembered, unforgotten **390 vantage** favorable opportunity **392 voice . . . more** vote will influence still others **393 presently** immediately

395 On on the basis of; on top of **397 put on** i.e., invested in royal office and so put to the test **398 passage** i.e., from life to death **400 Speak** (let them) speak **402 Becomes the field** suits the field of battle

---

SPOTLIGHT   SHAKESPEARE'S TWO THEATERS

Because it is the most famous theater in the world, there is a tendency to think of the Globe theater as the primary type of playhouse in Shakespeare's England. However, by 1600 English drama was in full blossom and London, a large capital city of about 150,000, had developed a variety of performance spaces for the many acting companies drawing enthusiastic crowds.

For simplicity's sake, Elizabethan public and private theaters can be divided into two categories, the indoor and the outdoor, that is, those with at least a portion of the roof open to the elements. There were four types of indoor theaters, all private:

1. Academic playhouses, such the Middle Temple, which were affixed to schools and used for student performances.
2. Nonscenic court playhouses, such as the great banqueting hall at Hampton Court, where plays were produced on an ad hoc basis and the playing space was adapted for the occasion.
3. Scenic court playhouses, such as the Great Hall at Whitechapel, where plays and masques were regularly performed in a space created to house scenery and other accoutrements of performance.
4. Private playhouses, which were fully functional theater spaces, usually within the city limits, where children's and professional acting companies performed for an exclusive clientele. There were four major private theaters: St. Paul's Boys Playhouse; the First Blackfriars; the Second Blackfriars; and the Whitefriars.

Two types of public outdoor theaters were used by professional adult acting companies:

1. Makeshift playhouses (e.g., the Boar's Head) which were adapted as permanent theaters from pre-existing spaces such as innyards or animal baiting rings.
2. Permanent public playhouses specifically constructed, usually beyond London's city limits, for the presentation of plays. The Globe is the best known of these, but there were six others: the Theatre; the Curtain; the Rose; the Swan; the Fortune; and the Red Bull. Of these, the Swan is most noteworthy because a Dutch traveler, Johannes de Witt, sketched its interior in his diary in 1596. De Witt's drawing was lost, but a copy by Arend van Buchell remains the only extant contemporary illustration of an Elizabethan public theater.

Shakespeare was a shareholder of both a public playhouse, the Globe, and a private theater, the Second Blackfriars. The original Blackfriars was converted from a monastery whose dining hall became a playing space for a boys' company that performed regularly for the queen. James Burbage constructed the Second Blackfriars in 1596, twenty years after he built London's first public theater, the Theatre. Burbage was the father of Shakespeare's principal actor, Richard Burbage; when the elder Burbage died in 1597, he willed the Blackfriars to his son, who leased it to a popular children's company. By 1608 the King's Men were performing at the Blackfriars from October through May, returning to the Globe only in the summer months. The company preferred the interior space for financial, artistic, and climatic reasons; its revenues more than doubled at the Blackfriars, which catered to a wealthier audience.

You have some familiarity with the Globe and its trappings (read the reconstruction of an early performance of *Hamlet* at The Globe Theater). The Blackfriars had some elements in common with the Globe: trapdoors in the stage floor; suspension gear for flying effects; an upper station for action above the stage level; and a "discovery space" located upstage center that was curtained off to reveal interior scenes. But each theater had distinctive features:

Public Theaters (The Globe, the Swan)	**Private Theaters** (Blackfriars)
Location	
Bankside; outside London's city limits.	Within the city limits; occasionally they were housed in private mansions.
Design and Configuration	
Open air; sunlit and exposed to the elements; daytime performances.	Enclosed and roofed; heated and lit by artificial means; evening performances.
Round or polygonal.	Rectangular or oblong.
Thrust stage.	Modified thrust stage with a modified proscenium arch.
Backed by a "tiring house" with (most likely) two entrance doors.	Classical three-door arrangement.
Dimensions and Capacity	
stage: c. 27' × 42'	18.5' × 29'
capacity: c. 2,500 spectators	c. 700 spectators
Audience-Actor Relationship	
Some spectators stood in the pit on three sides of the stage; galleries on three sides of stage with seating.	All audiences members seated, either on benches on the floor or in galleries; all seating in front of the stage.

The public theaters drew their audiences from the full spectrum of English society, while the private playhouses catered largely to a well-educated, aristocratic, socially homogenous clientele. Hence, the plays written for the private theaters are discernibly more literary. Because the private theaters were better equipped for scenic effects, plays in which environment and spectacle are important found their way into spaces like the Blackfriars. Shakespeare devoted his last years as a playwright to composing romances, such as *The Tempest*, partly because of the availability of a new type of theater and its technology. Still, whether public or private, indoor or out, the English theater relied principally on the evocative power of the word for impact.

CENTER STAGE · HAMLET AT THE GLOBE THEATER, 1601

Old Cade pauses to catch his breath; the long climb up four flights of wooden steps tires him. As he looks across the thatched roof, he can see London rising gloriously on the north bank of the Thames. Both the river and city flourish with activity on this warm June morning. Huge sailing ships, fresh from the Low Countries, the Mediterranean, and especially from the Indies, compete for space with small boats. Cade watches men and animals, carts and carriages, all bustling in the shadows of St. Paul's, the great cathedral that dominates the London skyline. To the east—just beyond London Bridge—stands Tower Hill, where men are hanged even as Londoners picnic on the green near the dreaded Tower of London. To the west, Westminster and Whitehall beckon proudly as England still basks in the glory of its victory over the Spanish Armada some 13 years ago.

Cade savors the view, and then turns to the flagpole to affix a white banner to its ropes. He tugs on the weathered line, and the flag unfurls to reveal the image of Hercules bearing the weight of the world on his shoulders. He lights the fuse on the old cannon, covers his ears, and awaits the flash and boom that tells the tradesmen across the river "Today, a play at the Globe!" Cade douses some smoldering straw on the roof with a bucket of water. "S'blood, that cannon shall burn this theatre to the ground one day," he grumbles as he hurries down the stairs to place props for the play.

By 1:30 the river is awash with boats ferrying people to the South Bank, as many more stream across the bridge, stopping to buy sweetmeats and baked goods from the merchants whose stalls line the bridge. The workday—which had begun at four—is done, and London's citizens, nobility and commoner, rich and poor, are coming to the Globe to see the Lord Chamberlain's Men perform their newest work, *Hamlet, Prince of Denmark*. Rumor, which races through London's crowded streets daily, has proclaimed the new tragedy perhaps

the best play yet by the Globe's popular playwright, Master William Shakespeare—even better than Thomas Kyd's bloody *The Spanish Tragedy*. (Rumor also suggests that Will Shakespeare may have borrowed more than a few plot elements, and even some characters, from Kyd's sensational play.) An apprentice in the company, who plays a small role in the play, bragged to his mates at Eastcheap Tavern, "By m' two thumbs, 'tis a most excellent and sorrowful tragedy."

As the Londoners walk along Bankside—amid the alehouses, the stews (where prostitutes beckon), the bear baiting rings, and the cockpits—they talk of ghosts and spirits wondrous strange, and of the young dramatist who has caught their imagination with such plays as *Henry V*, *Romeo and Juliet*, and *The Taming of the Shrew*. Over 2,000 spectators file into the theater through a small door, the commoners paying a penny to stand shoulder-to-shoulder on the ground around the great stage of the Globe. The wealthy offer an additional penny to sit in one of the three tiers of galleries that overlook the stage. Young girls wriggle their way through the crowd to sell oranges, oysters, and nuts to the carpenters, weavers, joiners, bellows menders, and tinkers.

Backstage two dozen members of the Lord Chamberlain's Men are dressing. Some wear clothing much like that of the workers in the pit; others attire themselves in handsome doublets and gowns bequeathed to them by nobles who boast that their garments can be seen at the Globe. Shakespeare himself, dressed in the warlike form of a warrior king, smears a paste of bleached wheat flour on his face, then turns and yells across the room, "D'ye think I look a proper ghost, Henry Condell?" "Aye, as frightful as any in England—or Denmark!" Condell laughs. In a far corner sits tall, portly Richard Burbage, the company's finest actor and son of the carpenter who built London's first public theater on the City's northern boundary in

1576. Burbage reviews Hamlet's many lines with young Richard Sharpe, a boy of 14 who has recently been hired from the Children of the Queen's Revels to play the fair Ophelia. Near them, several boy apprentices softly rehearse a snippet from an old play, *The Murder of Gonzago*, that Shakespeare has made an integral part of his new tragedy.

Cade makes his way to stage center and taps the hard wooden floor three times with his staff. The actors grow quiet, and 37-year-old Will Shakespeare gathers the company about him. "Speak your speeches as I told you; but if you mouth them I'll soon get the town crier to speak them. And you, Robert Armin, speak no more than is set down for you. The Gravedigger's part is written excellent well and needs not your saucy jests. Reform it well, Master Armin. Use all gently, my masters, and o'erstep not the modesty of nature. Now go make yourselves ready."

At precisely 2:00 the musicians play the opening sennet from a small gallery on the third floor. Their trumpets quiet the boisterous crowd, and a doorway at stage right opens for a boy carrying a large placard announcing the name of the play—"The Tragedie of Hamlete, Prince of Denmark." Another youth enters from the stage left door with a sign proclaiming "The Castle at Elsinore" as Cade settles onto a stool on the side stage, script in hand, ready to prompt any actor whose memory falters. Behind him, on a raised platform above the stage, two actors dressed as soldiers shiver to suggest a midnight cold. A third enters, and one calls out, "Who's there?" And thus begins a play that is filled with many questions.

The soldiers atop the inner above—as the actors call it—look down on the Globe's stage, and mysteriously a trapdoor in the stage floor opens to reveal a ghostly figure. Musicians in the upper gallery enhance the mood with the mournful, mystical music as the silent ghost disappears behind a curtain.

The scene shifts suddenly, effortlessly, as a dark curtain—hung to replace the multicolored one that is used only for comic plays—opens to reveal a large throne and a handsome young boy dressed as a Tudor noblewoman. Indeed, he looks like Elizabeth herself! On the throne sits William Ostler, "the Sole King of Actors," looking more like the renowned Sir Francis Drake in his doublet, hose, and ruff than a Danish king. Ostler speaks—"Though yet of Hamlet our dear brother's death…"—and the audience is transported to another kingdom years removed from the London of 1601. The audience nonetheless is keenly aware that the death of a king is indeed serious business. They have heard tales of the bloody Wars of the Roses that plunged England into chaos barely a century earlier, and they fear another civil war as Elizabeth, their beloved queen for over 40 years, is in ill health, and without a legitimate heir. *Hamlet*, which they know to be about the bloodshed that follows the death of a lawful king, has a message that is all too urgent for them.

The musicians play a lively gavotte as Claudius and Gertrude celebrate their recent marriage; colorfully dressed courtiers and ambassadors surround them. On the forestage nearest the audience sits Burbage dressed in black as Hamlet, an isolated figure against the revelry and color of the court. Although the platform is almost 30 feet deep, the actors prefer to play far downstage, especially in these first scenes so that the huge audience, still settling itself in the open-air theater for the afternoon's performance, can better hear these first crucial lines that set up the story. The Lord Chamberlain's Men are noted for their more natural, less bombastic acting, and the Globe's intimate stage allows them to speak more quietly to the audience. Gradually the stage empties, leaving only Burbage to address the audience in a soliloquy about his unhappy state. The mostly male audience is thoroughly hushed, absorbing every syllable of Hamlet's angry lamentation. The quiet is disrupted by the excited shouts of Hamlet's schoolmate, Horatio, who informs the prince that he and the soldiers have seen the very ghost of Old Hamlet stalking the castle battlements.

After a short scene of apparent domestic tranquility between Polonius and his children, Laertes and Ophelia, the stage is again transformed into a frightful place. A cannonball rolled across one of the upper floors of the tiring house supplies the thunder as the ghost again appears amid a cloud of gunpowder smoke that creates the fog. This time the ghost is lowered onto the stage from an opening in the roof covering the rearmost portion of the playing space. Backstage, two workers skillfully work the ropes that allow Shakespeare-as-Ghost to descend slowly from the machines room over the stage, the underside of its ceiling painted with astrological signs to signify "the Heavens." Later in the second act Burbage will point to the heavenly bodies on the ceiling when he refers to "this most excellent canopy, the air, look you, this brave o'erhanging firmament, this majestical roof fretted with golden fire."

The play moves swiftly, one set of actors entering even as another exits. Yet the spectators have no difficulty following the action despite the lack of scenery, lighting, or act curtains. They need only listen and let their minds create the details of each scene. Of course, the architecture of the Globe helps define locale. The two wooden posts that support the Heavens double, when necessary, as pillars for Claudius and Polonius to hide behind as they eavesdrop on Hamlet and Ophelia. Later they become trees that tower over Armin and another old actor who pretend to dig a hole at center stage. The trapdoor, which had been used for the ghost's first entrance, now suggests a grave, an apt passageway to the netherworld from whence the ghost came.

Without a break in the action, Shakespeare knows he must provide a bit of theatrical razzle-dazzle at the midpoint to please the groundlings that stand nearest the stage. Sure enough, in the second act the Lord Chamberlain's actors, posing as a traveling troupe of actors in Denmark, perform a sensational play, replete with masks and costumes, about the fall of Troy. The groundlings—whom Shakespeare gently chides in several speeches in *Hamlet*, much to their amusement—especially enjoy the bombastic performance of the actor playing King Priam.

The tragedy continues as Burbage-Hamlet unleashes his anger at the court that has wronged him. Polonius dies, stabbed as he hides behind the great curtain the separates the "discovery space" from the stage proper. The audience gasps as Polonius's blood oozes from a pig's bladder hidden in his costume. Later Burbage and the handsome young actor playing the fiery Laertes demonstrate their expert swordsmanship in a thrilling duel. Being so close to the swirling blades only adds to the excitement, and the audience clearly enjoys the fighting. They recall the superb fights between these same two actors as Mercutio and Tybalt in *Romeo and Juliet*.

The late afternoon shadows lengthen over the Globe's stage to increase the somber mood of the play's final moments. Burbage lays motionless as Horatio laments Hamlet's passing. The dead prince is surrounded by the lifeless bodies of Laertes, Gertrude, and Claudius, who sits slumped on the throne for which he murdered his brother. Fortinbras, splendid in plumes and armor, enters to discover the carnage of Elsinore's tragic court. Four captains pick up Burbage and carry him through the upstage darkness as the audience erupts into loud applause.

Seconds later the Chamberlain's Men again fill the stage to acknowledge their audience and treat them to a final song and dance—in this case, "Thumpkin and His Crying Mum." As the audience leaves the theater, excitedly talking about ghosts and bloody deeds, of Burbage's bravado performance, and of the horrible deaths they had witnessed, they are greeted by criers in the street who tell them that on Wednesday next, they can return to the Globe for a revival of the popular history play *Richard II*, another work about a fallen king. Atop the Globe, Old Cade lowers the flag and thinks

> Of carnal, bloody and unnatural acts
> Of accidental judgments, casual slaughters,
> Of deaths put on by cunning, and forc'd cause . . .

and of the delicate and tender prince who may have proved most royal had he not died in this woeful tragedy.

FORUMS

Hamlet in Production

Hamlet is among the most produced plays in the world, and its central character is perhaps the single most important test of an actor's mettle. In *Hamlet* at the Globe Theater, 1601, you read an imaginary account of Richard Burbage's performance in the original production at Shakespeare's Globe theater at Bankside. Here you may consider three additional versions of *Hamlet*:

- Edwin Booth revived his celebrated performance in New York in 1869. He first performed the role there in 1864, when it ran for 100 performances and began the vogue of "long-running" productions. In 1865 Booth's brother (John Wilkes) assassinated President Abraham Lincoln. The actor's courageous rendering of this play of "foul and unnatural murders" was thus all the more poignant when he returned to the stage after a self-imposed hiatus.

- Richard Burton's Hamlet was directed in New York in 1964 by the esteemed Shakespearean actor Sir John Gielgud, who had himself made a reputation as one of the twentieth century's finest Hamlets. Gielgud's staging is known as "the dress rehearsal *Hamlet*" because it was performed on a mostly bare stage and in contemporary street clothing because the director wanted to return the emphasis to the play's language.

- Grigori Kozintsev's 1966 film version of *Hamlet* is considered among the finest non-English renderings of the play, and it contained veiled political commentaries on Russia's system of government. Some people who speak both English and Russian claim the play sounds better in Boris Pasternak's translation into Russian.

"Hamlet: Picturesque and Refined"

Lucia Gilbert Calhoun

The Opening: As the curtain rose on the lonely sentinels pacing their beat before the castle, a wind seemed to blow across from the northern sea with premonition of death. There was terror in the tale of the night watchers shivering under the black skies. It was a relief when the scene shifted and the warm light glowed on the crimson audience chamber and the rich black dresses of the court. Before the splendid King and Queen bent a slight, lithe figure, robed in black, which cast a shadow on it—so sad, so desolate, so intense, so stricken it stood. When the King came toward it, with open palm and loud "And now, my cousin Hamlet, and my son," it started slightly and moved away; the scornful "A little more than kin and less than kind," falling in a half-whisper from its lips. While the Queen addressed to Hamlet her querulous commonplaces about death, he seemed to shake off a little forced respectfulness of manner, "Ay, madam, it is—common." But there was the agony of a deep heart in the "Seems, madam—nay, it is—I know not seems," and the lines that follow. Then one understood what his love for his father had been, and what his grief was. He heard the course harangue of the King with a courtier's silence, only the spasmodic closing of the hand at the words, "Our chiefest courtier, cousin, and our son," revealing the inward passion. He followed the departing court up the room, then returning, burst into the soliloquy, "O that this too, too solid flesh would melt." This he gave, moving from side to side of the stage, or half flung down upon his chair in an attitude of utter abandonment. But his soliloquy was most unequal. Sometimes it seemed the merest repetition of words to him. Sometimes it seemed to shake his being, and sometimes the lines

> O God, O God,
> *How weary, stale, flat, and unprofitable*
> *Seem to me all the uses of this world*

moaned themselves forth in tones so bitter and so hopeless, that one looked to see him end the scene with his bare bodkin. The instant change from the passionate desolation of his grief to the exquisite courtesy of the host, when the three young men approach—with his tender welcome to Horatio—was one of the finest of his transitions. . . .

With the Ghost: When the scene opens, the whole stage is disclosed. In the distance glows the grim castle, noisy with the orgies of the drunken King. The ghost stalks into the moonlight. Down the massive steps leading to the platform stumbles Hamlet, crying out hoarsely in the darkness, "Whither wilt thou lead me? Speak, I'll go no further;" and staggering forward, the moonlight falls on his ashen face, on his wild eyes, on his disheveled hair. "I am thy father's spirit," groans the ghost—in voice that seems to come from the lowest fires, wherein he is compelled to fast. Slowly, Hamlet sinks to his knees. There is no longer terror in his countenance. Infinite yearnings, infinite compassion, infinite tenderness, agonized longing to know the truth, look from his face. So intense is the feeling that moves him we, too, in the audience, yielding to his emotion, see, in the clumsy ghost—with his blue tarlatan diaphanousness, and his inhuman drawl, and his elocutionary nonsense, and his entire satisfaction with himself—the majesty of buried Denmark. Fierce and strong is the excitement which he cannot wholly overcome before his friends join him; wild and whirling his actions, yet controlled withal, as he puts off Marcellus; solemn his bearing as he offers them the oath; tenders his assurances of faith and friendship. . . .

With Ophelia: In the third act the scene is handsomely set as an audience chamber. A stately double staircase leads to a gallery, from which small doors open in the corridors without. In a deep embayed window Ophelia kneels—Hamlet is thus freed from the inconvenience of walking over her train without seeing her. . . . From a low-arched door beneath the stairway glides the Prince, his head bent, his hands clasped before him, his step slow and uncertain. He steadies himself by the balustrade, moves on mechanically, is stopped by a chair, sinks into it—still silent, still utterly abstracted. In another moment the "To be, or not to be," is uttered in a voice almost inaudible; and then, with intonations so wonderful and various that they will not be set down, followed the matchless soliloquy. The lines "For in that sleep of death what dreams may come;" and "From whose bourne no traveller returns," shuddered with vague but woeful foreboding. Rising suddenly and crossing toward the window he sees Ophelia. His whole face changes. A lovely tenderness suffuses it. Sweetness fills his tones as he addresses her. When, with exquisite softness of manner, he draws near to her, he catches glimpse of the "unlawful espials" in the gallery above. Why Mr. Booth should accept the adventitious aid of this stage usage, of which Shakespeare gives no hint, does not appear. His Hamlet is quite strong enough to dispense with it. He knows from Ophelia's manner that she is playing a part—she, the one being beside Horatio, in whose truth he believed. He knows that he is vowed to black revenge; must renounce all thoughts of love. He is half maddened with the secret of his thoughts. The cruel bitterness is not for her, but for women of whom she is one. Yet he makes an immense effect with this stage usage. When he suddenly says, "Where is your father!" he lays his hand on Ophelia's head, and turns her face up to his as he stands above her. She answers, looking straight into the eyes that love her, "At home, my lord."

No accusation, no reproach could be so terrible as the sudden plucking away of his hand, and the pain of the face he turns from her. The whole scene he plays like one distract. He is never still. He strides up and down the stage, in and out of the door, speaking outside with the same rapidity and vehemence. The speech, "I have heard of your paintings, too, well enough," he begins in the outer room and the tempestuous words hiss as they fall.

"It hath made me mad," was uttered with a flutter of the hand about the head more expressive than the words. As he turned towards Ophelia for the last time, all the bitterness, all the reckless violence seemed to die out of him; his voice was full

of unspeakable love, of appealing tenderness, of irrevocable doom, as he uttered the last "To a nunnery go, go, go!" and tottered from the room as one who could not see for tears. . . .

With the Queen: Into the Queen's closet, where a single light burns in the sumptuous gloom, and a crucifix gleams against the wall, comes Hamlet. There is no anger in him as he first accosts his mother. There is the awful obligation to tell her truths which are a horror to him and a shame to her. It is the terrible, intense quiet of his tone and manner which frightens her more than violence would have done. At the shout of old Polonius he leaps like lightening to the arras. The wild hope of the cry "Is it the King?" as he stands with the lamp he has snatched up flickering above his head and his hand on the parted arras, makes the air shudder. He cannot bring himself to murder with deliberate intent—this delicate, humane spirit. If but the deed be done in this heart of accident! Looking down at the old man he utters, "The wretched, rash intruding fool, farewell," with accumulating emphasis of bitterness, not more repenting the blow bestowed than the deploring the failure of the blow intended. His reproaches to the Queen are terrible; but never brutal, and never loud. He himself trembles and shudders with the pain he gives, but he never relents. He is pleading with her for her soul. Suddenly upon his sacred anger comes the ghost in whose name he has spoken. For an instant of time terror touches him. Then a passion of tenderness sweeps over him. He reaches out his hands to the shadowy figure. His tones vibrate with love. When the ghost says, "Speak to her, Hamlet," in the same state of double-consciousness which marked his first interview with the spirit, he puts his arm around the trembling woman of whose presence he has ceased to be aware. He is appalled to find that his mother sees nothing where stands this figure so real to him. He follows it with his eyes, and when it glides away he follows it as one who has no life apart from it—as it fades, falling like a dead thing across the threshold. Called back by his mother's voice to this hard life, a new pity for her softens his voice. He dismisses her with gentleness. He would bear the burden of her sin, if it could be. . . .

The Close: In the last scene the lithe grace, the elegance, the beauty, the electric swiftness of Booth make his the ideal Hamlet. In the last speech to Horatio his voice thrills with an unearthly sweetness, as he pleads with that sure friend to vindicate his name. And when silence falls we look as on our own dead in a sadness too deep for tears.

"*Hamlet:* Picturesque and Refined" by Lucia Gilbert Calhoun. *Galaxy*, January 1869.

"Richard Burton as Hamlet—Gielgud's Production at the Lunt-Fontanne"

Howard Taubman

The first and most important thing to be said about the "Hamlet" that opened last night at the Lunt-Fontanne Theater is that it is Shakespeare, not a self-indulgent holiday for a star.

Richard Burton dominates the drama, as Hamlet should. For his is a performance of electrical power and sweeping virility. But it does not burst the bounds of the framework set for it by John Gielgud's staging. It is not so much larger than life that it overwhelms the rest of the company. Nor does it demand attentions so fiercely for itself that the shape and poetry of the play are lost to the audience. Mr. Gielgud has pitched

(*continued*)

the performance to match Mr. Burton's range and intensity. The company for the most part has been well-chosen, though it is not and cannot be expected everywhere to approach the crispness of the Hamlet's attack, the scope of his voice, the peaks of his fury and remorse.

Mr. Gielgud's own Hamlet years ago was much different—more sinuous and refined. It is his merit that he has found a new way to look at the play to be in keeping with Mr. Burton's style and view of the role. This is no melancholy "Hamlet," no psychoanalytical or Oedipal "Hamlet," no effete or lackluster "Hamlet."

It is designed to look like a final run-through. The stage is bare, its brick walls and columns visible. A platform and a series of steps plus a few bits of furniture provide the setting. A clothes rack holding costumes—for some other "Hamlet," no doubt—is at the side and becomes the curtain behind which Polonius and the king hide and later the arras through which Polonius is gored.

The actors are in working clothes. Hamlet wears a black V-necked shirt and black trousers. Claudius and Polonius have on jackets and ties. The other men are in formal jackets, windbreakers, sweaters, slacks and jeans. Gertrude and Ophelia are in blouses and long skirts. Only the strolling players wear costumes when they are enacting the murder of Gonzago—a recognition that some differention in attire is useful.

Does this liberate the production from the weight of the customary trappings? If Mr. Burton and his companions think so, one should not quibble. My preference is for costumes, for there is a jarring note at the outset as the majestic Elizabethan language does not consort properly with rehearsal clothes. But as the performance progresses, one forgets about dress and moves into Shakespeare's magnificent imaginative world.

As for the lack of colorful scenery, one does not cavil. We have grown accustomed in recent years to open stages with little or no painted canvas, and the absence of the trumpery and machinery of lavish productions need not be mourned.

For it is liberating to the audience's imagination as well as the actor's to do without the gaudy stuff—at least when you have a play of the magnitude of "Hamlet." But it must be added that an uncluttered proscenium stage is not nearly the same thing as an open stage that becomes one with the audience.

It is clear that Mr. Burton means to play Hamlet with all the stops out—when power is wanted. He is aware of the risk of seeming to rant. For it is he who warns that the players must not tear a passion to tatters. But he is unafraid—and he is right.

I do not recall a Hamlet of such tempestuous manliness. In the first two soliloquies Mr. Burton does not hesitate to cry out as if his very soul were in torment, and the thunderous, wrenching climaxes do not ring false. But he reads the "to be or not to be" soliloquy with subdued anguish, like a man communing painfully with himself. Then in the scene that follows with Ophelia, he begins by being ineffably tender, but when he rails at her to get to a nunnery, his rage bespeaks his hatred for himself as well as for a base world.

Mr. Burton's Hamlet is full of pride and wit and mettle. He is warm and forthright with Horatio. As he listens to Polonius's windy craftiness a look of shrewd contempt hoods his eye. He trades quips with the first Gravedigger with gusto.

Mr. Burton's voice is not mellifluous like those of a few highly cultivated classic actors. It has a hardy ring and a rough edge, attributes that suit his interpretation. He does not, however, scant the poetry. He has a fine sense of rhythm. It is very much his own, with a flair for accenting words and phrases in unexpected ways. But the result, while personal, does no violence to sound or sense.

One has reservations about details. Hamlet prowls too restlessly during the performance of the players. His grabbing of the goblet from Claudius's hand is an effect that disturbs one's eagerness to believe. His standing with sword raised high only inches from the praying Claudius is another liberty that strikes at credibility.

As one sits through a long evening that seems all too short, one is humbled afresh by the surge of Shakespeare's poetry, by his tenderness and by his disillusioned awareness of man and his ways. It is the grandeur of "Hamlet," not of an actor or director, that prevails.

"Richard Burton as Hamlet—Gielgud's Production at the Lunt-Fontanne" by Howard Taubman. *New York Times*, 14 April 1964. Copyright © 1964 by the *New York Times*. Reprinted by permission.

"Shakespeare á la Russe: Kozintsev's *Hamlet*"

ARTHUR KNIGHT

Grigori Kozintsev, a veteran Russian director, is also a Shakespearean scholar with a book appearing later this year in English to prove it. Although his new version of *Hamlet* (or Gamlet, as the Russians say it) is based upon a translation by Boris Pasternak, the script is by Kozintsev himself, and one ventures to say that both the approach and the excision are pretty much his own.

This is an active Hamlet, not sicklied o'er by any pale cast of thought; he has almost too much to do just remaining alive to obey at once his father's ghostly command that he kill the usurping King. Unlike Olivier's version, which dwelt on every moment of doubt and indecision, this one actually prunes away such scenes as that in which Hamlet discovers Claudius at his prayers and will not kill him lest his soul go straight to heaven. "O what a rogue and peasant slave am I" is severely truncated (as are most of famous soliloquies) ; only the last few lines of "How all occasions do inform against me" remain. The result, of course, is a Hamlet far less complicated than Shakespeare's, but also a good deal more consistent. His hatred for the King is single-minded, with no Oedipal overtones to muddy its pursuit. He lacks not will, but opportunity; and when the opening at last presents itself in the climatic duel with Laertes, he seizes it with the desperation of one who knows both his doom and his destiny.

This is a virile Hamlet, a Hamlet who would truly merit the admiration of a solider like Fortinbras and the loyalty of an honest courtier like Horatio. It is also remarkably playable Hamlet, as cinematic a Hamlet as we are ever likely to see. From the first encounter with the Ghost, while the horses in the nearby stables break their traces and bolt in terror, it is evident that Kozintsev intends imagery to supplement the words, not merely to illustrate them. The wide screen fills with the Ghost's dark, windblown robes, and the evil deed that he recounts to Hamlet, and the evil deed that he demands, appear like a summons from Hell. Polonius is killed in the Queen's bedchamber and his falling body rips down a curtain to reveal her finery arrayed upon a row of dummies. When Ophelia dies, the corpse is discovered floating at the edge of a mist-filled lake. And the sea is a constantly recurring image, as if to stress the eternality of the tale.

Kozintsev, boldly cutting text to make way for pictures, at times seems to have gone too far. Why, for example, could not Polonius have said the whole of his famous farewell speech to his son? Hamlet's instructions to the players are glossed into a line or two. And whoever heard of a Hamlet without "to be or not to be"?

On the other hand, this production boasts a superb grave-digger's scene, a skilled staging of the play within the play and of the duel with Laertes, and innumerable touches such as playing Hamlet's death scene outside the gloomy castle so that he makes his affecting farewell to Horatio with hundreds of peasants looking on. Indeed, whenever possible, Kozintsev moves his cameras outside, thus dissipating still further the claustrophobic, gloomy Dane concept. Hamlet becomes, instead, a veritable "sweet prince." In this enterprise, the director has the advantage not only of a manly Hamlet and an exquisite Ophelia, but of an entire cast that plays with nuance and seems utterly at home in the rich costumes and vast halls of Elsinore; as well as an original score by no less a composer than Dmitri Shostakovich that aptly reflects the turbulent mood of the entire film. With all this excellence, it is unforgivable that the sub-titling has been so shabbily handled—neither good Shakespeare nor good English, and filled with typographical errors.

Another virtue of Kozintsev's *Hamlet* is the director's ability to discover a proper style for his work, and to sustain it. The camera plays close to his characters, making them larger than life, heroic; in the absence of much of The Bard's poetry, the thoughtfully chosen and composed images contribute poetry of their own.

SPAIN

Artistic and Cultural Events

c. 1490: First Spanish secular drama *(La Celestina)*

1579: Corral de la Cruz, first permanent theater in Spain

1605: *Don Quixote*

1627: Coliseo Theatre built in Mexico City

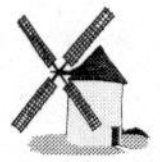

c. 1630: Lope de Vega dominates Spanish theater

1200 C.E. **1500 C.E.** **1600 C.E.**

Historical and Political Events

1200–1276: Christian war with Moors; Aztec civilization

1478: Inquisition begins

1492: Ferdinand and Isabella sponsor New World explorations

1519: King Carlos V becomes emperor of Holy Roman Empire

1588: Defeat of Spanish Armada

1609: Moors expelled from Spain

1621: Philip IV becomes king

Bay of
Biscay

ATLANTIC
OCEAN

SPAIN

Toledo Madrid

Barcelona

Granada

Mediterranean Sea

Despite their religious and political differences, the theaters of England and Spain had more in common during the sixteenth century than they did with those of Italy or France. From roughly the middle of the sixteenth century until the late seventeenth, Spanish drama equaled that of the English, and the period is referred to as the *Siglo d'Oro*, or "Golden Century." Today *Siglo d'Oro* theater festivals are held in such places as El Paso, Texas; Guanajuato, Mexico; and Lima, Peru; as well as in Spain.

Most significantly, neither England nor Spain was bound by the Neoclassic doctrines that thrived in most of Europe. In 1517 Bartolome de Torres Naharro wrote the first theoretical treatise on the drama in modern Europe, *Propolladia*, which decries the rules of antiquity. Thus began Spain's antipathy toward rules. In 1609 one of Spain's most influential playwrights and dramatic theorists, Lope de Vega, counseled his countrymen to follow their instincts and the will of the crowd rather than the rules of antiquity. The result was a national theater that freely mixed the comic with the tragic, the spiritual with the earthy, the regal with the common, the poetic with the colloquial, to create one of the most imaginative and completely theatrical bodies of dramatic literature in Western theater. Even today drama in Spain—and the many countries in the Americas whose theater tradition is traceable to Spanish colonization—remains among the most richly poetic in the West.

Like their European counterparts, the Spanish also created liturgical dramas during the Middle Ages. Sacred *entremeses* (interludes) were performed between courses of banquets, a custom that continued into the golden age, when they evolved into secular farces inserted between acts of longer plays. Lope de Rueda (c. 1510–1565), Spain's first great actor-playwright, cultivated *entremeses* (or *pasos*) that secularized Spanish drama. Though the overall tenor of Spanish drama remained theological, largely because Spain was Europe's most fiercely Catholic country, correspondingly, its drama was a means of manifesting the spiritual in concrete images and symbols.

Renaissance-era Spaniards retained the medieval notion of life as a pilgrimage toward eternity, and the majority of Spain's greatest comic and serious dramas explore the spiritual journey of people who seek *disengaño*, a term that literally means "disillusionment." However, this is not a pessimistic term. *Disengaño* actually means "to strip away the world's illusions" (or "deceptions") so that one can see more clearly the truly important things of the world in preparation for the greater journey to the next. Comic plays are totally immersed in the world of *engaño*, while the serious dramas—of which Calderón's *Life's a Dream* is the finest example (see below)—showed protagonists trapped in a world of deceptions that are gradually replaced by an awareness of the reality of the world. All this talk of "illusions," "deceptions," and "reality" suggests why the Spanish found the theater—a kingdom of illusions—the ideal vehicle for exploring these moral and philosophical questions.

Spanish plays of the golden age generally fall into one of two types:

- *Comedias*, a generic term for "play" that does not distinguish between the seriousness or lightness of the subject matter. Traditionally, a *comedia* was written in three acts of three to five scenes. Each act was composed of 1,000 lines of verse in a peculiarly Spanish meter. Like the English, the Spanish were indifferent to the unities of time and place, so the *comedias* were sprawling, unlocalized plays with vast numbers of people drawn from all strata of Spanish life. Because plotting took precedence over characterization, stock characters abounded—pairs of lovers, an old man (usually

Anne Bogart merged Spain's classical tradition (Calderón's play) and its modern sensibilities (a Salvador Dalí landscape) in Life's a Dream *at the American Repertory Company in Cambridge (1989).*

lecherous), kings and queens, and the Spanish version of the "wise fool," or *gracioso*, often a servant who stood outside the action and commented on the folly of his betters. An early-sixteenth-century *comedia*, *The Trickster of Seville* by Tirso de Molina, gave Western theater one of its most enduring characters, Don Juan.

- The *auto sacramental* ("sacramental act") is Spain's most distinctive dramatic form. Originally, an *auto* was a one-act verse play about the sacrament of the Eucharist. Presented as allegories in which professional actors personified abstractions, *autos* were elaborately staged, usually on large, spectacularly decorated carts (*carros*) pulled through flower-covered streets by enormous bulls with gilded horns. These wagons were fitted with ingenious machines to create stunning effects of transformation, a term that alludes to the sacred mystery of "transforming" bread and wine into the body and blood of Christ. Hundreds of such plays were written, often by village priests, during the second half of the sixteenth century and paved the way for the more sophisticated, secular dramas of Lope de Vega and especially Pedro Calderón de la Barca, whose *Life's a Dream* (1673) is the most famous and stageworthy of the *autos*. *The Divine Narcissus,* by the Mexican-born nun Juana Inés de la Cruz, also may be classified as an *auto* both in its form and content; it deals with Christian sacraments as they compare to indigenous rituals of Central America.

It was Spanish drama that first found its way to the New World. The first Spanish-language plays were performed in 1526 as part of a Corpus Christi festival in Mexico City, just five years after conquistadors permanently took command of that city. Missionary priests used the theater to convert indigenous peoples by writing catechetical plays in native tongues. Missionary theater declined by the end of the sixteenth century, subsumed by various folk entertainments in northern Mexico and the American Southwest. The Yaqui Easter rite (see Chapter 9, Center Stage box) might well be a remnant of such theatrical activity. By 1600 theater was well entrenched in Mexico City and Lima, and it was emerging in other corners of the new Spanish *colonias*. Most of the plays were variations on the *comedias* and *autos*, and future generations of Spanish-American playwrights would build on the fantastical, poetic forms that had thrilled audiences in the *corrales* of Madrid, Seville, and Toledo (see Spotlight box, The Spanish Theater: The *Corrales*).

Calderón and *Life's a Dream*

Pedro Calderón de la Barca (1600–1681) is considered Spain's greatest dramatist. Fittingly, he succeeded Lope de Vega (who wrote 1,800 *autos*) as the official court poet in 1635, but the variety and profundity of his work eclipse those of his chief rival. Calderón wrote more than 200 full-length plays (over 100 are extant) and a number of short works, and he invented the *zarzuela*, the spanish form of musical comedy. When he died at age 81 in Madrid, he is said to have been working on a new play at his writing table. Typical of gentlemen of his era, Calderón was not merely a writer but was actively involved in Spanish life, both secular (as an army officer and court diplomat) and religious (he became a Jesuit priest in 1651). Although they are rooted in the teachings of the Catholic Church, Calderón's best works transcend his Catholicism. The theater as a metaphor for life, which is merely a "rehearsal" for eternity, particularly fascinated Calderón. In *The Great Theatre of the World* (1649) a character says, "All men dream the lives they lead. Act well, for God is God." His dramatic talents earned him a knighthood in 1637.

Life's a Dream (1673) is the most admired drama of Spain's golden age. Like Shakespeare's *The Tempest*, it is a ro-mance, a genre that flourished in European theaters in the seventeenth century. Romances, a term that refers to mythological stories in the Italian or "Roman" style, are usually set in a remote locale and feature extraordinary events that suggest the potential for tragedy but end happily. The fantastical plots portray a king or powerful leader who commits a grievous error in judgement that brings chaos to his land; he is ultimately saved through acts of redemption and forgiveness, often prompted by a virginal heroine who restores goodness through acts of love and charity. Little wonder that Calderón was drawn to such fables as he wrote his dramas, equal parts secular adventure and Christian allegory.

Life's a Dream traces the maturation of Sigismund, son of Poland's King Basilio, who grows from a beastlike figure to a glorious king in his own right. Basilio, who believes omens that his son will one day overthrow him, places his infant son in a mountain cave. The king tests the prophecy by bringing Sigismund, now grown, in a drugged state (hence "the dream") to the palace, where he is dressed in golden clothing. Unaccustomed to court life and angered by his years of imprisonment, Sigismund rebels; he kills a servant and threatens his father's life. Sigismund is returned to his cave, where he awakens and declares that his visit to the court was only a dream. The people of Poland learn of Sigismund's plight and make him their king; he leads them in a rebellion against his father and his cousin Astolfo, the duke of Moscow. Sigismund refuses to kill his tyrant-father, and instead forgives him for his transgressions in a joyful finale. There is a subplot in which Rosaura, a good-hearted maiden who has been wronged by Astolfo, enlists Sigismund's aid. Her innate goodness helps transform the prince into a merciful and loving leader.

Calderón actually wrote two versions of *Life's a Dream*. The second, *(continued)*

(*continued*)

written in 1673, very late in his long life, represents a synthesis of his personal, theatrical, and philosophical growth. Drawing on the world of classic myth, the play reverberates with echoes of the Prometheus and Oedipus legends. Like Shakespeare, Calderón uses the romance device of the wronged woman who must disguise herself as a man to survive in a disordered masculine world. By fusing purely religious matters with secular subjects, Calderón crafted a more universal drama that is at once spiritual, humanist, political, moralistic, and more entertaining than his earlier work. Written about 1635, the earlier *Dream* was purely allegorical in its depiction of the four elements of Fire, Earth, Water, and Air arguing about the supremacy of each; the short play shows how God created order out of chaos.

To understand the implications of *Life's a Dream*, it is helpful to consider the central event of Calderón's life: his personal crisis of faith, which was precipitated by his father's deathbed wish that young Pedro become a priest. For 35 years Calderón rebelled against his father's will—which he equated with God's will—and suffered profound guilt as a consequence. The majority of Calderón's plays were an attempt by a tortured artist to reconcile his personal passions with the demands of duty and honor. Calderón felt himself tracked by the hounds of heaven as he fled through the labyrinthine ways of the world; for him, the labyrinth was like a carnival funhouse, filled with mirrors providing illusions about what was real and not real in this dreamlike world. Or as Sigismund states in act 2:

> . . . for we live in a world so strange
> That to live is only to dream.
> He who lives, dreams his life
> Until he wakes. . . .
> I dream that I am here,
> Loaded with chains, or dream
> That I saw myself in some other,
> More illustrious, part
> What is life? a delirium!
> What is life? an illusion,
> A shadow, a fiction,
> Whose greatest good is nothing,
> Because life is a dream!
> Even dreams are only dreams.

To make this incomprehensible world comprehensible, Calderón posits three principles—a trinity—upon which his philosophy and dramaturgy are based. First, one must accept the order of the world that permeates the universe, nature, political systems, and, especially for Calderón, the individual. One disturbs this order only at great peril to self and society, as King Basilio, Astolfo, and Sigismund learn. Calderón's second principle tells us that human passions must be controlled if they conflict with the order established by the cosmos, nature, and society. "He who hopes to master his fate," says Sigismund very late in the play, "should act with temperance and prudence." The third principle derives from the first two: self-denial—or to put it more positively, the freedom to choose to restrain one's worldly desires. Self-denial is predicated on another trinity sacred to the playwright: humility (i.e., the recognition of a higher authority), submission (the acceptance of authority), and obedience (the fulfillment of the law). Acceptance of this triad allows Sigismund to proclaim that he aims "at the highest triumph, that over myself."

But Sigismund's dilemma is only part of the play's equation. If Sigismund is an Everyman whom experience teaches the need for restraint, then Basilio is an "Every-God" who acquires hard-won knowledge about the nature of humanity. Calderón implies that God must respond to the will of humanity every bit as much as humans must submit to the order of God. The playwright goes to great lengths to establish the godlike nature of Basilio. In act 1, he is given an arialike speech that defines him as "Basilio the Sage" and "Basilio the Great." A 1984 production of *Life's a Dream*, staged by the Royal Shakespeare Company, effected this godliness in Basilio's costume: a cloak, literally covering the stage, that was embroidered with stars and other heavenly bodies. He looked like a walking universe, with a wizened gray head peering from the constellular cloak. More than his words, Basilio's actions proclaim him godlike: He manipulates Sigismund, first turning him into a captive beast. Basilio, like God before the Flood, laments what his creation has wrought. Experience also teaches Basilio that wrath and oppression only embitter humans and incite rebellion. Basilio recants his harsh treatment of his son, realizing that by depriving him of his "rights by laws both divine and human," he has acted intemperately. Basilio recognizes that he must act in consort with Sigismund, rather than tyrannically, and thus be becomes a more benevolent man, father, and king. He permits Sigismund to rise to his birth-given greatness and share in the governance of Poland. After considerable trial and error, Sigismund matures into "the mirror of Christian kings" when he performs the consummate godlike act: He forgives Basilio. The final moment of the play depicts a reconciliation between father and son, that most archetypal of images. A covenant of forgiveness and mutual respect is forged to make parent and progeny, God and Man, partners in the ordering of the world.

SPOTLIGHT — THE SPANISH THEATER: THE *CORRALES*

The Spanish developed a theater space quite unlike that found in Italy and France, although it shares some similarities with the English public theater, perhaps because both may have evolved from innyards. Spanish public theaters, as opposed to those of the court, were called *corrales* and were administered by charitable societies (*cofradías*), not by actors as was the English custom. This association with charities benefited the actors, who consequently enjoyed a greater degree of social acceptance than some of their European and English counterparts.

The earliest *corrales* were makeshift affairs, but in 1579 the Corral de la Cruz, the first permanent theater in Spain, was opened in Madrid. Four years later the famous Corral del Príncipe—the Madrid equivalent of the Globe—opened. Like the English public theater, the design of the Spanish *corrales* varied, but there were some common features. Most were square or rectangular because they were adapted from existing courtyards, which were unroofed. The central courtyard, or *patio*, was occupied by standing spectators, much as the groundlings occupied Shakespeare's theater; preening *mosqueteros* strutted about the *patio*, wanting to be seen, as much as wanting to see the plays. Elevated seating (*gradas*) lined two sides of the courtyard; at the back of the theater was a tavern and a *cazuela*, a segregated gallery for women (perhaps as much an influence of the Moorish occupation as a response to Christian scruples about women attending the theater). Above the tavern and *cazuela* were raised galleries or boxes (*aposentos*), complete with balconies, from which gentry could watch the plays performed on a raised stage equipped with trap doors and other stage machinery. Actors dressed and awaited entrances in the *vestuario*, which backed the playing area. The *corrales* could accommodate a total of about 2,000 spectators. Spanish audiences were quite vocal, shouting "Victor, Victor" when they approved of performances and playwrights, jangling keys or other noisemakers when they disapproved.

Touring professional acting companies were performing in the *corrales* of Madrid by 1560. These *garnachas*, led by an *autore* (actor-manager), consisted of five or six men, a woman who played the major female character, and a boy who played other women's roles. The standard repertory of such a company was four *comedias* (which could be serious or comic), three *autos sacramentales* (allegorical dramas), and numerous *entremeses* (short comedies, usually on topical matters). The *garnachas* customarily remained in a city or village for eight days. They shared accommodations, often sleeping four to a bed. Their costumes, properties, and personal belongings were transported by four-pack mules. The women rode the mules, while the men took turns riding for a quarter-league and walking. Larger companies (*farándulas* and *compañías*) employed carts and drivers for their properties. These companies could afford better meals and better quarters, and generally enjoyed more prestige than the *garnachas*. A contemporary wrote of these professionals, "Their labor is excessive because of the continuous amount of study, the continuous rehearsals." When Spanish explorers ventured into the Americas in the early sixteenth century, professional acting companies followed. There were *compañías* in Peru and in Mexico City in the 1520s.

Unfortunately, little is known about Spanish acting styles. The plays themselves and the *corrales* suggest a formal style emphasizing voice and gesture. However, Lope de Vega, a theorist as well as a superb playwright, wrote essays praising the naturalistic style used by his actors. But, as is always the case, such terms as "realistic" and "naturalistic" must be considered within the context of the time.

FRANCE

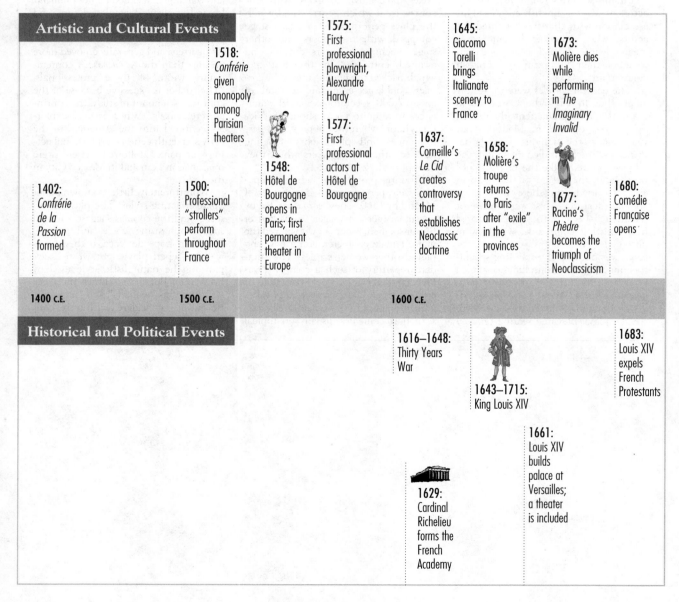

Artistic and Cultural Events

1402:
Confrérie de la Passion formed

1500:
Professional "strollers" perform throughout France

1518:
Confrérie given monopoly among Parisian theaters

1548:
Hôtel de Bourgogne opens in Paris; first permanent theater in Europe

1575:
First professional playwright, Alexandre Hardy

1577:
First professional actors at Hôtel de Bourgogne

1637:
Corneille's *Le Cid* creates controversy that establishes Neoclassic doctrine

1645:
Giacomo Torelli brings Italianate scenery to France

1658:
Molière's troupe returns to Paris after "exile" in the provinces

1673:
Molière dies while performing in *The Imaginary Invalid*

1677:
Racine's *Phèdre* becomes the triumph of Neoclassicism

1680:
Comédie Française opens

1400 C.E.　　　**1500 C.E.**　　　**1600 C.E.**

Historical and Political Events

1616–1648:
Thirty Years War

1629:
Cardinal Richelieu forms the French Academy

1643–1715:
King Louis XIV

1661:
Louis XIV builds palace at Versailles; a theater is included

1683:
Louis XIV expels French Protestants

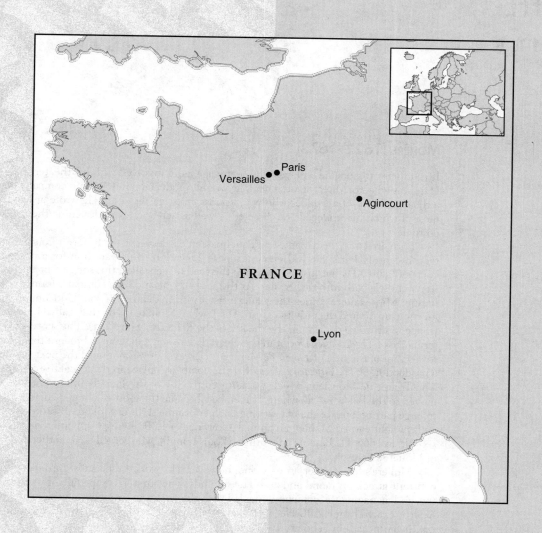

TARTUFFE

MOLIÈRE

MOLIÈRE (1622–1673)

It is difficult to imagine a playwright of any age more involved with his theater than Molière. Here was an actor, director, designer, playwright, producer, publicist, and company manager—a theatrical jack-of-all-trades who was, against type, master of all. He wrote at least 33 plays, most of which he produced and directed as well as acted in, even designing their scenery and costumes.

Born in 1622, Jean-Baptiste Poquelin seemed destined for life as a courtier in seventeenth-century Paris. He was given a superb education to prepare him for a position in the court of Louis XIV, but instead of taking the road to Versailles, this son of a prosperous upholsterer chose a path into the theater. At the age of 21 he and nine comrades formed the *Théâtre Illustre*, whose failure earned the young artist a stint in debtors' prison. Undaunted, the youthful company toured the provinces until 1658, when Molière (as he then called himself) and his troupe returned to perform in the theater of the *Roi Soleil* (Sun King). The success of their performance of *The Lovesick Doctor* in the Guard Room at Vieux Louvre brought the company the royal grant of the title of *Troupe de Monsieur*. However, it was not until the next year, thanks to a production of *The Affected Ladies*, that the company's place in theatrical history was assured. The Troupe de Monsieur, which was allowed the use of the Petit Bourbon until it was razed, moved to the Palais Royal, where its members became the most celebrated comedians in Paris, in large part because of the playwriting and performing skills of Molière. By 1663 his success as a playwright earned Molière an annual allowance of 1,000 livres, a stipend that was increased six-fold in 1665. He became a favorite of Louis himself, who served as godfather and namesake of Molière's first son.

Molière's lot was not an easy one, however. His work—especially *Tartuffe*—came under constant attack on moral and aesthetic grounds. The strenuous schedule of writing, performing, and managing the company, coupled with the deaths of two infant children and his failing health, exacted their toll. He was taken violently ill during a performance (ironically, *The Imaginary Invalid*) in February 1673 and died the same day.

Although Molière authored a number of farces patterned after the *commedia dell'arte* (*The Tricks of Scapin*), many comedic ballets for court performances (*The Forced Marriage*), and spectacular "machine plays" (*Amphitryon*), we think first of his satiric comedies: *Tartuffe*, *The Misanthrope*, *The Miser*, and *The Imaginary Invalid*. Characterized by intricate plots, archetypal characters, and social criticism, these works are invariably set in contemporary upper-class French society. Their action usually revolves around the archetypal pattern of young lovers who are separated by an older man—a blocking force—and often employ a *deus ex machina* to resolve the conflict.

While much of his subject matter is borrowed from Roman comedy and scenarios of the *commedia dell'arte* (his company shared a theater with a *commedia* troupe in the 1640s), his characters have a quality unique to Molière. Molière focuses most often not on traditional lovers, but on the blocking force, an older man, typically the father of one of the lovers who represents a conservative lifestyle and who is guided by a distinctive character flaw. In *Tartuffe*,

Orgon is gullible; in *The Miser*, Harpagon is greedy; in *The Imaginary Invalid*, Argan is the victim of his imagination and weak state of mind. These characters' names are variations of the French word *ogre*, a monster who devours children. The Molièrian father indeed devours his children, as you shall see in *Tartuffe*.

Unlike most other comic writers, Molière chooses not to have his aberrant characters rejoin the other, more sensible characters at the play's conclusion. With few exceptions, his miscreants do not overcome their deviant behavior and are not incorporated into the new society. And although Molière wrote in his preface to *Tartuffe* that "the duty of comedy is to correct men by entertaining them," it seems Molière believes that the rehabilitation of his misfits is mostly impossible. Rather than trying to reclaim them he seems content in the belief that, as eighteenth-century critic Gotthold Lessing famously observed, "it is enough for comedy that, if it cannot cure an incurable disease, it can confirm the healthy in their health."

TARTUFFE (1669)

The French philosopher Voltaire speaks for generations of *Tartuffe* admirers when he says that "as long as there are hypocrites and people who enjoy great art, *Tartuffe* will remain a masterpiece." What is it about this play that makes it a masterpiece? It appears, on first glance, to be a judicious comedy in which Molière gives us a plot that is easily followed, archetypal characters who are readily identifiable, and an obviously satiric theme. *Tartuffe* tells the story of a gullible man who is hoodwinked by a crafty hypocrite into sacrificing not only his daughter, his son, and his wife, but his good name and all that he owns. In addition to the fool (Orgon) and the charlatan (Tartuffe) there are obligatory young lovers (Mariane and Valère), a dutiful son (Damis), a loyal wife (Elmire), a saucy maid (Dorine), an imposing mother-in-law (Pernelle), and a voice of reason (Cléante). These rather conventional characters provide a scathing criticism of pretense and hypocrisy in a seventeenth-century bourgeois household. Indeed, the play's title is derived from *truffe* ("deception"), and *tartuffe* was a common epithet for schemers, connivers, and con men. So, if the play is so conventional, what makes it "a masterpiece"?

In this deceptively simple comedy, we see the nearly perfect interweaving of content and form—a dramatic criticism of pretense in the form of theatrical pretense. What Molière has given us is a plot, characters, and theme so expertly interwoven that at first reading we are not aware that such a tapestry exists. In addition, he has incorporated a metatheatrical (theater within theater) motif into his fabric and employed the comic mechanisms of jeopardy, fancy footwork, and exposure as the threads that bind it together. All of this leads to a conclusion that only "pretends" to be a *deus ex machina*.

The entire play is based on pretense—pretending to be something one is not or pretending that something is so when it is not. In its simplest form the audience is asked to observe a solo performance by a pretender (i.e., Tartuffe) who watches not only his own performance but its effect on his onstage audience and his audience's reaction as well. In its more complicated form the motif presents an ensemble performance, often scripted by the pretender, which involves other characters not only as performers but as audience.

Obviously, without Tartuffe's pretense of piety we have no play. But Molière is not content with a single pretense. Many other characters also resort to pretense. In act 2, Dorine pretends to agree with Orgon and encourages Mariane to marry Tartuffe. Shortly thereafter, Mariane and Valère, in the midst of their lovers' quarrel, pretend nonchalance as they try to convince each other of their ambivalence. In act 4, Elmire, with Tartuffe as her scene partner and Orgon as her audience, pretends to be genuinely interested in Tartuffe. In each case the pretense is prompted by personal gain. Tartuffe wants all he can get, Mariane and Valère want each other, and Elmire wants to rid her household of the imposter. Orgon, of course, wants to prove Elmire wrong so he will not be seen as a fool.

As is often the case, pretense precipitates comic action. First, the pretenders find themselves in jeopardy—the threat of exposure or physical violence. To avoid exposure, they each engage in fancy footwork—the literal or figurative evasion of danger—to rationalize their pretense. Such comic mechanisms are interrelated; their interplay propels the comic situation.

Throughout the play, Tartuffe is in jeopardy. When he is exposed by Damis at the end of act 3, he employs some figurative footwork to convince Orgon of his piety. In act 4, Elmire finds herself in jeopardy as her pretense of affection is called into question by Tartuffe's demands for proof and Orgon's inability to play his role as audience. Jeopardized, she must verbally placate Tartuffe while she physically avoids his advances in some of the play's fanciest footwork.

By act 5, it appears that Molière's various pretenses have created such an intricately complicated entanglement that the only way to untie the knot is through some outside help—a *deus ex machina*. When all appears lost, the Prince, in the form of the Officer, appears to expose Tartuffe's pretense and restore Orgon's property, thus insuring the Mariane-Valère marriage. And all live happily ever after—except Tartuffe. On closer examination, however, it may be that Molière's metatheatrical design extends beyond the dramatic world of the play, and that the *deus ex machina* is more than a convenient device for ending the play. Without question, the Prince represents Louis XIV, and given the Renaissance belief in the divine right of kings, it is logical that a "good" Prince, as God's emissary on earth, would be aware of evil in his realm and move to exorcise it. Given that Molière was indebted to his king for granting him permission to perform *Tartuffe*, it is also logical that he compliment Louis for his munificence. And since the purpose of a Neoclassic play was to teach proper moral (i.e., Christian) behavior, Molière presented "poetic justice" while reinforcing the omnipotence of God's emissary in France.

But Molière does not stop here. Clever playwright that he is, he takes his metatheatrics a step further. While he pretends to give us a vision of a righteous king watching the work of a hypocrite and then intervening to restore truth and goodness, what Molière actually presents is the portrait of a king who, as the ultimate censor, has allowed a noble citizen to suffer unduly at the hands of a scoundrel before rescuing him. Given the ending of the play, we can only believe that the Prince has not only been aware of everything that has transpired, but has been amused by the "play" he has been watching. What other explanation can there be for his delay in unmasking Tartuffe's pretense? It also appears that Molière may have been only pretending to pay a compliment to the king while he was, in fact, pointing out the pretentiousness of censorship. Remember, Louis waited nearly five years before granting Molière permission to produce the play. It may be that, by allowing the Prince to dawdle in his exposure of Tartuffe, Molière was indicting Louis for his delay. Although Molière states in his preface to *Tartuffe* that the play "in nowise tends to make sport for things that we must revere," he further notes that his work is "nothing other than a skillful poem which, by agreeable lessons, reprimands men's defects." Including those of the king?

Molière himself performed in the famous table scene in Tartuffe; a contemporary engraving suggests what his Parisian audience viewed in 1669.

LE TARTVFFE

TARTUFFE

MOLIÈRE

Translated by Richard Wilbur

CHARACTERS

MME PERNELLE, *Orgon's mother*
ORGON, *Elmire's husband*
ELMIRE, *Orgon's wife*

DAMIS, *Orgon's son, Elmire's stepson*
MARIANE, *Orgon's daughter, Elmire's stepdaughter, in love with Valère*
VALÈRE, *in love with Mariane*

CLÉANTE, *Orgon's brother-in-law*
TARTUFFE, *a hypocrite*
DORINE, *Mariane's lady's-maid*
M. LOYAL, *a bailiff*
A POLICE OFFICER
FLIPOTE, *Mme Pernelle's maid*

THE SCENE THROUGHOUT: *Orgon's house in Paris*

ACT ONE

SCENE ONE

*Madame Pernelle and Flipote, her maid, Elmire,
Mariane, Dorine, Damis, Cléante*

MADAME PERNELLE.
    Come, come, Flipote; it's time I left this place.
ELMIRE.
    I can't keep up, you walk at such a pace.
MADAME PERNELLE.
    Don't trouble, child; no need to show me out.
    It's not your manners I'm concerned about.
ELMIRE.
5   We merely pay you the respect we owe.
    But, Mother, why this hurry? Must you go?
MADAME PERNELLE.
    I must. This house appals me. No one in it
    Will pay attention for a single minute.
    Children, I take my leave much vexed in spirit.
10   I offer good advice, but you won't hear it.
    You all break in and chatter on and on.
    It's like a madhouse with the keeper gone.
DORINE.
    If . . .
MADAME PERNELLE.
        Girl, you talk too much, and I'm afraid
    You're far too saucy for a lady's-maid.
15   You push in everywhere and have your say.
DAMIS.
    But . . .
MADAME PERNELLE.
        You, boy, grow more foolish every day.
    To think my grandson should be such a dunce!
    I've said a hundred times, if I've said it once,
    That if you keep the course on which you've started,
20   You'll leave your worthy father broken-hearted.
MARIANE.
    I think . . .
MADAME PERNELLE.
        And you, his sister, seem so pure,
So shy, so innocent, and so demure.
But you know what they say about still waters.
I pity parents with secretive daughters.
ELMIRE.
    Now, Mother . . .
MADAME PERNELLE.
            And as for you, child, let me add   25
That your behavior is extremely bad,
And a poor example for these children, too.
Their dear, dead mother did far better than you.
You're much too free with money, and I'm distressed
To see you so elaborately dressed.   30
When it's one's husband that one aims to please,
One has no need of costly fripperies.
CLÉANTE.
    Oh, Madam, really . . .
MADAME PERNELLE.
                You are her brother, Sir,
And I respect and love you; yet if I were
My son, this lady's good and pious spouse,   35
I wouldn't make you welcome in my house.
You're full of worldly counsels which, I fear,
Aren't suitable for decent folk to hear.
I've spoken bluntly, Sir; but it behooves us
Not to mince words when righteous fervor moves us.   40
DAMIS.
    Your man Tartuffe is full of holy speeches . . .
MADAME PERNELLE.
    And practises precisely what he preaches.
    He's a fine man, and should be listened to.
    I will not hear him mocked by fools like you.
DAMIS.
    Good God! Do you expect me to submit   45
    To the tyranny of that carping hypocrite?
    Must we forgo all joys and satisfactions
    Because that bigot censures all our actions?
DORINE.
    To hear him talk—and he talks all the time—
    There's nothing one can do that's not a crime.   50
    He rails at everything, your dear Tartuffe.
MADAME PERNELLE.
    Whatever he reproves deserves reproof.
    He's out to save your souls, and all of you
    Must love him, as my son would have you do.
DAMIS.
    Ah no, Grandmother, I could never take   55
    To such a rascal, even for my father's sake.
    That's how I feel, and I shall not dissemble.
    His every action makes me seethe and tremble
    With helpless anger, and I have no doubt
    That he and I will shortly have it out.   60
DORINE.
    Surely it is a shame and a disgrace
    To see this man usurp the master's place—
    To see this beggar who, when first he came,

Had not a shoe or shoestring to his name
65 So far forget himself that he behaves
As if the house were his, and we his slaves.
MADAME PERNELLE.
Well, mark my words, your souls would fare far better
If you obeyed his precepts to the letter.
DORINE.
You see him as a saint. I'm far less awed;
70 In fact, I see right through him. He's a fraud.
MADAME PERNELLE.
Nonsense!
DORINE.
His man Laurent's the same, or worse;
I'd not trust either with a penny purse.
MADAME PERNELLE.
I can't say what his servant's morals may be;
His own great goodness I can guarantee.
75 You all regard him with distaste and fear
Because he tells you what you're loath to hear,
Condemns your sins, points out your moral flaws,
And humbly strives to further Heaven's cause.
DORINE.
If sin is all that bothers him, why is it
80 He's so upset when folk drop in to visit?
Is Heaven so outraged by a social call
That he must prophesy against us all?
I'll tell you what I think: if you ask me,
He's jealous of my mistress' company.
MADAME PERNELLE.
Rubbish! (To Elmire:) He's not alone, child, in com-
85   plaining
Of all your promiscuous entertaining.
Why, the whole neighborhood's upset, I know,
By all these carriages that come and go,
With crowds of guests parading in and out
90 And noisy servants loitering about.
In all of this, I'm sure there's nothing vicious;
But why give people cause to be suspicious?
CLÉANTE.
They need no cause; they'll talk in any case.
Madam, this world would be a joyless place
95 If, fearing what malicious tongues might say,
We locked our doors and turned our friends away.
And even if one did so dreary a thing,
D'you think those tongues would cease their chattering?
One can't fight slander; it's a losing battle;
100 Let us instead ignore their tittle-tattle.
Let's strive to live by conscience' clear decrees,
And let the gossips gossip as they please.
DORINE.
If there is talk against us, I know the source:
It's Daphne and her little husband, of course.
105 Those who have greatest cause for guilt and shame
Are quickest to besmirch a neighbor's name.
When there's a chance for libel, they never miss it;

When something can be made to seem illicit
They're off at once to spread the joyous news,
Adding to fact what fantasies they choose.   110
By talking up their neighbor's indiscretions
They seek to camouflage their own transgressions,
Hoping that others' innocent affairs
Will lend a hue of innocence to theirs,
Or that their own black guilt will come to seem   115
Part of a general shady color-scheme.
MADAME PERNELLE.
All that is quite irrelevant. I doubt
That anyone's more virtuous and devout
Than dear Orante; and I'm informed that she
Condemns your mode of life most vehemently.   120
DORINE.
Oh, yes, she's strict, devout, and has no taint
Of worldliness; in short, she seems a saint.
But it was time which taught her that disguise;
She's thus because she can't be otherwise.
So long as her attractions could enthrall,   125
She flounced and flirted and enjoyed it all,
But now that they're no longer what they were
She quits a world which fast is quitting her,
And wears a veil of virtue to conceal
Her bankrupt beauty and her lost appeal.   130
That's what becomes of old coquettes today:
Distressed when all their lovers fall away,
They see no recourse but to play the prude,
And so confer a style on solitude.
Thereafter, they're severe with everyone,   135
Condemning all our actions, pardoning none,
And claiming to be pure, austere and zealous
When, if the truth were known, they're merely jealous,
And cannot bear to see another know
The pleasures time has forced them to forgo.   140
MADAME PERNELLE (Initially to Elmire:).
That sort of talk is what you like to hear;
Therefore you'd have us all keep still, my dear,
While Madam rattles on the livelong day.
Nevertheless, I mean to have my say.
I tell you that you're blest to have Tartuffe   145
Dwelling, as my son's guest, beneath this roof;
That Heaven has sent him to forestall its wrath
By leading you, once more, to the true path;
That all he reprehends its reprehensible,
And that you'd better heed him, and be sensible.   150
These visits, balls, and parties in which you revel
Are nothing but inventions of the Devil.
One never hears a word that's edifying:
Nothing but chaff and foolishness and lying,
As well as vicious gossip in which one's neighbor   155
Is cut to bits with epee, foil, and saber.
People of sense are driven half-insane
At such affairs, where noise and folly reign
And reputations perish thick and fast.

160 As a wise preacher said on Sunday last,
Parties are Towers of Babylon, because
The guests all babble on with never a pause;
And then he told a story, which, I think . . .
(*To Cléante:*)
I heard that laugh, Sir, and I saw that wink!
165 Go find your silly friends and laugh some more!
Enough; I'm going; don't show me to the door.
I leave this household much dismayed and vexed;
I cannot say when I shall see you next.
(*Slapping Flipote:*)
Wake up, don't stand there gaping into space!
170 I'll slap some sense into that stupid face.
Move, move, you slut.

SCENE TWO

Cléante, Dorine

CLÉANTE.
                          I think I'll stay behind;
I want no further pieces of her mind.
How that old lady . . .
DORINE.
                          Oh, what wouldn't she say
If she could hear you speak of her that way!
175 She'd thank you for the *lady*, but I'm sure
She'd find the *old* a little premature.
CLÉANTE.
My, what a scene she made, and what a din!
And how this man Tartuffe has taken her in!
DORINE.
Yes, but her son is even worse deceived;
180 His folly must be seen to be believed.
In the late troubles, he played an able part
And served his king with wise and loyal heart,
But he's quite lost his senses since he fell
Beneath Tartuffe's infatuating spell.
185 He calls him brother, and loves him as his life,
Preferring him to mother, child, or wife.
In him and him alone will he confide;
He's made him his confessor and his guide;
He pets and pampers him with love more tender
190 Than any pretty mistress could engender,
Gives him the place of honor when they dine,
Delights to see him gorging like a swine,
Stuffs him with dainties till his guts distend,
And when he belches, cries "God bless you, friend!"
195 In short, he's mad; he worships him; he dotes,
His deeds he marvels at, his words he quotes,
Thinking each act a miracle, each word
Oracular as those that Moses heard.
Tartuffe, much pleased to find so easy a victim,

200 Has in a hundred ways beguiled and tricked him,
Milked him of money, and with his permission
Established here a sort of Inquisition.
Even Laurent, his lackey, dares to give
Us arrogant advice on how to live;
205 He sermonizes us in thundering tones
And confiscates our ribbons and colognes.
Last week he tore a kerchief into pieces
Because he found it pressed in a *Life of Jesus:*
He said it was a sin to juxtapose
210 Unholy vanities and holy prose.

SCENE THREE

Elmire, Mariane, Damis, Cléante, Dorine

ELMIRE (*To Cléante:*).
You did well not to follow; she stood in the door
And said *verbatim* all she'd said before.
I saw my husband coming. I think I'd best
Go upstairs now, and take a little rest.
CLÉANTE.
I'll wait and greet him here; then I must go.   215
I've really only time to say hello.
DAMIS.
Sound him about my sister's wedding, please.
I think Tartuffe's against it, and that he's
Been urging Father to withdraw his blessing.
As you well know, I'd find that most distressing.   220
Unless my sister and Valère can marry,
My hopes to wed *his* sister will miscarry,
And I'm determined . . .
DORINE.
                          He's coming.

SCENE FOUR

Orgon, Cléante, Dorine

ORGON.
                          Ah, Brother, good-day.
CLÉANTE.
Well, welcome back. I'm sorry I can't stay.
How was the country? Blooming, I trust, and green?   225
ORGON.
Excuse me, Brother; just one moment.
(*To Dorine:*)
                          Dorine . . .
(*To Cléante:*)
To put my mind at rest, I always learn
The household news the moment I return.
(*To Dorine:*)

Has all been well, these two days I've been gone?
How are the family? What's been going on?
DORINE.
    Your wife, two days ago, had a bad fever,
And a fierce headache which refused to leave her.
ORGON.
    Ah. And Tartuffe?
DORINE.
               Tartuffe? Why, he's round and red,
Bursting with health, and excellently fed.
ORGON.
    Poor fellow!
DORINE.
          That night, the mistress was unable
To take a single bite at the dinner-table.
Her headache-pains, she said, were simply hellish.
ORGON.
    Ah. And Tartuffe?
DORINE.
          He ate his meal with relish,
And zealously devoured in her presence
A leg of mutton and a brace of pheasants.
ORGON.
    Poor fellow!
DORINE.
        Well, the pains continued strong.
And so she tossed and tossed the whole night long,
Now icy-cold, now burning like a flame.
We sat beside her bed till morning came.
ORGON.
    Ah. And Tartuffe?
DORINE.
        Why, having eaten, he rose
And sought his room, already in a doze,
Got into his warm bed, and snored away
In perfect peace until the break of day.
ORGON.
    Poor fellow!
DORINE.
    After much ado, we talked her
Into dispatching someone for the doctor.
He bled her, and the fever quickly fell.
ORGON.
    Ah. And Tartuffe?
DORINE.
       He bore it very well.
To keep his cheerfulness at any cost,
And make up for the blood *Madame* had lost,
He drank, at lunch, four beakers full of port.
ORGON.
    Poor fellow!
DORINE.
     Both are doing well, in short.
I'll go and tell *Madame* that you've expressed
Keen sympathy and anxious interest.

SCENE FIVE

Orgon, Cléante

CLÉANTE.
    That girl was laughing in your face, and though
I've no wish to offend you, even so
I'm bound to say that she had some excuse.
How can you possibly be such a goose?
Are you so dazed by this man's hocus-pocus
That all the world, save him, is out of focus?
You've given him clothing, shelter, food, and care;
Why must you also . . .
ORGON.
         Brother, stop right there.
You do not know the man of whom you speak.
CLÉANTE.
    I grant you that. But my judgment's not so weak
That I can't tell, by his effect on others . . .
ORGON.
    Ah, when you meet him, you two will be like
      brothers!
There's been no loftier soul since time began.
He is a man who . . . a man who . . . an excellent man.
To keep his precepts is to be reborn,
And view this dunghill of a world with scorn.
Yes, thanks to him I'm a changed man indeed.
Under his tutelage my soul's been freed
From earthly loves, and every human tie:
My mother, children, brother, and wife could die,
And I'd not feel a single moment's pain.
CLÉANTE.
    That's a fine sentiment, Brother; most humane.
ORGON.
    Oh, had you seen Tartuffe as I first knew him,
Your heart, like mine, would have surrendered to him.
He used to come into our church each day
And humbly kneel nearby, and start to pray.
He'd draw the eyes of everybody there
By the deep fervor of his heartfelt prayer;
He'd sigh and weep, and sometimes with a sound
Of rapture he would bend and kiss the ground;
And when I rose to go, he'd run before
To offer me holy-water at the door.
His serving-man, no less devout than he,
Informed me of his master's poverty;
I gave him gifts, but in his humbleness
He'd beg me every time to give him less.
"Oh, that's too much," he'd cry, "too much by twice!
I don't deserve it. The half, Sir, would suffice."
And when I wouldn't take it back, he'd share
Half of it with the poor, right then and there.
At length, Heaven prompted me to take him in
To dwell with us, and free our souls from sin.
He guides our lives, and to protect my honor

Stays by my wife, and keeps an eye upon her;
He tells me whom she sees, and all she does,
And seems more jealous than I ever was!
305   And how austere he is! Why, he can detect
A mortal sin where you would least suspect;
In smallest trifles, he's extremely strict.
Last week, his conscience was severely pricked
Because, while praying, he had caught a flea
310   And killed it, so he felt, too wrathfully.

CLÉANTE.
Good God, man! Have you lost your common sense—
Or is this all some joke at my expense?
How can you stand there and in all sobriety . . .

ORGON.
Brother, your language savors of impiety.
315   Too much free-thinking's made your faith unsteady,
And as I've warned you many times already,
'Twill get you into trouble before you're through.

CLÉANTE.
So I've been told before by dupes like you:
Being blind, you'd have all others blind as well;
320   The clear-eyed man you call an infidel,
And he who sees through humbug and pretense
Is charged, by you, with want of reverence.
Spare me your warnings, Brother; I have no fear
Of speaking out, for you and Heaven to hear,
325   Against affected zeal and pious knavery.
There's true and false in piety, as in bravery,
And just as those whose courage shines the most
In battle, are the least inclined to boast,
So those who hearts are truly pure and lowly
330   Don't make a flashy show of being holy.
There's a vast difference, so it seems to me,
Between true piety and hypocrisy:
How do you fail to see it, may I ask?
Is not a face quite different from a mask?
335   Cannot sincerity and cunning art,
Reality and semblance, be told apart?
Are scarecrows just like men, and do you hold
That a false coin is just as good as gold?
Ah, Brother, man's a strangely fashioned creature
340   Who seldom is content to follow Nature,
But recklessly pursues his inclination
Beyond the narrow bounds of moderation,
And often, by transgressing Reason's laws,
Perverts a lofty aim or noble cause.
345   A passing observation, but it applies.

ORGON.
I see, dear Brother, that you're profoundly wise;
You harbor all the insight of the age.
You are our one clear mind, our only sage,
The era's oracle, its Cato too,
350   And all mankind are fools compared to you.

CLÉANTE.
Brother, I don't pretend to be a sage,
Nor have I all the wisdom of the age.
There's just one insight I would dare to claim:
I know that true and false are not the same;
355   And just as there is nothing I more revere
Than a soul whose faith is steadfast and sincere,
Nothing that I more cherish and admire
Than honest zeal and true religious fire,
So there is nothing that I find more base
360   Than specious piety's dishonest face—
Than these bold mountebanks, these histrios
Whose impious mummeries and hollow shows
Exploit our love of Heaven, and make a jest
Of all that men think holiest and best;
365   These calculating souls who offer prayers
Not to their Maker, but as public wares,
And seek to buy respect and reputation
With lifted eyes and sighs of exaltation;
These charlatans, I say, whose pilgrim souls
370   Proceed, by way of Heaven, toward earthly goals,
Who weep and pray and swindle and extort,
Who preach the monkish life, but haunt the court,
Who make their zeal the partner of their vice—
Such men are vengeful, sly, and cold as ice,
375   And when there is an enemy to defame
They cloak their spite in fair religion's name,
Their private spleen and malice being made
To seem a high and virtuous crusade,
Until, to mankind's reverent applause,
380   They crucify their foe in Heaven's cause.
Such knaves are all too common; yet, for the wise,
True piety isn't hard to recognize,
And, happily, these present times provide us
With bright examples to instruct and guide us.
385   Consider Ariston and Périandre;
Look at Oronte, Alcidamas, Clitandre;
Their virtue is acknowledged; who could doubt it?
But you won't hear them beat the drum about it.
They're never ostentatious, never vain,
390   And their religion's moderate and humane;
It's not their way to criticize and chide:
They think censoriousness a mark of pride,
And therefore, letting others preach and rave,
They show, by deeds, how Christians should behave.
395   They think no evil of their fellow man,
But judge of him as kindly as they can.
They don't intrigue and wangle and conspire;
To lead a good life is their one desire;
The sinner wakes no rancorous hate in them;
400   It is the sin alone which they condemn;
Nor do they try to show a fiercer zeal
For Heaven's cause than Heaven itself could feel.
These men I honor, these men I advocate
As models for us all to emulate.
405   Your man is not their sort at all, I fear:
And, while your praise of him is quite sincere,

I think that you've been dreadfully deluded.

ORGON.
  Now then, dear Brother, is your speech concluded?

CLÉANTE.
  Why, yes.

ORGON.
          Your servant, Sir. (*He turns to go.*)

CLÉANTE.
                          No, Brother; wait.
410 There's one more matter. You agreed of late
That young Valère might have your daughter's hand.

ORGON.
  I did.

CLÉANTE.
          And set the date, I understand.

ORGON.
  Quite so.

CLÉANTE.
          You've now postponed it; is that true?

ORGON.
  No doubt.

CLÉANTE.
          The match no longer pleases you?

ORGON.
  Who knows?

CLÉANTE.
415   D'you mean to go back on your word?

ORGON.
  I won't say that.

CLÉANTE.
                  Has anything occurred
Which might entitle you to break your pledge?

ORGON.
  Perhaps.

CLÉANTE.
          Why must you hem, and haw, and hedge?
The boy asked me to sound you in this affair . . .

ORGON.
  It's been a pleasure.

CLÉANTE.
                  But what shall I tell Valère?

420

ORGON.
  Whatever you like.

CLÉANTE.
                  But what have you decided?
What are your plans?

ORGON.
                  I plan, Sir, to be guided
By Heaven's will.

CLÉANTE.
                  Come, Brother, don't talk rot.
You've given Valère your word; will you keep it, or
  not?

ORGON.
  Good day.

CLÉANTE.
  This looks like poor Valère's undoing;   425
  I'll go and warn him that there's trouble brewing.

ACT TWO

SCENE ONE

Orgon, Mariane

ORGON.
  Mariane.

MARIANE.
          Yes, Father?

ORGON.
  A word with you; come here.

MARIANE.
  What are you looking for?

ORGON (*Peering into a small closet:*).
                          Eavesdroppers, dear.
  I'm making sure we shan't be overheard.
  Someone in there could catch our every word.
  Ah, good, we're safe. Now, Mariane, my child,   5
  You're a sweet girl who's tractable and mild,
  Whom I hold dear, and think most highly of.

MARIANE.
  I'm deeply grateful, Father, for your love.

ORGON.
  That's well said, Daughter; and you can repay me
  If, in all things, you'll cheerfully obey me.   10

MARIANE.
  To please you, Sir, is what delights me best.

ORGON.
  Good, good. Now, what d'you think of Tartuffe, our
    guest?

MARIANE.
  I, Sir?

ORGON.
          Yes. Weigh your answer; think it through.

MARIANE.
  Oh, dear. I'll say whatever you wish me to.

ORGON.
  That's wisely said, my Daughter. Say of him, then,   15
  That he's the very worthiest of men,
  And that you're fond of him, and would rejoice
  In being his wife, if that should be my choice.
  Well?

MARIANE.
      What?

ORGON.
          What's that?

MARIANE.
                  I . . .

ORGON.

                      Well?

MARIANE.

                          Forgive me, pray.

ORGON.

    Did you not hear me?

MARIANE.

20   Of *whom*, Sir, must I say
That I am fond of him, and would rejoice
In being his wife, if that should be your choice?

ORGON.

    Why, of Tartuffe.

MARIANE.

                But, Father, that's false, you know.
Why would you have me say what isn't so?

ORGON.

25   Because I am resolved it shall be true.
That it's my wish should be enough for you.

MARIANE.

    You can't mean, Father . . .

ORGON.

                   Yes, Tartuffe shall be
Allied by marriage to this family,
And he's to be your husband, is that clear?
It's a father's privilege . . .

SCENE TWO

Dorine, Orgon, Mariane

ORGON (*To Dorine:*).

30   What are you doing in here?
Is curiosity so fierce a passion
With you, that you must eavesdrop in this fashion?

DORINE.

    There's lately been a rumor going about—
Based on some hunch or chance remark, no doubt—
35   That you mean Mariane to wed Tartuffe.
I've laughed it off, of course, as just a spoof.

ORGON.

    You find it so incredible?

DORINE.

                    Yes, I do.
I won't accept that story, even from you.

ORGON.

    Well, you'll believe it when the thing is done.

DORINE.

40   Yes, yes, of course. Go on and have your fun.

ORGON.

    I've never been more serious in my life.

DORINE.

    Ha!

ORGON.

    Daughter, I mean it; you're to be his wife.

DORINE.

    No, don't believe your father; it's all a hoax.

ORGON.

    See here, young woman . . .

DORINE.

                  Come, Sir, no more jokes;
You can't fool us.

ORGON.

               How dare you talk that way?   45

DORINE.

    All right, then: we believe you, sad to say.
But how a man like you, who looks so wise
And wears a moustache of such splendid size,
Can be so foolish as to . . .

ORGON.

                  Silence, please!
My girl, you take too many liberties.   50
I'm master here, as you must not forget.

DORINE.

    Do let's discuss this calmly; don't be upset.
You can't be serious, Sir, about this plan.
What should that bigot want with Mariane?
Praying and fasting ought to keep him busy.   55
And then, in terms of wealth and rank, what is he?
Why should a man of property like you
Pick out a beggar son-in-law?

ORGON.

                 That will do.
Speak of his poverty with reverence.
His is a pure and saintly indigence.   60
Which far transcends all worldly pride and pelf.
He lost his fortune, as he says himself,
Because he cared for Heaven alone, and so
Was careless of his interests here below.
I mean to get him out of his present straits   65
And help him to recover his estates—
Which, in his part of the world, have no small fame.
Poor though he is, he's a gentleman just the same.

DORINE.

    Yes, so he tells us; and, Sir, it seems to me
Such pride goes very ill with piety.   70
A man whose spirit spurns this dungy earth
Ought not to brag of lands and noble birth;
Such worldly arrogance will hardly square
With meek devotion and the life of prayer.
. . . But this approach, I see, has drawn a blank;   75
Let's speak, then, of his person, not his rank.
Doesn't it seem to you a trifle grim
To give a girl like her to a man like him?
When two are so ill-suited, can't you see
What the sad consequence is bound to be?   80
A young girl's virtue is imperilled, Sir,
When such a marriage is imposed on her;

For if one's bridegroom isn't to one's taste,
It's hardly an inducement to be chaste,
85 And many a man with horns upon his brow
Has made his wife the thing that she is now.
It's hard to be a faithful wife, in short,
To certain husbands of a certain sort,
And he who gives his daughter to a man she hates
90 Must answer for her sins at Heaven's gates.
Think, Sir, before you play so risky a role.

ORGON.
This servant-girl presumes to save my soul!

DORINE.
You would do well to ponder what I've said.

ORGON.
Daughter, we'll disregard this dunderhead.
95 Just trust your father's judgment. Oh, I'm aware
That I once promised you to young Valère;
But now I hear he gambles, which greatly shocks me;
What's more, I've doubts about his orthodoxy.
His visits to church, I note, are very few.

DORINE.
100 Would you have him go at the same hours as you,
And kneel nearby, to be sure of being seen?

ORGON.
I can dispense with such remarks, Dorine.
(To Mariane:)
Tartuffe, however, is sure of Heaven's blessing,
And that's the only treasure worth possessing.
105 This match will bring you joys beyond all measure;
Your cup will overflow with every pleasure;
You two will interchange your faithful loves
Like two sweet cherubs, or two turtle-doves.
No harsh word shall be heard, no frown be seen,
110 And he shall make you happy as a queen.

DORINE.
And she'll make him a cuckold, just wait and see.

ORGON.
What language!

DORINE.
Oh, he's a man of destiny;
He's *made* for horns, and what the stars demand
Your daughter's virtue surely can't withstand.

ORGON.
115 Don't interrupt me further. Why can't you learn
That certain things are none of your concern?

DORINE.
It's for your own sake that I interfere.

(*She repeatedly interrupts Orgon just as he is turning
to speak to his daughter:*)

ORGON.
Most kind of you. Now, hold your tongue, d'you hear?

DORINE.
If I didn't love you . . .

ORGON.
Spare me your affection.

DORINE.
I'll love you, Sir, in spite of your objection. 120

ORGON.
Blast!

DORINE.
I can't bear, Sir, for your honor's sake,
To let you make this ludicrous mistake.

ORGON.
You mean to go on talking?

DORINE.
If I didn't protest
This sinful marriage, my conscience couldn't rest.

ORGON.
If you don't hold your tongue, you little shrew . . . 125

DORINE.
What, lost your temper? A pious man like you?

ORGON.
Yes! Yes! You talk and talk. I'm maddened by it.
Once and for all, I tell you to be quiet.

DORINE.
Well, I'll be quiet. But I'll be thinking hard.

ORGON.
Think all you like, but you had better guard 130
That saucy tongue of yours, or I'll . . .

(*Turning back to Mariane:*)
Now, child,
I've weighed this matter fully.

DORINE (*Aside:*).
It drives me wild
That I can't speak.

(*Orgon turns his head, and she is silent.*)

ORGON.
Tartuffe is no young dandy,
But, still, his person . . .

DORINE (*Aside:*).
Is as sweet as candy.

ORGON.
Is such that, even if you shouldn't care 135
For his other merits . . .

(*He turns and stands facing Dorine, arms crossed.*)

DORINE (*Aside:*).
They'll make a lovely pair.
If I were she, no man would marry me
Against my inclination, and go scot-free.
He'd learn, before the wedding-day was over,
How readily a wife can find a lover. 140

ORGON (*To Dorine:*).
It seems you treat my orders as a joke.

DORINE.
Why, what's the matter? 'Twas not to you I spoke.

ORGON.
What *were* you doing?

DORINE.
       Talking to myself, that's all.

ORGON.
Ah! (*Aside:*) One more bit of impudence and gall,
145 And I shall give her a good slap in the face.

(*He puts himself in position to slap her; Dorine, whenever
he glances at her, stands immobile and silent:*)

Daughter, you shall accept, and with good grace,
The husband I've selected . . . Your wedding-day . . .
(*To Dorine:*)
Why don't you talk to yourself?

DORINE.
        I've nothing to say.

ORGON.
Come, just one word.

DORINE.
      No, thank you, Sir. I pass.

ORGON.
Come, speak; I'm waiting.

DORINE.
150   I'd not be such an ass.

ORGON (*Turning to Mariane:*).
In short, dear Daughter, I mean to be obeyed,
And you must bow to the sound choice I've made.

DORINE (*Moving away:*).
I'd not wed such a monster, even in jest.

(*Orgon attempts to slap her, but misses.*)

ORGON.
Daughter, that maid of yours is a thorough pest;
155 She makes me sinfully annoyed and nettled.
I can't speak further; my nerves are too unsettled.
She's so upset me by her insolent talk,
I'll calm myself by going for a walk.

SCENE THREE

Dorine, Mariane

DORINE (*Returning:*).
 Well, have you lost your tongue, girl? Must I play
160 Your part, and say the lines you ought to say?
Faced with a fate so hideous and absurd,
Can you not utter one dissenting word?

MARIANE.
What good would it do? A father's power is great.

DORINE.
Resist him now, or it will be too late.

MARIANE.
But . . .

DORINE.
 Tell him one cannot love at a father's whim;   165
That you shall marry for yourself, not him;
That since it's you who are to be the bride,
It's you, not he, who must be satisfied;
And that if his Tartuffe is so sublime,
He's free to marry him at any time.   170

MARIANE.
I've bowed so long to Father's strict control,
I couldn't oppose him now, to save my soul.

DORINE.
Come, come, Mariane. Do listen to reason, won't you?
Valère has asked your hand. Do you love him, or don't
 you?

MARIANE.
Oh, how unjust of you! What can you mean   175
By asking such a question, dear Dorine?
You know the depth of my affection for him;
I've told you a hundred times how I adore him.

DORINE.
I don't believe in everything I hear;
Who knows if your professions were sincere?   180

MARIANE.
They were, Dorine, and you do me wrong to doubt it;
Heaven knows that I've been all too frank about it.

DORINE.
You love him, then?

MARIANE.
      Oh, more than I can express.

DORINE.
And he, I take it, cares for you no less?

MARIANE.
I think so.

DORINE.
    And you both, with equal fire,   185
Burn to be married?

MARIANE.
     That is our one desire.

DORINE.
What of Tartuffe, then? What of your father's plan?

MARIANE.
I'll kill myself, if I'm forced to wed that man.

DORINE.
I hadn't thought of that recourse. How splendid!
Just die, and all your troubles will be ended!   190
A fine solution. Oh, it maddens me
To hear you talk in that self-pitying key.

MARIANE.
Dorine, how harsh you are! It's most unfair.
You have no sympathy for my despair.

DORINE.
I've none at all for people who talk drivel   195
And, faced with difficulties, whine and snivel.

MARIANE.
No doubt I'm timid, but it would be wrong . . .

DORINE.
 True love requires a heart that's firm and strong.
MARIANE.
 I'm strong in my affection for Valère,
200 But coping with my father is his affair.
DORINE.
 But if your father's brain has grown so cracked
 Over his dear Tartuffe that he can retract
 His blessing, though your wedding-day was named,
 It's surely not Valère who's to be blamed.
MARIANE.
205 If I defied my father, as you suggest,
 Would it not seem unmaidenly, at best?
 Shall I defend my love at the expense
 Of brazenness and disobedience?
 Shall I parade my heart's desires, and flaunt . . .
DORINE.
210 No, I ask nothing of you. Clearly you want
 To be Madame Tartuffe, and I feel bound
 Not to oppose a wish so very sound.
 What right have I to criticize the match?
 Indeed, my dear, the man's a brilliant catch.
215 Monsieur Tartuffe! Now, there's a man of weight!
 Yes, yes, Monsieur Tartuffe, I'm bound to state,
 Is quite a person; that's not to be denied;
 'Twill be no little thing to be his bride.
 The world already rings with his renown;
220 He's a great noble—in his native town;
 His ears are red, he has a pink complexion,
 And all in all, he'll suit you to perfection.
MARIANE.
 Dear God!
DORINE.
   Oh, how triumphant you will feel
 At having caught a husband so ideal!
MARIANE.
225 Oh, do stop teasing, and use your cleverness
 To get me out of this appalling mess.
 Advise me, and I'll do whatever you say.
DORINE.
 Ah no, a dutiful daughter must obey
 Her father, even if he weds her to an ape.
230 You've a bright future; why struggle to escape?
 Tartuffe will take you back where his family lives,
 To a small town as warm with relatives—
 Uncles and cousins whom you'll be charmed to
   meet.
 You'll be received at once by the elite,
235 Calling upon the bailiff's wife, no less—
 Even, perhaps, upon the mayoress,
 Who'll sit you down in the *best* kitchen chair.
 Then, once a year, you'll dance at the village fair
 To the drone of bagpipes—two of them, in fact—
240 And see a puppet-show, or an animal act.
 Your husband . . .
MARIANE.
   Oh, you turn my blood to ice!
 Stop torturing me, and give me your advice.
DORINE (*threatening to go:*).
 Your servant, Madam.
MARIANE.
   Dorine, I beg of you . . .
DORINE.
 No, you deserve it; this marriage must go through.
MARIANE.
 Dorine!
DORINE.
  No.
MARIANE.
   Not Tartuffe! You know I think him . . . 245
DORINE.
 Tartuffe's your cup of tea, and you shall drink him.
MARIANE.
 I've always told you everything, and relied . . .
DORINE.
 No. You deserve to be tartuffified.
MARIANE.
 Well, since you mock me and refuse to care,
 I'll henceforth seek my solace in despair: 250
 Despair shall be my counsellor and friend,
 And help me bring my sorrows to an end.

(*She starts to leave.*)

DORINE.
 There now, come back; my anger has subsided.
 You do deserve some pity, I've decided.
MARIANE.
 Dorine, if Father makes me undergo 255
 This dreadful martyrdom, I'll die, I know.
DORINE.
 Don't fret; it won't be difficult to discover
 Some plan of action . . . But here's Valère, your lover.

SCENE FOUR

Valère, Mariane, Dorine

VALÈRE.
 Madam, I've just received some wondrous news
 Regarding which I'd like to hear your views. 260
MARIANE.
 What news?
VALÈRE.
   You're marrying Tartuffe.
MARIANE.
   I find
 That Father does have such a match in mind.

VALÈRE.
    Your father, Madam . . .
MARIANE.
                                    . . . has just this minute said
    That it's Tartuffe he wishes me to wed.
VALÈRE.
    Can he be serious?
MARIANE.
265   Oh, indeed he can;
    He's clearly set his heart upon the plan.
VALÈRE.
    And what position do you propose to take,
    Madam?
MARIANE.
                Why—I don't know.
VALÈRE.
                                    For heaven's sake—
    You don't know?
MARIANE.
                    No.
VALÈRE.
                        Well, well!
MARIANE.
                                    Advise me, do.
VALÈRE.
270   Marry the man. That's my advice to you.
MARIANE.
    That's your advice?
VALÈRE.
                        Yes.
MARIANE.
                            Truly?
VALÈRE.
                                    Oh, absolutely.
    You couldn't choose more wisely, more astutely.
MARIANE.
    Thanks for this counsel; I'll follow it, of course.
VALÈRE.
    Do, do; I'm sure 'twill cost you no remorse.
MARIANE.
275   To give it didn't cause your heart to break.
VALÈRE.
    I gave it, Madam, only for your sake.
MARIANE.
    And it's for your sake that I take it, Sir.
DORINE (*Withdrawing to the rear of the stage:*).
    Let's see which fool will prove the stubborner.
VALÈRE.
    So! I am nothing to you, and it was flat
    Deception when you . . .
MARIANE.
280   Please, enough of that.
    You've told me plainly that I should agree
    To wed the man my father's chosen for me,

And since you've deigned to counsel me so wisely,
    I promise, Sir, to do as you advise me.
VALÈRE.
    Ah, no, 'twas not by me that you were swayed.   285
    No, your decision was already made;
    Though now, to save appearances, you protest
    That you're betraying me at my behest.
MARIANE.
    Just as you say.
VALÈRE.
                    Quite so. And I now see
    That you were never truly in love with me.   290
MARIANE.
    Alas, you're free to think so if you choose.
VALÈRE.
    I choose to think so, and here's a bit of news:
    You've spurned my hand, but I know where to turn
    For kinder treatment, as you shall quickly learn.
MARIANE.
    I'm sure you do. Your noble qualities   295
    Inspire affection . . .
VALÈRE.
                    Forget my qualities, please.
    They don't inspire you overmuch, I find.
    But there's another lady I have in mind
    Whose sweet and generous nature will not scorn
    To compensate me for the loss I've borne.   300
MARIANE.
    I'm no great loss, and I'm sure that you'll transfer
    Your heart quite painlessly from me to her.
VALÈRE.
    I'll do my best to take it in my stride.
    The pain I feel at being cast aside
    Time and forgetfulness may put an end to.   305
    Or if I can't forget, I shall pretend to.
    No self-respecting person is expected
    To go on loving once he's been rejected.
MARIANE.
    Now, that's a fine, high-minded sentiment.
VALÈRE.
    One to which any sane man would assent.   310
    Would you prefer it if I pined away
    In hopeless passion till my dying day?
    Am I to yield you to a rival's arms
    And not console myself with other charms?
MARIANE.
    Go then: console yourself; don't hesitate.   315
    I wish you to; indeed, I cannot wait.
VALÈRE.
    You wish me to?
MARIANE.
                    Yes.
VALÈRE.
                        That's the final straw.

Madam, farewell. Your wish shall be my law.

(*He starts to leave, and then returns: this repeatedly:*)

MARIANE.

    Splendid.

VALÈRE (*Coming back again:*).

          This breach, remember, is of your making;
320   It's you who've driven me to the step I'm taking.

MARIANE.

    Of course.

VALÈRE (*Coming back again:*).

          Remember, too, that I am merely
Following your example.

MARIANE.

               I see that clearly.

VALÈRE.

    Enough. I'll go and do your bidding, then.

MARIANE.

    Good.

VALÈRE (*Coming back again:*).

        You shall never see my face again.

MARIANE.

    Excellent.

VALÈRE (*Walking to the door, then turning about:*).

          Yes?

MARIANE.

        What?

VALÈRE.

325   What's that? What did you say?

MARIANE.

    Nothing. You're dreaming.

VALÈRE.

          Ah. Well, I'm on my way.
Farewell, *Madame*.

(*He moves slowly away.*)

MARIANE.

        Farewell.

DORINE (*To Mariane:*).

          If you ask me,
Both of you are as mad as mad can be.
Do stop this nonsense, now. I've only let you
330   Squabble so long to see where it would get you.
Whoa there, Monsieur Valère!

(*She goes and seizes Valère by the arm; he makes a great show of resistance.*)

VALÈRE.

          What's this, Dorine?

DORINE.

    Come here.

VALÈRE.

    No, no, my heart's too full of spleen.
Don't hold me back; her wish must be obeyed.

DORINE.

    Stop!

VALÈRE.

    It's too late now; my decision's made.

DORINE.

    Oh, pooh!

MARIANE (*Aside:*).

        He hates the sight of me, that's plain. 335
I'll go, and so deliver him from pain.

DORINE (*Leaving Valère, running after Mariane:*).

    And now *you* run away! Come back.

MARIANE.

               No, no.
Nothing you say will keep me here. Let go!

VALÈRE (*Aside:*).

    She cannot bear my presence, I perceive.
To spare her further torment, I shall leave. 340

DORINE (*Leaving Mariane, running after Valère:*).

    Again! You'll not escape, Sir; don't you try it.
Come here, you two. Stop fussing, and be quiet.
(*She takes Valère by the hand, then Mariane, and draws them together.*)

VALÈRE (*To Dorine:*).

    What do you want of me?

MARIANE (*To Dorine:*).

          What is the point of this?

DORINE.

    We're going to have a little armistice.
(*To Valère:*).
Now, weren't you silly to get so overheated? 345

VALÈRE.

    Didn't you see how badly I was treated?

DORINE (*To Mariane:*).

    Aren't you a simpleton, to have lost your head?

MARIANE.

    Didn't you hear the hateful things he said?

DORINE (*To Valère:*).

    You're both great fools. Her sole desire, Valère,
Is to be yours in marriage. To that I'll swear. 350
(*To Mariane:*).
He loves you only, and he wants no wife
But you, Mariane. On that I'll stake my life.

MARIANE (*To Valère:*).

    Then why you advised me so, I cannot see.

VALÈRE (*To Mariane:*).

    On such a question, why ask advice of *me*?

DORINE.

    Oh, you're impossible. Give me your hands, you two. 355
(*To Valère:*).
Yours first.

VALÈRE (*Giving Dorine his hand:*).

        But why?

DORINE (*To Mariane:*).

          And now a hand from you.

MARIANE (*Also giving Dorine her hand:*).
　　What are you doing?
DORINE.
　　　　　　　　　There: a perfect fit.
　　You suit each other better than you'll admit.

(*Valère and Mariane hold hands for some time without
looking at each other.*)

VALÈRE (*Turning toward Mariane:*).
　　Ah, come, don't be so haughty. Give a man
360　　A look of kindness, won't you, Mariane?

(*Mariane turns toward Valère and smiles.*)

DORINE.
　　I tell you, lovers are completely mad!
VALÈRE (*To Mariane:*).
　　Now come, confess that you were very bad
　　To hurt my feelings as you did just now.
　　I have a just complaint, you must allow.
MARIANE.
365　　*You* must allow that you were most unpleasant . . .
DORINE.
　　Let's table that discussion for the present;
　　Your father has a plan which must be stopped.
MARIANE.
　　Advise us, then; what means must we adopt?
DORINE.
　　We'll use all manner of means, and all at once.
　　(*To Mariane:*).
370　　Your father's addled; he's acting like a dunce.
　　Therefore you'd better humor the old fossil.
　　Pretend to yield to him, be sweet and docile,
　　And then postpone, as often as necessary,
　　The day on which you have agreed to marry.
375　　You'll thus gain time, and time will turn the trick.
　　Sometimes, for instance, you'll be taken sick,
　　And that will seem good reason for delay;
　　Or some bad omen will make you change the day—
　　You'll dream of muddy water, or you'll pass
380　　A dead man's hearse, or break a looking-glass.
　　If all else fails, no man can marry you
　　Unless you take his ring and say "I do."
　　But now, let's separate. If they should find
　　Us talking here, our plot might be divined.
　　(*To Valère:*).
385　　Go to your friends, and tell them what's occurred,
　　And have them urge her father to keep his word.
　　Meanwhile, we'll stir her brother into action,
　　And get Elmire, as well, to join our faction.
　　Good-bye.
VALÈRE (*To Mariane:*).
　　　　　　　Though each of us will do his best,
390　　It's your true heart on which my hopes shall rest.
MARIANE (*To Valère:*).
　　Regardless of what Father may decide,
　　None but Valère shall claim me as his bride.

VALÈRE.
　　Oh, how those words content me! Come what will . . .
DORINE.
　　Oh, lovers, lovers! Their tongues are never still.
　　Be off, now.
VALÈRE (*Turning to go, then turning back:*).
　　　　　　　One last word . . .
DORINE.
　　　　　　　　　　　　　No time to chat:
　　You leave by this door; and *you* leave by that.　　395

(*Dorine pushes them, by the shoulders, toward
opposing doors.*)

ACT THREE

SCENE ONE

Damis, Dorine

DAMIS.
　　May lightning strike me even as I speak,
　　May all men call me cowardly and weak,
　　If any fear or scruple holds me back
　　From settling things, at once, with that great quack!
DORINE.
　　Now, don't give way to violent emotion.　　5
　　Your father's merely talked about this notion,
　　And words and deeds are far from being one.
　　Much that is talked about is left undone.
DAMIS.
　　No, I must stop that scoundrel's machinations;
　　I'll go and tell him off; I'm out of patience.　　10
DORINE.
　　Do calm down and be practical. I had rather
　　My mistress dealt with him—and with your father.
　　She has some influence with Tartuffe, I've noted.
　　He hangs upon her words, seems most devoted,
　　And may, indeed, be smitten by her charm.　　15
　　Pray Heaven it's true! 'Twould do our cause no harm.
　　She sent for him, just now, to sound him out
　　On this affair you're so incensed about;
　　She'll find out where he stands, and tell him, too,
　　What dreadful strife and trouble will ensue　　20
　　If he lends countenance to your father's plan.
　　I couldn't get in to see him, but his man
　　Says that he's almost finished with his prayers.
　　Go, now. I'll catch him when he comes downstairs.
DAMIS.
　　I want to hear this conference, and I will.　　25
DORINE.
　　No, they must be alone.
DAMIS.
　　　　　　　　　　　Oh, I'll keep still.

DORINE.
    Not you. I know your temper. You'd start a brawl,
    And shout and stamp your foot and spoil it all.
    Go on.
DAMIS.
                    I won't; I have a perfect right . . .
DORINE.
30   Lord, you're a nuisance! He's coming; get out of sight.

    (*Damis conceals himself in a closet at the rear of
    the stage.*)

SCENE TWO

Tartuffe, Dorine

TARTUFFE (*Observing Dorine, and calling to his manservant off-
stage:*).
    Hang up my hair-shirt, put my scourge in place,
    And pray, Laurent, for Heaven's perpetual grace.
    I'm going to the prison now, to share
    My last few coins with the poor wretches there.
DORINE (*Aside:*).
    Dear God, what affectation! What a fake!
TARTUFFE.
35   You wished to see me?
DORINE.
                    Yes . . .
TARTUFFE (*Taking a handkerchief from his pocket:*).
                                    For mercy's sake,
    Please take this handkerchief, before you speak.
DORINE.
    What?
TARTUFFE.
                Cover that bosom, girl. The flesh is weak,
    And unclean thoughts are difficult to control.
    Such sights as that can undermine the soul.
DORINE.
40   Your soul, it seems, has very poor defenses,
    And flesh makes quite an impact on your senses.
    It's strange that you're so easily excited;
    My own desires are not so soon ignited,
    And if I saw you naked as a beast,
    Not all your hide would tempt me in the least.
45 TARTUFFE.
    Girl, speak more modestly; unless you do,
    I shall be forced to take my leave of you.
DORINE.
    Oh, no, it's I who must be on my way;
    I've just one little message to convey.
    Madame is coming down, and begs you, Sir,
50   To wait and have a word or two with her.
TARTUFFE.
    Gladly.

DORINE (*Aside:*).
                That had a softening effect!
    I think my guess about him was correct.
TARTUFFE.
    Will she be long?
DORINE.
                    No: that's her step I hear.

    Ah, here she is, and I shall disappear.

                                                        55

SCENE THREE

Elmire, Tartuffe

TARTUFFE.
    May Heaven, whose infinite goodness we adore,
    Preserve your body and soul forevermore,
    And bless your days, and answer thus the plea
    Of one who is its humblest votary.
ELMIRE.
    I thank you for that pious wish. But please,   60
    Do take a chair and let's be more at ease.

    (*They sit down.*)

TARTUFFE.
    I trust that you are once more well and strong?
ELMIRE.
    Oh, yes: the fever didn't last for long.
TARTUFFE.
    My prayers are too unworthy, I am sure,
    To have gained from Heaven this most gracious cure; 65
    But lately, Madam, my every supplication
    Has had for objects your recuperation.
ELMIRE.
    You shouldn't have troubled so. I don't deserve it.
TARTUFFE.
    Your health is priceless, Madam, and to preserve it
    I'd gladly give my own, in all sincerity.   70
ELMIRE.
    Sir, you outdo us all in Christian charity.
    You've been most kind. I count myself your debtor.
TARTUFFE.
    'Twas nothing, Madam. I long to serve you better.
ELMIRE.
    There's a private matter I'm anxious to discuss.
    I'm glad there's no one here to hinder us.   75
TARTUFFE.
    I too am glad; it floods my heart with bliss
    To find myself alone with you like this.
    For just this chance I've prayed with all my power—
    But prayed in vain, until this happy hour.
ELMIRE.
    This won't take long, Sir, and I hope you'll be   80
    Entirely frank and unconstrained with me.

TARTUFFE.
    Indeed, there's nothing I had rather do
    Than bare my inmost heart and soul to you.
85   First, let me say that what remarks I've made
    About the constant visits you are paid
    Were prompted not by any mean emotion,
    But rather by a pure and deep devotion,
    A fervent zeal . . .
ELMIRE.
                No need for explanation.
90   Your sole concern, I'm sure, was my salvation.
TARTUFFE (*Taking Elmire's hand and pressing her
    fingertips:*).
    Quite so; and such great fervor do I feel . . .
ELMIRE.
    Ooh! Please! You're pinching!
TARTUFFE.
                    'Twas from excess of zeal.
    I never meant to cause you pain, I swear.
    I'd rather . . .

    (*He places his hand on Elmire's knee.*)

ELMIRE.
           What can your hand be doing there?
TARTUFFE.
95   Feeling your gown, what soft, fine-woven stuff.
ELMIRE.
    Please, I'm extremely ticklish. That's enough.

    (*She draws her chair away; Tartuffe pulls his after her.*)

TARTUFFE. (*Fondling the lace collar of her gown:*).
    My, my, what lovely lacework on your dress!
    The workmanship's miraculous, no less.
    I've not seen anything to equal it.
ELMIRE.
100   Yes, quite. But let's talk business for a bit.
    You say my husband means to break his word
    And give his daughter to you, Sir. Had you heard?
TARTUFFE.
    He did once mention it. But I confess
    I dream of quite a different happiness.
105   It's elsewhere, Madam, that my eyes discern
    The promise of that bliss for which I yearn.
ELMIRE.
    I see: you care for nothing here below.
TARTUFFE.
    Ah, well—my heart's not made of stone, you know.
ELMIRE.
    All your desires mount heavenward, I'm sure,
110   In scorn of all that's earthly and impure.
TARTUFFE.
    A love of heavenly beauty does not preclude
    A proper love for earthly pulchritude;
    Our senses are quite rightly captivated
    By perfect works our Maker has created.

    Some glory clings to all that Heaven has made;   115
    In you, all Heaven's marvels are displayed.
    On that fair face, such beauties have been lavished,
    The eyes are dazzled and the heart is ravished;
    How could I look on you, O flawless creature,
    And not adore the Author of all Nature,   120
    Feeling a love both passionate and pure
    For you, his triumph of self-portraiture?
    At first, I trembled lest that love should be
    A subtle snare that Hell had laid for me;
    I vowed to flee the sight of you, eschewing   125
    A rapture that might prove my soul's undoing;
    But soon, fair being, I became aware
    That my deep passion could be made to square
    With rectitude, and with my bounden duty.
    I thereupon surrendered to your beauty.   130
    It is, I know, presumptuous on my part
    To bring you this poor offering of my heart,
    And it is not my merit, Heaven knows,
    But your compassion on which my hopes repose.
    You are my peace, my solace, my salvation;   135
    On you depends my bliss—or desolation;
    I bide your judgment and, as you think best,
    I shall be either miserable or blest.
ELMIRE.
    Your declaration is most gallant, Sir,
    But don't you think it's out of character?   140
    You'd have done better to restrain your passion
    And think before you spoke in such a fashion.
    It ill becomes a pious man like you . . .
TARTUFFE.
    I may be pious, but I'm human too:
    With your celestial charms before his eyes,   145
    A man has not the power to be wise,
    I know such words sound strangely, coming from me,
    But I'm no angel, nor was meant to be,
    And if you blame my passion, you must needs
    Reproach as well the charms on which it feeds.   150
    Your loveliness I had no sooner seen
    Than you became my soul's unrivalled queen;
    Before your seraph glance, divinely sweet,
    My heart's defenses crumbled in defeat,
    And nothing fasting, prayer, or tears might do   155
    Could stay my spirit from adoring you.
    My eyes, my sighs have told you in the past
    What now my lips make bold to say at last,
    And if, in your great goodness, you will deign
    To look upon your slave, and ease his pain,—   160
    If, in compassion for my soul's distress,
    You'll stoop to comfort my unworthiness,
    I'll raise to you, in thanks for that sweet manna,
    An endless hymn, an infinite hosanna.
    With me, of course, there need be no anxiety,   165
    No fear of scandal or of notoriety.
    These young court gallants, whom all the ladies fancy,

Are vain in speech, in action rash and chancy;
When they succeed in love, the world soon knows it;
170 No favor's granted them but they disclose it
And by the looseness of their tongues profane
The very altar where their hearts have lain.
Men of my sort, however, love discreetly,
And one may trust our reticence completely.
175 My keen concern for my good name insures
The absolute security of yours;
In short, I offer you, my dear Elmire,
Love without scandal, pleasure without fear.

ELMIRE.
I've heard your well-turned speeches to the end,
180 And what you urge I clearly comprehend.
Aren't you afraid that I may take a notion
To tell my husband of your warm devotion,
And that, supposing he were duly told,
His feelings toward you might grow rather cold?

TARTUFFE.
185 I know, dear lady, that your exceeding charity
Will lead your heart to pardon my temerity;
That you'll excuse my violent affection
As human weakness, human imperfection;
And that—O fairest!—you will bear in mind
190 That I'm but flesh and blood, and am not blind.

ELMIRE.
Some women might do otherwise, perhaps,
But I shall be discreet about your lapse;
I'll tell my husband nothing of what's occurred
If, in return, you'll give your solemn word
195 To advocate as forcefully as you can
The marriage of Valère and Mariane,
Renouncing all desire to dispossess
Another of his rightful happiness,
And . . .

SCENE FOUR

Damis, Elmire, Tartuffe

DAMIS (*Emerging from the closet where he has been hiding:*).
            No! We'll not hush up this vile affair;
200 I heard it all inside that closet there,
Where Heaven, in order to confound the pride
Of this great rascal, prompted me to hide.
Ah, now I have my long-awaited chance
To punish his deceit and arrogance,
205 And give my father clear and shocking proof
Of the black character of his dear Tartuffe.

ELMIRE.
Ah no, Damis; I'll be content if he
Will study to deserve my leniency.
I've promised silence—don't make me break my word;

To make a scandal would be too absurd.   210
Good wives laugh off such trifles, and forget them;
Why should they tell their husbands, and upset them?

DAMIS.
You have your reasons for taking such a course,
And I have reasons, too, of equal force.
To spare him now would be insanely wrong.   215
I've swallowed my just wrath for far too long
And watched this insolent bigot bringing strife
And bitterness into our family life.
Too long he's meddled in my father's affairs,
Thwarting my marriage-hopes, and poor Valère's.   220
It's high time that my father was undeceived,
And now I've proof that can't be disbelieved—
Proof that was furnished me by Heaven above.
It's too good not to take advantage of.
This is my chance, and I deserve to lose it   225
If, for one moment, I hesitate to use it.

ELMIRE.
Damis . . .

DAMIS.
            No, I must do what I think right.
Madam, my heart is bursting with delight,
And, say whatever you will, I'll not consent
To lose the sweet revenge on which I'm bent.   230
I'll settle matters without more ado;
And here, most opportunely, is my cue.

SCENE FIVE

Orgon, Damis, Tartuffe, Elmire

DAMIS.
Father, I'm glad you've joined us. Let us advise you
Of some fresh news which doubtless will surprise you.
You've just now been repaid with interest   235
For all your loving-kindness to our guest.
He's proved his warm and grateful feelings toward you;
It's with a pair of horns he would reward you.
Yes, I surprised him with your wife, and heard
His whole adulterous offer, every word.   240
She, with her all too gentle disposition,
Would not have told you of his proposition;
But I shall not make terms with brazen lechery,
And feel that not to tell you would be treachery.

ELMIRE.
And I hold that one's husband's peace of mind   245
Should not be spoilt by tattle of this kind.
One's honor doesn't require it: to be proficient
In keeping men at bay is quite sufficient.
These are my sentiments, and I wish, Damis,
That you had heeded me and held your peace.   250

SCENE SIX

Orgon, Damis, Tartuffe

ORGON.
  Can it be true, this dreadful thing I hear?
TARTUFFE.
  Yes, Brother, I'm a wicked man, I fear:
  A wretched sinner, all depraved and twisted,
  The greatest villain that has ever existed.
  My life's one heap of crimes, which grows each
255   minute;
  There's naught but foulness and corruption in it;
  And I perceive that Heaven, outraged by me,
  Has chosen this occasion to mortify me.
  Charge me with any deed you wish to name;
260 I'll not defend myself, but take the blame.
  Believe what you are told, and drive Tartuffe
  Like some base criminal from beneath your roof;
  Yes, drive me hence, and with a parting curse:
  I shan't protest, for I deserve far worse.
ORGON (*To Damis:*).
265 Ah, you deceitful boy, how dare you try
  To stain his purity with so foul a lie?
DAMIS.
  What! Are you taken in by such a bluff?
  Did you not hear . . . ?
ORGON.
              Enough, you rogue, enough!
TARTUFFE.
  Ah, Brother, let him speak: you're being unjust.
270 Believe his story; the boy deserves your trust.
  Why, after all, should you have faith in me?
  How can you know what I might do, or be?
  Is it on my good actions that you base
  Your favor? Do you trust my pious face?
275 Ah, no, don't be deceived by hollow shows;
  I'm far, alas, from being what men suppose;
  Though the world takes me for a man of worth,
  I'm truly the most worthless man on earth.
  (*To Damis:*)
  Yes, my dear son, speak out now: call me the chief
280 Of sinners, a wretch, a murderer, a thief;
  Load me with all the names men most abhor;
  I'll not complain; I've earned them all, and more;
  I'll kneel here while you pour them on my head
  As a just punishment for the life I've led.
ORGON (*To Tartuffe:*).
  This is too much, dear Brother.
  (*To Damis:*)
                 Have you no heart?
285
DAMIS.
  Are you so hoodwinked by this rascal's art . . . ?
ORGON.
  Be still, you monster.

(*To Tartuffe:*)
              Brother, I pray you, rise.

(*To Damis:*)
  Villain!
DAMIS.
        But . . .
ORGON.
             Silence!
DAMIS.
                  Can't you realize . . . ?
ORGON.
  Just one word more, and I'll tear you limb from limb.
TARTUFFE.
  In God's name, Brother, don't be harsh with him.   290
  I'd rather far be tortured at the stake
  Than see him bear one scratch for my poor sake.
ORGON (*To Damis:*).
  Ingrate!
TARTUFFE.
       If I must beg you, on bended knee,
  To pardon him . . .
ORGON (*Falling to his knees, addressing Tartuffe:*).
             Such goodness cannot be!
(*To Damis:*).
  Now, *there's* true charity!
DAMIS.
              What, you . . . ?
ORGON.
                 Villain, be still!   295
  I know your motives; I know you wish him ill:
  Yes, all of you—wife, children, servants, all—
  Conspire against him and desire his fall,
  Employing every shameful trick you can
  To alienate me from this saintly man.   300
  Ah, but the more you seek to drive him away,
  The more I'll do to keep him. Without delay,
  I'll spite this household and confound its pride
  By giving him my daughter as his bride.
DAMIS.
  You're going to force her to accept his hand?   305
ORGON.
  Yes, and this very night, d'you understand?
  I shall defy you all, and make it clear
  That I'm the one who gives the orders here.
  Come, wretch, kneel down and clasp his blessed feet,
  And ask his pardon for your black deceit.   310
DAMIS.
  I ask that swindler's pardon? Why, I'd rather . . .
ORGON.
  So! You insult him, and defy your father!
  A stick! A stick! (*To Tartuffe:*) No, no—release me, do.
  (*To Damis:*)
  Out of my house this minute! Be off with you,
  And never dare set foot in it again.   315
DAMIS.
  Well, I shall go, but . . .

ORGON.

                Well, go quickly, then.
I disinherit you; an empty purse
Is all you'll get from me—except my curse!

SCENE SEVEN

Orgon, Tartuffe

ORGON.

    How he blasphemed your goodness! What a son!

TARTUFFE.

320   Forgive him, Lord, as I've already done.
    (To Orgon:)
    You can't know how it hurts when someone tries
    To blacken me in my dear Brother's eyes.

ORGON.

    Ahh!

TARTUFFE.

          The mere thought of such ingratitude
    Plunges my soul into so dark a mood . . .
325   Such horror grips my heart . . . I gasp for breath,
    And cannot speak, and feel myself near death.

ORGON.

    *(He runs, in tears, to the door through which he
    has just driven his son.)*

    You blackguard! Why did I spare you? Why did I not
    Break you in little pieces on the spot?
    Compose yourself, and don't be hurt, dear friend.

TARTUFFE.

330   These scenes, these dreadful quarrels, have got to end.
    I've much upset your household, and I perceive
    That the best thing will be for me to leave.

ORGON.

    What are you saying!

TARTUFFE.

             They're all against me here:
    They'd have you think me false and insincere.

ORGON.

335   Ah, what of that? Have I ceased believing in you?

TARTUFFE.

    Their adverse talk will certainly continue,
    And charges which you now repudiate
    You may find credible at a later date.

ORGON.

    No, Brother, never.

TARTUFFE.

          Brother, a wife can sway
    Her husband's mind in many a subtle way.

ORGON.

    No, no.

TARTUFFE.

         To leave at once is the solution;

    Thus only can I end their persecution.   340

ORGON.

    No, no, I'll not allow it; you shall remain.

TARTUFFE.

    Ah, well; 'twill mean much martyrdom and pain,
    But if you wish it . . .

ORGON.

              Ah!

TARTUFFE.

              Enough; so be it.   345
    But one thing must be settled, as I see it.
    For your dear honor, and for our friendship's sake,
    There's one precaution I feel bound to take.
    I shall avoid your wife, and keep away . . .

ORGON.

    No, you shall not, whatever they may say.   350
    It pleases me to vex them, and for spite
    I'd have them see you with her day and night.
    What's more, I'm going to drive them to despair
    By making you my only son and heir;
    This very day, I'll give to you alone   355
    Clear deed and title to everything I own.
    A dear, good friend and son-in-law-to-be
    Is more than wife, or child, or kin to me.
    Will you accept my offer, dearest son?

TARTUFFE.

    In all things, let the will of Heaven be done.   360

ORGON.

    Poor fellow! Come, we'll go draw up the deed,
    Then let them burst with disappointed greed!

ACT FOUR

SCENE ONE

Cléante, Tartuffe

CLÉANTE.

    Yes, all the town's discussing it, and truly,
    Their comments do not flatter you unduly.
    I'm glad we've met, Sir, and I'll give my view
    Of this sad matter in a word or two.
    As for who's guilty, that I shan't discuss;   5
    Let's say it was Damis who caused the fuss;
    Assuming, then, that you have been ill-used
    By young Damis, and groundlessly accused,
    Ought not a Christian to forgive, and ought
    He not to stifle every vengeful thought?   10
    Should you stand by and watch a father make
    His only son an exile for your sake?
    Again I tell you frankly, be advised:
    The whole town, high and low, is scandalized;
    This quarrel must be mended, and my advice is   15
    Not to push matters to a further crisis.
    No, sacrifice your wrath to God above,

And help Damis regain his father's love.
TARTUFFE.
    Alas, for my part I should take great joy
20   In doing so. I've nothing against the boy.
    I pardon all, I harbor no resentment;
    To serve him would afford me much contentment.
    But Heaven's interest will not have it so:
    If he comes back, then I shall have to go.
25   After his conduct—so extreme, so vicious—
    Our further intercourse would look suspicious.
    God knows what people would think! Why, they'd
       describe
    My goodness to him as a sort of bribe;
    They'd say that out of guilt I made pretense
30   Of loving-kindness and benevolence—
    That, fearing my accuser's tongue, I strove
    To buy his silence with a show of love.
CLÉANTE.
    Your reasoning is badly warped and stretched,
    And these excuses, Sir, are most far-fetched.
35   Why put yourself in charge of Heaven's cause?
    Does Heaven need our help to enforce its laws?
    Leave vengeance to the Lord, Sir; while we live,
    Our duty's not to punish, but forgive;
    And what the Lord commands, we should obey
40   Without regard to what the world may say.
    What! Shall the fear of being misunderstood
    Prevent our doing what is right and good?
    No, no; let's simply do what Heaven ordains,
    And let no other thoughts perplex our brains.
TARTUFFE.
45   Again, Sir, let me say that I've forgiven
    Damis, and thus obeyed the laws of Heaven;
    But I am not commanded by the Bible
    To live with one who smears my name with libel.
CLÉANTE.
    Were you commanded, Sir, to indulge the whim
50   Of poor Orgon, and to encourage him
    In suddenly transferring to your name
    A large estate to which you have no claim?
TARTUFFE.
    'Twould never occur to those who know me best
    To think I acted from self-interest.
55   The treasures of this world I quite despise;
    Their specious glitter does not charm my eyes;
    And if I have resigned myself to taking
    The gift which my dear Brother insists on making,
    I do so only, as he well understands,
60   Lest so much wealth fall into wicked hands,
    Lest those to whom it might descend in time
    Turn it to purposes of sin and crime,
    And not, as I shall do, make use of it
    For Heaven's glory and mankind's benefit.
CLÉANTE.
65   Forget these trumped-up fears. Your argument
    Is one the rightful heir might well resent;

    It *is* a moral burden to inherit
    Such wealth, but give Damis a chance to bear it.
    And would it not be worse to be accused
    Of swindling, than to see that wealth misused?   70
    I'm shocked that you allowed Orgon to broach
    This matter, and that you feel no self-reproach;
    Does true religion teach that lawful heirs
    May freely be deprived of what is theirs?
    And if the Lord has told you in your heart   75
    That you and young Damis must dwell apart,
    Would it not be the decent thing to beat
    A generous and honorable retreat,
    Rather than let the son of the house be sent,
    For your convenience, into banishment?   80
    Sir, if you wish to prove the honesty
    Of your intentions . . .
TARTUFFE.
                      Sir, it is half-past three.
    I've certain pious duties to attend to,
    And hope my prompt departure won't offend you.
CLÉANTE (*Alone:*).
    Damn.

SCENE TWO

Elmire, Mariane, Cléante, Dorine

DORINE.
          Stay, Sir, and help Mariane, for Heaven's sake!   85
    She's suffering so, I fear her heart will break.
    Her father's plan to marry her off tonight
    Has put the poor child in a desperate plight.
    I hear him coming. Let's stand together, now,
    And see if we can't change his mind, somehow,   90
    About this match we all deplore and fear.

SCENE THREE

Orgon, Elmire, Mariane, Cléante, Dorine

ORGON.
    Hah! Glad to find you all assembled here.
    (*To Mariane:*)
    This contract, child, contains your happiness,
    And what it says I think your heart can guess.
MARIANE (*Falling to her knees:*).
    Sir, by that Heaven which sees me here distressed,   95
    And by whatever else can move your breast,
    Do not employ a father's power, I pray you,
    To crush my heart and force it to obey you,
    Nor by your harsh commands oppress me so
    That I'll begrudge the duty which I owe—   100
    And do not so embitter and enslave me
    That I shall hate the very life you gave me.
    If my sweet hopes must perish, if you refuse
    To give me to the one I've dared to choose,

105 Spare me at least—I beg you, I implore—
The pain of wedding one whom I abhor;
And do not, by a heartless use of force,
Drive me to contemplate some desperate course.
ORGON (*Feeling himself touched by her:*).
Be firm, my soul. No human weakness, now.
MARIANE.
110 I don't resent your love for him. Allow
Your heart free rein, Sir; give him your property,
And if that's not enough, take mine from me;
He's welcome to my money; take it, do,
But don't, I pray, include my person too.
115 Spare me, I beg you; and let me end the tale
Of my sad days behind a convent veil.
ORGON.
A convent! Hah! When crossed in their amours,
All lovesick girls have the same thought as yours.
Get up! The more you loathe the man, and dread him,
120 The more ennobling it will be to wed him.
Marry Tartuffe, and mortify your flesh!
Enough; don't start that whimpering afresh.
DORINE.
But why . . . ?
ORGON.
                    Be still, there. Speak when you're spoken to.
Not one more bit of impudence out of you.
CLÉANTE.
125 If I may offer a word of counsel here . . .
ORGON.
Brother, in counseling you have no peer;
All your advice is forceful, sound, and clever;
I don't propose to follow it, however.
ELMIRE (*To Orgon:*).
I am amazed, and don't know what to say;
130 Your blindness simply takes my breath away.
You are indeed bewitched, to take no warning
From our account of what occurred this morning.
ORGON.
Madam, I know a few plain facts, and one
Is that you're partial to my rascal son;
135 Hence, when he sought to make Tartuffe the victim
Of a base lie, you dared not contradict him.
Ah, but you underplayed your part, my pet;
You should have looked more angry, more upset.
ELMIRE.
When men make overtures, must we reply
140 With righteous anger and a battle-cry?
Must we turn back their amorous advances
With sharp reproaches and with fiery glances?
Myself, I find such offers merely amusing,
And make no scenes and fusses in refusing;
145 My taste is for good-natured rectitude,
And I dislike the savage sort of prude
Who guards her virtue with her teeth and claws,
And tears men's eyes out for the slightest cause:
The Lord preserve me from such honor as that,

Which bites and scratches like an alley-cat! 150
I've found that a polite and cool rebuff
Discourages a lover quite enough.
ORGON.
I know the facts, and I shall not be shaken.
ELMIRE.
I marvel at your power to be mistaken.
Would it, I wonder, carry weight with you 155
If I could *show* you that our tale was true?
ORGON.
Show me?
ELMIRE.
                    Yes.
ORGON.
                              Rot.
ELMIRE.
                                        Come, what if I found a way
To make you see the facts as plain as day?
ORGON.
Nonsense.
ELMIRE.
                    Do answer me; don't be absurd.
I'm not now asking you to trust our word. 160
Suppose that from some hiding-place in here
You learned the whole sad truth by eye and ear—
What would you say of your good friend, after that?
ORGON.
Why, I'd say . . . nothing, by Jehoshaphat!
It can't be true.
ELMIRE.
                              You've been too long deceived, 165
And I'm quite tired of being disbelieved.
Come now: let's put my statements to the test,
And you shall see the truth made manifest.
ORGON.
I'll take that challenge. Now do your uttermost.
We'll see how you make good your empty boast. 170
ELMIRE (*To Dorine:*).
Send him to me.
DORINE.
                              He's crafty; it may be hard
To catch the cunning scoundrel off his guard.
ELMIRE.
No, amorous men are gullible. Their conceit
So blinds them that they're never hard to cheat.
Have him come down (*To Cléante & Mariane:*) Please
leave us, for a bit. 175

SCENE FOUR

Elmire, Orgon

ELMIRE.
Pull up this table, and get under it.
ORGON.
What?

ELMIRE.
        It's essential that you be well-hidden.
ORGON.
    Why there?
ELMIRE.
        Oh, Heaven's! Just do as you are bidden.
    I have my plans; we'll soon see how they fare.
180 Under the table, now; and once you're there,
    Take care that you are neither seen nor heard.
ORGON.
    Well, I'll indulge you, since I gave my word
    To see you through this infantile charade.
ELMIRE.
    Once it is over, you'll be glad we played.
    (*To her husband, who is now under the table:*)
185 I'm going to act quite strangely, now, and you
    Must not be shocked at anything I do.
    Whatever I may say, you must excuse
    As part of that deceit I'm forced to use.
    I shall employ sweet speeches in the task
190 Of making that imposter drop his mask;
    I'll give encouragement to his bold desires,
    And furnish fuel to his amorous fires.
    Since it's for your sake, and for his destruction,
    That I shall seem to yield to his seduction,
195 I'll gladly stop whenever you decide
    That all your doubts are fully satisfied.
    I'll count on you, as soon as you have seen
    What sort of man he is, to intervene,
    And not expose me to his odious lust
200 One moment longer than you feel you must.
    Remember: you're to save me from my plight
    Whenever . . . He's coming! Hush! Keep out of sight!

SCENE FIVE

Tartuffe, Elmire, Orgon

TARTUFFE.
    You wish to have a word with me, I'm told.
ELMIRE.
    Yes. I've a little secret to unfold.
205 Before I speak, however, it would be wise
    To close that door, and look about for spies.
    (*Tartuffe goes to the door, closes it, and returns.*)
    The very last thing that must happen now
    Is a repetition of this morning's row.
    I've never been so badly caught off guard.
210 Oh, how I feared for you! You saw how hard
    I tried to make that troublesome Damis
    Control his dreadful temper, and hold his peace.
    In my confusion, I didn't have the sense
    Simply to contradict his evidence;
215 But as it happened, that was for the best,
    And all has worked out in our interest.
    This storm has only bettered your position;

    My husband doesn't have the least suspicion,
    And now, in mockery of those who do,
220 He bids me be continually with you.
    And that is why, quite fearless of reproof,
    I now can be alone with my Tartuffe,
    And why my heart—perhaps too quick to yield—
    Feels free to let its passion be revealed.
TARTUFFE.
225 Madam, your words confuse me. Not long ago,
    You spoke in quite a different style, you know.
ELMIRE.
    Ah, Sir, if that refusal made you smart,
    It's little that you know of woman's heart,
    Or what that heart is trying to convey
230 When it resists in such a feeble way!
    Always, at first, our modesty prevents
    The frank avowal of tender sentiments;
    However high the passion which inflames us,
    Still, to confess its power somehow shames us.
235 Thus we reluct, at first, yet in a tone
    Which tells you that our heart is overthrown,
    That what our lips deny, our pulse confesses,
    And that, in time, all noes will turn to yesses.
    I fear my words are all too frank and free,
240 And a poor proof of woman's modesty;
    But since I'm started, tell me, if you will—
    Would I have tried to make Damis be still,
    Would I have listened, calm and unoffended,
    Until your lengthy offer of love was ended,
245 And been so very mild in my reaction,
    Had your sweet words not given me satisfaction?
    And when I tried to force you to undo
    The marriage-plans my husband has in view,
    What did my urgent pleading signify
250 If not that I admired you, and that I
    Deplored the thought that someone else might own
    Part of a heart I wished for mine alone?
TARTUFFE.
    Madam, no happiness is so complete
    As when, from lips we love, come words so sweet;
255 Their nectar floods my every sense, and drains
    In honeyed rivulets through all my veins.
    To please you is my joy, my only goal;
    Your love is the restorer of my soul;
    And yet I must beg leave, now, to confess
260 Some lingering doubts as to my happiness.
    Might this not be a trick? Might not the catch
    Be that you wish me to break off the match
    With Mariane, and so have feigned to love me?
    I shan't quite trust your fond opinion of me
265 Until the feelings you've expressed so sweetly
    Are demonstrated somewhat more concretely,
    And you have shown, by certain kind concessions,
    That I may put my faith in your professions.
ELMIRE (*She coughs, to warn her husband.*)
    Why be in such a hurry? Must my heart

270   Exhaust its bounty at the very start?
         To make that sweet admission cost me dear,
         But you'll not be content, it would appear,
         Unless my store of favors is disbursed
         To the last farthing, and at the very first.
      TARTUFFE.
275   The less we merit, the less we dare to hope,
         And with our doubts, mere words can never cope.
         We trust no promised bliss till we receive it;
         Not till a joy is ours can we believe it.
         I, who so little merit your esteem,
280   Can't credit this fulfillment of my dream,
         And shan't believe it, Madam, until I savor
         Some palpable assurance of your favor.
      ELMIRE.
         My, how tyrannical your love can be,
         And how it flusters and perplexes me!
285   How furiously you take one's heart in hand,
         And make your every wish a fierce command!
         Come, must you hound and harry me to death?
         Will you not give me time to catch my breath?
         Can it be right to press me with such force,
290   Give me no quarter, show me no remorse,
         And take advantage, by your stern insistence,
         Of the fond feelings which weaken my resistance?
      TARTUFFE.
         Well, if you look with favor upon my love,
         Why, then, begrudge me some clear proof thereof?
      ELMIRE.
295   But how can I consent without offense
         To Heaven, toward which you feel such reverence?
      TARTUFFE.
         If Heaven is all that holds you back, don't worry.
         I can remove that hindrance in a hurry.
         Nothing of that sort need obstruct our path.
      ELMIRE.
300   Must one not be afraid of Heaven's wrath?
      TARTUFFE.
         Madam, forget such fears, and be my pupil,
         And I shall teach you how to conquer scruple.
         Some joys, it's true, are wrong in Heaven's eyes;
         Yet Heaven is not averse to compromise;
305   There is a science, lately formulated,
         Whereby one's conscience may be liberated,
         And any wrongful act you care to mention
         May be redeemed by purity of intention.
         I'll teach you, Madam, the secrets of that science;
310   Meanwhile, just place on me your full reliance.
         Assuage my keen desires, and feel no dread:
         The sin, if any, shall be on my head.
         (Elmire coughs, this time more loudly.)
         You've a bad cough.
      ELMIRE.
                        Yes, yes. It's bad indeed.
      TARTUFFE (Producing a little brown bag:).
         A bit of licorice may be what you need.

      ELMIRE.
         No, I've a stubborn cold, it seems. I'm sure it   315
         Will take much more than licorice to cure it.
      TARTUFFE.
         How aggravating.
      ELMIRE.
                        Oh, more than I can say.
      TARTUFFE.
         If you're still troubled, think of things this way:
         No one shall know our joys, save us alone,
         And there's no evil till the act is known;   320
         It's scandal, Madam, which makes it an offense,
         And it's no sin to sin in confidence.
      ELMIRE (Having coughed once more:).
         Well, clearly I must do as you require,
         And yield to your importunate desire.
         It is apparent, now, that nothing less   325
         Will satisfy you, and so I acquiesce.
         To go so far is much against my will;
         I'm vexed that it should come to this; but still,
         Since you are so determined on it, since you
         Will not allow mere language to convince you,   330
         And since you ask for concrete evidence, I
         See nothing for it, now, but to comply.
         If this is sinful, if I'm wrong to do it,
         So much the worse for him who drove me to it.
         The fault can surely not be charged to me.   335
      TARTUFFE.
         Madam, the fault is mine, if fault there be,
         And . . .
      ELMIRE.
                  Open the door a little, and peek out;
         I wouldn't want my husband poking about.
      TARTUFFE.
         Why worry about the man? Each day he grows
         More gullible; one can lead him by the nose.   340
         To find us here would fill him with delight,
         And if he saw the worst, he'd doubt his sight.
      ELMIRE.
         Nevertheless, do step out for a minute
         Into the hall, and see that no one's in it.

                        SCENE SIX

      Orgon, Elmire

      ORGON (Coming out from under the table:).
         That man's a perfect monster, I must admit!   345
         I'm simply stunned. I can't get over it.
      ELMIRE.
         What, coming out so soon? How premature!
         Get back in hiding, and wait until you're sure.
         Stay till the end, and be convinced completely;
         We mustn't stop till things are proved concretely.   350
      ORGON.
         Hell never harbored anything so vicious!

ELMIRE.
    Tut, don't be hasty. Try to be judicious.
    Wait, and be certain that there's no mistake.
    No jumping to conclusions, for Heaven's sake!
    (*She places Orgon behind her, as Tartuffe re-enters.*)

SCENE SEVEN

Tartuffe, Elmire, Orgon

TARTUFFE (*Not seeing Orgon:*).
355   Madam, all things have worked out to perfection;
    I've given the neighboring rooms a full inspection;
    No one's about; and now I may at last . . .
ORGON (*Intercepting him:*).
    Hold on, my passionate fellow, not so fast!
    I should advise a little more restraint.
360   Well, so you thought you'd fool me, my dear saint!
    How soon you wearied of the saintly life—
    Wedding my daughter, and coveting my wife!
    I've long suspected you and had a feeling
    That soon I'd catch you at your double-dealing.
365   Just now, you've given me evidence galore;
    It's quite enough; I have no wish for more.
ELMIRE (*To Tartuffe:*).
    I'm sorry to have treated you so slyly,
    But circumstances forced me to be wily.
TARTUFFE.
    Brother, you can't think . . .
ORGON.
                    No more talk from you;
370   Just leave this household, without more ado.
TARTUFFE.
    What I intended . . .
ORGON.
              That seems fairly clear.
    Spare me your falsehoods and get out of here.
TARTUFFE.
    No, I'm the master, and you're the one to go!
    This house belongs to me, I'll have you know,
375   And I shall show you that you can't hurt *me*
    By this contemptible conspiracy,
    That those who cross me know not what they do,
    And that I've means to expose and punish you,
    Avenge offended Heaven, and make you grieve
380   That ever you dared order me to leave.

SCENE EIGHT

Elmire, Orgon

ELMIRE.
    What was the point of all that angry chatter?

ORGON.
    Dear God, I'm worried. This is no laughing matter.
ELMIRE.
    How so?
ORGON.
                      I fear I understood his drift.
    I'm much disturbed about that deed of gift.
ELMIRE.
    You gave him . . . ?
ORGON.
             Yes, it's all been drawn and signed.   385
    But one thing more is weighing on my mind.
ELMIRE.
    What's that?
ORGON.
             I'll tell you; but first let's see if there's
    A certain strong-box in his room upstairs.

ACT FIVE

SCENE ONE

Orgon, Cléante

CLÉANTE.
    Where are you going so fast?
ORGON.
                 God knows!
CLÉANTE.
                  Then wait;
    Let's have a conference, and deliberate
    On how this situation's to be met.
ORGON.
    That strong-box has me utterly upset;
    This is the worst of many, many shocks.   5
CLÉANTE.
    Is there some fearful mystery in that box?
ORGON.
    My poor friend Argas brought that box to me
    With his own hands, in utmost secrecy;
    'Twas on the very morning of his flight.
    It's full of papers which, if they came to light,   10
    Would ruin him—or such is my impression.
CLÉANTE.
    Then why did you let it out of your possession?
ORGON.
    Those papers vexed my conscience, and it seemed best
    To ask the counsel of my pious guest.
    The cunning scoundrel got me to agree   15
    To leave the strong-box in his custody,
    So that, in case of an investigation,
    I could employ a slight equivocation
    And swear I didn't have it, and thereby,
    At no expense to conscience, tell a lie.   20

CLÉANTE.
> It looks to me as if you're out on a limb.
> Trusting him with that box, and offering him
> That deed of gift, were actions of a kind
> 25 Which scarcely indicate a prudent mind.
> With two such weapons, he has the upper hand,
> And since you're vulnerable, as matters stand,
> You erred once more in bringing him to bay.
> You should have acted in some subtler way.

ORGON.
> Just think of it: behind that fervent face,
> 30 A heart so wicked, and a soul so base!
> I took him in, a hungry beggar, and then . . .
> Enough, by God! I'm through with pious men:
> Henceforth I'll hate the whole false brotherhood,
> And persecute them worse than Satan could.

CLÉANTE.
> 35 Ah, there you go—extravagant as ever!
> Why can you not be rational? You never
> Manage to take the middle course, it seems,
> But jump, instead, between absurd extremes.
> You've recognized your recent grave mistake
> 40 In falling victim to a pious fake;
> Now, to correct that error, must you embrace
> An even greater error in its place,
> And judge our worthy neighbors as a whole
> By what you've learned of one corrupted soul?
> 45 Come, just because one rascal made you swallow
> A show of zeal which turned out to be hollow,
> Shall you conclude that all men are deceivers,
> And that, today, there are no true believers?
> Let atheists make that foolish inference;
> 50 Learn to distinguish virtue from pretense,
> Be cautious in bestowing admiration,
> And cultivate a sober moderation.
> Don't humor fraud, but also don't asperse
> True piety; the latter fault is worse,
> 55 And it is best to err, if err one must,
> As you have done, upon the side of trust.

SCENE TWO

Damis, Orgon, Cléante

DAMIS.
> Father, I hear that scoundrel's uttered threats
> Against you; that he pridefully forgets
> How, in his need, he was befriended by you,
> 60 And means to use your gifts to crucify you.

ORGON.
> It's true, my boy. I'm too distressed for tears.

DAMIS.
> Leave it to me, Sir; let me trim his ears.
> Faced with such insolence, we must not waver.

> I shall rejoice in doing you the favor
> Of cutting short his life, and your distress.   65

CLÉANTE.
> What a display of young hotheadedness!
> Do learn to moderate your fits of rage.
> In this just kingdom, this enlightened age,
> One does not settle things by violence.

SCENE THREE

*Madame Pernelle, Mariane, Elmire, Dorine, Damis,
Orgon, Cléante*

MADAME PERNELLE.
> I hear strange tales of very strange events.   70

ORGON.
> Yes, strange events which these two eyes beheld.
> The man's ingratitude is unparalleled.
> I save a wretched pauper from starvation,
> House him, and treat him like a blood relation,
> Shower him every day with my largesse,   75
> Give him my daughter, and all that I possess;
> And meanwhile the unconscionable knave
> Tries to induce my wife to misbehave;
> And not content with such extreme rascality,
> Now threatens me with my own liberality,   80
> And aims, by taking base advantage of
> The gifts I gave him out of Christian love,
> To drive me from my house, a ruined man,
> And make me end a pauper, as he began.

DORINE.
> Poor fellow!

MADAME PERNELLE.
>   No, my son, I'll never bring   85
> Myself to think him guilty of such a thing.

ORGON.
> How's that?

MADAME PERNELLE.
>   The righteous always were maligned.

ORGON.
> Speak clearly, Mother. Say what's on your mind.

MADAME PERNELLE.
> I mean that I can smell a rat, my dear.
> You know how everybody hates him, here.   90

ORGON.
> That has no bearing on the case at all.

MADAME PERNELLE.
> I told you a hundred times, when you were small,
> That virtue in this world is hated ever;
> Malicious men may die, but malice never.

ORGON.
> No doubt that's true, but how does it apply?   95

MADAME PERNELLE.
> They've turned you against him by a clever lie.

ORGON.
　　I've told you, I was there and saw it done.
MADAME PERNELLE.
　　Ah, slanderers will stop at nothing, Son.
ORGON.
　　Mother, I'll lose my temper . . . For the last time,
100　　I tell you I was witness to the crime.
MADAME PERNELLE.
　　The tongues of spite are busy night and noon,
　　And to their venom no man is immune.
ORGON.
　　You're talking nonsense. Can't you realize
　　I saw it; saw it with my eyes?
105　　Saw, do you understand me? Must I shout it
　　Into your ears before you'll cease to doubt it?
MADAME PERNELLE.
　　Appearances can deceive, my son. Dear me,
　　We cannot always judge by what we see.
ORGON.
　　Drat! Drat!
MADAME PERNELLE.
　　　　　　　　One often interprets things awry;
110　　Good can seem evil to a suspicious eye.
ORGON.
　　Was I to see his pawing at Elmire
　　As an act of charity?
MADAME PERNELLE.
　　　　　　　　　　Till his guilt is clear,
　　A man deserves the benefits of the doubt.
　　You should have waited, to see how things turned out.
ORGON.
115　　Great God in Heaven, what more proof did I need?
　　Was I to sit there, watching, until he'd . . .
　　You drive me to the brink of impropriety.
MADAME PERNELLE.
　　No, no, a man of such surpassing piety
　　Could not do such a thing. You cannot shake me.
120　　I don't believe it, and you shall not make me.
ORGON.
　　You vex me so that, if you weren't my mother,
　　I'd say to you . . . some dreadful thing or other.
DORINE.
　　It's your turn now, Sir, not to be listened to;
　　You'd not trust us, and now she won't trust you.
CLÉANTE.
　　My friends, we're wasting time which should be
125　　　　spent
　　In facing up to our predicament.
　　I fear that scoundrel's threats weren't made in sport.
DAMIS.
　　Do you think he'd have the nerve to go to court?
ELMIRE.
　　I'm sure he won't: they'd find it all too crude
130　　A case of swindling and ingratitude.
CLÉANTE.
　　Don't be too sure. He won't be at a loss

To give his claims a high and righteous gloss;
And clever rogues with far less valid cause
Have trapped their victims in a web of laws.
I say again that to antagonize　　　　　　　135
A man so strongly armed was most unwise.
ORGON.
　　I know it; but the man's appalling cheek
　　Outraged me so, I couldn't control my pique.
CLÉANTE.
　　I wish to Heaven that we could devise
　　Some truce between you, or some compromise.　140
ELMIRE.
　　If I had known what cards he held, I'd not
　　Have roused his anger by my little plot.
ORGON (To Dorine, as M. Loyal enters:).
　　What is that fellow looking for? Who is he?
　　Go talk to him—and tell him that I'm busy.

SCENE FOUR

*Monsieur Loyal, Madame Pernelle, Orgon, Damis,
Mariane, Dorine, Elmire, Cléante*

MONSIEUR LOYAL.
　　Good day, dear sister. Kindly let me see　　　145
　　Your master.
DORINE.
　　　　　　　　He's involved with company,
　　And cannot be disturbed just now, I fear.
MONSIEUR LOYAL.
　　I hate to intrude; but what has brought me here
　　Will not disturb your master, in any event.
　　Indeed, my news will make him most content.　150
DORINE.
　　Your name?
MONSIEUR LOYAL.
　　　　　　　　Just say that I bring greetings from
　　Monsieur Tartuffe, on whose behalf I've come.
DORINE (To Orgon:).
　　Sir, he's a very gracious man, and bears
　　A message from Tartuffe, which, he declares,
　　Will make you most content.
CLÉANTE.
　　　　　　　　　　　　Upon my word,　　　155
　　I think this man had best be seen, and heard.
ORGON.
　　Perhaps he has some settlement to suggest.
　　How shall I treat him? What manner would be best?
CLÉANTE.
　　Control your anger, and if he should mention
　　Some fair adjustment, give him your full attention.　160
MONSIEUR LOYAL.
　　Good health to you, good Sir. May Heaven confound
　　Your enemies, and may your joys abound.
ORGON (Aside, to Cléante:).
　　A gentle salutation: it confirms

My guess that he is here to offer terms.
MONSIEUR LOYAL.
165   I've always held your family most dear;
    I served your father, Sir, for many a year.
ORGON.
    Sir, I must ask your pardon; to my shame,
    I cannot now recall your face or name.
MONSIEUR LOYAL.
    Loyal's my name; I come from Normandy,
170   And I'm a bailiff, in all modesty.
    For forty years, praise God, it's been my boast
    To serve with honor in that vital post,
    And I am here, Sir, if you will permit
    The liberty, to serve you with this writ . . .
ORGON.
    To—*what?*
MONSIEUR LOYAL.
175   Now, please, Sir, let us have no friction:
    It's nothing but an order of eviction.
    You are to move your goods and family out
    And make way for new occupants, without
    Deferment or delay, and give the keys . . .
ORGON.
    I? Leave this house?
MONSIEUR LOYAL.
180   Why yes, Sir, if you please.
    This house, Sir, from the cellar to the roof,
    Belongs now to the good Monsieur Tartuffe,
    And he is lord and master of your estate
    By virtue of a deed of present date,
185   Drawn in due form, with clearest legal phrasing . . .
DAMIS.
    Your insolence is utterly amazing!
MONSIEUR LOYAL.
    Young man, my business here is not with you,
    But with your wise and temperate father, who,
    Like every worthy citizen, stands in awe
190   Of justice, and would never obstruct the law.
ORGON.
    But . . .
MONSIEUR LOYAL.
          Not for a million, Sir, would you rebel
    Against authority; I know that well.
    You'll not make trouble, Sir, or interfere
    With the execution of my duties here.
DAMIS.
195   Someone may execute a smart tattoo
    On that black jacket of yours, before you're through.
MONSIEUR LOYAL.
    Sir, bid your son be silent. I'd much regret
    Having to mention such a nasty threat
    Of violence, in writing my report.
DORINE (*Aside:*).
200   This man Loyal's a most disloyal sort!
MONSIEUR LOYAL.
    I love all men of upright character,

And when I agreed to serve these papers, Sir,
    It was your feelings that I had in mind.
    I couldn't bear to see the case assigned
    To someone else, who might esteem you less
205   And so subject you to unpleasantness.
ORGON.
    What's more unpleasant than telling a man to leave
    His house and home?
MONSIEUR LOYAL.
          You'd like a short reprieve?
    If you desire it, Sir, I shall not press you,
    But wait until tomorrow to dispossess you.
210   Splendid. I'll come and spend the night here, then,
    Most quietly, with half a score of men.
    For form's sake, you might bring me, just before
    You go to bed, the keys to the front door.
    My men, I promise, will be on their best
215   Behavior, and will not disturb your rest.
    But bright and early, Sir, you must be quick
    And move out all your furniture, every stick:
    The men I've chosen are both young and strong,
220   And with their help it shouldn't take you long.
    In short, I'll make things pleasant and convenient,
    And since I'm being so extremely lenient,
    Please show me, Sir, a like consideration,
    And give me your entire cooperation.
ORGON (*Aside:*).
225   I may be all but bankrupt, but I vow
    I'd give a hundred louis, here and now,
    Just for the pleasure of landing one good clout
    Right on the end of that complacent snout.
CLÉANTE.
    Careful; don't make things worse.
DAMIS.
              My bootsole itches
230   To give that beggar a good kick in the breeches.
DORINE.
    Monsieur Loyal, I'd love to hear the whack
    Of a stout stick across your fine broad back.
MONSIEUR LOYAL.
    Take care: a woman too may go to jail if
    She uses threatening language to a bailiff.
CLÉANTE.
235   Enough, enough, Sir. This must not go on.
    Give me that paper, please, and then begone.
MONSIEUR LOYAL.
    Well, *au revoir*. God give you all good cheer!
ORGON.
    May God confound you, and him who sent you here!

SCENE FIVE

Orgon, Cléante, Mariane, Elmire, Madame Pernelle,
Dorine, Damis

ORGON.
    Now, Mother, was I right or not? This writ
240   Should change your notion of Tartuffe a bit.
    Do you perceive his villainy at last?
MADAME PERNELLE.
    I'm thunderstruck. I'm utterly aghast.
DORINE.
    Oh, come, be fair. You mustn't take offense
    At this new proof of his benevolence.
245   He's acting out of selfless love, I know.
    Material things enslave the soul, and so
    He kindly has arranged your liberation
    From all that might endanger your salvation.
ORGON.
    Will you not ever hold your tongue, you dunce?
CLÉANTE.
250   Come, you must take some action, and at once.
ELMIRE.
    Go tell the world of the low trick he's tried.
    The deed of gift is surely nullified
    By such behavior, and public rage will not
    Permit the wretch to carry out his plot.

SCENE SIX

Valère, Orgon, Cléante, Elmire, Mariane,
Madame Pernelle, Damis, Dorine

VALÈRE.
255   Sir, though I hate to bring you more bad news,
    Such is the danger that I cannot choose.
    A friend who is extremely close to me
    And knows my interest in your family
    Has, for my sake, presumed to violate
260   The secrecy that's due to things of state,
    And sends me word that you are in a plight
    From which your one salvation lies in flight.
    That scoundrel who's imposed upon you so
    Denounced you to the King an hour ago
265   And, as supporting evidence, displayed
    The strong-box of a certain renegade
    Whose secret papers, so he testified,
    You had disloyally agreed to hide.
    I don't know just what charges may be pressed,
270   But there's a warrant out for your arrest;
    Tartuffe has been instructed, furthermore,
    To guide the arresting officer to your door.
CLÉANTE.
    He's clearly done this to facilitate
    His seizure of your house and your estate.
ORGON.
275   That man, I must say, is a vicious beast!
VALÈRE.
    Quick, Sir; you mustn't tarry in the least.

    My carriage is outside, to take you hence;
    This thousand louis should cover all expense.
    Let's lose no time, or you shall be undone;
280   The sole defense, in this case, is to run.
    I shall go with you all the way, and place you
    In a safe refuge to which they'll never trace you.
ORGON.
    Alas, dear boy, I wish that I could show you
    My gratitude for everything I owe you.
285   But now is not the time; I pray the Lord
    That I may live to give you your reward.
    Farewell, my dears; be careful . . .
CLÉANTE.
                      Brother, hurry.
    We shall take care of things; you needn't worry.

SCENE SEVEN

The Officer, Tartuffe, Valère, Orgon, Elmire,
Mariane, Madame Pernelle, Dorine, Cléante, Damis

TARTUFFE.
    Gently, Sir, gently; stay right where you are.
    No need for haste; your lodging isn't far.
290   You're off to prison, by order of the Prince.
ORGON.
    This is the crowning blow, you wretch; and since
    It means my total ruin and defeat,
    Your villainy is now at last complete.
TARTUFFE.
    You needn't try to provoke me; it's no use.
295   Those who serve Heaven must expect abuse.
CLÉANTE.
    You are indeed most patient, sweet, and blameless.
DORINE.
    How he exploits the name of Heaven! It's shameless.
TARTUFFE.
    Your taunts and mockeries are all for naught;
300   To do my duty is my only thought.
MARIANE.
    Your love of duty is most meritorious,
    And what you've done is little short of glorious.
TARTUFFE.
    All deeds are glorious, Madam, which obey
    The sovereign prince who sent me here today.
ORGON.
305   I rescued you when you were destitute;
    Have you forgotten that, you thankless brute?
TARTUFFE.
    No, no, I well remember everything;
    But my first duty is to serve my King.
    That obligation is so paramount

310   That other claims, beside it, do not count;
    And for it I would sacrifice my wife,
    My family, my friend, or my own life.
ELMIRE.
    Hypocrite!
DORINE.
                All that we most revere, he uses
    To cloak his plots and camouflage his ruses.
CLÉANTE.
315   If it is true that you are animated
    By pure and loyal zeal, as you have stated,
    Why was this zeal not roused until you'd sought
    To make Orgon a cuckold, and been caught?
    Why weren't you moved to give your evidence
320   Until your outraged host had driven you hence?
    I shan't say that the gift of all his treasure
    Ought to have damped your zeal in any measure;
    But if he is a traitor, as you declare,
    How could you condescend to be his heir?
TARTUFFE (*To the Officer:*).
325   Sir, spare me all this clamor; it's growing shrill.
    Please carry out your orders, if you will.
OFFICER.
    Yes, I've delayed too long, Sir. Thank you kindly.
    You're just the proper person to remind me.
    Come, you are off to join the other boarders
330   In the King's prison, according to his orders.
TARTUFFE.
    Who? I, Sir?
OFFICER.
             Yes.
TARTUFFE.
                To prison? This can't be true!
OFFICER.
    I owe an explanation, but not to you.
(*To Orgon:*).
    Sir, all is well; rest easy, and be grateful.
    We serve a Prince to whom all sham is hateful,
335   A Prince who sees into our inmost hearts,
    And can't be fooled by any trickster's arts.
    His royal soul, though generous and human,
    Views all things with discernment and acumen;
    His sovereign reason is not lightly swayed,
340   And all his judgments are discreetly weighed.
    He honors righteous men of every kind,
    And yet his zeal for virtue is not blind,
    Nor does his love of piety numb his wits
    And make him tolerant of hypocrites.
345   'Twas hardly likely that this man could cozen
    A King who's foiled such liars by the dozen.
    With one keen glance, the King perceived the whole
    Perverseness and corruption of his soul,
    And thus high Heaven's justice was displayed:
350   Betraying you, the rogue stood self-betrayed.
    The King soon recognized Tartuffe as one

    Notorious by another name, who'd done
    So many vicious crimes that one could fill
    Ten volumes with them, and be writing still.
    But to be brief: our sovereign was appalled   355
    By this man's treachery toward you, which he called
    The last, worst villainy of a vile career,
    And bade me follow the impostor here
    To see how gross his impudence could be,
    And force him to restore your property.   360
    Your private papers, by the King's command,
    I hereby seize and give into your hand.
    The King, by royal order, invalidates
    The deed which gave this rascal your estates,
    And pardons, furthermore, your grave offense   365
    In harboring an exile's documents.
    By these decrees, our Prince rewards you for
    Your loyal deeds in the late civil war,
    And shows how heartfelt is his satisfaction
    In recompensing any worthy action,   370
    How much he prizes merit, and how he makes
    More of men's virtues than of their mistakes.
DORINE.
    Heaven be praised!
MADAME PERNELLE.
                I breathe again, at last.
ELMIRE.
    We're safe.
MARIANE.
            I can't believe the danger's past.
ORGON (*To Tartuffe:*).
    Well, traitor, now you see . . .
CLÉANTE.
                  Ah, Brother, please   375
    Let's not descend to such indignities.
    Leave the poor wretch to his unhappy fate,
    And don't say anything to aggravate
    His present woes; but rather hope that he
    Will soon embrace an honest piety,   380
    And mend his ways, and by a true repentance
    Move our just King to moderate his sentence.
    Meanwhile, go kneel before your sovereign's throne
    And thank him for the mercies he has shown.
ORGON.
    Well said: let's go at once and, gladly kneeling,   385
    Express the gratitude which all are feeling.
    Then, when that first great duty has been done,
    We'll turn with pleasure to a second one,
    And give Valère, whose love has proven so true,
    The wedded happiness which is his due.   390

SPOTLIGHT   THE FRENCH THEATER

Curiously, former playgrounds of the wealthy provided France with its distinctively shaped theaters. *Jeu des paumes*, or tennis courts, were converted into theaters. In 1634 the acclaimed French actor Montdory built such a theater in the Marais district of Paris; Richelieu frequently patronized the Thèâtre du Marais, which became the prototype for subsequent French theaters. Montdory placed a stage at one end of the long rectangle of the tennis court and used existing galleries that surrounded the courts for seating. Eventually, other spectators, primarily preening young men, sat on benches or stood on the floor (*parterre*) in front of the stage; some actually sat on the stage itself, the better to be seen. These theaters were about 100 feet long, and about 55 feet wide. The auditorium comprised roughly two-thirds of the theater, the stage-backstage area the remaining third. This configuration, which fully separates the actors from the audience, further increased the development of the proscenium stage and became the dominant architectural model throughout Europe and America until the twentieth century.

Play scripts and playhouses affected French acting styles, especially in tragedy. The philosophical ideal the French called *vraisemblance,* which sought to portray "idealized" life onstage, caused actors to adopt a heightened acting style. By today's standards it excessively emphasizes declaration and posing, but those were the means by which French actors signaled the heroic nature of the characters they portrayed. It is perhaps useful to think of the performance of a French tragedy in the seventeenth century as a recital in which the actors stood in a semicircle on the forestage and declaimed their lines. Characters also recited lengthy passionate speeches, which the French called *tirades.* (Today we still refer to a lengthy, angry outburst as a tirade, another example of how we appropriate the language of theater in our daily lives.) The *tirades* are as integral to French plays as the soliloquy is to Elizabethan drama. Like their English counterparts, the French enjoyed lengthy speeches because it was a means of celebrating the glory of the French language. John Dryden, the Restoration playwright and critic, complained that French actors spoke "by the hour-glass, as our parsons do; nay, they account it the grace of their parts, and think themselves disparaged by the poet, if they may not twice or thrice in a play entertain the audience with a speech of a hundred or two hundred lines." Such speeches naturally invited the more formal, grandiose acting style we associate with French Neoclassicism.

To heighten the heroic impact even more, French actors wore costumes that suggested Roman antiquity—the *habit à la romaine*—which were among the first attempts at historical costuming. Again we must remember that even this historical costuming was idealized and not an attempt at realism in costuming. Rather, realism made huge strides in the comic plays, such as Molière's, which reflect a conscious attempt to dress, behave, and talk like the actual people who watched the plays.

CENTER STAGE   THE (THIRD) OPENING NIGHT OF *TARTUFFE*

For the third time we await an "opening" of Molière's *Tartuffe*. Two previous presentations of the play have resulted in its being banned. The first, on May 12, 1664, concluded a two-week celebration entitled "The Pleasures of the Enchanted Island," which Louis XIV hosted for his court at Versailles. We heard that although the king enjoyed the performance, others did not, especially the queen mother, the archbishop of Paris, and the secret Company of the Holy Sacrament. This "cabal of the pious," as it is contemptuously known, wields great power and applied sufficient political pressure to draw a royal ban on the play. In their eyes *Tartuffe* was "absolutely harmful to religion and capable of producing very dangerous effects." Luckily for us, Monsieur Molière has no time for these hypocrites. Undaunted, he has continued to present the play in private readings and performances at various country estates of Parisian society. Ironically, the ban has only increased interest in the play. Following three years of such performances, Molière mounted the play publicly under a new title, *The Impostor*. Once more the censors prevailed; not only did the constabulary ban the play, the archbishop decreed excommunication for any who saw or read the "vile work." However, the valiant Monsieur Molière would not knuckle under to censorship and drafted a petition to the king pleading that he "need not think of writing comedies if the Tartuffes are triumphant." It is our good fortune that

Antony Sher (interviewed in the Spotlight box "The Secret Life of a Con Man") played the hypocritical Tartuffe at the Royal Shakespeare Company in 1983.

the king finally made public his private sentiments and authorized tonight's public performances of *Tartuffe*.

It is February 9, 1669, and we are in the Palais Royal. Soon we will be treated to our first glimpse of what will surely become the most celebrated comedy in all Europe. The Palais Royal provides a regal atmosphere, but attending plays here is always a peculiar experience. Built by Cardinal Richelieu in 1641 for elaborate spectacles like Molière's *Amphitryon*, the theater is not suited for the "daily life" comedies of the King's Troupe. Although the stage is well-equipped, it is too large—nearly 60 feet deep and over 45 feet wide—for intimate plays like *Tartuffe*. Also, the very low proscenium arch frames scenes of unpleasing proportions.

The theater holds about 1,000 spectators, most of whom sit in a stepped amphitheater. On the main floor, or *parterre*, other spectators stand to watch the play, though some sit on a few benches very near the stage. Surrounding us are three tiers of ornate

boxes, above which is an open gallery. Unlike many of the contemporary Italian theaters, the tiers form a V as they extend away from the proscenium, thus creating improved sightlines for those of us seated in the boxes. Though the view is good, the narrow amphitheater makes the boxes cramped.

The goings-on on the *parterre* are even more distracting than our uncomfortable seats. While it has been many years since Cyrano de Bergerac banished the fat, old Monfleury from the stage at the Hôtel de Bourgogne, much of our audience in the public theater is still rowdy. The jostling and camaraderie of the riff-raff on the *parterre*, coupled with the loud barking of the food and liquor vendors hawking their goods, often ruins a performance. Only slightly less irritating than these buffoons are the would-be courtiers who occupy the benches near the stage. Often they actually seat themselves on the stage itself so they can vie with the actors for the audience's attention. Fortunately Molière's entertaining come-

dies are so absorbing that distracting behaviors are kept to a minimum and we are able to enjoy his satires on Parisian life.

As the beginning of the show draws near, the sunlight that had earlier flooded through the windows that line the walls of the theater begins to fade and the great candelabra is lighted and raised into position over the auditorium and the stage. From offstage we hear the rhythmic banging of the stage manager's staff, and the theater falls silent as the curtain rises to reveal Orgon's unhappy family complaining about Tartuffe's hold on them.

We are soon rewarded for our five-year wait, as *Tartuffe* proves as wickedly funny as we have heard. Under the economical direction of Molière himself, the troupe succeeds in holding our attention by creating the ludicrous—yet believable—world of Orgon's household. The *Comédiens du Roi* are dressed in the high fashion of the day, and each intones in a beautiful voice the rich Alexandrines of Molière's verse. Their

(continued)

sense of language is inspiring, and their comic timing impeccable. They assume an exaggerated physical style that achieves a proper balance between the real and the ridiculous. Monsieur Molière, no doubt the greatest comic actor of our time, is amusingly gullible as Orgon. His work is nicely complemented by the women of the company, namely Madeleine Béjart as Dorine, Mlle. Hervé as Mariane, and his beautiful young wife, Armande Béjart, as Elmire. We are particularly amused by the bickering between Orgon and Elmire, as we have heard that Molière and Armande have a troubled marriage themselves.

While we enjoy the ready banter among the various characters, we most enjoy the scene in which Orgon hides under a small table to observe Tartuffe's despicable behavior toward Elmire. It is surely the funniest scene we have ever seen performed by Molière's troupe. And just when we think our favorite playwright cannot possibly top this scene, the old master triumphs with his marvelous ending. An officer of the prince, dressed in a shimmering costume so bright that it looks as if it has been lit by the sun itself, appears mysteriously to save Orgon's household and lead the hypocrite Tartuffe to the Bastille. His speech about his magnani-

mous prince fills us with pride because we know that Molière is praising our beloved King Louis. The king himself is obviously moved and rises from his seat at the center of the theater to lead the applause as Molière's company acknowledges our cheers.

As we leave the Palais Royal and step into the frigid night air, we are warmed by our thoughts of the comedy. We hope it will be performed again soon and often. (It was—it ran for a record-breaking thirty-three performances!—Eds.)

CENTER STAGE   *TARTUFFE* AT THE THÉÂTRE DU SOLEIL, 1995

Parisian director Arianne Mnouchkine undertook Molière's *Tartuffe* as the Théâtre du Soleil's artistic response to encroachments on citizens' rights throughout the world, terrorist violence, and the excesses of religious fundamentalism. The production played in Vienna in June 1995, at the Festival d'Avignon in July, and at the Théâtre du Soleil's Paris home, the Cartoucherie, throughout the fall. The Soleil's powerfully dark production exemplifies the company's stated goal of creating "a theatre taken directly from social reality, one which is not a simple account, but an encouragement to change the conditions in which we live. We want to recount our History to move it forward."

In August 1995 Mnouchkine and other French artists protested the inaction of the French government and the United Nations in Bosnia-Herzegovina with a hunger strike; similarly, the Soleil's *Tartuffe* depicted metaphorically what happens when the Western world, in Mnouchkine's words, "by a mixture of cowardice and alleged political lucidity, continues to discuss and negotiate with [the extremists]. . . . Like Orgon, the Occident is complicitous, and us with them. Every ten or fifteen

years this play dips back into our history due to current events which confirms its importance and insight" (Festival d'Avignon Program).

Mnouchkine set the play in the summer heat of an indeterminate Mediterranean locale. Blooming bougainvillea atop towering wrought-iron gates surrounded Orgon's bourgeois courtyard, itself bedecked with a stunning array of Byzantine doors and Middle Eastern carpets. Glass carafes of water, bowls of pistachios, bright oranges and green apples, and rows of well-worn leather slippers underneath two Indian cots rounded out the details of Orgon's spacious oasis. In light of France's complex sociopolitical relationship with its former North African colony Algeria, the Soleil's *Tartuffe* immediately called to mind modern-day Algiers and the terror that reigns there under the banner of Islamic fundamentalism. However, because Mnouchkine considers *Tartuffe* a timeless metaphor for societies in crisis, the overall setting was suggestive of diverse locations and political movements cross borders of time and place.

Molière's characters were also not clearly delineated as belonging to a specific time period, country, or religion;

rather, they existed as metaphors open to interpretation depending on the spectator's frame of reference. Madame Pernell conjured up "a mixture of a Mother Superior and a Muslim," as Mnouchkine characterized her in rehearsal. Orgon and Cléante, with their full goatees and mustaches, collarless white shirts, immaculate vests, and flowing black coats, suggested a Turkish-Mediterranean-European blend at the turn of various centuries. Tartuffe and his faithful followers wore long, sweeping black coats, skullcaps, and full beards inspired by (among other sources) seventeenth-century Islamic apparel to conjure images of a range of fundamentalist figures, of whatever century, who resort to violence in order to impose their philosophies on society.

In the opening scene, the family's fresh white linens sat in crisp, neat piles or hung along the gateposts of the courtyard; they suggested innocence in Orgon's warm, idyllic haven. It was a festive occasion at which Mariane and her lover, Valère, danced together to the undulating rhythms of *rai* music; they were goaded on by a graceful Cléante. The women of the house, Elmire and Dorine, watched in amusement while young Damis buried his

Tartuffe was transported to the modern Middle East in Arianne Mnouchkine's 1995 production for the Théâtre du Soleil.

head in a book he purchased from a local merchant peddling his wares from a colorful cart outside the gates. Madame Pernelle's servants, Flippe and Pote (formerly Flipote), were adorned from head to foot in black religious garments covered with white work aprons. They sneaked away from the house to purchase a record of forbidden music from the merchant. Madame Pernelle's emergence from the house was the first intrusion into this otherwise pleasant and protected world. Upon seeing the irreverent goings-on, her jaw dropped and she blew a silver whistle that hung about her neck to call the courtyard to order. She tossed Damis's book aside, chastised the servants as she flung their record—like a frisbee—into the wings, and sent Valère scampering over the gates. According to Mnouchkine, the material objects in this Eden "maintain an important role, and the family's treasures—the traces of paradise—transform themselves into hell." Madame Pernelle's vehement rejection and ceaseless criticism of free thought were not surprising (however annoying) to the assembled family who tried to placate her. However, it was her blind faith in the houseguest, Tartuffe, that re-

mained disquieting and suggested impending danger. Outnumbered and ignored, a frustrated Madame Pernelle collected herself and bopped the servants on their heads with her handbag to wake them from a catnap.

Wearing a fez, Orgon returned to his home to find the family worried about Tartuffe's encroachment upon their world. This threat took physical form as Tartuffe finally streamed onstage amid a thunderous roar of demonstrators and the strains of triumphant military music; he was flanked by four cohorts wearing pointed, black Ku Klux Klan–like hoods. Whereas Tartuffe is a convincing player "who forbids others to do what he himself is in the process of doing" (Mnouchkine), he is most dangerous when he is most sincere. By contrast, Orgon was prone to flare into physical bursts of anger when he was not obeyed. His instability and desperation were simultaneously droll and terrifying as he erupted into hysterics or smashed apples against his forehead in moments of crisis. For example, when Damis revealed that Tartuffe tried to seduce Elmire, Orgon commanded Tartuffe's men to drag the boy away on his heels; Damis cried out to his father who was busily

consoling a "wounded" Tartuffe. Later in act 4, Orgon brought in a team of notaries and their guards to sign away his daughter to Tartuffe forever. Only after Mariane pulled a knife and threatened to commit suicide did an embarrassed and shaken Orgon order them away. The issues surrounding a daughter's sacrifice as a tool to maintain the patriarchal order recalled images of the Soleil's recent production of Aeschylus's *Oresteia* in which Agamemnon sacrifices his daughter Iphigenia.

However, *Tartuffe* is a comedy, and the resistors inside Orgon's family would not let the patriarch get away with murder. Together, the clever Dorine-Elmire team mounted their defense despite the obvious risks involved. Both women (played by Nirupama Nitanyanden and Juliana Carnerio de Cunha) are consummate actors who strategically employ different tactics to undermine Orgon and Tartuffe. Throughout the production, the wise, witty, well-seasoned Dorine was the cement holding the family together as she gave courage to the children, and support to Elmire as she confronted Tartuffe. In contrast to her humor and high spirits, the gravity of the situation

(continued)

was heightened as Dorine broke down and cried when Tartuffe threatened to take Orgon's estate in act 5. As night fell and shadows flickered in the light of the candle that Elmire lit on the table while awaiting Tartuffe, the personal peril she was willing to face to prove his deceit was evident. Her forced enclosure in this unwanted nightmare was further underlined when an eager, smiling Tartuffe seductively, yet comically, set the scene by pulling down the linen

that lined the gates. He then rhythmically disrobed by tossing pieces of his clothing around the stage as he attempted to turn the entire courtyard into a bedroom.

The Soleil's reading of Molière's brilliantly wrought comedy offered a trenchant view of contemporary French society and its many contradictions by trusting the playwright's text *"au pied de la lattre"* ("to the word"). It revived the interplay of socially inscribed roles and

the incisive and potent political critique that initially caused the play to be banned in 1664 and again in 1667. The dexterity of the actors enabled Molière's characters—and the production as a whole—to dance along the narrow precipice between comedy and its chilly underside. The Théâtre du Soleil reinforced *Tartuffe's* relevance in 1995.

Lisa Jo Epstein
The University of Texas

SPOTLIGHT

THE SECRET LIFE OF A CON MAN: ANTONY SHER ON PLAYING TARTUFFE

(The following is an interview with Antony Sher, an actor with the Royal Shakespeare Company.)

"A man, or rather a demon disguised as a man, and the most notorious blasphemer and libertine who ever lived . . . He deserves to be tortured and burnt for this sacrilegious outrage," thundered a contemporary cleric at Molière after the one and only performance of *Tartuffe* in 1664. A modern audience seeing Molière's comedy about the unmasking of a religious hypocrite might well wonder what the uproar was about. To illuminate the furor surrounding *Tartuffe*, which opens at the Barbican this Thursday, the RSC has paired it with Bulgakov's *Molière*, about Molière's conflict with the Church over what has become the most performed French classical play.

The controversy centered on the character of Tartuffe, who impersonates a holy man and so bewitches a wealthy businessman, Orgon, that he has to catch Tartuffe *in flagrante* with his wife Elmire before realizing he has been duped. The French clergy were incensed, and *Tartuffe* was banned for five years until Molière did extensive rewriting.

In Bulgakov's not entirely factual account, Molière is persecuted by the Church both for *Tartuffe* and for his

marriage to a woman suspected of being his daughter. Although Louis XIV initially supports Molière against his clerical enemies, he arbitrarily withdraws his patronage and bans *Tartuffe*, a final blow which causes Molière to suffer a heart attack on stage.

Bulgakov's play is also a clever pastiche of Molière's plots. As in *Tartuffe*, sons are disinherited, old men deceived, and Molière's double-act with his servant Bouton mirrors the Master/Servant relationship of Orgon and Dorine.

Antony Sher, 34, plays both title roles, adding Tartuffe and his creator to a distinguished list of predatory manipulators (*The History Man*) and farcical anti-heroes (the Arab in *Goosepimples*; Clive in *Cloud 9*). "The great joy of doing the plays together is that *Tartuffe* is mentioned throughout *Molière* so that one approaches *Tartuffe* with all that background knowledge," says Sher. "Seeing *Molière* informs people about the religious issues behind *Tartuffe*: you see *Tartuffe* and then understand what the fuss is about in *Molière*."

Bulgakov's play exaggerates Molière's persecution by the Church and caricatures his sycophantic relationship with Louis. "Bulgakov hasn't written a biography," says Sher, "he has used the character of Molière and twisted the facts of his life to write a play about the artist in a repressive society."

Pairing *Tartuffe* and *Molière* sets up all sorts of political resonances. Molière was as dependent on Louis' support as Bulgakov was on Stalin's, and both plays were banned, ironically. *Tartuffe* ends with Louis saving Orgon, and Bulgakov's play with the King destroying Molière.

But Sher stresses that although links exist, "it could be about South Africa now, [where Sher was born] or any totalitarian society." Bulgakov charts the state's destruction of the individual because he's not fitting in. It becomes Kafkaesque: he's a man in a nightmare where everyone is after him.

"But it's a difficulty in the part that Bulgakov makes Molière much more neurotic than he probably was, a man who panics, who is desperate with fear and grief. Bulgakov puts him where the entire force of Church and state comes down on him, and then makes him behave like you or me rather than some super-hero."

Tartuffe, however, thrives on adversity, "a great improviser who thinks on his feet." But he is hardly a subtle portrait of a religious importer. He doesn't come on stage until Act 3, giving the other characters two acts to run him down. "Because of the objections that people wouldn't realize Tartuffe was a hypocrite, Molière had to do so much nudge-nudge, wink-wink to the audience that Tartuffe was a fraud that I think he came close to ruining the play," says Sher.

Molière explicitly made Tartuffe a scoundrel who says or does nothing that does not reveal his evil nature. Making Tartuffe one-dimensional may have partially appeased Molière's enemies, but it also makes the role difficult to play.

Sher explains; "There is actually no such man as Tartuffe; he's a criminal with a long record, and Tartuffe is just a role that he's playing. For rehearsal purposes, we have invented the real man, whom we call 'Eric.' 'Eric' is a con-man, who has done a lot of different cons, and this one happens to be a religious man called Tartuffe.

"And because it's a role he's playing, it doesn't have to be too fixed; he's a chameleon, constantly changing, he can go from full Rasputic powers to a lost little boy. He's got to have the ability to change and swop and surprise people at a rate of knots."

"Richard III is similar to Tartuffe. They're both manipulators, and very clever actors: they play whatever scene people want them to play. But the difference is that with Richard you do see

the man himself, in soliloquy. Because Molière hasn't given Tartuffe one bit of 'Eric' to do, it's frustrating; you can't investigate him at all as a human being." Even when Tartuffe is unmasked at the end, Molière has him "dragged off without a grace note or a final line. It's moments like that when you know there has been a lot of re-writing."

To counter-balance the odds Molière was obliged to stack against Tartuffe to get the play on, Sher's original idea was to fight tradition and go for "as pure an image as possible, young, Christ-like, and angelic." He discovered, however, that playing so much against the text didn't work.

"You can with Shakespeare: I think we have to some extent with *Lear* [Sher played the Fool as a double-act with Michael Gambon's King], but what Molière has written is very clear and clean . . . and it simply will not take such a drastic re-interpretation. Now I'm going towards something that is a bit creepier, more in keeping with the servant Dorine's comment that Tartuffe looks like a gargoyle off the side of Notre Dame. One must always remember that Molière started with *commedia dell'arte* stock characters. And although

he greatly improved on them that stock element must be there, though that doesn't mean they need to be cartoon people."

Sher points out that doing Molière's plays like pantomime is an exclusively English tradition. "Bill Alexander [who has directed both *Tartuffe* and *Molière*] and I went to Paris to see the *Comèdie Française* do *L'Avare* ("The Miser"), and it was a real eye-opener, because they do Molière terribly seriously. In England the plays become so thin they're like confections, but when you actually see them done with great seriousness, the comedy takes care of itself and the plays become rather rich and fascinating exposes of human weakness. I think that's especially true of *Tartuffe* because it's unsettling and quite frightening what's going on in Orgon's house. It's a black comedy."

"The Secret Life of a Con Man: Antony Sher on Playing Tartuffe" by Francesca Simon. *The Sunday Times*, 24 July 1983. Reprinted by permission of Antony Sher.

THE LATE SEVENTEENTH AND EIGHTEENTH CENTURIES

Artistic and Cultural Events

1660:
Theaters reopened in London

1660–1700:
Restoration theater

1677:
Aphra Behn's *The Rover*, first play by professional female playwright

1698:
Jeremy Collier attacks "immorality" on the English stage

1700:
William Congreve's *The Way of the World*; last great Restoration comedy

1722:
Richard Steel's *The Conscious Lovers*

1728:
John Gay's *The Beggar's Opera*, first ballad opera in English

1729–1739:
Reforms in German theater

1731:
George Lillo's *The London Merchant*, first domestic and prose tragedy

1743:
Teatro del Príncipe opens in Madrid

1752:
First theater company in Russia

1758:
Denis Diderot's "The Pardox of Acting"

1765:
Autos sacramentales prohibited in Spain

1767–1768:
Gotthold Lessing's *Hamburg Dramaturgy*

1772:
Oliver Goldsmith's *She Stoops to Conquer*

1777:
Richard B. Sheridan's *The School for Scandal*

1600 C.E.

1700 C.E.

Historical and Political Events

1660:
English monarchy restored

1688:
Glorious Revolution in England

1701–1713:
War of Spanish Succession

1789:
French Revolution

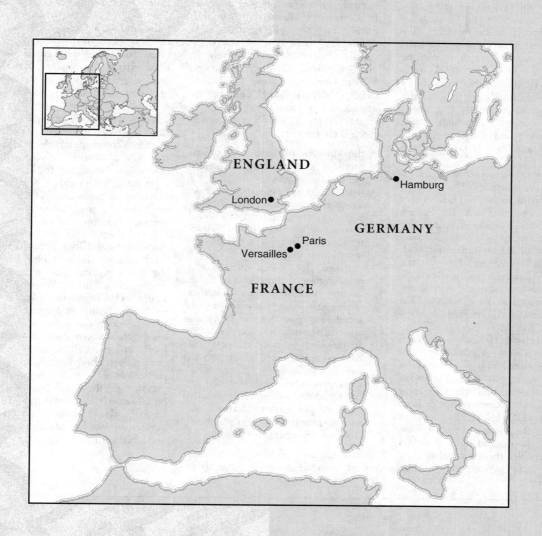

SPOTLIGHT — THE COMEDY OF MANNERS

Among the theater's most popular sub-genres of comedy is the Comedy of Manners, in which the manners, customs, and attitudes of a particular society are satirized. Though it can be found in novels (e.g., Jane Austen's *Pride and Prejudice*), the Comedy of Manners is especially at home in the theater because frequently it is about the way ("manner") in which people dress, behave, and talk—better yet, how they "act," in every sense of the term.

Its Western roots can be traced to Menander, the inventor of New Comedy and its emphasis on the daily behaviors of people in social situations. The Roman comedians, Plautus and Terence, also wrote plays that are akin to the Comedy of Manners, as did Shakespeare in such comedies as *Love's Labor's Lost*. But the Comedy of Manners is particularly associated with seventeenth- and eighteenth-century drama. In France, Molière (*The Learned Ladies*, 1659) and Pierre de Marivaux (*The False Confessions*, 1737) excelled in the form. The latter even lends his name to a term—*Maravaudage*—frequently associated with the Comedy of Manners; it suggests spirited plays in which young people fall in love (often at first sight), but modesty and pride keep them from acknowledging their feelings. Ultimately, the strength of their love, abetted by the machinations of skillful servants, enables them to profess their feelings in witty language and win their heart's desires.

However, we most closely associate the Comedy of Manners with English drama of the Restoration Era (1660–1700) and that of the eighteenth century. William Wycherly, John Dryden, George Etherege, William Congreve, Oliver Goldsmith, and especially Richard B. Sheridan are often cited as the exemplary playwrights of the Comedy of Manners, which is characterized by

- the amorous intrigues of sophisticated, upper-class people living in a tightly knit society.
- witty dialogue, especially *repartée*, which is a mainstay of such comedy. Repartee, a fencing term, is a verbal sparring contest in which a character attempts to top a rival through ingenious wordplay.
- violations of social norms and mores, often by those who lack true wit and grace. The fops and dandies of the Restoration excelled in such social faux pas, thereby providing much of the humor of the play.
- an emphasis on fashion, social behaviors, and speech, which can all too easily become "mannerisms" when people are blinded by their desire to advance themselves socially. Such people become "living lies," and laughter is the way in which society reforms or expels them.

The Comedy of Manners depends on an audience knowledgeable about the particulars of the society in question. Thus the audience becomes a kind of external character who judges the follies and social lapses of the characters being satirized. In the theater, directors often recontextualize a comedy of manners written for a particular society (e.g., the Restoration) by setting it in one with which an audience may more readily identify. The recent film *Clueless* provides a ready example; Austen's nineteenth-century novel *Emma* was reset in a contemporary American high school and satirized the dress, speech patterns, and especially the behaviors of a coterie of "valley girls."

In recent times England has continued to excel at the Comedy of Manners, particularly in the plays of Oscar Wilde, Bernard Shaw, and Noel Coward. Allen Ayckbourne and Tom Stoppard are currently among the best playwrights of the genre in England. In the United States, Neil Simon, Wendy Wasserstein, and Christopher Durang have written Comedies of Manners, though they are often quite dark and disturbing. Non-Western cultures also have their versions of the Comedy of Manners, though those unfamiliar with the particulars of the society being satirized may not "get the joke." There is a popular Chinese opera, *The Perfumed Handkerchief*, that satirizes a would-be mother-in-law, her daughter's suitor, and a blabbering old auntie.

In 1642 the Puritans, led by Oliver Cromwell, seized power in England and immediately closed the public theaters, which they had long considered "the devil's workshop." The supporters of King Charles I, who was executed on the steps of Parliament in 1649, fled England. Many went to the American colonies (the Carolinas were named for King Charles), where they eventually established theaters in Williamsburg, Jamestown, and Charleston. Others fled to Italy, where they were introduced to spectacular scenic effects and to the opera. But most royalists found refuge in France, where they attended the Parisian and court theaters, quite unlike those they left in London. They were enamored of the intimate, indoor French theaters, and they enjoyed the Neoclassic dramas of Corneille and the topical comedies of Molière. When the monarchists returned to England after the Interregnum (1642–1660), they demanded plays and playing conditions in keeping with the French fashion. And having seen women perform in France and Italy, they also made it possible for women to act in English theaters.

From 1660, when Charles II returned to the throne taken from his father, until 1700, the English theater presented heroic tragedies, such as Thomas Otway's *Venice Preserv'd*, and spectacles employing the new (to the English) Italian scenery. But the most popular plays were comedies portraying the affairs (sexual and otherwise) of the well-to-do who sought favor at Charles's court. Charles II attended the theater regularly and enjoyed a private box where he entertained his mistresses, one of whom was the popular actress Nell Gywnn. Courtiers wrote these plays about courtiers and for courtiers. (See Spotlight box, The Comedy of Manners.) At no other time in the history of the English theater has playwriting and performance been controlled by such a small, yet powerful, coterie. However, Restoration comedies retain a lasting appeal because of their wit and the brilliance of their satirical portraits of the manners and social customs of the society they mirrored. William Wycherly's *The Country Wife* (1675), Sir George Etherege's *The Man of Mode* (1676), and William Congreve's *The Way of the World* (1700) remain among the most popular Restoration comedies. Mrs. Aphra Behn, the first woman to achieve success as a professional playwright, wrote *The Rover*, which has enjoyed major revivals in the twentieth century.

After eighteen years of Puritanism, England's moral pendulum swung wildly in an opposite direction. Charles II and his courtiers (and would-be courtiers) were obsessed with the pursuit of material goods and sexual pleasure. Consequently, Restoration comedies are notoriously bawdy and amoral. Furthermore, they espouse one of the dominant philosophies of the age, as set forth in Thomas Hobbes's social tract *The Leviathan* (1651): "[Men] are in that condition which is called war; and such a war, as is of every man against every man." In the Restoration the battlefield became the boudoir, and those who survived were those who conquered through cunning, wit, deception, and charm. The hero of the Restoration play—"the rake"—is the antithesis of the conventional hero of serious drama. Whereas the latter idealistically pursues his goals (love and dignity) through honor and duty, the rake cynically pursues his (lust and self-indulgence) through deceit and sexual conquest. For the rake, it was a badge of honor to cuckold an enemy, a triumph to seduce a virtuous woman.

Within the comedies, the antithesis of the rake was the fop, one who lacks true wit and charm and who is excessive in dress and mannerisms. The grotesquely comical fop invariably steals the show in a Restoration comedy. Rakes especially enjoyed duping middle-class merchants and the nouveau riche. Whomever they attacked, rakes invariably bested because they were skillful at the most prized Restoration-era virtue: using one's wit (and therefore language) well.

Restoration comedies celebrate the game of love, and "the chase" is all in their plots. Those who play well—though not necessarily fairly—win; those who lack wit and invention, lose. In Restoration England, fidelity was not necessarily a virtue onstage or off. John Dryden, a fine playwright and a superb dramatic critic, captures such attitudes in the preface to his witty play, *Marriage à la Mode* (1672):

> *Why should a foolish marriage vow*
>
> *Which long ago was made*
>
> *Oblige us to each other now*
>
> *When passion is decayed?*
>
> *But our marriage is dead*
>
> *When the pleasure is fled. . . .*

Lest we be too shocked at such celebrations of adultery, we must remember that marriages, particularly among the nobility, were prearranged, usually for political and economic gain. Love was rarely the prime motivator for marriage. As audiences grew weary of the decadence exhibited in Restoration plays, and especially as the middle class (and its traditional morality) assumed greater economic and political power, there was a discernable shift in the attitudes expressed in Restoration plays. *The Way of the World* is generally considered the last true Restoration play; its

---

SPOTLIGHT **THE CONVENTIONS OF THE RESTORATION THEATER**

Because the Restoration theater was virtually the property of England's privileged class, it has peculiarities of style and performance. Reading a play from this era can be more entertaining if you imagine how *The Rover*, a popular comedy written by Mrs. Aphra Behn, might have been staged at the Dorset Garden Theater in March 1677, when King Charles II saw it performed.

Intimacy perhaps best characterizes Restoration plays in performance. Not only were the comedies about intimate relationships (i.e., sexual conquests), they were performed in an intimate space by actors who often had personal knowledge of the lives of their audience (and vice versa). In gossip-ridden London, courtiers and the wealthy seemingly had little to do but indulge themselves in intrigues when not attending the theater, which was itself among the most popular public meetingplaces of the time. Playhouses were a favorite rendezvous for assignations because ladies customarily wore vizards (masks) to protect their identities. Not surprisingly, the actions onstage often mirrored the offstage high jinks of the Dorset Garden's clientele—and everyone knew it. Except perhaps poor Lord So-and-So who was being cuckolded by Lady So-and-So and Sir You Know Who; Lord So-and-So was thereby the offstage butt of onstage jokes.

About 600 people could fill the new theaters being erected in London during the Restoration. The audience sat on benches on the floor (the "pit"), in elegant boxes located above the stage (the better to be seen at the play), or in galleries above the pit. No one was farther than about 35 feet from the stage, which itself was only about 12 feet deep (excluding the upstage scenic area). This meant that actors and audience, who were lit by a common candelabra, were very close to each other. Such intimacy encouraged frequent use of the aside, perhaps the most prominent convention of the Restoration theater. An aside occurs when a character speaks a short line directly to the audience (apparently) without the other characters hearing him or her. Although asides are not the exclusive property of Restoration comedy, they are used with greater frequency and effectiveness there than elsewhere (save perhaps the old-fashioned melodrama, where the villain's "Curses, foiled again" emerged as the most famous aside in Western theater). Asides actively involved the audience in the onstage intrigues. In Restoration comedies the audience is always "in" on the joke. Additionally, asides brought the reality of the onstage escapades into the auditorium, where the playgoers understood too well the implications of

the plot. Consider two asides taken from act 4 of *The Rover*. Imagine the effect if the actor playing the lover shares his exit line with a dandy in the pit who himself lives by a similar credo:

> I'm glad on this release. Now for my gipsy [sic]:
> For though to worse we change, yet still we find
> New joys, new charms, in a new miss that's kind.

Imagine how the fun is doubled if he says it to a friend with whom he has been out wenching. Consider the possibilities if he says it to an attractive young woman seated in a box above the stage as a flirtation. Or suppose he says it directly to the king, whom the entire audience knows to be interested in "a new miss that's kind." Now, look at the heroine's simple aside, "So, now is he [Willmore] for another woman." Again, consider the impact—not to mention the fun—if the line is shared with a lady in the audience whose own husband is "for another woman." What if she takes her case directly to the king? Or suppose she directs it to a notorious libertine in the third row? Such were the dynamics of a Restoration comedy in performance; when reading such plays, you can more easily enter into the spirit of the plays if you think of the asides as more than mere throwaways to the audience.

---

hero and heroine ultimately reject the wicked ways of the world and commit themselves to a new society. (See Spotlight box, The Conventions of the Restoration Theater.)

Sentimental Comedy

The licentiousness of Restoration comedies gave way to sentimental or "weeping" comedies popular among the new merchant class in the early eighteenth century. The new drama was shaped by the doctrine of benevolence, an outgrowth of the optimism engendered by the prosperity that accompanied colonialism. This philosophy claimed that God planted within humans the natural instinct to love others, and each person therefore had a moral responsibility to demonstrate this innate goodwill (i.e., benevolence) through acts of charity. Moral acts incited strong, positive feelings of virtue in both the doer and the observer, thereby engendering more acts of kindness. The theater became a temple where virtuous people congregated to

Not only did actors directly address the audience, but it was the practice of the time that some in the audience could actually rise and speak to the actors and others in the audience. The plays themselves, which are invariably filled with commentary about theater-going and behavior, evidence this. In William Wycherly's *The Country Wife* (1675) the doltish fop, Sparkish, brags that he and his fellow dandies go to a play as if they were going to a picnic:

I carry my own wine to one, and my own wit to t'other, or else I am sure I would not be merry at either; and the reason why we are so often louder than the players is because we think we speak more wit, and so become the [playwright's] rivals in the audience. For to tell you the truth, we hate the silly rogues; nay, so much that we find fault even with their bawdy upon the stage, whilst we talk nothing else in the pit as loud.

Actors no doubt had to be as quick-thinking and inventive to parry the thrusts of wits in the audience as modern standup comics working a room full of hecklers. To further add to the color of the event, wenches circulated throughout the audience selling oranges and other favors to the spectators. Clearly there was as much theater in the boxes, the pit, and the gallery as on the stage.

Perhaps you are familiar with the dress and wigs, physical posturing, and the use of such accoutrements as walking sticks, snuff boxes, and fans during this period in European history. They influenced the performance style required of Restoration comedy actors. In the late seventeenth century such things as "making a leg" or talking in "the language of the fan" were not the performance conventions they are today; rather, they were part of the social world the plays mirrored. A young man extended his ribbon-bedecked leg as a means of preening; such behavior was considered "sexy" and was part of a mating ritual. When a young woman demurely lowered her fan to reveal her eyes, it was not only a signal that she enjoyed a dandy's flirtations but an encouragement for him to continue. Should she place the fan over her lips, it meant that he was treading on thin ice and had better choose his words carefully. If she snapped it shut, it meant "end of conversation—now!" Though few of these societal conventions are scripted, actors must know when to use them to build their characters and enhance the interplay with other actors. When reading Restoration plays, it is easy to forget that such behaviors are as integral as any dialogue the playwright supplies. Aphra Behn alludes to those who carry social gestures to the point of mere affectation (a not uncommon occurrence of the time) in her epilogue to *The Rover*.

Both prologues and epilogues were *de rigueur* in the Restoration theater. Customarily, the prologue was delivered by the leading actor, and the epilogue by the favored actress. Like the aside, these lengthy, witty speeches heightened the interplay between stage and auditorium. Also, they were often topical and depended upon a sophisticated audience that understood the satirical barbs. Principal actors customarily bowed to the audience on their first entrances and only then assumed their characters. Orchestral music was played before the play, between its acts, and often as underscoring during the action. Thus, virtually every aspect of the Restoration theater was calculated to heighten the theatrical atmosphere of the event. Little wonder that the majority of plays of this time employ the artifice of theater and disguisings as a central component of the plot.

learn about virtue and sentiment. Richard Steele (1672–1729), who wrote England's most popular sentimental comedies, declared that "there is no human institution so aptly calculated for the forming of a free-born people as that of the theater." Steele wrote plays calculated to reward virtue and correct (as opposed to punishing) vices.

Consider a speech from Steele's *The Conscious Lovers*, the hit of the 1722 theater season in London. Here, the preeminently virtuous heroine, Indiana, describes the misfortunes of her infancy and childhood to her benefactor, a kindly old merchant named Sealand:

What have I to do but sigh, and weep, to rave, run wild, a lunatic in chains, or, hid in darkness, mutter in distracted starts and broken accents my strange, strange story! . . . All my comfort must be to expostulate in madness, to relieve with my frenzy and despair, and, shrieking, to demand of fate why—why was I born to such a variety of sorrows? . . . 'Twas heaven's high will I should be plundered in my cradle! Tossed on seas! And even there, an infant captive! To lose my mother, hear but of my father! To be adopted! To lose my adopter! Then plunged again in worse calamities!

But all is not lost for Indiana, who remained virtuous and true despite these severe tests. "Heaven's high will" rewards her by reuniting her with her lost and newly wealthy father, Sealand, whose real name is Danforth. (For good measure, kindly old Isabella, who has taken Indiana under her wing, is revealed as Sealand's long-lost sister!)

We may find such contrived playwriting laughable by our standards, but such plays dominated the English, French, and—quite significantly—early American stages because their simple lessons reflected middle-class morality. Two elements of sentimental comedy in particular influenced subsequent theater. First, drama turned its full attention to the daily problems of its middle-class audiences. Second, it provided the underpinnings of the full-fledged melodrama, which emerged by the end of the century.

The American theater, which emerged at precisely the time when sentimental comedies enjoyed their greatest popularity, has always had a pronounced strain of sentimentality running through it. Little Eva's famous deathbed speech in *Uncle Tom's Cabin* is a remarkable example of sentimentality fused with abolitionist propaganda. In our century Lorraine Hansberry's civil rights drama *A Raisin in the Sun* (1959) depends on sentimentality, although its issues are quite serious. Television sitcoms, especially in the 1950s, are sentimentalist at heart; *Father Knows Best* epitomized the genre. One of the most popular films in the history of American cinema, Stephen Spielberg's *E.T.*, is a thoroughly sentimental comedy. Recall the moment when Eliot revives E.T. by uttering the battle cry of the sentimentalists, "Love."

Laughing Comedy

In 1772 Oliver Goldsmith exposed the artificiality of "weeping comedies," which (in Steele's words) existed only "to introduce a joy too exquisite for laughter." He called for a return of "laughing comedy" to the stage. He wrote *She Stoops to Conquer* to satirize sentimentality and reestablish traditional comedy in the theater. Its success inspired Richard Brinsley Sheridan's *The School for Scandal*, which triumphed at London's Drury Lane Theater in 1777. These plays (with Sheridan's *The Rivals*) remain the preeminent examples of the eighteenth-century Comedy of Manners.

Bourgeois Tragedy

Though we remember the comedies of the late seventeenth and eighteenth centuries, we must not forget that there was a corresponding growth of serious plays depicting middle-class problems. "Domestic tragedy," "*le drame,*" and "*genre sérieux*" are terms variously used to describe such plays. In 1731 George Lillo (c. 1696–1739) wrote the first prose tragedy in English. Based on an actual murder, *The London Merchant* depicted the fall of a young man who murders his employer, the merchant, to get money for his lover, Mrs. Marwood. Lillo's preface to the play reveals much about the intent of bourgeois dramas. He claimed that his "private tale of woe" was an attempt to "accommodate tragedy to the circumstances of the generality of mankind" because all humans are prey to misfortune.

In the bourgeois tragedies of Europe, we see the precursors of the social realist drama that would emerge in the modern theater, but—like the sentimental comedies—these works were contrived, sensational, and too eager to preach moral lessons. Furthermore, purely external forces most often created the misfortune. Heroes were more victims than truly tragic beings. Nonetheless, the domestic tragedies placed common people at center stage and infused the theater with a concern for topical problems that would become the hallmark of the nineteenth century and ultimately the modern theater.

Samuel Beckett's tragicomedy Waiting for Godot *is among the most important plays in the modern theater; South African actors Winston Ntshona and John Kani performed it at the Long Wharf Theater in 1981.*

CHAPTER 5

THE MODERN THEATER

A cursory examination of most anthologies of Western drama suggests that very little theatrical activity occurred from the time of Molière and the Restoration to the emergence of Ibsen in the late nineteenth century. Relatively few plays from this nearly 200-year span are performed today (save the comedies of Goldsmith and Sheridan); nonetheless, major cultural changes during this time laid the foundation for the work of the early realists. In Asia, a similar upheaval was taking place as the Japanese Kabuki and the Peking Opera emerged, partly in response to middle-class calls for new entertainment. In more recent times, the theaters of Asia and Africa have also turned toward the social drama, sometimes portraying life in realistic terms and sometimes using the theatrical traditions that have served them well for centuries as they confront modern problems.

The Romantic melodramas of the early nineteenth century paved the way for the realistic dramas of Ibsen, Chekhov, and their successors. The novelist and playwright Émile Zola acknowledged this debt when he wrote, "Romanticism is the first step toward realism." In addition to realism (and its extension, naturalism), such theatrical styles as Expressionism, the epic theater of Brecht, and the theater of the absurd also evolved in the modern era. These various styles shared a common impulse: the desire to examine humans as social beings trapped in outmoded political, economic, and philosophical systems. While the spirit of Romanticism may be found, if darkly, in modern plays, its idealism has generally been supplanted by cynicism or—more accurately—a more "realistic" assessment of the human dilemma in a rapidly changing world.

ROMANTICISM

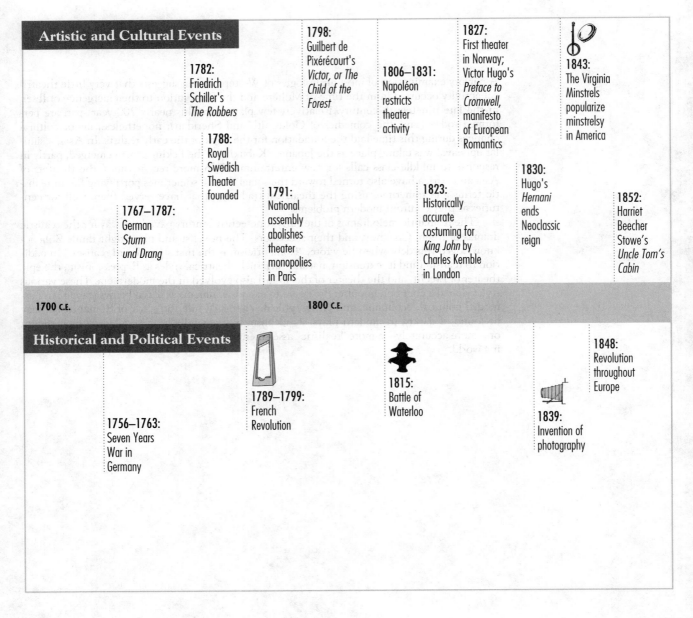

Artistic and Cultural Events

1767–1787:
German *Sturm und Drang*

1782:
Friedrich Schiller's *The Robbers*

1788:
Royal Swedish Theater founded

1791:
National assembly abolishes theater monopolies in Paris

1798:
Guilbert de Pixérécourt's *Victor, or The Child of the Forest*

1806–1831:
Napoléon restricts theater activity

1823:
Historically accurate costuming for *King John* by Charles Kemble in London

1827:
First theater in Norway; Victor Hugo's *Preface to Cromwell,* manifesto of European Romantics

1830:
Hugo's *Hernani* ends Neoclassic reign

1843:
The Virginia Minstrels popularize minstrelsy in America

1852:
Harriet Beecher Stowe's *Uncle Tom's Cabin*

1700 C.E.

1800 C.E.

Historical and Political Events

1756–1763:
Seven Years War in Germany

1789–1799:
French Revolution

1815:
Battle of Waterloo

1839:
Invention of photography

1848:
Revolution throughout Europe

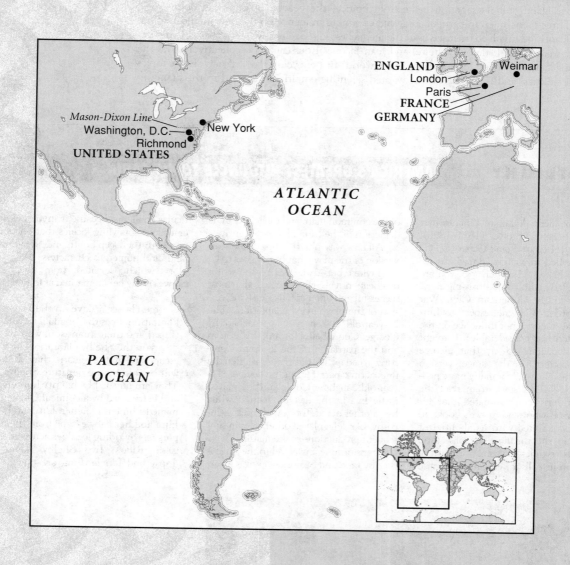

Romanticism was both an outgrowth of and a reaction to the Enlightenment, the eighteenth-century philosophical movement that extolled free thought, rationality, and scientific inquiry. The Enlightenment actually began in northwestern Europe in the mid–seventeenth century and spread to England, but its sanction came from France, the beacon of European culture and thought. Three Frenchmen in particular exerted enormous influence on the new intellectualism, and significantly all involved themselves in the media best suited to reach mass audiences: the theater. They were Denis Diderot, Voltaire, and Jean-Jacques Rousseau, who collectively bore the title of the *Philosophes*. They compiled one of the world's first encyclopedias on such diverse topics as science, politics, and the arts. Diderot wanted scientific empiricism applied to the drama to

SPOTLIGHT — AMERICA'S GREATEST HIT: *UNCLE TOM'S CABIN*

When President Abraham Lincoln met Harriet Beecher Stowe (1811–1896), whose novel *Uncle Tom's Cabin* (*UTC*) was published in March 1852, he is reported to have said to her, "So, you are the little lady who caused this big war," referring to the American Civil War (1861–1865). With all respect to Lincoln's assessment of her influence on the war (which was considerable), it might be more accurate to say that George Aiken's script for the stage version "caused the big war," for many more people saw *UTC* on stage than read the novel. It has been estimated that for every person who read Stowe's book, 50 became acquainted with its abolitionist message in the theater. The play (and novel) also typifies the romantic spirit of the age, in its calls for equality, its praise

of the common man, and especially in its depiction of the triumph over tyranny.

Aiken's was not the first American version of the play (that honor goes to C. W. Taylor), but it was this Boston writer of cheap novels who created the most successful and dramatically satisfying version of the play's many adaptations. The 22-year-old Aiken was approached by George Cunnabell Howard, his cousin and the patriarch of the Howard Company, to adapt *UTC* because it offered a fine acting part for his precocious 14-year-old daughter, Cordelia. (She played Little Eva in the first production while her mother acted Topsy with great sympathy; Cordelia played other roles in subsequent productions as she matured.)

Transforming any novel to the stage is no easy task, and Stowe's work was a par-

ticular challenge because it involves several plots, sprawling locales that encompass both the Deep South and New England, and numerous characters. Aiken's plot (which deviated from that of Stowe's) may be summarized as follows:

George Harris, a slave on the Haley Plantation, flees to Canada. His wife (Eliza) and their infant son, who are slaves on the Shelby plantation, also escape when they learn that they will be sold by the destitute Shelby. They are pursued by bounty hunters and befriended by a comical Quaker named Phineas Fletcher. Ultimately Eliza and her baby escape from their pursuers by riding ice floes across the Ohio River. Two Shelby slaves, Topsy and Uncle Tom, are bought

The most famous scene in the American theater: Eliza and her baby cross the ice floes of the Ohio River to escape slave trackers in the 1901 production of Uncle Tom's Cabin.

teach moral lessons. The theater, he argued, ought to be "a spectacle destined for bourgeois [i.e., middle-class] audiences, representing a striking moral picture of one's own social milieu." Diderot's call championed both the middle class as a subject for drama and realism as its artistic style. His essays prepared the way for Victor Hugo, Ibsen, and other nineteenth-century playwrights.

Voltaire (*nee* François-Marie Arouet, 1694–1778) was an outspoken critic of the French monarchy whose candor got him imprisoned in the infamous Bastille. In 1726 he was exiled to England, where he saw the plays of Shakespeare, which were unlike anything he had experienced in France. When he returned in 1729, he argued for political and artistic freedom of expression and even wrote tragedies whose style was Neoclassic but whose spirit was

by kindly Mr. St. Clare, who gives the former to his aunt Ophelia, a social reformer who lives in Vermont, and the latter to his sickly daughter, Little Eva. Tom is a good-hearted man loved by Little Eva, who, on her deathbed, begs her father to release Tom and other slaves. Unfortunately, St. Clare is killed before he can free Tom and the others, who are then purchased by the wicked slave owner, Simon Legree. Legree orders Tom to whip a young slave woman for refusing Legree's advances, but Tom refuses and is fatally beaten by Legree. Young Shelby arrives to accuse Legree of murdering St. Clare. Enraged, Legree threatens to kill his accuser, who is saved by a slave named Cassie, who had befriended Uncle Tom. Cassie stabs Legree, as Tom dies in Shelby's arms while the angelic spirit of Little Eva hovers above.

Aiken's first attempt included only those portions of the novel up to Little Eva's death (now in act 3); later it was he who added the killing of Tom, the reformation of Topsy (the play's most comical character), and the death of Legree. In the novel Legree is not punished for his crimes (in fact, he does not kill St. Clare), but the laws of melodrama demanded the triumph of poetic justice on which to ring down the curtain. The scene in which Eliza Harris and Little Harry are trapped on the ice floes of the Ohio is relatively minor in Stowe's novel (it merits two brief paragraphs and there are no bloodhounds). Realizing its the-

atrical potential—especially in an age of stage machinery—Aiken transforms the scene into what is arguably the most famous scene in the American theater (see photo). Most importantly, Aiken made the death of Uncle Tom the climax of the play (it is less dramatic in the novel), giving him a deathbed speech guaranteed to raise audience sympathies. Tom's dying words to his evil nemesis—". . . my troubles will be over soon, but if you don't repent yours will never end"—are typical of the sentimental reform dramas of the era. Aiken also added a stunning tableau with Little Eva, now an angel, descending to bless the play's martyrs, Tom and St. Clare. It was far more effective propaganda for the abolitionist cause than Stowe's lengthy antislavery debates because of its immediate emotional impact. While the tableau may have been a potent ending, there is something disturbing about Aiken's message that divine justice for slaves is perhaps more desirable than earthly justice.

The Howard version opened in Troy, New York, on September 27, 1852, at the Museum (a common euphemism for theaters in the Puritan North, where antitheater sentiment existed). It ran for 57 performances, easily the longest run of a play in a small town (c. 30,000) in the theater's history. In July 1853 it began a lengthy run at the National Theater in New York—and the rest, as they say, is history.

And what a history! The popularity of the play is unparalleled. Not only did it thrive throughout the Civil War, it was even more successful after the war and the

abolition of slavery. For instance, in 1879 the *Dramatic Mirror* listed 49 traveling companies who toured America with various versions of *UTC*; within a decade that number swelled tenfold as almost 500 companies criss-crossed America "tomming" in cities and towns that embraced the show as the year's biggest event. (The ultimate insult for actors was to be accused of "tomming the tanks," which implied that the actors were so bad they could perform *UTC* in only the tiniest towns.) The play was so popular with actors, as well as audiences, that it was not altogether uncommon to have "double shows" in which two actors played the same role. Lawyer Marks, Simon Legree, Uncle Tom, and especially Topsy were often played by two actors in the same show! The Tom shows grew in size and soon rivaled circuses as major attractions; in fact, showman P. T. Barnum mounted a Tom show that was equal parts theater and circus. By the time Stowe died in 1896, there had been—by a conservative estimate—some 250,000 performances of *UTC*. Ironically, this daughter of a New England clergyman (and wife to another) received no royalties because copyright laws had not been instituted.

Among the best accounts of the stage history of *UTC* is Harry Birdoff's *The World's Greatest Hit* (1947). The title is no exaggeration as adaptations of Stowe's anti-slavery novel were also an unequalled international success. We think of the play as an American entity, but there were no less than eight productions

(continued)

Romantic. Rousseau (1712–1778) was the most influential of the *Philosophes*. Although he wrote several treatises on dramatic theory and a short play (*Pygmalion*, 1775), it was Rousseau's political writings that, in part, inspired both the American and French Revolutions and the subsequent artistic movement that we call Romanticism. Rousseau wrote that we were born free but found ourselves shackled by tyrannical governments, science, and the new urbanization spreading across Europe. He called for a return to a natural state in which people were in harmony with nature. Rousseau admired the indigenous peoples of the Americas, whom Romantics called "noble savages," a term of respect for those uncorrupted by urban civilization.

Such thinking inspired a number of "antique plays" such as *Spartacus* (about a slave uprising in ancient Rome) and medieval plays that praised the glories of a country's historical past. Friedrich Schiller's *William Tell* (1804), a Robin Hood–like drama in which commoners fight tyranny from the shelter of the forest, is among the best of these. This fascination with history manifested itself in scenic design and, very importantly, costuming. "Setting" became central

---

(continued)

of *UTC* playing in London by the end of 1852, including puppet and "panto"—i.e., Christmas show—versions. The most prominent English *UTC* opened at the Olympic Theater in September (less than a month after the American premiere); it was subtitled "Negro Life in America," as opposed to the traditional "Life Among the Lowly." The Olympic version was rewritten to include a scene in which the slaves were freed (over a decade before Lincoln's Emancipation Proclamation!). British reviewers, conveniently forgetting that it was English traders who introduced slavery to their colonies, scolded Americans, saying that they hoped the play would "make America ashamed of herself for suffering such an anomaly in her institutions."

Versions of *UTC* could be found in German (*Onkle Tom's Hutte*), French (*Le Case de l'Oncle Tom*), Spanish (*La Cabana de Tom, o La Esclavitud de los Negros*), Polish (*Chata Wuja Tomasza*), Swedish (*Onkel Tom's Stuga*), Russian (*Khiszhina dyadi Toma*), Italian (*La Cappanna dello Zio Tommaso*), and even Finnish (*Seta Tumon Tupa*). In 1853 an actor was accidentally killed onstage in a gun accident in a Bade, Switzerland, production of the play. Gold miners in California were entertained by Charles R. Thorne's troupe, which was actually on its way to Australia.

The play retained its popularity well into the twentieth century. It was made into a silent film in 1903 by Thomas Edison's company, and again in 1916 (with Lillian Gish). A very young Spencer Tracy played St. Clare in a hometown production in Grand Rapids, Michigan. Child stars Shirley Temple and Judy Garland played Eva and Topsy, respectively, in musical films featuring scenes from *UTC*. Rogers and Hammerstein included a Siamese setting for "The Small House of Uncle Thomas" in their Broadway musical *The King and I*.

UTC is rarely performed in the post-civil rights era, although there was an admired revival in New York in 1998. However much we may sympathize with its antislavery message, we cannot deny its plotting is contrived, its language artificial, its characters stereotypical and too neatly divided into good and evil, and its propaganda blatant; the same charges may be made against numerous other Romantic dramas of the nineteenth century. And despite the best intentions of Stowe and Aiken, the portrait of the nonwhites is understandably offensive. The Negro dialect, while a then-honest attempt at realistic speech patterns, is crude and demeaning. Of greater concern are the stereotypical portraits of the slaves, especially Topsy, whose role was intended as comic relief (and no doubt embellished by actors going for the cheap laugh). Although Topsy is an ironist whose comments actually reveal a strong sense

of self-worth ("My name isn't Charcoal, it's Topsy" she declares in act 5), nineteenth-century audiences saw her as the stereotype of the uneducated, eye-rolling slave. The several songs she sings were derived from the minstrel show (see Spotlight box) and contributed to the stereotype. Much has been made of the character of Uncle Tom, who seems too much the faithful servant who willingly accepts the status quo. Only George Harris, who flees with wife (Eliza) and child (Harry) to Canada, emerges as an individual who takes his fate into his own hands. However, George and Eliza are of mixed race, which made them more sympathetic to white audiences, especially when George kills his pursuers.

For all its imperfections as literature and especially as social tract, *Uncle Tom's Cabin* remains the most important play in the history of the American theater. As a piece of mass entertainment, no other play offers a better sense of audience predilections for melodramas and minstrel shows in the nineteenth century. Of more importance, as a historical document no other play better reflects the country's attitudes—both positively and negatively—about slavery, about race relations, and about its destiny at a turning point in its development.

to the drama, while the move to historically accurate dress was intended to evoke the beauty of the past. Romantic dramas invariably portrayed common people as the saviors of their nations. Rousseau's countryman Pierre Caron de Beaumarchais (1732–1799), a fine playwright himself, argued that "the nearer the suffering [of the protagonist] is to my station, the greater his claim upon my sympathy. . . . We identify with people, not kings."

Although Romantic thought is multifaceted, three aspects in particular help define the impulse behind the Romantic Revolution:

- "Freedom" became the battle cry of the new thinkers of the mid–eighteenth century—freedom from political oppression, freedom to think for oneself, freedom to create art independent of stultifying rules and traditions.
- The heroes of the Romantic Revolution were the common man and woman. This was after all the age when Thomas Jefferson wrote that "all men are created equal" and French workers stormed the Bastille with the cry of "Liberty, Equality, Fraternity."
- Passion and feeling supplanted what the Romantics perceived to be the cold, analytical thought of the Enlightenment.

The Melodrama

Consequently, melodrama and its ringing passions became the theatrical embodiment of Romantic idealism. Melodrama is as old as Euripides, and Shakespeare wrote it, as did Lope de Vega in Spain. But melodrama as a full-fledged genre evolved in Europe in the late eighteenth century. By 1830 it was the dominant theatrical form in Europe and America. Though it is associated with the French theater during the years immediately after the 1789 Revolution, there was a significant German movement, the *Sturm und Drang* ("storm and stress"). In 1776 Friedrich Klinger wrote a drama expressing many of the same political sentiments that sparked the political revolutions in the American colonies and in France. Klinger called his play *Der Wirrwarr* (*The Hurly-Burly*), but retitled it *Sturm und Drang* because it reflected the "storm and stress" Germany was experiencing. The play's title was soon applied to a brigade of young intellectuals who wrote tumultuous dramas that rebelled against political, economic, and artistic tyranny. Their plays celebrated ordinary people in natural—even primitive—settings; they depicted heroic peasants overthrowing villainous land barons and tyrannical princes. Using the language of the common man and woman, the plays contained sensational action and elemental conflicts between the forces of good and evil. Schiller's *The Robbers* (1782) established the plot and character prototypes for the melodrama: the damsel in distress, the falsely accused hero, and the ruthless villain whose castle is filled with dungeons, secret passageways, and trap doors.

Historically, however, true melodrama was born on the boulevards of Paris after the Revolution. At this time, Parisian theaters were of two kinds: "restricted theaters" that were licensed to perform classical drama, and playhouses in working-class neighborhoods where laborers gathered to watch popular entertainments such as animal acts, prizefighting, and variety acts. Among the favorite diversions at these "boulevard theaters" were *pantomimes*, which appealed to a largely nonliterate audience. Pantomimes evolved into *tableaux vivants* ("living pictures") depicting spectacular scenes of violence and suspense (a hero dangling from a cliff) as well as historical events (the storming of the Bastille.) The finale of *Uncle Tom's Cabin* offers a stunning *tableau vivant*.

A young writer named Guilbert de Pixérécourt (1773–1844) frequented such theaters and began writing full-length plays that incorporated spectacles and violence, or at least dangerous situations. In 1796 he wrote *Victor, or The Child of the Forest*, generally regarded as the play that defines melodrama as an art form. Pixérécourt's melodramas gained international popularity as they championed justice and liberty. In Germany, August Iffland (1759–1814) wrote *Familienstücke*, middle-class dramas dealing with families in crisis (e.g., foreclosure on the old homestead by a heartless banker). August Kotzebue (1761–1819), the most popular playwright in the Western world by 1810, wrote melodramas that appealed to middle-class morality. William

SPOTLIGHT   THE MINSTREL SHOW

It has been said that the minstrel show is the unique contribution of the United States to world theater. Because of its sociological implications and its influence on the most popular theater piece in nineteenth-century America, *Uncle Tom's Cabin*, it is worth considering here.

The minstrel show evolved, almost by accident, out of a curious custom of nineteenth-century theater practice. To give their audiences a full evening's entertainment, theater managers regularly scheduled *entr'actes* and "after-pieces" on their bills. Between each act of a play, often a song or a dance was performed while scenery was changed; after the regular play was concluded, a short play, often a farce, was presented to showcase the actors' versatility and to send the audience home on an upbeat note. Thus, it was not unusual for an audience to spend five or more hours in the theater. *Uncle Tom's Cabin*, by the way, was the first major American stage play to be performed without an after-piece because of its length.

In 1827 a middling actor named Thomas D. Rice was walking to a theater in Louisville, Kentucky, when he heard an intriguing melody. He followed the sound to a stable where he saw a slave grooming a horse while singing a catchy little song that went:

> You wheel about and turn about and do just so,
>
> You wheel about and turn about and jump Jim Crow.

To accompany his singing, the stable hand danced a little shuffle step. Rice saw the potential of this song for an *entr'acte* piece and paid the man to teach him the song and the dance. Rice hurried to the theater, where he applied bootblack to his face and performed his "Jim Crow"

number. Audiences loved Rice's innovation, and soon scores of imitators were presenting their own "blackface" acts, usually within the context of a formal theater piece. In 1843 the first complete evening of blackface acts was performed in New York by the Virginia Minstrels, who took their name from a popular variety act from Austria, the Tyrolean Minstrels. Thus "minstrels" (or "minstrelsy") became the generic term for this form of entertainment. Historically, the more significant term was "Jim Crow"—which became a generic term applied to Africans brought to America as slaves. So-called Jim Crow laws, written to deny people of African descent their rights, were common until the mid–twentieth century, when the civil rights movement finally forced their repeal.

The typical American minstrel show was divided into two parts, three if the short comedy or farce performed as an afterpiece is counted. The first section was the actual minstrel show, in which about nine performers sat in a semicircle of chairs onstage. In the middle chair was the emcee for the show, Mr. Interlocutor, who introduced the various acts and asked the right questions of the two comic "sidemen" who sat at either end of the row: Mr. Tambo played a tambourine while Mr. Bones shook a percussive instrument. Tambo and Bones provided most of the humor, most of it racist stereotyping of the worst kind. The other performers played musical instruments as they sang and danced. Much of the music was derived from songs of the plantation slaves, though sentimentalized and filtered for white audience tastes. Stephen Foster, who wrote such songs as "Camp Town Races" and "My Old Kentucky Home," was the foremost composer of minstrel music. The minstrel shows purported to show audiences slices of plantation life, but the portrait was skewed and only preserved the myth of the "happy

slave." The first half of the minstrel show concluded with the "walk around," in which the individual performers displayed their specialty for a final time. The second half was called the olio, named after the colorfully painted backdrops that provided visual interest for what was essentially a conventional vaudeville show. It was not performed entirely in blackface.

In *Uncle Tom's Cabin* the character of Topsy, the comic relief, is derived from the minstrel show. If you read the play, note the songs she sings, most of which have nothing to do with the plot but were inserted to please audiences.

It should be noted that the popularity of minstrelsy also promoted the formation of African American troupes who also "blacked up" (the common term for applying makeup) to conform to audience expectations. Callender's Georgia Minstrels (and its superstar Billy Kersands) and Haverly's Colored Minstrels were among the most popular of these; there was even an all-female troupe of minstrels performing with Sam T. Jack's Creoles. Ironically, the minstrel show, despite its racist elements, provided employment for many black entertainers.

However entertaining and popular the minstrel shows may have been— and they were phenomenally popular, even into the twentieth century—they perpetuated racist stereotypes. Minstrel shows withered away in the early twentieth century, largely because of protests led by W. E. B. Du Bois, among the earliest and most influential civil rights leaders. Even after minstrel shows disappeared, their influence could still be detected. For instance, the popular Christmas film *Holiday Inn* (1944) features Bing Crosby and Fred Astaire in a blackface number. Few popular entertainments in the history of world theater have so influenced the social fabric of a country as did the minstrel show.

Dunlap, the "father of the American theater," imported many of Kotzebue's dramas and thus began America's long-standing fascination with the melodrama, the most popular of which was *Uncle Tom's Cabin*. (See Spotlight box, America's Greatest Hit: *Uncle Tom's Cabin*.)

Because melodramas emphasized plot over character development, the sensational over the profound, simple morality over complex issues, the quality of the playwriting diminished. "I write for those who cannot read," Pixérécourt once said. As a result, the scene designer, the technical wizard, and the costume designer became forces as powerful as the actor and the playwright. Scenery drew people into the theater because middle-class audiences were eager to escape into the magical illusions created by designers. The death-defying situations melodramatists imposed on their heroes and heroines necessitated the invention of new stage machinery—and vice versa. Dioramas, panoramas, treadmills, trapdoors, elevators for moving scenery on- and offstage, and flying devices were developed to stage train wrecks, horse races, apparitions, and disappearances. Playwrights and theater managers often incorporated special effects into the plays simply because the machinery existed. *Uncle Tom's Cabin*—which depicts a shipwreck, Eliza trapped on the ice floes of the Ohio River, and a concluding *tableau*—illustrates the kinds of effects audiences clamored to see in 1852, just as modern audiences thrill to the sinking of the great ship in *Titanic*.

The Romantic Revolution and *Hernani*

On February 25, 1830, Victor Hugo's *Hernani* premiered at Paris's Comédie Française in one of the most famous opening nights in the history of the theater. It was a defining moment for Western drama, as it incorporated true Romantic drama into the popular theater.

In 1827 actors from London's Covent Garden performed Shakespeare's plays in Paris, the bastion of Neoclassicism. Playgoers at the Odeon Theater were enthralled by the romantic drama of Shakespeare, who freely mixed comedy with tragedy while defying the classical unities in his sprawling epics. The English actors sparked the imaginations of young intellectuals, most notably the 25-year-old Victor Hugo (1802–1885), who hurriedly wrote a play, *Cromwell*, in the manner of Shakespearean drama. Though a flawed work, Hugo's preface to the play became the manifesto for a new generation of playwrights, and his next play, *Hernani*, became the most celebrated and controversial French drama since Corneille's *Le Cid*. The avant-garde clashed openly with traditionalists, brawls ensued, and the papers were filled with essays about the merits of Hugo's bold experiment. Audiences voted with their pocketbooks, and the phenomenal success of *Hernani* finally released the Neoclassic stranglehold on European drama and promoted experimentation with form and content. Furthermore, it represented the triumph of populism in the French theater, thus making the common voice a respectable, as well as an economically powerful, influence on subsequent drama. Note that Hugo remains "good box office" even today. *Les Misérables* (1989), among the most successful musical dramas in the world, was adapted from his 1862 novel.

REALISM AND NATURALISM

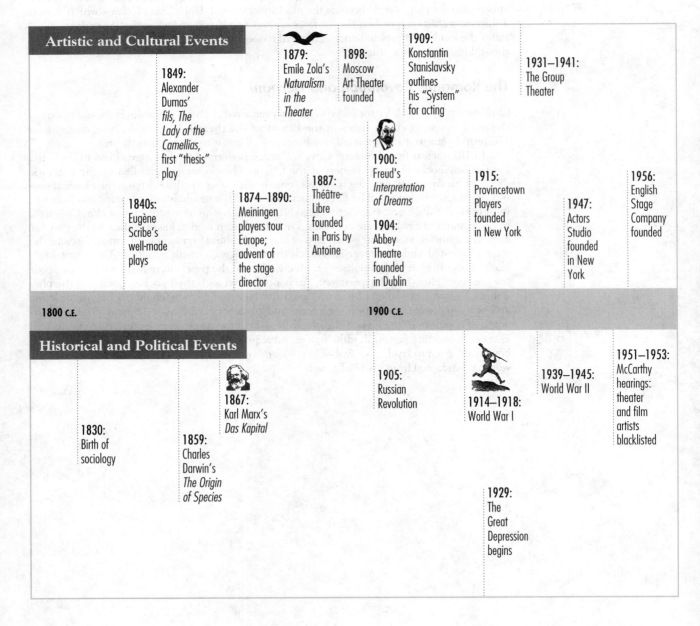

Artistic and Cultural Events

1849:
Alexander Dumas' *fils, The Lady of the Camellias,* first "thesis" play

1840s:
Eugène Scribe's well-made plays

1874–1890:
Meiningen players tour Europe; advent of the stage director

1879:
Emile Zola's *Naturalism in the Theater*

1887:
Théâtre-Libre founded in Paris by Antoine

1898:
Moscow Art Theater founded

1900:
Freud's *Interpretation of Dreams*

1904:
Abbey Theatre founded in Dublin

1909:
Konstantin Stanislavsky outlines his "System" for acting

1915:
Provincetown Players founded in New York

1931–1941:
The Group Theater

1947:
Actors Studio founded in New York

1956:
English Stage Company founded

1800 C.E.   1900 C.E.

Historical and Political Events

1830:
Birth of sociology

1859:
Charles Darwin's *The Origin of Species*

1867:
Karl Marx's *Das Kapital*

1905:
Russian Revolution

1914–1918:
World War I

1929:
The Great Depression begins

1939–1945:
World War II

1951–1953:
McCarthy hearings: theater and film artists blacklisted

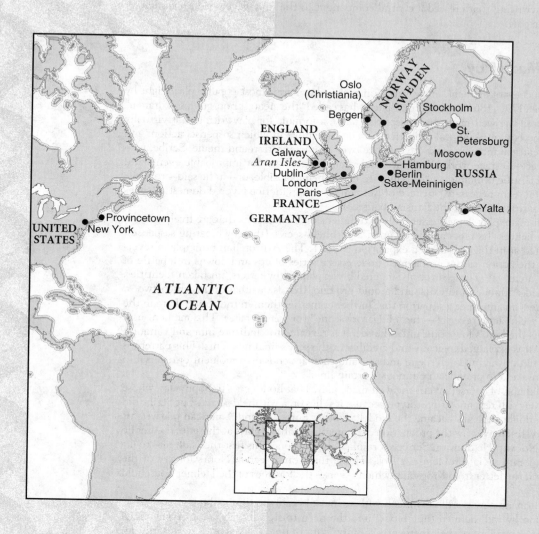

The Romantic spirit swept Europe and America amid the continuation of the scientific revolution fostered by the Enlightenment. It was spurred by empiricism, which placed a primary value on observation and experience. Consequently, this phenomenon inspired a new approach to playwriting that created a central component in the fully developed social drama: the well-made play.

The Well-Made Play

Despite the success of *Hernani*, Hugo was soon replaced as Paris's most popular playwright by Eugène Scribe (1791–1861), whom Eric Bentley has called "the greatest non-genius of drama." Scribe perfected the well-made play (*pièce bien faite*), a formula for playwriting that virtually guaranteed the box office appeal of intricate, believable plots in which suspense, action, and brilliantly theatrical moments take precedence over characterization and theme. Scribe, who composed over 400 stage works, disdained melodrama's penchant for improbable events and applied the scientific principles of "causality" to make them plausible, or—as he said—to make "the accidental seem necessary." Instead of Romantic settings, Scribe favored domestic scenes in his gently satiric dramas of the Parisian bourgeois.

The well-made play depicts essentially two-dimensional characters that are lively enough to engage audiences. Its plots are based upon a withheld secret (thereby creating suspense), which is hinted at in the well-crafted exposition of act 1. The Aristotelian principle of reversal advances the action as the protagonist undergoes a series of ups and downs in a battle of wits with an archrival. These reversals are credibly explained by letters, mistaken identities, carefully timed entrances and exits, and a quid pro quo, that is, a situation in which two or more characters misinterpret a situation that further enmeshes them in the action. Late in the play there is a climactic reversal—the "obligatory scene" (or *scène à faire*). This moment usually represents the hero's low point until the secret is revealed to vindicate him and vanquish the villain. All is explained logically and credibly in the play's final moments. This pattern is repeated in subtler ways in each scene and act, and each act ends on a moment of reversal to ensure suspense and to provide an ominous "curtain line."

Scribe did not, of course, invent the well-made play. That honor goes to Sophocles, whose *Oedipus the King* still remains its prototype because it relies on a withheld secret. But Scribe did perfect the formula and thus became the model for other European and American playwrights at midcentury. Ibsen oversaw the production of numerous Scribean plays at the state theater he managed in Norway. He drew on Scribe's formula as he fashioned his first thesis dramas to attack contemporary social problems. *A Doll's House* turns on a secret (Nora's forgery of the banknote) and the letter from Krogstad, which reverses the fortunes of the Helmer household forever.

The well-made play is still very much with us, most notably in film and television scriptwriting. Bound by well-defined time blocks and the need to stop the action for commercial messages (the equivalent of the nineteenth-century "curtain line"), TV writers necessarily adhere to the Scribean formula as they, too, write for mass audiences.

Influences on Realism

The new empiricism transformed society into a laboratory for sciences unknown to Galileo: sociology, economics, and especially psychology. Out of these would grow prescriptions for reordering human behavior, as the century's most provocative thinkers attempted to redress injustices spawned by outmoded beliefs about class, gender, and workers' rights. During the Industrial Revolution cities expanded to house factories and provide jobs for those who had previously tilled the soil. Some prospered, largely by exploiting workers, especially women and children, but many others were condemned to lives of poverty in teeming slums that bred disease and crime. Just as serfs rebelled against feudal lords and plebians toppled monarchs, so too would workers eventually rise against the captains of industry.

Predictably, a cultural revolution occurred in which the arts addressed social problems. The theater became a meetingplace in which audiences observed contemporary ills, live and close-up, considered arguments for their solution, and (in theory) returned to their communities to improve the world for all. Theater became a "here and now" enterprise, and no longer viewed the human situation through the Romantic past. A concern for social problems is hardly a new phenomenon emanating from Western stages. Because it is a communal activity, the theater has an innate social dimension. What made the social voice of the late nineteenth century so distinctive was its insistence on being heard in uncompromising and realistic terms.

While Romantic philosophers and literary artists laid much of the foundation for the socially conscious dramas, other important contributors also changed the theater, though they were not themselves artists. Six are noteworthy because they represent significant new disciplines that changed Western drama:

- **Auguste Comte** (1798–1857), often called the father of sociology, was a mathematician and philosopher who defined "the science of society." Comte and his disciples employed the empirical methodology of the hard sciences to social problems. Applying Comte's methods to the stage, artists saw the theater as a "bell jar" in which the precise conditions of a social problem (e.g., poverty) were re-created. The audience observed them with the detachment and rationality of a laboratory scientist as the problem was dissected and a cure was suggested.

- **Charles Darwin** (1809–1892) wrote *The Origin of Species* in 1859 and radically altered human thought. His studies of plant and animal life caused Darwin to conclude that beings (including humans) are products of their heredity and environment, and that life involves a perpetual battle in which only the "fittest" (i.e., those who adapt favorably) survive. Darwin's controversial theories, articulated by Herbert Spencer in his writings about "social Darwinism," had a number of implications for the theater. His emphasis on environment provoked theater artists to create, as faithfully as possible, the environment that created social problems. Whether it be the stultifying propriety of the Helmer household in Ibsen's *A Doll's House* or the dismal squalor of Maxim Gorky's Russian "flophouse" in *The Lower Depths*, playwrights, directors, and scene designers labored to create absolute worlds in which characters acted as their heredity and environments dictated.

- **Friedrich Nietzsche** (1844–1900), a German philosopher and theater critic, proclaimed "God is dead" in 1885. Because heredity and environment were viewed as determinants of human behavior, the role of divine providence was significantly reduced in dramatic literature. Miraculous endings and the *deus ex machina* disappeared. Tragic resolutions, which implied a kind of cosmic justice, gave way to the unhappy ending. Villainy diminished as moral absolutism was replaced by situational ethics because playwrights argued that miscreants were victims of forces beyond their control.

- **Karl Marx** (1818–1883) advanced socialism, a term that existed long before he wrote his famous manifesto, *Das Kapital*, in 1867. Like Darwin, Marx argued that change was inevitable and that workers could change their social and economic institutions by banding together to overthrow their oppressors. For Marx, art was the property of the bourgeois (which had usurped the monarchy) and must reflect the plight of the proletariat, which he esteemed as rulers in a classless society. Many early realistic plays, such as Gerhard Hauptman's *The Weavers* (1892), reflected Marx's attitude in their focus on the economic conditions that repressed workers. Dramatists, such as George Bernard Shaw in England and Eugene O'Neill in the United States, reflected many of the social concerns espoused by Europe's socialist reformers. Today Marxist and cultural materialist literary criticism considers art in terms of its class and economic issues.

- **Sigmund Freud** (1856–1939) and **Carl Jung** (1875–1961) studied the workings of the mind and popularized psychology. Though their approaches differed, both were concerned with motivations of human behavior. To Freud, actions were the result of a subconscious battle among the id (the agent of pleasure in the psyche), the ego (the ethical agent), and the superego (the "reality" or "parent" agent). Freud drew on classical mythology for his vocabulary. An ancient Greek might have argued that the id was the Dionysian force pulsing through a human, while the ego was the Apollonian. To Jung, the struggle was between one's conscious and the unconscious. While the ideas of these early psychologists are too complex to summarize here, their influence on drama and performance was enormous. Playwrights often dealt with abnormal states of mind, as in August Strindberg's *Miss Julie* and Eugene O'Neill's *The Hairy Ape*. Formerly taboo (a Freudian term) subjects, such as sexual frustration, became commonplace. Deviant behavior was no longer condemned, for behavior was now considered a product of a mental state over which one had little control. Most importantly, the old Aristotelian element of character usurped the primacy of plot in dramatic structure. Modern playwrights were—and still are—more concerned with the complexities of the human mind than with telling intricate stories. For actors, the psychologist's concern for the reasons behind human behavior was translated into a new acting style in which concepts like "subtext," "intentions," and "motivations" are paramount.

The Problem Play

Sociologists, evolutionists, philosophers, socialists, and psychologists created an atmosphere that precipitated radical changes in the drama in the late nineteenth century. But, as is often the case, an earlier dramatist anticipated such changes. In 1849 Alexander Dumas *fils* (1824–1895) wrote *La Dame aux Camellias* (*The Lady of the Camellias*), often regarded as the first *pièce à thèse* ("thesis" or "discussion" play). In it, he attempted to defend the dignity of the "fallen woman" as he portrayed a love affair between a respectable young man (Armande) and a courtesan (Marguerite). Though this much-imitated play, known as *Camille*, is a melodrama, Dumas' *fils* attempted to break new ground. He stated his intentions in a letter to a friend; the italicized portions here most directly reflect the spirit of the drama that followed:

> I realize the prime requisites of a play are laughter, tears, passion, emotion, interest, curiosity: to leave life at the cloak room. But I maintain that if, by means of all these ingredients and without minimizing one of them, I can exercise some influence over society; if, instead of treating effects, I can treat causes; if, for example, while I satirize and dramatize adultery, *I can find means to force people to discuss the problems* and the lawmakers to revise the law, I shall have done more than my part as a poet, I shall have done my duty as a man. . . . We need invent nothing, we have only to observe, remember, feel, coordinate, restore. *As for the basis, the real*; as for the facts, what is possible; as for means, what is ingenious: that is all that can be asked of us. [Emphasis added]

The decade of the 1870s was especially important in the Western theater's march toward realism. Although Ibsen wrote *The Pillars of Society* in 1877 and *A Doll's House* two years later—the works most often cited as the first genuine "problem plays"—events in Germany and France helped create the cultural atmosphere for Ibsen's daring new works.

The Rise of the Director

In 1874 Berlin hosted a provincial theater company, the Meiningen Players, who arrived in the capital for a four-week engagement. However, they extended their run by six weeks to satisfy audiences clamoring for the new "realism" they brought to the stage. The company derived its name from the small duchy of Saxe-Meiningen, where Duke Georg II indulged his passion for theater by mounting extraordinary productions in which all of the elements of scenery, custom, music, acting, and stage pictures were coordinated by a single vision: the duke's. Working with Ludwig Chronegk, his stage manager, the duke meticulously created realistic worlds for such plays as Shakespeare's *Julius Caeser* and Schiller's *William Tell*. He invented appropriate stage business for even the most faceless "extra," and grouped his crowds in aesthetically appealing compositions. The star system, which dominated Western theater in the nineteenth century, was replaced by an ensemble approach to performance. By 1880 the Meiningen Players were the most admired theatrical troupe in the Western world. They toured throughout Europe, Scandinavia, and eventually Russia, where the young Konstantin Stanislavsky saw them and was inspired to liberate the Russian theater from its ponderous acting techniques. The duke of Saxe-Meiningen is often referred to as the progenitor of the modern stage director because he transformed the theater by encouraging visual realism and ensemble performance.

Naturalism

Meanwhile, in France, Émile Zola (1840–1902), who had applied Comte's theories to the novel, turned the theater into a social laboratory where audiences could observe humans in the squalid environments that shaped their aberrant behaviors. Zola declared that he was "antiart" because art—especially in the French theater, now dominated by tawdry melodramas and farces—was too contrived to be effective. He wanted a theater that depicted random, mundane events: "One simply takes from life the history of a being, or a group of beings, whose acts one faithfully records." Zola referred to such actions, and the all-important environment in which they take place, as "*la tranche à vie*" ("slice of life"), a key term in the evolution of realistic drama.

Actually, Zola, like his countryman Henri Becque (1837–1899), and the Swedish playwright August Strindberg (1849–1912), was advancing an extreme form of realism: *naturalism*. The term defines both a philosophy and a theatrical style:

- Naturalism is a philosophy of determinism (derived from Darwin and Spencer) contending that humans are products of their heredity and their environment. Naturalistic plays are characterized by gloominess and pessimism because their characters are trapped in a world from which there is no escape.
- Naturalism, as a theatrical style, places a premium on actualistic details in scenery, costumes, and lighting, and it demands an acting style that is thoroughly lifelike. Naturalism is familiar, largely in the form of modern films about the "mean streets." Actors such as Al Pacino, Denzel Washington, Meryl Streep, and Edward James Olmos specialize in naturalistic films. Film accommodates naturalism especially well because the camera takes us into actual locations and captures their details with photographic precision.

At the risk of oversimplifying complex issues, one might say that naturalism places realism under a microscope in its quest to portray life onstage. Or as one wag put it, "Realism shows life as it is, while Naturalism shows life as it is—only worse."

Concerns with heredity and environment have lasted well into this century. The 1957 Broadway musical *West Side Story* illustrates these points in one of the play's most provocative songs, "Gee, Officer Krupke." The Jets, a street gang, satirize their frequent encounters with police officers, social workers, psychologists, and penologists. At one point they rationalize their delinquency with these lines:

> *Our mothers all are junkies,*
>
> *Our fathers all are drunks,*
>
> *Golly Moses, naturally we're punks.*

We might refer to this defense as the "hereditary principle." Later in the song, one of the Jets asserts that "I'm depraved on accounta I'm deprived." This is the other half of the equation, which we might call "the environmental principle." Although lyricist Stephen Sondheim and composer Leonard Bernstein were satirizing social problems in the 1950s, they echo the concerns of the early realists of the previous century.

While Zola was a visionary, he was more successful as a novelist than as a playwright because he found it difficult to reduce the random details of his novels on the stage. Despite his calls for reform, his plays, such as *Thérèse Raquin* (1873), retained an essentially melodramatic quality in which sensationalism supersedes logic. Zola's "Preface to *Thérèse Raquin*," a manifesto for the naturalists, is more important than the play. Zola's dreams of a "history of a group of beings" were realized by Anton Chekhov and his successors. His call for a theater language that replicates "spoken conversation . . . free from declamation, big words, and grand sentiments" manifests itself in the writings of such contemporaries as David Mamet and Marsha Norman. The triumph of Zola's ideal may be found in Norman's Pulitzer Prize–winning play, *'Night Mother*, which probes a woman's suicide in one lengthy act.

The Fathers of Realism: Ibsen, Strindberg, and Chekhov

Ironically, true realism in the modern theater sprang from the least likely places—Scandinavia and Russia. The geographical and cultural remoteness of Norway, Sweden, and czarist Russia allowed the Scandinavians Henrik Ibsen and August Strindberg and the Russians Anton Chekhov and Konstantin Stanislavsky the freedom to experiment with new forms, unfettered by the weight of long-standing dramatic traditions.

Ibsen's most famous works were shaped in no small part by popular Continental dramas, particularly Scribe's well-made plays. From Scribe he learned how to engage an audience through a well-structured play that builds to a satisfying climax. Ibsen's genius, as Bernard Shaw points out in his seminal essay "The Quintessence of Ibsenism" (1913), was the manner in which he inserted pointed discussions about social issues between the crisis and climax of the old Scribean formula. Shaw's analysis remains among the best explications of Ibsen's method:

> Formerly you had what was called a well-made play: an exposition in the first act, a situation in the second, an unraveling in the third. Now you have exposition, situation, and discussion; and the discussion is the test of the playwright. The critics protest in vain. They declare that discussions are not dramatic, and that art should not be didactic. Neither the playwrights nor the public take the smallest notice of them. The discussion conquered Europe in Ibsen's *A Doll's House* and now the serious playwright recognizes in the discussion not only the main test of his highest powers, but also the real center of the play's interest.

Ibsen's provocative dramas struck a chord as he outraged the old establishment, who considered him dangerous; he left Norway and wrote the majority of his works in Germany and Italy. The new generation saw in Ibsen's works a defiant voice that spoke for them: Hauptmann in Germany, Shaw in England, and James A. Herne in America. Women also emerged as important voices, both as characters in plays and, gradually, as writers. Susan Glaspell, instrumental in the emergence of a new American drama, wrote Ibsen-like plays as early as 1915. American actresses such as Minnie Maddern Fiske built their reputations, in part, by playing Ibsen's well-etched heroines.

In Sweden, Strindberg was also writing the new drama, though his plays are less concerned with the social implications of their protagonists' dilemmas. Strindberg, who suffered periods of mental illness, was drawn more to the inner workings of his characters' minds. If Ibsen was the most influential in portraying social dilemmas, Strindberg inspired modernists with his intense psychological portraits. In particular, the Swedish playwright had a profound effect on the style and thematic concerns of Eugene O'Neill, whose autobiographical play *Long Day's Journey into Night* is more aligned with Strindberg's dramaturgy than that of Ibsen's.

With the benefit of a hundred years of hindsight, we can now say that it was the Russian Anton Chekhov (1860–1904) who most fully portrayed realism onstage. Although Ibsen claimed that he wished "to produce the illusion of reality," his plays retain elements associated with nineteenth-century melodrama. Chekhov, however, devised a drama of what has been called "the action of inaction." In a letter to a friend, Chekhov defined his theatrical purpose:

Let the things that happen on stage be just as complex and yet as simple as they are in real life. For instance, people are having a meal at a table, just having a meal, but at the same time their happiness is being created or their lives are being smashed up.

Here Chekhov suggests one of the primary characteristics of his dramaturgy: the action most often occurs offstage, and his protagonists are most often unaware of the changes in their lives. Hence, Chekhovian plays are frequently considered "anticlimactic" because they do not build to a traditional climax and a resolution of the conflict. As so often happens in life, characters go on in ignorance, trapped by their own inertia. Sadly, they remain static in a world that is changing rapidly.

The typical Chekhov play consists primarily of a series of seemingly inconsequential conversations among a variety of characters. Rather than place an audience's emotional investment in a single character, Chekhov diffuses the sympathetic response to distance audiences from the dramatic action so they can see the folly (a comic response) of the frustrated, nearly tragic lives of his characters. For this reason, Chekhov's plays are customarily designated as tragicomedies. With its lack of discernible action, absence of theatrical climaxes, focus on the mundane, and refusal to resolve conflicts in either the traditional comedic or tragic ways, Chekhov invented a drama that is, in Francis Ferguson's estimation, "the closest to the reality of the human situation." Both realists (e.g., Tennessee Williams) and nonrealists (e.g., Samuel Beckett) have acknowledged their indebtedness to Chekhov's style.

Intimate Theaters

The new realism necessitated changes in theatrical architecture. Nineteenth-century playhouses across Europe and in America were cavernous because they were designed to house the elaborate scenery required by melodrama and to ensure enough seats to generate revenues to pay for the spectacles. These enormous spaces forced actors to enlarge gestures, to speak in thundering tones, and, in general, to portray characters in larger-than-life dimensions. (You can still see this style in many of the early silent movies that used actors trained in the older methods.) New theater spaces provided intimacy so actors could sit and talk in the natural tones ne-

Anton Chekhov reads one of his plays for Stanislavsky and the members of the Moscow Art Theater.

289

cessitated by the scripts. Furthermore, the controversial nature of the new works meant smaller audiences and the threat of censorship. Consequently, a number of intimate theaters sprang up that placed audiences, now numbering perhaps a hundred, closer to the actors, who could speak naturally and who no longer needed grand gestures and grimaces. Strindberg's own theater in Stockholm was aptly named the Intimate Theatre.

Among the most important of the new theaters was the Théâtre-Libre (Free Theatre), founded in Paris in May 1887 by André Antoine (1858–1941), a French civil servant whose interest in the new social dramas led him to transform performance modes. Antoine named his enterprise after Victor Hugo's Romantic essay "A Theatre Set Free." Like Hugo, Antoine wanted to free the theater from its old constraints by creating a new art for the commoner who could see plays addressing relevant social problems. To finance his venue, he sold season subscriptions to his "theater club," where he produced the new works of such dramatists as Zola, Ibsen, Strindberg, Tolstoy, and Hauptmann. Not only were the new scripts daring, the style in which they were presented was also innovative. Antoine insisted on new three-dimensional scenery for each production, and he advocated the use of natural light sources. He often brought "the real thing" onstage (he used actual beef carcasses in Fernand Icre's *The Butchers*). His actors stood with their backs to the audience and spoke in conversational tones. Everything about an Antoine production was calculated to suggest that the audience was watching real life through an invisible fourth wall.

The integrity and success of the Théâtre-Libre inspired imitators across Europe and, eventually, the United States and Latin America. In Germany, Otto Brahm created the *Frei Buhne* (Free Theatre) in 1889. In London, J. T. Grien opened the Independent Theater in March 1891 with a production of Ibsen's *Ghosts*. He soon persuaded one of London's most thoughtful critics and social thinkers, Bernard Shaw, to write plays for his avant-garde enterprise. In 1904 the Abbey Theatre opened in Dublin to encourage native voices, speaking in purely Irish accents. The poet-playwright William Butler Yeats, Lady Augusta Gregory (herself an excellent dramatist), and John Millington Synge founded the Abbey, which still flourishes today. The "little theater" movement arrived in the United States in 1915 when George Cram Cook and his wife, Susan Glaspell, founded the Provincetown Players on Cape Cod. In New York City, Cook and his company converted a stable on Macdougal Street into the Playwright's Theatre. In 1918 it became the Provincetown Playhouse, the site generally recognized as the birthplace of the modern American theater. Closer to our time, the Market Theatre in Johannesburg, South Africa, has captured the spirit of the independent theater; you may read about its inception and purpose in Chapter 8.

Whether in Paris, Berlin, Stockholm, Dublin, or Greenwich Village, the new independent theaters had common goals. All were committed to new works concerned with contemporary society. All were drawn to the new production style that sought to give the illusion of real life onstage (though they also experimented with Expressionism and symbolist drama). Perhaps most importantly, all disdained the commercial theater.

The Second Generation of Realists

Realism and naturalism have flourished in the West throughout much of the twentieth century, particularly in the United States, where the Group Theater and Actors Studio fostered actors and playwrights who were especially adept at realism. The period from 1930 through the 1950s might be considered the golden age of realistic drama. Playwrights such as O'Neill, Lillian Hellman, Clifford Odets, Tennessee Williams, and Arthur Miller were at the height of their powers. In turn, they influenced a new generation of American playwrights, including Lorraine Hansberry, Edward Albee, David Mamet, and even commercial playwrights such as Neil Simon.

As might be expected, a vibrant African American theater has emerged in response to problems created by segregation and racism. Most of these dramas tend toward the tradition of the social realists, though there have been attempts to incorporate traditional African theater modes in the writing and performance of the plays. Because so much African American theater is a product of the African diaspora, which uprooted people from their homeland, important plays by August Wilson and Derek Walcott are included in Chapter 8, as well as a Spotlight box on Hansberry's *A Raisin in the Sun*.

England, too, produced a number of significant realists, none more important than John Osborne (1929–1995), whose scathing social drama *Look Back in Anger* (1956) reinvigorated the British theater and yielded a new generation of angry young men and women such as John Arden, Edward Bond, Sheilah Delaney, and Caryl Churchill. Like their predecessor in social drama, Bernard Shaw, they questioned those institutions and social conventions that limited an individual's freedom and growth.

However, by midcentury social drama frequently was driven by a cynicism and hopelessness that was prompted by the cold war and atomic weapons, and that transcended the earlier realism of Ibsen, Shaw, and Odets. Compare two speeches by leading realists. In Odets's *Awake and Sing* (1936), a Depression-era youth vows to fight for a better world:

> Get teams [of workers] together all over. Spit on your hands and get to work. And with enough teams together maybe we'll get steam in the warehouse so our fingers don't freeze off. Maybe we'll fix it so life won't be printed on dollar bills.

In Osborne's drama, written only 20 years later, a spokesman for the postwar generation of disaffected youth laments that

> there aren't any good, brave causes left. If the big bang does come, and we all get killed off, it won't be in aid of the old-fashioned grand design. It'll just be for the Brave New-nothing-very-much-thank-you. About as pointless and inglorious as stepping in front of a bus.

As you read the varied social dramas herein, note those in which change seems possible and those in which the protagonists feel trapped by time and circumstance.

A DOLL'S HOUSE

HENRIK IBSEN

HENRIK IBSEN (1828–1906)

Ibsen, often called the father of modern drama, was born in the small village of Skien in southeastern Norway. The son of a prosperous merchant, he was raised in the relative comfort of a large mansion until 1836, when his father declared bankruptcy. The move to less plush environs and ostracism from the local community left a permanent mark on Ibsen. His bitterness is reflected in many of his early poems, his 1881 unfinished autobiography, and particularly in the thematic concerns of his great social dramas.

Working as an apprentice to an apothecary, the young Ibsen dreamed of becoming a doctor. When the qualifying exams proved too difficult for him, he immersed himself in the theater as both a scholar and manager. While he was a successful scholar, theater management was not his forte. At the age of 23 he accepted the position of stage manager at the new theater in Bergen, and six years later he was named artistic director of the Christiania [Oslo] Norway Theater. Neither venue proved successful, and when the Christiania Theater was closed in 1862, Ibsen began a self-imposed exile. He spent most of the remainder of his life in Italy and Germany, sharpening his critical vision of late-nineteenth-century Europe and honing his craft as a playwright. In 1891 he returned to his homeland, where, after being incapacitated by paralyzing strokes, he died in 1906.

His dramatic works may be divided into five distinct literary styles. His earliest works, completed between 1850 and 1865, consist of verse dramas such as *Cataline* (1850)—his first attempt at drama—and *The Pretenders* (1864), which dealt with Scandinavian history. Out of this period grew a series of dramatic poems, also based on his native history. They are epic tales of individual struggles, like *Brand* (1866) and *Peer Gynt* (1867). His next plays, usually called "social protest plays," include *The Pillars of Society* (1877), *A Doll's House* (1879), *Ghosts* (1881), and *An Enemy of the People* (1882). They deal with the social and economic inequities he observed throughout Europe. As he continued to mature, he moved to psychological dramas about interpersonal relationships: *The Wild Duck* (1885), *Rosmersholm* (1887), and *Hedda Gabler* (1890) typify these plays. He concluded his career deeply immersed in plays that were symbolist—*The Master Builder* (1892), *John Gabreil Bjorkman* (1896), and *When We Dead Awaken* (1900).

Bernard Shaw, his chief defender in England, saw Ibsen as an innovator who placed discussion at the heart of modern drama and as a courageous leader who tackled social injustice no matter how unpopular or offensive the subject matter. Indeed, it was not uncommon for critics to declare him vulgar and coarse. Witness a brief sampling of critical commentary that greeted *Ghosts*, which deals with venereal disease:

> Ibsen's positively abominable play entitled *Ghosts* [is a] disgusting representation. . . . An open drain; a loathsome sore unbandaged; a dirty act done publicly. . . . Absolutely loathsome and fetid . . . a mass of vulgarity, egotism, coarseness, and absurdity.

> As foul and filthy a concoction as has ever been allowed to disgrace the boards of an English theatre. . . . Dull and disgusting. . . . Nastiness and malodorousness laid on thickly as with a trowel.

> [A] Morbid, unhealthy, unwholesome and disgusting story.

In spite of this reception, Ibsen's work survives.

While his poetic dramas are marked by episodic plots, his social and psychological plays, generally considered to be his most important works, are essentially realistic. Their climactic plots grow from a gradual illumination of past transgressions, the discovery of which leads to the major reversal in the play. In *A Doll's House* the revelation of Nora's loan precipitates the climax of the play. In crafting these works, Ibsen employs the components of the well-made play: the withheld secret and the obligatory scene. Rather than using them as a springboard to move the action swiftly to its resolution, however, he suspends the action for an in-depth discussion of the play's social issues. Thus, his plays move from the realm of entertainment, sentimentality, and melodrama to genuine social commentary.

The conflicts between one's duty to self and one's duty to society, between social and moral restrictions and one's quest for personal sovereignty are Ibsen's primary thematic concerns. His leading characters, whether in pursuit of personal or political goals, invariably end up unfulfilled because they either sacrifice their own integrity or achieve success at the expense of others on whom they trample. *Brand* and *Peer Gynt* are excellent illustrations of this concept. Brand, uncompromising in his dedication to his ideal of what religion should be, sacrifices everything dear to him only to be destroyed by an avalanche that thunders, "God is love!" Peer follows a life of hedonism and compromise, only to find himself facing death with no sense of integrity, purpose, or accomplishment.

A DOLL'S HOUSE (1879)

Like many realistic plays, *A Doll's House* is based on an actual occurrence. A young mother named Laura Kieler illegally signed a large banknote to finance treatment for her tubercular husband. Trying to cash a forged check, she was apprehended, charged as an unfit mother by her husband, and committed to an asylum. Similarly, *A Doll's House* tells the simple story of a young wife, Nora Helmer, who appears to be the perfect model of a nineteenth-century homemaker. She is totally devoted to husband and children, but she unknowingly creates a potentially explosive situation. In borrowing money to finance a lifesaving trip for her sick husband, Torvald, Nora forges her father's name and thus violates both social customs and public statutes. After her husband's recovery, the Helmers are "one happy little family" until the loan's originator, Nils Krogstad, attempts to blackmail Nora. Assuming that Torvald will appreciate her lifesaving initiative when her secret is revealed, Nora is shattered when her husband castigates her as "a hypocrite, a liar—worse, worse—a criminal!" with "no religion, no morals, no sense of duty!" Horrified, Nora refuses to continue playing the "doll's role" and tells Torvald that she is leaving. When he reminds her that should she leave she would be neglecting her "most sacred duties"— her duties toward her husband and her children, she reveals that she must follow "another duty which is equally sacred. . . . My duty towards myself." As Nora exited, the reverberation of the heavy door closing was heard throughout the Western theatrical world.

The ending of the play was so shocking that many producers refused to stage the play and demanded that the ending be changed. (A leading actress of the day turned down the role of Nora for fear that her admirers might see her as one who supported Nora's "unwomanly" action.) To secure venues for his work, Ibsen wrote an alternate ending to the play in which Nora remains with Torvald, an outcome much more palatable to his conservative, Victorian audience.

Both the content and form of the play shocked nineteenth-century audiences. Accustomed to sentimental comedies, well-made plays, and melodramas wherein traditional values always triumphed, the original audiences of *A Doll's House* were taken aback by the effrontery of a woman who asserts her individuality at the expense of her family. As the climax of the play approached, they no doubt anticipated a contrite Nora who would win forgiveness from a benevolent Torvald, thereby ensuring a happy ending.

The dramatic form in which Ibsen's ideas were expressed was equally foreign to audiences in 1879. They were accustomed to plays in which the emotional intensity grew gradually from the exposition to the climax; Ibsen halted the action in midcrisis to discuss the reasons behind Nora's forgery and for her leaving. The audience was thus forced to hold its emotions in check and confront the social implications of her actions.

Beyond its revolutionary style, two problems arise when analyzing the play. First, Ibsen's basic premise was misunderstood. Original audiences mistakenly assumed, "much to Ibsen's chagrin," as theater historian Oscar Brockett has noted, that he was promoting a "feminist" point of view. True, the play served as a rallying point for early advocates of feminism who demanded suffrage and more legal rights. While considering this interpretation, we must remember that fundamentally the play advocates the sovereignty of the individual and is not a piece of feminist propaganda. Michael Meyer, among Ibsen's most respected biographers, argues that the play stresses "that the primary duty of anyone was to find out who he or she really was and to become that person." Indeed, Ibsen himself, in an address to the Norwegian Women's Rights League, stated that he "must disclaim the honor of having consciously worked for the women's rights movement. I am not even quite clear what this women's rights movement really is. To me it has seemed a problem of humanity in general."

Second, what we regard as a glaring error in Ibsen's craftsmanship went essentially unnoticed during early productions of the play. While those who debated the appropriateness of Nora's departure focused on her action, the most disconcerting aspect from the point of view of the play's construction is that in the discussion scene Nora, heretofore a rather sheltered "plaything" or "doll," suddenly metamorphoses into an articulate social advocate. She launches into an exquisite discourse on the new morality, which champions the rights of the individual over the expectations of society. Her sudden transformation seems an abrupt departure from the logic of the action which governed the play to that point.

Furthermore, the 1879 audience may have overlooked another innovative aspect of Ibsen's style: his use of the setting as an analogy for theme. Even contemporary audiences, predisposed to adopt a feminist reading of the play, might also overlook the significance of the setting so carefully described by Ibsen. While Neoclassic writers confined the action to a single location, and Romantic writers, who disdained the unity of place, presented their action as sprawling across a continent, Ibsen confined the action to a single setting to *enhance* his theme rather than to observe or oppose any "rules." In *A Doll's House*, Ibsen gives us the literal and figurative creation of Torvald's "doll house."

It is no accident that the play transpires in what Victorians called the "parlor" (literally, a room for talk or discussion). Today we might call it a "living room." The first words of the text describe it as "A comfortably and tastefully . . . furnished room," with all the amenities of the day—"a piano . . . a stove lined with porcelain . . . armchairs and a rocking chair"—a cozy home for a "twittering skylark," a safe habitat for a "rustling squirrel." In the opening scenes it is an ideal "doll's house." But before we are 20 minutes into the play, it is clear that this comfortable "living room" becomes an uncomfortable "dying room" in which Nora is incarcerated. She has been sentenced by Torvald and society to spend her life shuffling between the other important rooms—the bedroom, the kitchen, and the children's room—to carry out the traditional roles of the Victorian woman. Nora is confronted with the choice of accepting this fate or exerting her individuality.

Should she remain confined in this room where there is security without liberty? Or, should she liberate herself at the expense of security? While she initially accepts her imprisonment because she believes in the possibility of what Torvald calls "the miracle of miracles" happening in their marriage, her optimism is destroyed by Torvald's reaction to her secret. His selfishness, his preoccupation with his public reputation, and his attacks on her fitness as wife and mother expose him as a self-centered manipulator, not as a loving husband. Ironically, the living room eventually becomes not only a "liberating room" for Nora but a prison for Torvald, its former warden.

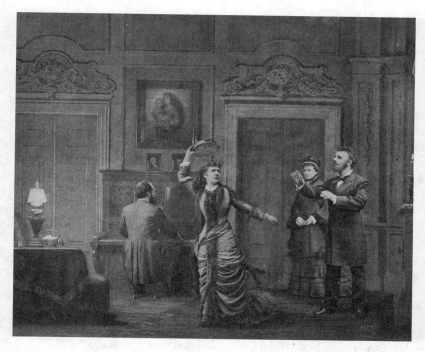

The original production (left) of A Doll's House (1879) and a recent version (right) of Ibsen's famous play as performed in India by actor-director Rudra Prasad Sen Gupta and his wife, Swatilekha Sen Gupta.

A DOLL'S HOUSE

HENRIK IBSEN

Translated by Michael Meyer

LIST OF CHARACTERS

TORVALD HELMER, *a lawyer*
NORA, *his wife*
DR. RANK
MRS. LINDE
NILS KROGSTAD, *also a lawyer*
The Helmers' three small children
ANNE-MARIE, *their nurse*
HELEN, *the maid*
A PORTER

SCENE: *The action takes place in the Helmers' apartment.*

ACT 1

A comfortably and tastefully, but not expensively furnished room. Backstage right a door leads out to the hall; backstage left, another door to Helmer's study. Between these two doors stands a piano. In the middle of the left-hand wall is a door, with a window downstage of it. Near the window, a round table with armchairs and a small sofa. In the right-hand wall, slightly upstage, is a door, downstage of this, against the same wall, a stove lined with porcelain tiles, with a couple of armchairs and a rocking-chair in front of it. Between the stove and the side door is a small table. Engravings on the wall. A what-not with china and other bric-a-brac; a small bookcase with leather-bound books. A carpet on the floor; a fire in the stove. A winter day.

A bell rings in the hall outside. After a moment, we hear the front door being opened. Nora enters the room, humming contentedly to herself. She is wearing outdoor clothes and carrying a lot of parcels, which she puts down on the table right. She leaves the door to the hall open; through it, we can see a Porter carrying a Christmas tree and a basket. He gives these to the Maid, who has opened the door for them.

NORA. Hide that Christmas tree away, Helen. The children mustn't see it before I've decorated it this evening. (*To the porter, taking out her purse.*) How much—?

PORTER. A shilling.

NORA. Here's half a crown. No, keep it.

The Porter touches his cap and goes. Nora closes the door. She continues to laugh happily to herself as she removes her coat, etc. She takes from her pocket a bag containing macaroons and eats a couple. Then, she tiptoes across and listens at her husband's door.

NORA. Yes, he's here. (*Starts humming again as she goes over to the table, right.*)

HELMER (*from his room*). Is that my skylark twittering out there?

NORA (*opening some of the parcels*). It is!

HELMER. Is that my squirrel rustling?

NORA. Yes!

HELMER. When did my squirrel come home?

NORA. Just now. (*Pops the bag of macaroons in her pocket and wipes her mouth.*) Come out here, Torvald, and see what I've bought.

HELMER. You mustn't disturb me! (*Short pause; then he opens the door and looks in, his pen in his hand.*) Bought, did you say? All that? Has my little squanderbird been overspending again?

NORA. Oh, Torvald, surely we can let ourselves go a little this year! It's the first Christmas we don't have to scrape.

HELMER. Well, you know, we can't afford to be extravagant.

NORA. Oh yes, Torvald, we can be a little extravagant now. Can't we? Just a tiny bit? You've got a big salary now, and you're going to make lots and lots of money.

HELMER. Next year, yes. But my new salary doesn't start till April.

NORA. Pooh; we can borrow till then.

HELMER. Nora! (*Goes over to her and takes her playfully by the ear.*) What a little spendthrift you are! Suppose I were to borrow fifty pounds today, and you spent it all over Christmas, and then on New Year's Eve a tile fell off a roof onto my head—

NORA (*puts her hand over his mouth*). Oh, Torvald! Don't say such dreadful things!

HELMER. Yes, but suppose something like that did happen? What then?

NORA. If anything as frightful as that happened, it wouldn't make much difference whether I was in debt or not.

HELMER. But what about the people I'd borrowed from?

NORA. Them? Who cares about them? They're strangers.

HELMER. Oh, Nora, Nora, how like a woman! No, but seriously, Nora, you know how I feel about this. No debts! Never borrow! A home that is founded on debts can never be a place of freedom and beauty. We two have stuck it out bravely up to now; and we shall continue to do so for the short time we still have to.

NORA (*goes over towards the stove*). Very well, Torvald. As you say.

HELMER (*follows her*). Now, now! My little songbird mustn't droop her wings. What's this? Is little squirrel sulking? (*Takes out his purse.*) Nora; guess what I've got here!

NORA (*turns quickly*). Money!

HELMER. Look. (*Hands her some banknotes.*) I know how these small expenses crop up at Christmas.

NORA (*counts them*). One—two—three—four. Oh, thank you, Torvald, thank you! I should be able to manage with this.

HELMER. You'll have to.

NORA. Yes, yes, of course I will. But come over here, I want to show you everything I've bought. And so cheaply! Look, here are new clothes for Ivar—and a sword. And a horse and a trumpet for Bob. And a doll and a cradle for Emmy—they're nothing much, but she'll pull them apart in a few days. And some bits of material and handkerchiefs for the maids. Old Anne-Marie ought to have had something better, really.

HELMER. And what's in that parcel?

NORA (*cries*). No, Torvald, you mustn't see that before this evening!

HELMER. Very well. But now, tell me, you little spendthrift, what do you want for Christmas?

NORA. Me? Oh, pooh, I don't want anything.

HELMER. Oh, yes, you do. Now tell me, what, within reason, would you most like?

NORA. No, I really don't know. Oh, yes—Torvald—!

HELMER. Well?

NORA (*plays with his coat-buttons; not looking at him*). If you really want to give me something, you could—you could—

HELMER. Come on, out with it.

NORA (*quickly*). You could give me money, Torvald. Only as much as you feel you can afford; then later I'll buy something with it.

HELMER. But, Nora—

NORA. Oh yes, Torvald dear, please! Please! Then I'll wrap up the notes in pretty gold paper and hang them on the Christmas tree. Wouldn't that be fun?

HELMER. What's the name of that little bird that can never keep any money?

NORA. Yes, yes, squanderbird; I know. But let's do as I say, Torvald; then I'll have time to think about what I need most. Isn't that the best way? Mm?

HELMER (*smiles*). To be sure it would be, if you could keep what I give you and really buy yourself something with it. But you'll spend it on all sorts of useless things for the house, and then I'll have to put my hand in my pocket again.

NORA. Oh, but Torvald—

HELMER. You can't deny it, Nora dear. (*Puts his arm round her waist.*) The squanderbird's a pretty little creature, but she gets through an awful lot of money. It's incredible what an expensive pet she is for a man to keep.

NORA. For shame! How can you say such a thing? I save every penny I can.

HELMER (*laughs*). That's quite true. Every penny you can. But you can't.

NORA (*hums and smiles, quietly gleeful*). Hm. If you only knew how many expenses we larks and squirrels have, Torvald.

HELMER. You're a funny little creature. Just like your father used to be. Always on the look-out for some way to get money, but as soon as you have any it just runs through your fingers, and you never know where it's gone. Well, I suppose I must take you as you are. It's in your blood. Yes, yes, yes, these things are hereditary, Nora.

NORA. Oh, I wish I'd inherited more of Papa's qualities.

HELMER. And I wouldn't wish my darling little songbird to be any different from what she is. By the way, that reminds me. You look awfully—how shall I put it?—awfully guilty today.

NORA. Do I?

HELMER. Yes, you do. Look me in the eyes.

NORA (*looks at him*). Well?

HELMER (*wags his finger*). Has my little sweet-tooth been indulging herself in town today, by any chance?

NORA. No, how can you think such a thing?

HELMER. Not a tiny little digression into a pastry shop?

NORA. No, Torvald, I promise—

HELMER. Not just a wee jam tart?

NORA. Certainly not.

HELMER. Not a little nibble at a macaroon?

NORA. No, Torvald—I promise you, honestly—

HELMER. There, there. I was only joking.

NORA (*goes over to the table, right*). You know I could never act against your wishes.

HELMER. Of course not. And you've given me your word—(*Goes over to her.*) Well, my beloved Nora, you keep your little Christmas secrets to yourself. They'll be revealed this evening, I've no doubt, once the Christmas tree has been lit.

NORA. Have you remembered to invite Dr. Rank?

HELMER. No. But there's no need; he knows he'll be dining with us. Anyway, I'll ask him when he comes this morning. I've ordered some good wine. Oh Nora, you can't imagine how I'm looking forward to this evening.

NORA. So am I. And, Torvald, how the children will love it!

HELMER. Yes, it's a wonderful thing to know that one's position is assured and that one has an ample income. Don't you agree? It's good to know that, isn't it?

NORA. Yes, it's almost like a miracle.

HELMER. Do you remember last Christmas? For three whole weeks you shut yourself away every evening to make flowers for the Christmas tree, and all those other things you were going to surprise us with. Ugh, it was the most boring time I've ever had in my life.

NORA. I didn't find it boring.

HELMER (*smiles*). But it all came to nothing in the end, didn't it?

NORA. Oh, are you going to bring that up again? How could I help the cat getting in and tearing everything to bits?

HELMER. No, my poor little Nora, of course you couldn't. You simply wanted to make us happy, and that's all that matters. But it's good that those hard times are past.

NORA. Yes, it's wonderful.

HELMER. I don't have to sit by myself and be bored. And you don't have to tire your pretty eyes and your delicate little hands—

NORA (*claps her hands*). No, Torvald, that's true, isn't it—I don't have to any longer? Oh, it's really all just like a miracle. (*Takes his arm.*) Now, I'm going to tell you what I thought we might do, Torvald. As soon as Christmas is over—(*A bell rings in the hall.*) Oh, there's the doorbell. (*Tidies up one or two things in the room.*) Someone's coming. What a bore.

HELMER. I'm not at home to any visitors. Remember!

MAID (*in the doorway*). A lady's called, madam. A stranger.

NORA. Well, ask her to come in.

MAID. And the doctor's here too, sir.

HELMER. Has he gone to my room?

MAID. Yes, sir.

Helmer goes into his room. The Maid shows in Mrs. Linde, who is dressed in traveling clothes, and closes the door.

MRS. LINDE (*shyly and a little hesitantly*). Good evening, Nora.

NORA (*uncertainly*). Good evening—

MRS. LINDE. I don't suppose you recognize me.

NORA. No, I'm afraid I—Yes, wait a minute—surely—(*Exclaims.*) Why, Christine! Is it really you?

MRS. LINDE. Yes, it's me.

NORA. Christine! And I didn't recognize you! But how could I—? (*More quietly.*) How you've changed, Christine!

MRS. LINDE. Yes, I know. It's been nine years—nearly ten—

NORA. Is it so long? Yes, it must be. Oh, these last eight years have been such a happy time for me! So you've come to town? All that way in winter! How brave of you!

MRS. LINDE. I arrived by the steamer this morning.

NORA. Yes, of course—to enjoy yourself over Christmas. Oh, how splendid! We'll have to celebrate! But take off your coat. You're not cold, are you? (*Helps her off with it.*) There! Now let's sit down here by the stove and be comfortable. No, you take the armchair. I'll sit here in the rocking-chair. (*Clasps Mrs. Linde's hands.*) Yes, now you look like your old self. It was just at first that—you've got a little paler, though, Christine. And perhaps a bit thinner.

MRS. LINDE. And older, Nora. Much, much older.

NORA. Yes, perhaps a little older. Just a tiny bit. Not much. (*Checks herself suddenly and says earnestly.*) Oh, but how thoughtless of me to sit here and chatter away like this! Dear, sweet Christine, can you forgive me?

MRS. LINDE. What do you mean, Nora?

NORA (*quietly*). Poor Christine, you've become a widow.

MRS. LINDE. Yes. Three years ago.

NORA. I know, I know—I read it in the papers. Oh, Christine, I meant to write to you so often, honestly. But I always put it off, and something else always cropped up.

MRS. LINDE. I understand, Nora dear.

NORA. No, Christine, it was beastly of me. Oh, my poor darling, what you've gone through! And he didn't leave you anything?

MRS. LINDE. No.

NORA. No children, either?

MRS. LINDE. No.

NORA. Nothing at all, then?

MRS. LINDE. Not even a feeling of loss or sorrow.

NORA (*looks incredulously at her*). But, Christine, how is that possible?

MRS. LINDE (*smiles sadly and strokes Nora's hair*). Oh, these things happen, Nora.

NORA. All alone. How dreadful that must be for you. I've three lovely children. I'm afraid you can't see them now, because they're out with nanny. But you must tell me everything—

MRS. LINDE. No, no, no. I want to hear about you.

NORA. No, you start. I'm not going to be selfish today, I'm just going to think about you. Oh, but there's one thing I *must* tell you. Have you heard of the wonderful luck we've just had?

MRS. LINDE. No. What?

NORA. Would you believe it—my husband's just been made manager of the bank!

MRS. LINDE. Your husband? Oh, how lucky—!

NORA. Yes, isn't it? Being a lawyer is so uncertain, you know, especially if one isn't prepared to touch any case that isn't—well—quite nice. And of course Torvald's been very firm about that—and I'm absolutely with him. Oh, you can imagine how happy we are! He's joining the bank in the New Year, and he'll be getting a big salary, and lots of percentages too. From now on we'll be able to live quite differently—we'll be able to do whatever we want. Oh, Christine, it's such a relief! I feel so happy! Well, I mean, it's lovely to have heaps of money and not to have to worry about anything. Don't you think?

MRS. LINDE. It must be lovely to have enough to cover one's needs, anyway.

NORA. Not just our needs! We're going to have heaps and heaps of money!

MRS. LINDE (*smiles*). Nora, Nora, haven't you grown up yet? When we were at school you were a terrible little spendthrift.

NORA (*laughs quietly*). Yes, Torvald still says that. (*Wags her finger.*) But "Nora, Nora" isn't as silly as you think. Oh, we've been in no position for me to waste money. We've both had to work.

MRS. LINDE. You too?

NORA. Yes, little things—fancy work, crocheting, embroidery and so forth. (*Casually.*) And other things too. I suppose you know Torvald left the Ministry when we got married? There were no prospects of promotion in his department, and of course he needed more money. But the first year he overworked himself quite dreadfully. He had to take on all sorts of extra jobs, and worked day and night. But it was too much for him, and he became frightfully ill. The doctors said he'd have to go to a warmer climate.

MRS. LINDE. Yes, you spent a whole year in Italy, didn't you?

NORA. Yes. It wasn't easy for me to get away, you know. I'd just had Ivar. But of course we had to do it. Oh, it was a marvelous trip! And it saved Torvald's life. But it cost an awful lot of money, Christine.

MRS. LINDE. I can imagine.

NORA. Two hundred and fifty pounds. That's a lot of money, you know.

MRS. LINDE. How lucky you had it.

NORA. Well, actually, we got it from my father.

MRS. LINDE. Oh, I see. Didn't he die just about that time?

NORA. Yes, Christine, just about then. Wasn't it dreadful, I couldn't go and look after him. I was expecting little Ivar any day. And then I had my poor Torvald to care for—we really didn't think he'd live. Dear, kind Papa! I never saw him again, Christine. Oh, it's the saddest thing that's happened to me since I got married.

MRS. LINDE. I know you were very fond of him. But you went to Italy—?

NORA. Yes. Well, we had the money, you see, and the doctors said we mustn't delay. So we went the month after Papa died.

MRS. LINDE. And your husband came back completely cured?

NORA. Fit as a fiddle!

MRS. LINDE. But—the doctor?

NORA. How do you mean?

MRS. LINDE. I thought the maid said that the gentleman who arrived with me was the doctor.

NORA. Oh yes, that's Doctor Rank, but he doesn't come because anyone's ill. He's our best friend, and he looks us up at least once every day. No, Torvald hasn't had a moment's illness since we went away. And the children are fit and healthy and so am I. (*Jumps up and claps her hands.*) Oh God, oh God, Christine, isn't it a wonderful thing to be alive and happy! Oh, but how beastly of me! I'm only talking about myself. (*Sits on a footstool and rests her arms on Mrs. Linde's knee.*) Oh, please don't be angry with me! Tell me, is it really true you didn't love your husband? Why did you marry him, then?

MRS. LINDE. Well, my mother was still alive; and she was helpless and bedridden. And I had my two little brothers to take care of. I didn't feel I could say no.

NORA. Yes, well, perhaps you're right. He was rich then, was he?

MRS. LINDE. Quite comfortably off, I believe. But his business was unsound, you see, Nora. When he died it went bankrupt, and there was nothing left.

NORA. What did you do?

MRS. LINDE. Well, I had to try to make ends meet somehow, so I started a little shop, and a little school, and anything else I could turn my hand to. These last three years have been just one endless slog for me, without a moment's rest. But now it's over, Nora. My poor dear mother doesn't need me any more; she's passed away. And the boys don't need me either; they've got jobs now and can look after themselves.

NORA. How relieved you must feel—

MRS. LINDE. No, Nora. Just unspeakably empty. No one to live for any more. (*Gets up restlessly.*) That's why I couldn't bear to stay out there any longer, cut off from the world. I thought it'd be easier to find some work here that will exercise and occupy my mind. If only I could get a regular job—office work of some kind—

NORA. Oh, but Christine, that's dreadfully exhausting; and you look practically finished already. It'd be much better for you if you could go away somewhere.

MRS. LINDE (*goes over to the window*). I have no Papa to pay for my holidays, Nora.

NORA (*gets up*). Oh, please don't be angry with me.

MRS. LINDE. My dear Nora, it's I who should ask you not to be angry. That's the worst thing about this kind of situation—it makes one so bitter. One has no one to work for; and yet one has to be continually sponging for jobs. One has to live; and so one becomes completely egocentric. When you told me about this luck you've just had with Torvald's new job—can you imagine?—I was happy not so much on your account, as on my own.

NORA. How do you mean? Oh, I understand. You mean Torvald might be able to do something for you?

MRS. LINDE. Yes, I was thinking that.

NORA. He will too, Christine. Just you leave it to me. I'll lead up to it so delicately, so delicately; I'll get him in the right mood. Oh, Christine, I do so want to help you.

MRS. LINDE. It's sweet of you to bother so much about me, Nora. Especially since you know so little of the worries and hardships of life.

NORA. I? You say I know little of—?

MRS. LINDE (*smiles*). Well, good heavens—those bits of fancy work of yours—well, really—! You're a child, Nora.

NORA (*tosses her head and walks across the room*). You shouldn't say that so patronizingly.

MRS. LINDE. Oh?

NORA. You're like the rest. You all think I'm incapable of getting down to anything serious—

MRS. LINDE. My dear—

NORA. You think I've never had any worries like the rest of you.

MRS. LINDE. Nora dear, you've just told me about all your difficulties—

NORA. Pooh—that! (*Quietly.*) I haven't told you about the big thing.

MRS. LINDE. What big thing? What do you mean?

NORA. You patronize me, Christine; but you shouldn't. You're proud that you've worked so long and so hard for your mother.

MRS. LINDE. I don't patronize anyone, Nora. But you're right—I am both proud and happy that I was able to make my mother's last months on earth comparatively easy.

NORA. And you're also proud of what you've done for your brothers.

MRS. LINDE. I think I have a right to be.

NORA. I think so too. But let me tell you something, Christine. I too have done something to be proud and happy about.

MRS. LINDE. I don't doubt it. But—how do you mean?

NORA. Speak quietly! Suppose Torvald should hear! He mustn't, at any price—no one must know, Christine—no one but you.

MRS. LINDE. But what is this?

NORA. Come over here. (*Pulls her down on to the sofa beside her.*) Yes, Christine—I too have done something to be happy and proud about. It was I who saved Torvald's life.

MRS. LINDE. Saved his—? How did you save it?

NORA. I told you about our trip to Italy. Torvald couldn't have lived if he hadn't managed to get down there—

MRS. LINDE. Yes, well—your father provided the money—

NORA (*smiles*). So Torvald and everyone else thinks. But—

MRS. LINDE. Yes?

NORA. Papa didn't give us a penny. It was I who found the money.

MRS. LINDE. You? All of it?

NORA. Two hundred and fifty pounds. What do you say to that?

MRS. LINDE. But Nora, how could you? Did you win a lottery or something?

NORA (*scornfully*). Lottery? (*Sniffs.*) What would there be to be proud of in that?

MRS. LINDE. But where did you get it from, then?

NORA (*hums and smiles secretively*). Hm; tra-la-la-la.

MRS. LINDE. You couldn't have borrowed it.

NORA. Oh? Why not?

MRS. LINDE. Well, a wife can't borrow money without her husband's consent.

NORA (*tosses her head*). Ah, but when a wife has a little business sense, and knows how to be clever—

MRS. LINDE. But Nora, I simply don't understand—

NORA. You don't have to. No one has said I borrowed the money. I could have got it in some other way. (*Throws herself back on the sofa.*) I could have got it from an admirer. When a girl's as pretty as I am—

MRS. LINDE. Nora, you're crazy!

NORA. You're dying of curiosity now, aren't you, Christine?

MRS. LINDE. Nora dear, you haven't done anything foolish?

NORA (*sits up again*). Is it foolish to save one's husband's life?

MRS. LINDE. I think it's foolish if without his knowledge, you—

NORA. But the whole point was that he mustn't know! Great heavens, don't you see? He hadn't to know how dangerously ill he was. I was the one they told that his life was in danger and that only going to a warm climate could save him. Do you suppose I didn't try to think of other ways of getting him down there? I told him how wonderful it would be for me to go abroad like other young wives; I cried and prayed; I asked him to remember my condition, and said he ought to be nice and tender to me; and then I suggested he might quite easily borrow the money. But then he got almost angry with me, Christine. He said I was frivolous, and that it was his duty as a husband not to pander to my moods and caprices—I think that's what he called them. Well, well, I thought, you've got to be saved somehow. And then I thought of a way—

MRS. LINDE. But didn't your husband find out from your father that the money hadn't come from him?

NORA. No, never. Papa died just then. I'd thought of letting him into the plot and asking him not to tell. But since he was so ill—! And as things turned out, it didn't become necessary.

MRS. LINDE. And you've never told your husband about this?

NORA. For heaven's sake, no! What an idea! He's frightfully strict about such matters. And besides—he's so proud of being a *man*—it'd be so painful and humiliating for him to know that he owed anything to me. It'd completely wreck our relationship. This life we have built together would no longer exist.

MRS. LINDE. Will you never tell him?

NORA (*thoughtfully, half-smiling*). Yes—some time, perhaps. Years from now, when I'm no longer pretty. You mustn't laugh! I mean of course, when Torvald no longer loves me as he does now; when it no longer amuses him to see me dance and dress up and play the fool for him. Then it might be useful to have something up my sleeve. (*Breaks off.*) Stupid, stupid, stupid! That time will never come. Well, what do you think of my big secret, Christine? I'm not completely useless, am I? Mind you, all this has caused me a frightful lot of worry. It hasn't been easy for me to meet my obligations punctually. In case you don't know, in the world of business there are things called quarterly installments and interest, and they're a terrible problem to cope with. So I've had to scrape a little here and save a little there as best I can. I haven't been able to save much on the housekeeping money, because Torvald likes to live well; and I couldn't let the children go short of clothes—I couldn't take anything out of what he gives me for them. The poor little angels!

MRS. LINDE. So you've had to stint yourself, my poor Nora?

NORA. Of course. Well, after all, it was my problem. Whenever Torvald gave me money to buy myself new clothes, I never used more than half of it; and I always bought what was cheapest and plainest. Thank heaven anything suits me, so that Torvald's never noticed. But it made me a bit sad sometimes, because it's lovely to wear pretty clothes. Don't you think?

MRS. LINDE. Indeed it is.

NORA. And then I've found one or two other sources of income. Last winter I managed to get a lot of copying to do. So I shut myself away and wrote every evening, late into the night. Oh, I often got so tired, so tired. But it was great fun, though, sitting there working and earning money. It was almost like being a man.

MRS. LINDE. But how much have you managed to pay off like this?

NORA. Well, I can't say exactly. It's awfully difficult to keep an exact check on these kind of transactions. I only know I've paid everything I've managed to scrape together. Sometimes I really didn't know where to turn. (*Smiles.*) Then I'd sit here and imagine some rich old gentleman had fallen in love with me—

MRS. LINDE. What! What gentleman?

NORA. Silly! And that now he'd died and when they opened his will it said in big letters: "Everything I possess is to be paid forthwith to my beloved Mrs. Nora Helmer in cash."

MRS. LINDE. But, Nora dear, who was this gentleman?

NORA. Great heavens, don't you understand? There wasn't any old gentleman, he was just something I used to dream up as I sat here evening after evening wondering how on earth I could raise some money. But what does it matter? The old bore can stay imaginary as far as I'm concerned, because now I don't have to worry any longer! (*Jumps up.*) Oh, Christine, isn't it wonderful? I don't have to worry any more! No more troubles! I can play all day with the children, I can fill the house with pretty things, just the way Torvald likes. And, Christine, it will soon be spring, and the air will be fresh and the skies blue—and then perhaps we'll be able to take a little trip somewhere. I shall be able to see the sea again. Oh, yes, yes, it's a wonderful thing to be alive and happy!

The bell rings in the hall.

MRS. LINDE (*gets up*). You've a visitor. Perhaps I'd better go.

NORA. No stay. It won't be for me. It's someone for Torvald—

MAID (*in the doorway*). Excuse me, madam, a gentleman's called who says he wants to speak to the master. But I didn't know—seeing as the doctor's with him—

NORA. Who is this gentleman?

KROGSTAD (*in the doorway*). It's me, Mrs. Helmer.

Mrs. Linde starts, composes herself; and turns away to the window.

NORA (takes a step toward him and whispers tensely). You? What is it? What do you want to talk to my husband about?

KROGSTAD. Business—you might call it. I hold a minor post in the bank, and I hear your husband is to become our new chief—

NORA. Oh—then it isn't—?

KROGSTAD. Pure business, Mrs. Helmer. Nothing more.

NORA. Well, you'll find him in his study.

Nods indifferently as she closes the hall door behind him. Then she walks across the room and sees to the stove.

MRS. LINDE. Nora, who was that man?

NORA. A lawyer called Krogstad.

MRS. LINDE. It was him, then.

NORA. Do you know that man?

MRS. LINDE. I used to know him—some years ago. He was a solicitor's clerk in our town, for a while.

NORA. Yes, of course, so he was.

MRS. LINDE. How he's changed!

NORA. He was very unhappily married, I believe.

MRS. LINDE. Is he a widower now?

NORA. Yes, with a lot of children. Ah, now it's alight.

She closes the door of the stove and moves the rocking-chair a little to one side.

MRS. LINDE. He does—various things now, I hear?

NORA. Does he? It's quite possible—I really don't know. But don't let's talk about business. It's so boring.

Dr. Rank enters from Helmer's study.

RANK (*still in the doorway*). No, no, my dear chap, don't see me out. I'll go and have a word with your wife. (*Closes the door and notices Mrs. Linde.*) Oh, I beg your pardon. I seem to be *de trop* here too.

NORA. Not in the least. (*Introduces them.*) Dr. Rank. Mrs. Linde.

RANK. Ah! A name I have often heard in this house. I believe I passed you on the stairs as I came up.

MRS. LINDE. Yes. Stairs tire me; I have to take them slowly.

RANK. Oh, have you hurt yourself?

MRS. LINDE. No, I'm just a little run down.

RANK. Ah, is that all? Then I take it you've come to town to cure yourself by a round of parties?

MRS. LINDE. I have come here to find work.

RANK. Is that an approved remedy for being run down?

MRS. LINDE. One has to live, Doctor.

RANK. Yes, people do seem to regard it as a necessity.

NORA. Oh, really, Dr. Rank. I bet you want to stay alive.

RANK. You bet I do. However miserable I sometimes feel, I still want to go on being tortured for as long as possible. It's the same with all my patients; and with people who are morally sick, too. There's a moral cripple in with Helmer at this very moment—

MRS. LINDE (*softly*). Oh!

NORA. Whom do you mean?

RANK. Oh, a lawyer fellow called Krogstad—you wouldn't know him. He's crippled all right; morally twisted. But even he started off by announcing, as though it were a matter of enormous importance, that he had to live.

NORA. Oh? What did he want to talk to Torvald about?

RANK. I haven't the faintest idea. All I heard was something about the bank.

NORA. I didn't know that Krog—that this man Krogstad had any connection with the bank.

RANK. Yes, he's got some kind of job down there. (*To Mrs. Linde.*) I wonder if in your part of the world you too have a species of human being that spends its time fussing around trying to smell out moral corruption? And when they find a case they give him some nice, comfortable position so that they can keep a good watch on him. The healthy ones just have to lump it.

MRS. LINDE. But surely it's the sick who need care most?

RANK (*shrugs his shoulders*). Well, there we have it. It's that attitude that's turning human society into a hospital.

Nora, lost in her own thoughts, laughs half to herself and claps her hands.

RANK. Why are you laughing? Do you really know what society is?

NORA. What do I care about society? I think it's a bore. I was laughing at something else—something frightfully funny. Tell me, Dr. Rank—will everyone who works at the bank come under Torvald now?

RANK. Do you find that particularly funny?

NORA (*smiles and hums*). Never you mind! Never you mind! (*Walks around the room.*) Yes, I find it very amusing to think that we—I mean, Torvald—has obtained so much influence over so many people. (*Takes the paper bag from her pocket.*) Dr. Rank, would you like a small macaroon?

RANK. Macaroons! I say! I thought they were forbidden here.

NORA. Yes, well, these are some Christine gave me.

MRS. LINDE. What? I—?

NORA. All right, all right, don't get frightened. You weren't to know Torvald had forbidden them. He's afraid they'll ruin my teeth. But, dash it—for once—! Don't you agree, Dr. Rank? Here! (*Pops a macaroon into his mouth.*) You too, Christine. And I'll have one too. Just a little one. Two at the most. (*Begins to walk round again.*) Yes, now I feel really, really happy. Now there's just one thing in the world I'd really love to do.

RANK. Oh? And what is that?

NORA. Just something I'd love to say to Torvald.

RANK. Well, why don't you say it?

NORA. No, I daren't. It's too dreadful.

MRS. LINDE. Dreadful?

RANK. Well, then, you'd better not. But you can say it to us. What is it you'd so love to say to Torvald?

NORA. I've the most extraordinary longing to say: "Bloody hell!"

RANK. Are you mad?

MRS. LINDE. My dear Nora—!

RANK. Say it. Here he is.

NORA (*hiding the bag of macaroons*). Ssh! Ssh!

Helmer, with his overcoat on his arm and his hat in his hand, enters from his study.

NORA (*goes to meet him*). Well, Torvald dear, did you get rid of him?

HELMER. Yes, he's just gone.

NORA. May I introduce you—? This is Christine. She's just arrived in town.

HELMER. Christine—? Forgive me, but I don't think—

NORA. Mrs. Linde, Torvald dear. Christine Linde.

HELMER. Ah. A childhood friend of my wife's, I presume?

MRS. LINDE. Yes, we knew each other in earlier days.

NORA. And imagine, now she's traveled all this way to talk to you.

HELMER. Oh?

MRS. LINDE. Well, I didn't really—

NORA. You see, Christine's frightfully good at office work, and she's mad to come under some really clever man who can teach her even more than she knows already—

HELMER. Very sensible, madam.

NORA. So when she heard you'd become head of the bank—it was in her local paper—she came here as quickly as she could and—Torvald, you will, won't you? Do a little something to help Christine? For my sake?

HELMER. Well, that shouldn't be impossible. You are a widow, I take it, Mrs. Linde?

MRS. LINDE. Yes.

HELMER. And you have experience of office work?

MRS. LINDE. Yes, quite a bit.

HELMER. Well then, it's quite likely I may be able to find some job for you—

NORA (*claps her hands*). You see, you see!

HELMER. You've come at a lucky moment, Mrs. Linde.

MRS. LINDE. Oh, how can I ever thank you—?

HELMER. There's absolutely no need. (*Puts on his overcoat.*) But now I'm afraid I must ask you to excuse me—

RANK. Wait. I'll come with you.

He gets his fur coat from the hall and warms it at the stove.

NORA. Don't be long, Torvald dear.

HELMER. I'll only be an hour.

NORA. Are you going too, Christine?

MRS. LINDE (*puts on her outdoor clothes*). Yes, I must start to look round for a room.

HELMER. Then perhaps we can walk part of the way together.

NORA (*helps her*). It's such a nuisance we're so cramped here—I'm afraid we can't offer to—

MRS. LINDE. Oh, I wouldn't dream of it. Goodbye, Nora dear, and thanks for everything.

NORA. *Au revoir.* You'll be coming back this evening, of course. And, you too, Dr. Rank. What? If you're well enough? Of course you'll be well enough. Wrap up warmly, though.

They go out, talking, into the hall. Children's voices are heard from the stairs.

NORA. Here they are! Here they are!

She runs out and opens the door. Anne-Marie, the nurse, enters with the children.

NORA. Come in, come in! (*Stoops down and kisses them.*) Oh, my sweet darlings—! Look at them, Christine! Aren't they beautiful?

RANK. Don't stand here chattering in this draught!

HELMER. Come, Mrs. Linde. This is for mothers only.

Dr. Rank, Helmer, and Mrs. Linde go down the stairs. The Nurse brings the children into the room. Nora follows, and closes the door to the hall.

NORA. How well you look! What red cheeks you've got! Like apples and roses! (*The children answer her inaudibly as she talks to them.*) Have you had fun? That's splendid. You gave Emmy and Bob a ride on the sledge? What, both together? I say! What a clever boy you are, Ivar! Oh, let me hold her for a moment, Anne-Marie! My sweet little baby doll! (*Takes the smallest child from the nurse and dances with her.*) Yes, yes, Mummy will dance with Bob too. What? Have you been throwing snowballs? Oh, I wish I'd been there! No, don't—I'll undress them myself, Anne-Marie. No, please let me; it's such fun. Go inside and warm yourself; you look frozen. There's some hot coffee on the stove. (*The nurse goes into the room on the left. Nora takes off the children's outdoor clothes and throws them anywhere while they all chatter simultaneously.*) What? A big dog ran after you? But he didn't bite you? No, dogs don't bite lovely little baby dolls. Leave those parcels alone, Ivar. What's in them? Ah, wouldn't you like to know! No, no; it's nothing nice. Come on, let's play a game. What shall we play? Hide and seek. Yes, let's play hide and seek. Bob shall hide first. You want me to? All right, let me hide first.

Nora and the children play around the room, and in the adjacent room to the left, laughing and shouting. At length Nora hides under the table. The children rush in, look, but cannot find her. Then they hear her half-stifled laughter, run to the table, lift up the cloth, and see her. Great excitement. She crawls out as though to frighten them. Further excitement. Meanwhile, there has been a knock on the door leading from the hall, but no one has noticed it. Now the door is half-opened and Krogstad enters. He waits for a moment; the game continues.

KROGSTAD. Excuse me, Mrs. Helmer—

NORA (*turns with a stifled cry and half jumps up*). Oh! What do you want?

KROGSTAD. I beg your pardon; the front door was ajar. Someone must have forgotten to close it.

NORA (*gets up*). My husband is not at home, Mr. Krogstad.

KROGSTAD. I know.

NORA. Well, what do want here, then?

KROGSTAD. A word with you.

NORA. With—? (*To the children, quietly.*) Go inside to Anne-Marie. What? No, the strange gentleman won't do anything to hurt Mummy. When he's gone we'll start playing again.

She takes the children into the room on the left and closes the door behind them.

NORA (*uneasy, tense*). You want to speak to me?

KROGSTAD. Yes.

NORA. Today? But it's not the first of the month yet.

KROGSTAD. No, it is Christmas Eve. Whether or not you have a merry Christmas depends on you.

NORA. What do you want? I can't give you anything today—

KROGSTAD. We won't talk about that for the present. There's something else. You have a moment to spare?

NORA. Oh, yes. Yes, I suppose so; though—

KROGSTAD. Good. I was sitting in the café down below and I saw your husband cross the street—

NORA. Yes.

KROGSTAD. With a lady.

NORA. Well?

KROGSTAD. Might I be so bold as to ask: was not that lady a Mrs. Linde?

NORA. Yes.

KROGSTAD. Recently arrived in town?

NORA. Yes, today.

KROGSTAD. She is a good friend of yours, is she not?

NORA. Yes, she is. But I don't see—

KROGSTAD. I used to know her too once.

NORA. I know.

KROGSTAD. Oh? You've discovered that. Yes, I thought you would. Well then, may I ask you a straight question: is Mrs. Linde to be employed at the bank?

NORA. How dare you presume to cross-examine me, Mr. Krogstad? You, one of my husband's employees? But since you ask, you shall have an answer. Yes, Mrs. Linde is to be employed by the bank. And I arranged it, Mr. Krogstad. Now you know.

KROGSTAD. I guessed right, then.

NORA (*walks up and down the room*). Oh, one has a little influence, you know. Just because one's a woman it doesn't necessarily mean that—When one is in a humble position, Mr. Krogstad, one should think twice before offending someone who—hm—

KROGSTAD. —who has influence?

NORA. Precisely.

KROGSTAD (*changes his tone*). Mrs. Helmer, will you have the kindness to use your influence on my behalf?

NORA. What? What do you mean?

KROGSTAD. Will you be so good as to see that I keep my humble position at the bank?

NORA. What do you mean? Who is thinking of removing you from your position?

KROGSTAD. Oh, you don't need to play innocent with me. I realize it can't be very pleasant for your friend to risk bumping into me; and now I also realize whom I have to thank for being hounded out like this.

NORA. But I assure you—

KROGSTAD. Look, let's not beat about the bush. There's still time, and I'd advise you to use your influence to stop it.

NORA. But, Mr. Krogstad, I have no influence—

KROGSTAD. Oh? I thought you just said—

NORA. But I didn't mean it like that! I? How on earth could you imagine that I would have any influence over my husband?

KROGSTAD. Oh, I've known your husband since we were students together. I imagine he has his weaknesses like other married men.

NORA. If you speak impertinently of my husband, I shall show you the door.

KROGSTAD. You're a bold woman, Mrs. Helmer.

NORA. I'm not afraid of you any longer. Once the New Year is in, I'll soon be rid of you.

KROGSTAD (*more controlled*). Now listen to me, Mrs. Helmer. If I'm forced to, I shall fight for my little job at the bank as I would fight for my life.

NORA. So it sounds.

KROGSTAD. It isn't just the money; that's the last thing I care about. There's something else—well, you might as well know. It's like this, you see. You know of course, as every one else does, that some years ago I committed an indiscretion.

NORA. I think I did hear something—

KROGSTAD. It never came into court; but from that day, every opening was barred to me. So I turned my hand to the kind of business you know about. I had to do something; and I don't think I was one of the worst. But now I want to give up all that. My sons are growing up; for their sake, I must try to regain what respectability I can. This job in the bank was the first step on the ladder. And now your husband wants to kick me off that ladder back into the dirt.

NORA. But my dear Mr. Krogstad, it simply isn't in my power to help you.

KROGSTAD. You say that because you don't want to help me. But I have the means to make you.

NORA. You don't mean you'd tell my husband that I owe you money?

KROGSTAD. And if I did?

NORA. That'd be a filthy trick! (*Almost in tears.*) This secret that is my pride and my joy—that he should hear about it in such a filthy, beastly way—hear about it from you! It'd involve me in the most dreadful unpleasantness—

KROGSTAD. Only—unpleasantness?

NORA (*vehemently*). All right, do it! You'll be the one who'll suffer. It'll show my husband the kind of man you are, and then you'll never keep your job.

KROGSTAD. I asked you whether it was merely domestic unpleasantness you were afraid of.

NORA. If my husband hears about it, he will of course immediately pay you whatever is owing. And then we shall have nothing more to do with you.

KROGSTAD (*takes a step closer*). Listen, Mrs. Helmer. Either you've a bad memory or else you know very little about financial transactions. I had better enlighten you.

NORA. What do you mean?

KROGSTAD. When your husband was ill, you came to me to borrow two hundred and fifty pounds.

NORA. I didn't know anyone else.

KROGSTAD. I promised to find that sum for you—

NORA. And you did find it.

KROGSTAD. I promised to find that sum for you on certain conditions. You were so worried about your husband's illness and so keen to get the money to take him abroad that I don't think you bothered much about the details. So it won't be out of place if I refresh your memory. Well—I promised to get you the money in exchange for an I.O.U., which I drew up.

NORA. Yes, and which I signed.

KROGSTAD. Exactly. But then I added a few lines naming your father as security for the debt. This paragraph was to be signed by your father.

NORA. Was to be? He did sign it.

KROGSTAD. I left the date blank for your father to fill in when he signed this paper. You remember, Mrs. Helmer?

NORA. Yes, I think so—

KROGSTAD. Then I gave you back this I.O.U. for you to post to your father. Is that not correct?

NORA. Yes.

KROGSTAD. And of course you posted it at once; for within five or six days you brought it along to me with your father's signature on it. Whereupon I handed you the money.

NORA. Yes, well. Haven't I repaid the installments as agreed?

KROGSTAD. Mm—yes, more or less. But to return to what we were speaking about—that was a difficult time for you just then, wasn't it, Mrs. Helmer?

NORA. Yes, it was.

KROGSTAD. And your father was very ill, if I am not mistaken.

NORA. He was dying.

KROGSTAD. He did in fact die shortly afterwards?

NORA. Yes.

KROGSTAD. Tell me, Mrs. Helmer, do you by any chance remember the date of your father's death? The day of the month, I mean.

NORA. Papa died on the twenty-ninth of September.

KROGSTAD. Quite correct; I took the trouble to confirm it. And that leaves me with a curious little problem—(*Takes out a paper.*)—which I simply cannot solve.

NORA. Problem? I don't see—

KROGSTAD. The problem, Mrs. Helmer, is that your father signed this paper three days after his death.

NORA. What? I don't understand—

KROGSTAD. Your father died on the twenty-ninth of September. But look at this. Here your father has dated his signature the second of October. Isn't that a curious little problem, Mrs. Helmer? (*Nora is silent.*) Can you suggest any explanation? (*She remains silent.*) And there's another curious thing. The words "second of October" and the year are written in a hand which is not your father's, but which I seem to know. Well, there's a simple explanation to that. Your father could have forgotten to write in the date when he signed, and someone else could have added it before the news came of his death. There's nothing criminal about that. It's the signature itself I'm wondering about. It is genuine, I suppose, Mrs. Helmer? It was your father who wrote his name here?

NORA (*after a short silence, throws back her head and looks defiantly at him*). No, it was not. It was I who wrote Papa's name there.

KROGSTAD. Look, Mrs. Helmer, do you realize this is a dangerous admission?

NORA. Why? You'll get your money.

KROGSTAD. May I ask you a question? Why didn't you send this paper to your father?

NORA. I couldn't. Papa was very ill. If I'd asked him to sign this, I'd have had to tell him what the money was for. But I couldn't have told him in his condition that my husband's life was in danger. I couldn't have done that!

KROGSTAD. Then you would have been wiser to have given up your idea of a holiday.

NORA. But I couldn't! It was to save my husband's life. I couldn't put it off.

KROGSTAD. But didn't it occur to you that you were being dishonest towards me?

NORA. I couldn't bother about that. I didn't care about you. I hated you because of all the beastly difficulties you'd put in my way when you knew how dangerously ill my husband was.

KROGSTAD. Mrs. Helmer, you evidently don't appreciate exactly what you have done. But I can assure you that it is no bigger nor worse a crime than the one I once committed, and thereby ruined my whole social position.

NORA. You? Do you expect me to believe that you would have taken a risk like that to save your wife's life?

KROGSTAD. The law does not concern itself with motives.

NORA. Then the law must be very stupid.

KROGSTAD. Stupid or not, if I show this paper to the police, you will be judged according to it.

NORA. I don't believe that. Hasn't a daughter the right to shield her father from worry and anxiety when he's old and dying? Hasn't a wife the right to save her husband's life? I don't know much about the law but there must be something somewhere that says that such things are allowed. You ought to know about that, you're meant to be a lawyer, aren't you? You can't be a very good lawyer, Mr. Krogstad.

KROGSTAD. Possibly not. But business, the kind of business we two have been transacting—I think you'll admit I understand something about that? Good. Do as you please. But I tell you this. If I get thrown into the gutter for a second time, I shall take you with me.

He bows and goes out through the hall.

NORA (*stands for a moment in thought, then tosses her head*). What nonsense! He's trying to frighten me! I'm not that stupid. (*Busies herself gathering together the children's clothes; then she suddenly stops.*) But—? No, it's impossible. I did it for love, didn't I?

CHILDREN (*in the doorway, left*). Mummy, the strange gentleman's gone out into the street.

NORA. Yes, yes, I know. But don't talk to anyone about the strange gentleman. You hear? Not even to Daddy.

CHILDREN. No, Mummy. Will you play with us again now?

NORA. No, no. Not now.

CHILDREN. Oh but, Mummy, you promised!

NORA. I know, but I can't just now. Go back to the nursery. I've a lot to do. Go away, my darlings, go away. (*She pushes them gently into the other room and closes the door behind them. She sits on the sofa, takes up her embroidery, stitches for a few moments, but soon stops.*) No! (*Throws the embroidery aside, gets up, goes to the door leading to the hall, and calls.*) Helen! Bring in the Christmas tree! (*She goes to the table on the left and opens the drawer in it; then pauses again.*) No, but it's utterly impossible!

MAID (*enters with the tree*). Where shall I put it, madam?

NORA. There, in the middle of the room.

MAID. Will you be wanting anything else?

NORA. No, thank you, I have everything I need.

The Maid puts down the tree and goes out.

NORA (*busy decorating the tree*). Now—candles here—and flowers here. That loathsome man! Nonsense, nonsense, there's nothing to be frightened about. The Christmas tree must be beautiful. I'll do everything that you like, Torvald. I'll sing for you, dance for you—

Helmer, with a bundle of papers under his arm, enters.

NORA. Oh—are you back already?

HELMER. Yes. Has anyone been here?

NORA. Here? No.

HELMER. That's strange. I saw Krogstad come out of the front door.

NORA. Did you? Oh yes, that's quite right—Krogstad was here for a few minutes.

HELMER. Nora, I can tell from your face, he's been here and asked you to put in a good word for him.

NORA. Yes.

HELMER. And you were to pretend you were doing it of your own accord? You weren't going to tell me he'd been here? He asked you to do that too, didn't he?

NORA. Yes, Torvald. But—

HELMER. Nora, Nora! And you were ready to enter into such a conspiracy? Talking to a man like that, and making him promises—and then, on top of it all, to tell me an untruth!

NORA. An untruth?

HELMER. Didn't you say no one had been here? (*Wags his finger.*) My little songbird must never do that again. A songbird must have a clean beak to sing with; otherwise she'll start twittering out of tune. (*Puts his arm round her waist.*) Isn't that the way we want things? Yes, of course it is. (*Lets go of her.*) So let's hear no more about that. (*Sits down in front of the stove.*) Ah, how cozy and peaceful it is here. (*Glances for a few moments at his papers.*)

NORA (*busy with the tree; after a short silence*). Torvald.

HELMER. Yes.

NORA. I'm terribly looking forward to that fancy dress ball at the Stenborgs on Boxing Day.

HELMER. And I'm terribly curious to see what you're going to surprise me with.

NORA. Oh, it's so maddening.

HELMER. What is?

NORA. I can't think of anything to wear. It all seems so stupid and meaningless.

HELMER. So my little Nora's come to that conclusion, has she?

NORA (*behind his chair, resting her arms on its back*). Are you very busy, Torvald?

HELMER. Oh—

NORA. What are those papers?

HELMER. Just something to do with the bank.

NORA. Already?

HELMER. I persuaded the trustees to give me authority to make certain immediate changes in the staff and organization. I want to have everything straight by the New Year.

NORA. Then that's why this poor man Krogstad—

HELMER. Hm.

NORA (*still leaning over his chair, slowly strokes the back of his head*). If you hadn't been so busy, I was going to ask you an enormous favor, Torvald.

HELMER. Well, tell me. What was it to be?

NORA. You know I trust your taste more than anyone's. I'm so anxious to look really beautiful at the fancy dress ball. Torvald, couldn't you help me to decide what I shall go as, and what kind of costume I ought to wear?

HELMER. Aha! So little Miss Independent's in trouble and needs a man to rescue her, does she?

NORA. Yes, Torvald. I can't get anywhere without your help.

HELMER. Well, well, I'll give the matter thought. We'll find something.

NORA. Oh, how kind of you! (*Goes back to the tree. Pause.*)

How pretty these red flowers look! But, tell me, is it so dreadful, this thing that Krogstad's done?

HELMER. He forged someone else's name. Have you any idea what that means?

NORA. Mightn't he have been forced to do it by some emergency?

HELMER. He probably just didn't think—that's what usually happens. I'm not so heartless as to condemn a man for an isolated action.

NORA. No, Torvald, of course not!

HELMER. Men often succeed in re-establishing themselves if they admit their crime and take their punishment.

NORA. Punishment?

HELMER. But Krogstad didn't do that. He chose to try and trick his way out of it; and that's what has morally destroyed him.

NORA. You think that would—?

HELMER. Just think how a man with that load on his conscience must always be lying and cheating and dissembling; how he must wear a mask even in the presence of those who are dearest to him, even his own wife and children! Yes, the children. That's the worst danger, Nora.

NORA. Why?

HELMER. Because an atmosphere of lies contaminates and poisons every corner of the home. Every breath that the children draw in such a house contains the germs of evil.

NORA (comes closer behind him). Do you really believe that?

HELMER. Oh, my dear, I've come across it so often in my work at the bar. Nearly all young criminals are the children of mothers who are constitutional liars.

NORA. Why do you say mothers?

HELMER. It's usually the mother; though of course the father can have the same influence. Every lawyer knows that only too well. And yet this fellow Krogstad has been sitting at home all these years poisoning his children with his lies and pretenses. That's why I say that, morally speaking, he is dead. (Stretches out his hands towards her.) So my pretty little Nora must promise me not to plead his case. Your hand on it. Come, come, what's this? Give me your hand. There. That's settled, now. I assure you it'd be quite impossible for me to work in the same building as him. I literally feel physically ill in the presence of a man like that.

NORA (draws her hand from his and goes over to the other side of the Christmas tree). How hot it is in here! And I've so much to do.

HELMER (gets up and gathers his papers). Yes, and I must try to get some of this read before dinner. I'll think about your costume too. And I may even have something up my sleeve to hang in gold paper on the Christmas tree. (Lays his hand on her head.) My precious little songbird!

He goes into his study and closes the door.

NORA (softly, after a pause). It's nonsense. It must be. It's impossible. It must be impossible!

NURSE (in the doorway, left). The children are asking if they can come in to Mummy.

NORA. No, no, no; don't let them in! You stay with them, Anne-Marie.

NURSE. Very good, madam. (Closes the door.)

NORA (pale with fear). Corrupt my little children—! Poison my home! (Short pause. She throws back her head.) It isn't true! It couldn't be true!

ACT 2

The same room. In the corner by the piano the Christmas tree stands, stripped and disheveled, its candles burned to their sockets. Nora's outdoor clothes lie on the sofa. She is alone in the room, walking restlessly to and fro. At length she stops by the sofa and picks up her coat.

NORA (drops the coat again). There's someone coming! (Goes to the door and listens.) No, it's no one. Of course—no one'll come today, it's Christmas Day. Nor tomorrow. But perhaps—! (Opens the door and looks out.) No. Nothing in the letter-box. Quite empty. (Walks across the room.) Silly, silly. Of course he won't do anything. It couldn't happen. It isn't possible. Why, I've three small children.

The Nurse, carrying a large cardboard box, enters from the room on the left.

NURSE. I found those fancy dress clothes at last, madam.

NORA. Thank you. Put them on the table.

NURSE (does so). They're all rumpled up.

NORA. Oh, I wish I could tear them into a million pieces!

NURSE. Why, madam! They'll be all right. Just a little patience.

NORA. Yes, of course. I'll go and get Mrs. Linde to help me.

NURSE. What, out again? In this dreadful weather? You'll catch a chill, madam.

NORA. Well, that wouldn't be the worst. How are the children?

NURSE. Playing with their Christmas presents, poor little dears. But—

NORA. Are they still asking to see me?

NURSE. They're so used to having their Mummy with them.

NORA. Yes, but, Anne-Marie, from now on I shan't be able to spend so much time with them.

NURSE. Well, children get used to anything in time.

NORA. Do you think so? Do you think they'd forget their mother if she went away from them—for ever?

NURSE. Mercy's sake, madam! For ever!

NORA. Tell me, Anne-Marie—I've so often wondered. How could you bear to give your child away—to strangers?

NURSE. But I had to when I came to nurse my little Miss Nora.

NORA. Do you mean you wanted to?

NURSE. When I had the chance of such a good job? A poor girl what's got into trouble can't afford to pick and choose. That good-for-nothing didn't lift a finger.

NORA. But your daughter must have completely forgotten you.

NURSE. Oh no, indeed she hasn't. She's written to me twice, once when she got confirmed and then again when she got married.

NORA (*hugs her*). Dear old Anne-Marie, you were a good mother to me.

NURSE. Poor little Miss Nora, you never had any mother but me.

NORA. And if my little ones had no one else, I know you would—no, silly, silly, silly! (*Opens the cardboard box.*) Go back to them, Anne-Marie. Now I must—Tomorrow you'll see how pretty I shall look.

NURSE. Why, there'll be no one at the ball as beautiful as my Miss Nora.

She goes into the room, left.

NORA (*begins to unpack the clothes from the box, but soon throws them down again*). Oh, if only I dared to go out! If I could be sure no one would come, and nothing would happen while I was away! Stupid, stupid! No one will come. I just mustn't think about it. Brush this muff. Pretty gloves, pretty gloves! Don't think about it, don't think about it! One, two, three, four, five, six—(*Cries.*) Ah—they're coming—!

She begins to run toward the door, but stops uncertainly. Mrs. Linde enters from the hall, where she has been taking off her outdoor clothes.

NORA. Oh, it's you, Christine. There's no one else out there, is there? Oh, I'm so glad you've come.

MRS. LINDE. I hear you were at my room asking for me.

NORA. Yes, I just happened to be passing. I want to ask you to help me with something. Let's sit down here on the sofa. Look at this. There's going to be a fancy dress ball tomorrow night upstairs at Consul Stenborg's, and Torvald wants me to go as a Neapolitan fisher-girl and dance the tarantella. I learned it on Capri.

MRS. LINDE. I say, are you going to give a performance?

NORA. Yes, Torvald says I should. Look, here's the dress. Torvald had it made for me in Italy; but now it's all so torn, I don't know—

MRS. LINDE. Oh, we'll soon put that right; the stitching's just come away. Needle and thread? Ah, here we are.

NORA. You're being awfully sweet.

MRS. LINDE (*sews*). So you're going to dress up tomorrow, Nora? I must pop over for a moment to see how you look. Oh, but I've completely forgotten to thank you for that nice evening yesterday.

NORA (*gets up and walks across the room*). Oh, I didn't think it was as nice as usual. You ought to have come to town a little earlier, Christine. . . . Yes, Torvald understands how to make a home look attractive.

MRS. LINDE. I'm sure you do, too. You're not your father's daughter for nothing. But, tell me. Is Dr. Rank always in such low spirits as he was yesterday?

NORA. No, last night it was very noticeable. But he's got a terrible disease; he's got spinal tuberculosis, poor man. His father was a frightful creature who kept mistresses and so on. As a result Dr. Rank has been sickly ever since he was a child—you understand—

MRS. LINDE (*puts down her sewing*). But, my dear Nora, how on earth did you get to know about such things?

NORA (*walks about the room*). Oh, don't be silly, Christine— when one has three children, one comes into contact with women who—well, who know about medical matters, and they tell one a thing or two.

MRS. LINDE (*sews again; a short silence*). Does Dr. Rank visit you every day?

NORA. Yes, every day. He's Torvald's oldest friend, and a good friend to me too. Dr. Rank's almost one of the family.

MRS. LINDE. But, tell me—is he quite sincere? I mean, doesn't he rather say the sort of thing he thinks people want to hear?

NORA. No, quite the contrary. What gave you that idea?

MRS. LINDE. When you introduced me to him yesterday, he said he'd often heard my name mentioned here. But later I noticed your husband had no idea who I was. So how could Dr. Rank—?

NORA. Yes, that's quite right, Christine. You see, Torvald's so hopelessly in love with me that he wants to have me all to himself—those were his very words. When we were first married, he got quite jealous if I as much as mentioned any of my old friends back home. So naturally, I stopped talking about them. But I often chat with Dr. Rank about that kind of thing. He enjoys it, you see.

MRS. LINDE. Now listen, Nora. In many ways you're still a child; I'm a bit older than you and have a little more experience of the world. There's something I want to say to you. You ought to give up this business with Dr. Rank.

NORA. What business?

MRS. LINDE. Well, everything. Last night you were speaking about this rich admirer of yours who was going to give you money—

NORA. Yes, and who doesn't exist—unfortunately. But what's that got to do with—?

MRS. LINDE. Is Dr. Rank rich?

NORA. Yes.

MRS. LINDE. And he has no dependents?

NORA. No, no one. But—

MRS. LINDE. And he comes here to see you every day?

NORA. Yes, I've told you.

MRS. LINDE. But how dare a man of his education be so forward?

NORA. What on earth are you talking about?

MRS. LINDE. Oh, stop pretending, Nora. Do you think I haven't guessed who it was who lent you that two hundred pounds?

NORA. Are you out of your mind? How could you imagine

such a thing? A friend, someone who comes here every day! Why, that'd be an impossible situation!

MRS. LINDE. Then it really wasn't him?

NORA. No, of course not. I've never for a moment dreamed of—anyway, he hadn't any money to lend then. He didn't come into that till later.

MRS. LINDE. Well, I think that was a lucky thing for you, Nora dear.

NORA. No, I could never have dreamed of asking Dr. Rank—Though I'm sure that if I ever did ask him—

MRS. LINDE. But of course you won't.

NORA. Of course not. I can't imagine that it should ever become necessary. But I'm perfectly sure that if I did speak to Dr. Rank—

MRS. LINDE. Behind your husband's back?

NORA. I've got to get out of this other business; and *that's* been going on behind his back. I've *got* to get out of it.

MRS. LINDE. Yes, well, that's what I told you yesterday. But—

NORA (*walking up and down*). It's much easier for a man to arrange these things than a woman—

MRS. LINDE. One's own husband, yes.

NORA. Oh, bosh. (*Stops walking.*) When you've completely repaid a debt, you get your I.O.U. back, don't you?

MRS. LINDE. Yes, of course.

NORA. And you can tear it into a thousand pieces and burn the filthy, beastly thing!

MRS. LINDE (*looks hard at her, puts down her sewing, and gets up slowly*). Nora, you're hiding something from me.

NORA. Can you see that?

MRS. LINDE. Something has happened since yesterday morning. Nora, what is it?

NORA (*goes toward her*). Christine! (*Listens.*) Ssh! There's Torvald. Would you mind going into the nursery for a few minutes? Torvald can't bear to see sewing around. Anne-Marie'll help you.

MRS. LINDE (*gathers some of her things together*). Very well. But I shan't leave this house until we've talked this matter out.

She goes into the nursery, left. As she does so, Helmer enters from the hall.

NORA (*runs to meet him*). Oh, Torvald dear, I've been so longing for you to come back!

HELMER. Was that the dressmaker?

NORA. No, it was Christine. She's helping me mend my costume. I'm going to look rather splendid in that.

HELMER. Yes, that was quite a bright idea of mine, wasn't it?

NORA. Wonderful! But wasn't it nice of me to give in to you?

HELMER (*takes her chin in his hand*). Nice—to give in to your husband? All right, little silly, I know you didn't mean it like that. But I won't disturb you. I expect you'll be wanting to try it on.

NORA. Are you going to work now?

HELMER. Yes. (*Shows her a bundle of papers.*) Look at these. I've been down to the bank—(*Turns to go into his study.*)

NORA. Torvald.

HELMER (*stops*). Yes.

NORA. If little squirrel asked you really prettily to grant her a wish—

HELMER. Well?

NORA. Would you grant it to her?

HELMER. First I should naturally have to know what it was.

NORA. Squirrel would do lots of pretty tricks for you if you granted her wish.

HELMER. Out with it, then.

NORA. Your little skylark would sing in every room—

HELMER. My little skylark does that already.

NORA. I'd turn myself into a little fairy and dance for you in the moonlight, Torvald.

HELMER. Nora, it isn't that business you were talking about this morning?

NORA (*comes closer*). Yes, Torvald—oh, please! I beg of you!

HELMER. Have you really the nerve to bring that up again?

NORA. Yes, Torvald, yes, you must do as I ask! You must let Krogstad keep his place at the bank!

HELMER. My dear Nora, his is the job I'm giving to Mrs. Linde.

NORA. Yes, that's terribly sweet of you. But you can get rid of one of the other clerks instead of Krogstad.

HELMER. Really, you're being incredibly obstinate. Just because you thoughtlessly promised to put in a word for him, you expect me to—

NORA. No, it isn't that, Helmer. It's for your own sake. That man writes for the most beastly newspapers—you said so yourself. He could do you tremendous harm. I'm so dreadfully frightened of him—

HELMER. Oh, I understand. Memories of the past. That's what's frightening you.

NORA. What do you mean?

HELMER. You're thinking of your father, aren't you?

NORA. Yes, yes. Of course. Just think what those dreadful men wrote in the papers about Papa! The most frightful slanders. I really believe it would have lost him his job if the Ministry hadn't sent you down to investigate, and you hadn't been so kind and helpful to him.

HELMER. But my dear little Nora, there's a considerable difference between your father and me. Your father was not a man of unassailable reputation. But I am; and I hope to remain so all my life.

NORA. But no one knows what spiteful people may not dig up. We could be so peaceful and happy now, Torvald—we could be free from every worry—you and I and the children. Oh, please, Torvald, please—!

HELMER. The very fact of your pleading his cause makes it impossible for me to keep him. Everyone at the bank already knows that I intend to dismiss Krogstad. If the rumor got about that the new manager had allowed his wife to persuade him to change his mind—

NORA. Well, what then?

HELMER. Oh, nothing, nothing. As long as my little Miss Obstinate gets her way—Do you expect me to make a laughing-stock of myself before my entire staff—give people the idea that I am open to outside influence? Believe me, I'd soon feel the consequences! Besides—there's something else that makes it impossible for Krogstad to remain in the bank while I am its manager.

NORA. What is that?

HELMER. I might conceivably have allowed myself to ignore his moral obloquies—

NORA. Yes, Torvald, surely?

HELMER. And I hear he's quite efficient at his job. But we—well, we were school friends. It was one of those friendships that one enters into over hastily and so often comes to regret later in life. I might as well confess the truth. We—well, we're on Christian name terms. And the tactless idiot makes no attempt to conceal it when other people are present. On the contrary, he thinks it gives him the right to be familiar with me. He shows off the whole time, with "Torvald this," and "Torvald that." I can tell you, I find it damned annoying. If he stayed, he'd make my position intolerable.

NORA. Torvald, you can't mean this seriously.

HELMER. Oh? And why not?

NORA. But it's so petty.

HELMER. What did you say? Petty? You think I am petty?

NORA. No, Torvald dear, of course you're not. That's just why—

HELMER. Don't quibble! You call my motives petty. Then I must be petty too. Petty! I see. Well, I've had enough of this. (Goes to the door and calls into the hall.) Helen!

NORA. What are you going to do?

HELMER (searching among his papers). I'm going to settle this matter once and for all. (The Maid enters.) Take this letter downstairs at once. Find a messenger and see that he delivers it. Immediately! The address is on the envelope. Here's the money.

MAID. Very good, sir. (Goes out with the letter.)

HELMER (putting his papers in order). There now, little Miss Obstinate.

NORA (tensely). Torvald—what was in that letter?

HELMER. Krogstad's dismissal.

NORA. Call her back, Torvald! There's still time. Oh, Torvald, call her back! Do it for my sake—for your own sake—for the children! Do you hear me, Torvald? Please do it! You don't realize what this may do to us all!

HELMER. Too late.

NORA. Yes. Too late.

HELMER. My dear Nora, I forgive you this anxiety. Though it is a bit of an insult to me. Oh, but it is! Isn't it an insult to imply that I should be frightened by the vindictiveness of a depraved hack journalist? But I forgive you, because it so charmingly testifies to the love you bear me. (Takes her in his arms.) Which is as it should be, my own dearest Nora. Let what will happen, happen. When the real crisis comes, you will not find me lacking in strength or courage. I am man enough to bear the burden for us both.

NORA (fearfully). What do you mean?

HELMER. The whole burden, I say—

NORA (calmly). I shall never let you do that.

HELMER. Very well. We shall share it, Nora—as man and wife. And that is as it should be. (Caresses her.) Are you happy now? There, there, there; don't look at me with those frightened little eyes. You're simply imagining things. You go ahead now and do your tarantella, and get some practice on that tambourine. I'll sit in my study and close the door. Then I won't hear anything, and you can make all the noise you want. (Turns in the doorway.) When Dr. Rank comes, tell him where to find me. (He nods to her, goes into his room with his papers, and closes the door.)

NORA (desperate with anxiety, stands as though transfixed, and whispers). He said he'd do it. He will do it. He will do it, and nothing'll stop him. No, never that. I'd rather anything. There must be some escape—Some way out—! (The bell rings in the hall.) Dr. Rank—! Anything but that! Anything, I don't care—!

She passes her hand across her face, composes herself, walks across, and opens the door to the hall. Dr. Rank is standing there, hanging up his fur coat. During the following scene, it begins to grow dark.

NORA. Good evening, Dr. Rank. I recognized your ring. But you mustn't go to Torvald yet. I think he's busy.

RANK. And—you?

NORA (as he enters the room and she closes the door behind him). Oh, you know very well I've always time to talk to you.

RANK. Thank you. I shall avail myself of that privilege as long as I can.

NORA. What do you mean by that? As long as you can?

RANK. Yes. Does that frighten you?

NORA. Well, it's rather a curious expression. Is something going to happen?

RANK. Something I've been expecting to happen for a long time. But I didn't think it would happen quite so soon.

NORA (seizes his arm). What is it? Dr. Rank, you must tell me!

RANK (sits down by the stove). I'm on the way out. And there's nothing to be done about it.

NORA (sighs with relief). Oh, it's you—?

RANK. Who else? No, it's no good lying to oneself. I am the most wretched of all my patients, Mrs. Helmer. These last few days I've been going through the books of this poor body of mine, and I find I am bankrupt. Within a month I may be rotting up there in the churchyard.

NORA. Ugh, what a nasty way to talk!

RANK. The facts aren't exactly nice. But the worst is that there's so much else that's nasty to come first. I've only one more test to make. When that's done I'll have a pretty accurate idea of when the final disintegration is likely to begin. I want to ask you a favour. Helmer's a sensitive chap, and I know how he hates anything ugly. I don't want him to visit me when I'm in hospital—

NORA. Oh but, Dr. Rank—

RANK. I don't want him there. On any pretext. I shan't have him allowed in. As soon as I know the worst, I'll send you my visiting card with a black cross on it, and then you'll know that the final filthy process has begun.

NORA. Really, you're being quite impossible this evening. And I did hope you'd be in a good mood.

RANK. With death on my hands? And all this to atone for someone else's sin? Is there justice in that? And in every single family, in one way or another, the same merciless law of retribution is at work—

NORA (*holds her hands to her ears*). Nonsense! Cheer up! Laugh!

RANK. Yes, you're right. Laughter's all the damned thing's fit for. My poor innocent spine must pay for the fun my father had as a gay young lieutenant.

NORA (*at the table, left*). You mean he was too fond of asparagus and *foie gras*?

RANK. Yes, and truffles too.

NORA. Yes, of course, truffles, yes. And oysters too, I suppose?

RANK. Yes, oysters, oysters. Of course.

NORA. And all that port and champagne to wash them down. It's too sad that all those lovely things should affect one's spine.

RANK. Especially a poor spine that never got any pleasure out of them.

NORA. Oh yes, that's the saddest thing of all.

RANK (*looks searchingly at her*). Hm—

NORA (*after a moment*). Why did you smile?

RANK. No, it was you who laughed.

NORA. No, it was you who smiled, Dr. Rank!

RANK (*gets up*). You're a worse little rogue than I thought.

NORA. Oh, I'm full of stupid tricks today.

RANK. So it seems.

NORA (*puts both her hands on his shoulders*). Dear, dear Dr. Rank, you mustn't die and leave Torvald and me.

RANK. Oh, you'll soon get over it. Once one is gone, one is soon forgotten.

NORA (*looks at him anxiously*). Do you believe that?

RANK. One finds replacements, and then—

NORA. Who will find a replacement?

RANK. You and Helmer both will, when I am gone. You seem to have made a start already, haven't you? What was this Mrs. Linde doing here yesterday evening?

NORA. Aha! But surely you can't be jealous of poor Christine?

RANK. Indeed I am. She will be my successor in this house. When I have moved on, this lady will—

NORA. Ssh—don't speak so loud! She's in there!

RANK. Today again? You see!

NORA. She's only come to mend my dress. Good heavens, how unreasonable you are! (*Sits on the sofa.*) Be nice now, Dr. Rank. Tomorrow you'll see how beautifully I shall dance; and you must imagine that I'm doing it just for you. And for Torvald of course; obviously. (*Takes some things out of the box.*) Dr. Rank, sit down here and I'll show you something.

RANK (*sits*). What's this?

NORA. Look here! Look!

RANK. Silk stockings!

NORA. Flesh-colored. Aren't they beautiful? It's very dark in here now, of course, but tomorrow—No, no, no; only the soles. Oh well, I suppose you can look a bit higher if you want to.

RANK. Hm—

NORA. Why are you looking so critical? Don't you think they'll fit me?

RANK. I can't really give you a qualified opinion on that.

NORA (*looks at him for a moment*). Shame on you! (*Flicks him on the ear with the stockings.*) Take that. (*Puts them back in the box.*)

RANK. What other wonders are to be revealed to me?

NORA. I shan't show you anything else. You're being naughty.

She hums a little and looks among the things in the box.

RANK (*after a short silence*). When I sit here like this being so intimate with you, I can't think—I cannot imagine what would have become of me if I had never entered this house.

NORA (*smiles*). Yes, I think you enjoy being with us, don't you?

RANK (*more quietly, looking into the middle distance*). And now to have to leave it all—

NORA. Nonsense. You're not leaving us.

RANK (*as before*). And not to be able to leave even the most wretched token of gratitude behind; hardly even a passing sense of loss; only an empty place, to be filled by the next comer.

NORA. Suppose I were to ask you to—? No—

RANK. To do what?

NORA. To give me proof of your friendship—

RANK. Yes, yes?

NORA. No, I mean—to do me a very great service—

RANK. Would you really for once grant me that happiness?

NORA. But you've no idea what it is.

RANK. Very well, tell me, then.

NORA. No, but, Dr. Rank, I can't. It's far too much—I want your help and advice, and I want you to do something for me.

RANK. The more the better. I've no idea what it can be. But tell me. You do trust me, don't you?

NORA. Oh, yes, more than anyone. You're my best and truest friend. Otherwise I couldn't tell you. Well then, Dr. Rank—there's something you must help me to prevent. You know how much Torvald loves me—he'd never hesitate for an instant to lay down his life for me—

RANK (*leans over towards her*). Nora—do you think he is the only one—?

NORA (*with a slight start*). What do you mean?

RANK. Who would gladly lay down his life for you?

NORA (*sadly*). Oh, I see.

RANK. I swore to myself I would let you know that before I go. I shall never have a better opportunity. . . . Well, Nora, now you know that. And now you also know that you can trust me as you can trust nobody else.

NORA (*rises; calmly and quietly*). Let me pass, please.

RANK (*makes room for her but remains seated*). Nora—

NORA (*in the doorway to the hall*). Helen, bring the lamp. (*Goes over to the stove.*) Oh, dear Dr. Rank, this was really horrid of you.

RANK (*gets up*). That I have loved you as deeply as anyone else has? Was that horrid of me?

NORA. No—but that you should go and tell me. That was quite unnecessary—

RANK. What do you mean? Did you know, then—?

The Maid enters with the lamp, puts it on the table, and goes out.

RANK. Nora—Mrs. Helmer—I am asking you, did you know this?

NORA. Oh, what do I know, what did I know, what didn't I know—I really can't say. How could you be so stupid, Dr. Rank? Everything was so nice.

RANK. Well, at any rate now you know that I am ready to serve you, body and soul. So—please continue.

NORA (*looks at him*). After this?

RANK. Please tell me what it is.

NORA. I can't possibly tell you now.

RANK. Yes, yes! You mustn't punish me like this. Let me be allowed to do what I can for you.

NORA. You can't do anything for me now. Anyway; I don't need any help. It was only my imagination—you'll see. Yes, really. Honestly. (*Sits in the rocking-chair, looks at him, and smiles.*) Well, upon my word you *are* a fine gentleman, Dr. Rank. Aren't you ashamed of yourself, now that the lamp's been lit?

RANK. Frankly, no. But perhaps I ought to say—*adieu*?

NORA. Of course not. You will naturally continue to visit us as before. You know quite well how Torvald depends on your company.

RANK. Yes, but you?

NORA. Oh, I always think it's enormous fun having you here.

RANK. That was what misled me. You're a riddle to me, you know. I'd often felt you'd just as soon be with me as with Helmer.

NORA. Well, you see, there are some people whom one loves, and others whom it's almost more fun to be with.

RANK. Oh yes, there's some truth in that.

NORA. When I was at home, of course I loved Papa best. But I always used to think it was terribly amusing to go down and talk to the servants; because they never told me what I ought to do; and they were such fun to listen to.

RANK. I see. So I've taken their place?

NORA (*jumps up and runs over to him*). Oh, dear, sweet Dr. Rank, I didn't mean that at all. But I'm sure you understand—I feel the same about Torvald as I did about Papa.

MAID (*enters from the hall*). Excuse me, madam. (*Whispers to her and hands her a visiting card.*)

NORA (*glances at the card*). Oh! (*Puts it quickly in her pocket.*)

RANK. Anything wrong?

NORA. No, no, nothing at all. It's just something that—it's my new dress.

RANK. What? But your costume is lying over there.

NORA. Oh—that, yes—but there's another—I ordered it specially—Torvald mustn't know—

RANK. Ah, so that's your big secret?

NORA. Yes, yes. Go in and talk to him—he's in his study—keep him talking for a bit—

RANK. Don't worry. He won't get away from me. (*Goes into Helmer's study.*)

NORA (*to the Maid*). Is he waiting in the kitchen?

MAID. Yes, madam, he came up the back way—

NORA. But didn't you tell him I had a visitor?

MAID. Yes, but he wouldn't go.

NORA. Wouldn't go?

MAID. No, madam, not until he'd spoken with you.

NORA. Very well, show him in; but quietly. Helen, you mustn't tell anyone about this. It's a surprise for my husband.

MAID. Very good, madam. I understand. (*Goes.*)

NORA. It's happening. It's happening after all. No, no, no, it can't happen, it mustn't happen.

She walks across and bolts the door of Helmer's study. The Maid opens the door from the hall to admit Krogstad, and closes it behind him. He is wearing an overcoat, heavy boots, and a fur cap.

NORA (*goes towards him*). Speak quietly. My husband's at home.

KROGSTAD. Let him hear.

NORA. What do you want from me?

KROGSTAD. Information.

NORA. Hurry up, then. What is it?

KROGSTAD. I suppose you know I've been given the sack.

NORA. I couldn't stop it, Mr. Krogstad. I did my best for you, but it didn't help.

KROGSTAD. Does your husband love you so little? He knows what I can do to you, and yet he dares to—

NORA. Surely you don't imagine I told him?

KROGSTAD. No. I didn't really think you had. It wouldn't have been like my old friend Torvald Helmer to show that much courage—

NORA. Mr. Krogstad, I'll trouble you to speak respectfully of my husband.

KROGSTAD. Don't worry, I'll show him all the respect he deserves. But since you're so anxious to keep this matter hushed up, I presume you're better informed than you were yesterday of the gravity of what you've done?

NORA. I've learned more than you could ever teach me.

KROGSTAD. Yes, a bad lawyer like me—

NORA. What do you want from me?

KROGSTAD. I just wanted to see how things were with you, Mrs. Helmer. I've been thinking about you all day. Even duns and hack journalists have hearts, you know.

NORA. Show some heart, then. Think of my little children.

KROGSTAD. Have you and your husband thought of mine? Well, let's forget that. I just wanted to tell you, you don't need to take this business too seriously. I'm not going to take any action, for the present.

NORA. Oh, no—you won't, will you? I knew it.

KROGSTAD. It can all be settled quite amicably. There's no need for it to become public. We'll keep it among the three of us.

NORA. My husband must never know about this.

KROGSTAD. How can you stop him? Can you pay the balance of what you owe me?

NORA. Not immediately.

KROGSTAD. Have you any means of raising the money during the next few days?

NORA. None that I would care to use.

KROGSTAD. Well, it wouldn't have helped anyway. However much money you offered me now I wouldn't give you back that paper.

NORA. What are you going to do with it?

KROGSTAD. Just keep it. No one else need ever hear about it. So in case you were thinking of doing anything desperate—

NORA. I am.

KROGSTAD. Such as running away—

NORA. I am.

KROGSTAD. Or anything more desperate—

NORA. How did you know?

KROGSTAD. —just give up the idea.

NORA. How did you know?

KROGSTAD. Most of us think of that at first. I did. But I hadn't the courage—

NORA (dully). Neither have I.

KROGSTAD (relieved). It's true, isn't it? You haven't the courage either?

NORA. No. I haven't. I haven't.

KROGSTAD. It'd be a stupid thing to do anyway. Once the first little domestic explosion is over. . . . I've got a letter in my pocket here addressed to your husband—

NORA. Telling him everything?

KROGSTAD. As delicately as possible.

NORA (quickly). He must never see that letter. Tear it up. I'll find the money somehow—

KROGSTAD. I'm sorry, Mrs. Helmer, I thought I'd explained—

NORA. Oh, I don't mean the money I owe you. Let me know how much you want from my husband, and I'll find it for you.

KROGSTAD. I'm not asking your husband for money.

NORA. What do you want, then?

KROGSTAD. I'll tell you. I want to get on my feet again, Mrs. Helmer. I want to get to the top. And your husband's going to help me. For eighteen months now my record's been clean. I've been in hard straits all that time; I was content to fight my way back inch by inch. Now I've been chucked back into the mud, and I'm not going to be satisfied with just getting back my job. I'm going to get to the top, I tell you. I'm going to get back into the bank, and it's going to be higher up. Your husband's going to create a new job for me—

NORA. He'll never do that!

KROGSTAD. Oh, yes he will. I know him. He won't dare to risk a scandal. And once I'm in there with him, you'll see! Within a year I'll be his right-hand man. It'll be Nils Krogstad who'll be running that bank, not Torvald Helmer!

NORA. That will never happen.

KROGSTAD. Are you thinking of—?

NORA. Now I have the courage.

KROGSTAD. Oh, you can't frighten me. A pampered little pretty like you—

NORA. You'll see! You'll see!

KROGSTAD. Under the ice? Down in the cold, black water? And then, in the spring, to float up again, ugly, unrecognizable, hairless—?

NORA. You can't frighten me.

KROGSTAD. And you can't frighten me. People don't do such things, Mrs. Helmer. And anyway, what'd be the use? I've got him in my pocket.

NORA. But afterwards? When I'm no longer—?

KROGSTAD. Have you forgotten that then your reputation will be in my hands? (She looks at him speechlessly.) Well, I've warned you. Don't do anything silly. When Helmer's read my letter, he'll get in touch with me. And remember, it's your husband who's forced me to act like this. And for that I'll never forgive him. Goodbye, Mrs. Helmer. (He goes out through the hall.)

NORA (runs to the hall door, opens it a few inches, and listens). He's going. He's not going to give him the letter. Oh, no, no, it couldn't possibly happen. (Opens the door a little wider.) What's he doing? Standing outside the front door. He's not going downstairs. Is he changing his mind? Yes, he—!

A letter falls into the letter-box. Krogstad's footsteps die away down the stairs.

NORA (with a stifled cry runs across the room towards the table by the sofa. A pause). In the letter-box. (Steals timidly over towards the hall door.) There it is! Oh, Torvald, Torvald! Now we're lost!

MRS. LINDE (enters from the nursery with Nora's costume). Well, I've done the best I can. Shall we see how it looks—?

NORA (whispers hoarsely). Christine, come here.

MRS. LINDE (*throws the dress on the sofa*). What's wrong with you? You look as though you'd seen a ghost!

NORA. Come here. Do you see that letter? There—look—through the glass of the letter-box.

MRS. LINDE. Yes, yes, I see it.

NORA. That letter's from Krogstad—

MRS. LINDE. Nora! It was Krogstad who lent you the money!

NORA. Yes. And now Torvald's going to discover everything.

MRS. LINDE. Oh, believe me, Nora, it'll be best for you both.

NORA. You don't know what's happened. I've committed a forgery—

MRS. LINDE. But, for heaven's sake—!

NORA. Christine, all I want is for you to be my witness.

MRS. LINDE. What do you mean? Witness what?

NORA. If I should go out of my mind—and it might easily happen—

MRS. LINDE. Nora!

NORA. Or if anything else should happen to me—so that I wasn't here any longer—

MRS. LINDE. Nora, Nora, you don't know what you're saying!

NORA. If anyone should try to take the blame, and say it was all his fault—you understand—?

MRS. LINDE. Yes, yes—but how can you think?

NORA. Then you must testify that it isn't true, Christine. I'm not mad—I know exactly what I'm saying—and I'm telling you, no one else knows anything about this. I did it entirely on my own. Remember that.

MRS. LINDE. All right. But I simply don't understand—

NORA. Oh, how could you understand? A—miracle—is about to happen.

MRS. LINDE. Miracle?

NORA. Yes. A miracle. But it's so frightening, Christine. It *mustn't* happen, not for anything in the world.

MRS. LINDE. I'll go over and talk to Krogstad.

NORA. Don't go near him. He'll only do something to hurt you.

MRS. LINDE. Once upon a time he'd have done anything for my sake.

NORA. He?

MRS. LINDE. Where does he live?

NORA. Oh, how should I know—? Oh, yes, wait a moment—! (*Feels in her pocket.*) Here's his card. But the letter, the letter—!

HELMER (*from his study, knocks on the door*). Nora!

NORA (*cries in alarm*). What is it?

HELMER. Now, now, don't get alarmed. We're not coming in; you've closed the door. Are you trying on your costume?

NORA. Yes, yes—I'm trying on my costume. I'm going to look so pretty for you, Torvald.

MRS. LINDE (*who has been reading the card*). Why, he lives just around the corner.

NORA. Yes; but it's no use. There's nothing to be done now. The letter's lying there in the box.

MRS. LINDE. And your husband has the key?

NORA. Yes, he always keeps it.

MRS. LINDE. Krogstad must ask him to send the letter back unread. He must find some excuse—

NORA. But Torvald always opens the box at just about this time—

MRS. LINDE. You must stop him. Go in and keep him talking. I'll be back as quickly as I can.

She hurries out through the hall.

NORA (*goes over to Helmer's door, opens it and peeps in*). Torvald!

HELMER (*offstage*). Well, may a man enter his own drawing-room again? Come on, Rank, now we'll see what—(*In the doorway.*) But what's this?

NORA. What, Torvald dear?

HELMER. Rank's been preparing me for some great transformation scene.

RANK (*in the doorway*). So I understood. But I seem to have been mistaken.

NORA. Yes, no one's to be allowed to see me before tomorrow night.

HELMER. But, my dear Nora, you look quite worn out. Have you been practicing too hard?

NORA. No, I haven't practiced at all yet.

HELMER. Well, you must.

NORA. Yes, Torvald, I must, I know. But I can't get anywhere without your help. I've completely forgotten everything.

HELMER. Oh, we'll soon put that to rights.

NORA. Yes, help me, Torvald. Promise me you will? Oh, I'm so nervous. All those people—! You must forget everything except me this evening. You mustn't think of business—I won't even let you touch a pen. Promise me, Torvald?

HELMER. I promise. This evening I shall think of nothing but you—my poor, helpless little darling. Oh, there's just one thing I must see to—(*Goes towards the hall door.*)

NORA. What do you want out there?

HELMER. I'm only going to see if any letters have come.

NORA. No, Torvald, no!

HELMER. Why, what's the matter?

NORA. Torvald, I beg you. There's nothing there.

HELMER. Well, I'll just make sure.

He moves towards the door. Nora runs to the piano and plays the first bars of the tarantella.

HELMER (*at the door, turns*). Aha!

NORA. I can't dance tomorrow if I don't practice with you now.

HELMER (*goes over to her*). Are you really so frightened, Nora dear?

NORA. Yes, terribly frightened. Let me start practicing now, at once—we've still time before dinner. Oh, do sit down and play for me, Torvald dear. Correct me, lead me, the way you always do.

HELMER. Very well, my dear, if you wish it.

He sits down at the piano. Nora seizes the tambourine and a long multi-colored shawl from the cardboard box, wraps the latter hastily around her, then takes a quick leap into the center of the room.

NORA. Play for me! I want to dance!

Helmer plays and Nora dances. Dr. Rank stands behind Helmer at the piano and watches her.

HELMER (*as he plays*). Slower, slower!

NORA. I can't!

HELMER. Not so violently, Nora.

NORA. I must!

HELMER (*stops playing*). No, no, this won't do at all.

NORA (*laughs and swings her tambourine*). Isn't that what I told you?

RANK. Let me play for her.

HELMER (*gets up*). Yes, would you? Then it'll be easier for me to show her.

Rank sits down at the piano and plays. Nora dances more and more wildly. Helmer has stationed himself by the stove and tries repeatedly to correct her, but she seems not to hear him. Her hair works loose and falls over her shoulders; she ignores it and continues to dance. Mrs. Linde enters.

MRS. LINDE (*stands in the doorway as though tongue-tied*). Ah—!

NORA (*as she dances*). Oh, Christine, we're having such fun!

HELMER. But, Nora darling, you're dancing as if your life depended on it.

NORA. It does.

HELMER. Rank, stop it! This is sheer lunacy. Stop it, I say!

Rank ceases playing. Nora suddenly stops dancing.

HELMER (*goes over to her*). I'd never have believed it. You've forgotten everything I taught you.

NORA (*throws away the tambourine*). You see!

HELMER. I'll have to show you every step.

NORA. You see how much I need you! You must show me every step of the way. Right to the end of the dance. Promise me you will, Torvald?

HELMER. Never fear. I will.

NORA. You mustn't think about anything but me—today or tomorrow. Don't open any letters—don't even open the letter-box—

HELMER. Aha, you're still worried about that fellow—

NORA. Oh, yes, yes, him too.

HELMER. Nora, I can tell from the way you're behaving, there's a letter from him already lying there.

NORA. I don't know. I think so. But you mustn't read it now. I don't want anything ugly to come between us till it's all over.

RANK (*quietly, to Helmer*). Better give her her way.

HELMER (*puts his arm round her*). My child shall have her way. But tomorrow night, when your dance is over—

NORA. Then you will be free.

MAID (*appears in the doorway, right*). Dinner is served, madam.

NORA. Put out some champagne, Helen.

MAID. Very good, madam. (*Goes.*)

HELMER. I say! What's this, a banquet?

NORA. We'll drink champagne until dawn! (*Calls.*) And, Helen! Put out some macaroons! Lots of macaroons—for once!

HELMER (*takes her hands in his*). Now, now, now. Don't get so excited. Where's my little songbird, the one I know?

NORA. All right. Go and sit down—and you too, Dr. Rank. I'll be with you in a minute. Christine, you must help me put my hair up.

RANK (*quietly, as they go*). There's nothing wrong, is there? I mean, she isn't—er—expecting—?

HELMER Good heavens no, my dear chap. She just gets scared like a child sometimes—I told you before—

They go out right.

NORA. Well?

MRS. LINDE. He's left town.

NORA. I saw it from your face.

MRS. LINDE. He'll be back tomorrow evening. I left a note for him.

NORA. You needn't have bothered. You can't stop anything now. Anyway, it's wonderful really, in a way—sitting here and waiting for the miracle to happen.

MRS. LINDE. Waiting for what?

NORA. Oh, you wouldn't understand. Go in and join them. I'll be with you in a moment.

Mrs. Linde goes into the dining-room.

NORA (*stands for a moment as though collecting herself. Then she looks at her watch*). Five o'clock. Seven hours till midnight. Then another twenty-four hours till midnight tomorrow. And then the tarantella will be finished. Twenty-four and seven? Thirty-one hours to live.

HELMER (*appears in the doorway, right*). What's happened to my little songbird?

NORA (*runs to him with her arms wide*). Your songbird is here!

ACT 3

The same room. The table which was formerly by the sofa has been moved into the center of the room; the chairs surround it as before. The door to the hall stands open. Dance music can be heard from the floor above. Mrs. Linde is seated at the table, absent-mindedly glancing through a book. She is trying to read, but seems unable to keep her mind on it. More than once she turns and listens anxiously towards the front door.

MRS. LINDE (*looks at her watch*). Not here yet. There's not much time left. Please God he hasn't—! (*Listens again.*) Ah, here he is. (*Goes out into the hall and cautiously opens the front door. Footsteps can be heard softly ascending the stairs. She whispers.*) Come in. There's no one here.

KROGSTAD (*in the doorway*). I found a note from you at my lodgings. What does this mean?

MRS. LINDE. I must speak with you.

KROGSTAD. Oh? And must our conversation take place in this house?

MRS. LINDE. We couldn't meet at my place; my room has no separate entrance. Come in. We're quite alone. The maid's asleep, and the Helmers are at the dance upstairs.

KROGSTAD (*comes into the room*). Well, well! So the Helmers are dancing this evening? Are they indeed?

MRS. LINDE. Yes, why not?

KROGSTAD. True enough. Why not?

MRS. LINDE. Well, Krogstad. You and I must have a talk together.

KROGSTAD. Have we two anything further to discuss?

MRS. LINDE. We have a great deal to discuss.

KROGSTAD. I wasn't aware of it.

MRS. LINDE. That's because you've never really understood me.

KROGSTAD. Was there anything to understand? It's the old story, isn't it—a woman chucking a man because something better turns up?

MRS. LINDE. Do you really think I'm so utterly heartless? You think it was easy for me to give you up?

KROGSTAD. Wasn't it?

MRS. LINDE. Oh, Nils, did you really believe that?

KROGSTAD. Then why did you write to me the way you did?

MRS. LINDE. I had to. Since I had to break with you, I thought it my duty to destroy all the feelings you had for me.

KROGSTAD (*clenches his fists*). So that was it. And you did this for money!

MRS. LINDE. You mustn't forget I had a helpless mother to take care of, and two little brothers. We couldn't wait for you, Nils. It would have been so long before you'd had enough to support us.

KROGSTAD. Maybe. But you had no right to cast me off for someone else.

MRS. LINDE. Perhaps not. I've often asked myself that.

KROGSTAD (*more quietly*). When I lost you, it was just as though all solid ground had been swept from under my feet. Look at me. Now I am a shipwrecked man, clinging to a spar.

MRS. LINDE. Help may be near at hand.

KROGSTAD. It was near. But then you came, and stood between it and me.

MRS. LINDE. I didn't know, Nils. No one told me till today that this job I'd found was yours.

KROGSTAD. I believe you, since you say so. But now you know, won't you give it up?

MRS. LINDE. No—because it wouldn't help you even if I did.

KROGSTAD. Wouldn't it? I'd do it all the same.

MRS. LINDE. I've learned to look at things practically. Life and poverty have taught me that.

KROGSTAD. And life has taught me to distrust fine words.

MRS. LINDE. Then it's taught you a useful lesson. But surely you still believe in actions?

KROGSTAD. What do you mean?

MRS. LINDE. You said you were like a shipwrecked man clinging to a spar.

KROGSTAD. I have good reason to say it.

MRS. LINDE. I'm in the same position as you. No one to care about, no one to care for.

KROGSTAD. You made your own choice.

MRS. LINDE. I had no choice—then.

KROGSTAD. Well?

MRS. LINDE. Nils, suppose we two shipwrecked souls could join hands?

KROGSTAD. What are you saying?

MRS. LINDE. Castaways have a better chance of survival together than on their own.

KROGSTAD. Christine!

MRS. LINDE. Why do you suppose I came to this town?

KROGSTAD. You mean—you came because of me?

MRS. LINDE. I must work if I'm to find life worth living. I've always worked, for as long as I can remember; it's been the greatest joy of my life—my only joy. But now I'm alone in the world, and I feel so dreadfully lost and empty. There's no joy in working just for oneself. Oh, Nils, give me something—someone—to work for.

KROGSTAD. I don't believe all that. You're just being hysterical and romantic. You want to find an excuse for self-sacrifice.

MRS. LINDE. Have you ever known me to be hysterical?

KROGSTAD. You mean you really—? Is it possible? Tell me—you know all about my past?

MRS. LINDE. Yes.

KROGSTAD. And you know what people think of me here?

MRS. LINDE. You said just now that with me you might have become a different person.

KROGSTAD. I know I could have.

MRS. LINDE. Couldn't it still happen?

KROGSTAD. Christine—do you really mean this? Yes—you do—I see it in your face. Have you really the courage—?

MRS. LINDE. I need someone to be a mother to; and your children need a mother. And you and I need each other. I believe in you, Nils. I am afraid of nothing—with you.

KROGSTAD (*clasps her hands*). Thank you, Christine—thank you! Now I shall make the world believe in me as you do! Oh—but I'd forgotten—

MRS. LINDE (*listens*). Ssh! The tarantella! Go quickly, go!

KROGSTAD. Why? What is it?

MRS. LINDE. You hear that dance? As soon as it's finished, they'll be coming down.

KROGSTAD. All right, I'll go. It's no good, Christine. I'd forgotten—you don't know what I've just done to the Helmers.

MRS. LINDE. Yes, Nils. I know.

KROGSTAD. And yet you'd still have the courage to—?

MRS. LINDE. I know what despair can drive a man like you to.

KROGSTAD. Oh, if only I could undo this!

MRS. LINDE. You can. Your letter is still lying in the box.

KROGSTAD. Are you sure?

MRS. LINDE. Quite sure. But—

KROGSTAD (*looks searchingly at her*). Is that why you're doing this? You want to save your friend at any price? Tell me the truth. Is that the reason?

MRS. LINDE. Nils, a woman who has sold herself once for the sake of others doesn't make the same mistake again.

KROGSTAD. I shall demand my letter back.

MRS. LINDE. No, no.

KROGSTAD. Of course I shall. I shall stay here till Helmer comes down. I'll tell him he must give me back my letter—I'll say it was only to do with my dismissal, and that I don't want him to read it—

MRS. LINDE. No, Nils, you mustn't ask for that letter back.

KROGSTAD. But—tell me—wasn't that the real reason you asked me to come here?

MRS. LINDE. Yes—at first, when I was frightened. But a day has passed since then, and in that time I've seen incredible things happen in this house. Helmer must know the truth. This unhappy secret of Nora's must be revealed. They must come to a full understanding; there must be an end of all these shiftings and evasions.

KROGSTAD. Very well. If you're prepared to risk it. But one thing I can do—and at once—

MRS. LINDE (*listens*). Hurry! Go, go! The dance is over. We aren't safe here another moment.

KROGSTAD. I'll wait for you downstairs.

MRS. LINDE. Yes, do. You can see me home.

KROGSTAD. I've never been so happy in my life before!

He goes out through the front door. The door leading from the room into the hall remains open.

MRS. LINDE (*tidies the room a little and gets her hat and coat*). What a change! Oh, what a change! Someone to work for—to live for! A home to bring joy into! I won't let this chance of happiness slip through my fingers. Oh, why don't they come? (*Listens.*) Ah, here they are. I must get my coat on.

She takes her hat and coat. Helmer's and Nora's voices become audible outside. A key is turned in the lock and Helmer leads Nora almost forcibly into the hall. She is dressed in an Italian costume with a large black shawl. He is in evening dress, with a black cloak.

NORA (*still in the doorway, resisting him*). No, no, no—not in here! I want to go back upstairs. I don't want to leave so early.

HELMER. But my dearest Nora—

NORA. Oh, please, Torvald, please! Just another hour!

HELMER. Not another minute, Nora, my sweet. You know what we agreed. Come along, now. Into the drawing-room. You'll catch cold if you stay out here.

He leads her, despite her efforts to resist him, gently into the room.

MRS. LINDE. Good evening.

NORA. Christine!

HELMER. Oh, hullo, Mrs. Linde. You still here?

MRS. LINDE. Please forgive me. I did so want to see Nora in her costume.

NORA. Have you been sitting here waiting for me?

MRS. LINDE. Yes. I got here too late, I'm afraid. You'd already gone up. And I felt I really couldn't go back home without seeing you.

HELMER (*takes off Nora's shawl*). Well, take a good look at her. She's worth looking at, don't you think? Isn't she beautiful, Mrs. Linde?

MRS. LINDE. Oh, yes, indeed—

HELMER. Isn't she unbelievably beautiful? Everyone at the party said so. But dreadfully stubborn she is, bless her pretty little heart. What's to be done about that? Would you believe it, I practically had to use force to get her away!

NORA. Oh, Torvald, you're going to regret not letting me stay—just half an hour longer.

HELMER. Hear that, Mrs. Linde? She dances her tarantella—makes a roaring success—and very well deserved—though possibly a trifle too realistic—more so than was aesthetically necessary, strictly speaking. But never mind that. Main thing is—she had a success—roaring success. Was I going to let her stay on after that and spoil the impression? No, thank you. I took my beautiful little Capri signorina—my capricious little Capricienne, what?—under my arm—a swift round of the ballroom, a curtsey to the company, and, as they say in novels, the beautiful apparition disappeared! An exit should always be dramatic, Mrs. Linde. But unfortunately that's just what I can't get Nora to realize. I say, it's hot in here. (*Throws his cloak on a chair and opens the door to his study.*) What's this? It's dark in here. Ah, yes, of course—excuse me. (*Goes in and lights a couple of candles.*)

NORA (*whispers swiftly, breathlessly*). Well?

MRS. LINDE (*quietly*). I've spoken to him.

NORA. Yes?

MRS. LINDE. Nora—you must tell your husband everything.

NORA (*dully*). I knew it.

MRS. LINDE. You've nothing to fear from Krogstad. But you must tell him.

NORA. I shan't tell him anything.

MRS. LINDE. Then the letter will.

NORA. Thank you, Christine. Now I know what I must do. Ssh!

HELMER (*returns*). Well, Mrs. Linde, finished admiring her?

MRS. LINDE. Yes. Now I must say good night.

HELMER. Oh, already? Does this knitting belong to you?

MRS. LINDE (*takes it*). Thank you, yes. I nearly forgot it.

HELMER. You knit, then?

MRS. LINDE. Why?

HELMER. Know what? You ought to take up embroidery.

MRS. LINDE. Oh? Why?

HELMER. It's much prettier. Watch me, now. You hold the embroidery in your left hand, like this, and then you take the needle in your right hand and go in and out in a slow, easy movement—like this. I am right, aren't I?

MRS. LINDE. Yes, I'm sure—

HELMER. But knitting, now—that's an ugly business—can't help it. Look—arms all huddled up—great clumsy needles going up and down—makes you look like a damned Chinaman. I say, that really was a magnificent champagne they served us.

MRS. LINDE. Well, good night, Nora. And stop being stubborn. Remember!

HELMER. Quite right, Mrs. Linde!

MRS. LINDE. Good night, Mr. Helmer.

HELMER (*accompanies her to the door*). Good night, good night! I hope you'll manage to get home all right? I'd gladly—but you haven't far to go, have you? Good night, good night. (*She goes. He closes the door behind her and returns.*) Well, we've got rid of her at last. Dreadful bore that woman is!

NORA. Aren't you very tired, Torvald?

HELMER. No, not in the least.

NORA. Aren't you sleepy?

HELMER. Not a bit. On the contrary, I feel extraordinarily exhilarated. But what about you? Yes, you look very sleepy and tired.

NORA. Yes, I am very tired. Soon I shall sleep.

HELMER. You see, you see! How right I was not to let you stay longer!

NORA. Oh, you're always right, whatever you do.

HELMER (*kisses her on the forehead*). Now my little songbird's talking just like a real big human being. I say, did you notice how cheerful Rank was this evening?

NORA. Oh? Was he? I didn't have a chance to speak with him.

HELMER. I hardly did. But I haven't seen him in such a jolly mood for ages. (*Looks at her for a moment, then comes closer.*) I say, it's nice to get back to one's home again, and be all alone with you. Upon my word, you're a distractingly beautiful young woman.

NORA. Don't look at me like that, Torvald!

HELMER. What, not look at my most treasured possession? At all this wonderful beauty that's mine, mine alone, all mine.

NORA (*goes round to the other side of the table*). You mustn't talk to me like that tonight.

HELMER (*follows her*). You've still the tarantella in your blood, I see. And that makes you even more desirable. Listen! Now the other guests are beginning to go. (*More quietly.*) Nora—soon the whole house will be absolutely quiet.

NORA. Yes, I hope so.

HELMER. Yes, my beloved Nora, of course you do! Do you know—when I'm out with you among other people like we were tonight, do you know why I say so little to you, why I keep so aloof from you, and just throw you an occasional glance? Do you know why I do that? It's because I pretend to myself that you're my secret mistress, my clandestine little sweetheart, and that nobody knows there's anything at all between us.

NORA. Oh, yes, yes, yes—I know you never think of anything but me.

HELMER. And then when we're about to go, and I wrap the shawl round your lovely young shoulders, over this wonderful curve of your neck—then I pretend to myself that you are my young bride, that we've just come from the wedding, that I'm taking you to my house for the first time—that, for the first time, I am alone with you—quite alone with you, as you stand there young and trembling and beautiful. All evening I've had no eyes for anyone but you. When I saw you dance the tarantella, like a huntress, a temptress, my blood grew hot, I couldn't stand it any longer! That was why I seized you and dragged you down here with me—

NORA. Leave me, Torvald! Get away from me! I don't want all this.

HELMER. What? Now, Nora, you're joking with me. Don't want, don't want—? Aren't I your husband—?

There is a knock on the front door.

NORA (*starts*). What was that?

HELMER (*goes towards the hall*). Who is it?

RANK (*outside*). It's me. May I come in for a moment?

HELMER (*quietly, annoyed*). Oh, what does he want now? (*Calls.*) Wait a moment. (*Walks over and opens the door.*) Well! Nice of you not to go by without looking in.

RANK. I thought I heard your voice, so I felt I had to say goodbye. (*His eyes travel swiftly around the room.*) Ah, yes—these dear rooms, how well I know them. What a happy, peaceful home you two have.

HELMER. You seemed to be having a pretty happy time yourself upstairs.

RANK. Indeed I did. Why not? Why shouldn't one make the most of this world? As much as one can, and for as long as one can. The wine was excellent—

HELMER. Especially the champagne.

RANK. You noticed that too? It's almost incredible how much I managed to get down.

NORA. Torvald drank a lot of champagne too, this evening.

RANK. Oh?

NORA. Yes. It always makes him merry afterwards.

RANK. Well, why shouldn't a man have a merry evening after a well-spent day?

HELMER. Well-spent? Oh, I don't know that I can claim that.

RANK (*slaps him across the back*). I can though, my dear fellow!

NORA. Yes, of course, Dr. Rank—you've been carrying out a scientific experiment today, haven't you?

RANK. Exactly.

HELMER. Scientific experiment! Those are big words for my little Nora to use!

NORA. And may I congratulate you on the finding?

RANK. You may indeed.

NORA. It was good, then?

RANK. The best possible finding—both for the doctor and the patient. Certainty.

NORA (*quickly*). Certainty?

RANK. Absolute certainty. So aren't I entitled to have a merry evening after that?

NORA. Yes, Dr. Rank. You were quite right to.

HELMER. I agree. Provided you don't have to regret it tomorrow.

RANK. Well, you never get anything in this life without paying for it.

NORA. Dr. Rank—you like masquerades, don't you?

RANK. Yes, if the disguises are sufficiently amusing.

NORA. Tell me. What shall we two wear at the next masquerade?

HELMER. You little gadabout! Are you thinking about the next one already?

RANK. We two? Yes, I'll tell you. You must go as the Spirit of Happiness—

HELMER. You try to think of a costume that'll convey that.

RANK. Your wife need only appear as her normal, everyday self—

HELMER. Quite right! Well said! But what are you going to be? Have you decided that?

RANK. Yes, my dear friend. I have decided that.

HELMER. Well?

RANK. At the next masquerade, I shall be invisible.

HELMER. Well, that's a funny idea.

RANK. There's a big, black hat—haven't you heard of the invisible hat? Once it's over your head, no one can see you any more.

HELMER (*represses a smile*). Ah yes, of course.

RANK. But I'm forgetting what I came for. Helmer, give me a cigar. One of your black Havanas.

HELMER. With the greatest pleasure. (*Offers him the box.*)

RANK (*takes one and cuts off the tip*). Thank you.

NORA (*strikes a match*). Let me give you a light.

RANK. Thank you. (*She holds out the match for him. He lights his cigar.*) And now—goodbye.

HELMER. Goodbye, my dear chap, goodbye.

NORA. Sleep well, Dr. Rank.

RANK. Thank you for that kind wish.

NORA. Wish me the same.

RANK. You? Very well—since you ask. Sleep well. And thank you for the light. (*He nods to them both and goes.*)

HELMER (*quietly*). He's been drinking too much.

NORA (*abstractedly*). Perhaps.

Helmer takes his bunch of keys from his pocket and goes out into the hall.

NORA. Torvald, what do you want out there?

HELMER. I must empty the letter-box. It's absolutely full. There'll be no room for the newspapers in the morning.

NORA. Are you going to work tonight?

HELMER. You know very well I'm not. Hullo, what's this? Someone's been at the lock.

NORA. At the lock—?

HELMER. Yes, I'm sure of it. Who on earth—? Surely not one of the maids? Here's a broken hairpin. Nora, it's yours—

NORA (*quickly*). Then it must have been the children.

HELMER. Well, you'll have to break them of that habit. Hm, hm. Ah, that's done it. (*Takes out the contents of the box and calls into the kitchen.*) Helen! Put out the light on the staircase. (*Comes back into the drawing-room with the letters in his hand and closes the door to the hall.*) Look at this! You see how they've piled up? (*Glances through them.*) What on earth's this?

NORA (*at the window*). The letter! Oh, no, Torvald, no!

HELMER. Two visiting cards—from Rank.

NORA. From Dr. Rank?

HELMER (*looks at them*). Peter Rank, M.D. They were on top. He must have dropped them in as he left.

NORA. Has he written anything on them?

HELMER. There's a black cross above his name. Look. Rather gruesome, isn't it? It looks just as though he was announcing his death.

NORA. He is.

HELMER. What? Do you know something? Has he told you anything?

NORA. Yes. When these cards come, it means he's said goodbye to us. He wants to shut himself up in his house and die.

HELMER. Ah, poor fellow. I knew I wouldn't be seeing him for much longer. But so soon—! And now he's going to slink away and hide like a wounded beast.

NORA. When the time comes, it's best to go silently. Don't you think so, Torvald?

HELMER (*walks up and down*). He was so much a part of our life. I can't realize that he's gone. His suffering and loneliness seemed to provide a kind of dark background to the happy sunlight of our marriage. Well, perhaps it's best this way. For him, anyway. (*Stops walking.*) And perhaps for us too, Nora. Now we have only each other. (*Embraces her.*) Oh, my beloved wife—I feel as though I could never hold you close enough. Do you know, Nora, often I wish some terrible danger might threaten you, so that I could offer my life and my blood, everything, for your sake.

NORA (*tears herself loose and says in a clear, firm voice*). Read your letters now, Torvald.

HELMER. No, no. Not tonight. Tonight I want to be with you, my darling wife—

NORA. When your friend is about to die—?

HELMER. You're right. This news has upset us both. An ugliness has come between us; thoughts of death and dissolution. We must try to forget them. Until then—you go to your room; I shall go to mine.

NORA (*throws her arms around his neck*). Good night, Torvald! Good night!

HELMER (*kisses her on the forehead*). Good night, my darling little songbird. Sleep well, Nora. I'll go and read my letters.

He goes into the study with the letters in his hand, and closes the door.

NORA (*wild-eyed, fumbles around, seizes Helmer's cloak, throws it round herself and whispers quickly, hoarsely*). Never see him again. Never. Never. Never. (*Throws the shawl over her head.*) Never see the children again. Them too. Never. Never. Oh—the icy black water! Oh—that bottomless—that—! Oh, if only it were all over! Now he's got it—he's reading it. Oh, no, no! Not yet! Goodbye, Torvald! Goodbye, my darlings!

She turns to run into the hall. As she does so, Helmer throws open his door and stands there with an open letter in his hand.

HELMER. Nora!

NORA (*shrieks*). Ah—!

HELMER. What is this? Do you know what is in this letter?

NORA. Yes, I know. Let me go! Let me go!

HELMER (*holds her back*). Go? Where?

NORA (*tries to tear herself loose*). You mustn't try to save me, Torvald!

HELMER (*staggers back*). Is it true? Is it true, what he writes? Oh, my God! No, no—it's impossible, it can't be true!

NORA. It *is* true. I've loved you more than anything else in the world.

HELMER. Oh, don't try to make silly excuses.

NORA (*takes a step towards him*). Torvald—

HELMER. Wretched woman! What have you done?

NORA. Let me go! You're not going to suffer for my sake. I won't let you!

HELMER. Stop being theatrical. (*Locks the front door.*) You're going to stay here and explain yourself. Do you understand what you've done? Answer me! Do you understand?

NORA (*looks unflinchingly at him and, her expression growing colder, says*). Yes. Now I am beginning to understand.

HELMER (*walking around the room*). Oh, what a dreadful awakening! For eight whole years—she who was my joy and my pride—a hypocrite, a liar—worse, worse—a criminal! Oh, the hideousness of it! Shame on you, shame!

Nora is silent and stares unblinkingly at him.

HELMER (*stops in front of her*). I ought to have guessed that something of this sort would happen. I should have foreseen it. All your father's recklessness and instability—be quiet!—I repeat, all your father's recklessness and instability he has handed on to you. No religion, no morals, no sense of duty! Oh, how I have been punished for closing my eyes to his faults! I did it for your sake. And now you reward me like this.

NORA. Yes. Like this.

HELMER. Now you have destroyed all my happiness. You have ruined my whole future. Oh, it's too dreadful to contemplate! I am in the power of a man who is completely without scruples. He can do what he likes with me, demand what he pleases, order me to do anything—I dare not disobey him. I am condemned to humiliation and ruin simply for the weakness of a woman.

NORA. When I am gone from this world, you will be free.

HELMER. Oh, don't be melodramatic. Your father was always ready with that kind of remark. How would it help me if you were "gone from this world," as you put it? It wouldn't assist me in the slightest. He can still make all the facts public; and if he does, I may quite easily be suspected of having been an accomplice in your crime. People may think that I was behind it—that it was I who encouraged you! And for all this I have to thank you, you whom I have carried on my hands through all the years of our marriage! Now do you realize what you've done to me?

NORA (*coldly calm*). Yes.

HELMER. It's so unbelievable I can hardly credit it. But we must try to find some way out. Take off that shawl. Take it off, I say! I must try to buy him off somehow. This thing must be hushed up at any price. As regards our relationship—we must appear to be living together just as before. Only *appear*, of course. You will therefore continue to reside here. That is understood. But the children shall be taken out of your hands. I dare no longer entrust them to you. Oh, to have to say this to the woman I once loved so dearly—and whom I still—! Well, all that must be finished. Henceforth there can be no question of happiness; we must merely strive to save what shreds and tatters— (*The front door bell rings. Helmer starts.*) What can that be? At this hour? Surely not—? He wouldn't—? Hide yourself, Nora. Say you're ill.

Nora does not move. Helmer goes to the door of the room and opens it. The Maid is standing half-dressed in the hall.

MAID. A letter for madam.

HELMER. Give it to me. (*Seizes the letter and shuts the door.*) Yes, it's from him. You're not having it. I'll read this myself.

NORA. Read it.

HELMER (*by the lamp*). I hardly dare to. This may mean the end for us both. No, I must know. (*Tears open the letter hastily; reads a few lines; looks at a piece of paper which is enclosed with it; utters a cry of joy.*) Nora! (*She looks at him questioningly.*) Nora! No—I must read it once more. Yes, yes, it's true! I am saved! Nora, I am saved!

NORA. What about me?

HELMER. You too, of course. We're both saved, you and I. Look! He's returning your I.O.U. He writes that he is sorry for what has happened—a happy accident has changed his life—oh, what does it matter what he writes? We are saved, Nora! No one can harm you now. Oh, Nora, Nora—no, first let me destroy this filthy thing. Let me see—! (*Glances at the I.O.U.*) No, I don't want to look at it. I shall merely regard the whole business as a dream. (*He tears the I.O.U. and both letters into pieces, throws them into the stove, and watches them burn.*) There. Now they're destroyed. He wrote that ever since Christmas Eve you've been—oh, these must have been three dreadful days for you, Nora.

NORA. Yes. It's been a hard fight.

HELMER. It must have been terrible—seeing no way out except—no, we'll forget the whole sordid business. We'll just be happy and go on telling ourselves over and over again: "It's over! It's over!" Listen to me, Nora. You don't seem to realize. It's over! Why are you looking so pale? Ah, my poor little Nora, I understand. You can't believe that I have forgiven you. But I have, Nora. I swear it to you. I have forgiven you everything. I know that what you did you did for your love of me.

NORA. That is true.

HELMER. You have loved me as a wife should love her husband. It was simply that in your inexperience you chose the wrong means. But do you think I love you any the less because you don't know how to act on your own initiative? No, no. Just lean on me. I shall counsel you. I shall guide you. I would not be a true man if your feminine helplessness did not make you doubly attractive in my eyes. You mustn't mind the hard words I said to you in those first dreadful moments when my whole world seemed to be tumbling about my ears. I have forgiven you, Nora. I swear it to you; I have forgiven you.

NORA. Thank you for your forgiveness.

She goes out through the door, right.

HELMER. No, don't go—(*Looks in.*) What are you doing there?

NORA (*offstage*). Taking off my fancy dress.

HELMER (*by the open door*). Yes, do that. Try to calm yourself and get your balance again, my frightened little songbird. Don't be afraid. I have broad wings to shield you. (*Begins to walk around near the door.*) How lovely and peaceful this little home of ours is, Nora. You are safe here; I shall watch over you like a hunted dove which I have snatched unharmed from the claws of the falcon. Your wildly beating little heart shall find peace with me. It will happen, Nora; it will take time, but it will happen, believe me. Tomorrow all this will seem quite different. Soon everything will be as it was before. I shall no longer need to remind you that I have forgiven you; your own heart will tell you that it is true. Do you really think I could ever bring myself to disown you, or even to reproach you? Ah, Nora, you don't understand what goes on in a husband's heart. There is something indescribably wonderful and satisfying for a husband in knowing that he has forgiven his wife—forgiven her unreservedly, from the bottom of his heart. It means that she has become his property in a double sense; he has, as it were, brought her into the world anew; she is now not only his wife but also his child. From now on that is what you shall be to me, my poor, helpless, bewildered little creature. Never be frightened of anything again, Nora. Just open your heart to me. I shall be both your will and your conscience. What's this? Not in bed? Have you changed?

NORA (*in her everyday dress*). Yes, Torvald. I've changed.

HELMER. But why now—so late—?

NORA. I shall not sleep tonight.

HELMER. But, my dear Nora—

NORA (*looks at her watch*). It isn't that late. Sit down here, Torvald. You and I have a lot to talk about.

She sits down on one side of the table.

HELMER. Nora, what does this mean? You look quite drawn—

NORA. Sit down. It's going to take a long time. I've a lot to say to you.

HELMER (*sits down on the other side of the table*). You alarm me, Nora. I don't understand you.

NORA. No, that's just it. You don't understand me. And I've never understood you—until this evening. No, don't interrupt me. Just listen to what I have to say. You and I have got to face facts, Torvald.

HELMER. What do you mean by that?

NORA (*after a short silence*). Doesn't anything strike you about the way we're sitting here?

HELMER. What?

NORA. We've been married for eight years. Does it occur to you that this is the first time that we two, you and I, man and wife, have ever had a serious talk together?

HELMER. Serious? What do you mean, serious?

NORA. In eight whole years—no, longer—ever since we first met—we have never exchanged a serious word on a serious subject.

HELMER. Did you expect me to drag you into all my worries—worries you couldn't possibly have helped me with?

NORA. I'm not talking about worries. I'm simply saying that we have never sat down seriously to try to get to the bottom of anything.

HELMER. But, my dear Nora, what on earth has that got to do with you?

NORA. That's just the point. You have never understood me. A great wrong has been done to me, Torvald. First by Papa, and then by you.

HELMER. What? But we two have loved you more than anyone in the world!

NORA (*shakes her head*). You have never loved me. You just thought it was fun to be in love with me.

HELMER. Nora, what kind of a way is this to talk?

NORA. It's the truth, Torvald. When I lived with Papa, he used to tell me what he thought about everything, so that I never had any opinions but his. And if I did have any of my own, I kept them quiet, because he wouldn't have liked them. He called me his little doll, and he played with me just the way I played with my dolls. Then I came here to live in your house—

HELMER. What kind of a way is that to describe our marriage?

NORA (*undisturbed*). I mean, then I passed from Papa's hands into yours. You arranged everything the way you wanted it, so that I simply took over your taste in everything—or pretended I did—I don't really know—I think it was a little of both—first one and then the other. Now I look back on it, it's as if I've been living here like a pauper, from hand to mouth. I performed tricks for you, and you gave me food and drink. But that was how you wanted it. You and Papa have done me a great wrong. It's your fault that I have done nothing with my life.

HELMER. Nora, how can you be so unreasonable and ungrateful? Haven't you been happy here?

NORA. No; never. I used to think I was; but I haven't ever been happy.

HELMER. Not—not happy?

NORA. No. I've just had fun. You've always been very kind to me. But our home has never been anything but a playroom. I've been your doll-wife, just as I used to be Papa's doll-child. And the children have been my dolls. I used to think it was fun when you came in and played with me, just as they think it's fun when I go in and play games with them. That's all our marriage has been, Torvald.

HELMER. There may be a little truth in what you say, though you exaggerate and romanticize. But from now on it'll be different. Playtime is over. Now the time has come for education.

NORA. Whose education? Mine or the children's?

HELMER. Both yours and the children's, my dearest Nora.

NORA. Oh, Torvald, you're not the man to educate me into being the right wife for you.

HELMER. How can you say that?

NORA. And what about me? Am I fit to educate the children?

HELMER. Nora!

NORA. Didn't you say yourself a few minutes ago that you dare not leave them in my charge?

HELMER. In a moment of excitement. Surely you don't think I meant it seriously?

NORA. Yes. You were perfectly right. I'm not fitted to educate them. There's something else I must do first. I must educate myself. And you can't help me with that. It's something I must do by myself. That's why I'm leaving you.

HELMER (*jumps up*). What did you say?

NORA. I must stand on my own feet if I am to find out the truth about myself and about life. So I can't go on living here with you any longer.

HELMER. Nora, Nora!

NORA. I'm leaving you now, at once. Christine will put me up for tonight—

HELMER. You're out of your mind! You can't do this! I forbid you!

NORA. It's no use your trying to forbid me any more. I shall take with me nothing but what is mine. I don't want anything from you, now or ever.

HELMER. What kind of madness is this?

NORA. Tomorrow I shall go home—I mean, to where I was born. It'll be easiest for me to find some kind of a job there.

HELMER. But you're blind! You've no experience of the world—

NORA. I must try to get some, Torvald.

HELMER. But to leave your home, your husband, your children! Have you thought what people will say?

NORA. I can't help that. I only know that I must do this.

HELMER. But this is monstrous! Can you neglect your most sacred duties?

NORA. What do you call my most sacred duties?

HELMER. Do I have to tell you? Your duties towards your husband, and your children.

NORA. I have another duty which is equally sacred.

HELMER. You have not. What on earth could that be?

NORA. My duty towards myself.

HELMER. First and foremost you are a wife and a mother.

NORA. I don't believe that any longer. I believe that I am first and foremost a human being, like you—or anyway, that I must try to become one. I know most people think as you do, Torvald, and I know there's something of the sort to be found in books. But I'm no longer prepared to accept what people say and what's written in books. I must think things out for myself, and try to find my own answer.

HELMER. Do you need to ask where your duty lies in your own home? Haven't you an infallible guide in such matters—your religion?

NORA. Oh, Torvald, I don't really know what religion means.

HELMER. What are you saying?

NORA. I only know what Pastor Hansen told me when I went to confirmation. He explained that religion meant this and that. When I get away from all this and can think things out on my own, that's one of the questions I want to look into. I want to find out whether what Pastor Hansen said was right—or anyway, whether it is right for me.

HELMER. But it's unheard of for so young a woman to behave

like this! If religion cannot guide you, let me at least appeal to your conscience. I presume you have some moral feelings left? Or—perhaps you haven't? Well, answer me.

NORA. Oh, Torvald, that isn't an easy question to answer. I simply don't know. I don't know where I am in these matters. I only know that these things mean something quite different to me from what they do to you. I've learned now that certain laws are different from what I'd imagined them to be; but I can't accept that such laws can be right. Has a woman really not the right to spare her dying father pain, or save her husband's life? I can't believe that.

HELMER. You're talking like a child. You don't understand how society works.

NORA. No, I don't. But now I intend to learn. I must try to satisfy myself which is right, society or I.

HELMER. Nora, you're ill; you're feverish. I almost believe you're out of your mind.

NORA. I've never felt so sane and sure in my life.

HELMER. You feel sure that it is right to leave your husband and your children?

NORA. Yes. I do.

HELMER. Then there is only one possible explanation.

NORA. What?

HELMER. That you don't love me any longer.

NORA. No, that's exactly it.

HELMER. Nora! How can you say this to me?

NORA. Oh, Torvald, it hurts me terribly to have to say it, because you've always been so kind to me. But I can't help it. I don't love you any longer.

HELMER (controlling his emotions with difficulty). And you feel quite sure about this too?

NORA. Yes, absolutely sure. That's why I can't go on living here any longer.

HELMER. Can you also explain why I have lost your love?

NORA. Yes, I can. It happened this evening, when the miracle failed to happen. It was then that I realized you weren't the man I'd thought you to be.

HELMER. Explain more clearly. I don't understand you.

NORA. I've waited so patiently, for eight whole years—well, good heavens, I'm not such a fool as to suppose that miracles occur every day. Then this dreadful thing happened to me, and then I knew: "Now the miracle will take place!" When Krogstad's letter was lying out there, it never occurred to me for a moment that you would let that man trample over you. I knew that you would say to him: "Publish the facts to the world." And when he had done this—

HELMER. Yes, what then? When I'd exposed my wife's name to shame and scandal—

NORA. Then I was certain that you would step forward and take all the blame on yourself, and say: "I am the one who is guilty!"

HELMER. Nora!

NORA. You're thinking I wouldn't have accepted such a sacrifice from you? No, of course I wouldn't! But what would my word have counted for against yours? That was the miracle I was hoping for, and dreading. And it was to prevent it happening that I wanted to end my life.

HELMER. Nora, I would gladly work for you night and day, and endure sorrow and hardship for your sake. But no man can be expected to sacrifice his honor, even for the person he loves.

NORA. Millions of women have done it.

HELMER. Oh, you think and talk like a stupid child.

NORA. That may be. But you neither think nor talk like the man I could share my life with. Once you'd got over your fright—and you weren't frightened of what might threaten me, but only of what threatened you—once the danger was past, then as far as you were concerned it was exactly as though nothing had happened. I was your little songbird just as before—your doll whom henceforth you would take particular care to protect from the world because she was so weak and fragile. (Gets up.) Torvald, in that moment I realized that for eight years I had been living here with a complete stranger, and had borne him three children—! Oh, I can't bear to think of it! I could tear myself to pieces!

HELMER (sadly). I see it, I see it. A gulf has indeed opened between us. Oh, but Nora—couldn't it be bridged?

NORA. As I am now, I am no wife for you.

HELMER. I have the strength to change.

NORA. Perhaps—if your doll is taken from you.

HELMER. But to be parted—to be parted from you! No, no, Nora, I can't conceive of it happening!

NORA (goes into the room, right). All the more necessary that it should happen.

She comes back with her outdoor things and a small traveling-bag, which she puts down on a chair by the table.

HELMER. Nora, Nora, not now! Wait till tomorrow!

NORA (puts on her coat). I can't spend the night in a strange man's house.

HELMER. But can't we live here as brother and sister, then—?

NORA (fastens her hat). You know quite well it wouldn't last. (Puts on her shawl.) Goodbye, Torvald. I don't want to see the children. I know they're in better hands than mine. As I am now, I can be nothing to them.

HELMER. But some time, Nora—some time—?

NORA. How can I tell? I've no idea what will happen to me.

HELMER. But you are my wife, both as you are and as you will be.

NORA. Listen, Torvald. When a wife leaves her husband's house, as I'm doing now, I'm told that according to the law he is freed of any obligations towards her. In any case, I release you from any such obligations. You mustn't feel bound to me in any way, however small, just as I shall not feel bound to you. We must both be quite free. Here is your ring back. Give me mine.

HELMER. That too?

NORA. That too.

HELMER. Here it is.

NORA. Good. Well, now it's over. I'll leave the keys here. The servants know about everything to do with the house—much better than I do. Tomorrow, when I have left town, Christine will come to pack the things I brought here from home. I'll have them sent on after me.

HELMER. This is the end then! Nora, will you never think of me any more?

NORA. Yes, of course. I shall often think of you and the children and this house.

HELMER. May I write to you, Nora?

NORA. No, never. You mustn't do that.

HELMER. But at least you must let me send you—

NORA. Nothing. Nothing.

HELMER. But if you should need help?—

NORA. I tell you, no. I don't accept things from strangers.

HELMER. Nora—can I never be anything but a stranger to you?

NORA (*picks up her bag*). Oh, Torvald! Then the miracle of miracles would have to happen.

HELMER. The miracle of miracles?

NORA. You and I would both have to change so much that—oh, Torvald, I don't believe in miracles any longer.

HELMER. But I want to believe in them. Tell me. We should have to change so much that—?

NORA. That life together between us two could become a marriage. Goodbye.

She goes out through the hall.

HELMER (*sinks down on a chair by the door and buries his face in his hands*). Nora! Nora! (*Looks round and gets up.*) Empty! She's gone! (*A hope strikes him.*) The miracle of miracles—?

The street door is slammed shut downstairs.

CENTER STAGE   THE TARANTELLA AND OTHER HEALING DANCES

Nora's frenzied tarantella in the second act of *A Doll's House* derives from a centuries-old Italian "healing dance" in which the dancer performs convulsive movements in frenetic 6/8 time. In the Late Middle Ages, Italy was afflicted with tarantism, an epidemic illness associated with the venomous bite of a spider (the tarantula—hence the name tarantella). The poison caused the bite victim to lapse into a hysterical fury, often foaming at the mouth, and the cure—or so it was believed—was to perform a violent, swirling dance that distributed the poison throughout the body and forced the dancer to "sweat out" the venom. The town of Taranto, in Italy's southern Puglia region, became most closely associated with the tarantella. It is also the title of one of the most famous Italian folk songs and remains a vestige of this folk ritual of healing. Incidentally, such acclaimed European composers as Chopin, Liszt, and Carl Maria von Weber wrote tarantellas for the piano. Ibsen, of course, lived in Italy while in self-imposed exile from Norway and doubtlessly saw the tarantella per-

formed there. Thus, he wisely scripted the tarantella into his most famous play, for Nora is indeed trying to exorcise the "poison" that has infected the Helmer household. The dance not only enhances the play's central theme, but is a remarkably theatrical moment in an otherwise realistic play.

Healing dances are virtually as old as humanity itself, and considerable evidence suggests that the theater grew from various forms of ecstatic dancing, many in worship of gods (e.g., the Dionysian rites described in Chapter 3), others specifically intended to "cast out" evil spirits. Often, of course, the two functions were combined.

The Early Middle Ages in Europe were a particularly fertile time for ecstatic dances that grew out of the Catholic mass. Some dealt with death, a very real presence to the plague-ridden medievals. The Dance of Death, also known as the *danse macabre* or *totentanz*, was especially popular. A dancer playing death seized onlookers, regardless of their age or social status, and led them in a frenzied dance that reminded all that Death was

indiscriminate. The renowned Swedish filmmaker Ingmar Bergman uses this dance to great effect in his allegorical movie *The Seventh Seal*. Ibsen, also a Scandinavian, surely knew the dance.

The St. Vitus' dance, which dates from the eleventh and twelfth centuries in northern Europe, may be the forerunner of the tarantella (versions of the St. Vitus' dance could be found in Italy in the fourteenth century). It was performed by masses of people, all dancing and screaming hysterically, often in response to the epileptic-like seizures associated with the Black Death, the plague that periodically ravaged Europe. Like the tarantella, the St. Vitus' dance was intended to purge illness from the dancers by forcing them to sweat out impurities. Such healing dances "purge" the body, and we must remember the Greek word for purgation was *catharsis*, the cornerstone of Aristotle's theory of the restorative powers of drama and theater (see Chapter 2). Once again a folk rite invests the theater with its power to heal the illnesses of both the individual and society.

323

THE CHERRY ORCHARD

ANTON CHEKHOV

ANTON CHEKHOV (1860–1904)

Few other playwrights have achieved such an exalted reputation on the basis of so few plays. Other than a number of short plays and farces (e.g., *The Marriage Proposal* and *The Boor*), Chekhov's place in the pantheon of the world's finest dramatists rests on four principal works: *The Seagull* (1895), *Uncle Vanya* (1899), *The Three Sisters* (1901), and *The Cherry Orchard* (1904). Perhaps more than his contemporaries in realism, Ibsen and Strindberg, Chekhov has inspired subsequent generations of writers who attempt to capture the ease with which he captures the day-to-day drama of life in all its simplicity. Tennessee Williams, William Inge, Samuel Beckett, and Wendy Wasserstein, to name but a few, are among the many playwrights who have acknowledged Chekhov as their mentor. Even Bernard Shaw attempted to write "a fantasia in the Russian manner" (*Heartbreak House*, 1918) and produced the kind of play Chekhov might have written were he Ibsen.

The son of a despotic storekeeper from the seaport village of Taganrog, Chekhov wrote to support himself while studying medicine at the University of Moscow. He wrote superb short stories and "vaudevilles," many based on his observations as a doctor. His daily rounds permitted him to see firsthand the rhythms of life: birth, death, recovery, lingering illness, despair, joy, uncertainty, and faith. These became the subjects of his stories and particularly his dramatic masterpieces. His own life was marked by many of these universal difficulties. His first attempts at serious drama were rejected, largely because they were misunderstood. He was chronically ill and spent his last years in the warm-weather city of Yalta, struggling against the tuberculosis that eventually killed him in 1904. (He did not see his plays performed successfully until Stanislavsky and the Moscow Art Theater toured the Crimea in 1900.) And like many of his characters, he was victimized by unrequited love. In 1890 he trekked to the Sakhalin gulag to study penal conditions, motivated in part by his immense humanitarianism and in part to forget the woman who had spurned him. In 1901 he married a leading actress of the MAT, Olga Knipper, only to die three years later. Despite the disappointments that plagued him, he remained a lover of humanity, however imperfect. In *The Seagull*, Nina perhaps comes closer than any of his characters to articulating Chekhov's credo: "What matters most for us, whether we're writers or actors, isn't fame or glamour, or any of the things I used to dream of. What matters most is knowing how to endure, knowing how to bear your cross and still have faith. I have faith now and I can stand my suffering. . . I am not afraid of life."

Chekhov's distinctive techniques have been discussed in conjunction with the rise of realistic drama. His use of the anticlimax, his focus on a number of individuals rather than a central protagonist, and his depiction of trivial actions and seemingly inconsequential exchanges among his characters are trademarks of his dramaturgy. Perhaps the most innovative aspect of the four great seriocomic dramas, however, is the use of the parallel monologue. His subtle plots are structured around a series of shared monologues in which characters voice their innermost desires, fears, and delusions. In this sense he is among the foremost psychological realists. But in these ongoing monologues, which are interspersed with those of the other characters, there is a failure to communicate. Chekhov depicts individuals trapped in an isolated universe in a manner that anticipates the work of the absurdists in the mid–twentieth century.

Unfortunately, Chekhov's plays are misinterpreted, and even a source of embarrassment among the Russian people. Too often they are presented as exercises in gloomy melancholy, largely because the monologues are rendered as angst-ridden laments by actors who take Chekhov's description of his plays as showing too literally "all the grayness of everyday life." Chekhov and Stanislavsky clashed over the MAT's overly somber treatment of his plays, which the writer believed turned his characters into pathetic whiners. For Chekhov, the plays were comedies, albeit serious ones, in which his characters (among whom there are no villains) are like so many people in life: destined to fail, partly because of the inexorable march of time, mostly because of the folly of their misguided aspirations.

Prior to Chekhov, the theater had faced neither characters such as these nor the unflinching realism in which their predicaments were handled. Fortunately, his friend and literary colleague Count Leo Tolstoy, Russia's leading novelist, accurately predicted his legacy: "It is possible that in the future, perhaps a hundred years hence, people will be amazed at what they find in Chekhov about the inner workings of the human soul."

THE CHERRY ORCHARD (1904)

The Breaking String (Maurice Valency, 1966) remains among the finest studies of Chekhov's dramaturgy. The title is taken from a stage direction found in act 2 of *The Cherry Orchard*:

> All sit lost in thought. The silence is broken only by the subdued muttering of Firs. Suddenly a distant sound is heard, as if from the sky, like the sound of a snapped string mournfully dying away.

It is fitting that Valency selects this moment because it crystallizes the whole of Chekhov's drama. Here we see a cluster of people on a remote Russian estate, so typical of the "ensemble pathos" that typifies Chekhov's style. Though they sit together, each is very much alone, "lost in thought." In the distance we see telegraph poles (the new technology), and beyond them the skyline of a growing city. Clearly the landscape of Mother Russia is changing, for it, too, is "mournfully dying away." Note that the play premiered in the year of the first of two great revolutions that transformed Russia between 1903 and 1917. Significantly, old Firs is a link to the 1862 revolution that overthrew feudalism. Though Chekhov was not a political writer in the manner of Ibsen or Shaw, *The Cherry Orchard* resonates with the social tensions of its time. The orchard itself, which is being chopped down as the final curtain falls, is emblematic of the outmoded aristocratic order.

Whatever its social relevance in 1904, the play, like each of Chekhov's major works, transcends the particulars of time and place and remains a universal study of the human dilemma, even a century after its composition. *The Cherry Orchard* is a four-act study of frustrated human aspirations, the dominant theme in each of the playwright's four masterpieces. His characters consistently demonstrate an uncanny ability to desire most that which they are least likely to obtain, and they do little to help themselves realize their dreams. Lopakhin is perhaps the most notable exception to this Chekhovian law. While he does indeed attain the estate and the revered orchard upon which his ancestors had toiled, he never quite gets around to marrying Varya, the object of his affection.

As detached observers, we see the absurdity of his characters' futile quests for the unachievable. Unlike the similarly delusional Don Quixote, who also chased impossible dreams, Chekhov's characters are trapped by their own inertia (and folly) as much as any external force. Thus Chekhov's plays are simultaneously amusing and pathetic, even nearly tragic. Real lives are "being smashed up" (to use Chekhov's own phrase), but there is invariably something oddly absurd, even silly, about the characters' dilemmas. Evidence of such folly abounds throughout *The Cherry Orchard*:

- Madame Ranevskaya desperately wants to retain her estate, but she fritters away her money, most notably by throwing a lavish ball even as the estate is being sold to the very man (Lopakhin) who has provided sound business advice that would permit her to salvage the cherry orchard. Of her mother's profligacy, Anya says, "Dear Mother, the same as ever. Hasn't changed a bit. If you let her, she'd give everything away."

- Gayev, her silly, sentimental brother, clings to the past while refusing to adjust to the present. He is too settled into a way of life in which "I keep thinking, racking my brains, I have many remedies, a great many, and that means, in effect, I have none."
- In contrast to Gayev, Trofimov expounds loftily about his visions for the future, but his credibility is undermined as we learn that he is little more than a professional student who will not venture out into the "real" world.
- Madame Ranevskaya's daughters, Anya and Varya, are ineffectual in their pursuit of love—the former too eager to involve herself in irresponsible relationships, the latter too bound by her work to feel genuine emotions.
- Even the parlormaid, Dunyasha, falls in love with the one person least likely to return her love: the self-absorbed valet, Yasha.
- And there is Yepikhodov, the bumbling bookkeeper whose very nickname epitomizes Chekhovian pathos: "Two-and-twenty Troubles."

It is perhaps natural for us to assign blame for the various predicaments of Chekhov's characters. In the tradition of melodrama, in which the family estate is lost, Lopakhin, the newly rich landowner, might be something of a villain. But here we are actually pleased that he gains the estate because it affirms his family's progress from serfdom to respectability. In Chekhov's world, however, there is truly only one villain: time. In the world of Sophocles or Ibsen, time abets change, reveals truths, and ultimately liberates (and frequently vindicates) protagonists from their ordeals. In time, Oedipus learns his identity and is thus liberated from the lie of his past; and in time, Nora Helmer (of *A Doll's House*) realizes that "I must stand on my own feet if I am to find out the truth about myself and about life." But in Chekhov's world, time only further entraps the characters because past, present, and future are virtually interchangeable. Note that Lopakhin opens the play with the question "What time is it?" And throughout the action, such as there is in this drama of "inaction," each character dwells on the inexorable passage of time, most notably in Uncle Gayev's famed speech to the bookcase in act 1. But perhaps the most telling reference to time is found in the play's finale. As the family leaves the estate for the last time, and as Firs settles onto the sofa for a nap—or death?—we again hear the sound of the breaking string, backed by the metronomic thud of an ax on the cherry trees, like the ticking of a cosmic clock.

Samuel Beckett (perhaps the dramatist most often aligned with Chekhov by modern critics) also meditates on the villainy of time in plays such as his masterpiece, *Waiting for Godot*. One of the characters explodes in a tirade against time: "Time! Time! Will you not stop tormenting me with your cursed Time? One day we are born, one day we die . . . that's how it is on this bitch of an earth." (Compare the exchange about death between Trofimov and Gayev near the end of act 2.) The inexorable march of time invests Chekhov's plays with their characteristic melancholy, far more than any of the lamentations of the characters. And it is here that Chekhov emerges as the most unflinchingly realistic of dramatists.

Andrei Serban's 1977 production of The Cherry Orchard *at Lincoln Center is considered among the finest interpretations of Chekhov's comedy; the director and designers intentionally poeticized this customarily realistic play.*

THE CHERRY ORCHARD

ANTON CHEKHOV

Translated by Ann Dunnigan

CHARACTERS

RANEVSKAYA, LYUBOV ANDREYEVNA, *a landowner*
ANYA, *her daughter, seventeen years old*
VARYA, *her adopted daughter, twenty-four years old*
GAYEV, LEONID ANDREYEVICH, *Madame Ranevskaya's brother*
LOPAKHIN, YERMOLAI ALEKSEYEVICH, *a merchant*
TROFIMOV, PYOTR SERGEYEVICH, *a student*
SEMYONOV-PISHCHIK, BORIS BORISOVICH, *a landowner*
CHARLOTTA IVANOVNA, *a governess*
YEPIKHODOV, SEMYON PANTELEYEVICH, *a clerk*
DUNYASHA, *a maid*
FIRS, *an old valet, eighty-seven years old*
YASHA, *a young footman*
A STRANGER
THE STATIONMASTER
A POST OFFICE CLERK
GUESTS, SERVANTS

The action takes place on Madame Ranevskaya's estate.

ACT I

(*A room that is still called the nursery. One of the doors leads into Anya's room. Dawn; the sun will soon rise. It is May, the cherry trees are in bloom, but it is cold in the orchard; there is a morning frost. The windows in the room are closed. Enter Dunyasha with a candle, and Lopakhin with a book in his hand.*)

LOPAKHIN. The train is in, thank God. What time is it?

DUNYASHA. Nearly two. (*Blows out the candle.*) It's already light.

LOPAKHIN. How late is the train, anyway? A couple of hours at least. (*Yawns and stretches.*) I'm a fine one! What a fool I've made of myself! Came here on purpose to meet them at the station, and then overslept. . . . Fell asleep in the chair. It's annoying. . . . You might have waked me.

DUNYASHA. I thought you had gone. (*Listens.*) They're coming now, I think!

LOPAKHIN. (*listens*). No . . . they've got to get the luggage and one thing and another. (*Pause.*) Lyubov Andreyevna has lived abroad for five years, I don't know what she's like now. . . . She's a fine person. Sweet-tempered, simple. I remember when I was a boy of fifteen, my late father—he had a shop in the village then—gave me a punch in the face and made my nose bleed. . . . We had come into the yard here for some reason or other, and he'd had a drop too much. Lyubov Andreyevna—I remember as if it were yesterday—still young, and so slender, led me to the washstand in this very room, the nursery. "Don't cry, little peasant," she said, "it will heal in time for your wedding. . . ." (*Pause.*) Little peasant . . . my father was a peasant, it's true, and here I am in a white waistcoat and tan shoes. Like a pig in a pastry shop. . . . I may be rich, I've made a lot of money, but if you think about it, analyze it, I'm a peasant through and through. (*Turning pages of the book.*) Here I've been reading this book, and I didn't understand a thing. Fell asleep over it. (*Pause.*)

DUNYASHA. The dogs didn't sleep all night: They can tell that their masters are coming.

LOPAKHIN. What's the matter with you, Dunyasha, you're so . . .

DUNYASHA. My hands are trembling. I'm going to faint.

LOPAKHIN. You're much too delicate, Dunyasha. You dress like a lady, and do your hair like one, too. It's not right. You should know your place.

(*Enter Yepikhodov with a bouquet; he wears a jacket and highly polished boots that squeak loudly. He drops the flowers as he comes in.*)

YEPIKHODOV (*picking up the flowers*). Here, the gardener sent these. He says you're to put them in the dining room. (*Hands the bouquet to Dunyasha.*)

LOPAKHIN. And bring me some kvas.[1]

DUNYASHA. Yes, sir. (*Goes out.*)

YEPIKHODOV. There's a frost this morning—three degrees—and the cherry trees are in bloom. I cannot approve of our climate. (*Sighs.*) I cannot. Our climate is not exactly conducive. And now, Yermolai Alekseyevich, permit me to append: The day before yesterday I bought myself a pair of boots, which, I venture to assure you, squeak so that it's quite infeasible. What should I grease them with?

LOPAKHIN. Leave me alone. You make me tired.

YEPIKHODOV. Every day some misfortune happens to me. But I don't complain, I'm used to it, I even smile.

(*Dunyasha enters, serves Lopakhin the kvas.*)

YEPIKHODOV. I'm going. (*Stumbles over a chair and upsets it.*) There! (*As if in triumph.*) Now you see, excuse the expression . . . the sort of circumstances, incidentally. . . . It's really quite remarkable! (*Goes out.*)

DUNYASHA. You know, Yermolai Alekseyich, I have to confess that Yepikhodov has proposed to me.

LOPAKHIN. Ah!

DUNYASHA. And I simply don't know. . . . He's a quiet man, but sometimes, when he starts talking, you can't understand a thing he says. It's nice, and full of feeling, only it doesn't make sense. I sort of like him. He's madly in love with me. But he's an unlucky fellow: Every day something happens to him. They tease him about it around here; they call him Two-and-twenty Troubles.

LOPAKHIN (*listening*). I think I hear them coming . . .

DUNYASHA. They're coming! What's the matter with me? I'm cold all over.

LOPAKHIN. They're really coming. Let's go and meet them. Will she recognize me? It's five years since we've seen each other.

DUNYASHA (*agitated*). I'll faint this very minute . . . oh, I'm going to faint!

(*Two carriages are heard driving up to the house. Lopakhin and Dunyasha go out quickly. The stage is empty. There is a hubbub in the adjoining rooms. Firs hurriedly crosses the stage leaning on a stick. He has been to meet Lyubov Andreyevna and wears old-fashioned livery and a high hat. He mutters something to himself, not a word of which can be understood. The noise offstage grows louder and louder. A voice: "Let's go through here. . . ." Enter Lyubov Andreyevna, Anya, Charlotta Ivanovna with a little dog on a chain, all in traveling dress; Varya wearing a coat and kerchief; Gayev, Semyonov-Pishchik, Lopakhin, Dunyasha with a bundle and parasol; servants with luggage—all walk through the room.*)

ANYA. Let's go this way. Do you remember, Mama, what room this is?

LYUBOV ANDREYEVNA (*joyfully, through tears*). The nursery!

VARYA. How cold it is! My hands are numb. (*To Lyubov Andreyevna.*) Your rooms, both the white one and the violet one, are just as you left them, Mama.

LYUBOV ANDREYEVNA. The nursery . . . my dear, lovely nursery. . . . I used to sleep here when I was little. . . . (*Weeps.*) And now, like a child, I . . . (*Kisses her brother, Varya, then her brother again.*) Varya hasn't changed; she still looks like a nun. And I recognized Dunyasha. . . . (*Kisses Dunyasha.*)

GAYEV. The train was two hours late. How's that? What kind of management is that?

CHARLOTTA (*to Pishchik*). My dog even eats nuts.

PISHCHIK (*amazed*). Think of that now!

(*They all go out except Anya and Dunyasha.*)

[1]**kvas** beer

DUNYASHA. We've been waiting and waiting for you. . . . (*Takes off Anya's coat and hat.*)

ANYA. I didn't sleep for four nights on the road . . . now I feel cold.

DUNYASHA. It was Lent when you went away, there was snow and frost then, but now? My darling! (*Laughs and kisses her.*) I've waited so long for you, my joy, my precious . . . I must tell you at once, I can't wait another minute. . . .

ANYA (*listlessly*). What now?

DUNYASHA. The clerk, Yepikhodov, proposed to me just after Easter.

ANYA. You always talk about the same thing. . . . (*Straightening her hair.*) I've lost all my hairpins. . . . (*She is so exhausted she can hardly stand.*)

DUNYASHA. I really don't know what to think. He loves me—he loves me so!

ANYA (*looking through the door into her room, tenderly*). My room, my windows . . . it's just as though I'd never been away. I am home! Tomorrow morning I'll get up and run into the orchard. . . . Oh, if I could only sleep! I didn't sleep during the entire journey, I was so tormented by anxiety.

DUNYASHA. Pyotr Sergeich arrived the day before yesterday.

ANYA (*joyfully*). Petya!

DUNYASHA. He's asleep in the bathhouse, he's staying there. "I'm afraid of being in the way," he said. (*Looks at her pocket watch.*) I ought to wake him up, but Varvara Mikhailovna told me not to. "Don't you wake him," she said.

(*Enter Varya with a bunch of keys at her waist.*)

VARYA. Dunyasha, coffee, quickly . . . Mama's asking for coffee.

DUNYASHA. This very minute. (*Goes out.*)

VARYA. Thank God, you've come! You're home again. (*Caressing her.*) My little darling has come back! My pretty one is here!

ANYA. I've been through so much.

VARYA. I can imagine!

ANYA. I left in Holy Week, it was cold then. Charlotta never stopped talking and doing her conjuring tricks the entire journey. Why did you saddle me with Charlotta?

VARYA. You couldn't have traveled alone, darling. At seventeen!

ANYA. When we arrived in Paris, it was cold, snowing. My French is awful. . . . Mama was living on the fifth floor, and when I got there, she had all sorts of Frenchmen and ladies with her, and an old priest with a little book, and it was full of smoke, dismal. Suddenly I felt sorry for Mama, so sorry. I took her head in my arms and held her close and couldn't let her go. Afterward she kept hugging me and crying. . . .

VARYA. (*through her tears*). Don't talk about it, don't talk about it. . . .

ANYA. She had already sold her villa near Mentone, and she had nothing left, nothing. And I hadn't so much as a kopeck left, we barely managed to get there. But Mama doesn't understand! When we had dinner in a station restaurant, she always ordered the most expensive dishes and tipped each of the waiters a ruble. Charlotta is the same. And Yasha also ordered a dinner, it was simply awful. You know, Yasha is Mama's footman; we brought him with us.

VARYA. I saw the rogue.

ANYA. Well, how are things? Have you paid the interest?

VARYA. How could we?

ANYA. Oh, my God, my God!

VARYA. In August the estate will be put up for sale.

ANYA. My God!

(*Lopakhin peeps in at the door and moos like a cow.*)

LOPAKHIN. Moo-o-o! (*Disappears.*)

VARYA. (*through her tears*). What I couldn't do to him! (*Shakes her fist.*)

ANYA. (*embracing Varya, softly*). Varya, has he proposed to you? (*Varya shakes her head.*) But he loves you. . . . Why don't you come to an understanding, what are you waiting for?

VARYA. I don't think anything will ever come of it. He's too busy, he has no time for me . . . he doesn't even notice me. I've washed my hands of him, it makes me miserable to see him. . . . Everyone talks of our wedding, they all congratulate me, and actually there's nothing to it—it's like a dream. . . . (*In a different tone.*) You have a brooch like a bee.

ANYA. (*sadly*). Mama bought it. (*Goes into her own room; speaks gaily, like a child.*) In Paris I went up in a balloon!

VARYA. My darling is home! My pretty one has come back!

(*Dunyasha has come in with the coffeepot and prepares coffee.*)

VARYA (*stands at the door of Anya's room*). You know, darling, all day long I'm busy looking after the house, but I keep dreaming. If we could marry you to a rich man I'd be at peace. I could go into a hermitage, then to Kiev, to Moscow, and from one holy place to another. . . . I'd go on and on. What a blessing!

ANYA. The birds are singing in the orchard. What time is it?

VARYA. It must be after two. Time you were asleep, darling. (*Goes into Anya's room.*) What a blessing!

(*Yasha enters with a lap robe and a traveling bag.*)

YASHA (*crosses the stage mincingly*). May one go through here?

DUNYASHA. A person would hardly recognize you, Yasha. Your stay abroad has done wonders for you.

YASHA. Hm. . . . And who are you?

DUNYASHA. When you left here I was only that high—(*indi-

cating with her hand). I'm Dunyasha, Fyodor Kozoyedov's daughter. You don't remember?

YASHA. Hm. . . . A little cucumber! (*Looks around, then embraces her; she cries out and drops a saucer. He quickly goes out.*)

VARYA (*in a tone of annoyance, from the doorway*). What's going on here?

DUNYASHA (*tearfully*). I broke a saucer.

VARYA. That's good luck.

ANYA. We ought to prepare Mama: Petya is here. . . .

VARYA. I gave orders not to wake him.

ANYA (*pensively*). Six years ago Father died, and a month later brother Grisha drowned in the river . . . a pretty little seven-year-old boy. Mama couldn't bear it and went away . . . went without looking back. . . . (*Shudders.*) How I understand her, if she only knew! (*Pause.*) And Petya Trofimov was Grisha's tutor, he may remind her. . . .

(*Enter Firs wearing a jacket and a white waistcoat.*)

FIRS (*goes to the coffeepot, anxiously*). The mistress will have her coffee here. (*Puts on white gloves.*) Is the coffee ready? (*To Dunyasha, sternly.*) You! Where's the cream?

DUNYASHA. Oh, my goodness! (*Quickly goes out.*)

FIRS (*fussing over the coffeepot*). Ah, what an addlepate! (*Mutters to himself.*) They've come back from Paris. . . . The master used to go to Paris . . . by carriage. . . . (*Laughs.*)

VARYA. What is it, Firs?

FIRS. If you please? (*Joyfully.*) My mistress has come home! At last! Now I can die. . . . (*Weeps with joy.*)

(*Enter Lyubov Andreyevna, Gayev, and Semyonov-Pishchik, the last wearing a sleeveless peasant coat of fine cloth and full trousers. Gayev, as he comes in, goes through the motions of playing billiards.*)

LYUBOV ANDREYEVNA. How does it go? Let's see if I can remember . . . cue ball into the corner! Double the rail to center table.

GAYEV. Cut shot into the corner! There was a time, sister, when you and I used to sleep here in this very room, and now I'm fifty-one, strange as it may seem. . . .

LOPAKHIN. Yes, time passes.

GAYEV. How's that?

LOPAKHIN. Time I say, passes.

GAYEV. It smells of patchouli here.

ANYA. I'm going to bed. Good night, Mama. (*Kisses her mother.*)

LYUBOV ANDREYEVNA. My precious child. (*Kisses her hands.*) Are you glad to be home? I still feel dazed.

ANYA. Good night, Uncle.

GAYEV (*kisses her face and hands*). God bless you. How like your mother you are! (*To his sister.*) At her age you were exactly like her, Lyuba.

(*Anya shakes hands with Lopakhin and Pishchik and goes out, closing the door after her.*)

LYUBOV ANDREYEVNA. She's exhausted.

PISHCHIK. Must have been a long journey.

VARYA. Well, gentlemen? It's after two, high time you were going.

LYUBOV ANDREYEVNA (*laughs*). You haven't changed, Varya. (*Draws Varya to her and kisses her.*) I'll just drink my coffee and then we'll all go. (*Firs places a cushion under her feet.*) Thank you, my dear. I've got used to coffee. I drink it day and night. Thanks, dear old man. (*Kisses him.*)

VARYA. I'd better see if all the luggage has been brought in.

LYUBOV ANDREYEVNA. Is this really me sitting here? (*Laughs.*) I feel like jumping about and waving my arms. (*Buries her face in her hands.*) What if it's only a dream! God knows I love my country, love it dearly. I couldn't look out the train window, I was crying so! (*Through tears.*) But I must drink my coffee. Thank you, Firs, thank you, my dear old friend. I'm so glad you're still alive.

FIRS. The day before yesterday.

GAYEV. He's hard of hearing.

LOPAKHIN. I must go now, I'm leaving for Kharkov about five o'clock. It's so annoying! I wanted to have a good look at you, and have a talk. You're as splendid as ever.

PISHCHIK (*breathing heavily*). Even more beautiful. . . . Dressed like a Parisienne. . . . There goes my wagon, all four wheels!

LOPAKHIN. Your brother here, Leonid Andreich, says I'm a boor, a moneygrubber, but I don't mind. Let him talk. All I want is that you should trust me as you used to, and that your wonderful, touching eyes should look at me as they did then. Merciful God! My father was one of your father's serfs, and your grandfather's, but you yourself did so much for me once, that I've forgotten all that and love you as if you were my own kin—more than my kin.

LYUBOV ANDREYEVNA. I can't sit still, I simply cannot. (*Jumps up and walks about the room in great excitement.*) I cannot bear this joy. . . . Laugh at me, I'm silly. . . . My dear little bookcase . . . (*kisses bookcase*) my little table . . .

GAYEV. Nurse died while you were away.

LYUBOV ANDREYEVNA (*sits down and drinks coffee*). Yes, God rest her soul. They wrote me.

GAYEV. And Anastasy is dead. Petrushka Kosoi left me and is now with the police inspector in town. (*Takes a box of hard candies from his pocket and begins to suck one.*)

PISHCHIK. My daughter, Dashenka . . . sends her regards . . .

LOPAKHIN. I wish I could tell you something very pleasant and cheering. (*Glances at his watch.*) I must go directly, there's no time to talk, but . . . well, I'll say it in a couple of words. As you know, the cherry orchard is to be sold to pay your debts. The auction is set for August twenty-second, but you need not worry, my dear, you can sleep in peace, there is a way out. This is my plan. Now, please listen! Your estate is only twenty versts[2] from town, the railway runs close by, and if the cherry orchard and the land along the river were cut up into lots and leased for summer cottages, you'd have, at the very least, an income of twenty-five thousand a year.

GAYEV. Excuse me, what nonsense!

LYUBOV ANDREYEVNA. I don't quite understand you, Yermolai Alekseich.

LOPAKHIN. You will get, at the very least, twenty-five rubles a year for a two-and-half-acre lot, and if you advertise now, I guarantee you won't have a single plot of ground left by autumn, everything will be snapped up. In short, I congratulate you, you are saved. The site is splendid, the river is deep. Only, of course, the ground must be cleared . . . you must tear down all the old outbuildings, for instance, and this house, which is worthless, cut down the old cherry orchard—

LYUBOV ANDREYEVNA. Cut it down? Forgive me, my dear, but you don't know what you are talking about. If there is one thing in the whole province that is interesting, not to say remarkable, it's our cherry orchard.

LOPAKHIN. The only remarkable thing about this orchard is that it is very big. There's a crop of cherries every other year, and then you can't get rid of them, nobody buys them.

GAYEV. This orchard is even mentioned in the *Encyclopedia*.

LOPAKHIN (*glancing at his watch*). If we don't think of something and come to a decision, on the twenty-second of August the cherry orchard, and the entire estate, will be sold at auction. Make up your minds! There is no other way out, I swear to you. None whatsoever.

FIRS. In the old days, forty or fifty years ago, the cherries were dried, soaked, marinated, and made into jam, and they used to—

GAYEV. Be quiet, Firs.

FIRS. And they used to send cartloads of dried cherries to Moscow and Kharkov. And that brought in money! The dried cherries were soft and juicy in those days, sweet, fragrant. . . . They had a method then . . .

LYUBOV ANDREYEVNA. And what has become of that method now?

FIRS. Forgotten. Nobody remembers. . . .

PISHCHIK. How was it in Paris? What's it like there? Did you eat frogs?

LYUBOV ANDREYEVNA. I ate crocodiles.

PISHCHIK. Think of that now!

LOPAKHIN. There used to be only the gentry and the peasants living in the country, but now these summer people have appeared. All the towns, even the smallest ones, are surrounded by summer cottages. And it is safe to say that in another twenty years these people will multiply enormously. Now the summer resident only drinks tea on his porch, but it may well be that he'll take to cultivating his acre, and then your cherry orchard will be a happy, rich, luxuriant—

GAYEV (*indignantly*). What nonsense!

(*Enter Varya and Yasha.*)

VARYA. There are two telegrams for you, Mama. (*Picks out a key and with a jingling sound opens an old-fashioned bookcase.*) Here they are.

LYUBOV ANDREYEVNA. From Paris. (*Tears up the telegrams without reading them.*) That's all over. . . .

GAYEV. Do you know, Lyuba, how old this bookcase is? A week ago I pulled out the bottom drawer, and what do I see? Some figures burnt into it. The bookcase was made exactly a hundred years ago. What do you think of that? Eh? We could have celebrated its jubilee. It's an inanimate object, but nevertheless, for all that, it's a bookcase.

PISHCHIK. A hundred years . . . think of that now!

GAYEV. Yes . . . that is something. . . . (*Feeling the bookcase.*) Dear, honored bookcase. I salute thy existence, which for over one hundred years has served the glorious ideals of goodness and justice; thy silent appeal to fruitful endeavor, unflagging in the course of a hundred years, tearfully sustaining through generations of our family, courage and faith in a better future, and fostering in us ideals of goodness and social consciousness. . . .

(*A pause.*)

LOPAKHIN. Yes . . .

LYUBOV ANDREYEVNA. You are the same as ever, Lyonya.

GAYEV (*somewhat embarrassed*). Carom into the corner, cut shot to center table.

LOPAKHIN (*looks at his watch*). Well, time for me to go.

YASHA (*hands medicine to Lyubov Andreyevna*). Perhaps you will take your pills now.

PISHCHIK. Don't take medicaments, dearest lady, they do neither harm nor good. Let me have them, honored lady. (*Takes the pillbox, shakes the pills into his hand, blows on them, puts them into his mouth, and washes them down with kvas.*) There!

LYUBOV ANDREYEVNA (*alarmed*). Why, you must be mad!

PISHCHIK. I've taken all the pills.

LOPAKHIN. What a glutton!

(*Everyone laughs.*)

FIRS. The gentleman stayed with us during Holy Week . . . ate half a bucket of pickles. . . . (*Mumbles.*)

LYUBOV ANDREYEVNA. What is he saying?

VARYA. He's been muttering like that for three years now. We've grown used to it.

YASHA. He's in his dotage.

(*Charlotta Ivanovna, very thin, tightly laced, in a white dress with a lorgnette at her belt, crosses the stage.*)

---

[2]**versts** A verst is a little more than half a mile.

LOPAKHIN. Forgive me, Charlotta Ivanovna, I haven't had a chance to say how do you do to you. (*Tries to kiss her hand.*)

CHARLOTTA (*pulls her hand away*). If I permit you to kiss my hand you'll be wanting to kiss my elbow next, then my shoulder.

LOPAKHIN. I have no luck today. (*Everyone laughs.*) Charlotta Ivanovna, show us a trick!

LYUBOV ANDREYEVNA. Charlotta, show us a trick!

CHARLOTTA. No. I want to sleep. (*Goes out.*)

LOPAKHIN. In three weeks we'll meet again. (*Kisses Lyubov Andreyevna's hand.*) Good-bye till then. Time to go. (*To Gayev.*) Good-bye. (*Kisses Pishchik.*) Good-bye. (*Shakes hands with Varya, then with Firs and Yasha.*) I don't feel like going. (*To Lyubov Andreyevna.*) If you make up your mind about the summer cottages and come to a decision, let me know; I'll get you a loan of fifty thousand or so. Think it over seriously.

VARYA (*angrily*). Oh, why don't you go!

LOPAKHIN. I'm going, I'm going. (*Goes out.*)

GAYEV. Boor. Oh, pardon. Varya's going to marry him, he's Varya's young man.

VARYA. Uncle dear, you talk too much.

LYUBOV ANDREYEVNA. Well, Varya, I shall be very glad. He's a good man.

PISHCHIK. A man, I must truly say . . . most worthy. . . . And my Dashenka . . . says, too, that . . . says all sorts of things. (*Snores but wakes up at once.*) In any case, honored lady, oblige me . . . a loan of two hundred and forty rubles . . . tomorrow the interest on my mortgage is due. . . .

VARYA (*in alarm*). We have nothing, nothing at all!

LYUBOV ANDREYEVNA. I really haven't any money.

PISHCHIK. It'll turn up. (*Laughs.*) I never lose hope. Just when I thought everything was lost, that I was done for, lo and behold—the railway line ran through my land . . . and they paid me for it. And before you know it, something else will turn up, if not today—tomorrow. . . . Dashenka will win two hundred thousand . . . she's got a lottery ticket.

LYUBOV ANDREYEVNA. The coffee is finished, we can go to bed.

FIRS (*brushing Gayev's clothes, admonishingly*). You've put on the wrong trousers again. What am I to do with you!

VARYA (*softly*). Anya's asleep. (*Quietly opens the window.*) The sun has risen, it's no longer cold. Look, Mama dear, what wonderful trees! Oh, Lord, the air! The starlings are singing!

GAYEV (*opens another window*). The orchard is all white. You haven't forgotten, Lyuba? That long avenue there that runs straight—straight as a stretched-out strap; it gleams on moonlight nights. Remember? You've not forgotten?

LYUBOV ANDREYEVNA (*looking out the window at the orchard*). Oh, my childhood, my innocence! I used to sleep in this nursery, I looked out from here into the orchard, happi-ness awoke with me each morning, it was just as it is now, nothing has changed. (*Laughing with joy.*) All, all white! Oh, my orchard! After the dark, rainy autumn and the cold winter, you are young again, full of happiness, the heavenly angels have not forsaken you. . . . If I could cast off this heavy stone weighing on my breast and shoulders, if I could forget my past!

GAYEV. Yes, and the orchard will be sold for our debts, strange as it may seem. . . .

LYUBOV ANDREYEVNA. Look, our dead mother walks in the orchard . . . in a white dress! (*Laughs with joy.*) It is she!

GAYEV. Where?

VARYA. God be with you, Mama dear.

LYUBOV ANDREYEVNA. There's no one there, I just imagined it. To the right, as you turn to the summerhouse, a slender white sapling is bent over . . . it looks like a woman.

(*Enter Trofimov wearing a shabby student's uniform and spectacles.*)

LYUBOV ANDREYEVNA. What a wonderful orchard! The white masses of blossoms, the blue sky—

TROFIMOV. Lyubov Andreyevna! (*She looks around at him.*) I only want to pay my respects, then I'll go at once. (*Kisses her hand ardently.*) I was told to wait until morning, but I hadn't the patience.

(*Lyubov Andreyevna looks at him, puzzled.*)

VARYA (*through tears*). This is Petya Trofimov.

TROFIMOV. Petya Trofimov, I was Grisha's tutor. . . . Can I have changed so much?

(*Lyubov Andreyevna embraces him, quietly weeping.*)

GAYEV (*embarrassed*). There, there, Lyuba.

VARYA (*crying*): Didn't I tell you, Petya, to wait till tomorrow?

LYUBOV ANDREYEVNA. My Grisha . . . my little boy . . . Grisha . . . my son. . . .

VARYA. What can we do, Mama dear? It's God's will.

TROFIMOV (*gently, through tears*). Don't, don't. . . .

LYUBOV ANDREYEVNA (*quietly weeping*). My little boy dead, drowned. . . . Why? Why, my friend? (*In a lower voice.*) Anya is sleeping in there, and I'm talking loudly . . . making all this noise. . . . But Petya, why do you look so bad? Why have you grown so old?

TROFIMOV. A peasant woman in the train called me a mangy gentleman.

LYUBOV ANDREYEVNA. You were just a boy then, a charming little student, and now your hair is thin—and spectacles! Is it possible you are still a student? (*Goes toward the door.*)

TROFIMOV. I shall probably be an eternal student.

LYUBOV ANDREYEVNA (*kisses her brother, then Varya*). Now, go to bed. . . . You've grown older too, Leonid.

PISHCHIK (*follows her*). Well, seems to be time to sleep. . . . Oh, my gout! I'm staying the night. Lyubov Andreyevna, my soul, tomorrow morning . . . two hundred and forty rubles. . . .

GAYEV. He keeps at it.

PISHCHIK. Two hundred and forty rubles . . . to pay the interest on my mortgage.

LYUBOV ANDREYEVNA. I have no money, my friend.

PISHCHIK. My dear, I'll pay it back. . . . It's a trifling sum.

LYUBOV ANDREYEVNA. Well, all right, Leonid will give it to you. . . . Give it to him, Leonid.

GAYEV. Me give it to him! . . . Hold out your pocket!

LYUBOV ANDREYEVNA. It can't be helped, give it to him. . . . He needs it. . . . He'll pay it back.

(Lyubov Andreyevna, Trofimov, Pishchik, and Firs go out. Gayev, Varya, and Yasha remain.)

GAYEV. My sister hasn't yet lost her habit of squandering money. *(To Yasha.)* Go away, my good fellow, you smell of the henhouse.

YASHA *(with a smirk)*. And you, Leonid Andreyevich, are just the same as ever.

GAYEV. How's that? *(To Varya.)* What did he say?

VARYA. Your mother has come from the village; she's been sitting in the servants' room since yesterday, waiting to see you. . . .

YASHA. Let her wait, for God's sake!

VARYA. Aren't you ashamed?

YASHA. A lot I need her! She could have come tomorrow. *(Goes out.)*

VARYA. Mama's the same as ever, she hasn't changed a bit. She'd give away everything, if she could.

GAYEV. Yes. . . . *(A pause.)* If a great many remedies are suggested for a disease, it means that the disease is incurable. I keep thinking, racking my brains, I have many remedies, a great many, and that means, in effect, that I have none. It would be good to receive a legacy from someone, good to marry our Anya to a very rich man, good to go to Yaroslav and try our luck with our aunt, the Countess. She is very, very rich, you know.

VARYA *(crying)*. If only God would help us!

GAYEV. Stop bawling. Auntie's very rich, but she doesn't like us. In the first place, sister married a lawyer, not a nobleman . . . *(Anya appears in the doorway.)* She married beneath her, and it cannot be said that she has conducted herself very virtuously. She is good, kind, charming, and I love her dearly, but no matter how much you allow for extenuating circumstances, you must admit she leads a sinful life. You feel it in her slightest movement.

VARYA *(in a whisper)*. Anya is standing in the doorway.

GAYEV. What? *(Pause.)* Funny, something got into my right eye . . . I can't see very well. And Thursday, when I was in the district court . . .

(Anya enters.)

VARYA. Why aren't you asleep, Anya?

ANYA. I can't get to sleep. I just can't.

GAYEV. My little one! *(Kisses Anya's face and hands.)* My child. . . . *(Through tears.)* You are not my niece, you are my angel, you are everything to me. Believe me, believe . . .

ANYA. I believe you, Uncle. Everyone loves you and respects you, but, Uncle dear, you must keep quiet, just keep quiet. What were you saying just now about my mother, about your own sister? What made you say that?

GAYEV. Yes, yes. . . . *(Covers his face with her hand.)* Really, it's awful! My God! God help me! And today I made a speech to the bookcase . . . so stupid! And it was only when I had finished that I realized it was stupid.

VARYA. It's true, Uncle dear, you ought to keep quiet. Just don't talk, that's all.

ANYA. If you could keep from talking, it would make things easier for you, too.

GAYEV. I'll be quiet. *(Kisses Anya's and Varya's hands.)* I'll be quiet. Only this is about business. On Thursday I was in the district court, well, a group of us gathered together and began talking about one thing and another, this and that, and it seems it might be possible to arrange a loan on a promissory note to pay the interest at the bank.

VARYA. If only God would help us!

GAYEV. On Tuesday I'll go and talk it over again. *(To Varya.)* Stop bawling. *(To Anya.)* Your mama will talk to Lopakhin; he, of course, will not refuse her. . . . And as soon as you've rested, you will go to Yaroslav to the Countess, your great-aunt. In that way we shall be working from three directions—and our business is in the hat. We'll pay the interest, I'm certain of it. . . . *(Puts a candy in his mouth.)* On my honor, I'll swear by anything you like, the estate shall not be sold. *(Excitedly.)* By my happiness, I swear it! Here's my hand on it, call me a worthless, dishonorable man if I let it come to auction! I swear by my whole being!

ANYA *(a calm mood returns to her, she is happy)*. How good you are, Uncle, how clever! *(Embraces him.)* Now I am at peace! I'm at peace! I'm happy!

(Enter Firs.)

FIRS *(reproachfully)*. Leonid Andreich, have you no fear of God? When are you going to bed?

GAYEV. Presently, presently. Go away, Firs. I'll . . . all right, I'll undress myself. Well, children, bye-bye. . . . Details tomorrow, and now go to sleep. *(Kisses Anya and Varya.)* I am a man of the eighties. . . . They don't think much of that period today, nevertheless, I can say that in the course of my life I have suffered not a little for my convictions. It is not for nothing that the peasant loves me. You have to know the peasant! You have to know from what—

ANYA. There you go again, Uncle!

VARYA. Uncle dear, do be quiet.

FIRS *(angrily)*. Leonid Andreich!

GAYEV. I'm coming, I'm coming. . . . Go to bed. A clean

double rail shot to center table.... (*Goes out; Firs hobbles after him.*)

ANYA. I'm at peace now. I would rather not go to Yaroslav, I don't like my great-aunt, but still, I'm at peace, thanks to Uncle. (*She sits down.*)

VARYA. We must get some sleep. I'm going now. Oh, something unpleasant happened while you were away. In the old servants' quarters, as you know, there are only the old people: Yefimushka, Polya, Yevstignei, and, of course, Karp. They began letting in all sorts of rogues to spend the night—I didn't say anything. But then I heard they'd been spreading a rumor that I'd given an order for them to be fed nothing but dried peas. Out of stinginess, you see.... It was all Yevstignei's doing.... Very well, I think, if that's how it is, you just wait. I send for Yevstignei ... (*yawning*) he comes.... "How is it, Yevstignei," I say, "that you could be such a fool...." (*Looks at Anya.*) She's fallen asleep. (*Takes her by the arm.*) Come to your little bed.... Come along. (*Leading her.*) My little darling fell asleep. Come.... (*They go.*)

(*In the distance, beyond the orchard, a shepherd is playing on a reed pipe. Trofimov crosses the stage and, seeing Varya and Anya, stops.*)

VARYA. Sh! She's asleep ... asleep.... Come along, darling.

ANYA (*softly, half-asleep*). I'm so tired.... Those bells ... Uncle ... dear ... Mama and Uncle ...

VARYA. Come, darling, come along. (*They go into Anya's room.*)

TROFIMOV (*deeply moved*). My sunshine! My spring!

ACT II

(*A meadow. An old, lopsided, long-abandoned little chapel; near it a well, large stones that apparently were once tombstones, and an old bench. A road to the Gayev manor house can be seen. On one side, where the cherry orchard begins, tall poplars loom. In the distance a row of telegraph poles, and far, far away, on the horizon, the faint outline of a large town, which is visible only in very fine, clear weather. The sun will soon set. Charlotta, Yasha, and Dunyasha are sitting on the bench; Yepikhodov stands near playing something sad on the guitar. They are all lost in thought. Charlotta wears an old forage cap; she has taken a gun from her shoulder and is addressing the buckle on the sling.*)

CHARLOTTA (*reflectively*). I haven't got a real passport, I don't know how old I am, but it always seems to me that I'm quite young. When I was a little girl, my father and mother used to travel from one fair to another giving performances—very good ones. And I did the *salto mortale* and all sorts of tricks. Then when Papa and Mama died, a German lady took me to live with her and began teaching me. Good. I grew up and became a governess. But where I come from and who I am—I do not know.... Who my parents were—perhaps they weren't even married—I don't know. (*Takes a cucumber out of her pocket and eats it.*) I don't know anything. (*Pause.*) One wants so much to talk, but there isn't anyone to talk to ... I have no one.

YEPIKHODOV (*plays the guitar and sings*). "What care I for the clamorous world, what's friend or foe to me?" ... How pleasant it is to play a mandolin!

DUNYASHA. That's a guitar, not a mandolin. (*Looks at herself in a hand mirror and powders her face.*)

YEPIKHODOV. To a madman, in love, it is a mandolin.... (*Sings.*) "Would that the heart were warmed by the flame of required love ..."

(*Yasha joins in.*)

CHARLOTTA. How horribly these people sing? ... Pfui! Like jackals!

DUNYASHA (*to Yasha*). Really, how fortunate to have been abroad!

YASHA. Yes, to be sure. I cannot but agree with you there. (*Yawns, then lights a cigar.*)

YEPIKHODOV. It stands to reason. Abroad everything has long since been fully constituted.

YASHA. Obviously.

YEPIKHODOV. I am a cultivated man, I read all sorts of remarkable books, but I am in no way able to make out my own inclinations, what it is I really want, whether, strictly speaking, to live or to shoot myself; nevertheless, I always carry a revolver on me. Here it is. (*Shows revolver.*)

CHARLOTTA. Finished. Now I'm going. (*Slings the gun over her shoulder.*) You're a very clever man, Yepikhodov, and quite terrifying; women must be mad about you. Brrr! (*Starts to go.*) These clever people are all so stupid, there's no one for me to talk to.... Alone, always alone, I have no one ... and who I am, and why I am, nobody knows.... (*Goes out unhurriedly.*)

YEPIKHODOV. Strictly speaking, all else aside, I must state regarding myself, that fate treats me unmercifully, as a storm does a small ship. If, let us assume, I am mistaken, then why, to mention a single instance, do I wake up this morning, and there on my chest see a spider of terrifying magnitude? ... Like that. (*Indicates with both hands.*) And likewise, I take up some kvas to quench my thirst, and there see something in the highest degree unseemly, like a cockroach. (*Pause.*) Have you read Buckle?[3] (*Pause.*) If I may trouble you, Avdotya Fedorovna, I should like to have a word or two with you.

DUNYASHA. Go ahead.

[3]**Buckle** Thomas Henry Buckle (1821–1862) an historian; he formulated a scientific basis for history emphasizing the interrelationship of climate, food production, population, and wealth.

YEPIKHODOV. I prefer to speak with you alone. . . . (*Sighs.*)

DUNYASHA (*embarrassed*). Very well . . . only first bring me my little cape . . . you'll find it by the cupboard. . . . It's rather damp here. . . .

YEPIKHODOV. Certainly, ma'am . . . I'll fetch it, ma'am. . . . Now I know what to do with my revolver. . . . (*Takes the guitar and goes off playing it.*)

YASHA. Two-and-twenty Troubles! Between ourselves, a stupid fellow. (*Yawns.*)

DUNYASHA. God forbid that he should shoot himself. (*Pause.*) I've grown so anxious, I'm always worried. I was only a little girl when I was taken into the master's house, and now I'm quite unused to the simple life, and my hands are white as can be, just like a lady's. I've become so delicate, so tender and ladylike, I'm afraid of everything. . . . Frightfully so. And, Yasha, if you deceive me, I just don't know what will become of my nerves.

YASHA (*kisses her*). You little cucumber! Of course, a girl should never forget herself. What I dislike above everything is when a girl doesn't conduct herself properly.

DUNYASHA. I'm passionately in love with you, you're educated, you can discuss anything. (*Pause.*)

YASHA (*yawns*). Yes. . . . As I see it, it's like this: If a girl loves somebody, that means she's immoral. (*Pause.*) Very pleasant smoking a cigar in the open air. . . . (*Listens.*) Someone's coming this way. . . . It's the masters. (*Dunyasha impulsively embraces him.*) You go home, as if you'd been to the river to bathe; take that path, otherwise they'll see you and suspect me of having a rendezvous with you. I can't endure that sort of thing.

DUNYASHA (*with a little cough*). My head is beginning to ache from your cigar. . . . (*Goes out.*)

(*Yasha remains, sitting near the chapel. Lyubov Andreyevna, Gayev, and Lopakhin enter.*)

LOPAKHIN. You must make up your mind once and for all—time won't stand still. The question, after all, is quite simple. Do you agree to lease the land for summer cottages or not? Answer in one word: Yes or no? Only one word!

LYUBOV ANDREYEVNA. Who is it that smokes those disgusting cigars out here? (*Sits down.*)

GAYEV. Now that the railway line is so near, it's made things convenient. (*Sits down.*) We went to town and had lunch . . . cue ball to the center! I feel like going to the house first and playing a game.

LYUBOV ANDREYEVNA. Later.

LOPAKHIN. Just one word! (*Imploringly.*) Do give me an answer.

GAYEV (*yawning*). How's that?

LYUBOV ANDREYEVNA (*looks into her purse*). Yesterday I had a lot of money, and today there's hardly any left. My poor Varya tries to economize by feeding everyone milk soup, and in the kitchen the old people get nothing but dried peas, while I squander money foolishly. . . . (*Drops the purse, scattering gold coins.*) There they go. . . . (*Vexed.*)

YASHA. Allow me, I'll pick them up in an instant. (*Picks up the money.*)

LYUBOV ANDREYEVNA. Please do, Yasha. And why did I go to town for lunch? . . . That miserable restaurant of yours with its music, and tablecloths smelling of soap. . . . Why drink so much, Lyonya? Why eat so much? Why talk so much? Today in the restaurant again you talked too much, and it was all so pointless. About the seventies, about the decadents. And to whom? Talking to waiters about the decadents!

LOPAKHIN. Yes.

GAYEV (*waving his hand*). I'm incorrigible, that's evident. . . . (*Irritably to Yasha.*) Why do you keep twirling about in front of me?

YASHA (*laughs*). I can't help laughing when I hear your voice.

GAYEV (*to his sister*). Either he or I—

LYUBOV ANDREYEVNA. Go away, Yasha, run along.

YASHA (*hands Lyubov Andreyevna her purse*): I'm going, right away. (*Hardly able to contain his laughter.*) This very instant. . . . (*Goes out.*)

LOPAKHIN. That rich man, Deriganov, is prepared to buy the estate. They say he's coming to the auction himself.

LYUBOV ANDREYEVNA. Where did you hear that?

LOPAKHIN. That's what they're saying in town.

LYUBOV ANDREYEVNA. Our aunt in Yaroslav promised to send us something, but when and how much, no one knows.

LOPAKHIN. How much do you think she'll send? A hundred thousand? Two hundred?

LYUBOV ANDREYEVNA. Oh . . . ten or fifteen thousand, and we'll be thankful for that.

LOPAKHIN. Forgive me, but I have never seen such frivolous, such queer, unbusinesslike people as you, my friends. You are told in plain language that your estate is to be sold, and it's as though you don't understand it.

LYUBOV ANDREYEVNA. But what are we to do? Tell us what to do.

LOPAKHIN. I tell you every day. Every day I say the same thing. Both the cherry orchard and the land must be leased for summer cottages, and it must be done now, as quickly as possible—the auction is close at hand. Try to understand! Once you definitely decide on the cottages, you can raise as much money as you like, and then you are saved.

LYUBOV ANDREYEVNA. Cottages, summer people—forgive me, but it's so vulgar.

GAYEV. I agree with you, absolutely.

LOPAKHIN. I'll either burst into tears, start shouting, or fall into a faint! I can't stand it! You've worn me out! (*To Gayev.*) You're an old woman!

GAYEV. How's that?

LOPAKHIN. An old woman! (*Starts to go.*)

LYUBOV ANDREYEVNA (*alarmed*). No, don't go, stay, my dear. I beg you. Perhaps we'll think of something!

LOPAKHIN. What is there to think of?

LYUBOV ANDREYEVNA. Don't go away, please. With you here it's more cheerful somehow. . . . (*Pause.*) I keep expecting something to happen, like the house caving in on us.

GAYEV (*in deep thought*). Double rail shot into the corner. . . . Cross table to the center. . . .

LYUBOV ANDREYEVNA. We have sinned so much. . . .

LOPAKHIN. What sins could you have—

GAYEV (*puts a candy into his mouth*). They say I've eaten up my entire fortune in candies. . . . (*Laughs.*)

LYUBOV ANDREYEVNA. Oh, my sins. . . . I've always squandered money recklessly, like a madwoman, and I married a man who did nothing but amass debts. My husband died from champagne—he drank terribly—then, to my sorrow, I fell in love with another man, lived with him, and just at that time—that was my first punishment, a blow on the head—my little boy was drowned . . . here in the river. And I went abroad, went away for good, never to return, never to see this river. . . . I closed my eyes and ran, beside myself, and *he* after me . . . callously, without pity. I bought a villa near Mentone, because he fell ill there, and for three years I had no rest, day or night. The sick man wore me out, my soul dried up. Then last year, when the villa was sold to pay my debts, I went to Paris, and there he stripped me of everything, and left me for another woman; I tried to poison myself. . . . So stupid, so shameful. . . . And suddenly I felt a longing for Russia, for my own country, for my little girl. . . . (*Wipes away her tears.*) Lord, Lord, be merciful, forgive my sins! Don't punish me anymore! (*Takes a telegram out of her pocket.*) This came today from Paris. . . . He asks my forgiveness, begs me to return. . . . (*Tears up telegram.*) Do I hear music? (*Listens.*)

GAYEV. That's our famous Jewish band. You remember, four violins, a flute, and double bass.

LYUBOV ANDREYEVNA. It's still in existence? We ought to send for them sometime and give a party.

LOPAKHIN (*listens*). I don't hear anything. . . . (*Sings softly.*) "The Germans, for pay, will turn Russians into Frenchmen, they say." (*Laughs.*) What a play I saw yesterday at the theater—very funny!

LYUBOV ANDREYEVNA. There was probably nothing funny about it. Instead of going to see plays you ought to look at yourselves a little more often. How drab your lives are, how full of futile talk!

LOPAKHIN. That's true. I must say, this life of ours is stupid. . . . (*Pause.*) My father was a peasant, an idiot; he understood nothing, taught me nothing; all he did was beat me when he was drunk, and always with a stick. As a matter of fact, I'm as big a blockhead and idiot as he was. I never learned anything, my handwriting's disgusting, I write like a pig—I'm ashamed to have people see it.

LYUBOV ANDREYEVNA. You ought to get married, my friend.

LOPAKHIN. Yes . . . that's true.

LYUBOV ANDREYEVNA. To our Varya. She's a nice girl.

LOPAKHIN. Yes.

LYUBOV ANDREYEVNA. She's a girl who comes from simple people, works all day long, but the main thing is she loves you. Besides, you've liked her for a long time now.

LOPAKHIN. Well? I've nothing against it. . . . She's a good girl. (*Pause.*)

GAYEV. I've been offered a place in the bank. Six thousand a year. . . . Have you heard?

LYUBOV ANDREYEVNA. How could you! You stay where you are. . . .

(*Firs enters carrying an overcoat.*)

FIRS (*to Gayev*). If you please, sir, put this on, it's damp.

GAYEV (*puts on the overcoat*). You're a pest, old man.

FIRS. Never mind. . . . You went off this morning without telling me. (*Looks him over.*)

LYUBOV ANDREYEVNA. How you have aged, Firs!

FIRS. What do you wish, madam?

LOPAKHIN. She says you've grown very old!

FIRS. I've lived a long time. They were arranging a marriage for me before your papa was born. . . . (*Laughs.*) I was already head footman when the emancipation came. At that time I wouldn't consent to my freedom, I stayed with the masters. . . . (*Pause.*) I remember, everyone was happy, but what they were happy about, they themselves didn't know.

LOPAKHIN. It was better in the old days. At least they flogged them.

FIRS (*not hearing*). Of course. The peasants kept to the masters, the masters kept to the peasants; but now they have all gone their own ways, you can't tell about anything.

GAYEV. Be quiet, Firs. Tomorrow I must go to town. I've been promised an introduction to a certain general who might let us have a loan.

LOPAKHIN. Nothing will come of it. And you can rest assured, you won't even pay the interest.

LYUBOV ANDREYEVNA. He's raving. There is no such general.

(*Enter Trofimov, Anya, and Varya.*)

GAYEV. Here come our young people.

ANYA. There's Mama.

LYUBOV ANDREYEVNA (*tenderly*). Come, come along, my darlings. (*Embraces Anya and Varya.*) If you only knew how I love you both! Sit here beside me—there, like that.

(*They all sit down.*)

LOPAKHIN. Our eternal student is always with the young ladies.

TROFIMOV. That's none of your business.

LOPAKHIN. He'll soon be fifty, but he's still a student.

TROFIMOV. Drop your stupid jokes.

LOPAKHIN. What are you so angry about, you queer fellow?

TROFIMOV. Just leave me alone.

LOPAKHIN (*laughs*). Let me ask you something: What do you make of me?

TROFIMOV. My idea of you, Yermolai Alekseich, is this:

You're a rich man, you will soon be a millionaire. Just as the beast of prey, which devours everything that crosses its path, is necessary in the metabolic process, so are you necessary.

(*Everybody laughs.*)

VARYA. Petya, you'd better tell us something about the planets.

LYUBOV ANDREYEVNA. No, let's go on with yesterday's conversation.

TROFIMOV. What was it about?

GAYEV. About the proud man.

TROFIMOV. We talked a long time yesterday, but we didn't get anywhere. In the proud man, in your sense of the word, there's something mystical. And you may be right from your point of view, but if you look at it simply, without being abstruse, why even talk about pride? Is there any sense in it if, physiologically, man is poorly constructed, if, in the vast majority of cases, he is coarse, ignorant, and profoundly unhappy? We should stop admiring ourselves. We should just work, and that's all.

GAYEV. You die, anyway.

TROFIMOV. Who knows? And what does it mean—to die? It may be that man has a hundred senses, and at his death only the five that are known to us perish, and the other ninety-five go on living.

LYUBOV ANDREYEVNA. How clever you are, Petya!

LOPAKHIN (*ironically*). Terribly clever!

TROFIMOV. Mankind goes forward, perfecting its powers. Everything that is now unattainable will some day be comprehensible and within our grasp, only we must work, and help with all our might those who are seeking the truth. So far, among us here in Russia, only a very few work. The great majority of the intelligentsia that I know seek nothing, do nothing, and as yet are incapable of work. They call themselves the intelligentsia, yet they belittle their servants, treat the peasants like animals, are wretched students, never read anything serious, and do absolutely nothing; they only talk about science and know very little about art. They all look serious, have grim expressions, speak of weighty matters, and philosophize; and meanwhile anyone can see that the workers eat abominably, sleep without pillows, thirty or forty to a room, and everywhere there are bedbugs, stench, dampness, and immorality. . . . It's obvious that all our fine talk is merely to delude ourselves and others. Show me the day nurseries they are always talking about—and where are the reading rooms? They only write about them in novels, but in reality they don't exist. There is nothing but filth, vulgarity, asiaticism.[4] . . . I'm afraid of those very serious countenances, I don't like them, I'm afraid of serious conversations. We'd do better to remain silent.

LOPAKHIN. You know, I get up before five in the morning, and I work from morning to night; now, I'm always handling money, my own and other people's, and I see what people around me are like. You have only to start doing something to find out how few honest, decent people there are. Sometimes, when I can't sleep, I think: "Lord, Thou gavest us vast forests, boundless fields, broad horizons, and living in their midst we ourselves ought truly to be giants. . . ."

LYUBOV ANDREYEVNA. Now you want giants! They're good only in fairy tales, otherwise they're frightening.

(*Yepikhodov crosses at the rear of the stage, playing the guitar.*)

LYUBOV ANDREYEVNA (*pensively*). There goes Yepikhodov . . .

ANYA (*pensively*). There goes Yepikhodov . . .

GAYEV. The sun has set, ladies and gentlemen.

TROFIMOV. Yes.

GAYEV (*in a low voice, as though reciting*). Oh, Nature, wondrous Nature, you shine with eternal radiance, beautiful and indifferent; you, whom we call mother, unite within yourself both life and death, giving life and taking it away. . . .

VARYA (*beseechingly*). Uncle dear!

ANYA. Uncle, you're doing it again!

TROFIMOV. You'd better cue ball into the center.

GAYEV. I'll be silent, silent.

(*All sit lost in thought. The silence is broken only by the subdued muttering of Firs. Suddenly a distant sound is heard, as if from the sky, like the sound of a snapped string mournfully dying away.*)

LYUBOV ANDREYEVNA. What was that?

LOPAKHIN. I don't know. Somewhere far off in a mine shaft a bucket's broken loose. But somewhere very far away.

GAYEV. It might be a bird of some sort . . . like a heron.

TROFIMOV. Or an owl . . .

LYUBOV ANDREYEVNA (*shudders*). It's unpleasant somehow. . . . (*Pause.*)

FIRS. The same thing happened before the troubles: An owl hooted and the samovar hissed continually.

GAYEV. Before what troubles?

FIRS. Before the emancipation.

LYUBOV ANDREYEVNA. Come along, my friends, let us go, evening is falling. (*To Anya.*) There are tears in your eyes—what is it, my little one?

(*Embraces her.*)

ANYA. It's all right, Mama. It's nothing.

TROFIMOV. Someone is coming.

(*A Stranger appears wearing a shabby white forage cap and an overcoat. He is slightly drunk.*)

---

[4]**asiaticism** Trofimov is referring to Asian apathy; a common Russian prejudice of the time.

STRANGER. Permit me to inquire, can I go straight through here to the station?

GAYEV. You can follow the road.

STRANGER. I am deeply grateful to you. (*Coughs.*) Splendid weather. . . . (*Reciting.*) "My brother, my suffering brother . . . come to the Volga, whose groans" . . . (*To Varya.*) Mademoiselle, will you oblige a hungry Russian with thirty kopecks?

(*Varya, frightened, cries out.*)

LOPAKHIN (*angrily*). There's a limit to everything.

LYUBOV ANDREYEVNA (*panic-stricken*). Here you are—take this . . . (*Fumbles in her purse.*) I have no silver. . . . Never mind, here's a gold piece for you. . . .

STRANGER. I am deeply grateful to you. (*Goes off.*)

(*Laughter.*)

VARYA (*frightened*). I'm leaving . . . I'm leaving. . . . Oh, Mama, dear, there's nothing in the house for the servants to eat, and you give him a gold piece!

LYUBOV ANDREYEVNA. What's to be done with such a silly creature? When we get home I'll give you all I've got. Yermolai Alekseyevich, you'll lend me some more!

LOPAKHIN. At your service.

LYUBOV ANDREYEVNA. Come, my friends, it's time to go. Oh, Varya, we have definitely made a match for you. Congratulations!

VARYA (*through tears*). Mama, that's not something to joke about.

LOPAKHIN. "Aurelia, get thee to a nunnery . . . "[5]

GAYEV. Look, my hands are trembling: It's a long time since I've played a game of billiards.

LOPAKHIN. "Aurelia, O Nymph, in thy orisons, be all my sins remember'd!"

LYUBOV ANDREYEVNA. Let us go, my friends, it will soon be suppertime.

VARYA. He frightened me. My heart is simply pounding.

LOPAKHIN. Let me remind you, ladies and gentlemen: On the twenty-second of August the cherry orchard is to be sold. Think about that!—Think!

(*All go out except Trofimov and Anya.*)

ANYA (*laughs*). My thanks to the stranger for frightening Varya, now we are alone.

TROFIMOV. Varya is so afraid we might suddenly fall in love with each other that she hasn't left us alone for days. With her narrow mind she can't understand that we are above love. To avoid the petty and the illusory, which prevent our being free and happy—that is the aim and meaning of life. Forward! We are moving irresistibly toward the bright star that burns in the distance! Forward! Do not fall behind, friends!

ANYA (*clasping her hands*). How well you talk! (*Pause.*) It's marvelous here today!

TROFIMOV. Yes, the weather is wonderful.

ANYA. What have you done to me, Petya, that I no longer love the cherry orchard as I used to? I loved it so tenderly, it seemed to me there was no better place on earth than our orchard.

TROFIMOV. All Russia is our orchard. It is a great and beautiful land, and there are many wonderful places in it. (*Pause.*) Just think, Anya: Your grandfather, your great-grandfather, and all your ancestors were serf-owners, possessors of living souls. Don't you see that from every cherry tree, from every leaf and trunk, human beings are peering out at you? Don't you hear their voices? To possess living souls—that has corrupted all of you, those who lived before and you who are living now, so that your mother, you, your uncle, no longer perceive that you are living in debt, at someone else's expense, at the expense of those whom you wouldn't allow to cross your threshold. . . . We are at least two hundred years behind the times, we have as yet absolutely nothing, we have no definite attitude toward the past, we only philosophize, complain of boredom, or drink vodka. Yet it's quite clear that to begin to live we must first atone for the past, be done with it, and we can atone for it only by suffering, only by extraordinary, unceasing labor. Understand this, Anya.

ANYA. The house we live in hasn't really been ours for a long time, and I shall leave it, I give you my word.

TROFIMOV. If you have the keys of the household, throw them into the well and go. Be as free as the wind.

ANYA (*ecstasy*). How well you put that!

TROFIMOV. Believe me, Anya, believe me! I am not yet thirty, I am young, still a student, but I have already been through so much! As soon as winter comes, I am hungry, sick, worried, poor as a beggar, and—where has not fate driven me! Where have I not been? And yet always, every minute of the day and night, my soul was filled with inexplicable premonitions. I have a premonition of happiness, Anya, I can see it . . .

ANYA. The moon is rising.

(*Yepikhodov is heard playing the same melancholy song on the guitar. The moon rises. Somewhere near the poplars Varya is looking for Anya and calling: "Anya, where are you?"*)

TROFIMOV. Yes, the moon is rising. (*Pause.*) There it is—happiness . . . it's coming, nearer and nearer, I can hear its footsteps. And if we do not see it, if we do not recognize it, what does it matter? Others will see it.

VARYA'S VOICE. Anya! Where are you?

TROFIMOV. That Varya again! (*Angrily.*) It's revolting!

ANYA. Well? Let's go down to the river. It's lovely there.

TROFIMOV. Come on. (*They go.*)

VARYA'S VOICE. Anya! Anya!

---

[5]**"Aurelia . . . nunnery"** Lopakhin misquotes Hamlet's famous line rejecting Ophelia. His next line is also from *Hamlet*).

ACT III

(The drawing room, separated by an arch from the ball-room. The chandelier is lighted. The Jewish band that was mentioned in act II is heard playing in the hall. It is evening. In the ballroom they are dancing a grand rond. The voice of Semyonov-Pishchik: "Promenade à une paire!"[6] They all enter the drawing room: Pishchik and Charlotta Ivanovna are the first couple, Trofimov and Lyubov Andreyevna the second, Anya and the Post-Office Clerk the third, Varya and the Stationmaster the fourth, etc. Varya, quietly weeping, dries her tears as she dances. Dunyasha is in the last couple. As they cross the drawing room Pishchik calls: "Grand rond, balancez!" and "Les cavaliers à genoux et remercier vos dames!"[7] Firs, wearing a dress coat, brings in a tray with seltzer water. Pishchik and Trofimov come into the drawing room.)

PISHCHIK. I'm a full-blooded man, I've already had two strokes, and dancing's hard work for me, but as they say, "If you run with the pack, you can bark or not, but at least wag your tail." At that, I'm as strong as a horse. My late father—quite a joker he was, God rest his soul—used to say, talking about our origins, that the ancient line of Se-myonov-Pishchik was descended from the very horse that Caligula had seated in the Senate.[8] . . . *(Sits down.)* But the trouble is—no money! A hungry dog believes in nothing but meat. . . . *(Snores but wakes up at once.)* It's the same with me—I can think of nothing but money. . . .

TROFIMOV. You know, there really is something equine about your figure.

PISHCHIK. Well, a horse is a fine animal. . . . You can sell a horse.

(There is the sound of a billiard game in the next room. Varya appears in the archway.)

TROFIMOV *(teasing her):* Madame Lopakhina! Madame Lopakhina!

VARYA *(angrily).* Mangy gentleman!

TROFIMOV. Yes, I am a mangy gentleman, and proud of it!

VARYA *(reflecting bitterly).* Here we've hired musicians, and what are we going to pay them with? *(Goes out.)*

TROFIMOV *(to Pishchik).* If the energy you have expended in the course of your life trying to find money to pay interest had gone into something else, ultimately, you might very well have turned the world upside down.

PISHCHIK. Nietzsche . . . the philosopher . . . the greatest, most renowned . . . a man of tremendous intellect . . . says in his works that it is possible to forge banknotes.

TROFIMOV. And have you read Nietzsche?

PISHCHIK. Well . . . Dashenka told me. I'm in such a state now that I'm just about ready for forging. . . . The day after tomorrow I have to pay three hundred and ten rubles . . . I've got a hundred and thirty. . . . *(Feels in his pocket, grows alarmed.)* The money is gone! I've lost the money! *(Tearfully.)* Where is my money? *(Joyfully.)* Here it is, inside the lining. . . . I'm all in a sweat. . . .

(Lyubov Andreyevna and Charlotta Ivanovna come in.)

LYUBOV ANDREYEVNA *(humming a Lezginka).*[9] Why does Leonid take so long? What is he doing in town? *(To Dun-yasha.)* Dunyasha, offer the musicians some tea.

TROFIMOV. In all probability, the auction didn't take place.

LYUBOV ANDREYEVNA. It was the wrong time to have the musicians, the wrong time to give a dance. . . . Well, never mind. . . . *(Sits down and hums softly.)*

CHARLOTTA *(gives Pishchik a deck of cards).* Here's a deck of cards for you. Think of a card.

PISHCHIK. I've thought of one.

CHARLOTTA. Now shuffle the pack. Very good. And now, my dear Mr. Pishchik, hand it to me. *Ein, zwei, drei!* Now look for it—it's in your side pocket.

PISHCHIK. *(takes the card out of his side pocket).* The eight of spades—absolutely right! *(Amazed.)* Think of that, now!

CHARLOTTA. *(holding the deck of cards in the palm of her hand, to Trofimov).* Quickly, tell me, which card is on top?

TROFIMOV. What? Well, the queen of spades.

CHARLOTTA. Right! *(To Pishchik.)* Now which card is on top?

PISHCHIK. The ace of hearts.

CHARLOTTA. Right! *(Claps her hands and the deck of cards disappears.)* What lovely weather we're having today! *(A mysterious feminine voice, which seems to come from under the floor, answers her: "Oh, yes, splendid weather, madam.")* You are so nice, you're my ideal. . . . *(The voice: "And I'm very fond of you, too, madam.")*

STATIONMASTER *(applauding).* Bravo, Madame Ventrilo-quist!

PISHCHIK *(amazed).* Think of that, now! Most enchanting Charlotta Ivanovna . . . I am simply in love with you. . . .

CHARLOTTA. In love? *(Shrugs her shoulders.)* Is it possible that you can love? *Guter Mensch, aber schlechter Musikant.*[10]

TROFIMOV *(claps Pishchik on the shoulder).* You old horse, you!

CHARLOTTA. Attention, please! One more trick. *(Takes a lap robe from a chair.)* Here's a very fine lap robe; I should like to sell it. *(Shakes it out.)* Doesn't anyone want to buy it?

---

[6]**"Promenade à une paire!"** promenade in pairs.   [7]**"Grand rond . . . dames!"** "Large circle!" and "Gentlemen, kneel down and thank our ladies!"   [8]**Caligula . . . Senate:** Caligula (A.D. 12–41), a Roman cavalry soldier; Roman emperor (A.D. 37–41) said to have appointed a horse to the Senate.

[9]**Lezginka** a lively Russian tune for a dance   [10]**Guter Mensch, aber schlechter Musikant:** "Good man, but poor musician"

PISHCHIK (*amazed*). Think of that, now!

CHARLOTTA. *Ein, zwei, drei!* (*Quickly raises the lap robe; behind it stands Anya, who curtsies, runs to her mother, embraces her, and runs back into the ballroom amid the general enthusiasm.*)

LYUBOV ANDREYEVNA (*applauding*). Bravo, bravo!

CHARLOTTA. Once again! *Ein, zwei, drei.* (*Raises the lap robe; behind it stands Varya, who bows.*)

PISHCHIK. (*amazed*). Think of that, now!

CHARLOTTA. The end! (*Throws the robe at Pishchik, makes a curtsy, and runs out of the room.*)

PISHCHIK (*hurries after her*). The minx! . . . What a woman! What a woman! (*Goes out.*)

LYUBOV ANDREYEVNA. And Leonid still not here. What he is doing in town so long, I do not understand! It must be all over by now. Either the estate is sold, or the auction didn't take place—but why keep us in suspense so long!

VARYA (*trying to comfort her*). Uncle has bought it, I am certain of that.

TROFIMOV (*mockingly*). Yes.

VARYA. Great-aunt sent him power of attorney to buy it in her name and transfer the debt. She's doing it for Anya's sake. And I am sure, with God's help, Uncle will buy it.

LYUBOV ANDREYEVNA. Our great-aunt in Yaroslav sent fifteen thousand to buy the estate in her name—she doesn't trust us—but that's not even enough to pay the interest. (*Covers her face with her hands.*) Today my fate will be decided, my fate . . .

TROFIMOV (*teasing Varya*). Madame Lopakhina!

VARYA (*angrily*). Eternal student! Twice already you've been expelled from the university.

LYUBOV ANDREYEVNA. Why are you so cross, Varya? If he teases you about Lopakhin, what of it? Go ahead and marry Lopakhin if you want to. He's a nice man, he's interesting. And if you don't want to, don't. Nobody's forcing you, my pet.

VARYA. To be frank, Mama dear, I regard this matter seriously. He is a good man, I like him.

LYUBOV ANDREYEVNA. Then marry him. I don't know what you're waiting for!

VARYA. Mama, I can't propose to him myself. For the last two years everyone's been talking to me about him; everyone talks, but he is either silent or he jokes. I understand. He's getting rich, he's absorbed in business, he has no time for me. If I had some money, no matter how little, if it were only a hundred rubles, I'd drop everything and go far away. I'd go into a nunnery.

TROFIMOV. A blessing!

VARYA (*to Trofimov*). A student ought to be intelligent! (*In a gentle tone, tearfully.*) How homely you have grown, Petya, how old! (*To Lyubov Andreyevna, no longer crying.*) It's just that I cannot live without work, Mama. I must be doing something every minute.

(*Yasha enters.*)

YASHA (*barely able to suppress his laughter.*) Yepikhodov has broken a billiard cue! (*Goes out.*)

VARYA. But why is Yepikhodov here? Who gave him permission to play billiards? I don't understand these people. . . . (*Goes out.*)

LYUBOV ANDREYEVNA. Don't tease her, Petya. You can see she's unhappy enough without that.

TROFIMOV. She's much too zealous, always meddling in other people's affairs. All summer long she's given Anya and me no peace—afraid a romance might develop. What business is it of hers? Besides, I've given no occasion for it, I am far removed from such banality. We are above love!

LYUBOV ANDREYEVNA. And I suppose I am beneath love. (*In great agitation.*) Why isn't Leonid here? If only I knew whether the estate had been sold or not! The disaster seems to me so incredible that I don't even know what to think, I'm lost. . . . I could scream this very instant . . . I could do something foolish. Save me, Petya. Talk to me, say something. . . .

TROFIMOV. Whether or not the estate is sold today—does it really matter? That's all done with long ago; there's no turning back, the path is overgrown. Be calm, my dear. One must not deceive oneself; at least once in one's life one ought to look the truth straight in the eye.

LYUBOV ANDREYEVNA. What truth? You can see where there is truth and where there isn't, but I seem to have lost my sight, I see nothing. You boldly settle all the important problems, but tell me, my dear boy, isn't it because you are young and have not yet had to suffer for a single one of your problems? You boldly look ahead, but isn't it because you neither see nor expect anything dreadful, since life is still hidden from your young eyes? You're bolder, more honest, deeper than we are, but think about it, be just a little bit magnanimous, and spare me. You see, I was born here, my mother and father lived here, and my grandfather. I love this house, without the cherry orchard my life has no meaning for me, and if it must be sold, then sell me with the orchard. . . . (*Embraces Trofimov and kisses him on the forehead.*) And my son was drowned here. . . . (*Weeps.*) Have pity on me, you good, kind man.

TROFIMOV. You know I feel for you with all my heart.

LYUBOV ANDREYEVNA. But that should have been said differently, quite differently. . . . (*Takes out her handkerchief and a telegram falls to the floor.*) My heart is heavy today, you can't imagine. It's so noisy here, my soul quivers at every sound, I tremble all over, and yet I can't go to my room. When I am alone the silence frightens me. Don't condemn me, Petya . . . I love you as if you were my own. I would gladly let you marry Anya, I swear it, only you must study, my dear, you must get your degree. You do nothing, fate simply tosses you from place to place—it's so strange. . . . Isn't that true? Isn't it? And you must do something about your beard, to make it grow somehow. . . . (*Laughs.*) You're so funny!

TROFIMOV (*picks up the telegram*). I have no desire to be an Adonis.

LYUBOV ANDREYEVNA. That's a telegram from Paris. I get them every day. One yesterday, one today. That wild man has fallen ill again, he's in trouble again. . . . He begs my forgiveness, implores me to come, and really, I ought to go to Paris to be near him. Your face is stern, Petya, but what can one do, my dear? What am I to do? He is ill, he's alone and unhappy, and who will look after him there, who will keep him from making mistakes, who will give him his medicine on time? And why hide it or keep silent, I love him, that's clear. I love him, love him. . . . It's a millstone round my neck, I'm sinking to the bottom with it, but I love that stone, I cannot live without it. (*Presses Trofimov's hand.*) Don't think badly of me, Petya, and don't say anything to me, don't say anything. . . .

TROFIMOV (*through tears*). For God's sake, forgive my frankness: You know that he robbed you!

LYUBOV ANDREYEVNA. No, no, no, you mustn't say such things! (*Covers her ears.*)

TROFIMOV. But he's a scoundrel! You're the only one who doesn't know it! He's a petty scoundrel, a nonentity—

LYUBOV ANDREYEVNA (*angry, but controlling herself*). You are twenty-six or twenty-seven years old, but you're still a schoolboy!

TROFIMOV. That may be!

LYUBOV ANDREYEVNA. You should be a man, at your age you ought to understand those who love. And you ought to be in love yourself. (*Angrily.*) Yes, yes! It's not purity with you, it's simply prudery, you're a ridiculous crank, a freak—

TROFIMOV (*horrified*). What is she saying!

LYUBOV ANDREYEVNA. "I am above love!" You're not above love, you're just an addlepate, as Firs would say. Not to have a mistress at your age!

TROFIMOV (*in horror*). This is awful! What is she saying! . . . (*Goes quickly toward the ballroom.*) This is awful . . . I can't . . . I won't stay here. . . . (*Goes out, but immediately returns.*) All is over between us! (*Goes out to the hall.*)

LYUBOV ANDREYEVNA (*calls after him*). Petya, wait! You absurd creature, I was joking! Petya!

(*In the hall there is the sound of someone running quickly downstairs and suddenly falling with a crash. Anya and Varya scream, but a moment later laughter is heard.*)

LYUBOV ANDREYEVNA. What was that?

(*Anya runs in.*)

ANYA (*laughing*). Petya fell down the stairs! (*Runs out.*)

LYUBOV ANDREYEVNA. What a funny boy that Petya is!

(*The Stationmaster stands in the middle of the ballrrom and recites A. Tolstoy's[11] "The Sinner." Everyone listens*

to him, but he has no sooner spoken a few lines than the sound of a waltz is heard from the hall and the recitation is broken off. They all dance. Trofimov, Anya, Varya, and Lyubov Andreyevna come in from the hall.)

LYUBOV ANDREYEVNA. Come, Petya . . . come, you pure soul . . . please, forgive me. . . . Let's dance. . . . (*They dance.*)

(*Anya and Varya dance. Firs comes in, puts his stick by the side door. Yasha also comes into the drawing room and watches the dancers.*)

YASHA. What is it, grandpa?

FIRS. I don't feel well. In the old days, we used to have generals, barons, admirals, dancing at our balls, but now we send for the post office clerk and the stationmaster, and even they are none too eager to come. Somehow I've grown weak. The late master, their grandfather, dosed everyone with sealing wax, no matter what ailed them. I've been taking sealing wax every day for twenty years or more; maybe that's what's kept me alive.

YASHA. You bore me, grandpa. (*Yawns.*) High time you croaked.

FIRS. Ah, you . . . addlepate! (*Mumbles.*)

(*Trofimov and Lyubov Andreyevna dance from the ballroom into the drawing room.*)

LYUBOV ANDREYEVNA. *Merci.* I'll sit down a while. (*Sits.*) I'm tired.

(*Anya comes in.*)

ANYA (*excitedly*). There was a man in the kitchen just now saying that the cherry orchard was sold today.

LYUBOV ANDREYEVNA. Sold to whom?

ANYA. He didn't say. He's gone. (*Dances with Trofimov; they go into the ballroom.*)

YASHA. That was just some old man babbling. A stranger.

FIRS. Leonid Andreich is not back yet, still hasn't come. And he's wearing the light, between-seasons overcoat; like enough he'll catch cold. Ah, when they're young they're green.

LYUBOV ANDREYEVNA. This is killing me. Yasha, go and find out who it was sold to.

YASHA. But that old man left long ago. (*Laughs.*)

LYUBOV ANDREYEVNA (*slightly annoyed*). Well, what are you laughing at? What are you so happy about?

YASHA. That Yepikhodov is very funny! Hopeless! Two-and-twenty Troubles.

LYUBOV ANDREYEVNA. Firs, if the estate is sold, where will you go?

FIRS. Wherever you tell me to go, I'll go.

LYUBOV ANDREYEVNA. Why do you look like that? Aren't you well? You ought to go to bed.

FIRS. Yes. . . . (*With a smirk.*) Go to bed, and without me who will serve, who will see to things? I'm the only one in the whole house.

YASHA (*to Lyubov Andreyevna*). Lyubov Andreyevna! Per-

---

[11]**A. Tolstoy** Aleksey Konstantinovich Tolstoy (1817–1875), Russian novelist, dramatist, and poet

mit me to make a request, be so kind! If you go back to Paris again, do me the favor of taking me with you. It is positively impossible for me to stay here. (*Looking around, then in a low voice.*) There's no need to say it, you can see for yourself, it's an uncivilized country, the people have no morals, and the boredom! The food they give us in the kitchen is unmentionable, and besides, there's this Firs who keeps walking about mumbling all sorts of inappropriate things. Take me with you, be so kind!

(*Enter Pishchik.*)

PISHCHIK. May I have the pleasure of a waltz with you, fairest lady? (*Lyubov Andreyevna goes with him.*) I really must borrow a hundred and eighty rubles from you, my charmer . . . I really must. . . . (*Dancing.*) Just a hundred and eighty rubles. . . . (*They pass into the ballroom.*)

YASHA (*softly sings*). "Wilt thou know my soul's unrest . . ."

(*In the ballroom a figure in a gray top hat and checked trousers is jumping about, waving its arms; there are shouts of "Bravo, Charlotta Ivanovna!"*)

DUNYASHA (*stopping to powder her face*). The young mistress told me to dance—there are lots of gentlemen and not enough ladies—but dancing makes me dizzy, and my heart begins to thump. Firs Nikolayevich, the post office clerk just said something to me that took my breath away.

(*The music grows more subdued.*)

FIRS. What did he say to you?

DUNYASHA. "You," he said, "are like a flower."

YASHA (*yawns*). What ignorance. . . . (*Goes out.*)

DUNYASHA. Like a flower. . . . I'm such a delicate girl, I just adore tender words.

FIRS. You'll get your head turned.

(*Enter Yepikhodov.*)

YEPIKHODOV. Avdotya Fyodorovna, you are not desirous of seeing me. . . . I might also be some sort of insect. (*Sighs.*) Ah, life!

DUNYASHA. What is it you want?

YEPIKHODOV. Indubitably, you may be right. (*Sighs.*) But, of course, if one looks at it from a point of view, then, if I may so express myself, and you will forgive my frankness, you have completely reduced me to a state of mind. I know my fate, every day some misfortune befalls me, but I have long since grown accustomed to that; I look upon my fate with a smile. But you gave me your word, and although I—

DUNYASHA. Please, we'll talk about it later, but leave me in peace now. Just now I'm dreaming. . . . (*Plays with her fan.*)

YEPIKHODOV. Every day, a misfortune, and yet, if I may so express myself, I merely smile, I even laugh.

(*Varya enters from the ballroom.*)

VARYA. Are you still here, Semyon? What a disrespectful man you are, really! (*To Dunyasha.*) Run along, Dunyasha. (*To Yepikhodov.*) First you play billiards and break a cue, then you wander about the drawing room as though you were a guest.

YEPIKHODOV. You cannot, if I may so express myself, penalize me.

VARYA. I am not penalizing you, I'm telling you. You do nothing but wander from one place to another, and you don't do your work. We keep a clerk, but for what, I don't know.

YEPIKHODOV (*offended*). Whether I work, or wander about, or eat, or play billiards, these are matters to be discussed only by persons of discernment, and my elders.

VARYA. You dare say that to me! (*Flaring up.*) You dare? You mean to say I have no discernment? Get out of here! This instant!

YEPIKHODOV (*intimidated*). I beg you to express yourself in a more delicate manner.

VARYA (*beside herself*). Get out, this very instant! Get out! (*He goes to the door, she follows him.*) Two-and-twenty Troubles! Don't let me set eyes on you again!

YEPIKHODOV (*goes out, his voice is heard behind the door*). I shall lodge a complaint against you!

VARYA. Oh, you're coming back? (*Seizes the stick left near the door by Firs.*) Come, come on. . . . Come, I'll show you. . . . Ah, so you're coming, are you? Then take that— (*Swings the stick just as Lopakhin enters.*)

LOPAKHIN. Thank you kindly.

VARYA (*angrily and mockingly*). I beg your pardon.

LOPAKHIN. Not at all. I humbly thank you for your charming reception.

VARYA. Don't mention it. (*Walks away, then looks back and gently asks.*) I didn't hurt you, did I?

LOPAKHIN. No, it's nothing. A huge bump coming up, that's all.

(*Voices in the ballroom: "Lopakhin has come! Yermolai Alekseich!" Pishchik enters.*)

PISHCHIK. As I live and breathe! (*Kisses Lopakhin.*) There is a whiff of cognac about you, dear soul. And we've been making merry here, too.

(*Enter Lyubov Andreyevna.*)

LYUBOV ANDREYEVNA. Is that you, Yermolai Alekseich? What kept you so long? Where's Leonid?

LOPAKHIN. Leonid Andreich arrived with me, he's coming . . .

LYUBOV ANDREYEVNA (*agitated*). Well, what happened? Did the sale take place? Tell me!

LOPAKHIN (*embarrased, fearing to reveal his joy*). The auction was over by four o'clock. . . . We missed the train, had to wait till half past nine. (*Sighing heavily.*) Ugh! My head is swimming. . . .

(*Enter Gayev; he carries his purchases in one hand and wipes away his tears with the other.*)

LYUBOV ANDREYEVNA. Lyonya, what happened? Well, Lyonya? (*Impatiently, through tears.*) Be quick, for God's sake!

GAYEV (*not answering her, simply waves his hand. To Firs, weeping*). Here, take these.... There's anchovies, Kerch herrings.... I haven't eaten anything all day.... What I have been through! (*The click of billiard balls is heard through the open door to the billiard room, and Yasha's voice: "Seven and eighteen!" Gayev's expression changes, he is no longer weeping.*) I'm terribly tired. Firs, help me change. (*Goes through the ballroom to his own room, followed by Firs.*)

PISHCHIK. What happened at the auction? Come on, tell us!

LYUBOV ANDREYEVNA. Is the cherry orchard sold?

LOPAKHIN. It's sold.

LYUBOV ANDREYEVNA. Who bought it?

LOPAKHIN. I bought it. (*Pause.*)

(*Lyubov Andreyevna is overcome; she would fall to the floor if it were not for the chair and table near which she stands. Varya takes the keys from her belt and throws them on the floor in the middle of the drawing room and goes out.*)

LOPAKHIN. I bought it! Kindly wait a moment, ladies and gentlemen, my head is swimming. I can't talk.... (*Laughs.*) We arrived at the auction, Deriganov was already there. Leonid Andreich had only fifteen thousand, and straight off Deriganov bid thirty thousand over and above the mortgage. I saw how the land lay, so I got into the fight and bid forty. He bid forty-five. I bid fifty-five. In other words, he kept raising it by five thousand, and I by ten. Well, it finally came to an end. I bid ninety thousand above the mortgage, and it was knocked down to me. The cherry orchard is now mine! Mine! (*Laughs uproariously.*) Lord! God in heaven! The cherry orchard is mine! Tell me I'm drunk, out of my mind, that I imagine it.... (*Stamps his feet.*) Don't laugh at me! If my father and my grandfather could only rise from their graves and see all that has happened, how their Yermolai, their beaten, half-literate Yermolai, who used to run about barefoot in winter, how that same Yermolai has bought an estate, the most beautiful estate in the whole world! I bought the estate where my father and grandfather were slaves, where they weren't even allowed in the kitchen. I'm asleep, this is just some dream of mine, it only seems to be.... It's the fruit of your imagination, hidden in the darkness of uncertainty.... (*Picks up the keys, smiling tenderly.*) She threw down the keys, wants to show that she's not mistress here anymore.... (*Jingles the keys.*) Well, no matter. (*The orchestra is heard tuning up.*) Hey, musicians, play, I want to hear you! Come on, everybody, and see how Yermolai Lopakhin will lay the ax to the cherry orchard, how the trees will fall to the ground! We're going to build summer cottages and our grandsons and great-grandsons will see a new life here.... Music! Strike up!

(*The orchestra plays. Lyubov Andreyevna sinks into a chair and weeps bitterly.*)

LOPAKHIN (*reproachfully*). Why didn't you listen to me, why? My poor friend, there's no turning back now. (*With tears.*) Oh, if only all this could be over quickly, if somehow our discordant, unhappy life could be changed!

PISHCHIK (*takes him by the arm; speaks in an undertone*). She's crying. Let's go into the ballroom, let her be alone.... Come on.... (*Leads him into the ballroom.*)

LOPAKHIN. What's happened? Musicians, play so I can hear you! Let everything be as I want it! (*Ironically.*) Here comes the new master, owner of the cherry orchard! (*Accidentally bumps into a little table, almost upsetting the candelabrum.*) I can pay for everything! (*Goes out with Pishchik.*)

(*There is no one left in either the drawing room or the ballroom except Lyubov Andreyevna, who sits huddled up and weeping bitterly. The music plays softly. Anya and Trofimov enter hurriedly. Anya goes to her mother and kneels before her. Trofimov remains in the doorway of the ballroom.*)

ANYA. Mama!... Mama, you're crying! Dear, kind, good Mama, my beautiful one, I love you ... I bless you. The cherry orchard is sold, it's gone, that's true, true, but don't cry, Mama, life is still before you, you still have your good, pure soul.... Come with me, come, darling, we'll go away from here!... We'll plant a new orchard, more luxuriant than this one. You will see it and understand; and joy, quiet, deep joy, will sink into your soul, like the evening sun, and you will smile, Mama! Come, darling, let us go....

ACT IV

(*The scene is the same as act I. There are neither curtains on the windows nor pictures on the walls, and only a little furniture piled up in one corner, as if for sale. There is a sense of emptiness. Near the outer door, at the rear of the stage, suitcases, traveling bags, etc., are piled up. Through the open door on the left the voices of Varya and Anya can be heard. Lopakhin stands waiting. Yasha is holding a tray with little glasses of champagne. In the hall, Yepikhodov is tying up a box. Offstage, at the rear, there is a hum of voices. It is the peasants who have come to say good-bye. Gayev's voice: "Thanks, brothers, thank you."*)

YASHA. The peasants have come to say good-bye. In my opinion, Yermolai Alekseich, peasants are good-natured, but they don't know much.

(*The hum subsides. Lyubov Andreyevna enters from the hall with Gayev. She is not crying, but she is pale, her face twitches, and she cannot speak.*)

GAYEV. You gave them your purse, Lyuba. That won't do! That won't do!

LYUBOV ANDREYEVNA. I couldn't help it! I couldn't help it! (*They both go out.*)

LOPAKHIN (*in the doorway, calls after them*). Please, do me the honor of having a little glass at parting. I didn't think of bringing champagne from town, and at the station I found only one bottle. Please! What's the matter, friends, don't you want any? (*Walks away from the door.*) If I'd known that, I wouldn't have bought it. Well, then I won't drink any either. (*Yasha carefully sets the tray down on a chair.*) At least you have a glass, Yasha.

YASHA. To those who are departing! Good luck! (*Drinks.*) This champagne is not the real stuff, I can assure you.

LOPAKHIN. Eight rubles a bottle. (*Pause.*) It's devilish cold in here.

YASHA. They didn't light the stoves today; it doesn't matter, since we're leaving. (*Laughs.*)

LOPAKHIN. Why are you laughing?

YASHA. Because I'm pleased.

LOPAKHIN. It's October, yet it's sunny and still outside, like summer. Good for building. (*Looks at his watch, then calls through the door.*) Bear in mind, ladies and gentlemen, only forty-six minutes till train time! That means leaving for the station in twenty minutes. Better hurry up!

(*Trofimov enters from outside wearing an overcoat.*)

TROFIMOV. Seems to me it's time to start. The carriages are at the door. What the devil has become of my rubbers? They're lost. (*Calls through the door.*) Anya, my rubbers are not here. I can't find them.

LOPAKHIN. I've got to go to Kharkov. I'm taking the same train you are. I'm going to spend the winter in Kharkov. I've been hanging around here with you, and I'm sick and tired of loafing. I can't live without work, I don't know what to do with my hands; they dangle in some strange way, as if they didn't belong to me.

TROFIMOV. We'll soon be done, then you can take up your useful labors again.

LOPAKHIN. Here, have a little drink.

TROFIMOV. No, I don't want any.

LOPAKHIN. So you're off for Moscow?

TROFIMOV. Yes, I'll see them into town, and tomorrow I'll go to Moscow.

LOPAKHIN. Yes. . . . Well, I expect the professors haven't been giving any lectures: They're waiting for you to come!

TROFIMOV. That's none of your business.

LOPAKHIN. How many years is it you've been studying at the university?

TROFIMOV. Can't you think of something new? That's stale and flat. (*Looks for his rubbers.*) You know, we'll probably never see each other again, so allow me to give you one piece of advice at parting: Don't wave your arms about! Get out of that habit—of arm-waving. And another thing, building cottages and counting on the summer res-

idents in time becoming independent farmers—that's just another form of arm-waving. Well, when all's said and done, I'm fond of you anyway. You have fine, delicate fingers, like an artist; you have a fine delicate soul.

LOPAKHIN (*embraces him*). Good-bye, my dear fellow. Thank you for everything. Let me give you some money for the journey, if you need it.

TROFIMOV. What for? I don't need it.

LOPAKHIN. But you haven't any!

TROFIMOV. I have. Thank you. I got some money for a translation. Here it is in my pocket. (*Anxiously.*) But where are my rubbers?

VARYA (*from the next room*). Here, take the nasty things! (*Flings a pair of rubbers onto the stage.*)

TROFIMOV. What are you so cross about, Varya? Hm. . . . But these are not my rubbers.

LOPAKHIN. In the spring I sowed three thousand acres of poppies, and now I've made forty thousand rubles clear. And when my poppies were in bloom, what a picture it was! So, I'm telling you, I've made forty thousand, which means I'm offering you a loan because I can afford to. Why turn up your nose? I'm a peasant—I speak bluntly.

TROFIMOV. Your father was a peasant, mine was a pharmacist—which proves absolutely nothing. (*Lopakhin takes out his wallet.*) No, don't—even if you gave me two hundred thousand I wouldn't take it. I'm a free man. And everything that is valued so highly and held so dear by all of you, rich and poor alike, has not the slightest power over me—it's like a feather floating in the air. I can get along without you, I can pass you by, I'm strong and proud. Mankind is advancing toward the highest truth, the highest happiness attainable on earth, and I am in the front ranks!

LOPAKHIN. Will you get there?

TROFIMOV. I'll get there. (*Pause.*) I'll either get there or I'll show others the way to get there.

(*The sound of axes chopping down trees is heard in the distance.*)

LOPAKHIN. Well, good-bye, my dear fellow. It's time to go. We turn up our noses at one another, but life goes on just the same. When I work for a long time without stopping, my mind is easier, and it seems to me that I, too, know why I exist. But how many there are in Russia, brother, who exist nobody knows why. Well, it doesn't matter, that's not what makes the wheels go round. They say Leonid Andreich has taken a position in the bank, six thousand a year. . . . Only, of course, he won't stick it out, he's too lazy. . . .

ANYA (*in the doorway*). Mama asks you not to start cutting down the cherry orchard until she's gone.

TROFIMOV. Yes, really, not to have had the tact . . . (*Goes out through the hall.*)

LOPAKHIN. Right away, right away. . . . Ach, what people. . . . (*Follows Trofimov out.*)

ANYA. Has Firs been taken to the hospital?

YASHA. I told them this morning. They must have taken him.

ANYA (*to Yepikhodov, who is crossing the room*). Semyon Panteleich, please find out if Firs has been taken to the hospital.

YASHA (*offended*). I told Yegor this morning. Why ask a dozen times?

YEPIKHODOV. It is my conclusive opinion that the venerable Firs is beyond repair; it's time he was gathered to his fathers. And I can only envy him. (*Puts a suitcase down on a hatbox and crushes it.*) There you are! Of course! I knew it! (*Goes out.*)

YASHA (*mockingly*). Two-and-twenty Troubles!

VARYA (*through the door*). Has Firs been taken to the hospital?

ANYA. Yes, he has.

VARYA. Then why didn't they take the letter to the doctor?

ANYA. We must send it on after them. . . . (*Goes out.*)

VARYA (*from the adjoining room*). Where is Yasha? Tell him his mother has come to say good-bye to him.

YASHA (*waves his hand*). They really try my patience.

(*Dunyasha has been fussing with the luggage; now that Yasha is alone she goes up to him.*)

DUNYASHA. You might give me one little look, Yasha. You're going away . . . leaving me. . . . (*Cries and throws herself on his neck.*)

YASHA. What's there to cry about? (*Drinks champagne.*) In six days I'll be in Paris again. Tomorrow we'll take the express, off we go, and that's the last you'll see of us. I can hardly believe it. *Vive la France!* This place is not for me, I can't live here. . . . It can't be helped. I've had enough of this ignorance—I'm fed up with it. (*Drinks champagne.*) What are you crying for? Behave yourself properly, then you won't cry.

DUNYASHA (*looks into a small mirror and powders her face*). Send me a letter from Paris. You know, I love you, Yasha, how I loved you! I'm such a tender creature, Yasha!

YASHA. Here they come. (*Busies himself with the luggage, humming softly.*)

(*Enter Lyubov Andreyevna, Gayev, Charlotta Ivanovna.*)

GAYEV. We ought to be leaving. There's not much time now. (*Looks at Yasha.*) Who smells of herring?

LYUBOV ANDREYEVNA. In about ten minutes we should be getting into the carriages. (*Glances around the room.*) Good-bye, dear house, old grandfather. Winter will pass, spring will come, and you will no longer be here, they will tear you down. How much these walls have seen! (*Kisses her daughter warmly.*) My treasure, you are radiant, your eyes are sparkling like two diamonds. Are you glad? Very?

GAYEV (*cheerfully*). Yes, indeed, everything is all right now. Before the cherry orchard was sold we were all worried and miserable, but afterward, when the question was finally settled once and for all, everybody calmed down and felt quite cheerful. . . . I'm in a bank now, a financier

. . . cue ball into the center . . . and you, Lyuba, say what you like, you look better, no doubt about it.

LYUBOV ANDREYEVNA. Yes. My nerves are better, that's true. (*Her hat and coat are handed to her.*) I sleep well. Carry out my things, Yasha, it's time. (*To Anya.*) My little girl, we shall see each other soon. . . . I shall go to Paris and live there on the money your great-aunt sent to buy the estate—long live Auntie!—but that money won't last long.

ANYA. You'll come back soon, Mama, soon . . . won't you? I'll study hard and pass my high school examinations, and then I can work and help you. We'll read all sorts of books together, Mama. . . . Won't we? (*Kisses her mother's hand.*) We'll read in the autumn evenings, we'll read lots of books, and a new and wonderful world will open up before us. . . . (*Dreaming.*) Mama, come back. . . .

LYUBOV ANDREYEVNA. I'll come, my precious. (*Embraces her.*)

(*Enter Lopakhin, Charlotta Ivanovna is softly humming a song.*)

GAYEV. Happy Charlotta: She's singing!

CHARLOTTA (*picks up a bundle and holds it like a baby in swaddling clothes*). Bye, baby, bye. . . . (*A baby's crying is heard, "Wah Wah!"*) Be quiet, my darling, my dear little boy. (*"Wah! Wah!"*) I'm so sorry for you! (*Throws the bundle down.*) You will find me a position, won't you? I can't go on like this.

LOPAKHIN. We'll find something, Charlotta Ivanovna, don't worry.

GAYEV. Everyone is leaving us, Varya's going away . . . all of a sudden nobody needs us.

CHARLOTTA. I have nowhere to go in town. I must go away. (*Hums.*) It doesn't matter . . .

(*Enter Pishchik.*)

LOPAKHIN. Nature's wonder!

PISHCHIK (*panting*). Ugh! Let me catch my breath. . . . I'm exhausted. . . . My esteemed friends. . . . Give me some water. . . .

GAYEV. After money, I suppose? Excuse me, I'm fleeing from temptation. . . . (*Goes out.*)

PISHCHIK. It's a long time since I've been to see you . . . fairest lady. . . . (*To Lopakhin*) So you're here. . . . Glad to see you, you intellectual giant. . . . Here . . . take it . . . four hundred rubles . . . I still owe you eight hundred and forty . . .

LOPAKHIN (*shrugs his shoulders in bewilderment*). I must be dreaming. . . . Where did you get it?

PISHCHIK. Wait . . . I'm hot. . . . A most extraordinary event. Some Englishmen came to my place and discovered some kind of white clay on my land. (*To Lyubov Andreyevna*) And four hundred for you . . . fairest, most wonderful lady. . . . (*Hands her the money.*) The rest later. (*Takes a drink of water.*) Just now a young man in the train was saying that a certain . . . great philosopher recommends jumping off roofs. . . . "Jump!" he says, and therein lies the whole problem. (*In amazement.*) Think of that, now! . . . Water!

LOPAKHIN. Who were those Englishmen?

PISHCHIK. I leased them the tract of land with the clay on it for twenty-four years. . . . And now, excuse me, I have no time . . . I must be trotting along . . . I'm going to Znoikov's . . . to Kardamanov's . . . I owe everybody. (*Drinks.*) Keep well . . . I'll drop in on Thursday . . .

LYUBOV ANDREYEVNA. We're just moving into town, and tomorrow I go abroad . . .

PISHCHIK. What? (*Alarmed.*) Why into town? That's why I see the furniture . . . suitcases. . . . Well, never mind. . . . (*Through tears.*) Never mind. . . . Men of the greatest intellect, those Englishmen. . . . Never mind. . . . Be happy . . . God will help you. . . . Never mind. . . . Everything in this world comes to an end. . . . (*Kisses Lyubov Andreyevna's hand.*) And should the news reach you that my end has come, just remember this old horse, and say: "There once lived a certain Semyonov-Pishchik, God rest his soul." . . . Splendid weather. . . . Yes. . . . (*Goes out greatly disconcerted, but immediately returns and speaks from the doorway.*) Dashenka sends her regards. (*Goes out.*)

LYUBOV ANDREYEVNA. Now we can go. I am leaving with two things on my mind. First—that Firs is sick. (*Looks at her watch.*) We still have about five minutes. . . .

ANYA. Mama, Firs has already been taken to the hospital. Yasha sent him there this morning.

LYUBOV ANDREYEVNA. My second concern is Varya. She's used to getting up early and working, and now, with no work to do, she's like a fish out of water. She's grown pale and thin, and cries all the time, poor girl. . . . (*Pauses.*) You know very well, Yermolai Alekseich, that I dreamed of marrying her to you, and everything pointed to your getting married. (*Whispers to Anya, who nods to Charlotta, and they both go out.*) She loves you, you are fond of her, and I don't know—I don't know why it is you seem to avoid each other. I can't understand it!

LOPAKHIN. To tell you the truth, I don't understand it myself. The whole thing is strange, somehow. . . . If there's still time, I'm ready right now. . . . Let's finish it up—and basta,[12] but without you I feel I'll never be able to propose to her.

LYUBOV ANDREYEVNA. Splendid! After all, it only takes a minute. I'll call her in at once. . . .

LOPAKHIN. And we even have the champagne. (*Looks at the glasses.*) Empty! Somebody's already drunk it. (*Yasha coughs.*) That's what you call lapping it up.

LYUBOV ANDREYEVNA (*animatedly*). Splendid! We'll leave you. . . . Yasha, *allez*![13] I'll call her. . . . (*At the door.*) Varya, leave everything and come here. Come! (*Goes out with Yasha.*)

LOPAKHIN. (*looking at his watch*). Yes. . . . (*Pause.*)

(*Behind the door there is smothered laughter and whispering; finally Varya enters.*)

VARYA (*looking over the luggage for a long time*). Strange, I can't seem to find it . . .

LOPAKHIN. What are you looking for?

VARYA. I packed it myself, and I can't remember . . . (*Pause.*)

LOPAKHIN. Where are you going now, Varya Mikhailovna?

VARYA. I? To the Ragulins'. . . . I've agreed to go there to look after the house . . . as a sort of housekeeper.

LOPAKHIN. At Yashnevo? That would be about seventy versts from here. (*Pause.*) Well, life in this house has come to an end. . . .

VARYA (*examining the luggage*). Where can it be? . . . Perhaps I put it in the trunk. . . . Yes, life in this house has come to an end . . . there'll be no more . . .

LOPAKHIN. And I'm off for Kharkov . . . by the next train. I have a lot to do. I'm leaving Yepikhodov here . . . I've taken him on.

VARYA. Really!

LOPAKHIN. Last year at this time it was already snowing, if you remember, but now it's still and sunny. It's cold though . . . About three degrees of frost.

VARYA. I haven't looked. (*Pause.*) And besides, our thermometer's broken. (*Pause.*)

(*A voice from the yard calls: "Yermolai Alekseich!"*)

LOPAKHIN (*as if he had been waiting for a long time for the call*). Coming! (*Goes out quickly.*)

(*Varya sits on the floor, lays her head on a bundle of clothes, and quietly sobs. The door opens and Lyubov Andreyevna enters cautiously.*)

LYUBOV ANDREYEVNA. Well? (*Pause.*) We must be going.

VARYA (*no longer crying, dries her eyes*). Yes, it's time, Mama dear. I can get to the Ragulins' today, if only we don't miss the train.

LYUBOV ANDREYEVNA (*in the doorway*). Anya, put your things on!

(*Enter Anya, then Gayev and Charlotta Ivanovna. Gayev wears a warm overcoat with a hood. The servants and coachmen come in. Yepikhodov bustles about the luggage.*)

LYUBOV ANDREYEVNA. Now we can be on our way.

ANYA (*joyfully*). On our way!

GAYEV. My friends, my dear, cherished friends! Leaving this house forever, can I pass over in silence, can I refrain from giving utterance, as we say farewell, to those feelings that now fill my whole being—

ANYA (*imploringly*). Uncle!

VARYA. Uncle dear, don't!

GAYEV (*forlornly*). Double the rail off the white to center table . . . yellow into the side pocket. . . . I'll be quiet. . . .

(*Enter Trofimov, then Lopakhin.*)

---

[12]*basta* "enough" in Italian   [13]*allez* "go" in French

TROFIMOV. Well, ladies and gentlemen, it's time to go!

LOPAKHIN. Yepikhodov, my coat!

LYUBOV ANDREYEVNA. I'll sit here just one more minute. It's as though I had never before seen what the walls of this house were like, what the ceilings were like, and now I look at them hungrily, with such tender love . . .

GAYEV. I remember when I was six years old, sitting on this windowsill on Whitsunday, watching my father going to church . . .

LYUBOV ANDREYEVNA. Have they taken all the things?

LOPAKHIN. Everything, I think. (*Puts on his overcoat.*) Yepikhodov, see that everything is in order.

YEPIKHODOV (*in a hoarse voice*). Rest assured, Yermolai Alekseich!

LOPAKHIN. What's the matter with your voice?

YEPIKHODOV. Just drank some water . . . must have swallowed something.

YASHA (*contemptuously*). What ignorance!

LYUBOV ANDREYEVNA. When we go—there won't be a soul left here. . . .

LOPAKHIN. Till spring.

VARYA (*pulls an umbrella out of a bundle as though she were going to hit someone; Lopakhin pretends to be frightened*). Why are you—I never thought of such a thing!

TROFIMOV. Ladies and gentlemen, let's get into the carriages—it's time now! The train will soon be in!

VARYA. Petya, there they are—your rubbers, by the suitcase. (*Tearfully.*) And what dirty old things they are!

TROFIMOV (*putting on his rubbers*). Let's go, ladies and gentlemen!

GAYEV (*extremely upset, afraid of bursting into tears*). The train . . . the station. . . . Cross table to the center, double the rail . . . on the white into the corner.

LYUBOV ANDREYEVNA. Let us go!

GAYEV. Are we all here? No one in there? (*Locks the side door on the left.*) There are some things stored in there, we must lock up. Let's go!

ANYA. Good-bye, house! Good-bye, old life!

TROFIMOV. Hail to the new life! (*Goes out with Anya.*)

(*Varya looks around the room and slowly goes out. Yasha and Charlotta with her dog go out.*)

LOPAKHIN. And so, till spring. Come along, my friends. . . . Till we meet! (*Goes out.*)

(*Lyubov Andreyevna and Gayev are left alone. As though they had been waiting for this, they fall onto each other's necks and break into quiet, restrained sobs, afraid of being heard.*)

GAYEV (*in despair*). My sister, my sister. . . .

LYUBOV ANDREYEVNA. Oh, my dear, sweet, lovely orchard! . . . My life, my youth, my happiness, good-bye! . . . Good-bye!

ANYA'S VOICE (*gaily calling*). Mama!

TROFIMOV'S VOICE (*gay and excited*). Aa-oo!

LYUBOV ANDREYEVNA. One last look at these walls, these windows. . . . Mother loved to walk about in this room. . . .

GAYEV. My sister, my sister!

ANYA'S VOICE. Mama!

TROFIMOV'S VOICE. Aa-oo!

LYUBOV ANDREYEVNA. We're coming! (*They go out.*)

(*The stage is empty. There is the sound of doors being locked, then of the carriages driving away. It grows quiet. In the stillness there is the dull thud of an ax on a tree, a forlorn, melancholy sound. Footsteps are heard. From the door on the right Firs appears. He is dressed as always in a jacket and white waistcoat, and wears slippers. He is ill.*)

FIRS (*goes to the door and tries the handle*). Locked. They have gone. . . . (*Sits down on the sofa.*) They've forgotten me. . . . Never mind. . . . I'll sit here awhile. . . . I expect Leonid Andreich hasn't put on his fur coat and has gone off in his overcoat. (*Sighs anxiously.*) And I didn't see to it. . . . When they're young, they're green! (*Mumbles something which cannot be understood.*) I'll lie down awhile. . . . There's no strength left in you, nothing's left, nothing. . . . Ach, you . . . addlepate! (*Lies motionless.*)

(*A distant sound is heard that seems to come from the sky, the sound of a snapped string mournfully dying away. A stillness falls, and nothing is heard but the thud of an ax on a tree far away in the orchard.*)

EXPRESSIONISM AND THE EPIC THEATER

Artistic and Cultural Events

1901:
Expressionist paintings by Van Gogh and Gauguin appear in Paris

1902:
Strindberg's *A Dream Play*

1900–1924:
German Expressionism

1920:
Erwin Piscator's theater experiments in Berlin

1922:
Eugene O'Neill's *The Hairy Ape*

1926:
Bertolt Brecht initiates the epic theater with *A Man's a Man*

1935:
Chinese actors perform in Russia, where Brecht conceives "the alienation effect"

1938–1940:
Brecht's *The Good Woman of Setzuan*

1949:
Arthur Miller's *Death of a Salesman*

Berliner Ensemble formed

1956:
Berliner Ensemble performs in London

1900 C.E.

Historical and Political Events

1914–1918:
World War 1

1929:
The Great Depression begins

1939–1945:
World War II

1945:
U.S. drops atomic bomb on Hiroshima

1945–1989:
Cold War era

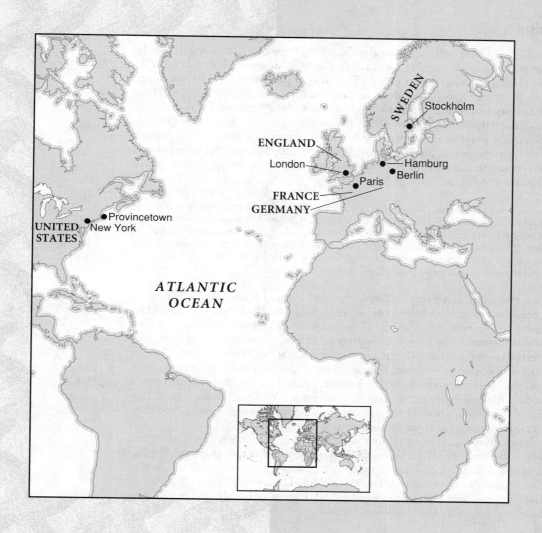

Realism, once intended as an antidote to the drama that preceded it, was itself challenged by subsequent theater artists. Even as Ibsen was writing his realistic social dramas, Expressionism was being cultivated in Sweden and Germany. It paved the way for Brecht's epic theater, and soon other "Isms"—Surrealism, Formalism, Futurism—would usurp realism's hold on the modern theater. Of these antirealist movement, Expressionism and the epic theater have enjoyed the greatest longevity and subsequent influence.

Expressionism

As effective as he was in his naturalistic works, Strindberg's greatest achievements can be found in his experimental works, notably a series of Expressionist dramas such as *A Dream Play* (1903) and *The Ghost* (or *Spook*) *Sonata* (1907). The titles of these works suggest an unreal, dreamlike, or, more accurately, nightmarish depiction of human existence. Strindberg and the subsequent Expressionists sought to portray subjective states of the human mind realistically. This is, of course, a contradiction in terms (have you ever tried to explain a dream to someone?). Nonetheless, the Expressionists attempted to construct authentic dream worlds onstage through the use of distorted scenic pictures, bizarre lighting effects, dialogue that defined logic, and nonrealistic acting. Strindberg defines some of the characteristics of Expressionistic drama in notes accompanying *A Dream Play*, which he wrote to

> imitate the incoherent but ostensibly logical form of our dreams. Anything can happen; everything is possible and probable. Time and space do not exist. Working with some insignificant real events as a background, the imagination spins out its threads of thoughts and weaves them into new patterns—a mixture of memories, experiences, spontaneous ideas, impossibilities and improbabilities. The characters split, double, multiply, dissolve, condense, float apart, coalesce. But one mind stands over and above them all, the mind of the dreamer.

Expressionism thrived in Germany during the early years of the twentieth century (1910–1924), partly as a means by which young writers, disillusioned by World War I, could attack the old order. Unlike Strindberg, who sought to project "dream states" onstage, the German Expressionists resorted to an intense subjectivism—that is, externalization of their most private inner feelings—to illustrate their outrage at a society that had betrayed them. German Expressionism used characters to symbolize abstractions of social vices rather than psychological realities, lyrical dialogue that superseded the logic of plot, and scenery that reflected purely subjective realities in concrete terms. Writers such as Frank Wedekind, Georg Kaiser, Paul Kornfeld, and Karl Sternheim represent the best of German Expressionism. Bertolt Brecht inherited their tradition when he entered the theater in the 1920s.

Expressionism had an impact on early cinema, such as the great German films *The Cabinet of Doctor Caligari* and *Metropolis*. The tricks of the moviemaker—crosscuts, dissolves, superimpositions, and bizarre camera angles—lent themselves to Expressionistic storytelling. Some of the most admired American playwrights, including O'Neill, Tennessee Williams, and Arthur Miller, freely used Expressionist elements in their dramas. Expressionism also did much to restore theatricality and poetry to drama that was becoming increasingly obsessed with putting real life onstage.

The Epic Theater

The creativity of the early German Expressionists notwithstanding, it was Bertolt Brecht (1898–1956) who most transformed the German and consequently Western theater. It can be argued that Brecht is the most influential artist in the modern theater. He radically altered the means by which artists use the theater as a political instrument. Today we frequently employ the term "Brechtian" to denote a particular style that can be found in both Western (e.g., *Angels in America*) and non-Western (e.g., *Woza Albert!*) dramas, musical theater (e.g., *Cabaret*), and even opera (e.g., *Nixon in China*). Even classical plays have been presented in a Brechtian style (e.g., the Royal Shakespeare Company's acclaimed 1963 production of the *Henry VI* cycle). Although it might be argued with good reason that Brecht initiated "postmodern" theater (see Chapter 6), he was, like Ibsen and Shaw, committed to transforming society through didactic theater, and he is discussed within the context of modern drama.

Brecht began writing for the theater at the height of the German Expressionist movement in 1922. He was not so much an antirealist as he was against any form of drama that sought to engage an audience's emotions. For Brecht, this traditional approach—which he called the Aristotelian or dramatic theater—erred on two counts:

- An audience aroused to an emotional state might not make rational decisions that could amend the problem presented in the play;
- By solving the problem onstage, the audience might not feel compelled to attack the problem in the streets.

Brecht's solution was an "epic theater," which would

> not only release the feelings, insights, and impulses possible within the particular historical field of human relations in which the action takes place, but [employ] and [encourage] those thoughts and feelings which help transform the field itself.

The epic theater rejected the Aristotelian catharsis, which implied a release of emotions. Instead, he sought to use the stage to provoke audiences into action. Specifically, the theater must "criticize constructively from a social point of view." Brecht constructed the following comparison between his epic theater and the dramatic theater:

Dramatic Theater	Epic Theater
plot	narrative
implicates spectator in stage situation	turns spectator into an observer
wears down his capacity for action	arouses his capacity for action
provides him with sensations	forces him to make decisions
experience	picture of the world
spectator is involved in something	spectator is made to face something
suggestion	argument
instinctive feelings are preserved	brought to point of recognition
spectator is in the thick of it, shares the experience	spectator stands outside, studies the experience
human being is taken for granted	human being is the subject of inquiry
eyes on the finish	eyes on the course
one scene makes another	each scene for itself
growth	montage
linear development	in curves (ups/down)
evolutionary determinism	jumps
man as a fixed point	man as a process
thought determines being	social being determines thought
feeling	reason*

To discourage the audience's emotional involvement with the characters, Brecht developed the *Verfremdungseffekt* ("alienation effect"), which is derived from the German verb *verfremden* ("to make strange"). In Brechtian terms, the "A-effect" (as it is now called) challenges audi-

*From "The Modern Theatre Is the Epic" by Bertolt Brecht, from *Brecht on Theatre*, edited and translated by John Willet, © 1964. Reprinted by permission of Methuen Publishing, Ltd.

ences to see a social problem as if for the first time, evaluate the issues, and devise solutions to correct it. Hence, the epic theater is didactic because it educates and arouses an audience to action, however entertaining its means.

To achieve the A-effect, Brecht resorted to a purposeful theatricality that reminds audiences that they are only watching a play, not real life. He admits the influence of such diverse and nonrealistic entertainments as folk plays, medieval dramas, cabaret and vaudeville, the films of Charlie Chaplin, Elizabethan stagecraft, court trials, and even boxing matches. Brecht returned the theater to the art of storytelling, frequently using narrators or singers to tell episodic tales. Between episodes, Brecht inserted speeches, songs, and visual devices such as signboards to instruct audiences about the play's intent. He rejected romantic lighting in favor of harsh, white lighting (inspired by the boxing arena) to "illuminate" the action; he rejected pretty scenery in favor of curtains that merely suggested locale and ambience; and he rejected beautiful costumes in favor of worn, used clothing made by the proletariat. Ironically, his costumes were quite often realistic.

Primarily, Brecht used *historification* to show how time and people can change societies and institutions. He set his plays in remote times and places. In *The Good Woman of Setzuan*, Brecht places his exposé of modern capitalism in provincial China. In every case he asks his audiences to judge the "pastness" of an action that clearly parallels a modern situation. Brecht was, of course, borrowing from earlier theater traditions, most notably the medieval and Elizabethan theaters, which also used history as a parallel for contemporary social problems.

Not only did Brecht—and those whom he inspired—revolutionize playwriting, he offered an alternative to realistic acting. Whereas Stanislavskian actors sought to identify with their characters through introspection and psychological motivation, Brechtian actors were taught to "quote" their characters' social essence (a boss, a worker, the oppressed, a soldier, etc.). If the Stanislavskian actor used a superobjective to get at a character's soul, the Brechtian actor defined character in terms of its *gestus* (i.e., social function). Brecht was influenced by Chinese actors he saw in Moscow in 1935, especially the great Mei Lan-fang, a man whose specialty was female roles. Brecht noted that Chinese actors sought not to become their characters, but rather to manifest the social essence of their characters.

Brecht has often been accused or being antiemotional, yet a look at his plays (especially *Mother Courage*, in which a mother loses three children to the war) suggests that he could summon up an audience's emotions as well as any "dramatic" playwright. Brecht frequently employs traditional devices, particularly those of the melodrama, to arouse emotions in his audience. However, he "short-circuits" the emotional response to keep audiences from achieving the catharsis of the Aristotelian theater (which Brecht called "barbaric" because it allowed the slaughter of noble beings like Oedipus). At an emotional crest, Brecht inserted one of his A-effects—a speech, joke, or signboard—to challenge audiences to evaluate why they felt so strongly about the issues. He asked them to consider alternatives to the social problems that created the dilemma. As you read *The Good Woman of Setzuan, No saca nada de la escuela, Top Girls*, and *Ti-Jean and His Brothers* you will observe these theories in practice.

SPOTLIGHT   THEATER IN THE INDUSTRIAL AGE

Just as realism necessitated new approaches to acting and playing spaces, so, too, was the stage refashioned to reflect an age in which science and industry affected virtually every facet of life in the West. Among many visionaries who boldly experimented with performance spaces, scenery, and even performance styles in the industrial age, four in particular merit attention here: Vesold Meyerhold, Erwin Piscator, Leopold Jessner, and Walter Gropius.

Ironically, the Russian Meyerhold (1874–1940) began his assault on the realistic theater by staging Ibsen's most realistic psychological drama, *Hedda Gabler*. In 1906 he staged the play in an intimate space with the audience seated only 7 feet from the actors. Dissatisfied with naturalistic acting techniques, Meyerhold first used an almost robotic style to force audiences to see the inner truth of characters stripped of outer realism. From this radical approach, Meyerhold developed *biomechanics*, a style in which actors performed either on an empty stage or—more likely—in a space reflecting the machinery fostered by the Industrial Revolution. To encourage his actors to distance themselves from realistic techniques, Meyerhold adapted styles drawn from a variety of theatrical performance modes: the *commedia dell'arte* and pantomime, cabaret, modern dance, ballet, and frozen tableaux. Think, for instance, of break dancing or Michael Jackson's "moon walk," both of which use techniques that Meyerhold would recognize.

Jessner (1878–1945), a German director, created a scenic structure—*Jessnersteppen* (Jessner-steps)—that manipulated both the playing arena and the acting style. He fashioned enormous steps leading from the forestage to the rear wall of the theater to create dynamic and impressive compositions. Jessner's actors had to learn to use these steps—horizontally and vertically—in order to appear in three-dimensional positions. Like Meyerhold, Jessner forced the actors into a style that was antithetical to the principles set forth by realism and naturalism. The styles reflected the modern industrial world in which workers were robotic parts of a great machine.

In Germany, Piscator and Gropius did much to transform theater spaces, production methods, and acting styles to create a total theater experience beyond the boundaries of realism and naturalism. Piscator (1893–1966), who influenced Brecht, designed a playing space incorporating large projection screens and revolving nonrealistic sets using noisy machinery. He introduced film and slide projections to create *total theater*, a presentational style that appealed to all of the audience's senses.

The concept of total theater actually originated as a part of a Bauhaus experiment. Bauhaus refers to a post–World War I architectural school founded by Gropius (1883–1969) that synthesized technology, craftsmanship, and design aesthetics. In consultation with Piscator, Gropius designed a theater that brought together audience, actor, designer, and technician in a brave new world of surprises and possibilities. Both artists migrated to the United States, where their "high tech" experiments influenced both theater architecture and production practice after World War II. Postmodernism is among the significant developments derived from the work of Gropius and others. Central Europeans, especially the Czechs and Romanians, are especially accomplished in the presentation of total theater.

THE GOOD WOMAN OF SETZUAN

BERTOLT BRECHT

BERTOLT BRECHT (1898–1956)

The son of a prosperous factory manager in Augsberg, Bavaria, Bertolt Brecht established himself as a controversial writer at an early age. As a high school student, he was nearly expelled for writing antiwar poetry in the midst of World War I. His intentions to pursue a medical career were cut short when he was conscripted into the German army in 1918 to serve as a medic. He observed firsthand the carnage and misery of war, and his subsequent writings—poetry, drama, song lyrics, and essays—are devoted to the eradication of all institutions that contribute to human suffering and indignity. In addition to his protest of war and the governments that wage it, Brecht's political satires expose corrupt social, economic, spiritual, and cultural institutions that oppress the common man. In this sense, Brecht is properly a Romantic writer, however modern and "antiemotional" the methods he employs.

Like so many young artists who lived in economically depressed postwar Germany, Brecht held a cynical, even nihilistic, view of society. And like many of his contemporaries, he gravitated to communism, whose philosophy of dialectical materialism provided him with both the subject matter and the methodology for his plays. Brecht's plays transcend mere propaganda, and he is arguably the most admired and imitated Marxist playwright of the twentieth century. Brecht was too much the humanist to write only ideological tracts, and his plays manifest a universality that transcends the particulars of Marxism. Ever the individualist aligned with no country or party, Brecht spent much of World War II writing film scripts in Santa Monica, California. When he returned to East Berlin in 1948 he obtained Austrian citizenship to skirt state censorship, and he retained a publisher in the West to protect the copyrights on his literary work. When he received the Stalin Peace Prize shortly before his death, he promptly invested the financial portion of his award in a Swiss bank account.

Brecht's first attempts at playwriting were in the Expressionist mode popular among young Germans during the war years. Such works as *Baal* (1918) and *Drums in the Night* (1918) are among his darkest efforts and reflect the angst of young Germans who realized that "the Great War" was not worth fighting. Gradually he turned to satire to vent his anger; in the early 1920s Brecht gained a reputation as a witty cabaret artist who sang politically caustic songs to the accompaniment of his own guitar. His subsequent plays are liberally sprinkled with such songs, an integral part of his *Verfremdungseffekt*. "The Song of the Smoke" in scene 1 of *The Good Woman of Setzuan* is an especially useful example.

In 1928 Brecht collaborated with composer Kurt Weill to write *The Threepenny Opera*, a contemporary retelling of John Gay's 1728 ballad opera, *The Beggar's Opera*. Largely because of its musical comedy nature, it is Brecht's most often performed work, also released as a feature film starring Raul Julia as the notorious MacHeath, about whom the popular song "Mack the Knife" was written. (Sting played the role in a New York revival in 1992.) You have no doubt heard "Mack the Knife" in either the Bobby Darin or Louis Armstrong versions, neither of which is like the Brecht-Weill arrangement. The point is made here because the song was intended to be harsh, dissonant, and even unpleasant, quite unlike the catchy, up-tempo recording heard in pop music venues. Brecht wanted his music to be much like the plays he wrote—unsettling, antiromantic, emotionally "cool"—so that audiences would listen to the message rather than the melody.

As he was defining his methodology for an "epic theater," Brecht discovered the Japanese Noh theater and found in this ancient masked drama, like the Chinese drama he saw in Russia in 1935, an acting style that accommodated his performance theory. Brecht wanted his actors to portray the social status (or "gestus") of his dramatic creations rather than become one with the emotional life of a character. This synthesis of an antirealistic approach to playwriting and performance can be found in his masterworks: *Mother Courage and Her Children* (1938), *The Good Woman of Setzuan* (1939), *Galileo* (1938), and *The Caucasian Chalk Circle* (1944).

Between 1933 and 1948 Brecht lived in exile because his procommunist, anti-Fascist politics made him a target of the Nazi Party. He first fled to Switzerland, and subsequently spent time in Finland, Sweden, Denmark, Russia, and ultimately the United States. The anticommunist purges of the McCarthy era forced him to return to Germany in 1948, but not before he turned his hearing before the House Un-American Activities Committee into a comical piece of Brechtian theater.

In East Berlin, Brecht founded the Berliner Ensemble, a state-supported theater dedicated to the production of his works and those of similar ideology. The Ensemble production of *Mother Courage* in January 1949 (in which Brecht's wife, Helene Weigel, played the title role to great acclaim) made the Ensemble one of Europe's most respected theater companies. The Berliner Ensemble performed in Paris in 1954 and in London during the summer of 1956. These engagements captivated the postwar generation of theater artists and the Ensemble became the model for mainstream companies (e.g., the Royal Shakespeare Company) and also many of the alternative theater collectives that proliferated during the 1950s and 1960s. Both as playwright and performance theorist, Brecht remains among the most imitated artists of the twentieth century. It is likely that no other single artist has exerted as much influence on the antirealist movement as Brecht.

THE GOOD WOMAN OF SETZUAN (1938–1939)

Most anthologies title this play *The Good Woman of Setzuan*, largely because its central character, Shen Te, is indeed a good and honest woman who struggles to survive in a corrupt world. However, Brecht's German title was *Der Gute Mensch von Setzuan. Mensch* is derived from an Old High German word (*mennisco*) meaning "man" in the most generic sense, that is, "humanity" or "human being." Hence, the word *person* instead of *woman* in the title is actually the more accurate translation. It is also worth noting that a *mensch* in the Yiddish idiom is "a person of integrity and honor"; Brecht may have known this meaning as Yiddish (another Germanic language) was commonly spoken in Germany. Furthermore, *mensch* is often used cynically to refer to "the little guy" whose integrity is constantly challenged by the unscrupulous. In this sense, a *mensch* is a "sucker" who is easily preyed upon by con artists.

These distinctions are significant because they help us understand Brecht's intentions. Shen Te is more than a former prostitute who comes into some money and opens a small tobacco shop to earn an honest living. (Brecht frequently uses such irony in his plays: the prostitute is ultimately the most moral person in the society.) To her dismay Shen Te soon discovers that she can survive in her honest trade only when she assumes the role of a nefarious male cousin, Shui Ta, who is as ruthless as he is callous. In this sense Shen Te is neither woman nor man, and the generic *mensch*—a person, irrespective of gender—is appropriate.

Mensch, in its Yiddish sense, is also applicable because Shen Te, without her mean-spirited alter ego, is very much a sucker. Her innate goodness and her propensity to see others as honest first earns her money (when she provides shelter to the three gods who seek an honest human), but later brings her misery. She is exploited by the wealthy, by her poor neighbors, and most importantly by her lover, the penniless pilot who is after her money. Only in the guise of Shui Ta can she protect herself, her fortune, and finally her child. Her confession in the final scene crystallizes her dilemma:

To be good to others and myself—

I couldn't do both at the same time.

To help others and myself was too hard.

Alas! Your world is difficult! Too much misery! too much despair!

The hand that is extended to a beggar, the beggar at once tears off!

Whoever helps the lost is lost himself!

That Brecht indicts ruthless exploiters like the factory owner Shui Ta and his equally corrupt manager Yang Sun is to be expected; they epitomize the capitalist bosses who were skewered in many agit-prop dramas of the 1930s. But Brecht is also as acidic in his treatment of the poor. Mrs. Shin, although comical, is every bit as greedy and exploitive as Shui Ta. Brecht is not indifferent to the plight of the poor and oppressed; rather, he scolds them (and the audiences that identify with them) for not taking matters into their own hands to make changes to improve their lot.

The Good Woman of Setzuan seems to suggest that change is impossible in this world as it is currently arranged. The play ends without a satisfactory resolution as the very gods who can effect change abandon Shen Te and float back to heaven on a pink cloud with the admonition that "The world should *not* be changed!" This ending, a perverse parody of the ancient *deus ex machina*, in which gods were literally lowered onto the stage to resolve human problems, further complicates the situation. Little wonder Shen Te can only scream "Help!" as the curtain falls. Brecht's ending for *The Good Woman of Setzuan* is as contrived as that of the old nineteenth-century melodrama, which dispensed poetic justice to all. Like Shaw, to whom he is a kindred spirit, Brecht also liked to take well-known theater forms and subvert them to challenge audiences' attitudes. *The Good Woman of Setzuan* is a parody of the rags-to-riches melodrama, with elements of the damsel-in-distress generously incorporated. That his refashioned melodrama ends without resolution should not imply pessimism on Brecht's part. Rather, the ending represents the quintessentially Brechtian technique of depriving the audience of a catharsis in order to provoke them, instead, to action. He says, in effect, that it is pointless to ask for divine assistance; humans must do the work, and his innovative ending drives this point home well. Brecht believed that the theater was not the place to solve worldly problems by punishing transgressors (which is why he condemned the old Aristotelian theater as "barbaric"). His purpose was to identify social ills and arouse the audience's indignation at them. He challenges them to return to the streets to eradicate injustice through political action. Herein lies the optimism of Brecht's works, however cynical they may appear. Throughout the play Brecht uses techniques central to his epic theater. First, he purposefully sets the action of his "parable" in remote and distant Setzuan, which for him stands "for all places where men are exploited by men." This typifies Brecht's concept of "historification"—that is, removing a play's action from contemporary life so that audiences may compare their circumstances with those of the past. Furthermore, Setzuan is an intriguing choice for locale; identifying the setting with ancient China, Brecht encourages his actors to use the acting techniques of the Chinese opera, which influenced his methodology. The fact that the actor who plays Shen Te must also play Shui Ta in a mask creates a "distancing" effect.

The play is structured in 10 scenes and a prologue. Although there is a discernible plot line, it is not based on causality in the traditional sense. Rather, the 10 scenes exist independently of one another and are unified thematically by their exploration of the play's central question: To what extent is morality defined by one's economic status? Most scenes are followed by a short subscene (e.g., 1-A, 2-A, etc.) in which a comical water seller, Wong, engages the three gods in satiric banter. The water seller is a variant on the "storyteller" that Brecht favors in his works. Wong provides a critical context from which to judge the story of Shen Te. Note that he frequently addresses the audience directly (as does Shen Te); his speeches are elaborate, Westernized versions of the *yin tzu* of the ancient Chinese opera, in which a character describes his social status and dramatic purpose to the audience. Brecht, the old cabaret balladeer, interpolates a half-dozen songs throughout the play, each commenting satirically on the action and themes.

That the final scene (10) takes place in a courtroom is no accident. The trial was among Brecht's favorite devices because, he argued, the theater itself should function as a court in which the audience/jury dispassionately examines evidence, hears opposing arguments, and renders judgement. In *The Good Woman of Setzuan* the gods refuse to issue a verdict or "renounce the rules" that permit the Shui Tas of the world to hold sway. But, in Brecht's estimation, the gods sitting in the seats beyond the stage can—and must.

American composer and playwright Elizabeth Swados wrote an original score for the American Repertory Theater's 1986 production of The Good Woman of Setzuan, *directed by Andrei Serban.*

THE GOOD WOMAN OF SETZUAN

BERTOLT BRECHT

Translated by Eric Bentley

CHARACTERS

WONG, *a water seller*
THREE GODS
SHEN TE, *a prostitute, later a shopkeeper*
MRS. SHIN, *former owner of Shen Te's shop*
A FAMILY OF EIGHT (*husband, wife, brother, sister-in-law,
    grandfather, nephew, niece, boy*)
AN UNEMPLOYED MAN
A CARPENTER
MRS. MI TZU, *Shen Te's landlady*
YANG SUN, *an unemployed pilot, later a factory manager*
AN OLD WHORE
A POLICEMAN
AN OLD MAN
AN OLD WOMAN, *his wife*
MR. SHU FU, *a barber*
MRS. YANG, *mother of Yang Sun*
GENTLEMEN, VOICES, CHILDREN (*three*), *etc.*

PROLOGUE

(*At the gates of the half-westernized city of Setzuan.*
Evening. Wong the Water Seller introduces himself to the
audience.*)

WONG. I sell water here in the city of Setzuan. It isn't easy.
When water is scarce, I have long distances to go in
search of it, and when it is plentiful, I have no income.
But in our part of the world there is nothing unusual
about poverty. Many people think only the gods can save
the situation. And I hear from a cattle merchant—who

**"So Brecht's first manuscript. Brecht must later have learned that
Setzuan (usually spelled Szechwan) is not a city but a province, and
he adjusted the printed German text. I have kept the earlier reading
since such mythology seems to me more Brechtian than Brecht's
own second thoughts."—E.B.

travels a lot—that some of the highest gods are on their way here at this very moment. Informed sources have it that heaven is quite disturbed at all the complaining. I've been coming out here to the city gates for three days now to bid these gods welcome. I want to be the first to greet them. What about those fellows over there? No, no, they *work*. And that one there has ink on his fingers, he's no god, he must be a clerk from the cement factory. *Those* two are another story. They look as though they'd like to beat you. But gods don't need to beat you, do they? (*Enter Three Gods.*) What about those three? Old-fashioned clothes—dust on their feet—they *must* be gods! (*He throws himself at their feet.*) Do with me what you will, illustrious ones!

FIRST GOD (*with an ear trumpet*). Ah! (*He is pleased.*) So we were expected?

WONG (*giving them water*). Oh, yes. And I *knew* you'd come.

FIRST GOD. We need somewhere to stay the night. You know of a place?

WONG. The whole town is at your service, illustrious ones! What sort of a place would you like?

(*The Gods eye each other.*)

FIRST GOD. Just try the first house you come to, my son.

WONG. That would be Mr. Fo's place.

FIRST GOD. Mr. Fo.

WONG. One moment! (*He knocks at the first house.*)

VOICE FROM MR. FO'S. No!

(*Wong returns a little nervously.*)

WONG. It's too bad. Mr. Fo isn't in. And his servants don't dare do a thing without his consent. He'll have a fit when he finds out who they turned away, won't he?

FIRST GOD (*smiling*). He will, won't he?

WONG. One moment! The next house is Mr. Cheng's. Won't he be thrilled?

FIRST GOD. Mr. Cheng.

(*Wong knocks.*)

VOICE FROM MR. CHENG'S. Keep your gods. We have our own troubles!

WONG (*back with the Gods*). Mr. Cheng is very sorry, but he has a houseful of relations. I think some of them are a bad lot, and naturally, he wouldn't like you to see them.

THIRD GOD. Are we so terrible?

WONG. Well, only with bad people, of course. Everyone knows the province of Kwan is always having floods.

SECOND GOD. Really? How's *that*?

WONG. Why, because they're so irreligious.

SECOND GOD. Rubbish. It's because they neglected the dam.

FIRST GOD (*to Second*). Sh! (*To Wong.*) You're still in hopes, aren't you, my son?

WONG. Certainly. All Setzuan is competing for the honor! What happened up to now is pure coincidence. I'll be back. (*He walks away, but then stands undecided.*)

SECOND GOD. What did I tell you?

THIRD GOD. It *could* be pure coincidence.

SECOND GOD. The same coincidence in Shun, Kwan, and Setzuan? People just aren't religious any more, let's face the fact. Our mission has failed!

FIRST GOD. Oh come, we might run into a good person any minute.

THIRD GOD. How did the resolution read? (*Unrolling a scroll and reading from it.*) "The world can stay as it is if enough people are found living lives worthy of human beings." Good people, that is. Well, what about this Water Seller himself? *He's* good, or I'm very much mistaken.

SECOND GOD. You're very much mistaken. When he gave us a drink, I had the impression there was something odd about the cup. Well, look! (*He shows the cup to the First God.*)

FIRST GOD. A false bottom!

SECOND GOD. The man is a swindler.

FIRST GOD. Very well, count *him* out. That's one man among millions. And as a matter of fact, we only need one on *our* side. These atheists are saying, "The world must be changed because no one can *be* good and *stay* good." No one, eh? I say: let us find one—just one—and we have those fellows where we want them!

THIRD GOD (*to Wong*). Water Seller, is it so hard to find a place to stay?

WONG. Nothing could be easier. It's just me. I don't go about it right.

THIRD GOD. Really? (*He returns to the others. A Gentleman passes by.*)

WONG. Oh dear, they're catching on. (*He accosts the Gentleman.*) Excuse the intrusion, dear sir, but three Gods have just turned up. Three of the very highest. They need a place for the night. Seize this rare opportunity—to have real gods as your guests!

GENTLEMAN (*laughing*). A new way of finding free rooms for a gang of crooks.

(*Exit Gentleman.*)

WONG (*shouting at him*). Godless rascal! Have you no religion, gentlemen of Setzuan? (*Pause.*) Patience, illustrious ones! (*Pause.*) There's only one person left. Shen Te, the prostitute. She can't say no. (*Calls up to a window.*) Shen Te!

(*Shen Te opens the shutters and looks out.*)

WONG. *They're* here, and nobody wants them. Will you take them?

SHEN TE. Oh, no, Wong, I'm expecting a gentleman.

WONG. Can't you forget about him for tonight?

SHEN TE. The rent has to be paid by tomorrow or I'll be out on the street.

WONG. This is no time for calculation, Shen Te.

SHEN TE. Stomachs rumble even on the Emperor's birthday, Wong.

WONG. Setzuan is one big dung hill!

SHEN TE. Oh, very well! I'll hide till my gentleman has come and gone. Then I'll take them. (*She disappears.*)

WONG. They mustn't see her gentleman or they'll know what she is.
FIRST GOD (*who hasn't heard any of this*). I think it's hopeless.

(*They approach Wong.*)

WONG. (*jumping, as he finds them behind him*). A room has been found, illustrious ones! (*He wipes sweat off his brow.*)
SECOND GOD. Oh, good.
THIRD GOD. Let's see it.
WONG (*nervously*). Just a minute. It has to be tidied up a bit.
THIRD GOD. Then we'll sit down here and wait.
WONG (*still more nervous*). No, no! (*Holding himself back.*) Too much traffic, you know.
THIRD GOD (*with a smile*). Of course, if you *want* us to move.

(*They retire a little. They sit on a doorstep. Wong sits on the ground.*)

WONG (*after a deep breath*). You'll be staying with a single girl—the finest human being in Setzuan!
THIRD GOD. That's nice.
WONG (*to the audience*). They gave me such a look when I picked up my cup just now.
THIRD GOD. You're worn out, Wong.
WONG. A little, maybe.
FIRST GOD. Do people here have a hard time of it?
WONG. The good ones do.
FIRST GOD. What about yourself?
WONG. You mean I'm not good. That's true. And I don't have an easy time either!

(*During this dialogue, a Gentleman has turned up in front of Shen Te's house, and has whistled several times. Each time Wong has given a start.*)

THIRD GOD (*to Wong, softly*). Psst! I think he's gone now.
WONG (*confused and surprised*). Ye-e-es.

(*The Gentleman has left now, and Shen Te has come down to the street.*)

SHEN TE (*softly*). Wong!

(*Getting no answer, she goes off down the street. Wong arrives just too late, forgetting his carrying pole.*)

WONG (*softly*). Shen Te! Shen Te! (*To himself.*) So she's gone off to earn the rent. Oh dear, I can't go to the gods again with no room to offer them. Having failed in the service of the gods, I shall run to my den in the sewer pipe down by the river and hide from their sight!

(*He rushes off. Shen Te returns, looking for him, but finding the gods. She stops in confusion.*)

SHEN TE. You are the illustrious ones? My name is Shen Te. It would please me very much if my simple room could be of use to you.
THIRD GOD. Where is the Water Seller, Miss . . . Shen Te?
SHEN TE. I missed him, somehow.

FIRST GOD. Oh, he probably thought you weren't coming, and was afraid of telling us.
THIRD GOD (*picking up the carrying pole*). We'll leave this with you. He'll be needing it.

(*Led by Shen Te, they go into the house. It grows dark, then light. Dawn. Again escorted by Shen Te, who leads them through the half-light with a little lamp, the Gods take their leave.*)

FIRST GOD. Thank you, thank you, dear Shen Te, for your elegant hospitality! We shall not forget! And give our thanks to the Water Seller—he showed us a good human being.
SHEN TE. Oh, I'm not good. Let me tell you something: when Wong asked me to put you up, I hesitated.
FIRST GOD. It's all right to hesitate if you then go ahead! And in giving us that room you did much more than you knew. You proved that good people still exist, a point that has been disputed of late—even in heaven. Farewell!
SECOND GOD. Farewell!
THIRD GOD. Farewell!
SHEN TE. Stop, illustrious ones! I'm not sure you're right. I'd like to be good, it's true, but there's the rent to pay. And that's not all: I sell myself for a living. Even so I can't make ends meet, there's too much competition. I'd like to honor my father and mother and speak nothing but the truth and not covet my neighbor's house. I should love to stay with one man. But how? How is it done? Even breaking only a *few* of your commandments, I can hardly manage.
FIRST GOD (*clearing his throat*). These thoughts are but, um, the misgivings of an unusually good woman!
THIRD GOD. Goodbye, Shen Te! Give our regards to the Water Seller!
SECOND GOD. And above all: be good! Farewell!
FIRST GOD. Farewell!
THIRD GOD. Farewell!

(*They start to wave good-bye.*)

SHEN TE. But everything is so expensive, I don't feel sure I can do it!
SECOND GOD. That's not in our sphere. We never meddle with economics.
THIRD GOD. One moment.

(*They stop.*)

Isn't it true she might do better if she had more money?

SECOND GOD. Come, come! How could we ever account for it Up Above?
FIRST GOD. Oh, there are ways.

(*They put their heads together and confer in dumb show.*)

(*To Shen Te, with embarrassment.*) As you say you can't pay your rent, well, um, we're not paupers, so of course we insist on paying for our room. (*Awkwardly thrusting money into her hands.*) There! (*Quickly.*) But don't tell anyone! The incident is open to misinterpretation.

SECOND GOD. It certainly is!
FIRST GOD (*defensively*). But there's no law against it! It was never decreed that a god mustn't pay hotel bills!

(*The Gods leave.*)

SCENE 1

(*A small tobacco shop. The shop is not as yet completely furnished and hasn't started doing business.*)

SHEN TE (*to the audience*). It's three days now since the gods left. When they said they wanted to pay for the room, I looked down at my hand, and there was more than a thousand silver dollars! I bought a tobacco shop with the money, and moved in yesterday. I don't own the building, of course, but I can pay the rent, and I hope to do a lot of good here. Beginning with Mrs. Shin, who's just coming across the square with her pot. She had the shop before me, and yesterday she dropped in to ask for rice for her children.

(*Enter Mrs. Shin. Both women bow.*)

How do you do, Mrs. Shin.
MRS. SHIN. How do you do, Miss Shen Te. You like your new home?
SHEN TE. Indeed, yes. Did your children have a good night?
MRS. SHIN. In that hovel? The youngest is coughing already.
SHEN TE. Oh, dear!
MRS. SHIN. You're going to learn a thing or two in these slums.
SHEN TE. Slums? That's not what you said when you sold me the shop!
MRS. SHIN. Now don't start nagging! Robbing me and my innocent children of their home and then calling it a slum! That's the limit! (*She weeps.*)
SHEN TE (*tactfully*). I'll get your rice.
MRS. SHIN. And a little cash while you're at it.
SHEN TE. I'm afraid I haven't sold anything yet.
MRS. SHIN (*screeching*). I've got to have it. Strip the clothes from my back and then cut my throat, will you? I know what I'll do: I'll leave my children on your doorstep! (*She snatches the pot out of Shen Te's hands.*)
SHEN TE. Please don't be angry. You'll spill the rice.

(*Enter an elderly Husband and Wife with their shabbily-dressed Nephew.*)

WIFE. Shen Te, dear! You've come into money, they tell me. And we haven't a roof over our heads! A tobacco shop. We had one too. But it's gone. Could we spend the night here, do you think?

NEPHEW (*appraising the shop*). Not bad!
WIFE. He's our nephew. We're inseparable!
MRS. SHIN. And who are these . . . ladies and gentlemen?
SHEN TE. They put me up when I first came in from the country. (*To the audience.*) Of course, when my small purse was empty, they put me out on the street, and they may be afraid I'll do the same to them. (*To the newcomers, kindly.*) Come in, and welcome, though I've only one little room for you—it's behind the shop.
HUSBAND. That'll do. Don't worry.
WIFE (*bringing Shen Te some tea*). We'll stay over here, so we won't be in your way. Did you make it a tobacco shop in memory of your first real home? We can certainly give you a hint or two! That's one reason we came.
MRS. SHIN (*to Shen Te*). Very nice! As long as you have a few customers too!
HUSBAND. Sh! A customer!

(*Enter an Unemployed Man, in rags.*)

UNEMPLOYED MAN. Excuse me. I'm unemployed.

(*Mrs. Shin laughs.*)

SHEN TE. Can I help you?
UNEMPLOYED MAN. Have you any damaged cigarettes? I thought there might be some damage when you're unpacking.
WIFE. What nerve, begging for tobacco! (*Rhetorically.*) Why don't they ask for bread?
UNEMPLOYED MAN. Bread is expensive. One cigarette butt and I'll be a new man.
SHEN TE (*giving him cigarettes*). That's very important—to be a new man. You'll be my first customer and bring me luck.

(*The Unemployed Man quickly lights a cigarette, inhales, and goes off, coughing.*)

WIFE. Was that right, Shen Te, dear?
MRS. SHIN. If this is the opening of a shop, you can hold the closing at the end of the week.
HUSBAND. I bet he had money on him.
SHEN TE. Oh, no, he said he hadn't!
NEPHEW. How d'you know he wasn't lying?
SHEN TE (*angrily*). How do you know he was?
WIFE (*wagging her head*). You're too good, Shen Te, dear. If you're going to keep this shop, you'll have to learn to say No.
HUSBAND. Tell them the place isn't yours to dispose of. Belongs to . . . some relative who insists on all accounts being strictly in order . . .
MRS. SHIN. That's right! What do you think you are—a philanthropist?
SHEN TE (*laughing*). Very well, suppose I ask you for my rice back, Mrs. Shin?
WIFE (*combatively, at Mrs. Shin*). So that's *her* rice?

(*Enter the Carpenter, a small man.*)

MRS. SHIN (*who, at the sight of him, starts to hurry away*). See you tomorrow, Miss Shen Te! (*Exit Mrs. Shin.*)

CARPENTER. Mrs. Shin, it's you I want!

WIFE (*to Shen Te*). Has she some claim on you?

SHEN TE. She's hungry. That's a claim.

CARPENTER. Are you the new tenant? And filling up the shelves already? Well, they're not yours, till they're paid for, ma'am. I'm the carpenter, so I should know.

SHEN TE. I took the shop "furnishings included."

CARPENTER. You're in league with that Mrs. Shin, of course. All right: I demand my hundred silver dollars.

SHEN TE. I'm afraid I haven't got a hundred silver dollars.

CARPENTER. Then you'll find it. Or I'll have you arrested.

WIFE (*whispering to Shen Te*). That relative: make it a cousin.

SHEN TE. Can't it wait till next month?

CARPENTER. No!

SHEN TE. Be a little patient, Mr. Carpenter, I can't settle all claims at once.

CARPENTER. Who's patient with me? (*He grabs a shelf from the wall.*) Pay up—or I take the shelves back!

WIFE. Shen Te! Dear! Why don't you let your . . . cousin settle this affair? (*To Carpenter.*) Put your claim in writing. Shen Te's cousin will see you get paid.

CARPENTER (*derisively*). Cousin, eh?

HUSBAND. Cousin, yes.

CARPENTER. I know these cousins!

NEPHEW. Don't be silly. He's a personal friend of mine.

HUSBAND. What a man! Sharp as a razor!

CARPENTER. All right. I'll put my claim in writing. (*Puts shelf on floor, sits on it, writes out bill.*)

WIFE (*to Shen Te*). He'd tear the dress off your back to get his shelves. Never recognize a claim! That's my motto.

SHEN TE. He's done a job, and wants something in return. It's shameful that I can't give it to him. What will the gods say?

HUSBAND. You did your bit when you took *us* in.

(*Enter the Brother, limping, and the Sister-in-Law, pregnant.*)

BROTHER (*to Husband and Wife*). So this is where you're hiding out! There's family feeling for you! Leaving us on the corner!

WIFE (*embarrassed, to Shen Te*). It's my brother and his wife. (*To them.*) Now stop grumbling, and sit quietly in that corner. (*To Shen Te.*) It can't be helped. She's in her fifth month.

SHEN TE. Oh, yes. Welcome!

WIFE (*to the couple*). Say thank you.

(*They mutter something.*)
The cups are there. (*To Shen Te.*) Lucky you bought this shop when you did!

SHEN TE (*laughing and bringing tea*). Lucky indeed!

(*Enter Mrs. Mi Tzu, the landlady.*)

MRS. MI TZU. Miss Shen Te? I am Mrs. Mi Tzu, your landlady. I hope our relationship will be a happy one? I like to think I give my tenants modern, personalized service. Here is your lease. (*To the others, as Shen Te reads the lease.*) There's nothing like the opening of a little shop, is there? A moment of true beauty! (*She is looking around.*) Not very much on the shelves, of course. But everything in the gods' good time! Where are your references, Miss Shen Te?

SHEN TE. Do I *have* to have references?

MRS. MI TZU. After all, I haven't a notion who you are!

HUSBAND. Oh, *we'd* be glad to vouch for Miss Shen Te! We'd go through fire for her!

MRS. MI TZU. And who may *you* be?

HUSBAND (*stammering*). Ma Fu, tobacco dealer.

MRS. MI TZU. Where is your shop, Mr. . . . Ma Fu?

HUSBAND. Well, um, I haven't a shop—I've just sold it.

MRS. MI TZU. I see. (*To Shen Te.*) Is there no one else that knows you?

WIFE (*whispering to Shen Te*). Your cousin! Your cousin!

MRS. MI TZU. This is a respectable house, Miss Shen Te. I never sign a lease without certain assurances.

SHEN TE (*slowly, her eyes downcast*). I have . . . a cousin.

MRS. MI TZU. On the square? Let's go over and see him. What does he do?

SHEN TE (*as before*). He lives . . . in another city.

WIFE (*prompting*). Didn't you say he was in Shung?

SHEN TE. That's right. Shung.

HUSBAND (*prompting*). I had his name on the tip of my tongue. Mr. . . .

SHEN TE (*with an effort*). Mr. . . . Shui . . . Ta.

HUSBAND. That's it! Tall, skinny fellow!

SHEN TE. Shui Ta!

NEPHEW (*to Carpenter*). You were in touch with him, weren't you? About the shelves?

CARPENTER (*surlily*). Give him this bill. (*He hands it over.*) I'll be back in the morning. (*Exit Carpenter.*)

NEPHEW (*calling after him, but with his eyes on Mrs. Mi Tzu*). Don't worry! Mr. Shui Ta pays on the nail!

MRS. MI TZU (*looking closely at Shen Te*). I'll be happy to make his acquaintance, Miss Shen Te. (*Exit Mrs. Mi Tzu.*)

(*Pause.*)

WIFE. By tomorrow morning she'll know more about you than you do yourself.

SISTER-IN-LAW (*to Nephew*). This thing isn't built to last.

(*Enter Grandfather.*)

WIFE. It's Grandfather! (*To Shen Te.*) Such a good old soul!

(*The Boy enters.*)

BOY (*over his shoulder*). Here they are!

WIFE. And the boy, how he's grown! But he always could eat enough for ten.

(*Enter the Niece.*)

WIFE (*to Shen Te*). Our little niece from the country. There are more of us now than in your time. The less we had, the more there were of us; the more there were of us, the less we had. Give me the key. We must protect ourselves from unwanted guests. (*She takes the key and locks the door.*) Just make yourself at home. I'll light the little lamp.

NEPHEW (*a big joke*). I hope her cousin doesn't drop in tonight! The strict Mr. Shui Ta!

(*Sister-in-Law laughs.*)

BROTHER (*reaching for a cigarette*). One cigarette more or less . . .

HUSBAND. One cigarette more or less.

(*They pile into the cigarettes. The Brother hands a jug of wine round.*)

NEPHEW. Mr. Shui Ta'll pay for it!

GRANDFATHER (*gravely, to Shen Te*). How do you do?

(*Shen Te, a little taken aback by the belatedness of the greeting, bows. She has the Carpenter's bill in one hand, the landlady's lease in the other.*)

WIFE. How about a bit of a song? To keep Shen Te's spirits up?

NEPHEW. Good idea. Grandfather: you start!

SONG OF THE SMOKE

GRANDFATHER.
    I used to think (before old age beset me)
      That brains could fill the pantry of the poor.
    But where did all my cerebration get me?
    I'm just as hungry as I was before.
          So what's the use?
            See the smoke float free
          Into ever colder coldness!
             It's the same with me.

HUSBAND.
    The straight and narrow path leads to disaster
      And so the crooked path I tried to tread.
    That got me to disaster even faster.
      (They say we shall be happy when we're dead.)
          So what's the use, etc.

NIECE.
    You older people, full of expectation,
      At any moment now you'll walk the plank!
    The future's for the younger generation!
      Yes, even if that future is a blank.
          So what's the use, etc.

NEPHEW (*to the Brother*). Where'd you get that wine?

SISTER-IN-LAW (*answering for the Brother*). He pawned the sack of tobacco.

HUSBAND (*stepping in*). What? That tobacco was all we had to fall back on! You pig!

BROTHER. *You'd* call a man a pig because your wife was frigid! Did you refuse to drink it?

(*They fight. The shelves fall over.*)

SHEN TE (*imploringly*). Oh, don't! Don't break everything! Take it, take it all, but don't destroy a gift from the gods!

WIFE (*disparagingly*). This shop isn't big enough. I should never have mentioned it to Uncle and the others. When *they* arrive, it's going to be disgustingly overcrowded.

SISTER-IN-LAW. And did you hear our gracious hostess? She cools off quick!

(*Voices outside. Knocking at the door.*)

UNCLE'S VOICE. Open the door!

WIFE. Uncle? Is that you, Uncle?

UNCLE'S VOICE. Certainly, it's me. Auntie says to tell you she'll have the children here in ten minutes.

WIFE (*to Shen Te*). I'll have to let him in.

SHEN TE (*who scarcely hears her*).
    The little lifeboat is swiftly sent down
    Too many men too greedily
    Hold on to it as they drown.

SCENE 1A

(*Wong's den in a sewer pipe.*)

WONG (*crouching there*). All quiet! It's four days now since I left the city. The gods passed this way on the second day. I heard their steps on the bridge over there. They must be a long way off by this time, so I'm safe.

(*Breathing a sigh of relief, he curls up and goes to sleep. In his dream the pipe becomes transparent, and the Gods appear.*)
(*Raising an arm, as if in self-defense.*) I know, I know, illustrious ones! I found no one to give you a room—not in all Setzuan! There, it's out. Please continue on your way!

FIRST GOD (*mildly*). But you did find someone. Someone who took us in for the night, watched over us in our sleep, and in the early morning lighted us down to the street with a lamp.

WONG. It was . . . Shen Te, that took you in?

THIRD GOD. Who else?

WONG. And I ran away! "She isn't coming," I thought, "she just can't afford it."

GODS (*singing*).
    O you feeble, well-intentioned, and yet feeble chap!
    Where there's need the fellow thinks there is no
      goodness!
    When there's danger he thinks courage starts to ebb
      away!
    Some people only see the seamy side!
    What hasty judgment! What premature desperation!

WONG. I'm *very* ashamed, illustrious ones.

FIRST GOD. Do us a favor, Water Seller. Go back to Setzuan. Find Shen Te, and give us a report on her. We hear that she's come into a little money. Show interest in her goodness—for no one can be good for long if goodness is not in demand. Meanwhile we shall continue the search, and find other good people. After which, the idle chatter about the impossibility of goodness will stop!

(*The Gods vanish.*)

SCENE 2

(*A knocking.*)

WIFE. Shen Te! Someone at the door. Where is she anyway?

NEPHEW. She must be getting the breakfast. Mr. Shui Ta will pay for it.

(*The Wife laughs and shuffles to the door. Enter Mr. Shui Ta and the Carpenter.*)

WIFE. Who is it?

SHUI TA. I am Miss Shen Te's cousin.

WIFE. What?

SHUI TA. My name is Shui Ta.

WIFE. Her cousin?

NEPHEW. Her cousin?

NIECE. But that was a joke. She hasn't got a cousin.

HUSBAND. So early in the morning?

BROTHER. What's all the noise?

SISTER-IN-LAW. This fellow says he's her cousin.

BROTHER. Tell him to prove it.

NEPHEW. Right. If you're Shen Te's cousin, prove it by getting the breakfast.

SHUI TA (*whose regime begins as he puts out the lamp to save oil. Loudly, to all present, asleep or awake*). Would you all please get dressed! Customers will be coming! I wish to open my shop!

HUSBAND. *Your* shop? Doesn't it belong to our good friend Shen Te?

(*Shui Ta shakes his head.*)

SISTER-IN-LAW. So we've been cheated. Where *is* the little liar?

SHUI TA. Miss Shen Te has been delayed. She wishes me to tell you there will be nothing she can do—now I am here.

WIFE (*bowled over*). I thought she was *good!*

NEPHEW. Do you have to believe *him?*

HUSBAND. *I* don't.

NEPHEW. Then do something.

HUSBAND. Certainly! I'll send out a search party at once. You, you, you, and you, go out and look for Shen Te.

(*As the Grandfather rises and makes for the door.*)

Not you, Grandfather, you and I will hold the fort.

SHUI TA. You won't find Miss Shen Te. She has suspended her hospitable activity for an unlimited period. There are too many of you. She asked me to say: this is a tobacco shop, not a gold mine.

HUSBAND. Shen Te never said a thing like that. Boy, food! There's a bakery on the corner. Stuff your shirt full when they're not looking!

SISTER-IN-LAW. Don't overlook the raspberry tarts.

HUSBAND. And don't let the policeman see you.

(*The Boy leaves.*)

SHUI TA. Don't you depend on this shop now? Then why give it a bad name, by stealing from the bakery?

NEPHEW. Don't listen to him. Let's find Shen Te. She'll give him a piece of her mind.

SISTER-IN-LAW. Don't forget to leave us some breakfast.

(*Brother, Sister-in-Law, and Nephew leave.*)

SHUI TA (*to the Carpenter*). You see, Mr. Carpenter, nothing has changed since the poet, eleven hundred years ago, penned these lines:
    A governor was asked what was needed
    To save the freezing people in the city.
    He replied:
    "A blanket ten thousand feet long
    To cover the city and all its suburbs."

(*He starts to tidy up the shop.*)

CARPENTER. Your cousin owes me money. I've got witnesses. For the shelves.

SHUI TA. Yes, I have your bill. (*He takes it out of his pocket.*) Isn't a hundred silver dollars rather a lot?

CARPENTER. No deductions! I have a wife and children.

SHUI TA. How many children?

CARPENTER. Three.

SHUI TA. I'll make you an offer. Twenty silver dollars.

(*The Husband laughs.*)

CARPENTER. You're crazy. Those shelves are real walnut.

SHUI TA. Very well. Take them away.

CARPENTER. What?

SHUI TA. They cost too much. Please take them away.

WIFE. Not bad! (*And she, too, is laughing.*)

CARPENTER (*a little bewildered*). Call Shen Te, someone! (*To Shui Ta.*) She's good!

SHUI TA. Certainly. She's ruined.

CARPENTER (*provoked into taking some of the shelves*). All right, you can keep your tobacco on the floor.

SHUI TA (*to the Husband*). Help him with the shelves.

HUSBAND (*grins and carries one shelf over to the door where the Carpenter now is*). Goodbye, shelves!

CARPENTER (*to the Husband*). You dog! You want my family to starve?

SHUI TA. I repeat my offer. I have no desire to keep my tobacco on the floor. Twenty silver dollars.

CARPENTER (*with desperate aggressiveness*). One hundred!

(Shui Ta shows indifference, looks through the window. The Husband picks up several shelves.)

(To Husband.) You needn't smash them against the doorpost, you idiot! *(To Shui Ta.)* These shelves were made to measure. They're no use anywhere else!

SHUI TA. Precisely.

(The Wife squeals with pleasure.)

CARPENTER *(giving up, sullenly)*. Take the shelves. Pay what you want to pay.

SHUI TA *(smoothly)*. Twenty silver dollars.

(He places two large coins on the table. The Carpenter picks them up.)

HUSBAND *(brings the shelves back in)*. And quite enough too!

CARPENTER *(slinking off)*. Quite enough to get drunk on.

HUSBAND *(happily)*. Well, we got rid of *him!*

WIFE *(weeping with fun, gives a rendition of the dialogue just spoken)*. "Real walnut," says he. "Very well, take them away," says his lordship. "I have children," says he. "Twenty silver dollars," says his lordship. "They're no use anywhere else," says he. "Precisely," said his lordship!

(She dissolves into shrieks of merriment.)

SHUI TA. And now: go!

HUSBAND. What's that?

SHUI TA. You're thieves, parasites. I'm giving you this chance. Go!

HUSBAND *(summoning all his ancestral dignity)*. That sort deserves no answer. Besides, one should never shout on an empty stomach.

WIFE. Where's that boy?

SHUI TA. Exactly. The boy. I want no stolen goods in this shop. *(Very loudly.)* I strongly advise you to leave! *(But they remain seated, noses in the air. Quietly.)* As you wish.

(Shui Ta goes to the door. A Policeman appears. Shui Ta bows.)

I am addressing the officer in charge of this precinct?

POLICEMAN. That's right, Mr., um . . . what was the name, sir?

SHUI TA. Mr. Shui Ta.

POLICEMAN. Yes, of course, sir.

(They exchange a smile.)

SHUI TA. Nice weather we're having.

POLICEMAN. A little on the warm side, sir.

SHUI TA. Oh, a little on the warm side.

HUSBAND *(whispering to the Wife)*. If he keeps it up till the boy's back, we're done for. *(Tries to signal Shui Ta.)*

SHUI TA *(ignoring the signal)*. Weather, of course, is one thing indoors, another out on the dusty street!

POLICEMAN. Oh, quite another, sir!

WIFE *(to the Husband)*. It's all right as long as he's standing in the doorway—the boy will see him.

SHUI TA. Step inside for a moment! It's quite cool indoors. My cousin and I have just opened the place. And we attach the greatest importance to being on good terms with the, um, authorities.

POLICEMAN *(entering)*. Thank you, Mr. Shui Ta. It *is* cool!

HUSBAND *(whispering to the Wife)*. And now the boy won't see him.

SHUI TA *(showing Husband and Wife to the Policeman)*. Visitors, I think my cousin knows them. They were just leaving.

HUSBAND *(defeated)*. Ye-e-es, we were . . . just leaving.

SHUI TA. I'll tell my cousin you couldn't wait.

(Noise from the street. Shouts of "Stop, thief!")

POLICEMAN. What's that?

(The Boy is in the doorway with cakes and buns and rolls spilling out of his shirt. The Wife signals desperately to him to leave. He gets the idea.)

No, you don't! *(He grabs the Boy by the collar.)* Where's all this from?

BOY *(vaguely pointing)*. Down the street.

POLICEMAN *(grimly)*. So that's it. *(Prepares to arrest the Boy.)*

WIFE *(stepping in)*. And *we* knew nothing about it. *(To the Boy.)* Nasty little thief!

POLICEMAN *(dryly)*. Can you clarify the situation, Mr. Shui Ta?

(Shui Ta is silent.)

POLICEMAN *(who understands silence)*. Aha. You're all coming with me—to the station.

SHUI TA. I can hardly say how sorry I am that *my* establishment . . .

WIFE. Oh, he saw the boy leave not ten minutes ago!

SHUI TA. And to conceal the theft asked a policeman in?

POLICEMAN. Don't listen to her, Mr. Shui Ta, I'll be happy to relieve you of their presence one and all! *(To all three.)* Out! *(He drives them before him.)*

GRANDFATHER *(leaving last. Gravely)*. Good morning!

POLICEMAN. Good morning!

(Shui Ta, left alone, continues to tidy up. Mrs. Mi Tzu breezes in.)

MRS. MI TZU. You're her cousin, are you? Then have the goodness to explain what all this means—police dragging people from a respectable house! By what right does your Miss Shen Te turn my property into a house of assignation?—Well, as you see, I know all!

SHUI TA. Yes. My cousin has the worst possible reputation: that of being poor.

MRS. MI TZU. No sentimental rubbish, Mr. Shui Ta. Your cousin was a common . . .

SHUI TA. Pauper. Let's use the uglier word.

MRS. MI TZU. I'm speaking of her conduct, not her earnings. But there must have *been* earnings, or how did she buy all this? Several elderly gentlemen took care of it, I suppose. I repeat: this is a respectable house! I have tenants who prefer not to live under the same roof with such a person.

SHUI TA (*quietly*). How much do you want?

MRS. MI TZU (*he is ahead of her now*). I beg your pardon.

SHUI TA. To reassure yourself. To reassure your tenants. How much will it cost?

MRS. MI TZU. You're a cool customer.

SHUI TA (*picking up the lease*). The rent is high. (*He reads on.*) I assume it's payable by the month?

MRS. MI TZU. Not in her case.

SHUI TA (*looking up*). What?

MRS. MI TZU. Six months rent payable in advance. Two hundred silver dollars.

SHUI TA. Six . . . ! Sheer usury! And where am I to find it?

MRS. MI TZU. You should have thought of that before.

SHUI TA. Have you no heart, Mrs. Mi Tzu? It's true Shen Te acted foolishly, being kind to all those people, but she'll improve with time. I'll see to it she does. She'll work her fingers to the bone to pay her rent, and all the time be as quiet as a mouse, as humble as a fly.

MRS. MI TZU. Her social background . . .

SHUI TA. Out of the depths! She came out of the depths! And before she'll go back there, she'll work, sacrifice, shrink from nothing. . . . Such a tenant is worth her weight in gold, Mrs. Mi Tzu.

MRS. MI TZU. It's silver we were talking about, Mr. Shui Ta. Two hundred silver dollars or . . .

(*Enter the Policeman.*)

POLICEMAN. Am I intruding, Mr. Shui Ta?

MRS. MI TZU. This tobacco shop is well-known to the police, I see.

POLICEMAN. Mr. Shui Ta has done us a service, Mrs. Mi Tzu. I am here to present our official felicitations!

MRS. MI TZU. That means less than nothing to me, sir. Mr. Shui Ta, all I can say is: I hope your cousin will find my terms acceptable. Good day, gentlemen. (*Exit.*)

SHUI TA. Good day, ma'am.

(*Pause.*)

POLICEMAN. Mrs. Mi Tzu a bit of a stumbling block, sir?

SHUI TA. She wants six months' rent in advance.

POLICEMAN. And you haven't got it, eh?

(*Shui Ta is silent.*)
But surely you can get it, sir? A man like you?

SHUI TA. What about a woman like Shen Te?

POLICEMAN. You're not staying, sir?

SHUI TA. No, and I won't be back. Do you smoke?

POLICEMAN (*taking two cigars, and placing them both in his pocket*). Thank you, sir—I see your point. Miss Shen

Te—let's mince no words—Miss Shen Te lived by selling herself. "What else could she have done?" you ask. "How else was she to pay the rent?" True. But the fact remains, Mr. Shui Ta, it is not respectable. Why not? A very deep question. But, in the first place, love—love isn't bought and sold like cigars, Mr. Shui Ta. In the second place, it isn't respectable to go waltzing off with someone that's paying his way, so to speak—it must be for love! Thirdly and lastly, as the proverb has it: not for a handful of rice but for love! (*Pause. He is thinking hard.*) "Well," you may say, "and what good is all this wisdom if the milk's already spilt?" Miss Shen Te is what she is. Is *where* she is. We have to face the fact that if she doesn't get hold of six months' rent pronto, she'll be back on the streets. The question then as I see it—everything in this world is a matter of opinion—the question as I see it is: *how* is she to get hold of this rent? How? Mr. Shui Ta: I don't know. (*Pause.*) I take that back, sir. It's just come to me. A husband. We must find her a husband!

(*Enter a little Old Woman.*)

OLD WOMAN. A good cheap cigar for my husband, we'll have been married forty years tomorrow and we're having a little celebration.

SHUI TA. Forty years? And you still want to celebrate?

OLD WOMAN. As much as we can afford to. We have the carpet shop across the square. We'll be good neighbors, I hope?

SHUI TA. I hope so too.

POLICEMAN (*who keeps making discoveries*). Mr. Shui Ta, you know what we need? We need capital. And how do we acquire capital? We get married.

SHUI TA (*to Old Woman*). I'm afraid I've been pestering this gentleman with my personal worries.

POLICEMAN (*lyrically*). We can't pay six months' rent, so what do we do? We marry money.

SHUI TA. That might not be easy.

POLICEMAN. Oh, I don't know. She's a good match. Has a nice, growing business. (*To the Old Woman.*) What do you think?

OLD WOMAN (*undecided*). Well—

POLICEMAN. Should she put an ad in the paper?

OLD WOMAN (*not eager to commit herself*). Well, if she agrees—

POLICEMAN. I'll write it for her. *You* lend us a hand, and *we* write an ad for you! (*He chuckles away to himself, takes out his notebook, wets the stump of a pencil between his lips, and writes away.*)

SHUI TA (*slowly*). Not a bad idea.

POLICEMAN. "What . . . *respectable* . . . man . . . with small capital . . . widower . . . not excluded . . . desires . . . marriage . . . into flourishing . . . tobacco shop?" And now let's add: "am . . . pretty . . ." No! . . . "Prepossessing appearance."

SHUI TA. If you don't think that's an exaggeration?

OLD WOMAN. Oh, not a bit. I've seen her.

(*The Policeman tears the page out of his notebook, and hands it over to Shui Ta.*)

SHUI TA (*with horror in his voice*). How much luck we need to keep our heads above water! How many ideas! How many friends! (*To the Policeman.*) Thank you, sir. I think I see my way clear.

SCENE 3

(*Evening in the municipal park. Noise of a plane overhead. Yang Sun, a young man in rags, is following the plane with his eyes: one can tell that the machine is describing a curve above the park. Yang Sun then takes a rope out of his pocket, looking anxiously about him as he does so. He moves toward a large willow. Enter Two Prostitutes, one old, the other the Niece whom we have already met.*)

NIECE. Hello. Coming with me?

YANG SUN (*taken aback*). If you'd like to buy me a dinner.

OLD WHORE. Buy you a dinner! (*To the Niece.*) Oh, we know him—it's the unemployed pilot. Waste no time on him!

NIECE. But he's the only man left in the park. And it's going to rain.

OLD WHORE. Oh, how do you know?

(*And they pass by. Yang Sun again looks about him, again takes his rope, and this time throws it round a branch of the willow tree. Again he is interrupted. It is the Two Prostitutes returning—and in such a hurry they don't notice him.*)

NIECE. It's going to pour!

(*Enter Shen Te.*)

OLD WHORE. There's that *gorgon* Shen Te! That *drove* your family out into the cold!

NIECE. It wasn't her. It was that cousin of hers. She offered to *pay* for the cakes. I've nothing against her.

OLD WHORE. I have, though. (*So that Shen Te can hear.*) Now where could the little lady be off to? She may be rich now but that won't stop her snatching our young men, will it?

SHEN TE. I'm going to the tearoom by the pond.

NIECE. Is it true what they say? You're marrying a widower—with three children?

SHEN TE. Yes. I'm just going to see him.

YANG SUN (*his patience at breaking point*). Move on there! This is a park, not a whorehouse!

OLD WHORE. Shut your mouth!

(*But the Two Prostitutes leave.*)

YANG SUN. Even in the farthest corner of the park, even when it's raining, you can't get rid of them! (*He spits.*)

SHEN TE (*overhearing this*). And what right have you to scold them? (*But at this point she sees the rope.*) Oh!

YANG SUN. Well, what are you staring at?

SHEN TE. That rope. What is it for?

YANG SUN. Think! Think! I haven't a penny. Even if I had, I wouldn't spend it on you. I'd buy a drink of water.

(*The rain starts.*)

SHEN TE (*still looking at the rope*). What is the rope for? You mustn't!

YANG SUN. What's it to you? Clear out!

SHEN TE (*irrelevantly*). It's raining.

YANG SUN. Well, don't try to come under this tree.

SHEN TE. Oh, no. (*She stays in the rain.*)

YANG SUN. Now go away. (*Pause.*) For one thing, I don't like your looks, you're bow-legged.

SHEN TE (*indignantly*). That's not true!

YANG SUN. Well, don't show 'em to me. Look, it's raining. You better come under this tree.

(*Slowly, she takes shelter under the tree.*)

SHEN TE. Why did you want to do it?

YANG SUN. You really want to know? (*Pause.*) To get rid of you! (*Pause.*) You know what a flyer is?

SHEN TE. Oh yes, I've met a lot of pilots. At the tearoom.

YANG SUN. You call *them* flyers? Think they know what a machine *is*? Just 'cause they have leather helmets? They gave the airfield director a bribe, that's the way *those* fellows got up in the air! Try one of them out sometime. "Go up to two thousand feet," tell him, "then let it fall, then pick it up again with a flick of the wrist at the last moment." Know what he'll say to that? "It's not in my contract." Then again, there's the landing problem. It's like landing on your own backside. It's no different, planes are human. Those fools don't understand. (*Pause.*) And I'm the biggest fool for reading the book on flying in the Peking school and skipping the page where it says: "We've got enough flyers and we don't need you." I'm a mail pilot and no mail. You understand that?

SHEN TE (*shyly*). Yes. I do.

YANG SUN. No, you don't. You'd never understand that.

SHEN TE. When we were little we had a crane with a broken wing. He made friends with us and was very good-natured about our jokes. He would strut along behind us and call out to stop us going too fast for him. But every spring and autumn when the cranes flew over the villages in great swarms, he got quite restless. (*Pause.*) I understood that. (*She bursts out crying.*)

YANG SUN. Don't!

SHEN TE (*quieting down*). No.

YANG SUN. It's bad for the complexion.

SHEN TE (*sniffing*). I've stopped.

(*She dries her tears on her big sleeve. Leaning against the tree, but not looking at her, he reaches for her face.*)

YANG SUN. You can't even wipe your own face. (*He is wiping it for her with his handkerchief. Pause.*)

SHEN TE (*still sobbing*). I don't know *anything!*

YANG SUN. You interrupted me! What for?

SHEN TE. It's such a rainy day. You only wanted to do . . . *that* because it's such a rainy day.

(*To the audience.*)

> In our country
> The evenings should never be somber
> High bridges over rivers
> The grey hour between night and morning
> And the long, long winter:
> Such things are dangerous
> For, with all the misery,
> A very little is enough
> And men throw away an unbearable life.

(*Pause.*)

YANG SUN. Talk about yourself for a change.

SHEN TE. What about me? I have a shop.

YANG SUN (*incredulous*). You have a shop, do you? Never thought of walking the streets?

SHEN TE. I *did* walk the streets. Now I have a shop.

YANG SUN (*ironically*). A gift of the gods, I suppose!

SHEN TE. How did you know?

YANG SUN (*even more ironical*). One fine evening the gods turned up saying: here's some money!

SHEN TE (*quickly*). One fine morning.

YANG SUN (*fed up*). This isn't much of an entertainment.

(*Pause.*)

SHEN TE. I can play the zither a little. (*Pause.*) And I can mimic men. (*Pause.*) I got the shop, so the first thing I did was to give my zither away. I can be as stupid as a fish now, I said to myself, and it won't matter.

> I'm rich now, I said
> I walk alone, I sleep alone
> For a whole year, I said
> I'll have nothing to do with a man.

YANG SUN. And now you're marrying one! The one at the tearoom by the pond?

(*Shen Te is silent.*)

YANG SUN. What do you know about love?

SHEN TE. Everything.

YANG SUN. Nothing. (*Pause.*) Or d'you just mean you enjoyed it?

SHEN TE. No.

YANG SUN (*again without turning to look at her, he strokes her cheek with his hand*). You like that?

SHEN TE. Yes.

YANG SUN (*breaking off*). You're easily satisfied, I must say. (*Pause.*) What a town!

SHEN TE. You have no friends?

YANG SUN (*defensively*). Yes, I have! (*Change of tone.*) But they don't want to hear I'm still unemployed. "What?" they ask. "Is there still water in the sea?" You have friends?

SHEN TE (*hesitating*). Just a . . . cousin.

YANG SUN. Watch him carefully.

SHEN TE. He only came once. Then he went away. He won't be back.

(*Yang Sun is looking away.*)

But to be without hope, they say, is to be without goodness!

(*Pause.*)

YANG SUN. Go on talking. A voice is a voice.

SHEN TE. Once, when I was a little girl, I fell, with a load of brushwood. An old man picked me up. He gave me a penny too. Isn't it funny how people who don't have very much like to give some of it away? They must like to show what they can do, and how could they show it better than by being kind? Being wicked is just like being clumsy. When we sing a song, or build a machine, or plant some rice, we're being kind. You're kind.

YANG SUN. You make it sound easy.

SHEN TE. Oh, no. (*Little pause.*) Oh! A drop of rain!

YANG SUN. Where'd you feel it?

SHEN TE. Between the eyes.

YANG SUN. Near the right eye? Or the left?

SHEN TE. Near the left eye.

YANG SUN. Oh, good. (*He is getting sleepy.*) So you're through with men, eh?

SHEN TE (*with a smile*). But I'm not bow-legged.

YANG SUN. Perhaps not.

SHEN TE. Definitely not.

(*Pause.*)

YANG SUN (*leaning wearily against the willow*). I haven't had a drop to drink all day, I haven't eaten anything for *two* days. I couldn't love you if I tried.

(*Pause.*)

SHEN TE. I like it in the rain.

(*Enter Wong the Water Seller, singing.*)

THE SONG OF THE WATER SELLER IN THE RAIN
"Buy my water," I am yelling
And my fury restraining
For no water I'm selling
'Cause it's raining, 'cause it's raining!
    I keep yelling: "Buy my water!"
    But no one's buying
    Athirst and dying
    And drinking and paying!
    Buy water!
    Buy water, you dogs!

Nice to dream of lovely weather!
Think of all the consternation
Were there no precipitation
Half a dozen years together!
Can't you hear them shrieking: "Water!"
Pretending they adore me!
They all would go down on their knees before me!
Down on your knees!
Go down on your knees, you dogs!
What are lawns and hedges thinking?
What are fields and forests saying?
"At the cloud's breast we are drinking!
And we've no idea who's paying!"
>I keep yelling: "Buy my water!"
>But no one's buying
>Athirst and dying
>And drinking and paying!
>Buy water!
>Buy water, you dogs!

(The rain has stopped now. Shen Te sees Wong and runs toward him.)

SHEN TE. Wong! You're back! Your carrying pole's at the shop.

WONG. Oh, thank you, Shen Te. And how is life treating *you?*

SHEN TE. I've just met a brave and clever man. And I want to buy him a cup of your water.

WONG (*bitterly*). Throw back your head and open your mouth and you'll have all the water you need—

SHEN TE (*tenderly*).
>I want *your* water, Wong
>The water that has tired you so
>The water that you carried all this way
>The water that is hard to sell because it's been raining
>I need it for the young man over there—he's a flyer!
>>A flyer is a bold man:
>>Braving the storms
>>In company with the clouds
>>He crosses the heavens
>>And brings to friends in far-away lands
>>The friendly mail!

(She pays Wong, and runs over to Yang Sun with the cup. But Yang Sun is fast asleep.)

(Calling to Wong, with a laugh.) He's fallen asleep! Despair and rain and I have worn him out!

SCENE 3A

(Wong's den. The sewer pipe is transparent, and the Gods again appear to Wong in a dream.)

WONG (*radiant*). I've seen her, illustrious ones! And she hasn't changed!

FIRST GOD. That's good to hear.

WONG. She loves someone.

FIRST GOD. Let's hope the experience gives her the strength to stay good!

WONG. It does. She's doing good deeds all the time.

FIRST GOD. Ah? What sort? What sort of good deeds, Wong?

WONG. Well, she has a kind word for everybody.

FIRST GOD (*eagerly*). And then?

WONG. Hardly anyone leaves her shop without tobacco in his pocket—even if he can't pay for it.

FIRST GOD. Not bad at all. Next?

WONG. She's putting up a family of eight.

FIRST GOD (*gleefully, to the Second God*). Eight! (*To Wong.*) And that's not all, of course!

WONG. She bought a cup of water from me even though it was raining.

FIRST GOD. Yes, yes, yes, all these smaller good deeds!

WONG. Even they run into money. A little tobacco shop doesn't make so much.

FIRST GOD (*sententiously*). A prudent gardener works miracles on the smallest plot.

WONG. She hands out rice every morning. That eats up half her earnings.

FIRST GOD (*a little disappointed*). Well, as a beginning . . .

WONG. They call her the Angel of the Slums—whatever the Carpenter may say!

FIRST GOD. What's this? A carpenter speaks ill of her?

WONG. Oh, he only says her shelves weren't paid for in full.

SECOND GOD (*who has a bad cold and can't pronounce his n's and m's*). What's this? Not paying a carpenter? Why was that?

WONG. I suppose she didn't have the money.

SECOND GOD (*severely*). One pays what one owes, that's in our book of rules! First the letter of the law, then the spirit!

WONG. But it wasn't Shen Te, illustrious ones, it was her cousin. She called *him* in to help.

SECOND GOD. Then her cousin must never darken her threshold again!

WONG. Very well, illustrious ones! But in fairness to Shen Te, let me say that her cousin is a businessman.

FIRST GOD. Perhaps we should inquire what is customary? I find business quite unintelligible. But everybody's doing it. Business! Did the Seven Good Kings do business? Did Kung the Just sell fish?

SECOND GOD. In any case, such a thing must not occur again!

(The Gods start to leave.)

THIRD GOD. Forgive us for taking this tone with you, Wong, we haven't been getting enough sleep. The rich recommend us to the poor, and the poor tell us they haven't enough room.

SECOND GOD. Feeble, feeble, the best of them!

FIRST GOD. No great deeds! No heroic daring!

THIRD GOD. On such a *small* scale!

SECOND GOD. Sincere, yes, but what is actually *achieved?*
(One can no longer hear them.)

WONG (*calling after them*). I've thought of something, illustrious ones: Perhaps you shouldn't ask—too—much—all—at—once!

SCENE 4

(*The square in front of Shen Te's tobacco shop. Beside Shen Te's place, two other shops are seen: the carpet shop and a barber's. Morning. Outside Shen Te's the Grandfather, the Sister-in-Law, the Unemployed Man, and Mrs. Shin stand waiting.*)

SISTER-IN-LAW. She's been out all night again.

MRS. SHIN. No sooner did we get rid of that crazy cousin of hers than Shen Te herself starts carrying on! Maybe she does give us an ounce of rice now and then, but can you depend on her? Can you depend on her?

(*Loud voices from the Barber's.*)

VOICE OF SHU FU. What are you doing in my shop? Get out—at once!

VOICE OF WONG. But sir. They all let me sell . . .

(*Wong comes staggering out of the barber's shop pursued by Mr. Shu Fu, the barber, a fat man carrying a heavy curling iron.*)

SHU FU. Get out, I said! Pestering my customers with your slimy old water! Get out! Take your cup!

(*He holds out the cup. Wong reaches out for it. Mr. Shu Fu strikes his hand with the curling iron, which is hot. Wong howls.*)

You had it coming, my man!

(*Puffing, he returns to his shop. The Unemployed Man picks up the cup and gives it to Wong.*)

UNEMPLOYED MAN. You can report that to the police.

WONG. My hand! It's smashed up!

UNEMPLOYED MAN. Any bones broken?

WONG. I can't move my fingers.

UNEMPLOYED MAN. Sit down. I'll put some water on it.

(*Wong sits.*)

MRS. SHIN. The water won't cost you anything.

SISTER-IN-LAW. You might have got a bandage from Miss Shen Te till she took to staying out all night. It's a scandal.

MRS. SHIN (*despondently*). If you ask me, she's forgotten we ever existed!

(*Enter Shen Te down the street, with a dish of rice.*)

SHEN TE (*to the audience*). How wonderful to see Setzuan in the early morning! I always used to stay in bed with my dirty blanket over my head afraid to wake up. This morning I saw the newspapers being delivered by little boys, the streets being washed by strong men, and fresh vegetables coming in from the country on ox carts. It's a long walk from where Yang Sun lives, but I feel lighter at every step. They say you walk on air when you're in love, but it's even better walking on the rough earth, on the hard cement. In the early morning, the old city looks like a great rubbish heap. Nice, though—with all its little lights. And the sky, so pink, so transparent, before the dust comes and muddies it! What a lot you miss if you never see your city rising from its slumbers like an honest old craftsman pumping his lungs full of air and reaching for his tools, as the poet says! (*Cheerfully, to her waiting guests.*) Good morning, everyone, here's your rice! (*Distributing the rice, she comes upon Wong.*) Good morning, Wong, I'm quite lightheaded today. On my way over, I looked at myself in all the shop windows. I'd love to be beautiful.

(*She slips into the carpet shop. Mr. Shu Fu has just emerged from his shop.*)

SHU FU (*to the audience*). It surprises me how beautiful Miss Shen Te is looking today! I never gave her a passing thought before. But now I've been gazing upon her comely form for exactly three minutes! I begin to suspect I am in love with her. She is overpoweringly attractive! (*Crossly, to Wong.*) Be off with you, rascal!

(*He returns to his shop. Shen Te comes back out of the carpet shop with the Old Man, its proprietor, and his wife—whom we have already met—the Old Woman. Shen Te is wearing a shawl. The Old Man is holding up a looking glass for her.*)

OLD WOMAN. Isn't it lovely? We'll give you a reduction because there's a little hole in it.

SHEN TE (*looking at another shawl on the Old Woman's arm*). The other one's nice too.

OLD WOMAN (*smiling*). Too bad there's no hole in that!

SHEN TE. That's right. My shop doesn't make very much.

OLD WOMAN. And your good deeds eat it all up! Be more careful, my dear . . .

SHEN TE (*trying on the shawl with the hole*). Just now, I'm lightheaded! Does the color suit me?

OLD WOMAN. You'd better ask a man.

SHEN TE (*to the Old Man*). Does the color suit me?

OLD MAN. You'd better ask your young friend.

SHEN TE. I'd like to have your opinion.

OLD MAN. It suits you, very well. But wear it this way: the dull side out.

(*Shen Te pays up.*)

OLD WOMAN. If you decide you don't like it, you can exchange it. (*She pulls Shen Te to one side.*) Has he got money?

SHEN TE (*with a laugh*). Yang Sun? Oh, no.

OLD WOMAN. Then how're you going to pay your rent?

SHEN TE. I'd forgotten about that.

OLD WOMAN. And next Monday is the first of the month! Miss Shen Te, I've got something to say to you. After we (*indicating her husband*) got to know you, we had our doubts about that marriage ad. We thought it would be better if you'd let *us* help you. Out of our savings. We reckon we could lend you two hundred silver dollars. We don't need anything in writing—you could pledge us your tobacco stock.

SHEN TE. You're prepared to lend money to a person like me?

OLD WOMAN. It's folks like you that need it. We'd think twice about lending anything to your cousin.

OLD MAN (*coming up*). All settled, my dear?

SHEN TE. I wish the gods could have heard what your wife was just saying, Mr. Ma. They're looking for good people who're happy—and helping me makes you happy because you know it was love that got me into difficulties!

(*The old couple smile knowingly at each other.*)

OLD MAN. And here's the money, Miss Shen Te.

(*He hands her an envelope. Shen Te takes it. She bows. They bow back. They return to their shop.*)

SHEN TE (*holding up her envelope*). Look, Wong, here's six months' rent! Don't you believe in miracles now? And how do you like my new shawl?

WONG. For the young fellow I saw you with in the park?

(*Shen Te nods.*)

MRS. SHIN. Never mind all that. It's time you took a look at his hand!

SHEN TE. Have you hurt your hand?

MRS. SHIN. That barber smashed it with his hot curling iron. Right in front of our eyes.

SHEN TE (*shocked at herself*). And I never noticed! We must get you to a doctor this minute or who knows what will happen?

UNEMPLOYED MAN. It's not a doctor he should see, it's a judge. He can ask for compensation. The barber's filthy rich.

WONG. You think I have a chance?

MRS. SHIN (*with relish*). If it's really good and smashed. But is it?

WONG. I think so. It's very swollen. Could I get a pension?

MRS. SHIN. You'd need a witness.

WONG. Well, you all saw it. You could all testify.

(*He looks round. The Unemployed Man, the Grandfather, and the Sister-in-Law are all sitting against the wall of the shop eating rice. Their concentration on eating is complete.*)

SHEN TE (*to Mrs. Shin*). You saw it yourself.

MRS. SHIN. I want nothin' to do with the police. It's against my principles.

SHEN TE (*to Sister-in-Law*). What about you?

SISTER-IN-LAW. Me? I wasn't looking.

SHEN TE (*to the Grandfather, coaxingly*). Grandfather, *you'll* testify, won't you?

SISTER-IN-LAW. And a lot of good that will do. He's simple-minded.

SHEN TE (*to the Unemployed Man*). You seem to be the only witness left.

UNEMPLOYED MAN. My testimony would only hurt him. I've been picked up twice for begging.

SHEN TE. Your brother is assaulted, and you shut your eyes?

He is hit, cries out in pain, and you are silent?
The beast prowls, chooses and seizes his victim, and you say:
"Because we showed no displeasure, he has spared us."
If no one present will be a witness, I will. I'll say I saw it.

MRS. SHIN (*solemnly*). The name for that is perjury.

WONG. I don't know if I can accept that. Though maybe I'll have to. (*Looking at his hand.*) Is it swollen enough, do you think? The swelling's not going down?

UNEMPLOYED MAN. No, no, the swelling's holding up well.

WONG. Yes. It's *more* swollen if anything. Maybe my wrist is broken after all. I'd better see a judge at once.

(*Holding his hand very carefully, and fixing his eyes on it, he runs off. Mrs. Shin goes quickly into the barber's shop.*)

UNEMPLOYED MAN (*seeing her*). She is getting on the right side of Mr. Shu Fu.

SISTER-IN-LAW. You and I can't change the world, Shen Te.

SHEN TE. Go away! Go away all of you!

(*The Unemployed Man, the Sister-in-Law, and the Grandfather stalk off, eating and sulking.*)

(*To the audience.*)

They've stopped answering
They stay put
They do as they're told
They don't care
Nothing can make them look up
But the smell of food.

(*Enter Mrs. Yang, Yang Sun's mother, out of breath.*)

MRS. YANG. Miss. Shen Te. My son has told me everything. I am Mrs. Yang, Sun's mother. Just think. He's got an offer. Of a job as a pilot. A letter has just come. From the director of the airfield in Peking!

SHEN TE. So he can fly again? Isn't that wonderful!

MRS. YANG (*less breathlessly all the time*). They won't give him the job for nothing. They want five hundred silver dollars.

SHEN TE. We can't let money stand in his way, Mrs. Yang!

MRS. YANG. If only you could help him out!

SHEN TE. I have the shop. I can try! (*She embraces Mrs. Yang.*) I happen to have two hundred with me now. Take it. (*She gives her the old couple's money.*) It was a loan but they said I could repay it with my tobacco stock.

MRS. YANG. And they were calling Sun the Dead Pilot of Setzuan! A friend in need!

SHEN TE. We must find another three hundred.

MRS. YANG. How?

SHEN TE. Let me think. (*Slowly.*) I know someone who can help. I didn't want to call on his services again, he's hard and cunning. But a flyer must fly. And I'll make this the last time.

(*Distant sound of a plane.*)

MRS. YANG. If the man you mentioned can do it. . . . Oh, look, there's the morning mail plane, heading for Peking!

SHEN TE. The pilot can see us, let's wave!

(*They wave. The noise of the engine is louder.*)

MRS. YANG. You know that pilot up there?

SHEN TE. Wave, Mrs. Yang! I know the pilot who *will* be up there. He gave up hope. But he'll do it now. One man to raise himself above the misery, above us all.

(*To the audience.*)

> Yang Sun, my lover:
> Braving the storms
> In company with the clouds
> Crossing the heavens
> And bringing to friends in far-away lands
> The friendly mail!

SCENE 4A

(*In front of the inner curtain. Enter Shen Te, carrying Shui Ta's mask. She sings.*)

THE SONG OF DEFENSELESSNESS

> In our country
> A useful man needs luck
> Only if he finds strong backers can he prove himself
>   useful
> The good can't defend themselves and
> Even the gods are defenseless.
>
> Oh, why don't the gods have their own ammunition
> And launch against badness their own expedition
> Enthroning the good and preventing sedition
> And bringing the world to a peaceful condition?
>
> Oh, why don't the gods do the buying and selling
> Injustice forbidding, starvation dispelling
> Give bread to each city and joy to each dwelling?
> Oh, why don't the gods do the buying and selling?

(*She puts on Shui Ta's mask and sings in his voice.*)

> You can only help one of your luckless brothers
> By trampling down a dozen others
>
> Why is it the gods do not feel indignation
> And come down in fury to end exploitation
> Defeat all defeat and forbid desperation

Refusing to tolerate such toleration?
Why is it?

SCENE 5

(*Shen Te's tobacco shop. Behind the counter, Mr. Shui Ta, reading the paper. Mrs. Shin is cleaning up. She talks and he takes no notice.*)

MRS. SHIN. And when certain' rumors get about, what *happens* to a little place like this? It goes to pot. *I* know. So, if you want my advice, Mr. Shui Ta, find out just what exactly has been going on between Miss Shen Te and that Yang Sun from Yellow Street. And remember: a certain interest in Miss Shen Te has been expressed by the barber next door, a man with twelve houses and only one wife, who, for that matter, is likely to drop off at any time. A certain interest has been expressed. (*She relishes the phrase.*) He was even inquiring about her means and, if *that* doesn't prove a man is getting serious, what would? (*Still getting no response, she leaves with her bucket.*)

YANG SUN'S VOICE. Is that Miss Shen Te's tobacco shop?

MRS. SHIN'S VOICE. Yes, it is, but it's Mr. Shui Ta who's here today.

(*Shui Ta runs to the looking glass with the short, light steps of Shen Te, and is just about to start primping, when he realizes his mistake, and turns away, with a short laugh. Enter Yang Sun. Mrs. Shin enters behind him and slips into the back room to eavesdrop.*)

YANG SUN. I am Yang Sun.

(*Shui Ta bows.*)

Is Miss Shen Te in?

SHUI TA. No.

YANG SUN. I guess you know our relationship? (*He is inspecting the stock.*) Quite a place! And I thought she was just talking big. I'll be flying again, all right. (*He takes a cigar, solicits and receives a light from Shui Ta.*) You think we can squeeze the other three hundred out of the tobacco stock?

SHUI TA. May I ask if it is your intention to sell at once?

YANG SUN. It was decent of her to come out with the two hundred but they aren't much use with the other three hundred still missing.

SHUI TA. Shen Te was overhasty promising so much. She might have to sell the shop itself to raise it. Haste, they say, is the wind that blows the house down.

YANG SUN. Oh, she isn't a girl to keep a man waiting. For one thing or the other, if you take my meaning.

SHUI TA. I take your meaning.

YANG SUN (*leering*). Uh, huh.

SHUI TA. Would you explain what the five hundred silver dollars are for?

YANG SUN. Trying to sound me out? Very well. The director of the Peking airfield is a friend of mine from flying school. I give him five hundred: he gets me the job.

SHUI TA. The price is high.

YANG SUN. Not as these things go. He'll have to fire one of the present pilots—for negligence. Only the man he has in mind isn't negligent. Not easy, you understand. You needn't mention that part of it to Shen Te.

SHUI TA (*looking intently at Yang Sun*). Mr. Yang Sun, you are asking my cousin to give up her possessions, leave her friends, and place her entire fate in your hands. I presume you intend to marry her?

YANG SUN. I'd be prepared to.

(*Slight pause.*)

SHUI TA. Those two hundred silver dollars would pay the rent here for six months. If you were Shen Te wouldn't you be tempted to continue in business?

YANG SUN. What? Can you imagine Yang Sun the Flyer behind a counter? (*In an oily voice.*) "A strong cigar or a mild one, worthy sir?" Not in this century!

SHUI TA. My cousin wishes to follow the promptings of her heart, and, from her own point of view, she may even have what is called the right to love. Accordingly, she has commissioned me to help you to this post. There is nothing here that I am not empowered to turn immediately into cash. Mrs. Mi Tzu, the landlady, will advise me about the sale.

(*Enter Mrs. Mi Tzu.*)

MRS. MI TZU. Good morning, Mr. Shui Ta, you wish to see me about the rent? As you know it falls due the day after tomorrow.

SHUI TA. Circumstances have changed, Mrs. Mi Tzu: my cousin is getting married. Her future husband here, Mr. Yang Sun, will be taking her to Peking. I am interested in selling the tobacco stock.

MRS. MI TZU. How much are you asking, Mr. Shui Ta?

YANG SUN. Three hundred sil—

SHUI TA. Five hundred silver dollars.

MRS. MI TZU. How much did she pay for it, Mr. Shui Ta?

SHUI TA. A thousand. And very little has been sold.

MRS. MI TZU. She was robbed. But I'll make you a special offer if you'll promise to be out by the day after tomorrow. Three hundred silver dollars.

YANG SUN (*shrugging*). Take it, man, take it.

SHUI TA. It is not enough.

YANG SUN. Why not? Why not? Certainly, it's enough.

SHUI TA. Five hundred silver dollars.

YANG SUN. But why? We only need three!

SHUI TA (*to Mrs. Mi Tzu*). Excuse me. (*Takes Yang Sun on one side.*) The tobacco stock is pledged to the old couple who gave my cousin the two hundred.

YANG SUN. Is it in writing?

SHUI TA. No.

YANG SUN (*to Mrs. Mi Tzu*). Three hundred will do.

MRS. MI TZU. Of course, I need an assurance that Miss Shen Te is not in debt.

YANG SUN. Mr. Shui Ta?

SHUI TA. She is not in debt.

YANG SUN. When can you let us have the money?

MRS. MI TZU. The day after tomorrow. And remember: I'm doing this because I have a soft spot in my heart for young lovers! (*Exit.*)

YANG SUN (*calling after her*). Boxes, jars and sacks—three hundred for the lot and the pain's over! (*To Shui Ta.*) Where else can we raise money by the day after tomorrow?

SHUI TA. Nowhere. Haven't you enough for the trip and the first few weeks?

YANG SUN. Oh, certainly.

SHUI TA. How much, exactly?

YANG SUN. Oh, I'll dig it up, if I have to steal it.

SHUI TA. I see.

YANG SUN. Well, don't fall off the roof. I'll get to Peking somehow.

SHUI TA. Two people can't travel for nothing.

YANG SUN (*not giving Shui Ta a chance to answer*). I'm leaving *her* behind. No millstones round *my* neck!

SHUI TA. Oh.

YANG SUN. Don't look at me like that!

SHUI TA. How precisely is my cousin to live?

YANG SUN. Oh, you'll think of something.

SHUI TA. A small request, Mr. Yang Sun. Leave the two hundred silver dollars here until you can show me two tickets for Peking.

YANG SUN. You learn to mind your own business, Mr. Shui Ta.

SHUI TA. I'm afraid Miss Shen Te may not wish to sell the shop when she discovers that . . .

YANG SUN. You don't know women. She'll want to. Even then.

SHUI TA (*a slight outburst*). She is a human being, sir! And not devoid of common sense!

YANG SUN. Shen Te is a woman: she *is* devoid of common sense. I only have to lay my hand on her shoulder, and church bells ring.

SHUI TA (*with difficulty*). Mr. Yang Sun!

YANG SUN. Mr. Shui Whatever-it-is!

SHUI TA. My cousin is devoted to you . . . because . . .

YANG SUN. Because I have my hands on her breasts. Give me a cigar. (*He takes one for himself, stuffs a few more in his pocket, then changes his mind and takes the whole box.*) Tell her I'll marry her, then bring me the three hundred. Or let her bring it. One or the other. (*Exit.*)

MRS. SHIN (*sticking her head out of the back room*). Well, he has your cousin under his thumb, and doesn't care if all Yellow Street knows it!

SHUI TA (*crying out*). I've lost my shop! And he doesn't love me! (*He runs berserk through the room, repeating these lines incoherently. Then stops suddenly, and addresses Mrs. Shin.*) Mrs. Shin, you grew up in the gutter, like me. Are we lacking in hardness? I doubt it. If you steal a penny from me,

I'll take you by the throat till you spit it out! You'd do the same to me. The times are bad, this city is hell, but we're like ants, we keep coming, up and up the walls, however smooth! Till bad luck comes. Being in love, for instance. *One* weakness is enough, and love is the deadliest.

MRS. SHIN (*emerging from the back room*). You should have a little talk with Mr. Shu Fu the Barber. He's a real gentleman and just the thing for your cousin. (*She runs off.*)

SHUI TA.

A caress becomes a stranglehold
A sigh of love turns to a cry of fear
Why are there vultures circling in the air?
A girl is going to meet her lover.

(*Shui Ta sits down and Mr. Shu Fu enters with Mrs. Shin.*)

Mr. Shu Fu?

SHU FU. Mr. Shui Ta.

(*They both bow.*)

SHUI TA. I am told that you have expressed a certain interest in my cousin Shen Te. Let me set aside all propriety and confess: she is at this moment in grave danger.

SHU FU. Oh, dear!

SHUI TA. She has lost her shop, Mr. Shu Fu.

SHU FU. The charm of Miss Shen Te, Mr. Shui Ta, derives from the goodness, not of her shop, but of her heart. Men call her the Angel of the Slums.

SHUI TA. Yet her goodness has cost her two hundred silver dollars in a single day: we must put a stop to it.

SHU FU. Permit me to differ, Mr. Shui Ta. Let us rather, open wide the gates to such goodness! Every morning, with pleasure tinged by affection, I watch her charitable ministrations. For they are hungry, and she giveth them to eat! Four of them, to be precise. Why only four? I ask. Why not four hundred? I hear she has been seeking shelter for the homeless. What about my humble cabins behind the cattle run? They are at her disposal. And so forth. And so on. Mr. Shui Ta, do you think Miss Shen Te could be persuaded to listen to certain ideas of mine? Ideas like these?

SHUI TA. Mr. Shu Fu, she would be honored.

(*Enter Wong and the Policeman. Mr. Shu Fu turns abruptly away and studies the shelves.*)

WONG. Is Miss Shen Te here?

SHUI TA. No.

WONG. I am Wong the Water Seller. You are Mr. Shui Ta?

SHUI TA. I am.

WONG. I am a friend of Shen Te's.

SHUI TA. An intimate friend, I hear.

WONG (*to the Policeman*). You see? (*To Shui Ta.*) It's because of my hand.

POLICEMAN. He hurt his hand, sir, that's a fact.

SHUI TA (*quickly*). You need a sling, I see. (*He takes a shawl from the back room, and throws it to Wong.*)

WONG. But that's her new shawl!

SHUI TA. She has no more use for it.

WONG. But she bought it to please someone!

SHUI TA. It happens to be no longer necessary.

WONG (*making the sling*). She is my only witness.

POLICEMAN. Mr. Shui Ta, your cousin is supposed to have seen the Barber hit the Water Seller with a curling iron.

SHUI TA. I'm afraid my cousin was not present at the time.

WONG. But she was, sir! Just ask her! Isn't she in?

SHUI TA (*gravely*). Mr. Wong, my cousin has her own troubles. You wouldn't wish her to add to them by committing perjury?

WONG. But it was she that told me to go to the judge!

SHUI TA. Was the judge supposed to heal your hand?

(*Mr. Shu Fu turns quickly around. Shui Ta bows to Shu Fu, and vice versa.*)

WONG (*taking the sling off, and putting it back*). I see how it is.

POLICEMAN. Well, I'll be on my way. (*To Wong.*) And you be careful. If Mr. Shu Fu wasn't a man who tempers justice with mercy, as the saying is, you'd be in jail for libel. Be off with you!

(*Exit Wong, followed by Policeman.*)

SHUI TA. Profound apologies, Mr. Shu Fu.

SHU FU. Not at all, Mr. Shui Ta. (*Pointing to the shawl.*) The episode is over?

SHUI TA. It may take her time to recover. There are some fresh wounds.

SHU FU. We shall be discreet. Delicate. A short vacation could be arranged . . .

SHUI TA. First, of course, you and she would have to talk things over.

SHU FU. At a small supper in a small, but high-class, restaurant.

SHUI TA. I'll go and find her. (*Exit into back room.*)

MRS. SHIN (*sticking her head in again*). Time for congratulations, Mr. Shu Fu?

SHU FU. Ah, Mrs. Shin! Please inform Miss Shen Te's guests they may take shelter in the cabins behind the cattle run!

(*Mrs. Shin nods, grinning.*)

(*To the audience.*) Well? What do you think of me, ladies and gentlemen? What could a man do more? Could he be less selfish? More farsighted? A small supper in a small but . . . Does that bring rather vulgar and clumsy thoughts into your mind? Ts, ts, ts. Nothing of the sort will occur. She won't even be touched. Not even accidentally while passing the salt. An exchange of ideas only. Over the flowers on the table— white chrysanthemums, by the way (He writes down a note of this.)—yes, over the white chrysanthemums, two young souls will . . . shall I say "find each other"? We shall NOT exploit the misfortune of others. Understanding? Yes. An offer of assistance? Certainly. But quietly. Almost inaudibly. Perhaps with a single glance. A glance that could also—mean more.

MRS. SHIN (*coming forward*). Everything under control, Mr. Shu Fu?

SHU FU. Oh, Mrs. Shin, what do you know about this worthless rascal Yang Sun?

MRS. SHIN. Why, he's the most worthless rascal . . .

SHU FU. Is he really? You're sure? (*As she opens her mouth.*) From now on, he doesn't exist! Can't be found anywhere!

(*Enter Yang Sun.*)

YANG SUN. What's been going on here?

MRS. SHIN. Shall I call Mr. Shui Ta, Mr. Shu Fu? He wouldn't want strangers in here!

SHU FU. Mr. Shui Ta is in conference with Miss Shen Te. Not to be disturbed!

YANG SUN. Shen Te here? I didn't see her come in. What kind of conference?

SHU FU (*not letting him enter the back room*). Patience, dear sir! And if by chance I have an inkling who you are, pray take note that Miss Shen Te and I are about to announce our engagement.

YANG SUN. What?

MRS. SHIN. You didn't expect that, did you?

(*Yang Sun is trying to push past the barber into the back room when Shen Te comes out.*)

SHU FU. My dear Shen Te, ten thousand apologies! Perhaps you . . .

YANG SUN. What is it, Shen Te? Have you gone crazy?

SHEN TE (*breathless*). My cousin and Mr. Shu Fu have come to an understanding. They wish me to hear Mr. Shu Fu's plans for helping the poor.

YANG SUN. Your cousin wants to part us.

SHEN TE. Yes.

YANG SUN. And you've agreed to it?

SHEN TE. Yes.

YANG SUN. They told you I was bad.

(*Shen Te is silent.*)

And suppose I am. Does that make me need you less? I'm low, Shen Te, I have no money, I don't do the right thing but at least I put up a fight! (*He is near her now, and speaks in an undertone.*) Have you no eyes? Look at him. Have you forgotten already?

SHEN TE. No.

YANG SUN. How it was raining?

SHEN TE. No.

YANG SUN. How you cut me down from the willow tree? Bought me water? Promised me money to fly with?

SHEN TE (*shakily*). Yang Sun, what do you want?

YANG SUN. I want you to come with me.

SHEN TE (*in a small voice*). Forgive me, Mr. Shu Fu, I want to go with Mr. Yang Sun.

YANG SUN. We're lovers you know. Give me the key to the shop.

(*Shen Te takes the key from around her neck. Yang Sun puts it on the counter. To Mrs. Shin.*)

Leave it under the mat when you're through. Let's go, Shen Te.

SHU FU. But this is rape! Mr. Shui Ta!!

YANG SUN (*to Shen Te*). Tell him not to shout.

SHEN TE. Please don't shout for my cousin, Mr. Shu Fu. He doesn't agree with me, I know, but he's wrong. (*To the audience.*)

I want to go with the man I love
I don't want to count the cost
I don't want to consider if it's wise
I don't want to know if he loves me
I want to go with the man I love.

YANG SUN. That's the spirit.

(*And the couple leave.*)

SCENE 5A

(*In front of the inner curtain. Shen Te in her wedding clothes, on the way to her wedding.*)

SHEN TE. Something terrible has happened. As I left the shop with Yang Sun, I found the old carpet dealer's wife waiting in the street, trembling all over. She told me her husband had taken to his bed—sick with all the worry and excitement over the two hundred silver dollars they lent me. She said it would be best if I gave it back now. Of course, I had to say I would. She said she couldn't quite trust my cousin Shui Ta or even my fiancé Yang Sun. There were tears in her eyes. With my emotions in an uproar, I threw myself into Yang Sun's arms, I couldn't resist him. The things he'd said to Shui Ta had taught Shen Te nothing. Sinking into his arms, I said to myself:

To let no one perish, not even oneself
To fill everyone with happiness, even oneself
Is so good

How could I have forgotten those two old people? Yang Sun swept me away like a small hurricane. But he's not a bad man, and he loves me. He'd rather work in the cement factory than owe his flying to a crime. Though, of course, flying is a great passion with Sun. Now, on the way to my wedding, I waver between fear and joy.

SCENE 6

(*The "private dining room" on the upper floor of a cheap restaurant in a poor section of town. With Shen Te: the*

Grandfather, the Sister-in-Law, the Niece, Mrs. Shin, the Unemployed Man. In a corner, alone, a Priest. A Waiter pouring wine. Downstage, Yang Sun talking to his mother. He wears a dinner jacket.)

YANG SUN. Bad news, Mamma. She came right out and told me she can't sell the shop for me. Some idiot is bringing a claim because he lent her the two hundred she gave you.

MRS. YANG. What did *you* say? Of course, you can't marry her now.

YANG SUN. It's no use saying anything to *her*. I've sent for her cousin, Mr. Shui Ta. He said there was nothing in writing.

MRS. YANG. Good idea. I'll go out and look for him. Keep an eye on things.

(*Exit Mrs. Yang. Shen Te has been pouring wine.*)

SHEN TE (*to the audience, pitcher in hand*). I wasn't mistaken in him. He's bearing up well. Though it must have been an awful blow—giving up flying. I do love him so. (*Calling across the room to him.*) Sun, you haven't drunk a toast with the bride!

YANG SUN. What do we drink to?

SHEN TE. Why, to the future!

YANG SUN. When the bridegroom's dinner jacket won't be a hired one!

SHEN TE. But when the bride's dress will still get rained on sometimes!

YANG SUN. To everything we ever wished for!

SHEN TE. May all our dreams come true!

(*They drink.*)

YANG SUN (*with loud conviviality*). And now, friends, before the wedding gets under way, I have to ask the bride a few questions. I've no idea what kind of a wife she'll make, and it worries me. (*Wheeling on Shen Te.*) For example. Can you make five cups of tea with three tea leaves?

SHEN TE. No.

YANG SUN. So I won't be getting very much tea. Can you sleep on a straw mattress the size of that book? (*He points to the large volume the Priest is reading.*)

SHEN TE. The two of us?

YANG SUN. The one of you.

SHEN TE. In that case, no.

YANG SUN. What a wife! I'm shocked!

(*While the audience is laughing, his mother returns. With a shrug of her shoulders, she tells Yang Sun the expected guest hasn't arrived. The Priest shuts the book with a bang, and makes for the door.*)

MRS. YANG. Where are *you* off to? It's only a matter of minutes.

PRIEST (*watch in hand*). Time goes on, Mrs. Yang, and I've another wedding to attend to. Also a funeral.

MRS. YANG (*irately*). D'you think we planned it this way? I was hoping to manage with one pitcher of wine, and we've run through two already. (*Points to empty pitcher.*

Loudly.) My dear Shen Te, I don't know where your cousin can be keeping himself!

SHEN TE. My cousin?

MRS. YANG. Certainly. I'm old fashioned enough to think such a close relative should attend the wedding.

SHEN TE. Oh, Sun, is it the three hundred silver dollars?

YANG SUN (*not looking her in the eye*). Are you deaf? Mother says she's old fashioned. And I say I'm considerate. We'll wait another fifteen minutes.

HUSBAND. Another fifteen minutes.

MRS. YANG (*addressing the company*). Now you all know, don't you, that my son is getting a job as a mail pilot?

SISTER-IN-LAW. In Peking, too, isn't it?

MRS. YANG. In Peking, too! The two of us are moving to Peking!

SHEN TE. Sun, tell your mother Peking is out of the question now.

YANG SUN. Your cousin'll tell her. If he agrees. I don't agree.

SHEN TE (*amazed, and dismayed*). Sun!

YANG SUN. I hate this godforsaken Setzuan. What people! Know what they look like when I half close my eyes? Horses! Whinnying, fretting, stamping, screwing their necks up! (*Loudly.*) And what is it the thunder says? They are su-per-flu-ous! (*He hammers out the syllables.*) They've run their last race! They can go trample themselves to death! (*Pause.*) I've got to get out of here.

SHEN TE. But I've promised the money to the old couple.

YANG SUN. And since you always do the wrong thing, it's lucky your cousin's coming. Have another drink.

SHEN TE (*quietly*). My cousin can't be coming.

YANG SUN. How d'you mean?

SHEN TE. My cousin can't be where I am.

YANG SUN. Quite a conundrum!

SHEN TE (*desperately*). Sun, I'm the one that loves you. Not my cousin. He was thinking of the job in Peking when he promised you the old couple's money—

YANG SUN. Right. And that's why he's bringing the three hundred silver dollars. Here—to my wedding.

SHEN TE. He is not bringing the three hundred silver dollars.

YANG SUN. Huh? What makes you think that?

SHEN TE (*looking into his eyes*). He says you only bought one ticket to Peking.

(*Short pause.*)

YANG SUN. That was yesterday. (*He pulls two tickets part way out of his inside pocket, making her look under his coat.*) Two tickets. I don't want Mother to know. She'll get left behind. I sold her furniture to buy these tickets, so you see . . .

SHEN TE. But what's to become of the old couple?

YANG SUN. What's to become of me? Have another drink. Or do you believe in moderation? If I drink, I fly again. And if you drink, you may learn to understand me.

SHEN TE. You want to fly. But I can't help you.

YANG SUN. "Here's a plane, my darling—but it's only got one wing!"

(The Waiter enters.)

WAITER. Mrs. Yang! Mrs. Yang!

MRS. YANG. Yes?

WAITER. Another pitcher of wine, ma'am?

MRS. YANG. We have enough, thanks. Drinking makes me sweat.

WAITER. Would you mind paying, ma'am?

MRS. YANG *(to everyone)*. Just be patient a few moments longer, everyone, Mr. Shui Ta is on his way over! *(To the Waiter.)* Don't be a spoilsport.

WAITER. I can't let you leave till you've paid your bill, ma'am.

MRS. YANG. But they know me here!

WAITER. That's just it.

PRIEST *(ponderously getting up)*. I humbly take my leave. *(And he does.)*

MRS. YANG *(to the others, desperately)*. Stay where you are, everybody! The priest says he'll be back in two minutes!

YANG SUN. It's no good, Mamma. Ladies and gentlemen, Mr. Shui Ta still hasn't arrived and the priest has gone home. We won't detain you any longer.

(They are leaving now.)

GRANDFATHER *(in the doorway, having forgotten to put his glass down)*. To the bride! *(He drinks, puts down the glass, and follows the others.)*

(Pause.)

SHEN TE. Shall I go too?

YANG SUN. You? Aren't you the bride? Isn't this your wedding? *(He drags her across the room, tearing her wedding dress.)* If we can wait, you can wait. Mother calls me her falcon. She wants to see me in the clouds. But I think it may be St. Nevercome's Day before she'll go to the door and see my plane thunder by. *(Pause. He pretends the guests are still present.)* Why such a lull in the conversation, ladies and gentlemen? Don't you like it here? The ceremony is only slightly postponed—because an important guest is expected at any moment. Also because the bride doesn't know what love is. While we're waiting, the bridegroom will sing a little song. *(He does so.)*

THE SONG OF ST. NEVERCOME'S DAY

On a certain day, as is generally known,
  One and all will be shouting: Hooray, hooray!
For the beggar maid's son has a solid-gold throne
  And the day is St. Nevercome's Day
  On St. Nevercome's, Nevercome's, Nevercome's Day
He'll sit on his solid-gold throne

Oh, hooray, hooray! That day goodness will pay!
  That day badness will cost you your head!
And merit and money will smile and be funny
  While exchanging salt and bread
On St. Nevercome's, Nevercome's, Nevercome's Day
  While exchanging salt and bread

And the grass, oh, the grass will look down at the sky
  And the pebbles will roll up the stream
And all men will be good without batting an eye
  They will make of our earth a dream
On St. Nevercome's, Nevercome's, Nevercome's Day
  They will make of our earth a dream

And as for me, that's the day I shall be
  A flyer and one of the best
Unemployed man, you will have work to do
  Washerwoman, you'll get your rest
On St. Nevercome's, Nevercome's, Nevercome's Day
  Washerwoman, you'll get your rest

MRS. YANG. It looks like he's not coming.

(The three of them sit looking at the door.)

SCENE 6A

(Wong's den. The sewer pipe is again transparent and again the Gods appear to Wong in a dream.)

WONG. I'm so glad you've come, illustrious ones. It's Shen Te. She's in great trouble from following the rule about loving thy neighbor. Perhaps she's *too* good for this world!

FIRST GOD. Nonsense! You are eaten up by lice and doubts!

WONG. Forgive me, illustrious one, I only meant you might deign to intervene.

FIRST GOD. Out of the question! My colleague here intervened in some squabble or other only yesterday. *(He points to the Third God who has a black eye.)* The results are before us!

WONG. She had to call on her cousin again. But not even he could help. I'm afraid the shop is done for.

THIRD GOD *(a little concerned)*. Perhaps we should help after all?

FIRST GOD. The gods help those that help themselves.

WONG. What if we *can't* help ourselves, illustrious ones?

(Slight pause.)

SECOND GOD. Try, anyway! Suffering ennobles!

FIRST GOD. Our faith in Shen Te is unshaken!

THIRD GOD. We certainly haven't found any *other* good people. You can see where we spend our nights from the straw on our clothes.

WONG. You might help her find her way by—

FIRST GOD. The good man finds his own way here below!

SECOND GOD. The good woman too.

FIRST GOD. The heavier the burden, the greater her strength!

THIRD GOD. We're only onlookers, you know.

FIRST GOD. And everything will be all right in the end, O ye of little faith!

(They are gradually disappearing through these last lines.)

SCENE 7

(*The yard behind Shen Te's shop. A few articles of furniture on a cart. Shen Te and Mrs. Shin are taking the washing off the line.*)

MRS. SHIN. If you ask me, you should fight tooth and nail to keep the shop.

SHEN TE. How can I? I have to sell the tobacco to pay back the two hundred silver dollars today.

MRS. SHIN. No husband, no tobacco, no house and home! What are you going to live on?

SHEN TE. I can work. I can sort tobacco.

MRS. SHIN. Hey, look, Mr. Shui Ta's trousers! He must have left here stark naked!

SHEN TE. Oh, he may have another pair, Mrs. Shin.

MRS. SHIN. But if he's gone for good as you say, why has he left his pants behind?

SHEN TE. Maybe he's thrown them away.

MRS. SHIN. Can I take them?

SHEN TE. Oh, no.

(*Enter Mr. Shu Fu, running.*)

SHU FU. Not a word! Total silence! I know all. You have sacrificed your own love and happiness so as not to hurt a dear old couple who had put their trust in you! Not in vain does this district—for all its malevolent tongues!—call you the Angel of the Slums! That young man couldn't rise to your level, so you left him. And now, when I see you closing up the little shop, that veritable haven of rest for the multitude, well, I cannot, I cannot let it pass. Morning after morning I have stood watching in the doorway not unmoved—while you graciously handed out rice to the wretched. Is that never to happen again? Is the good woman of Setzuan to disappear? If only you would allow *me* to assist you! Now don't say anything! No assurances, no exclamations of gratitude! (*He has taken out his check book.*) Here! A blank check. (*He places it on the cart.*) Just my signature. Fill it out as you wish. Any sum in the world. I herewith retire from the scene, quietly, unobtrusively, making no claims, on tiptoe, full of veneration, absolutely selflessly . . . (*He has gone.*)

MRS. SHIN. Well! You're saved. There's always some idiot of a man . . . Now hurry! Put down a thousand silver dollars and let me fly to the bank before he comes to his senses.

SHEN TE. I can pay you for the washing without any check.

MRS. SHIN. What? You're not going to cash it just because you might have to marry him? Are you crazy? Men like him *want* to be led by the nose! Are you still thinking of that flyer? All Yellow Street knows how he treated you!

SHEN TE.

When I heard his cunning laugh, I was afraid
But when I saw the holes in his shoes, I loved him
dearly.

MRS. SHIN. Defending that good for nothing after all that's happened!

SHEN TE (*staggering as she holds some of the washing*). Oh!

MRS. SHIN (*taking the washing from her, dryly*). So you feel dizzy when you stretch and bend? There couldn't be a little visitor on the way? If that's it, you can forget Mr. Shu Fu's blank check: it wasn't meant for a christening present!

(*She goes to the back with a basket. Shen Te's eyes follow Mrs. Shin for a moment. Then she looks down at her own body, feels her stomach, and a great joy comes into her eyes.*)

SHEN TE. O joy! A new human being is on the way. The world awaits him. In the cities the people say: he's got to be reckoned with, this new human being! (*She imagines a little boy to be present, and introduces him to the audience.*)

This is my son, the well-known flyer!
Say: Welcome
To the conqueror of unknown mountains and
unreachable regions
Who brings us our mail across the impassable deserts!

(*She leads him up and down by the hand.*) Take a look at the world, my son. That's a tree. Tree, yes. Say: "Hello, tree!" And bow. Like this. (*She bows.*) Now you know each other. And, look, here comes the Water Seller. He's a friend, give him your hand. A cup of fresh water for my little son, please. Yes, it is a warm day. (*Handing the cup.*) Oh dear, a policeman, we'll have to make a circle round him. Perhaps we can pick a few cherries over there in the rich Mr. Pung's garden. But we mustn't be seen. You want cherries? Just like children with fathers. No, no, you can't go straight at them like that. Don't pull. We must learn to be reasonable. Well, have it your own way. (*She has let him make for the cherries.*) Can you reach? Where to put them? Your mouth is the best place. (*She tries one herself.*) Mmm, they're good. But the policeman, we must run! (*They run.*) Yes, back to the street. Calm now, so no one will notice us. (*Walking the street with her child, she sings.*)

Once a plum—'twas in Japan—
Made a conquest of a man
But the man's turn soon did come
For he gobbled up the plum

(*Enter Wong, with a Child by the hand. He coughs.*)

SHEN TE. Wong!

WONG. It's about the Carpenter, Shen Te. He's lost his shop, and he's been drinking. His children are on the streets. This is one. Can you help?

SHEN TE (*to the child*). Come here, little man. (*Takes him down to the footlights. To the audience.*)

You there! A man is asking you for shelter!
A man of tomorrow says: what about today?
His friend the conqueror, whom you know,
Is his advocate!

(*To Wong.*) He can live in Mr. Shu Fu's cabins. I may have to go there myself. I'm going to have a baby. That's a secret—don't tell Yang Sun—we'd only be in his way. Can you find the Carpenter for me?

WONG. I knew you'd think of something. (*To the Child.*) Goodbye, son, I'm going for your father.

SHEN TE. What about your hand, Wong? I wanted to help, but my cousin . . .

WONG. Oh, I can get along with one hand, don't worry. (*He shows how he can handle his pole with his left hand alone.*)

SHEN TE. But your right hand! Look, take this cart, sell everything that's on it, and go to the doctor with the money . . .

WONG. She's still good. But first I'll bring the Carpenter. I'll pick up the cart when I get back. (*Exit Wong.*)

SHEN TE (*to the Child*). Sit down over here, son, till your father comes.

(*The Child sits crosslegged on the ground. Enter the Husband and Wife, each dragging a large, full sack.*)

WIFE (*furtively*). You're alone, Shen Te, dear?

(*Shen Te nods. The Wife beckons to the Nephew offstage. He comes on with another sack.*)

Your cousin's away?

(*Shen Te nods.*)

He's not coming back?

SHEN TE. No. I'm giving up the shop.

WIFE. That's why we're here. We want to know if we can leave these things in your new home. Will you do us this favor?

SHEN TE. Why, yes, I'd be glad to.

HUSBAND (*cryptically*). And if anyone asks about them, say they're yours.

SHEN TE. Would anyone ask?

WIFE (*with a glance back at her Husband*). Oh, someone might. The police, for instance. They don't seem to like us. Where can we put it?

SHEN TE. Well, I'd rather not get in any more trouble . . .

WIFE. Listen to her! The good woman of Setzuan!

(*Shen Te is silent.*)

HUSBAND. There's enough tobacco in those sacks to give us a new start in life. We could have our own tobacco factory!

SHEN TE (*slowly*). You'll have to put them in the back room.

(*The sacks are taken offstage, where the Child is left alone. Shyly glancing about him, he goes to the garbage can, starts playing with the contents, and eating some of the scraps. The others return.*)

WIFE. We're counting on you, Shen Te!

SHEN TE. Yes. (*She sees the Child and is shocked.*)

HUSBAND. We'll see you in Mr. Shu Fu's cabins.

NEPHEW. The day after tomorrow.

SHEN TE. Yes. Now, go. Go! I'm not feeling well.
                    (*Exeunt all three, virtually pushed off.*)
He is eating the refuse in the garbage can!
Only look at his little grey mouth!

(*Pause. Music.*)

As this is the world my son will enter
I will study to defend him.
To be good to you, my son,
I shall be a tigress to all others
If I have to.
And I shall have to.

(*She starts to go.*) One more time, then. I hope really the last.

(*Exit Shen Te, taking Shui Ta's trousers. Mrs. Shin enters and watches her with marked interest. Enter the Sister-in-Law and the Grandfather.*)

SISTER-IN-LAW. So it's true, the shop has closed down. And the furniture's in the back yard. It's the end of the road!

MRS. SHIN (*pompously*). The fruit of high living, selfishness, and sensuality! Down the primrose path to Mr. Shu Fu's cabins—with you!

SISTER-IN-LAW. Cabins? Rat holes! He gave them to us because his soap supplies only went mouldy there!

(*Enter the Unemployed Man.*)

UNEMPLOYED MAN. Shen Te is moving?

SISTER-IN-LAW. Yes. She was sneaking away.

MRS. SHIN. She's ashamed of herself, and no wonder!

UNEMPLOYED MAN. Tell her to call Mr. Shui Ta or she's done for this time!

SISTER-IN-LAW. Tell her to call Mr. Shui Ta or *we're* done for this time!

(*Enter Wong and Carpenter, the latter with a Child on each hand.*)

CARPENTER. So we'll have a roof over our heads for a change!

MRS. SHIN. Roof? Whose roof?

CARPENTER. Mr. Shu Fu's cabins. And we have little Feng to thank for it. (*Feng, we find, is the name of the child already there; his Father now takes him. To the other two.*) Bow to your little brother, you two! (*The Carpenter and the two new arrivals bow to Feng.*)

(*Enter Shui Ta.*)

UNEMPLOYED MAN. Sst! Mr. Shui Ta!

(*Pause.*)

SHUI TA. And what is this crowd here for, may I ask?

WONG. How do you do, Mr. Shui Ta? This is the Carpenter. Miss Shen Te promised him space in Mr. Shu Fu's cabins.

SHUI TA. That will not be possible.

CARPENTER. We can't go there after all?

SHUI TA. All the space is needed for other purposes.

SISTER-IN-LAW. You mean we have to get out? But we've got nowhere to go.

SHUI TA. Miss Shen Te finds it possible to provide employment. If the proposition interests you, you may stay in the cabins.

SISTER-IN-LAW (*with distaste*). You mean *work?* Work for Miss Shen Te?

SHUI TA. Making tobacco, yes. There are three bales here already. Would you like to get them?

SISTER-IN-LAW (*trying to bluster*). We have our own tobacco! We were in the tobacco business before you were born!

SHUI TA (*to the Carpenter and the Unemployed Man*). You don't have your own tobacco. What about you?

(*The Carpenter and the Unemployed Man get the point, and go for the sacks. Enter Mrs. Mi Tzu.*)

MRS. MI TZU. Mr. Shui Ta? I've brought you your three hundred silver dollars.

SHUI TA. I'll sign your lease instead. I've decided not to sell.

MRS. MI TZU. What? You don't need the money for that flyer?

SHUI TA. No.

MRS. MI TZU. And you can pay six months' rent?

SHUI TA (*takes the barber's blank check from the cart and fills it out*). Here is a check for ten thousand silver dollars. On Mr. Shu Fu's account. Look! (*He shows her the signature on the check.*) Your six months' rent will be in your hands by seven this evening. And now, if you'll excuse me.

MRS. MI TZU. So it's Mr. Shu Fu now. The flyer has been given his walking papers. These modern girls! In my day they'd have said she was flighty. That poor, deserted Mr. Yang Sun!

(*Exit Mrs. Mi Tzu. The Carpenter and the Unemployed Man drag the three sacks back on the stage.*)

CARPENTER (*to Shui Ta*). I don't know why I'm doing this for you.

SHUI TA. Perhaps your children want to eat, Mr. Carpenter.

SISTER-IN-LAW (*catching sight of the sacks*). Was my brother-in-law here?

MRS. SHIN. Yes, he was.

SISTER-IN-LAW. I thought as much. I know those sacks! That's our tobacco!

SHUI TA. Really? I thought it came from my back room? Shall we consult the police on the point?

SISTER-IN-LAW (*defeated*). No.

SHUI TA. Perhaps you will show me the way to Mr. Shu Fu's cabins?

(*Shui Ta goes off, followed by the Carpenter and his two older children, the Sister-in-Law, the Grandfather, and the Unemployed Man. Each of the last three drags a sack. Enter Old Man and Old Woman.*)

MRS. SHIN. A pair of pants—missing from the clothes line one minute—and next minute on the honorable backside of Mr. Shui Ta!

OLD WOMAN. We thought Miss Shen Te was here.

MRS. SHIN (*preoccupied*). Well, she's not.

OLD MAN. There was something she was going to give us.

WONG. She was going to help me too. (*Looking at his hand.*) It'll be too late soon. But she'll be back. This cousin has never stayed long.

MRS. SHIN (*approaching a conclusion*). No, he hasn't, has he?

SCENE 7A

(*The sewer pipe: Wong asleep. In his dream, he tells the Gods his fears. The Gods seem tired from all their travels. They stop for a moment and look over their shoulders at the Water Seller.*)

WONG. Illustrious ones, I've been having a bad dream. Our beloved Shen Te was in great distress in the rushes down by the rivers—the spot where the bodies of suicides are washed up. She kept staggering and holding her head down as if she was carrying something and it was dragging her down into the mud. When I called out to her, she said she had to take your Book of Rules to the other side, and not get it wet, or the ink would all come off. You had talked to her about the virtues, you know, the time she gave you shelter in Setzuan.

THIRD GOD. Well, but what do you suggest, my dear Wong?

WONG. Maybe a little relaxation of the rules, Benevolent One, in view of the bad times.

THIRD GOD. As for instance?

WONG. Well, um, good-will, for instance, might do instead of love?

THIRD GOD. I'm afraid that would create new problems.

WONG. Or, instead of justice, good sportsmanship?

THIRD GOD. That would only mean more work.

WONG. Instead of honor, outward propriety?

THIRD GOD. Still more work! No, no! The rules will have to stand, my dear Wong!

(*Wearily shaking their heads, all three journey on.*)

SCENE 8

(*Shui Ta's tobacco factory in Shu Fu's cabins. Huddled together behind bars, several families, mostly women and children. Among these people the Sister-in-Law, the Grandfather, the Carpenter, and his three children. Enter Mrs. Yang followed by Yang Sun.*)

MRS. YANG (*to the audience*). There's something I just *have* to tell you: strength and wisdom are wonderful things. The strong and wise Mr. Shui Ta has transformed my son from a dissipated good-for-nothing into a model citizen. As you may have heard, Mr. Shui Ta opened a small tobacco factory near the cattle runs. It flourished. Three months ago—I shall never forget it—I asked for an appointment, and Mr. Shui Ta agreed to see us—me and my son. I can see him now as he came through the door to meet us . . .

(*Enter Shui Ta, from a door.*)

SHUI TA. What can I do for you, Mrs. Yang?

MRS. YANG. This morning the police came to the house. We find you've brought an action for breach of promise of marriage. In the name of Shen Te. You also claim that Sun came by two hundred silver dollars by improper means.

SHUI TA. That is correct.

MRS. YANG. Mr. Shui Ta, the money's all gone. When the Peking job didn't materialize, he ran through it all in three days. I know he's a good-for-nothing. He sold my furniture. He was moving to Peking without me. Miss Shen Te thought highly of him at one time.

SHUI TA. What do *you* say, Mr. Yang Sun?

YANG SUN. The money's gone.

SHUI TA (*to Mrs. Yang*). Mrs. Yang, in consideration of my cousin's incomprehensible weakness for your son, I am prepared to give him another chance. He can have a job—here. The two hundred silver dollars will be taken out of his wages.

YANG SUN. So it's the factory or jail?

SHUI TA. Take your choice.

YANG SUN. May I speak with Shen Te?

SHUI TA. You may not.

(*Pause.*)

YANG SUN (*sullenly*). Show me where to go.

MRS. YANG. Mr. Shui Ta, you are kindness itself: the gods will reward you! (*To Yang Sun.*) And honest work will make a man of you, my boy.

(*Yang Sun follows Shui Ta into the factory. Mrs. Yang comes down again to the footlights.*)

Actually, honest work didn't agree with him—at first. And he got no opportunity to distinguish himself till— in the third week—when the wages were being paid. . . .

(*Shui Ta has a bag of money. Standing next to his foreman—the former Unemployed Man—he counts out the wages. It is Yang Sun's turn.*)

UNEMPLOYED MAN (*reading*). Carpenter, six silver dollars. Yang Sun, six silver dollars.

YANG SUN (*quietly*). Excuse me, sir. I don't think it can be more than five. May I see? (*He takes the foreman's list.*) It says six working days. But that's a mistake, sir. I took a day off for court business. And I won't take what I haven't earned, however miserable the pay is!

UNEMPLOYED MAN. Yang Sun. Five silver dollars. (*To Shui Ta.*) A rare case, Mr. Shui Ta!

SHUI TA. How is it the book says six when it should say five?

UNEMPLOYED MAN. I must've made a mistake, Mr. Shui Ta. (*With a look at Yang Sun.*) It won't happen again.

SHUI TA (*taking Yang Sun aside*). You don't hold back, do you? You give your all to the firm. You're even honest. Do the foreman's mistakes always favor the workers?

YANG SUN. He does have . . . friends.

SHUI TA. Thank you. May I offer you any little recompense?

YANG SUN. Give me a trial period of one week, and I'll prove my intelligence is worth more to you than my strength.

MRS. YANG (*still down at the footlight*). Fighting words, fighting words! That evening, I said to Sun: "If you're a flyer, then fly, my falcon! Rise in the world!" And he got to be foreman. Yes, in Mr. Shui Ta's tobacco factory, he worked real miracles.

(*We see Yang Sun with his legs apart standing behind the workers who are handing along a basket of raw tobacco above their heads.*)

YANG SUN. Faster! Faster! You there, d'you think you can just stand around now you're not foreman any more? It'll be your job to lead us in song. Sing!

(*Unemployed Man starts singing. The others join in the refrain.*)

SONG OF THE EIGHTH ELEPHANT

Chang had seven elephants—all much the same—
    But then there was Little Brother
The seven, they were wild, Little Brother, he was
    tame
And to guard them Chang chose Little Brother
        Run faster!
        Mr. Chang has a forest park
        Which must be cleared before tonight
        And already it's growing dark!
When the seven elephants cleared that forest park
    Mr. Chang rode high on Little Brother
While the seven toiled and moiled till dark
    On his big behind sat Little Brother
        Dig faster!
        Mr. Chang has a forest park
        Which must be cleared before tonight
        And already it's growing dark!

And the seven elephants worked many an hour
    Till none of them could work another
Old Chang, he looked sour, on the seven, he did
    glower
    But gave a pound of rice to Little Brother
        What was that?
        Mr. Chang has a forest park
        Which must be cleared before tonight
        And already it's growing dark!

And the seven elephants hadn't any tusks
    The one that had the tusks was Little Brother!

Seven are no match for one, if the one has a gun!
How old Chang did laugh at Little Brother!
Keep on digging!
Mr. Chang has a forest park
Which must be cleared before tonight
And already it's growing dark!

(*Smoking a cigar, Shui Ta strolls by. Yang Sun, laughing, has joined in the refrain of the third stanza and speeded up the tempo of the last stanza by clapping his hands.*)

MRS. YANG. And that's why I say: strength and wisdom are wonderful things. It took the strong and wise Mr. Shui Ta to bring out the best in Yang Sun. A real superior man is like a bell. If you ring it, it rings, and if you don't, it don't, as the saying is.

SCENE 9

(*Shen Te's shop, now an office with club chairs and fine carpets. It is raining. Shui Ta, now fat, is just dismissing the Old Man and Old Woman. Mrs. Shin, in obviously new clothes, looks on, smirking.*)

SHUI TA. No! I can NOT tell you when we expect her back.
OLD WOMAN. The two hundred silver dollars came today. In an envelope. There was no letter, but it must be from Shen Te. We want to write and thank her. May we have her address?
SHUI TA. I'm afraid I haven't got it.
OLD MAN (*pulling Old Woman's sleeve*). Let's be going.
OLD WOMAN. She's got to come back some time! (*They move off, uncertainly, worried. Shui Ta bows.*)
MRS. SHIN. They lost the carpet shop because they couldn't pay their taxes. The money arrived too late.
SHUI TA. They could have come to me.
MRS. SHIN. People don't like coming to you.
SHUI TA (*sits suddenly, one hand to his head*). I'm dizzy.
MRS. SHIN. After all, you *are* in your seventh month. But old Mrs. Shin will be there in your hour of trial! (*She cackles feebly.*)
SHUI TA (*in a stifled voice*). Can I count on that?
MRS. SHIN. We all have our price, and mine won't be too high for the great Mr. Shui Ta! (*She opens Shui Ta's collar.*)
SHUI TA. It's for the child's sake. All of this.
MRS. SHIN. "All for the child," of course.
SHUI TA. I'm so fat. People must notice.
MRS. SHIN. Oh no, they think it's 'cause you're rich.
SHUI TA (*more feelingly*). What will happen to the child?
MRS. SHIN. You ask that nine times a day. Why, it'll have the best that money can buy!
SHUI TA. He must never see Shui Ta.
MRS. SHIN. Oh, no. Always Shen Te.
SHUI TA. What about the neighbors? There are rumors, aren't there?

MRS. SHIN. As long as Mr. Shu Fu doesn't find out, there's nothing to worry about. Drink this.

(*Enter Yang Sun in a smart business suit, and carrying a businessman's brief case. Shui Ta is more or less in Mrs. Shin's arms.*)

YANG SUN (*surprised*). I seem to be in the way.
SHUI TA (*ignoring this, rises with an effort*). Till tomorrow, Mrs. Shin.

(*Mrs. Shin leaves with a smile, putting her new gloves on.*)

YANG SUN. Gloves now! She couldn't be fleecing you? And since when did *you* have a private life? (*Taking a paper from the brief case.*) You haven't been at your best lately, and things are getting out of hand. The police want to close us down. They say that at the most they can only permit twice the lawful number of workers.
SHUI TA (*evasively*). The cabins are quite good enough.
YANG SUN. For the workers maybe, not for the tobacco. They're too damp. We must take over some of Mrs. Mi Tzu's buildings.
SHUI TA. Her price is double what I can pay.
YANG SUN. Not unconditionally. If she has me to stroke her knees she'll come down.
SHUI TA. I'll never agree to that.
YANG SUN. What's wrong? Is it the rain? You get so irritable whenever it rains.
SHUI TA. Never! I will never . . .
YANG SUN. Mrs. Mi Tzu'll be here in five minutes. *You* fix it. And Shu Fu will be with her. . . . What's all that noise?

(*During the above dialogue, Wong is heard off stage calling: "The good Shen Te, where is she? Which of you has seen Shen Te, good people? Where is Shen Te?" A knock. Enter Wong.*)

WONG. Mr. Shui Ta, I've come to ask when Miss Shen Te will be back, it's six months now . . . There are rumors. People say something's happened to her.
SHUI TA. I'm busy. Come back next week.
WONG (*excited*). In the morning there was always rice on her doorstep—for the needy. It's been there again lately!
SHUI TA. And what do people conclude from this?
WONG. That Shen Te is still in Setzuan! She's been . . . (*He breaks off.*)
SHUI TA. She's been what? Mr. Wong, if you're Shen Te's friend, talk a little less about her, that's my advice to you.
WONG. I don't want your advice! Before she disappeared, Miss Shen Te told me something very important—she's pregnant!
YANG SUN. What? What was that?
SHUI TA (*quickly*). The man is lying.
WONG. A good woman isn't so easily forgotten, Mr. Shui Ta.

(*He leaves. Shui Ta goes quickly into the back room.*)

YANG SUN (*to the audience*). Shen Te pregnant? So that's why. Her cousin sent her away, so I wouldn't get wind of it. I have a son, a Yang appears on the scene, and what happens? Mother and child vanish into thin air! That scoundrel, that unspeakable . . . (*The sound of sobbing is heard from the back room.*) What was that? Someone sobbing? Who was it? Mr. Shui Ta the Tobacco King doesn't weep his heart out. And where does the rice come from that's on the doorstep in the morning?

(*Shui Ta returns. He goes to the door and looks out into the rain.*)

Where is she?

SHUI TA. Sh! It's nine o'clock. But the rain's so heavy, you can't hear a thing.

YANG SUN. What do you want to hear?

SHUI TA. The mail plane.

YANG SUN. What?

SHUI TA. I've been told *you* wanted to fly at one time. Is that all forgotten?

YANG SUN. Flying mail is night work. I prefer the daytime. And the firm is very dear to me—after all it belongs to my ex-fiancée, even if she's not around. And she's not, is she?

SHUI TA. What do you mean by that?

YANG SUN. Oh, well, let's say I haven't altogether—lost interest.

SHUI TA. My cousin might like to know that.

YANG SUN. I might not be indifferent—if I found she was being kept under lock and key.

SHUI TA. By whom?

YANG SUN. By you.

SHUI TA. What could you do about it?

YANG SUN. I could submit for discussion—my position in the firm.

SHUI TA. You are now my Manager. In return for a more appropriate position, you might agree to drop the enquiry into your ex-fiancée's whereabouts?

YANG SUN. I might.

SHUI TA. What position *would* be more appropriate?

YANG SUN. The one at the top.

SHUI TA. My own? (*Silence.*) And if I preferred to throw you out on your neck?

YANG SUN. I'd come back on my feet. With suitable escort.

SHUI TA. The police?

YANG SUN. The police.

SHUI TA. And when the police found no one?

YANG SUN. I might ask them not to overlook the back room. (*Ending the pretense.*) In short, Mr. Shui Ta, my interest in this young woman has not been officially terminated. I should like to see more of her. (*Into Shui Ta's face.*) Besides, she's pregnant and needs a friend. (*He moves to the door.*) I shall talk about it with the Water Seller.

(*Exit.*)

(*Shui Ta is rigid for a moment, then he quickly goes into the back room. He returns with Shen Te's belongings: underwear, etc. He takes a long look at the shawl of the previous scene. He then wraps the things in a bundle which,*

upon hearing a noise, he hides under the table. Enter Mrs. Mi Tzu and Mr. Shu Fu. They put away their umbrellas and galoshes.*)

MRS. MI TZU. I thought your manager was here, Mr. Shui Ta. He combines charm with business in a way that can only be to the advantage of all of us.

SHU FU. You sent for us, Mr. Shui Ta?

SHUI TA. The factory is in trouble.

SHU FU. It always is.

SHUI TA. The police are threatening to close us down unless I can show that the extension of our facilities is imminent.

SHU FU. Mr. Shui Ta, I'm sick and tired of your constantly expanding projects. I place cabins at your cousin's disposal; you make a factory of them. I hand your cousin a check; you present it. Your cousin disappears and you find the cabins too small and talk of yet more . . .

SHUI TA. Mr. Shu Fu, I'm authorized to inform you that Miss Shen Te's return is now imminent.

SHU FU. Imminent? It's becoming his favorite word.

MRS. MI TZU. Yes, what does it mean?

SHUI TA. Mrs. Mi Tzu, I can pay you exactly half what you asked for your buildings. Are you ready to inform the police that I am taking them over?

MRS. MI TZU. Certainly, if I can take over your manager.

SHU FU. What?

MRS. MI TZU. He's so efficient.

SHUI TA. I'm afraid I need Mr. Yang Sun.

MRS. MI TZU. So do I.

SHUI TA. He will call on you tomorrow

SHU FU. So much the better. With Shen Te likely to turn up at any moment, the presence of that young man is hardly in good taste.

SHUI TA. So we have reached a settlement. In what was once the good Shen Te's little shop we are laying the foundations for the great Mr. Shui Ta's twelve magnificent super tobacco markets. You will bear in mind that though they call me the Tobacco King of Setzuan, it is my cousin's interests that have been served . . .

VOICES (*off*). The police, the police! Going to the tobacco shop! Something must have happened! (*et cetera.*)

(*Enter Yang Sun, Wong, and the Policeman.*)

POLICEMAN. Quiet there, quiet, quiet! (*They quiet down.*) I'm sorry, Mr. Shui Ta, but there's a report that you've been depriving Miss Shen Te of her freedom. Not that I believe all I hear, but the whole city's in an uproar.

SHUI TA. That's a lie.

POLICEMAN. Mr. Yang Sun has testified that he heard someone sobbing in the back room.

SHU FU. Mrs. Mi Tzu and myself will testify that no one here has been sobbing.

MRS. MI TZU. We have been quietly smoking our cigars.

POLICEMAN. Mr. Shui Ta, I'm afraid I shall have to take a look at that room. (*He does so. The room is empty.*) No one there, of course, sir.

YANG SUN. But I hear sobbing. What's that? (*He finds the clothes.*)

WONG. Those are Shen Te's things. (*To crowd.*) Shen Te's clothes are here!

VOICES (*Off. In sequence*). Shen Te's clothes! They've been found under the table! Body of murdered girl still missing! Tobacco King suspected!

POLICEMAN. Mr. Shui Ta, unless you can tell us where the girl is, I'll have to ask you to come along.

SHUI TA. I do not know.

POLICEMAN. I can't say how sorry I am, Mr. Shui Ta. (*He shows him the door.*)

SHUI TA. Everything will be cleared up in no time. There are still judges in Setzuan.

YANG SUN. I heard sobbing!

SCENE 9 A

(*Wong's den. For the last time, the Gods appear to the Water Seller in his dream. They have changed and show signs of a long journey, extreme fatigue, and plenty of mishaps. The First no longer has a hat; the Third has lost a leg; all Three are barefoot.*)

WONG. Illustrious ones, at last you're here. Shen Te's been gone for months and today her cousin's been arrested. They think he murdered her to get the shop. But I had a dream and in this dream Shen Te said her cousin was keeping her prisoner. You must find her for us, illustrious ones!

FIRST GOD. We've found very few good people anywhere, and even they didn't keep it up. Shen Te is still the only one that stayed good.

SECOND GOD. If she *has* stayed good.

WONG. Certainly she has. But she's vanished.

FIRST GOD. That's the last straw. All is lost!

SECOND GOD. A little moderation, dear colleague!

FIRST GOD (*plaintively*). What's the good of moderation now? If she can't be found, we'll have to resign! The world is a terrible place! Nothing but misery, vulgarity, and waste! Even the countryside isn't what it used to be. The trees are getting their heads chopped off by telephone wires, and there's such a noise from all the gunfire, and I can't stand those heavy clouds of smoke, and—

THIRD GOD. The place is absolutely unlivable! Good intentions bring people to the brink of the abyss, and good deeds push them over the edge. I'm afraid our book of rules is destined for the scrap heap—

SECOND GOD. It's people! They're a worthless lot!

THIRD GOD. The world is too cold!

SECOND GOD. It's people! They are too weak!

FIRST GOD. Dignity, dear colleagues, dignity! Never despair! As for this world, didn't we agree that we only have to find one human being who can stand the place? Well, we

found her. True, we lost her again. We must find her again, that's all! And at once!

(*They disappear.*)

SCENE 10

(*Courtroom. Groups: Shu Fu and Mrs. Mi Tzu; Yang Sun and Mrs. Yang; Wong, the Carpenter, the Grandfather, the Niece, the Old Man, the Old Woman; Mrs. Shin, the Policeman; the Unemployed Man, the Sister-in-Law.*)

OLD MAN. So much power isn't good for one man.

UNEMPLOYED MAN. And he's going to open twelve super tobacco markets!

WIFE. One of the judges is a friend of Mr. Shu Fu's.

SISTER-IN-LAW. Another one accepted a present from Mr. Shui Ta only last night. A great fat goose.

OLD WOMAN (*to Wong*). And Shen Te is nowhere to be found.

WONG. Only the gods will ever know the truth.

POLICEMAN. Order in the court! My lords the judges!

(*Enter the Three Gods in judges' robes. We overhear their conversation as they pass along the footlights to their bench.*)

THIRD GOD. We'll never get away with it, our certificates were so badly forged.

SECOND GOD. My predecessor's "sudden indigestion" will certainly cause comment.

FIRST GOD. But he *had* just eaten a whole goose.

UNEMPLOYED MAN. Look at that! *New* judges!

WONG. New judges. And what good ones!

(*The Third God hears this, and turns to smile at Wong. The Gods sit. The First God beats on the bench with his gavel. The Policeman brings in Shui Ta who walks with lordly steps. He is whistled at.*)

POLICEMAN (*to Shui Ta*). Be prepared for a surprise. The judges have been changed.

(*Shui Ta turns quickly round, looks at them, and staggers.*)

NIECE. What's the matter now?

WIFE. The great Tobacco King nearly fainted.

HUSBAND. Yes, as soon as he saw the new judges.

WONG. Does *he* know who they are?

(*Shui Ta picks himself up, and the proceedings open.*)

FIRST GOD. Defendant Shui Ta, you are accused of doing away with your cousin Shen Te in order to take possession of her business. Do you plead guilty or not guilty?

SHUI TA. Not guilty, my lord.

FIRST GOD (*thumbing through the documents of the case*). The first witness is the Policeman. I shall ask him to tell us something of the respective reputations of Miss Shen Te and Mr. Shui Ta.

POLICEMAN. Miss Shen Te was a young lady who aimed to please, my lord. She liked to live and let live, as the saying goes. Mr. Shui Ta, on the other hand, is a man of principle. Though the generosity of Miss Shen Te forced him at times to abandon half measures, unlike the girl, he was always on the side of the law, my lord. One time, he even unmasked a gang of thieves to whom his too trustful cousin had given shelter. The evidence, in short, my lord, proves that Mr. Shui Ta was *incapable* of the crime of which he stands accused!

FIRST GOD. I see. And are there others who could testify along, shall we say, the same lines?

(*Shu Fu rises.*)

POLICEMAN (*whispering to Gods*). Mr. Shu Fu—a very important person.

FIRST GOD (*inviting him to speak*). Mr. Shu Fu!

SHU FU. Mr. Shui Ta is a businessman, my lord. Need I say more?

FIRST GOD. Yes.

SHU FU. Very well, I will. He is Vice President of the Council of Commerce and is about to be elected a Justice of the Peace. (*He returns to his seat.*)

WONG. Elected! *He* gave him the job!

(*With a gesture the First God asks who Mrs. Mi Tzu is.*)

POLICEMAN. Another very important person. Mrs. Mi Tzu.

FIRST GOD (*inviting her to speak*). Mrs. Mi Tzu!

MRS. MI TZU. My lord, as Chairman of the Committee on Social Work, I wish to call attention to just a couple of eloquent facts: Mr. Shui Ta not only has erected a model factory with model housing in our city, he is a regular contributor to our home for the disabled. (*She returns to her seat.*)

POLICEMAN (*whispering*). And she's a great friend of the judge that ate the goose!

FIRST GOD (*to the Policeman*). Oh, thank you. What next? (*To the Court, genially.*) Oh, yes. We should find out if any of the evidence is less favorable to the Defendant.

(*Wong, the Carpenter, the Old Man, the Old Woman, the Unemployed Man, the Sister-in-Law, and the Niece come forward.*)

POLICEMAN (*whispering*). Just the riff raff, my lord.

FIRST GOD (*addressing the "riff raff"*). Well, um, riff raff—do you know anything of the Defendant, Mr. Shui Ta?

WONG. Too much, my lord.

UNEMPLOYED MAN. What don't we know, my lord?

CARPENTER. He ruined us.

SISTER-IN-LAW. He's a cheat.

NIECE. Liar.

WIFE. Thief.

BOY. Blackmailer.

BROTHER. Murderer.

FIRST GOD. Thank you. We should now let the Defendant state his point of view.

SHUI TA. I only came on the scene when Shen Te was in danger of losing what I had understood was a gift from the gods. Because I did the filthy jobs which someone had to do, they hate me. My activities were held down to the minimum, my lord.

SISTER-IN-LAW. He had us arrested!

SHUI TA. Certainly. You stole from the bakery!

SISTER-IN-LAW. Such concern for the bakery! You didn't want the shop for yourself, I suppose!

SHUI TA. I didn't want the shop overrun with parasites.

SISTER-IN-LAW. We had nowhere else to go.

SHUI TA. There were too many of you.

WONG. What about this old couple: Were *they* parasites?

OLD MAN. We lost our shop because of you!

SISTER-IN-LAW. And we gave your cousin money!

SHUI TA. My cousin's fiancé was a flyer. The money had to go to *him*.

WONG. Did you care whether he flew or not? Did you care whether she married him or not? You wanted her to marry someone else! (*He points at Shu Fu.*)

SHUI TA. The flyer unexpectedly turned out to be a scoundrel.

YANG SUN (*jumping up*). Which was the reason you made him your Manager?

SHUI TA. Later on he improved.

WONG. And when he improved, you sold him to her? (*He points out Mrs. Mi Tzu.*)

SHUI TA. She wouldn't let me have her premises unless she had him to stroke her knees!

MRS. MI TZU. What? The man's a pathological liar. (*To him.*) Don't mention my property to me as long as you live! Murderer! (*She rustles off, in high dudgeon.*)

YANG SUN (*pushing in*). My lord, I wish to speak for the Defendant.

SISTER-IN-LAW. Naturally. He's your employer.

UNEMPLOYED MAN. And the worst slave driver in the country.

MRS. YANG. That's a lie! My lord, Mr. Shui Ta is a great man. He . . .

YANG SUN. He's this and he's that, but he is not a murderer, my lord. Just fifteen minutes before his arrest I heard Shen Te's voice in his own back room.

FIRST GOD. Oh? Tell us more!

YANG SUN. I heard sobbing, my lord!

FIRST GOD. But lots of women sob, we've been finding.

YANG SUN. Could I fail to recognize her voice?

SHU FU. No, you made her sob so often yourself, young man!

YANG SUN. Yes. But I also made her happy. Till he (*pointing at Shui Ta*) decided to sell her to you!

SHUI TA. Because you didn't love her.

WONG. Oh, no: it was for the money, my lord!

SHUI TA. And what was the money for, my lord? For the poor! And for Shen Te so she could go on being good!

WONG. For the poor? That he sent to his sweatshops? And why didn't you let Shen Te be good when you signed the big check?

SHUI TA. For the child's sake, my lord.

CARPENTER. What about *my* children? What did he do about them?

(*Shui Ta is silent.*)

WONG. The shop was to be a fountain of goodness. That was the gods' idea. You came and spoiled it!

SHUI TA. If I hadn't, it would have run dry!

MRS. SHIN. There's a lot in that, my lord.

WONG. What have you done with the good Shen Te, bad man? She *was* good, my lords, she was, I swear it! (*He raises his hand in an oath.*)

THIRD GOD. What's happened to your hand, Water Seller?

WONG (*pointing to Shui Ta*). It's all his fault, my lord, *she* was going to send me to a doctor—(*To Shui Ta.*) You were her worst enemy!

SHUI TA. I was her only friend!

WONG. Where is she then? Tell us where your good friend is!

(*The excitement of this exchange has run through the whole crowd.*)

ALL. Yes, where is she? Where is Shen Te? (*et cetera.*)

SHUI TA. Shen Te had to go.

WONG. Where? Where to?

SHUI TA. I cannot tell you! I cannot tell you!

ALL. Why? Why did she have to go away? (*et cetera.*)

WONG (*into the din with the first words, but talking on beyond the others*). Why not, why not? Why did she have to go away?

SHUI TA (*shouting*). Because you'd all have torn her to shreds, that's why! My lords, I have a request. Clear the court! When only the judges remain, I will make a confession.

ALL (*except Wong, who is silent, struck by the new turn of events*). So he's guilty? He's confessing! (*et cetera.*)

FIRST GOD (*using the gavel*). Clear the court!

POLICEMAN. Clear the court!

WONG. Mr. Shui Ta has met his match this time.

MRS. SHIN (*with a gesture toward the judges*). You're in for a little surprise.

(*The court is cleared. Silence.*)

SHUI TA. Illustrious ones!

(*The Gods look at each other, not quite believing their ears.*)

SHUI TA. Yes, I recognize you!

SECOND GOD (*taking matters in hand, sternly*). What have you done with our good woman of Setzuan?

SHUI TA. I have a terrible confession to make: I am she! (*He takes off his mask, and tears away his clothes. Shen Te stands there.*)

SECOND GOD. Shen Te!

SHEN TE. Shen Te, yes. Shui Ta *and* Shen Te. Both.
　Your injunction
　To be good and yet to live
　Was a thunderbolt:
　It has torn me in two
　I can't tell how it was
　But to be good to others
　And myself at the same time
　I could not do it
　Your world is not an easy one, illustrious ones!
　When we extend our hand to a beggar, he tears it off
　　for us
　When we help the lost, we are lost ourselves.
　And so
　Since not to eat is to die
　Who can long refuse to be bad?
　As I lay prostrate beneath the weight of good
　　intentions
　Ruin stared me in the face
　It was when I was unjust that I ate good meat
　And hobnobbed with the mighty
　Why?
　Why are bad deeds rewarded?
　Good ones punished?
　I enjoyed giving
　I truly wished to be the Angel of the Slums
　But washed by a foster-mother in the water of the
　　gutter
　I developed a sharp eye
　The time came when pity was a thorn in my side
　And, later, when kind words turned to ashes in my
　　mouth
　And anger took over
　I became a wolf
　Find me guilty, then, illustrious ones,
　But know:
　All that I have done I did
　To help my neighbor
　To love my lover
　And to keep my little one from want
　For your great, godly deeds, I was too poor, too small.

(*Pause.*)

FIRST GOD (*shocked*). Don't go on making yourself miserable, Shen Te! We're overjoyed to have found you!

SHEN TE. I'm telling you I'm the bad man who committed all those crimes!

FIRST GOD (*using—or failing to use—his ear trumpet*). The good woman who did all those good deeds?

SHEN TE. Yes, but the bad man too!

FIRST GOD (*as if something had dawned*). Unfortunate coincidences! Heartless neighbors!

THIRD GOD (*shouting in his ear*). But how is she to continue?

FIRST GOD. Continue? Well, she's a strong, healthy girl . . .

SECOND GOD. You didn't hear what she said!

FIRST GOD. I heard every word! She is confused, that's all!
(*He begins to bluster.*) And what about this book of
rules—we can't renounce our rules, can we? (*More quietly.*) Should the world be changed? How? By whom? The
world should *not* be changed! (*At a sign from him, the lights
turn pink, and music plays.*)

> And now the hour of parting is at hand.
> Dost thou behold, Shen Te, yon fleecy cloud?
> It is our chariot. At a sign from me
> 'Twill come and take us back from whence we came
> Above the azure vault and silver stars . . .

SHEN TE. No! Don't go, illustrious ones!

FIRST GOD.

> Our cloud has landed now in yonder field
> From whence it will transport us back to heaven.
> Farewell, Shen Te, let not thy courage fail thee . . .

(*Exeunt Gods.*)

SHEN TE. What about the old couple? They've lost their
shop! What about the Water Seller and his hand? And
I've got to defend myself against the barber, because I
don't love him! And against Sun, because I do love him!
How? How?

(*Shen Te's eyes follow the Gods as they are imagined to
step into a cloud which rises and moves forward over the
orchestra and up beyond the balcony*)

FIRST GOD (*from on high*). We have faith in you, Shen Te!

SHEN TE. There'll be a child. And he'll have to be fed. I
can't stay here. Where shall I go?

FIRST GOD. Continue to be good, good woman of Setzuan!

SHEN TE. I need my bad cousin!

FIRST GOD. But not very often!

SHEN TE. Once a week at least!

FIRST GOD. Once a month will be quite enough!

SHEN TE (*shrieking*). No, no! Help!

(*But the cloud continues to recede as the Gods sing.*)

VALEDICTORY HYMN

> What rapture, oh, it is to know
>   A good thing when you see it
> And having seen a good thing, oh,
>   What rapture 'tis to flee it
> Be good, sweet maid of Setzuan
>   Let Shui Ta be clever
> Departing, we forget the man
>   Remember your endeavor
> Ò Because through all the length of days
>   Her goodness faileth never
> Sing hallelujah! May Shen Te's
>   Good name live on forever!

SHEN TE. Help!

Epilogue

> You're thinking, aren't you, that this is no right
> Conclusion to the play you've seen tonight?
> After a tale, exotic, fabulous,
> A nasty ending was slipped up on us.
> We feel deflated too. We too are nettled
> To see the curtain down and nothing settled.
> How could a better ending be arranged?
> Could one change people? Can the world be
>   changed?
> Would new gods do the trick? Will atheism?
> Moral rearmament? Materialism?
> It is for you to find a way, my friends,
> To help good men arrive at happy ends.
> *You* write the happy ending to the play!
> There must, there must, there's got to be a way!

DEATH OF A SALESMAN

Certain Private Conversations in Two Acts and a Requiem

ARTHUR MILLER

ARTHUR MILLER (1915–)

While Eugene O'Neill was the first American playwright to be widely accepted outside the United States, Arthur Miller is better known internationally and is the most widely produced American playwright.

Born in Harlem, the son of hard-working Jewish immigrants, Miller's early life provided much of the thematic material for his plays. Achieving financial success and then losing it in the stock market crash of 1929, his father's career epitomized the roller coaster ride of the free enterprise system. When the family recovered from the crash, Miller enrolled in the University of Michigan, where his playwriting career began. Among the awards his early work received was the 1937 Theater Guild National Award, which he shared with the man who was to become the chief rival to his popularity from 1945 until the early 1960s, Tennessee Williams. In 1944, following a brief stint with the Federal Theater Project, he wrote his first Broadway play, entitled *The Man Who Had All the Luck,* which—ironically—closed after only four performances. His next play, *All My Sons,* proved to be much more successful both commercially and critically, earning him the New York Drama Critics Award as the most promising playwright of the 1947 season and his first New York Drama Critics Circle Award. Two years later his most famous play, *Death of a Salesman,* earned him not only his second New York Drama Critics Circle Award, but the Tony Award for best play and the Pulitzer Prize in drama. Although his later plays—the most well known of which are *The Crucible* (1952), *A View from the Bridge* (1955), *After the Fall* (1964), *Incident at Vichy* (1964), *The Price* (1968), *The Creation of the World and Other Business* (1973), *American Clock* (1980), *Broken Glass* (1993), and *The Ride Down Mount Morgan* (1998)—rarely achieved the commercial success or the critical acclaim of the early plays, he has continued to write and his plays have been produced in the United States and throughout Europe. Interestingly, his plays were among the first works to be performed in China after normalization of diplomatic relations began in the 1970s.

Shortly after his early success, he was called before the infamous House Un-American Activities Committee. Like many artists of his day, he was grilled mercilessly about his past and his relationship with the American Communist Party. Unlike many others, he managed to salvage his career. Cited for contempt of court for refusing to "name names" (the citation was later reversed), he was gallant in his stand for the rights of the individual. This episode in his life provided material for *The Crucible*, generally viewed as his indictment of the HUAC hearings.

As a playwright, Miller is an exceptional craftsman. His plays are marked by well-constructed plots; intriguing, highly motivated characters; and brutally honest social themes. Many of his plays, most notably *All My Sons* and *The Price*, are modern versions of the well-made play. In these plays the combination of the withheld secret and the obligatory scene are superbly crafted. However, his work is not limited to this traditional, realistic form. In *Death of a Salesman, After the Fall,* and *American Clock* he intricately combines realism and Expressionism as his characters freely bound, sometimes in their own minds and sometimes in ours, from one time and place to another, exploring the past and its effects on the present and the future.

His characters are usually strong-willed members of a dysfunctional, middle-class American family. Motivated primarily by materialism, the Kellers in *All My Sons*, the Lomans in *Death of a Salesman*, the Franzes in *The Price,* and the Gellburgs in *Broken Glass* are all so caught up in the struggle to fulfill their individual and collective duties to self, family, and society that they betray not only one another but the values and ethics they so strongly profess.

Thematically, Miller displays two basic concerns: the ruin and disaster precipitated by materialistic evils and the individual's struggle with conscience. Invariably the family father lives a life of lies and delusions as he struggles to obtain the material trappings of the American dream for his family. He grapples with a past error in judgement or unethical action which, unknown to him, has shaped his life. The individual's social and moral responsibilities are examined through such battles.

At the heart of many Miller dramas is also his quest to deal with "Tragedy and the Common Man," which is included as a Forum after this play.

DEATH OF A SALESMAN: CERTAIN PRIVATE CONVERSATIONS IN TWO ACTS AND A REQUIEM (1949)

Death of a Salesman is Miller's most widely produced play, staged frequently not only throughout the United States and Canada, but in Latin America and as a popular example of American drama in Europe. In 1983 it was directed by Miller himself in the People's Republic of China.

The play embodies nearly all the components of Miller's writing style: a tightly constructed plot reminiscent of the well-made play; well-rounded, believable characters drawn from the American middle class; and a seamless blending of realism and Expressionism. Thematically, it relies on most of Miller's recurring concerns: a secret past action that plants the seeds of the destruction of the dysfunctional family and its individual members; a father who lives a lie; and the struggle of facing one's responsibility to family and society. Miller accomplishes this by creating a play based, in both content and form, on seeming contradictions. Using what in 1949 were regarded as antithetical styles—realism and Expressionism—Miller portrays the simultaneous development and destruction of the American family and the American dream. These contradictions are exemplified by the most powerful image in the play, that of Willy and his sample cases.

As the play opens we see a defeated Willy lugging his worn and shabby sample cases back into the house after yet another failed day on the road. In Miller's words, "his exhaustion is apparent." He is a traveling salesman who can no longer travel and who can no longer sell. Our first glimpse of Willy prepares us for the drama that follows, for it is these cases, symbols of a salesman's life, that will be the death of Willy Loman. What does Willy sell? We are never told. We are told that he has the "best eye for color in the business," that he "open[ed] up unheard of territories," and that "he's vital in New England," but we never know what it is that he sells.

What is in the cases? Willy Loman himself. The cases contain the many contradictory aspects of his life. Contained in one case is what he says and in the other is what he does. In one case are his dreams and in the other is his reality. In one case is the disappearing pastoral environment for which he longs and in the other the encroaching urban society driving him to his grave. In one case are the sons whose potential has been the joy of his life, in the other the sons whose failures have become the bane of his existence. Together, the cases and their contents become Willy's coffin—the means of his livelihood has become the means of his death. He has spent his life living one lie, and he goes to his death believing another. Why do these cases contain so many contradictions? Because Willy himself is a constant contradiction.

Within minutes of the opening curtain we hear Willy ask Linda, "Why am I always being contradicted?" He is contradicted because those around him are reflecting what is happening in "the inside of his head," Miller's original title of the play. His contradictory nature permeates the play. He describes Biff as "a lazy bum!" then, within minutes, claims, "There's one thing about Biff—he's not lazy." Regarding his car, he says, the "Chevrolet, Linda, is the greatest car ever built!" A moment later he castigates the same vehicle: "They ought to prohibit the manufacture of that automobile." And, when schooling Biff to request a business loan from Bill

Oliver, Willy first cautions his son not "to crack any jokes" because "everybody likes a kidder but nobody lends him money." In the next breath he advises him to "walk in with a big laugh" and "start off with a couple of your best stories."

These verbal contradictions are indicative of Willy's actions throughout the play—he says one thing and then does another. For example, he indicts the boys for the lack of respect they show Linda: "Since when do you let your mother carry the wash up the stairs?" At the same time he is involved with other women on the road. Similarly, he chastises Linda for mending her old stockings while he lavishes new hosiery on secretaries. While he claims that he does not need nor cannot take Charley's money, he does so repeatedly.

Such dichotomies reflect the chasm between his dreams of success and the reality of his mediocrity. In both the past and the present episodes, his dreams of prosperity are belied by the reality of his failure. In the "old days" he dreamed of having "Knocked 'em cold in Providence" and "slaughtered 'em in Boston!," yet it is clear that he was always struggling to make ends meet. In addition to dreaming of sales success, Willy dreams of being not only liked but "well liked." Yet casual acquaintances, friends, business associates, and even his family only tolerate him. His neighbor, Charley, and his boss, Howard, befriend him not so much because they like him but because they pity him. And Howard's secretary, Jenny, "can't deal with him anymore." His family's impressions of him are not much better. At the moment when Willy needs him most, his son Happy acknowledges Willy not as his father but as "just a guy." Biff, the son he worshipped, is so repulsed by him that he returns home only on rare occasions, reunions that end in quarrels. Even the loyal Linda, while noting that "attention must be finally paid to such a person," concedes that "he's not easy to get along with" and that "no one knows him any more, no one welcomes him."

The contradictions within Willy might be seen as manifestations of a more deeply rooted paradox—Willy's consuming desire to return to the past versus his burning aspirations to be successful in the present. His yearning for days gone by is a quest for simplicity and serenity; his obsession with the present is a quest for "being well liked." These polar quests are incompatible; pursued simultaneously, they turn the present into a vacuum.

The past, which exists only in Willy's memory, is a disappearing pastoral landscape. He remembers when the trees were so thick and the sun so warm that he "opened the windshield and just let the warm air bathe" him. At home he recalls the "lilac and wisteria," the "peonies and the daffodils," and "the fragrance in this room." He reminisces about the backyard graced by stately elms where he and Biff once hung the hammock and watched it "just swingin' there under those branches." And he wonders, "How do we get back to all the great times?" His recollections of the beauty of the past only feed his anger that all the trees are gone and that "they boxed in the whole goddam neighborhood" so that "you can't raise a carrot in the back yard."

The present is a hostile, competitive, urban world where "business is definitely business" and "everybody's gotta pull his own weight." Willy finds "the competition is maddening," and admits that he is "tired to death." He is mystified by the present. Even when Charley tells him "the only thing you got in this world is what you can sell . . . and you don't know that," Willy cannot comprehend this primary tenet of the business world.

The contradictions between Willy's words and his actions, his dreams and his reality, the past and the present are more easily understood if we remember that the play depicts the death of two antithetical salesmen. The first is the "salesman's salesman," the man Willy would like to be—Dave Singleman. The other is the mediocre salesman, the man Willy cannot escape being—Willy Loman. As their names imply, one is a "Singleman," a man who is "one in a million," while the other is a "Lo[w]man," a man who is "a dime a dozen." The death and funeral of the former is a "singular" event attended by hundreds, while the funeral of the other is a common affair attended only by the family, only one of whom is brought to tears by the death of a salesman.

Willy's preoccupation with being another "Singleman" is symbolic of Miller's exploration of the American dream. To Willy, Dave Singleman and his brother Ben personify the American dream, and he envisions himself raising a family that will inhabit this dreamworld. Realizing that he will never achieve this dream, Willy projects this vision onto his sons, who represent the two parts of their father. Biff, the laborer, appreciates the beauty of nature and bygone days, while Happy, the businessman, possesses an "overdeveloped sense of competition." These young men, whom Willy regarded as "Adonises" when they were teens, are now disappointments to him. One is a philanderer and the other a kleptomaniac. Though Willy claims, "I never in my life told [them] anything but decent things," it is he who is responsible for their lifestyles. He not only condoned their thievery, but bragged about it in front of them. As a result, Happy has become another Willy, a man with no awareness of his plight. Because he is his father's son, Happy's pursuit of the American dream is as blind and fruitless as his attempts to gain his father's attention. "I'm losing weight, Pop!" and "I'm gonna be getting married, Mom!" are hollow echoes of Willy's "knocked 'em cold in Providence . . . slaughtered 'em in Boston." Though Biff at first appears headed in the same direction, it is he who evolves into the realist by virtue of two discoveries. First, he realizes that "all I want is out there, waiting for me the minute I say I know who I am!" Equally important is the revelation that not only did Willy have "all the wrong dreams," but the Loman family was "a dime a dozen" and "a dollar an hour," all "hard working drummers who landed in the ash can like all the rest of them."

Sometimes lost in the contradictions surrounding this death of this salesman are the facts that Willy's dreams were not all bad and that the play is not a condemnation of the free enterprise system. We must remember that while Willy sought success, he also wanted a good life for his family. What he sees in Dave Singleman, although sentimentalized, is the notion that personality, respect, comradeship, and gratitude are worthwhile goals. But unfortunately, Willy sees them as the end rather than as means to and end. He is seemingly ignorant of the fact that it was personality, respect, comradeship, and gratitude that made Dave Singleman successful and not success that made him personable, respected, friendly, and worthy of gratitude. And we must remember that while much that troubles Willy arises out of the notion that sometimes one *does* "eat the orange and throw away the peel," the play also portrays the success of Charley and Bernard, which is in no way indicted as being unethical, evil, or immoral.

Thus, through the use of contradictory styles and images, Miller succeeds in arousing the contradictory feelings of pity for and disgust with the people and events which surround and precipitate *The Death of a Salesman*.

Jo Mielziner's acclaimed Expressionistic setting for the Loman household in the 1949 production of Death of a Salesman; *note the sagging roofline—dwarfed by the New York skyline—that mirrors Willy's own exasperation.*

DEATH OF A SALESMAN

Certain Private Conversations in Two Acts and a Requiem

ARTHUR MILLER

CHARACTERS
WILLY LOMAN
LINDA
BIFF
HAPPY
BERNARD
THE WOMAN

CHARLEY
UNCLE BEN
HOWARD WAGNER
JENNY
STANLEY
MISS FORSYTHE
LETTA

SCENE: *The action takes place in Willy Loman's house and yard and in various places he visits in the New York and Boston of today.*

ACT 1

SCENE: *A melody is heard, played upon a flute. It is small and fine, telling of grass and trees and the horizon. The curtain rises.*

Before us is the Salesman's house. We are aware of towering, angular shapes behind it, surrounding it on all sides. Only the blue light of the sky falls upon the house and forestage; the surrounding area shows an angry glow of orange. As more light appears, we see a solid vault of apartment houses around the small, fragile-seeming home. An air of the dream clings to the place, a dream rising out of reality. The kitchen at center seems actual enough, for there is a kitchen table with three chairs, and a refrigerator. But no other fixtures are seen. At the back of the kitchen there is a draped entrance, which leads to the living room. To the right of the kitchen, on a level raised two feet, is a bedroom furnished only with a brass bedstead and a straight chair. On a shelf over the bed a silver athletic trophy stands. A window opens onto the apartment house at the side.

Behind the kitchen, on a level raised six and a half feet, is the boys' bedroom, at present barely visible. Two beds are dimly seen, and at the back of the room a dormer window. (This bedroom is above the unseen living room.) At the left a stairway curves up to it from the kitchen.

The entire setting is wholly or, in some places, partially transparent. The roof-line of the house is one-dimensional; under and over it we see the apartment buildings. Before the house lies an apron, curving beyond the forestage into the orchestra. This forward area serves as the back yard as well as the locale of all Willy's imaginings and of his city scenes. Whenever the action is in the present the actors observe the imaginary wall-lines, entering the house only through its door at the left. But in the scenes of the past these boundaries are broken, and characters enter or leave a room by stepping "through" a wall onto the forestage.

From the right, Willy Loman, the Salesman, enters, carrying two large sample cases. The flute plays on. He hears but is not aware of it. He is past sixty years of age, dressed quietly. Even as he crosses the stage to the doorway of the house, his exhaustion is apparent. He unlocks the door, comes into the kitchen, and thankfully lets his burden down, feeling the soreness of his palms. A word-sigh escapes his lips—it might be "Oh, boy, oh, boy." He closes the door, then carries his cases out into the living room, through the draped kitchen doorway.

Linda, his wife, has stirred in her bed at the right. She gets out and puts on a robe, listening. Most often jovial, she has developed an iron repression of her exceptions to Willy's behavior—she more than loves him, she admires him, as though his mercurial nature, his temper, his massive dreams and little cruelties, served her only as sharp reminders of the turbulent longings within him, longings which she shares but lacks the temperament to utter and follow to their end.

LINDA [*hearing Willy outside the bedroom, calls with some trepidation*]. Willy!

WILLY. It's all right. I came back.

LINDA. Why? What happened? (*Slight pause.*) Did something happen, Willy?

WILLY. No, nothing happened.

LINDA. You didn't smash the car, did you?

WILLY (*with casual irritation*). I said nothing happened. Didn't you hear me?

LINDA. Don't you feel well?

WILLY. I'm tired to the death. (*The flute has faded away. He sits on the bed beside her, a little numb.*) I couldn't make it. I just couldn't make it, Linda.

LINDA (*very carefully, delicately*). Where were you all day? You look terrible.

WILLY. I got as far as a little above Yonkers. I stopped for a cup of coffee. Maybe it was the coffee.

LINDA. What?

WILLY (*after a pause*). I suddenly couldn't drive any more. The car kept going off onto the shoulder, y'know?

LINDA (*helpfully*). Oh. Maybe it was the steering again. I don't think Angelo knows the Studebaker.

WILLY. No, it's me, it's me. Suddenly I realize I'm goin' sixty miles an hour and I don't remember the last five minutes. I'm—I can't seem to—keep my mind to it.

LINDA. Maybe it's your glasses. You never went for your new glasses.

WILLY. No, I see everything. I came back ten miles an hour. It took me nearly four hours from Yonkers.

LINDA (*resigned*). Well, you'll just have to take a rest, Willy, you can't continue this way.

WILLY. I just got back from Florida.

LINDA. But you didn't rest your mind. Your mind is overactive, and the mind is what counts, dear.

WILLY. I'll start out in the morning. Maybe I'll feel better in the morning. (*She is taking off his shoes.*) These goddam arch supports are killing me.

LINDA. Take an aspirin. Should I get you an aspirin? It'll soothe you.

WILLY (*with wonder*). I was driving along, you understand? And I was fine. I was even observing the scenery. You can imagine, me looking at scenery, on the road every week of my life. But it's so beautiful up there, Linda, the trees are so thick, and the sun is warm. I opened the windshield and just let the warm air bathe over me. And then all of a sudden I'm goin' off the road! I'm tellin' ya, I absolutely forgot I was driving. If I'd've gone the other way over the white line I might've killed somebody. So I went on again—and five minutes later I'm dreamin' again, and I nearly . . . (*He presses two fingers against his eyes.*) I have such thoughts, I have such strange thoughts.

LINDA. Willy, dear. Talk to them again. There's no reason why you can't work in New York.

WILLY. They don't need me in New York. I'm the New England man. I'm vital in New England.

LINDA. But you're sixty years old. They can't expect you to keep traveling every week.

WILLY. I'll have to send a wire to Portland. I'm supposed to see Brown and Morrison tomorrow morning at ten o'clock to show the line. Goddammit, I could sell them! (*He starts putting on his jacket.*)

LINDA (*taking the jacket from him*). Why don't you go down to the place tomorrow and tell Howard you've simply got to work in New York? You're too accommodating, dear.

WILLY. If old man Wagner was alive I'd a been in charge of New York now! That man was a prince, he was a masterful man. But that boy of his, that Howard, he don't appreciate. When I went north the first time, the Wagner Company didn't know where New England was!

LINDA. Why don't you tell those things to Howard, dear?

WILLY (*encouraged*). I will, I definitely will. Is there any cheese?

LINDA. I'll make you a sandwich.

WILLY. No, go to sleep. I'll take some milk. I'll be up right away. The boys in?

LINDA. They're sleeping. Happy took Biff on a date tonight.

WILLY (*interested*). That so?

LINDA. It was so nice to see them shaving together, one behind the other, in the bathroom. And going out together. You notice? The whole house smells of shaving lotion.

WILLY. Figure it out. Work a lifetime to pay off a house. You finally own it, and there's nobody to live in it.

LINDA. Well, dear, life is a casting off. It's always that way.

WILLY. No, no, some people—some people accomplish something. Did Biff say anything after I went this morning?

LINDA. You shouldn't have criticized him, Willy, especially after he just got off the train. You mustn't lose your temper with him.

WILLY. When the hell did I lose my temper? I simply asked him if he was making any money. Is that a criticism?

LINDA. But, dear, how could he make any money?

WILLY (*worried and angered*). There's such an undercurrent in him. He became a moody man. Did he apologize when I left this morning?

LINDA. He was crestfallen, Willy. You know how he admires you. I think if he finds himself, then you'll both be happier and not fight any more.

WILLY. How can he find himself on a farm? Is that a life? A farm hand? In the beginning, when he was young, I thought, well, a young man, it's good for him to tramp around, take a lot of different jobs. But it's more than ten years now and he has yet to make thirty-five dollars a week!

LINDA. He's finding himself, Willy.

WILLY. Not finding yourself at the age of thirty-four is a disgrace!

LINDA. Shh!

WILLY. The trouble is he's lazy, goddammit!

LINDA. Willy, please!

WILLY. Biff is a lazy bum!

LINDA. They're sleeping. Get something to eat. Go on down.

WILLY. Why did he come home? I would like to know what brought him home.

LINDA. I don't know. I think he's still lost, Willy. I think he's very lost.

WILLY. Biff Loman is lost. In the greatest country in the world a young man with such—personal attractiveness, gets lost. And such a hard worker. There's one thing about Biff—he's not lazy.

LINDA. Never.

WILLY (*with pity and resolve*). I'll see him in the morning; I'll have a nice talk with him. I'll get him a job selling. He could be big in no time. My God! Remember how they used to follow him around in high school? When he smiled at one of them their faces lit up. When he walked down the street . . . (*He loses himself in reminiscences.*)

LINDA (*trying to bring him out of it*). Willy, dear, I got a new kind of American-type cheese today. It's whipped.

WILLY. Why do you get American when I like Swiss?

LINDA. I just thought you'd like a change . . .

WILLY. I don't want a change! I want Swiss cheese. Why am I always being contradicted?

LINDA (*with a covering laugh*). I thought it would be a surprise.

WILLY. Why don't you open a window in here, for God's sake?

LINDA (*with infinite patience*). They're all open, dear.

WILLY. The way they boxed us in here. Bricks and windows, windows and bricks.

LINDA. We should've bought the land next door.

WILLY. The street is lined with cars. There's not a breath of fresh air in the neighborhood. The grass don't grow any more, you can't raise a carrot in the back yard. They should've had a law against apartment houses. Remember those two beautiful elm trees out there? When I and Biff hung the swing between them?

LINDA. Yeah, like being a million miles from the city.

WILLY. They should've arrested the builder for cutting those down. They massacred the neighborhood. (*Lost.*) More and more I think of those days, Linda. This time of year it was lilac and wisteria. And then the peonies would come out, and the daffodils. What fragrance in this room!

LINDA. Well, after all, people had to move somewhere.

WILLY. No, there's more people now.

LINDA. I don't think there's more people. I think . . .

WILLY. There's more people! That's what's ruining this country! Population is getting out of control. The competition is maddening! Smell the stink from that apartment house! And another one on the other side . . . How can they whip cheese?

On Willy's last line, Biff and Happy raise themselves up in their beds, listening.

LINDA. Go down, try it. And be quiet.

WILLY (*turning to Linda, guiltily*). You're not worried about me, are you, sweetheart?

BIFF. What's the matter?

HAPPY. Listen!

LINDA. You've got too much on the ball to worry about.

WILLY. You're my foundation and my support, Linda.

LINDA. Just try to relax, dear. You make mountains out of molehills.

WILLY. I won't fight with him any more. If he wants to go back to Texas, let him go.

LINDA. He'll find his way.

WILLY. Sure. Certain men just don't get started till later in life. Like Thomas Edison, I think. Or B. F. Goodrich. One of them was deaf. (*He starts for the bedroom doorway.*) I'll put my money on Biff.

LINDA. And Willy—if it's warm Sunday we'll drive in the country. And we'll open the windshield, and take lunch.

WILLY. No, the windshields don't open on the new cars.

LINDA. But you opened it today.

WILLY. Me? I didn't. (*He stops.*) Now isn't that peculiar! Isn't that a remarkable . . . (*He breaks off in amazement and fright as the flute is heard distantly.*)

LINDA. What, darling?

WILLY. That is the most remarkable thing.

LINDA. What, dear?

WILLY. I was thinking of the Chevvy. (*Slight pause.*) Nineteen twenty-eight . . . when I had that red Chevvy . . . (*Breaks off:*) That funny? I coulda sworn I was driving that Chevvy today.

LINDA. Well, that's nothing. Something must've reminded you.

WILLY. Remarkable. Ts. Remember those days? The way Biff used to simonize that car? The dealer refused to believe there was eighty thousand miles on it. (*He shakes his head.*) Heh! (*To Linda.*) Close your eyes, I'll be right up. (*He walks out of the bedroom.*)

HAPPY (*to Biff*). Jesus, maybe he smashed up the car again!

LINDA (*calling after Willy*). Be careful on the stairs, dear! The cheese is on the middle shelf. (*She turns, goes over to the bed, takes his jacket, and goes out of the bedroom.*)

Light has risen on the boys' room. Unseen, Willy is heard talking to himself; "Eighty thousand miles," and a little laugh. Biff gets out of bed, comes downstage a bit, and

stands attentively. Biff is two years older than his brother Happy, well built, but in these days bears a worn air and seems less self-assured. He has succeeded less, and his dreams are stronger and less acceptable than Happy's. Happy is tall, powerfully made. Sexuality is like a visible color on him, or a scent that many women have discovered. He, like his brother, is lost, but in a different way, for he has never allowed himself to turn his face toward defeat and is thus more confused and hard-skinned, although seemingly more content.

HAPPY (*getting out of bed*). He's going to get his license taken away if he keeps that up. I'm getting nervous about him, y'know, Biff?

BIFF. His eyes are going.

HAPPY. No, I've driven with him. He sees all right. He just doesn't keep his mind on it. I drove into the city with him last week. He stops at a green light and then it turns red and he goes. (*He laughs.*)

BIFF. Maybe he's color-blind.

HAPPY. Pop? Why he's got the finest eye for color in the business. You know that.

BIFF (*sitting down on his bed*). I'm going to sleep.

HAPPY. You're not still sour on Dad, are you, Biff?

BIFF. He's all right, I guess.

WILLY (*underneath them, in the living room*). Yes, sir, eighty thousand miles—eighty-two thousand!

BIFF. You smoking?

HAPPY (*holding out a pack of cigarettes*). Want one?

BIFF (*taking a cigarette*). I can never sleep when I smell it.

WILLY. What a simonizing job, heh!

HAPPY (*with deep sentiment*). Funny, Biff, y'know? Us sleeping in here again? The old beds. (*He pats his bed affectionately.*) All the talk that went across those beds, huh? Our whole lives.

BIFF. Yeah. Lotta dreams and plans.

HAPPY (*with a deep and masculine laugh*). About five hundred women would like to know what was said in this room. (*They share a soft laugh.*)

BIFF. Remember that big Betsy something—what the hell was her name—over on Bushwick Avenue?

HAPPY (*combing his hair*). With the collie dog!

BIFF. That's the one. I got you in there, remember?

HAPPY. Yeah, that was my first time—I think. Boy, there was a pig. (*They laugh, almost crudely.*) You taught me everything I know about women. Don't forget that.

BIFF. I bet you forgot how bashful you used to be. Especially with girls.

HAPPY. Oh, I still am, Biff.

BIFF. Oh, go on.

HAPPY. I just control it, that's all. I think I got less bashful and you got more so. What happened, Biff? Where's the old humor, the old confidence? (*He shakes Biff's knee. Biff gets up and moves restlessly about the room.*) What's the matter?

BIFF. Why does Dad mock me all the time?

HAPPY. He's not mocking you, he . . .

BIFF. Everything I say there's a twist of mockery on his face. I can't get near him.

HAPPY. He just wants you to make good, that's all. I wanted to talk to you about Dad for a long time, Biff. Something's—happening to him. He—talks to himself.

BIFF. I noticed that this morning. But he always mumbled.

HAPPY. But not so noticeable. It got so embarrassing I sent him to Florida. And you know something? Most of the time he's talking to you.

BIFF. What's he say about me?

HAPPY. I can't make it out.

BIFF. What's he say about me?

HAPPY. I think the fact that you're not settled, that you're still kind of up in the air . . .

BIFF. There's one or two other things depressing him, Happy.

HAPPY. What do you mean?

BIFF. Never mind. Just don't lay it all to me.

HAPPY. But I think if you just got started—I mean—is there any future for you out there?

BIFF. I tell ya, Hap, I don't know what the future is. I don't know—what I'm supposed to want.

HAPPY. What do you mean?

BIFF. Well, I spent six or seven years after high school trying to work myself up. Shipping clerk, salesman, business of one kind or another. And it's a measly manner of existence. To get on that subway on the hot mornings in summer. To devote your whole life to keeping stock, or making phone calls, or selling or buying. To suffer fifty weeks of the year for the sake of a two-week vacation, when all you really desire is to be outdoors, with your shirt off. And always to have to get ahead of the next fella. And still—that's how you build a future.

HAPPY. Well, you really enjoy it on a farm? Are you content out there?

BIFF (*with rising agitation*). Hap, I've had twenty or thirty different kinds of jobs since I left home before the war, and it always turns out the same. I just realized it lately. In Nebraska when I herded cattle, and the Dakotas, and Arizona, and now in Texas. It's why I came home now, I guess, because I realized it. This farm I work on, it's spring there now, see? And they've got about fifteen new colts. There's nothing more inspiring or—beautiful than the sight of a mare and a new colt. And it's cool there now, see? Texas is cool now, and it's spring. And whenever spring comes to where I am, I suddenly get the feeling, my God, I'm not gettin' anywhere! What the hell am I doing, playing around with horses, twenty-eight dollars a week! I'm thirty-four years old, I oughta be makin' my future. That's when I come running home. And now, I get here, and I don't know what to do with myself. (*After a pause.*) I've always made a point of not wasting my life, and everytime I come back here I know that all I've done is to waste my life.

HAPPY. You're a poet, you know that, Biff? You're a—you're an idealist!

BIFF. No, I'm mixed up very bad. Maybe I oughta get married. Maybe I oughta get stuck into something. Maybe that's my trouble. I'm like a boy. I'm not married, I'm not in business, I just—I'm like a boy. Are you content, Hap? You're a success, aren't you? Are you content?

HAPPY. Hell, no!

BIFF. Why? You're making money, aren't you?

HAPPY (*moving about with energy, expressiveness*). All I can do now is wait for the merchandise manager to die. And suppose I get to be merchandise manager? He's a good friend of mine, and he just built a terrific estate on Long Island. And he lived there about two months and sold it, and now he's building another one. He can't enjoy it once it's finished. And I know that's just what I would do. I don't know what the hell I'm workin' for. Sometimes I sit in my apartment—all alone. And I think of the rent I'm paying. And it's crazy. But then, it's what I always wanted. My own apartment, a car, and plenty of women. And still, goddammit, I'm lonely.

BIFF (*with enthusiasm*). Listen, why don't you come out West with me?

HAPPY. You and I, heh?

BIFF. Sure, maybe we could buy a ranch. Raise cattle, use our muscles. Men built like we are should be working out in the open.

HAPPY (*avidly*). The Loman Brothers, heh?

BIFF (*with vast affection*). Sure, we'd be known all over the counties!

HAPPY (*enthralled*). That's what I dream about, Biff. Sometimes I want to just rip my clothes off in the middle of the store and outbox that goddam merchandise manager. I mean I can outbox, outrun, and outlift anybody in that store, and I have to take orders from those common, petty sons-of-bitches till I can't stand it any more.

BIFF. I'm tellin' you, kid, if you were with me I'd be happy out there.

HAPPY (*enthused*). See, Biff, everybody around me is so false that I'm constantly lowering my ideals . . .

BIFF. Baby, together we'd stand up for one another, we'd have someone to trust.

HAPPY. If I were around you . . .

BIFF. Hap, the trouble is we weren't brought up to grub for money. I don't know how to do it.

HAPPY. Neither can I!

BIFF. Then let's go!

HAPPY. The only thing is—what can you make out there?

BIFF. But look at your friend. Builds an estate and then hasn't the peace of mind to live in it.

HAPPY. Yeah, but when he walks into the store the waves part in front of him. That's fifty-two thousand dollars a year coming through the revolving door, and I got more in my pinky finger than he's got in his head.

BIFF. Yeah, but you just said . . .

HAPPY. I gotta show some of those pompous, self-important executives over there that Hap Loman can make the grade. I want to walk into the store the way he walks in.

Then I'll go with you, Biff. We'll be together yet, I swear. But take those two we had tonight. Now weren't they gorgeous creatures?

BIFF. Yeah, yeah, most gorgeous I've had in years.

HAPPY. I get that any time I want, Biff. Whenever I feel disgusted. The only trouble is, it gets like bowling or something. I just keep knockin' them over and it doesn't mean anything. You still run around a lot?

BIFF. Naa. I'd like to find a girl—steady, somebody with substance.

HAPPY. That's what I long for.

BIFF. Go on! You'd never come home.

HAPPY. I would! Somebody with character, with resistance! Like Mom, y'know? You're gonna call me a bastard when I tell you this. That girl Charlotte I was with tonight is engaged to be married in five weeks. (*He tries on his new hat.*)

BIFF. No kiddin'!

HAPPY. Sure, the guy's in line for the vice-presidency of the store. I don't know what gets into me, maybe I just have an over-developed sense of competition or something, but I went and ruined her, and furthermore I can't get rid of her. And he's the third executive I've done that to. Isn't that a crummy characteristic? And to top it all, I go to their weddings! (*Indignantly, but laughing.*) Like I'm not supposed to take bribes. Manufacturers offer me a hundred-dollar bill now and then to throw an order their way. You know how honest I am, but it's like this girl, see. I hate myself for it. Because I don't want the girl, and, still, I take it and—I love it!

BIFF. Let's go to sleep.

HAPPY. I guess we didn't settle anything, heh?

BIFF. I just got one idea that I think I'm going to try.

HAPPY. What's that?

BIFF. Remember Bill Oliver?

HAPPY. Sure, Oliver is very big now. You want to work for him again?

BIFF. No, but when I quit he said something to me. He put his arm on my shoulder, and he said, "Biff, if you ever need anything, come to me."

HAPPY. I remember that. That sounds good.

BIFF. I think I'll go to see him. If I could get ten thousand or even seven or eight thousand dollars I could buy a beautiful ranch.

HAPPY. I bet he'd back you. 'Cause he thought highly of you, Biff. I mean, they all do. You're well liked, Biff. That's why I say to come back here, and we both have the apartment. And I'm tellin' you, Biff, any babe you want . . .

BIFF. No, with a ranch I could do the work I like and still be something. I just wonder though. I wonder if Oliver still thinks I stole that carton of basketballs.

HAPPY. Oh, he probably forgot that long ago. It's almost ten years. You're too sensitive. Anyway, he didn't really fire you.

BIFF. Well, I think he was going to. I think that's why I quit. I was never sure whether he knew or not. I know he thought the world of me, though. I was the only one he'd let lock up the place.

WILLY (*below*). You gonna wash the engine, Biff?

HAPPY. Shh!

Biff looks at Happy, who is gazing down, listening. Willy is mumbling in the parlor.

HAPPY. You hear that?

They listen. Willy laughs warmly.

BIFF (*growing angry*). Doesn't he know Mom can hear that?

WILLY. Don't get your sweater dirty, Biff!

A look of pain crosses Biff's face.

HAPPY. Isn't that terrible? Don't leave again, will you? You'll find a job here. You gotta stick around. I don't know what to do about him, it's getting embarrassing.

WILLY. What a simonizing job!

BIFF. Mom's hearing that!

WILLY. No kiddin', Biff, you got a date? Wonderful!

HAPPY. Go on to sleep. But talk to him in the morning, will you?

BIFF (*reluctantly getting into bed*). With her in the house. Brother!

HAPPY (*getting into bed*). I wish you'd have a good talk with him.

The light on their room begins to fade.

BIFF (*to himself in bed*). That selfish, stupid . . .

HAPPY. Sh . . . Sleep, Biff.

Their light is out. Well before they have finished speaking, Willy's form is dimly seen below in the darkened kitchen. He opens the refrigerator, searches in there, and takes out a bottle of milk. The apartment houses are fading out, and the entire house and surroundings become covered with leaves. Music insinuates itself as the leaves appear.

WILLY. Just wanna be careful with those girls, Biff, that's all. Don't make any promises. No promises of any kind. Because a girl, y'know, they always believe what you tell 'em, and you're very young, Biff, you're too young to be talking seriously to girls.

Light rises on the kitchen. Willy, talking, shuts the refrigerator door and comes downstage to the kitchen table. He pours milk into a glass. He is totally immersed in himself, smiling faintly.

WILLY. Too young entirely, Biff. You want to watch your schooling first. Then when you're all set, there'll be plenty of girls for a boy like you. (*He smiles broadly at a kitchen chair.*) That so? The girls pay for you? (*He laughs.*) Boy, you must really be makin' a hit.

Willy is gradually addressing—physically—a point off-stage, speaking through the wall of the kitchen, and his voice has been rising in volume to that of a normal conversation.

WILLY. I been wondering why you polish the car so careful. Ha! Don't leave the hubcaps, boys. Get the chamois to the hubcaps. Happy, use newspaper on the windows, it's the easiest thing. Show him how to do it, Biff! You see, Happy? Pad it up, use it like a pad. That's it, that's it, good work. You're doin' all right, Hap. (*He pauses, then nods in approbation for a few seconds, then looks upward.*) Biff, first thing we gotta do when we get time is clip that big branch over the house. Afraid it's gonna fall in a storm and hit the roof. Tell you what. We get a rope and sling her around, and then we climb up there with a couple of saws and take her down. Soon as you finish the car, boys, I wanna see ya. I got a surprise for you, boys.

BIFF (*offstage*). Whatta ya got, Dad?

WILLY. No, you finish first. Never leave a job till you're finished—remember that. (*Looking toward the "big trees."*) Biff, up in Albany I saw a beautiful hammock. I think I'll buy it next trip, and we'll hang it right between those two elms. Wouldn't that be something? Just swingin' there under those branches. Boy, that would be . . .

Young Biff and Young Happy appear from the direction Willy was addressing. Happy carries rags and a pail of water. Biff, wearing a sweater with a block "S," carries a football.

BIFF (*pointing in the direction of the car offstage*). How's that, Pop, professional?

WILLY. Terrific. Terrific job, boys. Good work, Biff.

HAPPY. Where's the surprise, Pop?

WILLY. In the back seat of the car.

HAPPY. Boy! (*He runs off.*)

BIFF. What is it, Dad? Tell me, what'd you buy?

WILLY (*laughing, cuffs him*). Never mind, something I want you to have.

BIFF (*turns and starts off*). What is it, Hap?

HAPPY (*offstage*). It's a punching bag!

BIFF. Oh, Pop!

WILLY. It's got Gene Tunney's signature on it!

Happy runs onstage with a punching bag.

BIFF. Gee, how'd you know we wanted a punching bag?

WILLY. Well, it's the finest thing for the timing.

HAPPY (*lies down on his back and pedals with his feet*). I'm losing weight, you notice, Pop?

WILLY (*to Happy*). Jumping rope is good too.

BIFF. Did you see the new football I got?

WILLY (*examining the ball*). Where'd you get a new ball?

BIFF. The coach told me to practice my passing.

WILLY. That so? And he gave you the ball, heh?

BIFF. Well, I borrowed it from the locker room. (*He laughs confidentially.*)

WILLY (*laughing with him at the theft*). I want you to return that.

HAPPY. I told you he wouldn't like it!

BIFF (*angrily*). Well, I'm bringing it back!

WILLY (*stopping the incipient argument, to Happy*). Sure, he's gotta practice with a regulation ball, doesn't he? (*To Biff.*) Coach'll probably congratulate you on your initiative!

BIFF. Oh, he keeps congratulating my initiative all the time, Pop.

WILLY. That's because he likes you. If somebody else took that ball there'd be an uproar. So what's the report, boys, what's the report?

BIFF. Where'd you go this time, Dad? Gee we were lonesome for you.

WILLY (*pleased, puts an arm around each boy and they come down to the apron*). Lonesome, heh?

BIFF. Missed you every minute.

WILLY. Don't say? Tell you a secret, boys. Don't breathe it to a soul. Someday I'll have my own business, and I'll never have to leave home any more.

HAPPY. Like Uncle Charley, heh?

WILLY. Bigger than Uncle Charley! Because Charley is not—liked. He's liked, but he's not—well liked.

BIFF. Where'd you go this time, Dad?

WILLY. Well, I got on the road, and I went north to Providence. Met the Mayor.

BIFF. The Mayor of Providence!

WILLY. He was sitting in the hotel lobby.

BIFF. What'd he say?

WILLY. He said, "Morning!" And I said, "Morning!" And I said, "You got a fine city here, Mayor." And then he had coffee with me. And then I went to Waterbury. Waterbury is a fine city. Big clock city, the famous Waterbury clock. Sold a nice bill there. And then Boston—Boston is the cradle of the Revolution. A fine city. And a couple of other towns in Mass., and on to Portland and Bangor and straight home!

BIFF. Gee, I'd love to go with you sometime, Dad.

WILLY. Soon as summer comes.

HAPPY. Promise?

WILLY. You and Hap and I, and I'll show you all the towns. America is full of beautiful towns and fine, upstanding people. And they know me, boys, they know me up and down New England. The finest people. And when I bring you fellas up, there'll be open sesame for all of us, 'cause one thing, boys: I have friends. I can park my car in any street in New England, and the cops protect it like their own. This summer, heh?

BIFF AND HAPPY (*together*). Yeah! You bet!

WILLY. We'll take our bathing suits.

HAPPY. We'll carry your bags, Pop!

WILLY. Oh, won't that be something! Me comin' into the Boston stores with you boys carryin' my bags. What a sensation!

Biff is prancing around, practicing passing the ball.

WILLY. You nervous, Biff, about the game?

BIFF. Not if you're gonna be there.

WILLY. What do they say about you in school, now that they made you captain?

HAPPY. There's a crowd of girls behind him everytime the classes change.

BIFF (*taking Willy's hand*). This Saturday, Pop, this Saturday—just for you, I'm going to break through for a touchdown.

HAPPY. You're supposed to pass.

BIFF. I'm takin' one play for Pop. You watch me, Pop, and when I take off my helmet, that means I'm breakin' out. Then you watch me crash through that line!

WILLY (*kisses Biff*). Oh, wait'll I tell this in Boston!

Bernard enters in knickers. He is younger than Biff, earnest and loyal, a worried boy.

BERNARD. Biff, where are you? You're supposed to study with me today.

WILLY. Hey, looka Bernard. What're you lookin' so anemic about, Bernard?

BERNARD. He's gotta study, Uncle Willy. He's got Regents next week.

HAPPY (*tauntingly, spinning Bernard around*). Let's box, Bernard!

BERNARD. Biff! (*He gets away from Happy.*) Listen, Biff, I heard Mr. Birnbaum say that if you don't start studyin' math he's gonna flunk you, and you won't graduate. I heard him!

WILLY. You better study with him, Biff. Go ahead now.

BERNARD. I heard him!

BIFF. Oh, Pop, you didn't see my sneakers! (*He holds up a foot for Willy to look at.*)

WILLY. Hey, that's a beautiful job of printing!

BERNARD (*wiping his glasses*). Just because he printed University of Virginia on his sneakers doesn't mean they've got to graduate him, Uncle Willy!

WILLY (*angrily*). What're you talking about? With scholarships to three universities they're gonna flunk him?

BERNARD. But I heard Mr. Birnbaum say . . .

WILLY. Don't be a pest, Bernard! (*To his boys.*) What an anemic!

BERNARD. Okay, I'm waiting for you in my house, Biff.

Bernard goes off. The Lomans laugh.

WILLY. Bernard is not well liked, is he?

BIFF. He's liked, but he's not well liked.

HAPPY. That's right, Pop.

WILLY. That's just what I mean. Bernard can get the best marks in school, y'understand, but when he gets out in the business world, y'understand, you are going to be five times ahead of him. That's why I thank Almighty God you're both built like Adonises. Because the man who makes an appearance in the business world, the man who creates personal interest, is the man who gets ahead. Be liked and you will never want. You take me, for instance. I never have to wait in line to see a buyer. "Willy Loman is here!" That's all they have to know, and I go right through.

BIFF. Did you knock them dead, Pop?

WILLY. Knocked 'em cold in Providence, slaughtered 'em in Boston.

HAPPY (*on his back, pedaling again*). I'm losing weight, you notice, Pop?

Linda enters as of old, a ribbon in her hair, carrying a basket of washing.

LINDA. (*with youthful energy*). Hello, dear!

WILLY. Sweetheart!

LINDA. How'd the Chevvy run?

WILLY. Chevrolet, Linda, is the greatest car ever built. (*To the boys.*) Since when do you let your mother carry wash up the stairs?

BIFF. Grab hold there, boy!

HAPPY. Where to, Mom?

LINDA. Hang them up on the line. And you better go down to your friends, Biff. The cellar is full of boys. They don't know what to do with themselves.

BIFF. Ah, when Pop comes home they can wait!

WILLY (*laughs appreciatively*). You better go down and tell them what to do, Biff.

BIFF. I think I'll have them sweep out the furnace room.

WILLY. Good work, Biff.

BIFF (*goes through wall-line of kitchen to doorway at back and calls down*). Fellas! Everybody sweep out the furnace room! I'll be right down!

VOICES. All right! Okay, Biff.

BIFF. George and Sam and Frank, come out back! We're hangin' up the wash! Come on, Hap, on the double! (*He and Happy carry out the basket.*)

LINDA. The way they obey him!

WILLY. Well, that's training, the training. I'm tellin' you, I was sellin' thousands and thousands, but I had to come home.

LINDA. Oh, the whole block'll be at that game. Did you sell anything?

WILLY. I did five hundred gross in Providence and seven hundred gross in Boston.

LINDA. No! Wait a minute. I've got a pencil. (*She pulls pencil and paper out of her apron pocket.*) That makes your commission . . . Two hundred—my God! Two hundred and twelve dollars!

WILLY. Well, I didn't figure it yet, but . . .

LINDA. How much did you do?

WILLY. Well, I—I did—about a hundred and eighty gross in Providence. Well, no—it came to—roughly two hundred gross on the whole trip.

LINDA (*without hesitation*). Two hundred gross. That's . . . (*She figures.*)

WILLY. The trouble was that three of the stores were half-closed for inventory in Boston. Otherwise I woulda broke records.

LINDA. Well, it makes seventy dollars and some pennies. That's very good.

WILLY. What do we owe?

LINDA. Well, on the first there's sixteen dollars on the refrigerator . . .

WILLY. Why sixteen?

LINDA. Well, the fan belt broke, so it was a dollar eighty.

WILLY. But it's brand new.

LINDA. Well, the man said that's the way it is. Till they work themselves in, y'know.

They move through the wall-line into the kitchen.

WILLY. I hope we didn't get stuck on that machine.

LINDA. They got the biggest ads of any of them!

WILLY. I know, it's a fine machine. What else?

LINDA. Well, there's nine-sixty for the washing machine. And for the vacuum cleaner there's three and a half due on the fifteenth. Then the roof, you got twenty-one dollars remaining.

WILLY. It don't leak, does it?

LINDA. No, they did a wonderful job. Then you owe Frank for the carburetor.

WILLY. I'm not going to pay that man! That goddam Chevrolet, they ought to prohibit the manufacture of that car!

LINDA. Well, you owe him three and a half. And odds and ends, comes to around a hundred and twenty dollars by the fifteenth.

WILLY. A hundred and twenty dollars! My God, if business don't pick up I don't know what I'm gonna do!

LINDA. Well, next week you'll do better.

WILLY. Oh, I'll knock 'em dead next week. I'll go to Hartford. I'm very well liked in Hartford. You know, the trouble is, Linda, people don't seem to take to me.

They move onto the forestage.

LINDA. Oh, don't be foolish.

WILLY. I know it when I walk in. They seem to laugh at me.

LINDA. Why? Why would they laugh at you? Don't talk that way, Willy.

Willy moves to the edge of the stage. Linda goes into the kitchen and starts to darn stockings.

WILLY. I don't know the reason for it, but they just pass me by. I'm not noticed.

LINDA. But you're doing wonderful, dear. You're making seventy to a hundred dollars a week.

WILLY. But I gotta be at it ten, twelve hours a day. Other men—I don't know—they do it easier. I don't know why—I can't stop myself—I talk too much. A man oughta come in with a few words. One thing about Charley. He's a man of few words, and they respect him.

LINDA. You don't talk too much, you're just lively.

WILLY (*smiling*). Well, I figure, what the hell, life is short, a couple of jokes. (*To himself:*) I joke too much! (*The smile goes.*)

LINDA. Why? You're . . .

WILLY. I'm fat. I'm very—foolish to look at, Linda. I didn't tell you, but Christmas time I happened to be calling on F. H. Stewarts, and a salesman I know, as I was going in to see the buyer I heard him say something about—walrus. And I—I cracked him right across the face. I won't take that. I simply will not take that. But they do laugh at me. I know that.

LINDA. Darling . . .

WILLY. I gotta overcome it. I know I gotta overcome it. I'm not dressing to advantage, maybe.

LINDA. Willy, darling, you're the handsomest man in the world . . .

WILLY. Oh, no, Linda.

LINDA. To me you are. (*Slight pause.*) The handsomest.

From the darkness is heard the laughter of a woman. Willy doesn't turn to it, but it continues through Linda's lines.

LINDA. And the boys, Willy. Few men are idolized by their children the way you are.

Music is heard as behind a scrim, to the left of the house; The Woman, dimly seen, is dressing.

WILLY (*with great feeling*). You're the best there is. Linda, you're a pal, you know that? On the road—on the road I want to grab you sometimes and just kiss the life outa you.

The laughter is loud now, and he moves into a brightening area at the left, where The Woman has come from behind the scrim and is standing, putting on her hat, looking into a "mirror" and laughing.

WILLY. 'Cause I get so lonely—especially when business is bad and there's nobody to talk to. I get the feeling that I'll never sell anything again, that I won't make a living for you, or a business, a business for the boys. (*He talks through The Woman's subsiding laughter; The Woman primps at the "mirror."*) There's so much I want to make for . . .

THE WOMAN. Me? You didn't make me, Willy. I picked you.

WILLY (*pleased*). You picked me?

THE WOMAN (*who is quite proper-looking, Willy's age*). I did. I've been sitting at that desk watching all the salesmen go by, day in, day out. But you've got such a sense of humor, and we do have such a good time together, don't we?

WILLY. Sure, sure. (*He takes her in his arms.*) Why do you have to go now?

THE WOMAN. It's two o'clock . . .

WILLY. No, come on in! (*He pulls her.*)

THE WOMAN. . . . my sisters'll be scandalized. When'll you be back?

WILLY. Oh, two weeks about. Will you come up again?

THE WOMAN. Sure thing. You do make me laugh. It's good for me. (*She squeezes his arm, kisses him.*) And I think you're a wonderful man.

WILLY. You picked me, heh?

THE WOMAN. Sure. Because you're so sweet. And such a kidder.

WILLY. Well, I'll see you next time I'm in Boston.

THE WOMAN. I'll put you right through to the buyers.

WILLY (*slapping her bottom*). Right. Well, bottoms up!

THE WOMAN (*slaps him gently and laughs*). You just kill me, Willy. (*He suddenly grabs her and kisses her roughly.*) You kill me. And thanks for the stockings. I love a lot of stockings. Well, good night.

WILLY. Good night. And keep your pores open!

THE WOMAN. Oh, Willy!

The Woman bursts out laughing, and Linda's laughter blends in. The Woman disappears into the dark. Now the area at the kitchen table brightens. Linda is sitting where she was at the kitchen table, but now is mending a pair of her silk stockings.

LINDA. You are, Willy. The handsomest man. You've got no reason to feel that . . .

WILLY (*coming out of The Woman's dimming area and going over to Linda*). I'll make it all up to you, Linda, I'll . . .

LINDA. There's nothing to make up, dear. You're doing fine, better than . . .

WILLY (*noticing her mending*). What's that?

LINDA. Just mending my stockings. They're so expensive . . .

WILLY (*angrily, taking them from her*). I won't have you mending stockings in this house! Now throw them out!

Linda puts the stockings in her pocket.

BERNARD (*entering on the run*). Where is he? If he doesn't study!

WILLY (*moving to the forestage, with great agitation*). You'll give him the answers!

BERNARD. I do, but I can't on a Regents! That's a state exam! They're liable to arrest me!

WILLY. Where is he? I'll whip him, I'll whip him!

LINDA. And he'd better give back that football, Willy, it's not nice.

WILLY. Biff! Where is he? Why is he taking everything?

LINDA. He's too rough with the girls, Willy. All the mothers are afraid of him!

WILLY. I'll whip him!

BERNARD. He's driving the car without a license!

The Woman's laugh is heard.

WILLY. Shut up!

LINDA. All the mothers . . .

WILLY. Shut up!

BERNARD (*backing quietly away and out*). Mr. Birnbaum says he's stuck up.

WILLY. Get outa here!

BERNARD. If he doesn't buckle down he'll flunk math! (*He goes off.*)

LINDA. He's right, Willy, you've gotta . . .

WILLY (*exploding at her*). There's nothing the matter with him! You want him to be a worm like Bernard? He's got spirit, personality . . .

As he speaks, Linda, almost in tears, exits into the living room. Willy is alone in the kitchen, wilting and staring. The leaves are gone. It is night again, and the apartment houses look down from behind.

WILLY. Loaded with it. Loaded! What is he stealing? He's giving it back, isn't he? Why is he stealing? What did I tell him? I never in my life told him anything but decent things.

Happy in pajamas has come down the stairs; Willy suddenly becomes aware of Happy's presence.

HAPPY. Let's go now, come on.

WILLY (*sitting down at the kitchen table*). Huh! Why did she have to wax the floors herself? Everytime she waxes the floors she keels over. She knows that!

HAPPY. Shh! Take it easy. What brought you back tonight?

WILLY. I got an awful scare. Nearly hit a kid in Yonkers. God! Why didn't I go to Alaska with my brother Ben that time! Ben! That man was a genius, that man was success incarnate! What a mistake! He begged me to go.

HAPPY. Well, there's no use in . . .

WILLY. You guys! There was a man started with the clothes on his back and ended up with diamond mines!

HAPPY. Boy, someday I'd like to know how he did it.

WILLY. What's the mystery? The man knew what he wanted and went out and got it! Walked into a jungle, and comes out, the age of twenty-one, and he's rich! The world is an oyster, but you don't crack it open on a mattress!

HAPPY. Pop, I told you I'm gonna retire you for life.

WILLY. You'll retire me for life on seventy goddam dollars a week? And your women and your car and your apartment, and you'll retire me for life! Christ's sake, I couldn't get past Yonkers today! Where are you guys, where are you? The woods are burning! I can't drive a car!

Charley has appeared in the doorway. He is a large man, slow of speech, laconic, immovable. In all he says, despite what he says, there is pity, and, now, trepidation. He has a robe over pajamas, slippers on his feet. He enters the kitchen.

CHARLEY. Everything all right?

HAPPY. Yeah, Charley, everything's . . .

WILLY. What's the matter?

CHARLEY. I heard some noise. I thought something happened. Can't we do something about the walls? You sneeze in here, and in my house hats blow off.

HAPPY. Let's go to bed, Dad. Come on.

Charley signals to Happy to go.

WILLY. You go ahead, I'm not tired at the moment.

HAPPY (*to Willy*). Take it easy, huh? (*He exits.*)

WILLY. What're you doin' up?

CHARLEY (*sitting down at the kitchen table opposite Willy*). Couldn't sleep good. I had a heartburn.

WILLY. Well, you don't know how to eat.

CHARLEY. I eat with my mouth.

WILLY. No, you're ignorant. You gotta know about vitamins and things like that.

CHARLEY. Come on, let's shoot. Tire you out a little.

WILLY (*hesitantly*). All right. You got cards?

CHARLEY (*taking a deck from his pocket*). Yeah, I got them. Someplace. What is it with those vitamins?

WILLY (*dealing*). They build up your bones. Chemistry.

CHARLEY. Yeah, but there's no bones in a heartburn.

WILLY. What are you talkin' about? Do you know the first thing about it?

CHARLEY. Don't get insulted.

WILLY. Don't talk about something you don't know anything about.

They are playing. Pause.

CHARLEY. What're you doin' home?

WILLY. A little trouble with the car.

CHARLEY. Oh. (*Pause.*) I'd like to take a trip to California.

WILLY. Don't say.

CHARLEY. You want a job?

WILLY. I got a job, I told you that. (*After a slight pause.*) What the hell are you offering me a job for?

CHARLEY. Don't get insulted.

WILLY. Don't insult me.

CHARLEY. I don't see no sense in it. You don't have to go on this way.

WILLY. I got a good job. (*Slight pause.*) What do you keep comin' in here for?

CHARLEY. You want me to go?

WILLY (*after a pause, withering*). I can't understand it. He's going back to Texas again. What the hell is that?

CHARLEY. Let him go.

WILLY. I got nothin' to give him, Charley, I'm clean, I'm clean.

CHARLEY. He won't starve. None a them starve. Forget about him.

WILLY. Then what have I got to remember?

CHARLEY. You take it too hard. To hell with it. When a deposit bottle is broken you don't get your nickel back.

WILLY. That's easy enough for you to say.

CHARLEY. That ain't easy for me to say.

WILLY. Did you see the ceiling I put up in the living room?

CHARLEY. Yeah, that's a piece of work. To put up a ceiling is a mystery to me. How do you do it?

WILLY. What's the difference?

CHARLEY. Well, talk about it.

WILLY. You gonna put up a ceiling?

CHARLEY. How could I put up a ceiling?

WILLY. Then what the hell are you bothering me for?

CHARLEY. You're insulted again.

WILLY. A man who can't handle tools is not a man. You're disgusting.

CHARLEY. Don't call me disgusting, Willy.

Uncle Ben, carrying a valise and an umbrella, enters the forestage from around the right corner of the house. He is a stolid man, in his sixties, with a mustache and an authoritative air. He is utterly certain of his destiny, and there is an aura of far places about him. He enters exactly as Willy speaks.

WILLY. I'm getting awfully tired, Ben.

Ben's music is heard. Ben looks around at everything.

CHARLEY. Good, keep playing; you'll sleep better. Did you call me Ben?

Ben looks at his watch.

WILLY. That's funny. For a second there you reminded me of my brother Ben.

BEN. I only have a few minutes. (*He strolls, inspecting the place. Willy and Charley continue playing.*)

CHARLEY. You never heard from him again, heh? Since that time?

WILLY. Didn't Linda tell you? Couple of weeks ago we got a letter from his wife in Africa. He died.

CHARLEY. That so.

BEN (*chuckling*). So this is Brooklyn, eh?

CHARLEY. Maybe you're in for some of his money.

WILLY. Naa, he had seven sons. There's just one opportunity I had with that man . . .

BEN. I must make a train, William. There are several properties I'm looking at in Alaska.

WILLY. Sure, sure! If I'd gone with him to Alaska that time, everything would've been totally different.

CHARLEY. Go on, you'd froze to death up there.

WILLY. What're you talking about?

BEN. Opportunity is tremendous in Alaska, William. Surprised you're not up there.

WILLY. Sure, tremendous.

CHARLEY. Heh?

WILLY. There was the only man I ever met who knew the answers.

CHARLEY. Who?

BEN. How are you all?

WILLY (*taking a pot, smiling*). Fine, fine.

CHARLEY. Pretty sharp tonight.

BEN. Is Mother living with you?

WILLY. No, she died a long time ago.

CHARLEY. Who?

BEN. That's too bad. Fine specimen of a lady, Mother.

WILLY (*to Charley*). Heh?

BEN. I'd hoped to see the old girl.

CHARLEY. Who died?

BEN. Heard anything from Father, have you?

WILLY (*unnerved*). What do you mean, who died?

CHARLEY (*taking a pot*). What're you talkin' about?

BEN (*looking at his watch*). William, it's half-past eight!

WILLY (*as though to dispel his confusion he angrily stops Charley's hand*). That's my build!

CHARLEY. I put the ace . . .

WILLY. If you don't know how to play the game I'm not gonna throw my money away on you!

CHARLEY (*rising*). It was my ace, for God's sake!

WILLY. I'm through, I'm through!

BEN. When did Mother die?

WILLY. Long ago. Since the beginning you never knew how to play cards.

CHARLEY (*picks up the cards and goes to the door*). All right! Next time I'll bring a deck with five aces.

WILLY. I don't play that kind of game!

CHARLEY (*turning to him*). You ought to be ashamed of yourself!

WILLY. Yeah?

CHARLEY. Yeah! (*He goes out.*)

WILLY (*slamming the door after him*). Ignoramus!

BEN (*as Willy comes toward him through the wall-line of the kitchen*). So you're William.

WILLY (*shaking Ben's hand*). Ben! I've been waiting for you so long! What's the answer? How did you do it?

BEN. Oh, there's a story in that.

Linda enters the forestage, as of old, carrying the wash basket.

LINDA. Is this Ben?

BEN (*gallantly*). How do you do, my dear.

LINDA. Where've you been all these years? Willy's always wondered why you . . .

WILLY (*pulling Ben away from her impatiently*). Where is Dad? Didn't you follow him? How did you get started?

BEN. Well, I don't know how much you remember.

WILLY. Well, I was just a baby, of course, only three or four years old . . .

BEN. Three years and eleven months.

WILLY. What a memory, Ben!

BEN. I have many enterprises, William, and I have never kept books.

WILLY. I remember I was sitting under the wagon in—was it Nebraska?

BEN. It was South Dakota, and I gave you a bunch of wild flowers.

WILLY. I remember you walking away down some open road.

BEN (*laughing*). I was going to find Father in Alaska.

WILLY. Where is he?

BEN. At that age I had a very faulty view of geography, William. I discovered after a few days that I was heading due south, so instead of Alaska, I ended up in Africa.

LINDA. Africa!

WILLY. The Gold Coast!

BEN. Principally diamond mines.

LINDA. Diamond mines!

BEN. Yes, my dear. But I've only a few minutes . . .

WILLY. No! Boys! Boys! (*Young Biff and Happy appear.*) Listen to this. This is your Uncle Ben, a great man! Tell my boys, Ben!

BEN. Why, boys, when I was seventeen I walked into the jungle, and when I was twenty-one I walked out. (*He laughs.*) And by God I was rich.

WILLY (*to the boys*). You see what I been talking about? The greatest things can happen!

BEN (*glancing at his watch*). I have an appointment in Ketchikan Tuesday week.

WILLY. No, Ben! Please tell about Dad. I want my boys to hear. I want them to know the kind of stock they spring from. All I remember is a man with a big beard, and I was in Mamma's lap, sitting around a fire, and some kind of high music.

BEN. His flute. He played the flute.

WILLY. Sure, the flute, that's right!

New music is heard, a high, rollicking tune.

BEN. Father was a very great and a very wild-hearted man. We would start in Boston, and he'd toss the whole family into the wagon, and then he'd drive the team right across the country; through Ohio, and Indiana, Michigan, Illinois, and all the Western states. And we'd stop in the towns and sell the flutes that he'd made on the way. Great inventor, Father. With one gadget he made more in a week than a man like you could make in a lifetime.

WILLY. That's just the way I'm bringing them up, Ben—rugged, well liked, all-around.

BEN. Yeah? (*To Biff.*) Hit that, boy—hard as you can. (*He pounds his stomach.*)

BIFF. Oh, no, sir!

BEN (*taking boxing stance*). Come on, get to me! (*He laughs.*)

WILLY. Go to it. Biff! Go ahead, show him!

BIFF. Okay! (*He cocks his fists and starts in.*)

LINDA (*to Willy*). Why must he fight, dear?

BEN (*sparring with Biff*). Good boy! Good boy!

WILLY. How's that, Ben, heh?

HAPPY. Give him the left, Biff!

LINDA. Why are you fighting?

BEN. Good boy! (*Suddenly comes in, trips Biff, and stands over him, the point of his umbrella poised over Biff's eye.*)

LINDA. Look out, Biff!

BIFF. Gee!

BEN (*patting Biff's knee*). Never fight fair with a stranger, boy. You'll never get out of the jungle that way. (*Taking Linda's hand and bowing.*) It was an honor and a pleasure to meet you, Linda.

LINDA (*withdrawing her hand coldly, frightened*). Have a nice—trip.

BEN (*to Willy*). And good luck with your—what do you do?

WILLY. Selling.

BEN. Yes. Well . . . (*He raises his hand in farewell to all.*)

WILLY. No, Ben, I don't want you to think . . . (*He takes Ben's arm to show him.*) It's Brooklyn, I know, but we hunt too.

BEN. Really, now.

WILLY. Oh, sure, there's snakes and rabbits and—that's why I moved out here. Why, Biff can fell any one of these trees in no time! Boys! Go right over to where they're building the apartment house and get some sand. We're gonna rebuild the entire front stoop right now! Watch this, Ben!

BIFF. Yes, sir! On the double, Hap!

HAPPY (*as he and Biff run off*). I lost weight, Pop, you notice?

Charley enters in knickers, even before the boys are gone.

CHARLEY. Listen, if they steal any more from that building the watchman'll put the cops on them!

LINDA (*to Willy*). Don't let Biff . . .

Ben laughs lustily.

WILLY. You shoulda seen the lumber they brought home last week. At least a dozen six-by-tens worth all kinds a money.

CHARLEY. Listen, if that watchman . . .

WILLY. I gave them hell, understand. But I got a couple of fearless characters there.

CHARLEY. Willy, the jails are full of fearless characters.

BEN (*clapping Willy on the back, with a laugh at Charley*). And the stock exchange, friend!

WILLY (*joining in Ben's laughter*). Where are the rest of your pants?

CHARLEY. My wife bought them.

WILLY. Now all you need is a golf club and you can go upstairs and go to sleep. (*To Ben.*) Great athlete! Between him and his son Bernard they can't hammer a nail!

BERNARD (*rushing in*). The watchman's chasing Biff!

WILLY (*angrily*). Shut up! He's not stealing anything!

LINDA (*alarmed, hurrying off left*). Where is he? Biff, dear! (*She exits.*)

WILLY (*moving toward the left, away from Ben*). There's nothing wrong. What's the matter with you?

BEN. Nervy boy. Good!

WILLY (*laughing*). Oh, nerves of iron, that Biff!

CHARLEY. Don't know what it is. My New England man comes back and he's bleedin', they murdered him up there.

WILLY. It's contacts, Charley, I got important contacts!

CHARLEY (*sarcastically*). Glad to hear it, Willy. Come in later, we'll shoot a little casino. I'll take some of your Portland money. (*He laughs at Willy and exits.*)

WILLY (*turning to Ben*). Business is bad, it's murderous. But not for me, of course.

BEN. I'll stop by on my way back to Africa.

WILLY (*longingly*). Can't you stay a few days? You're just what I need, Ben, because I—I have a fine position here,

but I—well, Dad left when I was such a baby and I never had a chance to talk to him and I still feel—kind of temporary about myself.

BEN. I'll be late for my train.

They are at opposite ends of the stage.

WILLY. Ben, my boys—can't we talk? They'd go into the jaws of hell for me, see, but I . . .

BEN. William, you're being first-rate with your boys. Outstanding, manly chaps!

WILLY (*hanging on to his words*). Oh, Ben, that's good to hear! Because sometimes I'm afraid that I'm not teaching them the right kind of—Ben, how should I teach them?

BEN (*giving great weight to each word, and with a certain vicious audacity*). William, when I walked into the jungle, I was seventeen. When I walked out I was twenty-one. And, by God, I was rich! (*He goes off into darkness around the right corner of the house.*)

WILLY. . . . was rich! That's just the spirit I want to imbue them with! To walk into a jungle! I was right! I was right! I was right!

Ben is gone, but Willy is still speaking to him as Linda, in nightgown and robe, enters the kitchen, glances around for Willy, then goes to the door of the house, looks out and sees him. Comes down to his left. He looks at her.

LINDA. Willy, dear? Willy?

WILLY. I was right!

LINDA. Did you have some cheese? (*He can't answer.*) It's very late, darling. Come to bed, heh?

WILLY (*looking straight up*). Gotta break your neck to see a star in this yard.

LINDA. You coming in?

WILLY. Whatever happened to that diamond watch fob? Remember? When Ben came from Africa that time? Didn't he give me a watch fob with a diamond in it?

LINDA. You pawned it, dear. Twelve, thirteen years ago. For Biff's radio correspondence course.

WILLY. Gee, that was a beautiful thing. I'll take a walk.

LINDA. But you're in your slippers.

WILLY (*starting to go around the house at the left*). I was right! I was! (*Half to Linda, as he goes, shaking his head.*) What a man! There was a man worth talking to. I was right!

LINDA (*calling after Willy*). But in your slippers, Willy!

Willy is almost gone when Biff, in his pajamas, comes down the stairs and enters the kitchen.

BIFF. What is he doing out there?

LINDA. Sh!

BIFF. God Almighty, Mom, how long has he been doing this?

LINDA. Don't, he'll hear you.

BIFF. What the hell is the matter with him?

LINDA. It'll pass by morning.

BIFF. Shouldn't we do anything?

LINDA. Oh, my dear, you should do a lot of things, but there's nothing to do, so go to sleep.

Happy comes down the stair and sits on the steps.

HAPPY. I never heard him so loud, Mom.

LINDA. Well, come around more often; you'll hear him. (*She sits down at the table and mends the lining of Willy's jacket.*)

BIFF. Why didn't you ever write me about this, Mom?

LINDA. How would I write to you? For over three months you had no address.

BIFF. I was on the move. But you know I thought of you all the time. You know that, don't you, pal?

LINDA. I know, dear, I know. But he likes to have a letter. Just to know that there's still a possibility for better things.

BIFF. He's not like this all the time, is he?

LINDA. It's when you come home he's always the worst.

BIFF. When I come home?

LINDA. When you write you're coming, he's all smiles, and talks about the future, and—he's just wonderful. And then the closer you seem to come, the more shaky he gets, and then, by the time you get here, he's arguing, and he seems angry at you. I think it's just that maybe he can't bring himself to—to open up to you. Why are you so hateful to each other? Why is that?

BIFF (*evasively*). I'm not hateful, Mom.

LINDA. But you no sooner come in the door than you're fighting!

BIFF. I don't know why. I mean to change. I'm tryin', Mom, you understand?

LINDA. Are you home to stay now?

BIFF. I don't know. I want to look around, see what's doin'.

LINDA. Biff, you can't look around all your life, can you?

BIFF. I just can't take hold, Mom. I can't take hold of some kind of a life.

LINDA. Biff, a man is not a bird, to come and go with the spring time.

BIFF. Your hair . . . (*He touches her hair.*) Your hair got so gray.

LINDA. Oh, it's been gray since you were in high school. I just stopped dyeing it, that's all.

BIFF. Dye it again, will ya? I don't want my pal looking old.

(*He smiles.*)

LINDA. You're such a boy! You think you can go away for a year and . . . You've got to get it into your head now that one day you'll knock on this door and there'll be strange people here . . .

BIFF. What are you talking about? You're not even sixty, Mom.

LINDA. But what about your father?

BIFF (*lamely*). Well, I meant him too.

HAPPY. He admires Pop.

LINDA. Biff, dear, if you don't have any feeling for him, then you can't have any feeling for me.

BIFF. Sure I can, Mom.

LINDA. No. You can't just come to see me, because I love him. (*With a threat, but only a threat, of tears.*) He's the dearest man in the world to me, and I won't have anyone making him feel unwanted and low and blue. You've got to make up your mind now, darling, there's no leeway any more. Either he's your father and you pay him that respect, or else you're not to come here. I know he's not easy to get along with—nobody knows that better than me—but . . .

WILLY (*from the left, with a laugh*). Hey, hey, Biffo!

BIFF (*starting to go out after Willy*). What the hell is the matter with him? (*Happy stops him.*)

LINDA. Don't—don't go near him!

BIFF. Stop making excuses for him! He always, always wiped the floor with you. Never had an ounce of respect for you.

HAPPY. He's always had respect for . . .

BIFF. What the hell do you know about it?

HAPPY (*surlily*). Just don't call him crazy!

BIFF. He's got no character—Charley wouldn't do this. Not in his own house—spewing out that vomit from his mind.

HAPPY. Charley never had to cope with what he's got to.

BIFF. People are worse off than Willy Loman. Believe me, I've seen them!

LINDA. Then make Charley your father, Biff. You can't do that, can you? I don't say he's a great man. Willy Loman never made a lot of money. His name was never in the paper. He's not the finest character that ever lived. But he's a human being, and a terrible thing is happening to him. So attention must be paid. He's not to be allowed to fall into his grave like an old dog. Attention, attention must be finally paid to such a person. You called him crazy . . .

BIFF. I didn't mean . . .

LINDA. No, a lot of people think he's lost his—balance. But you don't have to be very smart to know what his trouble is. The man is exhausted.

HAPPY. Sure!

LINDA. A small man can be just as exhausted as a great man. He works for a company thirty-six years this March, opens up unheard-of territories to their trademark, and now in his old age they take his salary away.

HAPPY (*indignantly*). I didn't know that, Mom.

LINDA. You never asked, my dear! Now that you get your spending money someplace else you don't trouble your mind with him.

HAPPY. But I gave you money last . . .

LINDA. Christmas time, fifty dollars! To fix the hot water it cost ninety-seven fifty! For five weeks he's been on straight commission, like a beginner, an unknown!

BIFF. Those ungrateful bastards!

LINDA. Are they any worse than his sons? When he brought them business, when he was young, they were glad to see him. But now his old friends, the old buyers that loved him so and always found some order to hand him in a pinch—they're all dead, retired. He used to be able to make six, seven calls a day in Boston. Now he takes his valises out of the car and puts them back and takes them out again and he's exhausted. Instead of walking he talks now. He drives seven hundred miles, and when he gets there no one knows him any more, no one welcomes him. And what goes through a man's mind, driving seven hundred miles home without having earned a cent? Why shouldn't he talk to himself? Why? When he has to go to Charley and borrow fifty dollars a week and pretend to me that it's his pay? How long can that go on? How long? You see what I'm sitting here and waiting for? And you tell me he has no character? The man who never worked a day but for your benefit? When does he get the medal for that? Is this his reward—to turn around at the age of sixty-three and find his sons, who he loved better than his life, one a philandering bum . . .

HAPPY. Mom!

LINDA. That's all you are, my baby! (*To Biff.*) And you! What happened to the love you had for him? You were such pals! How you used to talk to him on the phone every night! How lonely he was till he could come home to you!

BIFF. All right, Mom. I'll live here in my room, and I'll get a job. I'll keep away from him, that's all.

LINDA. No, Biff. You can't stay here and fight all the time.

BIFF. He threw me out of this house, remember that.

LINDA. Why did he do that? I never knew why.

BIFF. Because I know he's a fake and he doesn't like anybody around who knows!

LINDA. Why a fake? In what way? What do you mean?

BIFF. Just don't lay it all at my feet. It's between me and him—that's all I have to say. I'll chip in from now on. He'll settle for half my paycheck. He'll be all right. I'm going to bed. (*He starts for the stairs.*)

LINDA. He won't be all right.

BIFF (*turning on the stairs, furiously*). I hate this city and I'll stay here. Now what do you want?

LINDA. He's dying, Biff.

Happy turns quickly to her, shocked.

BIFF (*after a pause*). Why is he dying?

LINDA. He's been trying to kill himself.

BIFF (*with great horror*). How?

LINDA. I live from day to day.

BIFF. What're you talking about?

LINDA. Remember I wrote you that he smashed up the car again? In February?

BIFF. Well?

LINDA. The insurance inspector came. He said that they have evidence. That all these accidents in the last year—weren't—weren't—accidents.

HAPPY. How can they tell that? That's a lie.

LINDA. It seems there's a woman . . . (*She takes a breath as:*)

BIFF (*sharply but contained*). What woman?

LINDA (*simultaneously*). . . . and this woman . . .

LINDA. What?

BIFF. Nothing. Go ahead.

LINDA. What did you say?

BIFF. Nothing. I just said what woman?

HAPPY. What about her?

LINDA. Well, it seems she was walking down the road and saw his car. She says that he wasn't driving fast at all, and that he didn't skid. She says he came to that little bridge, and then deliberately smashed into the railing, and it was only the shallowness of the water that saved him.

BIFF. Oh, no, he probably just fell asleep again.

LINDA. I don't think he fell asleep.

BIFF. Why not?

LINDA. Last month . . . (*With great difficulty.*) Oh, boys, it's so hard to say a thing like this! He's just a big stupid man to you, but I tell you there's more good in him than in many other people. (*She chokes, wipes her eyes.*) I was looking for a fuse. The lights blew out, and I went down the cellar. And behind the fuse box—it happened to fall out—was a length of rubber pipe—just short.

HAPPY. No kidding!

LINDA. There's a little attachment on the end of it. I knew right away. And sure enough, on the bottom of the water heater there's a new little nipple on the gas pipe.

HAPPY (*angrily*). That—jerk.

BIFF. Did you have it taken off?

LINDA. I'm—I'm ashamed to. How can I mention it to him? Every day I go down and take away that little rubber pipe. But, when he comes home, I put it back where it was. How can I insult him that way? I don't know what to do. I live from day to day, boys. I tell you, I know every thought in his mind. It sounds so old-fashioned and silly, but I tell you he put his whole life into you and you've turned your backs on him. (*She is bent over in the chair, weeping, her face in her hands.*) Biff, I swear to God! Biff, his life is in your hands!

HAPPY (*to Biff*). How do you like that damned fool!

BIFF (*kissing her*). All right, pal, all right. It's all settled now. I've been remiss. I know that, Mom. But now I'll stay, and I swear to you, I'll apply myself. (*Kneeling in front of her, in a fever of self-reproach.*) It's just—you see, Mom, I don't fit in business. Not that I won't try. I'll try, and I'll make good.

HAPPY. Sure you will. The trouble with you in business was you never tried to please people.

BIFF. I know, I . . .

HAPPY. Like when you worked for Harrison's. Bob Harrison said you were tops, and then you go and do some damn fool thing like whistling whole songs in the elevator like a comedian.

BIFF (*against Happy*). So what? I like to whistle sometimes.

HAPPY. You don't raise a guy to a responsible job who whistles in the elevator!

LINDA. Well, don't argue about it now.

HAPPY. Like when you'd go off and swim in the middle of the day instead of taking the line around.

BIFF (*his resentment rising*). Well, don't you run off? You take off sometimes, don't you? On a nice summer day?

HAPPY. Yeah, but I cover myself!

LINDA. Boys!

HAPPY. If I'm going to take a fade the boss can call any number where I'm supposed to be and they'll swear to him that I just left. I'll tell you something that I hate to say, Biff, but in the business world some of them think you're crazy.

BIFF (*angered*). Screw the business world!

HAPPY. All right, screw it! Great, but cover yourself!

LINDA. Hap, Hap!

BIFF. I don't care what they think! They've laughed at Dad for years, and you know why? Because we don't belong in this nuthouse of a city! We should be mixing cement on some open plain or—or carpenters. A carpenter is allowed to whistle!

Willy walks in from the entrance of the house, at left.

WILLY. Even your grandfather was better than a carpenter. (*Pause. They watch him.*) You never grew up. Bernard does not whistle in the elevator, I assure you.

BIFF (*as though to laugh Willy out of it*). Yeah, but you do, Pop.

WILLY. I never in my life whistled in an elevator! And who in the business world thinks I'm crazy?

BIFF. I didn't mean it like that, Pop. Now don't make a whole thing out of it, will ya?

WILLY. Go back to the West! Be a carpenter, a cowboy, enjoy yourself!

LINDA. Willy, he was just saying . . .

WILLY. I heard what he said!

HAPPY (*trying to quiet Willy*). Hey, Pop, come on now . . .

WILLY (*continuing over Happy's line*). They laugh at me, heh? Go to Filene's, go to the Hub, go to Slattery's, Boston. Call out the name Willy Loman and see what happens! Big shot!

BIFF. All right, Pop.

WILLY. Big!

BIFF. All right!

WILLY. Why do you always insult me?

BIFF. I didn't say a word. (*To Linda.*) Did I say a word?

LINDA. He didn't say anything, Willy.

WILLY (*going to the doorway of the living room*). All right, good night, good night.

LINDA. Willy, dear, he just decided . . .

WILLY (*to Biff*). If you get tired hanging around tomorrow, paint the ceiling I put up in the living room.

BIFF. I'm leaving early tomorrow.

HAPPY. He's going to see Bill Oliver, Pop.

WILLY (*interestedly*). Oliver? For what?

BIFF (*with reserve, but trying; trying*). He always said he'd stake me. I'd like to go into business, so maybe I can take him up on it.

LINDA. Isn't that wonderful?

WILLY. Don't interrupt. What's wonderful about it? There's fifty men in the City of New York who'd stake him. (*To Biff.*) Sporting goods?

BIFF. I guess so. I know something about it and . . .

WILLY. He knows something about it! You know sporting goods better than Spalding, for God's sake! How much is he giving you?

BIFF. I don't know, I didn't even see him yet, but . . .

WILLY. Then what're you talkin' about?

BIFF (*getting angry*). Well, all I said was I'm gonna see him, that's all!

WILLY (*turning away*). Ah, you're counting your chickens again.

BIFF (*starting left for the stairs*). Oh, Jesus, I'm going to sleep!

WILLY (*calling after him*). Don't curse in this house!

BIFF (*turning*). Since when did you get so clean?

HAPPY (*trying to stop them*). Wait a . . .

WILLY. Don't use that language to me! I won't have it!

HAPPY (*grabbing Biff, shouts*). Wait a minute! I got an idea. I got a feasible idea. Come here, Biff, let's talk this over now, let's talk some sense here. When I was down in Florida last time, I thought of a great idea to sell sporting goods. It just came back to me. You and I, Biff—we have a line, the Loman Line. We train a couple of weeks, and put on a couple of exhibitions, see?

WILLY. That's an idea!

HAPPY. Wait! We form two basketball teams, see? Two water-polo teams. We play each other. It's a million dollars' worth of publicity. Two brothers, see? The Loman Brothers. Displays in the Royal Palms—all the hotels. And banners over the ring and the basketball court: "Loman Brothers." Baby, we could sell sporting goods!

WILLY. That is a one-million-dollar idea!

LINDA. Marvelous!

BIFF. I'm in great shape as far as that's concerned.

HAPPY. And the beauty of it is, Biff, it wouldn't be like a business. We'd be out playin' ball again.

BIFF (*enthused*). Yeah, that's . . .

WILLY. Million-dollar . . .

HAPPY. And you wouldn't get fed up with it, Biff. It'd be the family again. There'd be the old honor, and comradeship, and if you wanted to go off for a swim or somethin'—well, you'd do it! Without some smart cooky gettin' up ahead of you!

WILLY. Lick the world! You guys together could absolutely lick the civilized world.

BIFF. I'll see Oliver tomorrow. Hap, if we could work that out . . .

LINDA. Maybe things are beginning to . . .

WILLY (*widely enthused, to Linda*). Stop interrupting! (*To Biff.*) But don't wear sport jacket and slacks when you see Oliver.

BIFF. No, I'll . . .

WILLY. A business suit, and talk as little as possible, and don't crack any jokes.

BIFF. He did like me. Always liked me.

LINDA. He loved you!

WILLY (*to Linda*). Will you stop! (*To Biff.*) Walk in very serious. You are not applying for a boy's job. Money is to pass. Be quiet, fine, and serious. Everybody likes a kidder, but nobody lends him money.

HAPPY. I'll try to get some myself, Biff. I'm sure I can.

WILLY. I see great things for you kids, I think your troubles are over. But remember, start big and you'll end big. Ask for fifteen. How much you gonna ask for?

BIFF. Gee, I don't know . . .

WILLY. And don't say "Gee." "Gee" is a boy's word. A man walking in for fifteen thousand dollars does not say "Gee!"

BIFF. Ten, I think, would be top though.

WILLY. Don't be so modest. You always started too low. Walk in with a big laugh. Don't look worried. Start off with a couple of your good stories to lighten things up. It's not what you say, it's how you say it—because personality always wins the day.

LINDA. Oliver always thought the highest of him . . .

WILLY. Will you let me talk?

BIFF. Don't yell at her, Pop, will ya?

WILLY (*angrily*). I was talking, wasn't I?

BIFF. I don't like you yelling at her all the time, and I'm tellin' you, that's all.

WILLY. What're you, takin' over this house?

LINDA. Willy . . .

WILLY (*turning to her*). Don't take his side all the time, goddammit!

BIFF (*furiously*). Stop yelling at her!

WILLY (*suddenly pulling on his cheek, beaten down, guilt ridden*). Give my best to Bill Oliver—he may remember me. (*He exits through the living room doorway.*)

LINDA (*her voice subdued*). What'd you have to start that for? (*Biff turns away.*) You see how sweet he was as soon as you talked hopefully? (*She goes over to Biff.*) Come up and say good night to him. Don't let him go to bed that way.

HAPPY. Come on, Biff, let's buck him up.

LINDA. Please, dear. Just say good night. It takes so little to make him happy. Come. (*She goes through the living room doorway, calling upstairs from within the living room.*) Your pajamas are hanging in the bathroom, Willy!

HAPPY (*looking toward where Linda went out*). What a woman! They broke the mold when they made her. You know that, Biff.

BIFF. He's off salary. My God, working on commission!

HAPPY. Well, let's face it: he's no hot-shot selling man. Except that sometimes, you have to admit, he's a sweet personality.

BIFF (*deciding*). Lend me ten bucks, will ya? I want to buy some new ties.

HAPPY. I'll take you to a place I know. Beautiful stuff. Wear one of my striped shirts tomorrow.

BIFF. She got gray. Mom got awful old. Gee, I'm gonna go in to Oliver tomorrow and knock him for a . . .

HAPPY. Come on up. Tell that to Dad. Let's give him a whirl. Come on.

BIFF (*steamed up*). You know, with ten thousand bucks, boy!

HAPPY (*as they go into the living room*). That's the talk, Biff, that's the first time I've heard the old confidence out of you! (*From within the living room, fading off*) You're gonna live with me, kid, and any babe you want just say the word . . . (*The last lines are hardly heard. They are mounting the stairs to their parents' bedroom.*)

LINDA (*entering her bedroom and addressing Willy, who is in the bathroom. She is straightening the bed for him*). Can you do anything about the shower? It drips.

WILLY (*from the bathroom*). All of a sudden everything falls to pieces. Goddam plumbing, oughta be sued, those people. I hardly finished putting it in and the thing . . . (*His words rumble off.*)

LINDA. I'm just wondering if Oliver will remember him. You think he might?

WILLY (*coming out of the bathroom in his pajamas*). Remember him? What's the matter with you, you crazy? If he'd've stayed with Oliver he'd be on top by now! Wait'll Oliver gets a look at him. You don't know the average caliber any more. The average young man today—(*he is getting into bed*)—is got a caliber of zero. Greatest thing in the world for him was to bum around.

Biff and Happy enter the bedroom. Slight pause.

WILLY (*stops short, looking at Biff*). Glad to hear it, boy.

HAPPY. He wanted to say good night to you, sport.

WILLY (*to Biff*). Yeah. Knock him dead, boy. What'd you want to tell me?

BIFF. Just take it easy, Pop. Good night. (*He turns to go.*)

WILLY (*unable to resist*). And if anything falls off the desk while you're talking to him—like a package or something—don't you pick it up. They have office boys for that.

LINDA. I'll make a big breakfast . . .

WILLY. Will you let me finish? (*To Biff.*) Tell him you were in the business in the West. Not farm work.

BIFF. All right, Dad.

LINDA. I think everything . . .

WILLY (*going right through her speech*). And don't undersell yourself. No less than fifteen thousand dollars.

BIFF (*unable to bear him*). Okay. Good night, Mom. (*He starts moving.*)

WILLY. Because you got a greatness in you, Biff, remember that. You got all kinds of greatness . . . (*He lies back, exhausted. Biff walks out.*)

LINDA (*calling after Biff*). Sleep well, darling!

HAPPY. I'm gonna get married, Mom. I wanted to tell you.

LINDA. Go to sleep, dear.

HAPPY (*going*). I just wanted to tell you.

WILLY. Keep up the good work. (*Happy exits.*) God . . . remember that Ebbets Field game? The championship of the city?

LINDA. Just rest. Should I sing to you?

WILLY. Yeah. Sing to me. (*Linda hums a soft lullaby.*) When that team came out—he was the tallest, remember?

LINDA. Oh, yes. And in gold.

Biff enters the darkened kitchen, takes a cigarette, and leaves the house. He comes downstage into a golden pool of light. He smokes, staring at the night.

WILLY. Like a young god. Hercules—something like that. And the sun, the sun all around him. Remember how he waved to me? Right up from the field, with the representatives of three colleges standing by? And the buyers I brought, and the cheers when he came out—Loman, Loman, Loman! God Almighty, he'll be great yet. A star like that, magnificent, can never really fade away!

The light on Willy is fading. The gas heater begins to glow through the kitchen wall, near the stairs, a blue flame beneath red coils.

LINDA (*timidly*). Willy dear, what has he got against you?

WILLY. I'm so tired. Don't talk any more.

Biff slowly returns to the kitchen. He stops, stares toward the heater.

LINDA. Will you ask Howard to let you work in New York?

WILLY. First thing in the morning. Everything'll be all right.

Biff reaches behind the heater and draws out a length of rubber tubing. He is horrified and turns his head toward Willy's room, still dimly lit, from which the strains of Linda's desperate but monotonous humming rise.

WILLY (*staring through the window into the moonlight*). Gee, look at the moon moving between the buildings! Biff wraps the tubing around his hand and quickly goes up the stairs.*

ACT 2

SCENE: *Music is heard, gay and bright. The curtain rises as the music fades away. Willy, in shirt sleeves, is sitting at the kitchen table, sipping coffee, his hat in his lap. Linda is filling his cup when she can.*

WILLY. Wonderful coffee. Meal in itself.

LINDA. Can I make you some eggs?

WILLY. No. Take a breath.

LINDA. You look so rested, dear.

WILLY. I slept like a dead one. First time in months. Imagine, sleeping till ten on a Tuesday morning. Boys left nice and early, heh?

LINDA. They were out of here by eight o'clock.

WILLY. Good work!

LINDA. It was so thrilling to see them leaving together. I can't get over the shaving lotion in this house!

WILLY (*smiling*). Mmm . . .

LINDA. Biff was very changed this morning. His whole attitude seemed to be hopeful. He couldn't wait to get downtown to see Oliver.

WILLY. He's heading for a change. There's no question, there simply are certain men that take longer to get—solidified. How did he dress?

LINDA. His blue suit. He's so handsome in that suit. He could be a—anything in that suit!

Willy gets up from the table. Linda holds his jacket for him.

WILLY. There's no question, no question at all. Gee, on the way home tonight I'd like to buy some seeds.

LINDA (*laughing*). That'd be wonderful. But not enough sun gets back there. Nothing'll grow any more.

WILLY. You wait, kid, before it's all over we're gonna get a little place out in the country, and I'll raise some vegetables, a couple of chickens . . .

LINDA. You'll do it yet, dear.

Willy walks out of his jacket. Linda follows him.

WILLY. And they'll get married, and come for a weekend. I'd build a little guest house. 'Cause I got so many fine tools, all I'd need would be a little lumber and some peace of mind.

LINDA (*joyfully*). I sewed the lining . . .

WILLY. I could build two guest houses, so they'd both come. Did he decide how much he's going to ask Oliver for?

LINDA (*getting him into the jacket*). He didn't mention it, but I imagine ten or fifteen thousand. You going to talk to Howard today?

WILLY. Yeah. I'll put it to him straight and simple. He'll just have to take me off the road.

LINDA. And Willy, don't forget to ask for a little advance, because we've got the insurance premium. It's the grace period now.

WILLY. That's a hundred . . . ?

LINDA. A hundred and eight, sixty-eight. Because we're a little short again.

WILLY. Why are we short?

LINDA. Well, you had the motor job on the car . . .

WILLY. That goddam Studebaker!

LINDA. And you got one more payment on the refrigerator . . .

WILLY. But it just broke again!

LINDA. Well, it's old, dear.

WILLY. I told you we should've bought a well-advertised machine. Charley bought a General Electric and it's twenty years old and it's still good, that son-of-a-bitch.

LINDA. But, Willy . . .

WILLY. Whoever heard of a Hastings refrigerator? Once in my life I would like to own something outright before it's broken! I'm always in a race with the junkyard! I just finished paying for the car and it's on its last legs. The refrigerator consumes belts like a goddam maniac. They time those things. They time them so when you finally paid for them, they're used up.

LINDA (*buttoning up his jacket as he unbuttons it*). All told, about two hundred dollars would carry us, dear. But that includes the last payment on the mortgage. After this payment, Willy, the house belongs to us.

WILLY. It's twenty-five years!

LINDA. Biff was nine years old when we bought it.

WILLY. Well, that's a great thing. To weather a twenty-five year mortgage is . . .

LINDA. It's an accomplishment.

WILLY. All the cement, the lumber, the reconstruction I put in this house! There ain't a crack to be found in it any more.

LINDA. Well, it served its purpose.

WILLY. What purpose? Some stranger'll come along, move in, and that's that. If only Biff would take this house, and raise a family . . . (*He starts to go.*) Good-by, I'm late.

LINDA (*suddenly remembering*). Oh, I forgot! You're supposed to meet them for dinner.

WILLY. Me?

LINDA. At Frank's Chop House on Forty-eighth near Sixth Avenue.

WILLY. Is that so! How about you?

LINDA. No, just the three of you. They're gonna blow you to a big meal!

WILLY. Don't say! Who thought of that?

LINDA. Biff came to me this morning, Willy, and he said, "Tell Dad, we want to blow him to a big meal." Be there six o'clock. You and your two boys are going to have dinner.

WILLY. Gee whiz! That's really somethin'. I'm gonna knock Howard for a loop, kid. I'll get an advance, and I'll come home with a New York job. Goddammit, now I'm gonna do it!

LINDA. Oh, that's the spirit, Willy!

WILLY. I will never get behind a wheel the rest of my life!

LINDA. It's changing, Willy, I can feel it changing!

WILLY. Beyond a question. G'by, I'm late. (*He starts to go again.*)

LINDA (*calling after him as she runs to the kitchen table for a handkerchief*). You got your glasses?

WILLY (*feels for them, then comes back in*). Yeah, yeah, got my glasses.

LINDA (*giving him the handkerchief*). And a handkerchief.

WILLY. Yeah, handkerchief.

LINDA. And your saccharine?

WILLY. Yeah, my saccharine.

LINDA. Be careful on the subway stairs.

She kisses him, and a silk stocking is seen hanging from her hand. Willy notices it.

WILLY. Will you stop mending stockings? At least while I'm in the house. It gets me nervous. I can't tell you. Please.

Linda hides the stocking in her hand as she follows Willy across the forestage in front of the house.

LINDA. Remember, Frank's Chop House.

WILLY (*passing the apron*). Maybe beets would grow out there.

LINDA (*laughing*). But you tried so many times.

WILLY. Yeah. Well, don't work hard today. (*He disappears around the right corner of the house.*)

LINDA. Be careful!

As Willy vanishes, Linda waves to him. Suddenly the phone rings. She runs across the stage and into the kitchen and lifts it.

LINDA. Hello? Oh, Biff! I'm so glad you called, I just . . . Yes, sure, I just told him. Yes, he'll be there for dinner at six o'clock, I didn't forget. Listen, I was just dying to tell you. You know that little rubber pipe I told you about? That he connected to the gas heater? I finally decided to go down the cellar this morning and take it away and destroy it. But it's gone! Imagine? He took it away himself, it isn't there! (*She listens.*) When? Oh, then you took it. Oh—nothing, it's just that I'd hoped he'd taken it away himself. Oh, I'm not worried, darling, because this morning he left in such high spirits, it was like the old days! I'm not afraid any more. Did Mr. Oliver see you? . . . Well, you wait there then. And make a nice impression on him, darling. Just don't perspire too much before you see him. And have a nice time with Dad. He may have big news too! . . . That's right, a New York job. And be sweet to him tonight, dear. Be loving to him. Because he's only a little boat looking for a harbor. (*She is trembling with sorrow and joy.*) Oh, that's wonderful, Biff, you'll save his life. Thanks, darling. Just put your arm around him when he comes into the restaurant. Give him a smile. That's the boy . . . Good-by, dear. . . . You got your comb? . . . That's fine. Good-by, Biff dear.

In the middle of her speech, Howard Wagner, thirty-six, wheels in a small typewriter table on which is a wire-recording machine and proceeds to plug it in. This is on the left forestage. Light slowly fades on Linda as it rises on Howard. Howard is intent on threading the machine and only glances over his shoulder as Willy appears.

WILLY. Pst! Pst!

HOWARD. Hello, Willy, come in.

WILLY. Like to have a little talk with you, Howard.

HOWARD. Sorry to keep you waiting. I'll be with you in a minute.

WILLY. What's that, Howard?

HOWARD. Didn't you ever see one of these? Wire recorder.

WILLY. Oh. Can we talk a minute?

HOWARD. Records things. Just got delivery yesterday. Been driving me crazy, the most terrific machine I ever saw in my life. I was up all night with it.

WILLY. What do you do with it?

HOWARD. I bought it for dictation, but you can do anything with it. Listen to this. I had it home last night. Listen to what I picked up. The first one is my daughter. Get this. (*He flicks the switch and "Roll Out the Barrel" is heard being whistled.*) Listen to that kid whistle.

WILLY. That is lifelike, isn't it?

HOWARD. Seven years old. Get that tone.

WILLY. Ts, ts. Like to ask a little favor if you . . .

The whistling breaks off, and the voice of Howard's daughter is heard.

HIS DAUGHTER. "Now you, Daddy."

HOWARD. She's crazy for me! (*Again the same song is whistled.*) That's me! Ha! (*He winks.*)

WILLY. You're very good!

The whistling breaks off again. The machine runs silent for a moment.

HOWARD. Sh! Get this now, this is my son.

HIS SON. "The capital of Alabama is Montgomery; the capital of Arizona is Phoenix; the capital of Arkansas is Little Rock; the capital of California is Sacramento . . ." (*and on, and on.*)

HOWARD (*holding up five fingers*). Five years old, Willy!

WILLY. He'll make an announcer some day!

HIS SON (*continuing*). "The capital . . ."

HOWARD. Get that—alphabetical order! (*The machine breaks off suddenly.*) Wait a minute. The maid kicked the plug out.

WILLY. It certainly is a . . .

HOWARD. Sh, for God's sake!

HIS SON. "It's nine o'clock, Bulova watch time. So I have to go to sleep."

WILLY. That really is . . .

HOWARD. Wait a minute! The next is my wife.

They wait.

HOWARD'S VOICE. "Go on, say something." (*Pause.*) "Well, you gonna talk?"

HIS WIFE. "I can't think of anything."

HOWARD'S VOICE. "Well, talk—it's turning."

HIS WIFE (*shyly, beaten*). "Hello." (*Silence.*) "Oh, Howard, I can't talk into this . . . "

HOWARD (*snapping the machine off*). That was my wife.

WILLY. That is a wonderful machine. Can we . . .

HOWARD. I tell you, Willy, I'm gonna take my camera, and my bandsaw, and all my hobbies, and out they go. This is the most fascinating relaxation I ever found.

WILLY. I think I'll get one myself.

HOWARD. Sure, they're only a hundred and a half. You can't do without it. Supposing you wanna hear Jack Benny, see? But you can't be at home at that hour. So you tell the maid to turn the radio on when Jack Benny comes on, and this automatically goes on with the radio . . .

WILLY. And when you come home you . . .

HOWARD. You can come home twelve o'clock, one o'clock, any time you like, and you get yourself a Coke and sit yourself down, throw the switch, and there's Jack Benny's program in the middle of the night!

WILLY. I'm definitely going to get one. Because lots of times I'm on the road, and I think to myself, what I must be missing on the radio!

HOWARD. Don't you have a radio in the car?

WILLY. Well, yeah, but who ever thinks of turning it on?

HOWARD. Say, aren't you supposed to be in Boston?

WILLY. That's what I want to talk to you about, Howard. You got a minute? (*He draws a chair in from the wing.*)

HOWARD. What happened? What're you doing here?

WILLY. Well . . .

HOWARD. You didn't crack up again, did you?

WILLY. Oh, no. No . . .

HOWARD. Geez, you had me worried there for a minute. What's the trouble?

WILLY. Well, tell you the truth, Howard. I've come to the decision that I'd rather not travel any more.

HOWARD. Not travel! Well, what'll you do?

WILLY. Remember, Christmas time, when you had the party here? You said you'd try to think of some spot for me here in town.

HOWARD. With us?

WILLY. Well, sure.

HOWARD. Oh, yeah, yeah. I remember. Well, I couldn't think of anything for you, Willy.

WILLY. I tell ya, Howard. The kids are all grown up, y'know. I don't need much any more. If I could take home—well, sixty-five dollars a week, I could swing it.

HOWARD. Yeah, but Willy, see I . . .

WILLY. I tell ya why, Howard. Speaking frankly and between the two of us, y'know—I'm just a little tired.

HOWARD. Oh, I could understand that, Willy. But you're a road man, Willy, and we do a road business. We've only got a half-dozen salesmen on the floor here.

WILLY. God knows, Howard. I never asked a favor of any man. But I was with the firm when your father used to carry you in here in his arms.

HOWARD. I know that, Willy, but . . .

WILLY. Your father came to me the day you were born and asked me what I thought of the name Howard, may he rest in peace.

HOWARD. I appreciate that, Willy, but there just is no spot here for you. If I had a spot I'd slam you right in, but I just don't have a single solitary spot.

He looks for his lighter. Willy has picked it up and gives it to him. Pause.

WILLY (*with increasing anger*). Howard, all I need to set my table is fifty dollars a week.

HOWARD. But where am I going to put you, kid?

WILLY. Look, it isn't a question of whether I can sell merchandise, is it?

HOWARD. No, but it's business, kid, and everybody's gotta pull his own weight.

WILLY (*desperately*). Just let me tell you a story, Howard . . .

HOWARD. 'Cause you gotta admit, business is business.

WILLY (*angrily*). Business is definitely business, but just listen for a minute. You don't understand this. When I was a boy—eighteen, nineteen—I was already on the road. And there was a question in my mind as to whether selling had a future for me. Because in those days I had a yearning to go to Alaska. See, there were three gold strikes in one month in Alaska, and I felt like going out. Just for the ride, you might say.

HOWARD (*barely interested*). Don't say.

WILLY. Oh, yeah, my father lived many years in Alaska. He was an adventurous man. We've got quite a little streak of self-reliance in our family. I thought I'd go out with my older brother and try to locate him, and maybe settle in the North with the old man. And I was almost decided to go, when I met a salesman in the Parker House. His name was Dave Singleman. And he was eighty-four years old, and he'd drummed merchandise in thirty-one states. And old Dave, he'd go up to his room, y'understand, put on his green velvet slippers—I'll never forget—and pick up his phone and call the buyers, and without ever leaving his room, at the age of eighty-four, he made his living. And when I saw that, I realized that selling was the greatest career a man could want. 'Cause what could be more satisfying than to be able to go, at the age of eight-four, into twenty or thirty different cities, and pick up a phone, and be remembered and loved and helped by so many different people? Do you know? when he died—and by the way he died the death of a salesman, in his green velvet slippers in the smoker of the New York, New Haven and Hartford, going into Boston—when he died, hundreds of salesmen and buyers were at his funeral. Things were sad on a lotta trains for months after that. (*He stands up, Howard has not looked at him.*) In those days there was personality in it, Howard. There was respect, and comradeship, and gratitude in it. Today, it's all cut and dried, and there's no chance for bringing friendship to bear—or personality. You see what I mean? They don't know me any more.

HOWARD (*moving away, to the right*). That's just the thing, Willy.

WILLY. If I had forty dollars a week—that's all I'd need. Forty dollars, Howard.

HOWARD. Kid, I can't take blood from a stone, I . . .

WILLY (*desperation is on him now*). Howard, the year Al Smith was nominated, your father came to me and . . .

HOWARD (*starting to go off*). I've got to see some people, kid.

WILLY (*stopping him*). I'm talking about your father! There were promises made across this desk! You mustn't tell me you've got people to see—I put thirty-four years into this firm, Howard, and now I can't pay my insurance! You can't eat the orange and throw the peel away—a man is not a piece of fruit! (*After a pause.*) Now pay attention. Your father—in 1928 I had a big year. I averaged a hundred and seventy dollars a week in commissions.

HOWARD (*impatiently*). Now, Willy, you never averaged . . .

WILLY (*banging his hand on the desk*). I averaged a hundred and seventy dollars a week in the year of 1928! And your father came to me—or rather, I was in the office here—it was right over this desk—and he put his hand on my shoulder . . .

HOWARD (*getting up*). You'll have to excuse me, Willy, I gotta see some people. Pull yourself together. (*Going out.*) I'll be back in a little while.

On Howard's exit, the light on his chair grows very bright and strange.

WILLY. Pull myself together! What the hell did I say to him? My God, I was yelling at him! How could I? (*Willy breaks off, staring at the light, which occupies the chair, animating it. He approaches this chair, standing across the desk from it.*) Frank, Frank, don't you remember what you told me that time? How you put your hand on my shoulder, and Frank . . . (*He leans on the desk and as he speaks the dead man's name he accidentally switches on the recorder, and instantly*)

HOWARD'S SON. ". . . of New York is Albany. The capital of Ohio is Cincinnati, the capital of Rhode Island is . . ." (*The recitation continues.*)

WILLY (*leaping away with fright, shouting*). Ha! Howard! Howard! Howard!

HOWARD (*rushing in*). What happened?

WILLY (*pointing at the machine, which continues nasally, childishly, with the capital cities*). Shut it off! Shut it off!

HOWARD (*pulling the plug out*). Look, Willy . . .

WILLY (*pressing his hands to his eyes*). I gotta get myself some coffee. I'll get some coffee . . .

Willy starts to walk out. Howard stops him.

HOWARD (*rolling up the cord*). Willy, look . . .

WILLY. I'll go to Boston.

HOWARD. Willy, you can't go to Boston for us.

WILLY Why can't I go?

HOWARD. I don't want you to represent us. I've been meaning to tell you for a long time now.

WILLY. Howard, are you firing me?

HOWARD. I think you need a good long rest, Willy.

WILLY. Howard . . .

HOWARD. And when you feel better, come back, and we'll see if we can work something out.

WILLY. But I gotta earn money, Howard. I'm in no position to . . .

HOWARD. Where are your sons? Why don't your sons give you a hand?

WILLY. They're working on a very big deal.

HOWARD. This is no time for false pride, Willy. You go to

your sons and you tell them that you're tired. You've got two great boys, haven't you?

WILLY. Oh, no question, no question, but in the meantime . . .

HOWARD. Then that's that, heh?

WILLY. All right, I'll go to Boston tomorrow.

HOWARD. No, no.

WILLY. I can't throw myself on my sons. I'm not a cripple!

HOWARD. Look, kid, I'm busy this morning.

WILLY (*grasping Howard's arm*). Howard, you've got to let me go to Boston!

HOWARD (*hard, keeping himself under control*). I've got a line of people to see this morning. Sit down, take five minutes, and pull yourself together, and then go home, will ya? I need the office, Willy. (*He starts to go, turns, remembering the recorder, starts to push off the table holding the recorder.*) Oh, yeah. Whenever you can this week, stop by and drop off the samples. You'll feel better, Willy, and then come back and we'll talk. Pull yourself together, kid, there's people outside.

Howard exits, pushing the table off left. Willy stares into space, exhausted. Now the music is heard—Ben's music—first distantly, then closer, closer. As Willy speaks, Ben enters from the right. He carries valise and umbrella.

WILLY. Oh, Ben, how did you do it? What is the answer? Did you wind up the Alaska deal already?

BEN. Doesn't take much time if you know what you're doing. Just a short business trip. Boarding ship in an hour. Wanted to say good-by.

WILLY. Ben, I've got to talk to you.

BEN (*glancing at his watch*). Haven't the time, William.

WILLY (*crossing the apron to Ben*). Ben, nothing's working out. I don't know what to do.

BEN. Now, look here, William. I've bought timberland in Alaska and I need a man to look after things for me.

WILLY. God, timberland! Me and my boys in those grand outdoors!

BEN. You've a new continent at your doorstep, William. Get out of these cities, they're full of talk and time payments and courts of law. Screw on your fists and you can fight for a fortune up there.

WILLY. Yes, yes! Linda, Linda!

Linda enters as of old, with the wash.

LINDA. Oh, you're back?

BEN. I haven't much time.

WILLY. No, wait! Linda, he's got a proposition for me in Alaska.

LINDA. But you've got . . . (*To Ben.*) He's got a beautiful job here.

WILLY. But in Alaska, kid, I could . . .

LINDA. You're doing well enough, Willy!

BEN (*to Linda*). Enough for what, my dear?

LINDA (*frightened of Ben and angry at him*). Don't say those things to him! Enough to be happy right here, right now. (*To Willy, while Ben laughs.*) Why must everybody conquer the world? You're well liked, and the boys love you, and someday—(*To Ben*)—why, old man Wagner told him just the other day that if he keeps it up he'll be a member of the firm, didn't he, Willy?

WILLY. Sure, sure. I am building something with this firm, Ben, and if a man is building something he must be on the right track, mustn't he?

BEN. What are you building? Lay your hand on it. Where is it?

WILLY (*hesitantly*). That's true, Linda, there's nothing.

LINDA. Why? (*To Ben.*) There's a man eighty-four years old . . .

WILLY. That's right, Ben, that's right. When I look at that man I say, what is there to worry about?

BEN. Bah!

WILLY. It's true, Ben. All he has to do is go into any city, pick up the phone, and he's making his living and you know why?

BEN (*picking up his valise*). I've got to go.

WILLY (*holding Ben back*). Look at this boy!

Biff, in his high school sweater, enters carrying suitcase. Happy carries Biff's shoulder guards, gold helmet, and football pants.

WILLY. Without a penny to his name, three great universities are begging for him, and from there the sky's the limit, because it's not what you do, Ben. It's who you know and the smile on your face! It's contacts, Ben, contacts! The whole wealth of Alaska passes over the lunch table at the Commodore Hotel, and that's the wonder, the wonder of this country, that a man can end with diamonds here on the basis of being liked! (*He turns to Biff.*) And that's why when you get out on that field today it's important. Because thousands of people will be rooting for you and loving you. (*To Ben, who has again begun to leave.*) And Ben! when he walks into a business office his name will sound out like a bell and all the doors will open to him! I've seen it, Ben, I've seen it a thousand times! You can't feel it with your hand like timber, but it's there!

BEN. Good-by, William.

WILLY. Ben, am I right? Don't you think I'm right? I value your advice.

BEN. There's a new continent at your doorstep, William. You could walk out rich. Rich! (*He is gone.*)

WILLY. We'll do it here, Ben! You hear me? We're gonna do it here!

Young Bernard rushes in. The gay music of the Boys is heard.

BERNARD. Oh, gee, I was afraid you left already!

WILLY. Why? What time is it?

BERNARD. It's half-past one!

WILLY. Well, come on, everybody! Ebbets Field next stop! Where's the pennants? (*He rushes through the wall-line of the kitchen and out into the living room.*)

LINDA (*to Biff*). Did you pack fresh underwear?

BIFF (*who has been limbering up*). I want to go!

BERNARD. Biff, I'm carrying your helmet, ain't I?

HAPPY. No, I'm carrying the helmet.

BERNARD. Oh, Biff, you promised me.

HAPPY. I'm carrying the helmet.

BERNARD. How am I going to get in the locker room?

LINDA. Let him carry the shoulder guards. (*She puts her coat and hat on in the kitchen.*)

BERNARD. Can I, Biff? 'Cause I told everybody I'm going to be in the locker room.

HAPPY. In Ebbets Field it's the clubhouse.

BERNARD. I meant the clubhouse. Biff!

HAPPY. Biff!

BIFF (*grandly, after a slight pause*). Let him carry the shoulder guards.

HAPPY (*as he gives Bernard the shoulder guards*). Stay close to us now.

Willy rushes in with the pennants.

WILLY (*handing them out*). Everybody wave when Biff comes out on the field. (*Happy and Bernard run off.*) You set now, boy?

The music has died away.

BIFF. Ready to go, Pop. Every muscle is ready.

WILLY (*at the edge of the apron*). You realize what this means?

BIFF. That's right, Pop.

WILLY (*feeling Biff's muscles*). You're comin' home this afternoon captain of the All-Scholastic Championship Team of the City of New York.

BIFF. I got it, Pop. And remember, pal, when I take off my helmet, that touchdown is for you.

WILLY. Let's go! (*He is starting out, with his arm around Biff, when Charley enters, as of old, in knickers.*) I got no room for you, Charley.

CHARLEY. Room? For what?

WILLY. In the car.

CHARLEY. You goin' for a ride? I wanted to shoot some casino.

WILLY (*furiously*). Casino! (*Incredulously.*) Don't you realize what today is?

LINDA. Oh, he knows, Willy. He's just kidding you.

WILLY. That's nothing to kid about!

CHARLEY. No, Linda, what's goin' on?

LINDA. He's playing in Ebbets Field.

CHARLEY. Baseball in this weather?

WILLY. Don't talk to him. Come on, come on! (*He is pushing them out.*)

CHARLEY. Wait a minute, didn't you hear the news?

WILLY. What?

CHARLEY. Don't you listen to the radio? Ebbets Field just blew up.

WILLY. You go to hell! (*Charley laughs. Pushing them out.*) Come on, come on! We're late.

CHARLEY (*as they go*). Knock a homer, Biff, knock a homer!

WILLY (*the last to leave, turning to Charley*). I don't think that was funny, Charley. This is the greatest day of his life.

CHARLEY. Willy, when are you going to grow up?

WILLY. Yeah, heh? When this game is over, Charley, you'll be laughing out of the other side of your face. They'll be calling him another Red Grange. Twenty-five thousand a year.

CHARLEY (*kidding*). Is that so?

WILLY. Yeah, that's so.

CHARLEY. Well, then, I'm sorry, Willy. But tell me something.

WILLY. What?

CHARLEY. Who is Red Grange?

WILLY. Put up your hands. Goddam you, put up your hands!

Charley, chuckling, shakes his head and walks away, around the left corner of the stage. Willy follows him. The music rises to a mocking frenzy.

WILLY. Who the hell do you think you are, better than everybody else? You don't know everything, you big, ignorant, stupid . . . Put up your hands!

Light rises, on the right side of the forestage, on a small table in the reception room of Charley's office. Traffic sounds are heard. Bernard, now mature, sits whistling to himself. A pair of tennis rackets and an old overnight bag are on the floor beside him.

WILLY (*offstage*). What are you walking away for? Don't walk away! If you're going to say something say it to my face! I know you laugh at me behind my back. You'll laugh out of the other side of your goddam face after this game. Touchdown! Touchdown! Eighty thousand people! Touchdown! Right between the goal posts.

Bernard is a quiet, earnest, but self-assured young man. Willy's voice is coming from right upstage now. Bernard lowers his feet off the table and listens. Jenny, his father's secretary, enters.

JENNY (*distressed*). Say, Bernard, will you go out in the hall?

BERNARD. What is that noise? Who is it?

JENNY. Mr. Loman. He just got off the elevator.

BERNARD (*getting up*). Who's he arguing with?

JENNY. Nobody. There's nobody with him. I can't deal with him any more, and your father gets all upset every time he comes. I've got a lot of typing to do, and your father's waiting to sign it. Will you see him?

WILLY (*entering*). Touchdown! Touch—(*He sees Jenny.*) Jenny, Jenny, good to see you. How're ya? Workin'? Or still honest?

JENNY. Fine. How've you been feeling?

WILLY. Not much any more, Jenny. Ha, ha! (*He is surprised to see the rackets.*)

BERNARD. Hello, Uncle Willy.

WILLY (*almost shocked*). Bernard! Well, look who's here! (*He comes quickly, guiltily, to Bernard and warmly shakes his hand.*)

BERNARD. How are you? Good to see you.

WILLY. What are you doing here?

BERNARD. Oh, just stopped by to see Pop. Get off my feet till my train leaves. I'm going to Washington in a few minutes.

WILLY. Is he in?

BERNARD. Yes, he's in his office with the accountant. Sit down.

WILLY (*sitting down*). What're you going to do in Washington?

BERNARD. Oh, just a case I've got there, Willy.

WILLY. That so? (*Indicating the rackets.*) You going to play tennis there?

BERNARD. I'm staying with a friend who's got a court.

WILLY. Don't say. His own tennis court. Must be fine people, I bet.

BERNARD. They are, very nice. Dad tells me Biff's in town.

WILLY (*with a big smile*). Yeah, Biff's in. Working on a very big deal, Bernard.

BERNARD. What's Biff doing?

WILLY. Well, he's been doing very big things in the West. But he decided to establish himself here. Very big. We're having dinner. Did I hear your wife had a boy?

BERNARD. That's right. Our second.

WILLY. Two boys! What do you know!

BERNARD. What kind of a deal has Biff got?

WILLY. Well, Bill Oliver—very big sporting-goods man—he wants Biff very badly. Called him in from the West. Long distance, carte blanche, special deliveries. Your friends have their own private tennis court?

BERNARD. You still with the old firm, Willy?

WILLY (*after a pause*). I'm—I'm overjoyed to see how you made the grade, Bernard, overjoyed. It's an encouraging thing to see a young man really—really . . . Looks very good for Biff—very . . . (*He breaks off, then.*) Bernard . . . (*He is so full of emotion, he breaks off again.*)

BERNARD. What is it, Willy?

WILLY (*small and alone*). What—what's the secret?

BERNARD. What secret?

WILLY. How—how did you? Why didn't he ever catch on?

BERNARD. I wouldn't know that, Willy.

WILLY (*confidentially, desperately*). You were his friend, his boyhood friend. There's something I don't understand about it. His life ended after that Ebbets Field game. From the age of seventeen nothing good ever happened to him.

BERNARD. He never trained himself for anything.

WILLY. But he did, he did. After high school he took so many correspondence courses. Radio mechanics; television; God knows what, and never made the slightest mark.

BERNARD (*taking off his glasses*). Willy, do you want to talk candidly?

WILLY (*rising, faces Bernard*). I regard you as a very brilliant man, Bernard. I value your advice.

BERNARD. Oh, the hell with the advice, Willy. I couldn't advise you. There's just one thing I've always wanted to ask you. When he was supposed to graduate, and the math teacher flunked him . . .

WILLY. Oh, that son-of-a-bitch ruined his life.

BERNARD. Yeah, but, Willy, all he had to do was go to summer school and make up that subject.

WILLY. That's right, that's right.

BERNARD. Did you tell him not to go to summer school?

WILLY. Me? I begged him to go. I ordered him to go!

BERNARD. Then why wouldn't he go?

WILLY. Why? Why! Bernard, that question has been trailing me like a ghost for the last fifteen years. He flunked the subject, and laid down and died like a hammer hit him!

BERNARD. Take it easy, kid.

WILLY. Let me talk to you—I got nobody to talk to. Bernard, Bernard, was it my fault? Y'see? It keeps going around in my mind, maybe I did something to him. I got nothing to give him.

BERNARD. Don't take it so hard.

WILLY. Why did he lay down? What is the story there? You were his friend!

BERNARD. Willy, I remember, it was June, and our grades came out. And he'd flunked math.

WILLY. That son-of-a-bitch!

BERNARD. No, it wasn't right then. Biff just got very angry, I remember, and he was ready to enroll in summer school.

WILLY (*surprised*). He was?

BERNARD. He wasn't beaten by it at all. But then, Willy, he disappeared from the block for almost a month. And I got the idea that he'd gone up to New England to see you. Did he have a talk with you then?

Willy stares in silence.

BERNARD. Willy?

WILLY (*with a strong edge of resentment in his voice*). Yeah, he came to Boston. What about it?

BERNARD. Well, just that when he came back—I'll never forget this, it always mystifies me. Because I'd thought so well of Biff, even though he'd always taken advantage of me. I loved him, Willy, y'know? And he came back after that month and took his sneakers—remember those sneakers with "University of Virginia" printed on them? He was so proud of those, wore them every day. And he took them down in the cellar, and burned them up in the furnace. We had a fist fight. It lasted at least half an hour. Just the two of us, punching each other down the cellar, and crying right through it. I've often thought of how strange it was that I knew he'd given up his life. What happened in Boston, Willy?

Willy looks at him as at an intruder.

BERNARD. I just bring it up because you asked me.

WILLY (*angrily*). Nothing. What do you mean, "What happened?" What's that got to do with anything?

BERNARD. Well, don't get sore.

WILLY. What are you trying to do, blame it on me? If a boy lays down is that my fault?

BERNARD. Now, Willy, don't get . . .

WILLY. Well, don't—don't talk to me that way! What does that mean, "What happened?"

Charley enters. He is in his vest, and he carries a bottle of bourbon.

CHARLEY. Hey, you're going to miss that train. (*He waves the bottle.*)

BERNARD. Yeah, I'm going. (*He takes the bottle.*) Thanks, Pop. (*He picks up his rackets and bag.*) Good-by, Willy, and don't worry about it. You know, "If at first you don't succeed . . ."

WILLY. Yes, I believe in that.

BERNARD. But sometimes, Willy, it's better for a man just to walk away.

WILLY. Walk away?

BERNARD. That's right.

WILLY. But if you can't walk away?

BERNARD (*after a slight pause*). I guess that's when it's tough. (*Extending his hand.*) Good-by, Willy.

WILLY (*shaking Bernard's hand*). Good-by, boy.

CHARLEY (*an arm on Bernard's shoulder*). How do you like this kid? Gonna argue a case in front of the Supreme Court.

BERNARD (*protesting*). Pop!

WILLY (*genuinely shocked, pained, and happy*). No! The Supreme Court!

BERNARD. I gotta run. 'By, Dad!

CHARLEY. Knock 'em dead, Bernard!

Bernard goes off.

WILLY (*as Charley takes out his wallet*). The Supreme Court! And he didn't even mention it!

CHARLEY (*counting out money on the desk*). He don't have to—he's gonna do it.

WILLY. And you never told him what to do, did you? You never took any interest in him.

CHARLEY. My salvation is that I never took any interest in anything. There's some money—fifty dollars. I got an accountant inside.

WILLY. Charley, look . . . (*with difficulty.*) I got my insurance to pay. If you can manage it—I need a hundred and ten dollars.

Charley doesn't reply for a moment; merely stops moving.

WILLY. I'd draw it from my bank but Linda would know, and I . . .

CHARLEY. Sit down, Willy.

WILLY (*moving toward the chair*). I'm keeping an account of everything, remember. I'll pay every penny back. (*He sits.*)

CHARLEY. Now listen to me, Willy.

WILLY. I want you to know I appreciate . . .

CHARLEY (*sitting down on the table*). Willy, what're you doin'? What the hell is going on in your head?

WILLY. Why? I'm simply . . .

CHARLEY. I offered you a job. You make fifty dollars a week. And I won't send you on the road.

WILLY. I've got a job.

CHARLEY. Without pay? What kind of a job is a job without pay? (*He rises.*) Now, look, kid, enough is enough. I'm no genius but I know when I'm being insulted.

WILLY. Insulted!

CHARLEY. Why don't you want to work for me?

WILLY. What's the matter with you? I've got a job.

CHARLEY. Then what're you walkin' in here every week for?

WILLY (*getting up*). Well, if you don't want me to walk in here . . .

CHARLEY. I'm offering you a job.

WILLY. I don't want your goddam job!

CHARLEY. When the hell are you going to grow up?

WILLY (*furiously*). You big ignoramus, if you say that to me again I'll rap you one! I don't care how big you are! (*He's ready to fight.*)

Pause.

CHARLEY (*kindly, going to him*). How much do you need, Willy?

WILLY. Charley, I'm strapped. I'm strapped. I don't know what to do. I was just fired.

CHARLEY. Howard fired you?

WILLY. That snotnose. Imagine that? I named him. I named him Howard.

CHARLEY. Willy, when're you gonna realize that them things don't mean anything? You named him Howard, but you can't sell that. The only thing you got in this world is what you can sell. And the funny thing is that you're a salesman, and you don't know that.

WILLY. I've always tried to think otherwise, I guess. I always felt that if a man was impressive, and well liked, that nothing . . .

CHARLEY. Why must everybody like you? Who liked J. P. Morgan? Was he impressive? In a Turkish bath he'd look like a butcher. But with his pockets on he was very well liked. Now listen, Willy, I know you don't like me, and nobody can say I'm in love with you, but I'll give you a job because—just for the hell of it, put it that way. Now what do you say?

WILLY. I—I just can't work for you, Charley.

CHARLEY. What're you, jealous of me?

WILLY. I can't work for you, that's all, don't ask me why.

CHARLEY (*angered, takes out more bills*). You been jealous of me all your life, you damned fool! Here, pay your insurance. (*He puts the money in Willy's hand.*)

WILLY. I'm keeping strict accounts.

CHARLEY. I've got some work to do. Take care of yourself. And pay your insurance.

WILLY (*moving to the right*). Funny, y'know? After all the highways, and the trains, and the appointments, and the years, you end up worth more dead than alive.

CHARLEY. Willy, nobody's worth nothin' dead. (*After a slight pause.*) Did you hear what I said?

Willy stands still, dreaming.

CHARLEY. Willy!

WILLY. Apologize to Bernard for me when you see him. I didn't mean to argue with him. He's a fine boy. They're all fine boys, and they'll end up big—all of them. Someday they'll all play tennis together. Wish me luck, Charley. He saw Bill Oliver today.

CHARLEY. Good luck.

WILLY (*on the verge of tears*). Charley, you're the only friend I got. Isn't that a remarkable thing? (*He goes out.*)

CHARLEY. Jesus!

Charley stares after him a moment and follows. All light blacks out. Suddenly raucous music is heard, and a red glow rises behind the screen at right. Stanley, a young waiter, appears, carrying a table, followed by Happy, who is carrying two chairs.

STANLEY (*putting the table down*). That's all right, Mr. Loman. I can handle it myself. (*He turns and takes the chairs from Happy and places them at the table.*)

HAPPY (*glancing around*). Oh, this is better.

STANLEY. Sure, in the front there you're in the middle of all kinds of noise. Whenever you got a party, Mr. Loman, you just tell me and I'll put you back here. Y'know, there's a lotta people they don't like it private, because when they go out they like to see a lotta action around them because they're sick and tired to stay in the house by theirself. But I know you, you ain't from Hackensack. You know what I mean?

HAPPY (*sitting down*). So how's it coming, Stanley?

STANLEY. Ah, it's a dog's life. I only wish during the war they'd a took me in the Army. I coulda been dead by now.

HAPPY. My brother's back, Stanley.

STANLEY. Oh, he come back, heh? From the Far West.

HAPPY. Yeah, big cattle man, my brother, so treat him right. And my father's coming too.

STANLEY. Oh, your father too!

HAPPY. You got a couple of nice lobsters?

STANLEY. Hundred per cent, big.

HAPPY. I want them with the claws.

STANLEY. Don't worry, I don't give you no mice. (*Happy laughs.*) How about some wine? It'll put a head on the meal.

HAPPY. No. You remember, Stanley, that recipe I brought you from overseas? With the champagne in it?

STANLEY. Oh, yeah, sure. I still got it tacked up yet in the kitchen. But that'll have to cost a buck apiece anyways.

HAPPY. That's all right.

STANLEY. What'd you, hit a number or somethin'?

HAPPY. No, it's a little celebration. My brother is—I think he pulled off a big deal today. I think we're going into business together.

STANLEY. Great! That's the best for you. Because a family business, you know what I mean?—that's the best.

HAPPY. That's what I think.

STANLEY. 'Cause what's the difference? Somebody steals? It's in the family. Know what I mean? (*Sotto voce.*) Like this bartender here. The boss is goin' crazy what kinda leak he's got in the cash register. You put it in but it don't come out.

HAPPY (*raising his head*). Sh!

STANLEY. What?

HAPPY. You notice I wasn't lookin' right or left, was I?

STANLEY. No.

HAPPY. And my eyes are closed.

STANLEY. So what's the . . . ?

HAPPY. Strudel's comin'.

STANLEY (*catching on, looks around*). Ah, no, there's no . . .

He breaks off as a furred, lavishly dressed Girl enters and sits at the next table. Both follow her with their eyes.

STANLEY. Geez, how'd ya know?

HAPPY. I got radar or something. (*Staring directly at her profile.*) Oooooooo . . . Stanley.

STANLEY. I think that's for you, Mr. Loman.

HAPPY. Look at that mouth. Oh, God. And the binoculars.

STANLEY. Geez, you got a life, Mr. Loman.

HAPPY. Wait on her.

STANLEY (*going to the Girl's table*). Would you like a menu, ma'am?

GIRL. I'm expecting someone, but I'd like a . . .

HAPPY. Why don't you bring her—excuse me, miss, do you mind? I sell champagne, and I'd like you to try my brand. Bring her a champagne, Stanley.

GIRL. That's awfully nice of you.

HAPPY. Don't mention it. It's all company money. (*He laughs.*)

GIRL. That's a charming product to be selling, isn't it?

HAPPY. Oh, gets to be like everything else. Selling is selling, y'know.

GIRL. I suppose.

HAPPY. You don't happen to sell, do you?

GIRL. No, I don't sell.

HAPPY. Would you object to a compliment from a stranger? You ought to be on a magazine cover.

GIRL (*looking at him a little archly*). I have been.

Stanley comes in with a glass of champagne.

HAPPY. What'd I say before, Stanley? You see? She's a cover girl.

STANLEY. Oh, I could see, I could see.

HAPPY (*to the Girl*). What magazine?

GIRL. Oh, a lot of them. (*She takes the drink.*) Thank you.

HAPPY. You know what they say in France, don't you? "Champagne is the drink of the complexion"—Hya, Biff!

Biff has entered and sits with Happy.

BIFF. Hello, kid. Sorry I'm late.

HAPPY. I just got here. Uh, Miss . . . ?

GIRL. Forsythe.

HAPPY. Miss Forsythe, this is my brother.

BIFF. Is Dad here?

HAPPY. His name is Biff. You might've heard of him. Great football player.

GIRL. Really? What team?

HAPPY. Are you familiar with football?

GIRL. No, I'm afraid I'm not.

HAPPY. Biff is quarterback with the New York Giants.

GIRL. Well, that is nice, isn't it? (*She drinks.*)

HAPPY. Good health.

GIRL. I'm happy to meet you.

HAPPY. That's my name. Hap. It's really Harold, but at West Point they called me Happy.

GIRL (*now really impressed*). Oh, I see. How do you do? (*She turns her profile.*)

BIFF. Isn't Dad coming?

HAPPY. You want her?

BIFF. Oh, I could never make that.

HAPPY. I remember the time that idea would never come into your head. Where's the old confidence, Biff?

BIFF. I just saw Oliver . . .

HAPPY. Wait a minute. I've got to see that old confidence again. Do you want her? She's on call.

BIFF. Oh, no. (*He turns to look at the Girl.*)

HAPPY. I'm telling you. Watch this. (*Turning to the Girl.*) Honey? (*She turns to him.*) Are you busy?

GIRL. Well, I am . . . but I could make a phone call.

HAPPY. Do that, will you, honey? And see if you can get a friend. We'll be here for a while. Biff is one of the greatest football players in the country.

GIRL (*standing up*). Well, I'm certainly happy to meet you.

HAPPY. Come back soon.

GIRL. I'll try.

HAPPY. Don't try, honey, try hard.

The Girl exits. Stanley follows, shaking his head in bewildered admiration.

HAPPY. Isn't that a shame now? A beautiful girl like that? That's why I can't get married. There's not a good woman in a thousand. New York is loaded with them, kid!

BIFF. Hap, look . . .

HAPPY. I told you she was on call!

BIFF (*strangely unnerved*). Cut it out, will ya? I want to say something to you.

HAPPY. Did you see Oliver?

BIFF. I saw him all right. Now look, I want to tell Dad a couple of things and I want you to help me.

HAPPY. What? Is he going to back you?

BIFF. Are you crazy? You're out of your goddam head, you know that?

HAPPY. Why? What happened?

BIFF (*breathlessly*). I did a terrible thing today, Hap. It's been the strangest day I ever went through. I'm all numb, I swear.

HAPPY. You mean he wouldn't see you?

BIFF. Well, I waited six hours for him, see? All day. Kept sending my name in. Even tried to date his secretary so she'd get me to him, but no soap.

HAPPY. Because you're not showin' the old confidence, Biff. He remembered you, didn't he?

BIFF (*stopping Happy with a gesture*). Finally, about five o'clock, he comes out. Didn't remember who I was or anything. I felt like such an idiot, Hap.

HAPPY. Did you tell him my Florida idea?

BIFF. He walked away. I saw him for one minute. I got so mad I could've torn the walls down! How the hell did I ever get the idea I was a salesman there? I even believed myself that I'd been a salesman for him! And then he gave me one look and—I realized what a ridiculous lie my whole life has been! We've been talking in a dream for fifteen years. I was a shipping clerk.

HAPPY. What'd you do?

BIFF (*with great tension and wonder*). Well, he left, see. And the secretary went out. I was all alone in the waiting room. I don't know what came over me, Hap. The next thing I know I'm in his office—paneled walls, everything. I can't explain it. I—Hap. I took his fountain pen.

HAPPY. Geez, did he catch you?

BIFF. I ran out. I ran down all eleven flights. I ran and ran and ran.

HAPPY. That was an awful dumb—what'd you do that for?

BIFF (*agonized*). I don't know, I just—wanted to take something, I don't know. You gotta help me, Hap. I'm gonna tell Pop.

HAPPY. You crazy? What for?

BIFF. Hap, he's got to understand that I'm not the man somebody lends that kind of money to. He thinks I've been spiting him all these years and it's eating him up.

HAPPY. That's just it. You tell him something nice.

BIFF. I can't.

HAPPY. Say you got a lunch date with Oliver tomorrow.

BIFF. So what do I do tomorrow?

HAPPY. You leave the house tomorrow and come back at night and say Oliver is thinking it over. And he thinks it over for a couple of weeks, and gradually it fades away and nobody's the worse.

BIFF. But it'll go on forever!

HAPPY. Dad is never so happy as when he's looking forward to something!

Willy enters.

HAPPY. Hello, scout!

WILLY. Gee, I haven't been here in years!

Stanley has followed Willy in and sets a chair for him. Stanley starts off but Happy stops him.

HAPPY. Stanley!

Stanley stands by, waiting for an order.

BIFF (*going to Willy with guilt, as to an invalid*). Sit down, Pop. You want a drink?

WILLY. Sure, I don't mind.

BIFF. Let's get a load on.

WILLY. You look worried.

BIFF. N-no. (*To Stanley.*) Scotch all around. Make it doubles.

STANLEY. Doubles, right. (*He goes.*)

WILLY. You had a couple already, didn't you?

BIFF. Just a couple, yeah.

WILLY. Well, what happened, boy? (*Nodding affirmatively, with a smile.*) Everything go all right?

BIFF (*takes a breath, then reaches out and grasps Willy's hand*). Pal . . . (*He is smiling bravely, and Willy is smiling too.*) I had an experience today.

HAPPY. Terrific, Pop.

WILLY. That so? What happened?

BIFF (*high, slightly alcoholic, above the earth*). I'm going to tell you everything from first to last. It's been a strange day. (*Silence. He looks around, composes himself as best he can, but his breath keeps breaking the rhythm of his voice.*) I had to wait quite a while for him, and . . .

WILLY. Oliver?

BIFF. Yeah, Oliver. All day, as a matter of cold fact. And a lot of—instances—facts, Pop, facts about my life came back to me. Who was it, Pop? Who ever said I was a salesman with Oliver?

WILLY. Well, you were.

BIFF. No, Dad, I was a shipping clerk.

WILLY. But you were practically . . .

BIFF (*with determination*). Dad, I don't know who said it first, but I was never a salesman for Bill Oliver.

WILLY. What're you talking about?

BIFF. Let's hold on to the facts tonight, Pop. We're not going to get anywhere bullin' around. I was a shipping clerk.

WILLY (*angrily*). All right, now listen to me . . .

BIFF. Why don't you let me finish?

WILLY. I'm not interested in stories about the past or any crap of that kind because the woods are burning, boys, you understand? There's a big blaze going on all around. I was fired today.

BIFF (*shocked*). How could be be?

WILLY. I was fired, and I'm looking for a little good news to tell your mother, because the woman has waited and the woman has suffered. The gist of it is that I haven't got a story left in my head, Biff. So don't give me a lecture about facts and aspects. I am not interested. Now what've you got to say to me?

Stanley enters with three drinks. They wait until he leaves.

WILLY. Did you see Oliver?

BIFF. Jesus, Dad!

WILLY. You mean you didn't go up there?

HAPPY. Sure he went up there.

BIFF. I did. I—saw him. How could they fire you?

WILLY (*on the edge of his chair*). What kind of a welcome did he give you?

BIFF. He won't even let you work on commission?

WILLY. I'm out! (*Driving.*) So tell me, he gave you a warm welcome?

HAPPY. Sure, Pop, sure!

BIFF (*driven*). Well, it was kind of . . .

WILLY. I was wondering if he'd remember you. (*To Happy.*) Imagine, man doesn't see him for ten, twelve years and gives him that kind of a welcome!

HAPPY. Damn right!

BIFF (*trying to return to the offensive*). Pop, look . . .

WILLY. You know why he remembered you, don't you? Because you impressed him in those days.

BIFF. Let's talk quietly and get this down to the facts, huh?

WILLY (*as though Biff had been interrupting*). Well, what happened? It's great news, Biff. Did he take you into his office or'd you talk in the waiting room?

BIFF. Well, he came in, see, and . . .

WILLY (*with a big smile*). What'd he say? Betcha he threw his arm around you.

BIFF. Well, he kinda . . .

WILLY. He's a fine man. (*To Happy.*) Very hard man to see, y'know.

HAPPY (*agreeing*). Oh, I know.

WILLY (*to Biff*). Is that where you had the drinks?

BIFF. Yeah, he gave me a couple of—no, no!

HAPPY (*cutting in*). He told him my Florida idea.

WILLY. Don't interrupt. (*To Biff.*) How'd he react to the Florida idea?

BIFF. Dad, will you give me a minute to explain?

WILLY. I've been waiting for you to explain since I sat down here! What happened? He took you into his office and what?

BIFF. Well—I talked. And—and he listened, see.

WILLY. Famous for the way he listens, y'know. What was his answer?

BIFF. His answer was—(*He breaks off, suddenly angry.*) Dad, you're not letting me tell you what I want to tell you!

WILLY (*accusing, angered*). You didn't see him, did you?

BIFF. I did see him!

WILLY. What'd you insult him or something? You insulted him, didn't you?

BIFF. Listen, will you let me out of it, will you just let me out of it!

HAPPY. What the hell!
WILLY. Tell me what happened!
BIFF (*to Happy*). I can't talk to him!

A single trumpet note jars the ear. The light of green leaves stains the house, which holds the air of night and a dream. Young Bernard enters and knocks on the door of the house.

YOUNG BERNARD (FRANTICALLY). Mrs. Loman, Mrs. Loman!
HAPPY. Tell him what happened!
BIFF (*to Happy.*). Shut up and leave me alone!
WILLY. No, no! You had to go and flunk math!
BIFF. What math? What're you talking about?
YOUNG BERNARD. Mrs. Loman, Mrs. Loman!

Linda appears in the house, as of old.

WILLY (*wildly*). Math, math, math!
BIFF. Take it easy, Pop!
YOUNG BERNARD. Mrs. Loman!
WILLY (*furiously*). If you hadn't flunked you'd've been set by now!
BIFF. Now, look, I'm gonna tell you what happened, and you're going to listen to me.
YOUNG BERNARD. Mrs. Loman!
BIFF. I waited six hours . . .
HAPPY. What the hell are you saying?
BIFF. I kept sending in my name but he wouldn't see me. So finally he . . . (*He continues unheard as light fades low on the restaurant.*)
YOUNG BERNARD. Biff flunked math!
LINDA. No!
YOUNG BERNARD. Birnbaum flunked him! They won't graduate him!
LINDA. But they have to. He's gotta go to the university. Where is he? Biff! Biff!
YOUNG BERNARD. No, he left. He went to Grand Central.
LINDA. Grand—You mean he went to Boston!
YOUNG BERNARD. Is Uncle Willy in Boston?
LINDA. Oh, maybe Willy can talk to the teacher. Oh, the poor, poor boy!

Light on house area snaps out.

BIFF (*at the table, now audible, holding up a gold fountain pen*). . . . so I'm washed up with Oliver, you understand? Are you listening to me?
WILLY (*at a loss*). Yeah, sure. If you hadn't flunked . . .
BIFF. Flunked what? What're you talking about?
WILLY. Don't blame everything on me! I didn't flunk math—you did! What pen?
HAPPY. That was awful dumb, Biff, a pen like that is worth—
WILLY (*seeing the pen for the first time*). You took Oliver's pen?
BIFF (*weakening*). Dad, I just explained it to you.
WILLY. You stole Bill Oliver's fountain pen!

BIFF. I didn't exactly steal it! That's just what I've been explaining to you!
HAPPY. He had it in his hand and just then Oliver walked in, so he got nervous and stuck it in his pocket!
WILLY. My God, Biff!
BIFF. I never intended to do it, Dad!
OPERATOR'S VOICE. Standish Arms, good evening!
WILLY (*shouting*). I'm not in my room!
BIFF (*frightened*). Dad, what's the matter? (*He and Happy stand up.*)
OPERATOR. Ringing Mr. Loman for you!
WILLY. I'm not there, stop it!
BIFF (*horrified, gets down on one knee before Willy*). Dad, I'll make good, I'll make good. (*Willy tries to get to his feet. Biff holds him down.*) Sit down now.
WILLY. No, you're no good, you're no good for anything.
BIFF. I am, Dad, I'll find something else, you understand? Now don't worry about anything. (*He holds up Willy's face.*) Talk to me, Dad.
OPERATOR. Mr. Loman does not answer. Shall I page him?
WILLY (*attempting to stand, as though to rush and silence the Operator*). No, no, no!
HAPPY. He'll strike something, Pop.
WILLY. No, no . . .
BIFF (*desperately, standing over Willy*). Pop, listen! Listen to me! I'm telling you something good. Oliver talked to his partner about the Florida idea. You listening? He—he talked to his partner, and he came to me . . . I'm going to be all right, you hear? Dad, listen to me, he said it was just a question of the amount!
WILLY. Then you . . . got it?
HAPPY. He's gonna be terrific, Pop!
WILLY (*trying to stand*). Then you got it, haven't you? You got it! You got it!
BIFF (*agonized, holds Willy down*). No, no. Look, Pop. I'm supposed to have lunch with them tomorrow. I'm just telling you this so you'll know that I can still make an impression, Pop. And I'll make good somewhere, but I can't go tomorrow, see.
WILLY. Why not? You simply . . .
BIFF. But the pen, Pop!
WILLY. You give it to him and tell him it was an oversight!
HAPPY. Sure, have lunch tomorrow!
BIFF. I can't say that . . .
WILLY. You were doing a crossword puzzle and accidentally used his pen!
BIFF. Listen, kid, I took those balls years ago, now I walk in with his fountain pen? That clinches it, don't you see? I can't face him like that! I'll try elsewhere.
PAGE'S VOICE. Paging Mr. Loman!
WILLY. Don't you want to be anything?
BIFF. Pop, how can I go back?
WILLY. You don't want to be anything, is that what's behind it?
BIFF (*now angry at Willy for not crediting his sympathy*). Don't

take it that way! You think it was easy walking into that office after what I'd done to him? A team of horses couldn't have dragged me back to Bill Oliver!

WILLY. Then why'd you go?

BIFF. Why did I go? Why did I go! Look at you! Look at what's become of you!

Off left, The Woman laughs.

WILLY. Biff, you're going to go to that lunch tomorrow, or . . .

BIFF. I can't go. I've got no appointment!

HAPPY. Biff, for . . . !

WILLY. Are you spiting me?

BIFF. Don't take it that way! Goddammit!

WILLY (*strikes Biff and falters away from the table*). You rotten little louse! Are you spiting me?

THE WOMAN. Someone's at the door, Willy!

BIFF. I'm no good, can't you see what I am?

HAPPY (*separating them*). Hey, you're in a restaurant! Now cut it out, both of you! (*The girls enter.*) Hello, girls, sit down.

The Woman laughs, off left.

MISS FORSYTHE. I guess we might as well. This is Letta.

THE WOMAN. Willy, are you going to wake up?

BIFF (*ignoring Willy*). How're ya, miss, sit down. What do you drink?

MISS FORSYTHE. Letta might not be able to stay long.

LETTA. I gotta get up very early tomorrow. I got jury duty. I'm so excited! Were you fellows ever on a jury?

BIFF. No, but I been in front of them! (*The girls laugh.*) This is my father.

LETTA. Isn't he cute? Sit down with us, Pop.

HAPPY. Sit him down, Biff!

BIFF (*going to him*). Come on, slugger, drink us under the table. To hell with it! Come on, sit down, pal.

On Biff's last insistence, Willy is about to sit.

THE WOMAN (*now urgently*). Willy, are you going to answer the door!

The Woman's call pulls Willy back. He starts right, befuddled.

BIFF. Hey, where are you going?

WILLY. Open the door.

BIFF. The door?

WILLY. The washroom . . . the door . . . where's the door?

BIFF (*leading Willy to the left*). Just go straight down.

Willy moves left.

THE WOMAN. Willy, Willy, are you going to get up, get up, get up, get up?

Willy exits left.

LETTA. I think it's sweet you bring your daddy along.

MISS FORSYTHE. Oh, he isn't really your father!

BIFF (*at left, turning to her resentfully*). Miss Forsythe, you've just seen a prince walk by. A fine, troubled prince. A hardworking, unappreciated prince. A pal, you understand? A good companion. Always for his boys.

LETTA. That's so sweet.

HAPPY. Well, girls, what's the program? We're wasting time. Come on, Biff. Gather round. Where would you like to go?

BIFF. Why don't you do something for him?

HAPPY. Me!

BIFF. Don't you give a damn for him, Hap?

HAPPY. What're you talking about? I'm the one who . . .

BIFF. I sense it, you don't give a good goddam about him. (*He takes the rolled-up hose from his pocket and puts it on the table in front of Happy.*) Look what I found in the cellar, for Christ's sake. How can you bear to let it go on?

HAPPY. Me? Who goes away? Who runs off and . . .

BIFF. Yeah, but he doesn't mean anything to you. You could help him—I can't! Don't you understand what I'm talking about? He's going to kill himself, don't you know that?

HAPPY. Don't know it! Me!

BIFF. Hap, help him! Jesus . . . help him . . . Help me, help me, I can't bear to look at his face! (*Ready to weep, he hurries out, up right.*)

HAPPY (*starting after him*). Where are you going?

MISS FORSYTHE. What's he so mad about?

HAPPY. Come on, girls, we'll catch up with him.

MISS FORSYTHE (*as Happy pushes her out*). Say, I don't like that temper of his!

HAPPY. He's just a little overstrung, he'll be all right!

WILLY (*off left, as The Woman laughs*). Don't answer! Don't answer!

LETTA. Don't you want to tell your father . . .

HAPPY. No, that's not my father. He's just a guy. Come on, we'll catch Biff, and, honey, we're going to paint this town! Stanley, where's the check! Hey, Stanley!

They exit. Stanley looks toward left.

STANLEY (*calling to Happy indignantly*). Mr. Loman! Mr. Loman!

Stanley picks up a chair and follows them off. Knocking is heard off left. The Woman enters, laughing. Willy follows her. She is in a black slip; he is buttoning his shirt. Raw, sensuous music accompanies their speech:

WILLY. Will you stop laughing? Will you stop?

THE WOMAN. Aren't you going to answer the door? He'll wake the whole hotel.

WILLY. I'm not expecting anybody.

THE WOMAN. Whyn't you have another drink, honey, and stop being so damn self-centered?

WILLY. I'm so lonely.

THE WOMAN. You know you ruined me, Willy? From now on, whenever you come to the office, I'll see that you go right through to the buyers. No waiting at my desk any-more, Willy. You ruined me.

WILLY. That's nice of you to say that.

THE WOMAN. Gee, you are self-centered! Why so sad? You are the saddest, self-centeredest soul I ever did see-saw. (*She laughs. He kisses her.*) Come on inside, drummer boy. It's silly to be dressing in the middle of the night. (*As knocking is heard.*) Aren't you going to answer the door?

WILLY. They're knocking on the wrong door.

THE WOMAN. But I felt the knocking. And he heard us talking in here. Maybe the hotel's on fire!

WILLY (*his terror rising*). It's a mistake.

THE WOMAN. Then tell him to go away!

WILLY. There's nobody there.

THE WOMAN. It's getting on my nerves, Willy. There's somebody standing out there and it's getting on my nerves!

WILLY (*pushing her away from him*). All right, stay in the bathroom here, and don't come out. I think there's a law in Massachusetts about it, so don't come out. It may be that new room clerk. He looked very mean. So don't come out. It's a mistake, there's no fire.

The knocking is heard again. He takes a few steps away from her, and she vanishes into the wing. The light follows him, and now he is facing Young Biff, who carries a suit-case. Biff steps toward him. The music is gone.

BIFF. Why didn't you answer?

WILLY. Biff! What are you doing in Boston?

BIFF. Why didn't you answer? I've been knocking for five minutes, I called you on the phone . . .

WILLY. I just heard you. I was in the bathroom and had the door shut. Did anything happen home?

BIFF. Dad—I let you down.

WILLY. What do you mean?

BIFF. Dad . . .

WILLY. Biffo, what's this about? (*Putting his arm around Biff.*) Come on, let's go downstairs and get you a malted.

BIFF. Dad, I flunked math.

WILLY. Not for the term?

BIFF. The term. I haven't got enough credits to graduate.

WILLY. You mean to say Bernard wouldn't give you the an-swers?

BIFF. He did, he tried, but I only got a sixty-one.

WILLY. And they wouldn't give you four points?

BIFF. Birnbaum refused absolutely. I begged him, Pop, but he won't give me those points. You gotta talk to him before they close the school. Because if he saw the kind of man you are, and you just talked to him in your way, I'm sure he'd come through for me. The class came right before practice, see, and I didn't go enough. Would you talk to him? He'd like you, Pop. You know the way you could talk.

WILLY. You're on. We'll drive right back.

BIFF. Oh, Dad, good work! I'm sure he'll change it for you!

WILLY. Go downstairs and tell the clerk I'm checkin' out. Go right down.

BIFF. Yes, sir! See, the reason he hates me, Pop—one day he was late for class so I got up at the blackboard and imi-tated him. I crossed my eyes and talked with a lithp.

WILLY (*laughing*). You did? The kids like it?

BIFF. They nearly died laughing!

WILLY. Yeah? What'd you do?

BIFF. The thquare root of thixthy twee is . . . (*Willy bursts out laughing; Biff joins.*) And in the middle of it he walked in!

Willy laughs and The Woman joins in offstage.

WILLY (*without hesitation*). Hurry downstairs and . . .

BIFF. Somebody in there?

WILLY. No, that was next door.

The Woman laughs offstage.

BIFF. Somebody got in your bathroom!

WILLY. No, it's the next room, there's a party . . .

THE WOMAN (*enters, laughing; she lisps this*). Can I come in? There's something in the bathtub, Willy, and it's moving!

Willy looks at Biff; who is staring open-mouthed and horri-fied at The Woman.

WILLY. Ah—you better go back to your room. They must be finished painting by now. They're painting her room so I let her take a shower here. Go back, go back . . . (*He pushes her.*)

THE WOMAN (*resisting*). But I've got to get dressed, Willy, I can't . . .

WILLY. Get out of here! Go back, go back . . . (*Suddenly striving for the ordinary.*) This is Miss Francis, Biff, she's a buyer. They're painting her room. Go back, Miss Francis, go back . . .

THE WOMAN. But my clothes, I can't go out naked in the hall!

WILLY (*pushing her offstage*). Get outa here! Go back, go back!

Biff slowly sits down on his suitcase as the argument con-tinues offstage.

THE WOMAN. Where's my stockings? You promised me stockings, Willy!

WILLY. I have no stockings here!

THE WOMAN. You had two boxes of size nine sheers for me, and I want them!

WILLY. Here, for God's sake, will you get outa here!

THE WOMAN (*enters holding a box of stockings*). I just hope there's nobody in the hall. That's all I hope. (*To Biff.*) Are you football or baseball?

BIFF. Football.

THE WOMAN (*angry, humiliated*). That's me too. G'night. (*She snatches her clothes from Willy, and walks out.*)

WILLY (*after a pause*). Well, better get going. I want to get to the school first thing in the morning. Get my suits out of the closet. I'll get my valise. (*Biff doesn't move.*) What's the matter! (*Biff remains motionless, tears falling.*) She's a buyer. Buys for J. H. Simmons. She lives down the hall—they're painting. You don't imagine—(*He breaks off. After a pause.*) Now listen, pal, she's just a buyer. She sells merchandise in her room and they have to keep it looking just so . . . (*Pause. Assuming command.*) All right, get my suits. (*Biff doesn't move.*) Now stop crying and do as I say. I gave you an order. Biff, I gave you an order! Is that what you do when I give you an order? How dare you cry! (*Putting his arm around Biff.*) Now look, Biff, when you grow up you'll understand about these things. You mustn't—you mustn't overemphasize a thing like this. I'll see Birnbaum first thing in the morning.

BIFF. Never mind.

WILLY (*getting down beside Biff*). Never mind! He's going to give you those points. I'll see to it.

BIFF. He wouldn't listen to you.

WILLY. He certainly will listen to me. You need those points for the U. of Virginia.

BIFF. I'm not going there.

WILLY. Heh? If I can't get him to change that mark you'll make it up in summer school. You've got all summer to . . .

BIFF (*his weeping breaking from him*). Dad . . .

WILLY (*infected by it*). Oh, my boy . . .

BIFF. Dad . . .

WILLY. She's nothing to me, Biff. I was lonely, I was terribly lonely.

BIFF. You—you gave her Mama's stockings! (*His tears break through and he rises to go.*)

WILLY (*grabbing for Biff*). I gave you an order!

BIFF. Don't touch me, you—liar!

WILLY. Apologize for that!

BIFF. You fake! You phony little fake! You fake! (*Overcome, he turns quickly and weeping fully goes out with his suitcase. Willy is left on the floor on his knees.*)

WILLY. I gave you an order! Biff, come back here or I'll beat you! Come back here! I'll whip you!

Stanley comes quickly in from the right and stands in front of Willy.

WILLY (*shouts at Stanley*). I gave you an order . . .

STANLEY. Hey, let's pick it up, pick it up, Mr. Loman. (*He helps Willy to his feet.*) Your boys left with the chippies. They said they'll see you home.

A second waiter watches some distance away.

WILLY. But we were supposed to have dinner together.

Music is heard, Willy's theme.

STANLEY. Can you make it?

WILLY. I'll—sure, I can make it. (*Suddenly concerned about his clothes.*) Do I—I look all right?

STANLEY. Sure, you look all right. (*He flicks a speck off Willy's lapel.*)

WILLY. Here—here's a dollar.

STANLEY. Oh, your son paid me. It's all right.

WILLY (*putting it in Stanley's hand*). No, take it. You're a good boy.

STANLEY. Oh, no, you don't have to . . .

WILLY. Here—here's some more, I don't need it any more. (*After a slight pause.*) Tell me—is there a seed store in the neighborhood?

STANLEY. Seeds? You mean like to plant?

As Willy turns, Stanley slips the money back into his jacket pocket.

WILLY. Yes. Carrots, peas . . .

STANLEY. Well, there's hardware stores on Sixth Avenue, but it may be too late now.

WILLY (*anxiously*). Oh, I'd better hurry. I've got to get some seeds. (*He starts off to the right.*) I've got to get some seeds, right away. Nothing's planted. I don't have a thing in the ground.

Willy hurries out as the light goes down. Stanley moves over to the right after him, watches him off. The other waiter has been staring at Willy.

STANLEY (*to the waiter*). Well, whatta you looking at?

The waiter picks up the chairs and moves off right. Stanley takes the table and follows him. The light fades on this area. There is a long pause, the sound of the flute coming over. The light gradually rises on the kitchen, which is empty. Happy appears at the door of the house, followed by Biff. Happy is carrying a large bunch of long-stemmed roses. He enters the kitchen, looks around for Linda. Not seeing her, he turns to Biff, who is just outside the house door, and makes a gesture with his hands, indicating "Not here, I guess." He looks into the living room and freezes. Inside, Linda, unseen, is seated, Willy's coat on her lap. She rises ominously and quietly and moves toward Happy, who backs up into the kitchen, afraid.

HAPPY. Hey, what're you doing up? (*Linda says nothing but moves toward him implacably.*) Where's Pop? (*He keeps backing to the right, and now Linda is in full view in the doorway to the living room.*) Is he sleeping?

LINDA. Where were you?

HAPPY (*trying to laugh it off*). We met two girls, Mom, very fine types. Here, we brought you some flowers. (*Offering them to her.*) Put them in your room, Ma.

She knocks them to the floor at Biff's feet. He has now come inside and closed the door behind him. She stares at Biff, silent.

HAPPY. Now what'd you do that for? Mom, I want you to have some flowers . . .

LINDA (*cutting Happy off, violently to Biff*). Don't you care whether he lives or dies?

HAPPY (*going to the stairs*). Come upstairs, Biff.

BIFF (*with a flare of disgust, to Happy*). Go away from me! (*To Linda.*) What do you mean, lives or dies? Nobody's dying around here, pal.

LINDA. Get out of my sight! Get out of here!

BIFF. I wanna see the boss.

LINDA. You're not going near him!

BIFF. Where is he? (*He moves into the living room and Linda follows.*)

LINDA (*shouting after Biff.*). You invite him for dinner. He looks forward to it all day—(*Biff appears in his parents' bedroom, looks around, and exits*)—and then you desert him there. There's no stranger you'd do that to!

HAPPY. Why? He had a swell time with us. Listen, when I—(*Linda comes back into the kitchen*)—desert him I hope I don't outlive the day!

LINDA. Get out of here!

HAPPY. Now look, Mom . . .

LINDA. Did you have to go to women tonight? You and your lousy rotten whores!

Biff re-enters the kitchen.

HAPPY. Mom, all we did was follow Biff around trying to cheer him up! (*To Biff.*) Boy, what a night you gave me!

LINDA. Get out of here, both of you, and don't come back! I don't want you tormenting him any more. Go on now, get your things together! (*To Biff.*) You can sleep in his apartment. (*She starts to pick up the flowers and stops herself.*) Pick up this stuff, I'm not your maid any more. Pick it up, you bum, you!

Happy turns his back to her in refusal. Biff slowly moves over and gets down on his knees, picking up the flowers.

LINDA. You're a pair of animals! Not one, not another living soul would have had the cruelty to walk out on that man in a restaurant!

BIFF (*not looking at her*). Is that what he said?

LINDA. He didn't have to say anything. He was so humiliated he nearly limped when he came in.

HAPPY. But, Mom, he had a great time with us . . .

BIFF (*cutting him off violently*). Shut up!

Without another word, Happy goes upstairs.

LINDA. You! You didn't even go in to see if he was all right!

BIFF (*still on the floor in front of Linda, the flowers in his hand; with self-loathing*). No. Didn't. Didn't do a damned thing. How do you like that, heh? Left him babbling in a toilet.

LINDA. You louse. You . . .

BIFF. Now you hit it on the nose! (*He gets up, throws the flowers in the wastebasket.*) The scum of the earth, and you're looking at him!

LINDA. Get out of here!

BIFF. I gotta talk to the boss, Mom. Where is he?

LINDA. You're not going near him. Get out of this house!

BIFF (*with absolute assurance, determination*). No. We're gonna have an abrupt conversation, him and me.

LINDA. You're not talking to him.

Hammering is heard from outside the house, off right. Biff turns toward the noise.

LINDA (*suddenly pleading*). Will you please leave him alone?

BIFF. What's he doing out there?

LINDA. He's planting the garden!

BIFF (*quietly*). Now? Oh, my God!

Biff moves outside, Linda following. The light dies down on them and comes up on the center of the apron as Willy walks into it. He is carrying a flashlight, a hoe, and a handful of seed packets. He raps the top of the hoe sharply to fix it firmly, and then moves to the left, measuring off the distance with his foot. He holds the flashlight to look at the seed packets, reading off the instructions. He is in the blue of night.

WILLY. Carrots . . . quarter-inch apart. Rows . . . one-foot rows. (*He measures it off.*) One foot. (*He puts down a package and measures off.*) Beets. (*He puts down another package and measures again.*) Lettuce. (*He reads the package, puts it down.*) One foot—(*He breaks off as Ben appears at the right and moves slowly down to him.*) What a proposition, ts, ts. Terrific, terrific. 'Cause she's suffered, Ben, the woman has suffered. You understand me? A man can't go out the way he came in, Ben, a man has got to add up to something. You can't, you can't—(*Ben moves toward him as though to interrupt.*) You gotta consider now. Don't answer so quick. Remember, it's a guaranteed twenty-thousand-dollar proposition. Now look, Ben, I want you to go through the ins and outs of this thing with me. I've got nobody to talk to, Ben, and the woman has suffered, you hear me?

BEN (*standing still, considering*). What's the proposition?

WILLY. It's twenty thousand dollars on the barrelhead. Guaranteed, gilt-edged, you understand?

BEN. You don't want to make a fool of yourself. They might not honor the policy.

WILLY. How can they dare refuse? Didn't I work like a coolie to meet every premium on the nose? And now they don't pay off? Impossible!

BEN. It's called a cowardly thing, William.

WILLY. Why? Does it take more guts to stand here the rest of my life ringing up a zero?

BEN (*yielding*). That's a point, William. (*He moves, thinking, turns.*) And twenty thousand—that is something one can feel with the hand, it is there.

WILLY (*now assured, with rising power*). Oh, Ben, that's the whole beauty of it! I see it like a diamond, shining in the dark, hard and rough, that I can pick up and touch in my hand. Not like—like an appointment! This would not be another damned-fool appointment, Ben, and it changes all the aspects. Because he thinks I'm nothing, see, and so he spites me. But the funeral . . . (*Straightening up.*) Ben, that funeral will be massive! They'll come from Maine, Massachusetts, Vermont, New Hampshire! All the old-timers with the strange license plates—that boy will be thunderstruck, Ben, because he never realized—I am known! Rhode Island, New York, New Jersey—I am known, Ben, and he'll see it with his eyes once and for all. He'll see what I am, Ben! He's in for a shock, that boy!

BEN (*coming down to the edge of the garden*). He'll call you a coward.

WILLY (*suddenly fearful*). No, that would be terrible.

BEN. Yes. And a damned fool.

WILLY. No, no, he mustn't, I won't have that! (*He is broken and desperate.*)

BEN. He'll hate you, William.

The gay music of the Boys is heard.

WILLY. Oh, Ben, how do we get back to all the great times? Used to be so full of light, and comradeship, the sleigh-riding in winter, and the ruddiness on his cheeks. And always some kind of good news coming up, always something nice coming up ahead. And never even let me carry the valises in the house, and simonizing, simonizing that little red car! Why, why can't I give him something and not have him hate me?

BEN. Let me think about it. (*He glances at his watch.*) I still have a little time. Remarkable proposition, but you've got to be sure you're not making a fool of yourself.

Ben drifts off upstage and goes out of sight. Biff comes down from the left.

WILLY (*suddenly conscious of Biff, turns and looks up at him, then begins picking up the packages of seeds in confusion*). Where the hell is that seed? (*Indignantly.*) You can't see nothing out here! They boxed in the whole goddam neighborhood!

BIFF. There are people all around here. Don't you realize that?

WILLY. I'm busy. Don't bother me.

BIFF (*taking the hoe from Willy*). I'm saying good-by to you, Pop. (*Willy looks at him, silent, unable to move.*) I'm not coming back any more.

WILLY. You're not going to see Oliver tomorrow?

BIFF. I've got no appointment, Dad.

WILLY. He put his arm around you, and you've got no appointment?

BIFF. Pop, get this now, will you? Everytime I've left it's been a—fight that sent me out of here. Today I realized something about myself and I tried to explain it to you and I—I think I'm just not smart enough to make any sense out of it for you. To hell with whose fault it is or anything like that. (*He takes Willy's arm.*) Let's just wrap it up, heh? Come on in, we'll tell Mom. (*He gently tries to pull Willy to left.*)

WILLY (*frozen, immobile, with guilt in his voice*). No, I don't want to see her.

BIFF. Come on! (*He pulls again, and Willy tries to pull away.*)

WILLY (*highly nervous*). No, no, I don't want to see her.

BIFF (*tries to look into Willy's face, as if to find the answer there*). Why don't you want to see her?

WILLY (*more harshly now*). Don't bother me, will you?

BIFF. What do you mean, you don't want to see her? You don't want them calling you yellow, do you? This isn't your fault; it's me, I'm a bum. Now come inside! (*Willy strains to get away.*) Did you hear what I said to you?

Willy pulls away and quickly goes by himself into the house. Biff follows.

LINDA (*to Willy*). Did you plant, dear?

BIFF (*at the door, to Linda*). All right, we had it out. I'm going and I'm not writing any more.

LINDA (*going to Willy in the kitchen*). I think that's the best way, dear. 'Cause there's no use drawing it out, you'll just never get along.

Willy doesn't respond.

BIFF. People ask where I am and what I'm doing, you don't know, and you don't care. That way it'll be off your mind and you can start brightening up again. All right? That clears it, doesn't it? (*Willy is silent, and Biff goes to him.*) You gonna wish me luck, scout? (*He extends his hand.*) What do you say?

LINDA. Shake his hand, Willy.

WILLY (*turning to her, seething with hurt*). There's no necessity—to mention the pen at all, y'know.

BIFF (*gently*). I've got no appointment, Dad.

WILLY (*erupting fiercely*). He put his arm around . . . ?

BIFF. Dad, you're never going to see what I am, so what's the use of arguing? If I strike oil I'll send you a check. Meantime forget I'm alive.

WILLY (*to Linda*). Spite, see?

BIFF. Shake hands, Dad.

WILLY. Not my hand.

BIFF. I was hoping not to go this way.

WILLY. Well, this is the way you're going. Good-by.

Biff looks at him a moment, then turns sharply and goes to the stairs.

WILLY (*stops him with*). May you rot in hell if you leave this house!

BIFF (*turning*). Exactly what is it that you want from me?

WILLY. I want you to know, on the train, in the mountains, in the valleys, wherever you go, that you cut down your life for spite!

BIFF. No, no.

WILLY. Spite, spite, is the word of your undoing! And when you're down and out, remember what did it. When you're rotting somewhere beside the railroad tracks, remember, and don't you dare blame it on me!

BIFF. I'm not blaming it on you!

WILLY. I won't take the rap for this, you hear?

Happy comes down the stairs and stands on the bottom step, watching.

BIFF. That's just what I'm telling you!

WILLY (*sinking into a chair at a table, with full accusation*). You're trying to put a knife in me—don't think I don't know what you're doing!

BIFF. All right, phony! Then let's lay it on the line. (*He whips the rubber tube out of his pocket and puts it on the table.*)

HAPPY. You crazy . . .

LINDA. Biff! (*She moves to grab the hose, but Biff holds it down with his hand.*)

BIFF. Leave it there! Don't move it!

WILLY (*not looking at it*). What is that?

BIFF. You know goddam well what that is.

WILLY (*caged, wanting to escape*). I never saw that.

BIFF. You saw it. The mice didn't bring it into the cellar! What is this supposed to do, make a hero out of you? This supposed to make me sorry for you?

WILLY. Never heard of it.

BIFF. There'll be no pity for you, you hear it? No pity!

WILLY (*to Linda*). You hear the spite!

BIFF. No, you're going to hear the truth—what you are and what I am!

LINDA. Stop it!

WILLY. Spite!

HAPPY (*coming down toward Biff*). You cut it now!

BIFF (*to Happy*). The man don't know who we are! The man is gonna know! (*To Willy.*) We never told the truth for ten minutes in this house!

HAPPY. We always told the truth!

BIFF (*turning on him*). You big blow, are you the assistant buyer? You're one of the two assistants to the assistant, aren't you?

HAPPY. Well, I'm practically . . .

BIFF. You're practically full of it! We all are! and I'm through with it. (*To Willy.*) Now hear this, Willy, this is me.

WILLY. I know you!

BIFF. You know why I had no address for three months? I stole a suit in Kansas City and I was in jail. (*To Linda, who is sobbing.*) Stop crying. I'm through with it.

Linda turns away from them, her hands covering her face.

WILLY. I suppose that's my fault!

BIFF. I stole myself out of every good job since high school!

WILLY. And whose fault is that?

BIFF. And I never got anywhere because you blew me so full of hot air I could never stand taking orders from anybody! That's whose fault it is!

WILLY. I hear that!

LINDA. Don't, Biff!

BIFF. It's goddam time you heard that! I had to be boss big shot in two weeks, and I'm through with it!

WILLY. Then hang yourself! For spite, hang yourself!

BIFF. No! Nobody's hanging himself, Willy! I ran down eleven flights with a pen in my hand today. And suddenly I stopped, you hear me? And in the middle of that office building, do you hear this? I stopped in the middle of that building and I saw—the sky. I saw the things that I love in this world. The work and the food and time to sit and smoke. And I looked at the pen and said to myself, what the hell am I grabbing this for? Why am I trying to become what I don't want to be? What am I doing in an office, making a contemptuous, begging fool of myself, when all I want is out there, waiting for me the minute I say I know who I am! Why can't I say that, Willy? (*He tries to make Willy face him, but Willy pulls away and moves to the left.*)

WILLY (*with hatred, threateningly*). The door of your life is wide open!

BIFF. Pop! I'm a dime a dozen, and so are you!

WILLY (*turning on him now in an uncontrolled outburst*). I am not a dime a dozen! I am Willy Loman, and you are Biff Loman!

Biff starts for Willy, but is blocked by Happy. In his fury, Biff seems on the verge of attacking his father.

BIFF. I am not a leader of men, Willy, and neither are you. You were never anything but a hard-working drummer who landed in the ash can like all the rest of them! I'm one dollar an hour, Willy! I tried seven states and couldn't raise it. A buck an hour! Do you gather my meaning? I'm not bringing home any prizes any more, and you're going to stop waiting for me to bring them home!

WILLY (*directly to Biff*). You vengeful, spiteful mutt!

Biff breaks from Happy. Willy, in fright, starts up the stairs. Biff grabs him.

BIFF (*at the peak of his fury*). Pop! I'm nothing! I'm nothing, Pop. Can't you understand that? There's no spite in it any more. I'm just what I am, that's all.

Biff's fury has spent itself and he breaks down, sobbing, holding on to Willy, who dumbly fumbles for Biff's face.

WILLY (*astonished*). What're you doing? What're you doing? (*To Linda.*) Why is he crying?

BIFF (*crying, broken*). Will you let me go, for Christ's sake? Will you take that phony dream and burn it before something happens? (*Struggling to contain himself, he pulls away and moves to the stairs.*) I'll go in the morning. Put him—put him to bed. (*Exhausted, Biff moves up the stairs to his room.*)

WILLY (*after a long pause, astonished, elevated*). Isn't that—isn't that remarkable? Biff—he likes me!

LINDA. He loves you, Willy!

HAPPY (*deeply moved*). Always did, Pop.

WILLY. Oh, Biff! (*Staring wildly.*) He cried! Cried to me. (*He is choking with his love, and now cries out his promise.*) That boy—that boy is going to be magnificent!

Ben appears in the light just outside the kitchen.

BEN. Yes, outstanding, with twenty thousand behind him.

LINDA (*sensing the racing of his mind, fearfully, carefully*). Now come to bed, Willy. It's all settled now.

WILLY (*finding it difficult not to rush out of the house*). Yes, we'll sleep. Come on. Go to sleep, Hap.

BEN. And it does take a great kind of a man to crack the jungle.

In accents of dread, Ben's idyllic music starts up.

HAPPY (*his arm around Linda*). I'm getting married, Pop, don't forget it. I'm changing everything. I'm gonna run that department before the year is up. You'll see, Mom. (*He kisses her.*)

BEN. The jungle is dark but full of diamonds, Willy.

Willy turns, moves, listening to Ben.

LINDA. Be good. You're both good boys, just act that way, that's all.

HAPPY. 'Night, Pop. (*He goes upstairs.*)

LINDA (*to Willy*). Come, dear.

BEN (*with greater force*). One must go in to fetch a diamond out.

WILLY (*to Linda, as he moves slowly along the edge of the kitchen, toward the door*). I just want to get settled down, Linda. Let me sit alone for a little.

LINDA (*almost uttering her fear*). I want you upstairs.

WILLY (*taking her in his arms*). In a few minutes, Linda. I couldn't sleep right now. Go on, you look awful tired. (*He kisses her.*)

BEN. Not like an appointment at all. A diamond is rough and hard to the touch.

WILLY. Go on now. I'll be right up.

LINDA. I think this is the only way, Willy.

WILLY. Sure, it's the best thing.

BEN. Best thing!

WILLY. The only way. Everything is gonna be—go on, kid, get to bed. You look so tired.

LINDA. Come right up.

WILLY. Two minutes.

Linda goes into the living room, then reappears in her bedroom. Willy moves just outside the kitchen door.

WILLY. Loves me. (*Wonderingly.*) Always loved me. Isn't that a remarkable thing? Ben, he'll worship me for it!

BEN (*with promise*). It's dark there, but full of diamonds.

WILLY. Can you imagine that magnificence with twenty thousand dollars in his pocket?

LINDA (*calling from her room*). Willy! Come up!

WILLY (*calling into the kitchen*). Yes! Yes. Coming! It's very smart, you realize that, don't you, sweetheart? Even Ben sees it. I gotta go, baby. 'By! 'By! (*Going over to Ben, almost dancing.*) Imagine? When the mail comes he'll be ahead of Bernard again!

BEN. A perfect proposition all around.

WILLY. Did you see how he cried to me? Oh, if I could kiss him, Ben!

BEN. Time, William, time!

WILLY. Oh, Ben, I always knew one way or another we were gonna make it, Biff and I.

BEN (*looking at his watch*). The boat. We'll be late. (*He moves slowly off into the darkness.*)

WILLY (*elegiacally, turning to the house*). Now when you kick off, boy, I want a seventy-yard boot, and get right down the field under the ball, and when you hit, hit low and hit hard, because it's important, boy. (*He swings around and faces the audience.*) There's all kinds of important people in the stands, and the first thing you know . . . (*Suddenly realizing he is alone.*) Ben! Ben, where do I . . . ? (*He makes a sudden movement of search.*) Ben, how do I . . . ?

LINDA (*calling*). Willy, you coming up?

WILLY (*uttering a gasp of fear, whirling about as if to quiet her*). Sh! (*He turns around as if to find his way; sounds, faces, voices, seem to be swarming in upon him and he flicks at them, crying.*) Sh! Sh! (*Suddenly music, faint and high, stops him. It rises in intensity, almost to an unbearable scream. He goes up and down on his toes, and rushes off around the house.*) Shhh!

LINDA. Willy?

There is no answer. Linda waits. Biff gets up off his bed. He is still in his clothes. Happy sits up. Biff stands listening.

LINDA (*with real fear*). Willy, answer me! Willy!

There is the sound of a car starting and moving away at full speed.

LINDA. No!

BIFF (*rushing down the stairs*). Pop!

As the car speeds off the music crashes down in a frenzy of sound, which becomes the soft pulsation of a single cello string. Biff slowly returns to his bedroom. He and Happy gravely don their jackets. Linda slowly walks out of her room. The music has developed into a dead march. The leaves of day are appearing over everything. Charley and Bernard, somberly dressed, appear and knock on the kitchen door. Biff and Happy slowly descend the stairs to the kitchen as Charley and Bernard enter. All stop a moment when Linda, in clothes of mourning, bearing a little bunch of roses, comes through the draped doorway into the kitchen. She goes to Charley and takes his arm. Now all move toward the audience, through the wall-line of the kitchen. At the limit of the apron, Linda lays down the flowers, kneels, and sits back on her heels. All stare down at the grave.

REQUIEM

CHARLEY. It's getting dark, Linda.

Linda doesn't react. She stares at the grave.

BIFF. How about it, Mom? Better get some rest, heh? They'll be closing the gate soon.

Linda makes no move. Pause.

HAPPY (*deeply angered*). He had no right to do that. There was no necessity for it. We would've helped him.

CHARLEY (*grunting*). Hmmm.

BIFF. Come along, Mom.

LINDA. Why didn't anybody come?

CHARLEY. It was a very nice funeral.

LINDA. But where are all the people he knew? Maybe they blame him.

CHARLEY. Naa. It's a rough world, Linda. They wouldn't blame him.

LINDA. I can't understand it. At this time especially. First time in thirty-five years we were just about free and clear. He only needed a little salary. He was even finished with the dentist.

CHARLEY. No man only needs a little salary.

LINDA. I can't understand it.

BIFF. There were a lot of nice days. When he'd come home from a trip; or on Sundays, making the stoop; finishing the cellar; putting on the new porch; when he built the extra bathroom; and put up the garage. You know something, Charley, there's more of him in that front stoop than in all the sales he ever made.

CHARLEY. Yeah. He was a happy man with a batch of cement.

LINDA. He was so wonderful with his hands.

BIFF. He had the wrong dreams. All, all, wrong.

HAPPY (*almost ready to fight Biff*). Don't say that!

BIFF. He never knew who he was.

CHARLEY (*stopping Happy's movement and reply; to Biff*). Nobody dast blame this man. You don't understand: Willy was a salesman. And for a salesman, there is no rock bottom to the life. He don't put a bolt to a nut, he don't tell you the law or give you medicine. He's a man way out there in the blue, riding on a smile and a shoeshine. And when they start not smiling back—that's an earthquake.

And then you get yourself a couple of spots on your hat, and you're finished. Nobody dast blame this man. A salesman is got to dream, boy. It comes with the territory.

BIFF. Charley, the man didn't know who he was.

HAPPY (*infuriated*). Don't say that!

BIFF. Why don't you come with me, Happy?

HAPPY. I'm not licked that easily. I'm staying right in this city, and I'm gonna beat this racket! (*He looks at Biff, his chin set.*) The Loman Brothers!

BIFF. I know who I am, kid.

HAPPY. All right, boy. I'm gonna show you and everybody else that Willy Loman did not die in vain. He had a good dream. It's the only dream you can have—to come out number-one man. He fought it out here, and this is where I'm gonna win it for him.

BIFF (*with a hopeless glance at Happy, bends toward his mother*). Let's go, Mom.

LINDA. I'll be with you in a minute. Go on, Charley. (*He hesitates.*) I want to, just for a minute. I never had a chance to say good-by.

Charley moves away, followed by Happy. Biff remains a slight distance up and left of Linda. She sits there, summoning herself. The flute begins, not far away, playing behind her speech.

LINDA. Forgive me, dear. I can't cry. I don't know what it is, but I can't cry. I don't understand it. Why did you ever do that? Help me, Willy, I can't cry. It seems to me that you're just on another trip. I keep expecting you. Willy, dear, I can't cry. Why did you do it? I search and search and I search, and I can't understand it, Willy. I made the last payment on the house today. Today, dear. And there'll be nobody home. (*A sob rises in her throat.*) We're free and clear. (*Sobbing mournfully, released.*) We're free. (*Biff comes slowly toward her.*) We're free . . . We're free . . .

Biff lifts her to her feet and moves out up right with her in his arms. Linda sobs quietly. Bernard and Charley come together and follow them, followed by Happy. Only the music of the flute is left on the darkening stage as over the house the hard towers of the apartment buildings rise into sharp focus and the curtain falls.

F O R U M S

Following the essay "Tragedy and the Common Man" by Arthur Miller are three reviews of productions of *Death of a Salesman*. Each one illustrates a distinct type of journalistic criticism. The first, by William Hawkins, is a "morning after" review and represents a critic's spontaneous impressions of the play. John Mason Brown, one of the most admired critics in the American theater, wrote his review almost two weeks after the play opened. His commentary benefits from additional reflection and focuses more on the play's thematic concerns. Thirty-five years later, Christopher Wren described Miller's production of his play in Beijing. While it, too, is a type of "first night" review, it also reflects the long history of the play. Note that Wren legitimately incorporated Miller's commentary into his review as the play was an established masterpiece in the American theater by 1983.

"Tragedy and the Common Man"

ARTHUR MILLER

In this age few tragedies are written. It has often been held that the lack is due to a paucity of heroes among us, or else that modern man has had the blood drawn out of his organs of belief by the skepticism of science, and the heroic attack on life cannot feed on an attitude of reserve and circumspection. For one reason or another, we are often held to be below tragedy—or tragedy above us. The inevitable conclusion is, of course, that the tragic mode is archaic, fit only for the very highly placed, the kings or the kingly, and where this admission is not made in so many words it is most often implied.

I believe that the common man is as apt a subject for tragedy in its highest sense as kings were. On the face of it this ought to be obvious in the light of modern psychiatry, which bases its analysis upon classic formulations, such as the Oedipus and Orestes complexes, for instances, which were enacted by royal beings, but which apply to everyone in similar emotional situations.

More simply, when the question of tragedy in art is not at issue, we never hesitate to attribute to the well-placed and the exalted the very same mental processes as the lowly. And finally, if the exaltation of tragic action were truly a property of the high-bred character alone, it is inconceivable that the mass of mankind should cherish tragedy above all other forms, let alone be capable of understanding it.

As a general rule, to which there may be exceptions unknown to me, I think the tragic feeling is evoked in us when we are in the presence of a character who is ready to lay down his life, if need be, to secure one thing—his sense of personal dignity. From Orestes to Hamlet, Medea to Macbeth, the underlying struggle is that of the individual attempting to gain his "rightful" position in his society.

Sometimes he is one who has been displaced from it, sometimes one who seeks to attain it for the first time, but the fateful wound from which the inevitable events spiral is the wound of indignity, and its dominant force is indignation. Tragedy, then, is the consequence of a man's total compulsion to evaluate himself justly.

In the sense of having been initiated by the hero himself, the tale always reveals what has been called his "tragic flaw," a failing that is not peculiar to grand or elevated characters. Nor is it necessarily a weakness. The flaw, or crack in the character, is really nothing—and need be nothing—but his inherent unwillingness to remain passive in the face of what he conceives to be a challenge to his dignity, has image of his rightful status. Only the passive, only those who accept their lot without active retaliation, are "flawless." Most of us are in that category.

But there are among us today, as there always have been, those who act against the scheme of things that degrades them, and in the process of action everything we have accepted out of fear or insensitivity or ignorance is shaken before us and examined, and from this total onslaught by an individual against the seemingly stable cosmos surrounding us—from this total examination of the "unchangeable" environment—comes the terror and the fear that is classically associated with tragedy.

More important, from this total questioning of what has previously been unquestioned, we learn. And such a process is not beyond the common man. In revolutions around the world, these past thirty years, he has demonstrated again and again this inner dynamic of all tragedy.

Insistence upon the rank of the tragic hero, or the so-called nobility of his character, is really but a clinging to the outward forms of tragedy. If rank or nobility of character was indispensable, then it would follow that the problems of those with rank were the particular problems of tragedy. But surely the right of one monarch to capture the domain from another no longer raises our passions, nor are our concepts of justice what they were to the mind of an Elizabethan king.

The quality in such plays that does shake us, however, derives from the underlying fear of being displaced, the disaster inherent in being torn away from our chosen image of what and who we are in this world. Among us today this fear is as strong, and perhaps stronger, than it ever was. In fact, it is the common man who knows this fear best.

(continued)

Now, if it is true that tragedy is the consequence of a man's total compulsion to evaluate himself justly, his destruction in the attempt posits a wrong or an evil in his environment. And this is precisely the morality of tragedy and its lesson. The discovery of the moral law, which is what the enlightenment of tragedy consists of, is not the discovery of some abstract or metaphysical quantity.

The tragic right is a condition of life, a condition in which the human personality is able to flower and realize itself. The wrong is the condition which suppresses man, perverts the flowing out of his love and creative instinct. Tragedy enlightens— and it must, in that it points the heroic finger at the enemy of man's freedom. The thrust for freedom is the quality in tragedy which exalts. The revolutionary questioning of the stable environment is what terrifies. In no way is the common man debarred from such thoughts or such actions.

Seen in the light, our lack of tragedy may be partially accounted for by the turn which modern literature has taken toward the purely psychiatric view of life, or the purely sociological. If all our miseries, our indignities, are born and bred within our minds, then all action, let alone the heroic action, is obviously impossible.

And if society alone is responsible for the cramping of our lives, then the protagonist must needs be so pure and faultless as to force us to deny his validity as a character. From neither of these views can tragedy derive, simply because neither represents a balanced concept of life. Above all else, tragedy requires the finest appreciation by the writer of cause and effect.

No tragedy can therefore come about when its author fears to question absolutely everything, when he regards any institution, habit or custom as being either everlasting, immutable or inevitable. In the tragic view the need of man to wholly realize himself is the only fixed star, and whatever it is that hedges his nature and lowers it is ripe for attack and examination. Which is not to say that tragedy must preach revolution.

The Greeks could probe the very heavenly origin of their ways and return to confirm the rightness of laws. And Job could face God in anger, demanding his right and end in submission.

But for a moment everything is in suspension, nothing is accepted, and in this stretching and tearing apart of the cosmos, in the very action of so doing, the character gains "size," the tragic stature which is spuriously attached to the royal or the highborn in our minds. The commonest of men may take on that stature to the extent of his willingness to throw all he has into the contest, the battle to secure his rightful place in his world.

There is a misconception of tragedy with which I have been struck in review after review, and in many conversations with writers and readers alike. It is the idea that tragedy is of necessity allied to pessimism. Even the dictionary says nothing more about the word than that it means a story with a sad or unhappy ending. This impression is so firmly fixed that I almost hesitate to claim that in truth tragedy implies more optimism in its author than does comedy, and that its final result ought to be the reinforcement of the onlooker's brightest opinions of the human animal.

For, if it is true to say that in essence the tragic hero is intent upon claiming his whole due as a personality, and if this struggle must be total and without reservation, then it automatically demonstrates the indestructible will of man to achieve his humanity.

The possibility of victory must be there in tragedy. Where pathos rules, where pathos is finally derived, a character has fought a battle he could not possibly have won. The pathetic is achieved when the protagonist is, by virtue of his witlessness, his insensitivity or the very air he gives off, incapable of grappling with a much superior force.

Pathos truly is the mode for the pessimist. But tragedy requires a nicer balance between what is possible and what is impossible. And it is curious, although edifying, that the plays we revere, century after century, are the tragedies. In them, and in them alone, lies the belief—optimistic, if you will, in the perfectability of man.

It is time, I think, that we who are without kings, took up this bright thread of our history and followed it to the only place it can possibly lead in our time—the heart and spirit of the average man.

"Death of a Salesman: Powerful Tragedy"

WILLIAM HAWKINS

Death of a Salesman is a play written along the lines of the finest classical tragedy. It is the revelation of a man's downfall, in destruction whose roots are entirely in his own soul. The play builds to an immutable conflict where there is no resolution for this man in this life.

"Death of a Salesman: Powerful Tragedy" by William Hawkins. *New York World-Telegram*, 11 February 1949. Reprinted by permission.

The play is a fervent query into the great American competitive dream of success, as it strips to the core a castaway from the race for recognition and money.

The failure of a great potential could never be so moving or so universally understandable as is the fate of Willy Loman, because his complete happiness could have been so easy to attain. He is an artisan who glories in manual effort and can be proud of the sturdy fine things he puts together out of wood and cement.

At eighteen he is introduced to the attention he might receive and the financial vistas he might travel by selling on the road. This original deception dooms him to a life of touring and a habit of prideful rationalization, until at sixty he is so far along his tangent that his efforts not to admit his resultant mediocrity are fatal.

Through most of this career runs the insistent legacy of "amounting to something" on his adopted terms, which he forces on his favorite son. With indulgent adoration he unbalances the boy, demanding a mutual idolatry which he himself inevitably fails. If young Biff steals, it is courage. If he captains a football team, the world is watching.

In the end, after repeated failure, Biff sees the truth, too late to really penetrate his father's mind. The boy's tortured efforts to explain his own little true destiny can only crack open the years-long rift, and the salesman, with all his dream's lost shadows, has no alternative to death for his peace.

Often plays have been written that crossed beyond physical actuality into the realm of memory and imagination, but it is doubtful if any has so skillfully transcended the limits of real time and space. One cannot term the chronology here a flashback technique, because the transitions are so immediate and logical.

As Willy's mind wavers under the strain of his own failure and the antagonism of his boy, he recalls the early hopeful days. The course of the play runs so smoothly that it seems one moment the two sons have gone to bed upstairs in plain sight, weary and cynical, and an instant later they are tumbling in youthful exuberance to the tune of their father's delighted flattery.

Sometimes Willy recalls the chance he once had to join his rich adventurous brother, and as his desperation increases he begs Ben for some explanation of his deep confusion.

These illuminations of the man are so exquisitely molded into the form of the play that it sweeps along like a powerful tragic symphony. The actors are attuned to the text as if they were distinct instruments. Themes rise and fade, are varied and repeated. Again as in music, an idea may be introduced as a faint echo, and afterwards developed to its fullest part in the big scheme.

It is hard to imagine anyone more splendid than Lee J. Cobb is as Willy Loman, the salesman. To be big and broken is so contradictory. The actor subtly moves from the first realizations of defeat, into a state of stubborn jauntiness alternating with childlike fear in a magnificent portrait of obsolescence.

Only the rare young actor can sustain a role of hysterical intensity with any dignity, but Arthur Kennedy does it with the utmost taste and strength. It is a complicated role, now joyous, now bitter, sometimes surly then passionately outspoken. Kennedy rings these changes without faltering.

Willy's wife Linda is a truthfully blocked out character, gentle and delicate, yet fiercely loving and fiercely loyal.

Mildred Dunnock plays her with sincerity that comes only with surface simplicity and penetrating comprehension. The scenes where she defends and explains the father to her sons are done with heart-wringing reality.

"Even as You and I"

JOHN MASON BROWN

George Jean Nathan once described a certain actress's Camille as being the first Camille he had ever seen who had died of catarrh. This reduction in scale of a major disease to an unpleasant annoyance is symptomatic of more than the acting practice of the contemporary stage. Even our dramatists, at least most of them, tend in their writing, so to speak, to turn t.b. into a sniffle. They seem ashamed of the big things, embarrassed by the raw emotions, afraid of the naked passions, and unaware of life's brutalities and tolls.

Of understatement they make a fetish. They have all the reticences and timidities of the overcivilized and undemonstrative.

"Even as You and I" by John Mason Brown. From *Saturday Review of Literature*, 32 (26 February 1949), pp. 30–32. Reprinted by permission of *The Saturday Review*, © 1979, General Media International, Inc.

They pride themselves upon writing around a scene rather than from or to it; upon what they hold back instead of upon what they release. They paint with pastels, not oils, and dodge the primary anguishes as they would the primary colors.

Their characters belong to an anemic brood. Lacking blood, they lack not only violence but humanity. They are the puppets of contrivance, not the victims of circumstance or themselves. They are apt to be shadows without substance, surfaces without depths. They can be found in the *dramatis personae* but not in the telephone book. If they have hearts, their murmurings are seldom audible. They neither hear nor allow us to hear those inner whisperings of hope, fear, despair, or joy, which are the true accompaniment to spoken words. Life may hurt them, but they do not suffer from the wounds it gives them so that we watching them, are wounded ourselves and suffer with them.

(continued)

This willingness, this ability, to strike unflinchingly upon the anvil of human sorrow is one of the reasons for O'Neill's pre-eminence and for the respect in which we hold the best work of Clifford Odets and Tennessee Williams. It is also the source of Arthur Miller's unique strength and explains why his fine new play, *Death of a Salesman,* is an experience at once pulverizing and welcome.

Mr. Miller is, of course, remembered as the author of *Focus,* a vigorous and terrifying novel about anti-Semitism, and best known for *All My Sons,* which won the New York Critics Award two seasons back. Although that earlier play lacked the simplicity, hence the muscularity, of Mr. Miller's novel, it was notable for its force. Overelaborate as it may have been, it introduced a new and unmistakable talent. If as a young man's script it took advantage of its right to betray influences, these at least were of the best. They were Ibsen and Chekhov. The doctor who wandered in from next door might have been extradited from *The Three Sisters.* The symbolical use to which the apple tree was put was pure Ibsen. So, too, was the manner in which the action was maneuvered from the present back into the past in order to rush forward. Even so, Mr. Miller's own voice could be heard in *All My Sons,* rising strong and clear above those other voices. It was a voice that deserved the attention and admiration it won. It was not afraid of being raised. It spoke with heat, fervor, and compassion. Moreover, it had something to say.

In *Death of a Salesman* this same voice can be heard again. It has deepened in tone, developed wonderfully in modulation, and gained in carrying power. Its authority has become full grown. Relying on no borrowed accents, it now speaks in terms of complete accomplishment rather than exciting promise. Indeed, it is released in a play which provides one of the modern theatre's most overpowering evenings.

How good the writing of this or that of Mr. Miller's individual scenes may be, I do not know. Nor do I really care. When hit in the face, you do not bother to count the knuckles which strike you. All that matters, all you remember, is the staggering impact of the blow. Mr. Miller's is a terrific wallop, as furious in its onslaught on the heart as on the head. His play is the most poignant statement of man as he must face himself to have come out of our theatre. It finds the stuffs of life so mixed with the stuffs of the stage that they become one and indivisible.

If the proper study of mankind is man, man's inescapable problem is himself—what he would like to be, what he is, what he is not, and yet what he must live and die with. These are the moving, everyday, all-inclusive subjects with which Mr. Miller deals in *Death of a Salesman.* He handles them unflinchingly, with enormous sympathy, with genuine imagination, and in a mood which neither the prose of his dialogue nor the reality of his probing can rob of its poetry. Moreover, he has the wisdom and the insight not to blame the "system," in Mr. Odets' fashion, for what are the inner frailties and shortcomings of the individual. His rightful concern is with the dilemmas which are timeless in the drama because they are timeless in life.

Mr. Miller's play is a tragedy modern and personal, not classic and heroic. Its central figure is a little man sentenced to discover his smallness rather than a big man undone by his greatness. Although he happens to be a salesman tested and found wanting by his own very special crises, all of us sitting out front are bound to be shaken, long before the evening is over, by finding something of ourselves in him.

Mr. Miller's Willy Loman is a family man, father of two sons. He is sixty-three and has grubbed hard all his life. He has never possessed either the daring or the gold-winning luck of his prospector brother, who wanders through the play as a somewhat shadowy symbol of success but a necessary contrast. Stupid, limited, and confused as Willy Loman may have been, however, no one could have questioned his industry or his loyalty to his firm and his firm. He has loved his sons and, when they were growing up, been rewarded by the warmth of their returned love. He loves his wife, too, and has been unfaithful to her only because of his acute, aching loneliness when on the road.

He has lived on his smile and on his hopes; survived from sale to sale; been sustained by the illusion that he has countless friends in his territory, that everything will be all right, that he is a success, and that his boys will be successes also. His misfortune is that he has gone through life as an eternal adolescent, as someone who has not dared to take stock, as someone who never knew who he was. His personality has been his profession; his energy, his protection. His major ambition has been not only to be liked, but well liked. His ideal for himself and for his sons has stopped with an easy, back-slapping, sports-loving, locker-room popularity. More than ruining his sons so that one has become a woman chaser and the other a thief, his standards have turned both boys against their father.

When Mr. Miller's play begins, Willy Loman has reached the ebb-tide years. He is too old and worn out to continue traveling. His back aches when he stoops to lift the heavy sample cases that were once his pride. His tired, wandering mind makes it unsafe for him to drive the car which has carried him from one town and sale to the next. His sons see through him and despise him. His wife sees through him and defends him, knowing him to be better than most and, at any rate, well intentioned. What is far worse, when he is fired from his job he begins to see through himself. He realizes he is, and has been, a failure. Hence his deliberate smashup in his car in order to bring in some money for his family and make the final payment on his home when there is almost no one left who wants to live in it.

Although *Death of a Salesman* is set in the present, it finds time and space to include the past. It plays the agonies of the moment of collapse against the pleasures and sorrows of recollected episodes. Mr. Miller is interested in more than the life and fate of his central character. His scene seems to be Willy Loman's mind and heart no less than his home. What we see might just as well be that Willy Loman thinks, feels, fears, or remembers as what we see him doing. This gives the play a double and successful exposure in time. It makes possible the constant fusion of what has been and what is. It also enables it to achieve a greater reality by having been freed from the fetters of realism.

Once again Mr. Miller shows how fearless and perceptive an emotionalist he is. He writes boldly and brilliantly about the way in which we disappoint those we love by having disappointed ourselves. He knows the torment of family tensions, the compensations of friendship, and the heartbreak that goes with broken pride and lost confidence. He is aware of the loyalties, not blind but open-eyed, which are needed to support mortals in their loneliness. The anatomy of failure, the pathos of age, and the tragedy of those years when a life begins to slip down the hill it has labored to climb are subjects at which he excels.

The quality and intensity of his writing can perhaps best be suggested by letting Mr. Miller speak for himself, or rather by allowing his characters to speak for him, in a single scene, in fact, in the concluding one. It is then that Willy's wife, his two sons, and his old friend move away from Jo Mielziner's brilliantly simple and imaginative multiple setting, and advance to the footlights. It is then that Mr. Miller's words supply a scenery of their own. Willy Loman, the failure and suicide, has supposedly just been buried, and all of us are at his grave, including his wife who wants to cry but cannot and who keeps thinking that it is just as if he were off on another trip.

"You don't understand," says Willy's friend, defending Willy from one of his sons. "Willy was a salesman. And for a salesman, there is no rock bottom to the life. He don't put a bolt to a nut, he don't tell you the law or give you medicine. He's a man way out there in the blue, ridin' on a smile and a shoeshine. And then they start not smilin' back—that's an earthquake. And then you get yourself a couple spots on your hat, and you're finished. Nobody dast blame this man. A salesman is got to dream, boy. It comes with the territory."

The production of *Death of a Salesman* is as sensitive, human, and powerful as the writing. Elia Kazan has solved, and solved superbly, what must have been a difficult and challenging problem. He captures to the full the mood and heartbreak of the script. He does this without ever surrendering to sentimentality. He manages to mingle the present and the past, the moment and his memory, so that their intertwining raises no questions and causes no confusions. His direction, so glorious in its vigor, is no less considerate of those small details which can be both mountainous and momentous in daily living.

It would be hard to name a play more fortunate in its casting than *Death of a Salesman*. All its actors—especially Arthur Kennedy and Cameron Mitchell as the two sons, and Howard Smith as the friend—act with such skill and conviction that the line of demarcation between being and pretending seems abolished. The script's humanity has taken possession of their playing and is an integral part of their performances.

Special mention must be made of Lee J. Cobb and Mildred Dunnock as the salesman, Willy Loman, and his wife, Linda. Miss Dunnock is all heart, devotion, simplicity. She is unfooled but unfailing. She is the smiling, mothering, hard-worked, good wife, the victim of her husband's budget. She is the nourisher of his dreams, even when she knows they are only dreams; the feeder of his self-esteem. If she is beyond whining or nagging, she is above self-pity. She is the marriage vow—"for better for worse, for richer for poorer, in sickness and in health"—made flesh, slight of body but strong of faith.

Mr. Cobb's Willy Loman is irresistibly touching and wonderfully unsparing. He is a great shaggy bison of a man seen at that moment of defeat when he is deserted by the herd and can no longer run with it. Mr. Cobb makes clear the pathetic extent to which the herd has been Willy's life. He also communicates the fatigue of Willy's mind and body and that boyish hope and buoyancy which his heart still retains. Age, however, is his enemy. He is condemned by it. He can no more escape from it than he can from himself. The confusions, the weakness, the goodness, the stupidity, and the self-sustaining illusions which are Willy—all these are established by Mr. Cobb. Seldom has an average man at the moment of his breaking been characterized with such exceptional skill.

Did Willy Loman, so happy with a batch of cement when puttering around the house, or when acquaintances on the road smiled back at him, fail to find out who he was? Did this man, who worked so hard and meant so well, dream the wrong dream? At least he was willing to die by that dream, even when it had collapsed for him. He was a breadwinner almost to the end, and a breadwinner even in his death. Did the world walk out on him, and his sons see through him? At any rate he could boast one friend who believed in him and thought his had been a good dream, "the only dream you can have." Who knows? Who can say? One thing is certain. No one could have raised the question more movingly or compassionately than Arthur Miller.

"Willy Loman Gets China Territory"

CHRISTOPHER S. WREN

The salesman shuffled on stage into the exposed skeleton of his small house and wearily handed his hat to his solicitous wife, who cast about for some place to put it.

"Let's get a shelf or a bench upstage of the bed," interrupted Arthur Miller from the dark of the deserted audience. "She can stash it right there and no one will ever know the difference." Ying Ruocheng, the Chinese actor who is also his liaison, nodded and translated to the stage manager.

Nearly 35 years after it opened on Broadway with Lee J. Cobb playing Willy Loman, the salesman "riding on a smile and a shoeshine to self-destruction," *Death of a Salesman* has come to China. Translated into Chinese, it is being directed by the playwright with a cast from the Peking People's Art Theater.

The revival could prove one of the most significant events for the Chinese theater since the end of a Cultural Revolution [1965–1975], when the tedious repertory of Maoist plays got jettisoned. Many in the Chinese audiences raised on prim Socialist morality plays will get their first acquaintance with the more ambiguous nature of contemporary Western drama.

(continued)

It is customary here to allocate tickets to foreign plays to Government offices and factories, where officials will decide who gets them. Mr. Ying has appealed, however, for the Government to release one-half of the tickets for *Death of a Salesman* for public sale.

He doesn't normally like directing his plays, Mr. Miller explained, because he would rather be home writing. He said he consented to devote nearly two months to this project because, "It seemed like an adventure to me—a window into China that is without parallel."

Though the story of a man made superfluous under capitalism would appeal to China's cultural commissars, there was still apparent hesitation about allowing in *Death of a Salesman* and its flawed hero.

"My impression is that they had long and strenuous debates about it, and those who backed the idea have a lot riding on it," Mr. Miller said. "That's why I wanted to do it."

The playwright, who has visited China twice before, is already popular for *The Crucible*. When it was staged [in Peking] several years ago, the Chinese saw the Salem witch hunts of seventeenth century New England as an allegory of their capriciously cruel Cultural Revolution. *All My Sons* was performed in China, too, though the playwright isn't sure where.

To transport Willy Loman from Brooklyn to Peking, the Chinese painstakingly reconstructed the original 1949 set from plans Mr. Miller sent over earlier. Whether Chinese audiences can as easily empathize with a traveling salesman defeated by the American dream will become clear after the play opens. [N.B.: The production was given a standing ovation by Chinese audiences.—Eds.]

Mr. Miller said: "*Salesman* represents a challenge they didn't think they could meet because they didn't think the audience would get it. About a year and half ago, they decided to risk it. I have to remind you that when the play opened originally in New York, there was also a question whether the audience was going to follow Willy through the corridors of his mind."

The Chinese, with their tradition of closely knit family, should have no trouble recognizing Willy Loman's frictions with his sons or Linda Loman's inability to save her husband. [Miller's wife] recalled that one woman came to watch a rehearsal, broke down, and sobbed, "It's the same situation."

Mr. Miller said: "The play is really about morality and leaving something behind. Willy Loman is trying to write his name on a cake of ice on a hot July day, and they know all about that."

Chinese who have grown up with a centrally planned state-run economy may be confused about how a salesman earns his living, though the Government's recent encouragement of private enterprise has made Miller's job easier.

"I thought we'd have to write a big essay explaining what salesman are and put it in the program," Mr. Miller said, "but Willy explains in the course of the play what a salesman does. In 1983, they know all about that. There are now people selling stuff on commission. There are now traveling buyers going from place to place to buy materials. There are factories loaded with surplus goods that are selling them in distant places. It may have not been a known profession, but it sure as hell is now."

Mr. Miller's liaison, Ying Ruocheng, is a distinguished actor who played the Mongol emperor, Kublai Khan, in the television series *Marco Polo* last year. Mr. Ying not only plays the part of Willy Loman, he also interprets Mr. Miller's directions to the actors. And he translated *Death of a Salesman* into Chinese, doing it so deftly that Mr. Miller said he could follow the script by listening to the cadence of the language.

Mr. Miller wasn't sure that Mr. Ying realized beforehand how strenuous playing Willy Loman would be. "He's rarely off stage and the scenes when he is on are at very high intensity." Mr. Ying said he agreed that the role was "one of the toughest anywhere."

A more difficult task has been getting the other actors to drop stylized gestures characteristic of Chinese Socialist drama and to behave naturally. They are used to exaggerating their emotions as stereotypes of good and evil to hammer across the play's message.

"I kill it every time it starts," Mr. Miller said of their mannerisms, though he sighed that "it crops up in different disguises."

The actor playing Howard Wagner, the employer who discharges Willy Loman, was dissuaded from making the character hateful. "I had to work longer with him than with anyone else to break the villainy out of him," Mr. Miller said. "He's quite affable now."

The actors, who wear 1940s Western clothing, have also been crammed with such details as the popularity of American football. "I've had to indoctrinate them with a lot of American folklore and stories," said Mr. Miller, who believes that a director must be a teacher too. "You have to do it with American actors, too, but they have the American references at their fingertips."

The greatest leap for the Chinese may be accepting a play without the customary Marxist moralistic didacticism. "The first thing they ask of anything, whether it's a bridge or a pair of shoes, is 'What's the message?'" Mr. Miller said.

The play has not been affected by the Chinese Government's move to suspend cultural and sports exchanges with the United States for the rest of [1983] to protest the political asylum given Hu Na, the tennis player. The project is sponsored by the United States–China Arts Exchange, a nongovernmental program run out of Columbia University. "That's why we weren't shut down," Mr. Miller said.

Except for Mr. Ying, who has visited the United States and Europe, Mr. Miller has found most Chinese uninformed about Western theater. When actors ask him what they can learn, Mr. Miller says: "I disappoint them by saying the West is in turmoil as far as the theater is concerned. There is only experimentation, and much of it isn't any good. But I tell them they might have to go through this experimentation."

Mr. Miller believes that the contemporary repertory already familiar in the West is a good place for Chinese theater to begin after the long years of isolation. "They're really coming out of a cave and blinking their eyes," the playwright said.

ABSURDISM

Artistic and Cultural Events

1916:
Tristan Tzara
begins Dadaism
in Switzerland

1930s:
Symbolist
drama in
Spain

1950:
Eugène
Ionesco's
*The Bald
Soprano*

1836:
Georg Buchner's
Woyzeck

1896:
Alfred Jarry's
Ubu Roi,
first
absurdist
play

1902:
Filippo
Marinetti
initiates
futurism
in Italy

1923:
André Breton
initiates
surrealism

1944:
Jean-Paul
Sartre's
No Exit

1953:
Samuel
Beckett's
*Waiting for
Godot*

1956:
Osvaldo
Dragún's
*Stories
to Be
Told*

1961:
Edward
Albee's
*The
American
Dream*

1800 C.E.

1900 C.E.

Historical and Political Events

1914–1918:
World War I

1939–1945:
World War II

1960s:
Counter-
revolution

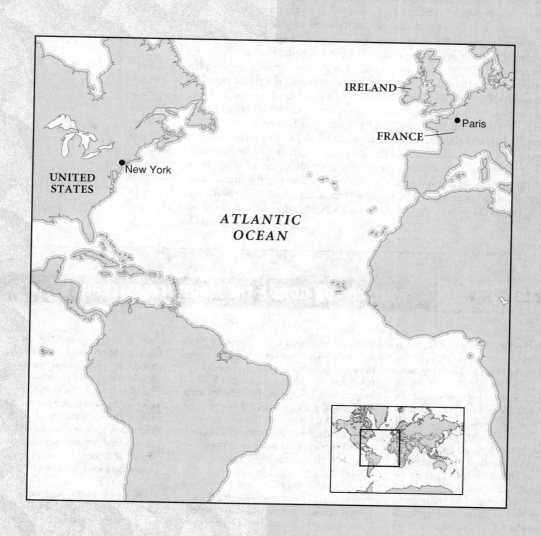

Whether they used realistic or other means in their exploration of social issues, most writers and artists in the modern theater shared the optimistic belief that change is possible, that social dilemmas can be solved if people are made aware of the problems that create them. Others, however, were less hopeful. Like Chekhov, they believed that time and institutions are indifferent to the human condition and that we are trapped by our circumstances and inertia. One of the most famous plays of the mid–twentieth century, Jean Paul Sartre's *No Exit* (*Huis Clos*, 1944), argues that there is no escape from the pain of being human.

Out of the ashes of the two great wars of the last century arose a philosophy—and a related theater movement—that challenged optimistic assumptions about people and institutions. The philosophy, existentialism, is manifested in a number of types of drama and production styles. Osborne's *Look Back in Anger*, although realistic, depicts Jimmy Porter's existential dilemma: How does a common man educated by the Establishment survive in a social system that is still rooted in the old class structure? "He doesn't," in Jimmy's estimation, and there is a fundamental absurdity to his dilemma. But the inherent rationality of the realistic theater was dismissed as inadequate as a means of portraying the senselessness of contemporary society. The theater of the absurd, as much a philosophical worldview as a theatrical style, developed primarily in France, which was scarred by years of Nazi occupation. Importantly, the theater of Latin America, especially South America, has also been a fertile source of absurdist and

---

SPOTLIGHT *WAITING FOR GODOT:* THE MODERN MASTERPIECE

Samuel Beckett's *Waiting for Godot* is among the most remarkable plays in the history of world theater. Nothing quite like it preceded its arrival in Paris in 1953, and it has since become one of the most imitated (if indirectly) and analyzed plays of the twentieth century. It stands as the epitome of the theater of the absurd, yet it has transcended the limitations of absurdism and remains a metaphysical landmark of the late twentieth century. Ironically, its status as a masterwork has curtailed its publication rights, so we may offer only this synopsis of the play and a brief assessment of its impact on the modern theater.

The story of *Waiting for Godot* is as sparse as the landscape in which it takes place: Two tramps (Gogo and Didi) wait under a barren tree for "Godot." They "improvise life" as they wait, and we watch them quarreling about seemingly insignificant matters, eating carrots and chicken bones, adjusting their ill-fitted shoes, and attempting suicide (unsuccessfully—fitting in a play about futility). Their wait is interrupted by two strangers, Pozzo (a master) and Lucky (his slave). The tramps engage in pseudophilosophic discourse with Pozzo,

who proclaims that we live on a "bitch of an earth." The tree sprouts a few leaves between acts, and Pozzo and Lucky return, this time blind and dumb. Finally, a boy arrives to inform the tramps that Godot will not come, and they continue to wait "in the midst of nothingness." The mundane routines with which Gogo and Didi occupy themselves as they wait reinforce the play's most quoted line: "Habit is the great deadener."

While "nothing" seems to happen during the play and in its seemingly incoherent conversations, in actuality everything happens. Virtually every aspect of the human condition is addressed—birth, death, suffering, redemption, salvation, loss, freedom, slavery, free will, isolation, companionship, hope, and despair. Midway through the play, Lucky—who speaks only once—delivers a long monologue (in the stream-of-consciousness style of Beckett's countryman James Joyce) that seems to summarize the history of humanity as it sits perched "astride of a grave and a difficult birth":

. . . but time will tell I resume alas alas on on in short in fine on on abode of stones who can doubt it I resume but

not so fast I resume the skull fading fading fading and concurrently simultaneously what is more for reasons unknown in spite for the tennis on on the beard the flames the tears the stones so blue so calm alas alas on on the skull the skull the skull the skull in Connemara in spite of the tennis the labors abandoned left unfinished graver still abode of stones in a word I resume alas alas abandoned unfinished . . .

So what does *Godot* mean? Indeed, who/what is Godot? Until his dying day Beckett steadfastly refused to reveal his intentions, saying only that "perhaps" is the most important word in the play. In the spirit of the absurdist movement, the playwright thus forces audiences—as they have been forced since 1953—to assign meaning to the play, if there is indeed meaning. Critics, scholars, philosophers, directors, actors, and general audiences have all attempted to assign meaning to Beckett's enigmatic play:

- It portrays humanity's fruitless search for someone or something that gives meaning to life.

grotesque drama as its artists, such as Osvaldo Dragún, turned to dark humor to depict the senselessness of their existence in oppressive societies.

While we can find moments that an absurdist would recognize in the plays of Aristophanes, the clowning of the *commedia dell'arte*, and even in the plays of Shakespeare (the Polish critic Jan Kott makes a compelling argument that there are moments in *King Lear* that might have been written by Samuel Beckett), there are more recent antecedents to the theater of the absurd. In the nineteenth century a German medical student, Georg Büchner (1813–1837), wrote plays such as *Woyzeck* (1836) that showed humans trapped in intolerable situations from which there was no escape. Some have called *Woyzeck* the first truly absurdist work; others cite Alfred Jarry's *Ubu Roi* (1896), a grotesque version of the Macbeth story that exposes all that the playwright found irrational about the bourgeois society in which he lived. It is among the darkest comedies composed in the preabsurdist era. The anti-art movement known as Dadaism also was a legitimate precursor to absurdism. In 1916 the original Dadaists, a group of young artists disillusioned by the brutality of World War I, conceived of a "negative art" that would destroy the apparently senseless values—promulgated by literature and art—of modern society. To create poetry they selected random words from a dictionary, wrote them on slips of paper, and cast them to the wind. (The term "dada" itself was randomly picked from a French dictionary; it is a word used by infants to describe horses.) Paintings were created by tossing paint at a canvas.

- It attempts to bridge the gap between human hopes and human futility.
- It is a modern myth, grounded in archetypal characters and situations, about "the suffering of being."
- It shows that humans "act out" life rather than live it; that is, we are actors in a cosmic drama, yet we do not know our lines, much less the character we are asked to play.
- It is a meaningless exercise that mirrors the meaningless of all human activity.

Despite its cryptic themes, *Godot* transformed the contemporary theater by loosening the grip of realism and absolute logic on dramaturgy. It returned the language of the theater to the realm of the evocative and symbolic, rather than the literal, and it released characterization from the particulars of psychology and sociology, thus making stage characters again mythic. Gogo and Didi, by the way, are rooted in that most elemental theater character: the hapless clown. For all its modernity, *Godot* is theater at its most essential—an empty space, a universal question, and skilled actors who bring it to life.

Godot was first staged by Roger Blin at the Théâtre de Babylon in Paris, where it ran for over 400 performances. Like *Hernani*, it provoked heated discussion; some in the opening-night audience felt they had been duped by this "nonplay." Like Gogo, they, too, believed the play was an event in which "nothing happens, nobody comes, nobody goes, it's awful." Others saw it as a theatrical Second Coming that would free the theater from the snares of realism just as *Hernani* had overthrown the Neoclassic codes 120 years earlier. News of Beckett's audacious work spread, and the play was performed at the Arts Theatre in London in 1955. It was directed by Peter Hall, fresh out of Cambridge University, who would found the Royal Shakespeare Company five years later. Harold Pinter and Tom Stoppard would be among the prominent British playwrights drawn to Beckett's new style. Stoppard wrote *Rosencrantz and Guildenstern Are Dead,* a dark comedy in which *Hamlet*'s Rosencrantz and Guildenstern resemble Beckett's tramps more than Shakespeare's creations.

The American premiere of *Godot* also stunned its audience, but for somewhat different reasons: Hearing that the play was a popular French comedy, an impresario booked it into a tourist resort theater in Florida. It has since been performed in hundreds of theaters by some of the American theater's most important actors: Bert Lahr, E. G. Marshall, and George C. Scott, to name but a few. A recent production at New York's Lincoln Center featured two of the most popular American comedians, Steve Martin and Robin Williams. *Godot* has been performed around the world; in 1979, for instance, Gogo and Didi were played in the Australian Academy of Dramatic Art by student actors Mel Gibson and Geoffrey Rush.

For almost a half-century actors, audiences, and critics have responded to Beckett's central question, spoken by Didi:

What are we doing here, *that* is the question? And we are blessed in this, that we happen to know the answer. Yes, in the immense confusion one thing alone is clear. We are waiting for Godot to come—

Theater was represented, in a famous French example, by a bicycle wheel, a clothesline on which signs were hung, and a series of insults exchanged between actors and audience. By 1922 Dadaism had lost much of its appeal, but it planted the seeds of an "anti-art" and skepticism that would resurface in the 1940s as the theater of the absurd.

During and immediately after World War II a group of international writers and philosophers flourished in Paris: Sartre and Albert Camus (France), Eugène Ionesco (Romania), and Samuel Beckett (Ireland) (see Spotlight box, *Waiting for Godot:* The Modern Masterpiece). Appalled by German atrocities, they embraced a philosophy that argued that there was no longer a system of order in the world (how else could one explain the Holocaust?) and that one was responsible for defining one's existence through personal choices. Disillusioned by the horrors of war, the economic depression of the 1930s, and other modern catastrophes, these nihilistic existentialists asserted that "the world is irrational and the truth unknowable."

If the world was indeed senseless, then it followed that art itself should mirror that senselessness. Traditional theater had to be transformed to reflect this condition. Conventional plots, dependent on causality and resolution, were abandoned in favor of cyclic plots that rarely resolved conflicts. Borrowing from the Expressionists and symbolists, the absurdists drew characters who were poetic abstractions. They were given generalized names (A and B, He and She, Gogo and Didi) and placed in unspecified time and space, often against dark curtains symbolizing the black void of existence. To illustrate lack of communication, language was frequently reduced to nonsensical utterings, non sequiturs, or mechanically repeated phrases. This dialogue from Ionesco's *The Bald Soprano* (1950) parodies the discussion drama of polite society. The speakers are indistinguishable from one another:

> MR. MARTIN. One doesn't polish spectacles with black wax.
> MRS. SMITH. Yes, but with money one can buy anything.
> MR. MARTIN. I'd rather kill a rabbit than sing in the garden.
> MR. SMITH. Cockatoos, cockatoos, cockatoos, cockatoos, cockatoos, cockatoos, cockatoos, cockatoos, cockatoos, cockatoos.
> MRS. SMITH. Such caca, such caca, such caca, such caca, such caca, such caca, such caca, such caca, such caca.
> MR. MARTIN. Such cascades of cacas, such cascades of cacas . . .

Traditional distinctions among the genres blur in the absurdist world: the comic frequently becomes serious, even near tragic, while the serious becomes laughable. Most absurdist plays are essentially comic, partly because they are satirical and partly because we are not engaged in the dramatic life of the characters. We laugh, albeit uncomfortably, at the enormous gap between human aspirations and the reality of existence. Edward Albee, whose early plays (e.g., *The American Dream*) are often categorized as absurdist, is perhaps the most successful playwright to have fused the philosophical concerns of the absurdists with traditional dramatic forms. His assessment of absurdism identifies the movement's concerns:

> As I get it, the Theatre of the Absurd is an absorption-in-art of certain existentialist and post-existentialist philosophical concepts having to do, in the main, with man's attempts to make sense of his senseless position in a world which makes no sense—which makes no sense because the moral, religious, political and social structures man has erected to "illusion" himself have collapsed.

In short, the theater of the absurd attempts to "make sense through nonsense." Unlike Ibsen, Shaw, and Brecht, absurdist playwrights refuse to suggest solutions to human problems. Meaning in this senseless world is derived solely by the audience, and in absurdist drama the discussion takes place long after the inevitable fade to black.

Many of the newer, antirealistic forms of drama have had a salutary effect on the theater. First, they have returned the art to its poetic roots. Theater began not as an imitation of real life but as a metaphor for life. Second, the social concerns voiced by both realists and antirealists exposed the plight of marginalized people throughout the world and opened the door to new writers. Consequently, the theater has been enriched in word and action by an infusion of new voices previously unheard in the mainstream.

THE AMERICAN DREAM

A Play in One Scene (1959–1960)

EDWARD ALBEE

EDWARD ALBEE (1928 –)

The winner of three Pulitzer Prizes in drama, Edward Albee has emerged as one of the finest American playwrights of the twentieth century. He bridges the early generation of admired playwrights (O'Neill, Miller, Williams) and the current one (Sam Shepard, August Wilson). No other playwright dominated the American theater in the 1960s as did Albee, who pioneered American absurdism in *The American Dream* and *The Sandbox*. After his initial exploration of absurdist drama, Albee took psychological realism to uncommon heights, tempering it with an almost surrealistic overlay. And he has emerged as one of the most articulate and candid spokespersons for the arts in America.

It is fitting that Albee should have pursued a life in the theater. His adoptive parents were heirs to the Albee-Keith fortune established in 1885 by Edward Franklin Albee II and B. F. Keith, who built a vaudeville empire that eventually stretched across America. Upon his adoption from a home for foundlings in Washington, D.C., Albee was christened Edward F. Albee III in memory of his adoptive grandfather. Though Albee's early life seems to have been charmed, his childhood was troubled and rancorous. His antipathy to his parents, especially his domineering mother, has been well publicized, and it appears that the domestic battles of the Albee household provided him with material for such plays as *Who's Afraid of Virginia Woolf?* and *The American Dream*, both of which are concerned with the disintegration of the contemporary family.

His parents' prosperity allowed Albee to attend the finest prep schools in the East, including Choate, followed by a brief stint at Trinity College in 1946–1947. His grandmother—a model for the Grandmother in *The Sandbox* and *The American Dream*—bequeathed him sufficient money to escape his home life. After a series of odd jobs, Albee achieved his first playwriting success when *The Zoo Story* was performed in New York (but only after proving itself in a West Berlin production in 1959). Performed on a bill with Beckett's *Krapp's Last Tape*, *The Zoo Story* was generously praised by Tennessee Williams. In May 1960 Albee wrote a short one-act, *The Sandbox*, whose principal characters reappeared the following year in *The American Dream*. In these works we see several Albee motifs: the impossibility of honest, open communication; emasculated father-figures embattled in a war of words with overbearing wives; the callous rejection of the older generation; masking reality with illusions (or delusions); and violence lurking beneath the surface of modern life.

In 1962 *Who's Afraid of Virginia Woolf?* premiered on Broadway, and its two-year run validated the critical praise it earned. It received the Drama Critics Circle Award and a Tony as best play of the season, but it failed to win the Pulitzer Prize because of a dispute among the trustees over the play's sexual references. Nonetheless, the play remains arguably Albee's finest drama in its devastating depiction of a psychological exorcism. Despite its patina of contemporary realism, the play is part Sartrean existentialism ("Hell is other people") and part Artaudian theater of cruelty as its characters "signal through the flames" of their personal hell. Albee did receive Pulitzer Prizes for *A Delicate Balance* (1966) and *Seascape* (1975). In the latter play,

Albee experimented with fantasy as a middle-aged couple encounters two prehistoric creatures from the sea; the play is a witty, philosophical discussion of mortality and human progress.

Despite his reputation as a superior playwright, whose dialogue is admired for its caustic wit and sophistication, Albee has had a curious relationship with critics. Like Williams, Albee was rejected by critics after his initial successes, partly because he tried to be too thoughtful in his works, and because he never measured up to the exacting standards he set for himself with *Virginia Woolf*, *Tiny Alice* (1964), and *A Delicate Balance*. In 1994 Albee was redeemed by *Three Tall Women*, a poetic look at immortality; the play won him a third Pulitzer Prize. In addition to playwriting, Albee also directs his own works. When not in New York, he teaches playwriting at the University of Houston and is an associate artist at Houston's Alley Theater.

THE AMERICAN DREAM: A PLAY IN ONE SCENE (1959–1960)

Because the centerpiece of this play is a lengthy story (an Albee trademark) about the adoption of "a little bumble of joy" by overbearing parents, it is tempting to regard *The American Dream* as an autobiographical piece in which the playwright exorcises the demons of his troubled youth. While this reading has some validity, the play transcends the particulars of Albee's life and remains among the most disturbing depictions of American culture in the postwar era. Furthermore, it provides insights into Albee's more mature, full-length works, such as *Who's Afraid of Virginia Woolf?* and *A Delicate Balance*. It can be argued that this one-act was a "first draft" of *Virginia Woolf*, just as *The Sandbox* was a precursor to *The American Dream*.

First, consider the play as an example of absurdist drama, the kind that emanated from Europe in the late 1940s and throughout the 1950s. In spirit and content, it is indebted to Eugène Ionesco's seminal absurdist drama, *The Bald Soprano* (1950). As in Ionesco's parody of banal small talk that precludes meaningful communication, *The American Dream* also relies on hilarious non sequiturs, the inversion of normal social exchanges (e.g., "What a dreadful apartment you have here," followed by "Yes, but you don't know what trouble it is"), gross violations of decorum (e.g., when Mrs. Barker removes her dress at Mommy's too-polite invitation), and the reduction of adult conversation to infantile prattling ("try to get the leak in the johnny fixed"). Albee's characters make self-canceling statements ("She's just a dreadful woman . . . so naturally I'm terribly fond of her") and elevate the most trivial elements of human endeavors (e.g., the color of a hat) to nearly cosmic significance. This was very much the arsenal of early absurdists who lamented the impossibility of communication in an increasingly illogical world; for them, language is reduced to a mechanical process of thoughtless noncommunication. Eventually, playwrights, led by Albee and Pinter, turned to a language of evasion and subterfuge to show lack of communication. More accurately, their characters refuse to communicate in a threatening world without verifiable meaning.

Also typical of absurdist comedy, the characters here are ciphers, nonentities in and of themselves but provocative symbols of the world at large. Only Mrs. Barker is given an actual name, yet in the context of this play it seems thoroughly generic. The bland box set described in the opening stage direction is peopled by the prototypical antiheroes of Albee's urban, WASP-ish wasteland. Daddy is the archetypal Albee male: emasculated, ineffectual, unable to commit himself to anything. Mommy is predictably domineering, stifling, sexually repressed. These are the parents of the American household at midcentury. In *Who's Afraid of Virginia Woolf?* the playwright fleshes them out with greater psychological complexity and, ominously, names them George and Martha (a macabre joke about the "first parents" of America?). Only Grandma is presented sympathetically, yet even she is just another discard in our disposable society. Early in the play, Mommy and Daddy threaten to "call the van man and have her taken away," and by the end of the play, when Grandma "disappears," Mrs. Barker tells us "the van man was here." Albee seems less interested in exposing the plight of the elderly than in examining America's preoccupation with the cult of youth. Even as Albee wrote the play in 1960, America was electing its youngest president (John Kennedy) and the baby boomer generation was entering adolescence.

Enter "the Young Man," a virile, narcissistic youth who, we are told, is "the American dream." Who is he, this identical twin of a child earlier adopted (and subsequently destroyed) by Mommy and Daddy? Is he the "American dream"—that is, the handsome, charming youth who seems immortal? Is he "the Angel of Death," as Albee called virtually the same character in *The Sandbox*? (Albee returned to the Angel of Death in his 1979 play, *The Lady from Dubuque*.) Albee challenges the audience to ascertain the symbolic value of this enigmatic character. Whatever he represents, the Young Man's most compelling line captures the ultimate dilemma in Albee's world. He tells Grandma, with whom he has a sympathetic covenant, that "I have been unable to love." The Young Man, it needs saying, is one of the first sympathetic portraits of a homosexual in the American theater as he recounts his plight as a male prostitute. Here Albee opened vistas for a subsequent generation of playwrights, including Harvey Fierstein and Terrence McNally.

Despite its grim portrait of contemporary life, the play is a comedy in its satirical portrait of the manners of a bourgeois family. In this sense it is kin to such works as *Tartuffe*. Significantly, Albee ends his play with the staple of comedies since Aristophanes: the *komos*, or "joyful ending," in which opposing parties unite to celebrate a new order. Albee's absurdly dysfunctional family, joined by Mrs. Barker and the mysterious Young Man, gather together "while everybody's happy" to drink "dreadful sauterne" in what appears to be a harmonious conclusion. Grandma breaks the illusion of the fourth wall to tell the audience that it is time to end the comedy "while everybody's got what he wants . . . or what he thinks he wants." And getting what one "wants" is, of course, the American dream. For Albee, the American dream seems to be as hollow and artificial as the contrived and sentimental ending of his play.

The Young Man stands before pictures of American icons (for example, Babe Ruth) in a 1975 Stevens Theatre Company production of Edward Albee's The American Dream.

THE AMERICAN DREAM

A Play in One Scene (1959–1960)

EDWARD ALBEE

For David Diamond

THE PLAYERS
MOMMY
DADDY
GRANDMA
MRS. BARKER
YOUNG MAN

THE SCENE: *A living room. Two armchairs, one toward either side of the stage, facing each other diagonally out toward the audience. Against the rear wall, a sofa. A door, leading out from the apartment, in the rear wall, far stage-right. An archway, leading to other rooms, in the side wall, stage-left.*
At the beginning, Mommy and Daddy are seated in the armchairs, Daddy in the armchair stage-left, Mommy in the other.
Curtain up. A silence. Then:

MOMMY. I don't know what can be keeping them.
DADDY. They're late, naturally.
MOMMY. Of course, they're late; it never fails.

DADDY. That's the way things are today, and there's nothing you can do about it.

MOMMY. You're quite right.

DADDY. When we took this apartment, they were quick enough to have me sign the lease; they were quick enough to take my check for two months' rent in advance . . .

MOMMY. And one month's security . . .

DADDY. . . . and one month's security. They were quick enough to check my references; they were quick enough about all that. But now! But now, try to get the icebox fixed, try to get the doorbell fixed, try to get the leak in the johnny fixed! Just try it . . . they aren't so quick about *that*.

MOMMY. Of course not; it never fails. People think they can get away with anything these days . . . and, of course they can. I went to buy a new hat yesterday.

(*Pause*)

I said, I went to buy a new hat yesterday.

DADDY. Oh! Yes . . . yes.

MOMMY. Pay attention.

DADDY. I *am* paying attention, Mommy.

MOMMY. Well, be sure you do.

DADDY. Oh, I am.

MOMMY. All right, Daddy; now listen.

DADDY. I'm listening, Mommy.

MOMMY. You're sure!

DADDY. Yes . . . yes, I'm sure, I'm all ears.

MOMMY (*Giggles at the thought; then*). All right, now. I went to buy a new hat yesterday and I said, "I'd like a new hat, please." And so, they showed me a few hats, green ones and blue ones, and I didn't like any of them, not one bit. What did I say? What did I just say?

DADDY. You didn't like any of them, not one bit.

MOMMY. That's right; you just keep paying attention. And then they showed me one that I did like. It was a lovely little hat, and I said, "Oh, this is a lovely little hat; I'll take this hat; oh my, it's lovely. What color is it?" And they said, "Why, this is beige; isn't it a lovely little beige hat?" And I said, "Oh, it's just lovely." And so, I bought it.

(*Stops, looks at Daddy*)

DADDY. (*To show he is paying attention*). And so you bought it.

MOMMY. And so I bought it, and I walked out of the store with the hat right on my head, and I ran spang into the chairman of our woman's club, and she said, "Oh, my dear, isn't that a lovely little hat? Where did you get that lovely little hat? It's the loveliest little hat; I've always wanted a wheat-colored hat *myself*." And, I said, "Why, no, my dear; this hat is beige; beige." And she laughed and said, "Why no, my dear, that's a wheat-colored hat . . . wheat. I know beige from wheat." And I said, "Well, my dear, I know beige from wheat, too." What did I say? What did I just say?

DADDY (*Tonelessly*). Well, my dear, I know beige from wheat, too.

MOMMY. That's right. And she laughed, and she said, "Well, my dear, they certainly put one over on you. That's wheat if I ever saw wheat. But it's lovely, just the same." And then she walked off. She's a dreadful woman, you don't know her; she has dreadful taste, two dreadful children, a dreadful house, and an absolutely adorable husband who sits in a wheel chair all the time. You don't know him. You don't know anybody, do you? She's just a dreadful woman, but she *is* chairman of our woman's club, so naturally I'm terribly fond of her. So, I went right back into the hat shop, and I said, "Look here; what do you mean selling me a hat that you say is beige, when it's wheat all the time . . . wheat! I can tell beige from wheat any day in the week, but not in this artificial light of yours." They have artificial light, Daddy.

DADDY. Have they!

MOMMY. And I said, "The minute I got outside I could tell that it wasn't a beige hat at all; it was a wheat hat." And they said to me, "How could you tell that when you had the hat on the top of your head?" Well, that made me angry, and so I made a scene right there; I screamed as hard as I could; I took my hat off and I threw it down on the counter, and oh, I made a terrible scene. I said, I made a terrible scene.

DADDY (*Snapping to*). Yes . . . yes . . . good for you!

MOMMY. And I made an absolutely terrible scene; and they became frightened, and they said, "Oh, madam; oh, madam." But I kept right on, and finally they admitted that they might have made a mistake; so they took my hat into the back, and then they came out again with a hat that looked exactly like it. I took one look at it, and I said, "This hat is wheat-colored; wheat." Well, of course, they said, "Oh, no, madam, this hat is beige; you go outside and see." So, I went outside, and lo and behold, it *was* beige. So I bought it.

DADDY (*Clearing his throat*). I would imagine that it was the same hat they tried to sell you before.

MOMMY (*With a little laugh*). Well, of course it was!

DADDY. That's the way things are today; you just can't get satisfaction; you just try.

MOMMY. Well, *I* got satisfaction.

DADDY. That's right, Mommy. *You did* get satisfaction, didn't you?

MOMMY. Why are they so late? I don't know what can be keeping them.

DADDY. I've been trying for two weeks to have the leak in the johnny fixed.

MOMMY. You can't get satisfaction; just try. *I* can get satisfaction, but you can't.

DADDY. I've been trying for two weeks and it isn't so much for my sake; I can always go to the club.

MOMMY. It isn't so much for my sake, either; I can always go shopping.

Edward Albee

DADDY. It's really for Grandma's sake.

MOMMY. Of course it's for Grandma's sake. Grandma cries every time she goes to the johnny as it is; but now that it doesn't work it's even worse, it makes Grandma think she's getting feeble-headed.

DADDY. Grandma *is* getting feeble-headed.

MOMMY. Of course Grandma is getting feeble-headed, but not about her johnny-do's.

DADDY. No; that's true. I must have it fixed.

MOMMY. WHY are they so late? I don't know what can be keeping them.

DADDY. When they came here the first time, they were ten minutes early; they were quick enough about it then.

(*Enter Grandma from the archway, stage left. She is loaded down with boxes, large and small, neatly wrapped and tied.*)

MOMMY. Why Grandma, look at you! What *is* all that you're carrying?

GRANDMA. They're boxes. What do they look like?

MOMMY. Daddy! Look at Grandma; look at all the boxes she's carrying!

DADDY. My goodness, Grandma; look at those boxes.

GRANDMA. Where'll I put them?

MOMMY. Heavens! I don't know. Whatever are they for?

GRANDMA. That's nobody's damn business.

MOMMY. Well, in that case, put them down next to Daddy; there.

GRANDMA (*Dumping the boxes down, on and around* Daddy's *feet*). I sure wish you'd get the john fixed.

DADDY. Oh, I do wish they'd come and fix it. We hear you . . . for hours . . . whimpering away . . .

MOMMY. Daddy! What a terrible thing to say to Grandma!

GRANDMA. Yeah. For shame, talking to me that way.

DADDY. I'm sorry, Grandma.

MOMMY. Daddy's sorry, Grandma.

GRANDMA. Well, all right. In that case I'll go get the rest of the boxes. I suppose I deserve being talked to that way. I've gotten so old. Most people think that when you get so old, you either freeze to death or you burn up. But you don't. When you get so old, all that happens is that people talk to you that way.

DADDY (*Contrite*). I said I'm sorry, Grandma.

MOMMY. Daddy said he was sorry.

GRANDMA. Well, that's all that counts. People being sorry. Makes you feel better; gives you a sense of dignity, and that's all that's important . . . a sense of dignity. And it doesn't matter if you don't care, or not, either. You got to have a sense of dignity, even if you don't care, 'cause, if you don't have that, civilization's doomed.

MOMMY. You've been reading my book club selections again!

DADDY. How dare you read Mommy's book club selections, Grandma!

GRANDMA. Because I'm old! When you're old you gotta do something. When you get old, you can't talk to people because people snap at you. When you get so old, people talk to you that way. That's why you become deaf, so you won't be able to hear people talking to you that way. And that's why you go and hide under the covers in the big soft bed, so you won't feel the house shaking from people talking to you that way. That's why old people die, eventually. People talk to them that way. I've got to go and get the rest of the boxes.

(*Grandma exits*)

DADDY. Poor Grandma, I didn't mean to hurt her.

MOMMY. Don't you worry about it; Grandma doesn't know what she means.

DADDY. She knows what she says, though.

MOMMY. Don't you worry about it; she won't know that soon. I love Grandma.

DADDY. I love her, too. Look how nicely she wrapped these boxes.

MOMMY. Grandma has always wrapped boxes nicely. When I was a little girl, I was very poor, and Grandma was very poor, too, because Grandpa was in heaven. And every day, when I went to school, Grandma used to wrap a box for me, and I used to take it with me to school; and when it was lunchtime, all the little boys and girls used to take out their boxes of lunch, and they weren't wrapped nicely at all, and they used to open them and eat their chicken legs and chocolate cakes; and I used to say, "Oh, look at my lovely lunch box; it's so nicely wrapped it would break my heart to open it." And so, I wouldn't open it.

DADDY. Because it was empty.

MOMMY. Oh no. Grandma always filled it up, because she never ate the dinner she cooked the evening before; she gave me all her food for my lunch box the next day. After school, I'd take the box back to Grandma, and she'd open it and eat the chicken legs and chocolate cake that was inside. Grandma used to say, "I love day-old cake." That's where the expression day-old cake came from. Grandma always ate everything a day late. I used to eat all the other little boys' and girls' food at school, because they thought my lunch box was empty. They thought my lunch box was empty, and that's why I wouldn't open it. They thought I suffered from the sin of pride, and since that made them better than me, they were very generous.

DADDY. You were a very deceitful little girl.

MOMMY. We were very poor! But then I married you, Daddy, and now we're very rich.

DADDY. Grandma isn't rich.

MOMMY. No, but you've been so good to Grandma she feels rich. She doesn't know you'd like to put her in a nursing home.

DADDY. I wouldn't!

MOMMY. Well, heaven knows, I would! I can't stand it, watching her do the cooking and the housework, polishing the silver, moving the furniture. . . .

DADDY. She likes to do that. She says it's the least she can do to earn her keep.

MOMMY. Well, she's right. You can't live off people. I can live off you, because I married you. And aren't you lucky all I brought with me was Grandma. A lot of women I know would have brought their whole families to live off you. All I brought was Grandma. Grandma is all the family I have.

DADDY. I feel very fortunate.

MOMMY. You should. I have a right to live off of you because I married you, and because I used to let you get on top of me and bump your uglies; and I have a right to all your money when you die. And when you do, Grandma and I can live by ourselves . . . if she's still here. Unless you have her put away in a nursing home.

DADDY. I have no intention of putting her in a nursing home.

MOMMY. Well, I wish somebody would do something with her!

DADDY. At any rate, you're very well provided for.

MOMMY. You're my sweet Daddy; that's very nice.

DADDY. I love my Mommy.

(*Enter Grandma again,* laden with more boxes)

GRANDMA (*Dumping the boxes on and around* Daddy's *feet*). There; that's the lot of them.

DADDY. They're wrapped so nicely.

GRANDMA (*To Daddy*). You won't get on my sweet side that way . . .

MOMMY. Grandma!

GRANDMA. . . . telling me how nicely I wrap boxes. Not after what you said: how I whimpered for hours. . . .

MOMMY. Grandma!

GRANDMA (*To Mommy*). Shut up!

(*To Daddy*)

You don't have any feelings, that's what's wrong with you. Old people make all sorts of noises, half of them they can't help. Old people whimper, and cry, and belch, and make great hollow rumbling sounds at the table; old people wake up in the middle of the night screaming, and find out they haven't even been asleep; and when old people *are* asleep, they try to wake up, and they can't . . . not for the longest time.

MOMMY. Homilies, homilies!

GRANDMA. And there's more, too.

DADDY. I'm really very sorry, Grandma.

GRANDMA. I know you are, Daddy; it's Mommy over there makes all the trouble. If you'd listened to me, you wouldn't have married her in the first place. She was a tramp and a trollop and a trull to boot, and she's no better now.

MOMMY. Grandma!

GRANDMA (*To Mommy*). Shut up!

(*To Daddy*)

When she was no more than eight years old she used to climb up on my lap and say, in a sickening little voice, "When I gwo up, I'm going to mahwy a wich old man; I'm going to set my wittle were end right down in a tub o' butter, that's what I'm going to do." And I warned you,

Daddy; I told you to stay away from her type. I told you to. I did.

MOMMY. You stop that! You're my mother, not his!

GRANDMA. I am?

DADDY. That's right, Grandma. Mommy's right.

GRANDMA. Well, how would you expect somebody as old as I am to remember a thing like that? You don't make allowances for people. I want an allowance. I want an allowance!

DADDY. All right, Grandma; I'll see to it.

MOMMY. Grandma! I'm ashamed of you.

GRANDMA. Humf! It's a fine time to say that. You should have gotten rid of me a long time ago if that's the way you feel. You should have had Daddy set me up in business somewhere . . . I could have gone into the fur business, or I could have been a singer. But no; not you. You wanted me around so you could sleep in my room when Daddy got fresh. But now it isn't important, because Daddy doesn't want to get fresh with you any more, and I don't blame him. You'd rather sleep with me, wouldn't you, Daddy?

MOMMY. Daddy doesn't want to sleep with anyone. Daddy's been sick.

DADDY. I've been sick. I don't even want to sleep in the apartment.

MOMMY. You see? I told you.

DADDY. I just want to get everything over with.

MOMMY. That's right. Why are they so late? Why can't they get here on time?

GRANDMA (*An owl*). Who? Who? . . . Who? Who?

MOMMY. You know, Grandma.

GRANDMA. No, I don't.

MOMMY. Well, it doesn't really matter whether you do or not.

DADDY. Is that true?

MOMMY. Oh, more or less. Look how pretty Grandma wrapped these boxes.

GRANDMA. I didn't really like wrapping them; it hurt my fingers, and it frightened me. But it had to be done.

MOMMY. Why, Grandma?

GRANDMA. None of your damn business.

MOMMY. Go to bed.

GRANDMA. I don't want to go to bed. I just got up. I want to stay here and watch. Besides . . .

MOMMY. Go to bed.

DADDY. Let her stay up, Mommy; it isn't noon yet.

GRANDMA. I want to watch; besides . . .

DADDY. Let her watch, Mommy.

MOMMY. Well all right, you can watch; but don't you dare say a word.

GRANDMA. Old people are very good at listening; old people don't like to talk; old people have colitis and lavender perfume. Now I'm going to be quiet.

DADDY. She never mentioned she wanted to be a singer.

MOMMY. Oh, I forgot to tell you, but it was ages ago.

(*The doorbell rings*)

Edward Albee

Oh, goodness! Here they are!

GRANDMA. Who? Who?

MOMMY. Oh, just some people.

GRANDMA. The van people? Is it the van people? Have you finally done it? Have you called the van people to come and take me away?

DADDY. Of course not, Grandma!

GRANDMA. Oh, don't be too sure. She'd have you carted off too, if she thought she could get away with it.

MOMMY. Pay no attention to her, Daddy.

(An aside to Grandma)

My God, you're ungrateful!

(The doorbell rings again)

DADDY (*Wringing his hands*). Oh dear; oh dear.

MOMMY (*Still to Grandma*). Just you wait; I'll fix your wagon.

(Now to Daddy)

Well, go let them in Daddy. What are you waiting for?

DADDY. I think we should talk about it some more. Maybe we've been hasty . . . a little hasty, perhaps.

(Doorbell rings again)

I'd like to talk about it some more.

MOMMY. There's no need. You made up your mind; you were firm; you were masculine and decisive.

DADDY. We might consider the pros and the . . .

MOMMY. I won't argue with you; it has to be done; you were right. Open the door.

DADDY. But I'm not sure that . . .

MOMMY. Open the door.

DADDY. Was I firm about it?

MOMMY. Oh, so firm; so firm.

DADDY. And was I decisive?

MOMMY. SO decisive! Oh, I shivered.

DADDY. And masculine? Was I really masculine?

MOMMY. Oh, Daddy, you were so masculine; I shivered and fainted.

GRANDMA. Shivered and fainted, did she? Humf!

MOMMY. You be quiet.

GRANDMA. Old people have a right to talk to themselves; it doesn't hurt the gums, and it's comforting.

(Doorbell rings again)

DADDY. I shall now open the door.

MOMMY. WHAT a masculine Daddy! Isn't he a masculine Daddy?

GRANDMA. Don't expect me to say anything. Old people are obscene.

MOMMY. Some of your opinions aren't so bad. You know that?

DADDY (*Backing off from the door*). Maybe we can send them away.

MOMMY. Oh, look at you! You're turning into jelly; you're indecisive; you're a woman.

DADDY. All right. Watch me now; I'm going to open the door. Watch. Watch!

MOMMY. We're watching; we're watching.

GRANDMA. *I'm* not.

DADDY. Watch now; it's opening.

(He opens the door)

It's open!

(Mrs. Barker steps into the room)

Here they are!

MOMMY. Here they are!

GRANDMA. Where?

DADDY. Come in. You're late. But, of course, we expected you to be late; we were saying that we expected you to be late.

MOMMY. Daddy, don't be rude! We were saying that you just can't get satisfaction these days, and we were talking about you, of course. Won't you come in?

MRS. BARKER. Thank you. I don't mind if I do.

MOMMY. We're very glad that you're here, late as you are. You do remember us, don't you? You were here once before. I'm Mommy, and this is Daddy, and that's Grandma, doddering there in the corner.

MRS. BARKER. Hello, Mommy; hello, Daddy; and hello there, Grandma.

DADDY. Now that you're here, I don't suppose you could go away and maybe come back some other time.

MRS. BARKER. Oh no; we're much too efficient for that. I said, hello there, Grandma.

MOMMY. Speak to them, Grandma.

GRANDMA. I don't see them.

DADDY. For shame, Grandma; they're here.

MRS. BARKER. Yes, we're here, Grandma. I'm Mrs. Barker. I remember you; don't you remember me?

GRANDMA. I don't recall. Maybe you were younger, or something.

MOMMY. Grandma! What a terrible thing to say!

MRS. BARKER. Oh no, don't scold her, Mommy; for all she knows she may be right.

DADDY. Uh . . . Mrs. Barker, is it? Won't you sit down?

MRS. BARKER. I don't mind if I do.

MOMMY. Would you like a cigarette, and a drink, and would you like to cross your legs?

MRS. BARKER. You forget yourself, Mommy; I'm a professional woman. But I will cross my legs.

DADDY. Yes, make yourself comfortable.

MRS. BARKER. I don't mind if I do.

GRANDMA. Are they still here?

MOMMY. Be quiet, Grandma.

MRS. BARKER. Oh, we're still here. My, what an unattractive apartment you have!

MOMMY. Yes, but you don't know what a trouble it is. Let me tell you . . .

DADDY. I was saying to Mommy . . .

MRS. BARKER. Yes, I know. I was listening outside.

DADDY. About the icebox, and . . . the doorbell . . . and the . . .

MRS. BARKER. . . . and the johnny. Yes, we're very efficient; we have to know everything in our work.

DADDY. Exactly what do you do?

MOMMY. Yes, what is your work?

MRS. BARKER. Well, my dear, for one thing, I'm chairman of your woman's club.

MOMMY. Don't be ridiculous. I was talking to the chairman of my woman's club just yester—Why, so you are. You remember, Daddy, the lady I was telling you about? The lady with the husband who sits in the *swing*? Don't you remember?

DADDY. No . . . no.

MOMMY. Of course you do. I'm sorry, Mrs. Barker. I would have known you anywhere, except in this artificial light. And look! You have a hat just like the one I bought yesterday.

MRS. BARKER (*With a little laugh*). No, not really; this hat is cream.

MOMMY. Well, my dear, that may look like a cream hat to you, but I can . . .

MRS. BARKER. Now, now; you seem to forget who I am.

MOMMY. Yes, I do, don't I? Are you sure you're comfortable? Won't you take off your dress.

MRS. BARKER. I don't mind if I do.

(*She removes her dress*)

MOMMY. There. You must feel a great deal more comfortable.

MRS. BARKER. Well, I certainly *look* a great deal more comfortable.

DADDY. I'm going to blush and giggle.

MOMMY. Daddy's going to blush and giggle.

MRS. BARKER (*Pulling the hem of her slip above her knees*). You're lucky to have such a man for a husband.

MOMMY. Oh, don't I know it!

DADDY. I just blushed and giggled and went sticky wet.

MOMMY. Isn't Daddy a caution, Mrs. Barker?

MRS. BARKER. Maybe if I smoked . . . ?

MOMMY. Oh, that isn't necessary.

MRS. BARKER. I don't mind if I do.

MOMMY. No; no, don't. Really.

MRS. BARKER. I don't mind . . .

MOMMY. I won't have you smoking in my house, and that's that! You're a professional woman.

DADDY. Grandma drinks AND smokes; don't you, Grandma?

GRANDMA. No.

MOMMY. Well, now, Mrs. Barker; suppose you tell us why you're here.

GRANDMA (*As Mommy walks through the boxes*). The boxes . . . the boxes . . .

MOMMY. Be quiet, Grandma.

DADDY. What did you say, Grandma?

GRANDMA (*As Mommy steps on several of the boxes*). The boxes, damn it!

MRS. BARKER. Boxes; she said boxes. She mentioned the boxes.

DADDY. What about the boxes, Grandma? Maybe Mrs. Barker is here because of the boxes. Is that what you meant, Grandma?

GRANDMA. I don't know if that's what I meant or not. It's certainly not what I *thought* I meant.

DADDY. Grandma is of the opinion that . . .

MRS. BARKER. Can we assume that the boxes are for us? I mean, can we assume that you had us come here for the boxes?

MOMMY. Are you in the habit of receiving boxes?

DADDY. A very good question.

MRS. BARKER. Well, that would depend on the reason we're here. I've got my fingers in so many little pies, you know. Now, I can think of one of my little activities in which we are in the habit of receiving *baskets*; but more in a literary sense than really. We *might* receive boxes, though, under very special circumstances. I'm afraid that's the best answer I can give you.

DADDY. It's a very interesting answer.

MRS. BARKER. *I* thought so. But, does it help?

MOMMY. No; I'm afraid not.

DADDY. I wonder if it might help us any if I said I feel misgivings, that I have definite qualms.

MOMMY. Where, Daddy?

DADDY. Well, mostly right here, right around where the stitches were.

MOMMY. Daddy had an operation, you know.

MRS. BARKER. Oh, you poor Daddy! I didn't know; but then, how could I?

GRANDMA. You might have asked; it wouldn't have hurt you.

MOMMY. Dry up, Grandma.

GRANDMA. There you go. Letting your true feelings come out. Old people aren't dry enough, I suppose. My sacks are empty, the fluid in my eyeballs is all caked on the inside edges, my spine is made of sugar candy, I breathe ice; but you don't hear me complain. Nobody hears old people complain because people think that's all old people do. And *that's* because old people are gnarled and sagged and twisted into the shape of a complaint.

(*Signs off*)

That's all.

MRS. BARKER. What was wrong, Daddy?

DADDY. Well, you know how it is: the doctors took out something that was there and put in something that wasn't there. An operation.

MRS. BARKER. You're very fortunate, I should say.

MOMMY. Oh, he is; he is. All his life. Daddy has wanted to be a United States Senator; but now . . . why now he's changed his mind, and for the rest of his life he's going to want to be Governor . . . it would be nearer the apartment, you know.

MRS. BARKER. You *are* fortunate, Daddy.

DADDY. Yes, indeed; except that I get these qualms now and then, definite ones.

MRS. BARKER. Well, it's just a matter of things settling; you're like an old house.

MOMMY. Why Daddy, thank Mrs. Barker.

DADDY. Thank you.

MRS. BARKER. Ambition! That's the ticket. I have a brother who's very much like you, Daddy . . . ambitious. Of course, he's a great deal younger than you; he's even younger than I am . . . if such a thing is possible. He runs a little newspaper. Just a little newspaper . . . but he runs it. He's chief cook and bottle washer of that little newspaper, which he calls *The Village Idiot*. He has such a sense of humor; he's so self-deprecating, so modest. And he'd never admit it himself, but he *is* the Village Idiot.

MOMMY. Oh, I think that's just grand. Don't you think so, Daddy?

DADDY. Yes, just grand.

MRS. BARKER. My brother's a dear man, and he has a dear little wife, whom he loves, dearly. He loves her so much he just can't get a sentence out without mentioning her. He wants everybody to know he's married. He's really a stickler on that point; he can't be introduced to anybody and say hello without adding, "Of course, I'm married." As far as I'm concerned, he's the chief exponent of Women Love in this whole country; he's even been written up in psychiatric journals because of it.

DADDY. Indeed!

MOMMY. Isn't that lovely.

MRS. BARKER. Oh, I think so. There's too much woman hatred in this country, and that's a fact.

GRANDMA. Oh, I don't know.

MOMMY. Oh, I think that's just grand. Don't you think so, Daddy?

DADDY. Yes, just grand.

GRANDMA. In case anybody's interested . . .

MOMMY. Be quiet, Grandma.

GRANDMA. Nuts!

MOMMY. Oh, Mrs. Barker, you *must* forgive Grandma. She's rural.

MRS. BARKER. I don't mind if I do.

DADDY. Maybe Grandma has something to say.

MOMMY. Nonsense. Old people have nothing to say; and if old people *did* have something to say, nobody would listen to them.

(*To Grandma*)

You see? I can pull that stuff just as easy as you can.

GRANDMA. Well, you got the rhythm, but you don't really have the quality. Besides, you're middle-aged.

MOMMY. I'm proud of it.

GRANDMA. Look. I'll show you how it's really done. Middle-aged people think they can do anything, but the truth is that middle-aged people can't do most things as well as they used to. Middle-aged people think they're special be-cause they're like everybody else. We live in the age of deformity. You see? Rhythm *and* content. You'll learn.

DADDY. I do wish I weren't surrounded by women; I'd like some men around here.

MRS. BARKER. You can say that again!

GRANDMA. I don't hardly count as a woman, so can I say my piece?

MOMMY. Go on. Jabber away.

GRANDMA. It's very simple; the fact is, these boxes don't have anything to do with why this good lady is come to call. Now, if you're interested in knowing why these boxes *are* here . . .

DADDY. I'm sure that must be all very true, Grandma, but what does it have to do with why . . . pardon me, what is that name again?

MRS. BARKER. Mrs. Barker.

DADDY. Exactly. What does it have to do with why . . . that name again?

MRS. BARKER. Mrs. Barker.

DADDY. Precisely. What does it have to do with why what's-her-name is here?

MOMMY. They're here because we asked them.

MRS. BARKER. Yes. That's why.

GRANDMA. Now if you're interested in knowing why these boxes *are* here . . .

MOMMY. Well, nobody *is* interested!

GRANDMA. You can be as snippety as you like for all the good it'll do you.

DADDY. You two will have to stop arguing.

MOMMY. I don't argue with her.

DADDY. It will just have to stop.

MOMMY. Well, why don't you call a van and have her taken away?

GRANDMA. Don't bother; there's no need.

DADDY. No, now, perhaps I can go away myself. . . .

MOMMY. Well, one or the other; the way things are now it's impossible. In the first place, it's too crowded in this apartment.

(*To Grandma*)

And it's you that takes up all the space, with your enema bottles, and your Pekinese, and God-only-knows-what-else . . . and now all these boxes . . .

GRANDMA. These boxes are . . .

MRS. BARKER. I've never heard of enema *bottles*. . . .

GRANDMA. She means enema bags, but she doesn't know the difference. Mommy comes from extremely bad stock. And besides, when Mommy was born . . . well, it was a difficult delivery, and she had a head shaped like a banana.

MOMMY. You ungrateful— Daddy? Daddy, you see how ungrateful she is after all these years, after all the things we've done for her?

(*To Grandma*)

One of these days you're going away in a van; that's what's going to happen to you!

GRANDMA. Do tell!

MRS. BARKER. Like a banana?

GRANDMA. Yup, just like a banana.

MRS. BARKER. My word!

MOMMY. You stop listening to her; she'll say anything. Just the other night she called Daddy a hedgehog.

MRS. BARKER. She didn't!

GRANDMA. That's right, baby; you stick up for me.

MOMMY. I don't know where she gets the words; on the television, maybe.

MRS. BARKER. Did you really call him a hedgehog?

GRANDMA. Oh look; what difference does it make whether I did or not?

DADDY. Grandma's right. Leave Grandma alone.

MOMMY (*To* Daddy). How dare you!

GRANDMA. Oh, leave her alone, Daddy; the kid's all mixed up.

MOMMY. You see? I told you. It's all those television shows. Daddy, you go right into Grandma's room and take her television and shake all the tubes loose.

DADDY. Don't mention tubes to me.

MOMMY. Oh! Mommy forgot!

(*To* Mrs. *Barker*)

Daddy has tubes now, where he used to have tracts.

MRS. BARKER. Is that a fact!

GRANDMA. I know why this dear lady is here.

MOMMY. You be still.

MRS. BARKER. Oh, I do wish you'd tell me.

MOMMY. No! No! That wouldn't be fair at all.

DADDY. Besides, she knows why she's here; she's here because we called them.

MRS. BARKER. La! But that still leaves me puzzled. I know I'm here because you called us, but I'm such a busy girl, with this committee and that committee, and the Responsible Citizens Activities I indulge in.

MOMMY. Oh my; busy, busy.

MRS. BARKER. Yes, indeed. So I'm afraid you'll have to give me some help.

MOMMY. Oh, no. No, you must be mistaken. I can't believe we asked you here to give you any help. With the way taxes are these days, and the way you can't get satisfaction in ANYTHING . . . no, I don't believe so.

DADDY. And if you need help . . . why, I should think you'd apply for a Fulbright Scholarship.

MOMMY. And if not that . . . why, then a Guggenheim Fellowship. . . .

GRANDMA. Oh, come on; why not shoot the works and try for the Prix de Rome.

(*Under her breath to Mommy and Daddy*)

Beasts!

MRS. BARKER. Oh, what a jolly family. But let me think. I'm knee-deep in work these days; there's the Ladies' Auxiliary Air Raid Committee, for one thing; how do you feel about air raids?

MOMMY. Oh, I'd say we're hostile.

DADDY. Yes, definitely; we're hostile.

MRS. BARKER. Then, you'll be no help there. There's too much hostility in the world these days as it is; but I'll not badger you! There's a surfeit of badgers as well.

GRANDMA. While we're at it, there's been a run on old people, too. The Department of Agriculture, or maybe it wasn't the Department of Agriculture—anyway, it was some department that's run by a girl—put out figures showing that ninety per cent of the adult population of the country is over eighty years old . . . or eighty percent is over ninety years old . . .

MOMMY. You're such a liar! You just finished saying that everyone is middle-aged.

GRANDMA. I'm just telling you what the government says . . . that doesn't have anything to do with what . . .

MOMMY. It's that television! Daddy, go break her television.

GRANDMA. You won't find it!

DADDY (*Wearily getting up*). If I must . . . I must.

MOMMY. And don't step on the Pekinese; it's blind.

DADDY. It may be blind, but Daddy isn't.

(*He exits, through the archway, stage left*)

GRANDMA. You won't find *it*, either.

MOMMY. Oh, I'm so fortunate to have such a husband. Just think; I could have a husband who was poor, or argumentative, or a husband who sat in a wheel chair all day . . . OOOOHHHH! *What* have I said? What *have* I said?

GRANDMA. You said you could have a husband who sat in a wheel . . .

MOMMY. I'm mortified! I could die! I could cut my tongue out! I could . . .

MRS. BARKER (*Forcing a smile*). Oh, now . . . now . . . don't think about it . . .

MOMMY. I could . . . why, I could . . .

MRS. BARKER. . . . don't think about it . . . really. . . .

MOMMY. You're quite right. I won't think about it, and that way I'll forget that I ever said it, and that way it will be all right.

(*Pause*)

There . . . I've forgotten. Well, now, now that Daddy is out of the room we can have some girl talk.

MRS. BARKER. I'm not sure that I . . .

MOMMY. You *do* want to have some girl talk, don't you?

MRS. BARKER. I was going to say I'm not sure that I wouldn't care for a glass of water. I feel a little faint.

MOMMY. Grandma, go get Mrs. Barker a glass of water.

GRANDMA. Go get it yourself. I quit.

MOMMY. Grandma loves to do little things around the house; it gives her a false sense of security.

GRANDMA. I quit! I'm through!

MOMMY. Now, you be a good Grandma, or you know what will happen to you. You'll be taken away in a van.

Edward Albee

GRANDMA. You don't frighten me. I'm too old to be frightened. Besides . . .
MOMMY. WELL! I'll tend to you later. I'll hide your teeth . . . I'll . . .
GRANDMA. Everything's hidden.
MRS. BARKER. I *am* going to faint. I *am*.
MOMMY. Good heavens! I'll go myself.

(*As she exits, through the archway, stage-left*)

I'll fix you, Grandma. I'll take care of you later.

(*She exits*)

GRANDMA. Oh, go soak your head.

(*To Mrs. Barker*)

Well, dearie, how do you feel?
MRS. BARKER. A little better, I think. Yes, much better, thank you, Grandma.
Grandma. That's good.
MRS. BARKER. But . . . I feel so lost . . . not knowing why I'm here . . . . and, on top of it, they say I was here before.
GRANDMA. Well, you were. You weren't *here*, exactly, because we've moved around a lot, from one apartment to another, up and down the social ladder like mice, if you like similes.
MRS. BARKER. I don't . . . particularly.
GRANDMA. Well, then, I'm sorry.
MRS. BARKER (*Suddenly*). Grandma, I feel I can trust you.
GRANDMA. Don't be too sure; it's every man for himself around this place. . . .
MRS. BARKER. Oh . . . is it? Nonetheless, I really do feel that I can trust you. *Please* tell me why they called and asked us to come. I implore you!
GRANDMA. Oh my; that feels good. It's been so long since anybody implored me. Do it again. Implore me some more.
MRS. BARKER. You're your daughter's mother, all right!
GRANDMA. Oh, I don't mean to be hard. If you won't implore me, then beg me, or ask me, or entreat me . . . just anything like that.
MRS. BARKER. You're a dreadful old woman!
GRANDMA. You'll understand some day. Please!
MRS. BARKER. Oh, for heaven's sake! . . . I implore you . . . I beg you . . . I beseech you!
GRANDMA. Beseech! Oh, that's the nicest word I've heard in ages. You're a dear, sweet woman. . . . You . . . beseech . . . me. I can't resist that.
MRS. BARKER. Well, then . . . please tell me why they asked us to come.
GRANDMA. Well, I'll give you a hint. That's the best I can do, because I'm a muddleheaded old woman. Now listen, because it's important. Once upon a time, not too very long ago, but a long enough time ago . . . oh, about twenty years ago . . . there was a man very much like Daddy, and a woman very much like Mommy, who were

married to each other, very much like Mommy and Daddy are married to each other; and they lived in an apartment very much like one that's very much like this one, and they lived there with an old woman who was very much like yours truly, only younger, because it was some time ago; in fact, they were all somewhat younger.
MRS. BARKER. How fascinating!
GRANDMA. Now, at the same time, there was a dear lady very much like you, only younger then, who did all sorts of Good Works. . . . And one of the Good Works this dear lady did was in something very much like a volunteer capacity for an organization very much like the Bye-Bye Adoption Service, which is nearby and which was run by a terribly deaf old lady very much like the Miss Bye-Bye who runs the Bye-Bye Adoption Service nearby.
MRS. BARKER. How enthralling!
GRANDMA. Well, be that as it may. Nonetheless, one afternoon this man, who was very much like Daddy, and this woman who was very much like Mommy came to see this dear lady who did all the Good Works, who was very much like you, dear, and they were very sad and very hopeful, and they cried and smiled and bit their fingers, and they said all the most intimate things.
MRS. BARKER. How spellbinding! What did they say?
GRANDMA. Well, it was very sweet. The woman, who was very much like Mommy, said that she and the man who was very much like Daddy had never been blessed with anything very much like a bumble of joy.
MRS. BARKER. A what?
GRANDMA. A bumble; a bumble of joy.
MRS. BARKER. Oh, like bundle.
GRANDMA. Well, yes; very much like it. Bundle, bumble; who cares? At any rate, the woman, who was very much like Mommy, said that they wanted a bumble of their own, but that the man, who was very much like Daddy, couldn't have a bumble; and the man, who was very much like Daddy, said that yes, they had wanted a bumble of their own, but that the woman, who was very much like Mommy, couldn't have one, and that now they wanted to buy something very much like a bumble.
MRS. BARKER. How engrossing!
GRANDMA. Yes. And the dear lady, who was very much like you, said something that was very much like, "Oh, what a shame; but take heart . . . I think we have just the bumble *for* you." And, well, the lady, who was very much like Mommy, and the man, who was very much like Daddy, cried and smiled and bit their fingers, and said some more intimate things, which were totally irrelevant but which were pretty hot stuff, and so the dear lady, who was very much like you, and who had something very much like a penchant for pornography, listened with something very much like enthusiasm. "Whee," she said. "Whooooopeeeeee!" But that's beside the point.
MRS. BARKER. I suppose *so*. But how gripping!
GRANDMA. Anyway . . . they *bought* something very much

like a bumble, and they took it away with them. But . . . things didn't work out very well.

MRS. BARKER. You mean there was trouble?

GRANDMA. You got it.

(*With a glance through the archway*)

But, I'm going to have to speed up now because I think I'm leaving soon.

MRS. BARKER. Oh. Are you really?

GRANDMA. Yup.

MRS. BARKER. But old people don't go anywhere; they're either taken places, or put places.

GRANDMA. Well, this old person is different. Anyway . . . things started going badly.

MRS. BARKER. Oh yes. Yes.

GRANDMA. Weeeeelllll . . . in the first place, it turned out the bumble didn't look like either one of its parents. That was enough of a blow, but things got worse. One night, it cried its heart out, if you can imagine such a thing.

MRS. BARKER. Cried its heart out! Well!

GRANDMA. But that was only the beginning. Then it turned out it only had eyes for its Daddy.

MRS. BARKER. For its Daddy! Why, any self-respecting woman would have gouged those eyes right out of its head.

GRANDMA. Well, she did. that's exactly what she did. But then, it kept its nose up in the air.

MRS. BARKER. Ufggh! How disgusting!

GRANDMA. That's what they thought. But *then*, it began to develop an interest in its you-know-what.

MRS. BARKER. In its you-know-what! Well! I hope they cut its hands off at the wrists!

GRANDMA. Well, yes, they did that eventually. But first, they cut off its you-know-what.

MRS. BARKER. A much better idea!

GRANDMA. That's what they thought. But after they cut off its you-know-what, it *still* put its hands under the covers, *looking* for its you-know-what. So, finally, they *had* to cut off its hands at the wrists.

MRS. BARKER. Naturally!

GRANDMA. And it was such a resentful bumble. Why, one day it called its Mommy a dirty name.

MRS. BARKER. Well, I hope they cut its tongue out!

GRANDMA. Of course. And then, as it got bigger, they found out all sorts of terrible things about it, like: it didn't have a head on its shoulders, it had no guts, it was spineless, its feet were made of clay . . . just dreadful things.

MRS. BARKER. Dreadful!

GRANDMA. So you can understand how they became discouraged.

MRS. BARKER. I certainly can! And what did they do?

GRANDMA. What did they do? Well, for the last straw, it finally up and died; and you can imagine how *that* made them feel, their having paid for it, and all. So, they called up the lady who sold them the bumble in the first place

and told her to come right over to their apartment. They wanted satisfaction; they wanted their money back. That's what they wanted.

MRS. BARKER. My, my, my.

GRANDMA. How do you like *them* apples?

MRS. BARKER. My, my, my.

DADDY (*Off stage*). Mommy! I can't find Grandma's television, and I can't find the Pekinese, either.

MOMMY (*Off stage*). Isn't that funny! And I can't find the water.

GRANDMA. Heh, heh, heh. I told them everything was hidden.

MRS. BARKER. Did you hide the water, too?

GRANDMA (*Puzzled*). No. No, I didn't do *that*.

DADDY (*Off stage*). The truth of the matter is, I can't even find Grandma's room.

GRANDMA. Heh, heh, heh.

MRS. BARKER. My! You certainly did hide things, didn't you?

GRANDMA. Sure, kid, sure.

MOMMY (*Sticking her head in the room*). Did you ever hear of such a thing, Grandma? Daddy can't find your television, and he can't find the Pekinese, and the truth of the matter is he can't even find your room.

GRANDMA. I told you. I hid everything.

MOMMY. Nonsense, Grandma! Just wait until I get my hands on you. You're a troublemaker . . . that's what you are.

GRANDMA. Well, I'll be out of here pretty soon, baby.

MOMMY. Oh, you don't know how right you are! Daddy's been wanting to send you away for a long time now, but I've been restraining him. I'll tell you one thing, though . . . I'm getting sick and tired of this fighting, and I might just let him have his way. Then you'll see what'll happen. Away you'll go; in a van, too. I'll let Daddy call the van man.

GRANDMA. I'm away ahead of you.

MOMMY. How can you be so old and so smug at the same time? You have no sense of proportion.

GRANDMA. You just answered your own question.

MOMMY. Mrs. Barker, I'd much rather you came into the kitchen for that glass of water, what with Grandma out here, and all.

MRS. BARKER. I don't see what Grandma has to do with it; and besides, I don't think you're very polite.

MOMMY. You seem to forget that you're a guest in this house . . .

GRANDMA. Apartment!

MOMMY. Apartment! And that you're a professional woman. So, if you'll be so good as to come into the kitchen, I'll be more than happy to show you where the water is, and where the glass is, and then you can put two and two together, if you're clever enough.

(*She vanishes*)

MRS. BARKER. (*After a moment's consideration*). I suppose she's right.

Edward Albee

GRANDMA. Well, that's how it is when people call you up and ask you over to do something for them.

MRS. BARKER. I suppose you're right, too. Well, Grandma, it's been very nice talking to you.

GRANDMA. And I've enjoyed listening. Say, don't tell Mommy or Daddy that I gave you that hint, will you?

MRS. BARKER. Oh, dear me, the hint! I'd forgotten about it, if you can imagine such a thing. No, I won't breathe a word of it to them.

GRANDMA. I don't know if it helped you any . . .

MRS. BARKER. I can't tell, yet. I'll have to . . . what *is* the word I want? . . . I'll have to relate it . . . that's it . . . I'll have to relate it to certain things that I *know*, and . . . draw . . . conclusions. . . . What I'll really have to do is to see if it applies to anything. I mean, after all, I *do* do volunteer work for an adoption service, but it isn't very much *like* the Bye-Bye Adoption Service . . . . it *is* the Bye-Bye Adoption Service . . . and while I can remember Mommy and Daddy coming to see me, oh, about twenty years ago, about buying a bumble, I can't quite remember anyone very much *like* Mommy and Daddy coming to see me about buying a bumble. Don't you see? It really presents quite a problem. . . . I'll have to think about it . . . mull it . . . but at any rate, it was truly first-class of you to try to help me. Oh, will you still be here after I've had my drink of water?

GRANDMA. Probably . . . I'm not as spry as I used to be.

MRS. BARKER. Oh. Well, I won't say good-by then.

GRANDMA. No. Don't.

(*Mrs. Barker exits through the archway*)

People don't say good-by to old people because they think they'll frighten them. Lordy! If they only knew how awful "hello" and "My, you're looking chipper" sounded, they wouldn't say those things either. The truth is, there isn't much you *can* say to old people that doesn't sound just terrible.

(*The doorbell rings*)

Come on in!

(*The Young Man enters. Grandma looks him over*)

Well, now, aren't you a breath of fresh air!

YOUNG MAN. Hello there.

GRANDMA. My, my, my. Are you the van man?

YOUNG MAN. The what?

GRANDMA. The van man. The van man. Are you coming to take me away?

YOUNG MAN. I don't know what you're talking about.

GRANDMA. Oh.

(*Pause*)

Well.

(*Pause*)

My, my, aren't you something!

YOUNG MAN. Hm?

GRANDMA. I said, my, my, aren't you something.

YOUNG MAN. Oh. Thank you.

GRANDMA. You don't sound very enthusiastic.

YOUNG MAN. Oh, I'm . . . I'm used to it.

GRANDMA. Yup . . . yup. You know, if I were about a hundred and fifty years younger I could go for you.

YOUNG MAN. Yes, I imagine so.

GRANDMA. Unh-hunh . . . will you look at those muscles!

YOUNG MAN (*Flexing his muscles*). Yes, they're quite good, aren't they?

GRANDMA. Boy, they sure are. They natural?

YOUNG MAN. Well the basic structure was there, but I've done some work, too . . . you know, in a gym.

GRANDMA. I'll bet you have. You ought to be in the movies, boy.

YOUNG MAN. I know.

GRANDMA. Yup! Right up there on the old silver screen. But I suppose you've heard that before.

YOUNG MAN. Yes, I have.

GRANDMA. You ought to try out for them . . . the movies.

YOUNG MAN. Well, actually, I may have a career there yet. I've lived out on the West coast almost all my life . . . and I've met a few people who . . . might be able to help me. I'm not in too much of a hurry, though. I'm almost as young as I look.

GRANDMA. Oh, that's nice. And will you look at that face!

YOUNG MAN. Yes, it's quite good, isn't it? Clean-cut, midwest farm boy type, almost insultingly good-looking in a typically American way. Good profile, straight nose, honest eyes, wonderful smile . . .

GRANDMA. Yup. Boy, you know what you are, don't you? You're the American Dream, that's what you are. All those other people, they don't know what they're talking about. You . . . *you* are the American Dream.

YOUNG MAN. Thanks.

MOMMY (*Off stage*). Who rang the doorbell?

GRANDMA (*Shouting off-stage*). The American Dream!

MOMMY (*Off stage*). What? What was that, Grandma?

GRANDMA (*Shouting*). The American Dream! The American Dream! Damn it!

DADDY (*Off stage*). How's that, Mommy?

MOMMY (*Off stage*). Oh, some gibberish; pay no attention. Did you find Grandma's room?

DADDY (*Off stage*). No. I can't even find Mrs. Barker.

YOUNG MAN. What was all that?

GRANDMA. Oh, that was just the folks, but let's not talk about them, honey; let's talk about you.

YOUNG MAN. All right.

GRANDMA. Well, let's see. If you're not the van man, what are you doing here?

YOUNG MAN. I'm looking for work.

GRANDMA. Are you! Well, what kind of work?

YOUNG MAN. Oh, almost anything . . . almost anything that pays. I'll do almost anything for money.

GRANDMA. Will you . . . will you? Hmmmm. I wonder if there's anything you could do around here?

YOUNG MAN. There might be. It looked to be a likely building.

GRANDMA. It's always looked to be a rather unlikely building to me, but I suppose you'd know better than I.

YOUNG MAN. I can sense these things.

GRANDMA. There *might* be something you could do around here. Stay there! Don't come any closer.

YOUNG MAN. Sorry.

GRANDMA. I don't mean I'd *mind*. I don't know whether I'd mind, or not. . . . But it wouldn't look well; it would look just *awful*.

YOUNG MAN. Yes; I suppose so.

GRANDMA. Now, stay there, let me concentrate. What could you do? The folks have been in something of a quandary around here today, sort of a dilemma, and I wonder if you mightn't be some help.

YOUNG MAN. I hope so . . . if there's money in it. Do you have any money?

GRANDMA. Money! Oh, there's more money around here than you'd know what to do with.

YOUNG MAN. I'm not so sure.

GRANDMA. Well, maybe not. Besides, I've got money of my own.

YOUNG MAN. You have?

GRANDMA. Sure. Old people quite often have lots of money; more often than most people expect. Come here, so I can whisper to you . . . not too close. I might faint.

YOUNG MAN. Oh, I'm sorry.

GRANDMA. It's all right, dear. Anyway . . . have you ever heard of that big baking contest they run? The one where all the ladies get together in a big barn and bake away?

YOUNG MAN. I'm . . . not . . . sure. . . .

GRANDMA. Not so close. Well, it doesn't matter whether you've heard of it or not. The important thing is—and I don't want anybody to hear this . . . the folks think I haven't been out of the house in eight years—the important thing is that I won first prize in that baking contest this year. Oh, it was in all the papers; not under my own name, though. I used a *nom de boulangère;* I called myself Uncle Henry.

YOUNG MAN. Did you?

GRANDMA. Why not? I didn't see any reason not to. I look just as much like an old man as I do like an old woman. And you know what I called it . . . what I won for?

YOUNG MAN. No. What did you call it?

GRANDMA. I called it Uncle Henry's Day-Old Cake.

YOUNG MAN. That's a very nice name.

GRANDMA. And it wasn't any trouble, either. All I did was go out and get a store-bought cake, and keep it around for a while, and then slip it in, unbeknownst to anybody. Simple.

YOUNG MAN. You're a very resourceful person.

GRANDMA. Pioneer stock.

YOUNG MAN. Is all this true? Do you want me to believe all this?

GRANDMA. Well, you can believe it or not . . . it doesn't make any difference to me. All *I* know is, Uncle Henry's Day-Old Cake won me twenty-five thousand smackerolas.

YOUNG MAN. Twenty-five thou—

GRANDMA. Right on the old loggerhead. Now . . . how do you like them apples?

YOUNG MAN. Love 'em.

GRANDMA. I thought you'd be impressed.

YOUNG MAN. Money talks.

GRANDMA. Hey! You look familiar.

YOUNG MAN. Hm? Pardon?

GRANDMA. I said you look familiar.

YOUNG MAN. Well, I've done some modeling.

GRANDMA. No . . . no. I don't mean that. You look familiar.

YOUNG MAN. Well, I'm a type.

GRANDMA. Yup; you sure are. Why do you say you'd do anything for money . . . if you don't mind my being nosy?

YOUNG MAN. No, no. It's part of the interviews. I'll be happy to tell you. It's that I have no talents at all, except what you see . . . my person; my body, my face. In every other way I am incomplete, and I must therefore . . . compensate.

GRANDMA. What do you mean, incomplete? You look pretty complete to me.

YOUNG MAN. I think I can explain it to you, partially because you're very old, and very old people have perceptions they keep to themselves, because if they expose them to other people . . . well, you know what ridicule and neglect are.

GRANDMA. I do, child, I do.

YOUNG MAN. Then listen. My mother died the night that I was born, and I never knew my father; I doubt my mother did. But, I wasn't alone, because lying with me . . . in the placenta . . . there was someone else . . . my brother . . . my twin.

GRANDMA. Oh, my child.

YOUNG MAN. We were identical twins . . . he and I . . . not fraternal . . . identical; we were derived from the same ovum; and in *this,* in that we were twins not from separate ova but from the same one, we had a kinship such as you cannot imagine. We . . . we felt each other breathe . . . his heartbeats thundered in my temples . . . mine in his . . . our stomachs ached and we cried for feeding at the same time . . . are you old enough to understand?

GRANDMA. I think so, child; I think I'm nearly old enough.

YOUNG MAN. I hope so. But we were separated when we were still very young, my brother, my twin and I . . . inasmuch as you can separate one being. We were torn apart . . . thrown to opposite ends of the continent. I don't know what became of my brother . . . to the rest of myself . . . except that, from time to time, in the years that have passed, I have suffered losses . . . that I can't explain. A fall from grace . . . a departure of innocence . . . loss . . . loss. How can I put it to you? All right; like this: Once . . . it was as if all at once my heart . . . became numb . . . almost as though I . . . almost as though . . . just like that

. . . it had been wrenched from my body . . . and from that time I have been unable to love. Once . . . I was asleep at the time . . . I awoke, and my eyes were burning. And since that time I have been unable to see anything, *anything*, with pity, with affection . . . with anything but . . . cool disinterest. And my groin . . . even there . . . since one time . . . one specific agony . . . since then I have not been able to *love* anyone with my body. And even my hands . . . I cannot touch another person and feel love. And there is more . . . there are more losses, but it all comes down to this: I no longer have the capacity to feel anything. I have no emotions. I have been drained, torn asunder . . . disemboweled. I have, now, only my person . . . my body, my face. I use what I have . . . I let people love me . . . I accept the syntax around me, for while I know I cannot relate . . . I know I must be related *to*. I let people love me . . . I let people touch me . . . I let them draw pleasure from my groin . . . from my presence . . . from the fact of me . . . but, that is all it comes to. As I told you, I am incomplete . . . I can feel nothing. I can feel nothing. And so . . . here I am . . . as you see me. I am . . . but this . . . what you see. And it will always be thus.

GRANDMA. Oh, my child; my child.

(*Long pause; then*)

I was mistaken . . . before. I don't know you from somewhere, but I knew . . . once . . . someone very much like you . . . or, very much as perhaps you were.

YOUNG MAN. Be careful; be very careful. What I have told you may not be true. In my profession . . .

GRANDMA. Shhhhhh.

(*The Young Man bows his head, in acquiescence*)

Someone . . . to be more precise . . . who might have turned out to be very much like you might have turned out to be. And . . . unless I'm terribly mistaken . . . you've found yourself a job.

YOUNG MAN. What are my duties?

MRS. BARKER (*Off stage*). Yoo-hoo! Yoo-hoo!

GRANDMA. Oh-oh. You'll . . . you'll have to play it by ear, my dear . . . unless I get a chance to talk to you again. I've got to go into my act, now.

YOUNG MAN. But, I . . .

GRANDMA. Yoo-hoo!

MRS. BARKER (*Coming through archway*). Yoo-hoo . . . oh, there you are, Grandma. I'm glad to see somebody. I can't find Mommy or Daddy.

(*Double takes*)

Well . . . who's this?

GRANDMA. This? Well . . . un . . . oh, this is the . . . uh . . . the van man. That's who it is . . . the van man.

MRS. BARKER. So! It's true! They *did* call the van man. They *are* having you carted away.

GRANDMA (*Shrugging*). Well, you know. It figures.

MRS. BARKER (*To Young Man*). How dare you cart this poor old woman away!

YOUNG MAN (*After a quick look at* Grandma, *who nods*). I do what I'm paid to do. I don't ask any questions.

MRS. BARKER (*After a brief pause*). Oh.

(*Pause*)

Well, you're quite right, of course, and I shouldn't meddle.

GRANDMA (*To Young Man*). Dear, will you take my things out to the van? (*She points to the boxes*)

YOUNG MAN (*After only the briefest hesitation*). Why, certainly.

GRANDMA (*As the* Young Man *takes up half the boxes, exits by the front door*). Isn't that a nice young van man?

MRS. BARKER (*Shaking her head in disbelief, watching the* Young Man *exit*). Unh-hunh . . . some things have changed for the better. I remember when I had *my* mother carted off . . . the van man who came for her wasn't anything near as nice as this one.

GRANDMA. Oh, did you have your mother carted off, too?

MRS. BARKER (*Cheerfully*). Why certainly! Didn't you?

GRANDMA (*Puzzling*). No . . . no, I didn't. At least, I can't remember. Listen dear; I got to talk to you for a second.

MRS. BARKER. Why certainly, Grandma.

GRANDMA. Now, listen.

MRS. BARKER. Yes, Grandma. Yes.

GRANDMA. Now listen carefully. You got this dilemma here with Mommy and Daddy . . .

MRS. BARKER. Yes! I wonder where they've gone to?

GRANDMA. They'll be back in. Now, LISTEN!

MRS. BARKER. Oh, I'm sorry.

GRANDMA. Now, you got this dilemma here with Mommy and Daddy, and I think I got the way out for you.

(*The Young Man re-enters through the front door*)

Will you take the rest of my things out now, dear?

(*To Mrs. Barker, while the Young Man takes the rest of the boxes, exits again by the front door*)

Fine. Now listen, dear.

(*She begins to whisper in Mrs. Barker's ear*)

MRS. BARKER. Oh! Oh! Oh! I don't think I could . . . do you really think I could? Well, why not? What a wonderful idea . . . what an absolutely wonderful idea!

GRANDMA. Well, yes, I thought it was.

MRS. BARKER. And you so old!

GRANDMA. Heh, heh, heh.

MRS. BARKER. Well, I think it's absolutely marvelous, anyway. I'm going to find Mommy and Daddy right now.

GRANDMA. Good. You do that.

MRS. BARKER. Well, now. I think I will say good-by. I can't thank you enough.

(*She starts to exit through the archway*)

GRANDMA. You're welcome. Say it!

MRS. BARKER. Huh? What?

GRANDMA. Say good-by.
MRS. BARKER. Oh. Good-by.

(She exits)

Mommy! I say, Mommy! Daddy!
GRANDMA. Good-by.

(By herself now, she looks about)

Ah me.

(Shakes her head)

Ah me.

(Takes in the room)

Good-by.

(The Young Man re-enters)

GRANDMA. Oh, hello, there.
YOUNG MAN. All the boxes are outside.
GRANDMA (A little sadly). I don't know why I bother to take them with me. They don't have much in them . . . some old letters, a couple of regrets . . . Pekinese . . . blind at that . . . the television . . . my Sunday teeth . . . eighty-six years of living . . . some sounds . . . a few images, a little garbled by now . . . and, well . . .

(She shrugs)

. . . you know . . . the things one accumulates.
YOUNG MAN. Can I get you . . . a cab, or something?
GRANDMA. Oh no, dear . . . thank you just the same. I'll take it from here.
YOUNG MAN. And what shall I do now?
GRANDMA. Oh, you stay here, dear. It will all become clear to you. It will be explained. You'll understand.
YOUNG MAN. Very well.
GRANDMA (After one more look about). Well . . .
YOUNG MAN. Let me see you to the elevator.
GRANDMA. Oh . . . that would be nice, dear.

(They both exit by the front door, slowly)

(Enter Mrs. Barker, followed by Mommy and Daddy)

MRS. BARKER. . . . and I'm happy to tell you that the whole thing's settled. Just like that.
MOMMY. Oh, we're so glad. We were afraid there might be a problem, what with delays, and all.
DADDY. Yes, we're very relieved.
MRS. BARKER. Well, now; that's what professional women are for.
MOMMY. Why . . . where's Grandma? Grandma's not here! Where's Grandma? And look! The boxes are gone, too. Grandma's gone, and so are the boxes. She's taken off, and she's stolen something! Daddy!
MRS. BARKER. Why, Mommy, the van man was here.
MOMMY (Startled). The what?
MRS. BARKER. The van man. The van man was here.

(The lights might dim a little, suddenly)

MOMMY (Shakes her head). No, that's impossible.
MRS. BARKER. Why, I saw him with my own two eyes.
MOMMY (Near tears). No, no, that's impossible. No. There's no such thing as the van man. There is no van man. We . . . we made him up. Grandma? Grandma?
DADDY (Moving to Mommy). There, there, now.
MOMMY. Oh Daddy . . . where's Grandma?
DADDY. There, there, now.

(While Daddy is comforting Mommy, Grandma comes out, stage right, near the footlights)

GRANDMA (To the audience). Shhhhhh! I want to watch this.

(She motions to Mrs. Barker who, with a secret smile, tip-toes to the front door and opens it. The Young Man is framed therein. Lights up full again as he steps into the room)

MRS. BARKER. Surprise! Surprise! Here we are!
MOMMY. What? What?
DADDY. Hm? What?
MOMMY (Her tears merely sniffles now). What surprise?
MRS. BARKER. Why, I told you. The surprise I told you about.
DADDY. You . . . you know, Mommy.
MOMMY. Sur . . . prise?
DADDY (Urging her to cheerfulness). You remember, Mommy; why we asked . . . uh . . . what's-her-name to come here?
MRS. BARKER. Mrs. Barker, if you don't mind.
DADDY. Yes. Mommy? You remember now? About the bumble . . . about wanting satisfaction?
MOMMY (Her sorrow turning into delight). Yes. Why yes! Of course! Yes! Oh, how wonderful!
MRS. BARKER (To the Young Man). This is Mommy.
YOUNG MAN. How . . . how do you do?
MRS. BARKER (Stage whisper). Her name's Mommy.
YOUNG MAN. How . . . how do you do, Mommy?
MOMMY. Well! Hello there!
MRS. BARKER (To the Young Man). And that is Daddy.
YOUNG MAN. How do you do, sir?
DADDY. How do you do?
MOMMY (Herself again, circling the Young Man, feeling his arm, poking him). Yes, sir! Yes, sirree! Now this is more like it. Now this is a great deal more like it! Daddy! Come see. Come see if this isn't a great deal more like it.
DADDY. I . . . I can see from here, Mommy. It does look a great deal more like it.
MOMMY. Yes, sir. Yes sirree! Mrs. Barker, I don't know how to thank you.
MRS. BARKER. Oh, don't worry about that. I'll send you a bill in the mail.
MOMMY. What this really calls for is a celebration. It calls for a drink.
MRS. BARKER. Oh, what a nice idea.
MOMMY. There's some sauterne in the kitchen.

YOUNG MAN. I'll go.

MOMMY. Will you? Oh, how nice. The kitchen's through the archway there.

(As the Young Man exits: to Mrs. Barker)

He's very nice. Really top notch; much better than the other one.

MRS. BARKER. I'm glad you're pleased. And I'm glad everything's all straightened out.

MOMMY. Well, at least we know why we sent for you. We're glad that's cleared up. By the way, what's his name?

MRS. BARKER. Ha! Call him whatever you like. He's yours. Call him what you called the other one.

MOMMY. Daddy? What did we call the other one?

DADDY (Puzzles). Why . . .

YOUNG MAN (Re-entering with a tray on which are a bottle of sauterne and five glasses). Here we are!

MOMMY. Hooray! Hooray!

MRS. BARKER. Oh, good!

MOMMY (Moving to the tray). So, let's—Five glasses? Why five? There are only four of us. Why five?

YOUNG MAN (Catches Grandma's eye; Grandma indicates she is not there). Oh, I'm sorry.

MOMMY. You must learn to count. We're a wealthy family, and you must learn to count.

YOUNG MAN. I will.

MOMMY. Well, everybody take a glass.

(They do)

And we'll drink to celebrate. To satisfaction! Who says you can't get satisfaction these days!

MRS. BARKER. What dreadful sauterne!

MOMMY. Yes, isn't it?

(To Young Man, her voice already a little fuzzy from the wine)

You don't know how happy I am to see you! Yes sirree. Listen, that time we had with . . . with the other one. I'll tell you about it some time.

(Indicates Mrs. Barker)

After she's gone. She was responsible for all the trouble in the first place. I'll tell you all about it.

(Sidles up to him a little)

Maybe . . . maybe later tonight.

YOUNG MAN (Not moving away). Why yes. That would be very nice.

MOMMY (Puzzles). Something familiar about you . . . you know that? I can't quite place it.

GRANDMA (Interrupting . . . to audience). Well, I guess that just about wraps it up. I mean, for better or worse, this is a comedy, and I don't think we'd better go any further. No, definitely not. So, let's leave things as they are right now . . . while everybody's happy . . . while everybody's got what he wants . . . or everybody's got what he thinks he wants. Good night, dears.

CURTAIN

Arianne Mnouchkine's 1979 production of Klaus Mann's Mephisto used a curious blend of styles: a baroque proscenium fronts an industrial-steel setting as a contemporary man and a Victorian gentleman watch a grotesque vaudeville.

CHAPTER 6

THE CONTEMPORARY THEATER

As we enter the new millennium, the world provides us with extraordinary scenarios that reflect a new reality:

- Late at night in a provincial Chinese village, where running water and indoor toilets are rare, flickering lights emanate from virtually every small house and store. The lights are produced by 13-inch color television sets that broadcast John Forsythe apparently speaking fluent Mandarin on *Falcon Crest*.
- The Los Angeles Dodgers, among the most traditional baseball organizations, features starting pitchers born in Japan, South Korea, the Dominican Republic, and Mexico. Between innings, fans—many of whom were born in Asia, Africa, and Latin America—rise to dance the macarena from South America, while their images are projected by a giant television screen made in Japan. Many listen to the game they are watching on transistor radios manufactured under the new capitalism of Communist China.
- Women now routinely run for—and are elected to—high political office, even as the military debates whether women should be allowed in combat. Openly gay and lesbian activists hold prominent positions in the Congress of the United States, as well as in such countries as Germany and Italy.

Our rapidly changing world has truly become, in Marshall McLuhan's words, a "global village," and the tension between the beliefs of an older, more absolute order and those of a more pluralistic, democratic, and ambiguous order is evident in the theater as well as in politics, commerce, and education. Contemporary thought has been shaped by any number of thinkers and historical events, each of which has prompted us to reevaluate the way in which we perceive the world.

Artistic and Cultural Events

1934:
"Postmodern" describes new era of art

1938:
Antonin Artaud's *The Theatre and Its Double*

1948:
The Living Theatre founded, New York

1949:
Simone de Beauvoir's *The Second Sex*

1950s:
Beat generation influences art

1958:
Off-off Broadway theater movement

1960:
Royal Shakespeare Company founded

1964:
Théâtre du Soleil founded, Paris

1965:
Jerzy Grotowski founds the Polish Lab Theatre

1969:
Woodstock Music Festival, New York

1979:
Jean-François Lyotard's *The Post modern Condition*

1982:
Caryle Churchill's *Top Girls*

1990–1993:
Tony Kushner's *Angels in America*

Pre-1960 C.E.   **1960 C.E.**   **1970 C.E.**

Historical and Political Events

1945:
United Nations founded

1945:
Advent of atomic warfare and cold war

1963:
John F. Kennedy assassinated

1965–1973:
Vietnam war; Anti-war movement

1980:
Solidarity Movement, Poland

1991:
Gulf War; Rodney King beating, Los Angeles

Late 1980s:
Collapse of Communism in Europe

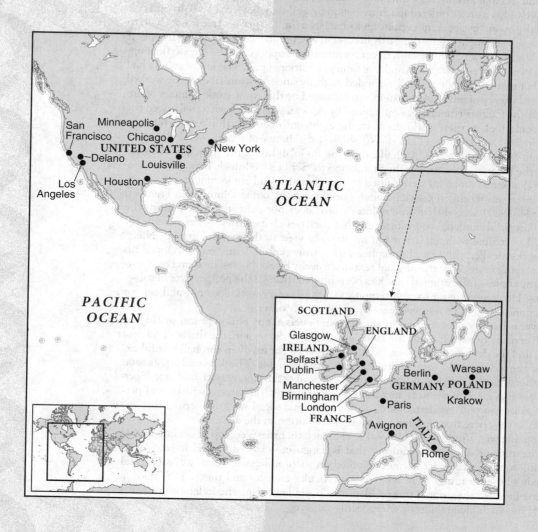

Influences on Contemporary Thought

We can find parallels to the changes in contemporary thought in the challenges to the Enlightenment and its emphasis on rationality and absolute values. In the eighteenth century the universe was viewed as a great, ordered machine bound by well-defined, fixed laws. In Sir Isaac Newton's world—bound by apparent certainties formed by a limited perspective from which to view the universe—an apple fell to the earth because it obeyed the laws of gravity. In Albert Einstein's world at the dawn of the twentieth century that same apple could be seen to float upward if it were twelve miles above earth and free from gravitational pull. The law of gravity had not changed, but human perceptions had expanded mightily since Newton's day. As he worked on his celebrated theory of relativity, Einstein was facinated by the avant-garde painters of Europe, especially the Cubists (themselves influenced by African sculpture), who challenged the way humans could look at their world. Even in the eighteenth century, thinkers such as the Scottish empiricist David Hume (1711–1776) showed the limits of reason—and the absolutism in much Western thought—by challenging the inviolability of the principle of cause-and-effect. In the theater, causality was the foundation for Scribe's well-made play and the naturalists' belief that social problems were caused by one's heredity and environment.

Even as Ibsen was writing his social dramas questioning the old absolute order, Friedrich Nietzsche (1844–1900) argued that an absolute "truth" does not exist, that a search for the truth was an "artificial burden," and ultimately that societies change their belief systems (or "perspectives") over time without arriving at an absolute view of the world. Fittingly, Nietzsche, who has been called the first philosopher with a truly postmodern view, developed his theories while trying to discover the original text of a tragedy by Sophocles; he found only various, conflicting copies of the original that had been filtered through the perspectives of subsequent cultures. He argued that a fixed interpretation of a literary work does not and cannot exist, and that one's subjective response is as "truthful" as any other is.

World events have been as forceful in altering our beliefs as any philosophical writing. In the twentieth century two world wars, the Holocaust, a global depression, the threat of nuclear annihilation, and the decline of the so-called superpowers taught us, often through painful experience, that the old absolutes were no longer necessarily operable. Thinkers and artists soon challenged other apparent certainties about language, social organisms, gender, and race. Such challenges were also made *in* theaters and *about* the way in which theater is written and performed. And as we saw with modern drama, philosophers and social scientists–critics fostered an intellectual atmosphere that inspired yet another revolution in the arts.

In Austria, Ludwig Wittgenstein (1889–1951) argued that the West was in decline largely because our instrument of communication—that is, language—was faulty and imprecise. In particular, philosophy was suspect because it relied on such ambiguous terms as "good" and "moral," words whose meanings were relative to particular cultures and times. T. S. Eliot, a playwright and literary critic, noted this problem in a poem lamenting the indeterminacy of a modern world in which old absolutes were suddenly suspect:

> . . . *Words strain*
>
> *Crack and sometimes break under the burden,*
>
> *Under the pressure, slip, slide, perish,*
>
> *Decay with imprecision, will not stay in place,*
>
> *Will not stay still.*

Therefore, the limits and liabilities of language necessarily redefined human perceptions of the world. Each person was, in essence, free to define "reality" according to her or his perceptions of the truth behind the language. Perception became reality, a concept captured by the title of Luigi Pirandello's play *Right You Are, If You Think You Are* (or, *It Is So If You Think So*, 1917). Playwrights such as Harold Pinter applied these principles to dramaturgy. Classical texts have been given new, ironic readings by actors and directors versed in new language theories represented by the French critic-philosopher Jacques Derrida, who argues that "there is nothing outside the text." This proposition encourages the reader/interpreter/viewer to participate actively in creating whatever meaning or message one finds in the text, whatever the author's intentions. Other stage artists, such as Robert Wilson and Heiner Müller, have virtually abandoned language as an integral part of the theater experience and use an almost exclusively visual vocabulary.

Not only language but human institutions have been reassessed in contemporary thought. In 1966 Peter Berger and Thomas Luckmann wrote *The Social Construction of Reality* in which they argued that society, culture, and even the roles we play in our daily lives are created by humans. We routinely forget that we ourselves have created these structures and live in a world we have forgotten we made. We err in assuming that our social organizations, our culture and its myths, and especially the societal roles we play cannot be re-created. Their thesis challenged individuals to re-create not only social institutions but themselves. Contemporaneously, the feminist and civil rights movements sought to redefine the roles imposed on women and minorities by traditional social systems.

In 1949 Simone de Beauvoir (1908–1986) wrote *The Second Sex,* an argument that women were treated as "the Other," an anthropological term used to describe those who are different from or who are not included in a majority culture. She claimed that men often accord women a different and inferior existence than themselves and advised women to seek independence from the old patriarchy by creating their own identity. Betty Friedan (1921–) initiated the modern American feminist movement with the publication of *The Feminine Mystique* (1963), which articulated the politics of gender. Coincidentally, 1963 was the year in which the African American civil rights movement triumphed as Martin Luther King Jr. led a march of hundreds of thousands of activists in Washington, D.C., where he delivered his famous "I Have a Dream" speech. Perhaps the most famous example of how language, social structures, and individual worth were redefined is the "Black Is Beautiful" slogan of the civil rights movement. Though they do not eradicate racism, such reconfigurations of language encouraged people of all colors to think—and perhaps act—more positively about people of African descent.

Social change precipitated by the feminist and the civil rights movements gave new voices and power to previously marginalized social groups such as Latinos, Asians, indigenous peoples, and homosexuals. Correspondingly, the theater has become a major outlet through which the new pluralism expresses itself. You will find many recent dramas that reflect the diversity of voices and ideologies of the pluralistic culture in which we now live.

Postmodernism and the Theater

Though we think of this as the contemporary era, it is often referred to as *postmodern* (i.e., "after the modern"), an often controversial term that describes a less Eurocentric culture than that which dominated the world for the past 400 years. The contemporary culture is decidedly more pluralistic and multicultural than at any other time in human history.

In keeping with this shift in thought, a postmodern style has emerged in the arts. Whether postmodernism will survive and become a long-lived artistic movement, or whether it is merely a transitional period (such as those that typically appear at the turn of a century), remains to be seen.

Though the concept of postmodernism was first defined in the 1930s (first by Federico de Onis in his 1934 study of Spanish-language poetry, then in 1938 in Arnold Toynbee's *A Study of History*), postmodernism as a bona fide movement in the arts evolved from architects who rebelled against the stark, sterile, purely functional and thereby "inhuman" designs of the so-called modernists. The new school of architects, exemplified by Robert Venturi (1925–), who favored "messy vitality over obvious unity," playfully fused elements of contemporary "pop" (or "democratic" as opposed to the old aristocratic) culture with traditional styles. In a spirit of global unity encouraged by the founding of the United Nations in 1945, architects looked to the Third World for inspiration. For example, they fronted a Neoclassic building with the silhouette of an African hut. These deliberate contrasts of style are hallmarks of postmodernism, and words such as *pastiche* and *collage* are central to its vocabulary and its practice. (Architects, by the way, write the term as "post-modern," with the hyphen. "Postmodern" is usually applied to literature and the other arts. This quibble suggests that the term is still being defined and that there is appreciable disagreement among postmodernism's practitioners, as well as its critics.)

Contradictions in artwork can create a playful irony that encourages people to look at the world from new perspectives. The imaginative blend of materials drawn from cultures beyond Europe and America is integral to postmoderns who, like the modernists, seek a more equitable world. Richard Rorty is an influential American philosopher whose writings (e.g., *Contingency, Irony, Solidarity*, 1989) envision a truly democratic world committed to universal freedom, creativity, and the elimination of cruelty. This new utopia is achieved by "poeticizing" human experience rather than "rationalizing" it. By recasting traditional forms through the inclusion of material drawn from a truly pluralistic society, new wave creator-artists shatter what they perceive as an oppressive power aligned with the older Eurocentric order. The Canadian Jean François Lyotard, whose study *The Postmodern Condition: A Report on Knowledge* (1979) laid the foundation for much of the critical thinking of the phenomenon, describes what he considers the appeal of postmodernism: "One listens to reggae [music], watches a Western, eats McDonald's food for lunch and local cuisine for dinner, wears Paris perfume in Tokyo and 'retro' clothes in Hong Kong." Similarly, Peter Sellars, the theater and opera director whose work is unmistakably postmodern, told the *New York Times* in 1984:

> We're living in a culture that is incredibly multifaceted. I grew up with [avant-garde composer] John Cage and [modern dancer] Merce Cunningham as old masters. But while they were giving birth to something, [painter] Norman Rockwell was also in his prime. With the push of a button we can choose some 18th century Chinese lute music, the Mahler 6th [symphony], or [the artist formerly known as] Prince.

In *Postmodernism and the Social Sciences* (1992), Pauline Marie Rosenau identifies two approaches to postmodernism. The first, skeptical postmodernism, was inspired by Nietzsche and is akin to the absurdist movement, which is pessimistic and steeped in malaise. In general, these skeptics are Europeans, scarred by the memories of World War II and communism. The second approach, called affirmative postmodernism, more indigenous to the Anglo–North American culture, seeks a harmonious world in which traditional distinctions between genders, races, nations, and cultural biases are dismissed as relative constructs. Rorty typifies the latter strain in his belief that freedom occurs when the individual can live and create without being obsessed by universal truths and rules that all rational beings must follow.

In addition to Lyotard's "healthy pluralism," spiritualism underlies some elements of the postmodern movement, though it is not necessarily rooted in traditional Judeo-Christian religions. Whereas modernists looked to science and technology as means to eradicate social ills, many postmoderns distrust unbridled technology, which they argue gave the world the atomic age and its threat of instant annihilation, pollution, and a greater disparity between the "haves" and the "have nots." In its place they have turned to ancient religions (such as Taoism), the occult, and mysticism to fill the void left by the "religion of science." Though it borrows freely from ancient religions, rituals, and musical practice, "New Age" is the term most closely associated with the new spiritualism. Nonetheless, it suggests a deeply rooted quest for something that transcends the particulars of sociology, psychology, politics, and contemporary mass-produced culture. The theories of the French anthropologist Claude Lévi-Strauss helped define this worldview, which maintains that innate—archetypal—mental patterns of all humans, irrespective of historical period or social setting, cause them to interact with nature and one another in recurring ways. In particular, Lévi-Strauss examined ritual activities around the world, and his findings have influenced Western theater practice, which in many instances has returned to a ritualistic—as opposed to realistic—depiction of human activity. Most theater in Asia, Africa, and much of Latin America never completely abandoned its ritual heritage.

Needless to say, postmodernism in the theater has been criticized, partly because it energetically and often irreverently challenges old systems, partly because it is perceived to be a license for indulgence among artists who, some would say, can now do anything they want and call it art. Walter D. Bannard, writing for *Arts Magazine* in 1983, dismissed postmodernism as "aimless, anarchic, amorphous, self-indulgent, inclusive, horizontally structured, and aim[ing] for the popular." It can be, and it has done so. Yet postmodernism, a constellation of many legitimate styles, seems to be the prevailing style of our age. To put Bannard's critique in perspective (or to "relativize" it), his comments might well have been penned by a member of the French Academy in 1830 as a response to Hugo's *Hernani*.

Artaud and the Theater of Cruelty

Such attitudes concerning cultural diversity have affected the theater and drama. The re-creation of ritual has been espoused as a primary component of the contemporary theater experience. Antonin Artaud (1895–1948) foreshadowed the new theater practice with his bold visions and experiments in Paris. Theater historian Margaret Croyden has written that "more than any other theorist of his generation, Artaud set the tone for the theater of the 1960s," and consequently for much postmodern theater. In 1933 Artaud, an actor frustrated by the limitations of the realistic theater, which emphasized a rational depiction of life, saw a Balinese theater company performing the Barong trance dance (see Chapter 1) at an international exhibition in Paris. Based on this experience, Artaud envisioned what he called a *theater of cruelty* that would, in his words, "link the theater to the expressive possibilities of forms, to everything in the domain of gestures, noises, colors, movements [in order] to restore it to its original direction, to reinstate it in its religious and metaphysical aspect, to reconcile it with the universe." By "cruelty" Artaud meant that artists should force audiences to confront their basest instincts and crimes, which, he believed, promoted the horrors of modern civilization. The theater, he argued, must compel humans to unmask themselves through "cries, groans, apparitions, surprises, theatricalities of all kinds, resplendent lighting, sudden changes of lights, masks, and effigies." Artaud's theater assaulted the senses to break down audiences' defenses and force them to confront the "plague," his metaphor for modern atrocities. The Romantics sought an intensely emotional reaction to societal ills, Brecht an intellectual detachment in his spectators; Artaud craved a thoroughly visceral response that transcends sentiment and rationality.

Though Artaud's own theater work failed to achieve his ends, he has had an extraordinary influence on production style, playwrights, and theater companies. In its early years, for instance, the Royal Shakespeare Company devoted its 1962–1963 seasons to an exploration of Artaud's theories on both classical and modern texts. Peter Brook directed the "cruelty seasons," staging *King Lear* and Peter Weiss's *The Persecution and Assassination of Jean-Paul Marat as Performed by the Inmates of the Asylum of Charenton Under the Direction of the Marquis de Sade* (or *Marat/Sade*). Even Broadway and London musicals, such as *Hair* (1967) and *Jesus Christ Superstar* (1970), employed techniques espoused by Artaud. Curiously, among the most successful derivatives of Artaud's theories, whether by design or accident, have been modern rock concerts and MTV videos. Pulsing lights, heavily amplified music, scenic effects such as towers of flame, stage actions such as smashing cars and guitars, and—in the case of videos—rapid cutting and overlapping of highly sensory images all are techniques espoused by Artaud, though they lack the spiritual foundation of his new theater.

In addition to Artaud's encounter with the Balinese dancers, other postmodern theater artists have looked to the East in their attempt to return the theater to its spiritual roots. Arianne Mnouchkine's Théâtre du Soleil regularly employs Asian dance and gesture in her refashioning of classical Western myths, as did Brook's eight-hour multinational production of India's sacred *Mahabharata* (1983). The first act of Sue Townsend's 1984 play, *The Great Celestial Cow,* ends with an Indian goddess and the protagonists celebrating a mystical dance. Stylized gesture and dance are again central to many contemporary plays and productions of earlier works. The diminution of language, the new spirituality, and—as significantly—music videos as typified by MTV have all conspired to return theater to many of its original performance modes. Ironically, through rituals, dance and gesture, and especially powerful and provocative images that transcend purely intellectual and emotional responses the theater has to some degree come full circle by returning to its most elemental means of communication.

Theater Collectives and Alternative Theater

Inspired by the theory and practice of Brecht and Artaud (both of whom are legitimate precursors of the postmodern theater), the *theater collective* has become one of the most notable phenomena of contemporary theater. Collectives are companies that frequently live together and share a sociopolitical ideology; they experiment with theater forms and collectively create a play and its production. To some degree the modern theater collective functions much like the "tribe" of older civilizations in that its members are bound spiritually (though not necessarily religiously) by common beliefs and goals that transcend commercialism and even art itself. Theodore Shank, who has studied collectives at some length, offers a useful description of both the philosophy and the techniques of these experimental (or alternative) theater companies:

> The artists who comprise alternative theater explore the relationship of the artist and the performance to the spectator. They attempt to discover the possibilities of live theater, and they seek ways of extending the uses of theater beyond its entertainment and financial functions. . . . They set out to articulate what they know about being alive in changing times, about society, about perceiving, feeling, and knowing. Of necessity, they find new materials, develop new techniques, and create new forms to hold and express this knowledge because the theatrical conventions cannot express the concepts they consider important.

If this sounds familiar, perhaps it is because Dumas *fils*, Ibsen, Strindberg, Shaw, Brecht, and so many of the other social revolutionaries in the theater have said much the same thing at various times.

The prototype of the modern theater collective in the West was the Group Theater, founded in 1931 by Harold Clurman, Cheryl Crawford, and Lee Strasberg to promote leftist causes in new works performed in the then-new realist style. They inspired subsequent generations of artists who also experimented with theater forms, especially those that are nonrealistic.

In the West, two companies merit particular attention because of their influence: the Living Theatre of Judith Malina (1926–) and Julian Beck (1925–1994) and the Polish Laboratory Theatre of Jerzy Grotowski. The Living Theatre was founded in 1947, ostensibly to perform poetic dramas such as Federico García Lorca's *Blood Wedding*. After a period in the late 1950s of experimentation with improvisational realism (*The Connection*, 1959), the Living Theatre turned to the work for which it was best known: highly ritualized performance pieces critical of institutions that the company considered "antihuman." The Living Theatre, like so many other alternative companies, emphasized physicality, rhythm, and chanting (among other things) instead of characterization and literary scripts. The company perhaps came closest to realizing Artaud's vision for a modern theater steeped in ritual and archetypal images to exorcise modern demons.

In Wroclaw, Poland, Jerzy Grotowski (1933–1999) founded the Polish Laboratory Theatre in 1965. His company experimented with performance styles while addressing the many social issues that have plagued Poland for hundreds of years. Out of this work came Grotowski's vision of a "poor theater," the concept that perhaps most significantly influenced the many socially conscious theater collectives in the 1960s and 1970s. In essence Grotowski wanted to return the theater to its spiritual roots by creating a ritualistic experience in which spectators and performers together could achieve a "collective introspection" of the social and philosophical problems confronting society. To achieve these ends, Grotowski and his colleagues reduced the theater experience to its most essential elements—actors in a space before an audience. The motto *via negativa* ("to refrain from doing") dictated the poor theater's production choices. Grotowski and his disciples avoided all elaborate lighting effects and performed in intimate spaces that were created for each play. The audience was invariably interspersed in the acting area to reinforce their roles as "privileged participants in a ritual." There was no scenery as such, and all props were multifunctional and made of "found" objects. Actors wore no makeup but learned to transform their faces into masks through arduous physical training. Productions such as *Akropolis* (about Nazi concentration camps) and an adaptation of Calderón's *The Constant Prince* gained renown for their ritualistic simplicity and the physical discipline of Grotowski's superbly trained actors. For Grotowski, actors were the equivalent of modern shamans who took on the suffering of the community; hence, they were trained as artist-priests who practiced self-denial and physical hardship for the good of the community.

Much of the most compelling experimental theater was produced in Third World countries where the lack of economic resources necessarily promoted creative, as opposed to financial, solutions to problems. In South Africa, Mbogeni Ngema founded Committed Artists in 1984 to develop scripts about the problems of apartheid and township life. Township theater has by necessity put many of the ideas espoused by Grotowski in practice; found objects such as old tires, corrugated tin panels, and packing crates customarily form the scenic backdrop for the plays. *Woza Albert!* is typical of the work produced by Committed Artists, as was the 1993 film *Sarafina!*, based on an Ngema musical. In Latin America Augusto Boal's Teatro de Arena (Brazil) has produced socially relevant works that could, by their ingenuity and simplicity, be taken into remote villages to educate people, much like Sergio Corrieri's Grupo Teatro Escambray in Cuba. Like Brecht, Boal rejects Aristotelian theater, which he perceives as coercive in its punishment of wrongdoers, whom he regards as oppressed. Boal actually takes Brecht a step further by actively engaging members of his audiences and prompting them to discover how they might rectify social problems. In the United States a similar phenomenon occurred with the founding of the Teatro Campesino by Luis Valdez in 1965; Valdez's accomplishments are discussed with *No saco nada de la escuela*, a play that vividly illustrates the philosophy and practice of the political theater collective (see Chapter 9).

In the past quarter-century there has been a proliferation of theaters that target specific audiences that have traditionally been outside the mainstream. An admittedly random sampling of such enterprises will give you some sense of the scope of the theater's newest constituencies. The Women's Playwright Project and Women's Interart, among others, have provided a theatrical platform for feminist issues. In 1974 a women's theater collective called At the Foot of the Mountain was formed in Minneapolis, Minnesota, to create new, ritual-based works drawn from their personal experiences (e.g., abuse) and the issues that confronted them directly (e.g., the challenges of motherhood). Audience members were invited to assist in the creation of a piece that, naturally, changed from one performance to the next. Gay and lesbian issues are argued by such companies as Rhinoceros, the Cockettes, and Split Britches; the AIDS crisis has understandably been a central concern of many gay theater companies. The National Theatre of the Deaf, which employs both hearing and hearing-impaired actors, depicts the needs of the physically disadvantaged; it also creates extraordinary productions of classical and poetic texts such as Ben Jonson's *Volpone* and Dylan Thomas's *Under Milkwood*; some members speak the lines while others "sign" them with a physicality that is as poetic as the spoken word.

Contemporary Playwriting

This discussion of visionary directors (now sometimes referred to as *auteurs* because theirs is a more creative than interpretive role) and theater collectives suggests a diminution of the role of the playwright. Playwrights are still very much the cornerstone of the theater process, though the lure of the television and film industries (and their lucrative contracts) has created something of a crisis. Nonetheless, plays are still being written though their form has changed considerably since Scribe's well-made play or Ibsen's discussion drama.

Because of the reassessment of purely rational communication (i.e., language and the well-structured plot), "ambiguity"—some would say "incomprehensibility"—is a term often applied to much contemporary theater. Plot, character, and meaning cannot be readily fathomed because we lack a single, consistent perspective from which to view them. Contemporary artists—playwrights and collectives—deconstruct social myths, or *metanarratives* (a term preferred by postmodernists), that reflect the pluralism of the world. Lyotard, in fact, defined postmodern as an "incredulity towards metanarratives" and suggested that the old myths had lost their legitimacy in a world in which traditional truths were challenged. As we have seen often throughout our study of the theater, the form of a play often reflects its content. The Greeks and Neoclassicists believed in a harmonious universe, and their plays were carefully structured affairs in which problems were resolved (although not always happily) in five compact acts. By contrast, the absurdists wrote about the great "rut of existence" and devised cyclic plots to show the meaningless of our actions. Because they see the world as a series of artificial constructs whose meanings change according to time, circumstance, and personal experience, many contemporary dramatists resist a single explanation for issues, characters, and plots, and thus *fragmentation* is often a characteristic of postmodern plays.

Plots are rarely linear; instead of lengthy acts with a well-defined beginning, middle, and end, we are given a series of scenes, often in markedly contrasting styles and moods (a technique used by Brecht, and even Shakespeare, though for different reasons). Many plays, in fact, are bereft of traditional exposition and denouements to heighten their ambiguity. The plays of Pinter and Sam Shepard are particularly representative of this technique ("I write stories without endings," says the latter). All is calculated to force audiences to assign meanings based on one's particular perception of reality, sometimes whimsically referred to as the MYOM ("Make Your Own Meaning") syndrome.

Some theorists, especially those aligned with postmodernism, argue that originality in art is a Romantic myth and that all art—indeed, all human endeavor—is influenced by myriad cultures and consciousness. Hence, art in our postmodern age is achieved by freely integrating styles and subject matter from across the spectrum of time and place. To achieve this spirit of *pastiche* (or *collage*), scripts frequently incorporate (or "quote") material from other periods and pieces of literature. Because of its pervasive influence on world culture and economics, material drawn from America's pop culture is especially popular. This often contradictory, purposefully disorienting style of playwriting is intended to challenge our beliefs about the way we perceive the world and the manner in which artists can represent it. As with all art, reinventing forms can have both salutary and controversial effects. Shepard regularly intersperses pop icons, such as comic book characters and cowboy heroes, with "real" characters throughout his innovative and much-praised work. In one of the most controversial examples of the pastiche script, Arthur Miller sued Elizabeth LeCompte and the Wooster Group, among New York's most controversial experimental theatrical companies, for using material from his play *The Crucible* in their 1984 collectively created "intertextual" work, *L.S.D. (or, Just the High Points)*.

Time and space are malleable concepts in postmodern plays, an outgrowth of the argument that history is suspect because it has been written by those in power to protect their base; like literature, history itself must be deconstructed. Scripts freely commingle historical periods and even reconstruct time lines. Caryl Churchill's *Top Girls* portrays women from five different historical periods meeting a contemporary "top girl" for lunch; the play ends with a scene that takes place one year *before* the first scene.

Whatever quibbles people may have about contemporary dramatic literature, there is considerable agreement that the movement has revitalized theater. By emphasizing the purely visual aspects of performance, the theater has reestablished itself as "the seeing place." Ironically, much of this has been accomplished by the very technology that postmodernists disdain. The realistic setting and the overused box set are now passé and best left to film and television, which handle the realistic style more convincingly. The conceptually stunning and purely theatrical images created by such directors as Peter Brook, Peter Stein, Anne Bogart, Tadashi Suzuki, Joanne Akalitis, Julie Taymor, and especially Robert Wilson reaffirm the theater's ability to create stunning effects live and before a living audience in imaginative ways that film cannot. After years of stark, minimalist designs reflecting the modernist preoccupation with a "less is more" philosophy, the designs of Joseph Svoboda, Maria Bjornson, and Ming Cho Lee commonly blend multiple styles, periods, and media to create haunting, archetypal images that transcend time and place.

Acting in Contemporary Plays

With its current focus on the multiple roles we play in our lives, as well as the "gamesmanship" that is required to survive in this world of artificial constructs, the theater itself has become a leading metaphor for contemporary philosophy (Shakespeare notwithstanding; proclaiming that "All the world's a stage . . . ," he used the "play-life" metaphor in virtually every play he wrote). The actor has become a favorite metaphor for artists. In 1921 Luigi Pirandello defined this theme in *Six Characters in Search of an Author,* which remains the prototype of the life-as-theater playscript. The English social satirist Tom Stoppard echoes Pirandello in *Rosencrantz and Guildenstern Are Dead* (1967), a retelling of Hamlet from the bit-players' point of view. In that play he reminds us that in our day-to-day existence, "every entrance is an exit, and every exit is an entrance." How adroitly we shift from one role to another as we make those entrances and exits is a predominant theme of the contemporary theater.

Actors themselves have had to adjust to the texts of contemporary scripts. Like the characters they portray, actors are often required to play multiple roles, literally and figuratively. It is not uncommon—as in Churchill's *Top Girls*—for an actor to be assigned several roles in a single play to underscore the fragmentation of personality. Often actors cross-dress to call attention to gender issues. Anna Deavere Smith's *Twilight: Los Angeles, 1992* is more than a one-woman show in which she skillfully plays different women and men of many races. Hers is the quintessential postmodern performance. Even when an actor plays a single character, the old notion of the Stanislavskian "spine" or "through line"—which suggests a consistency of character and motivation—is now less applicable. In the postmodern theater, characters are the sum of their inconsistencies, each determined by the multiple roles they play in society. The postmodern actor must be extraordinarily versatile and able to mix styles (e.g., realism with the New Vaudeville, or the classical with Expressionism) in a heartbeat. Furthermore, postmodern actors are more frequently asked to perform in a presentational style, unlike method actors who are grounded in an essentially representational style that ignores the presence of the audience.

Contemporary Dramatic Criticism: Deconstructionism and Others

Postmodernism has fostered various approaches to dramatic theory and criticism. Among the most prominent is *deconstructionist criticism,* which "constructs" new meanings through the "destruction" of old ones based on (arguably) erroneous perceptions of language and ideologies imposed by older hierarchies. Many detractors of deconstructionism claim it is less a critical tool than an ideological movement intended to undermine Western orthodoxy. Though deconstructionism and Jacques Derrida, its principal voice, have lost some of the appeal they had a decade ago, they have left two important legacies.

First, deconstructionist thought made possible, and even respectable, ironist readings of a text; that is, an interpreter could argue with the text in an essay or in a production by playing against its traditional historical and cultural meaning. This encouraged a debate between our society and the one that originally produced the work. For instance, Peter Stein, an Austrian director known for his provocative stagings of classical texts, applied deconstructionist theory and practice to his treatment of *Othello* in the 1980s. Othello was played by a Caucasian actor in blackface to underscore the obviousness of his ethnicity; by design, his makeup rubbed off on all those with whom he came in contact. Desdemona was dressed in a bikini to show that she was little more than a sex object over whom the men fought. Much of the play was acted as a cheap vaudeville sketch to undercut its romantic foundation. These theatrical choices were conspicuously at variance with our perceptions of Shakespeare's intentions, but their very audacity forced audiences to reconsider the racism and sexism inherent in our culture.

Secondly, deconstructionism's commitment to an "openness to the other"—that is, an acceptance of a multiplicity of perspectives—has enlarged the arena for criticism. Derrida argues that this is deconstructionism's most affirmative project. Evolving with deconstructionism, and perhaps to some degree because of it, have been gender studies, feminist criticism, gay and lesbian criticism, and multicultural criticism. All share the common impulse to expand the literary canon and theatrical criticism from the dominant perspective of the traditional patriarchy. Each is written in the belief that differences of sex, race, class, ethnicity, and other variables give us a sense of personal identity, both interiorly (how we see ourselves) and exteriorly (how others see us). Accordingly, specific strains of criticism have developed to accommodate these varied perspectives:

- feminist criticism, which critiques gender bias among male writers;
- gender criticism, which is less concerned with the distinction between "male" and "female" than with the examination of gender itself as a political system and as a cultural construct;
- gay and lesbian criticism, or "queer theory" (a term used by those within the movement) calls for an understanding of, and advocacy for, literature that sympathetically portrays homosexual lifestyles;
- multicultural criticism embraces race, economic class, ethnicity, and Third World cultures or some other variable to examine differences in perspective.

The common ground among these critical approaches is a belief that literary criticism, literature, and performance are inherently political and that the concerns of marginalized people can be best addressed when examined from perspectives other than traditional European and American cultures.

Some minority, as well as feminist and gay, critics argue that when whites attempt to speak for nonwhites (or men for women, or straights for gays), they are engaging in "ventriloquism," which is a form of cultural imperialism. To cite a prominent recent example: when Paul Simon, the pop singer-writer, wrote *The Capeman* (1997), a musical drama about Puerto Ricans in New York, he was criticized by some Latinos for appropriating their music and culture. All of this brings us to a very sensitive and much-discussed issue: political correctness. Surely there have been excesses that have provided critics with ripe material. Robert Brustein, among the American theater's most respected critics and directors, wrote in 1993 that "PC [political correctness] has crypto-Maoist roots and in extreme form is dedicated to a program not unlike that of the unlamented cultural revolution by the People's Republic of China—replacing an 'elite' system with a 'populist' agenda through egalitarian leveling." Brustein is not objecting to pluralism itself, which he embraces for the increased possibilities it brings to the creative experience. Rather, he fears that the increased focus on the particular concerns of a group or minority may "balkanize" theater audiences by turning them into "hostile self-absorbed enclaves in a disunited America" (and elsewhere). In January 1996 Brustein and African American playwright August Wilson (see *Fences* in Chapter 8) engaged in a controversial and much-publicized debate concerning these issues at New York's Town Hall; Wilson rebutted Brustein's arguments concerning the balkanization of American culture, noting that a vibrant African American theater provides a necessary voice for black concerns in a society that yet evidences racism.

If the theater continues to address fundamental human concerns at the highest aesthetic levels, there is nothing to fear in the work of contemporary artists. Such was the goal that guided Aeschylus in Greece, Kālidāsa in India, Ogun in West Africa, and Zeami in Japan. The advantage we have today is that we have never been so well equipped—mentally, artistically, and technically—to portray the triumphs and shortcomings of our species through such truly global means.

TOP GIRLS
CARYL CHURCHILL

CARYL CHURCHILL (1938–)

Caryl Churchill is the most frequently produced and critically admired female playwright of our time. She has written for several of England's most prestigious political theaters, primarily the Royal Court, the wellspring of contemporary British drama. She has also been affiliated with 7:84 Theater Company (whose name refers to the fact that 7 percent of Britain's population controls 84 percent of its wealth), Joint Stock, and Monstrous Regiment, a major feminist company. In America, her works have been produced by Joseph Papp's Public Theater (the American counterpart to the Royal Court) and with regularity in Off- and Off-Off-Broadway theaters. The production of *Top Girls*, for instance, won several Obie Awards in 1982 as the year's best Off-Broadway work.

Born in London, Churchill lived in Montreal, Canada, from 1949 to 1956, then returned to England to study at Oxford University. Though her primary field was English literature (which she uses frequently as source material for her works), Churchill was introduced to Buddhism and other Eastern religions such as Taoism, Jainism, and Hinduism at Oxford. Eastern philosophy and spirituality have influenced not only the themes of her plays (e.g., illusions, historical cycles, the transcendental nature of personality), but their very structure, as illustrated in *Top Girls*, where time is manipulated freely and is not bound by Western logic.

Churchill wrote several plays at Oxford, then several admired radio dramas in the 1960s, and in 1972 her first commercial stage play, *Owners*, was produced. Not until 1979, however, did she receive international recognition for *Cloud Nine*, which was written as part of a collective exploration of sexual identities for the Joint Stock Company. Produced by the Royal Court in 1979, it subsequently played in New York and other theater capitals. Her best works include *Vinegar Tom* (1977), *Top Girls* (1982), *Fen* (1983), *Softcops* (1984), and *Serious Money* (1987).

Although she is generally accepted as the world's foremost feminist playwright, Churchill describes herself as a socialist writer first who only later adopted the feminist cause. She now describes herself as a "socialist-feminist," noting that although "socialism and feminism aren't synonymous, . . . I feel strongly about both and wouldn't be interested in a form of one that didn't include the other." Though her later plays deal with feminist issues, they are equally bound by her critique of Western society, which she feels exploits its weakest individuals for monetary and political gain. Her plays often explore the friction between the "old world" colonial system and the new, pluralistic world in which women, gays, and non-Caucasians strive to overcome the strictures imposed by the old.

Not suprisingly, Churchill has adopted—and expanded on—many techniques associated with Brecht, himself a socialist who used the theater to advance his ideology. Like Brecht, Churchill writes plays that thrive on dialectical arguments that are often "historicized" to challenge modern assumptions about social, political, and economic issues. Act 1 of *Cloud Nine*, for instance, is set in a nineteenth-century British colonial outpost; in act 2, both the characters and the play's issues are hurled into the late twentieth century. *Serious Money* is written as a mock Restoration comedy in rhymed couplets, but set amid contemporary financial centers. *Top Girls*, perhaps Churchill's most innovative use of historification, opens with famous women of history and myth dining in a modern restaurant with a newly promoted executive of a personnel agency. The play's final scene takes place a year *prior* to the first scene, as Churchill boldly manipulates time to force her audience to confront the play's "frightening" issues.

Churchill often supersedes Brecht's techniques, particularly in her use of social *gestus* as the foundation of an actor's character. Not only does Churchill typically assign multiple roles to actors (as in *Top Girls*), she frequently specifies cross-gender casting (most notably in *Cloud Nine*) to undermine our preconceptions about sexual roles in society by naturally "alienating" actors from their characters. Churchill wittily illustrates that history itself does this—note that Pope Joan in *Top Girls* is the ultimate example of cross-gender casting. In Churchill's boldly theatrical world, disorientation rules to shake audiences from their bourgeois complacency. "Confusing" is a word often applied to her works by naïve critics—but confusion about time and history, sex and gender, and literary style itself is calculated to provoke the audience to find clarity in a world that confuses power and wealth with natural superiority.

TOP GIRLS (1982)

Here we find a decidedly feminist play—yet it satirically indicts much of the feminist movement. Here we meet women, both modern and historical, who appear to exemplify the "successful" woman—yet each is revealed as flawed, thus diminishing whatever admiration we first felt. The play opens with a fantasy about the past—yet it ends with a flashback that is an ironic preview of the future. Between these surreal sequences, Churchill scripts essentially realistic scenes from a contemporary society in which the only way to get ahead—for man and woman alike—is to "play the game" ruthlessly. This free mixture of historical periods, contrary ideologies, and assorted theatrical styles is, of course, typical of postmodern dramaturgy, and *Top Girls* represents some of the finest impulses of contemporary experimental drama. More importantly, the meaning of Churchill's play is best found in its provocative contradictions.

The play begins in that most mundane of modern meeting places—the chic restaurant (aptly named La Prima Donna) known for its Frascati wine and avocado vinaigrette. Into this world comes Marlene, the successful woman, newly appointed to an executive position in the Top Girls Employment Agency (where, ironically, women are "ordered up" like items on the restaurant's menu). Note, by the way, that Marlene is the only role that is not subsequently "doubled"; she is unalterably the prototype of the late-twentieth-century liberated woman. In a mood to celebrate, Marlene meets five celebrated women: Isabella Bird, the noted Victorian explorer who liberated herself from home and hearth as she trekked across the world; Lady Nijo, a medieval Japanese concubine who became a Buddhist nun; Dull Gret, an ax-wielding revolutionary from a Breughel canvas; Pope Joan, an actual woman who disguised herself as a man to ascend to the papacy in the ninth century; and Patient Griselda, the heroine of Chaucer's *Clerk's Tale*.

Churchill wryly implies that Marlene's promotion is the modern woman's triumphant equivalent of the more grandiose exploits of her famous foresisters ("It's not the Pope, but it is the managing director," she says to aggrandize herself). Here the playwright is attacking what has been called bourgeois feminism, that is, the notion that women succeed only when they assume the power and wealth afforded men. Yet in subsequent scenes in the employment agency, we see that Marlene and her staff advise would-be employees to mute their feminine roles. More tellingly, Marlene denigrates her own sister (Joyce) and her "niece" (Angie) as being inferior because they have not risen above their class status or mental states (Marlene is especially cruel in her rejection of the slow-witted Angie; "She's not going to make it," she tells her sister). Thus, Marlene epitomizes, in effect, the very aspects of the male-dominated socioeconomic system condemned by socialists such as Churchill. Marlene is so comfortable in her position as a "top girl" (the sexual innuendo is thematically significant) that she cannot attempt to change the hierarchical and exploitive structure of the capitalist world. She has become one of the "old boys" who sustain the status quo by using, even abusing, others to get "on top."

Isabella, Lady Nijo, Pope Joan, and Dull Gret can be aligned with aggressive feminists who posit the superiority of the feminine principal—and feminine principles. Each has charted her own destiny in male-dominated worlds, and each has triumphed (more or less) over male prejudices. But, again ironically, each has done so primarily by assuming a male identity (symbolized by clothing), or in Isabella's case by sealing herself off from the world to the extent that she is neither man nor woman, but only a solitary Scot trekking across the world. As strong and successful as these women are, each is flawed: Isabella is devoid of human feeling (save for her rather conventional sister, whom she never sees) and she retains a colonialist's attitude of superiority ("Buddhism is really most uncomfortable"); Lady Nijo loves the "thin silk" too much and dismisses her dead child as "only a girl"; Pope Joan wants the trappings of the papacy but none of its responsibilities; and Dull Gret (who has raised ten children—and a pig) assaults the demons of hell not for herself or her oppressed "sisters," but to protect the men and children who made her daily existence a hell. Significantly, Patient Griselda is the last to arrive at the dinner party. She has sacrificed her children and her life, all to prove her fealty to her demanding and abusive husband. The rapid-fire dinner conversation (note that lines overlap contrapuntally to heighten Churchill's critique of the women) shows the women to be self-centered egotists who seem more interested in personal aggrandizement than in addressing the collective problems they face as women. Thus, when Marlene toasts the gathering—"to our courage and the way we changed our lives and our extraordinary achievements"—her words ring hollow. We note that by the end of the first scene all the women are drunk (remember, Lady Nijo earlier mocks the men at court for being drunkards), and they are dutifully attended by the Waitress, a serving woman whose presence among these "top girls" is marked by an extraordinary silence.

Things are no better in the "real" world. Marlene's associates (Nell and Win) are supposed to represent the best that Top Girls has to offer; yet they thrive on banality and condescend to the women who seek employment (and empowerment). Marlene, we learn, has achieved her autonomy only by abandoning her roots and her literal and metaphorical sister(s). She spurns Angie as an unpleasant and unwanted memory of the past she tries to escape. Angie (quite appropriately played by the same actor who plays the battle-scarred Dull Gret) is socially maladjusted and homicidal, the by-product of that quintessential macho film, *The Exterminator*. Her best friend, Kit, we are assured, will make it because she has charm and beauty, the requisites of a "top girl" in the old patriarchal society. Only Joyce shows true heroism when she agrees to raise her sister's illegitimate child; she is motivated neither by economic nor material gain, but only by the will to do something "right" for her sister. Yet even Joyce is flawed; we might call her "Impatient Joyce" because of the way in which she wearily denigrates Angie in the ugliest of sexist terms ("fucking rotten little cunt"). Indeed, Churchill presents us with a "frightening" world, to borrow the play's last line.

While Churchill is clearly sympathetic to the plight of women, and while she knowingly writes for audiences conversant in feminist issues, she refuses to provide comfortable solutions to validate feminist beliefs. There is no preaching to the choir here. Rather, she raises questions, the answers to which may provide solutions to the greater problems created by outmoded systems in which women must become men—or at least male-like—to get "on top."

Dull Gret confronts a modern "top girl," Marlene, as Pope Joan and others look on; the New York Shakespeare Festival produced the American premiere of Caryl Churchill's play Top Girls.

TOP GIRLS

CARYL CHURCHILL

CHARACTERS
MARLENE
WAITRESS/KIT/SHONA
ISABELLA BIRD/JOYCE/MRS KIDD
LADY NIJO/WIN
DULL GRET/ANGIE
POPE JOAN/LOUISE
PATIENT GRISELDA/NELL/JEANINE

ACT I

Scene I: A Restaurant.
Scene II: Top Girls' Employment Agency, London.
Scene III: Joyce's backyard in Suffolk.

ACT II

Scene I: Top Girls' Employment Agency.
Scene II: A Year Earlier. Joyce's kitchen.

Production Note: *The seating order for Act I, Scene I in the original production at the Royal Court was (from right) Gret, Nijo, Marlene, Joan, Griselda, Isabella.*

THE CHARACTERS
ISABELLA BIRD (1831–1904): *Lived in Edinburgh, traveled extensively between the ages of forty and seventy.*
LADY NIJO (b. 1258): *Japanese, was an Emperor's courtesan and later a Buddhist nun who traveled on foot through Japan.*
DULL GRET: *Is the subject of the Brueghel painting Dulle Griet, in which a woman in an apron and armor leads a crowd of women charging through hell and fighting the devils.*
POPE JOAN: *Disguised as a man, is thought to have been pope between 854 and 856.*
PATIENT GRISELDA: *Is the obedient wife whose story is told by Chaucer in "The Clerk's Tale" of* The Canterbury Tales.

THE LAYOUT

A speech usually follows the one immediately before it but:

(1) *When one character starts speaking before the other has finished, the point of interruption is marked /. e.g.,*

ISABELLA. This is the Emperor of Japan? / I once met the Emperor of Morocco.

NIJO. In fact he was the ex-Emperor.

(2) *A character sometimes continues speaking right through another's speech, e.g.,*

ISABELLA. When I was forty I thought my life was over. / Oh I was pitiful. I was

NIJO. I didn't say I felt it for twenty years. Not every minute.

ISABELLA. sent on a cruise for my health and I felt even worse. Pains in my bones, pins and needles . . . etc.

(3) *Sometimes a speech follows on from a speech marked earlier than the one immediately before it, and continuity is marked*. e.g.,*

GRISELDA. I'd seen him riding by, we all had. And he'd seen me in the fields with the sheep.*

ISABELLA. I would have been well suited to minding sheep.

NIJO. And Mr. Nugent went riding by.

ISABELLA. Of course not, Nijo, I mean a healthy life in the open air.

JOAN. *He just rode up while you were minding the sheep and asked you to marry him?

where "in the fields with the sheep" is the cue to both "I would have been" and "He just rode up."

ACT I

SCENE I

(Restaurant. Saturday night. There is a table with a white cloth set for dinner with six places. The lights come up on Marlene and the Waitress.)

MARLENE. Excellent, yes, table for six. One of them's going to be late but we won't wait. I'd like a bottle of Frascati straight away if you've got one really cold. (*The Waitress goes. Isabella Bird arrives.*) Here we are, Isabella.

ISABELLA. Congratulations, my dear.

MARLENE. Well, it's a step. It makes for a party. I haven't time for a holiday. I'd like to go somewhere exotic like you but I can't get away. I don't know how you could bear to leave Hawaii. / I'd like to lie

ISABELLA. I did think of settling.

MARLENE. in the sun forever, except of course I can't bear sitting still.

ISABELLA. I sent for my sister Hennie to come and join me. I said, Hennie we'll live here forever and help the natives. You can buy two sirloins of beef for what a pound of chops costs in Edinburgh. And Hennie wrote back, the dear, that yes, she would come to Hawaii if I wished, but I said she had far better stay where she was. Hennie was suited to life in Tobermory.

MARLENE. Poor Hennie.

ISABELLA. Do you have a sister?

MARLENE. Yes in fact.

ISABELLA. Hennie was happy. She was good. I did miss its face, my own pet. But I couldn't stay in Scotland. I loathed the constant murk.

(Lady Nijo arrives)

MARLENE (*seeing her.*). Ah! Nijo! (*The Waitress enters with the wine.*)

NIJO. Marlene! (*To Isabella.*) So excited when Marlene told me / you were coming.

ISABELLA. I'm delighted / to meet you.

MARLENE. I think a drink while we wait for the others. I think a drink anyway. What a week. (*Marlene seats Nijo. The Waitress pours wine.*)

NIJO. It was always the men who used to get so drunk. I'd be one of the maidens, passing the sake.[1]

ISABELLA. I've had sake. Small hot drink. Quite fortifying after a day in the wet.

NIJO. One night my father proposed three rounds of three cups, which was normal, and then the Emperor should have said three rounds of three cups, but he said three rounds of nine cups, so you can imagine. Then the Emperor passed his sake cup to my father and said, "Let the wild goose come to me this spring."

MARLENE. Let the what?

NIJO. It's a literary allusion to a tenth-century epic, / His Majesty was very cultured.

ISABELLA. This is the Emperor of Japan? / I once met the Emperor of Morocco.

NIJO. In fact he was the ex-Emperor.

MARLENE. But he wasn't old? / Did you, Isabella?

NIJO. Twenty-nine.

ISABELLA. Oh it's a long story.

MARLENE. Twenty-nine's an excellent age.

NIJO. Well I was only fourteen and I knew he meant something but I didn't know what. He sent me an eight-layered gown and I sent it back. So when the time came I did nothing but cry. My thin gowns were badly ripped. But even that morning when he left / he'd a green

MARLENE. Are you saying he raped you.

NIJO. robe with a scarlet lining and very heavily embroidered trousers, I already felt different about him. It made me uneasy. No, of course not, Marlene, I belonged to

---

[1] **sake** a wine made from rice in Japan

him, it was what I was brought up for from a baby. I soon found I was sad if he stayed away. It was depressing day after day not knowing when he would come. I never enjoyed taking other women to him.

ISABELLA. I certainly never saw my father drunk. He was a clergyman. / And I didn't get married till I was fifty. (*The Waitress brings menus.*)

NIJO. Oh, my father was a very religious man. Just before he died he said to me, "Serve His Majesty, be respectful, if you lose his favour enter holy orders."

MARLENE. But he meant stay in a convent, not go wandering round the country.

NIJO. Priests were often vagrants, so why not a nun? You think I shouldn't? / I still did what my father wanted.

MARLENE. No, no, I think you should. / I think it was wonderful.

(*Dull Gret arrives.*)

ISABELLA. I tried to do what my father wanted.

MARLENE. Gret, good. Nijo. Gret / I know Griselda's going to be late, but should we wait for Joan? / Let's get you a drink.

ISABELLA. Hello Gret! (*She continues to Nijo:*) I tried to be a clergyman's daughter. Needlework, music, charitable schemes. I had a tumour removed from my spine and spent a great deal of time on the sofa. I studied the metaphysical poets and hymnology. / I thought I enjoyed intellectual pursuits.

NIJO. Ah, you like poetry. I come of a line of eight generations of poets. Father had a poem / in the anthology.

ISABELLA. My father taught me Latin although I was a girl. / But really I was

MARLENE. They didn't have Latin at my school.

ISABELLA. more suited to manual work. Cooking, washing, mending, riding horses. / Better than reading

NIJO. Oh but I'm sure you're very clever.

ISABELLA. books, eh Gret! A rough life in the open air.

NIJO. I can't say I enjoyed my rough life. What I enjoyed most was being the Emperor's favorite / and wearing thin silk.

ISABELLA. Did you have any horses, Gret?

GRET. Pig.

(*Pope Joan arrives.*)

MARLENE. Oh Joan, thank God, we can order. Do you know everyone? We were just talking about learning Latin and being clever girls. Joan was by way of an infant prodigy. Of course you were. What excited you when you were ten?

JOAN. Because angels are without matter they are not individuals. Every angel is a species.

MARLENE. There you are. (*They laugh. They look at menus.*)

ISABELLA. Yes, I forgot all my Latin. But my father was the mainspring of my life and when he died I was so grieved. I'll have the chicken, please, / and the soup.

NIJO. Of course you were grieved. My father was saying his prayers and he dozed off in the sun. So I touched his knee to rouse him. "I wonder what will happen," he said, and then he was dead before he finished the sentence. / If he'd

MARLENE. What a shock.

NIJO. died saying his prayers he would have gone straight to heaven. / Waldorf salad.

JOAN. Death is the return of all creatures to God.

NIJO. I shouldn't have woken him.

JOAN. Damnation only means ignorance of the truth. I was always attracted by the teachings of John the Scot, though he was inclined to confuse / God and the world.

ISABELLA. Grief always overwhelmed me at the time.

MARLENE. What I fancy is a rare steak. Gret?

ISABELLA. I am of course a member of the / Church of England.

MARLENE. Gret?

GRET. Potatoes.

MARLENE. I haven't been to church for years. / I like Christmas carols.

ISABELLA. Good works matter more than church attendance.

MARLENE. Make that two steaks and a lot of potatoes. Rare. But I don't do good works either.

JOAN. Canelloni, please, / and a salad.

ISABELLA. Well, I tried, but oh dear. Hennie did good works.

NIJO. The first half of my life was all sin and the second / all repentance.*

MARLENE. Oh what about starters?

GRET. Soup.

JOAN. *And which did you like best?

MARLENE. Were your travels just a penance? Avocado vinaigrette. Didn't you / enjoy yourself?

JOAN. Nothing to start with for me, thank you.

NIJO. Yes, but I was very unhappy. / It hurt to remember the past

MARLENE. And the wine list.

NIJO. I think that was repentance.

MARLENE. Well I wonder.

NIJO. I might have just been homesick.

MARLENE. Or angry.

NIJO. Not angry, no, / why angry?

GRET. Can we have some more bread?

MARLENE. Don't you get angry? I get angry.

NIJO. But what about?

MARLENE. Yes let's have two more Frascati. And some more bread, please. (*The Waitress exits.*)

ISABELLA. I tried to understand Buddhism when I was in Japan but all this birth and death succeeding each other through eternities just filled me with the most profound melancholy. I do like something more active.

NIJO. You couldn't say I was inactive. I walked every day for twenty years.

ISABELLA. I don't mean walking. / I mean in the head.

NIJO. I vowed to copy five Mahayana sutras. / Do you know how long they are?

MARLENE. I don't think religious beliefs are something we

have in common. Activity yes. (*Gret empties the bread basket into her apron.*)

NIJO. My head was active. / My head ached.

JOAN. It's no good being active in heresy.

ISABELLA. What heresy? She's calling the Church of England / a heresy.

JOAN. There are some very attractive / heresies.

NIJO. I had never heard of Christianity. Never / heard of it. Barbarians.

MARLENE. Well I'm not a Christian. / And I'm not a Buddhist.

ISABELLA. You have heard of it?

MARLENE. We don't all have to believe the same.

ISABELLA. I knew coming to dinner with a pope we should keep off religion.

JOAN. I always enjoy a theological argument. But I won't try to convert you, I'm not a missionary. Anyway I'm a heresy myself.

ISABELLA. There are some barbaric practices in the east.

NIJO. Barbaric?

ISABELLA. Among the lower classes.

NIJO. I wouldn't know.

ISABELLA. Well theology always made my head ache.

MARLENE. Oh good, some food. (*The Waitress brings the first course, serves it during the following, then exits.*)

NIJO. How else could I have left the court if I wasn't a nun? When father died I had only His Majesty. So when I fell out of favor I had nothing. Religion is a kind of nothing / and I dedicated what was left of me to nothing.

ISABELLA. That's what I mean about Buddhism. It doesn't brace.

MARLENE. Come on, Nijo, have some wine.

NIJO. Haven't you ever felt like that? You've all felt / like that. Nothing will ever happen again. I am dead already.

ISABELLA. You thought your life was over but it wasn't.

JOAN. You wish it was over.

GRET. Sad.

MARLENE. Yes, when I first came to London I sometimes . . . and when I got back from America I did. But only for a few hours. Not twenty years.

ISABELLA. When I was forty I thought my life was over. / Oh I was pitiful. I was sent

NIJO. I didn't say I felt it for twenty years. Not every minute.

ISABELLA. on a cruise for my health and I felt even worse. Pains in my bones, pins and needles in my hands, swelling behind the ears, and—oh, stupidity. I shook all over, indefinable terror. And Australia seemed to me a hideous country, the acacias stank like drains. / I

NIJO. You were homesick. (*Gret steals a bottle of wine.*)

ISABELLA. had a photograph taken for Hennie but I told her I wouldn't send it, my hair had fallen out and my clothes were crooked, I looked completely insane and suicidal.

NIJO. So did I, exactly, dressed as a nun. I was wearing walking shoes for the first time.

ISABELLA. I longed to go home, / but home to what? Houses are perfectly dismal.*

NIJO. I longed to go back ten years.

MARLENE. *I thought travelling cheered you both up.

ISABELLA. Oh it did / of course. It was on

NIJO. I'm not a cheerful person, Marlene. I just laugh a lot.

ISABELLA. the trip from Australia to the Sandwich Isles, I fell in love with the sea. There were rats in the cabin and ants in the food but suddenly it was like a new world. I woke up every morning happy, knowing there would be nothing to annoy me. No nervousness. No dressing.

NIJO. Don't you like getting dressed? I adored my clothes. / When I was chosen

MARLENE. You had prettier colours than Isabella.

NIJO. to give sake to His Majesty's brother, the Emperor Kameyana, on his formal visit, I wore raw silk pleated trousers and a seven-layered gown in shades of red, and two outer garments, / yellow lined with green

MARLENE. Yes, all that silk must have been very—

(*The Waitress enters, clears the first course and exits.*)

JOAN. I dressed as a boy when I left home.*

NIJO. and a light green jacket. Lady Betto had a five-layered gown in shades of green and purple.

ISABELLA. *You dressed as a boy?

MARLENE. Of course, / for safety.

JOAN. It was easy, I was only twelve. / Also women weren't allowed in the library. We wanted to study in Athens.

MARLENE. You ran away alone?

JOAN. No, not alone, I went with my friend. / He was

NIJO. Ah, an elopement.

JOAN. sixteen but I thought I knew more science than he did and almost as much philosophy.

ISABELLA. Well I always traveled as a lady and I repudiated strongly any suggestion in the press that I was other than feminine.

MARLENE. I don't wear trousers in the office. / I could but I don't.

ISABELLA. There was no great danger to a woman of my age and appearance.

MARLENE. And you got away with it, Joan?

JOAN. I did then. (*The Waitress brings the main course.*)

MARLENE. And nobody noticed anything?

JOAN. They noticed I was a very clever boy. / And

MARLENE. I couldn't have kept pretending for so long.

JOAN. when I shared a bed with my friend, that was ordinary—two poor students in a lodging house. I think I forgot I was pretending.

ISABELLA. Rocky Mountain Jim, Mr Nugent, showed me no disrespect. He found it interesting, I think, that I could make scones and also lasso cattle. Indeed he declared his love for me, which was most distressing.

NIJO. What did he say? / We always sent poems first.

MARLENE. What did you say?

ISABELLA. I urged him to give up whisky, / but he said it was too late.

MARLENE. Oh Isabella.

ISABELLA. He had lived alone in the mountains for many years.

MARLENE. But did you—? (*The Waitress goes.*)

ISABELLA. Mr Nugent was a man that any woman might love but none could marry. I came back to England.

NIJO. Did you write him a poem when you left? / Snow on the mountains. My sleeves

MARLENE. Did you never seen him again?

ISABELLA. No, never.

NIJO. are wet with tears. In England no tears, no snow.

ISABELLA. Well, I say never. One morning very early in Switzerland, it was a year later, I had a vision of him as I last saw him / in his trapper's clothes with his

NIJO. A ghost!

ISABELLA. hair round his face, and that was the day, / I learnt later, he died with a

NIJO. Ah!

ISABELLA. bullet in his brain. / He just bowed to me and vanished.

MARLENE. Oh Isabella.

NIJO. When your lover dies—One of my lovers died. / The priest Ariake.

JOAN. My friend died. Have we all got dead lovers?

MARLENE. Not me, sorry.

NIJO (*to Isabella*). I wasn't a nun, I was still at court, but he was a priest, and when he came to me he dedicated his whole life to hell. / He knew that when he died he would fall into one of the three lower realms. And he died, he did die.

JOAN (*to Marlene*). I'd quarrelled with him over the teachings of John the Scot, who held that our ignorance of God is the same as his ignorance of himself. He only knows what he creates because he creates everything he knows but he himself is above being—do you follow?

MARLENE. No, but go on.

NIJO. I couldn't bear to think / in what shape would he be reborn.*

JOAN. St. Augustine maintained that the Neo-Platonic Ideas are indivisible

ISABELLA. *Buddhism is really most uncomfortable.

JOAN. from God, but I agreed with John that the created world is essences derived from Ideas which derived from God. As Denys the Areopagite said—the pseudo-Denys—first we give God a name, then deny it / then reconcile the contradiction

NIJO. In what shape would he return?

JOAN. by looking beyond / those terms—

MARLENE. Sorry, what? Denys said what?

JOAN. Well we disagreed about it, we quarrelled. And next day he was ill, / I was so annoyed with him,

NIJO. Misery in this life and worse in the next, all because of me.

JOAN. all the time I was nursing him I kept going over the ar-

guments in my mind. Matter is not a means of knowing the essence. The source of the species is the Idea. But then I realised he'd never understand my arguments again, and that night he died. John the Scot held that the individual disintegrates / and there is no personal immortality.

ISABELLA. I wouldn't have you think I was in love with Jim Nugent. It was yearning to save him that I felt.

MARLENE (*to Joan*). So what did you do?

JOAN. First I decided to stay a man. I was used to it. And I wanted to devote my life to learning. Do you know why I went to Rome? Italian men didn't have beards.

ISABELLA. The loves of my life were Hennie, my own pet, and my dear husband the doctor, who nursed Hennie in her last illness. I knew it would be terrible when Hennie died but I didn't know how terrible. I felt half of myself had gone. How could I go on my travels without that sweet soul waiting at home for my letters? It was Doctor Bishop's devotion to her in her last illness that made me decide to marry him. He and Hennie had the same sweet character. I had not.

NIJO. I thought his majesty had sweet character because when he found out about Ariake he was so kind. But really it was because he no longer cared for me. One night he even sent me out to a man who had been pursuing me. / He lay awake on the other side of the screens and listened.

ISABELLA. I did wish marriage had seemed more of a step. I tried very hard to cope with the ordinary drudgery of life. I was ill again with carbuncles on the spine and nervous prostration. I ordered a tricycle, that was my idea of adventure then. And John himself fell ill, with erysipelas and anemia. I began to love him with my whole heart but it was too late. He was a skeleton with transparent white hands. I wheeled him on various seafronts in a bathchair. And he faded and left me. There was nothing in my life. The doctors said I had gout / and my heart was much affected.

NIJO. There was nothing in my life, nothing, without the Emperor's favor. The Empress had always been my enemy, Marlene, she said I had no right to wear three-layered gowns. / But I was the adopted daughter of my grandfather the Prime Minister. I had been publicly granted permission to wear thin silk.

JOAN. There was nothing in my life except my studies. I was obsessed with pursuit of the truth. I taught at the Greek School in Rome, which St. Augustine had made famous. I was poor, I worked hard. I spoke apparently brilliantly, I was still very young, I was a stranger; suddenly I was quite famous, I was everyone's favorite. Huge crowds came to hear me. The day after they made me cardinal I fell ill and lay two weeks without speaking, full of terror and regret. / But then I got up determined to

MARLENE. Yes, success is very . . .

JOAN. go on. I was seized again / with a desperate longing for the absolute.

ISABELLA. Yes, yes, to go on. I sat in Tobermory among Hennie's flowers and sewed a complete outfit in Jaeger flannel. / I was fifty-six years old.

NIJO. Out of favor but I didn't die. I left on foot, nobody saw me go. For the next twenty years I walked through Japan.

GRET. Walking is good. (*Meanwhile, the Waitress enters, pours lots of wine, then shows Marlene the empty bottle.*)

JOAN. Pope Leo died and I was chosen. All right then. I would be Pope. I would know God. I would know everything.

ISABELLA. I determined to leave my grief behind and set off for Tibet.

MARLENE. Magnificent all of you. We need some more wine, please, two bottles I think, Griselda isn't even here yet, and I want to drink a toast to you all. (*The Waitress exits*)

ISABELLA. To yourself surely, / we're here to celebrate your success.

NIJO. Yes, Marlene.

JOAN. Yes, what is it exactly, Marlene?

MARLENE. Well it's not Pope but it is managing director.*

JOAN. And you find work for people.

MARLENE. Yes, an employment agency.

NIJO. *Over all the women you work with. And the men.

ISABELLA. And very well deserved too. I'm sure it's just the beginning of something extraordinary.

MARLENE. Well it's worth a party.

ISABELLA. To Marlene.*

MARLENE. And all of us.

JOAN. *Marlene.

NIJO. Marlene.

GRET. Marlene.

MARLENE. We've all come a long way. To our courage and the way we changed our lives and our extraordinary achievements. (*They laugh and drink a toast.*)

ISABELLA. Such adventures. We were crossing a mountain pass at seven thousand feet, the cook was all to pieces, the muleteers suffered fever and snow blindness. But even though my spine was agony I managed very well.*

MARLENE. Wonderful.

NIJO. Once I was ill for four months lying alone at an inn. Nobody to offer a horse to Buddha. I had to live for myself, and I did live.

ISABELLA. Of course you did. It was far worse returning to Tobermory. I always felt dull when I was stationary. / That's why I could never stay anywhere.

NIJO. Yes, that's it exactly. New sights. The shrine by the beach, the moon shining on the sea. The goddess had vowed to save all living things. / She would even save the fishes. I was full of hope.

JOAN. I had thought the Pope would know everything. I thought God would speak to me directly. But of course he knew I was a woman.

MARLENE. But nobody else even suspected? (*The Waitress brings more wine and then exits.*)

JOAN. In the end I did take a lover again.*

ISABELLA. In the Vatican?

GRET. *Keep you warm.

NIJO. *Ah, lover.

MARLENE. *Good for you.

JOAN. He was one of my chamberlains. There are such a lot of servants when you're a Pope. The food's very good. And I realized I did know the truth. Because whatever the Pope says, that's true.

NIJO. What was he like, the chamberlain?*

GRET. Big cock.

ISABELLA. Oh Gret.

MARLENE. *Did he fancy you when he thought you were a fella?

NIJO. What was he like?

JOAN. He could keep a secret.

MARLENE. So you did know everything.

JOAN. Yes, I enjoyed being Pope. I consecrated bishops and let people kiss my feet. I received the King of England when he came to submit to the church. Unfortunately there were earthquakes, and some village reported it had rained blood, and in France there was a plague of giant grasshoppers, but I don't think that can have been my fault, do you?* (*Laughter.*)

The grasshoppers fell on the English Channel / and were washed up on shore

NIJO. I once went to sea. It was very lonely. I realised it made very little difference where I went.

JOAN. and their bodies rotted and poisoned the air and everyone in those parts died. (*Laughter.*)

ISABELLA. *Such superstition! I was nearly murdered in China by a howling mob. They thought the barbarians ate babies and put them under railway sleepers to make the tracks steady, and ground up their eyes to make the lenses of cameras. / So they were shouting,

MARLENE. And you had a camera!

ISABELLA. "child-eater, child-eater." Some people tried to sell girl babies to Europeans for cameras or stew! (*Laughter.*)

MARLENE. So apart from the grasshoppers it was a great success.

JOAN. Yes, if it hadn't been for the baby I expect I'd have lived to an old age like Theodora of Alexandria, who lived as a monk. She was accused by a girl / who fell in love with her of being the father of her child and—

NIJO. But tell us what happened to your baby. I had some babies.

MARLENE. Didn't you think of getting rid of it?

JOAN. Wouldn't that be a worse sin than having it? / But a Pope with a child was about as bad as possible.

MARLENE. I don't know, you're the Pope.

JOAN. But I wouldn't have known how to get rid of it.

MARLENE. Other Popes had children, surely.

JOAN. They didn't give birth to them.

NIJO. Well you were a woman.

JOAN. Exactly and I shouldn't have been a woman. Women, children and lunatics can't be Pope.

MARLENE. So the only thing to do / was to get rid of it some-how.

NIJO. You had to have it adopted secretly.

JOAN. But I didn't know what was happening. I thought I was getting fatter, but then I was eating more and sitting about, the life of a Pope is quite luxurious. I don't think I'd spoken to a woman since I was twelve. The chamberlain was the one who realized.

MARLENE. And by then it was too late.

JOAN. Oh I didn't want to pay attention. It was easier to do nothing.

NIJO. But you had to plan for having it. You had to say you were ill and go away.

JOAN. That's what I should have done I suppose.

MARLENE. Did you want them to find out?

NIJO. I too was often in embarrassing situations, there's no need for a scandal. My first child was His Majesty's, which unfortunately died, but my second was Akebono's. I was seventeen. He was in love with me when I was thirteen, he was very upset when I had to go to the Emperor, it was very romantic, a lot of poems. Now His Majesty hadn't been near me for two months so he thought I was four months pregnant when I was really six, so when I reached the ninth month / I announced I was seriously ill,

JOAN. I never knew what month it was.

NIJO. and Akebono announced he had gone on a religious retreat. He held me round the waist and lifted me up as the baby was born. He cut the cord with a short sword, wrapped the baby in white and took it away. It was only a girl but I was sorry to lose it. Then I told the Emperor that the baby had miscarried because of my illness, and there you are. The danger was past.

JOAN. But Nijo, I wasn't used to having a woman's body.

ISABELLA. So what happened?

JOAN. I didn't know of course that it was near the time. It was Rogation Day, there was always a procession. I was on the horse dressed in my robes and a cross was carried in front of me, and all the cardinals were following, and all the clergy of Rome, and a huge crowd of people. / We set off from St Peter's to go

MARLENE. Total Pope. (*Gret pours the wine and steals the bottle*)

JOAN. to St John's. I had felt a slight pain earlier, I thought it was something I'd eaten, and then it came back, and came back more often. I thought when this is over I'll go to bed. There were still long gaps when I felt perfectly all right and I didn't want to attract attention to myself and spoil the ceremony. Then I suddenly realized what it must be. I had to last out till I could get home and hide. Then something changed, my breath started to catch, I couldn't plan things properly any more. We were in a little street that goes between St Clement's and the Colosseum, and I just had to get off the horse and sit down for a minute. Great waves of pressure were gong through my body, I heard sounds like a cow lowing, they came out of my mouth. Far away I heard people screaming, "The Pope is ill, the Pope is dying." And the baby just slid out onto the road.*

482

MARLENE. The cardinals / won't have known where to put themselves.

NIJO. Oh dear, Joan, what a thing to do! In the street!

ISABELLA. *How embarrassing.

GRET. In a field, yah. (*They are laughing.*)

JOAN. One of the cardinals said, 'The Antichrist!' and fell over in a faint. (*They all laugh.*)

MARLENE. So what did they do? They weren't best pleased.

JOAN. They took me by the feet and dragged me out of town and stoned me to death. (*They stop laughing.*)

MARLENE. Joan, how horrible.

JOAN. I don't really remember.

NIJO. And the child died too?

JOAN. Oh yes, I think so, yes. (*The Waitress enters to clear the plates. They start talking quietly.*)

ISABELLA (*to Joan*). I never had any children. I was very fond of horses.

NIJO (*to Marlene*). I saw my daughter once. She was three years old. She wore a plum-red / small-sleeved gown. Akebono's wife

ISABELLA. Birdie was my favorite. A little Indian bay mare I rode in the Rocky Mountains.

NIJO. had taken the child because her own died. Everyone thought I was just a visitor. She was being brought up carefully so she could be sent to the palace like I was. (*Gret steals her empty plate.*)

ISABELLA. Legs of iron and always cheerful, and such a pretty face. If a stranger led her she reared up like a bronco.

NIJO. I never saw my third child after he was born, the son of Ariake the priest. Ariake held him on his lap the day he was born and talked to him as if he could understand, and cried. My fourth child was Ariake's too. Ariake died before he was born. I didn't want to see anyone, I stayed alone in the hills. It was a boy again, my third son. But oddly enough I felt nothing for him.

MARLENE. How many children did you have, Gret?

GRET. Ten.

ISABELLA. Whenever I came back to England I felt I had so much to atone for. Hennie and John were so good. I did no good in my life. I spent years in self-gratification. So I hurled myself into committees, I nursed the people of Tobermory in the epidemic of influenza, I lectured the Young Women's Christian Association on Thrift. I talked and talked explaining how the East was corrupt and vicious. My travels must do good to someone beside myself. I wore myself out with good causes.

MARLENE (*pause*). Oh God, why are we all so miserable?

JOAN (*pause*). The procession never went down that street again.

MARLENE. They rerouted it specially?

JOAN. Yes they had to go all round to avoid it. And they introduced a pierced chair.

MARLENE. A pierced chair?

JOAN. Yes, a chair made out of solid marble with a hole in the seat / and it was

MARLENE. You're not serious.

JOAN. in the Chapel of the Saviour, and after he was elected the Pope had to sit in it.

MARLENE. And someone looked up his skirts? / Not really?

ISABELLA. What an extraordinary thing.

JOAN. Two of the clergy / made sure he was a man.

NIJO. On their hands and knees!

MARLENE. A pieced chair!

GRET. Balls!

(Griselda arrives unnoticed.)

NIJO. Why couldn't he just pull up his robe?

JOAN. He had to sit there and look dignified.

MARLENE. You could have made all your chamberlains sit in it.*

GRET. Big one, small one.

NIJO. Very useful chair at court.

ISABELLA. *Or the laird of Tobermory in his kilt.

(They are quite drunk. They get the giggles. Marlene notices Griselda and gets up to welcome her. The others go on talking and laughing. Gret crosses to Joan and Isabella and pours them wine from her stolen bottles. The Waitress gives out the menus.)

MARLENE. Griselda! / There you are. Do you want to eat?

GRISELDA. I'm sorry I'm so late. No, no, don't bother.

MARLENE. Of course it's no bother. / Have you eaten?

GRISELDA. No really, I'm not hungry.

MARLENE. Well have some pudding.

GRISELDA. I never eat pudding.

MARLENE. Griselda, I hope you're not anorexic. We're having pudding, I am, and getting nice and fat.

GRISELDA. Oh if everyone is. I don't mind.

MARLENE. Now who do you know? This is Joan who was Pope in the ninth century, and Isabella Bird, the Victorian traveler, and Lady Nijo from Japan, Emperor's concubine and Buddhist nun, thirteenth century, nearer your own time, and Gret who was painted by Brueghel. Griselda's in Boccaccio and Petrarch and Chaucer because of her extraordinary marriage. I'd like profiteroles because they're disgusting.

JOAN. Zabaglione, please.

ISABELLA. Apple pie / and cream.

NIJO. What's this?

MARLENE. Zabaglione, it's Italian, it's what Joan's having, / it's delicious.

NIJO. A Roman Catholic / dessert? Yes please.

MARLENE. Gret?

GRET. Cake.

GRISELDA. Just cheese and biscuits, thank you. (The Waitress exits.)

MARLENE. Yes, Griselda's life is like a fairy story, except it starts with marrying the prince.

GRISELDA. He's only a marquis, Marlene.

MARLENE. Well everyone for miles around is his liege and he's absolute lord of life and death and you were the poor but beautiful peasant girl and he whisked you off. / Near enough a prince.

NIJO. How old were you?

GRISELDA. Fifteen.

NIJO. I was brought up in court circles and it was still a shock. Had you ever seen him before?

GRISELDA. I'd seen him riding by, we all had. And he'd seen me in the fields with the sheep.*

ISABELLA. I would have been well suited to minding sheep.

NIJO. And Mr. Nugent went riding by.

ISABELLA. Of course not, Nijo, I mean a healthy life in the open air.

JOAN. *He just rode up while you were minding the sheep and asked you to marry him?

GRISELDA. No, No, it was on the wedding day. I was waiting outside the door to see the procession. Everyone wanted him to get married so there'd be an heir to look after us when he died, / and at last he

MARLENE. I don't think Walter wanted to get married. It is Walter? Yes.

GRISELDA. announced a day for the wedding but nobody knew who the bride was, we thought it must be a foreign princess, we were longing to see her. Then the carriage stopped outside our cottage and we couldn't see the bride anywhere. And he came and spoke to my father.

NIJO. And your father told you to serve the Prince.

GRISELDA. My father could hardly speak. The Marquis said it wasn't an order, I could say not, but if I said yes I must always obey him in everything.

MARLENE. That's when you should have suspected.

GRISELDA. But of course a wife must obey her husband. / And of course I must obey the Marquis.*

ISABELLA. I swore to obey dear John, of course, but it didn't seem to arise. Naturally I wouldn't have wanted to go abroad while I was married.

MARLENE. *Then why bother to mention it at all? He'd got a thing about it, that's why.

GRISELDA. I'd rather obey the Marquis than a boy from the village.

MARLENE. Yes, that's a point.

JOAN. I never obeyed anyone. They all obeyed me.

NIJO. And what did you wear? He didn't make you get married in your own clothes? That would be perverse.*

MARLENE. Oh, you wait.

GRISELDA. *He had ladies with him who undressed me and they had a white silk dress and jewels for my hair.

MARLENE. And at first he seemed perfectly normal?

GRISELDA. Marlene, you're always so critical of him. / Of course he was normal, he was very kind.

MARLENE. But Griselda, come on, he took your baby.

GRISELDA. Walter found it hard to believe I loved him. He couldn't believe I would always obey him. He had to prove it.

MARLENE. I don't think Walter likes women.

GRISELDA. I'm sure he loved me, Marlene, all the time.

MARLENE. He just had a funny way / of showing it.

GRISELDA. It was hard for him too.

JOAN. How do you mean he took away your baby?

NIJO. Was it a boy?

GRISELDA. No, the first one was a girl.

NIJO. Even so it's hard when they take it away. Did you see it at all?

GRISELDA. Oh yes, she was six weeks old.

NIJO. Much better to do it straight away.

ISABELLA. But why did your husband take the child?

GRISELDA. He said all the people hated me because I was just one of them. And now I had a child they were restless. So he had to get rid of the child to keep them quiet. But he said he wouldn't snatch her, I had to agree and obey and give her up. So when I was feeding her a man came in and took her away. I thought he was going to kill her even before he was out of the room.

MARLENE. But you let him take her? You didn't struggle?

GRISELDA. I asked him to give her back so I could kiss her. And I asked him to bury her where no animals could dig her up. / It was Walter's child to do what he

ISABELLA. Oh my dear.

GRISELDA. liked with.*

MARLENE. Walter was bonkers.

GRET. Bastard.

ISABELLA. *But surely, murder.

GRISELDA. I had promised.

MARLENE. I can't stand this. I'm going for a pee.

(*Marlene goes out. The Waitress brings dessert, serves it during the following, then exits*)

NIJO. No, I understand. Of course you had to, he was your life. And were you in favor after that?

GRISELDA. Oh yes, we were very happy together. We never spoke about what had happened.

ISABELLA. I can see you were doing what you thought was your duty. But didn't it make you ill?

GRISELDA. No, I was very well, thank you.

NIJO. And you had another child?

GRISELDA. Not for four years, but then I did, yes, a boy.

NIJO. Ah a boy. / So it all ended happily.

GRISELDA. Yes he was pleased. I kept my son till he was two years old. A peasant's grandson. It made the people angry. Walter explained.

ISABELLA. But surely he wouldn't kill his children / just because—

GRISELDA. Oh it wasn't true. Walter would never give in to the people. He wanted to see if I loved him enough.

JOAN. He killed his children / to see if you loved him enough?

NIJO. Was it easier the second time or harder?

GRISELDA. It was always easy because I always knew I would do what he said. (*Pause. They start to eat.*)

ISABELLA. I hope you didn't have any more children.

GRISELDA. Oh no, no more. It was twelve years till he tested me again.

ISABELLA. So whatever did he do this time? / My poor John, I never loved him enough, and he would never have dreamt . . .

GRISELDA. He sent me away. He said the people wanted him to marry someone else who'd give him an heir and he'd got special permission from the Pope. So I said I'd go home to my father. I came with nothing / so I went with nothing. I took

NIJO. Better to leave if your master doesn't want you.

GRISELDA. off my clothes. He let me keep a slip so he wouldn't be shamed. And I walked home barefoot. My father came out in tears. Everyone was crying except me.

NIJO. At least your father wasn't dead. / I had nobody.

ISABELLA. Well it can be a relief to come home. I loved to see Hennie's sweet face again.

GRISELDA. Oh yes, I was perfectly content. And quite soon he sent for me again.

JOAN. I don't think I would have gone.

GRISELDA. But he told me to come. I had to obey him. He wanted me to help prepare his wedding. He was getting married to a young girl from France / and nobody except me knew how to arrange things the way he liked them.

NIJO. It's always hard taking him another woman. (*Marlene comes back.*)

JOAN. I didn't live a woman's life. I don't understand it.

GRISELDA. The girl was sixteen and far more beautiful than me. I could see why he loved her. / She had her younger brother with her as a page. (*The Waitress enters.*)

MARLENE. Oh God, I can't bear it. I want some coffee. Six coffees. Six brandies. / Double brandies. Straightaway. (*The Waitress exits.*)

GRISELDA. They all went in to the feast I'd prepared. And he stayed behind and put his arms round me and kissed me. / I felt half asleep with the shock.

NIJO. Oh, like a dream.

MARLENE. And he said, "This is your daughter and your son."

GRISELDA. Yes.

JOAN. What?

NIJO. Oh. Oh I see. You got them back.

ISABELLA. I did think it was remarkably barbaric to kill them but you learn not to say anything. / So he had them brought up secretly I suppose.

MARLENE. Walter's a monster. Weren't you angry? What did you do?

GRISELDA. Well I fainted. Then I cried and kissed the children. / Everyone was making a fuss of me.

NIJO. But did you feel anything for them?

GRISELDA. What?

NIJO. Did you feel anything for the children?

GRISELDA. Of course, I loved them.

JOAN. So you forgave him and lived with him?

GRISELDA. He suffered so much all those years.

ISABELLA. Hennie had the same sweet nature.

NIJO. So they dressed you again?

GRISELDA. Cloth of gold.

JOAN. I can't forgive anything.

MARLENE. You really are exceptional, Griselda.

NIJO. Nobody gave me back my children. (*She cries.*)

(*The Waitress brings the brandies and then exits. During the following, Joan goes to Nijo.*)

ISABELLA. I can never be like Hennie. I was always so busy in England, a kind of business I detested. The very presence of people exhausted my emotional reserves. I could not be like Hennie however I tried. I tried and was as ill as could be. The doctor suggested a steel net to support my head, the weight of my own head was too much for my diseased spine. It is dangerous to put oneself in depressing circumstances. Why should I do it?

JOAN (*to Nijo*). Don't cry.

NIJO. My father and the Emperor both died in the autumn. So much pain.

JOAN. Yes, but don't cry.

NIJO. They wouldn't let me into the palace when he was dying. I hid in the room with his coffin, then I couldn't find where I'd left my shoes, I ran after the funeral procession in bare feet, I couldn't keep up. When I got there it was over, a few wisps of smoke in the sky, that's all that was left of him. What I want to know is, if I'd still been at court, would I have been allowed to wear full mourning?

MARLENE. I'm sure you would.

NIJO. Why do you say that? You don't know anything about it. Would I have been allowed to wear full mourning?

ISABELLA. How can people live in this dim pale island and wear our hideous clothes? I cannot and will not live the life of a lady.

NIJO. I'll tell you something that made me angry. I was eighteen, at the Full Moon Ceremony. They make a special rice gruel and stir it with their sticks, and then they beat their women across the loins so they'll have sons and not daughters. So the Emperor beat us all / very hard as

MARLENE. What a sod. (*The Waitress enters with the coffees.*)

NIJO. usual—that's not it, Marlene, that's normal, what made us angry, he told his attendants they could beat us too. Well they had a wonderful time. / So Lady Genki and I made a plan, and the ladies

MARLENE. I'd like another brandy please. Better make it six. (*The Waitress exits.*)

NIJO. all hid in his rooms, and Lady Mashimizu stood guard with a stick at the door, and when His Majesty came in Genki seized him and I beat him till he cried out and promised he would never order anyone to hit us again. Afterward there was a terrible fuss. The nobles were horrified. "We wouldn't even dream of stepping on Your Majesty's shadow." And I had hit him with a stick. Yes, I hit him with a stick.

(*The Waitress brings the brandy bottle and tops up the glasses. Joan crosses in front of the table and back to her place while drunkenly reciting:*)

JOAN. Suave, mari magno turbantibus aequora ventis,

e terra magnum alterius spectare laborem;

non quia vexari quemquamst iucunda voluptas,

sed quibus ipse malis careas quia cernere suave est.

Suave etiam belli certamina magna tueri

per campos instructa tua sine parte pericli.

Sed nil dulcius est, bene quam munita tenere

edita doctrine sapientum templa serena, /

despicere uncle queas alios passimque videre

errare atque viam palantis quaerere vitae,

GRISELDA. I do think—I do wonder—it would have been nicer if Walter hadn't had to.

ISABELLA. Why should I? Why should I?

MARLENE. Of course not.

NIJO. I hit him with a stick.

JOAN. certare ingenio, contendere nobilitate,

noctes atque dies niti praestante labore

ad summas emergere opes retumque potiri.

O miseras hominum mentis, / o pectora caeca![2]

ISABELLA. Oh miseras!

NIJO. *Pectora caeca.

JOAN. qualibus in tenebris vitae quantisque periclis

degitur hoc aevi quodcumquest! / nonne videre

nil aliud sibi naturam latrare, nisi utqui

corpore seiunctus dolor absit, mente fruatur[3] . . .

(*She subsides.*)

GRET. We come to hell through a big mouth. Hell's black and red. / It's

MARLENE (*to Joan*). Shut up, pet.

GRISELDA. Hush, please.

ISABELLA. Listen, she's been to hell.

---

[2]**Suave, . . . o pectora caeca!** Joan is quoting a passage from Titus Lucretius Carus, a Roman philosopher, who wrote *On the Nature of Things* in the first century B.C.E. In English (by Cyril Bailey) the passage reads: Sweet it is, when on the great sea the winds are buffeting the waters, to gaze from the land on another's great struggles; not because it is pleasure or joy that any one should be distressed, but because it is sweet to perceive from what misfortune you yourself are free. Sweet is it too, to behold great contests of war in full array over the plains, when you have no part in the danger. But nothing is more gladdening than to dwell in the calm high places, firmly embattled on the heights by the teaching of the wise, whence you can look down on others, and see them wandering hither and thither, going astray as they seek the way of life, in strife matching their wits or rival claims of birth, struggling night and day by surpassing effort to rise up to the height of power and gain possession of the world. Ah! miserable minds of men, blind hearts!   [3]**qualibus.** In what darkness of life, in what great dangers ye spend this little span of years! to think that ye should not see that nature cries aloud for nothing else but that pain may be kept far sundered from the body, and that, withdrawn from care and fear, she may enjoy in mind the sense of pleasure!

GRET. like the village where I come from. There's a river and a bridge and houses. There's places on fire like when the soldiers come. There's a big devil sat on a roof with a big hole in his arse and he's scooping stuff out of it with a big ladle and it's falling down on us, and it's money, so a lot of the women stop and get some. But most of us is fighting the devils. There's lots of little devils, our size, and we get them down all right and give them a beating. There's lots of funny creatures round your feet, you don't like to look, like rats and lizards, and nasty things, a bum with a face, and fish with legs, and faces on things that don't have faces on. But they don't hurt, you just keep going. Well we'd had worse, you see, we'd had the Spanish. We'd all had family killed. My big son die on a wheel. Birds eat him. My baby, a soldier run her through with a sword. I'd had enough, I was mad, I hate the bastards. I come out my front door that morning and shout till my neighbors come out and I said, "Come on, we're going where the evil come from and pay the bastards out." And they all come out just as they was / from baking or

NIJO. All the ladies come.

GRET. washing in their aprons, and we push down the street and the ground opens up and we go through a big mouth into a street just like ours but in hell. I've got a sword in my hand from somewhere and I fill a basket with gold cups they drink out of down there. You just keep running on and fighting / you didn't stop for nothing. Oh we give them devils such a beating.*

NIJO. Take that, take that.

JOAN. *Something something something mortisque
    timores

tum vacuum pectus[4]—damn.

Quod si ridicula—
something something on and on and on
and something splendorem purpureai.

ISABELLA. I thought I would have a last jaunt up the west river in China. Why not? But the doctors were so very grave. I just went to Morocco. The sea was so wild I had to be landed by ship's crane in a coal bucket. / My horse was a terror to me, a powerful black charger.

GRET. Coal bucket, good.

JOAN. nos in luce timemus
    something
    terrorem.[5]

---

[4]**Something . . . pectus.** From Lucretius: "the dread of death leaves your heart empty . . . " [5]**Quod . . . purpureai. . . . nos in luce . . . terrorem.** Also from Lucretius: But if we see that these thoughts are mere mirth and mockery, and in very truth the fears of men and the cares that dog them fear not the clash of arms nor the weapons of war, but pass boldly among kings and lords of the world, nor dread the glitter that comes from gold nor the bright sheen of the purple robe, can you doubt that all such power belongs to reason alone, above all when the whole of life is but a struggle in darkness? For even as children tremble and fear everything in blinding darkness, so we sometimes dread in the light things that are no whit more to be feared than what chidren shudder at in the dark.

(Nijo is laughing and crying. Joan gets up and is sick. Griselda looks after her.)

GRISELDA. Can I have some water, please? (The Waitress exits.)

ISABELLA. So off I went to visit the Berber sheikhs in full blue trousers and great brass spurs. I was the only European woman ever to have seen the Emperor of Morocco. I was (the Waitress brings the water.) seventy years old. What lengths to go to for a last chance of joy. I knew my return of vigour was only temporary, but how marvellous while it lasted.

SCENE II

("Top Girls" Employment Agency. Monday morning. The lights come up on Marlene and Jeanine.)

MARLENE. Right Jeanine, you are Jeanine aren't you? Let's have a look. O's and A's.[6] / No A's, all those

JEANINE. Six O's.

MARLENE. O's you probably could have got an A. / Speeds, not brilliant, not too bad.

JEANINE. I wanted to go to work.

MARLENE. Well, Jeanine, what's your present job like?

JEANINE. I'm a secretary.

MARLENE. Secretary or typist?

JEANINE. I did start as a typist but the last six months I've been a secretary.

MARLENE. To?

JEANINE. To three of them, really, they share me. There's Mr. Ashford, he's the office manager, and Mr. Philby / is sales, and—

MARLENE. Quite a small place?

JEANINE. A bit small.

MARLENE. Friendly?

JEANINE. Oh it's friendly enough.

MARLENE. Prospects?

JEANINE. I don't think so, that's the trouble. Miss Lewis is secretary to the managing director and she's been there forever, and Mrs. Bradford / is—

MARLENE. So you want a job with better prospects?

JEANINE. I want a change.

MARLENE. So you'll take anything comparable?

JEANINE. No, I do want prospects. I want more money.

MARLENE. You're getting—?

JEANINE. Hundred.

MARLENE. It's not bad you know. You're what? Twenty?

JEANINE. I'm saving to get married.

MARLENE. Does that mean you don't want a long-term job, Jeanine?

---

[6]**O's and A's.** Examinations given in British school. O-levels are for basic knowledge skills, while A-levels are for more advanced skills learned in secondary schools.

JEANINE. I might do.

MARLENE. Because where do the prospects come in? No kids for a bit?

JEANINE. Oh no, not kids, not yet.

MARLENE. So you won't tell them you're getting married?

JEANINE. Had I better not?

MARLENE. It would probably help.

JEANINE. I'm not wearing a ring. We thought we wouldn't spend on a ring.

MARLENE. Saves taking it off.

JEANINE. I wouldn't take it off.

MARLENE. There's no need to mention it when you go for an interview. / Now Jeanine do you have a feel

JEANINE. But what if they ask?

MARLENE. for any particular kind of company?

JEANINE. I thought advertising.

MARLENE. People often do think advertising. I have got a few vacancies but I think they're looking for something glossier.

JEANINE. You mean how I dress? / I

MARLENE. I mean experience.

JEANINE. can dress different. I dress like this on purpose for where I am now.

MARLENE. I have a marketing department here of a knitwear manufacturer. / Marketing is near enough

JEANINE. Knitwear?

MARLENE. advertising secretary to the marketing manager, he's thirty-five, married, I've sent him a girl before and she was happy, left to have a baby, you won't want to mention marriage there. He's very fair I think, good at his job, you won't have to nurse him along. Hundred and ten, so that's better than you're doing now.

JEANINE. I don't know.

MARLENE. I've a fairly small concern here, father and two sons, you'd have more say potentially, secretarial and reception duties, only a hundred but the job's going to grow with the concern and then you'll be in at the top with new girls coming in underneath you.

JEANINE. What is it they do?

MARLENE. Lampshades. / This would be my first choice for you.

JEANINE. Just lampshades?

MARLENE. There's plenty of different kinds of lampshade. So we'll send you there, shall we, and the knitwear second choice. Are you free to go for an interview any day they call you?

JEANINE. I'd like to travel.

MARLENE. We don't have any foreign clients. You'd have to go elsewhere.

JEANINE. Yes I know. I don't really . . . I just mean . . .

MARLENE. Does your fiancé want to travel?

JEANINE. I'd like a job where I was here in London and with him and everything but now and then—I expect it's silly. Are there jobs like that?

MARLENE. There's personal assistant to a top executive in a

multinational. If that's the idea you need to be planning ahead. Is that where you want to be in ten years?

JEANINE. I might not be alive in ten years.

MARLENE. Yes but you will be. You'll have children.

JEANINE. I can't think about ten years.

MARLENE. You haven't got the speeds anyway. So I'll send you to these two shall I? You haven't been to any other agency? Just so we don't get crossed wires. Now Jeanine I want you to get one of these jobs, all right? If I send you that means I'm putting myself on the line for you. Your presentation's OK, you look fine, just be confident and go in there convinced that this is the best job for you and you're the best person for the job. If you don't believe it they won't believe it.

JEANINE. Do you believe it?

MARLENE. I think you could make me believe it if you put your mind to it.

JEANINE. Yes, all right.

SCENE III

(Joyce's back yard. Sunday afternoon. The house with a back door is upstage. Downstage is a shelter made of junk, made by children. The lights come up on two girls, Angie and Kit, who are squashed together in the shelter. Angie is sixteen, Kit is twelve. They cannot be seen from the house.)

JOYCE *(off, calling from the house)*. Angie. Angie are you out there?

(Silence. They keep still and wait. When nothing else happens they relax.)

ANGIE. Wish she was dead.

KIT. Wanna watch *The Exterminator*?

ANGIE. You're sitting on my leg.

KIT. There's nothing on telly. We can have an ice cream. Angie?

ANGIE. Shall I tell you something?

KIT. Do you wanna watch *The Exterminator*?

ANGIE. It's X, innit.

KIT. I can get into Xs.

ANGIE. Shall I tell you something?

KIT. We'll go to something else. We'll go to Ipswich. What's on the Odeon?

ANGIE. She won't let me, will she?

KIT. Don't tell her.

ANGIE. I've no money.

KIT. I'll pay.

ANGIE. She'll moan though, won't she?

KIT. I'll ask her for you if you like.

ANGIE. I've no money, I don't want you to pay.

KIT. I'll ask her.

ANGIE. She don't like you.

KIT. I still got three pounds birthday money. Did she say she don't like me? I'll go by myself then.

ANGIE. Your mum don't let you. I got to take you.

KIT. She won't know.

ANGIE. You'd be scared who'd sit next to you.

KIT. No I wouldn't. She does like me anyway. Tell me then.

ANGIE. Tell you what?

KIT. It's you she doesn't like.

ANGIE. Well I don't like her so tough shit.

JOYCE (off). Angie. Angie. Angie. I know you're out there. I'm not coming out after you. You come in here. (Silence. Nothing happens.)

ANGIE. Last night when I was in bed. I been thinking yesterday could I make things move. You know, make things move by thinking about them without touching them. Last night I was in bed and suddenly a picture fell down off the wall.

KIT. What picture?

ANGIE. My gran, that picture. Not the poster. The photograph in the frame.

KIT. Had you done something to make it fall down?

ANGIE. I must have done.

KIT. But were you thinking about it?

ANGIE. Not about it, but about something.

KIT. I don't think that's very good.

ANGIE. You know the kitten?

KIT. Which one?

ANGIE. There only is one. The dead one.

KIT. What about it?

ANGIE. I heard it last night.

KIT. Where?

ANGIE. Out here. In the dark. What if I left you here in the dark all night?

KIT. You couldn't. I'd go home.

ANGIE. You couldn't.

KIT. I'd / go home.

ANGIE. No you couldn't, not if I said.

KIT. I could.

ANGIE. Then you wouldn't see anything. You'd just be ignorant.

KIT. I can see in the daytime.

ANGIE. No you can't. You can't hear it in the daytime.

KIT. I don't want to hear it.

ANGIE. You're scared that's all.

KIT. I'm not scared of anything.

ANGIE. You're scared of blood.

KIT. It's not the same kitten anyway. You just heard an old cat, / you just heard some old cat.

ANGIE. You don't know what I heard. Or what I saw. You don't know nothing because you're a baby.

KIT. You're sitting on me.

ANGIE. Mind my hair / you silly cunt.

KIT. Stupid fucking cow, I hate you.

ANGIE. I don't care if you do.

KIT. You're horrible.

ANGIE. I'm going to kill my mother and you're going to watch.

KIT. I'm not playing.

ANGIE. You're scared of blood. (Kit puts her hand under her dress, brings it out with blood on her finger.)

KIT. There, see, I got my own blood, so. (Angie takes Kit's hand and licks her finger.)

ANGIE. Now I'm a cannibal. I might turn into a vampire now.

KIT. That picture wasn't nailed up right.

ANGIE. You'll have to do that when I get mine.

KIT. I don't have to.

ANGIE. You're scared.

KIT. I'll do it, I might do it. I don't have to just because you say. I'll be sick on you.

ANGIE. I don't care if you are sick on me, I don't mind sick. I don't mind blood. If I don't get away from here I'm going to die.

KIT. I'm going home.

ANGIE. You can't go through the house. She'll see you.

KIT. I won't tell her.

ANGIE. Oh great, fine.

KIT. I'll say I was by myself. I'll tell her you're at my house and I'm going there to get you.

ANGIE. She knows I'm here, stupid.

KIT. Then why can't I go through the house?

ANGIE. Because I said not.

KIT. My mum don't like you anyway.

ANGIE. I don't want her to like me. She's a slag.

KIT. She is not.

ANGIE. She does it with everyone.

KIT. She does not.

ANGIE. You don't even know what it is.

KIT. Yes I do.

ANGIE. Tell me then.

KIT. We get it all at school, cleverclogs. It's on television. You haven't done it.

ANGIE. How do you know?

KIT. Because I know you haven't.

ANGIE. You know wrong then because I have.

KIT. Who with?

ANGIE. I'm not telling you / who with.

KIT. You haven't anyway.

ANGIE. How do you know?

KIT. Who with?

ANGIE. I'm not telling you.

KIT. You said you told me everything.

ANGIE. I was lying wasn't I?

KIT. Who with? You can't tell me who with because / you never—

ANGIE. Sh.

(Joyce has come out of the house. She stops halfway across the yard and listens. They listen.)

JOYCE. You there Angie? Kit? You there Kitty? Want a cup of

tea? I've got some chocolate biscuits. Come on now I'll put the kettle on. Want a choccy biccy, Angie? (*They all listen and wait.*) Fucking rotten little cunt. You can stay there and die. I'll lock the door.

(*They all wait. Joyce goes back to the house. Angie and Kit sit in silence for a while.*)

KIT. When there's a war, where's the safest place?

ANGIE. Nowhere.

KIT. New Zealand is, my mum said. Your skin's burned right off. Shall we go to New Zealand?

ANGIE. I'm not staying here.

KIT. Shall we go to New Zealand?

ANGIE. You're not old enough.

KIT. You're not old enough.

ANGIE. I'm old enough to get married.

KIT. You don't want to get married.

ANGIE. No but I'm old enough.

KIT. I'd find out where they were going to drop it and stand right in the place.

ANGIE. You couldn't find out.

KIT. Better than walking round with your skin dragging on the ground. Eugh. / Would you like walking round with your skin dragging on the ground?

ANGIE. You couldn't find out, stupid, it's a secret.

KIT. Where are you going?

ANGIE. I'm not telling you.

KIT. Why?

ANGIE. It's a secret.

KIT. But you tell me all your secrets.

ANGIE. Not the true secrets.

KIT. Yes you do.

ANGIE. No I don't.

KIT. I want to go somewhere away from the war.

ANGIE. Just forget the war.

KIT. I can't.

ANGIE. You have to. It's so boring.

KIT. I'll remember it at night.

ANGIE. I'm going to do something else anyway.

KIT. What? Angie, come on. Angie.

ANGIE. It's a little secret.

KIT. It can't be worse than the kitten. And killing your mother. And the war.

ANGIE. Well I'm not telling you so you can die for all I care.

KIT. My mother says there's something wrong with you playing with someone my age. She says why haven't you got friends your own age. People your own age know there's something funny about you. She says you're a bad influence. She says she's going to speak to your mother. (*Angie twists Kit's arm till she cries out.*)

ANGIE. Say you're a liar.

KIT. She said it not me.

ANGIE. Say you eat shit.

KIT. You can't make me. (*Angie lets go.*)

ANGIE. I don't care anyway. I'm leaving.

KIT. Go on then.

ANGIE. You'll all wake up one morning and find I've gone.

KIT. Go on then.

ANGIE. You'll wake up one morning and find I've gone.

KIT. Good.

ANGIE. I'm not telling you when.

KIT. Go on then.

ANGIE. I'm sorry I hurt you.

KIT. I'm tired.

ANGIE. Do you like me?

KIT. I don't know.

ANGIE. You do like me.

KIT. I'm going home. (*She gets up.*)

ANGIE. No you're not.

KIT. I'm tired.

ANGIE. She'll see you.

KIT. She'll give me a chocolate biscuit.

ANGIE. Kitty.

KIT. Tell me where you're going.

ANGIE. Sit down.

KIT (*sittting down again*). Go on then.

ANGIE. Swear?

KIT. Swear.

ANGIE. I'm going to London. To see my aunt.

KIT. And what?

ANGIE. That's it.

KIT. I see my aunt all the time.

ANGIE. I don't see my aunt.

KIT. What's so special?

ANGIE. It is special. She's special.

KIT. Why?

ANGIE. She is.

KIT. Why?

ANGIE. She is.

KIT. Why?

ANGIE. My mother hates her.

KIT. Why?

ANGIE. Because she does.

KIT. Perhaps she's not very nice.

ANGIE. She is nice.

KIT. How do you know?

ANGIE. Because I know her.

KIT. You said you never see her.

ANGIE. I saw her last year. You saw her.

KIT. Did I?

ANGIE. Never mind.

KIT. I remember her. That aunt. What's so special?

ANGIE. She gets people jobs.

KIT. What's so special?

ANGIE. I think I'm my aunt's child. I think my mother's really my aunt.

KIT. Why?

ANGIE. Because she goes to America, now shut up.

KIT. I've been to London.

ANGIE. Now give us a cuddle and shut up because I'm sick.

KIT. You're sitting on my arm.

(They curl up in each other's arms. Silence. Joyce comes out and comes up to them quietly.)

JOYCE. Come on.

KIT. Oh hello.

JOYCE. Time you went home.

KIT. We want to go to the Odeon.

JOYCE. What time?

KIT. Don't know.

JOYCE. What's on?

KIT. Don't know.

JOYCE. Don't know much do you?

KIT. That all right then?

JOYCE. Angie's got to clean her room first.

ANGIE. No I don't.

JOYCE. Yes you do, it's a pigsty.

ANGIE. Well I'm not.

JOYCE. Then you're not going. I don't care.

ANGIE. Well I am going.

JOYCE. You've no money, have you?

ANGIE. Kit's paying anyway.

JOYCE. No she's not.

KIT. I'll help you with your room.

JOYCE. That's nice.

ANGIE. No you won't. You wait here.

KIT. Hurry then.

ANGIE. I'm not hurrying. You just wait. *(Angie goes into the house. Silence.)*

JOYCE. I don't know. *(Silence.)* How's school then?

KIT. All right.

JOYCE. What are you now? Third year?

KIT. Second year.

JOYCE. Your mum says you're good at English. *(Silence.)* Maybe Angie should've stayed on.

KIT. She didn't like it.

JOYCE. I didn't like it. And look at me. If your face fits at school it's going to fit other places too. It wouldn't make no difference to Angie. She's not going to get a job when jobs are hard to get. I'd be sorry for anyone in charge of her. She'd better get married. I don't know who'd have her, mind. She's one of those girls might never leave home. What do you want to be when you grow up, Kit?

KIT. Physicist.

JOYCE. What?

KIT. Nuclear physicist.

JOYCE. Whatever for?

KIT. I could, I'm clever.

JOYCE. I know you're clever, pet. *(Silence.)* I'll make a cup of tea. *(Silence.)* Looks like it's going to rain. *(Silence.)* Don't you have friends your own age?

KIT. Yes.

JOYCE. Well then.

KIT. I'm old for my age.

JOYCE. And Angie's simple is she? She's not simple.

KIT. I love Angie.

JOYCE. She's clever in her own way.

KIT. You can't stop me.

JOYCE. I don't want to.

KIT. You can't, so.

JOYCE. Don't be cheeky, Kitty. She's always kind to little children.

KIT. She's coming so you better leave me alone.

(Angie comes out. She has changed into an old best dress, slightly small for her.)

JOYCE. What you put that on for? Have you done your room? You can't clean your room in that.

ANGIE. I looked in the cupboard and it was there.

JOYCE. Of course it was there, it's meant to be there. Is that why it was a surprise, finding something in the right place? I should think she's surprised, wouldn't you Kit, to find something in her room in the right place.

ANGIE. I decided to wear it.

JOYCE. Not today, why? To clean your room? You're not going to the pictures till you've done your room. You can put your dress on after if you like. *(Angie picks up a brick.)* Have you done your room? You're not getting out of it, you know.

KIT. Angie, let's go.

JOYCE. She's not going till she's done her room.

KIT. It's starting to rain.

JOYCE. Come on, come on then. Hurry and do your room, Angie, and then you can go to the cinema with Kit. Oh it's wet, come on. We'll look up the time in the paper. Does your mother know, Kit, it's going to be a late night for you, isn't it? Hurry up, Angie. You'll spoil your dress. You make me sick. *(Joyce and Kit run into the house. Angie stays where she is. There is the sound of rain. Kit comes out of the house.)*

KIT *(shouting)*. Angie. Angie, come on, you'll get wet. *(She comes back to Angie.)*

ANGIE. I put on this dress to kill my mother.

KIT. I suppose you thought you'd do it with a brick.

ANGIE. You can kill people with a brick. *(She puts the brick down.)*

KIT. Well you didn't, so.

ACT II

SCENE I

("Top Girls" Employment Agency. Monday morning. There are three desks in the main office and a separate interviewing area. The lights come up in the main office on Win and Nell who have just arrived for work.)

NELL. Coffee coffee coffee coffee / coffee.

WIN. The roses were smashing. / Mermaid.

NELL. Ohhh.

WIN. Iceberg. He taught me all their names. (*Nell has some coffee now.*)

NELL. Ah. Now then.

WIN. He has one of the finest rose gardens in West Sussex. He exhibits.

NELL. He what?

WIN. His wife was visiting her mother. It was like living together.

NELL. Crafty, you never said.

WIN. He rang on Saturday morning.

NELL. Lucky you were free.

WIN. That's what I told him.

NELL. Did you hell.

WIN. Have you ever seen a really beautiful rose garden?

NELL. I don't like flowers. / I like swimming pools.

WIN. Marilyn. Esther's Baby. They're all called after birds.

NELL. Our friend's late. Celebrating all weekend I bet you.

WIN. I'd call a rose Elvis. Or John Conteh.

NELL. Is Howard in yet?

WIN. If he is he'll be bleeping us with a problem.

NELL. Howard can just hang on to himself.

WIN. Howard's really cut up.

NELL. Howard thinks because he's a fella the job was his as of right. Our Marlene's got far more balls than Howard and that's that.

WIN. Poor little bugger.

NELL. He'll live.

WIN. He'll move on.

NELL. I wouldn't mind a change of air myself.

WIN. Serious?

NELL. I've never been a staying put lady. Pastures new.

WIN. So who's the pirate?

NELL. There's nothing definite.

WIN. Inquiries?

NELL. There's always inquiries. I'd think I'd got bad breath if there stopped being inquiries. Most of them can't afford me. Or you.

WIN. I'm all right for the time being. Unless I go to Australia.

NELL. There's not a lot of room upward.

WIN. Marlene's filled it up.

NELL. Good luck to her. Unless there's some prospects moneywise.

WIN. You can but ask.

NELL. Can always but ask.

WIN. So what have we got? I've got a Mr. Holden I saw last week.

NELL. Any use?

WIN. Pushy. Bit of a cowboy.

NELL. Goodlooker?

WIN. Good dresser.

NELL. High flyer?

WIN. That's his general idea certainly but I'm not sure he's got it up there.

NELL. Prestel wants six high flyers and I've only seen two and a half.

WIN. He's making a bomb on the road but he thinks it's time for an office. I sent him to IBM but he didn't get it.

NELL. Prestel's on the road.

WIN. He's not overbright.

NELL. Can he handle an office?

WIN. Provided his secretary can punctuate he should go far.

NELL. Bear Prestel in mind then, I might put my head round the door. I've got that poor little nerd I should never have said I could help. Tender heart me.

WIN. Tender like old boots. How old?

NELL. Yes well forty-five.

WIN. Say no more.

NELL. He knows his place, he's not after calling himself a manager, he's just a poor little bod wants a better commission and a bit of sunshine.

WIN. Don't we all.

NELL. He's just got to relocate. He's got a bungalow in Dymchurch.

WIN. And his wife says.

NELL. The lady wife wouldn't care to relocate. She's going through the change.

WIN. It's his funeral, don't waste your time.

NELL. I don't waste a lot.

WIN. Good weekend you?

NELL. You could say.

WIN. Which one?

NELL. One Friday, one Saturday.

WIN. Aye—aye.

NELL. Sunday night I watched telly.

WIN. Which of them do you like best really?

NELL. Sunday was best, I liked the Ovaltine.

WIN. Holden, Barker, Gardner, Duke.

NELL. I've a lady here thinks she can sell.

WIN. Taking her on?

NELL. She's had some jobs.

WIN. Services?

NELL. No, quite heavy stuff, electric.

WIN. Tough bird like us.

NELL. We could do with a few more here.

WIN. There's nothing going here.

NELL. No but I always want the tough ones when I see them. Hang onto them.

WIN. I think we're plenty.

NELL. Derek asked me to marry him again.

WIN. He doesn't know when he's beaten.

NELL. I told him I'm not going to play house, not even in Ascot.

WIN. Mind you, you could play house.

NELL. If I chose to play house I would play house ace.

WIN. You could marry him and go on working.

NELL. I could go on working and not marry him.

(Marlene arrives.)

MARLENE. Morning ladies. (*Win and Nell cheer and whistle.*) Mind my head.

NELL. Coffee coffee coffee.

WIN. We're tactfully not mentioning you're late.

MARLENE. Fucking tube.

WIN. We've heard that one.

NELL. We've used that one.

WIN. It's the top executive doesn't come in as early as the poor working girl.

MARLENE. Pass the sugar and shut your face, pet.

WIN. Well I'm delighted.

NELL. Howard's looking sick.

WIN. Howard is sick. He's got ulcers and heart. He told me.

NELL. He'll have to stop then won't he?

WIN. Stop what?

NELL. Smoking, drinking, shouting. Working.

WIN. Well, working.

NELL. We're just looking through the day.

MARLENE. I'm doing some of Pam's ladies. They've been piling up while she's away.

NELL. Half a dozen little girls and an arts graduate who can't type.

WIN. I spent the whole weekend at his place in Sussex.

NELL. She fancies his rose garden.

WIN. I had to lie down in the back of the car so the neighbours wouldn't see me go in.

NELL. You're kidding.

WIN. It was funny.

NELL. Fuck that for a joke.

WIN. It was funny.

MARLENE. Anyway they'd see you in the garden.

WIN. The garden has extremely high walls.

NELL. I think I'll tell the wife.

WIN. Like hell.

NELL. She might leave him and you could have the rose garden.

WIN. The minute it's not a secret I'm out on my ear.

NELL. Don't know why you bother.

WIN. Bit of fun.

NELL. I think it's time you went to Australia.

WIN. I think it's pushy Mr. Holden time.

NELL. If you've any really pretty bastards, Marlene, I want some for Prestel.

MARLENE. I might have one this afternoon. This morning it's all Pam's secretarial.

NELL. Not long now and you'll be upstairs watching over us all.

MARLENE. Do you feel bad about it?

NELL. I don't like coming second.

MARLENE. Who does?

WIN. We'd rather it was you than Howard. We're glad for you, aren't we Nell.

NELL. Oh yes. Aces.

(Louise enters the interviewing area. The lights cross-fade to Win and Louise in the interviewing area. Nell exits.)

WIN. Now Louise, hello, I have your details here. You've been very loyal to the one job I see.

LOUISE. Yes I have.

WIN. Twenty-one years is a long time in one place.

LOUISE. I feel it is. I feel it's time to move on.

WIN. And you are what age now?

LOUISE. I'm in my early forties.

WIN. Exactly?

LOUISE. Forty-six.

WIN. It's not necessarily a handicap, well it is of course we have to face that, but it's not necessarily a disabling handicap, experience does count for something.

LOUISE. I hope so.

WIN. Now between ourselves is there any trouble, any reason why you're leaving that wouldn't appear on the form?

LOUISE. Nothing like that.

WIN. Like what?

LOUISE. Nothing at all.

WIN. No long term understandings come to a sudden end, making for an insupportable atmosphere?

LOUISE. I've always completely avoided anything like that at all.

WIN. No personality clashes with your immediate superiors or inferiors?

LOUISE. I've always taken care to get on very well with everyone.

WIN. I only ask because it can affect the reference and it also affects your motivation, I want to be quite clear why you're moving on. So I take it the job itself no longer satisfies you. Is it the money?

LOUISE. It's partly the money. It's not so much the money.

WIN. Nine thousand is very respectable. Have you dependants?

LOUISE. No, no dependants. My mother died.

WIN. So why are you making a change?

LOUISE. Other people make changes.

WIN. But why are you, now, after spending most of your life in the one place?

LOUISE. There you are, I've lived for that company, I've given my life really you could say because I haven't had a great deal of social life, I've worked in the evenings. I haven't had office entanglements for the very reason you just mentioned and if you are committed to your work you don't move in many other circles. I had management status from the age of twenty-seven and you'll appreciate what that means. I've built up a department. And there it is, it works extremely well, and I feel I'm stuck there. I've spent twenty years in middle management. I've seen young men who I trained go on, in my own company or elsewhere, to higher things. Nobody notices me, I don't expect it, I don't attract attention by making mistakes, everybody takes it for granted that my work is perfect.

They will notice me when I go, they will be sorry I think to lose me, they will offer me more money of course, I will refuse. They will see when I've gone what I was doing for them.

WIN. If they offer you more money you won't stay?

LOUISE. No I won't.

WIN. Are you the only woman?

LOUISE. Apart from the girls of course, yes. There was one, she was my assistant, it was the only time I took on a young woman assistant, I always had my doubts. I don't care greatly for working with women, I think I pass as a man at work. But I did take on this young woman, her qualifications were excellent, and she did well, she got a department of her own, and left the company for a competitor where she's now on the board and good luck to her. She has a different style, she's a new kind of attractive well-dressed—I don't mean I don't dress properly. But there is a kind of woman who is thirty now who grew up in a different climate. They are not so careful. They take themselves for granted. I have had to justify my existence every minute, and I have done so, I have proved—well.

WIN. Let's face it, vacancies are going to be ones where you'll be in competition with younger men. And there are companies that will value your experience enough you'll be in with a chance. There are also fields that are easier for a woman, there is a cosmetic company here where your experience might be relevant. It's eight and a half, I don't know if that appeals.

LOUISE. I've proved I can earn money. It's more important to get away. I feel it's now or never. I sometimes / think—

WIN. You shouldn't talk too much at an interview.

LOUISE. I don't. I don't normally talk about myself. I know very well how to handle myself in an office situation. I only talk to you because it seems to me this is different, it's your job to understand me, surely. You asked the questions.

WIN. I think I understand you sufficiently.

LOUISE. Well good, that's good.

WIN. Do you drink?

LOUISE. Certainly not. I'm not a teetotaller, I think that's very suspect, it's seen as being an alcoholic if you're teetotal. What do you mean? I don't drink. Why?

WIN. I drink.

LOUISE. I don't.

WIN. Good for you.

(The lights crossfade to the main office with Marlene sitting at her desk. Win and Louise exit. Angie arrives in the main office.)

ANGIE. Hello.

MARLENE. Have you an appointment?

ANGIE. It's me. I've come.

MARLENE. What? It's not Angie?

ANGIE. It was hard to find this place. I got lost.

MARLENE. How did you get past the receptionist? The girl on the desk, didn't she try to stop you?

ANGIE. What desk?

MARLENE. Never mind.

ANGIE. I just walked in. I was looking for you.

MARLENE. Well you found me.

ANGIE. Yes.

MARLENE. So where's your mum? Are you up in town for the day?

ANGIE. Not really.

MARLENE. Sit down. Do you feel all right?

ANGIE. Yes thank you.

MARLENE. So where's Joyce?

ANGIE. She's at home.

MARLENE. Did you come up on a school trip then?

ANGIE. I've left school.

MARLENE. Did you come up with a friend?

ANGIE. No. There's just me.

MARLENE. You came up by yourself, that's fun. What have you been doing? Shopping? Tower of London?

ANGIE. No, I just come here. I come to you.

MARLENE. That's very nice of you to think of paying your aunty a visit. There's not many nieces make that the first port of call. Would you like a cup of coffee?

ANGIE. No thank you.

MARLENE. Tea, orange?

ANGIE. No thank you.

MARLENE. Do you feel all right?

ANGIE. Yes thank you.

MARLENE. Are you tired from the journey?

ANGIE. Yes, I'm tired from the journey.

MARLENE. You sit there for a bit then. How's Joyce?

ANGIE. She's all right.

MARLENE. Same as ever.

ANGIE. Oh yes.

MARLENE. Unfortunately you've picked a day when I'm rather busy, if there's ever a day when I'm not, or I'd take you out to lunch and we'd go to Madame Tussaud's. We could go shopping. What time do you have to be back? Have you got a day return?

ANGIE. No.

MARLENE. So what train are you going back on?

ANGIE. I came on the bus.

MARLENE. So what bus are you going back on? Are you staying the night?

ANGIE. Yes.

MARLENE. Who are you staying with? Do you want me to put you up for the night, is that it?

ANGIE. Yes please.

MARLENE. I haven't got a spare bed.

ANGIE. I can sleep on the floor.

MARLENE. You can sleep on the sofa.

ANGIE. Yes please.

MARLENE. I do think Joyce might have phoned me. It's like her.

ANGIE. This is where you work is it?

MARLENE. It's where I have been working the last two years but I'm going to move into another office.

ANGIE. It's lovely.

MARLENE. My new office is nicer than this. There's just the one big desk in it for me.

ANGIE. Can I see it?

MARLENE. Not now, no, there's someone else in it now. But he's leaving at the end of next week and I'm going to do his job.

ANGIE. Is that good?

MARLENE. Yes, it's very good.

ANGIE. Are you going to be in charge?

MARLENE. Yes I am.

ANGIE. I knew you would be.

MARLENE. How did you know?

ANGIE. I knew you'd be in charge of everything.

MARLENE. Not quite everything.

ANGIE. You will be.

MARLENE. Well we'll see.

ANGIE. Can I see it next week then?

MARLENE. Will you still be here next week?

ANGIE. Yes.

MARLENE. Don't you have to go home?

ANGIE. No.

MARLENE. Why not?

ANGIE. It's all right.

MARLENE. Is it all right?

ANGIE. Yes, don't worry about it.

MARLENE. Does Joyce know where you are?

ANGIE. Yes of course she does.

MARLENE. Well does she?

ANGIE. Don't worry about it.

MARLENE. How long are you planning to stay with me then?

ANGIE. You know when you came to see us last year?

MARLENE. Yes, that was nice wasn't it?

ANGIE. That was the best day of my whole life.

MARLENE. So how long are you planning to stay?

ANGIE. Don't you want me?

MARLENE. Yes yes, I just wondered.

ANGIE. I won't stay if you don't want me.

MARLENE. No, of course you can stay.

ANGIE. I'll sleep on the floor. I won't be any bother.

MARLENE. Don't get upset.

ANGIE. I'm not, I'm not. Don't worry about it.

(*Mrs Kidd comes in.*)

MRS. KIDD. Excuse me.

MARLENE. Yes.

MRS KIDD. Excuse me.

MARLENE. Can I help you?

MRS KIDD. Excuse me bursting in on you like this but I have to talk to you.

MARLENE. I am engaged at the moment. / If you could go to reception—

MRS KIDD. I'm Rosemary Kidd, Howard's wife, you don't recognize me but we did meet, I remember you of course / but you wouldn't—

MARLENE. Yes of course, Mrs. Kidd, I'm sorry, we did meet. Howard's about somewhere I expect, have you looked in his office?

MRS KIDD. Howard's not about, no. I'm afraid it's you I've come to see if I could have a minute or two.

MARLENE. I do have an appointment in five minutes.

MRS KIDD. This won't take five minutes. I'm very sorry. It is a matter of some urgency.

MARLENE. Well of course. What can I do for you?

MRS KIDD. I just wanted a chat, an informal chat. It's not something I can simply—I'm sorry if I'm interrupting your work. I know office work isn't like housework / which is all interruptions.

MARLENE. No, no, this is my niece. Angie. Mrs. Kidd.

MRS KIDD. Very pleased to meet you.

ANGIE. Very well thank you.

MRS KIDD. Howard's not in today.

MARLENE. Isn't he?

MRS KIDD. He's feeling poorly.

MARLENE. I didn't know. I'm sorry to hear that.

MRS KIDD. The fact is he's in a state of shock. About what's happened.

MARLENE. What has happened?

MRS KIDD. You should know if anyone. I'm referring to you being appointed managing director instead of Howard. He hasn't been at all well all weekend. He hasn't slept for three nights. I haven't slept.

MARLENE. I'm sorry to hear that, Mrs. Kidd. Has he thought of taking sleeping pills?

MRS KIDD. It's very hard when someone has worked all these years.

MARLENE. Business life is full of little setbacks. I'm sure Howard knows that. He'll bounce back in a day or two. We all bounce back.

MRS KIDD. If you could see him you'd know what I'm talking about. What's it going to do to him working for a woman? I think if it was a man he'd get over it as something normal.

MARLENE. I think he's going to have to get over it.

MRS KIDD. It's me that bears the brunt. I'm not the one that's been promoted. I put him first every inch of the way. And now what do I get? You women this, you women that. It's not my fault. You're going to have to be very careful how you handle him. He's very hurt.

MARLENE. Naturally I'll be tactful and pleasant to him, you don't start pushing someone round. I'll consult him over any decisions affecting his department. But that's no different, Mrs. Kidd, from any of my other colleagues.

MRS KIDD. I think it is different, because he's a man.

MARLENE. I'm not quite sure why you came to see me.

MRS KIDD. I had to do something.

MARLENE. Well you've done it, you've seen me. I think

that's probably all we've time for. I'm sorry he's been taking it out on you. He really is a shit, Howard.

MRS KIDD. But he's got a family to support. He's got three
children. It's only fair.

MARLENE. Are you suggesting I give up the job to him then?

MRS KIDD. It had crossed my mind if you were unavailable
after all for some reason, he would be the natural second
choice I think, don't you? I'm not asking.

MARLENE. Good.

MRS KIDD. You mustn't tell him I came. He's very proud.

MARLENE. If he doesn't like what's happening here he can
go and work somewhere else.

MRS KIDD. Is that a threat?

MARLENE. I'm sorry but I do have some work to do.

MRS KIDD. It's not that easy, a man of Howard's age. You
don't care. I thought he was going too far but he's right.
You're one of these ballbreakers, / that's what you

MARLENE. I'm sorry but I do have some work to do.

MRS KIDD. are. You'll end up miserable and lonely. You're
not natural.

MARLENE. Could you please piss off?

MRS KIDD. I thought if I saw you at least I'd be doing something. (Mrs. Kidd goes.)

MARLENE. I've got to go and do some work now. Will you
come back later?

ANGIE. I think you were wonderful.

MARLENE. I've got to go and do some work now.

ANGIE. You told her to piss off.

MARLENE. Will you come back later?

ANGIE. Can't I stay here?

MARLENE. Don't you want to go sightseeing?

ANGIE. I'd rather stay here.

MARLENE. You can stay here I suppose, if it's not boring.

ANGIE. It's where I most want to be in the world.

MARLENE. I'll see you later then.

(Marlene goes. Shona and Nell enter the interviewing
area. Angie sits at Win's desk. The lights crossfade to Nell
and Shona in the interviewing area.)

NELL. Is this right? You are Shona?

SHONA. Yeh.

NELL. It says here you're twenty-nine.

SHONA. Yeh.

NELL. Too many late nights, me. So you've been where you
are for four years, Shona, you're earning six basic and
three commission. So what's the problem?

SHONA. No problem.

NELL. Why do you want a change?

SHONA. Just a change.

NELL. Change of product, change of area?

SHONA. Both.

NELL. But you're happy on the road?

SHONA. I like driving.

NELL. You're not after management status?

SHONA. I would like management status.

NELL. You'd be interested in titular management status but
not come off the road?

SHONA. I want to be on the road, yeh.

NELL. So how many calls have you been making a day?

SHONA. Six.

NELL. And what proportion of those are successful?

SHONA. Six.

NELL. That's hard to believe.

SHONA. Four.

NELL. You find it easy to get the initial interest do you?

SHONA. Oh yeh, I get plenty of initial interest.

NELL. And what about closing?

SHONA. I close, don't I?

NELL. Because that's what an employer is going to have
doubts about with a lady as I needn't tell you, whether
she's got the guts to push through to a closing situation.
They think we're too nice. They think we listen to the
buyer's doubts. They think we consider his needs and his
feelings.

SHONA. I never consider people's feelings.

NELL. I was selling for six years, I can sell anything, I've sold
in three continents, and I'm jolly as they come but I'm
not very nice.

SHONA. I'm not very nice.

NELL. What sort of time do you have on the road with the
other reps? Get on all right? Handle the chat?

SHONA. I get on. Keep myself to myself.

NELL. Fairly much of a loner are you?

SHONA. Sometimes.

NELL. So what field are you interested in?

SHONA. Computers.

NELL. That's a top field as you know and you'll be up against
some very slick fellas there, there's some very pretty boys
in computers, it's an American-style field.

SHONA. That's why I want to do it.

NELL. Video systems appeal? That's a high-flying situation.

SHONA. Video systems appeal OK.

NELL. Because Prestel have half a dozen vacancies I'm looking to fill at the moment. We're talking in the area of ten
to fifteen thousand here and upwards.

SHONA. Sounds OK.

NELL. I've half a mind to go for it myself. But it's good
money here if you've got the top clients. Could you fancy
it do you think?

SHONA. Work here?

NELL. I'm not in a position to offer, there's nothing officially
going just now, but we're always on the lookout. There's
not that many of us. We could keep in touch.

SHONA. I like driving.

NELL. So the Prestel appeals?

SHONA. Yeh.

NELL. What about ties?

SHONA. No ties.

NELL. So relocation wouldn't be a problem.

SHONA. No problem.

NELL. So just fill me in a bit more could you about what you've been doing.

SHONA. What I've been doing. It's all down there.

NELL. The bare facts are down here but I've got to present you to an employer.

SHONA. I'm twenty-nine years old.

NELL. So it says here.

SHONA. We look young. Youngness runs in the family in our family.

NELL. So just describe your present job for me.

SHONA. My present job at present. I have a car. I have a Porsche. I go up the M1 a lot. Burn up the M1 a lot. Straight up the M1 in the fast lane to where the clients are, Staffordshire, Yorkshire, I do a lot in Yorkshire. I'm selling electric things. Like dishwashers, washing machines, stainless steel tubs are a feature and the reliability of the program. After sales service, we offer a very good after sales service, spare parts, plenty of spare parts. And fridges, I sell a lot of fridges specially in the summer. People want to buy fridges in the summer because of the heat melting the butter and you get fed up standing the milk in a basin of cold water with a cloth over, stands to reason people don't want to do that in this day and age. So I sell a lot of them. Big ones with big freezers. Big freezers. And I stay in hotels at night when I'm away from home. On my expense account. I stay in various hotels. They know me, the ones I go to. I check in, have a bath, have a shower. Then I go down to the bar, have a gin and tonic, have a chat. Then I go into the dining room and have dinner. I usually have fillet steak and mushrooms, I like mushrooms. I like smoked salmon very much. I like having a salad on the side. Green salad. I don't like tomatoes.

NELL. Christ what a waste of time.

SHONA. Beg your pardon?

NELL. Not a word of this is true is it?

SHONA. How do you mean?

NELL. You just filled in the form with a pack of lies.

SHONA. Not exactly.

NELL. How old are you?

SHONA. Twenty-nine.

NELL. Nineteen?

SHONA. Twenty-one.

NELL. And what jobs have you done? Have you done any?

SHONA. I could though, I bet you.

(*The lights crossfade to the main office with Angie sitting as before. Win comes in to the main office. Shona and Nell exit.*)

WIN. Who's sitting in my chair?

ANGIE. What? Sorry.

WIN. Who's been eating my porridge?

ANGIE. What?

WIN. It's all right, I saw Marlene. Angie isn't it? I'm Win. And I'm not going out for lunch because I'm knackered.

I'm going to set me down here and have a yogurt. Do you like yogurt?

ANGIE. No.

WIN. That's good because I've only got one. Are you hungry?

ANGIE. No.

WIN. There's a cafe on the corner.

ANGIE. No thank you. Do you work here?

WIN. How did you guess?

ANGIE. Because you look as if you might work here and you're sitting at the desk. Have you always worked here?

WIN. No I was headhunted. That means I was working for another outfit like this and this lot came and offered me more money. I broke my contract, there was a hell of a stink. There's not many top ladies about. Your aunty's a smashing bird.

ANGIE. Yes I know.

MARLENE. Fan are you? Fan of your aunty's?

ANGIE. Do you think I could work here?

WIN. Not at the moment.

ANGIE. How do I start?

WIN. What can you do?

ANGIE. I don't know. Nothing.

WIN. Type?

ANGIE. Not very well. The letters jump up when I do capitals. I was going to do a CSE[7] in commerce but I didn't.

WIN. What have you got?

ANGIE. What?

WIN. CSE's, O's.

ANGIE. Nothing, none of that. Did you do all that?

WIN. Oh yes, all that, and a science degree funnily enough. I started out doing medical research but there's no money in it. I thought I'd go abroad. Did you know they sell Coca-Cola in Russia and Pepsi-Cola in China? You don't have to be qualified as much as you might think. Men are awful bullshitters, they like to make out jobs are harder than they are. Any job I ever did I started doing it better than the rest of the crowd and they didn't like it. So I'd get unpopular and I'd have a drink to cheer myself up. I lived with a fella and supported him for four years, he couldn't get work. After that I went to California. I like the sunshine. Americans know how to live. This country's too slow. Then I went to Mexico, still in sales, but it's no country for a single lady. I came home, went bonkers for a bit, thought I was five different people, got over that all right, the psychiatrist said I was perfectly sane and highly intelligent. Got married in a moment of weakness and he's inside now, he's been inside four years, and I've not been to see him too much this last year. I like this better than sales, I'm not really that aggressive. I started thinking sales was a good job if you want to meet people,

_____
[7]**CSE:** Certificate of Secondary Education.

but you're meeting people that don't want to meet you. It's no good if you like being liked. Here your clients want to meet you because you're the one doing them some good. They hope. (*Angie has fallen asleep. Nell comes in.*)

NELL. You're talking to yourself, sunshine.

WIN. So what's new?

NELL. Who is this?

WIN. Marlene's little niece.

NELL. What's she got, brother, sister? She never talks about her family.

WIN. I was telling her my life story.

NELL. Violins?

WIN. No, success story.

NELL. You've heard Howard's had a heart attack?

WIN. No, when?

NELL. I heard just now. He hadn't come in, he was at home, he's gone to hospital. He's not dead. His wife was here, she rushed off in a cab.

WIN. Too much butter, too much smoke. We must send him some flowers. (*Marlene comes in.*) You've heard about Howard?

MARLENE. Poor sod.

NELL. Lucky he didn't get the job if that's what his health's like.

MARLENE. Is she asleep?

WIN. She wants to work here.

MARLENE. Packer in Tesco more like.

WIN. She's a nice kid. Isn't she?

MARLENE. She's a bit thick. She's a bit funny.

WIN. She thinks you're wonderful.

MARLENE. She's not going to make it.

SCENE II

(*Joyce's kitchen. Sunday evening, a year earlier. The lights come up on Joyce, Angie, and Marlene. Marlene is taking presents out of bright carrier bag. Angie has already opened a box of chocolates.*)

MARLENE. Just a few little things. / I've

JOYCE. There's no need.

MARLENE. no memory for birthdays have I, and Christmas seems to slip by. So I think I owe Angie a few presents.

JOYCE. What do you say?

ANGIE. Thank you very much. Thank you very much, Aunty Marlene. (*She opens a present. It is the dress from Act I, new.*) Oh look, Mum, isn't it lovely?

MARLENE. I don't know if it's the right size. She's grown up since I saw her. / I knew she was always

ANGIE. Isn't it lovely?

MARLENE. tall for her age.

JOYCE. She's a big lump.

MARLENE. Hold it up, Angie, let's see.

ANGIE. I'll put it on, shall I?

MARLENE. Yes, try it on.

JOYCE. Go to your room then, we don't want / a strip show thank you.

ANGIE. Of course I'm going to my room, what do you think? Look Mum, here's something for you. Open it, go on. What is it? Can I open it for you?

JOYCE. Yes, you open it, pet.

ANGIE. Don't you want to open it yourself? / Go on.

JOYCE. I don't mind, you can do it.

ANGIE. It's something hard. It's—what is it? A bottle. Drink is it? No, it's what? Perfume, look. What a lot. Open it, look, let's smell it. Oh it's strong. It's lovely. Put it on me. How do you do it? Put it on me.

JOYCE. You're too young.

ANGIE. I can play wearing it like dressing up.

JOYCE. And you're too old for that. Here, give it here, I'll do it, you'll tip the whole bottle over yourself / and we'll have you smelling all summer.

ANGIE. Put it on you. Do I smell? Put it on Aunty too. Put it on Aunty too. Let's all smell.

MARLENE. I didn't know what you'd like.

JOYCE. There's no danger I'd have it already, / that's one thing.

ANGIE. Now we all smell the same.

MARLENE. It's a bit of nonsense.

JOYCE. It's very kind of you Marlene, you shouldn't.

ANGIE. Now I'll put on the dress and then we'll see. (*Angie goes.*)

JOYCE. You've caught me on the hop with the place in a mess. / If you'd let me

MARLENE. That doesn't matter.

JOYCE. know you was coming I'd have got something in to eat. We had our dinner dinnertime. We're just going to have a cup of tea. You could have an egg.

MARLENE. No, I'm not hungry. Tea's fine.

JOYCE. I don't expect you take sugar.

MARLENE. Why not?

JOYCE. You take care of yourself.

MARLENE. How do you mean you didn't know I was coming?

JOYCE. You could have written. I know we're not on the phone but we're not completely in the dark ages, / we do have a postman.

MARLENE. But you asked me to come.

JOYCE. How did I ask you to come?

MARLENE. Angie said when she phoned up.

JOYCE. Angie phoned up, did she?

MARLENE. Was it just Angie's idea?

JOYCE. What did she say?

MARLENE. She said you wanted me to come and see you. / It was a couple of

JOYCE. Ha.

MARLENE. weeks ago. How was I to know that's a ridiculous idea? My diary's always full a couple of weeks ahead so we fixed it for this weekend. I was meant to get here earlier but I was held up. She gave me messages from you.

JOYCE. Didn't you wonder why I didn't phone you myself.

MARLENE. She said you didn't like using the phone. You're shy on the phone and can't use it. I don't know what you're like, do I.

JOYCE. Are there people who can't use the phone?

MARLENE. I expect so.

JOYCE. I haven't met any.

MARLENE. Why should I think she was lying?

JOYCE. Because she's like what she's like.

MARLENE. How do I know / what she's like?

JOYCE. It's not my fault you don't know what she's like. You never come and see her.

MARLENE. Well I have now / and you don't seem over the moon.*

JOYCE. Good. *Well I'd have got a cake if she'd told me. (Pause.)

MARLENE. I did wonder why you wanted to see me.

JOYCE. I didn't want to see you.

MARLENE. Yes, I know. Shall I go?

JOYCE. I don't mind seeing you.

MARLENE. Great, I feel really welcome.

JOYCE. You can come and see Angie any time you like, I'm not stopping you. / You know where we are. You're the one went away, not me. I'm right here where I was. And will be a few years yet I shouldn't wonder.

MARLENE. All right. All right. (Joyce gives Marlene a cup of tea.)

JOYCE. Tea.

MARLENE. Sugar? (Joyce passes Marlene the sugar.) It's very quiet down here.

JOYCE. I expect you'd notice it.

MARLENE. The air smells different too.

JOYCE. That's the scent.

MARLENE. No, I mean walking down the lane.

JOYCE. What sort of air you get in London then?

(Angie comes in, wearing the dress. It fits.)

MARLENE. Oh, very pretty. / You do look pretty, Angie.

JOYCE. That fits all right.

MARLENE. Do you like the color?

ANGIE. Beautiful. Beautiful.

JOYCE. You better take it off, / you'll get it dirty.

ANGIE. I want to wear it. I want to wear it.

MARLENE. It is for wearing after all. You can't just hang it up and look at it.

ANGIE. I love it.

JOYCE. Well if you must you must.

ANGIE. If someone asks me what's my favorite colour I'll tell them it's this. Thank you very much, Aunty Marlene.

MARLENE. You didn't tell your mum you asked me down.

ANGIE. I wanted it to be a surprise.

JOYCE. I'll give you a surprise / one of these days.

ANGIE. I thought you'd like to see her. She hasn't been here since I was nine. People do see their aunts.

MARLENE. Is it that long? Doesn't time fly?

ANGIE. I wanted to.

JOYCE. I'm not cross.

ANGIE. Are you glad?

JOYCE. I smell nicer anyhow, don't I?

(Kit comes in without saying anything, as if she lived there.)

MARLENE. I think it was a good idea, Angie, about time. We are sisters after all. It's a pity to let that go.

JOYCE. This is Kitty, / who lives up the road. This is Angie's Aunty Marlene.

KIT. What's that?

ANGIE. It's a present. Do you like it?

KIT. It's all right. / Are you coming out?*

MARLENE. Hello, Kitty.

ANGIE. *No.

KIT. What's that smell?

ANGIE. It's a present.

KIT. It's horrible. Come on.*

MARLENE. Have a chocolate.

ANGIE. *No, I'm busy.

KIT. Coming out later?

ANGIE. No.

KIT (to Marlene). Hello. (Kit goes without a chocolate.)

JOYCE. She's a little girl Angie sometimes plays with because she's the only child lives really close. She's like a little sister to her really. Angie's good with little children.

MARLENE. Do you want to work with children, Angie? / Be a teacher or a nursery nurse?

JOYCE. I don't think she's ever thought of it.

MARLENE. What do you want to do?

JOYCE. She hasn't an idea in her head what she wants to do. / Lucky to get anything.

MARLENE. Angie?

JOYCE. She's not clever like you. (Pause.)

MARLENE. I'm not clever, just pushy.

JOYCE. True enough. (Marlene takes a bottle of whisky out of the bag.) I don't drink spirits.

ANGIE. You do at Christmas.

JOYCE. It's not Christmas, is it?

ANGIE. It's better than Christmas.

MARLENE. Glasses?

JOYCE. Just a small one then.

MARLENE. Do you want some, Angie?

ANGIE. I can't, can I?

JOYCE. Taste it if you want. You won't like it. (Angie tastes it.)

MARLENE. We got drunk together the night your grandfather died.

JOYCE. We did not get drunk.

MARLENE. I got drunk. You were just overcome with grief.

JOYCE. I still keep up the grave with flowers.

MARLENE. Do you really?

JOYCE. Why wouldn't I?

MARLENE. Have you seen Mother?

JOYCE. Of course I've seen Mother.

MARLENE. I mean lately.

JOYCE. Of course I've seen her lately, I go every Thursday.

MARLENE (to Angie). Do you remember your grandfather?

ANGIE. He got me out of the bath one night in a towel.

MARLENE. Did he? I don't think he ever gave me a bath. Did he give you a bath, Joyce? He probably got soft in his old age. Did you like him?

ANGIE. Yes of course.

MARLENE. Why?

ANGIE. What?

MARLENE. So what's the news? How's Mrs. Paisley? Still going crazily? / And Dorothy. What happened to Dorothy?*

ANGIE. Who's Mrs. Paisley?

JOYCE. *She went to Canada.

MARLENE. Did she? What to do?

JOYCE. I don't know. She just went to Canada.

MARLENE. Well / good for her.

ANGIE. Mr. Connolly killed his wife.

MARLENE. What, Connolly at Whitegates?

ANGIE. They found her body in the garden. / Under the cabbages.

MARLENE. He was always so proper.

JOYCE. Stuck up git. Connolly. Best lawyer money could buy but he couldn't get out of it. She was carrying on with Matthew.

MARLENE. How old's Matthew then?

JOYCE. Twenty-one. / He's got a motorbike.

MARLENE. I think he's about six.

ANGIE. How can he be six? He's six years older than me. / If he was six I'd be nothing, I'd be just born this minute.

JOYCE. Your aunty knows that, she's just being silly. She means it's so long since she's been here she's forgotten about Matthew.

ANGIE. You were here for my birthday when I was nine. I had a pink cake. Kit was only five then, she was four, she hadn't started school yet. She could read already when she went to school. You remember my birthday? / You remember me?

MARLENE. Yes, I remember the cake.

ANGIE. You remember me?

MARLENE. Yes, I remember you.

ANGIE. And Mum and Dad was there, and Kit was.

MARLENE. Yes, how is your dad? Where is he tonight? Up the pub?

JOYCE. No, he's not here.

MARLENE. I can see he's not here.

JOYCE. He moved out.

MARLENE. What? When did he? / Just recently?*

ANGIE. Didn't you know that? You don't know much.

JOYCE. *No, it must be three years ago. Don't be rude, Angie.

ANGIE. I'm not, am I Aunty? What else don't you know?

JOYCE. You was in America or somewhere. You sent a postcard.

ANGIE. I've got that in my room. It's the Grand Canyon. Do you want to see it? Shall I get it? I can get it for you.

MARLENE. Yes, all right. (Angie goes.)

JOYCE. You could be married with twins for all I know. You must have affairs and break up and I don't need to know about any of that so I don't see what the fuss is about.

MARLENE. What fuss? (Angie comes back with the postcard.)

ANGIE. "Driving across the states for a new job in L. A. It's a long way but the car goes very fast. It's very hot. Wish you were here. Love from Aunty Marlene."

JOYCE. Did you make a lot of money?

MARLENE. I spent a lot.

ANGIE. I want to go to America. Will you take me?

JOYCE. She's not going to America, she's been to America, stupid.

ANGIE. She might go again, stupid. It's not something you do once. People who go keep going all the time, back and forth on jets. They go on Concorde and Laker and get jet lag. Will you take me?

MARLENE. I'm not planning a trip.

ANGIE. Will you let me know?

JOYCE. Angie, / you're getting silly.

ANGIE. I want to be American.

JOYCE. It's time you were in bed.

ANGIE. No it's not. / I don't have to go to bed at all tonight.

JOYCE. School in the morning.

ANGIE. I'll wake up.

JOYCE. Come on now, you know how you get.

ANGIE. How do I get? / I don't get anyhow.*

JOYCE. Angie. *Are you staying the night?

MARLENE. Yes, if that's all right. / I'll see you in the morning.

ANGIE. You can have my bed. I'll sleep on the sofa.

JOYCE. You will not, you'll sleep in your bed. / Think

ANGIE. Mum.

JOYCE. I can't see through that? I can just see you going to sleep / with us talking.

ANGIE. I would, I would go to sleep, I'd love that.

JOYCE. I'm going to get cross, Angie.

ANGIE. I want to show her something.

JOYCE. Then bed.

ANGIE. It's a secret.

JOYCE. Then I expect it's in your room so off you go. Give us a shout when you're ready for bed and your aunty'll be up and see you.

ANGIE. Will you?

MARLENE. Yes of course. (Angie goes. Silence.) It's cold tonight.

JOYCE. Will you be all right on the sofa? You can / have my bed.

MARLENE. The sofa's fine.

JOYCE. Yes the forecast said rain tonight but it's held off.

MARLENE. I was going to walk down to the estuary but I've left it a bit late. Is it just the same?

JOYCE. They cut down the hedges a few years back. Is that since you were here?

MARLENE. But it's not changed down the end, all the mud? And the reeds? We used to pick them up when they were bigger than us. Are there still lapwings?

JOYCE. You get strangers walking there on a Sunday. I expect they're looking at the mud and the lapwings, yes.

MARLENE. You could have left.

JOYCE. Who says I wanted to leave?

MARLENE. Stop getting at me then, you're really boring.

JOYCE. How could I have left?

MARLENE. Did you want to?

JOYCE. I said how, / how could I?

MARLENE. If you'd wanted to you'd have done it.

JOYCE. Christ.

MARLENE. Are we getting drunk?

JOYCE. Do you want something to eat?

MARLENE. No, I'm getting drunk.

JOYCE. Funny time to visit, Sunday evening.

MARLENE. I came this morning. I spent the day—

ANGIE (off). Aunty! Aunty Marlene!

MARLENE. I'd better go.

JOYCE. Go on then.

MARLENE. All right.

ANGIE (off). Aunty! Can you hear me? I'm ready.

(Marlene goes. Joyce goes on sitting, clears up, sits again. Marlene comes back.)

JOYCE. So what's the secret?

MARLENE. It's a secret.

JOYCE. I know what it is anyway.

MARLENE. I bet you don't. You always said that.

JOYCE. It's her exercise book.

MARLENE. Yes, but you don't know what's in it.

JOYCE. It's some game, some secret society she has with Kit.

MARLENE. You don't know the password. You don't know the code.

JOYCE. You're really in it, aren't you. Can you do the handshake?

MARLENE. She didn't mention a handshake.

JOYCE. I thought they'd have a special handshake. She spends hours writing that but she's useless at school. She copies things out of books about black magic, and politicians out of the paper. It's a bit childish.

MARLENE. I think it's a plot to take over the world.

JOYCE. She's been in the remedial class the last two years.

MARLENE. I came up this morning and spent the day in Ipswich. I went to see mother.

JOYCE. Did she recognize you?

MARLENE. Are you trying to be funny?

JOYCE. No, she does wander.

MARLENE. She wasn't wandering at all, she was very lucid thank you.

JOYCE. You were very lucky then.

MARLENE. Fucking awful life she's had.

JOYCE. Don't tell me.

MARLENE. Fucking waste.

JOYCE. Don't talk to me.

MARLENE. Why shouldn't I talk? Why shouldn't I talk to you? / Isn't she my mother too?

JOYCE. Look, you've left, you've gone away, / we can do without you.

MARLENE. I left home, so what, I left home. People do leave home / it is normal.

JOYCE. We understand that, we can do without you.

MARLENE. We weren't happy. Were you happy?

JOYCE. Don't come back.

MARLENE. So it's just your mother is it, your child, you never wanted me round, / you were jealous

JOYCE. Here we go.

MARLENE. of me because I was the little one and I was clever.

JOYCE. I'm not clever enough for all this psychology / if that's what it is.

MARLENE. Why can't I visit my own family / without

JOYCE. Aah.

MARLENE. all this?

JOYCE. Just don't go on about Mum's life when you haven't been to see her for how many years. / I go

MARLENE. It's up to me.

JOYCE. and see her every week.

MARLENE. Then don't go and see her every week.

JOYCE. Somebody has to.

MARLENE. No they don't. / Why do they?

JOYCE. How would I feel if I didn't go?

MARLENE. A lot better.

JOYCE. I hope you feel better.

MARLENE. It's up to me.

JOYCE. You couldn't get out of here fast enough. (*Pause.*)

MARLENE. Of course I couldn't get out of here fast enough. What was I going to do? Marry a dairyman who'd come home pissed? / Don't you fucking this

JOYCE. Christ.

MARLENE. fucking that fucking bitch fucking tell me what to fucking do fucking.

JOYCE. I don't know how you could leave your own child.

MARLENE. You were quick enough to take her.

JOYCE. What does that mean?

MARLENE. You were quick enough to take her.

JOYCE. Or what? Have her put in a home? Have some stranger / take her would you rather?

MARLENE. You couldn't have one so you took mine.

JOYCE. I didn't know that then.

MARLENE. Like hell, / married three years.

JOYCE. I didn't know that. Plenty of people / take that long.

MARLENE. Well it turned out lucky for you, didn't it?

JOYCE. Turned out all right for you by the look of you. You'd be getting a few less thousand a year.

MARLENE. Not necessarily.

JOYCE. You'd be stuck here / like you said.

MARLENE. I could have taken her with me.

JOYCE. You didn't want to take her with you. It's no good coming back now, Marlene, / and saying—

MARLENE. I know a managing director who's got two children, she breast feeds in the board room, she pays a hundred pounds a week on domestic help alone and she can afford that because she's an extremely high-powered lady earning a great deal of money.

JOYCE. So what's that got to do with you at the age of seventeen?

MARLENE. Just because you were married and had somewhere to live—

JOYCE. You could have lived at home. / Or live

MARLENE. Don't be stupid.

JOYCE. with me and Frank. / You

MARLENE. You never suggested.

JOYCE. said you weren't keeping it. You shouldn't have had it / if you wasn't

MARLENE. Here we go.

JOYCE. going to keep it. You was the most stupid, / for someone so clever you was the most stupid, get yourself pregnant, not go to the doctor, not tell.

MARLENE. You wanted it, you said you were glad, I remember the day, you said I'm glad you never got rid of it, I'll look after it, you said that down by the river. So what are you saying, sunshine, you don't want her?

JOYCE. Course I'm not saying that.

MARLENE. Because I'll take her, / wake her up and pack now.

JOYCE. You wouldn't know how to begin to look after her.

MARLENE. Don't you want her?

JOYCE. Course I do, she's my child.

MARLENE. Then why are you going on about / why did I have her?

JOYCE. You said I got her off you / when you didn't—

MARLENE. I said you were lucky / the way it—

JOYCE. Have a child now if you want one. You're not old.

MARLENE. I might do.

JOYCE. Good. (Pause.)

MARLENE. I've been on the pill so long / I'm probably sterile.

JOYCE. Listen when Angie was six months I did get pregnant and I lost it because I was so tired looking after your fucking baby / because she cried so

MARLENE. You never told me.

JOYCE. much—yes I did tell you— / and the doctor

MARLENE. Well I forgot.

JOYCE. said if I'd sat down all day with my feet up I'd've kept it / and that's the only chance I ever had because after that—

MARLENE. I've had two abortions, are you interested? Shall I tell you about them? Well I won't, it's boring, it wasn't a problem. I don't like messy talk about blood / and what a bad time we all had.

JOYCE. If I hadn't had your baby. The doctor said.

MARLENE. I don't want a baby. I don't want to talk about gynaecology.

JOYCE. Then stop trying to get Angie off of me.

MARLENE. I come down here after six years. All night you've been saying I don't come often enough. If I don't come for another six years she'll be twenty-one, will that be OK?

JOYCE. That'll be fine, yes, six years would suit me fine. (Pause.)

MARLENE. I was afraid of this. I only came because I thought you wanted . . . I just want . . . (She cries.)

JOYCE. Don't grizzle, Marlene, for God's sake. Marly? Come on, pet. Love you really. Fucking stop it, will you? (She goes to Marlene.)

MARLENE. No, let me cry. I like it. (They laugh. Marlene begins to stop crying.) I knew I'd cry if I wasn't careful.

JOYCE. Everyone's always crying in this house. Nobody takes any notice.

MARLENE. You've been wonderful looking after Angie.

JOYCE. Don't get carried away.

MARLENE. I can't write letters but I do think of you.

JOYCE. You're getting drunk. I'm going to make some tea.

MARLENE. Love you. (Joyce gets up to make tea.)

JOYCE. I can see why you'd want to leave. It's a dump here.

MARLENE. So what's this about you and Frank?

JOYCE. He was always carrying on, wasn't he? And if I wanted to go out in the evening he'd go mad, even if it was nothing, a class, I was going to go to an evening class. So he had this girlfriend, only twenty-two poor cow, and I said go on, off you go, hoppit. I don't think he even likes her.

MARLENE. So what about money?

JOYCE. I've always said I don't want your money.

MARLENE. No, does he send you money?

JOYCE. I've got four different cleaning jobs. Adds up. There's not a lot round here.

MARLENE. Does Angie miss him?

JOYCE. She doesn't say.

MARLENE. Does she see him?

JOYCE. He was never that fond of her to be honest.

MARLENE. He tried to kiss me once. When you were engaged.

JOYCE. Did you fancy him?

MARLENE. No, he looked like a fish.

JOYCE. He was lovely then.

MARLENE. Ugh.

JOYCE. Well I fancied him. For about three years.

MARLENE. Have you got someone else?

JOYCE. There's not a lot round here. Mind you, the minute you're on your own, you'd be amazed how your friends' husbands drop by. I'd sooner do without.

MARLENE. I don't see why you couldn't take my money.

JOYCE. I do, so don't bother about it.

MARLENE. Only got to ask.

JOYCE. So what about you? Good job?

MARLENE. Good for a laugh. / Got back

JOYCE. Good for more than a laugh I should think.

MARLENE. from the US of A a bit wiped out and slotted into this speedy employment agency and still there.

JOYCE. You can always find yourself work then.

MARLENE. That's right.

JOYCE. And men?

MARLENE. Oh there's always men.

JOYCE. No one special?

MARLENE. There's fellas who like to be seen with a high-flying lady. Shows they've got something really good in their pants. But they can't take the day to day. They're waiting for me to turn into the little woman. Or maybe I'm just horrible of course.

JOYCE. Who needs them?

MARLENE. Who needs them? Well I do. But I need adventures more. So on on into the sunset. I think the eighties are going to be stupendous.

JOYCE. Who for?

MARLENE. For me. / I think I'm going up up up.

JOYCE. Oh for you. Yes, I'm sure they will.

MARLENE. And for the country, come to that. Get the economy back on its feet and whosh. She's a tough lady, Maggie. I'd give her a job. / She just needs to hang

JOYCE. You voted for them, did you?

MARLENE. in there. This country needs to stop whining. / Monetarism is not

JOYCE. Drink your tea and shut up, pet.

MARLENE. stupid. It takes time, determination. No more slop. / And

JOYCE. Well I think they're filthy bastards.

MARLENE. who's got to drive it on? First woman prime minister. Terrifico. Aces. Right on. / You must admit. Certainly gets my vote.

JOYCE. What good's first women if it's her? I suppose you'd have liked Hitler if he was a woman. Ms. Hitler. Got a lot done, Hitlerina. / Great adventures.

MARLENE. Bosses still walking on the workers' faces? Still Dadda's little parrot? Haven't you learned to think for yourself? I believe in the individual. Look at me.

JOYCE. I am looking at you.

MARLENE. Come on, Joyce, we're not going to quarrel over politics.

JOYCE. We are through.

MARLENE. Forget I mentioned it. Not a word about the slimy unions will cross my lips. (*Pause.*)

JOYCE. You say Mother had a wasted life.

MARLENE. Yes I do. Married to that bastard.

JOYCE. What sort of life did he have? /

MARLENE. Violent life?

JOYCE. Working in the fields like an animal. / Why

MARLENE. Come off it.

JOYCE. wouldn't he want a drink? You want a drink. He couldn't afford whisky.

MARLENE. I don't want to talk about him.

JOYCE. You started, I was talking about her. She had a rotten life because she had nothing. She went hungry.

MARLENE. She was hungry because he drank the money. / He used to hit her.

JOYCE. It's not all down to him. / Their

MARLENE. She didn't hit him.

JOYCE. lives were rubbish. They were treated like rubbish. He's dead and she'll die soon and what sort of life / did they have?

MARLENE. I saw him one night. I came down.

JOYCE. Do you think I didn't? / They

MARLENE. I still have dreams.

JOYCE. didn't get to America and drive across it in a fast car. / Bad nights, they had bad days. I knew when I

MARLENE. America, America, you're jealous. / I had to get out,

JOYCE. Jealous?

MARLENE. was thirteen, out of their house, out of them, never let that happen to me, / never let him, make my own way, out.

JOYCE. Jealous of what you've done, you'd be ashamed of me if I came to your office, your smart friends, wouldn't you, I'm ashamed of you, think of nothing but yourself, you've got on, nothing's changed for most people / has it?

MARLENE. I hate the working class / which is what

JOYCE. Yes you do.

MARLENE. you're going to go on about now, it doesn't exist any more, it means lazy and stupid. / I don't

JOYCE. Come on, now we're getting it.

MARLENE. like the way they talk. I don't like beer guts and football vomit and saucy tits / and brothers and sisters—

JOYCE. I spit when I see a Rolls Royce, scratch it with my ring / Mercedes it was

MARLENE. Oh very mature—

JOYCE. I hate the cows I work for / and their dirty dishes with blanquette of fucking veau.

MARLENE. and I will not be pulled down to their level by a flying picket and I won't be sent to Siberia / or a loony bin just because I'm original. And I support

JOYCE. No, you'll be on a yacht, you'll be head of Coca-Cola and you wait, the eighties is going to be stupendous all right because we'll get you lot off our backs—

MARLENE. Reagan even if he is a lousy movie star because the reds are swarming up his map and I want to be free in a free world—

JOYCE. What? / What?

MARLENE. I know what I mean / by that—not shut up here.

JOYCE. So don't be round here when it happens because if someone's kicking you I'll just laugh. (*Silence.*)

MARLENE. I don't mean anything personal. I don't believe in class. Anyone can do anything if they've got what it takes.

JOYCE. And if they haven't.

MARLENE. If they're stupid or lazy or frightened, I'm not going to help them get a job, why should I?

JOYCE. What about Angie?

MARLENE. What about Angie?

JOYCE. She's stupid, lazy and frightened, so what about her?

MARLENE. You run her down too much. She'll be all right.

Act 2, Scene 2

JOYCE. I don't expect so, no. I expect her children will say what a wasted life she had. If she has children. Because nothing's changed and it won't with them in.

MARLENE. Them, them. / Us and them?

JOYCE. And you're one of them.

MARLENE. And you're us, wonderful us, and Angie's us / and Mum and Dad's us.

JOYCE. Yes, that's right, and you're them.

MARLENE. Come on, Joyce, what a night. You've got what it takes.

JOYCE. I know I have.

MARLENE. I didn't really mean all that.

JOYCE. I did.

MARLENE. But we're friends anyway.

JOYCE. I don't think so, no.

MARLENE. Well it's lovely to be out in the country. I really must make the effort to come more often. I want to go to sleep. I want to go to sleep. (*Joyce gets blankets for the sofa.*)

JOYCE. Goodnight then. I hope you'll be warm enough.

MARLENE. Goodnight. Joyce—

JOYCE. No, pet. Sorry. (*Joyce goes. Marlene sits wrapped in a blanket and has another drink. Angie comes in.*)

ANGIE. Mum?

MARLENE. Angie? What's the matter?

ANGIE. Mum?

MARLENE. No, she's gone to bed. It's Aunty Marlene.

ANGIE. Frightening.

MARLENE. Did you have a bad dream? What happened in it? Well you're awake now, aren't you pet?

ANGIE. Frightening.

ANGELS IN AMERICA, PART ONE: MILLENNIUM APPROACHES
TONY KUSHNER

TONY KUSHNER (1956–)

Although he was born in Manhattan, Tony Kushner was raised in Lake Charles, Louisiana, a conservative southern town. As a Jew and a homosexual (which he did not openly acknowledge until he was in college), he knew too well the effects of prejudice against people who are "different." The son of classical musicians, Kushner found solace in the arts, especially the theater. Kushner left Louisiana to attend Columbia University in New York, where he studied medieval art, literature, and philosophy. As a student he attended the theater frequently and was drawn to the experimental work of such directors as Richard Foreman, JoAnne Akalaitis, and Charles Ludlam (an early champion of gay theater). From Foreman and Akalaitis he learned the power of the visual image; Ludlam's "theater of the ridiculous" taught him a freedom of form in which a variety of styles could be mixed to maximize theatrical effect. His work fuses Brecht's political theater with the narrative and psychological tradition of O'Neill and Williams. His universe extends from heaven to earth (including Antarctica), and mixes the metaphysical with the mundane to form what he calls "the theater of the fabulous."

While completing an MFA in stage direction at New York University, Kushner took a job as a switchboard operator. When not answering phones, he worked on a draft of his first play, *A Bright Room Called Day*, about the rise of Nazism. At the suggestion of his friend and mentor, Oskar Eustis (of San Francisco's Eureka Theater), Kushner began writing *Angels in America* in 1988. The first part, *Millennium Approaches*, won the Pulitzer Prize in drama in 1993; *Millennium Approaches* and *Perestroika*, a sequel, won successive Tony Awards (1993 and 1994) for best play, unprecedented in the history of the Tonys. The combined works have been performed throughout the world and have won virtually every accolade that can be given a play. The academic community has also canonized the play, about which at least two major compendiums of critical essays have already been published. Robert Altman, whose cinematic style is an admitted influence on Kushner, wishes to direct a film version of the work.

Kushner has continued his exploration of personal dilemmas amid global politics with *Slavs!* and *The Dybbuk*. He has also adapted Corneille's seventeenth-century drama *The Illusion*. Kushner lives in Manhattan, but the worldwide popularity of *Angels in America* has made him, in effect, an international citizen.

ANGELS IN AMERICA, PART ONE: MILLENNIUM APPROACHES (1992)

Although *Angels in America* has emerged as the most decorated and widely accepted play about gays, it is not the first to explore the subject sympathetically. As early as 1592 Christopher Marlowe wrote about the relationship between King Edward II and Piers Gaveston in *Edward II*. Shakespeare addresses the subject in *Troilus and Cressida* in the Achilles-Patroclus subplot, and a number of recent studies explore homoeroticism in his works. Subsequent playwrights, such as Oscar Wilde, Tennessee Williams, and Edward Albee (all known homosexuals), have included gays and gay issues in their works. But these works are not generally considered "gay plays" in the manner we recognize *Angels in America* as such.

Mart Crowley's *The Boys in the Band* (1968) was the first Broadway play to place the gay community and its distinctive subculture at center stage. Crowley's success paved the way for such respected playwrights as Terrence McNally, Harvey Fierstein, and Lanford Wilson. Gay musicals, such as *La Cage Aux Folles* (*The Bird Cage*, 1983), were also accepted within Broadway's mainstream. The AIDS crisis, which surfaced in the early 1980s, prompted several respected plays, most notably Larry Kramer's *The Normal Heart* and William Hoffman's *As Is*. By 1993 the American mainstream eagerly embraced *Angels in America*, not as a trailblazer, but as a necessary play about the state of the union as it entered the third millennium.

Kushner has subtitled his two-part, seven-hour epic "a gay fantasia on national themes." The themes in question concern the AIDS crisis; religious, racial, and sexual bigotry; drug addiction; and contemporary American politics, specifically the "conservative revolution" fostered by the Reagan presidency. Kushner attacks the belief that it is "OK to be AIDS-phobic and homophobic," and he advocates federal intervention to achieve equal rights for gays and lesbians. Although *Millennium Approaches* is a play about despair (and can be appreciated as a work unto itself), its sequel, *Perestroika*, ends with what Kushner calls "great quiet and hope." *Perestroika* is a Russian term coined by former premier Gorbachev to describe a major change in political attitudes. In it, Kushner has found "a more perfect metaphor for human change than it was in the heady days of 1990, when the world seemed to have miraculously transformed." Hence, the hope that pervades *Perestroika*.

The success of *Angels in America*, however, transcends its political message ("I don't think art is a public service announcement," Kushner says). Rather, its appeal is attributable to its audacious scope, its extraordinary mixture of styles, and ultimately its sympathetic portrait of people—straight as well as gay—who suffer unbearable loneliness, uncertainty, and pain.

Angels in America is a virtual casebook of contemporary—specifically postmodern—theatrical technique:

- It is episodic, even cinematic, in structure. Events fade, blur, and merge into one another, and often occur simultaneously. One set of characters discusses an issue that is echoed by another conversation in a different locale. See especially act 2, scene 9, which, according to Kushner, should be played "fast and obviously furious; overlapping is fine; the proceedings may be a little confusing but not the final result."
- Locales—Salt Lake City, Washington, D.C., the Arctic Circle, and Central Europe, even heaven itself—segue into one another almost seamlessly. One senses that the whole world, if not the universe, is in disarray.
- The public world of history overlaps the private world of the individual (a rather Shakespearean concept); ultimately, the history of America at the end of the millennium is the history of individuals in conflict with personal as well as larger social issues.
- Kushner freely mixes styles and genres. The issues are serious, nearly tragic, yet comedy in all its forms dominates the play. Even as Prior lies dying of AIDS, Belize, a campy ex–drag queen, upstages the action. Realism, Expressionism, fantasy, agitprop, vaudeville sketch, and—most importantly—grand theatricality meld to create one of the most ambitious plays in the history of the American theater.
- Actors are asked to play multiple roles. The actor who plays the angel is also seen, quite deliberately, as the homeless lady in the South Bronx, the grotesquely hilarious real estate saleswoman in Salt Lake City, and the nurse. One actor plays a man (Rabbi Chemelwitz) and a woman (Hannah), a Jew and a Christian. We see variants on the same character simultaneously: the dying Prior is visited by his ancestors, a medieval monk and a fop out of the Restoration theater.
- Pop culture (i.e., references to entertainers such as Judy Garland and Steven Spielberg) complements Marxist political tracts, biblical allusions, and other notable literature; vulgarity coexists with some of the most poetic stage language since Tennessee Williams. The result is a multilayered text that defies categorization.
- Despite its much-praised language, the play's most memorable moments are visual, even ritualistic: the descent of a single feather from on high, the eruption of a sacred book from the bowels of the earth, and, most famously, the apparition of the angel with "magnificent . . . steel-gray wings" in the final moment. Kushner's is very much "a theater of images."

Kushner's multifaceted dramaturgy, heightened by an inventive showmanship absent from most recent nonmusical theater, creates an ambience that transcends the particular "national themes" he explores. By mixing styles and theatrical effects, the play emerges as something more profound than a contemporary political tract. Its use of archetypes, most notably the Angel of Death and her intimations of "the Continental Principality of America," extends the parameters of the playwright's message that "everywhere things are collapsing."

For all its postmodern sensibilities, *Angels in America* emerges as a very traditional play in its treatment of human isolation. It is the legitimate successor of the works of O'Neill and Williams, especially in its psychological (and perhaps autobiographical) portraiture. Kushner's drama follows a cross-section of tormented Americans in the waning years of the millennium. Joe and Harper Pitt, staid Mormons, must confront their sexuality and mental deterioration (Harper's Valium-induced hallucinations are among the most troubling—and comic—in the play). Joe's mother, Hannah, can confront her son's dilemma only by denying it. Similarly, Louis, Prior's lover, chooses to leave his dying companion rather than face the reality of their situation. The scenes shared by this quartet of lovers are the most moving in the play.

The play is dominated by the specter of an actual historical figure, Roy Cohn (1927–1986), a lawyer who worked for the infamous Joseph McCarthy during the "Red scare" witch-hunts of the 1950s. Cohn was the prosecutor in the famous cold-war trial of Julius and Ethel Rosenberg, accused of treason; Cohn won his (still controversial) case, and the Rosenbergs were sentenced to death and executed. One of Kushner's masterstrokes is a scene in which Ethel Rosenberg's spirit visits Cohn as he is dying. Later Cohn worked in the Nixon administration and became a symbol among liberals of the cruel, dispassionate attitudes they associated with conservative Republicans. Kushner's Cohn—whom he describes as "a dramatic fiction"—is simultaneously the most reprehensible and pitiful character in the play. He is dying of AIDS, yet he denies reality ("It's just liver cancer"). He does not want to be branded as a homosexual because homosexuals are—in his mind—"only weak men who in fifteen years of trying cannot get a pissant antidiscrimination bill through City Council." In his twisted logic, he is "a heterosexual man . . . who fucks around with guys." In Kushner's mind, Cohn is the quintessential hypocrite who justifies his ruthless actions as serving the public good, even as he practices the very acts he condemns. Cohn is the dark angel hovering over the American landscape, and his hypocrisy is seen as more destructive than Harper's drug addiction, Joe's sexual ambiguity, Louis's callousness toward his dying lover, or the purportedly indecent acts committed by consenting adults. It is Cohn's ambiguity and contradictions that make his the most memorable and disturbing role in a memorable and disturbing play.

The Angel descends over Prior's deathbed in the theatrically stunning climax of Angels in America, *Part One:* Millennium Approaches.

ANGELS IN AMERICA, PART ONE: MILLENNIUM APPROACHES

—TONY KUSHNER—

THE CHARACTERS

ROY M. COHN, *a successful New York lawyer and unofficial power broker.*

JOSEPH PORTER PITT, *chief clerk for Justice Theodore Wilson of the Federal Court of Appeals, Second Circuit.*

HARPER AMATY PITT, *Joe's wife, an agoraphobic with a mild Valium addiction.*

LOUIS IRONSON, *a word processor working for the Second Circuit Court of Appeals.*

PRIOR WALTER, *Louis's boyfriend. Occasionally works as a club*

designer or caterer, otherwise lives very modestly but with great style off a small trust fund.

HANNAH PORTER PITT, *Joe's mother, currently residing in Salt Lake City, living off her deceased husband's army pension.*

BELIZE, *a former drag queen and former lover of Prior's. A registered nurse. Belize's name was originally Norman Arriaga; Belize is a drag name that stuck.*

THE ANGEL, *four divine emanations, Fluor, Phosphor, Lumen, and Candle; manifest in One: the Continental Principality of America. She was magnificent in steel-gray wings.*

OTHER CHARACTERS IN PART ONE

RABBI ISIDOR CHEMELWITZ, *an orthodox Jewish rabbi, played by the actor playing Hannah.*

MR. LIES, *Harper's imaginary friend, a travel agent, who in style of dress and speech suggests a jazz musician; he always wears a large lapel badge emblazoned "IOTA" (The International Order of Travel Agents). He is played by the actor playing Belize.*

THE MAN IN THE PARK, *played by the actor playing Prior.*

THE VOICE, *the voice of The Angel.*

HENRY, *Roy's doctor, played by the actor playing Hannah.*

EMILY, *a nurse, played by the actor playing The Angel.*

MARTIN HELLER, *a Reagan Administration Justice Department flackman, played by the actor playing Harper.*

SISTER ELLA CHAPTER, *a Salt Lake City real-estate saleswoman, played by the actor playing The Angel.*

PRIOR 1, *the ghost of a dead Prior Walter from the 13th century, played by the actor playing Joe. He is a blunt, gloomy medieval farmer with a guttural Yorkshire accent.*

PRIOR 2, *the ghost of a dead Prior Walter from the 17th century, played by the actor playing Roy. He is a Londoner, sophisticated, with a High British accent.*

THE ESKIMO, *played by the actor playing Joe.*

THE WOMAN IN THE SOUTH BRONX, *played by the actor playing The Angel.*

ETHEL ROSENBERG, *played by the actor playing Hannah.*

PLAYWRIGHT'S NOTES

A DISCLAIMER

Roy M. Cohn, the character, is based on the late Roy M. Cohn (1927–1986), who was all too real; for the most part the acts attributed to the character Roy, such as his illegal conferences with Judge Kaufmann during the trial of Ethel Rosenberg, are to be found in the historical record. But this Roy is a work of dramatic fiction; his words are my invention, and liberties have been taken.

A NOTE ABOUT THE STAGING

The play benefits from a pared-down style of presentation, with minimal scenery and scene shifts done rapidly (no blackouts!), employing the cast as well as stagehands—which make for an actor-driven event, as this must be. The moments of magic—the appearance and disappearance of Mr. Lies and the ghosts, the Book hallucination, and the ending—are to be fully realized, as bits of wonderful theatrical illusion—which means it's OK if the wires show, and maybe it's good that they do, but the magic should at the same time be thoroughly amazing.

In a murderous time
the heart breaks and breaks
and lives by breaking.
  —Stanley Kunitz, "The Testing-Tree"

ACT ONE: BAD NEWS

October–November 1985

SCENE 1

The last days of October. Rabbi Isidor Chemelwitz alone onstage with a small coffin. It is a rough pine box with two wooden pegs, one at the foot and one at the head, holding the lid in place. A prayer shawl embroidered with a Star of David is draped over the lid, and by the head a yarzheit candle is burning.

RABBI ISIDORE CHEMELWITZ (*He speaks sonorously, with a heavy Eastern European accent, unapologetically consulting a sheet of notes for the family names*). Hello and good morning. I am Rabbi Isidor Chemelwitz of the Bronx Home for Aged Hebrews. We are here this morning to pay respects at the passing of Sarah Ironson, devoted wife of Benjamin Ironson, also deceased, loving and caring mother of her sons Morris, Abraham, and Samuel, and her daughters Esther and Rachel; beloved grandmother of Max, Mark, Louis, Lisa, Maria . . . uh . . . Lesley, Angela, Doris, Luke and Eric. (*Looks more closely at paper*) Eric? This is a Jewish name? (*Shrugs*) Eric. A large and loving family. We assemble that we may mourn collectively this good and righteous woman.

(*He looks at the coffin*)

This woman. I did not know this woman. I cannot accurately described her attributes, nor do justice to her dimensions. She was. . . . Well, in the Bronx Home of Aged Hebrews are many like this, the old, and to many I speak but not to be frank with this one. She preferred silence. So I do not know her and yet I know her. She was . . .

(*He touches the coffin*)

. . . not a person but a whole kind of person, the ones who crossed the ocean, who brought with us to America the villages of Russia and Lithuania—and how we struggled, and how we fought, for the family, for the Jewish home, so that you would not grow up here, in this strange place, in the melting pot where nothing melted. Descendants of this immigrant woman, you do not grow up in America,

you and your children and their children with the goyis-
che names. You do not live in America. No such place
exists. Your clay is the clay of some Litvak shtetl, your air
the air of the steppes—because she carried the old world
on her back across the ocean, in a boat, and she put it
down on Grand Concourse Avenue, or in Flatbush, and
she worked that earth into your bones, and you pass it to
your children, this ancient, ancient culture and home.

(*Little pause*)

You can never make that crossing that she made, for such
Great Voyages in this world do not any more exist. But
every day of your lives the miles that voyage between that
place and this one you cross. Every day. You understand
me? In you that journey is.
    So . . .
    She was the last of the Mohicans, this one was. Pretty
soon . . . all the old will be dead.

SCENE 2

*Same day. Roy and Joe in Roy's office. Roy at an impres-
sive desk, bare except for a very elaborate phone system,
rows and rows of flashing buttons which bleep and beep
and whistle incessantly, making chaotic music underneath
Roy's conversations. Joe is sitting, waiting. Roy conducts
business with great energy, impatience and sensual abandon: gesticulating, shouting, cajoling, crooning, playing
the phone, receiver and hold button with virtuosity and
love.*

ROY (*Hitting a button*). Hold. (*To Joe*) I wish I was an octo-
    pus, a fucking octopus. Eight loving arms and all those
    suckers. Know what I mean?
JOE. No, I . . .
ROY (*Gesturing to a deli platter of little sandwiches on his desk*).
    You want lunch?
JOE. Not, that's OK really I just . . .
ROY (*Hitting a button*). Ailene? Roy Cohn. Now what kind of
    a greeting is. . . . I thought we were friends, Ai. . . . Look
    Mrs. Soffer, you don't have to get. . . . You're upset. You're
    yelling. You'll aggravate your condition, you shouldn't yell,
    you'll pop little blood vessels in your face if you yell. . . . No
    that was a joke, Mrs. Soffer, I was joking. . . . I already apol-
    ogized sixteen times for that, Mrs. Soffer, you . . . (*While
    she's fulminating, Roy covers the mouthpiece with his hand and
    talks to Joe*) This'll take a minute, *eat* already, what is this
    tasty sandwich here it's—(*He takes a bite of a sandwich*)
    Mmmmm, liver or some. . . . Here.

(*He pitches the sandwich to Joe, who catches it and
returns it to the platter.*)

ROY (*Back to Mrs. Soffer*). Uh huh, uh huh. . . . No, I al-
    ready told you, it wasn't a vacation, it was business, Mrs.
    Soffer, I have clients in Haiti, Mrs. Soffer, I. . . . Listen,
    AILENE, YOU THINK I'M THE ONLY GODDAM
    LAWYER IN HISTORY EVER MISSED A COURT
    DATE? Don't make such a big fucking. . . . Hold. (*He hits
    the hold button*) You HAG!
JOE. If this is a bad time . . .
ROY. *Bad* time? This is a good time! (*Button*) Baby doll, get
    me. . . . Oh fuck, wait . . . (*Button, button*) Hello? Yah.
    Sorry to keep you holding, Judge Hollins, I. . . . Oh Mrs.
    Hollins, sorry dear deep voice you got. Enjoying your
    visit? (*Hands over mouthpiece again, to Joe*) She sounds
    like a truckdriver and he sounds like Kate Smith, very
    confusing. Nixon appointed him, all the geeks are Nixon
    appointees . . . (*To Mrs. Hollins*) Yeah yeah right good so
    how many tickets dear? Seven. For what, *Cats, 42nd
    Street*, what? No you wouldn't like *La Cage*, trust me, I
    know. Oh for godsake. . . . Hold. (*Button, button*) Baby
    doll, seven for *Cats* or something, anything hard to get, I
    don't give a fuck what and neither will they. (*Button; to
    Joe*) You see *La Cage*?
JOE. No I . . .
ROY. Fabulous. Best thing on Broadway. Maybe ever. (*but-
    ton*) Who? Aw, Jesus H. Christ, Harry, *no*, Harry, Judge
    John Francis Grimes, Manhattan Family Court. Do I
    have to do every goddam thing myself? *Touch* the bastard,
    Harry, and don't call me on this line again, I told you not
    to . . .
JOE (*Starting to get up*). Roy, uh, should I wait outside or . . .
ROY (*To Joe*). Oh sit. (*To Harry*) You hold. I pay you to hold
    fuck you Harry you jerk. (*Button*) Half-wit dick-brain.
    (*Instantly philosophical*) I see the universe, Joe, as a kind of
    sandstorm in outer space with winds of mega-hurricane
    velocity, but instead of grains of sand it's shards and splin-
    ters of glass. You ever feel that way? Ever have one of
    those days?
JOE. I'm not sure I . . .
ROY. So how's life in Appeals? How's the Judge?
JOE. He sends his best.
ROY. He's a good man. Loyal. Not the brightest man on the
    bench, but he has manners. And a nice head of silver
    hair.
JOE. He gives me a lot of responsibility.
ROY. Yeah, like writing his decisions and signing his name.
JOE. Well . . .
ROY. He's a nice guy. And you cover admirably.
JOE. Well, thanks, Roy, I . . .
ROY (*Button*). Yah? Who is *this*? Well who the fuck are *you*?
    Hold—(*Button*) Harry? Eighty-seven grand, something
    like that. Fuck him. Eat me. New Jersey, chain of porno
    film stores in, uh, Weehawken. That's—Harry, that's the
    beauty of the law. (*Button*) So, baby doll, what? *Cats*?
    Bleah. (*Button*) *Cats*! It's about cats. Singing cats, you'll

love it. Eight o'clock, the theatre's always at eight. (*Button*) Fucking tourists. (*Button, then to Joe*) Oh live a little, Joe, *eat* something for Christ sake—

JOE. Um, Roy, could you . . .

ROY. What? (*To Harry*) Hold a minute. (*Button*) Mrs. Soffer? Mrs. . . . . (*Button*) God-fucking-dammit to hell, where is . . .

JOE (*Overlapping*). Roy, I'd really appreciate it if . . .

ROY (*Overlapping*). Well she was here a minute ago, baby doll, see if . . .

(*The phone starts making three different beeping sounds, all at once.*)

ROY (*Smashing buttons*). Jesus fuck this goddam thing . . .

JOE (*Overlapping*). I really wish you wouldn't . . .

ROY (*Overlapping*). Baby doll? Ring the *Post* get me Suzy see if . . .

(*The phone starts whistling loudly.*)

ROY. CHRIST!

JOE. *Roy.*

ROY (*Into receiver*). Hold. (*Button; to Joe*) What?

JOE. Could you please not take the Lord's name in vain?

(*Pause*)

I'm sorry. But please. At least while I'm . . .

ROY (*Laughs, then*). Right. Sorry. Fuck.

Only in America. (*Punches a button*) Baby doll, tell 'em all to fuck off. Tell 'em I died. You handle Mrs. Soffer. Tell her it's on the way. Tell her I'm schtupping the judge. I'll call her back. I *will* call her. I know how much I borrowed. She's got four hundred times that stuffed up her. . . . Yeah, tell her I said that. (*Button. The phone is silent*)

So, Joe.

JOE. I'm sorry Roy, I just . . .

ROY. No no no no, principles count, I respect principles, I'm not religious but I like God and God likes me. Baptist, Catholic?

JOE. Mormon.

ROY. Mormon. Delectable. Absolutely. Only in America. So, Joe. Whattya think?

JOE. It's . . . well . . .

ROY. Crazy life.

JOE. Chaotic.

ROY. Well but God bless chaos. Right?

JOE. Ummm . . .

ROY. Huh. Mormons. I knew Mormons, in um, Nevada.

JOE. Utah, mostly.

ROY. No, these Mormons were in Vegas.

So. So, how'd you like to go to Washington and work for the Justice Department?

JOE. Sorry?

ROY. How'd you like to go to Washington and work for the Justice Department? All I gotta do is pick up the phone, talk to Ed, and you're in.

JOE. In . . . what, exactly?

ROY. Associate Assistant Something Big. Internal Affairs, heart of the woods, something nice with clout.

JOE. Ed . . . ?

ROY. Meese. The Attorney General.

JOE. Oh.

ROY. I just have to pick up the phone . . .

JOE. I have to think.

ROY. Of course.

(*Pause*)

It's a great time to be in Washington, Joe.

JOE. Roy, it's incredibly exciting . . .

ROY. And it would mean something to me. You understand?

(*Little pause.*)

JOE. I . . . can't say how much I appreciate this Roy, I'm sort of . . . well, stunned, I mean. . . . Thanks, Roy. But I have to give it some thought. I have to ask my wife.

ROY. Your wife. Of course.

JOE. But I really appreciate . . .

ROY. Of course. Talk to your wife.

SCENE 3

Later that day. Harper at home, alone. She is listening to the radio and talking to herself, as she often does. She speaks to the audience.

HARPER. People who are lonely, people left alone, sit talking nonsense to the air, imagining . . . beautiful systems dying, old fixed orders spiraling apart . . .

When you look at the ozone layer, from outside, from a spaceship, it looks like a pale blue halo, a gentle, shimmering aureole encircling the atmosphere encircling the earth. Thirty miles above our heads, a thin layer of three-atom oxygen molecules, product of photosynthesis, which explains the fussy vegetable preference for visible light, its rejection of darker rays and emanations. Danger from without. It's a kind of gift, from God, the crowning touch to the creation of the world: guardian angel, hands linked, make a spherical net, a blue-green nesting orb, a shell of safety for itself. But everywhere, things are collapsing, lies surfacing, systems of defense giving way. . . . This is why, Joe, this is why I shouldn't be left alone.

(*Little pause*)

I'd like to go traveling. Leave you behind to worry. I'll send postcards with strange stamps and tantalizing messages on the back. "Later maybe." "Nevermore . . ."

(*Mr. Lies, a travel agent, appears.*)

HARPER. Oh! You startled me!

MR. LIES. Cash, check or credit card?

HARPER. I remember you. You're from Salt Lake. You sold us the plane tickets when we flew here. What are you doing in Brooklyn?

MR. LIES. You said you wanted to travel . . .

HARPER. And here you are. How thoughtful.

MR. LIES. Mr. Lies. Of the International Order of Travel Agents. We mobilize the globe, we set people adrift, we stir the populace and send nomads eddying across the planet. We are adepts of motion, acolytes of the flux. Cash, check or credit card. Name your destination.

HARPER. Antarctica, maybe. I want to see the hole in the ozone. I heard on the radio . . .

MR. LIES (*He has a computer terminal in his briefcase*). I can arrange a guided tour. Now?

HARPER. Soon. Maybe soon. I'm not safe here you see. Things aren't right with me. Weird stuff happens . . .

MR. LIES. Like?

HARPER. Well, like you, for instance. Just appearing. Or last week . . . well never mind. People are like planets, you need a thick skin. Things get to me, Joe stays away and now. . . . Well look. My dreams are talking back to me.

MR. LIES. It's the price of rootlessness. Motion sickness. The only cure: to keep moving.

HARPER. I'm undecided. I feel . . . that something's going to give. It's 1985. Fifteen years till the third millennium. Maybe Christ will come again. Maybe seeds will be planted, maybe there'll be harvest then, maybe early figs to eat, maybe new life, maybe fresh blood, maybe companionship and love and protection, safety from what's outside, maybe the door will hold, or maybe . . . maybe the troubles will come, and the end will come, and the sky will collapse and there will be terrible rains and showers of poison light, or maybe my life is really fine, maybe Joe loves me and I'm only crazy thinking otherwise, or maybe not, maybe it's even worse than I know, maybe . . . I want to know, maybe I don't. The suspense, Mr. Lies, it's killing me.

MR. LIES. I suggest a vacation.

HARPER (*Hearing something*). That was the elevator. Oh God, I should fix myself up, I. . . . You have to go, you shouldn't be here . . . you aren't even real.

MR. LIES. Call me when you decide . . .

HARPER. Go!

(*The Travel Agent vanishes as Joe enters.*)

JOE. Buddy?

Buddy? Sorry I'm late. I was just . . . out. Walking. Are you mad?

HARPER. I got a little anxious.

JOE. Buddy kiss.

(*They kiss.*)

JOE. Nothing to get anxious about.

So, So how'd you like to move to Washington?

SCENE 4

Same day. Louis and Prior outside the funeral home, sitting on a bench, both dressed in funereal finery, talking. The funeral service for Sarah Ironson had just concluded and Louis is about to leave for the cemetery.

LOUIS. My grandmother actually saw Emma Goldman speak. In Yiddish. But all Grandma could remember was that she spoke well and wore a hat.

What a weird service. That rabbi . . .

PRIOR. A definite find. Get his number when you go to the graveyard. I want him to bury me.

LOUIS. Better head out there. Everyone gets to put dirt on the coffin once it's lowered in.

PRIOR. Oooh. Cemetery fund. Don't want to miss that.

LOUIS. It's an old Jewish custom to express love. Here, Grandma, have a shovelful. Latecomers run the risk of finding the grave completely filled.

She was pretty crazy. She was up there in the home for ten years, talking to herself. I never visited. She looked too much like my mother.

PRIOR (*Hugs him*). Poor Louis. I'm sorry your grandma is dead.

LOUIS. Tiny little coffin, huh

Sorry I didn't introduce you to. . . . I always get so closety at these family things.

PRIOR. Butch. You get butch. (*Imitating*) "Hi Cousin Doris, you don't remember me I'm Lou, Rachel's boy." Lou, not Louis, because if you say Louis they'll hear the sibilant S.

LOUIS. I don't have a . . .

PRIOR. I don't blame you, hiding. Bloodlines, Jewish curses are the worst. I personally would dissolve if anyone ever looked me in the eye and said "Feh." Fortunately WASPs don't say "Feh." Oh and by the way, darling, cousin Doris is a dyke.

LOUIS. No.

Really?

PRIOR. You don't notice anything. If I hadn't spent the last four years fellating you I'd swear you were straight.

LOUIS. You're in a pissy mood. Cat still missing

(*Little pause.*)

PRIOR. Not a furball in sight. It's your fault.

LOUIS. It is?

PRIOR. I warned you, Louis. Names are important. Call an animal "Little Sheba" and you can't expect it to stick around. Besides, it's a dog's name.

LOUIS. I wanted a dog in the first place, not a cat. He sprayed my books.

PRIOR. He was a female cat.

LOUIS. Cats are stupid, high-strung predators, Babylonians sealed them up in bricks. Dogs have brains.

PRIOR. Cats have intuition.

LOUIS. A sharp dog is as smart as a really dull two-year-old child.

PRIOR. Cats know when something's wrong.

LOUIS. Only if you stop feeding them.

PRIOR. They know. That's why Sheba left, because she knew.

LOUIS. Knew what?

(Pause.)

PRIOR. I did my best Shirley Booth this morning, floppy slippers, housecoat, curlers, can of Little Friskies; "Come back, Little Sheba, come back. . . ." To no avail. Le chat, elle ne reviendra jamais, jamais . . .

(He removes his jacket, rolls up his sleeve, shows Louis a dark-purple spot on the underside of his arm near the shoulder)

See.

LOUIS. That's just a burst blood vessel.

PRIOR. Not according to the best medical authorities.

LOUIS. What?

(Pause)

Tell me.

PRIOR. K. S., baby. Lesion number one. Lookit. The wine-dark kiss of the angel of death.

LOUIS *(Very softly, holding Prior's arm)*. Oh please . . .

PRIOR. I'm a lesionnaire. The Foreign Lesion. The American Lesion. Lesionnaire's disease.

LOUIS. Stop.

PRIOR. My troubles are lesion.

LOUIS. Will you *stop*.

PRIOR. Don't you think I'm handling this well?
      I'm going to die.

LOUIS. Bullshit.

PRIOR. Let go of my arm.

LOUIS. No.

PRIOR. Let go.

LOUIS *(Grabbing Prior, embracing him ferociously)*. No.

PRIOR. I can't find a way to spare you baby. No wall like the wall of hard scientific fact. K. S. Wham. Bang your head on that.

LOUIS. Fuck you. *(Letting go)* Fuck you fuck you fuck you.

PRIOR. Now that's what I like to hear. A mature reaction. Let's go see if the cat's come home.
      Louis?

LOUIS. When did you find this?

PRIOR. I couldn't tell you.

LOUIS. Why?

PRIOR. I was scared, Lou.

LOUIS. Of what?

PRIOR. That you'll leave me.

LOUIS. Oh.

(Little pause.)

PRIOR. Bad timing, funeral and all, but I figured as long as we're on the subject of death . . .

LOUIS. I have to go bury my grandma.

PRIOR. Lou?

(Pause)

      Then you'll come home?

LOUIS. Then I'll come home.

SCENE 5

Same day, later on. Split scene: Joe and Harper at home; Louis at the cemetery with Rabbi Isidor Chemelwitz and the little coffin.

HARPER. Washington?

JOE. It's an incredible honor, buddy, and . . .

HARPER. I have to think.

JOE. Of course.

HARPER. Say no.

JOE. You said you were going to think about it.

HARPER. I don't want to move to Washington.

JOE. Well I do.

HARPER. It's a giant cemetery, huge white graves and mausoleums everywhere.

JOE. We could live in Maryland. Or Georgetown.

HARPER. We're happy here.

JOE. That's not really true, buddy, we . . .

HARPER. Well happy enough! Pretend happy. That's better than nothing.

JOE. It's time to make some changes, Harper.

HARPER. No changes. Why?

JOE. I've been chief clerk for four years. I make twenty-nine thousand dollars a year. That's ridiculous. I graduated fourth in my class and I make less than anyone I know. And I'm . . . I'm tired of being a clerk, I want to go where something good is happening.

HARPER. Nothing good happens in Washington. We'll forget church teachings and buy furniture at . . . at *Conran's* and become yuppies. I have too much to do here.

JOE. Like what?

HARPER. I *do* have things . . .

JOE. What things?

HARPER. I have to finish painting the bedroom.

JOE. You've been painting in there for over a year.

HARPER. I know, I. . . . It just isn't done because I never get time to finish it.

JOE. Oh that's . . . that doesn't make sense. You have all the time in the world. You could finish it when I'm at work.

HARPER. I'm afraid to go in there alone.

JOE. Afraid of what?

HARPER. I heard someone in there. Metal scraping on the wall. A man with a knife, maybe.

JOE. There's no one in the bedroom, Harper.

HARPER. Not now.

JOE. Not this morning either.

HARPER. How do you know? You were at work this morning. There's something creepy about this place. Remember *Rosemary's Baby*?

JOE. *Rosemary's Baby*?

HARPER. Our apartment looks like that one. Wasn't that apartment in Brooklyn?

JOE. No, it was . . .

HARPER. Well, it looked like this. It did.

JOE. Then let's move.

HARPER. Georgetown's worse. *The Exorcist* was in Georgetown.

JOE. The devil, everywhere you turn, huh, buddy.

HARPER. Yeah. Everywhere.

JOE. How many pills today, buddy?

HARPER. None. One. Three. Only three.

LOUIS (*Pointing at the coffin*). Why are there just two little wooden pegs holding the lid down?

RABBI ISIDOR CHEMELWITZ. So she can get out easier if she wants to.

LOUIS. I hope she stays put.

I pretended for years that she was already dead. When they called to say she had died it was a surprise. I abandoned her.

RABBI ISIDOR CHEMELWITZ. "Sharfer vi di tson fun a shlang iz n umdankbar kind!"

LOUIS. I don't speak Yiddish.

RABBI ISIDOR CHEMELWITZ. Sharper than the serpent's tooth is the ingratitude of children. Shakespeare. *King Lear*.

LOUIS. Rabbi, what does the Holy Writ say about someone who abandons someone he loves at a time of great need?

RABBI ISIDOR CHEMELWITZ. Why would a person do such a thing?

LOUIS. Because he has to.

Maybe because this person's sense of the world, that it will change for the better with struggle, maybe a person who has this neo-Hegelian positivist sense of constant historical progress towards happiness or perfection or something, who feels very powerful because he feels connected to these forces, moving uphill all the time . . . maybe that person can't, um, incorporate sickness into his sense of how things are supposed to go. Maybe vomit . . . and sores and disease . . . really frighten him, maybe . . . he isn't so good with death.

RABBI ISIDOR CHEMELWITZ. The Holy Scriptures have nothing to say about such a person.

LOUIS. Rabbi, I'm afraid of the crimes I may commit.

RABBI ISIDOR CHEMELWITZ. Please, mister. I'm a sick old rabbi facing a long drive home to the Bronx. You want to confess, better you should find a priest.

LOUIS. But I'm not a Catholic, I'm a Jew.

RABBI ISIDOR CHEMELWITZ. Worse luck for you, bubbulah. Catholics believe in foregiveness. Jews believe in Guilt. (*He pats the coffin tenderly*)

LOUIS. You just make sure those pegs are in good and tight.

RABBI ISIDOR CHEMELWITZ. Don't worry, mister. The life she had, she'll stay put. She's better off.

JOE. Look, I know this is scary for you. But try to understand what it means to me. Will you try?

HARPER. Yes.

JOE. Good. Really try.

I think things are starting to change in the world.

HARPER. But I don't want . . .

JOE. Wait. For the good. Change for the good. America has rediscovered itself. Its sacred position among nations. And people aren't ashamed of that like they used to be. This is a great thing. The truth restored. Law restored. That's what President Reagan's done, Harper. He says, "Truth exists and can be spoken proudly." And the country responds to him. We become better. More good. I need to be part of that, I need something big to lift me up. I mean, six years ago the world seemed in decline, horrible, hopeless, full of unsolvable problems and crime and confusion and hunger and . . .

HARPER. But it still seems that way. More now than before. They say the ozone layer is . . .

JOE. Harper . . .

HARPER. And today out the window on Atlantic Avenue there was a schizophrenic traffic cop who was making these . . .

JOE. Stop it! I'm trying to make a point.

HARPER. So am I.

JOE. You aren't even making sense, you . . .

HARPER. My point is the world seems just as . . .

JOE. It only seems that way to you because you never go out in the world, Harper, and you have emotional problems.

HARPER. I do so get out in the world.

JOE. You don't. You stay in all day, fretting about imaginary . . .

HARPER. I get out. I do. You don't know what I do.

JOE. You don't stay in all day.

HARPER. No.

JOE. Well. . . . Yes you do.

HARPER. That's what you think.

JOE. Where do you go?

HARPER. Where do *you* go? When you walk.

(*Pause, then angrily*) And I DO NOT have emotional problems.

JOE. I'm sorry.

HARPER. And if I do have emotional problems it's from living with you. Or . . .

JOE. I'm sorry buddy, I didn't mean to . . .

HARPER. Or if you do think I do then you should never have married me. You have all these secrets and lies.

JOE. I want to be married to you, Harper.

HARPER. You shouldn't. You never should.

(Pause)

>Hey buddy. Hey buddy.

JOE. Buddy kiss . . .

(They kiss.)

HARPER. I heard on the radio how to give a blowjob.

JOE. What?

HARPER. You want to try?

JOE. You really shouldn't listen to stuff like that.

HARPER. Mormons can give blowjobs.

JOE. *Harper.*

HARPER *(Imitating his tone)*. *Joe.*

>It was a little Jewish lady with a German accent. This is a good time. For me to make a baby.

(Little pause. Joe turns away.)

HARPER. Then they went on to a program about holes in the ozone layer. Over Antarctica. Skin burns, birds go blind, icebergs melt. The world's coming to an end.

SCENE 6

First week of November. In the men's room of the offices of the Brooklyn Federal Court of Appeals; Louis is crying over the sink; Joe enters.

JOE. Oh, um. . . . Morning.

LOUIS. Good morning, counselor.

JOE *(He watches Louis cry)*. Sorry, I. . . . I don't know your name.

LOUIS. Don't bother. Word processor. The lowest of the low.

JOE *(Holding out hand)*. Joe Pitt. I'm with Justice Wilson . . .

LOUIS. Oh, I know that. Counselor Pitt. Chief Clerk.

JOE. Were you . . . are you OK?

LOUIS. Oh, yeah. Thanks. What a nice man.

JOE. Not so nice.

LOUIS. What?

JOE. Not so nice. Nothing. You sure you're . . .

LOUIS. Life sucks shit. Life . . . just sucks shit.

JOE. What's wrong?

LOUIS. Run in my nylons.

JOE. Sorry . . . ?

LOUIS. Forget it. Look, thanks for asking.

JOE. Well . . .

LOUIS. I mean it really is nice of you.

>*(He starts crying again)*

>Sorry, sorry, sick friend . . .

JOE. Oh, I'm sorry.

LOUIS. Yeah, yeah, well, that's sweet.

>Three of your colleagues have preceded you to this baleful sight and you're the first one to ask. The others just opened the door, saw me, and fled. I hope they had to pee real bad.

JOE *(Handing him a wad of toilet paper)*. They just didn't want to intrude.

LOUIS. Hah. Reaganite heartless macho asshole lawyers.

JOE. Oh, that's unfair.

LOUIS. What is? Heartless? Macho? Reaganite? Lawyer?

JOE. I voted for Reagan.

LOUIS. You did?

JOE. Twice.

LOUIS. Twice? Well, oh boy. A Gay Republican.

JOE. Excuse me?

LOUIS. Nothing.

JOE. I'm not . . .

>Forget it.

LOUIS. Republican? Not Republican? Or . . .

JOE. What?

>Not gay. I'm not gay.

LOUIS. Oh, Sorry.

>*(Blows his nose loudly)* It's just . . .

JOE. Yes?

LOUIS. Well, sometimes you can tell from the way a person sounds that . . . I mean you *sound* like a . . .

JOE. No I don't. Like what?

LOUIS. Like a Republican.

(Little pause. Joe knows he's being teased; Louis knows he knows. Joe decides to be a little brave.)

JOE *(Making sure no one else is around)*. Do I? Sound like a . . . ?

LOUIS. What? Like a . . . ? Republican, or . . . ? Do I?

JOE. Do you what?

LOUIS. Sound like a . . . ?

JOE. Like a . . . ?

>I'm . . . confused.

LOUIS. Yes.

>My name is Louis. But all my friends call me Louise. I work in Word Processing. Thanks for the toilet paper.

(Louis offers Joe his hand, Joe reaches. Louis feints and pecks Joe on the cheek, then exits.)

SCENE 7

A week later. Mutual dream scene. Prior is at a fantastic makeup table, having a dream, applying the face. Harper is having a pill-induced hallucination. She has these from time to time. For some reason, Prior has appeared in this one. Or Harper has appeared in Prior's dream. It is bewildering.

PRIOR *(Alone, putting on makeup, then examining the results in the mirror; to the audience)*: "I'm ready for my closeup, Mr. DeMille."

>One wants to move through life with elegance and grace, blossoming infrequently but with exquisite taste, and perfect timing, like a rare bloom, a zebra orchid. . . .
>One wants. . . . But one so seldom gets what one wants,

does one? No. One does not. One gets fucked. Over. One . . . dies at thirty, robbed of . . . decades of majesty. Fuck this shit. Fuck this shit.

(*He almost crumbles; he pulls himself together; he studies his handiwork in the mirror*)

I look like a corpse. A corpsette. Oh my queen; you know you've hit rock-bottom when even drag is a drag.

(*Harper appears*)

HARPER. Are you. . . . Who are you?

PRIOR. Who are you?

HARPER. What are you doing in my hallucination?

PRIOR. I'm not in your hallucination. You're in my dream.

HARPER. You're wearing makeup.

PRIOR. So are you.

HARPER. But you're a man.

PRIOR (*Feigning dismay, shock, he mimes slashing his throat with his lipstick and dies, fabulously tragic. Then*). The hands and feet give it away.

HARPER. There must be some mistake here. I don't recognize you. You're not. . . . Are you my . . . some sort of imaginary friend?

PRIOR. No. Aren't you too old to have imaginary friends?

HARPER. I have emotional problems. I took too many pills. Why are you wearing makeup?

PRIOR. I was in the process of applying the face, trying to make myself feel better—I swiped the new fall colors at the Clinique counter at Macy's. (*Showing her*)

HARPER. You stole these?

PRIOR. I was out of cash; it was an emotional emergency!

HARPER. Joe will be so angry. I promised him. No more pills.

PRIOR. These pills you keep alluding to?

HARPER. Valium. I take Valium. Lots of Valium.

PRIOR. And you're dancing as fast as you can.

HARPER. I'm not *addicted*. I don't believe in addiction, and I never . . . well, I *never* drink. And I never take drugs.

PRIOR. Well, smell *you*, Nancy Drew.

HARPER. Except Valium.

PRIOR. Except Valium; in wee fistfuls.

HARPER. It's terrible. Mormons are not supposed to be addicted to anything. I'm a Mormon.

PRIOR. I'm a homosexual.

HARPER. Oh! In my church we don't believe in homosexuals.

PRIOR. In my church we don't believe in Mormons.

HARPER. What church do . . . oh! (*She laughs*) I get it.

I don't understand this. If I didn't ever see you before and I don't think I did then I don't think you should be here, in this hallucination, because in my experience the mind, which is where hallucinations come from, shouldn't be able to make up anything that wasn't there to start with, that didn't enter it from experience, from the real world. Imagination can't create anything new, can it? It only recycles bits and pieces from the world and reassembles them into visions. . . . Am I making sense right now?

PRIOR. Given the circumstances, yes.

HARPER. So when we think we've escaped the unbearable ordinariness and, well, untruthfulness of our lives, it's really only the same old ordinariness and falseness rearranged into the appearance of novelty and truth. Nothing unknown is knowable. Don't you think it's depressing?

PRIOR. The limitations of the imagination?

HARPER. Yes.

PRIOR. It's something you learn after your second theme party: It's All Been Done Before.

HARPER. The world. Finite. Terribly, terribly. . . . Well . . . This is the most depressing hallucination I've ever had.

PRIOR. Apologies. I do try to be amusing.

HARPER. Oh, well, don't apologize, you. . . . I can't expect someone who's really sick to entertain me.

PRIOR. How on earth did you know . . .

HARPER. Oh that happens. This is the very threshold of revelation sometimes. You can see things . . . how sick you are. Do you see anything about me?

PRIOR. Yes.

HARPER. What?

PRIOR. You are amazingly unhappy.

HARPER. Oh big deal. You meet a Valium addict and you figure out she's unhappy. That doesn't count. Of course I. . . . Something else. Something surprising.

PRIOR. Something surprising.

HARPER. Yes.

PRIOR. Your husband's a homo.

(*Pause.*)

HARPER. Oh, ridiculous.

(*Pause, then very quietly*)

Really?

PRIOR (*Shrugs*). Threshold of revelation.

HARPER. Well I don't like your revelations. I don't think you intuit well at all. Joe's a very normal man, he . . .

Oh God. Oh God. He. . . . Do homos take, like, lots of long walks?

PRIOR. Yes. We do. In stretch pants with lavender coifs. I just looked at you, and there was . . .

HARPER. A sort of blue streak of recognition.

PRIOR. Yes.

HARPER. Like you knew me incredibly well.

PRIOR. Yes.

HARPER. Yes.

I have to go now, get back, something just . . . fell apart.

Oh God, I feel so sad . . .

PRIOR. I . . . I'm sorry. I usually say, "Fuck the truth," but mostly, the truth fucks you.

HARPER. I see something else about you . . .

PRIOR. Oh?

HARPER. Deep inside you, there's a part of you, the most inner part, entirely free of disease. I can see that.

PRIOR. Is that. . . . That isn't true.

HARPER. Threshold of revelation.

Home . . .

(She vanishes.)

PRIOR. People come and go so quickly here . . .

(To himself in the mirror) I don't think there's any uninfected part of me. My heart is pumping polluted blood. I feel dirty.

(He begins to wipe makeup off with his hands, smearing it around. A large gray feather falls from up above. Prior stops smearing the makeup and looks at the feather. He goes to it and picks it up.)

A VOICE (It is an incredibly beautiful voice). Look up!

PRIOR (Looking up, not seeing anyone). Hello?

A VOICE. Look up!

PRIOR. Who is that?

A VOICE. Prepare the way!

PRIOR. I don't see any . . .

(There is a dramatic change in lighting, from above.)

A VOICE.

Look up, look up,
prepare the way
the infinite descent
A breath in air
floating down
Glory to . . .

(Silence.)

PRIOR. Hello? Is that it? Helloooo!

What the fuck . . . ? (He holds himself)
Poor me. Poor poor me. Why me? Why poor poor me?
Oh I don't feel good right now. I don't.

SCENE 8

That night. Split scene: Harper and Joe at home; Prior and Louis in bed.

HARPER. Where were you?

JOE. Out.

HARPER. Where?

JOE. Just out. Thinking.

HARPER. It's late.

JOE. I had a lot to think about.

HARPER. I burned dinner.

JOE. Sorry.

HARPER. Not my dinner. My dinner was fine. Your dinner. I put it back in the oven and turned everything up as high as it could go and I watched till it burned black. It's still hot. Very hot. Want it?

JOE. You didn't have to do that.

HARPER. I know. It just seemed like the kind of thing a mentally deranged sex-starved pill-popping housewife would do

JOE. Uh huh.

HARPER. So I did it. Who knows anymore what I have to do?

JOE. How many pills?

HARPER. A bunch. Don't change the subject.

JOE. I won't talk to you when you . . .

HARPER. No. No. Don't do that! I'm . . . I'm fine, pills are not the problem, not our problem, I WANT TO KNOW WHERE YOU'VE BEEN! I WANT TO KNOW WHAT'S GOING ON!

JOE. Going on with what? The job?

HARPER. Not the job.

JOE. I said I need more time.

HARPER. Not the job!

JOE. Mr. Cohn, I talked to him on the phone, he said I had to hurry . . .

HARPER. Not the . . .

JOE. But I can't get you to talk sensibly about anything so . . .

HARPER. SHUT UP!

JOE. Then what?

HARPER. Stick to the subject.

JOE. I don't know what that is. You have something you want to ask me? Ask me. Go.

HARPER. I . . . can't. I'm scared of you.

JOE. I'm tired, I'm going to bed.

HARPER. Tell me without making me ask. Please.

JOE. This is crazy, I'm not . . .

HARPER. When you come through the door at night your face is never exactly the way I remembered it. I get surprised by something . . . mean and hard about the way you look. Even the weight of you in the bed at night, the way you breathe in your sleep seems unfamiliar.

You terrify me.

JOE (Cold). I know who you are.

HARPER. Yes. I'm the enemy. That's easy. That doesn't change.

You think you're the only one who hates sex; I do; I hate it with you; I do. I dream that you batter away at me till all my joints come apart, like wax, and I fall into pieces. It's like a punishment. It was wrong of me to marry you. I knew you . . . (She stops herself) It's a sin, and it's killing us both.

JOE. I can always tell when you've taken pills, because it makes you red-faced and sweaty and frankly that's very often why I don't want to . . .

HARPER. Because . . .

JOE. Well, you aren't pretty. Not like this.

HARPER. I have something to ask you.

JOE. Then ASK! ASK! What in hell are you . . .

HARPER. Are you a homo?

(Pause)

Are you? If you try to walk out right now I'll put your dinner back in the oven and turn it up so high the whole building will fill with smoke and everyone in it will asphyxiate. So help me God I will.

Now answer the question.

JOE. What if I . . .

(Small pause.)

HARPER. Then tell me, please. And we'll see.

JOE. No, I'm not.

I don't see what difference it makes.

LOUIS. Jews don't have any clear textual guide to the afterlife; even that it exists. I don't think much about it. I see it as a perpetual rainy Thursday afternoon in March. Dead leaves.

PRIOR. Enough. Very Greco-Roman.

LOUIS. Well for us it's not the verdict that counts, it's the act of judgment. That's why I could never be a lawyer. In court all that matters is the verdict.

PRIOR. Your could never be a lawyer because you are oversexed. You're too distracted.

LOUIS. Not distracted: *ab*stracted. I'm trying to make a point:

PRIOR. Namely:

LOUIS. It's the judge in his or her chambers, weighing, books open, pondering the evidence, ranging freely over categories: good, evil, innocent, guilty; the judge in the chamber of circumspection, not the judge on the bench with the gavel. The shaping of the law, not its execution.

PRIOR. The point, dear, the point . . .

LOUIS. That it should be the questions and shape of a life, its total complexity gathered, arranged and considered, which matters in the end, not some stamp of salvation or damnation which disperses all the complexity in some unsatisfying decision—balancing of the scales . . .

PRIOR. I like this; very zen; it's . . . reassuringly incomprehensible and useless. We who are about to die thank you.

LOUIS. You are not about to die.

PRIOR. It's not going well, really . . . two new lesions. My leg hurts. There's protein in my urine, the doctor says, but who knows what the fuck that portends. Anyway it should be there, the protein. My butt is chapped from diarrhea and yesterday I shat blood.

LOUIS. I really hate this. You don't tell me . . .

PRIOR. You get too upset, I wind up comforting you. It's easier . . .

LOUIS. Oh thanks.

PRIOR. If it's bad I'll tell you.

LOUIS. Shitting blood sounds bad to me.

PRIOR. And I'm telling you.

LOUIS. And I'm handling it.

PRIOR. Tell me some more about justice.

LOUIS. I *am* handling it.

PRIOR. Well Louis you win Trooper of the Month.

(Louis starts to cry.)

PRIOR. I take it back. You aren't Trooper of the Month. This isn't working . . .

Tell me some more about justice.

LOUIS. You are not about to die.

PRIOR. Justice . . .

LOUIS. . . . is an immensity, a confusing vastness. Justice is God.

Prior?

PRIOR. Hmmm?

LOUIS. You love me.

PRIOR. Yes.

LOUIS. What if I walked out on this?

Would you hate me forever?

(Prior kisses Louis on the forehead.)

PRIOR. Yes.

JOE. I think we ought to pray. Ask God for help. Ask him together . . .

HARPER. God won't talk to me. I have to make up people to talk to me.

JOE. You have to keep asking.

HARPER. I forgot the question.

Oh yeah, God, is my husband a . . .

JOE *(Scary)*. Stop it, Stop it. I'm warning you.

Does it make any difference? That I might be one thing deep within, no matter how wrong or ugly that thing is, so long as I have fought, with everything I have, to kill it. What do you want from me? What do you want from me, Harper? More than that? For God's sake, there's nothing left, I'm a shell. There's nothing left to kill.

As long as my behavior is what I know it has to be. Decent. Correct. That alone in the eyes of God.

HARPER. No, no, not that, that's Utah talk, Mormon talk, I hate it, Joe tell me, say it . . .

JOE. All I will say is that I am a very good man who has worked very hard to become good and you want to destroy that. You want to destroy me, but I am not going to let you do that.

(Pause.)

HARPER. I'm going to have a baby.

JOE. Liar.

HARPER You liar.

A baby born addicted to pills. A baby who does not dream but who hallucinates, who stares up at us with big mirror eyes and who does not know who we are.

(Pause.)

JOE. Are you really . . .

HARPER. No. Yes. No. Yes. Get away from me.

Now we both have a secret.

PRIOR. One of my ancestors was a ship's captain who made money bringing whale oil to Europe and returning with immigrants—Irish mostly, packed in tight, so many dollars per head. The last ship he captained foundered off the coast of Nova Scotia in a winter tempest and sank to the bottom. He went down with the ship—la Grande Geste—but his crew took seventy women and kids in the ship's only longboat, this big, open rowboat, and when the weather got too rough, and they thought the boat was overcrowded, the crew started lifting people up and hurling them into the sea. Until they got the ballast right. They walked up and down the longboat, eyes to the waterline, and when the boat rode low in the water they'd grab the nearest passenger and throw them into the sea. The boat was leaky, see; seventy people; they arrived in Halifax with nine people on board.

LOUIS. Jesus.

PRIOR. I think about that story a lot now. People in a boat, waiting, terrified, while implacable, unsmiling men, irresistibly strong, seize . . . maybe the person next to you, maybe you, and with no warning at all, with time only for a quick intake of air you are pitched into freezing, turbulent water and salt and darkness to drown.

I like your cosmology, baby. While time is running out I find myself drawn to anything that's suspended, that lacks an ending—but it seems to me that it lets you off scot-free.

LOUIS. What do you mean?

PRIOR. No judgment, no guilt or responsibility.

LOUIS. For me.

PRIOR. For anyone. It was an editorial "you."

LOUIS. Please get better. Please.

Please don't get any sicker.

SCENE 9

Third week in November, Roy and Henry, his doctor, in Henry's office.

HENRY. Nobody knows what causes it. And nobody knows how to cure it. The best theory is that we blame a retrovirus, the Human Immunodeficiency Virus. Its presence is made known to us by the useless antibodies which appear in reaction to its entrance into the bloodstream through a cut, or an orifice. The antibodies are powerless to protect the body against it. Why, we don't know. The body's immune system ceases to function. Sometimes the body even attacks itself. At any rate it's left open to a whole horror house of infections from microbes which it usually defends against.

Like Kaposi's sarcomas. These lesions. Or your throat problem. Or the glands.

We think it may also be able to slip past the blood-brain barrier into the brain. Which is of course very bad news.

And it's fatal in we don't know what percent of people with suppressed immune responses.

(Pause.)

ROY. This is very interesting, Mr. Wizard, but why the fuck are you telling me this?

(Pause.)

HENRY. Well, I have just removed one of three lesions which biopsy results will probably tell us is a Kaposi's sarcoma lesion. And you have a pronounced swelling of glands in your neck, groin, and armpits—lymphadenopathy is another sign. And you have oral candidiasis and maybe a little more fungus under the fingernails of two digits on your right hand. So that's why . . .

ROY. This disease . . .

HENRY. Syndrome.

ROY. Whatever. It afflicts mostly homosexuals and drug addicts.

HENRY. Mostly. Hemophiliacs are also at risk.

ROY. Homosexuals and drug addicts. So why are you implying that I . . .

(Pause)

What are you implying, Henry?

HENRY. I don't . . .

ROY. I'm not a drug addict.

HENRY. Oh come on Roy.

ROY. What, what, come on Roy what? Do you think I'm a junkie, Henry, do you see tracks?

HENRY. This is absurd.

ROY. Say it.

HENRY. Say what?

ROY. Say, "Roy Cohn, you are a . . ."

HENRY. Roy.

ROY. "You are a. . . ." Go on. Not "Roy Cohn you are a drug fiend." "Roy Marcus Cohn, you are a . . ."

Go on, Henry, it starts with an "H."

HENRY. Oh I'm not going to . . .

ROY. *With an "H,"* Henry, and it isn't "Hemophiliac." Come on . . .

HENRY. What are you doing, Roy?

ROY. No, say it. I mean it. Say: "Roy Cohn, you are a homosexual."

(Pause)

And I will proceed, systematically, to destroy your reputation and your practice and your career in New York State, Henry. Which you know I can do.

(Pause.)

HENRY. Roy, you have been seeing me since 1958. Apart from the facelifts I have treated you for everything from syphilis . . .

ROY. From a whore in Dallas.

HENRY. From syphilis to venereal warts. In your rectum. Which you may have gotten from a whore in Dallas, but it wasn't a female whore.

(Pause.)

ROY. So say it.

HENRY. Roy Cohn, you are . . .

You have had sex with men, many many times, Roy, and one of them, or any number of them, has made you very sick. You have AIDS.

ROY. AIDS.

Your problem, Henry, is that you are hung up on words, on labels, that you believe they mean what they seem to mean. AIDS. Homosexual. Gay. Lesbian. You think these are names that tell you who someone sleeps with, but they don't tell you that.

HENRY. No?

ROY. No. Like all labels, they tell you one thing and one thing only: where does an individual so identified fit in the food chain, in the pecking order? Not ideology, or sexual taste, but something much simpler: clout. Not who I fuck or who fucks me, but who will pick up the phone when I call, who owes me favors. This is what a label refers to. Now to someone who does not understand this, homosexual is what I am because I have sex with men. But really this is wrong. Homosexuals are not men who sleep with other men. Homosexuals are men who in fifteen years of trying cannot get a pissant antidiscrimination bill through City Council. Homosexuals are men who know nobody and who nobody knows. Who have zero clout. Does this sound like me, Henry?

HENRY. No.

ROY. No. I have clout. A lot. I can pick up this phone, punch fifteen numbers, and you know who will be on the other end in under five minutes, Henry?

HENRY. The President.

ROY. Even better, Henry, His wife.

HENRY. I'm impressed.

ROY. I don't want you to be impressed. I want you to understand. This is not sophistry. And this is not hypocrisy. This is reality. I have sex with men. But unlike nearly every other man of whom this is true, I bring the guy I'm screwing to the White House and President Reagan smiles at us and shakes his hand. Because *what* I am is defined entirely by *who* I am. Roy Cohn is not a homosexual. Roy Cohn is a heterosexual man, Henry, who fucks around with guys.

HENRY. OK, Roy.

ROY. And what is my diagnosis, Henry?

HENRY. You have AIDS, Roy.

ROY. No, Henry, no. AIDS is what homosexuals have. I have liver cancer.

(Pause.)

HENRY. Well, whatever the fuck you have, Roy, it's very serious, and I haven't got a damn thing for you. The NIH in Bethesda has a new drug called AZT with a two-year waiting list that not even I can get you onto. So get on the phone, Roy, and dial the fifteen numbers, and tell the First Lady you need in on an experimental treatment for liver cancer, because you can call it any damn thing you want, Roy, but what it boils down to is very bad news.

ACT TWO: IN VITRO

December 1985–January 1986

SCENE 1

Night, the third week in December. Prior alone on the floor of his bedroom; he is much worse.

PRIOR. Louis, Louis, please wake up, oh God.

(Louis runs in.)

PRIOR. I think something horrible is wrong with me I can't breathe . . .

LOUIS *(Starting to exit)*. I'm calling the ambulance.

PRIOR. No, wait, I . . .

LOUIS. *Wait?* Are you fucking crazy? Oh God you're on fire, your head is on fire.

PRIOR. It hurts, it hurts . . .

LOUIS. I'm calling the ambulance.

PRIOR. I don't want to go to the hospital, I don't want to go to the hospital please let me lie here, just . . .

LOUIS. No, no, God, Prior, stand up . . .

PRIOR. DON'T TOUCH MY LEG!

LOUIS. We have to . . . oh God this is so crazy.

PRIOR. I'll be OK if I just lie here Lou, really, if I can only sleep a little . . .

(Louis exits.)

PRIOR. Louis?

No! No! Don't call, you'll send me there and I won't come back, please, please Louis I'm begging, baby, please . . .

(Screams) LOUIS!!

LOUIS *(From off; hysterical)*. WILL YOU SHUT THE FUCK UP!

PRIOR *(Trying to stand)*. Aaaah, I have . . . to go to the bathroom. Wait. Wait, just . . . oh. Oh God. *(He shits himself.)*

LOUIS *(Entering)*. Prior? They'll be here in . . .

Oh my God.

PRIOR. I'm sorry, I'm sorry.

LOUIS. What did . . . ? What?

PRIOR. I had an accident?

(Louis goes to him.)

LOUIS. This is blood.

PRIOR. Maybe you shouldn't touch it . . . me. . . . I . . . (*He faints*)

LOUIS (*Quietly*). Oh help. Oh help. Oh God oh God oh God help me I can't I can't I can't.

SCENE 2

Same night. Harper is sitting at home, all alone, with no lights on. We can barely see her. Joe enters, but he doesn't turn on the lights.

JOE. Why are you sitting in the dark? Turn on the light.

HARPER. *No.* I heard the sounds in the bedroom again. I know someone was in there.

JOE. No one was.

HARPER. Maybe actually in the bed, under the covers with a knife.

Oh, boy. Joe. I, um, I'm thinking of going away. By which I mean: I think I'm going off again. You . . . you know what I mean?

JOE. Please don't. Stay. We can fix it. I pray for that. This is my fault, but I can correct it. You have to try too . . .

(*He turns on the light. She turns it off again.*)

HARPER. When you pray, what do you pray for?

JOE. I pray for God to crush me, break me up into little pieces and start all over again.

HARPER. Oh. Please. Don't pray for that.

JOE. I had a book of Bible stories when I was a kid. There was a picture I'd look at twenty times every day: Jacob wrestles with the angel. I don't really remember the story, or why the wrestling—just the picture. Jacob is young and very strong. The angel is . . . a beautiful man, with golden hair and wings, of course. I still dream about it. Many nights, I'm . . . It's me. In that struggle. Fierce, and unfair. The angel is not human, and it holds nothing back, so how could anyone human win, what kind of a fight is that? It's not just. Losing means your soul thrown down in the dust, your heart torn out from God's. But you can't not lose.

HARPER. In the whole entire world, you are the only person, the only person I love or have ever loved. And I love you terribly. Terribly. That's what's so awfully, irreducibly real. I can make up anything but I can't dream that away.

JOE. Are you . . . are you really going to have a baby?

HARPER. It's my time, and there's no blood. I don't really know. I suppose it wouldn't be a great thing. Maybe I'm just not bleeding because I take too many pills. Maybe I'll give birth to a pill. That would give a new meaning to pill-popping, huh?

I think you should go to Washington. Alone. Change, like you said.

JOE. I'm not going to leave you, Harper.

HARPER. Well maybe not. But I'm going to leave you.

SCENE 3

One AM, the next morning. Louis and a nurse, Emily, are sitting in Prior's room in the hospital.

EMILY. He'll be all right now.

LOUIS. No he won't.

EMILY. No. I guess not. I gave him something that makes him sleep.

LOUIS. Deep asleep?

EMILY. Orbiting the moons of Jupiter.

LOUIS. A good place to be.

EMILY. Anyplace better than here. You his . . . uh?

LOUIS. Yes, I'm his uh.

EMILY. This must be hell for you.

LOUIS. It is. Hell. The After Life. Which is not at all like a rainy afternoon in March, by the way, Prior. A lot more vivid than I'd expected. Dead leaves, but the crunchy kind. Sharp, dry air. The kind of long, luxurious dying feeling that breaks your heart.

EMILY. Yeah, well we all get to break our hearts on this one. He seems like a nice guy. Cute.

LOUIS. Not like this.

Yes, he is. Was. Whatever.

EMILY. Weird name. Prior Walter. Like, "The Walter before this one."

LOUIS. Lots of Walters before this one. Prior is an old old family name in an old old family. The Walters go back to the Mayflower and beyond. Back to the Norman Conquest. He says there's a Prior Walter stitched into the Bayeux tapestry.

EMILY. Is that impressive?

LOUIS. Well, it's old. Very old. Which in some circles equals impressive.

EMILY. Not in my circle. What's the name of the tapestry?

LOUIS. The Bayeux tapestry. Embroidered by La Reine Mathilde.

EMILY. I'll tell my mother. She embroiders. Drives me nuts.

LOUIS. Manual therapy for anxious hands.

EMILY. Maybe you should try it.

LOUIS. Mathilde stitched while William the Conqueror was off to war. She was capable of . . . more than loyalty. Devotion.

She waited for him, she stitched for years. And if he had come back broken and defeated from war, she would have loved him even more. And if he had returned mutilated, ugly, full of infection and horror, she would still have loved him; fed by pity, by a sharing of pain, she would love him even more, and even more, and she would never, never have prayed to God, please let him die if he can't return to me whole and healthy and able to live a normal life . . . If he had died, she would have buried her heart with him.

So what the fuck is the matter with me?

(*Little pause*)

Will he sleep through the night?

EMILY. At least.

LOUIS. I'm going.

EMILY. It's one AM. Where do you have to go at . . .

LOUIS. I know what time it is. A walk. Night air, good for the. . . . The park.

EMILY. Be careful.

LOUIS. Yeah, Danger.

    Tell him, if he wakes up and you're still on, tell him goodbye, tell him I had to go.

SCENE 4

An hour later. Split scene: Joe and Roy in a fancy (straight) bar; Louis and a Man in the Rambles in Central Park, Joe and Roy are sitting at the bar; the place is brightly lit. Joe has a plate for food in front of him but he isn't eating. Roy occasionally reaches over the table and forks small bites off Joe's plate. Roy is drinking heavily. Joe not at all. Louis and the Man are eyeing each other, each alternating interest and indifference.

JOE. The pills were something she started when she miscarried or . . . no, she took some before that. She had a really bad time at home, when she was a kid, her home was really bad. I think a lot of drinking and physical stuff. She doesn't talk about that, instead she talks about . . . the sky falling down, people with knives hiding under sofas. Monsters. Mormons. Everyone thinks Mormons don't come from homes like that, we aren't supposed to behave that way, but we do. It's not lying, or being two-faced. Everyone tries very hard to live up to God's strictures, which are very . . . um . . .

ROY. Strict.

JOE. I shouldn't be bothering you with this.

ROY. No, please. Heart to heart. Want another. . . . What is that, seltzer?

JOE. The failure to measure up hits people hard. From such a strong desire to be good they feel very far from goodness when they fail.

    What scares me is that maybe what I really love in her is the part of her that's farthest from the light, from God's love; maybe I was drawn to that in the first place. And I'm keeping it alive because I need it.

ROY. Why would you need it?

JOE. There are things. . . . I don't know how well we know ourselves. I mean, what if? I know I married her because she . . . because I love it that she was always wrong, always doing something wrong, like one step out of step. In Salt Lake City that stands out. I never stood out, on the outside, but inside, it was hard for me. To pass.

ROY. Pass?

JOE. Yeah.

ROY. Pass as what?

JOE. Oh, Well. . . . As someone cheerful and strong. Those who love God with an open heart unclouded by secrets

and struggles are cheerful; God's easy simple love for them shows in how strong and happy they are. The saints.

ROY. But you had secrets? Secret struggles . . .

JOE. I wanted to be one of the elect, one of the Blessed. You feel you ought to be, that the blemishes are yours by choice, which of course they aren't. Harper's sorrow, that really deep sorrow, she didn't choose that. But it's there.

ROY. You didn't put it there.

JOE. No.

ROY. You sound like you think you did.

JOE. I am responsible for her.

ROY. Because she's your wife.

JOE. That. And I do love her.

ROY. Whatever. She's your wife. And so there are obligations. To her. But also to yourself.

JOE. She'd fall apart in Washington.

ROY. Then let her stay here.

JOE. She'll fall apart if I leave her.

ROY. Then bring her to Washington.

JOE. I just can't, Roy. She needs me.

ROY. Listen, Joe. I'm the best divorce lawyer in the business.

(Little pause.)

JOE. Can't Washington wait?

ROY. You do what you need to do, Joe. What *you* need. *You.* Let her life go where it wants to go. You'll be better for that. *Somebody* should get what they want.

MAN. What do you want?

LOUIS. I want you to fuck me, hurt me, make me bleed.

MAN. I want to.

LOUIS. Yeah?

MAN. I want to hurt you.

LOUIS. Fuck me.

MAN. Yeah?

LOUIS. Hard.

MAN. Yeah? You been a bad boy?

(Pause. Louis laughs, softly.)

LOUIS. Very bad. Very bad.

MAN. You need to be punished, boy?

LOUIS. Yes. I do.

MAN. Yes what?

(Little pause.)

LOUIS. Um, I . . .

MAN. Yes *what*, boy?

LOUIS. Oh. Yes sir.

MAN. I want you to take me to your place, boy.

LOUIS. No, I can't do that.

MAN. No *what*?

LOUIS. No sir, I can't, I . . .
    I don't live alone, sir.

MAN. Your lover know you're out with a man tonight, boy?

LOUIS. No sir, he . . .
    My lover doesn't know.

MAN. Your lover know you . . .

LOUIS. Let's change the subject, OK? Can we go to your place?

MAN. I live with my parents.

LOUIS. Oh.

ROY. Everyone who makes it in this world makes it because somebody older and more powerful takes an interest. The most precious asset in life, I think is the ability to be a good son. You have that, Joe. Somebody who can be a good son to a father who pushes them farther than they would otherwise go. I've had many fathers, I owe my life to them, powerful, powerful men. Walter Winchell, Edgar Hoover. Joe McCarthy most of all. He valued me because I am a good lawyer, but he loved me because I was and am a good son. He was a very difficult man, very guarded and cagey; I brought out something tender in him. He would have died for me. And me for him. Does this embarrass you?

JOE. I had a hard time with my father.

ROY. Well sometimes that's the way. Then you have to find other fathers, substitutes, I don't know. The father-son relationship is central to life. Women are for birth, beginning, but the father is continuance. The son offers the father his life as a vessel for carrying forth his father's dream. Your father's living?

JOE. Um, dead.

ROY. He was . . . what? A difficult man?

JOE. He was in the military. He could be very unfair. And cold.

ROY. But he loved you.

JOE. I don't know.

ROY. No, no, Joe, he did, I know this. Sometimes a father's love has to be very, very hard, unfair even, cold to make his son grow strong in a world like this. This isn't a good world.

MAN. Here, then.

LOUIS. I. . . . Do you have a rubber?

MAN. I don't use rubbers.

LOUIS. You should. (*He takes one from his coat pocket*) Here.

MAN. I don't use them.

LOUIS. Forget it, then. (*He starts to leave*)

MAN. No, wait.

Put it on me. Boy.

LOUIS. Forget it, I have to get back. Home. I must be going crazy.

MAN. Oh come on please he won't find out.

LOUIS. It's cold. Too cold.

MAN. It's never too cold, let me warm you up. Please?

(*They begin to fuck.*)

MAN. Relax.

LOUIS (*A small laugh*). Not a chance.

MAN. It . . .

LOUIS. What?

MAN. I think it broke. The rubber. You want me to keep going? (*Little pause*) Pull out? Should I . . .

LOUIS. Keep going.

Infect me.

I don't care. I don't care.

(*Pause. The Man pulls out.*)

MAN. I . . . um, look, I'm sorry, but I think I want to go.

LOUIS. Yeah.

Give my best to mom and dad.

(*The Man slaps him.*)

LOUIS. Ow!

(*They stare at each other.*)

LOUIS. It was a joke.

(*The Man leaves.*)

ROY. How long have we known each other?

JOE. Since 1980.

ROY. Right. A long time. I feel close to you, Joe. Do I advise you well?

JOE. You've been an incredible friend, Roy, I . . .

ROY. I want to be family. Familia, as my Italian friends call it. La Familia. A lovely word. It's important for me to help you, like I was helped.

JOE. I owe practically everything to you, Roy.

ROY. I'm dying, Joe. Cancer.

JOE. Oh my God.

ROY. Please. Let me finish.

Few people know this and I'm telling you this only because. . . . I'm not afraid of death. What can death bring that I haven't faced? I've lived; life is the worst. (*Gently mocking himself*) Listen to me, I'm a philosopher.

Joe. You must do this. You must must must. Love; that's a trap. Responsibility; that's a trap too. Like a father to a son I tell you this: Life is full of horror; nobody escapes, nobody; save yourself. Whatever pulls on you, whatever needs from you, threatens you. Don't be afraid; people are so afraid; don't be afraid to live in the raw wind, naked, alone. . . . Learn at least this: What you are capable of. Let nothing stand in your way.

SCENE 5

Three days later. Prior and Belize in Prior's hospital room. Prior is very sick but improving. Belize has just arrived.

PRIOR. Miss Thing.

BELIZE. Ma cherie bichete.

PRIOR. Stella.

BELIZE. Stella for star. Let me see. (*Scrutinizing Prior*) You look like shit, why yes indeed you do, comme la merde!

PRIOR. Merci.

BELIZE (*Taking little plastic bottles from his bag, handing them to Prior*). Not to despair, Belle Reeve. Lookie! Magic goop!

PRIOR (*Opening a bottle, sniffing*). Pooh! What kinda crap is that?

BELIZE. Beats me. Let's rub it on your poor blistered body and see what it does.

PRIOR. This is not Western medicine, these bottles . . .

BELIZE. Voodoo cream. From the botanica 'round the block.

PRIOR. And you a registered nurse.

BELIZE (*Sniffing it*). Beeswax and cheap perfume. Cut with Jergen's Lotion. Full of good vibes and love from some little black Cubana witch in Miami.

PRIOR. Get that trash away from me, I am immune-suppressed.

BELIZE. I *am* a health professional. I *know* what I'm doing.

PRIOR. It stinks. Any word from Louis?

(*Pause. Belize starts giving Prior a gentle massage.*)

PRIOR. Gone.

BELIZE. He'll be back. I know the type. Likes to keep a girl on edge.

PRIOR. It's been . . .

(*Pause.*)

BELIZE (*Trying to jog his memory*). How long?

PRIOR. I don't remember.

BELIZE. How long have you been here?

PRIOR (*Getting suddenly upset*). I don't remember, I don't give a fuck. I want Louis. I want my fucking boyfriend, where the fuck is he? I'm dying, I'm dying, where's Louis?

BELIZE. Shhhh, shhh . . .

PRIOR. This is a very strange drug, this drug. Emotional liability, for starters.

BELIZE. Save a tab or two for me.

PRIOR. Oh no, not this drug, ce n'est pas pour la joyeux noël et la bonne année, this drug she is serious poisonous chemistry, ma pauvre bichette.

And not just disorienting. I hear things. Voices.

BELIZE. Voices.

PRIOR. A voice.

BELIZE. Saying what?

(*Pause.*)

PRIOR. I'm not supposed to tell.

BELIZE. You better tell the doctor. Or I will.

PRIOR. No no don't. Please. I want the voice; it's wonderful. It's all that's keeping me alive. I don't want to talk to some intern about it.

You know what happens? When I hear it, I get hard.

BELIZE. Oh my.

PRIOR. Comme ça. (*He uses his arm to demonstrate*) And you know I am slow to rise.

BELIZE. My jaw aches at the memory.

PRIOR. And would you deny me this little solace—betray my concupiscence to Florence Nightingale's storm troopers?

BELIZE. Perish the thought, ma bébé.

PRIOR. They'd change the drug just to spoil the fun.

BELIZE. You and your boner can depend on me.

PRIOR. Je t'adore, ma belle nègre.

BELIZE. All this girl-talk shit is politically incorrect, you know. We should have dropped it back when we gave up drag.

PRIOR. I'm sick, I get to be politically incorrect if it makes me feel better. You sound like Lou.

(*Little pause*)

Well, at least I have the satisfaction of knowing he's in anguish somewhere. I loved his anguish. Watching him stick his head up his asshole and eat his guts out over some relatively minor moral conundrum—it was the best show in town. But Mother warned me: if they get overwhelmed by the little things . . .

BELIZE. They'll be belly-up bustville when something big comes along.

PRIOR. Mother warned me.

BELIZE. And they do come along.

PRIOR. But I didn't listen.

BELIZE. No. (*Doing Hepburn*) Men are beasts.

PRIOR (*Also Hepburn*). The absolute lowest.

BELIZE. I have to go. If I want to spend my whole lonely life looking after white people I can get underpaid to do it.

PRIOR. You're just a Christian martyr.

BELIZE. Whatever happens, baby, I will be here for you.

PRIOR. Je t'aime.

BELIZE. Je t'aime. Don't go crazy on me, girlfriend, I already got enough crazy queens for one lifetime. For two. I can't be bothering with dementia.

PRIOR. I promise.

BELIZE (*Touching him; softly*). Ouch.

PRIOR. Ouch. Indeed.

BELIZE. Why'd they have to pick on you?

And eat more, girlfriend, you really do look like shit.

(*Belize leaves.*)

PRIOR (*After waiting a beat*). He's gone.
Are you still . . .

VOICE. I can't stay. I will return.

PRIOR. Are you one of those "Follow me to the other side" voices?

VOICE. No. I am no nightbird. I am a messenger . . .

PRIOR. You have a beautiful voice, it sounds . . . like a viola, like a perfectly tuned, tight string, balanced, the truth. . . . Stay with me.

VOICE. Not now. Soon I will return, I will reveal myself to you; I am glorious, glorious; my heart, my countenance and my message. You must prepare.

PRIOR. For what? I don't want to . . .

VOICE. No death, no:
A marvelous work and a wonder we undertake, an edifice awry we sink plumb and straighten, a great Lie we abolish, a great error correct, with the rule, sword and broom of Truth!

PRIOR. What are you talking about, I . . .

VOICE.
I am on my way; when I am manifest, our Work begins:

Prepare for the parting of the air,
The breath, the ascent,
Glory to . . .

SCENE 6

The second week of January. Martin, Roy and Joe in a fancy Manhattan restaurant.

MARTIN. It's a revolution in Washington, Joe. We have a new agenda and finally a real leader. They got back the Senate but we have the courts. By the nineties the Supreme Court will be block-solid Republican appointees, and the Federal bench—Republican judges like land mines, everywhere, everywhere they turn. Affirmative action? Take it to court. Boom! Land mine. And we'll get our way on just about everything: abortion, defense, Central America, family values, a live investment climate. We have the White House locked till the year 2000. And beyond. A permanent fix on the Oval Office? It's possible. By '92 we'll get the Senate back, and in ten years the South is going to give us the House. It's really the end of Liberalism. The end of New Deal Socialism. The end of ipso facto secular humanism. The dawning of a genuinely American political personality. Modeled on Ronald Wilson Reagan.

JOE. It sounds great, Mr. Heller.

MARTIN. Martin. And Justice is the hub. Especially since Ed Meese took over. He doesn't specialize in Fine Points of the Law. He's a flatfoot, a cop. He reminds me of Teddy Roosevelt.

JOE. I can't wait to meet him.

MARTIN. Too bad, Joe, he's been dead for sixty years.

(There is a little awkwardness. Joe doesn't respond.)

MARTIN. Teddy Roosevelt. You said you wanted to. . . . Little joke. It reminds me of the story about the . . .

ROY *(Smiling, but nasty)*. Aw shut the fuck up Martin.
    (To Joe) You see that? Mr. Heller here is one of the mighty, Joseph, in D.C. He sitteth on the right hand of the man who sitteth on the right of The Man. And yet I can say "shut the fuck up" and he will take no offense. Loyalty. He . . .
    Martin?

MARTIN. Yes, Roy?

ROY. Rub my back.

MARTIN. Roy . . .

ROY. No no really, a sore spot, I get them all the time now, these. . . . Rub it for me darling, would you do that for me?

(Martin rubs Roy's back. They both look at Joe.)

ROY *(To Joe)*. How do you think a handful of Bolsheviks turned St. Petersburg into Leningrad in one afternoon? *Comrades*. Who do for each other. Marx and Engels.

Lenin and Trotsky. Josef Stalin and Franklin Delano Roosevelt.

(Martin laughs.)

ROY. *Comrades*, right, Martin?

MARTIN. This man, Joe, is a Saint of the Right.

JOE. I know, Mr. Heller, I . . .

ROY. And you see what I mean, Martin? He's special, right?

MARTIN. Don't embarrass him, Roy.

ROY. Gravity, decency, smarts! His strength is as the strength of ten because his heart is pure! *And* he's a Roy-boy, one hundred percent.

MARTIN. We're on the move, Joe. On the move.

JOE. Mr. Heller, I . . .

MARTIN *(Ending backrub)*. We can't wait any longer for an answer.

(Little pause.)

JOE. Oh. Um, I . . .

ROY. Joe's a married man, Martin.

MARTIN. Aha.

ROY. With a wife. She doesn't care to go to D.C., and so Joe cannot go. And keeps us dangling. We've seen that kind of thing before, haven't we? These men and their wives.

MARTIN. Oh yes. Beware.

JOE. I really can't discuss this under . . .

MARTIN. Then *don't* discuss. Say yes, Joe.

ROY. Now.

MARTIN. Say yes I will.

ROY. Now.
    Now. I'll hold my breath till you do, I'm turning blue waiting. . . . Now, goddammit!

MARTIN. Roy, calm down, it's not . . .

ROY. Aw, fuck it. *(He takes a letter from his jacket pocket, hands it to Joe.)*
    Read. Came today.

(Joe reads the first paragraph, then looks up.)

JOE. Roy. This is . . . Roy, this is terrible.

ROY. You're telling me.
    A letter from the New York State Bar Association, Martin.
    They're gonna try and disbar me.

MARTIN. Oh my.

JOE. Why?

ROY. Why, Martin?

MARTIN. Revenge.

ROY. The whole Establishment. Their little rules. Because I know no rules. Because I don't see the Law as a dead and arbitrary collection of antiquated dictums, thou shall, thou shalt not, because, because I know the Law's a pliable, breathing, sweating . . . *organ*, because, because . . .

MARTIN. Because he borrowed half a million from one of his clients.

ROY. Yeah, well, there's that.

MARTIN. *And* he forgot to *return* it.

JOE. Roy, that's. . . . You borrowed money from a client?

ROY. I'm deeply ashamed.

(Little pause.)

JOE *(Very sympathetic)*. Roy, you know how much I admire
you. Well I mean I know you have unorthodox ways, but
I'm sure you only did what you thought at the time you
needed to do. And I have faith that . . .

ROY. Not so damp, please. I'll deny it was a loan. She's got
no paperwork. Can't prove a fucking thing.

(Little pause. Martin studies the menu.)

JOE *(Handing back the letter, more official in tone)*. Roy I really
appreciate your telling me this, and I'll do whatever I can
to help.

ROY *(Holding up a hand, then, carefully)*. I'll tell you what
you can do.

I'm about to be tried, Joe, by a jury that is not a jury of
my peers. The disbarment committee: genteel gentleman
Brahmin lawyers, country-club men. I offend them, to
these men . . . I'm what, Martin, some sort of filthy little
Jewish troll?

MARTIN. Oh well, I wouldn't go so far as . . .

ROY. Oh well I would.

Very fancy lawyers, these disbarment committee
lawyers, fancy lawyers with fancy corporate clients and
complicated cases. Antitrust suits. Deregulation. Environmental control. Complex cases like these need Justice
Department cooperation like flowers need the sun.
Wouldn't you say that's an accurate assessment, Martin?

MARTIN. I'm not here, Roy. I'm not hearing any of this.

ROY. No. Of course not.

Without the light of the sun, Joe, these cases, and the
fancy lawyers who represent them, will wither and die.

A well-placed friend, someone in the Justice Department, say, can turn off the sun. Cast a deep shadow on my
behalf. Make them shiver in the cold. If they overstep.
They would fear that.

(Pause.)

JOE. Roy. I don't understand.

ROY. You do.

(Pause.)

JOE. You're not asking me to . . .

ROY. Ssshhhh. Careful.

JOE *(A beat, then)*. Even if I said yes to the job, it would be
illegal to interfere. With the hearings. It's unethical. No.
I can't.

ROY. Un-ethical.

Would you excuse us, Martin?

MARTIN. Excuse you?

ROY. Take a walk, Martin. For real.

(Martin leaves.)

ROY. Un-ethical. Are you trying to embarrass me in front of
my friend?

JOE. Well it is unethical, I can't . . .

ROY. Boy, you are really something. What the fuck do you
think this is, Sunday School?

JOE. No, but Roy this is . . .

ROY. This is . . . this is gastric juices churning, this is en-
zymes and acids, this is intestinal is what this is, bowel
movement and blood-red meat—this stinks, this is *politics*, Joe, the game of being alive. And you think you're
. . . . What? Above that? Above alive is what? Dead! In
the clouds! You're on earth, goddammit! Plant a foot, stay
a while.

I'm sick. They smell I'm weak. They want blood this
time. I must have eyes in Justice. In Justice you will protect me.

JOE. Why can't Mr. Heller . . .

ROY. Grow up, Joe. The administration can't get involved.

JOE. But I'd be part of the administration. The same as him.

ROY. Not the same. Martin's Ed's man. And Ed's Reagan's
man. So Martin's Reagan's man.

And you're mine.

(Little pause. He holds up the letter)

This will never be. Understand me?

(He tears the letter up)

I'm gonna be a lawyer, Joe, I'm gonna be a lawyer, Joe,
I'm gonna be a goddam motherfucking legally licensed
member of the bar lawyer, just like daddy was, till my last
bitter day on earth, Joseph, until the day I die.

(Martin returns.)

ROY. Ah, Martin's back.

MARTIN. So are we agreed?

ROY. Joe?

(Little pause.)

JOE. I will think about it.
(To Roy) I will.

ROY. Huh.

MARTIN. It's the fear of what comes after the doing that
makes the doing hard to do.

ROY. Amen.

MARTIN. But you can almost always live with the consequences.

SCENE 7

*That afternoon. On the granite steps outside the Hall of
Justice, Brooklyn. It is cold and sunny. A Sabrett wagon
is selling hot dogs. Louis, in a shabby overcoat, is sitting on*

the steps contemplatively eating one. Joe enters with three hot dogs and a can of Coke.

JOE. Can I . . . ?

LOUIS. Oh, sure. Sure. Crazy cold sun.

JOE (*Sitting*). Have to make the best of it.
     How's your friend?

LOUIS. My . . . ? Oh. He's worse. My friend is worse.

JOE. I'm sorry.

LOUIS. Yeah, well. Thanks for asking. It's nice, You're nice. I can't believe you voted for Reagan.

JOE. I hope he gets better.

LOUIS. Reagan?

JOE. Your friend.

LOUIS. He won't. Neither will Reagan.

JOE. Let's not talk politics, OK?

LOUIS (*Pointing to Joe's lunch*). You're eating *three* of those?

JOE. Well . . . I'm . . . hungry.

LOUIS. They're really terrible for you. Full of rat-poo and beetle legs and wood shavings 'n' shit.

JOE. Huh.

LOUIS. And . . . um . . . irridium, I think. Something toxic.

JOE. You're eating one.

LOUIS. Yeah, well, the shape, I can't help myself, plus I'm *trying* to commit suicide, what's your excuse?

JOE. I don't have an excuse. I just have Pepto-Bismol.

(*Joe takes a bottle of Pepto-Bismol and chugs it. Louis shudders audibly.*)

JOE. Yeah I know but then I wash it down with Coke.

(*He does this. Louis mimes barfing in Joe's lap. Joe pushes Louis's head away.*)

JOE. Are you *always* like this?

LOUIS. I've been worrying a lot about his kids.

JOE. Whose?

LOUIS. Reagan's. Maureen and Mike and little orphan Patti and Miss Ron Reagan Jr., the you-should-pardon-the-expression heterosexual.

JOE. Ron Reagan Jr. is *not*. . . . You shouldn't just make these assumptions about people. How do you know? About him? What he is? You don't know.

LOUIS (*Doing Tallulah*). Well darling he never sucked *my* cock but . . .

JOE. Look, if you're going to get vulgar . . .

LOUIS. No no really I mean. . . . What's it like to be the child of the Zeitgeist? To have the American Animus as your dad? It's not really a *family*, the Reagans. I read *People*, there aren't any connections there, no love, they don't even speak to each other except through their agents. So what's it like to be Reagan's kid? Enquiring minds want to know.

JOE. You can't believe everything you . . .

LOUIS (*Looking away*). But . . . I think we all know what that's like. Nowadays. No connections. No responsibili-

ties. All of us . . . falling through the cracks that separate what we owe to our selves and . . . and what we owe to love.

JOE. You just. . . . Whatever you feel like saying or doing, you don't care, you just . . . do it.

LOUIS. Do what?

JOE. It. Whatever. Whatever it is you want to do.

LOUIS. Are you trying to tell me something?

(*Little pause, sexual. They stare at each other. Joe looks away.*)

JOE. No, I'm just observing that you . . .

LOUIS. Impulsive.

JOE. Yes, I mean it must be scary, you . . .

LOUIS (*Shrugs*). Land of the free. Home of the brave. Call me irresponsible.

JOE. It's kind of terrifying.

LOUIS. Yeah, well, freedom is. Heartless, too.

JOE. Oh you're not heartless.

LOUIS. You don't know.
     Finish your weenie.

(*He pats Joe on the knee, starts to leave.*)

JOE. Um . . .

(*Louis turns, looks at him. Joe searches for something to say.*)

JOE. Yesterday was Sunday but I've been a little unfocused recently and I thought it was Monday. So I came here like I was going to work. And the whole place was empty. And at first I couldn't figure out why, and I had this moment of incredible . . . fear and also. . . . It just flashed through my mind: The whole Hall of Justice, it's empty, it's deserted, it's gone out of busines. Forever. The people that make it run have up and abandoned it.

LOUIS (*Looking at the building*). Creepy.

JOE. Well yes but. I felt that I was going to scream. Not because it was creepy, but because the emptiness felt so *fast*.
     And . . . well, good. A . . . happy scream.
     I just wondered what a thing it would be . . . if overnight everything you owe anything to, justice, or love, had really gone away. Free.
     It would be . . . heartless terror. Yes. Terrible, and . . .
     Very great. To shed your skin, every old skin, one by one then walk away, unencumbered, into the morning.

(*Little pause. He looks at the building*)

     I can't go in there today.

LOUIS. Then don't.

JOE (*Not really hearing Louis*). I can't go in, I need . . .

(*He looks for what he needs. He takes a swig of Pepto-Bismol*)

I can't *be* this anymore. I need . . . a change, I should just . . .

LOUIS (*Not a come-on, necessarily; he doesn't want to be alone*). Want some company? For whatever?

(*Pause. Joe looks at Louis and looks away, afraid. Louis shrugs.*)

LOUIS. Sometimes, even if it scares you to death, you have to be willing to break the law. Know what I mean?

(*Another little pause.*)

JOE. Yes.

(*Another little pause.*)

LOUIS. I moved out. I moved out on my . . .
  I haven't been sleeping well.

JOE. Me neither.

(*Louis goes up to Joe, licks his napkin and dabs at Joe's mouth.*)

LOUIS. Antacid moustache.
  (*Points to the building*) Maybe the court won't convene. Ever again. Maybe we are free. To do whatever.
  Children of the new morning, criminal minds. Selfish and greedy and loveless and blind. Reagan's children.
  You're scared. So am I. Everybody is in the land of the free. God help us all.

SCENE 8

Late that night. Joe at a payphone phoning Hannah at home in Salt Lake City.

JOE. Mom?

HANNAH. Joe?

JOE. Hi.

HANNAH. You're calling from the street. It's . . . it must be four in the morning. What's happened?

JOE. Nothing, nothing, I . . .

HANNAH. It's Harper. Is Harper. . . . Joe? Joe?

JOE. Yeah, hi. No, Harper's fine. Well, no, she's . . . not fine. How are you, Mom?

HANNAH. What's happened?

JOE. I just wanted to talk to you. I, uh, wanted to try something out on you.

HANNAH. Joe, you haven't . . . have you been drinking, Joe?

JOE. Yes ma'am. I'm drunk.

HANNAH. That isn't like you.

JOE. No. I mean, who's to say?

HANNAH. Why are you out on the street at four AM? In that crazy city. It's dangerous.

JOE. Actually, Mom, I'm not on the street. I'm near the boathouse in the park.

HANNAH. What park?

JOE. *Central Park.*

HANNAH. CENTRAL PARK! Oh my Lord. What on earth are you doing in Central Park at this time of night? Are you . . .
  Joe, I think you ought to go home right now. Call me from home.

(*Little pause*)
  Joe?

JOE. I come here to watch, Mom. Sometimes. Just to watch.

HANNAH. Watch what? What's there to watch at four in the . . .

JOE. Mom, did Dad Love me?

HANNAH. What?

JOE. Did he?

HANNAH. You ought to go home and call from there.

JOE. Answer.

HANNAH. Oh now really. This is maudlin. I don't like this conversation.

JOE. Yeah, well, it gets worse from here on.

(*Pause*)

HANNAH. Joe?

JOE. Mom. Momma. I'm a homosexual, Momma.
  Boy, did that come out awkward.

(*Pause*)
  Hello? Hello?
  I'm a homosexual.

(*Pause*)
  Please, Momma. Say something.

HANNAH. You're old enough to understand that your father didn't love you without being ridiculous about it.

JOE. What?

HANNAH. You're ridiculous. You're being ridiculous.

JOE. I'm . . .
  What?

HANNAH. You really ought to go home now to your wife. I need to go to bed. This phone call. . . . We will just forget this phone call.

JOE. Mom.

HANNAH. No more talk. Tonight. This . . .
  (*Suddenly very angry*) Drinking is a sin! A sin! I raised you better than that.

(*She hangs up*)

SCENE 9

The following morning, early. Split scene: Harper and Joe at home; Louis and Prior in Prior's hospital room. Joe and Louis have just entered. This should be fast and obviously furious; overlapping is fine; the proceedings may be a little confusing but not the final results.

HARPER. Oh God. Home. The moment of truth has arrived.

JOE. Harper.

LOUIS. I'm going to move out.

PRIOR. The fuck you are.

JOE. Harper. Please listen. I still love you very much. You're still my best buddy; I'm not going to leave you.

HARPER. No, I don't like the sound of this. I'm leaving.

LOUIS. I'm leaving.
        I already have.

JOE. Please listen. Stay. This is really hard. We have to talk.

HARPER. We are talking. Aren't we. Now please shut up. OK?

PRIOR. Bastard. Sneaking off while I'm flat out here, that's low.
        If I could get up now I'd beat the holy shit out of you.

JOE. Did you take pills? How many?

HARPER. No pills. Bad for the . . . (*Pats stomach*)

JOE. You aren't pregnant. I called your gynecologist.

HARPER. I'm seeing a new gynecologist.

PRIOR. You have no right to do this.

LOUIS. Oh, that's ridiculous.

PRIOR. No right. It's criminal.

JOE. Forget about that. Just listen. You want the truth. This is the truth.
        I knew this when I married you. I've known this I guess for as long as I've known anything, but . . . I don't know, I thought maybe that with enough effort and will I could change myself . . . but I can't . . .

PRIOR. Criminal.

LOUIS. There oughta be a law.

PRIOR. There is a law. You'll see.

JOE. I'm losing ground here, I go walking, you want to know where I walk, I . . . go to the park, or up and down 53rd Street, or places where. . . . And I keep swearing I won't go walking again, but I just can't.

LOUIS. I need some privacy.

PRIOR. That's new.

LOUIS. Everything's new, Prior.

JOE. I try to tighten my heart into a knot, a snarl, I try to learn to live dead, just numb, but then I see someone I want, and it's like a nail, like a hot spike through my chest, and I know I'm losing.

PRIOR. Apartment too small for three? Louis and Prior comfy but not Louis and Prior and Prior's disease?

LOUIS. Something like that.
        I won't be judged by you. This isn't a crime, just—the inevitable consequence of people who run out of—whose limitations . . .

PRIOR. Bang bang bang. The court will come to order.

LOUIS. I mean let's talk practicalities, schedules; I'll come over if you want, spend nights with you when I can, I can . . .

PRIOR. Has the jury reached a verdict?

LOUIS. I'm doing the best I can.

PRIOR. Pathetic. Who cares?

JOE. My whole life has conspired to bring me to this place, and I can't despise my whole life. I think I believed when I met you I could save you, you at least if not myself, but . . .
        I don't have any sexual feelings for you, Harper. And I don't think I ever did.

(*Little pause.*)

HARPER. I think you should go.

JOE. Where?

HARPER. Washington. Doesn't matter.

JOE. What are you talking about?

HARPER. Without me.
        Without me, Joe. Isn't that what you want to hear?

(*Little pause.*)

JOE. Yes.

LOUIS. You can love someone and fail them. You can love someone and not be able to . . .

PRIOR. You *can*, theoretically, yes. A person can, maybe an editorial "you" can love, Louis, but not *you*, specifically you, I don't know, I think you are excluded from that general category.

HARPER. You were going to save me, but the whole time you were spinning a lie. I just don't understand that.

PRIOR. A person could theoretically love and maybe many do but we both know now you can't.

LOUIS. I do.

PRIOR. You can't even say it.

LOUIS. I love you, Prior.

PRIOR. I repeat. Who cares?

HARPER. This is so scary, I want this to stop, to go back . . .

PRIOR. We have reached a verdict, your honor. This man's heart is deficient. He loves, but his love is worth nothing.

JOE. Harper . . .

HARPER. Mr. Lies, I want to get away from here. Far away. Right now. Before he starts talking again. Please, please . . .

JOE. As long as I've known you Harper you've been afraid of . . . of men hiding under the bed, men hiding under the sofa, men with knives.

PRIOR (*Shattered; almost pleading; trying to reach him*). I'm dying! You stupid fuck! Do you know what that is! Love! Do you know what love means? We lived together four-and-a-half years, you animal, you idiot.

LOUIS. I have to find some way to save myself.

JOE. Who are these men? I never understood it. Now I know.

HARPER. What?

JOE. It's me.

HARPER. It is?

PRIOR. GET OUT OF MY ROOM!

JOE. I'm the man with the knives.

HARPER. You are?

PRIOR. If I could get up now I'd kill you. I would. Go away. Go away or I'll scream.

HARPER. Oh God . . .

JOE. I'm sorry . . .

HARPER. It is you.

LOUIS. Please don't scream.

PRIOR. Go.

HARPER. I recognize you now.

LOUIS. Please . . .

JOE. Oh. Wait, I . . . . Oh!

(*He covers his mouth with his hand, gags, and removes his hand, red with blood*)

I'm bleeding.

(*Prior screams.*)

HARPER. Mr. Lies.

MR. LIES (*Appearing, dressed in antarctic explorer's apparel*). Right here.

HARPER. I want to go away. I can't see him anymore.

MR. LIES. Where?

HARPER. Anywhere. Far away.

MR. LIES. Absolutamento.

(*Harper and Mr. Lies vanish. Joe looks up, sees that she's gone.*)

PRIOR (*Closing his eyes*). When I open my eyes you'll be gone.

(*Louis leaves.*)

JOE. Harper?

PRIOR (*Opening his eyes*). Huh. It worked.

JOE (*Calling*). Harper?

PRIOR. I hurt all over. I wish I was dead.

SCENE 10

The same day, sunset. Hannah and Sister Ella Chapter, a real-estate saleswoman, Hannah Pitt's closest friend, in front of Hannah's house in Salt Lake City.

SISTER ELLA CHAPTER. Look at that view! A view of heaven. Like the living city of heaven, isn't it, it just fairly glimmers in the sun.

HANNAH. Glimmers.

SISTER ELLA CHAPTER. Even the stone and brick it just glimmers and glitters like heaven in the sunshine. Such a nice view you get, perched up on a canyon rim. Some kind of beautiful place.

HANNAH. It's just Salt Lake, and you're selling the house *for* me, not *to* me.

SISTER ELLA CHAPTER. I like to work up an enthusiasm for my properties.

HANNAH. Just get me a good price.

SISTER ELLA CHAPTER. Well, the market's off.

HANNAH. At least fifty.

SISTER ELLA CHAPTER. Forty'd be more like it.

HANNAH. Fifty.

SISTER ELLA CHAPTER. Wish you'd wait a bit.

HANNAH. Well I can't.

SISTER ELLA CHAPTER. Wish you would. You're about the only friend I got.

HANNAH. Oh well now.

SISTER ELLA CHAPTER. Know why I decided to like you? I decided to like you 'cause you're the only unfriendly Mormon I ever met.

HANNAH. Your wig is crooked.

SISTER ELLA CHAPTER. Fix it.

(*Hannah straightens Sister Ella's wig.*)

SISTER ELLA CHAPTER. New York City. All they got there is tiny rooms.

I always thought: People ought to stay put. That's why I got my license to sell real estate. It's a way of saying: Have a house! Stay put! It's a way of saying traveling's no good. Plus I needed the cash. (*She takes a pack of cigarettes out of her purse, lights one, offers pack to Hannah*).

HANNAH. Not out here, anyone could come by.

There's been days I've stood at this ledge and thought about stepping over.

It's a hard place, Salt Lake: baked dry. Abundant energy; not much intelligence. That's a combination that can wear a body out. No harm looking someplace else. I don't need much room.

My sister-in-law Libby thinks there's radon gas in the basement.

SISTER ELLA CHAPTER. Is there gas in the . . .

HANNAH. Of course not. Libby's a fool.

SISTER ELLA CHAPTER. 'Cause I'd have to include that in the description.

HANNAH. There's no gas, Ella. (*Little pause*) Give a puff. (*She takes a furtive drag of Ella's cigarette*) Put it away now.

SISTER ELLA CHAPTER. So I guess it's goodbye.

HANNAH. You'll be all right, Ella, I wasn't ever much of a friend.

SISTER ELLA CHAPTER. I'll say something but don't laugh, OK?

This is the home of saints, the godliest place on earth, they say, and I think they're right. That means there's no evil here? No. Evil's everywhere. Sin's everywhere. But this . . . is the spring of sweet water in the desert, the desert flower. Every step a Believer takes away from here is a step fraught with peril. I fear for you, Hannah Pitt, because you are my friend. Stay put. This is the right home of saints.

HANNAH. Latter-day saints.

SISTER ELLA CHAPTER. Only kind left.

HANNAH. But still. Late in the day . . . for saints and everyone. That's all. That's all. Fifty thousand dollars for the house, Sister Ella Chapter; don't undersell. It's an impressive view.

ACT THREE: NOT-YET-CONSCIOUS, FORWARD DAWNING

January 1986

SCENE 1

Late night, three days after the end of Act Two. The stage is completely dark. Prior is in bed in his apartment, having a nightmare. He wakes up, sits up and switches on a nightlight. He looks at his clock. Seated by the table near the bed is a man dressed in the clothing of a 13th-century British squire.

PRIOR (*Terrified*). Who are you?

PRIOR 1. My name is *Prior Walter*.

(*Pause.*)

PRIOR. My name is Prior Walter.

PRIOR 1. I know that.

PRIOR. Explain.

PRIOR 1. You're alive. I'm not. We have the same name. What do you want me to explain?

PRIOR. A ghost?

PRIOR 1. An ancestor.

PRIOR. Not *the* Prior Walter? The Bayeux tapestry Prior Walter?

PRIOR 1. His great-great grandson. The fifth of the name.

PRIOR. I'm the thirty-fourth, I think.

PRIOR 1. Actually the thirty-second.

PRIOR. Not according to Mother.

PRIOR 1. She's including the two bastards, then; I say leave them out. I say no room for bastards. The little things you swallow . . .

PRIOR. Pills.

PRIOR 1. Pills. For the pestilence. I too . . .

PRIOR. Pestilence. . . . You too what?

PRIOR 1. The pestilence in my time was much worse than now. Whole villages of empty houses. You could look outdoors and see Death walking in the morning, dew dampening the ragged hem of his black robe. Plain as I see you now.

PRIOR. You died of the plague.

PRIOR 1. The spotty monster. Like you, alone.

PRIOR. I'm not alone.

PRIOR 1. You have no wife, no children.

PRIOR. I'm gay.

PRIOR 1. So? Be gay, dance in your altogether for all I care, what's that to do with not having children?

PRIOR. Gay homosexual, not bonny, blithe and . . . never mind.

PRIOR 1. I had twelve. When I died.

(*The second ghost appears, this one dressed in the clothing of an elegant 17th-century Londoner.*)

PRIOR 1 (*Pointing to Prior 2*). And I was three years younger than him.

(*Prior sees the new ghost, screams.*)

PRIOR. Oh God another one.

PRIOR 2. Prior Walter. Prior to you by some seventeen others.

PRIOR 1. He's counting the bastards.

PRIOR. Are you having a convention?

PRIOR 2. We've been sent to declare her fabulous incipience. They love a well-paved entrance with lots of heralds, and . . .

PRIOR 1. The messenger come. Prepare the way. The infinite descent, a breath of in air . . .

PRIOR 2. They chose us, I suspect, because of the mortal affinities. In a family as long-descended as the Walters there are bound to be a few carried off by plague.

PRIOR 1. The spotty monster.

PRIOR 2. Black Jack. Came from a water pump, half the city of London, can you imagine? His came from fleas. Yours, I understand, is the lamentable consequence of venery . . .

PRIOR 1. Fleas on rats, but who knew that?

PRIOR. Am I going to die?

PRIOR 2. We aren't allowed to discuss . . .

PRIOR 1. When you do, you don't get ancestors to help you through it. You may be surrounded by children but you die alone.

PRIOR. I'm afraid.

PRIOR 1. You should be. There aren't even torches, and the path's rocky, dark and steep.

PRIOR 2. Don't alarm him. There's good news before there's bad.

We two come to strew rose petal and palm leaf before the triumphal procession. Prophet. Seer. Revelator. It's a great honor for the family.

PRIOR 1. He hasn't got a family.

PRIOR 2. I meant for the Walters, for the family in the larger sense.

PRIOR (*Singing*).
　　All I want is a room somewhere,
　　Far away from the cold night air . . .

PRIOR 2 (*Putting a hand on Prior's forehead*). Calm, calm, this is no brain fever . . .

(*Prior calms down, but keeps his eyes closed. The lights begin to change. Distant Glorious Music.*)

PRIOR 1 (*Low chant*).
　　Adonai, Adonai,
　　Olam ha-yichud,
　　Zefirot, Zazahot,
　　Ha-adam, ha-gadol

Daughter of Light,
Daughter of Splendors,
Fluor! Phosphor!
Lumen! Candle!
PRIOR 2 (*Simultaneously*).
Even now,
From the mirror-bright halls of heaven,
Across the cold and lifeless infinity of space,
The Messenger comes
Trailing orbs of light,
Fabulous, incipient,
Oh Prophet,
To you . . .
PRIOR 1 AND PRIOR 2.
Prepare, prepare,
The Infinite Descent,
A breath, a feather,
Glory to . . .

(They vanish.)

SCENE 2

The next day. Split scene: Louis and Belize in a coffee shop. Prior is at the outpatient clinic at the hospital with Emily, the nurse; she has him on a pentamidine IV drip.

LOUIS. Why has democracy succeeded in America? Of course by succeeded I mean comparatively, not literally, not in the present, but what makes for the prospect of some sort of radical democracy spreading outward and growing up? Why does the power that was once so carefully preserved at the top of the pyramid by the original framers of the Constitution seem drawn inexorably downward and outward in spite of the best effort of the Right to stop this? I mean it's the really hard thing about being Left in this country, the American Left can't help but trip over all these petrified little fetishes: freedom, that's the worst; you know, *Jeane Kirkpatrick* for God's sake will go on and on about freedom and so what does that mean, the word freedom, when she talks about it, or human rights; you have Bush talking about human rights, and so what are these people talking about, they might as well be talking about the mating habits of Venusians, these people don't begin to know what, ontologically, freedom is or human rights, like they see these bourgeois property-based Rights-of-Man-type rights but that's not enfranchisement, not democracy, not what's implicit, what's potential within the idea, not the idea with blood in it. That's just liberalism, the worst kind of liberalism, really, bourgeois tolerance, and what I think is that what AIDS shows us is the limits of tolerance, that it's not enough to be tolerated, because when the shit hits the fan you find out how much tolerance is worth. Nothing. And underneath all the tolerance is intense, passionate hatred.

BELIZE. Uh huh.
LOUIS. Well don't you think that's true?
BELIZE. Uh huh. It is.
LOUIS. *Power* is the object, not being tolerated. Fuck assimilation. But I mean in spite of all this the thing about America, I think, is that ultimately we're different from every other nation on earth, in that, with people here of every race, we can't. . . . Ultimately what defines us isn't race, but politics. Not like any European country where there's an insurmountable fact of a kind of racial, or ethnic, monopoly, or monolith, like all Dutchmen, I mean Dutch people, are well, Dutch, and the Jews of Europe were never Europeans, just a small problem. Facing the monolith. But here there are so many small problems, it's really just a collection of small problems, the monolith is missing. Oh, I mean, of course I suppose there's the monolith of White America. White Straight Male America.
BELIZE. Which is not unimpressive, even among monoliths.
LOUIS. Well, no, but when the race thing gets taken care of, and I don't mean to minimize how major it is, I mean I know it is, this is a really, really incredibly racist country but it's like, well, the British. I mean, all these blue-eyed pink people. And it's just weird, you know, I mean I'm not all that Jewish-looking, or . . . well, maybe I am but, you know, in New York, everyone is . . . well, not everyone, but so many are but so but in England, in London I walk into bars and I feel like Sid the Yid, you know I mean like Woody Allen in *Annie Hall*, with the payess and the gabardine coat, like never, never anywhere so much—I mean, not actively despised, not like they're Germans, who I think are still terribly anti-Semitic, and racist too, I mean black-racist, they pretend otherwise but, anyway, in London, there's just . . . and at one point I met this black gay guy from Jamaica who talked with a lilt but he said his family'd been living in London since before the Civil War—the American one—and how the English never let him forget for a minute that he wasn't blue-eyed and pink and I said yeah, me too, these people are anti-Semites and he said yeah but the British Jews have the clothing business all sewed up and blacks here can't get a foothold. And it was an incredibly awkward moment of just. . . . I mean here we were, in this bar that was gay but it was a *pub*, you know, the beams and the plaster and those horrible little, like, two-day-old fish and egg sandwiches—and just so British, so *old*, and I felt, well, there's no way out of this because both of us are, right now, too much immersed in this history, hope is dissolved in the sheer age of this place, where race is what counts and there's no real hope of change—it's the racial destiny of the Brits that matters to them, not their political destiny, whereas in America . . .
BELIZE. Here in America race doesn't count.
LOUIS. No, no, that's not. . . . I mean you *can't* be hearing that . . .

BELIZE. I . . .

LOUIS. It's—look, race, yes, but ultimately race here is a political question, right? Racists just try to use race here as a tool in a political struggle. It's not really about race. Like the spiritualists try to use that stuff, are you enlightened, are you centered, channeled, whatever, this reaching out for a spiritual past in a country where no indigenous spirits exist—only the Indians, I mean Native American spirits and we killed them off so now, there are no gods here, no ghosts and spirits in America, there are no angels in America, no spiritual past, no racial past, there's only the political, and the decoys and the ploys to maneuver around the inescapable battle of politics, the shifting downwards and outwards of political power to the people . . .

BELIZE. POWER to the People! AMEN! (*Looking at his watch*) OH MY GOODNESS! Will you look at the time. I gotta . . .

LOUIS. Do you. . . . You think this is, what, racist or naive or something?

BELIZE. Well it's certainly *something*. Look, I just remembered I have an appointment . . .

LOUIS. What? I mean I really don't want to, like, speak from some position of privilege and . . .

BELIZE. I'm sitting here, thinking, eventually he's *got* to run out of steam, so I let you rattle on and on saying about maybe seven or eight things I find really offensive.

LOUIS. What?

BELIZE. But I know you, Louis, and I know the guilt fueling this peculiar tirade is obviously already swollen bigger than your hemorrhoids.

LOUIS. I don't have hemorrhoids.

BELIZE. I hear different. May I finish?

LOUIS. Yes, but I don't have hemorrhoids.

BELIZE. So finally, when I . . .

LOUIS. Prior told you, he's an asshole, he should have . . .

BELIZE. You promised, Louis. Prior is not a subject.

LOUIS. You brought him up.

BELIZE. I brought up hemorrhoids.

LOUIS. So it's indirect. Passive-aggressive.

BELIZE. Unlike, I suppose, banging me over the head with your theory that America doesn't have a race problem.

LOUIS. Oh be fair I never said that.

BELIZE. Not exactly, but . . .

LOUIS. I said . . .

BELIZE. . . . but it was close enough, because if it'd been that blunt I'd've just walked out and . . .

LOUIS. You deliberately misinterpreted! I . . .

BELIZE. Stop interrupting! I haven't been able to . . .

LOUISE. Just let me . . .

BELIZE. NO! What, *talk*? You've been running your mouth nonstop since I got here, yaddadda yaddadda blah blah blah, up the hill, down the hill, playing with your MONOLITH . . .

LOUIS (*Overlapping*). Well, you could have joined in at any time instead of . . .

BELIZE (*Continuing over Louis*). . . . and girlfriend it is truly an *awesome* spectacle but I got better things to do with my time than sit here listening to this racist bullshit just because I feel sorry for you that . . .

LOUIS. I am not a racist!

BELIZE. Oh come on . . .

LOUIS. So maybe I am a racist but . . .

BELIZE. Oh I really hate that! It's no fun picking on you Louis; you're so guilty, it's like throwing darts at a glob of jello, there's no satisfying hits, just quivering, the darts just blop in and vanish.

LOUIS. I just think when you are discussing lines of oppression it gets very complicated and . . .

BELIZE. Oh is that a fact? You know, we black drag queens have a rather intimate knowledge of the complexity of the lines of . . .

LOUIS. *Ex*-black drag queen.

BELIZE. Actually ex-ex.

LOUIS. You're doing drag again?

BELIZE. I don't. . . . Maybe. I don't have to tell you. Maybe.

LOUIS. I think it's sexist.

BELIZE. I didn't ask you.

LOUIS. Well it is. The gay community, I think, has to adopt the same attitude towards drag as black women have to take towards black women blues singers.

BELIZE. Oh my we *are* walking dangerous tonight.

LOUIS. Well, it's all internalized oppression, right, I mean the masochism, the stereotypes, the . . .

BELIZE. Louis, are you deliberately trying to make me hate you?

LOUIS. No, I . . .

BELIZE. I mean, are you deliberately transforming yourself into an arrogant, sexual-political Stalinist-slash-racist flagwaving thug for my benefit?

(*Pause.*)

LOUIS. You know what I think?

BELIZE. What?

LOUIS. You hate me because I'm a Jew.

BELIZE. I'm leaving.

LOUIS. It's true.

BELIZE. You have no basis except your . . .
    Louis, it's good to know you haven't changed; you are still an honorary citizen of the Twilight Zone, and after your pale, pale white polemics on behalf of racial insensitivity you have a flaming *fuck* of a lot of nerve calling me an anti-Semite. Now I really gotta go.

LOUIS. You called me Lou the Jew.

BELIZE. That was a joke.

LOUIS. I didn't think it was funny. It was hostile.

BELIZE. It was three years ago.

LOUIS. So?

BELIZE. You just called yourself Sid the Yid.

LOUIS. That's not the same thing.

BELIZE. Sid the Yid is different from Lou the Jew.

LOUIS. Yes.

BELIZE. Someday you'll have to explain that to me, but right now . . .

    You hate me because you hate black people.

LOUIS. I do not. But I do think most black people are anti-Semitic.

BELIZE. "Most black people." *That's* racist, Louis, and *I* think most Jews . . .

LOUIS. Louis Farrakhan.

BELIZE. Ed Koch.

LOUIS. Jesse Jackson.

BELIZE. Jackson. Oh really, Louis, this is . . .

LOUIS. Hymietown! Hymietown!

BELIZE. Louis, you voted for Jesse Jackson. You send checks to the Rainbow Coalition.

LOUIS. I'm ambivalent. The checks bounced.

BELIZE. All your checks bounce, Louis; you're ambivalent about everything.

LOUIS. What's that supposed to mean?

BELIZE. You may be dumber than shit but I refuse to believe you can't figure it out. Try.

LOUIS. I was never ambivalent about Prior. I love him. I do. I really do.

BELIZE. Nobody said different.

LOUIS. Love and ambivalence are. . . . Real love isn't ambivalent.

BELIZE. "Real love isn't ambivalent." I'd swear that's a line from my favorite bestselling paperback novel, *In Love with the Night Mysterious*, except I don't think you ever read it.

    (*Pause.*)

LOUIS. I never read it, no.

BELIZE. You ought to. Instead of spending the rest of your life trying to get through *Democracy in America*. It's about this white woman whose Daddy owns a plantation in the Deep South in the years before the Civil War—the American one—and her name is Margaret, and she's in love with her Daddy's number-one slave, and his name is Thaddeus, and she's married but her white slave-owner husband has AIDS: Antebellum Insufficiently Developed Sexorgans. And there's a lot of hot stuff going down when Margaret and Thaddeus can catch a spare torrid ten under the cotton-picking moon, and then of course the Yankees come, and here they set the slaves free, and the slaves string up old Daddy, and so on. Historical fiction. Somewhere in there I recall Margaret and Thaddeus find the time to discuss the nature of love; her face is reflecting the flames of the burning plantation—you know, the way white people do—and his black face is dark in the night and she says to him, "Thaddeus, real love isn't ever ambivalent."

(*Little pause. Emily enters and turns off IV drip.*)

BELIZE. Thaddeus looks at her; he's contemplating her thesis; and he isn't sure he agrees.

EMILY (*Removing IV drip from Prior's arm*). Treatment number . . . (*Consulting chart*) four.

PRIOR. Pharmaceutical miracle. Lazarus breathes again.

LOUIS. Is he. . . . How bad is he?

BELIZE. You want the laundry list?

EMILY. Shirt off, let's check the . . .

(*Prior takes his shirt off. She examines his lesions.*)

BELIZE. There's the weight problem and the shit problem and the morale problem.

EMILY. Only six. That's good. Pants.

(*He drops his pants. He's naked. She examines.*)

BELIZE. And. He thinks he's going crazy.

EMILY. Looking good. What else?

PRIOR. Ankles sore and swollen, but the leg's better. The nausea's mostly gone with the little orange pills. BM's pure liquid but not bloody anymore, for now, my eye doctor says everything's OK, for now, my dentist says "Yuck!" when he sees my fuzzy tongue, and now he wears little condoms on his thumb and forefinger. And a mask. So what? My dermatologist is in Hawaii and my mother . . . well leave my mother out of it. Which is usually where my mother is, out of it. My glands are like walnuts, my weight's holding steady for week two, and a friend died two days ago of bird tuberculosis; bird tuberculosis; that scared me and I didn't go to the funeral today because he was an Irish Catholic and it's probably open casket and I'm afraid of . . . something, the bird TB or seeing him or. . . . So I guess I'm doing OK. Except for of course I'm going nuts.

EMILY. We ran the toxoplasmosis series and there's no indication . . .

PRIOR. I know, I know, but I feel like something terrifying is on its way, you know, like a missile from outer space, and its plummeting down towards the earth, and I'm ground zero, and . . . I am generally known where I am known as one cool, collected queen. And I am ruffled.

EMILY. There's really nothing to worry about. I think that shochen bamromim hamtzeh menucho nechono al kanfey haschino.

PRIOR. What?

EMILY. Everything's fine. Bemaalos k'doshim ut'horim kezohar horokeea mazhirim . . .

PRIOR. Oh I don't understand what you're . . .

EMILY. Es nishmas Prior sheholoch leolomoh, baavur shenodvoo z'dokoh b'ad hazkoras nishmosoh.

PRIOR. Why are you doing that? Stop it! Stop it!

EMILY. Stop what?

PRIOR. You were just . . . weren't you just speaking in Hebrew or something.

EMILY. *Hebrew?* (*Laughs*) I'm basically Italian-American. No. I didn't speak in Hebrew.

PRIOR. Oh no, oh God please I really think I . . .

EMILY. Look, I'm sorry, I have a waiting room full of. . . . I think you're one of the lucky ones, you'll live for years, probably—you're pretty healthy for someone with no immune system. Are you seeing someone? Loneliness is a danger. A therapist?

PRIOR. No, I don't need to see anyone, I just . . .

EMILY. Well think about it. You aren't going crazy. You're just under a lot of stress. No wonder . . . (*She starts to write in his chart*)

(*Suddenly there is an astonishing blaze of light, a huge chord sounded by a gigantic choir, and a great book with steel pages mounted atop a molten-red pillar pops up from the stage floor. The book opens; there is a large Aleph inscribed on its pages, which bursts into flames. Immediately the book slams shut and disappears instantly under the floor as the lights become normal again. Emily notices none of this, writing. Prior is agog.*)

EMILY (*Laughing, exiting*). Hebrew . . .

(*Prior flees.*)

LOUIS. Help me.

BELIZE. I beg your pardon?

LOUIS. You're a nurse, give me something, I . . . don't know what to do anymore, I. . . . Last week at work I screwed up the Xerox machine like permanently and so I . . . then I tripped on the subway steps and my glasses broke and I cut my forehead, here, see, and now I can't see much and my forehead . . . it's like the Mark of Cain, stupid, right, but it won't heal and every morning I see it and I think, Biblical things, Mark of Cain, Judas Iscariot and his silver and his noose, people who . . . in betraying what they love betray what's truest in themselves, I feel . . . nothing but cold for myself, just cold, and every night I miss him, I miss him so much but then . . . those sores, and the smell and . . . where I thought it was going. . . . I could be . . . I could be sick too, maybe I'm sick too. I don't know.

Belize. Tell him I love him. Can you do that?

BELIZE. I've thought about it for a long time, and I still don't understand what love is. Justice is simple. Democracy is simple. Those things are unambivalent. But love is very hard. And it goes bad for you if you violate the hard law of love.

LOUIS. I'm dying.

BELIZE. He's dying. You just wish you were.

Oh cheer up, Louis. Look at that heavy sky out there.

LOUIS. Purple.

BELIZE. *Purple?* Boy, what kind of a homosexual are you, anyway? That's not purple, Mary, that color up there is (*very grand*) mauve.

All day today it's felt like Thanksgiving. Soon, this . . . ruination will be blanketed white. You can smell it—can you smell it?

LOUIS. Smell what?

BELIZE. Softness, compliance, forgiveness, grace.

LOUIS. No . . .

BELIZE. I can't help you learn that. I can't help you, Louis. You're not my business. (*He exits*)

(*Louis puts his head in his hands, inadvertently touching his forehead.*)

LOUIS. Ow FUCK! (*He stands slowly, looks towards where Belize is seated*) Smell what?

(*He looks both ways to be sure no one is watching, then inhales deeply, and is surprised.*) Huh. Snow.

SCENE 3

Same day. Harper in a very white, cold place, with a brilliant sky above; a delicate snowfall. She is dressed in a beautiful snowsuit. The sound of the sea, faint.

HARPER. Snow! Ice! Mountains of ice! Where am I? I . . . I feel better, I do. I . . . feel better. There are ice crystals in my lungs, wonderful and sharp. And the snow smells like cold, crushed peaches. And there's something . . . some current of blood in the wind, how strange, it has that iron taste.

MR. LIES. Ozone.

HARPER. Ozone! Wow! Where am I?

MR. LIES. The Kingdom of Ice, the bottommost part of the world.

HARPER (*Looking around, then realizing*). Antarctica. This is Antarctica!

MR. LIES. Cold shelter for the shattered. No sorrow here, tears freeze.

HARPER. Antarctica, Antarctica, oh boy oh boy, LOOK at this, I. . . . Wow, I must've really snapped the tether, huh?

MR. LIES. Apparently . . .

HARPER. That's great. I want to stay here forever. Set up camp. Build things. Build a city, an enormous city made up of frontier forts, dark wood and green roofs and high gates made of pointed logs and bonfires burning on every street corner. I should build by a river. Where are the forests?

MR. LIES. No timber here. Too cold. Ice, no trees.

HARPER. Oh details! I'm sick of details! I'll plant them and grow them. I'll live off caribou fat, I'll melt it over the bonfires and drink it from long, curved goat-horn cups.

It'll be great. I want to make a new world here. So that I never have to go home again.

MR. LIES. As long as it lasts. Ice has a way of melting . . .

HARPER. No. Forever. I can have anything I want here—maybe even companionship, someone who has . . . desire for me. You, maybe.

MR. LIES. It's against the by-laws of the International Order of Travel Agents to get involved with clients. Rules are rules. Anyway, I'm not the one you really want.

HARPER. There isn't anyone . . . maybe an Eskimo. Who

could ice-fish for food. And help me build a nest for when the baby comes.

MR. LIES. There are no Eskimo in Antarctica. And you're not really pregnant. You made that up.

HARPER. Well all of this is made up. So if the snow feels cold I'm pregnant. Right? Here, I can be pregnant. And I can have any kind of a baby I want.

MR. LIES. This is a retreat, a vacuum, its virtue is that it lacks everything; deep-freeze for feelings. You can be numb and safe here, that's what you came for. Respect the delicate ecology of your delusions.

HARPER. You mean like no Eskimo in Antarctica.

MR. LIES. Correcto. Ice and snow, no Eskimo. Even hallucinations have laws.

HARPER. Well then who's that?

(The Eskimo appears.)

MR. LIES. An Eskimo.

HARPER. An antarctic Eskimo. A fisher of the polar deep.

MR. LIES. There's something wrong with this picture.

(The Eskimo beckons.)

HARPER. I'm going to like this place. It's my own National Geographic Special! Oh! Oh! *(She holds her stomach)* I think . . . I think I felt her kicking. Maybe I'll give birth to a baby covered with thick white fur, and that way she won't be cold. My breasts will be full of hot cocoa so she doesn't get chilly. And if it gets really cold, she'll have a pouch I can crawl into. Like a marsupial. We'll mend together. That's what we'll do; we'll mend.

SCENE 4

Same day. An abandoned lot in the South Bronx. A homeless Woman is standing near an oil drum in which a fire is burning. Snowfall. Trash around. Hannah enters dragging two heavy suitcases.

HANNAH. Excuse me? I said excuse me? Can you tell me where I am? Is this Brooklyn? Do you know a Pineapple Street? Is there some sort of bus or train or . . . ?
    I'm lost, I just arrived from Salt Lake. City. Utah? I took the bus that I was told to take and I got off—well it was the very last stop, so I had to get off, and I *asked* the driver was this Brooklyn, and he nodded yes but he was from one of those foreign countries where they think it's good manners to nod at everything even if you have no idea what it is you're nodding at, and in truth I think he spoke no English at all, which I think would make him ineligible for employment on public transportation. The public being English-speaking, mostly. Do you speak English?

(The Woman nods.)

HANNAH. I was supposed to be met at the airport by my son. He didn't show and I don't wait more than three and three-quarters hours for *anyone*. I should have been patient, I guess, I. . . . Is this . . .

WOMAN. Bronx.

HANNAH. Is that. . . . The *Bronx*? Well how in the name of Heaven did I get to the Bronx when the bus driver said . . .

WOMAN *(Talking to herself)*. Slurp slurp slurp will you STOP that disgusting slurping! YOU DISGUSTING SLURPING FEEDING ANIMAL! Feeding yourself, just feeding yourself, what would it matter, to you or to ANYONE, if you just stopped. Feeding. And DIED?

(Pause.)

HANNAH. Can you just tell me where I . . .

WOMAN. Why was the Kosciusko Bridge named after a Polack?

HANNAH. I don't know what you're . . .

WOMAN. That was a joke.

HANNAH. Well what's the punchline?

WOMAN. I don't know.

HANNAH *(Looking around desperately)*. Oh for pete's sake, is there anyone else who . . .

WOMAN *(Again, to herself)*. Stand further off you fat loathsome whore, you can't have any more of this soup, slurp slurp slurp you animal, and the—I know you'll just go pee it all away and where will you do that? Behind what bush? It's FUCKING COLD out here and I . . .
    Oh that's right, because it was supposed have been a tunnel!
    That's not very funny.
    Have you read the prophecies of Nostradamus?

HANNAH. Who?

WOMAN. Some guy I went out with once somewhere, Nostradamus. Prophet, outcast, eyes like. . . . Scary shit, he . . .

HANNAH. Shut up. Please. Now I want you to stop jabbering for a minute and pull your wits together and tell me how to get to Brooklyn. Because you know! And you are going to tell me! Because there is no one else around to tell me and I am wet and cold and I am very hungry! So I am sorry you're psychotic but just make the effort—take a deep breath—DO IT!

(Hannah and the Woman breathe together.)

HANNAH. That's good. Now exhale.

(They do.)

HANNAH. Good. Now how do I get to Brooklyn?

WOMAN. Don't know. Never been. Sorry. Want some soup?

HANNAH. Manhattan? Maybe you know . . . I don't suppose you know the location of the Mormon Visitor's . . .

WOMAN. 65th and Broadway.

HANNAH. How do you . . .

WOMAN. Go there all the time. Free movies. Boring, but you can stay all day.

HANNAH. Well. . . . So how do I . . .
WOMAN. Take the D Train. Next block make a right.
HANNAH. Thank you.
WOMAN. Oh yeah. In the next century I think we will all be insane.

SCENE 5

Same day. Joe and Roy in the study of Roy's brownstone. Roy is wearing an elegant bathrobe. He has made a considerable effort to look well. He isn't well, and he hasn't succeeded much in looking it.

JOE. I can't. The answer's no. I'm sorry.
ROY. Oh, well, apologies . . .
    I can't see that there's anyone asking for apologies.

(Pause.)

JOE. I'm sorry, Roy.
ROY. Oh, well, apologies.
JOE. My wife is missing, Roy. My mother's coming from Salt Lake to . . . to help look, I guess. I'm supposed to be at the airport now, picking her up but. . . . I just spent two days in a hospital, Roy, with a bleeding ulcer, I was spitting up blood.
ROY. Blood, huh? Look, I'm very busy here and . . .
JOE. It's just a job.
ROY. A job? A *job? Washington!* Dumb Utah Mormon hick shit!
JOE. Roy . . .
ROY. WASHINGTON! When Washington called me I was younger than you, you think I said, "Aw fuck no I can't go I got two fingers up my asshole and a little moral nosebleed to boot!" When Washington calls you my pretty young punk friend you go or you can go fuck yourself sideways 'cause the train has pulled out of the station, and you are *out*, nowhere, out in the cold. Fuck you, Mary Jane, get outta here.
JOE. Just let me . . .
ROY. Explain? Ephemera. You broke my heart. Explain that. Explain that.
JOE. I love you. Roy.
    There's so much that I want, to be . . . what you see in me, I want to be a participant in the world, in your world, Roy, I want to be capable of that, I've tried, really I have but . . . I can't do this. Not because I don't believe in you, but because I believe in you so much, in what you stand for, at heart, the order, the decency. I would give anything to protect you, but. . . . There are laws I can't break. It's too ingrained. It's not me. There's enough damage I've already done.
    Maybe you were right, maybe I'm dead.
ROY. You're not dead, boy, you're a sissy.
    You love me; that's moving, I'm moved. It's nice to be loved. I warned you about her, didn't I, Joe? But you don't listen to me, why, because you say Roy is smart and Roy's a friend but Roy . . . well, he isn't nice, and you wanna be nice. Right? A nice, nice man!

(Little pause)

    You know what my greatest accomplishment was, Joe, in my life, what I am able to look back on and be proudest of? And I have helped make Presidents and unmake them and mayors and more goddam judges than anyone in NYC ever—AND several million dollars, tax-free—and what do you think means the most to me?
    You ever hear of Ethel Rosenberg? Huh, Joe, huh?
JOE. Well, yeah, I guess I. . . . Yes.
ROY. Yes. Yes. You have heard of Ethel Rosenberg. Yes. Maybe you even read about her in the history books.
    If it wasn't for me, Joe, Ethel Rosenberg would be alive today, writing some personal-advice column for *Ms.* magazine. She isn't. Because during the trial, Joe, I was on the phone every day, talking with the judge . . .
JOE. Roy . . .
ROY. Every day, doing what I do best, talking on the telephone, making sure that timid Yid nebbish on the bench did his duty to America, to history. That sweet unprepossessing woman, two kids, boo-hoo-hoo, reminded us all of our little Jewish mamas—she came this close to getting life; I pleaded till I wept to put her in the chair. Me. I did that. I would have fucking pulled the switch if they'd have let me. Why? Because I fucking hate traitors. Because I fucking hate communists. Was it legal? Fuck legal. Am I a nice man? Fuck nice. They say terrible things about me in the *Nation.* Fuck the *Nation.* You want to be Nice, or you want to be Effective? Make the law, or subject to it. Choose. Your wife chose. A week from today, she'll be back. SHE knows how to get what SHE wants. Maybe I ought to send *her* to Washington.
JOE. I don't believe you.
ROY. Gospel.
JOE. You can't possibly mean what you're saying.
    Roy, you were the Assistant United States Attorney on the Rosenberg case, ex parte communication with the judge during the trial would be . . . censurable, at least, probably conspiracy and . . . in a case that resulted in execution, it's . . .
ROY. What? Murder?
JOE. You're not well is all.
ROY. What do you mean, not well? Who's not well?

(Pause.)

JOE. You said . . .
ROY. No I didn't. I said what?
JOE. Roy, you have cancer.
ROY. No I don't.

(Pause.)

JOE. You told me you were dying.

ROY. What the fuck are you talking about Joe? I never said that. I'm in perfect health. There's not a goddam thing wrong with me.

(He smiles)

Shake?

(Joe hesitates. He holds out his hand to Roy. Roy pulls Joe into a close, strong clinch.)

ROY *(More to himself than to Joe)*. It's OK that you hurt me because I love you, baby Joe. That's why I'm so rough on you.

(Roy releases Joe. Joe backs away a step or two.)

ROY. Prodigal son. The world will wipe its dirty hands all over you.

JOE. It already has, Roy.

ROY. Now go.

(Roy shoves Joe, hard. Joe turns to leave. Roy stops him, turns him around.)

ROY *(Smoothing Joe's lapels, tenderly)*. I'll always be here, waiting for you . . .

(Then again, with sudden violence, he pulls Joe close, violently)

What did you want from me, what was all this, what do you want, you treacherous ungrateful little . . .

(Joe, very close to belting Roy grabs him by the front of his robe, and propels him across the length of the room. He holds Roy at arm's length, the other arm ready to hit.)

ROY *(Laughing softly, almost pleading to be hit)*. Transgress a little, Joseph.

(Joe releases Roy.)

ROY. There are so many laws; find one you can break.

(Joe hesitates, then leaves, backing out. When Joe has gone, Roy doubles over in great pain, which he's been hiding throughout the scene with Joe.)

ROY. Ah, Christ . . .

Andy! Andy! Get in here! Andy!

(The door opens but it isn't Andy. A small Jewish Woman dressed modestly in a fifties hat and coat stands in the doorway. The room darkens.)

ROY. Who the fuck are you? The new nurse?

(The figure in the doorway says nothing. She stares at Roy. A pause. Roy looks at her carefully, gets up, crosses to her. He crosses back to the chair, sits heavily.)

ROY. Aw, fuck. Ethel.

ETHEL ROSENBERG *(Her manner is friendly, her voice is ice-cold)*. You don't look good, Roy.

ROY. Well, Ethel. I don't feel good.

ETHEL ROSENBERG. But you lost a lot of weight. That suits you. You were heavy back then. Zaftig, mit hips.

ROY. I haven't been that heavy since 1960. We were all heavier back then, before the body thing started. Now I look like a skeleton. They stare.

ETHEL ROSENBERG. That shit's really hit the fan, huh, Roy?

(Little pause. Roy nods.)

ETHEL ROSENBERG. Well, the fun's just started.

ROY. What is this, Ethel, Halloween? You trying to scare me?

(Ethel says nothing.)

ROY. Well you're wasting your time! I'm scarier than you any day of the week! So beat it, Ethel! BOOO! BETTER DEAD THAN RED! Somebody trying to shake me up? HAH HAH! From the throne of God in heaven to the belly of hell, you can all fuck yourselves and then go jump in the lake because I'M NOT AFRAID OF YOU OR DEATH OR HELL OR ANYTHING!

ETHEL ROSENBERG. Be seeing you soon, Roy. Julius sends his regards.

ROY. Yeah, well send this to Julius!

(He flips the bird in her direction, stands and moves towards her. Halfway across the room he slumps to the floor, breathing laboriously, in pain.)

ETHEL ROSENBERG. You're a very sick man, Roy.

ROY. Oh God . . . ANDY!

ETHEL ROSENBERG. Hmmm. He doesn't hear you, I guess. We should call the ambulance.

(She goes to the phone)

Hah! Buttons! Such things they got now. What do I dial, Roy?

(Pause. Roy looks at her, then)

ROY. 911.

ETHEL ROSENBERG. *(Dials the phone)*? It sings!

(Imitating dial tones) La la la . . .

Huh.

Yes, you should please send an ambulance to the home of Mister Roy Cohn, the famous lawyer.

What's the address, Roy?

ROY *(A beat, then)*. 244 East 87th.

ETHEL ROSENBERG. 244 East 87th Street. No apartment number, he's got the whole building.

My name? *(A beat)* Ethel Greenglass Rosenberg.

(Small smile) Me? No I'm not related to Mr. Cohn. An old friend.

(She hangs up)

They said a minute.

ROY. I have all the time in the world.

ETHEL ROSENBERG. You're immortal.

ROY. I'm immortal. Ethel. *(He forces himself to stand)*
I have forced my way into history. I ain't never gonna die.

ETHEL ROSENBERG *(A little laugh, then)*. History is about to crack wide open. Millennium approaches.

SCENE 6

Late that night. Prior's bedroom. Prior 1 watching Prior in bed, who is staring back at him, terrified. Tonight Prior 1 is dressed in weird alchemical robes and hat over his historical clothing and he carries a long palm-leaf bundle.

PRIOR 1. Tonight's the night! Aren't you excited? Tonight she arrives! Right through the roof! Ha-adam, Ha-gadol . . .

PRIOR 2 *(Appearing similarly attired)*. Lumen! Phosphor! Fluor! Candle! An unending billowing of scarlet and . . .

PRIOR. Look. Garlic. A mirror. Holy water. A crucifix. FUCK OFF! Get the fuck out of my room! GO!

PRIOR 1 *(To Prior 2)*. Hard as a hickory knob, I'll bet.

PRIOR 2. We all tumesce when they approach. We wax full, like moons.

PRIOR 1. Dance.

PRIOR. Dance?

PRIOR 1. Stand up, dammit, give us your hands, dance!

PRIOR 2. Listen . . .

(A lone oboe begins to play a little dance tune.)

PRIOR 2. Delightful sound. Care to dance?

PRIOR. Please leave me alone, please just let me sleep . . .

PRIOR 2. Ah, he wants someone familiar. A partner who knows his steps. *(To Prior)* Close your eyes. Imagine . . .

PRIOR. I don't . . .

PRIOR 2. Hush. Close your eyes.

(Prior does.)

PRIOR 2. Now open them.

(Prior does. Louis appears. He looks gorgeous. The music builds gradually into a full-blooded, romantic dance tune.)

PRIOR. Lou.

LOUIS. Dance with me.

PRIOR. I can't, my leg, it hurts at night . . .
Are you . . . a ghost, Lou?

LOUIS. No. Just spectral. Lost to myself. Sitting all day on cold park benches. Wishing I could be with you. Dance with me, babe . . .

(Prior stands up. The legs stop hurting. They begin to dance. The music is beautiful.)

PRIOR 1 *(To Prior 2)*. Hah. Now I see why he's got no children. He's a sodomite.

PRIOR 2. Oh be quiet, you medieval gnome, and let them dance.

PRIOR 1. I'm not interfering, I've done my bit. Hooray, hooray, the messenger's come, now I'm blowing off. I don't like it here.

(Prior 1 vanishes.)

PRIOR 2. The twentieth century. Oh dear, the world has gotten so terribly, terribly old.

(Prior 2 vanishes. Louis and Prior waltz happily. Lights fade back to normal. Louis vanishes.
Prior dances alone.
Then suddenly, the sound of wings fills the room.)

SCENE 7

Split scene: Prior alone in his apartment; Louis alone in the park.
Again, a sound of beating wings.

PRIOR. Oh don't come in here don't come in . . . LOUIS!!
No. My name is Prior Walter, I am . . . the scion of an ancient line, I am . . . abandoned I . . . no, my name is . . . is . . . Prior and I live . . . *here and now*, and . . . in the dark, in the dark, the Recording Angel opens its hundred eyes and snaps the spine of the Book of Life and . . . hush! Hush!
I'm talking nonsense, I . . .
No more mad scene, hush, hush . . .

(Louis in the park on a bench. Joe approaches, stands at a distance. They stare at each other, then Louis turns away.)

LOUIS. Do you know the story of Lazarus?

JOE. Lazarus?

LOUIS. Lazarus. I can't remember what happens, exactly.

JOE. I don't. . . . Well, he was dead, Lazarus, and Jesus breathed life into him. He brought him back from death.

LOUIS. Come here often?

JOE. No. Yes. Yes.

LOUIS. Back from the dead. You believe that really happened?

JOE. I don't know anymore what I believe.

LOUIS. This is quite a coincidence. Us meeting.

JOE. I followed you.
From work. I . . . followed you here.

(Pause.)

LOUIS. You followed me.
You probably saw me that day in the washroom and thought: there's a sweet guy, sensitive, cries for friends in trouble.

JOE. Yes.

LOUIS. Well I fooled you. Crocodile tears. Nothing . . . (*He touches his heart, shrugs*)

(*Joe reaches tentatively to touch Louis's face.*)

LOUIS (*Pulling back*). What are you doing? Don't do that.

JOE (*Withdrawing his hand*). Sorry. I'm sorry.

LOUIS. I'm . . . just not . . . I think, if you touch me, your hand might fall off or something. Worse things have happened to people who have touched me.

JOE. Please.

Oh, boy . . .

Can I . . .

I . . . want . . . to touch you. Can't I please just touch you . . . um, here?

(*He puts his hand on one side of Louis's face. He holds it there*)

I'm going to hell for doing this.

LOUIS. Big deal. You think it could be any worse than New York City?

(*He puts his hand on Joe's hand. He takes Joe's hand away from his face, holds it for a moment, then*) Come on.

JOE. Where?

LOUIS. Home. With me.

JOE. This makes no sense. I mean I don't know you.

LOUIS. Likewise.

JOE. And what you do know about me you don't like.

LOUIS. The Republican stuff?

JOE. Yeah, well for starters.

LOUIS. I don't not like that. I *hate* that.

JOE. So why on earth should we . . .

(*Louis goes to Joe and kisses him.*)

LOUIS. Strange bedfellows. I don't know. I never made it with one of the damned before. I would really rather not have to spend tonight alone.

JOE. I'm a pretty terrible person, Louis.

LOUIS. Lou.

JOE. No, I really am. I don't think I deserve being loved.

LOUIS. There? See? We already have a lot in common.

(*Louis stands, begins to walk away. He turns, looks back at Joe, Joe follows. They exit.*)

(*Prior listens. At first no sound, then once again, the sound of beating wings, frighteningly near.*)

PRIOR. That sound, that sound, it. . . . What is that, like birds or something, like a *really* big bird, I'm frightened, I . . . no, no fear, find the anger, find the . . . anger, my blood is clean, my brain is fine, I can handle pressure, I am a gay man and I am used to pressure, to trouble, I am tough and strong and. . . . Oh. Oh my goodness. I . . . (*He is washed over by an intense sexual feeling*) Ooohhhh. . . . I'm hot, I'm . . . so . . . aw Jeez what is going on here I . . . must have a fever I . . .

(*The bedside lamp flickers wildly as the bed begins to roll forward and back. There is a deep bass creaking and groaning from the bedroom ceiling, like the timbers of a ship under immense stress, and from above a fine rain of plaster dust.*)

PRIOR. OH!

PLEASE, OH PLEASE! Something's coming in here, I'm scared, I don't like this at all, something's approaching and I. . . . OH!

(*There is a great blaze of triumphal music, heralding. The light turns an extraordinary harsh, cold, pale blue, then a rich, brilliant warm golden color, then a hot bilious green, and then finally a spectacular royal purple. Then silence.*)

PRIOR (*An awestruck whisper*). God almighty . . .

Very Steven Spielberg.

(*A sound, like a plummeting meteor, tears down from very, very far above the earth, hurtling at an incredible velocity towards the bedroom; the light seems to be sucked out of the room as the projectile approaches; as the room reaches darkness, we hear a terrifying CRASH as something immense strikes earth; the whole building shudders and a part of the bedroom ceiling, lots of plaster and lathe and wiring, crashes to the floor. And then in a shower of unearthly white light, spreading great opalescent gray-silver wings, the Angel descends into the room and floats above the bed.*)

ANGEL.

Greetings, Prophet;

The Great Work begins:

The Messenger has arrived.

(*Blackout.*)

END OF PART ONE

FORUMS

"Embracing All Possibilities in Art and Life"

Frank Rich

"History is about to crack open," says Ethel Rosenberg, back from the dead, as she confronts a cadaverous Roy Cohn, soon to die of AIDS, in his East Side town house. "Something's going to give," says a Brooklyn housewife so addicted to Valium she thinks she's in Antarctica. The year is 1985. It is fifteen years until the millennium. And a young man drenched in death fevers in his Greenwich Village bedroom hears a persistent throbbing, a thunderous heartbeat, as if the heavens were about to give birth to a miracle so that he might be born again.

This is the astonishing theatrical landscape, intimate and epic, of Tony Kushner's "Angels in America." . . . This play has already been talked about so much that you may feel you have already seen it, but believe me, you haven't, even if you actually have. The New York production is the third I've seen of "Millennium Approaches," as the first self-contained, three-and-a-half-hour part of "Angels in America" is titled. . . . As directed with crystalline lucidity by George C. Wolfe and ignited by blood-churning performances by Ron Liebman and Stephen Spinella, this staging only adds to the impression that Mr. Kushner has written the most thrilling American play in years.

"Angels in America" is a work that never loses its wicked sense of humor or its wrenching grasp of such timeless dramatic matters as life, death and faith even as it ranges through territory as far-flung as the complex, plague-ridden nation Mr. Kushner wishes to survey and to address. Subtitled "A Gay Fantasia on National Themes," the play is a political call to arms for the age of AIDS, but it is no polemic. Mr. Kushner's convictions about power and justice are matched by his conviction that the stage, and perhaps the stage alone, is a space large enough to accommodate everything from precise realism to surrealistic hallucination, from black comedy to religious revelation. In "Angels in America," a true American work in its insistence on embracing all possibilities in art and life, he makes the spectacular case that they can all be brought into fusion in one play.

At center stage, "Angels" is a domestic drama, telling the story of two very different but equally troubled young New York couples, one gay and one nominally heterosexual, who intersect by chance. But the story of these characters soon proves inseparable from the way Mr. Kushner tells it. His play opens with a funeral led by an Orthodox rabbi and reaches its culmination with what might be considered the Second Coming. In between, it travels to Salt Lake City in search of latter-day saints and spirals into dreams and dreams-within-dreams where the languages spoken belong to the minority American cultures of drag and jazz. Hovering above it all is not only an Angel (Ellen McLaughlin) but also an Antichrist, Mr. Liebman's Roy Cohn,

an unreconstructed right-wing warrior who believes that "life is full of horror" from which no one can escape.

While Cohn is a villain, a hypocritical closet case and a corrupt paragon of both red-baiting and Reagan-era greed, his dark view of life is not immediately dismissed by Mr. Kushner. The America of "Angels in America" is riddled with cruelty. When a young WASP esthete named Prior Walter (Mr. Spinella) reveals his first lesions of Kaposi's sarcoma to his lover for four years, a Jewish clerical worker named Louis Ironson (Joe Mantello), he finds himself deserted in a matter of weeks. Harper Pitt (Marcia Gay Harden), pill-popping housewife and devout Mormon, has recurrent nightmares that a man with a knife is out to kill her; she also has real reason to fear that the man is her husband, Joe (David Marshall Grant), an ambitious young lawyer with a dark secret and aspirations to rise high in Ed Meese's Justice Department.

But even as Mr. Kushner portrays an America of lies and cowardice to match Cohn's cynical view, he envisions another America of truth and beauty, the paradise imagined by both his Jewish and Mormon characters' ancestors as they made their crossing to the new land. "Angels in America" not only charts the split of its two central couples but it also implicitly sets its two gay men with AIDS against each other in a battle over their visions of the future. While the fatalistic, self-loathing Cohn ridicules gay men as political weaklings with "zero clout" doomed to defeat, the younger, equally ill Prior sees the reverse. "I am a gay man, and I am used to pressure," he says from his sick bed. "I am tough and strong." Possessed by scriptural visions he describes as "very Steven Spielberg" even when in abject pain, Prior is Mr. Kushner's prophet of hope in the midst of apocalypse.

Though Cohn and Prior never have a scene together, they are the larger-than-life poles between which all of "Angels in America" swings. And they could not be more magnetically portrayed than they are in this production. Mr. Liebman, red-faced and cackling, is a demon of Shakespearean grandeur, an alternately hilarious and terrifying mixture of chutzpah and megalomania, misguided brilliance and relentless cunning. He turns the mere act of punching telephone buttons into a grotesque manipulation of the levers of power, and he barks out the most outrageous pronouncements ("I brought out something tender in him," he says of Joe McCarthy) with a shamelessness worthy of history's most incredible monsters.

Mr. Spinella is a boyish actor so emaciated that when he removes his clothes for a medical examination, some in the audience gasp. But he fluently conveys buoyant idealism and pungent drag-queen wit as well as the piercing, open-mouthed cries of fear and rage that arrive with the graphically dramatized collapse of his health. Mr. Spinella is also blessed with a superb acting partner in Mr. Mantello, who as his callow lover is a combustible amalgam of puppyish Jewish guilt and self-serving intellectual piety.

The entire cast, which includes Kathleen Chalfant and Jeffrey Wright in a variety of crisply observed comic cameos, is first rate. Ms. Harden's shattered, sleepwalking housewife is pure pathos, a figure of slurred thought, voice and emotions, while Mr. Grant fully conveys the internal warfare of her husband, torn between Mormon rectitude and uncontrollable sexual heat. When Mr. Wolfe gets both of the play's couples on stage simultaneously to enact their parallel, overlapping domestic crackups, "Angels in America" becomes a wounding fugue of misunderstanding and recrimination committed in the name of love.

But "Angels in America" is an ideal assignment for Mr. Wolfe because of its leaps beyond the bedroom into the fabulous realms of myth and American archetypes, which have preoccupied this director and playwright in such works as "The Colored Museum" and "Spunk." Working again with Robin Wagner, the designer who was an essential collaborator on "Jelly's Last Jam," Mr. Wolfe makes the action fly through the delicate, stylized heaven that serves as the evening's loose scenic environment, yet he also manages to make some of the loopier scenes, notably those involving a real-estate agent in Salt Lake City and a homeless woman in the South Bronx, sharper and far more pertinent than they have seemed before.

What has really affected "Angels in America" during the months of its odyssey to New York, however, is not so much its change of directors as Washington's change of Administrations. When first seen a year or so ago, the play seemed defined by its anger at the reigning political establishment, which tended to reward the Roy Cohns and ignore the Prior Walters. Mr. Kushner has not revised the text since—a crony of Cohn's still boasts of a Republican lock on the White House until the year 2000—but the shift in Washington has had the subliminal effect of making "Angels in America" seem more focused on what happens next than on the past.

This is why any debate about what this play means or does not mean for Broadway seems, in the face of the work itself, completely beside the point. "Angels in America" speaks so powerfully because something far larger and more urgent than the future of the theater is at stake. It really is history that Mr. Kushner intends to crack open. He sends his haunting messenger, a spindly, abandoned gay man with a heroic spirit and a ravaged body, deep into the audience's heart to ask just who we are and just what, as the plague continues and the millennium approaches, we intend this country to become.

"Tony Kushner Considers the Long-standing Problems of Virtue and Happiness"

DAVID SAVRAN

SAVRAN: **As the subtitle of *Angels* makes plain, this play recognized that gay men have been at the center of certain crucial themes and identities in our national life. How do you see *Angels* in relation to the development of queer politics?**
KUSHNER: I'm in my late thirties now and of the generation that made ACT UP and then Queer Nation—a generation stuck between the people who created the '60s and their children. I see traces of the Stonewall generation, of Larry Kramer and even, to a certain extent, Harvey Fierstein. . . . I feel like I'm part of a group of theatre people that includes Holly Hughes, David Greenspan, Paula Vogel. . . . As I've said in other interviews, I think of it as a change from the Theatre of the Ridiculous to the Theatre of the Fabulous.

The Queer Nation chant—"We're here. We're queer. We're fabulous. Get used to it!"—uses *fabulous* in two senses. First, there's *fabulous* as opposed to *ridiculous*. In *The Beautiful Room Is Empty*, Edmund White writes about the Stonewall rebellion being a "ridiculous" thing for the people who were involved: It was a political gesture, what Wayne Koestenbaum calls "retalia-

tory self-invention," a gesture of defiance. That's the essence of the ridiculous. And the drag gesture is still not completely capable of taking itself seriously. I don't want to talk in a judgmental way, but there's still a certain weight of self-loathing, I think that's caught up in it. We're the generation that grew up when homophobia wasn't axiomatic and universal, and when the closet wasn't nailed shut and had to be kicked open. . . .

It seemed to me that this development of queer politics has in part prepared for the success of *Angels in America*.
Absolutely. It kicked down the last door. The notion of acting up, much more than outing, is what really blew out liberal gay politics. I mean, you depend upon the work that's done by the slightly assimilationist but hard-working, libertarian, civil rights groups, like the NAACP, but then at some point you need the Panthers. The way *Angels in America* talks, and its complete lack of apology for that kind of fagginess, is something that would not have made sense before.

I keep thinking of that line from Walter Benjamin's: "Where we perceive a chain of events, [the angel] sees one single catastrophe which keeps piling wreckage upon wreckage and hurls it in front of his feet." The scene in heaven in *Perestroika* really took my breath away, seeing the wreckage behind the scrim.
And there's a whole scene that we didn't perform because it just didn't play. These very Benjaminian, Rilkean angels are listen-

(continued)

ing on an ancient radio to the first report of the disaster at Chernobyl. Benjamin's sense of utopianism is also so profoundly apocalyptic: a teleology, but not a guarantee, or a guarantee that Utopia will be as fraught and as infected with history. It's not pie in the sky at all.

I think that is also a very American trope. In *The American Religion*, Harold Bloom keeps referring to this country as the evening land, where the promise of Utopia is so impossibly remote that it brings one almost to grieving and despair. Seeing what heaven looks like from the depths of hell. It's the most excruciating pain. And even as one is murdering and rampaging and slashing and burning to achieve Utopia, one is aware that the possibility of attaining Utopia is being irreparably damaged. People in this country knew somewhere what they were doing, but as we moved into this century, we began to develop a mechanism for repressing that knowledge. There's a sense of progress, but at tremendous cost.

It's Prior who carries the burden of that in *Angels*. Embedded even in his name is the sense that he's out of step with time, both too soon and belated, connected to the past and future, to ancestors and what's to come.
He's also connected to Walter Benjamin. I've written about my friend Kimberly [Flynn], who is a profound influence on me. The line that Benjamin wrote that's most important to her—and is so true—is, "Even the dead will not be safe if the enemy wins." She said joking that at times she felt such an extraordinary kinship with him that she thought she was Walter Benjamin reincarnated. And so at one point in the conversation, when I was coming up with names for my characters, I said, "I had to look up something in Benjamin—not you, but the prior Walter." That's where the name came from. I had been looking for one of those WASP names that nobody gets called anymore.

Agnes and Louis are, in one way or another, liberals. In both plays you've well-intentioned liberals whose actions are at an extraordinary remove from their intentions. Why?
I've never thought of Louis and Agnes as a pair, but they really are. I think they're very American. American radicalism has always been anarchic as opposed to socialist. The socialist tradition in this country is so despised and has been blamed so much on immigrants. It's been constructed as a Jewish, alien thing, which is not the way socialism is perceived anywhere else in the world where there is a native sense of *communitas* that we don't share. What we have is a native tradition of anarchism, and that's a fraught, problematic tradition. Ronald Reagan is as much its true heir as Abbie Hoffman. Abbie Hoffman was an anarcho-communist and Ronald Reagan is an ego-anarchist, but they're both anarchists.

The strain in the American character I feel the most affection for and that has the most potential for growth is American liberalism, which is incredibly short of what it needs to be, incredibly limited and exclusionary and predicated on all sorts of racist, sexist, homophobic and classist prerogatives. And yet, as Louis asks, why has democracy succeeded in America? I really believe that there is the potential for radical democracy in this country, one of the few places on earth where I see it as a strong possibility. There is an American tradition of liberalism, of a kind of social justice, fair play and tolerance—and each of these things can certainly be played upon in the most horrid ways. (Reagan kept the most hair-raising anarchist aspects of his

agenda hidden, and presented himself as a good old-fashioned liberal who kept invoking FDR.) It may just be sentimentalism on my part because I am the child of liberal-pinko parents but I do believe in it—as much as I often find it despicable. . . .

None of the characters in *Angels*, though, is involved with mass-movement politics.
That's because the play is set—and I think is very important—at a time when there's no such thing in the United States for generally progressive people. For someone like Belize, there isn't anything. The Rainbow Coalition has started to waffle and fall apart. And there is nothing in the gay community—there's the Gay Pride parade, and Gay Men's Health Crisis getting humiliated at the City Council in Newark every year. 1984–85 was a horrible, horrible time. It really seemed as if the maniacs had won for good.

What Martin says in *Millennium* now seems like a joke that we can all snigger at, but at the time, I just wrote what I thought was most accurate. The Republicans had lost the Senate, but would eventually get that back because the South would go Republican. There would never be a Democratic President again, because Mondale was the best answer we could make to Ronald Reagan, the most popular President we've ever had. So none of these people had anything they could hook into, which is the history of the Left. When the moment comes, when the break happens and history can be made, do we step in and make it or do we flub and fail? As much as I am horrified by what Clinton does—and we could have had someone better—we didn't completely blow it this time.

I'm interested in father-son relationships in the play—the way that Roy Cohn is set up as the masochistic son of a sadistic father, Joseph McCarthy, and how he, in turn, is a sadistic father to Joe. Isn't a sadomasochistic dynamic really crucial for mapping so many of the relationships in the play? Both Louis and Harper seem amazingly masochistic, in very different ways.
I want to explore S&M more because I feel that it's an enormously pervasive dynamic, that it's inextricably wound up with the issue of patriarchy, and that there are ways in which it plays through every aspect of life. I think it's something that needs to be understood, thought about and spoken about more openly.

We subjects of capitalist societies have to talk about the ways in which we are constructed to eroticize and cathect pain, as well as the pain that is transformed into pleasure, and self-destruction into self-creation. What price must we finally pay for that? Until now, there's been a kind of dumb liberation policies—all forms of sexual practice are off-limits for analysis, and S&M that's acted out that needs to concern us. I think that sexuality should still be subject to analysis, including the question of why we're gay instead of straight, which I think has nothing to do with the hypothalamus or interstitial brain cells, but to do with trauma.

But isn't all sexuality rooted in trauma?
We're just good Freudians. Yes, it's all trauma and loss, and the question is, are there specific forms of trauma? I believe that there is an etiology of sexuality that's traceable if anybody wants to spend the money on an analyst. Oedipus is still legitimate grounds for exploration and inquiry. And I think that the notion of the cultural formation of personalities is of tremendous importance. Roy's generation of gay men, for example, had that kind of deeply patriarchal, gender-enforced notion of the seduc-

tion of youth—the ephebe and the elder man. That comes down from the Greeks, homosexuality being a form of tutelage, of transmission, of dominance and submission. It felt to me that that would absolutely be part of Roy's repressed, ardent desire for Joe. Then what you see replicated in the blessing scene is the form of love which has to flow through inherited structures of hierarchical power.

These are some of the oldest questions with which we've been torturing ourselves: What is the relationship between sexuality and power? Is there even such a thing as a "sexuality"? If we buy into the notion of the construction of these forms of behavior, and the construction of personalities that engage in these behaviors, do we believe in the deconstruction of these forms? What is that deconstruction? There's the issue of reforming the personality to become a socialist subject: By what process, other than submission, does the individual ego become part of a collective? Is there a process other than revolution, other than bloodshed, agony and pain—which is fundamentally masochistic—by which we can transform ourselves? That's a big question, and it turns you toward things like Zen.

That's the question of the play: What is there beyond pain? Is Utopia even imaginable?

If our lives are in fact shaped by trauma and loss—and as I get older it seems to me that life is very, very profoundly shaped by loss and death—how do you address that? How does one progress in the face of that? That's the question that the AIDS epidemic has asked. There is no place more optimistic than America, in the most awful way (like "Up with People!"). These questions make so many people queasy, and become the subject of so much sarcasm, but identity is shaped, even racial identity. If there weren't bigots, there wouldn't be a politics of a race. There has to be a politics of difference that speaks to the presence of enormous oppression and violence and terror. The more we know about history, the more we realize—and this is an important thing about sadomasochism—that it never ends. You can see in our present moment a thousand future Sarajevos. You know that when you're 90, if you live so long, they'll still be fighting. Even after the Holocaust, the monsters are still among

us. And can you forgive? That's why I ask this question of forgiveness, because it possibly, like that of Utopia, is under-theorized and under-expressed.

Relating to the question of forgiveness, why do you use Mormons in the play, along with Jews? The angels are so clearly Old Testament angels, angels of the vengeful God. How does that tie in with the Mormon Religion?

There are interesting similarities between Mormonism and Judaism. They both have a very elusive notion of damnation. It's always been unclear to me, as a Jew, what happens if you don't do good things. Presumably you don't go to Paradise. There is a Hell, but even among the Orthodox, there isn't an enormous body of literature about it—it's not like Catholicism. Mormonism has a Hell but it also has three or four layers of Heaven.

Also, like Judaism, Mormonism is a diasporic religion, and it is of the book. It draws its strength very much from the book. It draws its strength very much from a literal, physical volume, which isn't sacred like the Torah—but it's all about the discovery of a book. Neither religion is about redemption based on being sorry for what you've done and asking for forgiveness. The hallmark of Mormonism is, "By deeds ye shall be known." Ethics are defined by action, and that is also true in Judaism. Your intentions make very little difference to God. What counts is what you do and whether you're righteous in your life. That appeals to me. It also feels very American.

I started the play with an image of an angel crashing through a bedroom ceiling, and I knew that this play would have a connection to American themes. The title came from that, and I think the title, as much as anything else, suggested Mormonism because the prototypical American angel is the angel Moroni. It's of this continent, the place of Mormon mythology that Jesus visited after he was crucified. It's a great story—not the Book of Mormon, which, as Mark Twain said, is chloroform in print, but the story of Joseph Smith's life and the trek, the gathering of Zion. The idea of inventing a complete cosmology out of a personal vision is something I can't imagine a European doing. . . . It's like Grandma Moses, the celestial and the terrestrial heavens with all this masonry incorporated into it. It's American gothic.

PART III

An Anthology of Non-Western Drama

Mojin Shoka, *a contemporary Japanese play, was performed in Tokyo in 1973.*

CHAPTER 7

THE THEATER OF ASIA

Theater in the many countries of Asia also sprang from religious rites, shamanistic ceremonies (especially those devoted to healing), and sacred dances. In India the deity Brahma appeared to the mortal priest Bharata and instructed him in the ways of theater so humans might be enlightened about life in its sublime state. In China the first professional actors may have been priests employed by farmers to perform sacred dances that would insure a bountiful harvest. The Noh theater of Japan evolved from Buddhist temple dances and even today retains a spiritual dimension in its attempt to induce its audience into meditation. Even the more secular Kabuki originated with temple dancers. Today, the Japanese word for "festival," *matsuri* ("to be near a god or sacred thing"), reflects the spiritual roots of such events as the Tanabata festival (see Center Stage box, The Tanabata Festival of Japan).

Consider other examples of the spiritual origins of the theater in other Asian locales. As early as the twelfth century B.C.E., Koreans celebrated Yong-go, a religious festival not unlike the Greek Dionysia. During the tenth month of each year, Koreans gathered for singing, dancing, and wine drinking. A short play, *The Welcoming of the Drum*, was central to the Yong-go. By 100 C.E., numerous folk performances in Southeast Asia were associated with animal worship (especially sea creatures in this oceangoing culture). In Indonesia and Malaysia leather figures representing man, gods, and evil spirits were used as shadow puppets to enact the great myths of the people. The puppets were controlled by the *dalang* (an actor-shaman-storyteller) who was thought to be a god. Plays that lasted a full day were performed to depict the progress of a man from youth to spiritual harmony. Such plays were commonplace by 907 C.E. (near the advent of Christian drama in Europe), and they eventually evolved into *khon*, plays about human dilemmas performed by the *dalang* themselves. Similar progressions in the evolution of theater and drama can be found throughout the world.

While there exists a wealth of extraordinary theatrical activity throughout Asia—much of which has influenced contemporary Western performance—the best-known drama comes from India, China, and Japan. Specifically, we will look at the most representative forms of drama from those three cultures:

- The Sanskrit drama of India, which flourished for over a thousand years. You may read a summary of the greatest of the Sanskrit plays, a romance called *The Recognition of Śakuntalā*.
- The Chinese theater, which will be considered in two forms:
  - The Classical theater of the Yuan dynasty produced China's greatest literary drama.
  - The Peking Opera is arguably the most popular theater-form in the world as it is the national drama of the world's most populous country. *The Qing Ding Pearl*, a short melodrama, will allow you to experience the type of play the Chinese have been enjoying for 200 years.

- The Noh theater of Japan, which is perhaps most rooted in ritual and ceremony.
- The Kabuki, which was developed in the early seventeenth century, and remains Japan's most popular theater form. You will read one of the eighteen treasures of the Kabuki, *Kanjinchō* (*The Subscription List*), a tale of a loyal samurai warrior.
- Contemporary Japanese plays, which are called *shengeki* ("new plays").

Though these works come from differing cultures and performance traditions, some characteristics are common to most Asian theater:

- There is no pretense of realism in the performance of traditional Asian plays (though that is changing in the contemporary era). The Asian theater has always been presentational and highly theatrical.
- Consequently, there is a high degree of interaction among performers and spectators. While many periods of theater in the West enjoyed such interaction, it remains one of the most distinguishing characteristics of Asian theater. (Ironically, Western artists are rediscovering the appeal of this quality.)
- Dance, mime, and gesture are as important as the verbal aspects of Asian plays.
- Music is integral to the performance. Most Asian plays are sung or, at the very least, accompanied by music as the actors perform.
- Masks and painted faces are essential costume elements. Clothing is richly adorned, usually brightly colored, and rarely realistic as we understand the term.
- Most plays are episodic and reflect the Asian theater's indebtedness to storytelling.
- Though there may be moments of profound insight into human behavior, there is usually little attempt at psychological realism as it has been developed in the West. Characters are more archetypal than specific.
- Actors rarely try to "become" the character they portray. Rather, they "present" the character as a type.
- Though it may be hard for us to ascertain this when reading translations, Asian drama retains its poetic roots, even in nonmusical dialogue or recited passages.

In 1931 a young French actor, Antonin Artaud, saw a performance of the Balinese Barong described in Chapter 1. The experience transformed Artaud and he set out to revitalize the theater by returning it to its roots (see Chapter 6 for a discussion of Artaud's "theater of cruelty"). In his germinal work *The Theater and Its Double*, Artaud compares the theaters of the West and of the East, though his comments reflect a Western bias. He begins by noting that the Balinese theater revealed to him "a physical and non verbal idea of the theatre, in which the theatre is contained within the limits of everything that can happen on a stage, independently of the written text." Western theater, for Artaud, "declared its alliance with the text and finds itself limited by it." His ensuing discussion then contrasts the two worlds of theater:

Balinese (Asian) Theater	Western Theater
Mystical	Realistic
Gesture and Signs	Dialogue and Words
Ritual and Transcendence	Ethics and Morality
Metaphysical States	"The Here and Now"
Does Not Rely on Rational Continuity	Causality
Transcends Reality on Stage	Creates Reality on Stage
Abandons Illusion	Creates Realistic Illusions
Uses Platforms and Spaces	Uses Scenery and Settings
Sounds and Rhythms	Speech

Much contemporary Western theater has conscientiously adopted elements of Asian theater articulated in this analysis of the two cultures. It may prove useful as you read plays throughout this anthology. Conversely, contemporary writers in Asia have shown an increasing interest in Western methods, especially realism, in their works.

Let us begin our study of the theater of Asia by looking at the oldest surviving drama, the Sanskrit from India.

INDIA

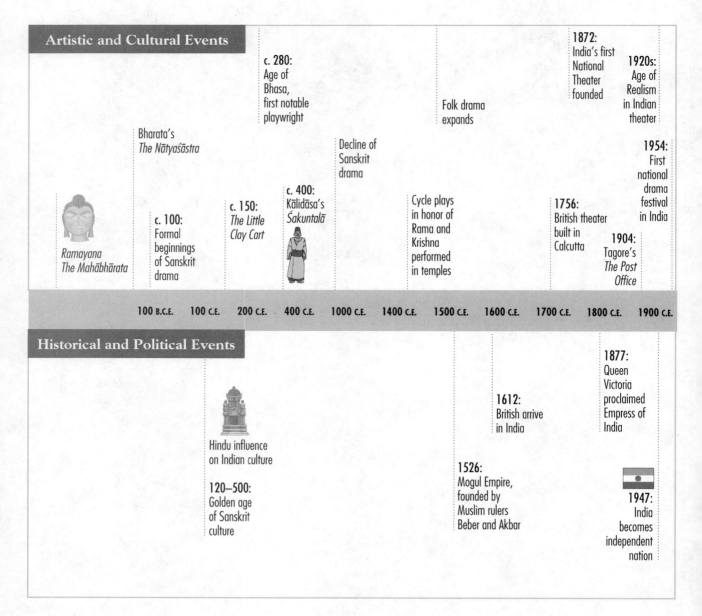

Artistic and Cultural Events

c. 280: Age of Bhasa, first notable playwright

Folk drama expands

1872: India's first National Theater founded

1920s: Age of Realism in Indian theater

Bharata's *The Nātyaśāstra*

Decline of Sanskrit drama

1954: First national drama festival in India

c. 100: Formal beginnings of Sanskrit drama

c. 150: *The Little Clay Cart*

c. 400: Kālidāsa's *Śakuntalā*

Cycle plays in honor of Rama and Krishna performed in temples

1756: British theater built in Calcutta

1904: Tagore's *The Post Office*

Ramayana The Mahābhārata

100 B.C.E.   100 C.E.   200 C.E.   400 C.E.   1000 C.E.   1400 C.E.   1500 C.E.   1600 C.E.   1700 C.E.   1800 C.E.   1900 C.E.

Historical and Political Events

1877: Queen Victoria proclaimed Empress of India

1612: British arrive in India

Hindu influence on Indian culture

120–500: Golden age of Sanskrit culture

1526: Mogul Empire, founded by Muslim rulers Beber and Akbar

1947: India becomes independent nation

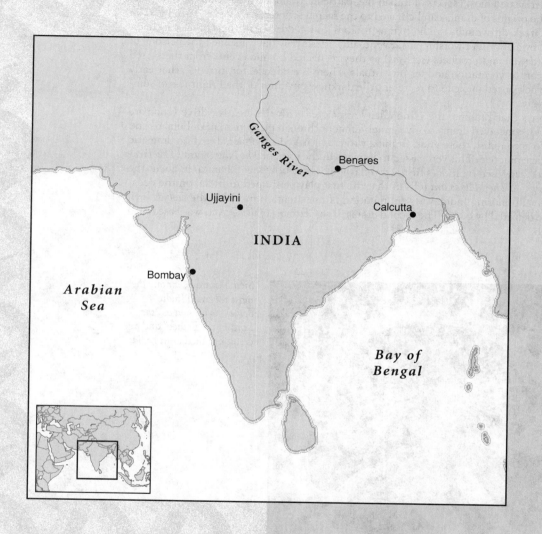

The Origins of Indian Drama

Theater and drama in the vast Asian subcontinent are as varied and ancient as India itself. As religion has permeated most aspects of Indian life, particularly among the Hindus, it is not surprising that the origins of drama can be traced to the sacred scriptures, or Vedas, of India. Like the ancient Greek dithyrambs, Vedic hymns to gods and goddesses in the Hindu pantheon were chanted by a chorus of worshippers. Eventually, priests may have assumed the persona of various gods (*devas*) and prophets (*sadhyas*) as they reenacted cosmic events from the sacred teachings as part of vegetation and fertility rituals. There is evidence, for instance, that early actors wore black or red makeup to represent the darkness of winter or the brightness of summer, respectively.

Legend says that Brahma, the Hindu deity associated with the creative drive (compare with Dionysus), conceived drama to give enlightenment through pleasure to both humans and other gods. To accomplish these ends, Brahma wrote a fifth Veda as a sacred text on dramatic theory and stage practice. This was passed to humans in the form of *The Nātyaśātra* (*The Treatise on Drama*) composed by India's first actor-playwright, the holy sage Bharata, in about the fourth century C.E. *The Nātyaśātra* tells us that the first play performed in India, on the occasion of a festival honoring Indra, was "an imitation of the situation in which the *daityas* [evil demons] were defeated by gods." The second drama, *The Churning of the Ocean*, was based on a creation myth.

Siva Nataraja, among the most revered Hindu deities, is known as "the Lord of the Dance" and a creator of theater in India.

In addition to Brahma's invention, Indian mythology claims that Siva brought dance, so indispensable to Indian theater, to the drama. Siva, known as Lord of the Dance, is associated with time and death and thus the length of his dance determines one's longevity. Another deity, Vishnu ("the Preserver") gave Indian drama its characteristic styles. Coincidentally, Vishnu—like Dionysus—was believed to immerse himself in the earth for four months, after which his triumphant resurrection was marked by rituals and theatrical celebrations.

Although stories recounting the divine sources of drama substantiate the sacred dimension of theater in India, we also know that historically theater and subsequently drama developed from a variety of sources. Dance, which remains perhaps Indian drama's dominant distinguishing feature, is one source. Another is the *bhuta* ritual, in which many men wearing massive costumes and armed with swords performed a "demon play" re-creating a cosmic battle between the goddess Kali and the sinister demon Darika. (It may have resembled the Balinese Barong dance described in Chapter 1.) *The Nātyaśātra* confirms this possible origin in its commentary about the "first play" in Indian drama. Indian theater may also have evolved from the *kuttiyattabm,* a form of shamanistic monologue in which a single shaman-actor created a number of characters while recounting mythic epics. Such narrators were known as a *sútradhara,* or "holder of the strings." The term is ambiguous: it may refer to puppets and their strings (puppetry is especially popular in almost all forms of Asian theater), or it may simply indicate that the storyteller holds the various strands of a story together. *Sútradhara* is a term that is still widely used to denote a playwright or storyteller.

The Types of Indian Drama

Whatever the precise origins of theater in India, several types of theatrical activity have resulted. In practice there is considerable overlap among the various forms. Sanskrit drama, of which *Śakuntalā* is the best-known example, was the formal drama of the court and thrived until the Muslim arrival in India in about 1000 C.E. Sanskrit drama is still regarded as India's premier literary drama. Sanskrit plays fall into two broad categories. *Nátaka* plays, such as *Śakuntalā,* are based on traditional mythology or history, and *prakarana* plays, such as *The Little Clay Cart,* are invented by the playwright and portray less exalted characters. *Nátaka* plays are traditionally five to seven acts in length, while the *prakarana* plays can be as long as ten acts. Both were traditionally performed in court theaters located near the temple, a reminder of the spiritual roots of Indian drama.

The Conventions of Classical Indian Theater

The ultimate goal of performance art in India is to produce *rasa,* or "flavor," an emotional state or mood, in each audience member. Whereas Western audiences concern themselves with the plot and character of a play, Indian audiences judge a production's success by its ability to induce a strong emotional response through the skillful integration of poetry, mime, dance, music, costume, and jewelry. Each play has a dominant *rasa*—for example, the erotic *rasa*—and each act within the larger play produces an individual rasa such as wonder, awe, dread, or love. There is a progression of moods, ultimately leading to serenity or peace. It may be useful to compare an Indian drama to a musical composition. In a symphony each movement exists to create a specific mood, although the entire piece has an identifiable sentiment. Audiences attending an Indian drama are cued to the proper emotional response by a variety of conventions and traditional devices. Words and music are the most obvious, but others include a very elaborate system of hand gestures (*mudras*), dance movements, and body attitudes that take years for the performer to master. A mere reading of a drama such as *Śakuntalā* can only hint at the subtleties of mood so integral to the experience of the Indian theater (see Spotlight box, The Sanskrit Masterpiece of India: *The Recognition of Śakuntalā*).

SPOTLIGHT

THE SANSKRIT MASTERPIECE OF INDIA: *THE RECOGNITION OF ŚAKUNTALĀ (ABHIJĀNAŚAKUNTĀLAM)*

The Recognition of Śakuntalā—or simply, *Śakuntalā*—remains the finest example of Indian Sanskrit drama, as revered as Western plays such as *Oedipus the King* or *Hamlet*. It is regularly performed by professional, amateur, and educational theater companies, and it is India's most discussed drama by scholars. Because of its unusual length—it uses the traditional seven-act structure, and a cast of over 60 characters—the text could not be included in a compact anthology. Still, it is a play worth knowing and reading in its entirety (see Kālidāsā: *The Loom of Time: A Selection of His Plays and Poems*, ed. Chandra Rajan, for an excellent introduction and annotation to the play).

The Playwright

Śakuntalā was written by Kālidāsā (373? –415? C.E.), the greatest poet-playwright of classical Sanskrit literature. Legend says that Kālidāsā—which means "the servant of time" or "servant of the creative powers"—was a simple Brahmin orphan possessing extraordinary beauty and grace who was raised by an ox driver. The youth devoted himself to the worship of the goddess Kali, the Absolute Being whose dance shapes all human life. Kali was taken by the young Brahmin's fidelity and blessed him with infinite knowledge and superior skills in the poetic arts. Though scholars have not been able to pinpoint Kālidāsā's dates, he is reputed to have been one of the nine jewels and official poet of the court of the nearly

mythical King Vikramaditya who ruled at Ujjayini in the first century B.C.E. Ujjayini was one of the twelve sacred cities of ancient India, the very place where Shiva descended into this universe; thus the city has long been a center for the arts, especially theater and dance. Referred to as "the Master of Poets," Kālidāsā is the greatest innovator among Sanskrit writers and the acknowledged master of the Sanskrit language, imbuing it with a rich variety, subtlety, and musicality; his status in India is comparable to that of Shakespeare in English-speaking countries.

The Play

The Recognition of Śakuntalā, based on a portion of India's national epic, the *Mahabharata*, seems strangely familiar to Western audiences. It resonates throughout with the "mythic bells" that are elemental to literature that is truly universal. The play is a romance, a universal genre that was popularized in the West during the Middle Ages. The Arthurian legends set down by Sir Thomas Mallory, Chaucer's *Knight's Tale*, and Shakespeare's last plays, especially *The Tempest*, are among the best-known romances in the Western canon. Like *Śakuntalā*, each is about a respected ruler who makes a grievous error in judgement, suffers the consequences, and is ultimately restored to a newfound knowledge that brings greater prosperity to his kingdom. A virginal heroine, usually wronged and isolated by male arro-

gance, is inevitably central to the action; her innate goodness and virtue ultimately triumph and traditionally there is a promise of a prosperous future symbolized by a wedding or a child. Romances, it has been said, are tragedies that end happily when the flawed king recognizes his error and reconciles with those whom he has wronged. Indeed, the very act of reconciliation provides the dramatic climax of most romances. Northrop Frye, who has extensively analyzed recurring patterns in romance literature, notes that "the renewing power of the final action [i.e., reconciliation] lifts us to a higher world." That higher world is one that transcends this earth; reconciliation approaches godhead because it promotes harmony and a new order.

Though the play is formally entitled *The Recognition of Śakuntalā*, it may be more apt to call it "Duhsanta's Recognition" for it is the noble king Duhsanta who undergoes the dramatic journey from ignorance to knowledge. As the play begins we see the king in his regal glory, hunting the sacred blackbuck, the revered antelope of Indian mythology. Hunting the blackbuck is a taboo, akin to killing a great bald eagle in America. The blackbuck leads the king to the sacred hermitage of Kanva, the wise seer so popular in romances (cf. Merlin). There, Duhsanta meets the pure and peerless beauty Śakuntalā, the daughter of an Apsara, one of the celestial dancers who guards the pools of water that sustain life. Śakuntalā, whose very name means "she who is protected by

The *Nātyaśātra* is very specific about the design and construction of the *natyamandapa*, or playhouse. It was required to be in the shape of a mountain cave, free from gusts of wind "so that the voices of the actors . . . will be resonant." Though the playhouse could be square or even triangular, Bharata suggests that the ideal configuration is a rectangle measuring 96 feet by 48 feet (about the size of a modern basketball court) to encourage an intimacy of playing between the actors and the audiences of some 400. The stage was raised 27 inches off the ground, and, in the days of the great courts, precious jewels were buried beneath the stage. The acting area was backed by a richly adorned curtain with two doors, one for entrances, the other for exits. The curtain was—and remains—an important convention of the Indian theater. It is shaken to create moods and denote emotional states; an actor may be wrapped in its folds to convey him to another locale. Very little scenery and few props were used. Like the Eliza-

Śakuntalā, the foremost Sanskrit drama of classical India, is still performed regularly by such companies as the Goa Hindu Association of Bombay; this 1985 production honored the tradition of simple staging practices used 1,600 years ago at Ujjaymi.

the birds," lives in an Edenic "green world," so loved by romanticists. At every turn Kālidasā reminds us that she is a child of Nature:

*If girls bred in a hermitage
can boast of such beauty rare in palaces,
is there any denying woodland vines
far surpass those nurtured in gardens?*

But Duhsanta mistakes lust for love. Erotic poetry marks the first meeting between the king and Śakuntalā ("with rounded breasts concealed by cloth bark . . . her youthful form enfolded like a flower . . ."). By falsely presenting himself as a "plain visitor," Duhsanta seduces Śakuntalā to satisfy his carnal desires, though he knows that his pleasure is momentary and that he must "wait seeking to know the truth."

Truth, the highest form of knowledge in Hindu theology, comes hard for Duhsanta. As he prepares to take Śakuntalā to his court, Durvasa, a foul-tempered sage who is furious that he has been ignored in the courtship, curses the new marriage. Duhsanta returns to the "golden world" of his court, which, despite its many earthly glories, is flawed because its unenlightened inhabitants are corruptible. True to Durvasa's curse, Duhsanta fails to recognize his bride when she arrives at court because she has lost the signet ring he gave her at their betrothal, and Duhsanta renounces

(continued)

bethan theater, the Sanskrit theater relied on language and the poetic imagination to create the many locales of the drama.

As befitting a theater form that evolved in a land where dance is supreme, movement and mimetic gesture were integral to performances; even today Indian actor-dancers spend many years perfecting the *mudras*, gestural grammar, of the Indian theater. *The Nātyaśātra* carefully catalogues these. In act 6 of *Śakuntalā*, for instance, Madhukarikā, one of the nymphs attending the sacred gardens, "folds her hands together in prayer." Specifically, she would use here a gesture in which the hands form the shape of a dove, a sign of supplication in which the doer's thoughts fly heavenward. Like the Chinese theater, the Indian theater also uses highly stylized movement as part of its conventions of performance. Actors frequently walk in a large circle about the stage to indicate a shift in locale, or enter with a toss of the curtain to suggest a state

(continued)

Śakuntalā. Miraculously, the gods intervene and produce the lost ring, which had been swallowed by a fish. This mystical revelation lifts the veil of doubt from Duhsanta's eyes and he and his bride are joyfully reconciled. To reaffirm his glory, Duhsanta defends his kingdom against invading Titans, for which he is rewarded at the beginning of the final act with a ride through the Hindu cosmos atop Indra's own chariot. This extraordinary stage picture of the renewed king reinforces his greatness and suggests the plenitude all in his kingdom will enjoy.

Śakuntalā, then, is much more than a secular romance. It is a spiritual journey in which unenlightened humans are led to sacred knowledge by forces greater than they are. Not uncoincidentally, the play is a highly structured religious ritual that mirrors the life cycle itself. As prescribed by the Nātyaśātra, the play opens with a benediction, one of eighteen preliminary steps of a Sanskrit performance meant to please the Hindu pantheon. Specifically, the banner of Indra, Lord of Heaven, is raised prior to the benediction as a reminder of the spiritual roots of the theater of India. The benediction not only purifies the actors and audience from any evil forces that may be present in the theater, it also elevates the performance to the status of a "special event" distinct from daily life.

Throughout the play there are other reminders that Sanskrit drama evolved from religious rituals marking the cycle of life. For instance, in act 4 Śakuntalā prepares to leave the sacred hermitage by undergoing an ancient purification as she walks "sun wise round the Sacrificial Fires." There is an autumnal quality about the ritual that marks Śakuntalā's leave-taking; one senses the blossom of spring giving way to the dying of the very trees, which were "kin to her during her woodland sojourn." Later, in act 6, King Duhsanta undergoes a symbolic death as he loses consciousness when overcome by sorrow at his cruel treatment of Śakuntalā. He—like so many real and fictional kings throughout the world's literature—is reborn to lead his country to a new prosperity, a triumph that Kālidasā equates with the very creation of the universe itself:

As the mountains rear upwards, the land climbs
precipitately down their great peaks, it seems;
trees whose forms were merged within the dense leafage
emerge distinct as their branching shoulders
thrust into view: those fine lines display themselves
as great rivers brimming with water:
see how the Earth looms at my side
as if some mighty hand had flung her up to me.

The play concludes with another benediction in which Marica, Indra's royal charioteer, asks "the god of gods" to insure that "both the worlds" (i.e., the heavens and the earth) enjoy glory and plenitude. If we remember that the-ater in many cultures developed from planting and harvest rituals—prayers for which surely echoed Marica's sentiments—Śakuntalā's relationship to the evolution of world theater quickly manifests itself.

We must not, however, ignore the play's distinctly Hindu strains. In addition to its universal appeals, Śakuntalā is very much a product of the fertile Indian imagination that has provided the world with a complex theology. In the final benediction King Duhsanta acknowledges the "Self-Existent Lord who unites in Himself the Dark and the Light." Conflict is central to the dramatic experience and polarities help define conflict. Throughout the play we are constantly aware of the dualities of Śakuntalā's world—the green (natural) world of the hermitage versus the gilded (cultivated) world of the court, love versus lust, Duhsanta's royal face versus his private face, appearances versus reality, isolation versus group harmony. Western writers and audiences have a tendency to see the world in terms of its polarities, but the Indian mind sees polarities as two aspects of a single whole that must be balanced. Life, in the Hindu worldview, is a struggle to reconcile these opposites into a harmonious whole. Thus in the final act—itself a celebration of the harmony of the world's many contraries—Duhsanta emerges as the complete king, tempered by his errors in judgement, enriched by his sorrow. His failures, as well as his triumphs, thus combine to make the whole person.

of agitation. Costuming, hairstyles, and a bold use of color—blue, red, yellow, and black—in masks and makeup further the metaphoric nature of Indian theatre. After Duhsanta has rebuked Śakuntalā, she returns to the stage with her hair in a single braid, a symbol of a woman's grief.

Like so much of the theater of Asia, the Sanskrit drama of classical India celebrates the human imagination. Unfettered by the particulars of realism and the mundane, Indian audiences are free to transport themselves from the limitations of this world to higher realms in which a "oneness" with the universe is possible.

Because India is a tradition-bound country that proudly reveres its past, modern Indian drama still uses many of the conventions of its classical theater, most notably song, dance, and mime. In the nineteenth century the Nawab of Oudh sponsored a national drama festival celebrating the cults of Krishna and Rama. The event, attended by thousands, helped resurrect older theatrical forms and inspired a new generation of Indians to pursue the theater as both a religious and an entertainment enterprise. Contemporary audiences still delight in spectacle that tends to dwarf a more literate drama. The Rajamanickam Company of Madras province is especially popular for its ability to present spectacular dramas based on mythological themes.

Dance and Folk Drama in India

There also exists a vibrant dance theater, which Indians claim is their supreme art form. Kathakali and Chhau are among the best-known forms of dance theater. In the twentieth century dance drama has remained popular, largely because of the work of Uday Shankar, the preeminent teacher of the modern era. Shankar studied in Europe and danced with the great Russian ballerina Irena Pavlova in a classical Indian piece. He used mythological characters such as Krishna and themes of ancient India in his modern works, which frequently combine racy folk dances with the more decorous temple dances. Also, Rabindranath Tagore (see below) composed several important dance dramas, although today he is best remembered as the patriarch of modern drama in India.

A variety of folk plays and entertainments associated with each of India's provinces constitutes the third major form of theatrical activity in this vast country. Often, they are propagandistic and deal with regional, as well as national, problems. For example, *Neel Darpana* (1872) by Dinabandhu Mitra is a Bengali play in the folk style that portrays the ordeals of plantation life in northern India. Because they are so completely indigenous to the provinces from which they spring, few folk plays exist in written form.

The Modern Theater of India

Modern theater in India is urban, not rural, and it is created primarily for the middle and upper classes (India yet retains its caste system). Because it was a British colony for several hundred years, Indian theater, like that of Africa, owes much of its impetus to European drama, largely because of the Eurocentric education system established at universities in Calcutta, Bombay, and Madras. Drama written in any of the hundreds of Indian languages and performed onstage by Indian actors did not emerge until the last years of the nineteenth century. The success of these native enterprises inspired others to construct public theaters that appealed to the tastes and languages of a variety of castes. Producers with nationalistic tendencies soon employed the theater as a means of propaganda that appealed to a growing concern for self-rule and the eradication of colonialism.

The artist most credited with bridging the gap between the traditional Indian theater and that of the modern era was the Bengali poet and dramatist Rabindranath Tagore (1861–1941). Some Indian scholars dispute Tagore's influence, arguing that he was too provincial and therefore failed to inspire many twentieth-century Indian dramatists. Nonetheless, it was Tagore who caught the attention of such Western theater artists as William Butler Yeats, who produced his work at Dublin's Abbey Theatre.

It is worth noting that the motion picture dominates Indian entertainment today; no country in the world produces more movies than does India. The popularity of cinema has had an adverse impact on live theater, forcing the closure of some companies. However, a modern Indian theater does exist in commercial, amateur, and educational venues. Calcutta is perhaps the dominant commercial theater center in all of India, and the Star (founded in 1888) is its best-known theater. Because of India's enormous size, and the hundreds of languages spoken by its diverse people, it is difficult to identify major national playwrights. Very few artists can actually make a living writing plays; in Bombay playwrights earn about $8 per performance. Few plays written in Hindi, one of the dominant languages, are translated into other languages, which makes the task of discussing modern Indian theater even more difficult. Ironically, many Western theater artists (Peter Brook and Arianne Mnouchkine are the most prominent) have incorporated elements of the classical Indian theater in their most admired "modern" works.

CHINA

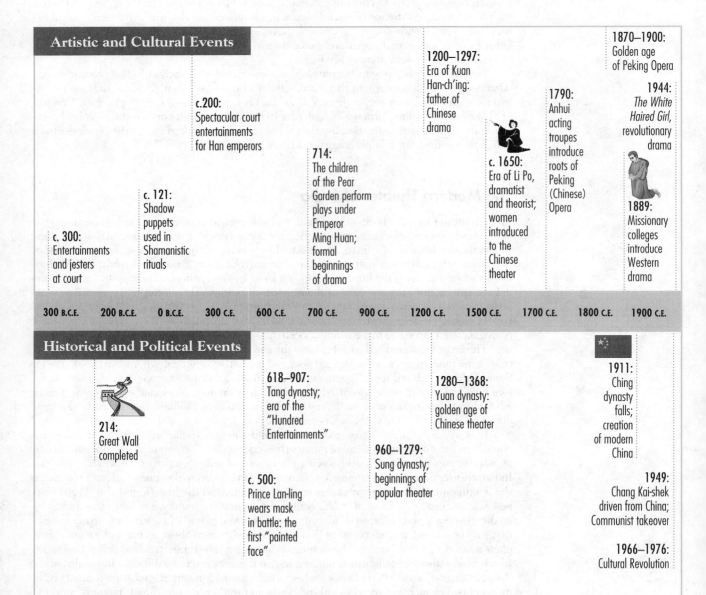

Artistic and Cultural Events

1870–1900:
Golden age
of Peking Opera

1200–1297:
Era of Kuan
Han-ch'ing:
father of
Chinese
drama

1944:
*The White
Haired Girl*,
revolutionary
drama

c.200:
Spectacular court
entertainments
for Han emperors

1790:
Anhui
acting
troupes
introduce
roots of
Peking
(Chinese)
Opera

714:
The children
of the Pear
Garden perform
plays under
Emperor
Ming Huan;
formal
beginnings
of drama

c. 1650:
Era of Li Po,
dramatist
and theorist;
women
introduced
to the
Chinese
theater

c. 121:
Shadow
puppets
used in
Shamanistic
rituals

1889:
Missionary
colleges
introduce
Western
drama

c. 300:
Entertainments
and jesters
at court

| 300 B.C.E. | 200 B.C.E. | 0 B.C.E. | 300 C.E. | 600 C.E. | 700 C.E. | 900 C.E. | 1200 C.E. | 1500 C.E. | 1700 C.E. | 1800 C.E. | 1900 C.E. |

Historical and Political Events

1911:
Ching
dynasty
falls;
creation
of modern
China

214:
Great Wall
completed

618–907:
Tang dynasty;
era of the
"Hundred
Entertainments"

1280–1368:
Yuan dynasty:
golden age of
Chinese theater

1949:
Chang Kai-shek
driven from China;
Communist takeover

960–1279:
Sung dynasty;
beginnings of
popular theater

c. 500:
Prince Lan-ling
wears mask
in battle: the
first "painted
face"

1966–1976:
Cultural Revolution

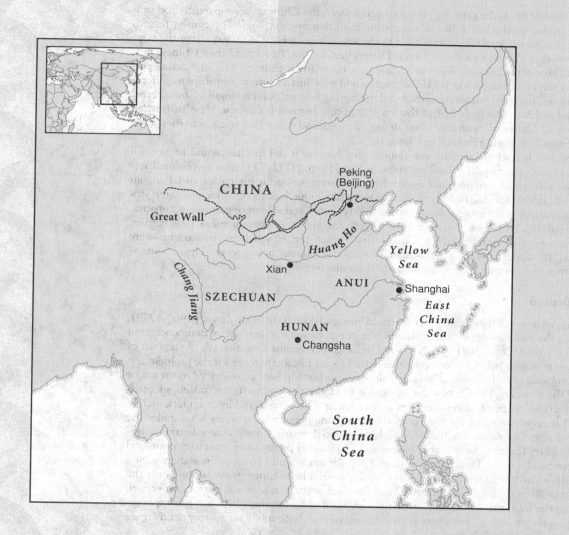

The History of Chinese Theater

Early Theater in China

To such inventions as the printing press and gunpowder, the Chinese can apparently add professional acting on the list of "firsts" emanating from that ancient land. The earliest records that mention an actor in China date back to the seventh century B.C.E.; if we accept the popular notion that in c. 534 B.C.E. the Greek Thespis became the "first actor," then Chinese professional theater predates its Western counterpart by nearly a century. The first actors performed as part of ceremonies in Buddhist temples and were hired by rural townships to perform at agricultural festivals. Such events included the Spring Festival, which remains China's most celebrated holiday. The highlight of the lengthy Spring Festival is Chinese New Year, when the streets of China fill with cavorting dragon dancers and other theatrical activities. (See Center Stage box, Spring Festival in China.)

However, literate theater did not flourish in China as it did in Greece and India until about the eighth century C.E. The Tang emperor Ming Huang (712–755) gave professional acting troupes his royal sanction and established a training school at his palace in Chang-an (modern Xian). Actors learned the skills that remain the foundations of Chinese theater: storytelling, musical performance, dance, and a highly specialized system of gestures, acrobatics, and martial arts. Tradition says that classes were conducted in the emperor's pear garden, which became the formal name for China's first known theater academy. Its students were known as "the children of the Pear Garden." Even today Chinese actors revere Ming Huang as their patron and burn incense to his image in their dressing rooms.

Yuan Drama

Although a variety of theatrical activities could be found during the Sung dynasty (960–1279), including the building of permanent theaters at court, China's golden age of drama occurred under the Yuan (1280–1368). China's most cherished plays come from this era. As a point of reference, it may be helpful to compare this period to the Elizabethan age for the proliferation and importance of its literature. Curiously, although authorship has been ascribed to the major plays of the Yuan era, the Chinese are not prone to idolize their playwrights; indeed, succeeding generations are free to adapt the plays as they see fit. The Yuan were Mongol rulers, such as Kublai Khan, whose thirst for theater made playwriting popular by scholars who, under the specter of strict Confucianism, had previously dismissed dramatic writing as a pedestrian activity. Yuan plays (*tsa chu*) were highly lyrical and emphasized poetry over dramatic action and character development. Playwrights employed popular music well known to the audience. Significantly, Yuan dramas are readily distinguishable from other Chinese plays because only the protagonist sings in them. Customarily Yuan drama is written in four acts with many scenes, including the *hsieh-tzu*, or "wedge," which was inserted as an interlude between acts or, occasionally, as the prologue. Dramatists gathered material from both myth and history to create six principal types of Yuan plays:

1. Love stories filled with intrigue;
2. Religious and supernatural tales;
3. Historical and pseudohistorical sagas;
4. Domestic dramas and comedies;
5. Crime (especially murder) and lawsuit dramas;
6. Bandit-hero plays.

The last, Robin Hood–type stories, were very popular and have been used centuries later by the Communist regime as propaganda pieces. Stock characters were integral to the Yuan dramas, and the varied styles that followed, though there is a remarkable degree of individuation and nuance within these characters. Heroic kings (*K'ung-meng*) and their wise counselors are confronted by the villainous *cao-cao*, while long-suffering wives and servants are tormented by tyrannical stepmothers. Certain features of costume and even voice production became the exclusive properties of such stock types. More famously, the colorful "painted faces" (*hua lien*) became the emblem of Chinese theater. Specific colors were assigned to virtues and vices: white for treachery, black for courage, red for loyalty. Other colors defined status: gods had gold faces, while demon spirits wore green. Colors could be combined on a single face to denote character complexity.

The Yuan elevated drama in China, largely because it was "democratic" in that it consciously appealed to the spectrum of Chinese society. Again, the Elizabethan theater serves as a comparable model to help us understand the popularity of Yuan drama.

Ming Drama

The succeeding Ming dynasty (1368–1644) overthrew the Mongols and returned "pure-blooded" Chinese emperors to the throne. Consequently, the dramas of the Ming dynasty were elitist and highly refined. These dramas, called *ch'uan-ch'i* because they were derived from the south, were written in many acts, and averaged about 40 scenes. Whereas only a single actor sang in Yuan drama, several actors sing in later drama. The instrumentation accompanying them became far more complex and relied heavily on the flute. Though there are a number of quality plays from this era, drama in China gradually lost its vitality under the Ming because it relinquished its contact with the masses.

Ultimately, theater activity during the Ming dynasty is best remembered for the critical writings of Li Yu (1611–1680), who might be called "the Aristotle of China." He was the first to systematically examine the art of playwriting. Ironically, Li Yu urged his fellow playwrights to write for the masses, and his own comedies featured original plots based on observations of daily life. It should also be noted that Li Yu—who had some 40 wives and numerous concubines!—helped legitimize the role of the actress in the Chinese theater.

Peking Opera

The Manchu of northeastern China assumed power in the mid–seventeenth century and established the Qing (Ch'ing) dynasty (1645–1912 C.E.). Qing emperors retained the popular, though less sophisticated, forms of folk drama (*hua pu*), though the older, elitist theater (*ya pu*) continued under courtly scholars. However, little drama of import was written as the Manchu often suppressed new works for political or moral reasons. Happily, the Manchu allowed the *hua pu* drama of the peasants gradually to infiltrate the court drama.

During the reign of Emperor Qian Lung (1736–1795), troupes from the central provinces, especially Anhui, appeared in Peking to celebrate the emperor's seventieth and eightieth birthdays. The provincial troupes remained in the capital, where audiences who enjoyed the simpler stories, the folk music, and especially the acrobatic performances favored them. By 1810 this new style of performance (*ching hsi*) dominated Chinese theater, and it has remained so to this day. Westerners know *ching hsi* by the generic term of Peking Opera, which represents the principal form of Chinese national theater. Like the many regional cuisines for which China is famous, most of China's provinces have retained their unique theatrical forms. For instance, in Hunan province in south central China, one can attend the *hua gu* (or "Flower Drum") opera, whose specialty is folk drama (see Center Stage box, A Night at the Chinese Opera: The *Hua-gu* Opera of Hunan).

The term "Chinese opera" should not evoke images of the grand opera of Western theater. Rather, it combines music, dance, acrobatics, and martial arts to create a spectacular entertainment that is exceptionally theatrical. Today Peking Opera is divided into two categories:

- the *wu-hsi* or military plays, which are based on legend and history;
- the *wen-hsi*, which are primarily love stories set amid daily social problems (not unlike the sentimental comedies or bourgeois dramas of eighteenth-century Europe).

Frequently the two styles are incorporated into a single play.

CENTER STAGE   SPRING FESTIVAL IN CHINA

In the West the term "Chinese New Year" prompts images of festive dragon dancers cavorting through crowded streets in "Chinatown," paper streamers and lanterns, and multicourse meals featuring delicacies such as Peking duck and egg drop soup. In China, Taiwan, and other Asian countries such as Vietnam, "New Year" is more commonly referred to as Spring Festival (or Tet in Vietnam), a weeks-long time of family reunions and ritual celebrations. It is a moveable feast celebrated in late January and early February, not on January 1, as in the West.

The actual day of the new year—called Yuan Day (*yuan* means "to begin")—is determined by an ingenious lunar-solar calendar that also absorbs the West's Gregorian calendar. The Chinese calendar (or Xia calendar, which dates back to roughly the twentieth century B.C.E.) acknowledges seasonal change and provides a useful tool for farmers who need to know the proper time for planting. The ancient Egyptians, Greeks, and Maya also had spring planting rituals that, like those of the Chinese, used theatrical means. The names of subsequent days in the Chinese calendar also reflect the close harmony between nature and the people: Rain Day, Waking of the Insects, Grain Full, Frost's Descent, and Great

Snow. Indeed each year in the Chinese calendar—which runs in twelve-year cycles—reflects the spirit of animism we see in many cultures; thus we have the Year of the Tiger, Ox, Rat, Monkey, and Dragon (considered the luckiest year and the year when Chinese couples are most eager to have a child).

And just as the Egyptians, Greeks, and Maya created myths about Osiris, Dionysus, and the Jaguar Twins to account for natural phenomena, so, too, did the Chinese. A mythological beast, Nian (which also means "year"), devoured people on the night beginning the new year. A wise old man—reverence for ancestors and the old is a primary virtue among the Chinese—convinced Nian that its appetite could be sated by devouring other beasts troublesome to humans. Nian complied and thus rid China of every manner of problems. The old man—in actuality an immortal god—mounted Nian and disappeared into the heavens. Before he left he told the people of China to live peacefully and to put red paper decorations on their doors at the end of each year to scare Nian away; red was the color Nian feared most and today it remains the "lucky color." Chinese brides wear red dresses and children are given red envelopes (*hongbao*) containing good luck money (*yasui qian*) on Guo

Nian, a term that originally meant "Surviving the Nian," but which now means "Celebrating the New Year." (Here it may be useful to remember Oedipus, who saved the people of Thebes from the Sphinx, another devouring monster.)

There is an alternate version of the Nian legend. Two brothers (Shennai and Yulei) grew large groves of peach trees whose leafless, grotesque shapes frightened away the Nian; the brothers were rewarded for their heroism by the gods who made them supreme deities charged with inflicting punishment on evildoers. Today the Chinese decorate their doorways during Spring Festival with poetic couplets (*duilian*) honoring the brothers and other gods, who are further glorified in song, dance, puppetry, and theatricals.

The entire Spring Festival is filled with events and rites that feature theatrical and symbolic elements. To prepare for Yuan Day, the Chinese fastidiously clean and even repaint their humble homes in the hope that all ill fortune will be replaced by good luck. There is both an actual sweeping of the home and a purely symbolic sweeping that dates back to the oldest agrarian calendars, which marked the twentieth day of the twelfth lunar month as the day for sweeping floors. The kitchen

---

As with Yuan drama, both Peking and regional operas depend on well-known, highly developed character types. Chinese actors specialize in a single role and spend their entire careers developing the complex system of hand gestures, physical attitudes, and especially vocal techniques associated with these roles. Audiences, who are familiar with the plots of the plays, attend to see how well the actor interprets the four principal roles in Peking Opera: the male (*sheng*), female (*tan*), painted-face (*jing*), and clown (*ch'ou*). It is not uncommon to find a 60-year-old actor still playing the acrobatic *ch'ou* or clown role.

Contemporary Chinese Drama

With the overthrow of the Qing dynasty in 1911, there was an increased assimilation of Western theater methods in China, particularly in Shanghai, the country's most Westernized city. With the rise of communism in the 1940s, drama became more ideological, especially in the works of China's most noted dramatist of the twentieth century, Cao Yu (b. 1910). During the Cultural Revolution (1966–1976), the Maoists resurrected classical drama, particularly those with themes

god (whose likeness dominates Chinese kitchens) reported the cleanliness of one's house to other deities; an unkempt house was a sure way to earn a year's bad luck from the gods. In addition to such cleansing rites, the Chinese pursue other forms of "cleansing": old debts are paid, transgressions against others are forgiven, and individuals reflect on their human failings. Ritual cleansing (purgation) is, as we have seen, a primary impulse behind many plays around the world.

Throughout China (and those places where the Chinese have settled), people return to their home villages to renew the bonds of family and friendship. In older times—and even today in China's most rural areas—the first day of the new year is the only day on which peasants allow themselves to rest and celebrate with magnificent meals, an Asian variant of the old *komos* of the Greek theaters. Ripe fruit (especially tiny oranges), fish and poultry (preferably duck), and various rice dishes abound. A special meat-filled dumpling (*jiaozi*) is eaten at midnight to insure good fortune; *jiaozi*, by the way, sounds like the Mandarin word for that moment when the last hour of the old year meets the first of the new. At first light, the Chinese unseal their doors (which have been sealed to keep Nian from en-

tering) and greet the new day with long rows of exploding firecrackers. In ancient China peasants used to burn bamboo, which crackled loudly, to frighten Nian; today firecrackers are lit at the moment of one's death to fend off evil spirits. In large cities—most notably Hong Kong—lengthy and spectacular fireworks displays light up the winter sky.

Spring Festival closes with the charming and symbolic Lantern Festival, which occurs on the fifteenth day of the first lunar month. Like the New Year ritual, the Yuanxiao, as it is called, has its roots in a popular legend that has provided many a theatrical troupe with a colorful plot and characters. During the Han dynasty a beautiful maiden named Yuanxiao was brought to live at the court of Emperor Wu Di in the ancient capital of Changan (now Xian). She became homesick for her native village and revealed her sorrow to the emperor's counselor, a wise elder named Dongfang Shuo. The counselor warned the emperor that the Supreme Deity was displeased and would command the God of Fire to burn the capital unless fireworks were set off and red lanterns were hung throughout the city to satisfy the god's desire to see a colorful burning scene. Coincidentally, the God of Fire loved to eat Yuanxiao's special rice

dumplings because he believed them magical conveyors of good luck. To appease the Supreme Deity, firecrackers were set off, red lanterns were lit, dumplings were eaten—and Yuanxiao returned to her family. Today each of these customs has become an integral part of the Spring Festival. In Guanzhou (formerly Canton) in southern China, the city park is filled with many thousands of beautiful light displays made from paper, glass (often discarded soft drink bottles), and other objects; it is truly one of the most beautiful spectacles one can behold in China.

Throughout this text, light is a primary symbol favored by playwrights. For the Greeks, Apollo was the god of light who brought wisdom to people, a universal goal of drama and theater. Aechylus's great trilogy, the *Oresteia*, begins with a watchman searching for light amid the darkness of a ten-year war, and ends with a processional of humans and gods following the new light brought to them by Athena. Such images are aligned with a basic human desire to seek the light against the darkness of winter (when the earth is, figuratively, dead), and China's Spring and Lantern Festivals attest to this universal impulse.

supporting the revolution, as part of their move to purge China of all foreign influences. Mostly, however, theater in Maoist China consisted of spectacular, state-produced song-and-dance extravaganzas that glorified the people and their Great Leader. *The White Haired Girl,* the most famous of these, is a melodrama glorifying the People's Army that liberated rural China from the Japanese; in spirit, it calls to mind the antislavery melodrama *Uncle Tom's Cabin* (see Chapter 5). After President Richard Nixon's visit and the ensuing cultural exchange of 1972, the Chinese renewed their interest in Western drama. In 1983 Arthur Miller staged a production of his play *Death of a Salesman* in Beijing (see Chapter 5). Today one can find a variety of theater forms, both classical and decidedly contemporary, performed in China's major cities. In 1988 a Shakespeare festival even enjoyed an 18-day run in Beijing and Shanghai. Twenty-two productions of the bard's plays were performed in both the classical Chinese style and in the traditional Western mode. The Chinese retain their affection for the Peking Opera, and in addition to performances in China's many theaters, elaborately mounted Peking Opera can be seen daily on Chinese national television. Because Chinese opera companies are state run, performances are inexpensive and well attended by workers, as well as by students and the emerging middle class.

China's Peking Opera, which derived from dance, music, storytelling, and martial arts, is among the most colorful forms of theater in the world.

The Conventions of Chinese Theater

The Chinese theater has never conspicuously attempted to portray life in realistic terms on its stages. It is a symbolic, exquisitely stylized theater that employs a sophisticated system of gestures, poses, stage properties, costumes, and musical accompaniment. The Chinese esteem art that places maximum value on the imagination and symbolic expression. Westerners accustomed to realism may find the Chinese theater noisy and overly "busy," but knowledge of some of its rudimentary conventions offers the potential for a fascinating theater experience.

Though there are specific differences among the many styles of Chinese theater, a knowledge of general conventions may help you understand this venerable theater form. The descriptions below are applicable, in varying degrees, to *The Qing Ding Pearl*.

Playwriting

Chinese audiences have not lost their fascination with plays that are centuries old, and consequently the repertory comprises a relatively small number of works. In fact, it is not uncommon for Chinese theater troupes to perform a series of acts taken from a variety of famous plays in an evening. Because the plots are well known, playwrights do not need to obey the laws of strict logic. Time and place are manipulated freely for dramatic effect, plays may contain scores of scenes, historical accuracy is not obligatory, and soliloquies, asides, and other presentational modes are commonplace. The plays of Chinese opera represent dramatic storytelling at its most flexible as readers and audiences alike are, according to Harold Acton, "translated into the Kingdom of the Imagination."

Confucianism is inherent in the Chinese culture and its literature. At the risk of oversimplifying a complex issue, Confucianism is a moralistic ideology that teaches correct codes of behavior. A well-defined sense of right and wrong gives rise to the principles of poetic justice. Virtue must be rewarded, particularly that of patience, the paramount virtue of the Confucianists; vice must be punished. Such beliefs are also embodied in the teachings of China's most notable spiritual movements, Buddhism and Taoism. Thus it is not surprising that retribution plays, such as *The Qing Ding Pearl*, should be integral to Chinese drama. There is no well-defined sense of tragedy in the Chinese theater, however, for it is the duty of the playwright to see that the truly good are rewarded and that the transgressors are punished by the final curtain. Liu Wu-chi notes that from the Chinese point of view "it would be a blemish in a literary work not to give its [audience] a sense of satisfaction in the ultimate vindication and triumph of the good and virtuous." Interestingly, contemporary Chinese scholars and theater artists invariably characterize their plays as "melodramas," an apt term because Western melodrama (particularly in the nineteenth century) also emphasized poetic justice.

The Stage

The earliest theaters in China were found in temples and were of simple design, little more than a raised platform with no curtain. Spectators stood on three sides. Variants of this design could be found in court theaters, though they were more elaborate and featured ornate roofs supported by four "posts" that—not unlike the famous posts that supported the roof of Shakespeare's Globe theater—could be used for a variety of scenic purposes. Frequently there were separate balconies from which women could watch the plays. Such a theater can be found in one of the old court palaces in modern Shanghai. In rural locales, itinerant acting troupes devised temporary theaters of planks, bamboo poles, and roofs made of grass mats, which gives them the generic term "mat-shed" theaters; similar theaters are still found in China and in Hong Kong's New Territories.

Most modern theaters are conventional Western-style proscenium arch theaters. In deference to the raucous musical accompaniment that permeates Chinese opera, lyrics to the songs,

The Guangdong Guild Hall in Tianjin is a traditional Chinese theater with its tea tables and elevated galleries surrounding the stage. The multipurpose red box and two chairs are visible at center stage.

CENTER STAGE

A NIGHT AT THE CHINESE OPERA: THE *HUA-GU* OPERA OF HUNAN

Hunan province in south-central China is famous to Westerners for its spicy food and its status as the birthplace of Chairman Mao Zedong. It also is the home of the *Hua-gu*—or "Flower Drum"—Opera, one of the many provincial styles of theater cultivated outside of Beijing. *Hua-gu* Opera has unique conventions, particularly of music and singing, that set it apart from that of China's other many provinces. Still, there are enough similarities between the provincial and Peking operas that a description of several productions by the *Hua-gu* Opera Company will suggest the performance conventions of Chinese opera.

The plays described here were performed in Changsha, the capital of Hunan, in late May 1989. Three short plays were given a private performance held at the company's rehearsal hall, located in a communal housing complex, where all actors, technicians, allied artists, and their families are provided accommodations by the Chinese government. Like most Chinese theater companies, the *Hua-gu* troupe is state supported and its members live, re-

hearse, and work together in a spacious facility on Renmen ("The People's") Road near downtown Changsha. Several blocks away is the Hunan Normal School, where Mao taught and articulated his vision for a new China in the 1920s. Later that evening the *Hua-gu* Company performed a fully mounted opera in its vast theater located on Wu-Yi ("May First") Road, Changsha's main thoroughfare. Farther down Wu-Yi Road is the provincial government headquarters, where students from Changsha's many universities had established a tent city in support of the prodemocracy movement in Tiananmen Square in Beijing, 800 miles to the north. Some students passed the time singing songs from Chinese opera.

The afternoon performance, arranged by a director (and principal actor) of the *Hua-gu* Company to honor an American visitor's request to see traditional provincial theater, consisted of three short plays acted on a proscenium stage. Black drapes defined the acting space. In the glow of a light emanating from behind the stage left proscenium, an orchestra of nine musicians set up

their instruments: the traditional two-stringed violin, a couple of woodwinds, and a variety of drums, gongs, cymbals, and wooden clappers. The orchestra, dressed in T-shirts and baggy shorts in deference to the late spring heat, played virtually nonstop throughout the three plays. Every physical action and verbal joke was punctuated by the percussive instruments, especially the cymbals.

The first play, *Picking Turnips*, was a comic romp in which a *ch'ou* (clown) tried to dupe a naïve young lady out of her turnip crop. As might be expected, she outwitted the cunning clown, who was left alone at the end to rue his roguery. Though there was dialogue and song in Hunan's distinctive dialect, the action was readily comprehensible because of the physicality of the performance. Exchange the *ch'ou*'s bright blue (to indicate his cunning) costume for a diamond-hued suit, replace his gaily painted face (with traditional white markings on his nose) for a dark mask, and put a slapstick in his hand instead of a bright orange fan, and a Western audience would immediately think of Arlecchino (Harlequin), the notorious

The Hua-gu *Opera of Hunan specializes in folktales. Here a cunning* ch'ou *(clown) attempts to steal turnips from a* hua tan *(flirtatious woman) in the short play* Picking Turnips. *(Photo reproduced from a video still.)*

trickster of the *commedia dell'arte*. To punctuate every action, the *ch'ou* struck an exaggerated, comical pose or leapt exuberantly (no easy task for the 57-year-old actor who played him). His gestures were highlighted by brightly colored balls of yarn affixed to his hat and shoe tops. His lines were delivered directly to the audience, even when answering the young woman. The maiden (a *hua-tan*, or "flirt" role) was dressed in a pink jacket and silk trousers, all covered by a festive blue smock with stunning floral embroidery. She sported three knee-length braids of hair and carried a small green basket of imaginary produce. She moved in short, mincing steps, always leading with her heels. Her lines were delivered in the shrill, nasal "singsong" unique to Chinese opera. Her hand movements and facial expressions were so graceful that spectators quickly succumbed to her charms. Certainly the *ch'ou* did. Although he tried to abscond with her harvest, he was quickly duped into pulling her turnips from the soil. His "picking turnips" was done in an exaggerated mime closer to dance than the miming Westerners associate with Marcel Marceau. The play featured several song and dance duets, the most interesting of which was one in which the *ch'ou* unfurled his fan to reveal shimmering feathers while the *hua-tan* expertly mimed chopsticks between the third and fourth fingers of her right hand. Given Hunan's importance as one of China's leading agricultural zones, the play's emphasis on harvests and eating was not surprising.

The second playlet was similar in plot, though less rustic in its setting. *The Tuition Fee* told the amusing story of a scheming teacher duped of his income by a quick-witted student. Judging by the reactions of the Chinese audience, wordplay was the source of much of the humor, although the physical comedy compensated for any language barriers. Performed with only the traditional red

box and two chairs as scenery, the play featured a comically dressed "professor" (*hsu sheng*) who wore an enormous, drooping mustache and a traditional scholar's hat. His pedantry generated much humor, not unlike that of the "pig Latin" lectures in the Italian *commedia* or, more recently, by the absurdist playwright Eugene Ionesco. The old scholar's delivery was more naturalistic sounding than that of the *ch'ou* in *Turnips*, although one could not mistake the comic intonations. While the particulars of his arguments may have been lost to non-Chinese speakers, the caricature of the teacher and the spirited "sendups" by his student were sufficiently universal that it was still a wonderfully funny play. Most of the action consisted of comic exchanges between student and teacher (with many asides), each of which climaxed with a comic chase and beating. She pursued him about the stage and forced him to leap into the audience, which delighted the children who had gathered near the forestage. Finally, she grabbed his long queue (the traditional hair braid of feudal China) and led him ceremoniously back to his "classroom" (which was always defined by stepping over its threshold). A source of amusement in this and the preceding play was the manner in which a woman outwitted the male. Given the low status China has traditionally afforded its women, such subversion of gender roles seems especially humorous to the Chinese.

The Sister-in-Law concluded the afternoon's bill. It was the most sumptuously mounted of the three works and employed a larger cast, each member of which was dressed in brightly colored silk hand-embroidered in exquisite detail. The story was universal in that it dealt with the impending marriage of a young couple whose love was thwarted by a tyrannical sister-in-law. Of course the play ended happily with a wedding. The termagant sister-in-law (though it is customarily the mother-in-law who

plays the comic villain in Chinese opera) was acted hilariously by an older gentleman whose facial features were reminiscent of the great silent film clown Buster Keaton. The actor was noted for his expert rendering of women's roles, and his colleagues in the *Hua-gu* Company affectionately referred to him as Hunan's Mei Lan-fang, a reference to the most famous actor in the Peking Opera. As with the other plays, each actor employed formal hand and body movements to define his or her character. It would take a Westerner considerably more exposure to fathom the nuances of these movements, but even an initial viewing made it apparent that there were distinct differences among the characters in their gestures and singing styles.

The *Hua-gu* Opera House is a large, gray edifice fronted by two columns, over which are hung three enormous gold ideograms that identify the building. The auditorium is spartan and contains wooden chairs for about 1,200 spectators. A velvet green curtain masks the proscenium opening. Unlike the simple folk plays of the afternoon, the evening performance, a tragic tale called *Under the Dragon Stick,* was accompanied by a full orchestra situated in a conventional Western-style pit beneath the forestage. Many children gathered around the orchestra as they tuned their instruments. Entire families attend the opera (at the cost of two or three cents a ticket, which is not inexpensive to laborers who earn about $30 a month). Children are free to roam the auditorium throughout the play, and they especially like to congregate near the stage to watch the actors or amuse themselves with their own games of make-believe. No one seems to mind as there is a festive air about theatergoing. Above all, an evening at the Chinese opera has little sense of the "dressing up" for a social event that one often

(continued)

(*continued*)

finds in the West. The audience attends in its blue or green work clothes, and women wear the brightly colored sleeve protectors on their otherwise drab Mao jackets.

As the house lights dimmed, the orchestra played a melodic overture (in contrast to the cacophony of the three folk plays) while the play's title and the names of its author and cast were projected onto the proscenium arch. A series of gongs and cymbals sounded, and *Under the Dragon Stick* began with a spectacular procession in which a large entourage filed into an ancient Chinese court. A huge walled city formed the permanent scenic backdrop for the opera; changes of locale were efficiently handled by placing smaller set units in front of this foreboding backdrop. Ten warriors in classical dress and helmets carried spears to escort the prince consort to the throne room. A retinue of older male citizens followed somberly, each dressed in richly embroidered gowns and headpieces. Throughout the opera, there was an unusually strong emphasis on pictorial composition; at any moment, the stage looked like one of the ancient water colors or wood prints so loved by the Chinese.

Under the Dragon Stick unfolded as a classical tragedy of court intrigue. An old emperor dies and his son inherits the throne. His queen is banished (only to return later as a vengeful ghost), while another warrior-son claims both his younger brother's throne and his wife. A villainous old counselor controls the action, and a beautiful princess adds romantic interest to the complex plot. Ultimately the brothers square off for a death duel, and in the finale the court reconvenes to mourn the loss of its youthful leaders. A new leader is named to inherit the "dragon stick" (i.e., a scepter) which has been cursed for generations. Aeschylus, Shakespeare, or Wagner might have written the script, and there were indeed moments when the heroes might have been called Orestes, Hamlet, or Siegfried.

As interesting as the plot may have been, the play—the equivalent of Western "grand opera"—was most memorable for its visual elements. In addition to the spectacular costumes (even the most lowly extra wore a richly detailed costume of hand-embroidered fabric), the scenery was impressive in its size and design. Settings were both elaborate (a tomb of the dead emperor nearly filled the proscenium opening) and simple (a sumptuously lit bedchamber was defined by glass beads and silk curtains). Legions of attendants, warriors, courtiers, and others added to the stage pictures. A half-

dozen ladies-in-waiting attended the princess and performed a graceful dance with the billowing "water sleeves" (*shui hsi*) of their crimson dresses. Ultimately, however, the most captivating visual elements were the beautifully stylized movements of the actors. Many gestures seemed melodramatic in the nineteenth-century sense of the term. When the warrior-son faced separation from his lover, he held the back of his hand to his forehead, grimaced sadly, and extended his free hand away from his lover, who clutched the draperies surrounding her bed and sank to the floor. Later, when he died, he lay on his back, raised his feet (thus exposing the elevated boots that are traditional in serious opera), and slowly lowered his legs to signify his death. Such melodramatic posing might seem comical in the age of realism, but given the size of the character's emotions, the theatricality of the costumes and setting, the florid music, and especially the skill with which the actor performed these long-established conventions, the gesture assumed an aesthetic that was harmonious to the overall tone of the play. The Chinese audience was thoroughly captivated by this ancient tale presented in a centuries-old tradition.

---

cast lists, and "coming attractions" are projected onto the walls of the proscenium so that audiences can read them. Gauzy silk curtains, colored by lights to indicate mood and locale changes, back the stage. Scenery is invariably painted in bright colors in a manner that Western audiences might equate with musical comedy. Even serious scenes are brightly colored and more lightly rendered than one would expect for a comparable scene in Western theater. Even in serious social dramas, there is picturesque idealization of the subject matter.

Staging Devices

Traditionally, the Chinese theater uses a minimum of scenery. Most stories are told with the aid of a couple of wooden chairs and a large box or table either painted red and gold or covered by a bright cloth. These few stage properties are all that is needed to tell even the most complex tales. An actor may sit on a chair, but can also jump from it to suggest a leap from a high place, or leap over it to suggest a suicide (i.e., jumping into a river or into a well). At other times the chair can suggest locale: the slats of the chair back can suggest a prison; tilted sideways it can represent a gate. The box serves as a desk, a throne, or a rock; it may also be a hiding place or a large object such as a wall.

More importantly, actors use movement and gesture to define locale. Perhaps the best known of these is the "threshold" effect (*kua men jian*): When actors want to suggest that they are entering a building, they lift their legs ceremoniously to step over the doorsill, which is customarily about eight inches high in Chinese houses. If they are moving from one locale to another, actors merely circle the stage; they circle it twice for longer journeys. A rider defines his horse by use of a whip and a ceremoniously lifted leg to suggest mounting the horse. An oar or long pole is sufficient to suggest the entirety of a boat (as in *The Qing Ding Pearl*).

Actors also employ simple, yet highly effective, emblems to further the color and invention of the Chinese theater. Black-clad actors (who are therefore not "seen" by the audience) wave blue silk scarves rhythmically to suggest water. Snowstorms are defined by tossing white confetti, while thunderstorms are created by billowing black cloth. Two yellow flags held horizontally define a chariot or cart; its passengers merely walk between the flags. Ghosts are identified by long strips of white paper affixed to an actor's right ear (and by the cacophony of fireworks set off by stagehands). Gods carry a horsehair switch and enter to the sound of a reverent gong. A yellow cloth over one's face denotes a sick person; the dead wear a red cloth.

A 1925 visitor to an opera in Peking recalls a particularly imaginative illustration of the power of Chinese staging conventions. The play required the slaughter of a pig onstage. An actor with a black cloth over his head mimed the movement of a pig, driven by another actor carrying a swineherd's stick. The actor-pig placed his head on the chair while the butcher mimed the beheading, after which the cloth was removed from the man's head. Now neither actor nor pig, the man simply walked upright offstage to conclude the scene.

Acting Technique

In addition to the many pantomimic gestures employed by actors, Chinese performers are bound by a number of highly refined body movements that denote character. To illustrate, consider hand gestures. Female roles (whether played by a woman or a man) require specialized pointing gestures; never is "she" permitted to expose her thumb, which is hidden by the middle finger. A male juvenile (the *hsiao-sheng*) makes his thumb as inconspicuous as possible, while the *lao-sheng* (a "painted face" depicting a warrior or bandit-hero) sticks his thumb up and extends both middle and index finger before him. A wide variety of walks and foot movements for specific character types must also be mastered. There is even a popular comic character known exclusively by his walk—the mischievous "hobbler" who drags a withered leg about the stage.

In addition to these essentially mimetic techniques, Chinese actors must learn to manipulate costumes and accessories. To cite but a single example, imagine the various uses of the *shui hsui* (or "water sleeves," because their movement suggests rippling water). The sleeves, which adorn traditional costumes, are about two feet long. They denote a variety of symbolic meanings, and they signal the orchestra that the actor will begin singing. Sleeve movements, performed rhythmically to musical accompaniment, suggest a variety of emotional states. For instance, when both arms are used simultaneously, the movement suggests worry. Similar movements apply to hats, fans, and warrior feathers.

Even stranger to non-Chinese audiences than the physical actions, which are usually recognizable to the most naïve visitor, are the vocal techniques. There is a specific vocal signature for each major character type. The dignified male roles (*lao sheng*) are softer and more pleasant to listen to, being neither too high-pitched nor too harsh. By contrast, the "young man" (*hsaio sheng*) must have a shrill, high-pitched voice to suggest the unchanged voice of adolescence. The *tan* (women's) roles are divided into a half-dozen types, each with a recognizable vocal quality. The virtuous woman (*jing i*) has a pure, high-pitched voice, while the flirtatious *hua-tan* sings in a nasal voice. Because the vocal qualities cannot be put into words, we encourage you to acquire recordings of Chinese operas and listen to the varied vocal techniques.

Because the Chinese language is tonal (i.e., the meaning of a word is determined by the voice inflection), there is an extraordinary musicality in Chinese speech. It is heightened in the theater by the use of meter and rhyme. Actors must learn some 13 different rhyming formulas for their work. Among the most popular is the *shu pan*, a comic tour de force. The *shu pan* is a gigantic tongue twister requiring accelerated speech and body movement. Specialized vocal effects mark entrances and exits. Upon entrance, all principal roles perform the *yin-zi*, a two- to four-line poem that is half-sung, half-recited, to introduce a character. The Yuan masterpiece *Autumn in the Palace of Han* provides a useful example of the *yin-zi* when the villainous counselor makes his first entrance:

> I am a man of a hawk's heart and a vulture's claw,
> My business swindling the great and oppressing the poor.
> All through flattery, cunning, treachery, and greed,
> I've got riches that one life is too short to exceed.
> I am none other than Mao Yen-shou . . .

Given the rigorous physical and vocal techniques demanded by the traditions of the Chinese theater, actors must spend up to seven years training for their profession.

Music and Sound

Perhaps no aspect of Chinese theater is more daunting to untrained ears than the cacophony of sound produced by the small orchestra (seven to nine musicians) that sits in "The Den of the Seven Dragons," a screened area "off left." Banging cymbals and gongs, the sharp retort of drums and percussive sticks (*pan*), and the shrill wail of the two-stringed fiddle (*hu qin*) can indeed be overwhelming to the uninitiated. Chinese opera music is not built on Western harmonic scales, but on those introduced by the Mongols in the eleventh century. Music and Chinese theater are inseparable: Without music the actors cannot function. Entrances and exits are ceremoniously heralded by music that defines character. The orchestra punctuates every piece of stage business, whether by a simple, reverent gong or a crescendo of all instruments. The musicians, by the way, do not use sheet music: They have memorized the entire repertory of the company, of which they are indispensable members.

THE QING DING PEARL
(THE LUCKY PEARL)
ANONYMOUS

THE QING DING PEARL

This popular play, the plot of which dates back to the Sung dynasty (960–1279 C.E.), is known to the Chinese by a variety of titles. It is best known as *The Qing Ding Pearl* (pronounced "chin deen"), a reference to the engagement pearl that Chinese maidens wear on the crown of their bridal headpieces. In this story the pearl takes on magic powers because it allows the wearer to cross through waters without getting wet. It is also known as *The Fisherman's Revenge*; *A Fisherman Kills a Family*; or *Collecting the Fishing Tax*, titles which suggest its plot line. It is a *xi-pi* play, which means that it was written to be accompanied by the *xi-pi*, or "Western skins," a reference to the percussive instruments (said to have been invented by the son of the first emperor).

The various titles and traditional instruments suggest that the play is a lively, robust piece loaded with romance, action, and violence. It is. It is also a farcical burlesque in its portrait of corrupt landowners and their bully henchmen. Furthermore, like Romantic melodramas in Western theater, it has characters molded in the Robin Hood tradition of the good-hearted bandits who take on the powerful land baron. To offset the merrymaking and physical humor, there is considerable sentimentality in the relationship of the long-suffering fisherman and his devoted daughter. Little wonder the play has become a favorite of the Peking Opera, as well as such regional operas as those from Hubei and Shaanxi provinces.

Perhaps *The Qing Ding Pearl* is best known beyond China because of its association with Mei Lan-fang, unquestionably the greatest performer in the Peking Opera in the twentieth century. Mei Lan-fang was particularly noted for his stunning portraits of women, and it was he who played Kuei-ying when the opera toured both the United States and the Soviet Union in the 1930s. Bertolt Brecht saw Mei Lan-fang's performance and was particularly taken by his masterful pantomime of Kuei-ying's paddling the boat across the river. Brecht cited this moment in his famous comparison between the acting style of the Chinese and that of the Stanislavsky school (see Chapter 5).

Because this charming play is so dependent on action and a variety of locales which would be challenging to define using conventional scenery, reading provides a good opportunity for you to apply what you have learned about the imaginative staging practices of the Chinese theater. As you read it, try to visualize how skillful actors, trained in dance, mime, and the martial arts, could create the many physical and scenic needs of the play. This is truly a play which must "on your imaginary forces work."

Much of the lasting popularity of *The Qing Ding Pearl* can be ascribed to its theme of the long-suffering "little man" overthrowing his tormentors. Given China's history of oppression under feudalism, the Japanese occupation, and, more recently, communism, one can understand why the Chinese would be drawn to this mostly comic tale. One can also understand why the ruling Communists themselves would sanction the play. The tyrannical landlord Ting could just as easily have been rendered by a Communist propagandist as by the play's creator. Compare Ting to the equally odious Simon Legree in *Uncle Tom's Cabin*; Ting may be more comical than Legree but he is no less grotesque.

In the final analysis, *The Qing Ding Pearl* is a revenge play, a commodity of the Western theater since Aeschylus. Its originality, however, comes from its free mixture of the grossly comical—the battle of the boxers is slapstick in the best Three Stooges tradition—and the deadly serious as the old fisherman, clearly a good and honest man throughout the play, is reduced to a ruthless killer. We are asked to recoil in horror at his bloodlust, just as his daughter does in their final, fateful boat trip down the river. Kuei-ying, of course, overcomes her revulsion—perhaps too quickly?—and the play ends with the violent murders of Ting and his men. All this after a rousing, knockabout farce! The neoclassic rules concerning unity of action and tone are not applicable to the Chinese opera.

Nor is subtlety of portraiture typically a virtue of the Peking Opera. The characters are servants to the plot and situation, and the playwright makes them only interesting enough to get them from one situation or song to the next. Li Chün, the swashbuckling hero, shows us little more than his derring-do and physical prowess, yet that is enough in the hands of a skilled and acrobatic actor specializing in the *wu sheng* roles. Think of such film actors as John Wayne, Arnold Schwarzenegger, or Chuck Norris: American movie audiences expected little virtuosity in either the playwriting or the acting in the majority of their works.

Motivation, often the obsession of contemporary actors trained in psychological realism, is hardly a concern of actors in the Peking Opera. Very late in the play, Kuei-ying asks her father if he actually intends to murder the tyrant-landlord, a most un-Confucian act. His daughter, horrified by his resolve, declares that she cannot accompany him on his murderous journey. As he turns the boat about in the swift river to return her to their home, she suddenly reconsiders: "I'll go with you, father. I don't want to return. I could not possibly part with you so!" There is a sentimental reconciliation between father and daughter, they find and quickly kill their prey, and the play ends abruptly (which is a typical feature of Chinese operas: There are no long, drawn-out denouements). A Western actor might well pester her director for clues about Kuei-ying's sudden about-face. "What's my motivation? What's happened to her scruples all of a sudden?" she might ask. And while answers such as "Well, in China a child's duty to the parents takes precedence over all else" or "She is duty-bound to show honor to her father" might go a long way to provide her with an objective for her about-face, the answer is much simpler. In the Chinese theater, according to Chinese scholar Huang Shang, the opera artist "may be likened to a connoisseur who has perceived in the vast and colorful and prolific field of life what is primary and what is indispensable and what is secondary and what may be passed by." For in this simple story of the dutiful maiden, the bandit-hero, and the fisherman who learns to say "Enough!", such psychological probing surely may be passed by.

THE QING DING PEARL
(THE LUCKY PEARL)

─A N O N Y M O U S─

Translated by L. C. Arlington and Harold Acton

PERIOD: *Northern Sung* (A.D. 960–1127).

DRAMATIS PERSONÆ

HSIAO ÊN, *a fisherman*	Lao-shêng
KUEI-YING, *his daughter*	Ch'ing-i
LI CHÜN, *a swashbuckler* ⎫	
NI JUNG, *another* ⎭	Erh-hua-lien
TING LANG, *a servant of the Ting household*	Ch'ou-êrh
TING YÜAN WAI, *a retired official*	Pai-ching
TA CHIAO SHIH, *a champion boxer*	
FOUR HSIAO CHIAO SHIH, *assistant boxers* ⎫	Ch'ou-êrh
KUO HSIEN SHÊNG, *secretary to Ting Yüan Wai* ⎭	

This play is partly a burlesque, holding rapacious officials up to scorn. The victims of oppression are a poor old fisherman and his attractive daughter who, taxed to the limits of endurance, bring retribution on the local bully and his satellites.

The prologue consists of the fisherman and his daughter singing as they cross the stage in a boat. As soon as they row out of sight two swashbucklers appear.

SCENE I

LI CHÜN. I've fought fierce tigers on the southern mountains.

NI JUNG. And I've kicked the scaly dragon that swims the northern seas.

LI CHÜN. My name's Li Chün. I'm known as "the Dragon that confuses the river currents."

NI JUNG. My name is Ni Jung, alias "the Curly-haired Tiger."

LI CHÜN. Since we have leisure to-day, let us take a stroll along the river-bank. (*Sings in hsi-p'i yao-pan*) I can remember when I exterminated the notorious rebel-brigand Fang La in years gone by.

NI JUNG (*also in hsi-p'i yao-pan*). You are truly a hero, Brother!

LI CHÜN (*sings*). I declined to wear the ceremonial robes and belt of jade (i.e., enter official life).

NI JUNG. I would rather join the braves of rivers and lakes (i.e., go about redressing wrongs, in Robin Hood style).

Exeunt.

SCENE II

KUEI-YING (*sings behind the curtain in hsi-p'i tao-pan*).
Onward the river rolls, and waves break high. (*Comes on stage and sings in k'uai-pan*) My father and I make our living on the turbulent waters. No painter's brush could depict the beauty of these verdant hills and waves. The home of every fisherman is his bark.

HSIAO ÊN (*enters and sings in hsi-p'i yao-pan*). Father and daughter catch fish in the river: we may be poor, but what do we care if people laugh at us? (*To Kuei-ying*) Hold fast the rudder! I am ready to cast the net. Alas, age is beginning to tell on me: my strength is failing.

KUEI-YING. If you are beginning to feel your age, Father, why not give up fishing?

HSIAO ÊN (*speaks*). If I did that, how could we live?

KUEI-YING (*weeps and sighs*). Alas!

HSIAO ÊN. Don't weep, my dear. The weather is too hot! Let us seek a cool nook under the trees to rest. I have already caught a few fish. Go and put them in the hold ready for sale so that I may procure some wine to cheer me.

Li Chün and Ni Jung appear, singing in hsi-p'i yao-pan.

LI. Idly we saunter by the riverside.

NI. Mightily ever eastwards roll the billows.

LI. I pause to view the prospect far and wide.

NI. I spy a bark beneath a fringe of willows.

LI (*speaking*). Now that I'm nearer I can discern a figure on board that looks remarkably like my old comrade, Brother Hsiao. I'll call out and make sure . . .

KUEI-YING. Father, somebody's calling you from the bank.

HSIAO ÊN. I'll see who it is. (*Stands up and gazes towards the newcomers*). Why yes, it's Brother Li! Are you coming on board, Brother?

LI AND NI (*in unison*). We were just on our way to see you.

HSIAO ÊN. Wait while your clumsy brother wipes and hands you the oar (*gestures accordingly*) . . . Who is this other

gentleman? I have not yet had the pleasure of his acquaintance.

LI. This is Mr. Ni Jung, the Curly-haired Tiger. Let me introduce you two brethren.

NI JUNG. You are too punctilious, Sir. (*He grasps Hsiao's hand and gives it a tight squeeze*).

HSIAO ÊN. Why do you grip me so hard, Brother?

NI JUNG. I was only testing your strength.

HSIAO ÊN. I am old and useless. (*Both laugh; Hsiao sings to Kuei-ying*) Come out of the hold and greet your two uncles. (*She obeys. Follows a characteristic specimen of Chinese polite conversation which we print as such rather than for any inherent interest*).

NI JUNG. Who is this maiden?

HSIAO ÊN. It's my little daughter, Kuei-ying.

LI CHÜN. How old is she?

HSIAO ÊN. Sixteen.

LI CHÜN. Is she engaged to anyone yet?

HSIAO ÊN. Yes, she's already betrothed.

LI CHÜN. To whom, may I ask?

HSIAO ÊN. To Hua P'êng-ch'un, the son of Mr. Hua Jung.

LI CHÜN. I hope the two families are well matched.

Li and Ni turn to take leave.

HSIAO ÊN. Don't go yet! I've caught a few fish to-day; stay and help me to digest them with some wine.

LI AND NI. We fear our visit has put you to a deal of trouble.

HSIAO ÊN. What sort of talk is this among brethren? (*To Kuei-ying*) Bring us the wine, dear. (*They sit down to drink*). Now, as I live on the produce of the waters, I dread the mention of two words: *kan* and *han* (i.e., to dry up, either through heavy frost or lack of rain). Whoever uses them is to drink three cups as forfeit.

LI CHÜN (*lifts his cup and says*). "Kan pei!" (*Chinese for "no heeltaps." He is promptly fined three cups*).

KUO (*enters while the party is thus engaged, and sings in hsi-p'i yao-pan*). While idly strolling by the shore, I spy a little boat. (*Speaks*) Hallo! I see there's a pretty wench on board. I'll take a few steps forward and snatch a furtive glance.

LI AND NI. Brother Hsiao, there's a fellow spying on us from the bank.

Hsiao steps on shore and asks him who he is.

KUO. I've only come to ask my way.

HSIAO ÊN. Whither?

KUO. To Mr. Ting's house.

HSIAO ÊN. Do you see that white wall like a figure eight just ahead of you there, with the big black varnished door and the two flag-poles? That's the Ting Mansion. (*Kuo pays no attention: his eyes are riveted on Kuei-ying*). How now! You are not even listening.

Exit Kuo in consternation.

HSIAO ÊN (*shouting after him*). Dog's head and brains!* I am sure you're up to no good! (*Returns to boat. Li and Ni inquire who it was and he tells them. Enter Ting Lang, Yüan Wai's servant, calling out for Hsiao En: Li Chün draws Hsiao's attention to the fact. Hsiao urges them to drink a little more, but they say they have tippled enough. He then steps on shore again.*) Well, well, if it isn't Ting Lang-êrh! And what has brought you hither?

TING LANG. I've come to collect the fishing-tax.

HSIAO ÊN. The river's almost dry for lack of rain and the nets have long been empty. Some other day when I am in funds I'll go along and pay the tax to the Ting family.

TING LANG. Although you offer fair words, I've worn out a pair of shoes on this errand. Who'll give me the money to buy new ones?

Hsiao Ên returns to his boat and tells his friends what Ting had come for.

LI CHÜN. I'll call him back and exchange a few words with him.

HSIAO ÊN. But don't cause a rumpus, whatever you do!

LI CHÜN. I quite understand! (*To Ting Lang*) Ho you, come here!

TING LANG. Oh, there's another of them. Well, I'll turn back.

LI CHÜN. What's your business?

TING LANG. To collect the tax on fishing.

LI CHÜN. Have you the Emperor's permission?

TING LANG. No.

LI CHÜN. Well, where did you get your authority from?

TING LANG. From His Honour the Magistrate.

LI CHÜN. It must be that Lü Tzŭ-ch'iu you refer to?

TING LANG. I refer to His Honour the Magistrate.†

LI CHÜN. Be off with you and tell him to abolish the fishing-tax. If he doesn't, there's a chance that something inconvenient may happen if we meet in the road.

TING LANG. You talk pretty big; what is your name anyway?

LI CHÜN. I'm the Dragon that confuses the Rivers.

TING LANG. You mean you're the stink-bug in a ball of dung.

LI CHÜN. Just wait till I give you a walloping, you eight days' spawn of a turtle! (*Here Hsiao Ên begs them to desist. But Ni Jung joins in the vituperation*).

NI (*to Ting Lang*). Roll back, and I'll gouge out your eyes and boil them in liquor! I'll flay your hide and mix it with dog-skin to make a plaster for carbuncles.

TING LANG. Stop bragging! What's your name I'd like to know?

NI JUNG. I'm Ni Jung, the Curly-haired Tiger.

TING LANG. What sort of louse in a mongrel's hair are you?

NI JUNG. Look out for a thrashing, you mouldy spawn of a turtle.

TING LANG. Just wait, don't be in such a hurry. I'll first take off my hat and gown . . .

Hsiao Ên attempts to dissuade them from fighting.

TING LANG (*to Hsiao*). You hold him while I run away.
                                                          (*Exit*).

LI AND NI. Why are you so feeble, Brother Hsiao?

HSIAO ÊN. The power and influence of the Ting family are very considerable.

LI AND NI. But they are not princes!

HSIAO ÊN. They have a quantity of retainers.

LI AND NI. But our brethren also are many.

HSIAO ÊN. They have abundance of riches.

LI AND NI. They cannot buy us over, though.

HSIAO ÊN. It's a very ticklish problem.

LI AND NI. You had better retire from this water business.

HSIAO. It's time I did, but then I'd have nothing to live on, I fear. I'd just become a beggar.

LI CHÜN. I'll present you with a hundred ounces of silver.

HSIAO. I'd be too ashamed to accept such a gift.

NI JUNG. And I'll present you with a thousand pounds of rice.

HSIAO. I could not accept, I would really feel ashamed!

LI AND NI. Never mind shame! We'll go and fetch the money and the rice.

Both depart. Hsiao sees them off with expressions of gratitude. Afterwards they discuss the appropriateness of Kuei-ying's engagement "as they are of equal status," and decide to send the wedding presents to her new home. Parallelwise the old fisherman and his daughter admiringly discuss the recent guests and their knight-errantry.

HSIAO ÊN (*sings*). Look yonder, the evening shades are falling fast. (*Speaks*) It is getting late; we had better steer for home. . . . (*Exeunt, after a refrain reminiscent of The Miller of Dee: "I care for nobody, no, not I," etc.*).

SCENE III

Enter Ting Yüan Wai and his secretary Kuo.

YÜAN WAI. I have stored a thousand piculs of grain.

KUO. Yes, all our granaries are full.

TING LANG (*enters and says*). I've just arrived from the river to report to you, Sir.

YÜAN WAI. Come to the point then. What about the fishing-tax I sent you to collect this morning?

Ting Lang reports his conversation with Hsiao En and trouble with the swashbucklers, after which he is told he may go.

---

*Epithet for one whose eyes are continually roving in all directions.
†Li Chün purposely pronounces the magistrate's name, while Ting refers to him as "His Honour," as it is not complimentary to use an official's cognomen.

KUO. This is a trifling affair: let me settle it.

Yüan Wai tells him to proceed with great circumspection.

Exit Ting Yüan Wai.

KUO (*to himself*). It seems to me that we had better send the boxers along. (*He shouts, and four boxers appear*). Where is your chief? (*They reply that he is practicing at the back*). Tell him to come here.

CHIEF BOXER (*appears saying*). It's good to gorge and good to booze but sleep is better fun. And when there is a fight, I am the very first to run. What's up, my lads?

THE FOUR BOXERS. Mr. Kuo wishes to see you.

Kuo tells them about the fracas with Hsiao Ên, etc., and that they are required to go and enforce payment of the tax and avenge their master's insult.

CHIEF BOXER. We are here to guard the mansion, not to collect taxes.

KUO (*persuasively*). But it's only for this once!

CHIEF BOXER. Well, we'll help you out this time, but mind there's to be no second time. Get the carts ready!

KUO. Are the carts to be used for transporting the money collected?

CHIEF BOXER. No, they're to carry our men, not the silver.

KUO. How ludicrous! (*Exit laughing*).

CHIEF BOXER. Are any of you fistical fellows acquainted with this Hsiao Ên?

FOUR BOXERS. Oh yes, we all know him by sight.

CHIEF BOXER. Capital! We'll pick up chicken's feathers as we go along.

FOUR BOXERS. What do you mean by that?

CHIEF BOXER. I mean we'll have more courage if we stick together.

(*Exeunt omnes*).

SCENE IV

HSIAO ÊN (*enters rather muzzily, singing in hsi-p'i man-pan*). Last night I got tippled and slept in my clothes. Already the cocks are crowing on the rafters. While I was dreaming they woke me up.

My two comrades advised me to have done with fishing. It's high time I did retire, to stay at home and rest. But I'm too poor and can think of no other means of supporting myself in old age. I have woken up early this morning. Is it not crows that I hear?* Hither and thither they fly calling to each other . . . I think I'll go into my grass hut and quench my thirst with tea.

Kuei-ying appears with a tea-tray.

KUEI-YING (*singing in hsi-p'i yao-pan*). How ill-fated am I to have lost my mother in early youth: only poor Father and I are left to fish by the river! (*Speaks*) Here's your tea, Father.

HSIAO ÊN (*takes the cup and drinks, then looking at Kuei-ying's*

*Unlucky omens.

clothes, says*). Didn't I tell you not to wear your fishing-clothes at home?

KUEI-YING. I was born and brought up in a fisherman's family. If you don't want me to dress like this, how am I to dress?

HSIAO ÊN. Not listening to your father's advice shows that you are unfilial.

KUEI-YING. There's no need to be angry, Father. I'll go and change.

HSIAO ÊN. Very well, see that you do so in future.

Here the boxers all strut in and a deal of irrelevant verbiage follows as to whether Hsiao is at home or not, and much dawdling for fear of being attacked by the fisherman's friends. Finally Hsiao opens his cottage door: the chief boxer, true to the universal conventions of farce, slips and stumbles. "Oh, I've slipped on a water-melon peel!" he observes. Pretending not to see Hsiao, one of his myrmidons then inquires: "Has Mr. Hsiao come out?"

CHIEF BOXER. So you are at home, Mr. Hsiao. I wish to see you about something. (*Examining him closely*). Why he's nothing but a feeble old man!

HSIAO ÊN. Where do you folks come from?

CHIEF BOXER. We're Mr. Ting's fine fistical fellows. *They tell him their mission; he makes the same excuses and says he will pay the tax on some future date at the Ting Mansion.*

CHIEF BOXER. Others have come and heard the same tale. I, the chief boxer, have come to-day to see that you pay up.

HSIAO ÊN. I had nothing for the others, and I have less for you. (*Inflates his chest and strikes a threatening attitude.*)

CHIEF BOXER. He's showing fight! Help me to get out of this quick before I lose any blood. We mustn't show any signs of weakness: we must resist him strength for strength. Have you brought the chains? Shackle him, and drag him away. (*To Hsiao*) Do you know what these things are?

HSIAO ÊN. Yes, they are instruments of Imperial law but what are you applying them to me for?

CHIEF BOXER. These chains are something that will shorten your wretched old life, let me tell you.

HSIAO ÊN. Quite useless! (*He throws them off and tramples on them. The chief boxer, too cowardly to go nearer and pick up the chains, orders his myrmidons to do so*).

BOXERS (*nervously*). You haven't taught us how to play this sort of trick.

CHIEF BOXER. What a pack of nincompoops! Just look at me! (*To Hsiao*) What ho, Hsiao Ên, have you ever seen a sight so strange as that?

HSIAO ÊN. Strange as what?

CHIEF BOXER. A bird with two polls.

HSIAO ÊN (*looking round*). Where?

CHIEF BOXER. Right here, in my hands: I picked it up while you were looking the other way. (*He begins to fasten the chain round Hsiao's neck*).

HSIAO ÊN. You sneak-thief, you worthless worm!

CHIEF BOXER. Remove him. If he has the money, well and good: if not, away with him!

An argument ensues as to whether he is to be shackled. Hsiao bursts the chains, throws them over the chief's head and shouts: "Haul him away!" The myrmidons start off with their chief in shackles instead of the fisherman.

CHIEF BOXER. Stop it. Where are you tugging me off to?

ASSISTANTS. Why, we've been heaving the wrong fellow!

CHIEF BOXER. There's not a single eye between the lot of you! This old codger's a wily one. We can't take him by force, better try persuasion. (*To Hsiao*) Your Honour, never mind if you have no cash. Come over the river with us and visit Ting Yüan Wai. Whether you pay or not is up to you; and whether he defers the tax is up to him. It has really nothing to do with us boxers anyway.

HSIAO ÊN. I catch your drift. You want me to cross the river with you to visit Ting Yüan Wai: whether he accepts the money or not rests with him, and not with you. Gentlemen, I have no leisure!

CHIEF BOXER. So you cold-shoulder my advances. You'll neither pay up nor come along with us. If you don't we are many against you . . .

HSIAO ÊN. A set of sucklings. You want a fight, do you? When I was young, I was as keen to fight as a child is to slip on a pair of new shoes on the first of the year: I rejoiced at the very idea. But now I am old and useless in a struggle.

CHIEF BOXER. I'd like to test you.

HSIAO ÊN. In what way?

CHIEF BOXER. Test *you*, you antiquated rat, licking a cat's whiskers right over its nose and waiting for death!

HSIAO ÊN. Are you really so anxious to fight me, baby? (*The dialogue continues in the same strain until the fisherman says*) All right then. Wait until I take off my coat and I'll show you something. (*Sings in hsi-p'i yao-pan*) May I expose the seven apertures of my body to fiery flames if I don't . . .

CHIEF BOXER. I'll go one better and riddle your carcass with eight holes until it smokes!

HSIAO ÊN. Old as I am, I'm in such a boiling rage that I could grind my teeth to powder! (*Starts fighting with the boxers and sings*) I'm the stalwart Hsiao En who roams the lakes and rivers.

CHIEF BOXER. And I'm the famous Tso T'ung-chui (Chief Brass-hammer).

HSIAO ÊN. How many battles have you fought, great and small? As for me, I'm the fierce lonely tiger of the mountains.

CHIEF BOXER. We'll see! I'll have a round with you. If you are the tiger, I am the hunter to kill it.

HSIAO ÊN (*sings*). Who's afraid of a mere domestic watchdog?

After further braggadocio, they butt into each other; the four boxers are beaten and quit the stage. The chief begs Hsiao on his knees to let him off.

HSIAO ÊN. It's easy enough to let you off, but first I'll give you three punches to remember me by.

CHIEF BOXER. Three punches! why I'll take three hundred if you let me off and consider myself in luck.

Hsiao continues to belabour him and Knei-ying joins in with a stick. The chief boxer bolts.

KUEI-YING. I can fight too!

HSIAO ÊN. You can! But this will only bring trouble on us. He is bound to tell the Ting family. Fetch my clothes quick; I'll go to the yamen before him and lodge a complaint.

KUEI-YING. He belongs to an official's household, better not go!

HSIAO ÊN. You are a child: what do you know of such things? You look after the home while I am away.

Exit Kuei-ying.

HSIAO ÊN (*solo*). Just as I am sitting quietly at home with the door closed, sudden calamity descends from Heaven upon me!

(*Exit*).

SCENE V

Enter the Boxers and Secretary Kuo.

KUO. So you have returned. Have you brought the money with you?

CHIEF BOXER. No. We were all routed by that old blackguard, Hsiao Ên.

KUO. To-morrow I'll have him taken to the yamen for punishment. That should appease your wrath.

CHIEF BOXER (*to his myrmidons*). Let's go and have our wounds dressed. (*Exeunt omnes*).

SCENE VI

Kuei-ying appears singing in hsi-p'i yao-pan to express her anxiety about her absent father: Father has been gone a long time, and still no tidings.

The hubbub of a magistrate's yamen is heard from behind the stage. Then voices counting ten, twenty, thirty, forty: Hsiao Ên is getting forty strokes of the bamboo. After which he totters on to the stage.

HSIAO ÊN. Curses on that Lü Tzǔ-ch'iu! He is not an honest and upright official. He had no right to punish me like that. A quiet and peaceful subject like me goes to complain at the yamen and the vicious curs, without a single word, set on me with forty strokes of the heavy bamboo and want me to apologize into the bargain! But there's no help for it. I can only gnash my teeth and hurry home. (*On arriving he sings out*) Kuei-ying, open the door!

KUEI-YING (*opening*). At last you've returned, Father! But why are you in such a dreadful state? (*Hsiao tells her. She bursts into tears*). You have been most barbarously treated!

HSIAO ÊN. I don't mind the pain so much as I resent being ordered to apologize to the Ting family.

KUEI-YING. Are you going to, Father?

HSIAO ÊN. I wish I could grow a pair of wings to fly across and kill the lot of them.

KUEI-YING. Father, you had better not go.

HSIAO ÊN. A mere child like you knows nothing of such matters. Make haste! fetch my coat and cap and the steel sword. (*She fetches them*). Stay here and look after the place in the meantime.

KUEI-YING. I'll accompany you, Father.

HSIAO ÊN. You are a girl and had better stay at home.

KUEI-YING. But isn't this a fine chance to show my courage?

HSIAO ÊN. All right. Get ready to come along with me.

KUEI-YING. What about our things here?

HSIAO ÊN. We don't need any of them. (*Kuei-ying fears they will be stolen during their absence and bursts into tears*). Don't cry so. Have you brought that lucky pearl (*Ch'ing Ting Chu*) with you? (*Kuei-ying says yes*). If anything untoward happens, you had better run off to your mother-in-law's, where you'll be safe.

KUEI-YING. What about you, Father?

HSIAO ÊN. Don't worry about me. (*They board the boat*). My child, sailing by night is not the same as by day: steady the rudder, you must be more cautious than usual. (*Sings in hsi-p'i k'uai-pan*) This affair is none of my seeking. I feel as if I were going through fire. I am crossing the river to-night to slay the whole family. If only I had wings to cross more swiftly! Why have you slackened the ropes, child?

KUEI-YING. Do you really mean to murder them, Father?

HSIAO ÊN. Of course, I am in earnest!

KUEI-YING. In that case I'll not go: I dare not.

HSIAO ÊN. Pah! When I didn't want you to, you insisted on coming: now that we're half-way, you want to turn back! Very well, I'll take you back.

KUEI-YING. I'll go with you, Father. I don't want to return. I could not possibly part with you so!

HSIAO ÊN (*sings and weeps*). Alas, my poor, dear daughter!

SCENE VII

They reach their destination, moor the boat and disembark.

HSIAO ÊN. My child, bear this in mind. Henceforth no matter where we are, if I upbraid, you too upbraid. If I say strike, you strike! We have now arrived at the Ting Mansion. Hey there! Anybody at home? (*The Chief Boxer appears and opens the door*). I've come to tender my apologies to Ting Yüan Wai. (*The Chief Boxer, after some conventional fooling, goes off to announce him*).

SCENE VIII

Enter Ting Yüan Wai and his secretary Kuo.

TING. Last night I had a very curious dream.

KUO. So had I! I dreamt that Yen Lo, King of the Underworld, had invited me to drink with him.

CHIEF BOXER. Hsiao Ên has come to offer his apologies.

TING. Show him in. (*Enter Hsiao, whom he addresses*) You impudent old wretch, what made you attack my employees as if they were wild beasts? And what have you to say in defence of such conduct?

HSIAO ÊN. With respect to this fishing-tax, have you the Imperial sanction?

TING. No.

HSIAO ÊN. Have you authority from the Six Boards?

TING. No.

HSIAO ÊN. By whose authority do you levy it, then?

TING. By His Honour the District Magistrate's.

HSIAO ÊN. Can you mean that Lü Tzŭ-ch'iu? (*Sings in hsi-p'i yao-pan*) Lü Tzŭ-ch'iu, you are far too avaricious! By what right did you sentence me to forty strokes of the bamboo? (*To Kuei-ying*) Curse him, denounce him, my dear!

KUEI-YING (*sings in hsi-p'i yao-pan*). The thieving cur and rebel! May Heaven utterly destroy him! He takes advantage of his official status to oppress the innocent. May he die without a clod of earth to cover his wretched carcass!*

TING (*to his servants*). Bring her here!

HSIAO ÊN. Ho, slowly there! We have, in the goodness of our hearts, brought you an offering.

TING. What is it?

HSIAO ÊN. We have come to present you with a pearl which we fished up out of the river.

TING. Let me see it.

HSIAO ÊN. There are too many eyes about.

TING (*to attendants*). Leave the room, all of you. (*Exeunt servants*). Where is it?

HSIAO ÊN. Here! (*Promptly draws his sword and kills Ting Yüan Wai and Kuo. He then says to Kuei-ying*) Daughter, help me to dispose of the rest.

The four assistant boxers come in and are slain. The Chief Boxer follows, and is likewise put to the sword.

Exeunt the fisherman and his daughter.

FINIS.

---

*The last is one of the worst maledictions that could blight a Chinese ear.

JAPAN

Artistic and Cultural Events

c. 550: Records of erotic dances in honor of sun goddess

c. 600: Records of *gigaku* and *bugaku* dances at court; antecedents of Noh drama

c. 1300: Musical storytelling; antecedents of *bunraku* and *kabuki* drama

c. 1350: Beginnings of Noh drama as Zeami writes the *Kadensho* and *Komachi* plays

c. 1490: Kyogen (farce) emerges

1586: Okuni performs dances that become basis for Kabuki theater

1617: Young Men's Kabuki

1629: Women banned from performing *kabuki*

1642: First *onnagata* Age of Chikamatsu (to 1725); golden age of *kabuki* and *bunraku* puppetry

1749: *The Actors Analects,* major treatise on performace

1881: Modern theater movement begins

c. 1890: New School of Art in Japan; favors Western realism

1930s: Shingeki theater popularized

1970s: Suzuki Tadeshi forms experimental theater companies

600 B.C.E.	500 C.E.	600 C.E.	1300 C.E.	1400 C.E.	1500 C.E.	1600 C.E.	1700 C.E.	1800 C.E.	1900 C.E.

Historical and Political Events

660: First earthly emperor of Japan: Jimmu Tenno

c. 525: Buddhism appears in Japan

Feudalism weakened

1603–1867: Tokugawa period; last shogunate rulers

1868: Meiji period

1945: Atomic bombs dropped on Hiroshima and Nagasaki

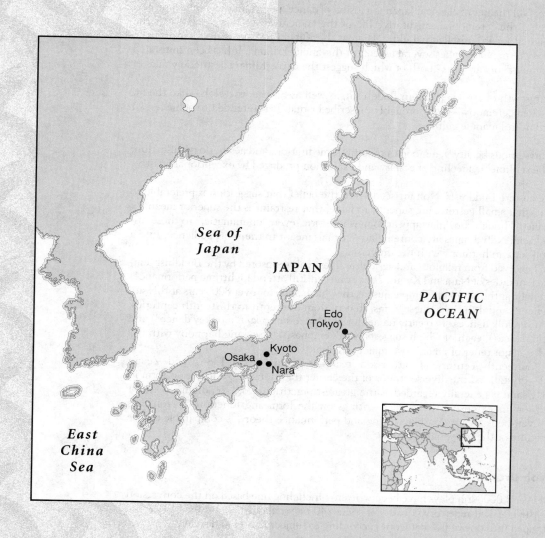

The Noh Theater

The Evolution of Noh Theater

The Noh (also: *Nō*) theater of classical Japan is a fusion of dance, poetry, music, mime, and acting that reflected the ceremonial, meditative life of the ancient aristocracy. Today, it is the drama of choice of Japan's intellectual elite, whereas the Kabuki theater is the drama of the masses. The very term *Noh* implies several aspects of this ancient drama. It has been translated as "accomplishment" or "art play," both of which suggest the extraordinary aesthetic values of the Noh theater.

As an outgrowth of Amida and Zen Buddhism, as well as Shinto, the Noh—like the famous Japanese tea ceremony—is a thoroughly prescribed ritual. It is intended to achieve two virtues important in Japanese culture:

- *yúgen* ("mysterious beauty"), a mood of quietness, meditation, and aesthetic gratification;
- *ran-i* ("the sublime"), a feeling of ecstasy and exaltation produced by exceptional artistry.

From the austere Buddhists, Noh artists derived the belief that suggestion is preferable to overstatement, that small gestures are superior to large, that restraint is the superior means of achieving beauty. Though they may appear somewhat static, even "undramatic," to those unfamiliar with them, Noh dramas are contemplative rituals meant to transport audiences into a transcendental state in harmony with the universe.

Noh itself evolved from religious and agricultural festivals sponsored by the Buddhist temples at the ancient cities of Nara and Kyoto. Today one can still attend nighttime performances of Noh by firelight at the Kofukuji Temple, just as they have done for over 800 years at this site of Japan's ancient capital. In its earliest forms, that is, from the tenth to thirteenth centuries, Noh evolved from folk dances. Two early names for Noh were *surugaku* ("monkey dance") and *dengaku* ("field dance"), each of which suggests Noh's emphasis on seeking harmony with the natural world, a major tenet of Japan's two major religions.

In the fourteenth century, a father-son team—Kan'ami (1333–1384) and Zeami (1363–1443)—crystallized the diverse strains of the earlier traditions into a major art form in Heian Japan. Zeami is generally regarded as the greatest practitioner of Noh drama, both for his plays and for his extensive theoretical writings on the form and function of Noh. His *Kadensho*, a seven-book treatise on playwriting and performance theory, is comparable to *The Poetics* of Aristotle or the *Nātyaśātra* of India.

Types of Noh Drama

Though well over 2,000 Noh plays have been written—including one based on the conversion of St. Paul—the classical repertory consists of some 240 plays, about half ascribed to Zeami. These are grouped into one of five categories according to subject matter and style:

1. god (*kami* or *waki*) plays celebrating an auspicious religious event;
2. warrior (*shura-mono*) plays in which the protagonist is usually a slain warrior whose ghost returns to relieve human suffering;
3. woman (*kazura*) plays, sometimes referred to as "wig plays" because they are acted by men in wigs;
4. "living person pieces" (*genzai*), which often deal with madness, obsessions, and unbridled passion;
5. demon (*kiri*) plays in which the protagonist is a demon, devil, or other supernatural figure, both good and evil.

Because most of the plays in the repertory are short, an evening of Noh theater usually consists of a sample of each of the five types of plays. Short farces (*kyógen*) are performed between the lofty dramas, much the way comic satyr plays were performed at the tragic festivals of ancient

The renowned Noh actor Sadayo Kita plays a noblewoman who is transformed into a demon to do battle with the warrior-prince Kan Hosh. Demon and god plays are staples of the Noh theater.

Athens. The Japanese respect for nature dictates that a play may not be performed out of its appropriate season: when spring comes to Japan the winter plays are put to rest for another year.

The Conventions of Noh Theater

Because its emphasis is not on an unfolding human action and the attendant suspense, Noh theater is not grounded in intricate plotting. Rather, Noh drama exists to create mood, emotion, and a spiritual state. Most Noh plays are dominated by a single, powerful emotion summoned by the harmony of instrumental and vocal music, dance and gesture, and poetry. Whatever their genre, subject matter, or emotional impact, the plots and characters of Noh plays are carefully structured according to ancient formulas. With only a few exceptions, the plays are in two parts. In the first section the central character, called the *shite* ("doer"), appears in disguise, customarily that of a humble person. In the second, the *shite* is transformed into a supernatural being: a god, a demon, or a ghostly specter who, in the tradition of Buddhism, repents past deeds. The *shite* is accompanied by a *tsure*. An objective third party—the *waki*, often a holy person—watches from the "side" and comments on the action. Other roles are often the *kokata*, or child, symbolizing a new order. A servant, or *kyógen* ("clown"), adds irony to the play. While the *kyógen* uses colloquial prose, the *shite* speaks in lofty, poetic language filled with obscure references to Japanese literature and religion. Thus Noh plays virtually defy translation. Imagine a Japanese visitor trying to watch a Western play filled with snippets from the Bible, Shakespeare, Homer, and the Arthurian legends. Still, the themes and emotions elicited by these plays are sufficiently universal that one need not be educated in Buddhist philosophy, classical Japanese literature, or the particulars of sacred gesture and dance.

The Noh theater's aversion to realistic representation is perhaps best manifested by the stage on which these spiritual rituals are enacted. In its earliest days, the Noh stage was perhaps more versatile, particularly as its first performers wandered from temple to temple, court to court, performing their plays. Today, however, the Noh stage has a standard size. The playing space is 19 feet, 5 inches square; it is always 2 feet, 7 inches high. It projects into the auditorium and is surrounded by the audience on three sides; customarily a small moat separates the forestage from the first row of spectators. The stage is constructed of highly polished wood that reflects the actors and enhances the aesthetics of the production. It is backed by a panel on which is painted an aged pine tree signifying natural beauty and eternity. A roof, supported by four 15-foot pillars, covers the playing space.

The actors enter from the audience's left via the *hashigakari*, a bridge lined by three small trees. Prior to their entrance, the actors sit in the *kagami no ma* ("mirror room") for hours contemplating the polished wooden masks they wear. Only the *shite* and *tsure* wear masks, hewn from a rare wood found in only one area of Japan; they are crafted by a single family that has performed this sacred duty for centuries. The other characters wear masklike makeup; the chorus and musicians wear none. Four musicians, who play three types of drums and a flute, sit in an alcove upstage, fully visible to the audience. A chorus chants the words of the play while sitting on the right side of the stage. Each of the principal actors, all male, has an assigned area where he sits or performs. The *shite* stands at the place where the *hashigakari* meets the stage, the *waki* at the pillar diagonally opposite the *shite*, and the *kyógen* at the rear of the stage. The very rigidity of this placement reinforces the ritualistic nature of Noh drama, as well as its presentational style of performance. The costumes are extraordinary works of art in themselves. Little wonder that Noh actors have been a favorite subject for Japanese artists for 600 years.

The performance techniques of Noh drama have been strictly codified in the *Kadensho* and are not subject to variation because the Japanese do not especially embrace innovation in art. According to the principle of *sabi*, they revere the past and judge a work by the exactness of its replication of ancient methods. Thus, each of the five major types of plays employs a particular music that is proper to it alone. A twentieth-century Noh actor must learn and recreate meticulously the gestures, intonations, and dance steps that were perfected in Zeami's age. The gestures and steps are executed with slow precision to enhance the meditative experience of the Noh theater; it is not uncommon for an actor to take many seconds to merely raise an arm. Because of its many conventions and traditions, only the barest elements of Noh performance can be described here. Of the many types of theater described in this text, perhaps none so completely demands a living example as Noh theater because of its stately aestheticism, which words cannot replicate.

The stage of the National Noh Theater of Japan with its traditional posts; the shite pillar is at the rear left. The image of the pine tree is considered sacred and is a fixture of the Noh stage.

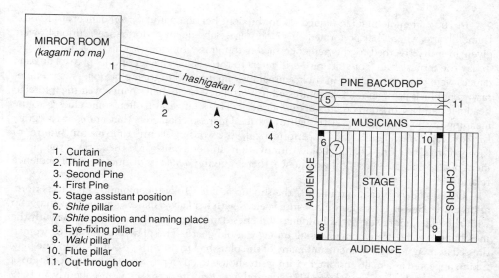

1. Curtain
2. Third Pine
3. Second Pine
4. First Pine
5. Stage assistant position
6. *Shite* pillar
7. *Shite* position and naming place
8. Eye-fixing pillar
9. *Waki* pillar
10. Flute pillar
11. Cut-through door

Diagram of a traditional Noh stage; note especially the bridge (hashikagari) linking the mirror room with the stage to facilitate ceremonial entrances for the principal actors.

The Influence of Noh Drama on the West

Many twentieth-century theater artists in the West have been attracted to the Noh theater, perhaps none more than Irish poet-playwright William Butler Yeats. He especially admired the poetic, antirealistic nature of the Japanese theater and in 1916 began a series of "Plays for Dancers" in which he fused ancient Celtic myth with Noh technique. "I have invented a form of drama, distinguished, indirect, and symbolic . . . an aristocratic form," he announced as he wrote *At the Hawk's Well*. Though more influenced by the Chinese theater, Bertolt Brecht adapted a Noh play in 1930 for his didactic theater, and the noted British composer Sir Benjamin Britten wrote the Noh-inspired *Curlew River* (1964) as "a parable for church performance." The minimalist plays of Samuel Beckett summon parallels with the Noh theater in both form and content. The formalist productions of director-*auteurs* such as Robert Wilson suggest a kinship with the stately, static aesthetics of the Noh. Even contemporary Japanese theater artists such as Tadashi Suzuki use the conventions of Noh (and often Kabuki) in their decidedly modern works, including those from the Western canon.

The Kabuki Theater

The Evolution of the Kabuki Theater

The Noh has largely been the theater of sophisticates and intellectuals. In the late sixteenth century Noh was given state sanction when the shogunate government made it the official drama of the court. At the same time Japan was being torn asunder by civil warfare and a dying feudalism. Under the Tokugawa shogunate (1603–1867), the merchant class gained influence, particularly as Portuguese, Spanish, and Dutch explorers opened trade routes between Asia and the West. Merchants sought their entertainment in places other than the court theaters, and they frequented shrines where they were entertained by temple maidens who performed graceful yet lively folk dances called *nembutsu odori*. The *odori* were quite unlike the solemn *mai* dances of the Noh theater.

In 1603 a temple maiden named Okuni brought her company of *odori* dancers to Kyoto's Izumo Shrine, where they performed on a Noh stage. Subsequent performances, curiously, were given in a dry riverbed as the audience sat on the grassy hillside to watch Okuni's troupe. Today the term *shibai* ("grass sitting") still refers to the Kabuki theater and its plays. The *odori* dances were provocative both in their sensual movements and in their clothing. A contemporary woodblock print shows Okuni dressed in Portuguese-style men's pants, wearing a foreign headpiece and a Christian crucifix about her neck. This strange garb offers some clues as to the meaning of the term *kabuki*. Although the three Japanese characters that are used to signify *kabuki* mean "song, dance, skill [in performance]," the word in Okuni's time meant "bizarre" or "avant-garde." Among Okuni's boldest innovations in her avant-garde theater was the placement of actors in the midst of the audience, thereby giving *kabuki* its distinctive actor-audience relationship.

Okuni's fame spread, and in 1607 the shogun at Edo (Tokyo) commanded her to perform at his castle. She enacted short plays, interspersed with her *kabuki* dances, on the same program with the older, more stately Noh dramas. Okuni's dances and plays were as popular with the merchants as they were controversial among the old guard. The plays often featured women dressed as men, men as women, and many of the plots had to do with prostitution; in one play, Okuni appeared as a male customer visiting a teahouse to buy a prostitute. The erotic nature of these early *kabuki* plays caused patrons to quarrel over favorite actresses. Consequently, in 1629 the shogunate forbade the appearance of women on the stage, not because of any moral scruples about prostitution (which thrived among the merchant class) but because any form of disorder—such as fights among *kabuki* spectators—was intolerable in the Japanese culture.

The popular new theater art continued as the Women's Kabuki (*onno*) was replaced by the Young Men's Kabuki (*wakashu*). There had been troupes of young male dancers prior to Okuni's time, but they fell out of favor when the Women's Kabuki became popular. The young males soon adopted the style of Okuni's troupe, and for the next 23 years they were the most popular stage entertainments in Japan. The boys, too, were involved in prostitution and once again quarrels among Kabuki patrons caused the shogunate to outlaw the Young Men's Kabuki. From 1653 only mature males (*yaro*), whose foreheads were shaved to make them less attractive, were allowed to perform Kabuki. The male-only custom continues today (with a few notable exceptions) and one can still see the shaved forelock wigs in many Kabuki costumes. Importantly, the ban on women gave rise to one of present-day Kabuki's most distinguishing features, the *onnagata* role in which a mature man meticulously creates the dress, dance, and manners of the idealized woman.

During the Genrouku period (1673 to 1735) Japanese arts, and consequently Kabuki, expanded and thrived in a manner comparable to that of the Elizabethan age. Power was passing from the feudal warlords to the newly monied class of merchants who fostered the arts. From the Genrouku era came Kabuki's first great actor, Ickikawa Danjúró I (whose descendant created the role of Benkei in *Kanjinchō* [*The Subscription List*]) and its greatest poet-playwright, Chikamatsu Monzaemon (1653–1724), whose stature is comparable to that of Shakespeare. Most of the conventions and form of the Kabuki were fixed during the Genrouku period. The adoption of the curtain and scenery, unthinkable in Noh theater, the emergence of the *hanamichi*, a lengthy ramp through the audience on which actors entered and exited the stage, and the primacy of literary texts were significant developments.

Types of Kabuki Drama

Kabuki plays traditionally comprise five acts, perhaps a remnant of the days in which five separate Noh plays made up a day's program. Traditionally, a Kabuki program lasted about 12 hours, although the length was reduced to 8 in 1868. Audiences are free to come and go as they please, and they often bring food and drink for the day-long event. A Kabuki program is divided into four distinct parts, beginning with a historical play (*jidaimono*) glorifying the samurai code. This is followed by a dance drama intended to be a mood piece. Next, a *sewamono* or domestic drama is presented; it invariably portrays the world of the merchant class that sup-

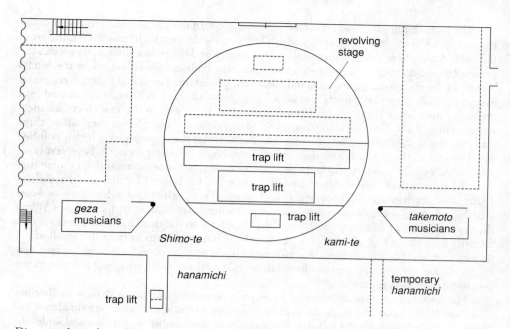

Diagram of a traditional Kabuki stage and its hanamichi *that allows actors to enter and exit through the audience.*

ports Kabuki and is (relatively) more realistic than the *jidaimono* plays. Although Kabuki can never be mistaken for realistic theater, there is an ongoing debate about the degree to which it should be "real." Chikamatsu's celebrated observation that "Art lies in the slender margin between the real and the unreal" suggests Kabuki's attempt to capture genuinely human dilemmas and their emotions in an exquisitely stylized manner. The final portion of a Kabuki program is a one-act dance drama, frequently humorous, like the farcical *kyōgen* of the Noh. Although it is a serious play, *Kanjinchō*, which follows later in this section, depends on an essentially comic structure. Today Kabuki programs are much shorter, usually comprised of scenes from longer plays and dances well known to Japanese audiences.

There have been some attempts to alter Kabuki's form and content to accommodate modern sensibilities. For instance, a more realistic format (the *Shin Kabuki*) uses more natural vocal patterns and naturalistic settings in a darkened auditorium. The *Ichikawa* (All-Girl) *Kabuki-za* was formed after World War II. Still, Kabuki remains tradition-bound and resistant to change. One of the liabilities of popular art, of course, is that it is susceptible to changing tastes. Just as the merchants of Kyoto were seduced by Okuni's daring dances in 1603, so, too, have their descendants been enticed by Western film, television, and pop music. At the same time many Western theater artists, such as France's Arianne Mnouchkine, are exploring the theatrical possibilities of Kabuki.

The Conventions of Kabuki

With its roots in middle-class tastes; its techniques drawn from an eclectic mixture of puppetry, song, music, and dance; and its subject matter derived from Japanese myth, folktales, and history, the Kabuki theater is more theatrical than literary. As with the Chinese theater and the older Noh, Kabuki makes no pretense at realism. It is, however, less poetic and abstract than the Noh, and though it uses some techniques similar to Chinese opera (e.g., painted faces), it relies on special effects and decor. As you read the Kabuki play, imagine how it might be performed at the *Kabuki-za*, the traditional home of Kabuki in Tokyo.

The modern Kabuki stage reveals influences of Western theater architecture, the most obvious of which is the large proscenium with a European-style curtain. In many ways, the art of Kabuki is dedicated to creating memorable stage images, and the proscenium arch provides the picture frame necessary to focus the picture. Stunning tableaux are enhanced by the formal parting of the traditional green, rust, and black-striped curtain. The Kabuki stage is enormous as it must house large casts, many "invisible" stage assistants clad in black, a full ensemble of orchestra and chorus (*naugata*), which are always visible, as well as the machinery for ingenious scenic effects. The *Kabuki-za* is over 90 feet wide and about 35 feet deep, about three times the size of the typical Western stage. The Kabuki stage floor, composed of highly polished wood to add to the aesthetics of the performance, has several trapdoors. A large revolving stage, which can be dated to the mid–eighteenth century, enhances scene shifts; in some theaters there are actually two revolves, a smaller one inside the larger. Elevators (used as early as 1736) abet apparitions, disappearances, and other effects, which are referred to as *keren* ("tricks"). Kabuki theaters are normally equipped with flying equipment for *chunori* ("riding the sky") effects that can lift an actor from the stage floor to the third balcony. There are also facilities for a number of water effects (*honmizu*). As one might expect from this small island nation, there exists a whole class of Kabuki plays known as water plays (*mizumono*). It has been suggested that water effects were instituted to provide audiences with images of coolness in the hot, humid Japanese summers.

The Kabuki fosters much interplay between actors and audience. A shallow auditorium (less than 60 feet) puts the audience in close proximity to the actors, who perform almost exclusively on the forestage. As you read *Kanjinchō* note the number of speeches and asides directed to the audience. In the Kabuki it is not uncommon to stop the action and make an announcement (*kojo*) about the accomplishments of an actor.

The most distinctive feature of the Kabuki stage is the *hanamichi* ("the flowery way"), a narrow 65-foot runway that leads from a dressing room behind the audience to the forestage. The actor enters and exits amid the spectators, who frequently shout his name in admiration. An actor does not merely walk the length of the *hanamichi*. He uses an extraordinary walk—part dance, part martial arts—called a *roppo* (or *tobiroppo* for exits). *Roppo* means "six directions," because the actor swings his arms and legs violently up, down, front, back, and side-to-side. The *tobiroppo* often occurs *after* the curtain has been lowered at the conclusion of the action, and the lone actor makes a grandly theatrical exit. For Japanese audiences, this is the true emotional climax of the play. Foreigners unaware of this tradition are occasionally embarrassed as they rise to leave when the curtain closes, only to discover that the Kabuki's grandest moment is yet to come.

Benkei (Danjuro XII) in mie *pose as he exits* Kanjinchō (The Subscription List); *note the* hanamichi *at the Kabuki-za, Japan's foremost theater.*

A blend of Eastern and Western traditions in the contemporary Japanese theater are found in Tadashi Suzuki's 1991 adaptation of Euripides' The Bacchae. *Agave cradles the head of her dead son as Cadmus looks on.*

While entering, the actor stops at a spot exactly seven-tenths down the *hanamichi* and freezes in an exaggerated pose called the *mie,* which he holds for several seconds. The *mie* allows the audience to study his colorful costume and to assess his psychological state, which is indicated by gestures, makeup, and grimaces. Perhaps you have seen pictures of Kabuki actors with what appear to be crossed eyes, a technique meant to suggest enormous emotional turmoil.

Despite its beginnings in "the Women's Kabuki," the Kabuki today is virtually a male-dominated institution. Among the principal roles, there are three styles of performance for male actors. First, the *aragoto,* or "rough" style, portrays thoroughly masculine virtues, such as power and courage, derived from the ancient *samurai* ("warrior") code. The *aragoto* paints his face in fantastic designs (*kumadori*) to show his manliness, and wears an oversized costume to emphasize his larger-than-life status. Vocally, the *aragoto* uses a high-pitched voice, and often resorts to nonsensical utterances to indicate strong emotion. In *Kanjinchō* Togashi, who guards the gates, is an *aragoto* role; as part of his ruse, Benkei assumes the *aragoto* style to gain Togashi's respect.

In contrast to the "rough" style is the *wagato,* which is much more refined and delicate. The *wagato* is customarily a handsome young lover. Though he is sought after for his looks and grace, he is usually depicted as cowardly and irresponsible. The more virile, harsher tones of the *aragoto* give way to a softer, more melodic vocal pattern in the *wagato.* Prince Yoshitsune (in *Kanjinchō*) is a *wagato.*

The *onnagata* is perhaps the most famous of the three classical Kabuki styles. In this style a man plays female roles, a convention that grew, of necessity, out of the shogunate's 1629 ban on women in theater. By the eighteenth century the techniques for playing women had been perfected, thanks largely to the efforts of the first great female impersonator of the Kabuki, Yoshizaw Ayame (1673–1729). He advocated that *onnagata* actors live their female roles both on and offstage, but the practice has been abandoned in the twentieth century. Because it is the duty of the *onnagata* to portray an idealized femininity, he must study and master many rigorous poses, gestures, and movements, as well as perfect Japanese ceremonial dances. The *onnagata* always appears in the traditional all-white makeup, and the vocal techniques of the role are much more delicate than that of the *wagato.* Obviously, there is no *onnagata* in *Kanjinchō.*

Kata, a term also used in the Noh theater, are the basic movements and vocal patterns that Kabuki actors must learn. The *mie* is a specialized *kata,* as is the *roppo.* Vocal patterning is

CENTER STAGE   THE TANABATA FESTIVAL OF JAPAN

Among the most prevalent archetypes in myth and literature is that of star-crossed lovers, a phrase taken from the most famous play about lovers who are forbidden to see each other, *Romeo and Juliet. A Midsummer Night's Dream*—perhaps written the same year as *Romeo and Juliet*—also portrays young lovers (Hermia and Lysander, Pyramis and Thisbe) who are separated by tyrannical fathers. The Chinese drama *Autumn in the Palace of Han* depicts the emperor's pain when he is forced to relinquish his favorite concubine. And think of the scores of pop ballads in which a singer laments that the world is cruel because he or she cannot be with a lover.

Life slows in Japan on July 7 as people, especially children, pause to remember the plight of Orihime (or Shokujo), a beautiful weaving girl, and her lover, the cowherd Hikoboshi (or Kengyu). Their story of frustrated love (appropri-

An audience watches young dancers at a Tanabata Festival in Sendai; the colorful banners display love poems in honor of the star-crossed lovers of Japanese mythology.

intended to create atmosphere through rhythmic, antiphonal patterns of sound. Obviously, *kata* cannot be adequately described and must be seen and heard to be appreciated. The Japanese, who revere the old (*sabi*), expect Kabuki actors to master centuries-old *kata*. Actors are judged not on their originality, but on their ability to raise traditional artistry to new levels and thus achieve *aware*, an appreciation of beauty in the familiar.

There are also scenic *kata*. If the Noh theater is a celebration of the imagination through suggestion, the Kabuki celebrates the ingenuity of its craftsmen to stimulate the senses through an array of sights, colors, and sounds. The Japanese love scenes in which vibrant cherry blossoms fill the stage to denote spring, or in which travelers circling the stage to suggest a long journey (*michiyuki*) are covered with softly falling snow. They also love sensational scenes, transformations, and battles. In one famous Kabuki play a seductive woman is transformed into an enormous spider before the delighted audience. Quick changes, among the Kabuki's supreme artistic accomplishments, are called *hayagawari*. (The transformation of "the Beast" into the handsome prince in the Broadway production of *Beauty and the Beast* is very much in the *hayagawari* tradition.) Unlike the Noh theater, Kabuki actors do not wear masks; in fact, the Kabuki (and, significantly, the women who invented it) placed a new emphasis on the human form in Japanese culture. However, warriors in battle scenes wear special masks which can be "cut open" by samurai swords to suggest a decapitation.

Because the Kabuki evolved from dance, music is as integral to its experience as its visual elements. Indeed, the heart of the Kabuki is the *naguata*, the ensemble of musicians who play the traditional *samisen* (a stringed instrument), flutes, and Noh drums. Kabuki music is livelier

ated from an ancient Chinese fairy tale) is set against the backdrop of the universe itself on this "Festival of the Stars." Legend says that when they fell in love and married eons ago, Orihime's father, a celestial king, was angered because she neglected her weaving and he his herd. He separated them on opposite sides of the Milky Way as the stars Vega and Altair and decreed that they might meet only one night a year. Customarily, the stars are aligned on the evening of July 7 (though the cities of Daito and Sendai actually celebrate Tanabata on August 6). Of course, the lovers may be reunited only on a clear night; if it is overcast or raining, they must wait another year for their night of love.

Tanabata is a major civic occasion, especially in Sendai, the city most closely associated with this festival (over 2 million people visit Sendai during the Tanabata). Children and young lovers write *haiku* and *tanka* poems, as well as wishes, on brightly colored paper (*tanzaku*). These are affixed to bamboo poles that have been placed in gardens. Shopping centers are decorated with the same enthusiasm Westerners see at Christmas. Offerings of food, especially corn and eggplant, are left for the lovers. Girls pray that their handiwork might be as beautiful as Orihime's. After they have been displayed, the *tanzaku* are burned so that the wishes may rise with the smoke into the heavens where Orihime and Hikobashi can read them. The lucky and the faithful have their wishes granted.

The highlight of the evening is a spectacular parade in which children, dressed in traditional Japanese costumes, march through town beating drums as they sing

Ten Ten Ten Ten,
Tentekoten-no-tanabatasan
Tanabatsan-o-okuwa.

The translation—"we are off to see the god Tanabata"—cannot capture the rhythmic joy of the song. The parade is climaxed by a fireworks show that lights the sky so that the lovers might find each other.

There is certainly great charm in this age-old story. In it we see yet another attempt by humans to explain natural phenomena through myth (i.e., the presence of stars), to reconcile life's bitter disappointments, and to control events through a ritual or—in this case—a ceremonial festival. Although the story that inspired the Tanabata is founded on an unhappy situation, the festival is predicated upon hope that lovers will be reunited, that wishes will be granted. The theatrical embellishments (costumes, decorations, parades, songs, and fireworks) elevate the festivities to something beyond ordinary life.

That Zeami should set his Noh drama *Komachi at Sekidira* against the background of the Tanabata is not surprising. The beautiful and talented Komachi was a great poet who, like Orihime and Hikoboshi, inspired generations of lovers.

Ayumi Kazama and Sayaka Sudo
Texas A&M University

---

than that of the meditative Noh theater. During dance plays, the *nagauta* sit on a raised platform at the rear of the stage; in other plays, they play offstage, though still highly visible in keeping with the theatricality of Kabuki. Two sets of wooden clappers (*ki*) provide the rhythmic accompaniment to the action, especially on entrances and exits. A chorus of eight sings while the actors mime vigorous movements. The *nagauta* music for *Kanjinchō*, composed by Kineya Rokusaburo for the play's premiere in 1840, is considered the finest in the Kabuki repertory.

The Contemporary Japanese Theater: Shingeki

Although the Noh and Kabuki are the best-known forms of theater outside Japan, there is also a vibrant contemporary theater in Japan, fueled in no small part by a younger generation that has rejected the country's traditional arts in favor of experimentation and current issues. As an alternative to Noh, Kabuki, and Bunraku puppetry, *Shingeki*—"new/other theater"—has evolved since 1868 with the concerted effort on the part of artists who reacted to the inundation of Western influence on Japan. Today the Shingeki thrives alongside the more venerable forms.

In 1873 the Kabuki Reform Movement was formed to "save" traditional Kabuki performances by investing them with Western-style fashions. Though well intentioned, the reforms diminished both the quality and the appeal of Kabuki, and, ironically, only furthered the vogue for Western-style drama. Soon Japanese began to consider Western theater as the model for which modern Japan ought to strive. In 1909 Tsubouchi Shoyo (1859–1935) formed the Literary Arts Society, a school committed to shaping a new theater and drama for Japan as it entered the twentieth century. Tsubouchi considered the Kabuki outmoded, even corrupt, and called for a theater based on such European models as Ibsen and Shakespeare (who is actually one of Japan's most revered playwrights; the Japanese publish more articles about Shakespeare than many English-speaking countries). Tsubouchi's experiments were successful, and Western-style theater became entrenched in Japan.

Japanese theater artists also founded a Free Theater based on Antoine's experiment in Paris. Osani Kaoru (1881–1928), who led this movement, did much to introduce naturalism to the Japanese theater. In particular, he wrote and staged Ibsen-like social dramas that attacked middle-class hypocrisy and corruption. It was Osani who coined the term *Shingeki*, and he promoted the motto "Ignore tradition" among young theater artists. Though Osani and other innovators called for young Japanese to write plays for Japan, the primary benefit of the Free Theater movement was the importation of popular Western plays by Ibsen, Chekhov, and other new realists from Europe.

By the 1920s Western plays were prominent in Japan, a situation that was as detrimental as it was inspiring. It took almost two decades before Japanese dramatists developed a modern style that was uniquely Japanese. Kishida Kunio (1890–1954), who studied in Paris, emerged as the most respected of the new Shingeki playwrights. In 1947 Morimoto Kaoru wrote *Onna no issho* (*A Woman's Life*), the play generally acknowledged as the work that brought contemporary Japanese playwriting to its maturity. The drama depicts the tragic experiences of a woman who sacrifices herself for her family and captures the angst of a nation devastated by World War II. Although it is decidedly modern, Morimoto's play nonetheless maintains a kinship to the older Noh and Kabuki traditions because it celebrates the inner strength of its central character, who endures the unendurable stoically.

Most Shingeki drama is concerned with a single theme: identity, both personal and national. Because Japan has undergone massive social, economic, and political changes in the wake of World War II, it has in many ways been forced to redefine itself. The tension between traditional virtues and modern values dominates contemporary Japanese literature. Japanese theater and stagecraft exhibit a similar duality. One finds a provocative blend of the naturalistic and the symbolic (a la the Noh theater) in many Japanese plays. Kobo Abe's *The Man Who Turned into a Stick* represents this phenomenon: the acting style is naturalistic, yet its visual imagery is metaphysical, even Noh-like in its classic simplicity.

Tadashi Suzuki's work, well known and much admired in the West, is especially apt at fusing the old and the new. Suzuki has stated that his mission is "to make traditional consciousness compatible with modern habits." In 1974 he staged Euripides' tragic war drama *The Trojan Women*; it moved freely from the ancient Greek world to modern Japan and employed Noh, Kabuki, and naturalistic theater styles.

Today the Shingeki is truly reflective of contemporary Japan. Having arrived at a point of healthy equilibrium between its own cultural traditions and those of the modern West, it is diverse, and represents a healthy fusion of new and old, Eastern and Western, social and metaphysical concerns.

KANJINCHŌ
(THE SUBSCRIPTION LIST)
NAMIKI GOHEI III

NAMIKI GOHEI III (1789–1855)

Little is known about Namiki Gohei III, one of four playwrights bearing that name. In Japan it is customary for artists—both writers and actors—to adopt the name of a renowned predecessor even though one is not related to another. Of the four writers named Namiki Gohei, only the first (1747–1808) was prolific enough to merit scholarly attention.

Namiki Gohei III (nee Shindo Soruku) was a disciple of Namiki Gohei II (1768–1819, nee Shinodo Kinji), a critic and author of a dance drama. Namiki Gohei III was the father of Namiki Gohei IV (1829–1901), and thus they are the only blood relatives among the four artists bearing that name.

Although Namiki Gohei III is actually a minor figure in the annals of Japanese theater, *Kanjinchō* assures that he will be remembered as the author of one of the most celebrated plays in the Kabuki repertory.

KANJINCHŌ (1841)

Kanjinchō is the last of the *juhachiban,* or "Eighteen Favorite Plays" of the Kabuki theater. The music of this play is considered the finest in the entire Kabuki repertory, and in terms of its stature, it is the equivalent of a work such as Verdi's *Otello* in its fusion of dramatic literature and music for the theater. Like Verdi's opera, *Kanjinchō* was adopted from an older and revered tradition, in this case the Noh theater. In 1841 Namiki refashioned the venerable Noh drama *Ataka* for the Kabuki; specifically, it was created for the premiere actor of the mid–nineteenth century, Ichikawa Danjúró VII, who played the role of Benkei, a popular character who appears in other Noh and Kabuki plays. The warrior-monk is a prized challenge for an actor because he portrays a broad range of emotions, as well as engaging in a clever battle of wits with a worthy opponent in Togashi, the protector of the bridge at Kaga. Though all principal Kabuki roles demand great physical and vocal virtuosity, Benkei is among the most difficult because of the extraordinary dance and martial arts movements. His exit down the *hanamichi* after the play is regarded as the most famous *tobiroppo* in all of Kabuki.

The Noh roots of *Kanjinchō* are readily apparent. Based on an actual event from the twelfth century, the play is composed in three movements, as were Noh plays: Benkei's cunning deception, which frees Prince Yoshitsune from Togashi's trap; the melancholy account of the prince's fall from power; and finally the "dance of longevity" Benkei performs to celebrate his triumph. Each of the three principal roles is aligned with a traditional Noh character: Benkei is the *shite* who is the focal point of the story; Togashi is the *waki,* or antagonist to the *shite;* and Prince Yoshitsune is the *kokata,* or child's role, here played as a young adult in the *wogata* style. Because it is derived from the sacred Noh theater, *Kanjinchō* is more dignified, less melodramatic, and certainly less spectacular than most Kabuki plays. Today it is performed, Noh-like, against a simple backdrop of the sacred pine tree. The drama's appeal derives from the skillful balance of its intellectual and emotional elements. In fact, the play's earliest audiences rejected it as being too lofty, and the play only became a classic as actors revived it in their eagerness to portray Benkei.

To audiences unfamiliar with Japanese thought and the nuances of the Kabuki, *Kanjinchō* might seem a comedy. Its central premise, in which a cunning underling disguises himself to dupe an adversary, is about as archetypal a comic situation as one can imagine. Add to this a drinking scene (which is intended to amuse) and the scene in which a servant beats his master, who cannot protest, and you have the stuff of a thousand comedies from around the world. But culture and context make *Kanjinchō* a dignified, even profound, play about duty and human feeling.

The plot of *Kanjinchō* is reminiscent of classical Roman comedy. A young man has an overpowering desire: Prince Yoshitsune wishes to escape from his brother's tyranny. He turns to a resourceful, cunning retainer for help: Benkei. Seemingly insurmountable barriers confront the schemers—Togashi's intelligence and suspicion, his guards, and especially the barrier that blocks the escape route. The serving man devises a brilliant, if deceitful, stratagem that not only thwarts the resistance but draws sympathy and cooperation from their opponents. The conflict is resolved by a disturbing breech of decorum: Benkei beats his master and even threatens him with death. The denouement features a union of the adversaries sharing food and drink.

Benkei appears every bit as Machiavellian as the servants of Roman and Renaissance Italian comedy. His lie about the subscription list—"he who contributes even a trifling amount shall live in ease in this world and shall sit among thousands of lotus in the next"—seems blasphemous. However, Namiki ennobles both Benkei and his adversary, Togashi. Benkei is not operating out of self-interest. He is no parasite, but one who is obligated, according to the *samurai* code, to protect his master at all costs. The Japanese ideogram for *samurai* is translated as "he who serves" and loyalty to one's master was the preeminent virtue expected of the servant-warrior. (Loyalty was, by the way, actually a Confucian concept imported from China and fused with Shintoism and Zen Buddhism.) To ensure his master's safety, Benkei lies because of his reverence for *giri* ("obligation"). He has no choice because he and his small band of retainers are outnumbered by Togashi's superior forces, and while the *samurai* would willingly fight to the death, combat is not an option because it would surely lead to Yoshitsune's death.

Benkei's beating of the prince actually represents the play's most dramatic moment, that is, the moment of greatest conflict. The conflict is internal, as Benkei must suppress his natural feelings of affection and unqualified respect for his prince. He thrashes him only to make the ruse succeed when one of the guards recognizes Yoshitsune. In true *samurai* fashion, he suppresses his *ninjo* (human feelings or sympathy) and performs an odious task. His remorse is clearly manifested in the last movement of the play: "I have struck my own dear Lord. The heavenly reprisals are frightening to contemplate!" And he weeps bitterly, perhaps even contemplating *seppuku*, the ritual suicide expected of the *samurai* who errs. But Benkei knows he has triumphed on a higher level by performing *giri*, and thus his "dance of the winding stream" becomes a celebration of duty over personal feelings.

Namiki explores the problem from another perspective as Togashi also faces the conflict between *giri* and *ninjo*. It is his obligation to protect the barrier at Kaga, which he states unequivocally in his opening speech. He, too, is a superb *samurai* who is loyal and unswerving in his duty to his lord, Prince Yoritomo. But he is equally loyal to his other lord, the Buddha. Benkei's arguments are cloaked in the authority of Buddhist teaching. The section concerning Buddhist orthodoxy was added by Danjúró (the actor who first played Benkei) after he heard a famous storyteller recite the exchange. Benkei's loyalty to his master is so compelling that Togashi—who has recognized Yoshitsune—has no choice but let his *ninjo* supersede his *giri*. In the Japanese mind Togashi is not duped; rather, he emerges as an honorable warrior with a good heart, just as Benkei emerges as an honorable man with a warrior's heart. And therein lies the lesson of the play: there are times when obligation takes precedence over sentiment, just as there are times when sympathy is more honorable than duty. The two resolutions need not be contradictory. Indeed, they are complementary, just as the *yin* (the feminine force, represented here by *ninjo*) and the *yang* (the masculine force, represented by *giri* and the *samurai* code) unite to complete the great circle that embraces all that comes to be in this world of paradoxes.

*Benkei (center) and his retinue protect their prince (right) in a Grand Kabuki Theater production of
Kanjinchō; the chorus and musicians, as well as the Noh pine trees, form a traditional background.*

KANJINCHŌ
(THE SUBSCRIPTION LIST)

A Kabuki Play

NAMIKI GOHEI III

Adapted by James R. Brandon and Tamako Niwa

As we enter the theater the traditional Kabuki curtain of broad
green, rust, and black stripes is closed; the house lights are partially dimmed. In a few moments two sharp claps are heard from
backstage, wood against wood, as the stage manager signals the
start of the performance with his Hyoshigi sticks. From off-stage
right comes the cry "Hoo-yoo!", and the three musicians in the
off-stage music cage (Geza) take up the opening music of Kanjinchō: first, the quavering, high pitched notes of flute, then the measured beating of drums. The sounds drift clearly through the light
silk curtain. The audience settles down. Then two more claps of
the stage manager's sticks signal that the cast is in place. The

drumming rapidly increases in tempo and a stage assistant (Kyogen Kata), kneeling beside the left proscenium arch, begins to
beat out a furious tatoo with two wood clappers on a board in
front of him. Just as the crescendo of sound reaches its peak another stage assistant, robed and hooded in black, runs swiftly
across the stage pushing the curtain before him.

Before us is revealed the sweeping expanse of the ninety-foot
wide Kabuki stage, its full area suffused with light and reflecting
warmly on the polished surface of the cypress dance floor. The setting is simple and stylized, representing as it does, the Noh stage.
On a backpiece and two side pieces, is painted a background of

light tan wooden planking, and a single gnarled pine tree flanked by bamboos. The series of slits in the scenery stage right show the location of the off-stage musicians' cage. Except for a small area upstage left, where a small group of hand properties is placed, partially covered by a purple silk cloth, the entire area of the stage is available for the action of the play. There are three entrances. A colorfully striped curtain (Kirimaku) covers the large entrance stage right. On the opposite side of the stage is a small door (Kirido-guchi), used by the stage assistants who are stationed on the left of the stage and by actors for less important exits. The main entrance, however, is the "flower way" or Hanamichi, a raised platform which leads from the rear of the auditorium, through the audience, to the right side of the stage, and which serves as an extension of the stage proper into the audience.

A "long-song," or Nagauta, orchestra of twenty-two men can be seen formally seated at the rear of the stage, singers and Samisen (a three stringed instrument) players in the top row, and the musicians who play the small hand-drums (Tsuzumi and Kotsuzumi), the larger stand drums (Taiko), and the flute (Yokobue) in the bottom row. They wear identical black kimonos and wide-shouldered outer garments of deep blue marked with the crest of the Ichikawa family, the famous Kabuki acting family that originally produced Kanjinchō.

There is a moment of silence as the off-stage music stops. Then slowly the "long-song" flutist lifts his instrument to his lips, a drummer deliberately raises his sticks and they begin to play. The curtain stage right flies open and Togashi, three soldiers, and a sword bearer enter in stately procession. They move slowly, deliberately, using the sliding step of Noh dance. The foot never leaves the floor. This style of movement is used by all the characters in Kanjinchō. Each controlled movement blends into the next, so that the character appears to glide, rather than walk.

When Togashi reaches center stage he stops, pivots slowly, and faces the audience. It is obvious that he is a Samurai, for he wears the sumptuous ceremonial dress of nobility. His outer kimono is a voluminous affair of pale blue brocade figured with white and silver cranes. Its sleeves almost touch the floor. His legs are encased in the long trousers of court dress (Nagabakama), which trail away a full four feet behind him. He carries a fan in his right hand. His face and hands are pure white except for black lip and eye markings. Togashi addresses the audience directly, in a stately, half-changing style of speech.

TOGASHI. I stand before you here at the Kaga barrier gate! I, Togashi-Zaemon! Our Lord Yoritomo has commanded barriers to be raised throughout the realm to apprehend his younger brother Yoshitsune now reported fleeing northward toward Michinoku. The rift between the brothers is deep and Yoshitsune is said to have disguised himself as a priest in order to escape. We are strictly ordered by Our Lord Yoritomo to stop and investigate every passing priest. In faithful duty I guard this barrier for Our Lord! I command you all to be of this same mind. (No

flicker of expression has crossed Togashi's face, composure being one of the highest virtues of the Samurai code.)

FIRST SOLDIER. (Replying strongly, but also without any visible expression.) Already the heads of three doubtful priests hang from the trees!

SECOND SOLDIER. As you command, every priest shall be brought before you!

THIRD SOLDIER. Captured! Bound on the spot!

FIRST SOLDIER. We are alert . . .

ALL THREE SOLDIERS. . . . ever on guard!

TOGASHI. Well spoken! Seize each and every priest who attempts to pass! We shall put at ease the mind of Our Lord of Kamakura.[1] Now, all of you to your posts!

ALL THREE SOLDIERS. As you command, sir!

(There is a shrill cry from the flute, followed by metallic beats on the Tsuzumi drum. Togashi turns and slowly leads his small procession across the stage, this movement symbolizing their arriving at the barrier. The soldiers kneel in a row upstage. The sword bearer kneels directly behind Togashi, holding the sword before him in readiness. From under the purple property cloth Togashi's personal stage assistant [Koken] brings out a black lacquered cask ornamented with gold. Togashi seats himself on it. Another stage assistant arranges the folds of his costume.)

FULL CHORUS. (To flute and drum accompaniment the eight singers seated at the rear of the stage tell the tale of Yoshitsune's wanderings.)

Their travel garments are those of a priest . . .
Their travel garments are those of a wandering priest,
    with sleeves wet by dew and tears.
The time is the tenth night of the second moon.
    The tenth night of the second moon.
And so having left the capital on a moonlit night . . .

CHORUS LEADER. (The lead singer continues the story of the past.)

Passed is the Mountain of Osaka,
    Before whom those coming and going part,
    Where friends and strangers meet.
Beautiful the hills,
    Shrouded by the mists of spring.

(The curtain at the rear of the Hanamichi flies up and Yoshitsune enters. Using quick sliding steps he moves down the Hanamichi toward the stage, then sees Togashi and the soldiers at the barrier. He stops and turns back toward the audience. For a moment he poses, a subdued tragic figure. He wears a dark purple kimono and pale green trousers. His long hair is gathered together and falls down his back. His face, hands, and dancing socks [tabi] are pure white. As

[1]Yoshitsune's brother Yoritomo had several titles. He was the Shogun, or supreme military ruler of Japan. He was also the Lord of Kamakura, for he ruled from the city of Kamakura.

part of his disguise he carries a large coolie's hat and a pilgrim's staff. The blue oi box strapped to his back supposedly contains Benkei's sutras and other religious objects; actually it contains Yoshitsune's armor. Next, Yoshitsune's four retainers stride purposefully down the Hanamichi one by one. They pass their master and form a line between him and the stage. They wear priests' vestments and carry Buddhist rosaries. Each has a short sword at his waist.)

FULL CHORUS. (Continuing the story of their journey.)
> By furtive ship,
>> Through distant paths of waves,
> Arriving, now at last,
>> At Kaizu Bay.

(At this point Benkei moves quickly down the Hanamichi. He wears a priest's pill-box hat and vestments. He is an imposing figure dressed entirely in black brocade silk figured with gold. As Yoshitsune turns to him, the retainers kneel.)

YOSHITSUNE. So, Benkei. The roads ahead are blocked as you say. And this was our last hope. I know now I shall never see the North. For myself I have decided: rather than suffer an ignoble death at the hand of some nameless soldier I shall take my own life first. But I must consider your wishes, too, as I did in disguising myself a common porter. At this crucial moment have you any suggestions?

FIRST RETAINER. My Lord, why do we carry these swords? When shall they be painted with blood? Now is the crucial moment of My Lord's life.

SECOND RETAINER. Let us resolve! Cut the soldiers down! We shall fight our way through this barrier!

THIRD RETAINER. The years of obligation to Our Lord shall be repaid today! We must pass through, My Lord!

FIRST, SECOND, AND THIRD RETAINERS. (They rise, hands on the hilts of their swords.) We shall pass through! (They turn to go, but the Fourth Retainer, an older man, blocks their path with an imperative gesture and Benkei speaks.)

BENKEI. Stop! Wait a moment! (Reluctantly the three retainers return to their kneeling positions.) A crisis is no time for rash action. If we fight now, even though we succeed, the news will travel ahead making it all the more difficult to pass further barriers. (Very respectfully to Yoshitsune.) It was with this in mind that My Lord was asked to remove his priest's vestments and assume the role of a mountain porter when first My Lord put this matter in my charge. And now, My Lord, I beg you, pull your hat low over your eyes and make a pretense of being exhausted. If you will but follow behind us, far in our rear, surely no one will suspect who My Lordship is.

YOSHITSUNE. You plan well, Benkei. (To the chaffing retainers.) We shall do exactly as Benkei says.

THE FOUR RETAINERS. (Bowing slightly.) As Our Lord commands.

BENKEI. Then pass peacefully on.

THE FOUR RETAINERS. We obey.

(Benkei passes Yoshitsune and moves onto the stage to the accompaniment of samisen music. The retainers follow closely behind.)

FULL CHORUS.
> And so the travelers,
>> Bent upon passing through,
>> Drew near the barrier gate.

(There are irregular metallic taps from the tsuzumi drum. Still on the Hanamichi, Yoshitsune ties his hat low over his eyes, then moves slowly onto the stage, taking a position between Benkei, who is almost center stage, and the retainers who are kneeling in a row upstage right. His personal stage assistant places a small stool for him to sit on, and arranges his costume. Yoshitsune poses with his head low, clasping the pilgrim's staff over his shoulder. Though he remains motionless in this position throughout most of the play, his noble bearing is such that we are always aware of his presence.

BENKEI. (Faces front and speaks in a dignified manner befitting a priest.) Ho there! We are priests who wish to pass!

TOGASHI. What's that? Priests, you say? (In all his dignity he rises, strides forward, and addresses Benkei in measured tones.) Now my friends, know that this is a barrier!

BENKEI. (Facing Togashi, but feigning deference.) I know, sir. Throughout the country priests are now soliciting contributions for the rebuilding of the temple Todaiji in the Southern Capital. It is our honored mission to be dispatched to the Northern Provinces.

TOGASHI. A praiseworthy project, indeed. However, the very purpose of this barrier is to stop priests like yourselves. You shall find it very difficult to pass.

BENKEI. This is hard to understand. What can it mean?

TOGASHI. Relations between Our Lord Yoritomo and the Hogan[2] having become strained, three years ago Yoshitsune left his brother's service. Now he flees to the north, disguised as a priest, to seek the aid of his friend Hidehira. Hearing this the Lord of Kamakura has caused these barriers to be raised. (He draws himself up and speaks deliberately.) Know you that I am in command of this barrier!

FIRST SOLDIER. We stand guard with orders to detain all priests!

SECOND SOLDIER. And now before us, behold, many priests!

THIRD SOLDIER. We shall not allow . . .

THE THREE SOLDIERS. . . . even one to pass!

BENKEI. Your orders are to stop all those disguised as priests, are they not? They surely say nothing of stopping real priests.

FIRST SOLDIER. (Not sharing Togashi's lofty politeness, he speaks roughly and to the point.) Say what you will. Yesterday we killed three priests!

----

[2] Another name for Yoshitsune.

SECOND SOLDIER. So your saying you are real priests will not excuse you!

THIRD SOLDIER. And if you try to pass by force . . .

FIRST, SECOND, AND THIRD SOLDIER. (*In unison.*) . . . not one of you will survive!

BENKEI. (*Reacting with mock horror.*) And these priests you beheaded . . . Was one Yoshitsune?

TOGASHI. Who can say? (*Speaks commandingly.*) It is useless for you to argue. No priest . . .

THE THREE SOLDIERS. (*With great force.*) . . . shall pass this barrier!

(*Togashi imperiously turns his back on Benkei, kicking the long trailing ends of his trousers as he does so. He strides back to his former position stage left and resumes his seat.*)

BENKEI. Monstrous horror! (*Turning to the retainers, but speaking loudly for Togashi's benefit.*) Why should such misfortune be ours? Human strength is powerless against such unforeseen fate! But at least we shall be killed with honor. Come, draw near. Let us perform our last rites!

THE FOUR RETAINERS. We shall, sir.

BENKEI. (*Gravely.*) This is our final rite! (*So saying he moves majestically up right where two stage assistants tie back the long sleeves of his kimono and hand him a scarlet Buddhist rosary. Meanwhile the retainers form a square center stage; they kneel, their hands folded in an attitude of meditation. With a quick glance at Togashi to see how he is taking all this, Benkei moves swiftly into the square, and as the chorus sings, dances a prayer to the gods.*)

FULL CHORUS. (*To full orchestra accompaniment.*)
> To detain here Yamabushi priests,
> > Who are versed in the austere teaching of *En no Ubazoku*,
> Whose bodies and spirit are one and the same with the Lord Buddha . . .
> > (*Benkei raises his arms in supplication to the heavens.*)
> Surely the Gods will look with disfavor upon this impious act,
> > The wrath of God
> Yuya Gongen shall strike this spot!
> > (*In simulated anger Benkei leaps high in the air and stamps loudly upon the floor.*)
> "On A Bi Ra Un Ken" . . .
> > So chanting they rubbed the beads of their rosaries in prayer.

(*Benkei rises to his full height and with a sweeping upward motion begins to rub the beads of his rosary. The others follow suit. The beads of the rosaries buzz and chatter. Then the retainers turn their backs to Benkei, clap their hands in unison, and kneel, hands still folded in prayer. The tableau thus formed is similar to a statue grouping seen in many temples, that of Buddha, protected on the four sides by his kneeling guardian angels, thus implying their closeness to Buddha. Fade music no. 5.*)

TOGASHI. (*Suspicious, he determines to test Benkei's story.*) A noble decision, to die. However, you mentioned a mission of soliciting for the Todaiji Temple. If this is so surely you cannot be without a list of contributors. (*An order.*) Bring out this *Kanjinchō!* I demand to hear it!

BENKEI. What? (*Momentarily stunned.*) You . . . you say read the *kanjinchō* list?

TOGASHI. Read it I say!

BENKEI. (*His confident voice betrays nothing.*) It shall be done. (*He moves up stage right, where a stage assistant hands him a scroll.*)

CHORUS LEADER.
> Ah, were there but a *kanjinchō!*
> > Instead, from the *oi* box he draws a single unused letter scroll,
> And calling it the *kanjinchō*,
> He boldly reads aloud.

BENKEI. (*Moving back to center stage, he unrolls the scroll and, holding it so Togashi cannot see it, pretends to read the dedicatory passage. As Benkei is a priest, he has a considerable knowledge of Buddhist ritual and is able to make up a plausible passage.*) Even Buddha, like the autumn moon, has taken refuge in the dark clouds of death. (*Togashi rises and stealthily begins edging toward Benkei.*) Who then, in this world, should be surprised that life is but a long night's dream! (*Suddenly Benkei senses Togashi's presence, and he whirls to face him. The two pose for a moment, glaring angrily at each other. Then Togashi, his suspicions confirmed, strides back to his position stage left and regally resumes his seat. Uncertain whether he has been found out or not, Benkei determines to brazen it out. With a flourish he unrolls the scroll once more and in even louder tones than before continues to "read" from the* kanjinchō.) In the Middle Ages, there once lived an Emperor whose name was Shomu! Having lost his beloved wife, his grief became too much for him to bear. The tears flowed from his eyes in a continuous chain; his cheeks were never dry. To aid her advance as a Bodhisattva, he then built in her memory the great Rushana Buddha, the same that burned to the ground in the era of Juei. I, the priest Chogen, lamenting the loss of this place of worship, have received the Imperial Order to solicit throughout the provinces to rebuild this holy temple. I appeal to priests, high and low, and to laymen alike. He who contributes even a trifling amount shall live in ease in this world and shall sit among thousands of lotus in the next. I address you most reverently!

CHORUS LEADER. He reads as if challenging the heavens to reverberate!

(*Benkei rolls up the scroll with utter composure and is about to turn away.*)

TOGASHI. (*There is little doubt in Togashi's mind that this is Yoshitsune's party, yet he is impressed by Benkei's bold improvisation. Rising, he decides to test Benkei further.*) I see. I have heard the *kanjinchō* now, and should have no further doubts. Nevertheless, let me put a few questions to you. In this world Buddha has many kinds of followers. There are some who show a warlike appearance, and who, it is difficult to believe, are true disciples of the religious austerities. Is there an explanation for this?

BENKEI. (*Without hesitation he fabricates a plausible answer.*) There is indeed a simple explanation. It is the stern prescript of the Shungen Order, in which the principles of Buddha and Shinto combine, that its followers should wander through the precipitous mountains, there to undergo hardship and pain, subduing wild beasts and poisonous reptiles which are harmful to the world, and showing compassion toward their fellow men. Thus do they accumulate meritorious works as was our Lord Buddha's command. Thus do they save evil and lost souls and show them the way toward Nirvana. They pray for purity; they pray for the brightness of the sun and moon and for the everlasting peace of the world. In this way, within themselves they nurture the twin virtues of stoicism and benevolence, while outwardly they conquer evil and subdue heretical doctrines in a warlike manner. All is Shinto and Buddha . . . the one-hundred-eight beads of the rosary representing the multitudinous blessings of the Gods!

TOGASHI. (*Pressing another question without pause.*) You appear to be followers of Buddha, wearing a priest's *kesa* vestment. Why then do you wear a pilgrim's *tokin* hat at the same time?

BENKEI. The *tokin* hat and the *suzukake* vestments are like the warrior's helmet and armor. With the sharp sword of Amida Buddha at his side, and breaking a path with the Kongo staff, the pilgrim crosses the highest mountains and the most dangerous places.

TOGASHI. I know that priests carry the Shakujo scepter, with its soft sounding bells. But how does carrying a Kongo staff protect a pilgrim's body and limbs?

BENKEI. A foolish question! The Kongo staff has been famous as the pilgrim's staff since first used by the Holy Arara, the divine being who lived in the Dantaloka Mountains in India, and under whose guidance our Buddha first accumulated meritorious deeds. It was this seer who gave to our Buddha the new name of Shofubiku in recognition of his pupil's great faith and strength of purpose. The spirit of Buddha dwells within the staff! As a child grows in his mother's womb, so the spirit of Buddha grows within us all!

TOGASHI. How has this tradition been handed down?

BENKEI. Our predecessors carried it as the holy staff of Our Lord Buddha when traveling in the mountains and valleys and this has become the practice down through the ages!

TOGASHI. Though a priest, you wear a sword. Is this merely a symbol of defense, or is it used to do physical harm?

BENKEI. Like the bow of the scarecrow, it serves to frighten our enemies. At the same time we do not hesitate to strike down those evil beasts and poisonous snakes, and human

beings as well, that violate Buddha's law or the Princely Way. For with one death many lives may be saved!

TOGASHI. One can, of course, cut down a solid object, that obstructs the eye, but what of those formless evils that may obstruct Buddha's law or the Princely Way? With what would you cut them down?

BENKEI. What difficulty is there in destroying formless evils? One would dispel them with the nine-word Shingon prayer!

TOGASHI. (*Moving in toward Benkei, he presses another series of questions without pause.*) Now tell me, what is the significance of your dress?

BENKEI. It is patterned in the likeness of the ferocious deity Fudo!

TOGASHI. What is the meaning of your *tokin* hat?

BENKEI. It is the headdress of the five wisdoms, its twelve folds symbolizing the affinity of cause and retribution!

TOGASHI. (*Moves in another step.*) And the *kesa* vestment you wear about your neck?

BENKEI. (*He moves in toward Togashi.*) It is a *suzukake* of persimmon in color, signifying the nine stages of Buddha's paradise!

TOGASHI. Why the bindings about your legs?

BENKEI. They are the black leggings of the Shingon Sect!

TOGASHI. And your eight-knobbed straw sandals?

BENKEI. In the spirit of treading on the eight-petaled lotus!

TOGASHI. (*Almost spitting it out.*) And the air you breathe?

BENKEI. (*They are face to face, just a few feet apart. Benkei controls himself, but he is trembling with anger. For a moment they glare at each other in tableau.*) In the holy sutras, the beginning and the end, the two reverend sounds—"A and UN"!

TOGASHI. (*Still pressing.*) And now one final question. What is the meaning of the nine-word Shingon prayer! (*For a moment Benkei cannot reply. Togashi senses the lapse he has been waiting for. He draws back a pace, and raises his fan in a commanding gesture. He speaks imperiously.*) Come, come! What do you say!

BENKEI. (*The question is far beyond Benkei's knowledge of Buddhism. He is furious with Togashi and being by nature an impetuous and proud man, he is sorely tempted to abandon his pose. Benkei is renowned as a warrior; he knows he could easily defeat Togashi. Nevertheless, he controls himself and launches into a brilliant improvisation of Buddhist jargon.*) This nine-word prayer is a precious secret of the Shingon faith and its meaning is most difficult to explain. But to still your doubt I shall undertake to do so. The nine words are: *Rin Byoh Toh Sha Kai Chin Retsu Zai Zen!* Before you draw your sword, first, you must strike your teeth thirty-six times with hands folded in supplication. Then, with the thumb of your right hand, you draw four lines from earth to sky and five lines from horizon to horizon. Simultaneously, you rapidly incant the blessing "*kyuu kyuu nyo ritsu ryoo.*" So doing, all evil—the evil of worldly passions and the devil of heresy—will disappear like frost before the vapors of steam. Sharp and shining, the prayer cuts through to the very heart of the world's darkness. In this it is beyond compare, even to the miraculous sword of Bakuya, and the warrior who utters it cannot fail to defeat his enemy! Now . . . have you any further questions regarding our religious practices? I shall reply to them all in full, that you may share in the power of their virtue, which is all-embracing and infinite! engrave these words on your heart, but reveal their secrets to no one! Oh, Gods and Bodhisattvas of Japan, I call upon you to witness the words I most reverently speak! I bow before you! (*He does, then turns to Togashi.*) I speak to you with utmost respect.

FULL CHORUS. (*To samisen music.*)
>The barrier guard seems impressed.

(*Benkei dances a few steps expressive of his success, then he and Togashi pose in tableau: Benkei with the scroll held high as in triumph, and Togashi with his fan held over his head. This is a high point of the play. From the audience come loud cries of "Well done!", "We've waited for this!", "Like your father before you!"*)

TOGASHI. (*Togashi is certain they are Benkei and Yoshitsune, yet Benkei has not faltered in his defense of his master. Impressed, Togashi decides to let them pass.*) That I should have doubted such honorable priests even for a moment. I should like to be added to your list of contributors. Guards, bring gifts for the priests!

THE THREE SOLDIERS. Yes, sir.

(*The mood relaxes perceptibly. Quiet samisen music underlies the following actions. Togashi returns to his seat stage left. Benkei gives the scroll to his stage assistant up right and receives a rosary. At the same time, The Three Soldiers pick up gift trays which have just been brought in through the small door stage left by Togashi's stage assistant. The soldiers place the trays center stage and return to their kneeling positions up stage of Togashi.*)

FULL CHORUS.
>On wide stands, brought forth by the guards,
>>A ceremonial skirt of pure white silk,
>>Many rolls of Kaga silk,
>>A mirror and golden coins.

TOGASHI. Though the gifts are small it would be accredited as a meritorious deed for me should you accept them on behalf of the priests of Todaiji. Respectfully, I beg you accept them.

BENKEI. (*Standing before the gifts, ready to receive them, he speaks impressively.*) You are indeed a benevolent Lord. There can be no doubt of your peaceful, happy existence in this world and the next. (*He rubs his rosary over the gifts in blessing.*) One thing more. We will be traveling through the neighboring provinces, not returning to the capital until the middle of the fourth moon. I beg you to keep the larger articles for us until then. (*He kneels before the gifts. When he rises he takes only the two bags of money from the center tray. These he gives to two of the retainers.*) Now, pass through!

THE FOUR RETAINERS. Yes, sir!

BENKEI. (*He take out his fan, flips it open, and holds it in front of him. His actions appear unconcerned, but his voice betrays his anxiety over their delicate situation.*) Go! Go now! Hurry!

THE FOUR RETAINERS. We go, sir!

CHORUS LEADER.
>Rejoicing within
>>The warrior-priests
>>Quietly rise and move away.

(*Benkei moves swiftly down the Hanamichi followed by the four retainers. Yoshitsune rises and, with head bent low, slowly begins to leave the stage. Suddenly one of the soldiers crosses to Togashi's side and whispers in his ear.*)

TOGASHI. (*Rises abruptly.*) What? That porter? (*With the help of his stage assistant, Togashi slips the kimono from his right shoulder, freeing his arm for action. Receiving his sword from the bearer, he takes two deliberate paces forward, and stops, hand poised on the hilt of his sword in a threatening gesture.*) Stop! Stop, I say! (*The action now is very rapid, Yoshitsune stops, and then as if pulled by invisible strings, he backs toward Togashi. He kneels again in the same position he was in previously, head low and staff held against one shoulder. At the same time, Benkei turns and rushes past the retainers toward the stage but before he can reach Yoshitsune, the retainers also turn and start toward the stage. They have their hands on their swords ready to draw, thinking their master is discovered. But with viciously twirling rosary and outstretched arms Benkei succeeds in blocking their headlong rush at the very end of the Hanamichi.*)

BENKEI. No! Rashness will lose it all!

FULL CHORUS.
>"Our Lord is suspected!
>>Now is the moment
>>Between sinking and floating!"
>These are their thoughts as they turn.

BENKEI. (*In feigned rage, shakes his head violently and stamps loudly on the floor. He twirls the rosary about his head in a sweeping arc, and crosses in swiftly to Yoshitsune, attempting to shield him from Togashi's searching gaze.*) You! Strong One! why haven't you passed through?

TOGASHI. (*In a fearsome voice.*) Because I have detained him!

BENKEI. Detained him? What for?

TOGASHI. There are those who say he resembles . . . a certain person. That is why I have detained him.

BENKEI. Well? What's strange about that? One person often resembles another! (*Brazening it out.*) Who do you think he resembles?

TOGASHI. My soldiers say the Hogan, Yoshitsune. He is to be held for questioning.

BENKEI. The Hogan? The Strong One resembles the *Hogan*, you say? (*Turning on Yoshitsune in feigned jury.*) This is something to remember a lifetime! Ohhhh! It's unendurable! We'd planned to reach Noto by sundown and now, just because of this lagging porter . . . *this* has happened! If people begin suspecting you of being the Hogan on the slightest provocation, you'll be the cause of the failure of our mission! (*Grinds his teeth as if in uncontrollable rage.*) The more I think of it the more despicable you become! (*He growls through clenched teeth; he leaps in the air and stamps on the floor.*) You are hateful I say! Hateful! Hateful!!

FULL CHORUS. (*To rapid and excited samisen music.*)
    Snatching up the Kongo staff,
    He strikes right . . .

(*Restraining the tears, Benkei raises the staff high, then strikes his master on the right shoulder. His whole body jerks as if he himself had been struck. Once again he raises the staff, hesitates, his face contorted with grief, then strikes his master on the left shoulder.*)
He strikes left!

BENKEI. Now, move on, I tell you!

CHORUS LEADER.
    He berates him soundly,
    Ordering him to pass through!

(*Shielding his face, Yoshitsune rises and quickly crosses up stage right and kneels with his back to the audience, in effect, removing himself from the scene which follows.*)

TOGASHI. No matter how you plead his case, he shall not . . .

THE THREE SOLDIERS. . . . pass through! (*The soldiers stand in a resolute row with their hands on their sword hilts. Yoshitsune's retainers reach for their swords and are about to attack. Still trying to avert a conflict, Benkei makes an excuse for the retainers' actions.*)

BENKEI. For you to eye the *oi* box as you do, you're not guards at all. You must be thieves! (*He strikes the staff loudly on the floor and poses with it threateningly. The retainers surge forward. Benkei quickly uses the staff to block their path.*) Here! Here!

(*Benkei forces the retainers back once, but they press forward again. He pushes them back a second time, holding them with the staff until they are calmed. Benkei now turns to face Togashi, holding the staff before him in both hands. The sight of Benkei striking his own master has come as a physical shock to Togashi. Impressed with Benkei's daring, momentarily he cannot bring himself to act. But now he dismisses such thoughts and resolves to attack.*)

FULL CHORUS. (*Accompanied by full orchestra.*)
    "How cowardly it is!
    To draw swords
    Against a lowly porter!"

    With such seeming thoughts,
    And god-frightening looks,
    The priests prepared for battle.

(*Slowly the two opposing groups move toward each other until they meet center stage. On each side the men press against their leader. Benkei and Togashi glare fiercely at each other. Then Togashi and the soldiers begin to advance. Slowly, deliberately, using the sliding dance step of Noh, they take one, two, three slow-motion strides forward. In unison, Benkei and the retainers take one, two, three strides backward. The two masses of men pivot and surge as one, bound together by their fierce antagonism. Now Benkei summons his last resources and halts Togashi. Holding the staff before him, he begins to push Togashi back. The soldiers and the retainers stand aside as Benkei forces Togashi back step by step to his original position. The implication is that Togashi can no longer bring himself to attack in the face of Benkei's great display of courage on behalf of Yoshitsune. Benkei has succeeded in preventing first his own men and now Togashi from launching an attack. The victory is his. Defiantly he faces Togashi. Twirling the rosary, he swings the staff about his head, and strikes it on the floor. He raises the staff over his head and poses. Togashi poses with his legs spread wide apart and his hand on the hilt of his sword. They hold their tableau for a moment.*)

BENKEI. If you still think this miserable creature is the Hogan, then hold him along with the gifts until our return! Investigate him any way you wish. Or would you rather I kill him with this now? (*He strikes the staff on the floor and brandishes it threateningly.*)

TOGASHI. You are too harsh!

BENKEI. Then why do you still doubt us?

TOGASHI. There is the complaint of my soldiers.

BENKEI. (*With grim determination.*) Then I shall kill him before your own eyes! Will that convince you?

TOGASHI. (*Togashi visibly recoils at the thought. He is caught up in conflicting emotions. He is aghast to think that Benkei would actually raise his hand against his own master, an unheard of act in feudal Japan. At the same time he recognizes this as an act of supreme devotion on Benkei's part and is overwhelmed with admiration. In Benkei he recognizes his moral superior. He makes his decision.*) Stop! Do not be hasty! Because of the baseless suspicions of my soldiers you have already severely beaten this person who . . . is not the Hogan. My doubts are now dispelled. (*Speaking brusquely to cover his emotions.*) Quickly now, pass through the barrier!

BENKEI. (*Continuing the pretense to the end.*) Were it not for the words of the Great Lord here, I should have killed you on the spot! You laggard, you've been lucky this time! Don't tempt the Gods again!

TOGASHI. From now on, it is my duty to maintain even stricter guard! (*His stage assistant fixes the sleeve of his kimono.*) Come with me, men!

THE THREE SOLDIERS. Yes, My Lord.

(*Benkei and Togashi face each other once more in tableau. The air fairly crackles with emotion. Benkei has succeeded; he knows this, yet cannot show it. For Togashi's part, he knows full well who Benkei and Yoshitsune are, yet he cannot show this. Further, there is the implication that, having failed his own master Yoritomo, the honorable course for him now would be to take his own life. He averts his face so the soldiers cannot see his struggle to maintain composure. Just as he is about to give way to tears, he shakes his head, dismissing the thought of death from his mind. He draws himself up to his full height, pivots regally about, kicking out the long trailing ends of his trousers, and strides off the stage.*)

FULL CHORUS.
　　Taking his soldiers with him,
　　　　The barrier guard enters within the gate.

(*Togashi and the soldiers exit through the small door stage left. Benkei looks after them. The music now becomes plaintive and halting in tempo. Yoshitsune's hat and oi box have been taken by his stage assistant and now he moves to left center stage where he kneels. Benkei slowly moves to center stage right. He kneels facing Yoshitsune, his head bent in grief. The retainers kneel in a line up stage between the two. They have symbolically passed through the barrier and are now stopping some distance beyond it.*)

YOSHITSUNE. (*He speaks quietly. In spite of their success he seems subdued and melancholy.*) Benkei, you acted with great presence of mind. Indeed no one but you could have succeeded with such a daring plan. Without hesitation you struck me as recklessly as though I were a lowly servant and so saved me. I stand in awe, for having received the divine protection of our patron, Sho Hachiman, the God of War.

FIRST RETAINER. The barrier guard stopped us and we all felt, "Now is the moment to fight for Our Lord's safety!"

SECOND RETAINER. It is a sign that Sho Hachiman is protecting Our Lord. Our trip from here on to Michinoku should be a swift one.

THIRD RETAINER. Yet without the quick thinking of our Priest of Musashi here, it would have been hard to escape.

FIRST RETAINER. We were . . .

ALL FOUR RETAINERS. . . . truly amazed!

BENKEI. (*Benkei's head is bent to the floor. He can scarcely speak for remorse.*) The seers have preached that the end of the world is soon at hand. Yet the sun and the moon have not yet fallen from their places in the heavens. Fate has been kind to Yoshitsune also. How grateful we all are. You speak of strategy, but the fact is I have *struck* my own dear Lord. The heavenly reprisals are frightening to con-

template. These two arms which can lift a thousand *kin* are as though benumbed. How wrong I have been! How wrong!

CHORUS LEADER.
　　How noble, now,
　　　　Even Benkei,
　　　　Who has never given way before,
　　Finally shed the tears of a lifetime.

(*His whole body shaking with grief, Benkei bows his head and holds his hand before his eyes in the symbolic gesture of weeping.*)

FULL CHORUS. The Hogan then took his hand.

(*Rising to one knee, Yoshitsune extends his right hand to Benkei in token of forgiveness. Benkei starts forward as if to accept his master's gesture, then is overcome with the enormity of his crime. He pulls back sharply, flings down his fan, and bows his head once more to the floor in remorse.*)

YOSHITSUNE. (*To see the rock-like Benkei reduced to tears on his behalf, brings home to Yoshitsune the full misery and the hopelessness of their position. He too raises his hand to his eyes to cover his tears.*) Why should it be? Why should Yoshitsune, nobly born, his whole life spent in devoted service to his brother, end his life as a corpse sinking unheralded beneath the waves of the Western Sea?

BENKEI. (*Picking up his fan, he holds it before him formally and begins to tell the story of Yoshitsune's wanderings.*)
　　Midst mountain places,
　　　　And rock-bound coasts,
　　　　Awake and asleep,
　　The warrior spends his lonely existence.

FULL CHORUS. As the chorus takes up the story, Benkei dances its meaning to the accompaniment of a plaintive melody played by the full orchestra. The pace is slow, the mood softly melancholy.)
　　The warrior,
　　　　With armor and sleeve-pillow
　　　　As sole companions . . .
(*Benkei mimes sleeping, his head cradled on his kimono sleeve.*)
　　Sometimes,
　　　　Adrift at sea,
　　　　At the mercy of wind and tide . . .
(*He sculls a boat; his open fan flutters overhead as in the wind.*)
　　Sometimes,
　　　　In mountain fastnesses,
　　　　Where no hoofprint breaks the white snow . . .
(*The upside-down fan becomes a mountain.*)
　　While he endures it all,
　　　　From small evening waves of the sea,
　　　　Come whispers of disgrace and banishment.

(*To emphasize the strength of the thought, Benkei draws the string of an imaginary bow. Then he gestures the throwing of a stone, indicating that Yoshitsune's fortunes* are being dashed to earth in the same way. For a moment he holds a powerful pose, right hand extended, left hand over his head. Then he slowly crosses his eyes, executing a "mie," the most expressive type of pose in Kabuki. Two sharp claps of the stage manager's hyoshigi sticks emphasize the emotional tension of the moment.)

> For three long years past,
>> Like the oniazami thistle,
>> Which has begun to wither and die,
>> Covered only by the frost and dew.
> How pitiful it is!

(Benkei indicates Yoshitsune with his closed fan. Then he and the four retainers bow low. Straightening up, they cover their eyes to hide their tears.)

THE FOUR RETAINERS. Quickly now, My Lord, let us withdraw!

FULL CHORUS.
> Pulling on each other's sleeves,
>> They seem anxious to be on their way.

(But Benkei does not move. The fan falls from his nerveless fingers, his head sinks to his chest.)

TOGASHI. (Off stage.) Wait. Wait a moment! (As Benkei rises instantly, prepared to meet whatever new challenge may come, Yoshitsune retires up stage right where he is covered from view by the four retainers. Togashi and the soldiers enter through the main entrance stage right and cross immediately to their original positions stage left.) Forgive my abruptness, but I have brought some sake, and though it is nothing much, I hope you will drink with me. (A small cup is placed on a tray before Togashi by one of the soldiers, and filled. As is the custom, Togashi, the host, drinks first. Then the cup on the tray is ceremoniously placed before Benkei, who accepts it center stage, kneeling facing the audience. The cup is filled and Benkei looks at it with undisguised pleasure.)

BENKEI. My kind Lord, I shall drink with you with pleasure!

CHORUS LEADER. (Accompanied by a single samisen.)
> Truly, truly, Benkei understands this gesture.
>> How can he ever forget,
>> Having received this cup of human sympathy?

(Benkei tosses off the drink in one swallow. In an expansive mood, now that the crisis is past, he laughingly gestures for the lid of the big lacquered cask stage left to be brought to him and filled with wine. Two soldiers do so, then watch in open-mouthed amazement as Benkei buries his face in the lid and downs an enormous draught. Benkei comes up for air, smacks his lips, and then with a sly chuckle points straight to the audience. The soldiers lean forward, straining to see what is out there, and as they do so, Benkei pushes them off balance and they tumble to the floor. Benkei roars with good natured laughter.)

And now for tales of the past . . .

(As a kind of counterpoint to Benkei's actions, the chorus leader tells of an early love affair Benkei once had as a priest, obliquely comparing the difficulties he faced then to the crossing of the barrier now.)
> What embarrassment
>> my heart
>> once met.
> Once met
>> a woman
>> and confusion.
> Along the road of confusion,
>> this barrier
>> once was crossed.
> Being crossed,
>> yet another now,
>> with difficulty passed.
> Ah, to pass the barrier
>> of people's eyes
>> is difficult to bear.
> It is a transient world!
>> We never know enlightenment!

(Benkei empties the lid, then gestures for it to be filled once more. The soldiers hesitate, afraid of the consequences, but a menacing glare and a roar of mock anger quickly convince them which is the lesser of the two evils. They fill the lid at once. His eyes gleaming with delight, Benkei raises the lid to his lips and drains the entire contents in a single, breathtaking swallow. The soldiers stand amazed. Now slightly tipsy, Benkei puts the lid on his head like a hat as a stage assistant removes the lid, he rises unsteadily to his feet to dance, beating time with the closed fan. Now the fan is flicked open and it becomes a sake cup; it sails in a graceful arc across the stage and it is a sake cup floating down a mountain stream.)

FULL CHORUS.
> How amusing,
>> Floating the wine cup
>> Down the mountain stream.
> The swirling water,
>> In eddies and currents,
> Splashes the sleeves
>> Covering the reaching hand.

(Benkei dances his unsteady way along the "river bank" after his "sake cup." He trips, stumbles, almost falls, then at the last moment recovers his balance. Then, the dance over, and his tipsiness gone, he retrieves the fan, folds it, and formally turns to face Togashi.)

> Now, let us perform a dance!

BENKEI. In gratitude, I come to offer you wine! (He holds out the open fan to Togashi, thus symbolizing an offering of drink.)

TOGASHI. Come, dance for us.

BENKEI. (*Benkei turns to the audience and kneels. When he speaks, it is with great emotion. The implied meaning is that he, Benkei, recognizes what Togashi has done for them, and that he wishes to express his gratitude. At the same time, it is implied that Togashi recognizes the true meaning of Benkei's words.*)

> Live myriad long years!
> > As the turtle dwells
> > On the rocks!
> *Aryu dondo!*

(*As further expression of his gratitude, Benkei now rises and performs a dance taken from the Noh drama. In the first section of the dance, he circles the stage twice with closed fan and three times with fan open, as the drums and flute play a lively rhythmic passage. This is a standard Noh dance pattern with no particular meaning. In the second section, the tempo becomes much slower, and a samisen joins the drums and flute. Benkei crosses the stage in a triangular figure. His foot movements remain the simple sliding steps they were in the first section, but his arm movements and gestures with the open fan become increasingly complicated. In the third and final section of the dance, the tempo quickens again and Benkei's dancing takes on an infectious, rhythmic quality. In a gold and red arc the open fan flashes through the air. Benkei leaps high and stamps loudly on the floor. With outstretched arms he twirls the long red rosary. The dance is concluded as he kneels and ceremoniously closes the fan.*)

FULL CHORUS.
> Originally Benkei was the Wandering Priest of Santo.
> As a youth he danced the Ennen dance.

(*Benkei now performs a short* ennen *dance, a dance of longevity, traditionally performed by priests. Inasmuch as Benkei was famous in his youth for his skill in this dance, and inasmuch as Togashi would be expected to know this, to dance it now is a daring and subtle way for Benkei to express his gratitude. The complex web of recognition is now complete: both Benkei and Togashi know that the other knows, yet neither can acknowledge the fact directly. At the conclusion of the dance Benkei kneels again. Once more playing the role, he comments politely on the beauty of the scene where they have stopped.*)

BENKEI.
> The sound of the falling mountain stream,
> > Reverberates on the rocks below.
> > > (*A piercing note is heard from the flute.*)
> That which roars is the waterfall!
> That which roars is the waterfall!

FULL CHORUS. (*With full orchestra accompaniment.*)

> The waterfall will roar,
> > The sun will shine
> Let us take our leave
> > Of the barrier guards!

(*As the music reaches a crescendo, Benkei rises and signals the party to leave with a single, sudden gesture of the fan. Yoshitsune and the retainers move swiftly down the* Hanamichi *and exit at the rear of the auditorium.*)

> So saying, Benkei
> > Shouldered the *oi* box.

(*Two stage assistants help Benkei into the oi box harness. Then as he moves quickly toward the* Hanamichi, *Togashi rises, following his progress with an intent gaze. At the* Hanamichi, *Benkei pauses, and stands with legs spread wide apart, the staff held over his head in both hands. Togashi steps forward a pace, twirls the long sleeve of his kimono over his left arm, and raises his closed fan high in the air. This climactic pose is held for a moment.*)

> Feeling as though,
> > They had trod on the tail of a tiger,
> > And slipped through the jaws of a dragon,
> They departed for the Province of Michinoku.

(*Benkei moves quickly onto the* Hanamichi, *and the curtain is run closed behind him. Again Benkei pauses; all is silence. He cannot but think of the great sacrifice Togashi has made on their behalf. His eyes are drawn back toward the place where Togashi was a moment ago. Then his thoughts abruptly return to the many difficulties still lying ahead. He resolutely faces front. He twirls the staff round his head, and poses again, eyes crossed in a "mie." Now he begins his famous "flying roppo," or "moving-in-six-directions-at-once," exit. He remains poised for a long instant on one leg, bending and flexing it. Then he makes a powerful leap forward onto the other leg. Bending and flexing again, he prepares for the next leap. With a twirl of the staff he makes another bound, landing on the opposite leg. Again the bending and flexing, then another leap, and another, and another. Faster and faster he goes, arms and legs flashing in all directions. By the time he reaches the end of the sixty-foot Hanamichi he is moving at full speed, in prodigious leaps and bounds, a brilliant and theatrical projection of masculine strength. As Benkei disappears from sight through the agemaku curtain, the music and clapping of the sticks reach a crescendo, then quickly taper off. The play ends as it began, with a few minutes of quiet drum and flute music played by the musicians off stage right.*)

Zambia's popular Chikwakwa Traveling Theater Company performs The Trial of Zwangendaba *(1976), which fuses contemporary politics and traditional African theater practice.*

CHAPTER 8

THE THEATER OF AFRICA AND THE AFRICAN DIASPORA

As it has been for thousands of years, contemporary African theater and drama is markedly functional (as opposed to diversionary) because within its many communities it serves a purpose beyond mere entertainment. While it may often draw upon the traditional forms and performance styles of its colonial past, African drama is a rich amalgam of ancient and modern influences. Because Africa is an enormous continent comprising many countries and distinct cultures, it is inaccurate to imply too homogeneous a view of African theater. Nevertheless, an indisputable vitality and urgency characterizes late-twentieth-century theater throughout Africa.

Colonial policies, especially in education, brought Western-style drama to Africa, but there has also been a fortuitous enrichment of Western culture by Africans displaced by the diaspora—the enforced resettlement of indigenous peoples through slavery. The diaspora is a name applied to the capture and redistribution of Africans during the seventeenth and eighteenth centuries. Traditionally, the Diaspora is the name given to the migration of the Jews from their homeland in biblical times, but today the word also refers to the dispersion of a variety of peoples because of political turmoil, war, or economic explotation. American playwright David Henry Hwang's play *The Dance and the Railroad* is based on the Chinese diaspora, when thousands of Chinese were imported as cheap labor for the American railroad. However, diaspora, as it is used here, refers specifically to the forced relocation of African slaves from the sub-Sahara.

Though the diaspora remains an ignoble tragedy for the continent, people of African heritage have significantly contributed to the arts and other endeavors wherever they were settled. Jazz (and its derivatives, rhythm and blues, and rock and roll) is perhaps the best-known by-product of the fusion of traditional African music and that of other cultures. Artists whose roots may be traced to Africa have particularly enriched theater in the United States, the Caribbean, and Latin America. Of late, the British theater has enjoyed the influence of writers and artists from Africa and the West Indies; Mustapha Matura from Trinidad has been especially successful at adapting European works, such as Synge's *The Playboy of the Western World*, to the idioms of the Caribbean.

Plays by August Wilson and Derek Walcott are included in this anthology to complement those of such admired African playwrights as Wole Soyinka and the white South African playwright Athol Fugard, who employs distinctly European forms in his passionately antiapartheid dramas. Fugard's plays have been produced throughout the world and are among the very best works in the contemporary theater.

AFRICA

Artistic and Cultural Events

2500 B.C.E.:
Abydos Passion Play; variety of rituals, ceremonies, masquerades, spirit cult performances throughout Africa

c. 3000 B.C.E.:
Pyramid texts

1801:
First European theater in Cape Town, South Africa

1880s:
Missionaries use theater for conversions

1930s:
First plays published by native black Africans

1947:
National Theater Organization founded in South Africa

1958:
Experimental theater in Ghana

1965:
Makerere Traveling Theater Company founded in East Africa

1966:
First African Arts and Cultural Festival

1970s:
Township theater flourishes in South Africa

1986:
Soyinka wins Nobel Prize

1976:
Market Theatre opens in Johannesburg

Pre-Nineteenth Century   1800 C.E.   1900 C.E.

Historical and Political Events

1844–1845:
European nations partition Africa in Berlin

1830s:
Africa opened for exploration by Europeans

1960:
Independence of Nigeria, Cameroon, and Mali

1957:
Independence of Ghana

1963:
Independence of Kenya

1976:
Soweto Riots in South Africa

1994:
Apartheid abolished in South Africa

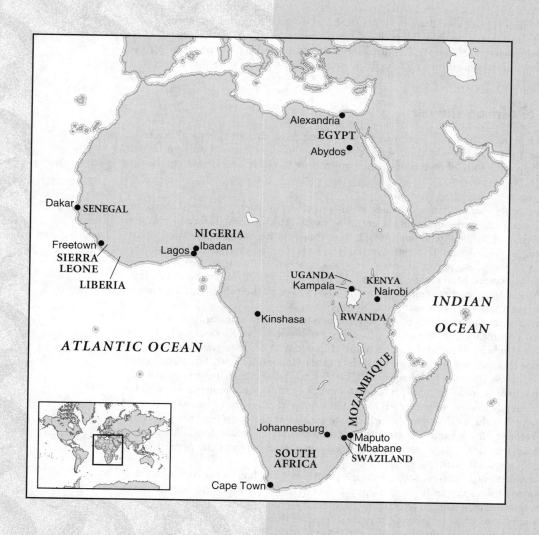

The history of the theater in Africa—particularly that of the sub-Sahara—is complex. Though its theatrical roots are ancient, written drama by black Africans is largely a twentieth-century phenomenon. Prior to this time, formal drama was largely the product of European colonists, but since the late 1950s, native black Africans (as opposed to Africans of European descent, such as Athol Fugard) have used drama as a political tool. Accordingly, the evolution of contemporary African theater parallels the political emancipation of much of the continent. As European colonists have relinquished control of Africa to its indigenous peoples, African drama has reasserted its own cultural and linguistic integrity by returning to its theatrical roots.

The Roots of African Theater

Africa remains perhaps the finest repository of the world's most ancient theatrical practices. Cultural historian E. T. Kirby identifies seven performance modes typical of African theater that, collectively, offer a useful review of the human instinct to create events that are theatrical:

1. *Storytelling performances:* African theater, both ancient and modern, is largely characterized by its emphasis on storytelling. Central to many African theatricals is a narrator, often the *griot,* or "healer," who improvises a story (however well known) to the accompaniment of song and dance. The narrator frequently assumes the voice and physical characteristics of the many people in his story, though occasionally others leap in to play particular characters. Masks and costume pieces may distinguish the characters. Contemporary African playwrights frequently employ storytellers in their dramas; for example, *Death and the King's Horseman* features a "Praise-Singer."

2. *Simple enactments:* Bushmen improvise performances in which hunting animals is the primary plot. For instance, a man wears a headpiece fashioned from a forked stick and impersonates a kudu antelope while others mime killing him. A group of young boys pretend to be dogs that accompany the men. Such hunting dances are both functional (they promise food for the tribe) and spiritual (they acknowledge higher powers in nature). Other enactments are more clearly social in scope. The Shona use simple plays in which a woman pretends to cook as part of an initiation rite for young girls. Other women scold her for sampling the food as they smear her face with flour and warn her that "You must not eat before your husband." These unscripted dramas are as basic a form of theater as can be found; at heart, they are imitation games such as children might perform while learning their roles in society.

3. *Ritualized enactments:* We have seen that the earliest rites often had an aura of magic about them. For instance, some cultures developed dances in which they imitated rain falling in the hope that nature would, in return, imitate them by sending rain. This is called *sympathetic* (or *homeopathic*) *magic,* one of the earliest forms of theatrical activity. Numerous examples of such ritual activity are found throughout Africa today. The Loga of Central Africa have a lengthy initiation ritual in which important artifacts are paraded through the village while proverbs are sung. A processional dance leads the villagers to a specially constructed initiation hut; the participants climb upon the roof while eight proverbs are chanted. The "magic" occurs when the malevolent spirits are driven from the hut and when good spirits enter the bodies of the Loga.

4. *Spirit cult performances:* A medium, thought to be possessed by spirits, assumes a "character" while in a trance. Dressed in striking costumes and speaking in a "spirit language," the medium performs gestures so extraordinary that they give the illusion that the spirit, or even a god, is actually present. There is strong dramatic interaction between the character and the audience, most of it improvised by the medium. Such performances are so common among the people of western Uganda that anthropologist John Beattie refers to them as their "traditional national theater." A spirit called a *shave,* recognizable by his white shirt, hat, and belt, possesses mediums of one East African community. Drinking, dancing, and dialogue mark the trance ceremony with the spirits. Slaves brought spirit

cult performances to the Americas. For instance, the Macumba of Brazil still use spirit performances in healing ceremonies. The medium customarily becomes one of four identifiable characters: an old slave (a reminder of past suffering); a native (who embodies pre-Columbian glory); a temptress (the spirit of fertility and pleasure); and, perhaps most intriguing, the trickster, a symbol of mischief who figures prominently in world drama.

5. *Masquerades:* Masquerades, evolved from ceremonials performed by secret societies to honor the dead, remain perhaps the most representative form of indigenous African theater. Enormous and colorful masks, large costumes (often made of wicker or grass), and vigorous dancing and other mimetic actions characterize masquerades. Frequently, a dramatic narrative holds them together. Ibibio masquerades even improvise comic skits. The costumes used at Carnival in Trinidad (see Center Stage box, The Trinidad Carnival, at the end of this chapter) are remnants of such masquerades, brought by slaves to the Americas.

6. *Ceremonial performances:* Like so many other indigenous theatricals in Africa, singing, dancing, and the beating of drums accompany ceremonial performances. The Dogon of West Africa celebrate a Festival of the Dead each year, a ceremony in which the feats of ancestors are recalled. There are nightlong mock battles, acrobatic dances, and a display of weapons meant to teach the Dogon respect for their past and acceptance of the inevitability of death.

7. *"Comedies":* Perhaps the theatrical activities most closely resembling a play as we understand the term are comedies performed in open spaces in the villages of many African tribes. These performances may have evolved from simple enactments or masquerades into plays with a discernible plot and characterization. Just when this happened we cannot ascertain, but the presence of these comic playlets suggests the process by which formal drama has developed around the world. Coincidentally, many of the characters appearing in these comedies are African versions of popular comic characters found in ancient Rome, Renaissance Italy, Chinese opera, and Japanese *kyōgen* (farces), not to mention American TV sitcoms. The Mande-speaking people of West Africa perform comedies portraying a deceiving wife, a gullible husband, a bragging warrior, and a trickster-thief. Though they are painted with clay or white ash, these village actors are no less appealing to their audiences than the comedians of Italy's *commedia dell'arte* or the *ch'ou* (clown) of Chinese opera. The comedies use dialogue, frequently improvised, and may be accompanied by singers and an orchestra. Men frequently play women's roles, a convention we find throughout world theater, particularly in those cultures in which women are not permitted to act. Like comedy everywhere, the African plays portray the social aspects of village life. In one comedy, a husband working in the fields with his wife burns a pile of stalks under which his wife's lover is hidden. The piece ends with a comic chase as the transgressor flees both the irate husband and the flames. Like all good comedy, the plays are intended, in Walter Kerr's words, "to show the cracks in the human façade."

Postcolonial Drama in Africa

By the 1880s sub-Saharan Africa was largely in the control of European powers including England, France, Germany, and the Netherlands. The British established colonies in South Africa much earlier in the nineteenth century, and by 1801 a theater had been established in what is now Cape Town. In 1884–1885 the Europeans divided their African colonies among themselves in Berlin. Consequently, formal drama in Africa was virtually a European enterprise, though records indicate native black Africans improvised plays in the nineteenth century. Christian missionaries also used drama as a means of converting black Africans; *The Redemption*, for instance, contributed to the Christianization of Rwanda. Amiri Baraka's *Slave Ship* (1969) attacks Christians for subverting traditional African religious practices.

We do not find plays published by native black Africans until the 1930s, and there is little significant publication and production of black African plays until the 1950s. The drama of black Africans developed in three significant stages:

CENTER STAGE   SOUTH AFRICAN TOWNSHIP THEATER

South African township theater typifies Jerzy Grotowski's vision of a "poor theater" because it is necessarily reduced to the essence of the theatrical act by stripping the performance of superfluous accoutrements. Grotowski argues and township theater proves that "theater *can* exist without makeup, without autonomic costume and scenography, without a separate performance area (stage), without lighting and sound effects, etc. It *cannot* exist without the actor-spectator relationship of perceptual, direct, live communion." The Polish artist envisioned a theater that becomes a "spiritual act" and South African township theater is that spiritual act. Its form develops out of the demands of its content and milieu, not a shaping of the content to fit an existing form. Township theater is about freedom. It is about poverty and oppression. It is about not only what is, but what could be. Township theater is presented with the barest essentials—the actor and the audience. It merely suggests scenery, properties, and costumes, all of which are usually "found" rather than "designed."

Township theater is, in the words of critic Keyan Tomaselli, "the most accessible and forceful medium . . . to articulate [black] ideology, expose the contradictions of apartheid, and communicate a more accurate portrayal of the actual conditions of existence." Playwright Matsemela Manaka says, "Our theater is here to search for the truth about the history of the dispossessed . . . [about] the liberation of the mind and the liberation of the body." In such a theater, David Coplan, author of *In the Township Tonight!*, declares, "The working class aesthetic of the township is that theater is a direct extension of the actual conditions of black existence, with no necessary boundaries between art and life, performer and audience."

Township theater, a relatively new form of South African theater, emerged within a decade of the formal establishment of apartheid in 1948. This dauntless and dynamic theater was spawned in the "locations" or "townships" (read ghettos) established by the government. As Pretoria gradually tightened the noose of apartheid and the suffering of the indigenous population grew, both the form and content of this so-called poor theater evolved.

Its development passed through four stages, each lasting about ten years. The early plays, essentially those of the 1950s, were largely escapist entertainments depicting daily life in the townships. During the 1960s the plays developed into pictures of the suffering of the blacks of South Africa, presenting the plight of those who were physically and psychologically maimed by the system. As an awareness of history and bitterness against imperialism grew in the 1970s, township theater evolved into a medium for the expression of the rage that accompanied the rise in black consciousness. The final stage, which began in the late 1970s and continued throughout the 1980s to the present, is almost celebratory. It is an affirmation of the noble spirit, the undying optimism, and the impending liberation of the people.

"Mistress It's A Pity": The teacher of Sarafina and her schoolmates leads the students in a rousing number from Mbongeni Ngema's internationally acclaimed musical hit Sarafina!

- Plays in which black Africans attempt to show they have assimilated the culture of the colonists; these dramas show an indebtedness to European dramaturgy. Popular European plays, such as those by Oscar Wilde, Bernard Shaw, and the operettists Gilbert and Sullivan, were often the staples of colonial African theater, whether performed by Europeans or black Africans.

Township theater is truly a theater of the people. Although it exemplifies Grotowski's poor theater, it also resembles other agitprop and revolutionary theaters, most notably Bertolt Brecht's epic theater (see Chapter 5). Township theater first exposes the transgressions of the oppressors and then infuses the oppressed with a sense of beauty and self-worth and imbues them with political power. "There is only one ally against the growth of barbarism," declares Brecht, "the people on whom it imposes these sufferings. Only the people offer any prospects. Thus it is natural to turn to them."

The leaders of township theater are the playwrights and directors, who most often take on both duties. The popular term for this combined role is "play-maker." Playmakers work improvisationally with their companies to develop new works that rely on the people in the townships for their experiences and stories. In fact, the plays are often cast first, and then the script is developed based on the lives and observations of the actors. For example, when Mbongeni Ngema developed his company, Committed Artists, he gathered the homeless of Durban, who knew firsthand the particulars of the rent strike. Their collective experience gave birth to the play *Asinamali!* (*We Have No Money!*). "If the actors didn't . . . get the spirit right," declares Ngema, "I would say, 'let's go to a funeral in Lamontville (where police were shooting people almost daily), so that we can experience running away from tear gas, how it is to be close to death.'"

This type of "patchy," pieced-together playmaking, which is the heart and soul of township theater, has led to the development of what might be called "motley theater"—motley venues, scripts, and performance styles. The venues for these performances consist of "found spaces" because few or no theaters exist in the townships. For example, the township of Soweto, a community of a million people, is served by a single theater—Deipkloof Hall, a performance space that more closely approximates a small high school gymnasium than a theater. The most popular performance spaces are the local churches, schoolyards, community halls, garages, and streets.

The scripts consist of collages of images portraying township life. Farcical comedy combines with pathetic tragedy; poignant sentimentalism freely mixes with cold documentary; the surreal and expressionistic is superimposed on the realistic and naturalistic. This eclectic mix of styles bombards the senses with striking images of township life. These seemingly plotless, episodic, improvisational plays often offend traditional theater connoisseurs and critics.

These unique plays are often presented on a bare stage with little costuming. A packing crate or two, a couple of chairs, and whatever discarded clothes can be found are the visual staples of these dramas. The opening description of *Woza Albert!* is an excellent illustration:

The set consists of two up-ended tea-chests side by side about center stage. Further upstage an old wooden plank, about ten feet long, is suspended horizontally on old ropes. From nails in the plank hang the ragged clothes that the actors will use for their transformation. The actors wear grey track-suit bottoms and running shoes. They are bare-chested.

Eclectic music is used to reinforce theme and mood. A single play may use music drawn from traditional African rhythms, Christian hymns, African choral songs, English secular compositions, Afro-American jazz, miners' chants and *mbaquanga*, the music of the inner city, so beautifully reflected in the score of *Sarafina!* The music, whether composed especially for the play or borrowed, is live, and the actors frequently sing a cappella in rich harmonies.

Township performers combine the skills of the actor, athlete, singer, dancer, mime, historian, impressionist, politician, and social commentator. Usually appearing on the stage as "themselves," these performers are specialists at "transformation"—the act of evolving spontaneously. Virtually an entire population can be played by a couple of actors using imaginative physical manipulation, clever vocal alteration, and a cacophony of sound effects. In *Woza Albert!*, for example, the two actors create people ranging from the homeless to the Prime Minister; they create machines such as cement mixers, garbage trucks, and helicopters; and they create an airport, a prison, a TV studio, and a nuclear explosion. In later plays, such as Ngema's *Sarafina!* and *Township Fever!*, the casts are expanded and there is far less use of transformation. Such plays resemble a more traditional Western musical.

- Plays in which the colonized dramatists display an uncertainty about their status and attempt to recover their native past and its forms. Because of a Eurocentric educational system, plays still rely on an essentially Old World dramaturgy.
- Plays that revolt against colonization, both politically and aesthetically. Here dramatists purposefully employ traditional African theater modes as they write plays designed to

Aided by a chorus of women bearing baskets, actors perform an antelope dance during a political rally in Mali. "Street theater" is common in African villages that may not have formal performance spaces.

rouse the people against colonization. In 1956 the West African playwright Aimé Césaaire wrote a play in which the central character, the Rebel, tells his oppressors: "Leave me alone, leave me to shout enough to intoxicate myself with that cry of revolt, I wish to be alone under my skin, I recognize no one's right to live in me."

Hubert Ogunde (Nigeria), Ngugiwa Thiong'o (Kenya), and Herbert Dholmo (South Africa) were among the first black African playwrights to achieve international respect for dramas about the liberation of Africa.

In 1966 the First World Festival of Negro Arts was held in Dakar, Senegal (formerly French West Africa), and in 1977 a Black and African Festival of Arts and Culture (FESTAC) convened in Lagos, Nigeria. In many ways, these events signaled the arrival of contemporary black African theater and arts as entities liberated from the Eurocentric tradition that dominated African stages for over a century. There exist relatively few outlets for contemporary African drama in the West because of translation and publication problems. The best-known work comes from Nigeria and South Africa, though playwrights such as Jacob Hemvi in Uganda are enjoying international publication and production. Within the next decade we can expect greater accessibility to contemporary African drama and theater.

While there is a distinctly commercial theater throughout Africa, the most famous of which is the Market Theatre in South Africa (see Spotlight box, South Africa's Market Theatre and the Independent Theater Phenomenon), much contemporary African drama emerges from three significant sources:

1. *Universities:* Although many African universities were established by colonialists and retain an educational system based on European models, the majority of Africa's most accomplished dramatists (and directors and actors) have emerged from such universities as Makerere University (Uganda), which served all of East Africa until the breakup of the East African com-

munity in the 1950s. Ibadan University (Nigeria) encouraged the early work of Soyinka and John Pepper Clark-Bekederemo. The University of Zimbabwe (formerly Rhodesia) introduced a full theater curriculum in 1984 and has produced much of that country's best drama, a phenomenon that has been repeated throughout much of modern Africa.

2. *Traveling theater companies:* Numerous companies, such as Zambia's Chikwakwa Theater (1971) and the Yoruba Traveling Theater (Nigeria, c. 1955), take plays into rural areas to entertain and, more importantly, to instruct villagers about a variety of social, political, and cultural issues. Often theater artists elicit commentary and solutions from the audience as they improvise their works.

3. *Village and community theater:* Although the roots of such enterprises may be traced to pre-colonial times, black Africans seeking to restore their culture have revitalized popular theater. To non-Africans, the township plays of South Africa (see Center Stage box, South African Township Theater) are the best-known forms of community-created theater, though numerous varieties can be cited throughout the continent. In Niger—formerly a French colony in West Africa that was liberated in 1960—youth groups (*samariyas*) who speak in their native Hausa perform "ballets." These dramas are performed in government-constructed youth centers or in open spaces in the villages. In Togo, once a German colony, "concert parties" are popular mass entertainments (despised by the literate elite). They are composed of "high-life" music, skits and storytelling, and improvised plays on topical issues; the language is a blend of native Ewe and pidgin colonial dialects.

The Conventions of African Theater

While realistic theater in the Euro-American mode exists in Africa, most African theater is presentational and uses conspicuously theatrical conventions. Narrators, storytellers, and praise singers guide the action; actors frequently play multiple roles and address the audience directly. African dramatists and performers do not distance themselves from their people, and they do not write abstruse material for the learned elite; rather, they continue the tradition of the *griot* as they chronicle the history and concerns of their audiences. There is often considerable interaction between performers and the audience, which is free to respond verbally to the action onstage. Song, dance, and poetry are used freely in both scripted and improvised performances. Traditional, as well as contemporary, masks remain central to much African theater. Scenery and costumes may be found, but financial constraints often require simple settings that use "found" objects and selective costuming. This is particularly apparent in community theater. It is the energy and vitality of the actors—and their interplay with the audience—that provides the appeal of African theater.

Theater throughout Africa is performed in a variety of spaces, from sophisticated, modern theaters that rival those found in Europe and America to open spaces in courtyards and platform stages erected in the round. Because African audiences are participating audiences, vocally and even physically, often no conspicuous attempt is made to separate the audience from the performers. To do so would kill the spirit of the theater whose very roots depended on the interaction between performer and audience.

"MASTER HAROLD" . . . and the boys

ATHOL FUGARD

ATHOL FUGARD (1932–)

Identified by *Time* as "the greatest active playwright in the English-speaking world," South African Harold Athol Lanning Fugard was born in Middleburg, Cape Province. When he was three, his family moved to Port Elizabeth in Eastern Province, where his mother was forced to be the family provider because of his father's heavy drinking and physical handicap. She ran the Jubilee Hotel and the Saint George's Park Tea Room. After graduation from the local technical high school, Fugard earned a scholarship to the University of Cape Town, where he studied philosophy for three years before dropping out to embark on a life as a sailor, journalist, and court clerk. In each job he was constantly confronted by the inequities, bigotry, and racism fostered by apartheid, South Africa's official policy of racial separation. As an adolescent he was subjected to his father's "pointless, unthought-out prejudices"; as the only white sailor on a voyage to Japan, he gained intimate knowledge of the plight of many blacks and Asians; and as a court clerk he saw firsthand the cruel effects of apartheid.

Unsatisfied and at the urging of his wife, actress Sheila Meiring, he turned to playwriting. A voracious reader, he was influenced by British playwright John Osborne and the American novelist William Faulkner. Following Osborne's lead as the outspoken "angry young man" and Faulkner's "unashamedly regional" preoccupation, he developed into a passionate, regional playwright whose insight and sensitivity spoke not only to his native land but to the world.

It is not only life in South Africa that is portrayed in a Fugard play, but the life of the playwright himself. An autobiographical thread runs through his major plays, which include *No-Good Friday* (1958), *Blood Knot* (1961), *Bosman and Lena* (1968), *The Island* and *Sizwe Bansi Is Dead* (1972, both written in collaboration with Winston Ntshona and John Kani), *Statements After an Arrest Under the Immorality Act* (1974), *A Lesson from Aloes* (1978), *"MASTER HAROLD" . . . and the boys* (1982), *The Road to Mecca* (1984), *My Children! My Africa!* (1989), *Playland* (1992), and *Valley Song* (1996).

His work as a dramatist began in Port Elizabeth with the Serpent Players, a company including white, black, and "colored" South Africans, many of whom became his lifelong friends. Two members, Zakes Mokae and John Kani—South Africa's leading black actors— have played many leading roles in his plays. His early works were developed as pieces-in-progress in which much of the action and the dialogue were created through improvisation. His later plays, though rooted in his apartheid experiences, are more the work of an individual voice.

Fugard's plots, reminiscent of Ibsen's great discussion dramas, develop painstakingly slowly. With exceptional care, he meticulously lays out the exposition so that as the action moves through its complications, a tremendous sense of rhythm and momentum carries the viewer to an unexpected and shattering conclusion. Because his works are usually populated by only two or three people, each character is well developed. Often the situations he creates reflect the mixed population of South Africa. For example, *Blood Knot* concerns Zack and Morrie, men of mixed race (or "coloreds," as apartheid classifies them) who are sons of the same mother and different fathers; *My Children! My Africa!* presents Mr. M., Thami, and Isabel, a black schoolmaster, his black male pupil, and a white female student; in *"MASTER HAROLD" . . . and the boys* we meet Hally, Sam, and Willie, a white adolescent and two older blacks. Whether his characters are tied together by a blood knot, a desire for learning, or sense of surrogate family, they form a bond that crosses racial and generational barriers only to be destroyed by the ingrained racism of which they are victims.

Thematically, Fugard's plays are an indictment of the ignorance, racism, and hatred that nourish apartheid. Calling for patience, tolerance, and understanding, his plays reveal not only the exploitation and victimization of the black and colored majority of South Africa, but the dehumanizing effects on the white minority. Quite often Fugard creates a peaceful world within a violent one. In *Blood Knot* it is the men's shanty hut; in *My Children! My Africa!*, the classroom; and in *"MASTER HAROLD" . . . and the boys*, the tea room. Inside, the dream of equality thrives and optimism rules, but outside a nightmare of separateness and injustice flourishes while despair reigns.

"MASTER HAROLD" . . . and the boys (1982)

For Fugard, the playwright's work begins not with ideas but with images. "From the very first, the generative—the seed of what energy's involved and goes on to produce a play—comes from images, not ideas," declares Fugard, " . . . something I have to see or hear, not think, but see or hear," that leads to crafting of the play. In *"MASTER HAROLD,"* Fugard has created images of sublime memories juxtaposed with those of grotesque reality. More specifically, the play is composed of a number of central images—ballroom dancing, kite making and flying, and teaching—each presented metatheatrically to create in the tea room a microcosm of a bigoted world.

The plot of the play is simple. "Master Harold" of the title is Hally, a precocious white South African teenager, and "the boys" are Willie and Sam, black men, both of whom work for Hally's family and are old enough to be his father. The action takes place in Port Elizabeth, South Africa, in 1950. On his way home from school, Hally stops by the family-owned tea room, where Willie and Sam are tidying up while they practice their ballroom dancing in preparation for the "event of the year"—the Eastern Province Ballroom Dancing Championships in New Brighton, a black township outside Port Elizabeth. A lifetime of camaraderie is apparent as Hally, Sam, and Willie talk, joke, and revel in fond memories. This cordial atmosphere is shattered, however, as Hally, via a telephone call from his mother, learns that his crippled, alcoholic father is about to be released from the hospital and will be home again, where his presence is painfully disruptive. Suddenly angry and afraid, Hallie turns viciously on Willie and Sam. For the father he cannot strike, Hally substitutes the fathers who cannot retaliate. As Hally lashes out at his two lifelong African friends, we understand how the underlying realities of time and place define who we are and dominate our actions. The play is based on an actual incident in Fugard's youth, and he presents an image of himself caught in emotional turmoil as he moved from the innocence of youth to the poisonous bigotry of adulthood.

Among Fugard's most obvious images is that of life as a dance—a vision of a world in which "accidents don't happen; a vision of a world without collisions." The play presents simultaneous images of rituals in the tea room—one a figurative dance, the other a literal one. We immediately see the figurative dance—the boys preparing the dilapidated tea room for the next business day. The establishment is a mess: chairs and tables piled atop one another, the floor half-scrubbed, the windows dirty. As the action proceeds, they ritualistically clean the room. At the same time, "the boys" prepare for the ballroom dancing contest by taking turns dancing around the room with their invisible partners. The play ends with the tea room neatly prepared for the next day's business, while "the boys" continue their dance, gliding effortlessly through the clutter of the tea room that represents their cluttered lives.

Sam's image of the dance as "a world without collisions" is displayed as Hally, Sam, and Willie dance and reminisce. Just before the climax of the play, the tea room is partially cleaned and arranged, Sam explains "a world without collisions" to Hally, and Willie weaves his way through the clutter. When the dreamworld is interrupted by the "bump" from Hally's mother, the dancing ceases and their peace is destroyed.

Though Fugard indicates that the boys are tidying the room and dancing, he mentions very little specific action. What is implied, however, is that in the course of rearranging the furniture, the boys have set up a difficult obstacle course, which only experienced dancers can negotiate. The tea room resembles a crowded ballroom dance floor; it is a safe world inhabited only by the boys, who, having violently bumped into Hally, continue to dream of a world without collisions. The final dance seems to be an image of harmony among men. Unfortunately, at the time the play is set (and even when it was written), harmony existed only among black men. However, we now know it was the white man, Hally (Fugard himself), who went on to write about Sam's dream. It was Hally who in the end learned the lesson that was being taught on that rainy afternoon.

Images of a kite also appear throughout the play. Kite making and kite flying are presented as accomplishments. "I wanted you to look up," says Sam, "[and] be proud of something, of yourself." The kite in this sublime memory is not store-bought fresh from the factory but a "homemade" kite constructed from the refuse of their lives. The memory of that kite in flight conjures up the image of freedom and of Sam, a man who, surrounded by a constricting society, is free only in his mind. Sam relinquished control of the kite that fateful day in hopes that Hally might see the beauty of freedom. In addition to the freedom implied by a soaring kite, there is also the sense of communion between the kite and its handler. Neither one can be successful, nor exist, without the other. Their kite is, of course, a phoenix—it flew once and, as we see in postapartheid South Africa, it may fly again.

Closely aligned with the image of the kite is that of the "whites-only bench." While the kite signifies togetherness, the bench epitomizes separateness—or to use the Afrikaans term, apartheid. As long as the "whites-only bench" exists and Hally continues to make use of it, the kite and its freedom will only be a vague memory of youth, a dream destined for oblivion. As Sam explains to Hally, "You're going to be sitting up there by yourself for a long time to come, and there won't be a kite in the sky."

Throughout the play Hally seems to be the teacher and Sam the student. At the conclusion, we realize that while Hally has led Sam on a journey through books, it is Sam who has worked tirelessly to teach Hally "what being a man means." In the end Hally declares: "I don't know. I don't know anything anymore." Sam reassures him, saying, "Are you sure of that, Hally? Because it would be hopeless if that was true. It would mean nothing has been learnt in here this afternoon, and there was a hell of a lot of teaching going on . . . one way or the other."

The characters move freely about the entire tea room, where, at least after hours, there are no "whites-only benches." Even as Sam and Willie dance, Hally stands behind the counter to make an ice cream soda. Not until the final moments are they separated, and we see an image of Sam and Willie as servants waiting to, in Hally's words, "get on with [their] job[s]." But even this picture changes as Sam reaches out one last time to Hally. When he asks Hally if they "should try again . . . [to] fly another kite," it is more than forgiveness, more than turning the other cheek he represents. He is the epitome of generosity, the ultimate act of humanity, which makes Sam the "man of magnitude" referred to in Hally's school lesson.

The images of the dancing, the kite, the "whites-only bench," and the teaching are presented through a metatheatrical motif—everything is acted out. Fugard's few stage directions demand that the characters "perform" for one another. For example, as Hally conjures up the memory of the old Jubilee Boarding House, he exclaims: "I bet I could still find my way to your room with my eye closed." To which Fugard adds, "(*He does exactly that.*)" Shortly thereafter, "using a few chairs [Hally] re-creates the room," and Willie, eager to partake in the drama, assumes the "boxing pose" of Joe Louis as Hally, now a director, works to bring the scene to life. Later, as Sam describes the finale to the ballroom dancing contest, Fugard places Sam "onto the chair to act out the M.C."

The "let's pretend" images of the play occur in the dialogue as well. As Hally completes his re-creation of the Old Jubilee Boarding House, he exclaims, "Right, so much for the stage directions. Now the characters." He proceeds to describe Sam and Willie, who "move to their appropriate positions in the bedroom." Certainly implied here are the directions for "Master Harold" and "the boys" to act out as much of the description in the text as possible—in short, to turn the narratives into dramatic performance.

The overriding reality of racism permeates the play's images, especially in Hally's dialogue. While his condescending "Don't be smart, Sam, it doesn't become you," "What does a black man know about flying a kite?" and "It's called bigotry, Sam" are attempts at humor, they are also signs of Hally's latent racism. Hally is his father's son, and the greatest irony of all is that while Hally is ashamed of his father's afflictions, his greatest disease is neither physical nor drug induced but his ignorant racism. The degrading racist lines we hear early in the play are actually figurative spits in the face as disturbing as the literal spit of the climax.

The world of the tea room is a microcosm of South Africa, which is itself a microcosm of the world. Fugard sees his hometown as representative of South Africa: "In Port Elizabeth, I think, you have a microcosm in a microcosm . . . black, white, Indian, Chinese, and Colored [mixed race]. It is also very representative of South Africa in the range of its social strata, from total affluence on the white side to the extremist poverty of the non-white." Fugard has written that the circumstances of his life have set him in opposition to apartheid and makes it clear that in his plays he is "judging my own people for what they have done to themselves, done to the Black people in that country, done to the Colored people in that country, done to the Indian people in that country, done to the Chinese people in that country. My sense of myself as judge came about without my realizing it; it came out of a sense of the common humanity of all people in that country." While apartheid has been "officially" banned in the Republic of South Africa and many other sovereign nations, a great deal of informal separateness lingers in our society, breeding the same kind of racism we see in Hally.

A young Master Harold (Damaso Rodriguez) shares his dreams with "the boys"—Sam (Rapulana Seiphemo) and Willie (Armando Garza) in this production staged by Roger Schultz at Texas A&M University in 1994.

"MASTER HAROLD" . . . and the boys

A T H O L   F U G A R D

The St. George's Park Tea Room on a wet and windy Port Elizabeth[1] afternoon.

Tables and chairs have been cleared and are stacked on one side except for one which stands apart with a single chair. On this table a knife, fork, spoon and side plate in anticipation of a simple meal, together with a pile of comic books.

Other elements: a serving counter with a few stale cakes under glass and a not very impressive display of sweets, cigarettes and cool drinks, etc.; a few cardboard advertising handouts—Cadbury's Chocolate, Coca-Cola—and a blackboard on which an untrained hand has chalked up the prices of Tea, Coffee, Scones, Milkshakes—all flavors—and Cool Drinks; a few sad ferns in pots; a telephone; an old-style jukebox.

There is an entrance on one side and an exit into a kitchen on the other.

Leaning on the solitary table, his head cupped in one hand as he pages through one of the comic books, is Sam. A black man in his mid-forties. He wears the white coat of a waiter. Behind him on his knees, mopping down the floor with a bucket of water and a rag, is Willie. Also black and about the same age as Sam. He has his sleeves and trousers rolled up.

The year: 1950

---

[1]**Port Elizabeth** city in South Africa

WILLIE (*singing as he works*).

> "She was scandalizin' my name,
> She took my money
> She called me honey
> But she was scandalizin' my name.
> Called it love but was playin' a game . . . "

He gets up and moves the bucket. Stands thinking for a moment, then, raising his arms to hold an imaginary partner, he launches into an intricate ballroom dance step. Although a mildly comic figure, he reveals a reasonable degree of accomplishment.

Hey, Sam.

Sam, absorbed in the comic book, does not respond.

Hey, Boet[2] Sam!

Sam looks up.

I'm getting it. The quickstep. Look now and tell me. (*He repeats the step.*) Well?

SAM (*encouragingly*). Show me again.

WILLIE. Okay, count for me.

SAM. Ready?

WILLIE. Ready.

SAM. Five, six, seven, eight . . . (*Willie starts to dance.*) A-n-d one two three four . . . and one two three four. . . . (*Ad libbing as Willie dances.*) Your shoulders, Willie . . . your shoulders! Don't look down! Look happy, Willie! Relax, Willie!

WILLIE (*desperate but still dancing*). I am relax.

SAM. No, you're not.

WILLIE. (*He falters.*) Ag no man, Sam! Mustn't talk. You make me make mistakes.

SAM. But you're too stiff.

WILLIE. Yesterday I'm not straight . . . today I'm too stiff!

SAM. Well, you are. You asked me and I'm telling you.

WILLIE. Where?

SAM. Everywhere. Try to glide through it.

WILLIE. Glide?

SAM. Ja, make it smooth. And give it more style. It must look like you're enjoying yourself.

WILLIE (*emphatically*). I wasn't.

SAM. Exactly.

WILLIE. How can I enjoy myself? Not straight, too stiff and now it's also glide, give it more style, make it smooth. . . . Haai! Is hard to remember all those things, Boet Sam.

SAM. That's your trouble. You're trying too hard.

WILLIE. I try hard because it *is* hard.

SAM. But don't let me see it. The secret is to make it look easy. Ballroom must look happy, Willie, not like hard work. It must . . . Ja! . . . it must look like romance.

WILLIE. Now another one! What's romance?

SAM. Love story with happy ending. A handsome man in tails, and in his arms, smiling at him, a beautiful lady in evening dress!

WILLIE. Fred Astaire, Ginger Rogers.

SAM. You got it. Tapdance or ballroom, it's the same. Romance. In two weeks' time when the judges look at you and Hilda, they must see a man and a woman who are dancing their way to a happy ending. What I saw was you holding her like you were frightened she was going to run away.

WILLIE. Ja! Because that is what she wants to do! I got no romance left for Hilda anymore, Boet Sam.

SAM. Then pretend. When you put your arms around Hilda, imagine she is Ginger Rogers.

WILLIE. With no teeth? You try.

SAM. Well, just remember, there's only two weeks left.

WILLIE. I know, I know! (*To the jukebox.*) I do it better with music. You got sixpence for Sarah Vaughan?[3]

SAM. That's a slow foxtrot. You're practicing the quickstep.

WILLIE. I'll practice slow foxtrot.

SAM (*shaking his head*). It's your turn to put money in the jukebox.

WILLIE. I only got bus fare to go home. (*He returns disconsolately to his work.*) Love story and happy ending! She's doing it all right, Boet Sam, but is not me she's giving happy endings. Fuckin' whore! Three nights now she doesn't come practice. I wind up gramophone, I get record ready and I sit and wait. What happens? Nothing. Ten o'clock I start dancing with my pillow. You try and practice romance by yourself, Boet Sam. Struesgod, she doesn't come tonight I take back my dress and ballroom shoes and I find me new partner. Size twenty-six. Shoes size seven. And now she's also making trouble for me with the baby again. Reports me to Child Wellfed, that I'm not giving her money. She lies! Every week I am giving her money for milk. And how do I know is my baby? Only his hair looks like me. She's fucking around all the time I turn my back. Hilda Samuels is a bitch! (*Pause.*) Hey, Sam!

SAM. Ja.

WILLIE. You listening?

SAM. Ja.

WILLIE. So what you say?

SAM. About Hilda?

WILLIE. Ja.

SAM. When did you last give her a hiding?

WILLIE (*reluctantly*). Sunday night.

SAM. And today is Thursday.

WILLIE. (*He knows what's coming.*) Okay.

SAM. Hiding on Sunday night, then Monday, Tuesday and Wednesday she doesn't come to practice . . . and you are asking me why?

WILLIE. I said okay, Boet Sam!

---

[2] **Boet** Buddy, Brother

[3] **Sarah Vaughan** (1924 – 1990) American jazz singer

SAM. You hit her too much. One day she's going to leave you for good.

WILLIE. So? She makes me the hell-in too much.

SAM (*emphasizing his point*). *Too* much and *too* hard. You had the same trouble with Eunice.

WILLIE. Because she also make the hell-in, Boet Sam. She never got the steps right. Even the waltz.

SAM. Beating her up every time she makes a mistake in the waltz? (*Shaking his head.*) No, Willie! That takes the pleasure out of ballroom dancing.

WILLIE. Hilda is not too bad with the waltz, Boet Sam. Is the quickstep where the trouble starts.

SAM (*teasing him gently*). How's your pillow with the quickstep?

WILLIE. (*ignoring the tease*). Good! And why? Because it got no legs. That's her trouble. She can't move them quick enough, Boet Sam. I start the record and before halfway Count Basie[4] is already winning. Only time we catch up with him is when gramophone runs down.

Sam laughs.

Haaikona, Boet Sam, is not funny.

SAM (*snapping his fingers*). I got it! Give her a handicap.

WILLIE. What's that?

SAM. Give her a ten-second start and then let Count Basie go. Then I put my money on her. Hot favorite in the Ballroom Stakes: Hilda Samuels ridden by Willie Malopo.

WILLIE (*turning away*). I'm not talking to you no more.

SAM (*relenting*). Sorry, Willie . . .

WILLIE. It's finish between us.

SAM. Okay, okay . . . I'll stop.

WILLIE. You can also fuck off.

SAM. Willie, listen! I want to help you!

WILLIE. No more jokes?

SAM. I promise.

WILLIE. Okay. Help me.

SAM (*his turn to hold an imaginary partner*). Look and learn. Feet together. Back straight. Body relaxed. Right hand placed gently in the small of her back and wait for the music. Don't start worrying about making mistakes or the judges or the other competitors. It's just you, Hilda and the music, and you're going to have a good time. What Count Basie do you play?

WILLIE. "You the cream in my coffee, you the salt in my stew."

SAM. Right. Give it to me in strict tempo.

WILLIE. Ready?

SAM. Ready.

WILLIE. A-n-d . . . (*Singing.*)
"You the cream in my coffee.
You the salt in my stew.

---

[4]**Count Basie** William Basie (1904–1984), American jazz pianist, and band leader

You will always be my necessity.
I'd be lost without you. . . ." (etc.)

Sam launches into the quickstep. He is obviously a much more accomplished dancer than Willie. Hally enters. A seventeen-year-old white boy. Wet raincoat and school case. He stops and watches Sam. The demonstration comes to an end with a flourish. Applause from Hally and Willie.

HALLY. Bravo! No question about it. First place goes to Mr. Sam Semela.

WILLIE (*in total agreement*). You was gliding with style, Boet Sam.

HALLY (*cheerfully*). How's it, chaps?

SAM. Okay, Hally.

WILLIE (*springing to attention like a soldier and saluting*). At your service, Master Harold!

HALLY. Not long to the big event, hey!

SAM. Two weeks.

HALLY. You nervous?

SAM. No.

HALLY. Think you stand a chance?

SAM. Let's just say I'm ready to go out there and dance.

HALLY. It looked like it. What about you, Willie?
Willie groans.
What's the matter?

SAM. He's got leg trouble.

HALLY (*innocently*). Oh, sorry to hear that, Willie.

WILLIE. Boet Sam! You promised. (*Willie returns to his work.*)

Hally deposits his school case and takes off his raincoat. His clothes are a little neglected and untidy: black blazer with school badge, gray flannel trousers in need of an ironing, khaki shirt and tie, black shoes. Sam has fetched a towel for Hally to dry his hair.

HALLY. God, what a lousy bloody day. It's coming down cats and dogs out there. Bad for business, chaps . . . (*Conspiratorial whisper.*) . . . but it also means we're in for a nice quiet afternoon.

SAM. You can speak loud, Your Mom's not here.

HALLY. Out shopping?

SAM. No. The hospital.

HALLY. But it's Thursday. There's no visiting on Thursday afternoons. Is my Dad okay?

SAM. Sounds like it. In fact, I think he's going home.

HALLY (*stopped short by Sam's remark*). What do you mean?

SAM. The hospital phoned.

HALLY. To say what?

SAM. I don't know. I just heard your Mom talking.

HALLY. So what makes you say he's going home?

SAM. It sounded as if they were telling her to come and fetch him.

Hally thinks about what Sam has said for a few seconds.

HALLY. When did she leave?

SAM. About an hour ago. She said she would phone you. Want to eat?

Hally doesn't respond.

Hally, want your lunch?

HALLY. I suppose so. (*His mood has changed.*) What's on the menu? . . . as if I don't know.

SAM. Soup, followed by meat pie and gravy.

HALLY. Today's?

SAM. No.

HALLY. And the soup?

SAM. Nourishing pea soup.

HALLY. Just the soup. (*The pile of comic books on the table.*) And these?

SAM. For your Dad. Mr. Kempston brought them.

HALLY. You haven't been reading them, have you?

SAM. Just looking.

HALLY (*examining the comics*). Jungle Jim . . . Batman and Robin . . . Tarzan . . . God, what rubbish! Mental pollution. Take them away.

Sam exits waltzing into the kitchen. Hally turns to Willie.

HALLY. Did you hear my Mom talking on the telephone, Willie?

WILLIE. No, Master Hally. I was at the back.

HALLY. And she didn't say anything to you before she left?

WILLIE. She said I must clean the floors.

HALLY. I mean about my Dad.

WILLIE. She didn't say nothing to me about him, Master Hally.

HALLY (*with conviction*). No! It can't be. They said he needed at least another three weeks of treatment. Sam's definitely made a mistake. (*Rummages through his school case, finds a book and settles down at the table to read.*) So, Willie!

WILLIE. Yes, Master Hally! Schooling okay today?

HALLY. Yes, okay. . . . (*He thinks about it.*) . . . No, not really. Ag, what's the difference? I don't care. And Sam says you've got problems.

WILLIE. Big problems.

HALLY. Which leg is sore?

Willie groans.

Both legs.

WILLIE. There is nothing wrong with my legs. Sam is just making jokes.

HALLY. So then you will be in the competition.

WILLIE. Only if I can find me a partner.

HALLY. But what about Hilda?

SAM (*returning with a bowl of soup*). She's the one who's got trouble with her legs.

HALLY. What sort of trouble, Willie?

SAM. From the way he describes it, I think the lady has gone a bit lame.

HALLY. Good God! Have you taken her to see a doctor?

SAM. I think a vet would be better.

HALLY. What do you mean?

SAM. What do you call it again when a racehorse goes very fast?

HALLY. Gallop?

SAM. That's it!

WILLIE. Boet Sam!

HALLY. "A gallop down the homestretch to the winning post." But what's that got to do with Hilda?

SAM. Count Basie always gets there first.

Willie lets fly with his slop rag. It misses Sam and hits Hally.

HALLY (*furious*). For Christ's sake, Willie! What the hell do you think you're doing!

WILLIE. Sorry, Master Hally, but it's him. . . .

HALLY. Act your bloody age! (*Hurls the rag back at Willie.*) Cut out the nonsense now and get on with your work. And you too, Sam. Stop fooling around.

Sam moves away.

No. Hang on. I haven't finished! Tell me exactly what my Mom said.

SAM. I have. "When Hally comes, tell him I've gone to the hospital and I'll phone him."

HALLY. She didn't say anything about taking my Dad home?

SAM. No. It's just that when she was talking on the phone . . .

HALLY (*interrupting him*). No, Sam. They can't be discharging him. She would have said so if they were. In any case, we saw him last night and he wasn't in good shape at all. Staff nurse even said there was talk about taking more X-rays. And now suddenly today he's better? If anything, it sounds more like a bad turn to me . . . which I sincerely hope it isn't. Hang on . . . how long ago did you say she left?

SAM. Just before two . . . (*His wrist watch.*) . . . hour and a half.

HALLY. I know how to settle it. (*Behind the counter to the telephone. Talking as he dials.*) Let's give her ten minutes to get to the hospital, ten minutes to load him up, another ten, at the most, to get home and another ten to get him inside. Forty minutes. They should have been home for at least half an hour already. (*Pause—he waits with the receiver to his ear.*) No reply, chaps. And you know why? Because she's at his bedside in hospital helping him pull through a bad turn. You definitely heard wrong.

SAM. Okay.

As far as Hally is concerned, the matter is settled. He returns to his table, sits down and divides his attention between the book and his soup. Sam is at his school case and picks up a textbook "Modern Graded Mathematics for Standards Nine and Ten." Opens it at random and laughs at something he sees.

Who is this supposed to be?

HALLY. Old fart-face Prentice.

SAM. Teacher?

HALLY. Thinks he is. And believe me, that is not a bad likeness.

SAM. Has he seen it?

HALLY. Yes.

SAM. What did he say?

HALLY. Tried to be clever, as usual. Said I was no Leonardo da Vinci and that bad art had to be punished. So, six of the best, and his are bloody good.

SAM. On your bum?

HALLY. Where else? The days when I got them on my hands are gone forever, Sam.

SAM. With your trousers down!

HALLY. No. He's not quite that barbaric.

SAM. That's the way they do it in jail.

HALLY (flicker of morbid interest). Really?

SAM. Ja. When the magistrate sentences you to "strokes with a light cane."

HALLY. Go on.

SAM. They make you lie down on a bench. One policeman pulls down your trousers and holds your ankles, another one pulls your shirt over your head and holds your arms . . .

HALLY. Thank you! That's enough.

SAM. . . . and the one that gives you the strokes talks to you gently and for a long time between each one. (He laughs.)

HALLY. I've heard enough, Sam! Jesus! It's a bloody awful world when you come to think of it. People can be real bastards.

SAM. That's the way it is, Hally.

HALLY. It doesn't have to be that way. There is something called progress, you know. We don't exactly burn people at the stake anymore.

SAM. Like Joan of Arc.

HALLY. Correct. If she was captured today, she'd be given a fair trial.

SAM. And then the death sentence.

HALLY (a world-weary sigh). I know, I know! I oscillate between hope and despair for this world as well, Sam. But things will change, you wait and see. One day somebody is going to get up and give history a kick up the backside and get it going again.

SAM. Like who?

HALLY (after thought). They're called social reformers. Every age, Sam, has got its social reformer. My history book is full of them.

SAM. So where's ours?

HALLY. Good question. And I hate to say it, but the answer is: I don't know. Maybe he hasn't even been born yet. Or is still only a babe in arms at his mother's breast. God, what a thought.

SAM. So we just go on waiting.

HALLY. Ja, looks like it. (Back to his soup and the book.)

SAM (reading from the textbook). "Introduction: In some mathematical problems only the magnitude . . ." (He mispronounces the word "magnitude.")

HALLY (correcting him without looking up). Magnitude.

SAM. What's it mean?

HALLY. How big it is. The size of the thing.

SAM (reading). ". . . a magnitude of the quantities is of importance. In other problems we need to know whether these quantities are negative or positive. For example, whether there is a debit or credit bank balance . . ."

HALLY. Whether you're broke or not.

SAM. ". . . whether the temperature is above or below Zero . . ."

HALLY. Naught degrees. Cheerful state of affairs! No cash and you're freezing to death. Mathematics won't get you out of that one.

SAM. "All these quantities are called . . ." (Spelling the word.) . . . s-c-a-l . . .

HALLY. Scalars.

SAM. Scalars! (Shaking his head with a laugh.) You understand all that?

HALLY (turning a page). No. And I don't intend to try.

SAM. So what happens when the exams come?

HALLY. Failing a maths exam isn't the end of the world, Sam. How many times have I told you that examination results don't measure intelligence?

SAM. I would say about as many times as you've failed one of them.

HALLY (mirthlessly). Ha, ha, ha.

SAM (simultaneously). Ha, ha, ha.

HALLY. Just remember Winston Churchill didn't do particularly well at school.

SAM. You've also told me that one many times.

HALLY. Well, it just so happens to be the truth.

SAM (enjoying the word). Magnitude! Magnitude! Show me how to use it.

HALLY (after thought). An intrepid social reformer will not be daunted by the magnitude of the task he has undertaken.

SAM (impressed). Couple of jaw-breakers in there!

HALLY. I gave you three for the price of one. Intrepid, daunted and magnitude. I did that once in an exam. Put five of the words I had to explain in one sentence. It was half a page long.

SAM. Well, I'll put my money on you in the English exam.

HALLY. Piece of cake. Eighty percent without even trying.

SAM (another textbook from Hally's case). And history?

HALLY. So-so. I'll scrape through. In the fifties if I'm lucky.

SAM. You didn't do too badly last year.

HALLY. Because we had World War One. That at least had some action. You try to find that in the South African Parliamentary system.

SAM (reading from the history textbook). "Napoleon and the

principle of equality." Hey! This sounds interesting. "After concluding peace with Britain in 1802, Napoleon used a brief period of calm to in-sti-tute . . . "

HALLY. Introduce.

SAM. " . . . many reforms. Napoleon regarded all people as equal before the law and wanted them to have equal opportunities for advancement. All ves-ti-ges of the feu-dal system with its oppression of the poor were abolished." Vestiges, feudal system and abolished. I'm all right on oppression.

HALLY. I'm thinking. He swept away . . . abolished . . . the last remains . . . vestiges . . . of the bad old days . . . feudal system.

SAM. Ha! There's the social reformer we're waiting for. He sounds like a man of some magnitude.

HALLY. I'm not so sure about that. It's a damn good title for a book, though. A man of magnitude!

SAM. He sounds pretty big to me, Hally.

HALLY. Don't confuse historical significance with greatness. But maybe I'm being a bit prejudiced. Have a look in there and you'll see he's two chapters long. And hell! . . . has he only got dates, Sam, all of which you've got to remember! This campaign and that campaign, and then, because of all the fighting, the next thing is we get Peace Treaties all over the place. And what's the end of the story? Battle of Waterloo, which he loses. Wasn't worth it. No, I don't know about him as a man of magnitude.

SAM. Then who would you say was?

HALLY. To answer that, we need a definition of greatness, and I suppose that would be somebody who . . . somebody who benefited all mankind.

SAM. Right. But like who?

HALLY. (*He speaks with total conviction.*) Charles Darwin. Remember him? That big book from the library. *The Origin of the Species.*

SAM. Him?

HALLY. Yes. For his Theory of Evolution.

SAM. You didn't finish it.

HALLY. I ran out of time. I didn't finish it because my two weeks was up. But I'm going to take it out again after I've digested what I read. It's safe. I've hidden it away in the Theology section. Nobody ever goes in there. And anyway who are you to talk? You hardly even looked at it.

SAM. I tried. I looked at the chapters in the beginning and I saw one called "The Struggle for an Existence." Ah ha, I thought. At last! But what did I get? Something called the mistletoe which needs the apple tree and there's too many seeds and all are going to die except one . . . ! No, Hally.

HALLY (*intellectually outraged*). What do you mean, No! The poor man had to start somewhere. For God's sake, Sam, he revolutionized science. Now we know.

SAM. What?

HALLY. Where we come from and what it all means.

SAM. And that's a benefit to mankind? Anyway, I still don't believe it.

HALLY. God, you're impossible. I showed it to you in black and white.

SAM. Doesn't mean I got to believe it.

HALLY. It's the likes of you that kept the Inquisition in business. It's called bigotry. Anyway, that's my man of magnitude. Charles Darwin! Who's yours?

SAM (*without hesitation*). Abraham Lincoln.

HALLY. I might have guessed as much. Don't get sentimental, Sam. You've never been a slave, you know. And anyway we freed your ancestors here in South Africa long before the Americans. But if you want to thank somebody on their behalf, do it to Mr. William Wilberforce.[5] Come on. Try again. I want a real genius. (*Now enjoying himself, and so is Sam. Hally goes behind the counter and helps himself to a chocolate.*)

SAM. William Shakespeare.

HALLY (*no enthusiasm*). Oh. So you're also one of them, are you? You're basing that opinion on only one play, you know. You've only read my *Julius Caesar* and even I don't understand half of what they're talking about. They should do what they did with the old Bible: bring the language up to date.

SAM. That's all you've got. It's also the only one you've read.

HALLY. I know. I admit it. That's why I suggest we reserve our judgment until we've checked up on a few others. I've got a feeling, though, that by the end of this year one is going to be enough for me, and I can give you the names of twenty-nine other chaps in the Standard Nine class of the Port Elizabeth Technical College who feel the same. But if you want him, you can have him. My turn now. (*Pacing.*) This is a damned good exercise, you know! It started off looking like a simple question and here it's got us really probing into the intellectual heritage of our civilization.

SAM. So who is it going to be?

HALLY. My next man . . . and he gets the title on two scores: social reform and literary genius . . . is Leo Nikolaevich Tolstoy.

SAM. That Russian.

HALLY. Correct. Remember the picture of him I showed you?

SAM. With the long beard.

HALLY (*trying to look like Tolstoy*). And those burning, visionary eyes. My God, the face of a social prophet if ever I saw one! And remember my words when I showed it to you? Here's a *man*, Sam!

SAM. Those were words, Hally.

HALLY. Not many intellectuals are prepared to shovel manure with the peasants and then go home and write a "little book" called *War and Peace*. Incidentally, Sam, he was

[5]**William Wilberforce** (1759–1833) English abolitionist

somebody else who, to quote, "... did not distinguish himself scholastically."

SAM. Meaning?

HALLY. He was also no good at school.

SAM. Like you and Winston Churchill.

HALLY. (*mirthlessly*). Ha, ha, ha.

SAM (*simultaneously*). Ha, ha, ha.

HALLY. Don't get clever, Sam. That man freed his serfs of his own free will.

SAM. No argument. He was a somebody, all right. I accept him.

HALLY. I'm sure Count Tolstoy will be very pleased to hear that. Your turn. Shoot. (*Another chocolate from behind the counter.*) I'm waiting, Sam.

SAM. I've got him.

HALLY. Good. Submit your candidate for examination.

SAM. Jesus.

HALLY (*stopped dead in his tracks*). Who?

SAM. Jesus Christ.

HALLY. Oh, come on, Sam!

SAM. The Messiah.

HALLY. Ja, but still ... No, Sam. Don't let's get started on religion. We'll just spend the whole afternoon arguing again. Suppose I turn around and say Mohammed?

SAM. All right.

HALLY. You can't have them both on the same list!

SAM. Why not? You like Mohammed, I like Jesus.

HALLY. I *don't* like Mohammed. I never have. I was merely being hypothetical. As far as I'm concerned, the Koran is as bad as the Bible. No. Religion is out! I'm not going to waste my time again arguing with you about the existence of God. You know perfectly well I'm an atheist ... and I've got homework to do.

SAM. Okay, I take him back.

HALLY. You've got time for one more name.

SAM (*after thought*). I've got one I know we'll agree on. A simple straightforward great Man of Magnitude ... and no arguments. And he really did benefit all mankind.

HALLY. I wonder. After your last contribution I'm beginning to doubt whether anything in the way of an intellectual agreement is possible between the two of us. Who is he?

SAM. Guess.

HALLY. Socrates? Alexandre Dumas? Karl Marx? Dostoevsky? Nietzsche?

Sam shakes his head after each name.

Give me a clue.

SAM. The letter P is important ...

HALLY. Plato!

SAM. ... and his name begins with an F.

HALLY. I've got it. Freud and Psychology.

SAM. No. I didn't understand him.

HALLY. That makes two of us.

SAM. Think of mouldy apricot jam.

HALLY (*after a delighted laugh*). Penicillin and Sir Alexander Fleming! And the title of the book: *The Microbe Hunters*. (*Delighted.*) Splendid, Sam! Splendid. For once we are in total agreement. The major breakthrough in medical science in the Twentieth Century. If it wasn't for him, we might have lost the Second World War. It's deeply gratifying, Sam, to know that I haven't been wasting my time in talking to you. (*Strutting around proudly.*) Tolstoy may have educated his peasants, but I've educated you.

SAM. Standard Four to Standard Nine.

HALLY. Have we been at it as long as that?

SAM. Yep. And my first lesson was geography.

HALLY (*intrigued*). Really? I don't remember.

SAM. My room there at the back of the old Jubilee Boarding House. I had just started working for your Mom. Little boy in short trousers walks in one afternoon and asks me seriously: "Sam, do you want to see South Africa?" Hey man! Sure I wanted to see South Africa!

HALLY. Was that me?

SAM. ... So the next thing I'm looking at a map you had just done for homework. It was your first one and you were very proud of yourself.

HALLY. Go on.

SAM. Then came my first lesson. "Repeat after me, Sam: Gold in the Transvaal, mealies in the Free State, sugar in Natal and grapes in the Cape." I still know it!

HALLY. Well, I'll be buggered. So that's how it all started.

SAM. And your next map was one with all the rivers and the mountains they came from. The Orange, the Vaal, the Limpopo, the Zambezi ...

HALLY. You've got a phenomenal memory!

SAM. You should be grateful. That is why you started passing your exams. You tried to be better than me.

They laugh together. Willie is attracted by the laughter and joins them.

HALLY. The old Jubilee Boarding House. Sixteen rooms with board and lodging, rent in advance and one week's notice. I haven't thought about it for donkey's years ... and I don't think that's an accident. God, was I glad when we sold it and moved out. Those years are not remembered as the happiest ones of an unhappy childhood.

WILLIE (*knocking on the table and trying to imitate a woman's voice*). "Hally, are you there?"

HALLY. Who's that supposed to be?

WILLIE. "What you doing in there, Hally? Come out at once!"

HALLY (*to Sam*). What's he talking about?

SAM. Don't you remember?

WILLIE. "Sam, Willie ... is he in there with you boys?"

SAM. Hiding away in our room when your mother was looking for you.

HALLY (*another good laugh*). Of course! I used to crawl and hide under your bed! But finish the story, Willie. Then what used to happen? You chaps would give the game away by telling her I was in there with you. So much for friendship.

SAM. We couldn't lie to her. She knew.

HALLY. Which meant I got another rowing for hanging around the "servants' quarters." I think I spent more time in there with you chaps than anywhere else in that dump. And do you blame me? Nothing but bloody misery wherever you went. Somebody was always complaining about the food, or my mother was having a fight with Micky Nash because she'd caught her with a petty officer in her room. Maud Meiring was another one. Remember those two? They were prostitutes, you know. Soldiers and sailors from the troopships. Bottom fell out of the business when the war ended. God, the flotsam and jetsam that life washed up on our shores! No joking, if it wasn't for your room, I would have been the first certified ten-year-old in medical history. Ja, the memories are coming back now. Walking home from school and thinking: "What can I do this afternoon?" Try out a few ideas, but sooner or later I'd end up in there with you fellows. I bet you I could still find my way to your room with my eyes closed. (*He does exactly that.*) Down the corridor . . . telephone on the right, which my Mom keeps locked because somebody is using it on the sly and not paying . . . past the kitchen and unappetizing cooking smells . . . around the corner into the backyard, hold my breath again because there are more smells coming when I pass your lavatory, then into that little passageway, first door on the right and into your room. How's that?

SAM. Good. But, as usual, you forgot to knock.

HALLY. Like that time I barged in and caught you and Cynthia . . . at it. Remember? God, was I embarrassed! I didn't know what was going on at first.

SAM. Ja, that taught you a lesson.

HALLY. And about a lot more than knocking on doors, I'll have you know, and I don't mean geography either. Hell, Sam, couldn't you have waited until it was dark?

SAM. No.

HALLY. Was it that urgent?

SAM. Yes, and if you don't believe me, wait until your time comes.

HALLY. No, thank you. I am not interested in girls. (*Back to his memories . . . Using a few chairs he recreates the room as he lists the items.*) A gray little room with a cold cement floor. Your bed against that wall . . . and I now know why the mattress sags so much! . . . Willie's bed . . . it's propped up on bricks because one leg is broken . . . that wobbly little table with the washbasin and jug of water . . . Yes! . . . stuck to the wall above it are some pin-up pictures from magazines. Joe Louis[6] . . .

[6] **Joe Louis** (1914–1981) African-American prizefighter known as the Brown Bomber

WILLIE. Brown Bomber. World Title. (*Boxing pose.*) Three rounds and knockout.

HALLY. Against who?

SAM. Max Schmeling.

HALLY. Correct. I can also remember Fred Astaire and Ginger Rogers, and Rita Hayworth in a bathing costume which always made me hot and bothered when I looked at it. Under Willie's bed is an old suitcase with all his clothes in a mess, which is why I never hide there. Your things are neat and tidy in a trunk next to your bed, and on it there is a picture of you and Cynthia in your ballroom clothes, your first silver cup for third place in a competition and an old radio which doesn't work anymore. Have I left out anything?

SAM. No.

HALLY. Right, so much for the stage directions. Now the characters. (*Sam and Willie move to their appropriate positions in the bedroom.*) Willie is in bed, under his blankets with his clothes on, complaining nonstop about something, but we can't make out a word of what he's saying because he's got his head under the blankets as well. You're on your bed trimming your toenails with a knife—not a very edifying sight—and as for me . . . What am I doing?

SAM. You're sitting on the floor giving Willie a lecture about being a good loser while you get the checker board and pieces ready for a game. Then you go to Willie's bed, pull off the blankets and make him play with you first because you know you're going to win, and that gives you the second game with me.

HALLY. And you certainly were a bad loser, Willie!

WILLIE. Haai!

HALLY. Wasn't he, Sam? And so slow! A game with you almost took the whole afternoon. Thank God I gave up trying to teach you how to play chess.

WILLIE. You and Sam cheated.

HALLY. I never saw Sam cheat, and mine were mostly the mistakes of youth.

WILLIE. Then how is it you two was always winning?

HALLY. Have you ever considered the possibility, Willie, that it was because we were better than you?

WILLIE. Every time better?

HALLY. Not every time. There were occasions when we deliberately let you win a game so that you would stop sulking and go on playing with us. Sam used to wink at me when you weren't looking to show me it was time to let you win.

WILLIE. So then you two didn't play fair.

HALLY. It was for your benefit, Mr. Malopo, which is more than being fair. It was an act of self-sacrifice. (*To Sam.*) But you know what my best memory is, don't you?

SAM. No.

HALLY. Come on, guess. If your memory is so good, you must remember it as well.

SAM. We got up to a lot of tricks in there, Hally.

HALLY. This one was special, Sam.

SAM. I'm listening.

HALLY. It started off looking like another of those useless nothing-to-do afternoons. I'd already been down to Main Street looking for adventure, but nothing had happened. I didn't feel like climbing trees in the Donkin Park or pretending I was a private eye and following a stranger . . . so as usual: See what's cooking in Sam's room. This time it was you on the floor. You had two thin pieces of wood and you were smoothing them down with a knife. It didn't look particularly interesting, but when I asked you what you were doing, you just said, "Wait and see, Hally. Wait . . . and see" . . . in that secret sort of way of yours, so I knew there was a surprise coming. You teased me, you bugger, by being deliberately slow and not answering my questions!

Sam laughs.

And whistling while you worked away! God, it was infuriating! I could have brained you! It was only when you tied them together in a cross and put that down on the brown paper that I realized what you were doing. "Sam is making a kite?" And when I asked you and you said "Yes" . . . ! (*Shaking his head with disbelief.*) The sheer audacity of it took my breath away. I mean, seriously, what the hell does a black man know about flying a kite? I'll be honest with you, Sam, I had no hopes for it. If you think I was excited and happy, you got another guess coming. In fact, I was shit-scared that we were going to make fools of ourselves. When we left the boarding house to go up onto the hill, I was praying quietly that there wouldn't be any other kids around to laugh at us.

SAM (*enjoying the memory as much as Hally*). Ja, I could see that.

HALLY. I made it obvious, did I?

SAM. Ja. You refused to carry it.

HALLY. Do you blame me? Can you remember what the poor thing looked like? Tomato-box wood and brown paper! Flour and water for glue! Two of my mother's old stockings for a tail, and then all those bits and pieces of string you made me tie together so that we could fly it! Hell, no, that was now only asking for a miracle to happen.

SAM. Then the big argument when I told you to hold the string and run with it when I let go.

HALLY. I was prepared to run, all right, but straight back to the boarding house.

SAM (*knowing what's coming*). So what happened?

HALLY. Come on, Sam, you remember as well as I do.

SAM. I want to hear it from you.

Hally pauses. He wants to be as accurate as possible.

HALLY. You went a little distance from me down the hill, you held it up ready to let it go. . . . "This is it," I thought. "Like everything else in my life, here comes another fiasco." Then you shouted, "Go, Hally!" and I started to run. (*Another pause.*) I don't know how to describe it, Sam. Ja! The miracle happened! I was running, waiting for it to crash to the ground, but instead suddenly there was something alive behind me at the end of the string, tugging at it as if it wanted to be free. I looked back . . . (*Shakes his head.*) . . . I still can't believe my eyes. It was flying! Looping around and trying to climb even higher into the sky. You shouted to me to let it have more string. I did, until there was none left and I was just holding that piece of wood we had tied it to. You came up and joined me. You were laughing.

SAM. So were you. And shouting, "It works, Sam! We've done it!"

HALLY. And we had! I was so proud of us! It was the most splendid thing I had ever seen. I wished there were hundreds of kids around to watch us. The part that scared me, though, was when you showed me how to make it dive down to the ground and then just when it was on the point of crashing, swoop up again!

SAM. You didn't want to try yourself.

HALLY. Of course not! I would have been suicidal if anything had happened to it. Watching you do it made me nervous enough. I was quite happy just to see it up there with its tail fluttering behind it. You left me after that, didn't you? You explained how to get it down, we tied it to the bench so that I could sit and watch it, and you went away. I wanted you to stay, you know. I was a little scared of having to look after it by myself.

SAM (*quietly*). I had work to do, Hally.

HALLY. It was sort of sad bringing it down, Sam. And it looked sad again when it was lying there on the ground. Like something that had lost its soul. Just tomato-box wood, brown paper and two of my mother's old stockings! But, hell, I'll never forget that first moment when I saw it up there. I had a stiff neck the next day from looking up so much.

Sam laughs. Hally turns to him with a question he never thought of asking before.

Why did you make that kite, Sam?

SAM (*evenly*). I can't remember.

HALLY. Truly?

SAM. Too long ago, Hally.

HALLY. Ja, I suppose it was. It's time for another one, you know.

SAM. Why do you say that?

HALLY. Because it feels like that. Wouldn't be a good day to fly it, though.

SAM. No. You can't fly kites on rainy days.

HALLY. (*He studies Sam. Their memories have made him conscious of the man's presence in his life.*) How old are you, Sam?

SAM. Two score and five.

HALLY. Strange, isn't it?

SAM. What?

HALLY. Me and you.

SAM. What's strange about it?

HALLY. Little white boy in short trousers and a black man old enough to be his father flying a kite. It's not every day you see that.

SAM. But why strange? Because the one is white and the other black?

HALLY. I don't know. Would have been just as strange, I suppose, if it had been me and my Dad . . . cripple man and a little boy! Nope! There's no chance of me flying a kite without it being strange. (*Simple statement of fact—no self-pity*.) There's a nice little short story there. "The Kite-Flyers." But we'd have to find a twist in the ending.

SAM. Twist?

HALLY. Yes. Something unexpected. The way it ended with us was too straightforward . . . me on the bench and you going back to work. There's no drama in that.

WILLIE. And me?

HALLY. You?

WILLIE. Yes me.

HALLY. You want to get into the story as well, do you? I got it! Change the title: "Afternoons in Sam's Room" . . . expand it and tell all the stories. It's on its way to being a novel. Our days in the old Jubilee. Sad in a way that they're over. I almost wish we were still in that little room.

SAM. We're still together.

HALLY. That's true. It's just that life felt the right size in there . . . not too big and not too small. Wasn't so hard to work up a bit of courage. It's got so bloody complicated since then.

The telephone rings. Sam answers it.

SAM. St. George's Park Tea Room . . . Hello, Madam . . . Yes, Madam, he's here . . . Hally, it's your mother.

HALLY. Where is she phoning from?

SAM. Sounds like the hospital. It's a public telephone.

HALLY (*relieved*). You see! I told you. (*The telephone.*) Hello, Mom . . . Yes . . . Yes no fine. Everything's under control here. How's things with poor old Dad? . . . Has he had a bad turn? . . . What? . . . Oh, God! . . . Yes, Sam told me, but I was sure he'd made a mistake. But what's this all about, Mom? He didn't look at all good last night. How can he get better so quickly? . . . Then very obviously you must say no. Be firm with him. You're the boss. . . . You know what it's going to be like if he comes home. . . . Well, then, don't blame me when I fail my exams at the end of the year. . . . Yes! How am I expected to be fresh for school when I spend half the night massaging his gammy leg? . . . So am I! . . . So tell him a white lie. Say Dr. Colley wants more X-rays of his stump. Or bribe him. We'll sneak in double tots of brandy in future. . . . What? . . . Order him to get back into bed at once! If he's going to behave like a child, treat him like one. . . . All right, Mom! I was just trying to . . . I'm sorry. . . . I said I'm sorry. . . . Quick, give me your number. I'll phone you

back. (*He hangs up and waits a few seconds.*) Here we go again! (*He dials.*) I'm sorry, Mom. . . . Okay . . . But now listen to me carefully. All it needs is for you to put your foot down. Don't take no for an answer. . . . Did you hear me? And whatever you do, don't discuss it with him. . . . Because I'm frightened you'll give in to him. . . . Yes, Sam gave me lunch. . . . I ate all of it! . . . No, Mom not a soul. It's still raining here. . . . Right, I'll tell them. I'll just do some homework and then lock up. . . . But remember now, Mom. Don't listen to anything he says. And phone me back and let me know what happens. . . . Okay. Bye, Mom. (*He hangs up. The men are staring at him.*) My Mom says that when you're finished with the floors you must do the windows. (*Pause.*) Don't misunderstand me, chaps. All I want is for him to get better. And if he was, I'd be the first person to say: "Bring him home." But he's not, and we can't give him the medical care and attention he needs at home. That's what hospitals are there for. (*Brusquely.*) So don't just stand there! Get on with it!

Sam clears Hally's table.

You heard right. My Dad wants to go home.

SAM. Is he better?

HALLY (*sharply*.). No! How the hell can he be better when last night he was groaning with pain? This is not an age of miracles!

SAM. Then he should stay in hospital.

HALLY (*seething with irritation and frustration*). Tell me something I don't know, Sam. What the hell do you think I was saying to my Mom? All I can say is fuck-it-all.

SAM. I'm sure he'll listen to your Mom.

HALLY. You don't know what she's up against. He's already packed his shaving kit and pajamas and is sitting on his bed with his crutches, dressed and ready to go. I know him when he gets in that mood. If she tries to reason with him, we've had it. She's no match for him when it comes to a battle of words. He'll tie her up in knots. (*Trying to hide his true feelings.*)

SAM. I suppose it gets lonely for him in there.

HALLY. With all the patients and nurses around? Regular visits from the Salvation Army? Balls! It's ten times worse for him at home. I'm at school and my mother is here in the business all day.

SAM. He's at least got you at night.

HALLY (*before he can stop himself*). And we've got him! Please! I don't want to talk about it anymore. (*Unpacks his school case, slamming down books on the table.*) Life is just a plain bloody mess, that's all. And people are fools.

SAM. Come on, Hally.

HALLY. Yes, they are! They bloody well deserve what they get.

SAM. Then don't complain.

HALLY. Don't try to be clever, Sam. It doesn't suit you. Anybody who thinks there's nothing wrong with this world needs to have his head examined. Just when things are going along all right, without fail someone or something will come along and spoil everything. Somebody should write that down as a fundamental law of the Universe. The principle of perpetual disappointment. If there is a God who created this world, he should scrap it and try again.

SAM. All right, Hally, all right. What you got for homework?

HALLY. Bullshit, as usual. (*Opens an exercise book and reads.*) "Write five hundred words describing an annual event of cultural or historical significance."

SAM. That should be easy enough for you.

HALLY. And also plain bloody boring. You know what he wants, don't you? One of their useless old ceremonies. The commemoration of the landing of the 1820 Settlers, or if it's going to be culture, Carols by Candlelight every Christmas.

SAM. It's an impressive sight. Make a good description, Hally. All those candles glowing in the dark and the people singing hymns.

HALLY. And it's called religious hysteria. (*Intense irritation.*) Please, Sam! Just leave me alone and let me get on with it. I'm not in the mood for games this afternoon. And remember my Mom's orders . . . you're to help Willie with the windows. Come on now, I don't want any more nonsense in here.

SAM. Okay, Hally, okay.

Hally settles down to his homework; determined preparations . . . pen, ruler, exercise book, dictionary, another cake . . . all of which will lead to nothing. (Sam waltzes over to Willie and starts to replace tables and chairs. He practices a ballroom step while doing so. Willie watches. When Sam is finished, Willie tries.)

Good! But just a little bit quicker on the turn and only move in to her after she's crossed over. What about this one?

Another step. When Sam is finished, Willie again has a go.

Much better. See what happens when you just relax and enjoy yourself? Remember that in two weeks' time and you'll be all right.

WILLIE. But I haven't got partner, Boet Sam.

SAM. Maybe Hilda will turn up tonight.

WILLIE. No, Boet Sam. (*Reluctantly.*) I gave her a good hiding.

SAM. You mean a bad one.

WILLIE. Good bad one.

SAM. Then you mustn't complain either. Now you pay the price for losing your temper.

WILLIE. I also pay two pounds ten shilling entrance fee.

SAM. They'll refund you if you withdraw now.

WILLIE (*appalled*). You mean, don't dance?

SAM. Yes.

WILLIE. No! I wait too long and I practice too hard. If I find me new partner, you think I can be ready in two weeks? I ask Madam for my leave now and we practice every day.

SAM. Quickstep non-stop for two weeks. World record, Willie, but you'll be mad at the end.

WILLIE. No jokes, Boet Sam.

SAM. I'm not joking.

WILLIE. So then what?

SAM. Find Hilda. Say you're sorry and promise you won't beat her again.

WILLIE. No.

SAM. Then withdraw. Try again next year.

WILLIE. No.

SAM. Then I give up.

WILLIE. Haaikona, Boet Sam, you can't.

SAM. What do you mean, I can't? I'm telling you: I give up.

WILLIE (*adamant*). No! (*Accusingly.*) It was you who start me ballroom dancing.

SAM. So?

WILLIE. Before that I use to be happy. And is you and Miriam who bring me to Hilda and say here's partner for you.

SAM. What are you saying, Willie?

WILLIE. You!

SAM. But me what? To blame?

WILLIE. Yes.

SAM. Willie . . . ? (*Bursts into laughter.*)

WILLIE. And now all you do is make jokes at me. You wait. When Miriam leaves you is my turn to laugh. Ha! Ha! Ha!

SAM. (*He can't take Willie seriously any longer.*) She can leave me tonight! I know what to do. (*Bowing before an imaginary partner*). May I have the pleasure? (*He dances and sings.*)

"Just a fellow with his pillow . . .
Dancin' like a willow . . .
In an autumn breeze . . . "

WILLIE. There you go again!

Sam goes on dancing and singing.

Boet Sam!

SAM. There's the answer to your problem! Judges' announcement in two weeks' time: "Ladies and gentlemen, the winner in the open section . . . Mr. Willie Malopo and his pillow!"

This is too much for a now really angry Willie. He goes for Sam, but the latter is too quick for him and puts Hally's table between the two of them.

HALLY (*exploding*). For Christ's sake, you two!

WILLIE (*still trying to get at Sam*). I donner you, Sam! Struesgod!

SAM (*still laughing*). Sorry, Willie . . . Sorry . . .

HALLY. Sam! Willie! (*Grabs his ruler and gives Willie a vicious whack on the bum.*) How the hell am I supposed to concentrate with the two of you behaving like bloody children!

WILLIE. Hit him too!

HALLY. Shut up, Willie.

WILLIE. He started jokes again.
HALLY. Get back to your work. You too, Sam. (*His ruler.*) Do you want another one, Willie?

Sam and Willie return to their work. Hally uses the opportunity to escape from his unsuccessful attempt at homework. He struts around like a little despot, ruler in hand, giving vent to his anger and frustration.

Suppose a customer had walked in then? Or the Park Superintendent. And seen the two of you behaving like a pair of hooligans. That would have been the end of my mother's license, you know. And your jobs! Well, this is the end of it. From now on there will be no more of your ballroom nonsense in here. This is a business establishment, not a bloody New Brighton dancing school. I've been far too lenient with the two of you. (*Behind the counter for a green cool drink and a dollop of ice cream. He keeps up his tirade as he prepares it.*) But what really makes me bitter is that I allow you chaps a little freedom in here when business is bad and what do you do with it? The foxtrot! Specially you, Sam. There's more to life than trotting around a dance floor and I thought at least you knew it.
SAM. It's a harmless pleasure, Hally. It doesn't hurt anybody.
HALLY. It's also a rather simple one, you know.
SAM. You reckon so? Have you ever tried?
HALLY. Of course not.
SAM. Why don't you? Now.
HALLY. What do you mean? Me dance?
SAM. Yes. I'll show you a simple step—the waltz—then you try it.
HALLY. What will that prove?
SAM. That it might not be as easy as you think.
HALLY. I didn't say it was easy. I said it was simple—like in simple-minded, meaning mentally retarded. You can't exactly say it challenges the intellect.
SAM. It does other things.
HALLY. Such as?
SAM. Make people happy.
HALLY (*the glass in his hand*). So do American cream sodas with ice cream. For God's sake, Sam, you're not asking me to take ballroom dancing serious, are you?
SAM. Yes.
HALLY (*sigh of defeat*). Oh, well, so much for trying to give you a decent education. I've obviously achieved nothing.
SAM. You still haven't told me what's wrong with admiring something that's beautiful and then trying to do it yourself.
HALLY. Nothing. But we happen to be talking about a foxtrot, not a thing of beauty.
SAM. But that is just what I'm saying. If you were to see two champions doing, two masters of the art . . . !
HALLY. Oh, God, I give up. So now it's also art!
SAM. Ja.
HALLY. There's a limit, Sam. Don't confuse art and entertainment.

SAM. So then what is art?
HALLY. You want a definition?
SAM. Ja.
HALLY. (*He realizes he has got to be careful. He gives the matter a lot of thought before answering.*) Philosophers have been trying to do that for centuries. What is Art? What is Life? But basically I suppose it's . . . the giving of meaning to matter.
SAM. Nothing to do with beautiful?
HALLY. It goes beyond that. It's the giving of form to the formless.
SAM. Ja, well, maybe it's not art, then. But I still say it's beautiful.
HALLY. I'm sure the word you mean to use is entertaining.
SAM (*adamant*). No. Beautiful. And if you want proof, come along to the Centenary Hall in New Brighton in two weeks' time.

The mention of the Centenary Hall draws Willie over to them.

HALLY. What for? I've seen the two of you prancing around in here often enough.
SAM. (*He laughs.*) This isn't the real thing, Hally. We're just playing around in here.
HALLY. So? I can use my imagination.
SAM. And what do you get?
HALLY. A lot of people dancing around and having a so-called good time.
SAM. That all?
HALLY. Well, basically it is that, surely.
SAM. No, it isn't. Your imagination hasn't helped you at all. There's a lot more to it than that. We're getting ready for the championships, Hally, not just another dance. There's going to be a lot of people, all right, and they're going to have a good time, but they'll only be spectators, sitting around and watching. It's just the competitors out there on the dance floor. Party decorations and fancy lights all around the walls! The ladies in beautiful evening dresses!
HALLY. My mother's got one of those, Sam, and quite frankly, it's an embarrassment every time she wears it.
SAM (*undeterred*). Your imagination left out the excitement.

Hally scoffs.

Oh, yes. The finalists are not going to be out there just to have a good time. One of those couples will be the 1950 Eastern Province Champions. And your imagination left out the music.
WILLIE. Mr. Elijah Gladman Guzana and his Orchestral Jazzonions.
SAM. The sound of the big band, Hally. Trombone, trumpet, tenor and alto sax. And then, finally, your imagination also left out the climax of the evening when the dancing is finished, the judges have stopped whispering among themselves and the Master of Ceremonies collects their scorecards and goes up onto the stage to announce the winners.

HALLY. All right. So you make it sound like a bit of a do. It's an occasion. Satisfied?

SAM (*victory*). So you admit that!

HALLY. Emotionally yes, intellectually no.

SAM. Well, I don't know what you mean by that, all I'm telling you is that it is going to be the event of the year in New Brighton. It's been sold out for two weeks already. There's only standing room left. We've got competitors coming from Kingwilliamstown, East London, Port Alfred.

Hally starts pacing thoughtfully.

HALLY. Tell me a bit more.

SAM. I thought you weren't interested . . . intellectually.

HALLY (*mysteriously*). I've got my reasons.

SAM. What do you want to know?

HALLY. It takes place every year?

SAM. Yes. But only every third year in New Brighton. It's East London's turn to have the championships next year.

HALLY. Which, I suppose, makes it an even more significant event.

SAM. Ah ha! We're getting somewhere. Our "occasion" is now a "significant event."

HALLY. I wonder.

SAM. What?

HALLY. I wonder if I would get away with it.

SAM. But what?

HALLY (*to the table and his exercise book*). "Write five hundred words describing an annual event of cultural or historical significance." Would I be stretching poetic license a little too far if I called your ballroom championships a cultural event?

SAM. You mean . . . ?

HALLY. You think we could get five hundred words out of it, Sam?

SAM. Victor Sylvester has written a whole book on ballroom dancing.

WILLIE. You going to write about it, Master Hally?

HALLY. Yes, gentlemen, that is precisely what I am considering doing. Old Doc Bromely—he's my English teacher—is going to argue with me, of course. He doesn't like natives. But I'll point out to him that in strict anthropological terms the culture of a primitive black society includes its dancing and singing. To put my thesis in a nutshell: The war-dance has been replaced by the waltz. But it still amounts to the same thing: the release of primitive emotions through movement. Shall we give it a go?

SAM. I'm ready.

WILLIE. Me also.

HALLY. Ha! This will teach the old bugger a lesson. (*Decision taken.*) Right. Let's get ourselves organized. (*This means another cake on the table. He sits.*) I think you've given me enough general atmosphere, Sam, but to build the tension and suspense I need facts. (*Pencil poised.*)

WILLIE. Give him facts, Boet Sam.

HALLY. What you called the climax . . . how many finalists?

SAM. Six couples.

HALLY (*making notes*). Go on. Give me the picture.

SAM. Spectators seated right around the hall. (*Willie becomes a spectator.*)

HALLY. . . . and it's a full house.

SAM. At one end, on the stage, Gladman and his Orchestral Jazzonions. At the other end is a long table with the three judges. The six finalists go onto the dance floor and take up their positions. When they are ready and the spectators have settled down, the Master of Ceremonies goes to the microphone. To start with, he makes some jokes to get the people laughing . . .

HALLY. Good touch! (*As he writes.*) ". . . creating a relaxed atmosphere which will change to one of tension and drama as the climax is approached."

SAM (*onto a chair to act out the M.C.*). "Ladies and gentlemen, we come now to the great moment you have all been waiting for this evening. . . . The finals of the 1950 Eastern Province Open Ballroom Dancing Championships. But first let me introduce the finalists! Mr. and Mrs. Welcome Tchabalala from Kingwilliamstown . . ."

WILLIE (*He applauds after every name*). Is when the people clap their hands and whistle and make a lot of noise, Master Hally.

SAM. "Mr. Mulligan Njikelane and Miss Nomhle Nkonyeni of Grahamstown; Mr. and Mrs. Norman Nchinga from Port Alfred; Mr. Fats Bokolane and Miss Dina Plaatjies from East London; Mr. Sipho Dugu and Mrs. Mable Magada from Peddie; and from New Brighton our very own Mr. Willie Malopo and Miss Hilda Samuels."

Willie can't believe his ears. He abandons his role as spectator and scrambles into position as a finalist.

WILLIE. Relaxed and ready to romance!

SAM. The applause dies down. When everybody is silent, Gladman lifts up his sax, nods at the Orchestral Jazzonions . . .

WILLIE. Play the jukebox please, Boet Sam!

SAM. I also only got bus fare, Willie.

HALLY. Hold it, everybody. (*Heads for the cash register behind the counter.*) How much is in the till, Sam?

SAM. Three shillings. Hally . . . your Mom counted it before she left.

Hally hesitates.

HALLY. Sorry, Willie. You know how she carried on the last time I did it. We'll just have to pool our combined imaginations and hope for the best. (*Returns to the table.*) Back to work. How are the points scored, Sam?

SAM. Maximum of ten points each for individual style, deportment, rhythm and general appearance.

WILLIE. Must I start?

HALLY. Hold it for a second, Willie. And penalties?

SAM. For what?

HALLY. For doing something wrong. Say you stumble or bump into somebody . . . do they take off any points?

SAM (*aghast*). Hally . . . !

HALLY. When you're dancing. If you and your partner collide into another couple.

Hally can get no further. Sam has collapsed with laughter. He explains to Willie.

SAM. If me and Miriam bump into you and Hilda . . .

Willie joins him in another good laugh.

Hally, Hally . . . !

HALLY. (*perplexed*). Why? What did I say?

SAM. There's no collisions out there, Hally. Nobody trips or stumbles or bumps into anybody else. That's what that moment is all about. To be one of those finalists on that dance floor is like . . . like being in a dream about a world in which accidents don't happen.

HALLY (*genuinely moved by Sam's image*). Jesus, Sam! That's beautiful!

WILLIE (*can endure waiting no longer*). I'm starting! (*Willie dances while Sam talks.*)

SAM. Of course it is. That's what I've been trying to say to you all afternoon. And it's beautiful because that is what we want life to be like. But instead, like you said, Hally, we're bumping into each other all the time. Look at the three of us this afternoon: I've bumped into Willie, the two of us have bumped into you, you've bumped into your mother, she bumping into your Dad. . . . None of us knows the steps and there's no music playing. And it doesn't stop with us. The whole world is doing it all the time. Open a newspaper and what do you read? America has bumped into Russia, England is bumping into India, rich man bumps into poor man. Those are big collisions, Hally. They make for a lot of bruises. People get hurt in all that bumping, and we're sick and tired of it now. It's been going on for too long. Are we never going to get it right? . . . Learn to dance life like champions instead of always being just a bunch of beginners at it?

HALLY (*deep and sincere admiration of the man*). You've got a vision, Sam!

SAM. Not just me. What I'm saying to you is that everybody's got it. That's why there's only standing room left for the Centenary Hall in two weeks' time. For as long as the music lasts, we are going to see six couples get it right, the way we want life to be.

HALLY. But is that the best we can do, Sam . . . watch six finalists dreaming about the way it should be?

SAM. I don't know. But it starts with that. Without the dream we won't know what we're going for. And anyway I reckon there are a few people who have got past just dreaming about it and are trying for something real. Remember that thing we read once in the paper about the Mahatma Gandhi? Going without food to stop those riots in India?

HALLY. You're right. He certainly was trying to teach people to get the steps right.

SAM. And the Pope.

HALLY. Yes, he's another one. Our old General Smuts as well, you know. He's also out there dancing. You know, Sam, when you come to think of it, that's what the United Nations boils down to . . . a dancing school for politicians!

SAM. And let's hope they learn.

HALLY (*a little surge of hope*). You're right. We mustn't despair. Maybe there's some hope for mankind after all. Keep it up, Willie. (*Back to his table with determination.*) This is a lot bigger than I thought. So what have we got? Yes, our title: "A World Without Collisions."

SAM. That sounds good! "A World Without Collisions."

HALLY. Subtitle: "Global Politics on the Dance Floor." No. A bit too heavy, hey? What about "Ballroom Dancing as a Political Vision"?

The telephone rings. Sam answers it.

SAM. St. George's Park Tea Room . . . Yes, Madam . . . Hally, it's your Mom.

HALLY (*back to reality*). Oh, God, yes! I'd forgotten all about that. Shit! Remember my words, Sam? Just when you're enjoying yourself, someone or something will come along and wreck everything.

SAM. You haven't heard what she's got to say yet.

HALLY. Public telephone?

SAM. No.

HALLY. Does she sound happy or unhappy?

SAM. I couldn't tell. (*Pause.*) She's waiting, Hally.

HALLY (*to the telephone*). Hello, Mom . . . No, everything is okay here. Just doing my homework. . . . What's your news? . . . You've what? . . . (*Pause. He takes the receiver away from his ear for a few seconds. In the course of Hally's telephone conversation, Sam and Willie discretely position the stacked tables and chairs. Hally places the receiver back to his ear.*) Yes, I'm still here. Oh, well, I give up now. Why did you do it, Mom? . . . Well, I just hope you know what you've let us in for. . . . (*Loudly.*) I said I hope you know what you've let us in for! It's the end of the peace and quiet we've been having. (*Softly.*) Where is he? (*Normal voice.*) He can't hear us from in there. But for God's sake, Mom, what happened? I told you to be firm with him. . . . Then you and the nurses should have held him down, taken his crutches away. . . . I know only too well he's my father! . . . I'm not being disrespectful, but I'm sick and tired of emptying stinking chamberpots full of phlegm and piss. . . . Yes, I do! When you're not there, he asks *me* to do it. . . . If you really want to know the truth, that's why I've got no appetite for my food. . . . Yes! There's a lot of things you don't know about. For your information, I still haven't got that science textbook I need. And you know why? He borrowed the money you gave me for it. . . . Because I didn't want to start another fight between you two. . . . He says that every time. . . . All right, Mom! (*Viciously.*) Then just remember to start hiding your bag away again, because he'll be at your purse before long for money for booze. And when he's well enough to come down here, you better keep an eye on the till as well, because that is also going to develop a leak. . . . Then don't complain to me when he starts his old tricks. . . . Yes, you do. I get it from you on one side and from him on the other, and it makes life hell for me. I'm not going to be the peacemaker anymore. I'm warning you now: when the two of you start fighting again, I'm leaving home. . . . Mom, if you start crying, I'm going to put down the receiver. . . . Okay . . . (*Lowering his voice to a vicious whisper.*) Okay, Mom. I heard you. (*Desperate.*) No. . . . Because I don't want to. I'll see him when I get home! Mom! . . . (*Pause. When he speaks again, his tone changes completely. It is not simply pretense. We sense a genuine emotional conflict.*) Welcome home, chum! . . . What's that? . . . Don't be silly, Dad. You being home is just about the best news in the world. . . . I bet you are. Bloody depressing there with everybody going on about their ailments, hey! . . . How you feeling? . . . Good . . . Here as well, pal. Coming down cats and dogs. . . . That's right. Just the day for a kip and a toss in your old Uncle Ned. . . . Everything's just hunky-dory on my side, Dad. . . . Well, to start with, there's a nice pile of comics for you on the counter. . . . Yes, old Kemple brought them in. *Batman and Robin, Submariner* . . . just your cup of tea . . . I will. . . . Yes, we'll spin a few yarns tonight. . . . Okay, chum, see you in a little while. . . . No, I promise. I'll come straight home. . . . (*Pause—his mother comes back on the phone.*) Mom? Okay. I'll lock up now. . . . What? . . . Oh, the brandy . . . Yes, I'll remember! . . . I'll put it in my suitcase now, for God's sake. I know well enough what will happen if he doesn't get it. . . . (*Places a bottle of brandy on the counter.*) I was kind to him, Mom. I didn't say anything nasty! . . . All right. Bye. (*End of telephone conversation. A desolate Hally doesn't move. A strained silence.*)

SAM (*quietly*). That sounded like a bad bump, Hally.

HALLY (*having a hard time controlling his emotions. He speaks carefully*). Mind your own business, Sam.

SAM. Sorry. I wasn't trying to interfere. Shall we carry on? Hally? (*He indicates the exercise book. No response from Hally.*)

WILLIE. (*also trying*). Tell him about when they give out the cups, Boet Sam.

SAM. Ja! That's another big moment. The presentation of the cups after the winners have been announced. You've got to put that in.

Still no response from Hally.

WILLIE. A big silver one, Master Hally, called floating trophy for the champions.

SAM. We always invite some big-shot personality to hand

them over. Guest of honor this year is going to be His Holiness Bishop Jabulani of the All African Free Zionist Church.

Hally gets up abruptly, goes to his table and tears up the page he was writing on.

HALLY. So much for a bloody world without collisions.

SAM. Too bad. It was on its way to being a good composition.

HALLY. Let's stop bullshitting ourselves, Sam.

SAM. Have we been doing that?

HALLY. Yes! That's what all our talk about a decent world has been . . . just so much bullshit.

SAM. We did say it was still only a dream.

HALLY. And a bloody useless one at that. Life's a fuck-up and it's never going to change.

SAM. Ja, maybe that's true.

HALLY. There's no maybe about it. It's a blunt and brutal fact. All we've done this afternoon is waste our time.

SAM. Not if we'd got your homework done.

HALLY. I don't give a shit about my homework, so, for Christ's sake, just shut up about it. (*Slamming books viciously into his school case.*) Hurry up now and finish your work. I want to lock up and get out of here. (*Pause.*) And then go where? Home-sweet-fucking-home. Jesus, I hate that word.

Hally goes to the counter to put the brandy bottle and comics in his school case. After a moment's hesitation, he smashes the bottle of brandy. He abandons all further attempts to hide his feelings. Sam and Willie work away as unobtrusively as possible.

Do you want to know what is really wrong with your lovely little dream, Sam? It's not just that we are all bad dancers. That does happen to be perfectly true, but there's more to it than just that. You left out the cripples.

SAM. Hally!

HALLY (*now totally reckless*). Ja! Can't leave them out, Sam. That's why we always end up on our backsides on the dance floor. They're also out there dancing . . . like a bunch of broken spiders trying to do the quickstep! (*An ugly attempt at laughter.*) When you come to think of it, it's a bloody comical sight. I mean, it's bad enough on two legs . . . but one and a pair of crutches! Hell, no, Sam. That's guaranteed to turn that dance floor into a shambles. Why you shaking your head? Picture it, man. For once this afternoon let's use our imaginations sensibly.

SAM. Be careful, Hally.

HALLY. Of what? The truth? I seem to be the only one around here who is prepared to face it. We've had the pretty dream, it's time now to wake up and have a good long look at the way things really are. Nobody knows the steps, there's no music, the cripples are also out there tripping up everybody and trying to get into the act, and it's all called the All-Comers-How-to-Make-a-Fuckup-of-

Life Championships. (*Another ugly laugh.*) Hang on, Sam! The best bit is still coming. Do you know what the winner's trophy is? A beautiful big chamber-pot with roses on the side, and it's full to the brim with piss. And guess who I think is going to be this year's winner.

SAM (*almost shouting*). Stop now!

HALLY (*suddenly appalled by how far he has gone*). Why?

SAM. Hally? It's your father you're talking about.

HALLY. So?

SAM. Do you know what you've been saying?

Hally can't answer. He is rigid with shame. Sam speaks to him sternly.

No, Hally, you mustn't do it. Take back those words and ask for forgiveness! It's a terrible sin for a son to mock his father with jokes like that. You'll be punished if you carry on. Your father is your father, even if he is a . . . cripple man.

WILLIE. Yes, Master Hally. Is true what Sam say.

SAM. I understand how you are feeling, Hally, but even so . . .

HALLY. No, you don't!

SAM. I think I do.

HALLY. And I'm telling you you don't. Nobody does. (*Speaking carefully as his shame turns to rage at Sam.*) It's your turn to be careful, Sam. Very careful! You're treading on dangerous ground. Leave me and my father alone.

SAM. I'm not the one who's been saying things about him.

HALLY. What goes on between me and my Dad is none of your business!

SAM. Then don't tell me about it. If that's all you've got to say about him, I don't want to hear.

For a moment Hally is at loss for a response.

HALLY. Just get on with your bloody work and shut up.

SAM. Swearing at me won't help you.

HALLY. Yes, it does! Mind your own fucking business and shut up!

SAM. Okay. If that's the way you want it, I'll stop trying.

He turns away. This infuriates Hally even more.

HALLY. Good. Because what you've been trying to do is meddle in something you know nothing about. All that concerns you in here, Sam, is to try and do what you get paid for—keep the place clean and serve the customers. In plain words, just get on with your job. My mother is right. She's always warning me about allowing you to get too familiar. Well, this time you've gone too far. It's going to stop right now.

No response from Sam.

You're only a servant in here, and don't forget it.

Still no response. Hally is trying hard to get one.

And as far as my father is concerned, all you need to remember is that he is your boss.

SAM (*needled at last*). No, he isn't. I get paid by your mother.

HALLY. Don't argue with me, Sam!

SAM. Then don't say he's my boss.

HALLY. He's a white man and that's good enough for you.

SAM. I'll try to forget you said that.

HALLY. Don't! Because you won't be doing me a favor if you do. I'm telling you to remember it.

A pause. Sam pulls himself together and makes one last effort.

SAM. Hally, Hally . . . ! Come on now. Let's stop before it's too late. You're right. We are on dangerous ground. If we're not careful, somebody is going to get hurt.

HALLY. It won't be me.

SAM. Don't be so sure.

HALLY. I don't know what you're talking about, Sam.

SAM. Yes, you do.

HALLY (*furious*). Jesus, I wish you would stop trying to tell me what I do and what I don't know.

Sam gives up. He turns to Willie.

SAM. Let's finish up.

HALLY. Don't turn your back on me! I haven't finished talking.

He grabs Sam by the arm and tries to make him turn around. Sam reacts with a flash of anger.

SAM. Don't do that, Hally! (*Facing the boy.*) All right, I'm listening. Well? What do you want to say to me?

HALLY (*pause as Hally looks for something to say*). To begin with, why don't you also start calling me Master Harold, like Willie.

SAM. Do you mean that?

HALLY. Why the hell do you think I said it?

SAM. And if I don't.

HALLY. You might just lose your job.

SAM (*quietly and very carefully*). If you make me say it once, I'll never call you anything else again.

HALLY. So? (*The boy confronts the man.*) Is that meant to be a threat?

SAM. Just telling you what will happen if you make me do that. You must decide what it means to you.

HALLY. Well, I have. It's good news. Because that is exactly what Master Harold wants from now on. Think of it as a little lesson in respect, Sam, that's long overdue, and I hope you remember it as well as you do your geography. I can tell you now that somebody who will be glad to hear I've finally given it to you will be my Dad. Yes! He agrees with my Mom. He's always going on about it as well. "You must teach the boys to show you more respect, my son."

SAM. So now you can stop complaining about going home. Everybody is going to be happy tonight.

HALLY. That's perfectly correct. You see, you mustn't get the wrong idea about me and my Dad, Sam. We also have our good times together. Some bloody good laughs. He's got a marvelous sense of humor. Want to know what our favorite joke is? He gives out a big groan, you see, and says: "It's not fair, is it, Hally?" Then I have to ask: "What, chum?" And then he says: "A nigger's arse" . . . and we both have a good laugh.

The men stare at him with disbelief.

What's the matter, Willie? Don't you catch the joke? You always were a bit slow on the uptake. It's what is called a pun. You see, fair means both light in color and to be just and decent. (*He turns to Sam.*) I thought *you* would catch it, Sam.

SAM. Oh ja, I catch it all right.

HALLY. But it doesn't appeal to your sense of humor.

SAM. Do you really laugh?

HALLY. Of course.

SAM. To please him? Make him feel good?

HALLY. No, for heaven's sake! I laugh because *I* think it's a bloody good joke.

SAM. You're really trying hard to be ugly, aren't you? And why drag poor old Willie into it? He's done nothing to you except show you the respect you want so badly. That's also not being fair, you know . . . and I mean just or decent.

WILLIE. It's all right, Sam. Leave it now.

SAM. It's me you're after. You should just have said "Sam's arse" . . . because that's the one you're trying to kick. Anyway, how do you know it's not fair? You've never seen it. Do you want to? (*He drops his trousers and underpants and presents his backside for Hally's inspection.*) Have a good look. A real Basuto arse . . . which is about as nigger as they can come. Satisfied? (*Trousers up.*) Now you can make your Dad even happier when you go home tonight. Tell him I showed you my arse and he is quite right. It's not fair. And if it will give him an even better laugh next time, I'll also let him have a look. Come, Willie, let's finish up and go.

Sam and Willie start to tidy up the tea room. Hally doesn't move. He waits for a moment when Sam passes him.

HALLY (*quietly*). Sam . . .

Sam stops and looks expectantly at the boy. Hally spits in his face. A long and heartfelt groan from Willie. For a few seconds Sam doesn't move.

SAM (*taking out a handkerchief and wiping his face*). It's all right, Willie.

To Hally.

Ja, well, you've done it . . . Master Harold. Yes, I'll start calling you that from now on. It won't be difficult anymore. You've hurt yourself, Master Harold. I saw it coming. I warned you, but you wouldn't listen. You've just

hurt yourself *bad.* And you're a coward, Master Harold. The face you should be spitting in is your father's . . . but you used mine, because you think you're safe inside your fair skin . . . and this time I don't mean just or decent. (*Pause, then moving violently towards Hally.*) Should I hit him, Willie?

WILLIE. (*stopping Sam*). No, Boet Sam.

SAM (*violently*). Why not?

WILLIE. It won't help, Boet Sam.

SAM. I don't want to help! I want to hurt him.

WILLIE. You also hurt yourself.

SAM. And if he had done it to you, Willie?

WILLIE. Me? Spit at me like I was a dog? (*A thought that had not occurred to him before. He looks at Hally.*) Ja. Then I want to hit him. I want to hit him hard!

A dangerous few seconds as the men stand staring at the boy. Willie turns away, shaking his head.

But maybe all I do is go cry at the back. He's little boy, Boet Sam. Little *white* boy. Long trousers now, but he's still little boy.

SAM (*his violence ebbing away into defeat as quickly as it flooded*). You're right. So go on, then: groan again, Willie. You do it better than me. (*To Hally.*) You don't know all of what you've just done . . . Master Harold. It's not just that you've made me feel dirtier than I've ever been in my life . . . I mean, how do I wash off yours and your father's filth? . . . I've also failed. A long time ago I promised myself I was going to try and do something, but you've just shown me . . . Master Harold . . . that I've failed. (*Pause.*) I've also got a memory of a little white boy when he was still wearing short trousers and a black man, but they're not flying a kite. It was the old Jubilee days, after dinner one night. I was in my room. You came in and just stood against the wall, looking down at the ground, and only after I'd asked you what you wanted, what was wrong, I don't know how many times, did you speak and even then so softly I almost didn't hear you. "Sam, please help me to go and fetch my Dad." Remember? He was dead drunk on the floor of the Central Hotel Bar. They'd phoned for your Mom, but you were the only one at home. And do you remember how we did it? You went in first by yourself to ask permission for me to go into the bar. Then I loaded him onto my back like a baby and carried him back to the boarding house with you following behind carrying his crutches. (*Shaking his head as he remembers.*) A crowded Main Street with all the people watching a little white boy following his drunk father on a nigger's back! I felt for that little boy . . . Master Harold. I felt for him. After that we still had to clean him up, remember? He'd messed in his trousers, so we had to clean him up and get him into bed.

HALLY (*great pain*). I love him, Sam.

SAM. I know you do. That's why I tried to stop you from saying these things about him. It would have been so simple if you could have just despised him for being a weak man. But he's your father. You love him and you're ashamed of him. You're ashamed of so much! . . . And now that's going to include yourself. That was the promise I made to myself: to try and stop that happening. (*Pause.*) After we got him to bed you came back with me to my room and sat in a corner and carried on just looking down at the ground. And for days after that! You hadn't done anything wrong, but you went around as if you owed the world an apology for being alive. I didn't like seeing that! That's not the way a boy grows up to be a man! . . . But the one person who should have been teaching you what that means was the cause of your shame. If you really want to know, that's why I made you that kite. I wanted you to look up, be proud of something, of yourself . . . (*Bitter smile at the memory.*) . . . and you certainly were that when I left you with it up there on the hill. Oh, ja . . . something else! . . . If you ever do write it as a short story, there *was* a twist in our ending. I couldn't sit down there and stay with you. It was a "Whites Only" bench. You were too young, too excited to notice then. But not anymore. If you're not careful . . . Master Harold . . . you're going to be sitting up there by yourself for a long time to come, and there won't be a kite in the sky. (*Sam has got nothing more to say. He exits into the kitchen, taking off his waiter's jacket.*)

WILLIE. Is bad. Is all all bad in here now.

HALLY (*books into his school case, raincoat on*). Willie . . . (*It is difficult to speak.*) Will you lock up for me and look after the keys?

WILLIE. Okay.

Sam returns. Hally goes behind the counter and collects the few coins in the cash register. As he starts to leave . . .

SAM. Don't forget the comic books.

Hally returns to the counter and puts them in his case. He starts to leave again.

SAM (*to the retreating back of the boy*). Stop . . . Hally . . .

Hally stops, but doesn't turn to face him.

Hally . . . I've got no right to tell you what being a man means if I don't behave like one myself, and I'm not doing so well at that this afternoon. Should we try again, Hally?

HALLY. Try what?

SAM. Fly another kite, I suppose. It worked once, and this time I need it as much as you do.

HALLY. It's still raining, Sam. You can't fly kites on rainy days, remember.

SAM. So what do we do? Hope for better weather tomorrow?

HALLY (*helpless gesture*). I don't know. I don't know anything anymore.

SAM. You sure of that, Hally? Because it would be pretty hopeless if that was true. It would mean nothing has been learnt in here this afternoon, and there was a hell of a lot of teaching going on . . . one way or the other. But anyway, I don't believe you. I reckon there's one thing you know. You don't *have* to sit up there by yourself. You know what that bench means now, and you can leave it any time you choose. All you've got to do is stand up and walk away from it.

Hally leaves. Willie goes up quietly to Sam.

WILLIE. Is okay, Boet Sam. You see. Is . . . (*He can't find any better words.*) . . . is going to be okay tomorrow. (*Changing his tone.*) Hey, Boet Sam! (*He is trying hard.*) You right. I think about it and you right. Tonight I find Hilda and say sorry. And make promise I won't beat her no more. You hear me, Boet Sam?

SAM. I hear you, Willie.

WILLIE. And when we practice I relax and romance with her from beginning to end. Non-stop! You watch! Two weeks' time: "First prize for promising newcomers: Mr. Willie Malopo and Miss Hilda Samuels." (*Sudden impulse.*) To hell with it! I walk home. (*He goes to the jukebox, puts in a coin and selects a record. The machine comes to life in the gray twilight, blushing its way through a spectrum of soft, romantic colors.*) How did you say it, Boet Sam? Let's dream. (*Willie sways with the music and gestures for Sam to dance.*)

Sarah Vaughan sings.

"Little man you're crying,
I know why you're blue,
Someone took your kiddy car away;
Better go to sleep now,
Little man you've had a busy day." (*etc. etc.*)
You lead. I follow.

The men dance together.

"Johnny won your marbles,
Tell you what we'll do;
Dad will get you new ones right away;
Better go to sleep now,
Little man you've had a busy day."

For more than 25 years the Market Theatre in Johannesburg has been the leading noncommercial theater in South Africa. It has produced new works by such prominent South African playwrights as Mbogeni Ngema and Athol Fugard, as well as classics by Shakespeare and Chekhov. Despite strict apartheid laws, its productions feature multiracial casts. In spirit and purpose since its inception, the Market Theatre truly reflects the vision of the late-nineteenth-century social realists, and its legacy is as important as that of Ibsen, Strindberg, and Antoine. The Market Theatre stands beside the Théâtre-Libre, the Intimate Theatre, and the Provincetown Playhouse as a space of extraordinary importance in the evolution of world theater.

The creation of the Market Theatre on June 21, 1976, was the dream of many, but two individuals are credited as the engineers of its development: Barney Simon and Mannie Manin. Each dreamed of creating a new theater for South Africa, though they came from different backgrounds. Manin had been working in South Africa's State Theater, where he produced plays in plush entertainment palaces, working with budgets of millions of rands. Simon found a condemned mansion and turned the dingy dining room into a theater to which he could invite black and white audiences alike. Manin grew increasingly frustrated working in a bureaucracy that did not understand theater or his pleas to expand the state's offerings of traditional European fare. He argued without success that in addition to the state's white audience there was also a black and colored audience to be served. Manin knew that Simon and others were working individually, but with little progress, to create a new theater that truly reflected South Africa's reality. So, in his words, "holding hands, we all decided to make the big jump," and with Manin's pension as the working capital, the Market Theatre was created in the shell of the old Indian Fruit Market in downtown Johannesburg. Coincidentally, its first effort was a Simon-directed production of Chekhov's *The Seagull*, the play that defined the Moscow Art Theater in 1898.

Under the leadership of Simon (artistic director) and Manin (managing trustee), the Market Theatre was established under the banner "Theatre with, by, and for all the people of South Africa." It was to be, according to Manin, "dedicated to a theater that would be relevant to and involved with the lives of the people." Simon wanted the new theater "to give a reflecting surface in which our community might find an image of itself and share images of each other."

From the beginning the major mission of the Market was—in the words of John Kani—"to create a situation where all people could come together, where all artists could share and give together." Kani, the Market's associate artistic director and most prominent actor, recalls that when the Market started "we wanted a space that could be available to all the artists of this country, irrespective of color, race, or creed. We wanted to promote a theater that was South African in identity. We are here to bring the South African different races together to share and to exchange ideas." Jon White-Spunner adds that "we have tried to do work that mirrors people's lives, work that looks at issues that are important to people." Under the strict apartheid laws of the time, however, that was a difficult, not to mention illegal, task.

Today the Market Theatre is Africa's foremost producer of new scripts by both black (e.g., Mbongeni Ngema) and white writers (e.g., Athol Fugard). *"MASTER HAROLD" . . . and the boys* is a product of the Market Theatre.

Other stories tell of similar theater ventures conceived by visionaries such as Antoine in Paris in 1888. The so-called Off-Broadway movement, begun in New York City in the 1950s, eventually spawned the fiercely independent "Off-off-Broadway" theaters (again, in Greenwich Village, the home of the Provincetown Players in 1915). In 1957 Joe Cino turned his coffeehouse, Café Cino, into a soundingboard for new playwrights, and several years later Ellen Stewart created La Mama Experimental Theater Club, still the model of such theaters in New York. London countered with its "fringe" theaters, also dedicated to producing new, socially relevant works. Today, the English Stage Company at the Royal Court Theatre, founded by George Divine in 1956, is Britain's preeminent home for new works.

Independent theaters also thrived in Latin America. From the 1930s to the mid-1950s, Argentina witnessed one of its most productive anticommercial theater movements. It portrayed the broken dreams of immigrants who moved to Argentina to escape the despair that plagued Europe following World War I. These dramas, performed in small theaters, parks, open markets, and streets, spoke of a nation transformed by a military regime that imperiled democracy. Highly influenced by European Expressionism, the theater of the grotesque, and Brecht's epic theater, playwrights such as Griselda Gambarro and Osvaldo Dragún—both of European lineage—created a radically new drama in opposition to the naturalistic tradition. Chile enjoyed a similar phenomenon, largely in response to its own oppressive military. In Cuba the Teatro de Arte La Cueva (The Cellar Art Theater) was founded in 1936 with a production of Pirandello's *Tonight We Improvise*. The event signaled a new experimentation with form and content in Cuban drama and eventually led to the creation of original Cuban dramas. In 1940 the Academy of the Dramatic Arts of the Free School of Havana was established to cultivate a specifically Cuban acting style, free of the old traditions of Spanish acting and vocal techniques. Brazil saw the formation of a dramatic training school in 1948 to foster a distinctively Brazilian style of theater and performance. Os Comediantes, an experimental group that used Rio de Janeiro's lower-class slang for the first time in Brazilian drama, prompted a drama that was distinct from the European style that pervaded that country's theater heritage.

DEATH AND THE KING'S HORSEMAN

WOLE SOYINKA

WOLE SOYINKA (1934–)

Born into the Yoruban culture of Abeokuta, Nigeria, Akinwande Oluwole Soyinka has emerged as Africa's most noteworthy playwright; he is as well a supremely accomplished poet, novelist, short-story writer, and literary theorist. He received his initial education at St. Peter's School and the Abeokuta Grammar School in his native city, then went to Ibadam, capital of Nigeria's Oyo state, where he studied at both the Government College and University College. From 1954 to 1957 he was a student at Leeds University in north-central England, where he earned honors in English and some renown as a short-story writer.

In 1957 he was attached to the newly founded Royal Court Theatre in London as a play reader, and it was there that his unpublished play *The Invention* was first performed in 1959. The Royal Court has continued to produce many of Soyinka's works, including *The Lion and the Jewel* (1963), *A Dance in the Forest* (1963), *The Road* (1965), *Kongi's Harvest* (1967), an adaptation of Euripides' *The Bacchae* (1973), *Death and the King's Horseman* (1975), *A Play of Giants* (1984), and most recently, *From Zia with Love* (1992). His novels include *The Interpreters* (1965) and *Seasons of Agony* (1973), and his poetry is collected as *Indare and Other Poems* (1967), *Ogun Abibiman* (1976), and *Mandela's Earth* (1996). Soyinka has written several autobiographical works, such as *Ake: The Years of Childhood* (1981) and *Ibadan* (1994). And he has excelled in critical writing, most notably *Myth, Literature, and the African World* (1976) and *Art, Dialogue, and Outrage* (1988). This prodigious outpouring of literature, which has inspired both praise and controversy, earned Soyinka the Nobel Prize in 1986; he was the first African writer to receive the world's most prestigious literary award.

Soyinka's critics—primarily Marxists and neo-Negritudists (those wanting to reclaim Africa for black Africans)—have attacked him on the grounds that his work lacks a specific political direction. Generally, such claims are accurate: Soyinka himself has frequently spoken out forcefully against imposing constraints on artistic exploration in favor of the hegemonic goals of a particular group. Yet, Soyinka is anything but apolitical. As early as 1965 he was arrested for pirating a radio broadcast of the Nigerian Broadcasting Corporation subsequent to the disputed elections in Nigeria's Western Regions. Though he was acquitted of this crime, he was later arrested and placed in solitary confinement for not being demonstrably anti-Biafran during the Nigerian civil war of the late 1960s (he recounted the terrors of this two-year imprisonment in his book *A Man Died*). Currently, Soyinka energetically (some have said recklessly) opposes the military dictatorship that rules Nigeria and names himself as one of the three most dangerous men in the world to that regime. The government has shown no reservation in silencing dissident voices within its borders, a point evidenced by the mock trial and execution of Soyinka's colleague and fellow playwright, Ken Saro-Wiwa, in November 1995. Were Soyinka not speaking about Nigeria's turmoil from the safety of exile, his fate would in all likelihood be the same as Saro-Wiwa's.

Wole Soyinka

Death and the King's Horseman (1975)

Soyinka's "Author's Note" to *Death and the King's Horseman* has drawn much attention from critics but little consensus about its meaning. To the Yoruba (or to many peoples whose religious life is animistic and therefore not separated from the natural world), Soyinka's instructions seem superfluous. But the playwright does not level his warnings to those who already understand them; rather, he admonishes those aspects of Western consciousness that he sees as ultimately prohibitive to the apprehension of Yoruban tragedy. For the Western reader steeped in "modernist" sensibilities, perhaps Soyinka's note should appear at the end of the play. Reading it subsequent to the actual text might prove useful in measuring the extent to which Soyinka is accurate in his assessment of how the play must be interpreted. Should readers ignore the "Author's Note" as a prologue (as some critics have suggested it is) and instead read it afterward as a commentary on a specific type of work, they may discover the trap which Soyinka identifies as "the bane of themes of this genre"—that is, the facile tag of a "clash of cultures" play. In fact, a real clash of cultures does occur when the Western mind attempts to analyze drama that does not conform to traditional forms or content. It is at precisely this point that Soyinka's poetic imagination comes into conflict with the Western-trained critic.

Soyinka's approach to tragic myth within the context of the Yoruban worldview can be found in his essay "The Fourth Stage," a piece heavily influenced by Friedrich Nietzsche's *The Birth of Tragedy* (1872). Nietzsche's work, among the most important in dramatic theory, explores the manner in which Greek tragedy developed through a marriage between the Apollonian (i.e., rationale) art of the sculptor and the nonvisual Dionysian (i.e., emotional) art of music. Though these two creative urges are often in violent opposition to each other, they are ultimately coupled to form tragedy, which was for Nietzsche the perfect synthesis of the Apollonian and Dionysian impulses in humans. Although Yoruban tragedy is not a copy of Greek tragedy, these Nietzschean images and those of the Yoruban myth lend themselves to a comparison that may lead us to an understanding of *Death and the King's Horseman*.

The same sense of duality that is found in Nietzsche's tragic schema can be found in the dyadic, self-contradictory nature of Ogun, a god seeking to rejoin himself to man. At the same time, humans attempt to elevate themselves to the stature of a god, as demonstrated by Elesin's desire to follow his king in death. Both god and humans reach for knowledge they do not possess, a daring and hubristic quest that challenges nature itself. Thus Soyinka sees Ogun as the embodiment of not only the Apollonian and Dionysian, but also the Promethean virtues. The tragic hero is one who confronts nature (often on his own) and thereby dares to enter the great abyss—what Soyinka calls "the gulf of transition"—and suffers whatever agony awaits him before achieving the ultimate reward: cosmic oneness. To the Yoruba and Soyinka, Ogun is the embodiment of the will, which originally overcame the forces of this abyss between being and nonbeing, and it is Ogun who reunited the gods with humans. When humans, in the world of the living, face a challenge of tragic proportion, it is seen as a vital manifestation, not merely a representation, of Ogun's self-sacrifice. Elesin's obsession with meeting his death as "the King's (first) Horseman" is best understood in this light: the horseman is re-creating Ogun's own act.

Ogun's tragic heroism restored the inseparability of the gods and man in nature (as seen in animism: Elesin, the rider, is an extension of the horse itself). By this means Ogun earned his most revered title, the Lord of the Road, the "road" being the means by which peoples of all times are connected. Consequently, there is no separation among the ancestors and the living and the unborn. After Ogun's sacrifice, "the gulf of transition" continuously connects the three realms of the dead, the living, and the unborn. But to pass from one realm to the next, one must brave the abyss after the manner of the hero-god Ogun. Thus, all transitions become rites of passage. Braving the abyss—as Prince Olunde does—demands the will of a true tragic hero. Soyinka's fourth stage is the abyss itself, the chthonic or underworld, realm of the immediate, physical, and animistic world of the Yoruba, for whom all things are potentially sacred.

In the "Author's Note" Soyinka insists that the play's "threnodic essence" be stressed. This relates to the rhythm and music of the dirge that provides the aural backdrop for *Death and the King's Horseman*. Music is an immediate and necessary element in tragedy, and for

Soyinka music is inseparable from the will. The Western mind cannot fully appreciate this concept of music-as-will without first shedding all notions of music as a commodity to be used for financial gain or diversion. To those for whom tragedy is a living product of natural forces, such as Soyinka and Nietzsche (and the ancient Greeks: recall that Aristotle identified music as an integral part of the tragic experience), music is the mournful lament (i.e., the threnody), as well as the solitary companion of the tragic hero at the moment of "self-individuation" on the brink of the abyss. Soyinka says that "if we agree that, in the European sense, music is the direct copy or the direct expression of the will, it is only because nothing rescues man (ancestral, living, or unborn) from loss of self within this abyss but a titanic resolution of the will whose ritual summons, response, and expression is the strange alien sound to which we give the name of Music." Music, then, is the creative essence, the will itself, and it both drives and accompanies the tragic hero—Ogun, Elesin, Olunde—into the abyss of transition. Ironically, the means by which Soyinka illustrates this in *Death and the King's Horseman* is largely through Apollonian means—words, symbols, argument. Herein lies the play's true "clash of cultures."

Allen Alford
Louisiana State University

Death and the King's Horseman *was revived in 1987 at New York's Lincoln Center with Earle Hyman as Elesin, shown here with the Praise-Singer.*

DEATH AND THE KING'S HORSEMAN

WOLE SOYINKA

CHARACTERS
PRAISE-SINGER
ELESIN, *Horseman of the King*
IYALOJA, *'Mother' of the market*
SIMON PILKINGS, *District Officer*
JANE PILKINGS, *his wife*
SERGEANT AMUSA

JOSEPH, *houseboy to the Pilkingses*
BRIDE
H.R.H. THE PRINCE
THE RESIDENT
AIDE-DE-CAMP
OLUNDE, *eldest son of Elesin*
DRUMMERS, WOMEN, YOUNG GIRLS, DANCERS AT THE BALL

AUTHOR'S NOTE

This play is based on events which took place in Oyo, ancient Yoruba city of Nigeria, in 1946. That year, the lives of Elesin (Olori Elesin), his son, and the Colonial District Officer intertwined with the disastrous results set out in the play. The changes I have made are in matters of detail, sequence and of course characterisation. The action has also been set back two or three years to when the war was still on, for minor reasons of dramaturgy.

The factual account still exists in the archives of the British Colonial Administration. It has already inspired a fine play in Yoruba (*Oba Wàjà*) by Duro Ladipo. It has also misbegotten a film by some German television company.

The bane of themes of this genre is that they are no sooner employed creatively than they acquire the facile tag of 'clash of cultures', a prejudicial label which, quite apart from its frequent misapplication, presupposes a potential equality *in every given situation* of the alien culture and the indigenous, on the actual soil of the latter. (In the area of misapplication, the overseas prize for illiteracy and mental conditioning undoubtedly goes to the blurb-writer for the American edition of my novel *Seasons of Agony* who unblushingly declares that this work portrays the 'clash between old values and new ways, between western methods and African traditions'!) It is thanks to this kind of perverse mentality that I find it necessary to caution the would-be producer of this play against a sadly familiar reductionist tendency, and to direct his vision instead to the far more difficult and risky task of eliciting the play's threnodic essence.

One of the more obvious alternative structures of the play would be to make the District Officer the victim of a cruel dilemma. This is not to my taste and it is not by chance that I have avoided dialogue or situation which would encourage this. No attempt should be made in production to suggest it. The Colonial Factor is an incident, a catalytic incident merely. The confrontation in the play is largely metaphysical, contained in the human vehicle which is Elesin and the universe of the Yoruba mind—the world of the living, the dead and the unborn, and the numinous passage which links all: transition. *Death and the King's Horseman* can be fully realised only through an evocation of music from the abyss of transition.

W.S.

1

A passage through a market in its closing stages. The stalls are being emptied, mats folded. A few women pass through on their way home, loaded with baskets. On a cloth-stand, bolts of cloth are taken down, display pieces folded and piled on a tray. Elesin Oba enters along a passage before the market, pursued by his drummers and praise-singers. He is a man of enormous vitality, speaks, dances and sings with that infectious enjoyment of life which accompanies all his actions.

PRAISE-SINGER. Elesin o! Elesin Oba! Howu! What tryst is this the cockerel goes to keep with such haste that he must leave his tail behind?

ELESIN (*slows down a bit, laughing*). A tryst where the cockerel needs no adornment.

PRAISE-SINGER. O-oh, you hear that my companions? That's the way the world goes. Because the man approaches a brand-new bride he forgets the long faithful mother of his children.

ELESIN. When the horse sniffs the stable does he not strain at the bridle? The market is the long-suffering home of my spirit and the women are packing up to go. That Esu-harrassed day slipped into the stewpot while we feasted. We ate it up with the rest of the meat. I have neglected my women.

PRAISE-SINGER. We know all that. Still it's no reason for shedding your tail on this day of all days. I know the women will cover you in damask and *alari* but when the wind blows cold from behind, that's when the fowl knows his true friends.

ELESIN. Olohun-iyo!

PRAISE-SINGER. Are you sure there will be one like me on the other side?

ELESIN. Olohun-iyo!

PRAISE-SINGER. Far be it for me to belittle the dwellers of that place but, a man is either born to his art or he isn't. And I don't know for certain that you'll meet my father, so who is going to sing these deeds in accents that will pierce the deafness of the ancient ones. I have prepared my going—just tell me: Olohun-iyo, I need you on this journey and I shall be behind you.

ELESIN. You're like a jealous wife. Stay close to me, but only on this side. My fame, my honour are legacies to the living; stay behind and let the world sip its honey from your lips.

PRAISE-SINGER. Your name will be like the sweet berry a child places under his tongue to sweeten the passage of food. The world will never spit it out.

ELESIN. Come then. This market is my roost. When I come among the women I am a chicken with a hundred mothers. I become a monarch whose palace is built with tenderness and beauty.

PRAISE-SINGER. They love to spoil you but beware. The hands of women also weaken the unwary.

ELESIN. This night I'll lay my head upon their lap and go to sleep. This night I'll touch feet with their feet in a dance that is no longer of this earth. But the smell of their flesh, their sweat, the smell of indigo on their cloth, this is the last air I wish to breathe as I go to meet my great forebears.

PRAISE-SINGER. In their time the world was never tilted from its groove, it shall not be in yours.

ELESIN. The gods have said No.

PRAISE-SINGER. In their time the great wars came and went, the little wars came and went; the white slavers came and went, they took away the heart of our race, they bore away the mind and muscle of our race. The city fell and was rebuilt; the city fell and our people trudged through mountain and forest to found a new home but—Elesin Oba do you hear me?

ELESIN. I hear your voice Olohun-iyo.

PRAISE-SINGER. Our world was never wrenched from its true course.

ELESIN. The gods have said No.

PRAISE-SINGER. There is only one home to the life of a river-mussel; there is only one home to the life of a tortoise; there is only one shell to the soul of man: there is only one world to the spirit of our race. If that world leaves its course and smashes on boulders of the great void, whose world will give us shelter?

ELESIN. It did not in the time of my forebears, it shall not in mine.

PRAISE-SINGER. The cockerel must not be seen without his feathers.

ELESIN. Nor will the Not-I bird be much longer without his nest.

PRAISE-SINGER (stopped in his lyric stride). The Not-I bird, Elesin?

ELESIN. I said, the Not-I bird.

PRAISE-SINGER. All respect to our elders but, is there really such a bird?

ELESIN. What! Could it be that he failed to knock on your door?

PRAISE-SINGER (smiling). Elesin's riddles are not merely the nut in the kernel that breaks human teeth; he also buries the kernel in hot embers and dares a man's fingers to draw it out.

ELESIN. I am sure he called on you, Olohun-iyo. Did you hide in the loft and push out the servant to tell him you were out?

(Elesin executes a brief, half-taunting dance. The drummer moves in and draws a rhythm out of his steps. Elesin dances towards the market-place as he chants the story of the Not-I bird, his voice changing dexterously to mimic his characters. He performs like a born raconteur, infecting his retinue with his humour and energy. More women arrive during his recital, including Iyaloja.)

Death came calling.
Who does not know his rasp of reeds?
A twilight whisper in the leaves before
The great araba falls? Did you hear it?

Not I! swears the farmer! He snaps
His fingers round his head, abandons

A hard-worn harvest and begins
A rapid dialogue with his legs.

'Not I,' shouts the fearless hunter, 'but—
It's getting dark, and this night-lamp
Has leaked out all its oil. I think
It's best to go home and resume my hunt
Another day.' But now he pauses, suddenly
Lets out a wail: 'Oh foolish mouth, calling
Down a curse on your own head!
    Your lamp
Has leaked out all its oil, has it?'
Forwards or backwards now he dare not move.
To search for leaves and make etutu
On that spot? Or race home to the safety
Of his hearth? Ten market-days have passed
My friends, and still he's rooted there
Rigid as the plinth of Orayan.

The mouth of the courtesan barely
Opened wide enough to take a ha'penny robo
When she wailed: 'Not I.' All dressed she was
To call upon my friend the Chief Tax Officer.
But now she sends her go-between instead:
'Tell him I'm ill: my period has come suddenly
But not—I hope—my time.'

Why is the pupil crying?
His hapless head was made to taste
The knuckles of my friend the Mallam:
'If you were then reciting the Koran
Would you have ears for idle noises
Darkening the trees, you child of ill omen?'
He shuts down school before its time
Runs home and rings himself with amulets.

And take my good kinsman Ifawomi.
His hands were like a carver's, strong
And true. I saw them
Tremble like wet wings of a fowl
One day he cast his time-smoothed opele
Across the divination board. And all because
The suppliant looked him in the eye and asked,
'Did you hear that whisper in the leaves?'
'Not I,' was his reply; 'perhaps I'm growing deaf—
Good-day.' And Ifa spoke no more that day
The priest locked fast his doors,
Sealed up his leaking roof—but wait!
This sudden care was not for Fawomi
But for Osanyin, courier-bird of Ifa's
Heart of wisdom. I did not know a kite
Was hovering in the sky
And Ifa now a twittering chicken in
The brood of Fawomi the Mother Hen.

Ah, but I must not forget my evening

Courier from the abundant palm, whose groan
Became Not I, as he constipated down
A wayside bush. He wonders if Elegbara
Has tricked his buttocks to discharge
Against a sacred grove. Hear him
Mutter spells to ward off penalties
For an abomination he did not intend.
If any here
Stumbles on a gourd of wine, fermenting
Near the road, and nearby hears a stream
Of spells issuing from a crouching form,
Brother to a *sigidi*, bring home my wine,
Tell my tapper I have ejected
Fear from home and farm. Assure him,
All is well.

PRAISE-SINGER. In your time we do not doubt the peace of
   farmstead and home, the peace of road and hearth, we do
   not doubt the peace of the forest.

ELESIN. There was fear in the forest too.
   Not-I was lately heard even in the lair
   Of beasts. The hyena cackled loud Not I,
   The civet twitched his fiery tail and glared:
   Not I. Not-I became the answering-name
   Of the restless bird, that little one
   Whom Death found nesting in the leaves
   When whisper of his coming ran
   Before him on the wind. Not-I
   Has long abandoned home. This same dawn
   I heard him twitter in the gods' abode.
   Ah, companions of this living world
   What a thing this is, that even those
   We call immortal
   Should fear to die.

IYALOJA. But you, husband of multitudes?

ELESIN. I, when that Not-I bird perched
   Upon my roof, bade him seek his nest again,
   Safe, without care or fear. I unrolled
   My welcome mat for him to see. Not-I
   Flew happily away, you'll hear his voice
   No more in this lifetime—You all know
   What I am.

PRAISE-SINGER. That rock which turns its open lodes
   Into the path of lightning. A gay
   Thoroughbred whose stride disdains
   To falter through an adder reared
   Suddenly in his path.

ELESIN. My rein is loosened.
   I am master of my Fate. When the hour comes
   Watch me dance along the narrowing path
   Glazed by the soles of my great precursors.
   My soul is eager. I shall not turn aside.

WOMEN. You will not delay?

ELESIN. Where the storm pleases, and when, it directs
   The giants of the forest. When friendship summons
   Is when the true comrade goes.

WOMEN. Nothing will hold you back?

ELESIN. Nothing. What! Has no one told you yet?
   I go to keep my friend and master company.
   Who says the mouth does not believe in
   'No, I have chewed all that before?' I say I have.
   The world is not a constant honey-pot.
   Where I found little I made do with little.
   Where there was plenty I gorged myself.
   My master's hands and mine have always
   Dipped together and, home or sacred feast,
   The bowl was beaten bronze, the meats
   So succulent our teeth accused us of neglect.
   We shared the choicest of the season's
   Harvest of yams. How my friend would read
   Desire in my eyes before I knew the cause—
   However rare, however precious, it was mine.

WOMEN. The town, the very land was yours.

ELESIN. The world was mine. Our joint hands
   Raised houseposts of trust that withstood
   The siege of envy and the termites of time.
   But the twilight hour brings bats and rodents—
   Shall I yield them cause to foul the rafters?

PRAISE-SINGER. Elesin Oba! Are you not that man who
   Looked out of doors that stormy day
   The god of luck limped by, drenched
   To the very lice that held
   His rags together? You took pity upon
   His sores and wished him fortune.
   Fortune was footloose this dawn, he replied,
   Till you trapped him in a heartfelt wish
   That now returns to you. Elesin Oba!
   I say you are that man who
   Chanced upon the calabash of honour
   You thought it was palm wine and
   Drained its contents to the final drop.

ELESIN. Life has an end. A life that will outlive
   Fame and friendship begs another name.
   What elder takes his tongue to his plate,
   Licks it clean of every crumb? He will encounter
   Silence when he calls on children to fulfill
   The smallest errand! Life is honour.
   It ends when honour ends.

WOMEN. We know you for a man of honour.

ELESIN. Stop! Enough of that!

WOMEN (*puzzled, they whisper among themselves, turning
   mostly to Iyaloja*). What is it? Did we say something to
   give offence? Have we slighted him in some way?

ELESIN. Enough of that sound I say. Let me hear no more in
   that vein. I've heard enough.

IYALOJA. We must have said something wrong. (*Comes forward a little.*) Elesin Oba, we ask forgiveness before you
   speak.

ELESIN. I am bitterly offended.

IYALOJA. Our unworthiness has betrayed us. All we can do is
   ask your forgiveness. Correct us like a kind father.

ELESIN. This day of all days . . .

IYALOJA. It does not bear thinking. If we offend you now we
have mortified the gods. We offend heaven itself. Father
of us all, tell us where we went astray. (*She kneels, the other
women follow.*)

ELESIN. Are you not ashamed? Even a tear-veiled
Eye preserves its function of sight.
Because my mind was raised to horizons
Even the boldest man lowers his gaze
In thinking of, must my body here
Be taken for a vagrant's?

IYALOJA. Horseman of the King, I am more baffled than ever.

PRAISE-SINGER. The strictest father unbends his brow when
the child is penitent, Elesin. When time is short, we do
not spend it prolonging the riddle. Their shoulders are
bowed with the weight of fear lest they have marred your
day beyond repair. Speak now in plain words and let us
pursue the ailment to the home of remedies.

ELESIN. Words are cheap. 'We know you for
A man of honour.' Well tell me, is this how
A man of honour should be seen?
Are these not the same clothes in which
I came among you a full half-hour ago?

(*He roars with laughter and the women, relieved, rise and
rush into stalls to fetch rich cloths.*)

WOMAN. The gods are kind. A fault soon remedied is soon
forgiven. Elesin Oba, even as we match our words with
deed, let your heart forgive us completely.

ELESIN. You who are breath and giver of my being
How shall I dare refuse you forgiveness
Even if the offence were real.

IYALOJA (*dancing round him. Sings*).
He forgives us. He forgives us.
What a fearful thing it is when
The voyager sets forth
But a curse remains behind.

WOMEN. For a while we truly feared
Our hands had wrenched the world adrift
In emptiness.

IYALOJA. Richly, richly, robe him richly
The cloth of honour is *alari*
Sanyan is the band of friendship
Boa-skin makes slippers of esteem

WOMEN. For a while we truly feared
Our hands had wrenched the world adrift
In emptiness.

PRAISE-SINGER. He who must, must voyage forth
The world will not roll backwards
It is he who must, with one
Great gesture overtake the world.

WOMEN. For a while we truly feared
Our hands had wrenched the world
In emptiness.

PRAISE-SINGER. The gourd you bear is no for shirking.
The gourd is not for setting down
At the first crossroad or wayside grove.
Only one river may know its contents

WOMEN. We shall all meet at the great market
We shall all meet at the great market
He who goes early takes the best bargains
But we shall meet, and resume our banter.

(*Elesin stands resplendent in rich clothes, cap, shawl, etc.
His sash is of a bright red alari cloth. The women dance
round him. Suddenly, his attention is caught by an object
off-stage.*)

ELESIN. The world I know is good.

WOMEN. We know you'll leave it so.

ELESIN. The world I know is the bounty
Of hives after bees have swarmed.
No goodness teems with such open hands
Even in the dreams of deities.

WOMEN. And we know you'll leave it so.

ELESIN. I was born to keep it so. A hive
Is never known to wander. An anthill
Does not desert its roots. We cannot see
The still great womb of the world—
No man beholds his mother's womb—
Yet who denies it's there? Coiled
To the navel of the world is that
Endless cord that links us all
To the great origin. If I lose my way
The trailing cord will bring me to the roots.

WOMEN. The world is in your hands.

(*The earlier distraction, a beautiful young girl, comes
along the passage through which Elesin first made his
entry.*)

ELESIN. I embrace it. And let me tell you, women—
I like this farewell that the world designed,
Unless my eyes deceive me, unless
We are already parted, the world and I,
And all that breeds desire is lodged
Among our tireless ancestors. Tell me friends,
Am I still earthed in that beloved market
Of my youth? Or could it be my will
Has outleapt the conscious act and I have come
Among the great departed?

PRAISE-SINGER. Elesin-Oba why do your eyes roll like a
bushrat who sees his fate like his father's spirit, mirrored
in the eye of a snake? And all these questions! You're
standing on the same earth you've always stood upon.
This voice you hear is mine, Oluhun-iyo, not that of an
acolyte in heaven.

ELESIN. How can that be? In all my life
As Horseman of the King, the juiciest
Fruit on every tree was mine. I saw,

I touched, I wooed, rarely was the answer No.
The honour of my place, the veneration I
Received in the eye of man or woman
Prospered my suit and
Played havoc with my sleeping hours.
And they tell me my eyes were a hawk
In perpetual hunger. Split an iroko tree
In two, hide a woman's beauty in its heartwood
And seal it up again—Elesin, journeying by,
Would make his camp beside that tree
Of all the shades in the forest.

PRAISE-SINGER. Who would deny your reputation, snake-on-the-loose in dark passages of the market! Bed-bug who wages war on the mat and receives the thanks of the vanquished! When caught with his bride's own sister he protested—but I was only prostrating myself to her as becomes a grateful in-law. Hunter who carries his powder-horn on the hips and fires crouching or standing! Warrior who never makes that excuse of the whining coward—but how can I go to battle without my trousers?—trouser-less or shirtless it's all one to him. Oka-rearing-from-a-camouflage-of-leaves, before he strikes the victim is already prone! Once they told him, Howu, a stallion does not feed on the grass beneath him: he replied, true, but surely he can roll on it!

WOMEN. Ba-a-a-ba O!

PRAISE-SINGER. Ah, but listen yet. You know there is the leaf-knibbling grub and there is the cola-chewing beetle; the leaf-nibbling grub lives on the leaf, the cola-chewing beetle lives in the colanut. Don't we know what our man feeds on when we find him cocooned in a woman's wrapper?

ELESIN. Enough, enough, you all have cause
To know me well. But, if you say this earth
Is still the same as gave birth to those songs,
Tell me who was that goddess through whose lips
I saw the ivory pebbles of Oya's riverbed.
Iyaloja, who is she? I saw her enter
Your stall; all your daughters I know well.
No, not even Ogun-of-the-farm toiling
Dawn till dusk on his tuber patch
Not even Ogun with the finest hoe he ever
Forged at the anvil could have shaped
That rise of buttocks, not though he had
The richest earth between his fingers.
Her wrapper was no disguise
For thighs whose ripples shamed the river's
Coils around the hills of Ilesi. Her eyes
Were new-laid eggs glowing in the dark.
Her skin . . .

IYALOJA. Elesin Oba . . .

ELESIN. What! Where do you all say I am?

IYALOJA. Still among the living.

ELESIN. And that radiance which so suddenly

Lit up this market I could boast
I knew so well?

IYALOJA. Has one step already in her husband's home. She is betrothed.

ELESIN (irritated). Why do you tell me that?

(Iyaloja falls silent. The women shuffle uneasily.)

IYALOJA. Not because we dare give you offence Elesin. Today is your day and the whole world is yours. Still, even those who leave town to make a new dwelling elsewhere like to be remembered by what they leave behind.

ELESIN. Who does not seek to be remembered?
Memory is Master of Death, the chink
In his armour of conceit. I shall leave
That which makes my going the sheerest
Dream of an afternoon. Should voyagers
Not travel light? Let the considerate traveller
Shed, of his excessive load, all
That may benefit the living.

WOMEN (relieved). Ah Elesin Oba, we knew you for a man of honour.

ELESIN. Then honour me. I deserve a bed of honour to lie upon.

IYALOJA. The best is yours. We know you for a man of honour. You are not one who eats and leaves nothing on his plate for children. Did you not say it yourself? Not one who blights the happiness of others for a moment's pleasure.

ELESIN. Who speaks of pleasure? O women, listen!
Pleasure palls. Our acts should have meaning.
The sap of the plantain never dries.
You have seen the young shoot swelling
Even as the parent stalk begins to wither.
Women, let my going be likened to
The twilight hour of the plantain.

WOMEN. What does he mean Iyaloja? This language is the language of our elders, we do not fully grasp it.

IYALOJA. I dare not understand you yet Elesin.

ELESIN. All you who stand before the spirit that dares
The opening of the last door of passage,
Dare to rid my going of regrets! My wish
Transcends the blotting out of thought
In one mere moment's tremor of the senses.
Do me credit. And do me honour.
I am girded for the route beyond
Burdens of waste and longing.
Then let me travel light. Let
Seed that will not serve the stomach
On the way remain behind. Let it take root
In the earth of my choice, in this earth
I leave behind.

IYALOJA (turns to women). The voice I hear is already touched by the waiting fingers of our departed. I dare not refuse.

WOMAN. But Iyaloja . . .

IYALOJA. The matter is no longer in our hands.

WOMAN. But she is betrothed to your own son. Tell him.

IYALOJA. My son's wish is mine. I did the asking for him, the loss can be remedied. But who will remedy the blight of closed hands on the day when all should be openness and light? Tell him, you say! You wish that I burden him with knowledge that will sour his wish and lay regrets on the last moments of his mind. You pray to him who is your intercessor to the other world—don't set this world adrift in your own time; would you rather it was my hand whose sacrilege wrenched it loose?

WOMAN. Not many men will brave the curse of a dispossessed husband.

IYALOJA. Only the curses of the departed are to be feared. The claims of one whose foot is on the threshold of their abode surpasses even the claims of blood. It is impiety even to place hindrances in their ways.

ELESIN. What do my mothers say? Shall I step Burdened into the unknown?

IYALOJA. Not we, but the very earth says No. The sap in the plantain does no dry. Let grain that will not feed the voyagers at his passage drop here and take root as he steps beyond this earth and us. Oh you who fill the home from hearth to threshold with the voices of children, you who now bestride the hidden gulf and pause to draw the right foot across and into the resting-home of the great forebears, it is good that your loins be drained into the earth we know, that your last strength be ploughed back into the womb that gave you being.

PRAISE-SINGER. Iyaloja, mother of multitudes in the teeming market of the world, how your wisdom transfigures you!

IYALOJA (smiling broadly, completely reconciled). Elesin, even at the narrow end of the passage I know you will look back and sigh a last regret for the flesh that flashed past your spirit in flight. You always had a restless eye. Your choice has my blessing. (To the women.) Take the good news to our daughter and make her ready. (Some women go off.)

ELESIN. Your eyes were clouded at first.

IYALOJA. Not for long. It is those who stand at the gateway of the great change to whose cry we must pay heed. And then, think of this—it makes the mind tremble. The fruit of such a union is rare. It will be neither of this world nor of the next. Nor of the one behind us. As if the timelessness of the ancestor world and the unborn have joined spirits to wring an issue of the elusive being of passage . . . Elesin!

ELESIN. I am here. What is it?

IYALOJA. Did you hear all I said just now?

ELESIN. Yes.

IYALOJA. The living must eat and drink. When the moment comes, don't turn the food to rodents' droppings in their mouth. Don't let them taste the ashes of the world when they step out at dawn to breathe the morning dew.

ELESIN. This doubt is unworthy of you Iyaloja.

IYALOJA. Eating the awusa nut is not so difficult as drinking water afterwards.

ELESIN. The waters of the bitter stream are honey to a man Whose tongue has savoured all.

IYALOJA. No one knows when the ants desert their home; they leave the mound intact. The swallow is never seen to peck holes in its nest when it is time to move with the season. There are always throngs of humanity behind the leave-taker. The rain should not come through the roof for them, the wind must not blow through the walls at night.

ELESIN. I refuse to take offence.

IYALOJA. You wish to travel light. Well, the earth is yours. But be sure the seed you leave in it attracts no curse.

ELESIN. You really mistake my person Iyaloja.

IYALOJA. I said nothing. Now we must go prepare your bridal chamber. Then these same hands will lay your shrouds.

ELESIN (exasperated). Must you be so blunt? (Recovers.) Well, weave your shrouds, but let the fingers of my bride seal my eyelids with earth and wash my body.

IYALOJA. Prepare yourself Elesin.

(She gets up to leave. At that moment the women return, leading the Bride. Elesin's face glows with pleasure. He flicks the sleeves of his agbada with renewed confidence and steps forward to meet the group. As the girl kneels before Iyaloja, lights fade out on the scene.)

2

The verandah of the District Officer's bungalow. A tango is playing from an old hand-cranked gramophone and, glimpsed through the wide windows and doors which open onto the forestage verandah are the shapes of Simon Pilkings and his wife, Jane, tangoing in and out of shadows in the living-room. They are wearing what is immediately apparent as some form of fancy-dress. The dance goes on for some moments and then the figure of a 'Native Administration' policeman emerges and climbs up the steps onto the verandah. He peeps through and observes the dancing couple, reacting with what is obviously a long-standing bewilderment. He stiffens suddenly, his expression changes to one of disbelief and horror. In his excitement he upsets a flower-pot and attracts the attention of the couple. They stop dancing.

PILKINGS. Is there anyone out there?

JANE. I'll turn off the gramophone.

PILKINGS (approaching the verandah). I'm sure I heard something fall over. (The constable retreats slowly, open-mouthed as Pilkings approaches the verandah.) Oh it's you Amusa. Why didn't you just knock instead of knocking things over?

AMUSA (*stammers badly and points a shaky finger at his dress*). Mista Pirinkin . . . Mista Pirinkin . . .

PILKINGS. What is the matter with you?

JANE (*emerging*). Who is it dear? Oh, Amusa . . .

PILKINGS. Yes its Amusa, and acting most strangely.

AMUSA (*his attention now transferred to Mrs Pilkings*). Mammadam . . . you too!

PILKINGS. What the hell is the matter with you man!

JANE. Your costume darling. Our fancy dress.

PILKINGS. Oh hell, I'd forgotten all about that. (*Lifts the face mask over his head showing his face. His wife follows suit.*)

JANE. I think you've shocked his big pagan heart bless him.

PILKINGS. Nonsense, he's a Moslem. Come on Amusa, you don't believe in all this nonsense do you? I thought you were a good Moslem.

AMUSA. Mista Pirinkin, I beg you sir, what you think you do with that dress? It belong to dead cult, not for human being.

PILKINGS. Oh Amusa, what a let down you are. I swear by you at the club you know—thank God for Amusa, he doesn't believe in any mumbo-jumbo. And now look at you!

AMUSA. Mista Pirinkin, I beg you, take it off. Is no good for man like you to touch that cloth.

PILKINGS. Well, I've got it on. And what's more Jane and I have bet on it we're taking first prize at the ball. Now, if you can just pull yourself together and tell me what you wanted to see me about . . .

AMUSA. Sir, I cannot talk this matter to you in that dress. I no fit.

PILKINGS. What's that rubbish again?

JANE. He is dead earnest too Simon. I think you'll have to handle this delicately.

PILKINGS. Delicately my . . . ! Look here Amusa, I think this little joke has gone far enough hm? Let's have some sense. You seem to forget that you are a police officer in the service of His Majesty's Government. I order you to report your business at once or face disciplinary action.

AMUSA. Sir, it is a matter of death. How can man talk against death to person in uniform of death? Is like talking against government to person in uniform of police. Please sir, I go and come back.

PILKINGS (*roars*). Now! (*Amusa switches his gaze to the ceiling suddenly, remains mute.*)

JANE. Oh Amusa, what is there to be scared of in the costume? You saw it confiscated last month from those *egungun* men who were creating trouble in town. You helped arrest the cult leaders yourself—if the juju didn't harm you at the time how could it possibly harm you now? And merely by looking at it?

AMUSA (*without looking down*). Madam, I arrest the ringleaders who make trouble but me I no touch *egungun*. That *egungun* itself, I no touch. And I no abuse 'am. I arrest ringleader but I treat *egungun* with respect.

PILKINGS. It's hopeless. We'll merely end up missing the best part of the ball. When they get this way there is nothing you can do. It's simply hammering against a brick wall. Write your report or whatever it is on that pad Amusa and take yourself out of here. Come on Jane. We only upset his delicate sensibilities by remaining here.

(*Amusa waits for them to leave, then writes in the notebook, somewhat laboriously. Drumming from the direction of the town wells up. Amusa listens, makes a movement as if he wants to recall Pilkings but changes his mind. Completes his note and goes. A few moments later Pilkings emerges, picks up the pad and reads.*)

PILKINGS. Jane!

JANE (*from the bedroom*). Coming darling. Nearly ready.

PILKINGS. Never mind being ready, just listen to this.

JANE. What is it?

PILKINGS. Amusa's report. Listen. 'I have to report that it come to my information that one prominent chief, namely, the Elesin Oba, is to commit death tonight as a result of native custom. Because this is criminal offence I await further instruction at charge office. Sergeant Amusa.'

(*Jane comes out onto the verandah while he is reading.*)

JANE. Did I hear you say commit death?

PILKINGS. Obviously he means murder.

JANE. You mean a ritual murder?

PILKINGS. Must be. You think you've stamped it all out but it's always lurking under the surface somewhere.

JANE. Oh. Does it mean we are not getting to the ball at all?

PILKINGS. No-o. I'll have the man arrested. Everyone remotely involved. In any case there may be nothing to it. Just rumours.

JANE. Really? I thought you found Amusa's rumours generally reliable.

PILKINGS. That's true enough. But who knows what may have been giving him the scare lately. Look at his conduct tonight.

JANE (*laughing*). You have to admit he had his own peculiar logic. (*Deepens her voice.*) How can man talk against death to person in uniform of death? (*Laughs.*) Anyway, you can't go into the police station dressed like that.

PILKINGS. I'll send Joseph with instructions. Damn it, what a confounded nuisance!

JANE. But don't you think you should talk first to the man, Simon?

PILKINGS. Do you want to go to the ball or not?

JANE. Darling, why are you getting rattled? I was only trying to be intelligent. It seems hardly fair just to lock up a man—and a chief at that—simply on the er . . . what is that legal word again?—uncorroborated word of a sergeant.

PILKINGS. Well, that's easily decided. Joseph!

JOSEPH (*from within*). Yes master.

PILKINGS. You're quite right of course, I am getting rattled. Probably the effect of those bloody drums. Do you hear how they go on and on?

JANE. I wondered when you'd notice. Do you suppose it has something to do with this affair?

PILKINGS. Who knows? They always find an excuse for making a noise . . . (*Thoughtfully.*) Even so . . .

JANE. Yes Simon?

PILKINGS. It's different Jane. I don't think I've heard this particular—sound—before. Something unsettling about it.

JANE. I thought all bush drumming sounded the same.

PILKINGS. Don't tease me now Jane. This may be serious.

JANE. I'm sorry. (*Gets up and throws her arms around his neck. Kisses him. The houseboy enters, retreats and knocks.*)

PILKINGS (*wearily*). Oh, come in Joseph! I don't know where you pick up all these elephantine notions of tact. Come over here.

JOSEPH. Sir?

PILKINGS. Joseph, are you a Christian or not?

JOSEPH. Yessir.

PILKINGS. Does seeing me in this outfit bother you?

JOSEPH. No sir, it has no power.

PILKINGS. Thank God for some sanity at last. Now Joseph, answer me on the honour of a christian—what is supposed to be going on in town tonight?

JOSEPH. Tonight sir? You mean that chief who is going to kill himself?

PILKINGS. What?

JANE. What do you mean, kill himself?

PILKINGS. You do mean he is going to kill somebody don't you?

JOSEPH. No master. He will not kill anybody and no one will kill him. He will simply die.

JANE. But why Joseph?

JOSEPH. It is native law and custom. The King die last month. Tonight is his burial. But before they can bury him, the Elesin must die so as to accompany him to heaven.

PILKINGS. I seem to be fated to clash more often with that man than with any of the other chiefs.

JOSEPH. He is the King's Chief Horseman.

PILKINGS (*in a resigned way*). I know.

JANE. Simon, what's the matter?

PILKINGS. It would have to be him!

JANE. Who is he?

PILKINGS. Don't you remember? He's that chief with whom I had a scrap some three or four years ago. I helped his son get to a medical school in England, remember? He fought tooth and nail to prevent it.

JANE. Oh now I remember. He was that very sensitive young man. What was his name again?

PILKINGS. Olunde. Haven't replied to his last letter come to think of it. The old pagan wanted him to stay and carry on some family tradition or the other. Honestly I couldn't understand the fuss he made. I literally had to help the boy escape from close confinement and load him onto the next boat. A most intelligent boy, really bright.

JANE. I rather thought he was much too sensitive you know. The kind of person you feel should be a poet munching rose petals in Bloomsbury.

PILKINGS. Well, he's going to make a first-class doctor. His mind is set on that. And as long as he wants my help he is welcome to it.

JANE (*after a pause*). Simon.

PILKINGS. Yes?

JANE. This boy, he was his eldest son wasn't he?

PILKINGS. I'm not sure. Who could tell with that old ram?

JANE. Do you know, Joseph?

JOSEPH. Oh yes madam. He was the eldest son. That's why Elesin cursed master good and proper. The eldest son is not supposed to travel away from the land.

JANE (*giggling*). Is that true Simon? Did he really curse you good and proper?

PILKINGS. By all accounts I should be dead by now.

JOSEPH. Oh no, master is white man. And good christian. Black man juju can't touch master.

JANE. If he was his eldest, it means that he would be the Elesin to the next king. It's a family thing isn't it Joseph?

JOSEPH. Yes madam. And if this Elesin had died before the King, his eldest son must take his place.

JANE. That would explain why the old chief was so mad you took the boy away.

PILKINGS. Well it makes me all the more happy I did.

JANE. I wonder if he knew.

PILKINGS. Who? Oh, you mean Olunde?

JANE. Yes. Was that why he was so determined to get away? I wouldn't stay if I knew I was trapped in such a horrible custom.

PILKINGS (*thoughtfully*). No, I don't think he knew. At least he gave no indication. But you couldn't really tell with him. He was rather close you know, quite unlike most of them. Didn't give much away, not even to me.

JANE. Aren't they all rather close, Simon?

PILKINGS. These natives here? Good gracious. They'll open their mouths and yap with you about their family secrets before you can stop them. Only the other day . . .

JANE. But Simon, do they really give anything away? I mean, anything that really counts. This affair for instance, we didn't know they still practised that custom did we?

PILKINGS. Ye-e-es, I suppose you're right there. Sly, devious bastards.

JOSEPH (*stiffly*). Can I go now master? I have to clean the kitchen.

PILKINGS. What? Oh, you can go. Forgot you were still here.

(*Joseph goes.*)

JANE. Simon, you really must watch your language. Bastard isn't just a simple swear-word in these parts, you know.

PILKINGS. Look, just when did you become a social anthropologist, that's what I'd like to know.

JANE. I'm not claiming to know anything. I just happen to have overheard quarrels among the servants. That's how I know they consider it a smear.

PILKINGS. I thought the extended family system took care of all that. Elastic family, no bastards.

JANE (shrugs). Have it your own way.

(Awkward silence. The drumming increases in volume. Jane gets up suddenly, restless.)

That drumming Simon, do you think it might really be connected with this ritual? It's been going on all evening.

PILKINGS. Let's ask our native guide. Joseph! Just a minute Joseph. (Joseph re-enters.) What's the drumming about?

JOSEPH. I don't know master.

PILKINGS. What do you mean you don't know? It's only two years since your conversion. Don't tell me all that holy water nonsense also wiped out your tribal memory.

JOSEPH (visibly shocked). Master!

JANE. Now you've done it.

PILKINGS. What have I done now?

JANE. Never mind. Listen Joseph, just tell me this. Is that drumming connected with dying or anything of that nature?

JOSEPH. Madam, this is what I am trying to say: I am not sure. It sounds like the death of a great chief and then, it sounds like the wedding of a great chief. It really mix me up.

PILKINGS. Oh get back to the kitchen. A fat lot of help you are.

JOSEPH. Yes master. (Goes.)

JANE. Simon . . .

PILKINGS. Alright, alright. I'm in no mood for preaching.

JANE. It isn't my preaching you have to worry about, it's the preaching of the missionaries who preceded you here. When they make converts they really convert them. Calling holy water nonsense to our Joseph is really like insulting the Virgin Mary before a Roman Catholic. He's going to hand in his notice tomorrow you mark my word.

PILKINGS. Now you're being ridiculous.

JANE. Am I? What are you willing to bet that tomorrow we are going to be without a steward-boy? Did you see his face?

PILKINGS. I am more concerned about whether or not we will be one native chief short by tomorrow. Christ! Just listen to those drums. (He strides up and down, undecided.)

JANE (getting up). I'll change and make up some supper.

PILKINGS. What's that?

JANE. Simon, it's obvious we have to miss this ball.

PILKINGS. Nonsense. It's the first bit of real fun the European club has managed to organise for over a year, I'm damned if I'm going to miss it. And it is a rather special occasion. Doesn't happen every day.

JANE. You know this business has to be stopped Simon. And you are the only man who can do it.

PILKINGS. I don't have to stop anything. If they want to throw themselves off the top of a cliff or poison themselves for the sake of some barbaric custom what is that to me? If it were ritual murder or something like that I'd be duty-bound to do something. I can't keep an eye on all the potential suicides in this province. And as for that man—believe me it's good riddance.

JANE (laughs). I know you better than that Simon. You are going to have to do something to stop it—after you've finished blustering.

PILKINGS (shouts after her). And suppose after all it's only a wedding. I'd look a proper fool if I interrupted a chief on his honeymoon, wouldn't I? (Resumes his angry stride, slows down.) Ah well, who can tell what those chiefs actually do on their honeymoon anyway? (He takes up the pad and scribbles rapidly on it.) Joseph! Joseph! Joseph! (Some moments later Joseph puts in a sulky appearance.) Did you hear me call you? Why the hell didn't you answer?

JOSEPH. I didn't hear master.

PILKINGS. You didn't hear me! How come you are here then?

JOSEPH (stubbornly). I didn't hear master.

PILKINGS (controls himself with an effort). We'll talk about it in the morning. I want you to take this note directly to Sergeant Amusa. You'll find him at the charge office. Get on your bicycle and race there with it. I expect you back in twenty minutes exactly. Twenty minutes, is that clear?

JOSEPH. Yes master. (Going.)

PILKINGS. Oh er . . . Joseph.

JOSEPH. Yes master?

PILKINGS (between gritted teeth). Er . . . forget what I said just now. The holy water is not nonsense. I was talking nonsense.

JOSEPH. Yes master. (Goes.)

JANE (pokes her head round the door). Have you found him?

PILKINGS. Found who?

JANE. Joseph. Weren't you shouting for him?

PILKINGS. Oh yes, he turned up finally.

JANE. You sounded desperate. What was it all about?

PILKINGS. Oh nothing. I just wanted to apologise to him. Assure him that the holy water isn't really nonsense.

JANE. Oh? And how did he take it?

PILKINGS. Who the hell gives a damn! I had a sudden vision of our Very Reverend Macfarlane drafting another letter of complaint to the Resident about my unchristian language towards his parishioners.

JANE. Oh I think he's given up on you by now.

PILKINGS. Don't be too sure. And anyway, I wanted to make sure Joseph didn't 'lose' my note on the way. He looked sufficiently full of the holy crusade to do some such thing.

JANE. If you've finished exaggerating, come and have something to eat.

PILKINGS. No, put it all way. We can still get to the ball.

JANE. Simon . . .

PILKINGS. Get your costume back on. Nothing to worry about. I've instructed Amusa to arrest the man and lock him up.

JANE. But that station is hardly secure Simon. He'll soon get his friends to help him escape.

PILKINGS. A-ah, that's where I have out-thought you. I'm not having him put in the station cell. Amusa will bring him right here and lock him up in my study. And he'll stay with him till we get back. No one will dare come here to incite him to anything.

JANE. How clever of you darling. I'll get ready.

PILKINGS. Hey.

JANE. Yes darling.

PILKINGS. I have a surprise for you. I was going to keep it until we actually got to the ball.

JANE. What is it?

PILKINGS. You know the Prince is on a tour of the colonies don't you? Well, he docked in the capital only this morning but he is already at the Residency. He is going to grace the ball with his presence later tonight.

JANE. Simon! Not really.

PILKINGS. Yes he is. He's been invited to give away the prizes and he has agreed. You must admit old Engleton is the best Club Secretary we ever had. Quick off the mark that lad.

JANE. But how thrilling.

PILKINGS. The other provincials are going to be damned envious.

JANE. I wonder what he'll come as.

PILKINGS. Oh I don't know. As a coat-of-arms perhaps. Anyway it won't be anything to touch this.

JANE. Well that's lucky. If we are to be presented I won't have to start looking for a pair of gloves. It's all sewn on.

PILKINGS (laughing). Quite right. Trust a woman to think of that. Come on, let's get going.

JANE (rushing off). Won't be a second. (Stops.) Now I see why you've been so edgy all evening. I thought you weren't handling this affair with your usual brilliance—to begin with that is.

PILKINGS (his mood is much improved). Shut up woman and get your things on.

JANE. Alright boss, coming.

(Pilkings suddenly begins to hum the tango to which they were dancing before. Starts to execute a few practice steps. Lights fade.)

3

A swelling, agitated hum of women's voices rises immediately in the background. The lights come on and we see the frontage of a converted cloth stall in the market. The floor leading up to the entrance is covered in rich velvets and woven cloth. The women come on stage, borne backwards by the determined progress of Sergeant Amusa and his two constables who already have their batons out and use them as a pressure against the women. At the edge of the cloth-covered floor, however, the women take a determined stand and block all further progress of the men. They begin to tease them mercilessly.

AMUSA. I am tell you women for last time to commot my road. I am here on official business.

WOMAN. Official business you white man's eunuch? Official business is taking place where you want to go and it's a business you wouldn't understand.

WOMAN (makes a quick tug at the constable's baton). That doesn't fool anyone you know. It's the one you carry under your government knickers that counts. (She bends low as if to peep under the baggy shorts. The embarrassed constable quickly puts his knees together. The women roar.)

WOMAN. You mean there is nothing there at all?

WOMAN. Oh there was something. You know that handbell which the whiteman uses to summon his servants . . . ?

AMUSA (he manages to preserve some dignity throughout). I hope you women know that interfering with officer in execution of his duty is criminal offence.

WOMAN. Interfere? He says we're interfering with him. You foolish man we're telling you there's nothing there to interfere with.

AMUSA. I am order you now to clear the road.

WOMAN. What road? The one your father built?

WOMAN. You are a Policeman not so? Then you know what they call trespassing in court. Or—(Pointing to the cloth-lined steps)—do you think that kind of road is built for every kind of feet.

WOMAN. Go back and tell the white man who sent you to come himself.

AMUSA. If I go I will come back with reinforcement. And we will all return carrying weapons.

WOMAN. Oh, now I understand. Before they can put on those knickers the white man first cuts off their weapons.

WOMAN. What a cheek! You mean you come here to show power to women and you don't even have a weapon.

AMUSA (shouting above the laughter). For the last time I warn you women to clear the road.

WOMAN. To where?

AMUSA. To that hut. I know he dey dere.

WOMAN. Who?

AMUSA. The chief who call himself Elesin Oba.

WOMAN. You ignorant man. It is not he who calls himself Elesin Oba, it is his blood that says it. As it called out to his father before him and will to his son after him. And that is in spite of everything your white man can do.

WOMAN. Is it not the same ocean that washes this land and the white man's land? Tell your white man he can hide our son away as long as he likes. When the time comes for him, the same ocean will bring him back.

AMUSA. The government say dat kin' ting must stop.

WOMAN. Who will stop it? You? Tonight our husband and father will prove himself greater than the laws of strangers.

AMUSA. I tell you nobody go prove anyting tonight or anytime. Is ignorant and criminal to prove dat kin' prove.

IYALOJA (*entering, from the hut. She is accompanied by a group of young girls who have been attending the Bride*). What is it Amusa? Why do you come here to disturb the happiness of others.

AMUSA. Madame Iyaloja, I glad you come. You know me. I no like trouble but duty is duty. I am here to arrest Elesin for criminal intent. Tell these women to stop obstructing me in the performance of my duty.

IYALOJA. And you? What gives you the right to obstruct our leader of men in the performance of his duty.

AMUSA. What kin' duty be dat one Iyaloja.

IYALOJA. What kin' duty? What kin' duty does a man have to his new bride?

AMUSA (*bewildered, looks at the women and at the entrance to the hut*). Iyaloja, is it wedding you call dis kin' ting?

IYALOJA. You have wives haven't you? Whatever the white man has done to you he hasn't stopped you having wives. And if he has, at least he is married. If you don't know what a marriage is, go and ask him to tell you.

AMUSA. This no to wedding.

IYALOJA. And ask him at the same time what he would have done if anyone had come to disturb him on his wedding night.

AMUSA. Iyaloja, I say dis no to wedding.

IYALOJA. You want to look inside the bridal chamber? You want to see for yourself how a man cuts the virgin knot?

AMUSA. Madam . . .

WOMAN. Perhaps his wives are still waiting for him to learn.

AMUSA. Iyaloja, make you tell dese women make den no insult me again. If I hear dat kin' insult once more . . .

GIRL (*pushing her way through*). You will do what?

GIRL. He's out of his mind. It's our mothers you're talking to, do you know that? Not to any illiterate villager you can bully and terrorise. How dare you intrude here anyway?

GIRL. What a cheek, what impertinence!

GIRL. You've treated them too gently. Now let them see what it is to tamper with the mothers of this market.

GIRLS. Your betters dare not enter the market when the women say no!

GIRL. Haven't you learnt that yet, you jester in khaki and starch?

IYALOJA. Daughters . . .

GIRL. No no Iyaloja, leave us to deal with him. He no longer knows his mother, we'll teach him.

(*With a sudden movement they snatch the batons of the two constables. They begin to hem them in.*)

GIRL. What next? We have your batons? What next? What are you going to do?

(*With equally swift movements they knock off their hats.*)

GIRL. Move if you dare. We have your hats, what will you do about it? Didn't the white man teach you to take off your hats before women?

IYALOJA. It's a wedding night. It's a night of joy for us. Peace . . .

GIRL. Not for him. Who asked him here?

GIRL. Does he dare go to the Residency without an invitation?

GIRL. Not even where the servants eat the left-overs.

GIRLS (*in turn. In an 'English' accent*). Well well it's Mister Amusa. Were you invited? (*Play-acting to one another. The older women encourage them with their titters.*)

—Your invitation card please?

—Who are you? Have we been introduced?

—And who did you say you were?

—Sorry, I didn't quite catch your name.

—May I take your hat?

—If you insist. May I take yours? (*Exchanging the policeman's hats.*)

—How very kind of you.

—Not at all. Won't you sit down?

—After you.

—Oh no.

—I insist.

—You're most gracious.

—And how do you find the place?

—The natives are alright.

—Friendly?

—Tractable.

—Not a teeny-weeny bit restless?

—Well, a teeny-weeny bit restless.

—One might even say, difficult?

—Indeed one might be tempted to say, difficult.

—But you do manage to cope?

—Yes indeed I do. I have a rather faithful ox called Amusa.

—He's loyal?

—Absolutely.

—Lay down his life for you what?

—Without a moment's thought.

—Had one like that once. Trust him with my life.

—Mostly of course they are liars.

—Never known a native tell the truth.

—Does it get rather close around here?

—It's mild for this time of the year.

—But the rains may still come.

—They are late this year aren't they?

—They are keeping African time.

—Ha ha ha ha

—Ha ha ha ha

—The humidity is what gets me.

—It used to be whisky.

—Ha ha ha ha

—Ha ha ha ha

—What's your handicap old chap?

—Is there racing by golly?

—Splendid golf course, you'll like it.

—I'm beginning to like it already.

—And a European club, exclusive.

—You've kept the flag flying.

—We do our best for the old country.

—It's a pleasure to serve.

—Another whisky old chap?

—You are indeed too too kind.

—Not at all sir. Where is that boy? (*With a sudden bellow.*) Sergeant!

AMUSA (*snaps to attention*). Yessir!

(*The women collapse with laughter.*)

GIRL. Take your men out of here.

AMUSA (*realising the trick, he rages from loss of face*). I'm give you warning . . .

GIRL. Alright then. Off with his knickers! (*They surge slowly forward.*)

IYALOJA. Daughters, please.

AMUSA (*squaring himself for defence*). The first woman wey touch me . . .

IYALOJA. My children, I beg of you . . .

GIRL. Then tell him to leave this market. This is the home of our mothers. We don't want the eater of white left-overs at the feast their hands have prepared.

IYALOJA. You heard them Amusa. You had better go.

GIRLS. Now!

AMUSA (*commencing his retreat*). We dey go now, but make you no say we no warn you.

GIRL. Now!

GIRL. Before we read the riot act—you should know all about that.

AMUSA. Make we go. (*They depart, more precipitately.*)

(*The women strike their palms across in the gesture of wonder.*)

WOMEN. Do they teach you all that at school?

WOMAN. And to think I nearly kept Apinke away from the place.

WOMAN. Did you hear them? Did you see how they mimicked the white man?

WOMAN. The voices exactly. Hey, there are wonders in this world!

IYALOJA. Well, our elders have said it: Dada may be weak, but he has a younger sibling who is truly fearless.

WOMAN. The next time the white man shows his face in this market I will set Wuraola on his tail.

(*A woman bursts into song and dance of euphoria—'Tani l'awa o l'ogbeja? Kayi! A l'ogbeja. Omo Kekere l'ogbeja.* The rest of the women join in, some placing the girls on their back like infants, other dancing round them. The dance becomes general, mounting in excitement. Elesin appears, in wrapper only. In his hands a white velvet cloth folded loosely as if it held some delicate object. He cries out.*)

ELESIN. Oh you mothers of beautiful brides! (*The dancing stops. They turn and see him, and the object in his hands. Iyaloja approaches and gently takes the cloth from him.*) Take it. It is no mere virgin stain, but the union of life and the seeds of passage. My vital flow, the last from this flesh is intermingled with the promise of future life. All is prepared. Listen! (*A steady drum-beat from the distance.*) Yes. It is nearly time. The King's dog has been killed. The King's favourite horse is about to follow his master. My brother chiefs know their task and perform it well. (*He listens again.*)

(*The Bride emerges, stands shyly by the door. He turns to her.*)

Our marriage is not yet wholly fulfilled. When earth and passage wed, the consummation is complete only when there are grains of earth on the eyelids of passage. Stay by me till then. My faithful drummers, do me your last service. This is where I have chosen to do my leave-taking, in this heart of life, this hive which contains the swarm of the world in its small compass. This is where I have known love and laughter away from the palace. Even the richest food cloys when eaten days on end; in the market, nothing ever cloys. Listen. (*They listen to the drums.*) They have begun to seek out the heart of the King's favourite horse. Soon it will ride in its bolt of raffia with the dog at its feet. Together they will ride on the shoulders of the King's grooms through the pulse centres of the town. They know it is here I shall await them. I have told them. (*His eyes appear to cloud. He passes his hand over them as if to clear his sight. He gives a faint smile.*) It promises well; just then I felt my spirit's eagerness. The kite makes for wide spaces and the wind creeps up behind its tail; can the kite say less than—thank you, the quicker the better? But wait a while my spirit. Wait. Wait for the coming of the courier of the King. Do you know friends, the horse is born to this one destiny, to bear the burden that is man upon its back. Except for this night, this night alone when the spotless stallion will ride in triumph on the back of man. In the time of my father I witnessed the strange sight. Perhaps tonight also I shall see it for the last time. If they arrive before the drums beat for me, I shall tell him to let the Alafin know I follow swiftly. If they come after the drums have sounded, why then, all is well for I have gone ahead. Our spirits shall fall in step along the great passage. (*He listens to the drums. He seems again to be falling into a state of semi-hypnosis; his eyes scan the sky but it is in a kind of daze. His voice is a little breathless.*) The moon has fed, a glow from its full stomach fills the sky and air, but I cannot tell where is that gateway through which I must pass. My faithful friends, let our feet touch together this last time, lead me into the other market with sounds that cover my

---

*Who says we haven't a defender? Silence! We have our defenders. Little children are our champions.

skin with down yet make my limbs strike earth like a thoroughbred. Dear mothers, let me dance into the passage even as I have lived beneath your roofs. (*He comes down progressively among them. They make a way for him, the drummers playing. His dance is one of solemn, regal motions, each gesture of the body is made with a solemn finality. The women join him, their steps a somewhat more fluid version of his. Beneath the Praise-Singer's exhortation the women dirge 'Alę, lę lę, awo mil lọ'.*)

PRAISE-SINGER. Elesin Alafin, can you hear my voice?

ELESIN. Faintly, my friend, faintly.

PRAISE-SINGER. Elesin Alafin, can you hear my call?

ELESIN. Faintly my king, faintly.

PRAISE-SINGER. Is your memory sound Elesin?
  Shall my voice be a blade of grass and
  Tickle the armpit of the past?

ELESIN. My memory needs no prodding but
  What do you wish to say to me?

PRAISE-SINGER. Only what has been spoken. Only
  what concerns
  The dying wish of the father of all.

ELESIN. It is buried like seed-yam in my mind
  This is the season of quick rains, the harvest
  Is this moment due for gathering.

PRAISE-SINGER. If you cannot come, I said, swear
  You'll tell my favourite horse. I shall
  Ride on through the gates alone.

ELESIN. Elesin's message will be read
  Only when his loyal heart no longer beats.

PRAISE-SINGER. If you cannot come Elesin, tell my dog.
  I cannot stay the keeper too long
  At the gate.

ELESIN. A dog does not outrun the hand
  That feeds it meat. A horse that throws its rider
  Slows down to a stop. Elesin Alafin
  Trusts no beasts with messages between
  A king and his companion.

PRAISE-SINGER. If you get lost my dog will track
  The hidden path to me.

ELESIN. The seven-way crossroads confuses
  Only the stranger. The Horseman of the King
  Was born in the recesses of the house.

PRAISE-SINGER. I know the wickedness of men. If there is
  Weight on the loose end of your sash, such weight
  As no mere man can shift; if your sash is earthed
  By evil minds who mean to part us at the last . . .

ELESIN. My sash is of the deep purple *alari*;
  It is no tethering-rope. The elephant
  Trails no tethering-rope; that king
  Is not yet crowned who will peg an elephant—
  Not even you my friend and King.

PRAISE-SINGER. And yet this fear will not depart from me
  The darkness of this new abode is deep—
  Will your human eyes suffice?

ELESIN. In a night which falls before our eyes
  However deep, we do not miss our way.

PRAISE-SINGER. Shall I now not acknowledge I have stood
  Where wonders met their end? The elephant deserves
  Better than that we say 'I have caught
  A glimpse of something'. If we see the tamer
  Of the forest let us say plainly, we have seen
  An elephant.

ELESIN (*his voice is drowsy*).
  I have freed myself of earth and now
  It's getting dark. Strange voices guide my feet.

PRAISE-SINGER. The river is never so high that the eyes
  Of a fish are covered. The night is not so dark
  That the albino fails to find his way. A child
  Returning homewards craves no leading by the hand.
  Gracefully does the mask regain his
     grove at the end of day . . .
  Gracefully. Gracefully does the mask dance
  Homeward at the end of day, gracefully . . .

(*Elesin's trance appears to be deepening, his steps heavier.*)

IYALOJA. It is the death of war that kills the valiant,
  Death of water is how the swimmer goes
  It is the death of markets that kills the trader
  And death of indecision takes the idle away
  The trade of the cutlass blunts its edge
  And the beautiful die the death of beauty.
  It takes an Elesin to die the death of death . . .
  Only Elesin . . . dies the unknowable death of death . . .
  Gracefully, gracefully does the horseman regain
  The stables at the end of day, gracefully . . .

PRAISE-SINGER. How shall I tell what my eyes have seen? The Horseman gallops on before the courier, how shall I tell what my eyes have seen? He says a dog may be confused by new scents of beings he never dreamt of, so he must precede the dog to heaven. He says a horse may stumble on strange boulders and be lamed, so he races on before the horse to heaven. It is best, he says, to trust no messenger who may falter at the outer gate; oh how shall I tell what my ears have heard? But do you hear me still Elesin, do you hear your faithful one?

(*Elesin in his motions appears to feel for a direction of sound, subtly, but he only sinks deeper into his trance-dance.*)

Elesin, Alafin, I no longer sense your flesh. The drums are changing now but you have gone far ahead of the world. It is not yet noon in heaven; let those who claim it is begin their own journey home. So why must you rush like an impatient bride: why do you race to desert your Olohun-iyo?

(*Elesin is now sunk fully deep in his trance, there is no longer sign of any awareness of his surroundings.*)

Does the deep voice of *gbedu* cover you then, like the passage of royal elephants? Those drums that brook no rivals, have they blocked the passage to your ears that my voice passes into wind, a mere leaf floating in the night? Is your flesh lightened Elesin, is that lump of earth I slid between your slippers to keep you longer slowly sifting from your feet? Are the drums on the other side no tuning skin to skin with ours in osugbo? are there sounds there I cannot hear, do footsteps surround you which pound the earth like *gbedu*, roll like thunder round the dome of the world? Is the darkness gathering in your head Elesin? Is there now a streak of light at the end of the passage, a light I dare not look upon? Does it reveal whose voices we often heard, whose touches we often felt, whose wisdoms come suddenly into the mind when the wisest have shaken their heads and murmured; It cannot be done? Elesin Alafin, don't think I do not know why your lips are heavy, why your limbs are drowsy as palm oil in the cold of harmattan. I would call you back but when the elephant heads for the jungle, the tail is too small a hand-hold for the hunter that would pull him back. The sun that heads for the sea no longer heeds the prayers of the farmer. When the river begins to taste the salt of the ocean, we no longer know what deity to call on, the river-god or Olokun. No arrow flies back to the string, the child does not return through the same passage that gave it birth. Elesin Oba, can you hear me at all? Your eyelids are glazed like a courtesan's, is it that you see the dark groom and master of life? And will you see my father? Will you tell him that I stayed with you to the last? Will my voice ring in your ears awhile, will you remember Olohun-iyo even if the music on the other side surpasses his mortal craft? But will they know you over there? Have they eyes to gauge your worth, have they the heart to love you, will they know what thoroughbred prances towards them in caparisons of honour? If they do not Elesin, if any there cuts your yam with a small knife, or pours you wine in a small calabash, turn back and return to welcoming hands. If the world were not greater than the wishes of Olohun-iyo, I would not let you go . . .

(*He appears to break down. Elesin dances on, completely in a trance. The dirge wells up louder and stronger. Elesin's dance does not lose its elasticity but his gestures become, if possible, even more weighty. Lights fade slowly on the scene.*)

4

A Masque. The front side of the stage is part of a wide corridor around the great hall of the Residency extending beyond vision into the rear and wings. It is redolent of the tawdry decadence of a far-flung but key imperial frontier. The couples in a variety of fancy-dress are ranged around the walls, gazing in the same direction. The guest-of-honour is about to make an appearance. A portion of the local police brass band with its white conductor is just visible. At last, the entrance of Royalty. The band plays 'Rule Britannia', badly, beginning long before he is visible. The couples bow and curtsey as he passes by them. Both he and his companions are dressed in seventeenth century European costume. Following behind are the Resident and his partner similarly attired. As they gain the end of the hall where the orchestra dais begins the music comes to an end. The Prince bows to the guests. The band strikes up a Viennese waltz and the Prince formally opens the floor. Several bars later the Resident and his companion follow suit. Others follow in appropriate pecking order. The orchestra's waltz rendition is not of the highest musical standard.

Some time later the Prince dances again into view and is settled into a corner by the Resident who then proceeds to select couples as they dance past for introduction, sometimes threading his way through the dancers to tap the lucky couple on the shoulder. Desperate efforts from many to ensure that they are recognised in spite of, perhaps, their costume. The ritual of introductions soon takes in Pilkings and his wife. The Prince is quite fascinated by their costume and they demonstrate the adaptations they have made to it, pulling down the mask to demonstrate how the egungun normally appears, then showing the various press-button controls they have innovated for the face flaps, the sleeves, etc. They demonstrate the dance steps and the guttural sounds made by the egungun, harass other dancers in the hall, Mrs Pilkings playing the 'restrainer' to Pilkings' manic darts. Everyone is highly entertained, the Royal Party especially who lead the applause.

At this point a liveried footman comes in with a note on a salver and is intercepted almost absent-mindedly by the Resident who takes the note and reads it. After polite coughs he succeeds in excusing the Pilkingses from the Prince and takes them aside. The Prince considerately offers the Resident's wife his hand and dancing is resumed.

On their way out the Resident gives an order to his Aide-De-Camp. They come into the side corridor where the Resident hands the note to Pilkings.

RESIDENT. As you see it says 'emergency' on the outside. I took the liberty of opening it because His Highness was obviously enjoying the entertainment. I didn't want to interrupt unless really necessary.

PILKINGS. Yes, yes of course sir.

RESIDENT. Is it really as bad as it says? What's it all about?

PILKINGS. Some strange custom they have sir. It seems because the King is dead some important chief has to commit suicide.

RESIDENT. The King? Isn't it the same one who died nearly a month ago?

PILKINGS. Yes sir.

RESIDENT. Haven't they buried him yet?

PILKINGS. They take their time about these things sir. The pre-burial ceremonies last nearly thirty days. It seems tonight is the final night.

RESIDENT. But what has it got to do with the market women? Why are they rioting? We've waived that troublesome tax haven't we?

PILKINGS. We don't quite know that they are exactly rioting yet sir. Sergeant Amusa is sometimes prone to exaggerations.

RESIDENT. He sounds desperate enough. That comes out even in his rather quaint grammar. Where is the man anyway? I asked my aide-de-camp to bring him here.

PILKINGS. They are probably looking in the wrong verandah. I'll fetch him myself.

RESIDENT. No no you stay here. Let your wife go and look for them. Do you mind my dear . . . ?

JANE. Certainly not, your Excellency. (Goes.)

RESIDENT. You should have kept me informed Pilkings. You realise how disastrous it would have been if things had erupted while His Highness was here.

PILKINGS. I wasn't aware of the whole business until tonight sir.

RESIDENT. Nose to the ground Pilkings, nose to the ground. If we all let these little things slip past us where would the empire be eh? Tell me that. Where would we all be?

PILKINGS (low voice). Sleeping peacefully at home I bet.

RESIDENT. What did you say Pilkings?

PILKINGS. It won't happen again sir.

RESIDENT. It mustn't Pilkings. It mustn't. Where is that damned sergeant? I ought to get back to His Highness as quickly as possible and offer him some plausible explanation for my rather abrupt conduct. Can you think of one Pilkings?

PILKINGS. You could tell him the truth sir.

RESIDENT. I could? No no no no no Pilkings, that would never do. What! Go and tell him there is a riot just two miles away from him? This is supposed to be a secure colony of His Majesty, Pilkings.

PILKINGS. Yes sir.

RESIDENT. Ah, there they are. No, these are not our native police. Are these the ring-leaders of the riot?

PILKINGS. Sir, these are my police officers.

RESIDENT. Oh, I beg your pardon officers. You do look a little . . . I say, isn't there something missing in their uniform? I think they used to have some rather colourful sashes. If I remember rightly I recommended them myself in my young days in the service. A bit of colour always appeals to the natives, yes, I remember putting that in my report. Well well well, where are we? Make your report man.

PILKINGS (moves close to Amusa, between his teeth). And let's have no more superstitious nonsense from your Amusa or I'll throw you in the guardroom for a month and feed you pork!

RESIDENT. What's that? What has pork to do with it?

PILKINGS. Sir, I was just warning him to be brief. I'm sure you are most anxious to hear his report.

RESIDENT. Yes yes yes of course. Come on man, speak up. Hey, didn't we give them some colourful fez hats with all those wavy things, yes, pink tassells . . .

PILKINGS. Sir, I think if he was permitted to make his report we might find that he lost his hat in the riot.

RESIDENT. Ah yes indeed. I'd better tell His Highness that. Lost his hat in the riot, ha ha. He'll probably say well, as long as he didn't lose his head. (Chuckles to himself.) Don't forget to send me a report first thing in the morning young Pilkings.

PILKINGS. No sir.

RESIDENT. And whatever you do, don't let things get out of hand. Keep a cool head and—nose to the ground Pilkings. (Wanders off in the general direction of the hall.)

PILKINGS. Yes sir.

AIDE-DE-CAMP. Would you be needing me sir?

PILKINGS. No thanks Bob. I think His Excellency's need of you is greater than ours.

AIDE-DE-CAMP. We have a detachment of soldiers from the capital sir. They accompanied His Highness up here.

PILKINGS. I doubt if it will come to that but, thanks, I'll bear it in mind. Oh, could you send an orderly with my cloak.

AIDE-DE-CAMP. Very good sir. (Goes.)

PILKINGS. Now Sergeant.

AMUSA. Sir . . . (Makes an effort, stops dead. Eyes to the ceiling.)

PILKINGS. Oh, not again.

AMUSA. I cannot against death to dead cult. This dress get power of dead.

PILKINGS. Alright, let's go. You are relieved of all further duty Amusa. Report to me first thing in the morning.

JANE. Shall I come Simon?

PILKINGS. No, there's no need for that. If I can get back later I will. Otherwise get Bob to bring you home.

JANE. Be careful Simon . . . I mean, be clever.

PILKINGS. Sure I will. You two, come with me. (As he turns to go, the clock in the Residency begins to chime. Pilkings looks at his watch then turns, horror-stricken, to stare at his wife. The same thought clearly occurs to her. He swallows hard. An orderly brings his cloak.) It's midnight. I had no idea it was that late.

JANE. But surely . . . they don't count the hours the way we do. The moon, or something . . .

PILKINGS. I am . . . not so sure.

(He turns and breaks into a sudden run. The two constables follow, also at a run. Amusa, who has kept his eyes on the ceiling throughout waits until the last of the footsteps has faded out of hearing. He salutes suddenly, but without once looking in the direction of the woman.)

AMUSA. Goodnight madam.

JANE. Oh. (She hesitates.) Amusa . . . (He goes off without seeming to have heard.) Poor Simon . . . (A figure emerges *from the shadows, a young black man dressed in a sober western suit. He peeps into the hall, trying to make out the figures of the dancers.)*

Who is that?

OLUNDE *(emerging into the light)*. I didn't mean to startle you madam. I am looking for the District Officer.

JANE. Wait a minute . . . don't I know you? Yes, you are Olunde, the young man who . . .

OLUNDE. Mrs Pilkings! How fortunate. I came here to look for your husband.

JANE. Olunde! Let's look at you. What a fine young man you've become. Grand but solemn. Good God, when did you return? Simon never said a word. But you do look well Olunde. Really!

OLUNDE. You are . . . well, you look quite well yourself Mrs Pilkings. From what little I can see of you.

JANE. Oh, this. It's caused quite a stir I assure you, and not all of it very pleasant. You are not shocked I hope?

OLUNDE. Why should I be? But don't you find it rather hot in there? Your skin must find it difficult to breathe.

JANE. Well, it is a little hot I must confess, but it's all in a good cause.

OLUNDE. What cause Mrs Pilkings?

JANE. All this. The ball. And His Highness being here in person and all that.

OLUNDE *(mildly)*. And that is the good cause for which you desecrate an ancestral mask?

JANE. Oh, so you are shocked after all. How disappointing.

OLUNDE. No I am not shocked Mrs Pilkings. You forget that I have now spent four years among your people. I discovered that you have no respect for what you do not understand.

JANE. Oh. So you've returned with a chip on your shoulder. That's a pity Olunde. I am sorry.

(An uncomfortable silence follows.)

I take it then that you did not find your stay in England altogether edifying.

OLUNDE. I don't say that. I found your people quite admirable in many ways, their conduct and courage in this war for instance.

JANE. Ah yes the war. Here of course it is all rather remote. From time to time we have a black-out drill just to remind us that there is a war on. And the rare convoy passes through on its way somewhere or on manoeuvres. Mind you there is the occasional bit of excitement like that ship that was blown up in the harbour.

OLUNDE. Here? Do you mean through enemy action?

JANE. Oh no, the war hasn't come that close. The captain did it himself. I don't quite understand it really. Simon tried to explain. The ship had to be blown up because it had become dangerous to the other ships, even to the city itself. Hundreds of the coastal population would have died.

OLUNDE. Maybe it was loaded with ammunition and had caught fire. Or some of those lethal gases they've been experimenting on.

JANE. Something like that. The captain blew himself up with it. Deliberately. Simon said someone had to remain on board to light the fuse.

OLUNDE. It must have been a very short fuse.

JANE *(shrugs)*. I don't know much about it. Only that there was no other way to save lives. No time to devise anything else. The captain took the decision and carried it out.

OLUNDE. Yes . . . I quite believe it. I met men like that in England.

JANE. Oh just look at me! Fancy welcoming you back with such morbid news. Stale too. It was at least six months ago.

OLUNDE. I don't find it morbid at all. I find it rather inspiring. It is an affirmative commentary on life.

JANE. What is?

OLUNDE. That captain's self-sacrifice.

JANE. Nonsense. Life should never be thrown deliberately away.

OLUNDE. And the innocent people round the harbour?

JANE. Oh, how does one know? The whole thing was probably exaggerated anyway.

OLUNDE. That was a risk the captain couldn't take. But please Mrs Pilkings, do you think you could find your husband for me? I have to talk to him.

JANE. Simon? Oh. *(As she recollects for the first time the full significance of Olunde's presence.)* Simon is . . . there is a little problem in town. He was sent for. But . . . when did you arrive? Does Simon know you're here?

OLUNDE *(suddenly earnest)*. I need your help Mrs Pilkings. I've always found you somewhat more understanding than your husband. Please find him for me and when you do, you must help me talk to him.

JANE. I'm afraid I don't quite . . . follow you. Have you seen my husband already?

OLUNDE. I went to your house. Your houseboy told me you were here. *(He smiles.)* He even told me how I would recognise you and Mr Pilkings.

JANE. Then you must know what my husband is trying to do for you.

OLUNDE. For me?

JANE. For you. For your people. And to think he didn't even know you were coming back! But how do you happen to be here? Only this evening we were talking about you. We thought you were still four thousand miles away.

OLUNDE. I was sent a cable.

JANE. A cable? Who did? Simon? The business of your father didn't begin till tonight.

OLUNDE. A relation sent it weeks ago, and it said nothing about my father. All it said was, Our King is dead. But I knew I had to return home at once so as to bury my father. I understood that.

JANE. Well, thank God you don't have to go through that agony. Simon is going to stop it.

OLUNDE. That's why I want to see him. He's wasting his time. And since he has been so helpful to me I don't want him to incur the enmity of our people. Especially over nothing.

JANE (*sits down open-mouthed*). You . . . you Olunde!

OLUNDE. Mrs Pilkings, I came home to bury my father. As soon as I heard the news I booked my passage home. In fact we were fortunate. We travelled in the same convoy as your Prince, so we had excellent protection.

JANE. But you don't think your father is also entitled to whatever protection is available to him?

OLUNDE. How can I make you understand? He *has* protection. No one can undertake what he does tonight without the deepest protection the mind can conceive. What can you offer him in place of his peace of mind, in place of the honour and veneration of his own people? What would you think of your Prince if he had refused to accept the risk of losing his life on this voyage? This . . . showing-the-flag tour of colonial possessions.

JANE. I see. So it isn't just medicine you studied in England.

OLUNDE. Yet another error into which your people fall. You believe that everything which appears to make sense was learnt from you.

JANE. Not so fast Olunde. You have learnt to argue I can tell that, but I never said you made sense. However cleverly you try to put it, it is still a barbaric custom. It is even worse—it's feudal! The king dies and a chieftain must be buried with him. How feudalistic can you get!

OLUNDE (*waves his hand towards the background. The Prince is dancing past again—to a different step—and all the guests are bowing and curtseying as he passes*). And this? Even in the midst of a devastating war, look at that. What name would you give to that?

JANE. Therapy, British style. The preservation of sanity in the midst of chaos.

OLUNDE. Others would call it decadence. However, it doesn't really interest me. You white races know how to survive; I've seen proof of that. By all logical and natural laws this war should end with all the white races wiping out one another, wiping out their so-called civilisation for all time and reverting to a state of primitivism the like of which has so far only existed in your imagination when you thought of us. I thought all that at the beginning. Then I slowly realised that your greatest art is the art of survival. But at least have the humility to let others survive in their own way.

JANE. Through ritual suicide?

OLUNDE. Is that worse than mass suicide? Mrs Pilkings, what do you call what those young men are sent to do by their generals in this war? Of course you have also mastered the art of calling things by names which don't remotely describe them.

JANE. You talk! You people with your long-winded, round-about way of making conversation.

OLUNDE. Mrs Pilkings, whatever we do, we never suggest that a thing is the opposite of which it really is. In your

newsreels I heard defeats, thorough, murderous defeats described as strategic victories. No wait, it wasn't just on your newsreels. Don't forget I was attached to hospitals all the time. Hordes of your wounded passed through those wards. I spoke to them. I spent long evenings by their bedside while they spoke terrible truths of the realities of that war. I know now how history is made.

JANE. But surely, in a war of this nature, for the morale of the nation you must expect . . .

OLUNDE. That a disaster beyond human reckoning be spoken of as a triumph? No. I mean, is there no mourning in the home of the bereaved that such blasphemy is permitted?

JANE (*after a moment's pause*). Perhaps I can understand you now. The time we picked for you was not really one for seeing us at our best.

OLUNDE. Don't think it was just the war. Before that even started I had plenty of time to study your people. I saw nothing, finally, that gave you the right to pass judgement on other peoples and their ways. Nothing at all.

JANE (*hesitantly*). Was it the . . . colour thing? I know there is some discrimination.

OLUNDE. Don't make it so simple, Mrs Pilkings. You make it sound as if when I left, I took nothing at all with me.

JANE. Yes . . . and to tell the truth, only this evening, Simon and I agreed that we never really knew what you left with.

OLUNDE. Neither did I. But I found out over there. I am grateful to your country for that. And I will never give it up.

JANE. Olunde, please . . . promise me something. Whatever you do, don't throw away what you have started to do. You want to be a doctor. My husband and I believe you will make an excellent one, sympathetic and competent. Don't let anything make you throw away your training.

OLUNDE (*genuinely surprised*). Of course not. What a strange idea. I intend to return and complete my training. Once the burial of my father is over.

JANE. Oh, please . . . !

OLUNDE. Listen! Come outside. You can't hear anything against that music.

JANE. What is it?

OLUNDE. The drums. Can you hear the change? Listen.

(*The drums come over, still distant but more distinct. There is a change of rhythm, it rises to a crescendo and then, suddenly, it is cut off. After a silence, a new beat begins, slow and resonant.*)

There. It's all over.

JANE. You mean he's . . .

OLUNDE. Yes Mrs Pilkings, my father is dead. His willpower has always been enormous; I know he is dead.

JANE (*screams*). How can you be so callous! So unfeeling! You announce your father's own death like a surgeon looking down on some strange . . . stranger's body! You're just a savage like all the rest.

Wole Soyinka

AIDE-DE-CAMP (*rushing out*). Mrs Pilkings. Mrs Pilkings. (*She breaks down, sobbing.*) Are you alright, Mrs Pilkings?

OLUNDE. She'll be alright. (*Turns to go.*)

AIDE-DE-CAMP. Who are you? And who the hell asked your opinion?

OLUNDE. You're quite right, nobody. (*Going.*)

AIDE-DE-CAMP. What the hell! Did you hear me ask you who you were?

OLUNDE. I have business to attend to.

AIDE-DE-CAMP. I'll give you business in a moment you impudent nigger. Answer my question!

OLUNDE. I have a funeral to arrange. Excuse me. (*Going.*)

AIDE-DE-CAMP. I said stop! Orderly!

JANE. No no, don't do that. I'm alright. And for heaven's sake don't act so foolishly. He's a family friend.

AIDE-DE-CAMP. Well he'd better learn to answer civil questions when he's asked them. These natives put a suit on and they get high opinions of themselves.

OLUNDE. Can I go now?

JANE. No no don't go. I must talk to you. I'm sorry about what I said.

OLUNDE. It's nothing Mrs Pilkings. And I'm really anxious to go. I couldn't see my father before, it's forbidden for me, his heir and successor to set eyes on him from the moment of the king's death. But now . . . I would like to touch his body while it is still warm.

JANE. You will. I promise I shan't keep you long. Only, I couldn't possibly let you go like that. Bob, please excuse us.

AIDE-DE-CAMP. If you're sure . . .

JANE. Of course I'm sure. Something happened to upset me just then, but I'm alright now. Really.

(*The Aide-De-Camp goes, somewhat reluctantly.*)

OLUNDE. I mustn't stay long.

JANE. Please, I promise not to keep you. It's just that . . . oh you saw yourself what happens to one in this place. The Resident's man thought he was being helpful, that's the way we all react. But I can't go in among that crowd just now and if I stay by myself somebody will come looking for me. Please, just say something for a few moments and then you can go. Just so I can recover myself.

OLUNDE. What do you want me to say?

JANE. Your calm acceptance for instance, can you explain that? It was so unnatural. I don't understand that at all. I feel a need to understand all I can.

OLUNDE. But you explained it yourself. My medical training perhaps. I have seen death too often. And the soldiers who returned from the front, they died on our hands all the time.

JANE. No. It has to be more than that. I feel it has to do with the many things we don't really grasp about your people. At least you can explain.

OLUNDE. All these things are part of it. And anyway, my father has been dead in my mind for nearly a month. Ever since I learnt of the King's death. I've lived with my be-reavement so long now that I cannot think of him alive. On that journey on the boat, I kept my mind on my duties as the one who must perform the rites over his body. I went through it all again and again in my mind as he himself had taught me. I didn't want to do anything wrong, something which might jeopardise the welfare of my people.

JANE. But he had disowned you. When you left he swore publicly you were no longer his son.

OLUNDE. I told you, he was a man of tremendous will. Sometimes that's another way of saying stubborn. But among our people, you don't disown a child just like that. Even if I had died before him I would still be buried like his eldest son. But it's time for me to go.

JANE. Thank you. I feel calmer. Don't let me keep you from your duties.

OLUNDE. Goodnight Mrs Pilkings.

JANE. Welcome home. (*She holds out her hand. As he takes it footsteps are heard approaching the drive. A short while later a woman's sobbing is also heard.*)

PILKINGS (*off*). Keep them here till I get back. (*He strides into view, reacts at the sight of Olunde but turns to his wife.*) Thank goodness you're still here.

JANE. Simon, what happened?

PILKINGS. Later Jane, please. Is Bob still here?

JANE. Yes, I think so. I'm sure he must be.

PILKINGS. Try and get him out here as quietly as you can. Tell him it's urgent.

JANE. Of course. Oh Simon, you remember . . .

PILKINGS. Yes yes. I can see who it is. Get Bob out here. (*She runs off.*) At first I thought I was seeing a ghost.

OLUNDE. Mr Pilkings, I appreciate what you tried to do. I want you to believe that. I can only tell you it would have been a terrible calamity if you'd succeeded.

PILKINGS (*opens his mouth several times, shuts it*). You . . . said what?

OLUNDE. A calamity for us, the entire people.

PILKINGS (*sighs*). I see. Hm.

OLUNDE. And now I must go. I must see him before he turns cold.

PILKINGS. Oh ah . . . em . . . but this is a shock to see you. I mean er thinking all this while you were in England and thanking God for that.

OLUNDE. I came on the mail boat. We travelled in the Prince's convoy.

PILKINGS. Ah yes, a-ah, hm . . . er well . . .

OLUNDE. Goodnight. I can see you are shocked by the whole business. But you must know by now there are things you cannot understand—or help.

PILKINGS. Yes. Just a minute. There are armed policemen that way and they have instructions to let no one pass. I suggest you wait a little. I'll er . . . yes, I'll give you an escort.

OLUNDE. That's very kind of you. But do you think it could be quickly arranged.

PILKINGS. Of course. In fact, yes, what I'll do is send Bob

over with some men to the er . . . place. You can go with them. Here he comes now. Excuse me a minute.

AIDE-DE-CAMP. Anything wrong sir?

PILKINGS (*takes him to one side*). Listen Bob, that cellar in the disused annex of the Residency, you know, where the slaves were stored before being taken down to the coast . . .

AIDE-DE-CAMP. Oh yes, we use it as a storeroom for broken furniture.

PILKINGS. But it's still got the bars on it?

AIDE-DE-CAMP. Oh yes, they are quite intact.

PILKINGS. Get the keys please. I'll explain later. And I want a strong guard over the Residency tonight.

AIDE-DE-CAMP. We have that already. The detachment from the coast . . .

PILKINGS. No, I don't want them at the gates of the Residency. I want you to deploy them at the bottom of the hill, a long way from the main hall so they can deal with any situation long before the sound carries to the house.

AIDE-DE-CAMP. Yes of course.

PILKINGS. I don't want His Highness alarmed.

AIDE-DE-CAMP. You think the riot will spread here?

PILKINGS. It's unlikely but I don't want to take a chance. I made them believe I was going to lock the man up in my house, which was what I had planned to do in the first place. They are probably assailing it by now. I took a roundabout route here so I don't think there is any danger at all. At least not before dawn. Nobody is to leave the premises of course—the native employees I mean. They'll soon smell something is up and they can't keep their mouths shut.

AIDE-DE-CAMP. I'll give instructions at once.

PILKINGS. I'll take the prisoner down myself. Two policemen will stay with him throughout the night. Inside the cell.

AIDE-DE-CAMP. Right sir. (*Salutes and goes off at the double.*)

PILKINGS. Jane. Bob is coming back in a moment with a detachment. Until he gets back please stay with Olunde. (*He makes an extra warning gesture with his eyes.*)

OLUNDE. Please Mr Pilkings . . .

PILKINGS. I hate to be stuffy old son, but we have a crisis on our hands. It has to do with your father's affair if you must know. And it happens also at a time when we have His Highness here. I am responsible for security so you'll simply have to do as I say. I hope that's understood. (*Marches off quickly, in the direction from which he made his first appearance.*)

OLUNDE. What's going on? All this can't be just because he failed to stop my father killing himself.

JANE. I honestly don't know. Could it have sparked off a riot?

OLUNDE. No. If he'd succeeded that would be more likely to start the riot. Perhaps there were other factors involved. Was there a chieftaincy dispute?

JANE. None that I know of.

ELESIN (*an animal bellow from off*). Leave me alone! Is it not

enough that you have covered me in shame! White man, take your hand from my body!

(*Olunde stands frozen on the spot. Jane understanding at last, tries to move him.*)

JANE. Let's go in. It's getting chilly out here.

PILKINGS (*off*). Carry him.

ELESIN. Give me back the name you have taken away from me you ghost from the land of the nameless!

PILKINGS. Carry him! I can't have a disturbance here. Quickly! stuff up his mouth.

JANE. Oh God! Let's go in. Please Olunde. (*Olunde does not move.*)

ELESIN. Take your albino's hand from me you . . .

(*Sounds of a struggle. His voice chokes as he is gagged.*)

OLUNDE (*quietly*). That was my father's voice.

JANE. Oh you poor orphan, what have you come home to?

(*There is a sudden explosion of rage from off-stage and powerful steps come running up the drive.*)

PILKINGS. You bloody fools, after him!

(*Immediately Elesin, in handcuffs, comes pounding in the direction of Jane and Olunde, followed some moments afterwards by Pilkings and the constables. Elesin confronted by the seeming statue of his son, stops dead. Olunde stares above his head into the distance. The constables try to grab him. Jane screams at them.*)

JANE. Leave him alone! Simon, tell them to leave him alone.

PILKINGS. All right, stand aside you. (*Shrugs.*) Maybe just as well. It might help to calm him down.

For several moments they hold the same position. Elesin moves a few steps forward, almost as if he's still in doubt.

ELESIN. Olunde! (*He moves his head, inspecting him from side to side.*) Olunde! (*He collapses slowly at Olunde's feet.*) Oh son, don't let the sight of your father turn you blind!

OLUNDE (*he moves for the first time since he heard his voice, brings his head slowly down to look on him*). I have no father, eater of left-overs.

(*He walks slowly down the way his father had run. Light fades out on Elesin, sobbing into the ground.*)

5

A wide iron-barred gate stretches almost the whole width of the cell in which Elesin is imprisoned. His wrists are encased in thick iron bracelets, chained together; he stands against the bars, looking out. Seated on the ground to one side on the outside is his recent bride, her eyes bent perpetually to the ground. Figures of the two guards can be seen

Wole Soyinka

deeper inside the cell, alert to every movement Elesin makes. Pilkings now in a police officer's uniform enters noiselessly, observes him for a while. Then he coughs ostentatiously and approaches. Leans against the bars near a corner, his back to Elesin. He is obviously trying to fall in mood with him. Some moments' silence.

PILKINGS. You seem fascinated by the moon.

ELESIN (*after a pause*). Yes, ghostly one. Your twin-brother up there engages my thoughts.

PILKINGS. It is a beautiful night.

ELESIN. Is that so?

PILKINGS. The light on the leaves, the peace of the night . . .

ELESIN. The night is not at peace, District Officer.

PILKINGS. No? I would have said it was. You know, quiet . . .

ELESIN. And does quiet mean peace for you?

PILKINGS. Well, nearly the same thing. Naturally there is a subtle difference . . .

ELESIN. The night is not at peace ghostly one. The world is not at peace. You have shattered the peace of the world for ever. There is no sleep in the world tonight.

PILKINGS. It is still a good bargain if the world should lose one night's sleep as the price of saving a man's life.

ELESIN. You did not save my life District Officer. You destroyed it.

PILKINGS. Now come on . . .

ELESIN. And not merely my life but the lives of many. The end of the night's work is not over. Neither this year nor the next will see it. If I wished you well, I would pray that you do not stay long enough on our land to see the disaster you have brought upon us.

PILKINGS. Well, I did my duty as I saw it. I have no regrets.

ELESIN. No. The regrets of life always come later.

(*Some moments' pause.*)

You are waiting for dawn white man. I hear you saying to yourself: only so many hours until dawn and then the danger is over. All I must do is keep him alive tonight. You don't quite understand it all but you know that tonight is when what ought to be must be brought about. I shall ease your mind even more, ghostly one. It is not an entire night but a moment of the night, and that moment is past. The moon was my messenger and guide. When it reached a certain gateway in the sky, it touched that moment for which my whole life has been spent in blessings. Even I do not know the gateway. I have stood here and scanned the sky for a glimpse of that door but, I cannot see it. Human eyes are useless for a search of this nature. But in the house of osugbo, those who keep watch through the spirit recognised the moment, they sent word to me through the voice of our sacred drums to prepare myself. I heard them and I shed all thoughts of earth. I began to follow the moon to the abode of gods . . . servant of the white king, that was when you entered my chosen place of departure on feet of desecration.

PILKINGS. I'm sorry, but we all see our duty differently.

ELESIN. I no longer blame you. You stole from me my first-born, sent him to your country so you could turn him into something in your own image. Did you plan it all beforehand? There are moments when it seems part of a larger plan. He who must follow my footsteps is taken from me, sent across the ocean. Then, in my turn, I am stopped from fulfilling my destiny. Did you think it all out before, this plan to push our world from its course and sever the cord that links us to the great origin?

PILKINGS. You don't really believe that. Anyway, if that was my intention with your son, I appear to have failed.

ELESIN. You did not fail in the main thing ghostly one. We know the roof covers the rafters, the cloth covers blemishes; who would have known that the white skin covered our future, preventing us from seeing the death our enemies had prepared for us. The world is set adrift and its inhabitants are lost. Around them, there is nothing but emptiness.

PILKINGS. Your son does not take so gloomy a view.

ELESIN. Are you dreaming now white man? Were you not present at my reunion of shame? Did you not see when the world reversed itself and the father fell before his son, asking forgiveness?

PILKINGS. That was in the heat of the moment. I spoke to him and . . . if you want to know, he wishes he could cut out his tongue for uttering the words he did.

ELESIN. No. What he said must never be unsaid. The contempt of my own son rescued something of my shame at your hands. You may have stopped me in my duty but I know now that I did give birth to a son. Once I mistrusted him for seeking the companionship of those my spirit knew as enemies of our race. Now I understand. One should seek to obtain the secrets of his enemies. He will avenge my shame, white one. His spirit will destroy you and yours.

PILKINGS. That kind of talk is hardly called for. If you don't want my consolation . . .

ELESIN. No white man, I do not want your consolation.

PILKINGS. As you wish. Your son anyway, sends his consolation. He asks your forgiveness. When I asked him not to despise you his reply was: I cannot judge him, and if I cannot judge him, I cannot despise him. He wants to come to you to say goodbye and to receive your blessing.

ELESIN. Goodbye? Is he returning to your land?

PILKINGS. Don't you think that's the most sensible thing for him to do? I advised him to leave at once, before dawn, and he agrees that is the right course of action.

ELESIN. Yes, it is best. And even if I did not think so, I have lost the father's place of honour. My voice is broken.

PILKINGS. Your son honours you. If he didn't he would not ask your blessing.

ELESIN. No. Even a thoroughbred is not without pity for the turf he strikes with his hoof. When is he coming?

PILKINGS. As soon as the town is a little quieter. I advised it.

ELESIN. Yes white man, I am sure you advised it. You advise all our lives although on the authority of what gods, I do not know.

PILKINGS (*opens his mouth to reply, then appears to change his mind. Turns to go. Hesitates and stops again*). Before I leave you, may I ask just one thing of you?

ELESIN. I am listening.

PILKINGS. I wish to ask you to search the quiet of your heart and tell me—do you not find great contradictions in the wisdom of your own race?

ELESIN. Make yourself clear, white one.

PILKINGS. I have lived among you long enough to learn a saying or two. One came to my mind tonight when I stepped into the market and saw what was going on. You were surrounded by those who egged you on with song and praises. I thought, are these not the same people who say: the elder grimly approaches heaven and you ask him to bear your greetings yonder; do you really think he makes the journey willingly? After that, I did not hesitate.

(*A pause. Elesin sighs. Before he can speak a sound of running feet is heard.*)

JANE (*off*). Simon! Simon!

PILKINGS. What on earth . . . ! (*Runs off.*)

(*Elesin turns to his new wife, gazes on her for some moments.*)

ELESIN. My young bride, did you hear the ghostly one? You sit and sob in your silent heart but say nothing to all this. First I blamed the white man, then I blamed my gods for deserting me. Now I feel I want to blame you for the mystery of the sapping of my will. But blame is a strange peace offering for a man to bring a world he has deeply wronged, and to its innocent dwellers. Oh little mother, I have taken countless women in my life but you were more than a desire of the flesh. I needed you as the abyss across which my body must be drawn, I filled it with earth and dropped my seed in it at the moment of preparedness for my crossing. You were the final gift of the living to their emissary to the land of the ancestors, and perhaps your warmth and youth brought new insights of this world to me and turned my feet leaden on this side of the abyss. For I confess to you, daughter, my weakness came not merely from the abomination of the white man who came violently into my fading presence, there was also a weight of longing on my earth-held limbs. I would have shaken it off, already my foot had begun to lift but then, the white ghost entered and all was defiled.

(*Approaching voices of Pilkings and his wife.*)

JANE. Oh Simon, you will let her in won't you?

PILKINGS. I really wish you'd stop interfering.

(*They come in view. Jane is in a dressing-gown. Pilkings is holding a note to which he refers from time to time.*)

JANE. Good gracious, I didn't initiate this. I was sleeping quietly, or trying to anyway, when the servant brought it. It's not my fault if one can't sleep undisturbed even in the Residency.

PILKINGS. He'd have done the same if we were sleeping at home so don't sidetrack the issue. He knows he can get round you or he wouldn't send you the petition in the first place.

JANE. Be fair Simon. After all he was thinking of your own interests. He is grateful you know, you seem to forget that. He feels he owes you something.

PILKINGS. I just wish they'd leave this man alone tonight, that's all.

JANE. Trust him Simon. He's pledged his word it will all go peacefully.

PILKINGS. Yes, and that's the other thing. I don't like being threatened.

JANE. Threatened? (*Takes the note.*) I didn't spot any threat.

PILKINGS. It's there. Veiled, but it's there. The only way to prevent serious rioting tomorrow—what a cheek!

JANE. I don't think he's threatening you Simon.

PILKINGS. He's picked up the idiom alright. Wouldn't surprise me if he's been mixing with commies or anarchists over there. The phrasing sounds too good to be true. Damn! If only the Prince hadn't picked this time for his visit.

JANE. Well, even so Simon, what have you got to lose? You don't want a riot on your hands, not with the Prince here.

PILKINGS (*going up to Elesin*). Let's see what he has to say. Chief Elesin, there is yet another person who wants to see you. As she is not a next-of-kin I don't really feel obliged to let her in. But your son sent a note with her, so it's up to you.

ELESIN. I know who that must be. So she found out your hiding-place. Well, it was not difficult. My stench of shame is so strong, it requires no hunter's dog to follow it.

PILKINGS. If you don't want to see her, just say so and I'll send her packing.

ELESIN. Why should I not want to see her? Let her come. I have no more holes in my rag of shame. All is laid bare.

PILKINGS. I'll bring her in. (*Goes off.*)

JANE (*hesitates, then goes to Elesin*). Please, try and understand. Everything my husband did was for the best.

ELESIN (*he gives her a long strange stare, as if he is trying to understand who she is*). You are the wife of the District Officer?

JANE. Yes. My name, is Jane.

ELESIN. That is my wife sitting down there. You notice how still and silent she sits? My business is with your husband.

(*Pilkings returns with Iyaloja.*)

PILKINGS. Here she is. Now first I want your word of honour that you will try nothing foolish.

ELESIN. Honour? White one, did you say you wanted my word of honour?

PILKINGS. I know you to be an honourable man. Give me your word of honour you will receive nothing from her.

ELESIN. But I am sure you have searched her clothing as you would never dare touch your own mother. And there are these two lizards of yours who roll their eyes even when I scratch.

PILKINGS. And I shall be sitting on that tree trunk watching even how you blink. Just the same I want your word that you will not let her pass anything to you.

ELESIN. You have my honour already. It is locked up in that desk in which you will put away your report of the night's events. Even the honour of my people you have taken already; it is tied together with those papers of treachery which make you masters in this land.

PILKINGS. Alright. I am trying to make things easy but if you must bring in politics we'll have to do it the hard way. Madam, I want you to remain along this line and move no nearer to that cell door. Guards! (*They spring to attention.*) If she moves beyond this point, blow your whistle. Come on Jane. (*They go off.*)

IYALOJA. How boldly the lizard struts before the pigeon when it was the eagle itself he promised us he would confront.

ELESIN. I don't ask you to take pity on me Iyaloja. You have a message for me or you would not have come. Even if it is the curses of the world, I shall listen.

IYALOJA. You made so bold with the servant of the white king who took your side against death. I must tell your brother chiefs when I return how bravely you waged war against him. Especially with words.

ELESIN. I more than deserve your scorn.

IYALOJA (*with sudden anger*). I warned you, if you must leave a seed behind, be sure it is not tainted with the curses of the world. Who are you to open a new life when you dared not open the door to a new existence? I say who are you to make so bold? (*The Bride sobs and Iyaloja notices her. Her contempt noticeably increases as she turns back to Elesin.*) Oh you self-vaunted stem of the plantain, how hollow it all proves. The pith is gone in the parent stem, so how will it prove with the new shoot? How will it go with that earth that bears it? Who are you to bring this abomination on us!

ELESIN. My powers deserted me. My charms, my spells, even my voice lacked strength when I made to summon the powers that would lead me over the last measure of earth into the land of the fleshless. You saw it, Iyaloja. You saw me struggle to retrieve my will from the power of the stranger whose shadow fell across the doorway and left me floundering and blundering in a maze I had never before encountered. My senses were numbed when the touch of cold iron came upon my wrists. I could do nothing to save myself.

IYALOJA. You have betrayed us. We fed your sweetmeats such as we hoped awaited you on the other side. But you said No, I must eat the world's left-overs. We said you

were the hunter who brought the quarry down; to you belonged the vital portions of the game. No, you said, I am the hunter's dog and I shall eat the entrails of the game and the faeces of the hunter. We said you were the hunter returning home in triumph, a slain buffalo pressing down on his neck; you said wait, I first must turn up this cricket hole with my toes. We said yours was the doorway at which we first spy the tapper when he comes down from the tree, yours was the blessing of the twilight wine, the purl that brings night spirits out of doors to steal their portion before the light of day. We said yours was the body of wine whose burden shakes the tapper like a sudden gust on his perch. You said, No, I am content to lick the dregs from each calabash when the drinkers are done. We said, the dew on earth's surface was for you to wash your feet along the slopes of honour. You said No, I shall step in the vomit of cats and the droppings of mice; I shall fight them for the left-overs of the world.

ELESIN. Enough Iyaloja, enough.

IYALOJA. We called you leader and oh, how you led us on. What we have no intention of eating should not be held to the nose.

ELESIN. Enough, enough. My shame is heavy enough.

IYALOJA. Wait. I came with a burden.

ELESIN. You have more than discharged it.

IYALOJA. I wish I could pity you.

ELESIN. I need neither your pity nor the pity of the world. I need understanding. Even I need to understand. You were present at my defeat. You were part of the beginnings. You brought about the renewal of my tie to earth, you helped in the binding of the cord.

IYALOJA. I gave you warning. The river which fills up before our eyes does not sweep us away in its flood.

ELESIN. What were warnings beside the moist contact of living earth between my fingers? What were warnings beside the renewal of famished embers lodged eternally in the heart of man. But even that, even if it overwhelmed one with a thousandfold temptations to linger a little while, a man could overcome it. It is when the alien hand pollutes the source of will, when a stranger force of violence shatters the mind's calm resolution, this is when a man is made to commit the awful treachery of relief, commit in his thought the unspeakable blasphemy of seeing the hand of the gods in this alien rupture of his world. I know it was this thought that killed me, sapped my powers and turned me into an infant in the hands of unnamable strangers. I made to utter my spells anew but my tongue merely rattled in my mouth. I fingered hidden charms and the contact was damp; there was no spark left to sever the life-strings that should stretch from every fingertip. My will was squelched in the spittle of an alien race, and all because I had committed this blasphemy of thought—that there might be the hand of the gods in a stranger's intervention.

IYALOJA. Explain it how you will, I hope it brings you peace of mind. The bush-rat fled his rightful cause, reached the market and set up a lamentation. 'Please save me!'—are these fitting words to hear from an ancestral mask? 'There's a wild beast at my heels' is not becoming language from a hunter.

ELESIN. May the world forgive me.

IYALOJA. I came with a burden I said. It approaches the gates which are so well guarded by those jackals whose spittle will from this day be on your food and drink. But first, tell me, you who were once Elesin Oba, tell me, you who know so well the cycle of the plantain: is it the parent shoot which withers to give sap to the younger or, does your wisdom see it running the other way?

ELESIN. I don't see your meaning Iyaloja?

IYALOJA. Did I ask you for a meaning? I asked a question. Whose trunk withers to give sap to the other? The parent shoot or the younger?

ELESIN. The parent.

IYALOJA. Ah. So you do know that. There are sights in this world which say different Elesin. There are some who choose to reverse this cycle of our being. Oh you emptied bark that the world once saluted for a pith-laden being, shall I tell you what the gods have claimed of you?

(In her agitation she steps beyond the line indicated by Pilkings and the air is rent by piercing whistles. The two Guards also leap forward and place safe-guarding hands on Elesin. Iyaloja stops, astonished. Pilkings comes racing in, followed by Jane.)

PILKINGS. What is it? Did they try something?

GUARD. She stepped beyond the line.

ELESIN *(in a broken voice)*. Let her alone. She meant no harm.

IYALOJA. Oh Elesin, see what you've become. Once you had no need to open your mouth in explanation because evil-smelling goats, itchy of hand and foot had lost their senses. And it was a brave man indeed who dared lay hands on you because Iyaloja stepped from one side of the earth onto another. Now look at the spectacle of your life. I grieve for you.

PILKINGS. I think you'd better leave. I doubt you have done him much good by coming here. I shall make sure you are not allowed to see him again. In any case we are moving him to a different place before dawn, so don't bother to come back.

IYALOJA. We foresaw that. Hence the burden I trudged here to lay beside your gates.

PILKINGS. What was that you said?

IYALOJA. Didn't our son explain? Ask that one. He knows what it is. At least we hope the man we once knew as Elesin remembers the lesser oaths he need not break.

PILKINGS. Do you know what she is talking about?

ELESIN. Go to the gates, ghostly one. Whatever you find there, bring it to me.

IYALOJA. Not yet. It drags behind me on the slow, weary feet of women. Slow as it is Elesin, it has long overtaken you. It rides ahead of your laggard will.

PILKINGS. What is she saying now? Christ! Must your people forever speak in riddles?

ELESIN. It will come white man, it will come. Tell your men at the gates to let it through.

PILKINGS *(dubiously)*. I'll have to see what it is.

IYALOJA. You will. *(Passionately.)* But this is one oath he cannot shirk. White one, you have a king here, a visitor from your land. We know of his presence here. Tell me, were he to die would you leave his spirit roaming restlessly on the surface of earth? Would you bury him here among those you consider less than human? In your land have you no ceremonies of the dead?

PILKINGS. Yes. But we don't make our chiefs commit suicide to keep him company.

IYALOJA. Child, I have not come to help your understanding. *(Points to Elesin.)* This is the man whose weakened understanding holds us in bondage to you. But ask him if you wish. He knows the meaning of a king's passage; he was not born yesterday. He knows the peril to the race when our dead father, who goes as intermediary, waits and waits and knows he is betrayed. He knows when the narrow gate was opened and he knows it will not stay for laggards who drag their feet in dung and vomit, whose lips are reeking of the left-overs of lesser men. He knows he has condemned our king to wander in the void of evil with beings who are enemies of life.

PILKINGS. Yes er . . . but look here . . .

IYALOJA. What we ask is little enough. Let him release our King so he can ride on homewards alone. The messenger is on his way on the backs of women. Let him send word through the heart that is folded up within the bolt. It is the least of all his oaths, it is the easiest fulfilled.

(The Aide-De-Camp runs in.)

PILKINGS. Bob?

AIDE-DE-CAMP. Sir, there's a group of women chanting up the hill.

PILKINGS *(rounding on Iyaloja)*. If you people want trouble . . .

JANE. Simon, I think that's what Olunde referred to in his letter.

PILKINGS. He knows damned well I can't have a crowd here! Damn it, I explained the delicacy of my position to him. I think it's about time I got him out of town. Bob, send a car and two or three soldiers to bring him in. I think the sooner he takes his leave of his father and gets out the better.

IYALOJA. Save your labour white one. If it is the father of your prisoner you want, Olunde, he who until this night we knew as Elesin's son, he comes soon himself to take his leave. He has sent the women ahead, so let them in.

(Pilkings remains undecided.)

AIDE-DE-CAMP. What do we do about the invasion? We can still stop them far from here.

PILKINGS. What do they look like?

AIDE-DE-CAMP. They're not many. And they seem quite peaceful.

PILKINGS. No men?

AIDE-DE-CAMP. Mm, two or three at the most.

JANE. Honestly, Simon, I'd trust Olunde. I don't think he'll deceive you about their intentions.

PILKINGS. He'd better not. Alright, let them in Bob. Warn them to control themselves. Then hurry Olunde here. Make sure he brings his baggage because I'm not returning him into town.

AIDE-DE-CAMP. Very good sir. (*Goes.*)

PILKINGS (*to Iyaloja*). I hope you understand that if anything goes wrong it will be on your head. My men have orders to shoot at the first sign of trouble.

IYALOJA. To prevent one death you will actually make other deaths? Ah, great is the wisdom of the white race. But have no fear. Your Prince will sleep peacefully. So at long last will ours. We will disturb you no further, servant of the white king. Just let Elesin fulfill his oath and we will retire home and pay homage to our King.

JANE. I believe her Simon, don't you?

PILKINGS. Maybe.

ELESIN. Have no fear ghostly one. I have a message to send my King and then you have nothing more to fear.

IYALOJA. Olunde would have done it. The chiefs asked him to speak the words but he said no, not while you lived.

ELESIN. Even from the depths to which my spirit has sunk, I find some joy that this little has been left to me.

(*The women enter, intoning the dirge 'Alẹ lẹ lẹ' and swaying from side to side. On their shoulders is borne a longish object roughly like a cylindrical bolt, covered in cloth. They set it down on the spot where Iyaloja had stood earlier, and form a semi-circle round it. The Praise-Singer and Drummer stand on the inside of the semi-circle but the drum is not used at all. The Drummer intones under the Praise-Singer's invocations.*)

PILKINGS (*as they enter*). What is that?

IYALOJA. The burden you have made white one, but we bring it in peace.

PILKINGS. I said *what* is it?

ELESIN. White man, you must let me out. I have a duty to perform.

PILKINGS. I most certainly will not.

ELESIN. There lies the courier of my King. Let me out so I can perform what is demanded of me.

PILKINGS. You'll do what you need to do from inside there or not at all. I've gone as far as I intend to with this business.

ELESIN. The worshipper who lights a candle in your church to bear a message to his god bows his head and speaks in a whisper to the flame. Have I not seen it ghostly one? His voice does not ring out to the world. Mine are no words

for anyone's ears. They are not words even for the bearers of this load. They are words I must speak secretly, even as my father whispered them in my ears and I in the ears of my first-born. I cannot shout them to the wind and the open night-sky.

JANE. Simon . . .

PILKINGS. Don't interfere. Please!

IYALOJA. They have slain the favourite horse of the king and slain his dog. They have borne them from pulse to pulse centre of the land receiving prayers for their king. But the rider has chosen to stay behind. Is it too much to ask that he speak his heart to heart of the waiting courier? (*Pilkings turns his back on her.*) So be it. Elesin Oba, you see how even the mere leavings are denied you. (*She gestures to the Praise-Singer.*)

PRAISE-SINGER. Elesin Oba! I call you by that name only this last time. Remember when I said, if you cannot come, tell my horse. (*Pause.*) What? I cannot hear you? I said, if you cannot come, whisper in the ears of my horse. Is your tongue severed from the roots Elesin? I can hear no response. I said, if there are boulders you cannot climb, mount my horse's back, this spotless black stallion, he'll bring you over them. (*Pauses.*) Elesin Oba, once you had a tongue that darted like a drummer's stick. I said, if you get lost my dog will track a path to me. My memory fails me but I think you replied: My feet have found the path, Alafin.

(*The dirge rises and falls.*)

I said at the last, if evil hands hold you back, just tell my horse there is weight on the hem of your smock. I dare not wait too long.

(*The dirge rises and falls.*)

There lies the swiftest ever messenger of a king, so set me free with the errand of your heart. There lie the head and heart of the favourite of the gods, whisper in his ears. Oh my companion, if you had followed when you should, we would not say that the horse preceded its rider. If you had followed when it was time, we would not say the dog has raced beyond and left his master behind. If you had raised your will to cut the thread of life at the summons of the drums, we would not say your mere shadow fell across the gateway and took its owner's place at the banquet. But the hunter, laden with a slain buffalo, stayed to root in the cricket's hole with his toes. What now is left? If there is a dearth of bats, the pigeon must serve us for the offering. Speak the words over your shadow which must now serve in your place.

ELESIN. I cannot approach. Take off the cloth. I shall speak my message from heart to heart of silence.

IYALOJA (*moves forward and removes the covering*). Your courier Elesin, cast your eyes on the favoured companion of the King.

(*Rolled up in the mat, his head and feet showing at either end is the body of Olunde.*)

There lies the honour of your household and of our race. Because he could not bear to let honour fly out of doors, he stopped it with his life. The son has proved the father Elesin, and there is nothing left in your mouth to gnash but infant gums.

PRAISE-SINGER. Elesin, we placed the reins of the world in your hands yet you watched it plunge over the edge of the bitter precipice. You sat with folded arms while evil strangers tilted the world from its course and crashed it beyond the edge of emptiness—you muttered, there is little that one man can do, you left us floundering on a blind future. Your heir has taken the burden on himself. What the end will be, we are not gods to tell. But this young shoot has poured its sap into the parent stalk, and we know this is not the way of life. Our world is tumbling in the void of strangers, Elesin.

(*Elesin has stood rock-still, his knuckles taut on the bars, his eyes glued to the body of his son. The stillness seizes and paralyses everyone, including Pilkings who has turned to look. Suddenly Elesin flings one arm round his neck, once, and with the loop of the chain, strangles himself in a swift, decisive pull. The guards rush forward to stop him but they are only in time to let his body down. Pilkings has leapt to the door at the same time and struggles with the lock. He rushes within, fumbles with the handcuffs and unlocks them, raises the body to a sitting position while he tries to give resuscitation. The women continue their dirge, unmoved by the sudden event.*)

IYALOJA. Why do you strain yourself? Why do you labour at tasks for which no one, not even the man lying there would give you thanks? He is gone at last into the passage but oh, how late it all is. His son will feast on the meat and throw him bones. The passage is clogged with droppings from the King's stallion; he will arrive all stained in dung.

PILKINGS (*in a tired voice*). Was this what you wanted?

IYALOJA. No child, it is what you brought to be, you who play with strangers' lives, who even usurp the vestments of our dead, yet believe that the stain of death will not cling to you. The gods demanded only the old expired plantain but you cut down the sap-laden shoot to feed your pride. There is your board, filled to overflowing. Feast on it. (*She screams at him suddenly, seeing that Pilkings is about to close Elesin's staring eyes.*) Let him alone! However sunk he was in debt he is no pauper's carrion abandoned on the road. Since when have strangers donned clothes of indigo before the bereaved cries out his loss?

(*She turns to the Bride who has remained motionless throughout.*)

CHILD.

(*The girl takes up a little earth, walks calmly into the cell and closes Elesin's eyes. She then pours some earth over each eyelid and comes out again.*)

Now forget the dead, forget even the living. Turn your mind only to the unborn.

(*She goes off, accompanied by the Bride. The dirge rises in volume and the women continue their sway. Lights fade to a black-out.*)

THE END

Though their roots are thousands of years old, Yoruban festivals have been continuously celebrated in late January in many Nigerian villages since the seventeenth century. The Yoruba use rituals to mark seasonal rhythms, religious beliefs, and cultural heritage. For the Yoruba contemporary theater remains directly related to the rituals and dance dramas from which it sprang. An understanding of their theology helps us understand why theater remains an intensely spiritual activity for the Yoruba.

The Yoruban Worldview
As one of Africa's most resilient people, the Yoruba can be traced throughout the Western world of the sub-Saharan diaspora. They are unusual among Africans because they have successfully adapted to large urban centers. Both Lagos and Ibadan lie within that part of southwest Nigeria known as Yorubaland, where currently 13 million Yoruba live. The Yoruba are animistic; that is, their existence is governed by a religion that abounds with gods and spirits that interact—usually in animal form—with humans. The actual number of deities within the Yoruban pantheon is virtually impossible to ascertain because the people within various regions in Yorubaland worship gods unique to themselves. There are, however, several major gods who are recognized and worshipped by all Yoruba in varying forms.

According to Yoruban myth, the gods and humans once dwelt on earth and shared the joys of comradeship and thereby a sense of wholeness. Each needed the other to exist. A "cosmic totality" (to apply Soyinka's phrase) can exist only when gods and humans share this wholeness; only when each seeks an interaction with the essential character of the other can either claim a complete personality. This bond was broken (either through sin or sacrilege, as various interpreters have suggested), and the gods sought new residence in the ethereal regions. Humans were then separated from the gods by death. It was the god Ogun, who is given to imperfection, as are all Yoruban gods, who felt the "anguish of incompleteness" and broke away from the other deities.

A wooden mask used in Yoruban Egungun festivals in Nigeria; such masks sustain a vital link between the wearer and his ancestors.

To bridge "the gulf of transition" between gods and humans, Ogun plunged hubristically into the *chthonic realm*. This act of self-sacrifice gives Ogun a heroic status that sets him apart from all other Yoruban deities.

In addition to being the god of iron and metallurgy, Ogun is also "the Creative Essence" (similar to the Greek Dionysus) and "the Lord of the Road" because he leads humans over the "way" that bridges the "gulf of transition." He is perhaps the favorite god of the Yoruba, and it is he with whom Soyinka most identifies because Ogun, by becoming human again, is "the first actor" (i.e., one who assumes an identity other than his own). Ogun was the first to confront nature and bend it to his will, even while suffering the pain of disintegration within the abyss of being and nonbeing. The communicant chorus in the ritual reenactments of Ogun's heroic act—the Ogun Mysteries—is, in itself, a physical manifestation of the god's spiritual reincarnation.

The Yoruban Festival
Thus, the Obatala Festival at Ede is an intense spiritual experience that employs such common ritualistic devices as symbolic sacrifice, prayers, drumming, singing, dancing, and storytelling that encourage worshippers to come closer to their gods through the enactment of their myths. After a day of sacred songs and dances, the second day of the festival features heroic epics handed down from generation to generation. The performance lasts for almost two weeks as solo maskers often take an entire day to tell stories of superhuman deeds that nourish the Yoruba. The festival begins with the women dancing into the playing space as they carry sacred masks (*eba*) to symbolize fertility and harmony. The men tell stories through songs, using bananas and oils derived from native plants to lubricate their throats and facilitate their incantations. The action is mimed by dancers in colorful costumes and enormous headpieces that not only disguise their human form but also transform them into godlike beings. Nonperformers are forbidden to touch these "gods" who sing and dance, or even to imitate their sounds.

The performers and their audience collectively relive the fabled battle between Ajagemo, the incarnation of Obatala, and another priest, Olunwi. Ajagemo is captured by Olunwi and carried off from the palace. The Oba (king), however, seeks his release. He pays ransom to Olunwi, and Ajagemo is freed and returns to the palace. His triumph is marked by a magnificent procession in which the performers and audience unite in celebration. *Death and the King's Horseman* is a contemporary play that retains elements of Yoruban ritual in its use of the Praise-Singer and especially in the costumes worn by the Pilkingtons to their masquerade. For a full account of Yoruban art and myth, see Femi Euba's *Archetypes, Imprecators, and Victims of Fate: Origins and Developments of Satire in Black Drama* (New York, 1989).

AFRICAN AMERICAN THEATER

Artistic and Cultural Events

1824:
Brown's *The Drama of King Shotaway*

1821:
W. H. Brown establishes the African Theatre in New York

1884:
Astor Place Company of Colored Tragedians

1915:
LaFayette Players, New York

1923:
Willis Richardson's *The Chip Woman's Fortune*, first play by African American on Broadway

1930s:
The Harlem Renaissance

1940:
American Negro Theatre

1959:
Lorraine Hansberry's *A Raisin in the Sun*

1964:
Black Arts Repertory Theatre

1967:
Negro Ensemble Company

1969:
Amiri Baraka's *Slave Ship*

1970:
Charles Gordone's *No Place to Be Somebody*; first Pulitzer Prize for African American playwright

1983:
August Wilson's *Fences*

1800 C.E.   **1900 C.E.**

Historical and Political Events

Slavery practiced in U.S.

1863:
Emancipation Proclamation abolishes slavery

1861–1865:
Civil War

1954:
U.S. Supreme Court desegregates schools

1963:
Civil rights March on Washington; "I Have a Dream" speech by Martin Luther King

1967:
"Summer of Rage," civil rights riots throughout U.S.A.

1968:
Martin Luther King assassinated

The Development of African American Theater

Seeking solace from their slavery and the continuity of an indigenous culture, Africans in America performed folktales (often about Anansi, the frail spider who survived by using his wits), songs, music, and dance in cabins and camp meetings, even in town parks such as Congo Square in New Orleans. Such performances eventually melded with, and were transformed by, the Euro-American culture. In 1821 William Henry Brown established the African Theatre in New York, an enterprise modeled after the white playhouses. Brown's company performed traditional European fare, particularly Shakespeare, but Brown also authored *The Drama of King Shotaway*, based on slavery; it is the first play by an author of African descent in the United States. Though Brown's enterprise was short-lived, it was a notable attempt to produce theater for and about African exiles. Ira Aldridge (1807–1867) emerged as the African Theatre's finest actor, and he is generally regarded as the first "star" actor of African descent in the American theater. Aldridge achieved his greatest fame in Europe, where he performed major Shakespearean roles; he was buried with state honors in Lodz, Poland.

After the demise of the African Theatre there was little theatrical activity by Africans in America (save the minstrel show, see Chapter 5) until after the Civil War (1861–1865). In New York the Astor Place Company of Colored Tragedians was founded by J. A. Arnaux in 1884 to perform mostly Shakespearean plays. Most performers of African descent were specialty artists, such as Henrietta Vinto Davies (an opera singer) and the popular stars of vaudeville and musical comedy, such as Bob Cole and Bert Williams.

In 1915 the Lafayette Players were founded in New York and became the preeminent outlet for African American dramatists in the early twentieth century. That year also saw the emergence of the Provincetown Players (see Chapter 5), which produced Eugene O'Neill's *The Emperor Jones* in 1922. Charles Gilpin played Brutus Jones to great acclaim and became the first prominent African American actor on Broadway.

In 1923 Willis Richardson's *The Chip Woman's Fortune* was the first nonmusical play written by an African American staged on Broadway. However, it was Lorraine Hansberry's *A Raisin in the Sun* (1959) that became the first Broadway "hit" written by an African American (see Spotlight box, *A Raisin in the Sun: Portrait of America in Transition*). Hansberry's drama was as significant a groundbreaker in its time as the dramas by Europe's early realists. Its title was taken from a poem by Langston Hughes, a leader of the 1930s Harlem Renaissance (an outpouring of poetry, fiction, and plays by and for African Americans). Hughes's own play *Mulatto* (1935) was among the finest achievements of the Harlem Renaissance. The play, which portrayed the lynching of a young man of mixed race, ran for almost 400 performances on Broadway, a testimony to the power of Hughes's writing and to the acting of Rose McClendon, among the first black women to achieve stardom in the New York theater. The play was later turned into an opera, *The Barrier* (1950). The American Negro Theatre, founded by Abram Hill and Frederick O'Neill in 1940, provided more opportunities for dramatists and actors to work in the American mainstream. Its most successful production, *Anna Lucasta* (1944), played for 957 performances on Broadway and became an international hit.

The civil rights movement in postwar America fostered more African American and integrated theater companies, most notably the Free Southern Theatre, founded by Gilbert Moses to develop African American drama "as unique to the Negro people as blues and jazz." Based in New Orleans, the FST was the first integrated theater company to perform in the American South; it produced both European dramas (e.g., *Waiting for Godot*) and works written expressly for African Americans (e.g., Ossie Davis's rousing comedy *Purlie Victorious*).

The civil rights movement also encouraged the development of playwrights writing from and about the black experience: Amiri Baraka (LeRoi Jones), Charles Gordone (the first Pulitzer Prize–winning dramatist of African descent), Ed Bullins, Adrienne Kennedy, Ntozaki Shange, Charles Fuller, and most recently Suzan Lori Parks. Small theaters such as the New Lafayette Playhouse emerged as showcases for African American writers. In 1967 the Negro Ensemble Company (NEC) was organized in New York by playwright Douglas Turner Ward and actor Robert Hooks to train young artists as performers and playwrights and especially to produce plays relevant to black Americans. It remains one of the most admired production companies in America, with over 50 productions of new plays, including the Pulitzer Prize–winning *A Soldier's Play* (1982). Curiously, the NEC turned down Gordone's Pulitzer Prize–winning play (*No Place to Be Somebody*, 1970).

African American theater artists are also thriving well beyond New York. Currently August Wilson, winner of two Pulitzer Prizes, is recognized as the foremost American playwright—as opposed to the foremost African American playwright. Wilson lives in St. Paul, and his plays usually receive their first productions at Yale's renowned School of Drama. His works have become mainstays of many professional regional companies, notably in Seattle, Houston, and Kansas City.

Among the most interesting and visible phenomena concerning African American performance has been the popularity of musicals based on the works of such pioneers in jazz as Fats Waller (*Ain't Misbehavin'*, 1979), Eubie Blake (*Bubblin' Brown Sugar*, 1976, and *Eubie*, 1978), and Jelly Roll Morton (*Jelly's Last Jam*, 1992). These reviews have introduced a new generation of Americans to the extraordinary contributions of African Americans to the country's culture.

A RAISIN IN THE SUN: PORTRAIT OF AMERICA IN TRANSITION

Although it was not the first play by and about African Americans produced on Broadway (Willis Richardson's *The Chip Woman's Fortune*, 1923, claimed that distinction), *A Raisin in the Sun*, however, is rightly recognized as the first commercially successful play written by an African American and performed on Broadway. There are two outstanding film versions of the play, a 1961 feature film with Sidney Poitier and a 1989 made-for-television version (available on video) with Danny Glover. The play represents a significant moment in American theater history, and you should familiarize yourself with it.

The play was written by Lorraine Hansberry (1930–1965), who was born into a prominent, middle-class African American family in Chicago (her father helped found one of the first banks for people of color in that city). However, the Hansberry world was not idyllic. Her father became disillusioned with the treatment of African Americans in the United States and migrated to Mexico to seek a more color-blind existence; his quest for interracial harmony instilled in his daughter a similar passion.

Hansberry attended the University of Wisconsin and Roosevelt College in Chicago, but her real education followed her move to New York City in 1950. She married a songwriter–music publisher (Bob Nemiroff) and lived in Greenwich Village, where liberal politics and an intellectual environment kindled her aspirations to become a writer. In 1955 she began to write *A Raisin in the Sun*. Because plays by and about African Americans were virtually nonexistent, it was difficult to raise funds for the play, but after successful out-of-town try-outs, which encouraged producers, the play eventually premiered at the Ethel Barrymore Theater on March 11, 1959. It was directed by a young African American, Lloyd Richards (currently noted for his association with August Wilson), and it starred an unknown Sidney Poitier as Walter Lee. Audiences embraced the play, and Hansberry was awarded the

New York Drama Critics Circle Award for the best play of the season, becoming the first African American woman to receive this prestigious award. Despite her short life and small output of works, Hansberry is recognized as a major force in the shaping of minority theater in the United States. Yet she always argued that she was not a black playwright. She maintained that she wrote about people, "some of whom happened to be black."

There are many reasons for the success of *A Raisin in the Sun*. First, it is useful to place the play in historical context. The legitimacy of African American literature and arts was established by the Harlem Renaissance of the 1930s, a movement that encouraged young African American writers and artists to cultivate work that reflected the American experience from the black point of view. Its leader was Langston Hughes, a fine playwright and a superb poet. It was Hughes who provided Hansberry with the title of her play in his most famous poem, which asks

What happens to a dream deferred?
Does it wither like a raisin in the sun?
. . . .
Or does it explode?

Hughes anticipated the "black rage" that erupted in America in the 1960s when anger at social injustices literally exploded in the streets of Watts, Detroit, and Newark.

But while repressed anger lurks beneath *A Raisin in the Sun*, it is not an angry play in the confrontational manner of many Black Power dramatists of the 1960s. In part, that is precisely why the play was embraced by Broadway audiences in 1959. White audiences entering the Barrymore Theater were far more sympathetic to the injustices suffered by African Americans than perhaps at any other time in the nation's history. In April 1947, Jackie Robinson had shown that African Americans could perform magnificently in a previously all-white world when he broke baseball's color barrier. Soon other

African Americans followed Robinson in baseball, as well as other major league sports. The nation had a new host of African American heroes to admire.

In 1954 the Supreme Court desegregated public schools, a move that emboldened the emerging civil rights movement. Even as Hansberry's play moved to Broadway, the Reverend Martin Luther King Jr. was leading marches through the South; his famous "I Have a Dream" speech was delivered just four years after *Raisin* opened. Rosa Parks defiantly refused to "move to the back of the bus" in Mobile, Alabama. Such events were duly recorded on television, a relatively new medium that allowed middle-class America to see firsthand the problems and poverty spawned by racism. A new consciousness about race relations was developing. Mama's eloquent reflection on her husband's dreams engaged Broadway audiences on a more personal level than was possible for previous generations: "Big Walter used to say . . . 'Seem like God didn't see fit to give the black man nothing but dreams—but He did give us children to make them dreams worthwhile.'"

Actually, the dreams that most affected audiences at the Barrymore—and in the theaters throughout the country that added *Raisin* to their repertory—was the American Dream of owning a house. Mama's argument that "it makes a difference in a man when he can walk on floors that belong to *him*" echoed any number of lines that had become the staple of American drama. In 1943 *Oklahoma* expressed the sentiment that "we know we belong to the land, and the land we belong to is grand." *Tobacco Road*, the longest-running Broadway play during the Great Depression, presented a dirt-poor farmer, Jeeter Lester, who eloquently defended his property to a banker who was attempting to evict him:

This was my Daddy's place and his Daddy's before him, and I don't know how many Lesters before that. There wasn't nothing here but the whole country before they came. . . . Now I don't own it and it belongs to a durn bank that ain't never had nothing to do with it even. By God, that ain't right, I tell you. God won't stand for such cheating much longer. He ain't so liking of the rich as people think He is. God, he likes the poor.

Or "plain people," to use Mama Hooker's term.

Despite its status as a seminal African American drama, *A Raisin in the Sun* is actually a rather conventional play. At its heart it is a mid-twentieth-century version of the German *familienstucke*, a brand of domestic melodrama pioneered by August Iffland early in the nineteenth century. Such plays, in which families were threatened by eviction if they did not raise money for the mortgage, became a staple of the American melodrama. Audiences understood the sanctity of the "old homestead." The irony of Hansberry's play, however, is that the Younger family actually has the mortgage money. It is not the greed of the heartless banker that threatens their new home; rather, it is the incipient racism expressed by Mr. Linder, the spokesman for the Homeowners Association: "Our Negro families are happier when they live in their *own* communities." Ironically, the greedy thief of the old melodrama is Walter Lee's friend Willy Harris, who dashes the Hooker dream when he absconds with the insurance money, a plot element that elevates Hansberry's play above the level of mere polemic.

Beneatha, Mama's daughter, offered white audiences an example of a newly emerging phenomenon among African Americans: the quest to recapture the pride and dignity of their cultural roots. (Less than two decades after *Raisin*, Arthur Hailey's epic novel *Roots* became the most popular miniseries in the history of American television.) She proclaims proudly and defiantly that she is looking for her identity. Furthermore, she is not an assimilationist, that is, one who gives up her cultural roots in favor of those of the country in which she lives. Hansberry invents Joseph Asagai, the immigrant student with aspirations to the American Dream, to underscore Beneatha's plight. He retains his "old country" prejudices against women ("For a woman [love and a family] should be enough"); ironically, Beneatha must fight biases among her own people as much as those of the white society. Again Hansberry raised issues beyond racial intolerance.

Despite its status as a groundbreaking work, *A Raisin in the Sun* has fallen into disrepute among some African Americans who criticize it for not being militant enough. Mama's dependence on religion ("There'll always be a God in this house!") is thus faulted as passivity; she relies on divine guidance rather than actively working to change her circumstances. These issues and others have been addressed by George C. Wolfe, the playwright and director who now heads the New York Free Shakespeare Theater and the Public Theater. Wolfe wrote *The Colored Museum* (1988), a collection of sketches, some fiercely satirical, others poignant vignettes, which attack stereotypical views of African Americans enshrined in "the colored museum" of white consciousness. One sketch, "The Last Mama-on-the-Couch Play," parodies *A Raisin in the Sun* (and Poitier's mannered acting). Because it critiques Hansberry's work from the perspective of African Americans in the late twentieth century, Wolfe's sketch creates a dialogue between his generation and that represented by Hansberry.

However much subsequent events in the civil rights movement may have altered the status of *A Raisin in the Sun*, it nonetheless remains among the most significant plays in the history of the American theater. It was an urgent play in 1959 and a necessary step in the evolution of African American literature and performance.

Walter Lee (Ossie Davis) lectures his wife Ruth (left) and his sister Beneatha (right), who prides herself on her traditional African dress in this Lincoln Center revival of A Raisin in the Sun.

FENCES
AUGUST WILSON

AUGUST WILSON (1945–)

Just as Arthur Miller and Tennessee Williams dominated the American theater in the years following World War II, August Wilson has become the most admired and decorated American playwright of the 1980s and 1990s. In little more than a decade he has already won two Pulitzer Prizes (*Fences*, 1987; *The Piano Lesson*, 1990); virtually all of his other works (see below) have won a "best of season" award from the New York Drama Critics. Given the esteem he has earned among critics and audiences, Wilson will likely emerge as one of America's most honored playwrights before his playwriting career is concluded.

Perhaps the most intriguing aspect of his collected plays is their organizational principle. Each play of a proposed ten-play cycle is set in a different decade of the twentieth century, and each is framed against the backdrop of a peculiarly American cultural icon ('20s jazz for *Ma Rainey's Black Bottom*, '50s baseball for *Fences*, and '40s delta blues for *Seven Guitars*). Collectively the plays chronicle the evolution of an authentic African American voice within the broader national culture. Though the past Wilson depicts painfully dramatizes racism and the residue of slavery, there nonetheless remains an undercurrent of optimism in Wilson's work. He has talked about "exorcising the demons of memory" so that African Americans can advance in the next century (in *Joe Turner's Come and Gone* an actual exorcism typifies his canon).

Many of Wilson's plays are set in Pittsburgh, where he was born to a white father and a black mother; he was raised in the Hill district, a ghetto for African Americans. His father was rarely around, and his strong-willed mother was determined that her son would succeed; she moved the family to a mostly white suburb. But social realities deterred Wilson. He left a Catholic school because of racial slurs; he deemed a vocational school academically worthless; and his brief experience in a public high school embittered him when a teacher falsely accused him of plagiarizing a 20-page paper on Napoleon. Wilson's rage at such injustices drew him to the Black Power movement of the 1960s. In Pittsburgh he helped found the Black Horizon on the Hill, a theater company that staged the plays of LeRoi Jones (Amiri Baraka), whose work inspired him to take up playwriting. At first he was discouraged because he "wasn't any good at dialogue," an ironic assessment from a man whose plays are praised for their lyrical, yet completely naturalistic, language.

In 1978 Wilson accepted an invitation to move to St. Paul, Minnesota, to write plays for a theater company founded by a former Pittsburgh colleague. Despite his success, he still maintains the same tiny apartment in St. Paul. In 1982 Wilson was a fellow-in-residence at a playwright-development program at the Eugene O'Neill Center in Connecticut. There he met Lloyd Richards, an African American director and head of the Yale School of Drama, who encouraged Wilson by producing his works. Today his plays are still tested at Yale prior to their New York opening. The Wilson-Richards collaboration has proven to be among the most fruitful in the history of the American theater.

Though Wilson's works are rooted in naturalism (heredity and environment are central to the lives of his characters), his works transcend the style and assume an aura of mystery and myth. Again we turn to his comments about the need to exorcise demons from American life as perhaps the source of the mystic in his plays. Ultimately, his collected works—from *Ma Rainey* in 1983 to *Seven Guitars* in 1996—have attracted audiences of all races and economic classes because they speak of universal suffering and hope. While the plays are unmistakably about the African American experience in a nation with a history of troubled race relations, they are also about human problems, which may account for their unprecedented success.

FENCES (1987)

Fences is in many ways similar to *Death of a Salesman*, particularly in its portrait of the clash between a domineering father and his athletically gifted son. Like Willy, Troy Maxson is a man who cannot adapt to a changing world, who is unfaithful to his wife and who ultimately drives his son away by his stubbornness. Furthermore, as in *Salesman*, we meet a ne'er-do-well son (cf. Happy and Lyons) and a long-suffering, dutiful wife (cf. Linda and Rose). And both plays are set in the so-called boom years after World War II, when many prospered while others were left behind.

But whereas Miller's near-tragic hero, Willy Loman, is the essence of "the little [low] man," Wilson invests Troy with a larger-than-life ("maximum") quality; like Prometheus, Troy is a titan who rails against the injustices heaped on the black man. Note that in virtually every confrontation in which Troy engages himself, his opponent is aligned with superhuman values: Mr. Death, the Devil, and "the Boss" for whom he works as a trash man (Troy's heroic stand at work is truly Promethean in its sheer audacity). Even the furniture salesman with whom he battles is described in supernatural terms ("devil standing there bigger than life"). The great baseball players with whom Troy aligns himself—Josh Gibson ("the Black Babe Ruth"), the ageless Satchel Paige, the trail-blazing Jackie Robinson, and the young Hank Aaron—emerge as godlike beings. Thus Wilson creates in Troy a modern mythic hero who tries to shake a universe filled with injustice and inequality. The playwright even assigns him a trumpet-playing brother, Gabriel, who tries to blow down the gates of heaven itself. Troy is Wilson's finest creation, and he stands among the most compelling characters to emerge in the contemporary American theater.

But Troy is as flawed as he is heroic. His "errors in judgement"—to use an apt Aristotelian term—are many. Because of his own failed career as an athlete, he stifles Cory's ambitions to escape the destitution in which he lives. Though he proclaims his love for Rose, he condemns her to a life of servitude ("You supposed to come when I call you, woman"); ironically, he treats her much as his boss treats him. In short, he doesn't let her "drive the truck." He possesses a destructive temper and a pride that ultimately destroys him—and his family. Wilson's refusal to render his protagonist in only heroic terms makes Troy all the more universal and sympathetic. Through Troy's weaknesses, Wilson argues that the most divisive and dangerous threats to the African American community stem from internal conflict. To be sure, they are exacerbated by the rage fostered by a racist society, but Wilson represents a new strain of African American playwriting. Unlike the works of Baraka, Ed Bullins, and other early Black Power dramatists, Wilson argues that the enemy is as often within as without the black community.

Rose Maxson also emerges as an extraordinary being, another in a long line of memorable American stage mothers such as Linda Loman. Rose is uncommonly heroic in her acceptance of Raynell and, of course, in the manner in which she preserves a quiet dignity in the face of Troy's chauvinism. Her monologue at the end of act 2, scene 1, is a masterpiece of self-realization, and her dismissal of Troy at the end of the next scene ("you a womanless man") is as powerful as Nora Helmer's famed door slam at the end of *A Doll's House*.

Cory, like Biff, is repulsed by his father's hypocrisy and heavy-handed justice; ironically, Troy is just as angered at the "unfairness" of his boss. And Cory, like Biff, is condemned to walk in his father's shoes (says Cory, "I got to the place where I could feel [Troy] kicking in my blood and knew that the only thing that separated us was the matter of a few years"). And, true to the form of dramas about generational warfare, Wilson provides us with an obligatory scene in which father and son square off in an archetypal battle in which a baseball bat is as potent a weapon as a broadsword.

It may be tempting to assume that Cory "wins" the battle because our final view of him is as a smartly dressed "corporal in the United States Marine Corps." He has escaped the "fence" of Pittsburgh's Hill, and he is clearly admired by Bono, Raynell, and Rose. But the reality is that Cory is a marine in 1965, and his escape from the Hill most likely will lead him to the rice paddies of Vietnam. For Wilson, although military service seemed an attractive alternative to life in the inner city, the reality was that "a whole bunch of blacks went over and died in the Vietnam War. The survivors came back to the same street corners and found nothing had changed. They still couldn't get a job." Cory, then, is also condemned to an institution, as are the other principal characters: Rose at her church, Lyons in jail, and Gabriel in a mental hospital. Even Bono remains trapped on the Hill, his only respite the Friday evening paycheck that brings a few hours' solace.

Despite the bleak ending, Wilson—as is typical of his work—intimates some hope throughout, largely in his well-chosen music. In addition to his use of baseball (along with boxing, the first mainstream sporting enterprise to employ African Americans and thus change perceptions about minorities in America), Wilson also uses the song of black Americans liberally throughout his scripts for both thematic and cultural purposes. Note that each song in *Fences* comments on the action just as the ancient Greek choral odes did. But the music is also a manifestation of the characters' ability to persevere amid hardship. In his earliest full-length play, *Ma Rainey's Black Bottom*, the title character (an actual historical figure who is recognized as "the mother of the blues") declares that "you don't sing to feel better—you sing because that's a way of understanding life." The line is an apt prologue to Wilson's ten-play cycle—especially *Fences*—in which he explores the black experience through the lens of various cultural phenomena that simultaneously enrich and exploit African Americans. To paraphrase Ma Rainey, Wilson doesn't write to entertain; he writes because it is a proven way for audiences of all colors to understand life. And in that understanding of the pain of rejection, injustice, and human error emerges a kind of hope that the world's imperfections, on the Hill and elsewhere, will diminish, just as surely as baseball's "color line" was broken in Brooklyn in 1947.

James Earl Jones created the role of Troy Maxson in the New York production of Fences; his baseball bat is the modern equivalent of a warrior's weapon as he battles the demons of racism.

FENCES

AUGUST WILSON

for Lloyd Richards,
who adds to whatever he touches.

When the sins of our fathers visit us
We do not have to play host.
We can banish them with forgiveness
As God, in His Largeness and Laws.
—August Wilson

LIST OF CHARACTERS

TROY MAXSON
JIM BONO, Troy's friend
ROSE, Troy's wife
LYONS, Troy's oldest son by previous marriage
GABRIEL, Troy's brother
CORY, Troy and Rose's son
RAYNELL, Troy's daughter

SETTING: *The setting is the yard which fronts the only entrance to the Maxson household, an ancient two-story brick house set back off a small alley in a big-city neighborhood. The entrance to the house is gained by two or three steps leading to a wooden porch badly in need of paint.*

A relatively recent addition to the house and running its full width, the porch lacks congruence. It is a sturdy porch with a flat roof. One or two chairs of dubious value sit at one end where the kitchen window opens onto the porch. An old-fashioned icebox stands silent guard at the opposite end.

The yard is a small dirt yard, partially fenced, except for the last scene, with a wooden saw horse, a pile of lumber, and other fence-building equipment set off to the side. Opposite is a tree from which hangs a ball made of rags. A baseball bat leans against the tree. Two oil drums serve as garbage receptacles and sit near the house at right to complete the setting.

THE PLAY: *Near the turn of the century, the destitute of Europe sprang on the city with tenacious claws and an honest and solid dream. The city devoured them. They swelled its belly until it burst into a thousand furnaces and sewing machines, a thousand butcher shops and bakers' ovens, a thousand churches and hospitals and funeral parlors and money-lenders. The city grew. It nourished itself and offered each man a partnership limited only by his talent, his guile, and his willingness and capacity for hard work. For the immigrants of Europe, a dream dared and won true.*

The descendants of African slaves were offered no such welcome or participation. They came from places called the Carolinas and the Virginias, Georgia, Alabama, Mississippi, and Tennessee. They came strong, eager, searching. The city rejected them and they fled and settled along the riverbanks and under bridges in shallow, ramshackle houses made of sticks and tarpaper. They collected rags and wood. They sold the use of their muscles and their bodies. They cleaned houses and washed clothes, they shined shoes, and in quiet desperation and vengeful pride, they stole, and lived in pursuit of their own dream. That they could breathe free, finally, and stand to meet life with the force of dignity and whatever eloquence the heart could call upon.

By 1957, the hard-won victories of the European immigrants had solidified the industrial might of America. War had been confronted and won with new energies that used loyalty and patriotism as its fuel. Life was rich, full, and flourishing. The Milwaukee Braves won the World Series, and the hot winds of change that would make the sixties a turbulent, racing, dangerous, and provocative decade had not yet begun to blow full.

ACT 1

SCENE 1

It is 1957. Troy and Bono enter the yard, engaged in conversation. Troy is fifty-three years old, a large man with thick, heavy hands; it is this largeness that he strives to fill out and make an accommodation with. Together with his blackness, his largeness informs his sensibilities and the choices he has made in his life.

Of the two men, Bono is obviously the follower. His commitment to their friendship of thirty-odd years is rooted in his admiration of Troy's honesty, capacity for hard work, and his strength, which Bono seeks to emulate.

It is Friday night, payday, and the one night of the week the two men engage in a ritual of talk and drink. Troy is usually the most talkative and at times he can be crude and almost vulgar, though he is capable of rising to profound heights of expression. The men carry lunch buckets and wear or carry burlap aprons and are dressed in clothes suitable to their jobs as garbage collectors.

BONO. Troy, you ought to stop that lying!

TROY. I ain't lying! The nigger had a watermelon this big. (*He indicates with his hands.*) Talking about . . . "What watermelon, Mr. Rand?" I liked to fell out! "What watermelon, Mr. Rand?" . . . And it sitting there big as life.

BONO. What did Mr. Rand say?

TROY. Ain't said nothing. Figure if the nigger too dumb to know he carrying a watermelon, he wasn't gonna get much sense out of him. Trying to hide that great big old watermelon under his coat. Afraid to let the white man see him carry it home.

BONO. I'm like you . . . I ain't got no time for them kind of people.

TROY. Now what he look like getting mad cause he see the man from the union talking to Mr. Rand?

BONO. He come to me talking about . . . "Maxson gonna get us fired." I told him to get away from me with that. He walked away from me calling you a troublemaker. What Mr. Rand say?

TROY. Ain't said nothing. He told me to go down the Commissioner's office next Friday. They called me down there to see them.

BONO. Well, as long as you got your complaint filed, they can't fire you. That's what one of them white fellows tell me.

TROY. I ain't worried about them firing me. They gonna fire me cause I asked a question? That's all I did. I went to Mr. Rand and asked him, "Why? Why you got the white mens driving and the colored lifting?" Told him, "what's the matter, don't I count? You think only white fellows got sense enough to drive a truck. That ain't no paper job!

Hell, anybody can drive a truck. How come you got all whites driving and the colored lifting?" He told me "take it to the union." Well, hell, that's what I done! Now they wanna come up with this pack of lies.

BONO. I told Brownie if the man come and ask him any questions . . . just tell the truth! It ain't nothing but something they done trumped up on you cause you filed a complaint on them.

TROY. Brownie don't understand nothing. All I want them to do is change the job description. Give everybody a chance to drive the truck. Brownie can't see that. He ain't got that much sense.

BONO. How you figure he be making out with that gal be up at Taylor's all the time . . . that Alberta gal?

TROY. Same as you and me. Getting just as much as we is. Which is to say nothing.

BONO. It is, huh? I figure you doing a little better than me . . . and I ain't saying what I'm doing.

TROY. Aw, nigger, look here . . . I know you. If you had got anywhere near that gal, twenty minutes later you be looking to tell somebody. And the first one you gonna tell . . . that you gonna want to brag to . . . is me.

BONO. I ain't saying that. I see where you be eyeing her.

TROY. I eye all the women. I don't miss nothing. Don't never let nobody tell you Troy Maxson don't eye the women.

BONO. You been doing more than eyeing her. You done bought her a drink or two.

TROY. Hell yeah, I bought her a drink! What that mean? I bought you one, too. What that mean cause I buy her a drink? I'm just being polite.

BONO. It's all right to buy her one drink. That's what you call being polite. But when you wanna be buying two or three . . . that's what you call eyeing her.

TROY. Look here, as long as you known me . . . you ever known me to chase after women?

BONO. Hell yeah! Long as I done known you. You forgetting I knew you when.

TROY. Naw, I'm talking about since I been married to Rose?

BONO. Oh, not since you been married to Rose. Now, that's the truth, there. I can say that.

TROY. All right then! Case closed.

BONO. I see you be walking up around Alberta's house. You supposed to be at Taylors' and you be walking up around there.

TROY. What you watching where I'm walking for? I ain't watching after you.

BONO. I seen you walking around there more than once.

TROY. Hell, you liable to see me walking anywhere! That don't mean nothing cause you see me walking around there.

BONO. Where she come from anyway? She just kinda showed up one day.

TROY. Tallahassee. You can look at her and tell she one of them Florida gals. They got some big healthy women down there. Grow them right up out the ground. Got a little bit of Indian in her. Most of them niggers down in Florida got some Indian in them.

BONO. I don't know about that Indian part. But she damn sure big and healthy. Woman wear some big stockings. Got them great big old legs and hips as wide as the Mississippi River.

TROY. Legs don't mean nothing. You don't do nothing but push them out of the way. But them hips cushion the ride!

BONO. Troy, you ain't got no sense.

TROY. It's the truth! Like you riding on Goodyears!

Rose enters from the house. She is ten years younger than Troy, her devotion to him stems from her recognition of the possibilities of her life without him: a succession of abusive men and their babies, a life of partying and running the streets, the Church, or aloneness with its attendant pain and frustration. She recognizes Troy's spirit as a fine and illuminating one and she either ignores or forgives his faults, only some of which she recognizes. Though she doesn't drink, her presence is an integral part of the Friday night rituals. She alternates between the porch and the kitchen, where supper preparations are under way.

ROSE. What you all out here getting into?

TROY. What you worried about what we getting into for? This is men talk, woman.

ROSE. What I care what you all talking about? Bono, you gonna stay for supper?

BONO. No, I thank you, Rose. But Lucille say she cooking up a pot of pigfeet.

TROY. Pigfeet! Hell, I'm going home with you! Might even stay the night if you got some pigfeet. You got something in there to top them pigfeet, Rose?

ROSE. I'm cooking up some chicken. I got some chicken and collard greens.

TROY. Well, go on back in the house and let me and Bono finish what we was talking about. This is men talk. I got some talk for you later. You know what kind of talk I mean. You go on and powder it up.

ROSE. Troy Maxson, don't you start that now!

TROY (*puts his arm around her*). Aw, woman . . . come here. Look here, Bono . . . when I met this woman . . . I got out that place, say, "Hitch up my pony, saddle up my mare . . . there's a woman out there for me somewhere. I looked here. Looked there. Saw Rose and latched on to her." I latched on to her and told her—I'm gonna tell you the truth—I told her, "Baby, I don't wanna marry, I just wanna be your man." Rose told me . . . tell him what you told me, Rose.

ROSE. I told him if he wasn't the marrying kind, then move out the way so the marrying kind could find me.

TROY. That's what she told me. "Nigger, you in my way. You blocking the view! Move out the way so I can find me a husband." I thought it over two or three days. Come back—

ROSE. Ain't no two or three days nothing. You was back the same night.

TROY. Come back, told her . . . "Okay, baby . . . but I'm gonna buy me a banty rooster and put him out there in the backyard . . . and when he see a stranger come, he'll flap his wings and crow. . . ." Look here, Bono, I could watch the front door by myself . . . it was that back door I was worried about.

ROSE. Troy, you ought not talk like that. Troy ain't doing nothing but telling a lie.

TROY. Only thing is . . . when we first got married . . . forget the rooster . . . we ain't had no yard!

BONO. I hear you tell it. Me and Lucille was staying down there on Logan Street. Had two rooms with the outhouse in the back. I ain't mind the outhouse none. But when that goddamn wind blow through there in the winter . . . that's what I'm talking about! To this day I wonder why in the hell I ever stayed down there for six long years. But see, I didn't know I could do no better. I thought only white folks had inside toilets and things.

ROSE. There's a lot of people don't know they can do no better than they doing now. That's just something you got to learn. A lot of folks still shop at Bella's.

TROY. Ain't nothing wrong with shopping at Bella's. She got fresh food.

ROSE. I ain't said nothing about if she got fresh food. I'm talking about what she charge. She charge ten cents more than the A&P.

TROY. The A&P ain't never done nothing for me. I spends my money where I'm treated right. I go down to Bella, say, "I need a loaf of bread, I'll pay you Friday." She give it to me. What sense that make when I got money to go and spend it somewhere else and ignore the person who done right by me? That ain't in the Bible.

ROSE. We ain't talking about what's in the Bible. What sense it make to shop there when she overcharge?

TROY. You shop where you want to. I'll do my shopping where the people been good to me.

ROSE. Well, I don't think it's right for her to overcharge. That's all I was saying.

BONO. Look here . . . I got to get on. Lucille going be raising all kind of hell.

TROY. Where you going, nigger? We ain't finished this pint. Come here, finish this pint.

BONO. Well, hell, I am . . . if you ever turn the bottle loose.

TROY (*hands him the bottle*). The only thing I say about the A&P is I'm glad Cory got that job down there. Help him take care of his school clothes and things. Gabe done moved out and things getting tight around here. He got that job. . . . He can start to look out for himself.

ROSE. Cory done went and got recruited by a college football team.

TROY. I told that boy about that football stuff. The white man ain't gonna let him get nowhere with that football. I told him when he first come to me with it. Now you come telling me he done went and got more tied up in it. He ought to go and get recruited in how to fix cars or something where he can make a living.

ROSE. He ain't talking about making no living playing football. It's just something the boys in school do. They gonna send a recruiter by to talk to you. He'll tell you he ain't talking about making no living playing football. It's a honor to be recruited.

TROY. It ain't gonna get him nowhere. Bono'll tell you that.

BONO. If he be like you in the sports . . . he's gonna be all right. Ain't but two men ever played baseball as good as you. That's Babe Ruth and Josh Gibson.[1] Them's the only two men ever hit more home runs than you.

TROY. What it ever get me? Ain't got a pot to piss in or a window to throw it out of.

ROSE. Times have changed since you was playing baseball, Troy. That was before the war. Times have changed a lot since then.

TROY. How in hell they done changed?

ROSE. They got lots of colored boys playing ball now. Baseball and football.

BONO. You right about that, Rose. Times have changed, Troy. You just come along too early.

TROY. There ought not never have been no time called too early! Now you take that fellow . . . what's that fellow they had playing right field for the Yankees back then? You know who I'm talking about, Bono. Used to play right field for the Yankees.

ROSE. Selkirk?

TROY. Selkirk! That's it! Man batting .269, understand? .269. What kind of sense that make? I was hitting .432 with thirty-seven home runs! Man batting .269 and playing right field for the Yankees! I saw Josh Gibson's daughter yesterday. She walking around with raggedy shoes on her feet. Now I bet you Selkirk's daughter ain't walking around with raggedy shoes on the feet! I bet you that!

ROSE. They got a lot of colored baseball players now. Jackie Robinson[2] was the first. Folks had to wait for Jackie Robinson.

TROY. I done seen a hundred niggers play baseball better than Jackie Robinson. Hell, I know some teams Jackie Robinson couldn't even make! What you talking about Jackie Robinson. Jackie Robinson wasn't nobody. I'm talking about if you could play ball then they ought to have let you play. Don't care what color you were. Come telling me I come along too early. If you could play . . . then they ought to have let you play.

[1]African American ballplayer (1911–1947), known as the Babe Ruth of the Negro leagues.
[2]In 1947 Robinson (1919–1972) became the first African American to play baseball in the major leagues.

Troy takes a long drink from the bottle.

ROSE. You gonna drink yourself to death. You don't need to be drinking like that.

TROY. Death ain't nothing. I done seen him. Done wrassled with him. You can't tell me nothing about death. Death ain't nothing but a fastball on the outside corner. And you know what I'll do to that! Lookee here, Bono . . . am I lying? You get one of them fastballs, about waist high, over the outside corner of the plate where you can get the meat of the bat on it . . . and good god! You can kiss it goodbye. Now, am I lying?

BONO. Naw, you telling the truth there. I seen you do it.

TROY. If I'm lying . . . that 450 feet worth of lying! (*Pause.*) That's all death is to me. A fastball on the outside corner.

ROSE. I don't know why you want to get on talking about death.

TROY. Ain't nothing wrong with talking about death. That's part of life. Everybody gonna die. You gonna die, I'm gonna die. Bono's gonna die. Hell, we all gonna die.

ROSE. But you ain't got to talk about it. I don't like to talk about it.

TROY. You the one brought it up. Me and Bono was talking about baseball . . . you tell me I'm gonna drink myself to death. Ain't that right, Bono? You know I don't drink this but one night out of the week. That's Friday night. I'm gonna drink just enough to where I can handle it. Then I cuts it loose. I leave it alone. So don't you worry about me drinking myself to death. 'Cause I ain't worried about Death. I done seen him. I done wrestled with him.

Look here, Bono . . . I looked up one day and Death was marching straight at me. Like Soldiers on Parade! The Army of Death was marching straight at me. The middle of July, 1941. It got real cold just like it be winter. It seem like Death himself reached out and touched me on the shoulder. He touch me just like I touch you. I got cold as ice and Death standing there grinning at me.

ROSE. Troy, why don't you hush that talk.

TROY. I say . . . what you want, Mr. Death? You be wanting me? You done brought your army to be getting me? I looked him dead in the eye. I wasn't fearing nothing. I was ready to tangle. Just like I'm ready to tangle now. The Bible say be ever vigilant. That's why I don't get but so drunk. I got to keep watch.

ROSE. Troy was right down there in Mercy Hospital. You remember he had pneumonia? Laying there with a fever talking plumb out of his head.

TROY. Death standing there staring at me . . . carrying that sickle in his hand. Finally he say, "You want bound over for another year?" See, just like that . . . "You want bound over for another year?" I told him, "Bound over hell! Let's settle this now!"

It seem like he kinda fell back when I said that, and all the cold went out of me. I reached down and grabbed that sickle and threw it just as far as I could throw it . . . and me and him commenced to wrestling.

We wrestled for three days and three nights. I can't say where I found the strength from. Everytime it seemed like he was gonna get the best of me, I'd reach way down deep inside myself and find the strength to do him one better.

ROSE. Everytime Troy tell that story he find different ways to tell it. Different things to make up about it.

TROY. I ain't making up nothing. I'm telling you the facts of what happened. I wrestled with Death for three days and three nights and I'm standing here to tell you about it. (*Pause.*) All right. At the end of the third night we done weakened each other to where we can't hardly move. Death stood up, throwed on his robe . . . had him a white robe with a hood on it. He throwed on that robe and went off to look for his sickle. Say, "I'll be back." Just like that. "I'll be back." I told him, say, "Yeah, but . . . you gonna have to find me!" I wasn't no fool. I wasn't going looking for him. Death ain't nothing to play with. And I know he's gonna get me. I know I got to join his army . . . his camp followers. But as long as I keep my strength and see him coming . . . as long as I keep up my vigilance . . . he's gonna have to fight to get me. I ain't going easy.

BONO. Well, look here, since you got to keep up your vigilance . . . let me have the bottle.

TROY. Aw hell, I shouldn't have told you that part. I should have left out that part.

ROSE. Troy be talking that stuff and half the time don't even know what he be talking about.

TROY. Bono know me better than that.

BONO. That's right. I know you. I know you got some Uncle Remus[3] in your blood. You got more stories than the devil got sinners.

TROY. Aw hell, I done seen him too! Done talked with the devil.

ROSE. Troy, don't nobody wanna be hearing all that stuff.

Lyons enters the yard from the street. Thirty-four years old, Troy's son by a previous marriage, he sports a neatly trimmed goatee, sport coat, white shirt, tieless and buttoned at the collar. Though he fancies himself a musician, he is more caught up in the rituals and "idea" of being a musician than in the actual practice of the music. He has come to borrow money from Troy, and while he knows he will be successful, he is uncertain as to what extent his lifestyle will be held up to scrutiny and ridicule.

LYONS. Hey, Pop.

TROY. What you come "Hey, Popping" me for?

LYONS. How you doing, Rose? (*He kisses her.*) Mr. Bono. How you doing?

---

[3]Narrator of traditional black tales in a book by Joel Chandler Harris.

BONO. Hey, Lyons . . . how you been?

TROY. He must have been doing all right. I ain't seen him around here last week.

ROSE. Troy, leave your boy alone. He come by to see you and you wanna start all that nonsense.

TROY. I ain't bothering Lyons. (*Offers him the bottle.*) Here . . . get you a drink. We got an understanding. I know why he come by to see me and he know I know.

LYONS. Come on, Pop . . . I just stopped by to say hi . . . see how you was doing.

TROY. You ain't stopped by yesterday.

ROSE. You gonna stay for supper, Lyons? I got some chicken cooking in the oven.

LYONS. No, Rose . . . thanks. I was just in the neighborhood and thought I'd stop by for a minute.

TROY. You was in the neighborhood all right, nigger. You telling the truth there. You was in the neighborhood cause it's my payday.

LYONS. Well, hell, since you mentioned it . . . let me have ten dollars.

TROY. I'll be damned! I'll die and go to hell and play black-jack with the devil before I give you ten dollars.

BONO. That's what I wanna know about . . . that devil you done seen.

LYONS. What . . . Pop done seen the devil? You too much, Pops.

TROY. Yeah, I done seen him. Talked to him too!

ROSE. You ain't seen no devil. I done told you that man ain't had nothing to do with the devil. Anything you can't understand, you want to call it the devil.

TROY. Look here, Bono . . . I went down to see Hertzberger about some furniture. Got three rooms for two-ninety-eight. That what it say on the radio. "Three rooms . . . two-ninety-eight." Even made up a little song about it. Go down there . . . man tell me I can't get no credit. I'm working every day and can't get no credit. What to do? I got an empty house with some raggedy furniture in it. Cory ain't got no bed. He's sleeping on a pile of rags on the floor. Working every day and can't get no credit. Come back here—Rose'll tell you—madder than hell. Sit down . . . try to figure what I'm gonna do. Come a knock on the door. Ain't been living here but three days. Who know I'm here? Open the door . . . devil standing there bigger than life. White fellow . . . white fellow . . . got on good clothes and everything. Standing there with a clipboard in his hand. I ain't had to say nothing. First words come out of his mouth was . . . "I understand you need some furniture and can't get no credit." I liked to fell over. He say, "I'll give you all the credit you want, but you got to pay the interest on it." I told him, "Give me three rooms worth and charge whatever you want." Next day a truck pulled up here and two men unloaded them three rooms. Man what drove the truck give me a book. Say send ten dollars, first of every month to the address in the book and everything will be all right. Say if I miss a pay-

ment the devil was coming back and it'll be hell to pay. That was fifteen years ago. To this day . . . the first of the month I send my ten dollars, Rose'll tell you.

ROSE. Troy lying.

TROY. I ain't never seen that man since. Now you tell me who else that could have been but the devil? I ain't sold my soul or nothing like that, you understand. Naw, I wouldn't have truck with the devil about nothing like that. I got my furniture and pays my ten dollars the first of the month just like clockwork.

BONO. How long you say you been paying this ten dollars a month?

TROY. Fifteen years!

BONO. Hell, ain't you finished paying for it yet? How much the man done charged you?

TROY. Ah hell, I done paid for it. I done paid for it ten times over! The fact is I'm scared to stop paying it.

ROSE. Troy lying. We got that furniture from Mr. Glickman. He ain't paying no ten dollars a month to nobody.

TROY. Aw hell, woman. Bono know I ain't that big a fool.

LYONS. I was just getting ready to say . . . I know where there's a bridge for sale.

TROY. Look here, I'll tell you this . . . it don't matter to me if he was the devil. It don't matter if the devil give credit. Somebody has got to give it.

ROSE. It ought to matter. You going around talking about having truck with the devil . . . God's the one you gonna have to answer to. He's the one gonna be at the Judgment.

LYONS. Yeah, well, look here, Pop . . . Let me have that ten dollars. I'll give it back to you. Bonnie got a job working at the hospital.

TROY. What I tell you, Bono? The only time I see this nigger is when he wants something. That's the only time I see him.

LYONS. Come on, Pop, Mr. Bono don't want to hear all that. Let me have the ten dollars. I told you Bonnie working.

TROY. What that mean to me? "Bonnie working." I don't care if she working. Go ask her for the ten dollars if she working. Talking about "Bonnie working." Why ain't you working?

LYONS. Aw, Pop, you know I can't find no decent job. Where am I gonna get a job at? You know I can't get no job.

TROY. I told you I know some people down there. I can get you on the rubbish if you want to work. I told you that the last time you came by here asking me for something.

LYONS. Naw, Pop . . . thanks. That ain't for me. I don't wanna be carrying nobody's rubbish. I don't wanna be punching nobody's time clock.

TROY. What's the matter, you too good to carry people's rubbish? Where you think that ten dollars you talking about come from? I'm just supposed to haul people's rubbish and give my money to you cause you too lazy to work. You too lazy to work and wanna know why you ain't got what I got.

ROSE. What hospital Bonnie working at? Mercy?

LYONS. She's down at Passavant working in the laundry.

TROY. I ain't got nothing as it is. I give you that ten dollars and I got to eat beans the rest of the week. Naw . . . you ain't getting no ten dollars here.

LYONS. You ain't got to be eating no beans. I don't know why you wanna say that.

TROY. I ain't got no extra money. Gabe done moved over to Miss Pearl's paying her the rent and things done got tight around here. I can't afford to be giving you every payday.

LYONS. I ain't asked you to give me nothing. I asked you to loan me ten dollars. I know you got ten dollars.

TROY. Yeah, I got it. You know why I got it? Cause I don't throw my money away out there in the streets. You living the fast life . . . wanna be a musician . . . running around in them clubs and things . . . then, you learn to take care of yourself. You ain't gonna find me going and asking nobody for nothing. I done spent too many years without.

LYONS. You and me is two different people, Pop.

TROY. I done learned my mistake and learned to do what's right by it. You still trying to get something for nothing. Life don't owe you nothing. You owe it to yourself. Ask Bono. He'll tell you I'm right.

LYONS. You got your way of dealing with the world . . . I got mine. The only thing that matters to me is the music.

TROY. Yeah, I can see that! It don't matter how you gonna eat . . . where your next dollar is coming from. You telling the truth there.

LYONS. I know I got to eat. But I got to live too. I need something that gonna help me to get out of the bed in the morning. Make me feel like I belong in the world. I don't bother nobody. I just stay with the music cause that's the only way I can find to live in the world. Otherwise there ain't no telling what I might do. Now I don't come criticizing you and how you live. I just come by to ask you for ten dollars. I don't wanna hear all that about how I live.

TROY. Boy, your mamma did a hell of a job raising you.

LYONS. You can't change me, Pop. I'm thirty-four years old. If you wanted to change me, you should have been there when I was growing up. I come by to see you . . . ask for ten dollars and you want to talk about how I was raised. You don't know nothing about how I was raised.

ROSE. Let the boy have ten dollars, Troy.

TROY (to Lyons). What the hell you looking at me for? I ain't got no ten dollars. You know what I do with my money. (To Rose.) Give him ten dollars if you want him to have it.

ROSE. I will. Just as soon as you turn it loose.

TROY (handing Rose the money). There it is. Seventy-six dollars and forty-two cents. You see this, Bono? Now, I ain't gonna get but six of that back.

ROSE. You ought to stop telling that lie. Here, Lyons. (She hands him the money.)

LYONS. Thanks, Rose. Look . . . I got to run . . . I'll see you later.

TROY. Wait a minute. You gonna say, "thanks, Rose" and ain't gonna look to see where she got that ten dollars from? See how they do me, Bono?

LYONS. I know she got it from you, Pop. Thanks. I'll give it back to you.

TROY. There he go telling another lie. Time I see that ten dollars . . . he'll be owing me thirty more.

LYONS. See you, Mr. Bono.

BONO. Take care, Lyons!

LYONS. Thanks, Pop. I'll see you again.

Lyons exits the yard.

TROY. I don't know why he don't go and get him a decent job and take care of that woman he got.

BONO. He'll be all right, Troy. The boy is still young.

TROY. The *boy* is thirty-four years old.

ROSE. Let's not get off into all that.

BONO. Look here . . . I got to be going. I got to be getting on. Lucille gonna be waiting.

TROY (*puts his arm around Rose*). See this woman, Bono? I love this woman. I love this woman so much it hurts. I love her so much . . . I done run out of ways of loving her. So I got to go back to basics. Don't you come by my house Monday morning talking about time to go to work . . . 'cause I'm still gonna be stroking!

ROSE. Troy! Stop it now!

BONO. I ain't paying him no mind, Rose. That ain't nothing but gin-talk. Go on, Troy. I'll see you Monday.

TROY. Don't you come by my house, nigger! I done told you what I'm gonna be doing.

The lights go down to black.

SCENE 2

The lights come up on Rose hanging up clothes. She hums and sings softly to herself. It is the following morning.

ROSE (*sings*).
    Jesus, be a fence all around me every day
    Jesus, I want you to protect me as I travel on my way.
    Jesus, be a fence all around me every day.

Troy enters from the house.

    Jesus, I want you to protect me
    As I travel on my way.

(*To Troy.*) 'Morning. You ready for breakfast? I can fix it soon as I finish hanging up these clothes?

TROY. I got the coffee on. That'll be all right. I'll just drink some of that this morning.

ROSE. That 651 hit yesterday. That's the second time this month. Miss Pearl hit for a dollar . . . seem like those that need the least always get lucky. Poor folks can't get nothing.

TROY. Them numbers don't know nobody. I don't know why you fool with them. You and Lyons both.

ROSE. It's something to do.

TROY. You ain't doing nothing but throwing your money away.

ROSE. Troy, you know I don't play foolishly. I just play a nickel here and a nickel there.

TROY. That's two nickels you done thrown away.

ROSE. Now I hit sometimes . . . that makes up for it. It always comes in handy when I do hit. I don't hear you complaining then.

TROY. I ain't complaining now. I just say it's foolish. Trying to guess out of six hundred ways which way the number gonna come. If I had all the money niggers, these Negroes, throw away on numbers for one week—just one week—I'd be a rich man.

ROSE. Well, you wishing and calling it foolish ain't gonna stop folks from playing numbers. That's one thing for sure. Besides . . . some good things come from playing numbers. Look where Pope done bought him that restaurant off of numbers.

TROY. I can't stand niggers like that. Man ain't had two dimes to rub together. He walking around with his shoes all run over bumming money for cigarettes. All right. Got lucky there and hit the numbers . . .

ROSE. Troy, I know all about it.

TROY. Had good sense, I'll say that for him. He ain't throwed his money away. I seen niggers hit the numbers and go through two thousand dollars in four days. Man bought him that restaurant down there . . . fixed it up real nice . . . and then didn't want nobody to come in it! A Negro go in there and can't get no kind of service. I seen a white fellow come in there and order a bowl of stew. Pope picked all the meat out of the pot for him. Man ain't had nothing but a bowl of meat! Negro come behind him and ain't got nothing but the potatoes and carrots. Talking about what numbers do for people, you picked a wrong example. Ain't done nothing but make a worser fool out of him than he was before.

ROSE. Troy, you ought to stop worrying about what happened at work yesterday.

TROY. I ain't worried. Just told me to be down there at the Commissioner's office on Friday. Everybody think they gonna fire me. I ain't worried about them firing me. You ain't got to worry about that. (*Pause.*) Where's Cory? Cory in the house? (*Calls.*) Cory?

ROSE. He gone out.

TROY. Out, huh? He gone out 'cause he know I want him to help me with this fence. I know how he is. That boy scared of work.

Gabriel enters. He comes halfway down the alley and, hearing Troy's voice, stops.

TROY (*continues*). He ain't done a lick of work in his life.

ROSE. He had to go to football practice. Coach wanted them to get in a little extra practice before the season start.

TROY. I got his practice . . . running out of here before he get his chores done.

ROSE. Troy, what is wrong with you this morning? Don't nothing set right with you. Go on back in there and go to bed . . . get up on the other side.

TROY. Why something got to be wrong with me? I ain't said nothing wrong with me.

ROSE. You got something to say about everything. First it's the numbers . . . then it's the way the man runs his restaurant . . . then you done got on Cory. What's it gonna be next? Take a look up there and see if the weather suits you . . . or is it gonna be how you gonna put up the fence with the clothes hanging in the yard.

TROY. You hit the nail on the head then.

ROSE. I know you like I know the back of my hand. Go on in there and get you some coffee . . . see if that straighten you up. 'Cause you ain't right this morning.

Troy starts into the house and sees Gabriel. Gabriel starts singing. Troy's brother, he is seven years younger than Troy. Injured in World War II, he has a metal plate in his head. He carries an old trumpet tied around his waist and believes with every fiber of his being that he is the Archangel Gabriel. He carries a chipped basket with an assortment of discarded fruits and vegetables he has picked up in the strip district and which he attempts to sell.

GABRIEL (*singing*).
　Yes, ma'am I got plums
　You ask me how I sell them
　Oh ten cents apiece
　Three for a quarter
　Come and buy now
　'Cause I'm here today
　And tomorrow I'll be gone

Gabriel enters.

　Hey, Rose!

ROSE. How you doing Gabe?

GABRIEL. There's Troy . . . Hey, Troy!

TROY. Hey, Gabe.

Exit into kitchen.

ROSE (*to Gabriel*). What you got there?

GABRIEL. You know what I got, Rose. I got fruits and vegetables.

ROSE (*looking in basket*). Where's all these plums you talking about?

GABRIEL. I ain't got no plums today, Rose. I was just singing that. Have some tomorrow. Put me in a big order for plums. Have enough plums tomorrow for St. Peter and everybody.

Troy reenters from kitchen, crosses to steps.

(*To Rose.*) Troy's mad at me.

TROY. I ain't mad at you. What I got to be mad at you about? You ain't done nothing to me.

GABRIEL. I just moved over to Miss Pearl's to keep out from in your way. I ain't mean no harm by it.

TROY. Who said anything about that? I ain't said anything about that.

GABRIEL. You ain't mad at me, is you?

TROY. Naw . . . I ain't mad at you, Gabe. If I was mad at you I'd tell you about it.

GABRIEL. Got me two rooms. In the basement. Got my own door too. Wanna see my key? (*He holds up a key.*) That's my own key! My two rooms!

TROY. Well, that's good, Gabe. You got your own key . . . that's good.

ROSE. You hungry, Gabe? I was just fixing to cook Troy his breakfast.

GABRIEL. I'll take some biscuits. You got some biscuits? Did you know when I was in heaven . . . every morning me and St. Peter would sit down by the gate and eat some big fat biscuits? Oh, yeah! We had us a good time. We'd sit there and eat us them biscuits and then St. Peter would go off to sleep and tell me to wake him up when it's time to open the gates for the judgment.

ROSE. Well, come on . . . I'll make up a batch of biscuits.

Rose exits into the house.

GABRIEL. Troy . . . St. Peter got your name in the book. I seen it. It say . . . Troy Maxson. I say . . . I know him! He got the same name like what I got. That's my brother!

TROY. How many times you gonna tell me that, Gabe?

GABRIEL. Ain't got my name in the book. Don't have to have my name. I done died and went to heaven. He got your name though. One morning St. Peter was looking at his book . . . marking it up for the judgment . . . and he let me see your name. Got it in there under M. Got Rose's name . . . I ain't seen it like I seen yours . . . but I know it's in there. He got a great big book. Got everybody's name what was ever been born. That's what he told me. But I seen your name. Seen it with my own eyes.

TROY. Go on in the house there. Rose going to fix you something to eat.

GABRIEL. Oh, I ain't hungry. I done had breakfast with Aunt Jemimah. She come by and cooked me up a whole mess of flapjacks. Remember how we used to eat them flapjacks?

TROY. Go on in the house and get you something to eat now.

GABRIEL. I got to sell my plums. I done sold some tomatoes. Got me two quarters. Wanna see? (*He shows Troy his quarters.*) I'm gonna save them and buy me a new horn so St. Peter can hear me when it's time to open the gates. (*Gabriel stops suddenly. Listens.*) Hear that? That's the

hellhounds. I got to chase them out of here. Go on get out of here! Get out!

Gabriel exits singing.

Better get ready for the judgment
Better get ready for the judgment
My Lord is coming down

Rose enters from the house.

TROY. He's gone off somewhere.

GABRIEL (*offstage*).

Better get ready for the judgment
Better get ready for the judgment morning
Better get ready for the judgment
My God is coming down

ROSE. He ain't eating right. Miss Pearl say she can't get him to eat nothing.

TROY. What you want me to do about it, Rose? I done did everything I can for the man. I can't make him get well. Man got half his head blown away . . . what you expect?

ROSE. Seem like something ought to be done to help him.

TROY. Man don't bother nobody. He just mixed up from that metal plate he got in his head. Ain't no sense for him to go back into the hospital.

ROSE. Least he be eating right. They can help him take care of himself.

TROY. Don't nobody wanna be locked up, Rose. What you wanna lock him up for? Man go over there and fight the war . . . messin' around with them Japs, get half his head blow off . . . and they give him a lousy three thousand dollars. And I had to swoop down on that.

ROSE. Is you fixing to go into that again?

TROY. That's the only way I got a roof over my head . . . cause of that metal plate.

ROSE. Ain't no sense you blaming yourself for nothing. Gabe wasn't in no condition to manage that money. You done what was right by him. Can't nobody say you ain't done what was right by him. Look how long you took care of him . . . till he wanted to have his own place and moved over there with Miss Pearl.

TROY. That ain't what I'm saying, woman! I'm just stating the facts. If my brother didn't have that metal plate in his head . . . I wouldn't have a pot to piss in or a window to throw it out of. And I'm fifty-three years old. Now see if you can understand that!

Troy gets up from the porch and starts to exit the yard.

ROSE. Where you going off to? You been running out of here every Saturday for weeks. I thought you was gonna work on this fence?

TROY. I'm gonna walk down to Taylor's. Listen to the ball game. I'll be back in a bit. I'll work on it when I get back.

He exits the yard. The lights go to black.

SCENE 3

The lights come up on the yard. It is four hours later. Rose is taking down the clothes from the line. Cory enters carrying his football equipment.

ROSE. Your daddy like to had a fit with you running out of here this morning without doing your chores.

CORY. I told you I had to go to practice.

ROSE. He say you were supposed to help him with this fence.

CORY. He been saying that the last four or five Saturdays, and then he don't never do nothing, but go down to Taylors'. Did you tell him about the recruiter?

ROSE. Yeah, I told him.

CORY. What he say?

ROSE. He ain't said nothing too much. You get in there and get started on your chores before he gets back. Go on and scrub down them steps before he gets back here hollering and carrying on.

CORY. I'm hungry. What you got to eat, Mama?

ROSE. Go on and get started on your chores. I got some meat loaf in there. Go on and make you a sandwich . . . and don't leave no mess in there.

Cory exits into the house. Rose continues to take down the clothes. Troy enters the yard and sneaks up and grabs her from behind.

Troy! Go on, now. You liked to scared me to death. What was the score of the game? Lucille had me on the phone and I couldn't keep up with it.

TROY. What I care about the game? Come here, woman. (*He tries to kiss her.*)

ROSE. I thought you went down Taylors' to listen to the game. Go on, Troy! You supposed to be putting up this fence.

TROY (*attempting to kiss her again*). I'll put it up when I finish with what is at hand.

ROSE. Go on, Troy. I ain't studying you.

TROY (*chasing after her*). I'm studying you . . . fixing to do my homework!

ROSE. Troy, you better leave me alone.

TROY. Where's Cory? That boy brought his butt home yet?

ROSE. He's in the house doing his chores.

TROY (*calling*). Cory! Get your butt out here, boy!

Rose exits into the house with the laundry. Troy goes over to the pile of wood, picks up a board, and starts sawing. Cory enters from the house.

TROY. You just now coming in here from leaving this morning?

CORY. Yeah, I had to go to football practice.

TROY. Yeah, what?

CORY. Yessir.

TROY. I ain't but two seconds off you noway. The garbage sitting in there overflowing . . . you ain't done none of your chores . . . and you come in here talking about "Yeah."

CORY. I was just getting ready to do my chores now, Pop . . .

TROY. Your first chore is to help me with this fence on Saturday. Everything else come after that. Now get that saw and cut them boards.

Cory takes the saw and begins cutting the boards. Troy continues working. There is a long pause.

CORY. Hey, Pop . . . why don't you buy a TV?

TROY. What I want with a TV? What I want one of them for?

CORY. Everybody got one. Earl, Ba Bra . . . Jesse!

TROY. I ain't asked you who had one. I say what I want with one?

CORY. So you can watch it. They got lots of things on TV. Baseball games and everything. We could watch the World Series.

TROY. Yeah . . . and how much this TV cost?

CORY. I don't know. They got them on sale for around two hundred dollars.

TROY. Two hundred dollars, huh?

CORY. That ain't that much, Pop.

TROY. Naw, it's just two hundred dollars. See that roof you got over your head at night? Let me tell you something about that roof. It's been over ten years since that roof was last tarred. See now . . . the snow come this winter and sit up there on that roof like it is . . . and it's gonna seep inside. It's just gonna be a little bit . . . ain't gonna hardly notice it. Then the next thing you know, it's gonna be leaking all over the house. Then the wood rot from all that water and you gonna need a whole new roof. Now, how much you think it cost to get that roof tarred?

CORY. I don't know.

TROY. Two hundred and sixty-four dollars . . . cash money. While you thinking about a TV, I got to be thinking about the roof . . . and whatever else go wrong here. Now if you had two hundred dollars, what would you do . . . fix the roof or buy a TV?

CORY. I'd buy a TV. Then when the roof started to leak . . . when it needed fixing . . . I'd fix it.

TROY. Where you gonna get the money from? You done spent it for a TV. You gonna sit up and watch the water run all over your brand new TV.

CORY. Aw, Pop. You got money. I know you do.

TROY. Where I got it at, huh?

CORY. You got it in the bank.

TROY. You wanna see my bankbook? You wanna see that seventy-three dollars and twenty-two cents I got sitting up in there?

CORY. You ain't got to pay for it all at one time. You can put a down payment on it and carry it on home with you.

TROY. Not me. I ain't gonna owe nobody nothing if I can help it. Miss a payment and they come and snatch it right out of your house. Then what you got? Now, soon as I get two hundred dollars clear, then I'll buy a TV. Right now, as soon as I get two hundred and sixty-four dollars, I'm gonna have this roof tarred.

CORY. Aw . . . Pop!

TROY. You go on and get you two hundred dollars and buy one if ya want it. I got better things to do with my money.

CORY. I can't get no two hundred dollars. I ain't never seen two hundred dollars.

TROY. I'll tell you what . . . you get you a hundred dollars and I'll put the other hundred with it.

CORY. All right, I'm gonna show you.

TROY. You gonna show me how you can cut them boards right now.

Cory begins to cut the boards. There is a long pause.

CORY. The Pirates won today. That makes five in a row.

TROY. I ain't thinking about the Pirates. Got an all-white team. Got that boy . . . that Puerto Rican boy . . . Clemente. Don't even half-play him. That boy could be something if they give him a chance. Play him one day and sit him on the bench the next.

CORY. He gets a lot of chances to play.

TROY. I'm talking about playing regular. Playing every day so you can get your timing. That's what I'm talking about.

CORY. They got some white guys on the team that don't play every day. You can't play everybody at the same time.

TROY. If they got a white fellow sitting on the bench . . . you can bet your last dollar he can't play! The colored guy got to be twice as good before he get on the team. That's why I don't want you to get all tied up in them sports. Man on the team and what it get him? They got colored on the team and don't use them. Same as not having them. All them teams the same.

CORY. The Braves got Hank Aaron and Wes Covington. Hank Aaron hit two home runs today. That makes forty-three.

TROY. Hank Aaron ain't nobody. That what you supposed to do. That's how you supposed to play the game. Ain't nothing to it. It's just a matter of timing . . . getting the right follow-through. Hell, I can hit forty-three home runs right now!

CORY. Not off no major-league pitching, you couldn't.

TROY. We had better pitching in the Negro leagues. I hit seven home runs off of Satchel Paige.[4] You can't get no better than that!

CORY. Sandy Koufax. He's leading the league in strikeouts.

TROY. I ain't thinking of no Sandy Koufax.

CORY. You got Warren Spahn and Lew Burdette. I bet you couldn't hit no home runs off of Warren Spahn.

TROY. I'm through with it now. You go on and cut them boards. (*Pause.*) Your mama tell me you done got recruited by a college football team? Is that right?

CORY. Yeah. Coach Zellman say the recruiter gonna be coming by to talk to you. Get you to sign the permission papers.

TROY. I thought you supposed to be working down there at the A&P. Ain't you suppose to be working down there after school?

CORY. Mr. Stawicki say he gonna hold my job for me until after the football season. Say starting next week I can work weekends.

TROY. I thought we had an understanding about this football stuff? You suppose to keep up with your chores and hold that job down at the A&P. Ain't been around here all day on a Saturday. Ain't none of your chores done . . . and now you telling me you done quit your job.

CORY. I'm going to be working weekends.

TROY. You damn right you are! And ain't no need for nobody coming around here to talk to me about signing nothing.

CORY. Hey, Pop . . . you can't do that. He's coming all the way from North Carolina.

TROY. I don't care where he coming from. The white man ain't gonna let you get nowhere with that football noway. You go on and get your book-learning so you can work yourself up in that A&P or learn how to fix cars or build houses or something, get you a trade. That way you have something can't nobody take away from you. You go on and learn how to put your hands to some good use. Besides hauling people's garbage.

CORY. I get good grades, Pop. That's why the recruiter wants to talk with you. You got to keep up your grades to get recruited. This way I'll be going to college. I'll get a chance . . .

TROY. First you gonna get your butt down there to the A&P and get your job back.

CORY. Mr. Stawicki done already hired somebody else 'cause I told him I was playing football.

TROY. You a bigger fool than I thought . . . to let somebody take away your job so you can play some football. Where you gonna get your money to take out your girlfriend and whatnot? What kind of foolishness is that to let somebody take away your job?

CORY. I'm still gonna be working weekends.

TROY. Naw . . . naw. You getting your butt out of here and finding you another job.

CORY. Come on, Pop! I got to practice. I can't work after school and play football too. The team needs me. That's what Coach Zellman say . . .

TROY. I don't care what nobody else say. I'm the boss . . . you understand? I'm the boss around here. I do the only saying what counts.

CORY. Come on, Pop!

TROY. I asked you . . . did you understand?

CORY. Yeah . . .

TROY. What?!

CORY. Yessir.

TROY. You go on down there to that A&P and see if you can get your job back. If you can't do both . . . then you quit the football team. You've got to take the crookeds with the straights.

---

[4]Paige (1906–1982) was a pitcher in the Negro leagues.

CORY. Yessir. (*Pause.*) Can I ask you a question?

TROY. What the hell you wanna ask me? Mr. Stawicki the one you got the questions for.

CORY. How come you ain't never liked me?

TROY. Liked you? Who the hell say I got to like you? What law is there say I got to like you? Wanna stand up in my face and ask a damn foolass question like that. Talking about liking somebody. Come here, boy, when I talk to you.

Cory comes over to where Troy is working. He stands slouched over and Troy shoves him on his shoulder.

Straighten up, goddammit! I asked you a question . . . what law is there say I got to like you?

CORY. None.

TROY. Well, all right then! Don't you eat every day? (*Pause.*) Answer me when I talk to you! Don't you eat every day?

CORY. Yeah.

TROY. Nigger, as long as you in my house, you put that sir on the end of it when you talk to me.

CORY. Yes . . . sir.

TROY. You eat every day.

CORY. Yessir!

TROY. Got a roof over your head.

CORY. Yessir!

TROY. Got clothes on your back.

CORY. Yessir.

TROY. Why you think that is?

CORY. Cause of you.

TROY. Ah, hell I know it's cause of me . . . but why do you think that is?

CORY (*hesitant*). Cause you like me.

TROY. Like you? I go out of here every morning . . . bust my butt . . . putting up with them crackers every day . . . cause I like you? You are the biggest fool I ever saw. (*Pause.*) It's my job. It's my responsibility! You understand that? A man got to take care of his family. You live in my house . . . sleep you behind on my bedclothes . . . fill you belly up with my food . . . cause you my son. You my flesh and blood. Not cause I like you! Cause it's my duty to take care of you. I owe a responsibility to you! Let's get this straight right here . . . before it go along any further . . . I ain't got to like you. Mr. Rand don't give me my money come payday cause he likes me. He gives me cause he owe me. I done give you everything I had to give you. I gave you your life! Me and your mama worked that out between us. And liking your black ass wasn't part of the bargain. Don't you try and go through life worrying about if somebody like you or not. You best be making sure they doing right by you. You understand what I'm saying boy?

CORY. Yessir.

TROY. Then get the hell out of my face, and get on down to that A&P.

Rose has been standing behind the screen door for much of the scene. She enters as Cory exits.

ROSE. Why don't you let the boy go ahead and play football, Troy? Ain't no harm in that. He's just trying to be like you with the sports.

TROY. I don't want him to be like me! I want him to move as far away from my life as he can get. You the only decent thing that ever happened to me. I wish him that. But I don't wish him a thing else from my life. I decided seventeen years ago that boy wasn't getting involved in no sports. Not after what they did to me in the sports.

ROSE. Troy, why don't you admit you was too old to play in the major leagues? For once . . . why don't you admit that?

TROY. What do you mean too old? Don't come telling me I was too old. I just wasn't the right color. Hell, I'm fifty-three years old and can do better than Selkirk's .269 right now!

ROSE. How's was you gonna play ball when you were over forty? Sometimes I can't get no sense out of you.

TROY. I got good sense, woman. I got sense enough not to let my boy get hurt over playing no sports. You been mothering that boy too much. Worried about if people like him.

ROSE. Everything that boy do . . . he do for you. He wants you to say "Good job, son." That's all.

TROY. Rose, I ain't got time for that. He's alive. He's healthy. He's got to make his own way. I made mine. Ain't nobody gonna hold his hand when he get out there in that world.

ROSE. Times have changed from when you was young, Troy. People change. The world's changing around you and you can't even see it.

TROY (*slow, methodical*). Woman . . . I do the best I can do. I come in here every Friday. I carry a sack of potatoes and a bucket of lard. You all line up at the door with your hands out. I give you the lint from my pockets. I give you my sweat and my blood. I ain't got no tears. I done spent them. We go upstairs in that room at night . . . and I fall down on you and try to blast a hole into forever. I get up Monday morning . . . find my lunch on the table. I go out. Make my way. Find my strength to carry me through to the next Friday. (*Pause.*) That's all I got, Rose. That's all I got to give. I can't give nothing else.

Troy exits into the house. The lights go down to black.

SCENE 4

It is Friday. Two weeks later. Cory starts out of the house with his football equipment. The phone rings.

CORY (*calling*). I got it! (*He answers the phone and stands in the screen door talking.*) Hello? Hey, Jesse. Naw . . . I was just getting ready to leave now.

ROSE (*calling*). Cory!

CORY. I told you, man, them spikes is all tore up. You can

use them if you want, but they ain't no good. Earl got some spikes.

ROSE (*calling*). Cory! Cory (*calling to Rose*). Mam? I'm talking to Jesse. (*Into phone.*) When she say that? (*Pause.*) Aw, you lying, man. I'm gonna tell her you said that.

ROSE (*calling*). Cory, don't you go nowhere!

CORY. I got to go to the game, Ma! (*Into the phone.*) Yeah, hey, look, I'll talk to you later. Yeah, I'll meet you over Earl's house. Later. Bye, Ma.

Cory exits the house. Starts out to the garden.

ROSE. Cory, where you going off to? You got that stuff all pulled out and thrown all over your room.

CORY (*in the yard*). I was looking for my spikes. Jesse wanted to borrow my spikes.

ROSE. Get up there and get that cleaned up before your daddy get back in here.

CORY. I got to go to the game! I'll clean it up *when I get back.*

Cory exits.

ROSE. That's all he need to do is see that room all messed up.

Rose exits into the house. Troy and Bono enter the yard. Troy is dressed in clothes other than his work clothes.

BONO. He told him the same thing he told you. Take it to the union.

TROY. Brownie ain't got that much sense. Man wasn't thinking about nothing. He wait until I confront them on it . . . then he wanna come crying seniority. (*Calls.*) Hey, Rose!

BONO. I wish I could have seen Mr. Rand's face when he told you.

TROY. He couldn't get it out of his mouth! Liked to bit his tongue! When they called me down there to the Commissioner's office . . . he thought they was gonna fire me. Like everybody else.

BONO. I didn't think they was gonna fire you. I thought they was gonna put you on the warning paper.

TROY. Hey, Rose! (*To Bono.*) Yeah, Mr. Rand like to bit his tongue.

Troy breaks the seal on the bottle, takes a drink, and hands it to Bono.

BONO. I see you run right down to Taylors' and told that Alberta gal.

TROY (*calling*). Hey Rose! (*To Bono.*) I told everybody. Hey, Rose! I went down there to cash my check.

ROSE (*entering from the house*). Hush all that hollering, man! I know you out here. What they say down there at the Commissioner's office?

TROY. You supposed to come when I call you, woman. Bono'll tell you that. (*To Bono.*) Don't Lucille come when you call her?

ROSE. Man, hush your mouth. I ain't no dog . . . talk about "come when you call me."

TROY (*puts his arm around Rose*). You hear this, Bono? I had me an old dog used to get uppity like that. You say, "C'mere, Blue!" . . . and he just lay there and look at you. End up getting a stick and chasing him away trying to make him come.

ROSE. I ain't studying you and your dog. I remember you used to sing that old song.

TROY (*he sings*).
     Hear it ring! Hear it ring! I had a dog his name was Blue.

ROSE. Don't nobody wanna hear you sing that old song.

TROY (*sings*).
     You know Blue was mighty true.

ROSE. Used to have Cory running around here singing that song.

BONO. Hell, I remember that song myself.

TROY (*sings*).
     You know Blue was a good old dog.

     Blue treed a possum in a hollow log.

That was my daddy's song. My daddy made up that song.

ROSE. I don't care who made it up. Don't nobody wanna hear you sing it.

TROY (*makes a song like calling a dog*). Come here, woman.

ROSE. You come in here carrying on, I reckon they ain't fired you. What they say down there at the Commissioner's office?

TROY. Look here, Rose . . . Mr. Rand called me into his office today when I got back from talking to them people down there . . . it come from up top . . . he called me in and told me they was making me a driver.

ROSE. Troy, you kidding!

TROY. No I ain't. Ask Bono.

ROSE. Well, that's great, Troy. Now you don't have to hassle them people no more.

Lyons enters from the street.

TROY. Aw hell, I wasn't looking to see you today. I thought you was in jail. Got it all over the front page of the *Courier* about them raiding Sefus's place . . . where you be hanging out with all them thugs.

LYONS. Hey, Pop . . . that ain't got nothing to do with me. I don't go down there gambling. I go down there to sit in with the band. I ain't got nothing to do with the gambling part. They got some good music down there.

TROY. They got some rogues . . . is what they got.

LYONS. How you been, Mr. Bono? Hi, Rose.

BONO. I see where you playing down at the Crawford Grill tonight.

ROSE. How come you ain't brought Bonnie like I told you? You should have brought Bonnie with you, she ain't been over in a month of Sundays.

LYONS. I was just in the neighborhood . . . thought I'd stop by.

TROY. Here he come . . .

BONO. Your daddy got a promotion on the rubbish. He's gonna be the first colored driver. Ain't got to do nothing but sit up there and read the paper like them white fellows.

LYONS. Hey, Pop . . . if you knew how to read you'd be all right.

BONO. Naw . . . naw . . . you mean if the nigger knew how to drive he'd be all right. Been fighting with them people about driving and ain't even got a license. Mr. Rand know you ain't got no driver's license?

TROY. Driving ain't nothing. All you do is point the truck where you want it to go. Driving ain't nothing.

BONO. Do Mr. Rand know you ain't got no driver's license? That's what I'm talking about. I ain't asked if driving was easy. I asked if Mr. Rand know you ain't got no driver's license.

TROY. He ain't got to know. The man ain't got to know my business. Time he find out, I have two or three driver's licenses.

LYONS (going into his pocket). Say, look here, Pop . . .

TROY. I knew it was coming. Didn't I tell you, Bono? I know what kind of "Look here, Pop" that was. The nigger fixing to ask me for some money. It's Friday night. It's my payday. All them rogues down there on the avenue . . . the ones that ain't in jail . . . and Lyons is hopping in his shoes to get down there with them.

LYONS. See, Pop . . . if you give somebody else a chance to talk sometimes, you'd see that I was fixing to pay you back your ten dollars like I told you. Here . . . I told you I'd pay you when Bonnie got paid.

TROY. Naw . . . you go ahead and keep that ten dollars. Put it in the bank. The next time you feel like you wanna come by here and ask me for something . . . you go on down there and get that.

LYONS. Here's your ten dollars, Pop. I told you I don't want you to give me nothing. I just wanted to borrow ten dollars.

TROY. Naw . . . you go on and keep that for the next time you want to ask me.

LYONS. Come on, Pop . . . here go your ten dollars.

ROSE. Why don't you go on and let the boy pay you back, Troy?

LYONS. Here you go, Rose. If you don't take it I'm gonna have to hear about it for the next six months. (He hands her the money.)

ROSE. You can hand yours over here too, Troy.

TROY. You see this, Bono. You see how they do me.

BONO. Yeah, Lucille do me the same way.

Gabriel is heard singing off stage. He enters.

GABRIEL. Better get ready for the Judgment! Better get ready for . . . Hey! . . . Hey! . . . There's Troy's boy!

LYONS. How are you doing, Uncle Gabe?

GABRIEL. Lyons . . . The King of the Jungle! Rose . . . hey, Rose. Got a flower for you. (He takes a rose from his pocket.) Picked it myself. That's the same rose like you is!

ROSE. That's right nice of you, Gabe.

LYONS. What you been doing, Uncle Gabe?

GABRIEL. Oh, I been chasing hellhounds and waiting on the time to tell St. Peter to open the gates.

LYONS. You been chasing hellhounds, huh? Well . . . you doing the right thing, Uncle Gabe. Somebody got to chase them.

GABRIEL. Oh, yeah . . . I know it. The devil's strong. The devil ain't no pushover. Hellhounds snipping at everybody's heels. But I got my trumpet waiting on the judgment time.

LYONS. Waiting on the Battle of Armageddon, huh?

GABRIEL. Ain't gonna be too much of a battle when God get to waving that Judgment sword. But the people's gonna have a hell of a time trying to get into heaven if them gates ain't open.

LYONS (putting his arm around Gabriel). You hear this, Pop. Uncle Gabe, you all right!

GABRIEL (laughing with Lyons). Lyons! King of the Jungle.

ROSE. You gonna stay for supper, Gabe? Want me to fix you a plate?

GABRIEL. I'll take a sandwich, Rose. Don't want no plate. Just wanna eat with my hands. I'll take a sandwich.

ROSE. How about you, Lyons? You staying? Got some short ribs cooking.

LYONS. Naw, I won't eat nothing till after we finished playing. (Pause.) You ought to come down and listen to me play, Pop.

TROY. I don't like that Chinese music. All that noise.

ROSE. Go on in the house and wash up, Gabe . . . I'll fix you a sandwich.

GABRIEL (to Lyons, as he exits). Troy's mad at me.

LYONS. What you mad at Uncle Gabe for, Pop?

ROSE. He thinks Troy's mad at him cause he moved over to Miss Pearl's.

TROY. I ain't mad at the man. He can live where he want to live at.

LYONS. What he move over there for? Miss Pearl don't like nobody.

ROSE. She don't mind him none. She treats him real nice. She just don't allow all that singing.

TROY. She don't mind that rent he be paying . . . that's what she don't mind.

ROSE. Troy, I ain't going through that with you no more. He's over there cause he want to have his own place. He can come and go as he please.

TROY. Hell, he could come and go as he please here. I wasn't stopping him. I ain't put no rules on him.

ROSE. It ain't the same thing, Troy. And you know it.

Gabriel comes to the door.

Now, that's the last I wanna hear about that. I don't wanna hear nothing else about Gabe and Miss Pearl. And next week . . .

GABRIEL. I'm ready for my sandwich, Rose.

ROSE. And next week . . . when that recruiter come from that school . . . I want you to sign that paper and go on and let Cory play football. Then that'll be the last I have to hear about that.

TROY (*to Rose as she exits into the house*). I ain't thinking about Cory nothing.

LYONS. What . . . Cory got recruited? What school he going to?

TROY. That boy walking around here smelling his piss . . . thinking he's grown. Thinking he's gonna do what he want, irrespective of what I say. Look here, Bono . . . I left the Commissioner's office and went down to the A&P . . . that boy ain't working down there. He lying to me. Telling me he got his job back . . . telling me he working weekends . . . telling me he working after school . . . Mr. Stawicki tell me he ain't working down there at all!

LYONS. Cory just growing up. He's just busting at the seams trying to fill out your shoes.

TROY. I don't care what he's doing. When he get to the point where he wanna disobey me . . . then it's time for him to move on. Bono'll tell you that. I bet he ain't never disobeyed his daddy without paying the consequences.

BONO. I ain't never had a chance. My daddy came on through . . . but I ain't never knew him to see him . . . or what he had on his mind or where he went. Just moving on through. Searching out the New Land. That's what the old folks used to call it. See a fellow moving around from place to place . . . woman to woman . . . called it searching out the New Land. I can't say if he ever found it. I come along, didn't want no kids. Didn't know if I was gonna be in one place long enough to fix on them right as their daddy. I figured I was going searching too. As it turned out I been hooked up with Lucille near about as long as your daddy been with Rose. Going on sixteen years.

TROY. Sometimes I wish I hadn't known my daddy. He ain't cared nothing about no kids. A kid to him wasn't nothing. All he wanted was for you to learn how to walk so he could start you to working. When it come time for eating . . . he ate first. If there was anything left over, that's what you got. Man would sit down and eat two chickens and give you the wing.

LYONS. You ought to stop that, Pop. Everybody feed their kids. No matter how hard times is . . . everybody care about their kids. Make sure they have something to eat.

TROY. The only thing my daddy cared about was getting them bales of cotton in to Mr. Lubin. That's the only thing that mattered to him. Sometimes I used to wonder why he was living. Wonder why the devil hadn't come and got him. "Get them bales of cotton in to Mr. Lubin" and find out he owe him money . . .

LYONS. He should have just went on and left when he saw he couldn't get nowhere. That's what I would have done.

TROY. How he gonna leave with eleven kids? And where he gonna go? He ain't knew how to do nothing but farm. No, he was trapped and I think he knew it. But I'll say this for him . . . he felt a responsibility toward us. Maybe he ain't treated us the way I felt he should have . . . but without that responsibility he could have walked off and left us . . . made his own way.

BONO. A lot of them did. Back in those days what you talking about . . . they walk out their front door and just take on down one road or another and keep on walking.

LYONS. There you go! That's what I'm talking about.

BONO. Just keep on walking till you come to something else. Ain't you never heard of nobody having the walking blues? Well, that's what you call it when you just take off like that.

TROY. My daddy ain't had them walking blues! What you talking about? He stayed right there with his family. But he was just as evil as he could be. My mama couldn't stand him. Couldn't stand that evilness. She run off when I was about eight. She sneaked off one night after he had gone to sleep. Told me she was coming back for me. I ain't never seen her no more. All his women run off and left him. He wasn't good for nobody.

When my turn come to head out, I was fourteen and got to sniffing around Joe Canewell's daughter. Had us an old mule we called Greyboy. My daddy sent me out to do some plowing and I tied up Greyboy and went to fooling around with Joe Canewell's daughter. We done found us a nice little spot, got real cozy with each other. She about thirteen and we done figured we was grown anyway . . . so we down there enjoying ourselves . . . ain't thinking about nothing. We didn't know Greyboy had got loose and wandered back to the house and my daddy was looking for me. We down there by the creek enjoying ourselves when my daddy come up on us. Surprised us. He had them leather straps off the mule and commenced to whupping me like there was no tomorrow. I jumped up, mad and embarrassed. I was scared of my daddy. When he commenced to whupping on me . . . quite naturally I run to get out of the way. (*Pause.*) Now I thought he was mad cause I ain't done my work. But I see where he was chasing me off so he could have the gal for himself. When I see what the matter of it was, I lost all fear of my daddy. Right there is where I become a man . . . at fourteen years of age. (*Pause.*) Now it was my turn to run him off. I picked up them same reins that he had used on me. I picked up them reins and commenced to whupping on him. The gal jumped up and run off . . . and when my daddy turned to face me, I could see why the devil had never come to get him . . . cause he was the devil himself. I don't know what happened. When I woke up, I was laying right there by the creek, and Blue . . . this old dog we had . . . was licking my face. I thought I was blind. I couldn't see nothing. Both my eyes were swollen shut. I laid there and cried. I didn't know what I was gonna do. The only thing I knew was the time had come for me to leave my daddy's house. And right there the world suddenly got big. And it was a long time before I could cut it down to where I could handle it.

Part of that cutting down was when I got to the place where I could feel him kicking in my blood and knew that the only thing that separated us was the matter of a few years.

Gabriel enters from the house with a sandwich.

LYONS. What you got there, Uncle Gabe?

GABRIEL. Got me a ham sandwich. Rose gave me a ham sandwich.

TROY. I don't know what happened to him. I done lost touch with everybody except Gabriel. But I hope he's dead. I hope he found some peace.

LYONS. That's a heavy story, Pop. I didn't know you left home when you was fourteen.

TROY. And didn't know nothing. The only part of the world I knew was the forty-two acres of Mr. Lubin's land. That's all I knew about life.

LYONS. Fourteen's kinda young to be out on your own. (*Phone rings.*) I don't even think I was ready to be out on my own at fourteen. I don't know what I would have done.

TROY. I got up from the creek and walked on down to Mobile. I was through with farming. Figured I could do better in the city. So I walked the two hundred miles to Mobile.

LYONS. Wait a minute . . . you ain't walked no two hundred miles, Pop. Ain't nobody gonna walk no two hundred miles. You talking about some walking there.

BONO. That's the only way you got anywhere back in them days.

LYONS. Shhh. Damn if I wouldn't have hitched a ride with somebody!

TROY. Who you gonna hitch it with? They ain't had no cars and things like they got now. We talking about 1918.

ROSE (*entering*). What you all out here getting into?

TROY (*to Rose*). I'm telling Lyons how good he got it. He don't know nothing about this I'm talking.

ROSE. Lyons, that was Bonnie on the phone. She say you supposed to pick her up.

LYONS. Yeah, okay, Rose.

TROY. I walked on down to Mobile and hitched up with some of them fellows that was heading this way. Got up here and found out . . . not only couldn't you get a job . . . you couldn't find no place to live. I thought I was in freedom. Shhh. Colored folks living down there on the riverbanks in whatever kind of shelter they could find for themselves. Right down there under the Brady Street Bridge. Living in shacks made of sticks and tarpaper. Messed around there and went from bad to worse. Started stealing. First it was food. Then I figured, hell, if I steal money I can buy me some food. Buy me some shoes too!

One thing led to another. Met your mama. I was young and anxious to be a man. Met your mama and had you. What I do that for? Now I got to worry about feeding you and her. Got to steal three times as much. Went out one day looking for somebody to rob . . . that's what I was, a robber. I'll tell you the truth. I'm ashamed of it today. But it's the truth. Went to rob this fellow . . . pulled out my knife . . . and he pulled out a gun. Shot me in the chest. I felt just like somebody had taken a hot branding iron and laid it on me. When he shot me I jumped at him with my knife. They told me I killed him and they put me in the penitentiary and locked me up for fifteen years. That's where I met Bono. That's where I learned how to play baseball. Got out that place and your mama had taken you and went on to make life without me. Fifteen years was a long time for her to wait. But that fifteen years cured me of that robbing stuff. Rose'll tell you. She asked me when I met her if I had gotten all that foolishness out of my system. And I told her, "Baby, it's you and baseball all what count with me." You hear me, Bono? I meant it too. She say, "Which one comes first?" I told her, "Baby, ain't no doubt it's baseball . . . but you stick and get old with me and we'll both outlive this baseball." Am I right, Rose? And it's true.

ROSE. Man, hush your mouth. You ain't said no such thing. Talking about, "Baby you know you'll always be number one with me." That's what you was talking.

TROY. You hear that, Bono. That's why I love her.

BONO. Rose'll keep you straight. You get off the track, she'll straighten you up.

ROSE. Lyons, you better get on up and get Bonnie. She waiting on you.

LYONS (*gets up to go*). Hey, Pop, why don't you come on down to the Grill and hear me play?

TROY. I ain't going down there. I'm too old to be sitting around in them clubs.

BONO. You got to be good to play down at the Grill.

LYONS. Come on, Pop . . .

TROY. I got to get up in the morning.

LYONS. You ain't got to stay long.

TROY. Naw, I'm gonna get my supper and go on to bed.

LYONS. Well, I got to go. I'll see you again.

TROY. Don't you come around my house on my payday.

ROSE. Pick up the phone and let somebody know you coming. And bring Bonnie with you. You know I'm always glad to see her.

LYONS. Yeah, I'll do that, Rose. You take care now. See you, Pop. See you, Mr. Bono. See you, Uncle Gabe.

GABRIEL. Lyons! King of the Jungle!

Lyons exits.

TROY. Is supper ready, woman? Me and you got some business to take care of. I'm gonna tear it up too.

ROSE. Troy, I done told you now!

TROY (*puts his arm around Bono*). Aw hell, woman . . . this is

Bono. Bono like family. I done known this nigger since . . . how long I done know you?

BONO. It's been a long time.

TROY. I done know this nigger since Skippy was a pup. Me and him done been through some times.

BONO. You sure right about that.

TROY. Hell, I done know him longer than I known you. And we still standing shoulder to shoulder. Hey, look here, Bono . . . a man can't ask for no more than that. (*Drinks to him.*) I love you, nigger.

BONO. Hell, I love you too . . . I got to get home see my woman. You got yours in hand. I got to get mine.

Bono starts to exit as Cory enters the yard, dressed in his football uniform. He gives Troy a hard, uncompromising look.

CORY. What you do that for, Pop?

He throws his helmet down in the direction of Troy.

ROSE. What's the matter? Cory . . . what's the matter?

CORY. Papa done went up to the school and told Coach Zellman I can't play football no more. Wouldn't even let me play the game. Told him to tell the recruiter not to come.

ROSE. Troy . . .

TROY. What you Troying me for. Yeah, I did it. And the boy know why I did it.

CORY. Why you wanna do that to me? That was the one chance I had.

ROSE. Ain't nothing wrong with Cory playing football, Troy.

TROY. The boy lied to me. I told the nigger if he wanna play football . . . to keep up his chores and hold down that job at the A&P. That was the conditions. Stopped down there to see Mr. Stawicki . . .

CORY. I can't work after school during the football season, Pop! I tried to tell you that Mr. Stawicki's holding my job for me. You don't never want to listen to nobody. And then you wanna go and do this to me!

TROY. I ain't done nothing to you. You done it to yourself.

CORY. Just cause you didn't have a chance! You just scared I'm gonna be better than you, that's all.

TROY. Come here.

ROSE. Troy . . .

Cory reluctantly crosses over to Troy.

TROY. All right! See. You done made a mistake.

CORY. I didn't even do nothing!

TROY. I'm gonna tell you what your mistake was. See . . . you swung at the ball and didn't hit it. That's strike one. See, you in the batter's box now. You swung and you missed. That's strike one. Don't you strike out!

Lights fade to black.

The following morning. Cory is at the tree hitting the ball with the bat. He tries to mimic Troy, but his swing is awkward, less sure. Rose enters from the house.

ROSE. Cory, I want you to help me with this cupboard.

CORY. I ain't quitting the team. I don't care what Poppa say.

ROSE. I'll talk to him when he gets back. He had to go see about your Uncle Gabe. The police done arrested him. Say he was disturbing the peace. He'll be back directly. Come on in here and help me clean out the top of this cupboard.

Cory exits into the house. Rose sees Troy and Bono coming down the alley.

Troy. . . . what they say down there?

TROY. Ain't said nothing. I give them fifty dollars and they let him go. I'll talk to you about it. Where's Cory?

ROSE. He's in there helping me clean out these cupboards.

TROY. Tell him to get his butt out here.

Troy and Bono go over to the pile of wood. Bono picks up the saw and begins sawing.

TROY (*to Bono*). All they want is the money. That makes six or seven times I done went down there and got him. See me coming they stick out their hands.

BONO. Yeah. I know what you mean. That's all they care about . . . that money. They don't care about what's right. (*Pause.*) Nigger, why you got to go and get some hard wood? You ain't doing nothing but building a little old fence. Get you some soft pine wood. That's all you need.

TROY. I know what I'm doing. This is outside wood. You put pine wood inside the house. Pine wood is inside wood. This here is outside wood. Now you tell me where the fence is gonna be?

BONO. You don't need this wood. You can put it up with pine wood and it'll stand as long as you gonna be here looking at it.

TROY. How you know how long I'm gonna be here, nigger? Hell, I might just live forever. Live longer than old man Horsely.

BONO. That's what Magee used to say.

TROY. Magee's damn fool. Now you tell me who you ever heard of gonna pull their own teeth with a pair of rusty pliers.

BONO. The old folks . . . my granddaddy used to pull his teeth with pliers. They ain't had no dentists for the colored folks back then.

TROY. Get clean pliers! You understand? Clean pliers! Sterilize them! Besides we ain't living back then. All Magee had to do was walk over to Doc Goldblum's.

BONO. I see where you and that Tallahassee gal . . . that Alberta . . . I see where you all done got tight.

TROY. What you mean "got tight"?

BONO. I see where you be laughing and joking with her all the time.

TROY. I laughs and jokes with all of them, Bono. You know me.

BONO. That ain't the kind of laughing and joking I'm talking about.

Cory enters from the house.

CORY. How you doing. Mr. Bono?

TROY. Cory? Get that saw from Bono and cut some wood. He talking about the wood's too hard to cut. Stand back there, Jim, and let that young boy show you how it's done.

BONO. He's sure welcome to it.

Cory takes the saw and begins to cut the wood.

Whew-e-e! Look at that. Big old strong boy. Look like Joe Louis. Hell, must be getting old the way I'm watching that boy whip through that wood.

CORY. I don't see why Mama want a fence around the yard noways.

TROY. Damn if I know either. What the hell she keeping out with it? She ain't got nothing nobody want.

BONO. Some people build fences to keep people out . . . and other people build fences to keep people in. Rose wants to hold on to you all. She loves you.

TROY. Hell, nigger, I don't need nobody to tell me my wife loves me. Cory . . . go on in the house and see if you can find that other saw.

CORY. Where's it at?

TROY. I said find it! Look for it till you find it!

Cory exits into the house.

What's that supposed to mean? Wanna keep us in?

BONO. Troy . . . I done known you seem like damn near my whole life. You and Rose both. I done know both of you all for a long time. I remember when you met Rose. When you was hitting them baseball out the park. A lot of them old gals was after you then. You had the pick of the litter. When you picked Rose, I was happy for you. That was the first time I knew you had any sense. I said . . . My man Troy knows what he's doing . . . I'm gonna follow this nigger . . . he might take me somewhere. I been following you too. I done learned a whole heap of things about life watching you. I done learned how to tell where the shit lies. How to tell it from the alfalfa. You done learned me a lot of things. You showed me how to not make the same mistakes . . . to take life as it comes along and keep putting one foot in front of the other. (*Pause.*) Rose a good woman, Troy.

TROY. Hell, nigger, I know she a good woman. I been married to her for eighteen years. What you got on your mind, Bono?

BONO. I just say she a good woman. Just like I say anything. I ain't got to have nothing on my mind.

TROY. You just gonna say she a good woman and leave it hanging out there like that? Why you telling me she a good woman?

BONO. She loves you, Troy. Rose loves you.

TROY. You saying I don't measure up. That's what you trying to say. I don't measure up cause I'm seeing this other gal. I know what you trying to say.

BONO. I know what Rose means to you, Troy. I'm just trying to say I don't want to see you mess up.

TROY. Yeah, I appreciate that, Bono. If you was messing around on Lucille I'd be telling you the same thing.

BONO. Well, that's all I got to say. I just say that because I love you both.

TROY. Hell, you know me . . . I wasn't out there looking for nothing. You can't find a better woman than Rose. I know that. But seems like this woman just stuck onto me where I can't shake her loose. I done wrestled with it, tried to throw her off me . . . but she just stuck on tighter. Now she's stuck on for good.

BONO. You's in control . . . that's what you tell me all the time. You responsible for what you do.

TROY. I ain't ducking the responsibility of it. As long as it sets right in my heart . . . then I'm okay. Cause that's all I listen to. It'll tell me right from wrong every time. And I ain't talking about doing Rose no bad turn. I love Rose. She done carried me a long ways and I love and respect her for that.

BONO. I know you do. That's why I don't want to see you hurt her. But what you gonna do when she find out? What you got then? If you try and juggle both of them . . . sooner or later you gonna drop one of them. That's common sense.

TROY. Yeah, I hear what you saying, Bono. I been trying to figure a way to work it out.

BONO. Work it out right, Troy. I don't want to be getting all up between you and Rose's business . . . but work it so it come out right.

TROY. Ah hell, I get all up between you and Lucille's business. When you gonna get that woman that refrigerator she been wanting? Don't tell me you ain't got no money now. I know who your banker is. Mellon don't need that money bad as Lucille want that refrigerator. I'll tell you that.

BONO. Tell you what I'll do . . . when you finish building this fence for Rose . . . I'll buy Lucille that refrigerator.

TROY. You done stuck your foot in your mouth now!

Troy grabs up a board and begins to saw. Bono starts to walk out the yard.

Hey, nigger . . . where you going?

BONO. I'm going home. I know you don't expect me to help you now. I'm protecting my money. I wanna see you put that fence up by yourself. That's what I want to see. You'll be here another six months without me.

TROY. Nigger, you ain't right.

BONO. When it comes to my money . . . I'm right as fireworks on the Fourth of July.

TROY. All right, we gonna see now. You better get out your bankbook.

Bono exits, and Troy continues to work. Rose enters from the house.

ROSE. What they say down there? What's happening with Gabe?

TROY. I went down there and got him out. Cost me fifty dollars. Say he was disturbing the peace. Judge set up a hearing for him in three weeks. Say to show cause why he shouldn't be recommitted.

ROSE. What was he doing that cause them to arrest him?

TROY. Some kids was teasing him and he run them off home. Say he was howling and carrying on. Some folks seen him and called the police. That's all it was.

ROSE. Well, what's you say? What'd you tell the judge?

TROY. Told him I'd look after him. It didn't make no sense to recommit the man. He stuck out his big greasy palm and told me to give him fifty dollars and take him on home.

ROSE. Where's he at now? Where'd he go off to?

TROY. He's gone about his business. He don't need nobody to hold his hand.

ROSE. Well, I don't know. Seem like that would be the best place for him if they did put him into the hospital. I know what you're gonna say. But that's what I think would be best.

TROY. The man done had his life ruined fighting for what? And they wanna take and lock him up. Let him be free. He don't bother nobody.

ROSE. Well, everybody got their own way of looking at it I guess. Come on and get your lunch. I got a bowl of lima beans and some cornbread in the oven. Come and get something to eat. Ain't no sense you fretting over Gabe.

Rose turns to go into the house.

TROY. Rose . . . got something to tell you.

ROSE. Well, come on . . . wait till I get this food on the table.

TROY. Rose!

She stops and turns around.

I don't know how to say this. (*Pause.*) I can't explain it none. It just sort of grows on you till it gets out of hand. It starts out like a little bush . . . and the next thing you know it's a whole forest.

ROSE. Troy . . . what is you talking about?

TROY. I'm talking, woman, let me talk. I'm trying to find a way to tell you . . . I'm gonna be a daddy. I'm gonna be somebody's daddy.

ROSE. Troy . . . you're not telling me this? You're gonna be . . . what?

TROY. Rose . . . now . . . see . . .

ROSE. You telling me you gonna be somebody's daddy? You telling your *wife* this?

Gabriel enters from the street. He carries a rose in his hand.

GABRIEL. Hey, Troy! Hey, Rose!

ROSE. I have to wait eighteen years to hear something like this.

GABRIEL. Hey, Rose . . . I got a flower for you. (*He hands it to her.*) That's a rose. Same rose like you is.

ROSE. Thanks, Gabe.

GABRIEL. Troy, you ain't mad at me is you? Them bad mens come and put me away. You ain't mad at me is you?

TROY. Naw, Gabe, I ain't mad at you.

ROSE. Eighteen years and you wanna come with this.

GABRIEL (*takes a quarter out of his pocket*). See what I got? Got a brand new quarter.

TROY. Rose . . . it's just . . .

ROSE. Ain't nothing you can say, Troy. Ain't no way of explaining that.

GABRIEL. Fellow that give me this quarter had a whole mess of them. I'm gonna keep this quarter till it stop shining.

ROSE. Gabe, go on in the house there. I got some watermelon in the Frigidaire. Go on and get you a piece.

GABRIEL. Say, Rose . . . you know I was chasing hellhounds and them bad mens come and get me and take me away. Troy helped me. He come down there and told them they better let me go before he beat them up. Yeah, he did!

ROSE. You go on and get you a piece of watermelon, Gabe. Them bad mens is gone now.

GABRIEL. Okay, Rose . . . gonna get me some watermelon. The kind with the stripes on it.

Gabriel exits into the house.

ROSE. Why, Troy? Why? After all these years to come dragging this in to me now. It don't make no sense at your age. I could have expected this ten or fifteen years ago, but not now.

TROY. Age ain't got nothing to do with it, Rose.

ROSE. I done tried to be everything a wife should be. Everything a wife could be. Been married eighteen years and I got to live to see the day you tell me you been seeing another woman and done fathered a child by her. And you know I ain't never wanted no half nothing in my family. My whole family is half. Everybody got different fathers and mothers . . . my two sisters and my brother. Can't hardly tell who's who. Can't never sit down and talk about Papa and Mama. It's your papa and your mama and my papa and my mama . . .

TROY. Rose . . . stop it now.

ROSE. I ain't never wanted that for none of my children. And now you wanna drag your behind in here and tell me something like this.

TROY. You ought to know. It's time for you to know.

ROSE. Well, I don't want to know, goddamn it!

TROY. I can't just make it go away. It's done now. I can't wish the circumstance of the thing away.

ROSE. And you don't want to either. Maybe you want to wish me and my boy away. Maybe that's what you want? Well, you can't wish us away. I've got eighteen years of my life invested in you. You ought to have stayed upstairs in my bed where you belong.

TROY. Rose . . . now listen to me . . . we can get a handle on this thing. We can talk this out . . . come to an understanding.

ROSE. All of a sudden it's "we." Where was "we" at when you was down there rolling around with some godforsaken woman? "We" should have come to an understanding before you started making a damn fool of yourself. You're a day late and a dollar short when it comes to an understanding with me.

TROY. It's just . . . She gives me a different idea . . . a different understanding about myself. I can step out of this house and get away from the pressures and problems . . . be a different man. I ain't got to wonder how I'm gonna pay the bills or get the roof fixed. I can just be a part of myself that I ain't never been.

ROSE. What I want to know . . . is do you plan to continue seeing her. That's all you can say to me.

TROY. I can sit up in her house and laugh. Do you understand what I'm saying. I can laugh out loud . . . and it feels good. It reaches all the way down to the bottom of my shoes. (*Pause.*) Rose, I can't give that up.

ROSE. Maybe you ought to go on and stay down there with her . . . if she's a better woman than me.

TROY. It ain't about nobody being a better woman or nothing. Rose, you ain't the blame. A man couldn't ask for no woman to be a better wife than you've been. I'm responsible for it. I done locked myself into a pattern trying to take care of you all that I forgot about myself.

ROSE. What the hell was I there for? That was my job, not somebody else's.

TROY. Rose, I done tried all my life to live decent . . . to live a clean . . . hard . . . useful life. I tried to be a good husband to you. In every way I knew how. Maybe I come into the world backwards, I don't know. But . . . you born with two strikes on you before you come to the plate. You got to guard it closely . . . always looking for the curve ball on the inside corner. You can't afford to let none get past you. You can't afford a call strike. If you going down . . . you going down swinging. Everything lined up against you. What you gonna do. I fooled them, Rose. I bunted. When I found you and Cory and a halfway decent job . . . I was safe. Couldn't nothing touch me. I wasn't gonna strike out no more. I wasn't going back to the penitentiary. I wasn't gonna lay in the streets with a bottle of wine. I was safe. I had me a family. A job. I wasn't gonna get that last strike. I was on first looking for one of them boys to knock me in. To get me home.

ROSE. You should have stayed in my bed, Troy.

TROY. Then when I saw that gal . . . she firmed up my backbone. And I got to thinking that if I tried . . . I just might be able to steal second. Do you understand after eighteen years I wanted to steal second.

ROSE. You should have held me tight. You should have grabbed me and held on.

TROY. I stood on first base for eighteen years and I thought . . . well, goddamn it . . . go on for it!

ROSE. We're not talking about baseball! We're talking about you going off to lay in bed with another woman . . . and then bring it home to me. That's what we're talking about. We ain't talking about no baseball.

TROY. Rose, you're not listening to me. I'm trying the best I can to explain it to you. It's not easy for me to admit that I been standing in the same place for eighteen years.

ROSE. I been standing with you! I been right here with you, Troy. I got a life too. I gave eighteen years of my life to stand in the same spot with you. Don't you think I ever wanted other things? Don't you think I had dreams and hopes? What about my life? What about me. Don't you think it ever crossed my mind to want to know other men? That I wanted to lay up somewhere and forget about my responsibilities? That I wanted someone to make me laugh so I could feel good? You not the only one who's got wants and needs. But I held on to you, Troy. I took all my feelings, my wants and needs, my dreams . . . and I buried them inside you. I planted a seed and watched and prayed over it. I planted myself inside you and waited to bloom. And it didn't take me no eighteen years to find out the soil was hard and rocky and it wasn't never gonna bloom.

But I held on to you, Troy. I held you tighter. You was my husband. I owed you everything I had. Every part of me I could find to give you. And upstairs in that room . . . with the darkness falling in on me . . . I gave everything I had to try and erase the doubt that you wasn't the finest man in the world. And wherever you was going . . . I wanted to be there with you. Cause you was my husband. Cause that's the only way I was gonna survive as your wife. You always talking about what you give . . . and what you don't have to give. But you take too. You take . . . and don't even know nobody's giving!

Rose turns to exit into the house; Troy grabs her arm.

TROY. You say I take and don't give!

ROSE. Troy! You're hurting me!

TROY. You say I take and don't give!

ROSE. Troy . . . you're hurting my arm! Let go!

TROY. I done give you everything I got. Don't you tell that lie on me.

ROSE. Troy!

TROY. Don't you tell that lie on me!

Cory enters from the house.

CORY. Mama!

ROSE. Troy. You're hurting me.

TROY. Don't you tell me about no taking and giving.

Cory comes up behind Troy and grabs him. Troy, surprised, is thrown off balance just as Cory throws a glancing blow that catches him on the chest and knocks him down. Troy is stunned, as is Cory.

ROSE. Troy. Troy. No!

Troy gets to his feet and starts at Cory.

Troy . . . no. Please! Troy!

Rose pulls on Troy to hold him back. Troy stops himself.

TROY (*to Cory*). All right. That's strike two. You stay away from around me, boy. Don't you strike out. You living with a full count. Don't you strike out.

Troy exits out the yard as the lights go down.

SCENE 2

It is six months later, early afternoon. Troy enters from the house and starts to exit the yard. Rose enters from the house.

ROSE. Troy, I want to talk to you.

TROY. All of a sudden, after all this time, you want to talk to me, huh? You ain't wanted to talk to me for months. You ain't wanted to talk to me last night. You ain't wanted no part of me then. What you wanna talk to me about now?

ROSE. Tomorrow's Friday.

TROY. I know what day tomorrow is. You think I don't know tomorrow's Friday? My whole life I ain't done nothing but look to see Friday coming and you got to tell me it's Friday.

ROSE. I want to know if you're coming home.

TROY. I always come home, Rose. You know that. There ain't never been a night I ain't come home.

ROSE. That ain't what I mean . . . and you know it. I want to know if you're coming straight home after work.

TROY. I figure I'd cash my check . . . hang out at Taylors' with the boys . . . maybe play a game of checkers . . .

ROSE. Troy, I can't live like this. I won't live like this. You livin' on borrowed time with me. It's been going on six months now you ain't been coming home.

TROY. I be here every night. Every night of the year. That's 365 days.

ROSE. I want you to come home tomorrow after work.

TROY. Rose . . . I don't mess up my pay. You know that now. I take my pay and I give it to you. I don't have no money but what you give me back. I just want to have a little time to myself . . . a little time to enjoy life.

ROSE. What about me? When's my time to enjoy life?

TROY. I don't know what to tell you, Rose. I'm doing the best I can.

ROSE. You ain't been home from work but time enough to change your clothes and run out . . . and you wanna call that the best you can do?

TROY. I'm going over to the hospital to see Alberta. She went into the hospital this afternoon. Look like she might have the baby early. I won't be gone long.

ROSE. Well, you ought to know. They went over to Miss Pearl's and got Gabe today. She said you told them to go ahead and lock him up.

TROY. I ain't said no such thing. Whoever told you that is telling a lie. Pearl ain't doing nothing but telling a big fat lie.

ROSE. She ain't had to tell me. I read it on the papers.

TROY. I ain't told them nothing of the kind.

ROSE. I saw it right there on the papers.

TROY. What it say, huh?

ROSE. It said you told them to take him.

TROY. Then they screwed that up, just the way they screw up everything. I ain't worried about what they got on the paper.

ROSE. Say the government send part of his check to the hospital and the other part to you.

TROY. I ain't got nothing to do with that if that's the way it works. I ain't made up the rules about how it work.

ROSE. You did Gabe just like you did Cory. You wouldn't sign the paper for Cory . . . but you signed for Gabe. You signed that paper.

The telephone is heard ringing inside the house.

TROY. I told you I ain't signed nothing, woman! The only thing I signed was the release form. Hell, I can't read, I don't know what they had on that paper! I ain't signed nothing about sending Gabe away.

ROSE. I said send him to the hospital . . . you said let him be free . . . now you done went down there and signed him to the hospital for half his money. You went back on yourself, Troy. You gonna have to answer for that.

TROY. See now . . . you been over there talking to Miss Pearl. She done got mad cause she ain't getting Gabe's rent money. That's all it is. She's liable to say anything.

ROSE. Troy, I seen where you signed the paper.

TROY. You ain't seen nothing I signed. What she doing got papers on my brother anyway? Miss Pearl telling a big fat lie. And I'm gonna tell her about it too! You ain't seen nothing I signed. Say . . . you ain't seen nothing I signed.

Rose exits into the house to answer the telephone. Presently she returns.

ROSE. Troy . . . that was the hospital. Alberta had the baby.

TROY. What she have? What is it?

ROSE. It's a girl.

TROY. I better get on down to the hospital to see her.

ROSE. Troy . . .

TROY. Rose . . . I got to go see her now. That's only right . . . what's the matter . . . the baby's all right, ain't it?

ROSE. Alberta died having the baby.

TROY. Died . . . you say she's dead? Alberta's dead?

ROSE. They said they done all they could. They couldn't do nothing for her.

TROY. The baby? How's the baby?

ROSE. They say it's healthy. I wonder who's gonna bury her.

TROY. She had family, Rose. She wasn't living in the world by herself.

ROSE. I know she wasn't living in the world by herself.

TROY. Next thing you gonna want to know if she had any insurance.

ROSE. Troy, you ain't got to talk like that.

TROY. That's the first thing that jumped out your mouth. "Who's gonna bury her?" Like I'm fixing to take on that task for myself.

ROSE. I am your wife. Don't push me away.

TROY. I ain't pushing nobody away. Just give me some space. That's all. Just give me some room to breathe.

Rose exits into the house. Troy walks about the yard.

TROY (*with a quiet rage that threatens to consume him*). All right . . . Mr. Death. See now . . . I'm gonna tell you what I'm gonna do. I'm gonna take and build me a fence around this yard. See? I'm gonna build me a fence around what belongs to me. And then I want you to stay on the other side. See? You stay over there until you're ready for me. Then you come on. Bring your army. Bring your sickle. Bring your wrestling clothes. I ain't gonna fall down on my vigilance this time. You ain't gonna sneak up on me no more. When you ready for me . . . when the top of your list say Troy Maxson . . . that's when you come around here. You come up and knock on the front door. Ain't nobody else got nothing to do with this. This is between you and me. Man to man. You stay on the other side of that fence until you ready for me. Then you come up and knock on the front door. Anytime you want. I'll be ready for you.

The lights go down to black.

SCENE 3

The lights come up on the porch. It is late evening three days later. Rose sits listening to the ball game waiting for Troy. The final out of the game is made and Rose switches off the radio. Troy enters the yard carrying an infant wrapped in blankets. He stands back from the house and calls.

Rose enters and stands on the porch. There is a long, awkward silence, the weight of which grows heavier with each passing second.

TROY. Rose . . . I'm standing here with my daughter in my arms. She ain't but a wee bittie little old thing. She don't know nothing about grownups' business. She innocent . . . and she ain't got no mama.

ROSE. What you telling me for, Troy?

She turns and exits into the house.

TROY. Well . . . I guess we'll just sit out here on the porch.

He sits down on the porch. There is an awkward indelicateness about the way he handles the baby. His largeness engulfs and seems to swallow it. He speaks loud enough for Rose to hear.

A man's got to do what's right for him. I ain't sorry for nothing I done. It felt right in my heart. (*To the baby.*) What you smiling at? Your daddy's a big man. Got these great big old hands. But sometimes he's scared. And right now your daddy's scared cause we sitting out here and ain't got no home. Oh, I been homeless before. I ain't had no little baby with me. But I been homeless. You just be out on the road by your lonesome and you see one of them trains coming and you just kinda go like this . . .

He sings as a lullaby.

Please, Mr. Engineer let a man ride the line
Please, Mr. Engineer let a man ride the line
I ain't got no ticket please let me ride the blinds.

Rose enters from the house. Troy, hearing her steps behind him, stands and faces her.

She's my daughter, Rose. My own flesh and blood. I can't deny her no more than I can deny them boys. (*Pause.*) You and them boys is my family. You and them and this child is all I got in the world. So I guess what I'm saying is . . . I'd appreciate it if you'd help me take care of her.

ROSE. Okay, Troy . . . you're right. I'll take care of your baby for you . . . cause . . . like you say . . . she's innocent . . . and you can't visit the sins of the father upon the child. A motherless child has got a hard time. (*She takes the baby from him.*) From right now . . . this child got a mother. But you a womanless man.

Rose turns and exits into the house with the baby. Lights go down to black.

SCENE 4

It is two months later. Lyons enters the street. He knocks on the door and calls.

LYONS. Hey, Rose! (*Pause.*) Rose!

ROSE (*from inside the house*). Stop that yelling. You gonna wake up Raynell. I just got her to sleep.

LYONS. I just stopped by to pay Papa this twenty dollars I owe him. Where's Papa at?

ROSE. He should be here in a minute. I'm getting ready to go down to the church. Sit down and wait on him.

LYONS. I got to go pick up Bonnie over her mother's house.

ROSE. Well, sit it down there on the table. He'll get it.

LYONS (*enters the house and sets the money on the table*). Tell Papa I said thanks. I'll see you again.

ROSE. All right, Lyons. We'll see you.

Lyons starts to exit as Cory enters.

CORY. Hey, Lyons.

LYONS. What's happening, Cory? Say man, I'm sorry I missed your graduation. You know I had a gig and couldn't get away. Otherwise, I would have been there, man. So what you doing?

CORY. I'm trying to find a job.

LYONS. Yeah I know how that go, man. It's rough out here. Jobs are scarce.

CORY. Yeah, I know.

LYONS. Look here, I got to run. Talk to Papa . . . he know some people. He'll be able to help get you a job. Talk to him . . . see what he say.

CORY. Yeah . . . all right, Lyons.

LYONS. You take care. I'll talk to you soon. We'll find some time to talk.

Lyons exits the yard. Cory wanders over to the tree, picks up the bat, and assumes a batting stance. He studies an imaginary pitcher and swings. Dissatisfied with the result, he tries again. Troy enters. They eye each other for a beat. Cory puts the bat down and exits the yard. Troy starts into the house as Rose exits with Raynell. She is carrying a cake.

TROY. I'm coming in and everybody's going out.

ROSE. I'm taking this cake down to the church for the bake sale. Lyons was by to see you. He stopped by to pay you your twenty dollars. It's laying in there on the table.

TROY (*going into his pocket*). Well . . . here go this money.

ROSE. Put it in there on the table, Troy. I'll get it.

TROY. What time you coming back?

ROSE. Ain't no use in you studying me. It don't matter what time I come back.

TROY. I just asked you a question, woman. What's the matter . . . can't I ask you a question?

ROSE. Troy, I don't want to go into it. Your dinner's in there on the stove. All you got to do is heat it up. And don't you be eating the rest of them cakes in there. I'm coming back for them. We having a bake sale at the church tomorrow.

Rose exits the yard. Troy sits down on the steps, takes a pint bottle from his pocket, opens it, and drinks. He begins to sing.

TROY.

Hear it ring! Hear it ring!
Had an old dog his name was Blue
You know Blue was mighty true
You know Blue as a good old dog

Blue trees a possum in a hollow log
You know from that he was a good old dog.

Bono enters the yard.

BONO. Hey, Troy.

TROY. Hey, what's happening, Bono?

BONO. I just thought I'd stop by to see you.

TROY. What you stop by and see me for? You ain't stopped by in a month of Sundays. Hell, I must owe you money or something.

BONO. Since you got your promotion I can't keep up with you. Used to see you every day. Now I don't even know what route you working.

TROY. They keep switching me around. Got me out in Greentree now . . . hauling white folks' garbage.

BONO. Greentree, huh? You lucky, at least you ain't got to be lifting them barrels. Damn if they ain't getting heavier. I'm gonna put in my two years and call it quits.

TROY. I'm thinking about retiring myself.

BONO. You got it easy. You can drive for another five years.

TROY. It ain't the same, Bono. It ain't like working the back of the truck. Ain't got nobody to talk to . . . feel like you working by yourself. Naw, I'm thinking about retiring. How's Lucille?

BONO. She all right. Her arthritis get to acting up on her sometime. Saw Rose on my way in. She going down to the church, huh?

TROY. Yeah, she took up going down there. All them preachers looking for somebody to fatten their pockets. (*Pause.*) Got some gin here.

BONO. Naw, thanks. I just stopped by to say hello.

TROY. Hell, nigger . . . you can take a drink. I ain't never known you to say no to a drink. You ain't got to work tomorrow.

BONO. I just stopped by. I'm fixing to go over to Skinner's. We got us a domino game going over his house every Friday.

TROY. Nigger, you can't play no dominoes. I used to whup you four games out of five.

BONO. Well, that learned me. I'm getting better.

TROY. Yeah? Well, that's all right.

BONO. Look here . . . I got to be getting on. Stop by sometime, huh?

TROY. Yeah, I'll do that, Bono. Lucille told Rose you bought her a new refrigerator.

BONO. Yeah, Rose told Lucille you had finally built your fence . . . so I figured we'd call it even.

TROY. I knew you would.

BONO. Yeah . . . okay. I'll be talking to you.

TROY. Yeah, take care, Bono. Good to see you. I'm gonna stop over.

BONO. Yeah. Okay, Troy.

Bono exits. Troy drinks from the bottle.

TROY.

> Old Blue died and I dig his grave
> Let him down with a golden chain
> Every night when I hear old Blue bark
> I know Blue treed a possum in Noah's Ark.
> Hear it ring! Hear it ring!

Cory enters the yard. They eye each other for a beat. Troy is sitting in the middle of the steps. Cory walks over.

CORY. I got to get by.

TROY. Say what? What's you say?

CORY. You in my way. I got to get by.

TROY. You got to get by where? This is my house. Bought and paid for. In full. Took me fifteen years. And if you wanna go in my house and I'm sitting on the steps . . . you say excuse me. Like your mama taught you.

CORY. Come on, Pop . . . I got to get by.

Cory starts to maneuver his way past Troy. Troy grabs his leg and shoves him back.

TROY. You just gonna walk over top of me?

CORY. I live here too!

TROY (*advancing toward him*). You just gonna walk over top of me in my own house?

CORY. I ain't scared of you.

TROY. I ain't asked if you was scared of me. I asked you if you was fixing to walk over top of me in my own house? That's the question. You ain't gonna say excuse me? You just gonna walk over top of me?

CORY. If you wanna put it like that.

TROY. How else am I gonna put it?

CORY. I was walking by you to go into the house cause you sitting on the steps drunk, singing to yourself. You can put it like that.

TROY. Without saying excuse me???

Cory doesn't respond.

I asked you a question. Without saying excuse me???

CORY. I ain't got to say excuse me to you. You don't count around here no more.

TROY. Oh, I see . . . I don't count around here no more. You ain't got to say excuse me to your daddy. All of a sudden you done got so grown that your daddy don't count around here no more . . . Around here in his own house and yard that he done paid for with the sweat of his brow. You done got so grown to where you gonna take over. You gonna take over my house. Is that right? You gonna wear my pants. You gonna go in there and stretch out on my bed. You ain't got to say excuse me cause I don't count around here no more. Is that right?

CORY. That's right. You always talking this dumb stuff. Now, why don't you just get out my way?

TROY. I guess you got someplace to sleep and something to put in your belly. You got that, huh? You got that? That's what you need. You got that, huh?

CORY. You don't know what I got. You ain't got to worry about what I got.

TROY. You right! You one hundred percent right! I done spent the last seventeen years worrying about what you got. Now it's your turn, see? I'll tell you what to do. You grown . . . we done established that. You a man. Now, let's see you act like one. Turn your behind around and walk out this yard. And when you get out there in the alley . . . you can forget about this house. See? Cause this is my house. You go on and be a man and get your own house. You can forget about this. Cause this is mine. You go on and get yours cause I'm through with doing for you.

CORY. You talking about what you did for me . . . what'd you ever give me?

TROY. Them feet and bones! That pumping heart, nigger! I give you more than anybody else is ever gonna give you.

CORY. You ain't never gave me nothing! You ain't never done nothing but hold me back. Afraid I was gonna be better than you. All you ever did was try and make me scared of you. I used to tremble every time you called my name. Every time I heard your footsteps in the house. Wondering all the time . . . what's Papa gonna say if I do this? . . . What's he gonna say if I do that? . . . What's Papa gonna say if I turn on the radio? And Mama, too . . . she tries . . . but she's scared of you.

TROY. You leave your mama out of this. She ain't got nothing to do with this.

CORY. I don't know how she stand you . . . after what you did to her.

TROY. I told you to leave your mama out of this!

He advances toward Cory.

CORY. What you gonna do . . . give me a whupping? You can't whup me no more. You're too old. You just an old man.

TROY (*shoves him on his shoulder*). Nigger! That's what you are. You just another nigger on the street to me!

CORY. You crazy! You know that?

TROY. Go on now! You got the devil in you. Get on away from me!

CORY. You just a crazy old man . . . talking about I got the devil in me.

TROY. Yeah, I'm crazy! If you don't get on the other side of that yard . . . I'm gonna show you how crazy I am! Go on . . . get the hell out of my yard.

CORY. It ain't your yard. You took Uncle Gabe's money he got from the army to buy this house and then you put him out.

TROY (*advances on Cory*). Get your black ass out of my yard!

Troy's advance backs Cory up against the tree. Cory grabs up the bat.

CORY. I ain't going nowhere! Come on . . . put me out! I ain't scared of you.

TROY. That's my bat!

CORY. Come on!

TROY. Put my bat down!

CORY. Come on, put me out.

Cory swings at Troy, who backs across the yard.

What's the matter? You so bad . . . put me out!

Troy advances toward Cory.

CORY (*backing up*). Come on! Come on!

TROY. You're gonna have to use it! You wanna draw that bat back on me . . . you're gonna have to use it.

CORY. Come on! . . . Come on!

Cory swings the bat at Troy a second time. He misses. Troy continues to advance toward him.

TROY. You're gonna have to kill me! You wanna draw that bat back on me. You're gonna have to kill me.

Cory, backed up against the tree, can go no farther. Troy taunts him. He sticks out his head and offers him a target.

Come on! Come on!

Cory is unable to swing the bat. Troy grabs it.

TROY. Then I'll show you.

Cory and Troy struggle over the bat. The struggle is fierce and fully engaged. Troy ultimately is the stronger and takes the bat from Cory and stands over him ready to swing. He stops himself.

Go on and get away from around my house.

Cory, stung by his defeat, picks himself up, walks slowly out of the yard and up the alley.

CORY. Tell Mama I'll be back for my things.

TROY. They'll be on the other side of that fence.

Cory exits.

TROY. I can't taste nothing. Helluljah! I can't taste nothing no more. (*Troy assumes a batting posture and begins to taunt Death, the fastball on the outside corner.*) Come on! It's between you and me now! Come on! Anytime you want! Come on! I be ready for you . . . but I ain't gonna be easy.

The lights go down on the scene.

SCENE 5

*The time is 1965. The lights come up in the yard. It is the morning of Troy's funeral. A funeral plaque with a light hangs beside the door. There is a small garden plot off to the side. There is noise and activity in the house as Rose, Lyons, and Bono have gathered. The door opens and Raynell, seven years old, enters dressed in a flannel night-*gown. *She crosses to the garden and pokes around with a stick. Rose calls from the house.*

ROSE. Raynell!

RAYNELL. Mam?

ROSE. What you doing out there?

RAYNELL. Nothing.

Rose comes to the door.

ROSE. Girl, get in here and get dressed. What you doing?

RAYNELL. Seeing if my garden growed.

ROSE. I told you it ain't gonna grow overnight. You got to wait.

RAYNELL. It don't look like it never gonna grow. Dag!

ROSE. I told you a watched pot never boils. Get in here and get dressed.

RAYNELL. This ain't even no pot, Mama.

ROSE. You just have to give it a chance. It'll grow. Now you come on and do what I told you. We got to be getting ready. This ain't no morning to be playing around. You hear me?

RAYNELL. Yes, mam.

Rose exits into the house. Raynell continues to poke at her garden with a stick. Cory enters. He is dressed in a Marine corporal's uniform, and carries a duffelbag. His posture is that of a military man, and his speech has a clipped sternness.

CORY (*to Raynell*). Hi. (*Pause.*) I bet your name is Raynell.

RAYNELL. Uh huh.

CORY. Is your mama home?

Raynell runs up on the porch and calls through the screen door.

RAYNELL. Mama . . . there's some man out here. Mama!

Rose comes to the door.

ROSE. Cory? Lord have mercy! Look here, you all!

Rose and Cory embrace in a tearful reunion as Bono and Lyons enter from the house dressed in funeral clothes.

BONO. Aw, looka here . . .

ROSE. Done got all grown up!

CORY. Don't cry, Mama. What you crying about?

ROSE. I'm just so glad you made it.

CORY. Hey Lyons. How you doing, Mr. Bono.

Lyons goes to embrace Cory.

LYONS. Look at you, man. Look at you. Don't he look good, Rose. Got them Corporal stripes.

ROSE. What took you so long?

CORY. You know how the Marines are, Mama. They got to get all their paperwork straight before they let you do anything.

ROSE. Well, I'm sure glad you made it. They let Lyons come.

Your Uncle Gabe's still in the hospital. They don't know if they gonna let him out or not. I just talked to them a little while ago.

LYONS. A Corporal in the United States Marines.

BONO. Your daddy knew you had it in you. He used to tell me all the time.

LYONS. Don't he look good, Mr. Bono?

BONO. Yeah, he remind me of Troy when I first met him. (*Pause.*) Say, Rose, Lucille's down at the church with the choir. I'm gonna go down and get the pallbearers lined up. I'll be back to get you all.

ROSE. Thanks, Jim.

CORY. See you, Mr. Bono.

LYONS (*with his arm around Raynell*). Cory . . . look at Raynell. Ain't she precious? She gonna break a whole lot of hearts.

ROSE. Raynell, come and say hello to your brother. This is your brother, Cory. You remember Cory.

RAYNELL. No, Mam.

CORY. She don't remember me, Mama.

ROSE. Well, we talk about you. She heard us talk about you. (*To Raynell.*) This is your brother, Cory. Come on and say hello.

RAYNELL. Hi.

CORY. Hi. So you're Raynell. Mama told me a lot about you.

ROSE. You all come on into the house and let me fix you some breakfast. Keep up your strength.

CORY. I ain't hungry, Mama.

LYONS. You can fix me something, Rose. I'll be in there in a minute.

ROSE. Cory, you sure you don't want nothing? I know they ain't feeding you right.

CORY. No, Mama . . . thanks. I don't feel like eating. I'll get something later.

ROSE. Raynell . . . get on upstairs and get that dress on like I told you.

Rose and Raynell exit into the house.

LYONS. So . . . I hear you thinking about getting married.

CORY. Yeah, I done found the right one, Lyons. It's about time.

LYONS. Me and Bonnie been split up about four years now. About the time Papa retired. I guess she just got tired of all them changes I was putting her through. (*Pause.*) I always knew you was gonna make something out yourself. Your head was always in the right direction. So . . . you gonna stay in . . . make it a career . . . put in your twenty years?

CORY. I don't know. I got six already, I think that's enough.

LYONS. Stick with Uncle Sam and retire early. Ain't nothing out here. I guess Rose told you what happened with me. They got me down the workhouse. I thought I was being slick cashing other people's checks.

CORY. How much time you doing?

LYONS. They give me three years. I got that beat now. I ain't got but nine more months. It ain't so bad. You learn to

deal with it like anything else. You got to take the crookeds with the straights. That's what Papa used to say. He used to say that when he struck out. I seen him strike out three times in a row . . . and the next time up he hit the ball over the grandstand. Right out there in Homestead Field. He wasn't satisfied hitting in the seats . . . he want to hit it over everything! After the game he had two hundred people standing around waiting to shake his hand. You got to take the crookeds with the straights. Yeah, Papa was something else.

CORY. You still playing?

LYONS. Cory . . . you know I'm gonna do that. There's some fellows down there we got us a band . . . we gonna try and stay together when we get out . . . but yeah, I'm still playing. It still helps me to get out of bed in the morning. As long as it do that I'm gonna be right there playing and trying to make some sense out of it.

ROSE (*calling*). Lyons, I got these eggs in the pan.

LYONS. Let me go on and get these eggs, man. Get ready to go bury Papa. (*Pause.*) How you doing? You doing all right?

Cory nods. Lyons touches him on the shoulder and they share a moment of silent grief. Lyons exits into the house. Cory wanders about the yard. Raynell enters.

RAYNELL. Hi.

CORY. Hi.

RAYNELL. Did you used to sleep in my room?

CORY. Yeah . . . that used to be my room.

RAYNELL. That's what Papa call it. "Cory's room." It got your football in the closet.

Rose comes to the door.

ROSE. Raynell, get in there and get them good shoes on.

RAYNELL. Mama, can't I wear these? Them other one hurt my feet.

ROSE. Well, they just gonna have to hurt your feet for a while. You ain't said they hurt your feet when you went down to the store and got them.

RAYNELL. They didn't hurt then. My feet done got bigger.

ROSE. Don't you give me no backtalk now. You get in there and get them shoes on.

Raynell exits into the house.

Ain't too much changed. He still got that piece of rag tied to that tree. He was out here swinging that bat. I was just ready to go back in the house. He swung that bat and then he just fell over. Seem like he swung it and stood there with this grin on his face . . . and then he just fell over. They carried him on down to the hospital, but I knew there wasn't no need . . . why don't you come on in the house?

CORY. Mama . . . I got something to tell you. I don't know how to tell you this . . . but I've got to tell you . . . I'm not going to Papa's funeral.

ROSE. Boy, hush your mouth. That's your daddy you talking

about. I don't want hear that kind of talk this morning. I done raised you to come to this? You standing there all healthy and grown talking about you ain't going to your daddy's funeral?

CORY. Mama . . . listen . . .

ROSE. I don't want to hear it, Cory. You just get that thought out of your head.

CORY. I can't drag Papa with me everywhere I go. I've got to say no to him. One time in my life I've got to say no.

ROSE. Don't nobody have to listen to nothing like that. I know you and your daddy ain't seen eye to eye, but I ain't got to listen to that kind of talk this morning. Whatever was between you and your daddy . . . the time has come to put it aside. Just take it and set it over there on the shelf and forget about it. Disrespecting your daddy ain't gonna make you a man, Cory. You got to find a way to come to that on your own. Not going to your daddy's funeral ain't gonna make you a man.

CORY. The whole time I was growing up . . . living in his house . . . Papa was like a shadow that followed you everywhere. It weighed on you and sunk into your flesh. It would wrap around you and lay there until you couldn't tell which one was you anymore. That shadow digging in your flesh. Trying to crawl in. Trying to live through you. Everywhere I looked, Troy Maxson was staring back at me . . . hiding under the bed . . . in the closet. I'm just saying I've got to find a way to get rid of that shadow, Mama.

ROSE. You just like him. You got him in you good.

CORY. Don't tell me that, Mama.

ROSE. You Troy Maxson all over again.

CORY. I don't want to be Troy Maxson. I want to be me.

ROSE. You can't be nobody but who you are, Cory. That shadow wasn't nothing but you growing into yourself. You either got to grow into it or cut it down to fit you. But that's all you got to make life with. That's all you got to measure yourself against that world out there. Your daddy wanted you to be everything he wasn't . . . and at the same time he tried to make you into everything he was. I don't know if he was right or wrong . . . but I do know he meant to do more good than he meant to do harm. He wasn't always right. Sometimes when he touched he bruised. And sometimes when he took me in his arms he cut.

When I first met your daddy I thought . . . Here is a man I can lay down with and make a baby. That's the first thing I thought when I seen him. I was thirty years old and had done seen my share of men. But when he walked up to me and said, "I can dance a waltz that'll make you dizzy," I thought, Rose Lee, here is a man that you can open yourself up to and be filled to bursting. Here is a man that can fill all them empty spaces you been tipping around the edges of. One of them empty spaces was being somebody's mother.

I married your daddy and settled down to cooking his supper and keeping clean sheets on the bed. When your daddy walked through the house he was so big he filled it up. That was my first mistake. Not to make him leave some room for me. For my part in the matter. But at that time I wanted that. I wanted a house that I could sing in. And that's what your daddy gave me. I didn't know to keep up his strength I had to give up little pieces of mine. I did that. I took on his life as mine and mixed up the pieces so that you couldn't hardly tell which was which anymore. It was my choice. It was my life and I didn't have to live it like that. But that's what life offered me in the way of being a woman and I took it. I grabbed hold of it with both hands.

By the time Raynell came into the house, me and your daddy had done lost touch with one another. I didn't want to make my blessing off of nobody's misfortune . . . but I took on to Raynell like she was all them babies I had wanted and never had.

The phone rings.

Like I'd been blessed to relive a part of my life. And if the Lord see fit to keep up my strength . . . I'm gonna do her just like your daddy did you . . . I'm gonna give her the best of what's in me.

RAYNELL (*entering, still with her old shoes*). Mama . . . Reverend Tollivier on the phone.

Rose exits into the house.

RAYNELL. Hi.

CORY. Hi.

RAYNELL. You in the Army or the Marines?

CORY. Marines.

RAYNELL. Papa said it was the Army. Did you know Blue?

CORY. Blue? Who's Blue?

RAYNELL. Papa's dog what he sing about all the time.

CORY (*singing*).

Hear it ring! Hear it ring!
I had a dog his name was Blue
You know Blue was mighty true
You know Blue was a good old dog
Blue treed a possum in a hollow log
You know from that he was a good old dog.
Hear it ring! Hear it ring!

Raynell joins in singing.

CORY and RAYNELL.

Blue treed a possum out on a limb
Blue looked at me and I looked at him
Grabbed that possum and put him in a sack
Blue stayed there till I came back
Old Blue's feets was big and round
Never allowed a possum to touch the ground.

Old Blue died and I dug his grave
I dug his grave with a silver spade
Let him down with a golden chain
And every night I call his name
Go on Blue, you good dog you

Go on Blue, you good dog you.

RAYNELL.

Blue laid down and died like a man
Blue laid down and died . . .

BOTH.

Blue laid down and died like a man
Now he's treeing possums in the Promised Land
I'm gonna tell you this to let you know
Blue's gone where the good dogs go
When I hear old Blue bark
When I hear old Blue bark
Blue treed a possum in Noah's Ark
Blue treed a possum in Noah's Ark.

Rose comes to the screen door.

ROSE. Cory, we gonna be ready to go in a minute.

CORY (*to Raynell*). You go on in the house and change them
shoes like Mama told you so we can go to Papa's funeral.

RAYNELL. Okay, I'll be back.

*Raynell exits into the house. Cory gets up and crosses over
to the tree. Rose stands in the screen door watching him.
Gabriel enters from the alley.*

GABRIEL (*calling*). Hey, Rose!

ROSE. Gabe?

GABRIEL. I'm here, Rose. Hey Rose, I'm here!

Rose enters from the house.

ROSE. Lord . . . Look here, Lyons!

LYONS. See, I told you, Rose . . . I told you they'd let him
come.

CORY. How you doing, Uncle Gabe?

LYONS. How you doing, Uncle Gabe?

GABRIEL. Hey, Rose. It's time. It's time to tell St. Peter to
open the gates. Troy, you ready? You ready, Troy. I'm
gonna tell St. Peter to open the gates. You get ready now.

*Gabriel, with great fanfare, braces himself to blow. The
trumpet is without a mouthpiece. He puts the end of it into
his mouth and blows with great force, like a man who has
been waiting some twenty-odd years for this single
moment. No sound comes out of the trumpet. He braces
himself and blows again with the same result. A third time
he blows. There is a weight of impossible description that
falls away and leaves him bare and exposed to a frightful
realization. It is a trauma that a sane and normal mind
would be unable to withstand. He begins to dance. A
slow, strange dance, eerie and life-giving. A dance of
atavistic signature and ritual. Lyons attempts to embrace
him. Gabriel pushes Lyons away. He begins to howl in
what is an attempt at song, or perhaps a song turning back
into itself in an attempt at speech. He finishes his dance
and the gates of heaven stand open as wide as God's closet.*

That's the way that go!

BLACKOUT

THE CARIBBEAN

Artistic and Cultural Events

c. 1570: Corpus Christi rites in Cuba

1826: Five professional theaters established in Trinidad

1941: Little Theater Movement, Jamaica

1955: Racially integrated plays in Trinidad

1968: Theatre Escambray, Cuba

1943–1945: Teatro Popular, Cuba

Areítos performed in Cuba and Puerto Rico

1590s: Spanish comedias performed in Cuba

1755: First Cuban play, *The Gardener Prince and Imagined Cloridano* (Santiago Pita y Borroto)

1866: First Grand Masquerade of Trinidad Carnival

1920: Paragon Players, Port-au-Prince Spain, Trinidad

1948: Little Carib Theater, Trinidad

1953: René Marqués's *The Ox Cart*, Puerto Rico

1959: Trinidad Theater Workshop

1500 C.E.	1600–1800 C.E.	1900 C.E.

Historical and Political Events

1834: Slaves emancipated in Trinidad

1898: Spanish-American War

1952: Puerto Rico becomes independent commonwealth

1959: Cuban Revolution

Spaniards in Hispaniola

African slaves brought to Caribbean by Europeans who govern islands

In his study of the history of the Caribbean, *The Repeating Island*, Antonio Benítez-Rojo articulates the present social, political, and economic realities of the region: "For it is certain that the Caribbean basin, although it includes the first American lands to be explored, conquered, and colonized by Europe, is still, especially in the discourse of the social sciences, one of the least known regions of the modern world." This archipelago, with its legacy of the diaspora, numerous languages, diverse histories of colonization, and cultural nuances is today one of the richest areas for the discovery and understanding of human creativity. Sadly and quite often, our impressions of the Caribbean are based on television commercials selling ocean cruises, people resting on a beach surrounded by exotic drinks, and the rhythmic movement of a "native" beckoning the viewer to travel to paradise. What these commercials do not reveal, however, is the Caribbean's relentless commitment to survive in the face of industrial global expansion, foreign intervention, unstable economies, and political turmoil. The Cuban writer Alejo Carpentier defines the problem: "Our cities, because they haven't yet entered our literature, are more difficult to handle than the jungles or the mountains."

Given its rich history of tradition, survival, and transition, the theatrical and dramatic productivity of the Caribbean is complex and diverse. As we have seen, theatrical expression often evolves from mimetic activity and the necessity for humans to express themselves through mime, dance, song, and the oral tradition. The first European-recorded signs of theatrical activity in the New World emanate from the late fifteenth century when Spanish colonizers witnessed performances of *areítos* in Cuba and Puerto Rico. These ritual-like activities, under the supervision of a choral leader, were performed by indigenous people to share their tribal history through music, dance, and the spoken word. Considered primitive and often blasphemous in the eyes of Catholic colonizers, these activities ceased by the sixteenth century. Similar activities took place in the Francophone islands of Haiti, Martinique, and French Guyana during the early seventeenth century when the African diaspora produced a multitude of slaves to serve the European plantations. These slaves, and their Creole descendants, devised ritualistic performances using music, dance, and storytelling that linked their new envi-

Contemporary issues are often presented with a playful theatricality in Caribbean theater. Here the Little Theater Movement and the National Pantomime Company of Jamaica lampoon the Y2K bug in a production of Bugsie the Millennium Bug *by Barbara Gloudon and Conliffe Wilmot-Simpson.*

ronment to their past heritage, religions, and cultural traditions, all of which were nearly destroyed by the slave trade.

Throughout the eighteenth and nineteenth centuries, many of the Caribbean islands witnessed theatrical fare imported from Europe, mostly from the Renaissance and Neoclassical perspective. In the nineteenth century, European Romantic drama and melodrama gave way to individual Caribbean dramatic voices that emphasized local social conditions, language, and ethnic heritage. Of particular importance in this artistic development are the islands of Cuba, Puerto Rico, Haiti, Jamaica, and Trinidad-Tobago, each of which paved the way for sophisticated twentieth-century theatrical endeavors and internationally respected playwrights, directors, and actors.

Cuba

Despite the current disenfranchisement caused by its socialist politics, the United States—imposed blockade, and Russia's inability to continue its economic assistance to the Castro regime, Cuba still maintains a strong commitment to theatrical exploration. Following Castro's revolution in 1959, Cuban theater saw the implementation of the National Council for Culture which augmented artistic activity throughout the island. Today, the well-established House of the Americas continues to produce Latin American theater festivals and frequently honors plays (e.g., Egon Wolff's *Paper Flowers*, Chapter 9) with its prestigious House of the Americas Prize.

Because of his international recognition, José Triana remains Cuba's most respected playwright, and his plays have been produced throughout the Americas and Europe; the most notable of these, *Night of the Assassins* (1965), is a violent, surrealistic work portraying three adolescents who kill their parents as a ritual exorcism. A protégé of Triana, Freddy Artiles also represents Cuba's most progressive and mature playwriting. The author of serious dramas and children's plays, Artiles is a product of Cuba's social revolution, whose best works examine Cuban social and political realities; for instance, *At the Station* (part of a 1977 trilogy, *At the End of Blood's Journey*) depicts two Cuban citizens attempting to depart their native land in 1959 because of repressive political policies. Artiles continues his work as a playwright, professor of theater, and dramaturg, and his workshops and lectures have been presented throughout Europe, Canada, the United States, Mexico, and Latin America.

Under the direction of the well-known actor and director Sergio Corrieri, Theatre Escambray (1968) has altered the aesthetics of Cuban theater. Its innovative staging techniques include interviews with audience members who are asked to provide solutions to local problems; postperformance discussions between actors and audiences are important features of Escambray's work. Presently the Galiano 108 Theatre is a collective dedicated to a new performance style using Expressionistic techniques. *Saint Cecilia*, a recent one-woman tour de force, has won wide recognition for the Galiano Company.

The contemporary press, preoccupied by the long-standing conflict between opposite political ideologies, often portrays Cuba in negative terms. Nevertheless, Cuba remains at the forefront of theatrical and dramatic productivity in the Caribbean.

Puerto Rico

Although this island has been an independent commonwealth of the United States since 1952, the spirit of Puerto Rico is rooted in the indigenous culture of the Taíno. For centuries the people of this historic island have sought to settle its national sense of belonging, and thus Puerto Rico's political winds have undergone massive changes. With its roots in the diasporic tradition and the Spanish-American War, it has attempted to become an independent nation. In spite of its political and economic shifts, Puerto Rico's theatrical culture has influenced dramatic activity in the Caribbean, the United States, Latin America, and Europe; it has also exerted an influence on the Hollywood cinema.

Contemporary Puerto Rican drama has been influenced by the likes of the brilliant René Marqués, who in 1953 wrote perhaps his most important play, *The Ox Cart*, a stinging, naturalistic critique of Puerto Rican immigration to the United States. The play depicts its characters' feelings as they rediscover their Caribbean roots. Significantly, Puerto Rican theater has opened many a door to women, most notably Rosa Luisa Márquez, a professor of theater and drama at the University of Puerto Rico. A director, actor, and playwright, she founded the Anamu Theater Collective and received the Puerto Rican Drama Critics Circle Award. Márquez, who is committed to the alternative theater movement, is an active participant of the Bread and Puppet Theater of Peter Schumann, and she is also a board member of the International School of Theater of Latin America and the Caribbean.

Regardless of its political future in the twenty-first century, it is clear that Puerto Rico will continue to be a dominant voice in Caribbean theater. Puerto Rico's centuries of creativity attest to the human will to survive in spite of social and political dichotomies.

Haiti and Jamaica

For two centuries, Haiti has also survived numerous social, economic, and political shifts. A product of French colonial occupation, invasion and occupation by the United States from 1915 to 1934, and the devastating consequences of the recent François Duvalier dictatorship, this Caribbean island has been fractured in its economic development. Although Haiti has been ignored by the world economy, it continues to exhibit a sound strength in her theatrical identity, which was originally based on religious voodoo ceremonies derived from African rituals in honor of their *orishas* (gods). These were later mixed with Catholic ceremonial traditions. Given its colonial nature, Haitian theater has always exhibited a mix of French popular offerings and the many Creole attempts to establish a national drama. Haiti's theatrical and dramatic maturity, however, occurred in the twentieth century, and it is best appreciated in the dramatic output of Mona Guérin, the author of numerous plays about the social conditions of her native land. The more contemporary plays of Frédéric Surpris, author of *Coup d'état*, speak of Haiti's immersion in poverty and the colonial mentality. Although Haiti appears politically stable despite its economic problems, its theater continues to explore the nation's vacillation between its Francophone past and its emerging Creole identity, both within the island and abroad. A massive Haitian migratory journey toward North America and Europe has carried Haitian drama beyond its Caribbean shores.

Caribbean theater boasts a unique form of expression found in the oral discourse of Jamaica. Such performances are usually acted out by a writer-actor who shares with the audience her/his perception of race, identity, and social status within the culture. Much like Homer's *Iliad*, these works link the entire island society to its national sense of belonging. Spoken in the Jamaican-Creole language, these oral performances help audiences realize that regional dialects are a valid—often superior—form of expression. Mixing poetry and the musical rhythms of reggae, well-known Jamaican performers (e.g., Michael Smith, Binta Breeze, and Oku Onuora) have brought a national consciousness to Jamaicans, as well as to people abroad. Like the rap music of the United States, these oral performances remind their audiences that the power of popular culture is not necessarily highbrow.

Trinidad-Tobago

Trinidad was seized from the indigenous Arawak Indians by Columbus in 1498, and for 300 years it remained a Spanish possession. The French and their African slaves arrived in 1783, and the British took control of the island in 1797 and retained it as a Crown colony until 1962. Nearby Tobago was first a Dutch colony, then French, and finally became a British colony in 1763. To replace African slaves who were freed in the 1830s, plantation owners imported Chinese, Muslim, Portuguese, and East Indians (who currently comprise about 40 percent of the islands' population). Given this diverse cultural mix, theater emanating from these sister islands is among the richest and most diverse in the Caribbean.

The most famous theatrical activity in Trinidad is the annual pre-Lenten Carnival, which is described in some detail in conjunction with *Ti-Jean and His Brothers* (see Center Stage box, The Trinidad Carnival, at the end of this chapter). There is also a major street festival (the *Hosay*) conducted by the islands' East Indian community to commemorate the Muslim battle of Karbala. Calypso plays, in which topical events are enacted in song and story to the rhythms of steel-drum bands, are especially popular among the locals, and lively calypso play competitions are held several times a year. In 1982 the Trinidad Tent Theater was founded to specialize in carnival theater with a political thrust; *King Jab Jab* was especially notable for its fierce political satire. Thus there is a rich and popular tradition of street theater in Trinidad-Tobago.

A thriving theater community produces some of the most compelling drama in the Caribbean. The roots of formal theater can be traced to 1826, when Port of Spain, the capital city, housed five professional theaters and three amateur companies. E. J. Joseph, a Scotsman, wrote some of the islands' first dramas (e.g., *Martial Law in Trinidad*, 1832), which are notable for their sympathetic and dignified portrayals of slaves and their dialects. After emancipation, there was a fallow period in Trinidad's theaters. In 1858, for example, there was only a single theater in the capital, and by 1866 no theaters existed. Though the Trinidad Drama Club revived theater in 1897, most work was imported and, of course, most of the plays performed were European and American.

In 1932 two schoolteachers, Arthur Roberts and De Wilton Rogers, began producing works on topical problems, such as race (*Blue Blood and Black*, 1936) and imperialism (*Silk Cotton Grove*, 1942). Such works showed the people of Trinidad-Tobago that the theater could be a weapon as the islands attempted to define themselves culturally and to become autonomous. In 1943 there was a concerted effort towards recognizing folk culture and island music when the respected musician Edric Connor delivered a powerful lecture on West Indian folk music and ethnography to the Music Association. This sparked a renewed interest in local heritage and customs that soon affected the theater. In 1948 Beryl McBurnie founded the Little Carib Theater in Port of Spain, primarily to promote dance, but it soon became the preeminent theater in Trinidad and sponsored an arts festival in which over 500 entries celebrated West Indian arts and entertainment. A number of Trinidad-Tobago's most prominent theater artists, including Errol Hill and Derek Walcott, tested their work at the Little Carib.

The University of the West Indies sponsored playwriting competitions in the 1950s that raised the quality of the region's drama. In 1955 John Ainsworth, an English actor, staged racially integrated plays, such as *Hamlet* and *Macbeth*, which further opened the possibilities for would-be artists in Trinidad-Tobago. And in 1959 Walcott—the first Caribbean literary artist to win a Nobel Prize—opened the Trinidad Theater Workshop, the most influential artistic enterprise on these islands.

In addition to Walcott, Trinidad-Tobago has produced a number of internationally respected dramatists (e.g., Lennox Brown, Mustapha Matura, and Pearl Springer), actors (Errol Jones and Jean Sue-Wing), and directors (Errol Sitahal and Ralph Maraj).

TI-JEAN AND HIS BROTHERS

DEREK WALCOTT

DEREK WALCOTT (1930–)

As a poet and a dramatist, Derek Walcott is among the most honored writers of the twentieth century. In 1992 he achieved the world's highest literary award, the Nobel Prize, and is thus one of the few dramatists to receive that honor (Soyinka is another).

Walcott and his twin brother and theater colleague, Roderick, were born on the Caribbean island of St. Lucia and reared by their mother after their father died. Because his mother was the headmistress of the local Methodist Infant School, Walcott received an excellent education and an uncommonly fine grounding in English, which was not available to other nonwhites on the island. His father had been a civil servant with a strong interest in the arts, particularly play reading and painting. The Walcott twins were encouraged to pursue these interests by their mother and family friends.

He studied at University College of the West Indies in Jamaica, where he continued the classical education begun in St. Lucia. The tension between his Euro-centered education and his desire to create a theater representative of his native West Indies has been a source of controversy for Walcott throughout his career. As a student Walcott distinguished himself as a poet, dramatist, and editor of a literary journal. He began writing plays in 1946, and his drama about Haiti's revolution, *Henri Christophe* (1949), earned him respect as a dramatist. In 1950 he cofounded the Arts Guild of St. Lucia as an outlet for native voices.

The Trinidad Theater Workshop, which evolved from his work with Little Carib Theater and the Basement Theater, was founded in the late 1950s and remains the legacy of Walcott's vision of a "little theater" devoted to the development of native Caribbean drama performed in a distinctive West Indian style. The TTW created works fusing native stories, music, and dance with such diverse non-Caribbean theater forms as Noh and Kabuki, classical European theater, American method acting, Brechtian epic theater, and Grotowski's poor theater. Walcott's best dramatic pieces were written for the TTW: *The Charlatan* (1962), *Dream on Monkey Mountain* (1968), *The Joker of Seville* (a work commissioned by the Royal Shakespeare Company in 1975), and *O! Babylon!* (1976). His works have been produced by Joseph Papp's New York Free Shakespeare Festival, the Mark Taper Forum in Los Angeles, and the Boston Playwright's Theater. In addition to his plays, Walcott has written volumes of poetry, including his lengthy autobiographical poem *Another Life*. He is among the most anthologized poets of the twentieth century.

TI-JEAN AND HIS BROTHERS (1958)

"Dancing with the devil" is a recurring image in our survey of global theatrical rituals and ceremonies. We see devils, actual and metaphorical, called the *Barong* in Bali, the *Chapayepkas* among the Yaqui Indians, *diablos* in Mexico and Latin America, and *diablesse* in Trinidad— where *Ti-Jean* is set. The need to exorcise the spirits of darkness so that life can proceed in harmony has been manifested in both ancient and advanced cultures, and it is not surprising that a significant body of the globe's dramatic literature portrays humans locked in combat with demons.

Derek Walcott's folk play *Ti-Jean and His Brothers* is simultaneously a contemporary work (1958) portraying modern political realities and a very ancient story, adapted from a St. Lucian legend, which uses archetypal characters engaged in battle with the devil himself. Its plotting and theatricality are primitive in the best sense because it is so fundamental. Yet there is sophistication in the way Walcott blends contemporary concerns with older traditions to create a new work that both entertains and instructs his West Indian audiences.

The play comprises three short scenes, which are preceded by a lengthy prologue. Actually, two prologues provide exposition. The first is purposely artificial and uses a chorus of forest creatures, the frog and his allies, to establish the story telling framework of the main plot. Furthermore, the prologue given by the creatures mythologizes Ti-Jean's exploits and raises him to hero status ("Ti-jean the hunter . . . he beat the devil"). This contrived prologue, very much in the storytelling tradition, allows the audience to accept more readily the play's extraordinary events.

The second prologue introduces us to the play's earthly characters, each an archetype found in folk plays. We meet the long-suffering mother, impoverished and anxious to feed and shelter her children. Through her, Walcott quickly enlists our sympathy. Mother has three sons, each an emblem of a particular human value. Gros ("Big") Jean, the oldest, relies solely on his physical powers, whereas the middle son, Mi(ddle)-Jean, is bookish and depends on his intelligence. The spirited rivalry between Gros Jean and Mi-Jean is more than a sibling rivalry: theirs is that ancient battle between brains and brawn. The little brother, Ti(ny)-Jean, has only a portion of his oldest brother's strength and his elder brother's wit; he possesses a greater strength, however, which enables him to triumph over the devil. Significantly, Ti-Jean aligns himself with the biblical David who slays Goliath, the quintessential archetype of the "little guy" who topples the giant-oppressor.

That Walcott resorts to a tripartite structure for his story is not surprising. The "rule of three" is a favorite tool of storytellers and playwrights everywhere (Shakespeare used it in *Hamlet,* in which three sons must avenge the deaths of three fathers). Think of how many fairy tales, folk stories, or jokes you know that begin with "there were three . . . ." There are several reasons for this universal plot structure. First, the two errant brothers become foils to Ti-Jean; that is, we judge his success against the failure of his brothers. The first prologue actually reveals the ending so that the audience may assess the choices each brother makes. Second, the tripartite structure builds suspense. The three-step build to a resolution has proven to be an ideal number for involving audiences, even when we know the eventual outcome as in *Ti-Jean.* A lesser number does not tease us quite enough, a larger one becomes cumbersome. Finally, the "rule of three" has a phenomenological significance. Something that happens once (Gros Jean is devoured by the devil) we think of as happenstance; if it happens twice (Mi-Jean's defeat) it is coincidence. A third occurrence, especially when resolved to our satisfaction, moves the problem into the realm of universal law.

Each of the three scenes has a well-defined point of attack: a brother encounters the devil. The rising action increases the tension as each brother "riles" at a different tempo. And finally, there is a well-marked climax to each sequence in which a brother is either devoured or triumphs. Playwriting does not get much clearer than this. Walcott's skill keeps us involved through the debate between each brother and the devil.

Thematically, the play works on two levels. First, it is a simple folktale, the roots of which can be found in many locales around the globe. We might refer to it as a "rite of passage play," in which three young men must go into the world to test themselves against the unknown. Gros Jean leaves his mother while singing

> *There's a time for every man*
> *To leave his mother and father*
> *To leave everybody he know*
> *And march to the grave me one!*

(The last line is a nice bit of poetry in which Walcott uses the West Indian dialect; it actually means "march to the grave on my own," but the playwright creates an ironic pun within the dialect.) Each brother ventures into the forest to use his particular strength to battle the devil. From the winner, we learn a lesson about the hierarchy of human virtues.

To this simple folk motif, however, Walcott adds contemporary political commentary. He aligns the devil with plantation owners, the old colonialists who used native and African labor for profit in Trinidad's troubled past. Carnival in Trinidad (see Center Stage box, The Trinidad Carnival, following the text of the play) traditionally begins with a *canboulay*, a mock military march that parodies the colonial guards who oversaw the slaves. *Canboulay* refers to "the burning of the cane," a nineteenth-century rebellion in which the slaves burned the sugar cane fields rather than submit to the horrible conditions to which they were subjected. In the final scene Walcott scripts a "cane burners chorus" that sings "Burn, burn, burn de cane!" The vestiges of this historical event, so central to the spirit of the people of the West Indies, is skillfully blended into the dramatic framework of the play and foreshadows Ti-Jean's triumph over his diabolical adversary. Some critics, by the way, have noted that *Ti-Jean* is a parable about the evolution of Africans in the Caribbean—that is, from exploited physical laborers (Gros Jean), to educated "Anglo-Africans" (Mi-Jean), to resourceful "natives" who remain true to their innate sense of self (Ti-Jean).

Whether we view it as a folktale or a political parable, *Ti-Jean and His Brothers* is superb theater by any criterion. It blends local dialects and speech rhythms to complement Walcott's own poetic talents. As is his custom, Walcott uses both Creole folk songs and Trinidad's popular calypso music to heighten the atmosphere and, on occasion, to make thematic points (e.g., the song of triumph that concludes the action). As you read the play, "hear" the infectious music that the people of the West Indies use to hearten themselves in the face of hardship.

You must also see this play in your mind's eye. At both the Little Carib Theater in Port of Spain and at Walcott's Trinidad Theater Workshop, where it was successfully revived as a "musical drama" in 1970, the play takes place on an open stage and uses little scenery. Colorfully dressed and masked actors (inspired by Walcott's contact with the Noh theater while in New York in the midfifties) created the environment through body language. Theatrically exciting scenes abound throughout the play: the invasion of the spirits midway through the prologue, the chorus of forest creatures, the literally explosive climax of each scene, the various transformations of the devil into old man and planter, and the final tableau in which the older brothers are seen passing through hell. Walcott uses little that has not been seen in theaters around the world; his ingenuity springs from the spirited manner in which he adapts older forms for his West Indian audiences, while addressing concerns that are universal.

Derek Walcott, dramatist and poet, is the first Nobel laureate from the Caribbean.

TI-JEAN AND HIS BROTHERS

DEREK WALCOTT

for Peter Walcott

CHARACTERS
CRICKET
FROG
FIREFLY
BIRD
GROS JEAN
MI-JEAN
TI-JEAN
MOTHER
BOLOM
{OLD MAN, OR PAPA BOIS
{PLANTER
{DEVIL

PROLOGUE

Evening. Rain. The heights of a forest. A Cricket, a Frog, a Firefly, a Bird. Left, a hut with bare table, an empty bowl, stools. The Mother waiting.

FROG.
    Greek-croak, Greek-croak.
CRICKET.
    Greek-croak, Greek-croak.
    [The others join.]
FROG.
    [Sneezing]

Aeschylus me!
All that rain and no moon tonight.

CRICKET.
The moon always there even fighting the rain
Creek-crak, it is cold, but the moon always there
And Ti-Jean in the moon just like the story.

[Bird passes.]

CRICKET.
Before you fly home, listen,
The cricket cracking a story
A story about the moon.

FROG.
If you look in the moon,
Though no moon is here tonight,
There is a man, no, a boy,
Bent by the weight of faggots
He carried on his shoulder,
A small dog trotting with him.
That is Ti-Jean the hunter,
He got the heap of sticks
From the old man of the forest
They calling Papa Bois,
Because he beat the devil,
God put him in that height
To be the sun's right hand
And light the evil dark,
But as the bird so ignorant
I will start the tale truly.

[Music]

Well, one time it had a mother,
That mother had three sons.
The first son was Gros Jean.
That son he was the biggest,
His arm was hard as iron,
But he was very stupid.

[Enter Gros Jean, a bundle of faggots in one hand, an axe
over his shoulder, moving in an exaggerated march to
music. The creatures laugh.]

FROG.
The name of the second son,
They was calling him Mi-Jean,
In size, the second biggest,
So only half as stupid; now,
He was a fisherman, but
Always studying book, and
What a fisherman; for
When he going and fish,
Always forgetting the bait,
So between de bait and debate . . .

CRICKET.
Mi boug qui tait cooyon!
(Look man who was a fool!)

[Roll of drums. Comic quatro, martial]

[Enter Mi-Jean from the opposite side, carrying a book in
one hand and a fishing net over his shoulder. Halfway
across the stage he flings the net casually, still reading]

BIRD.
How poor their mother was?

[Sad music on flute]

FROG.
Oh that was poverty, bird!
Old hands dried up like claws
Heaping old sticks on sticks,
Too weak to protect her nest.
Look, the four of that family

[Light shows the hut.]

Lived in a little house,
Made up of wood and thatch,
On the forehead of the mountain,
Where night and day was rain,
Mist, cloud white as cotton
Caught in the dripping branches;
Where sometimes it was so cold
The frog would stop its singing

[The Frog stops. Five beats. Resumes.]

The cricket would stop rattling
And the wandering firefly
That lights the tired woodsman
Home through the raining trees
Could not strike a damp light
To star the wanderer home!

[The music stops. The brothers Gros Jean and Mi-Jean
put their arms around each other, and to heavy drums
tramp home.]

CRICKET.
I damned sorry for that mother.
FROG.
Aie, cricket, you croak the truth!
The life of an old woman
With her husband cold in earth,
Where the bamboo leaves lie lightly,
And smell of mouldering flesh,
How well I know that story!
Near where the mother was,
Across the wet and melancholy
Mountain where her hut was, O God,
The Devil used to live!

[Crash of cymbals. Shrieks, thunder. The animals cower
as the Devil with his troop of fiends, the Werewolf, the
Diablesse, the Bolom, somersault and dance across the
stage. The sky is red.]

DEVIL.

Bai Diable-là manger un'ti mamaille!
(Give the Devil a child for dinner!)

DEVILS.

Un, deux, trois'ti mamaille!
(One, two, three little children!)

[*They whirl around the stage leaping, chanting, then as suddenly go off.*]

BIRD.

Wow!
Were they frightened of him?

FROG.

If they were frightened?
They were frightened of his skin,
Powdery as leprosy,
Like the pock-marked moon,
Afraid of his dead eye,
That had no fire in it . . .

CRICKET.

Of the terrible thunder
In his wood-shaking throat!

[*Roar of devils off-stage*]

FROG.

Just hear them in the hut . . .

[*Sad flute, as the light comes up on the three sons around the knees of the old woman*]

GROS JEAN.

One time again it have nothing to eat,
But one day bread to break;
I went out to chop some wood
To make a nice fire,
But the wood was too damp,
So I didn't use the axe
As I didn't want it to get wet;
If it get wet it get rusty.

MI-JEAN.

Sense!
I went out to do fishing
For crayfish by the cold stones,
In the cold spring in the ferns,
But when I get there so,
I find I lack bait,

[*Rising solemnly*]

Now for man to catch fish,
That man must have bait,
But the best bait is fish,
Yet I cannot catch no fish
Without I first have bait,
As the best bait for fish
Is to catch fish with fish,
So I . . .

GROS JEAN.

Mi-Jean is a fool,
Reading too much damn book.

MOTHER.

My sons, do not quarrel,
Here all of us are starving,
While the planter is eating
From plates painted golden,
Forks with silver tongues,
The brown flesh of birds,
And the white flesh of fish,
What did you do today,
My last son Ti-Jean?

TI-JEAN.

Maman, m'a fait un rien.
(Mama, I didn't do a thing.)

GROS JEAN.

We do all the damned work.

MI-JEAN.

We do all the damn thinking,

GROS JEAN.

And he sits there like a prince.

MI-JEAN.

As useless as a bone.

GROS JEAN and MI-JEAN

[*Jeering*]

Maman, m'a fait un rien!
Maman, m'a fait un rien!

MOTHER.

Wait, and God will send us something.

GROS JEAN.

God forget where he put us.

MI-JEAN.

God too irresponsible.

MOTHER.

Children!

[*Weird music. The Bolom or Foetus rolls in unheard, somersaults around the hut, then waits. Sound of wind, rain, shriek of insects.*]

Children, listen,
There is something listening
Outside of the door!

GROS JEAN.

I don't hear nothing.

MI-JEAN.

I hear only the rain,
Falling hard on the leaves,
And the wind down the throat
Of the gorge with the spring,
The crickets and the bull-frog,
And maybe one frightened bird.

MOTHER.

[*Standing*]

I tell you there is something
Outside of the door,
I tell you from experience
I know when evil comes.
It is not the wind, listen!

[The Bolom imitates a child crying.]

MI-JEAN.
A young child out in the forest.
GROS JEAN.
Looking for its mother.
MOTHER.
The Devil has sent us
Another of his angels!
I prayed to God all day,
While I scrubbed the hut bare,
On the knuckles of my knees
All day in the hungry house;
Now God has sent me evil,
Who can understand it?
Death, death is coming nearer.
GROS JEAN.
Line the step with fine sand
To keep the evil out!
MI-JEAN.
Turn over, Mother, the hem of your skirt!
GROS JEAN and MI-JEAN.
Let two of our fingers form in one crucifix!

[Ti-Jean steps outside.]

MOTHER.
Spirit that is outside,
With the voice of a child
Crying out in the rain,
What do you want from the poor?

[Ti-Jean searches carefully.]

BOLOM.
I have a message for a woman with three sons.
MOTHER.
Child of the Devil, what is your message?
BOLOM.
Send the first of your sons outside for it,
They must die in that order. And let the youngest
Return into the hut.

[Ti-Jean steps back into the hut.]

MOTHER.
We can hear you in the wind,
What do you want of me?

[A weird light shows the Bolom. Shrieks.]

ALL.
Where are you? Where is it?

Hit it! There! Where is it?
BOLOM.

[Leaping, hiding]

Here, in the bowl!
Here, sitting on a stool!
Here, turning in a cup!
Here, crawling up your skirt!
MOTHER.
I have done you no harm, child.
BOLOM.
A woman did me harm,
Called herself mother,
The fear of her hatred
A cord round my throat!
MOTHER.

[Turning, searching]

Look, perhaps it is luckiest
Never to be born,
To the horror of this life
Crowded with shadows,
Never to have known
That the sun will go out,
The green leaf rust,
The strong tree be stricken
And the roaring spring quail;
Peace to you, unborn,
You can find comfort here.
Let a mother touch you,
For the sake of her kind.
BOLOM.

[Shrieks, dancing back]

Whatever flesh touches me,
Withers me into mortality;
Not till your sons die, Mother,
Shall this shape feel this life.
GROS JEAN.

[Seizes axe]

Kill it, then, kill it.
MI-JEAN.
Curse it back to the womb.
DEMON'S VOICE.
Faire ça mwen di ous!
(Do what I commanded!)
BOLOM.
I hear the voice of my master.
DEMON'S VOICE.
Bolom, faire tout ça mwen dire ous!
(Child, do all that I ordered you!)
BOLOM.
Listen, creature of gentleness,
Old tree face marked with scars,

And the wounds of bearing children,
Whom the earth womb will swallow,
This is the shriek
Of a child which was strangled,
Who never saw the earth light
Through the hinge of the womb,
Strangled by a woman,
Who hated my birth,
Twisted out of shape,
Deformed past recognition,
Tell me then, Mother,
Would you care to see it?

[Bolom moves out of the light, shrieking.]

GROS JEAN.
    Let us see you!
MOTHER.
    The sight of such horror, though you are brave,
    Would turn you to stone, my strong son, Gros Jean.
MI-JEAN.
    Let us reason with you.
MOTHER.
    My son, the thing may be a ball of moving fire,
    A white horse in the leaves, or a clothful of skin,
    Found under a tree, you cannot explain that!
BOLOM.
    Save your understanding for the living,
    Save your pity for the dead,
    I am neither living nor dead,
    A puny body, a misshapen head.
MOTHER.
    What does your white master
    The Devil want from us?
BOLOM.
    The house looks warm, old woman,
    Love keeps the house warm,
    From the cold wind and cold rain;
    Though you bar up the door,
    I can enter the house.

[Thunder]

MOTHER.
    Enter! You are welcome.

[She flings open the door.]

GROS JEAN and MI-JEAN
    Shut the door, shut the door!

[Crash of cymbals. The Bolom rolls in a blue light towards
the hut, then enters; all freeze in fear.]

BOLOM.
    The Devil my master
    Who owns half the world,
    In the kingdom of night,

Has done all that is evil
Butchered thousands in war,
Whispered his diseases
In the ears of great statesmen,
Invented human justice,
Made anger, pride, jealousy,
And weakened prayer;
Still cannot enjoy
Those vices he created.
He is dying to be human.
So he sends you this challenge!
To all three of your sons,
He says through my voice,
That if anyone on earth

[Devils' Voices chanting].

Anyone human
Can make him feel anger,
Rage, and human weakness,
He will reward them,
He will fill that bowl,
With a shower of sovereigns,
You shall never more know hunger,
But fulfillment, wealth, peace.

[Increased drum roll to climax]

But if any of your sons
Fails to give him these feelings,
For he never was human,
Then his flesh shall be eaten,
For he is weary of the flesh
Of the fowls of the air,
And the fishes in the sea,
But whichever of your sons
Is brave enough to do this,
Then that one shall inherit
The wealth of my prince.
And once they are dead, woman,
I too shall feel life!

[Exit]

DEVILS' VOICES OFF.
Bai Diable-là manger un'ti mamaille,
Un, deux, trois'ti mamaille!
Bai Diable-là manger un'ti mamaille,
Un,
        deux,
            trois . . .
(Give the Devil a child for dinner,
One, two, three little children!
Give the Devil a child for dinner,
One,
        two,
            three . . .)

Fadeout

721

SCENE ONE

Daybreak. The hut. The Mother and her sons asleep. Gros Jean rises, packs a bundle. His Mother stirs and watches. He opens the door.

MOTHER.
    You will leave me just so,
    My eldest son?
GROS JEAN.
    Is best you didn't know.
MOTHER.
    Woman life is so. Watching and losing.
GROS JEAN.
    Maman, the time obliged to come I was to leave the house, go down the tall forest, come out on the high road, and find what is man work. Is big man I reach now, not no little boy again. Look, feel this arm, but to split trees is nothing. I have an arm of iron, and have nothing I fraid.
MOTHER.
    The arm which digs a grave
    Is the strongest arm of all.
    Your grandfather, your father,
    Their muscles like brown rivers
    Rolling over rocks.
    Now, they bury in small grass,
    Just the jaws of the ant
    Stronger than them now.
GROS JEAN.
    I not even fraid that. You see,
    Is best you still was sleeping?
    I don't want to wake my brothers.
    Ti-Jean love me and will frighten.
    Mi-Jean will argue and make me remain.
    The sun tapping me on my shoulder.
MOTHER.
    When you go down the tall forest, Gros Jean,
    Praise God who make all things; ask direction
    Of the bird, and the insects, imitate them;
    But be careful of the hidden nets of the devil,
    Beware of a wise man called Father of the Forest,
    The Devil can hide in several features,
    A woman, a white gentleman, even a bishop.
    Strength, *ça pas tout*, there is patience besides;
    There always is something stronger than you.
    If is not man, animal, is God or demon.
GROS JEAN.
    Maman, I know all that already.
MOTHER.
    Then God bless you, Gros Jean.
GROS JEAN.
    The world not the same it was in your time,
    Tell my brothers I gone. A man have to go.

[*Marches from hut*]

[*Martial flute, quatro, drum*]

GROS JEAN.

[*Sings*]

    There's a time for every man
    To leave his mother and father
    To leave everybody he know
    And march to the grave he one!

[*Enter the animals, hopping around him*]

    So the time has come for me
    To leave me mother and father
    To add my force to the world
    And go to the grave me one!

[*The Frog is in his path. He aims a kick.*]

Get out of my way, you slimy bastard! How God could make such things? Jump out under my foot, cricket, you know you have no bones! *Gibier! Gibier, montrez-moi sortir!* Bird-o, bird-o, show me a good short-cut, be quick!

[*Suddenly the Bird, Cricket and the Frog all scurry shrieking, croaking. The Old Man enters limping and rests a bundle of faggots down. Gros Jean watches. The Old Man lifts a corner of his robe to scratch a cloven, hairy hoof. Gros Jean emerges.*]

GROS JEAN.
    Bon jour, vieux papa.
OLD MAN.
    Bon matin, Gros Jean.
GROS JEAN.
    What you have with your foot?
OLD MAN.
    Fleas, fleas, boy.

[*Covers it quickly*]

GROS JEAN.
    Is man I am now. Chiggers in your flesh?
    Is man I am, papa, and looking for success.
OLD MAN.
    The flesh of the earth is rotting. Worms.
GROS JEAN.
    Which way, papa?
OLD MAN.
    I cannot tell you the way to success;
    I can only show you, Gros Jean,
    One path through the forest.
GROS JEAN.
    I have no time to waste. I have an arm of iron,
    It have nothing, I fraid, man, beast, or beast-man,
    And more quick I get what I want, more better.
OLD MAN.
    I think strength should have patience. Look at me today.

I was a strong woodman, now I burn coals,
I'm as weak as ashes. And nearly deaf. Come nearer.

GROS JEAN.

[Advances calmly]

What you would say is the quickest way?

OLD MAN.

The quickest way to what?

GROS JEAN.

To what counts in this world.

OLD MAN.

What counts in this world is money and power.

GROS JEAN.

I have an arm of iron, only money I missing.

OLD MAN.

Then I can't advise you.

GROS JEAN.

You old and you have experience.
So don't be selfish with it.
Or you know what I'll do.

[Grabs him, hurls him down, axe uplifted]

Chop you and bury you in the bamboo leaves!

OLD MAN.

With your arm of iron, the first thing to kill is wisdom?

GROS JEAN.

That's right, papa.

OLD MAN.

Well, the Devil always wants help.

GROS JEAN.

The Devil boasts that he never get vex.

OLD MAN.

[Rising]

Easy, easy son, I'll help you if you wait,
Just let me adjust the edge of my skirt.
Well, I was coming through the forest now
And I passed by the white spring, and I saw
Some poor souls going to work for the white planter.
He'll work you like the devil, but that's what you want,
You and your impatience and arm cast in iron,
So turn to the right, go through the bamboo forest,
Over the black rocks, then the forest will open,
And you will see the sky, below that a valley,
And smoke, and a white house that is empty,
The old fellow is hiring harvesters today.
Remember an iron arm may rust, flesh is deciduous.
There's your short-cut, Gros Jean, make the most of it.

GROS JEAN.

Next time don't be so selfish.

[Exit Gros Jean, marching]

OLD MAN.

[Sings, gathering bundle]

Who is the man who can speak to the strong?

Where is the fool who can talk to the wise?
Men who are dead now have learnt this long,
Bitter is wisdom that fails when it tries.
[To the audience] Ah well, there's wood to cut, fires to light, smoke to wrinkle an old man's eyes, and a shrivelling skin to keep warm. There went the spirit of war: an iron arm and a clear explanation, and might is still right, thank God, for God is the stronger. But get old father forest from the path of the fable, for there's wood to cut, a nest of twittering beaks to feed with world-eating worms. Oh, oh, oh.

[The creatures creep after him timidly.]

For they all eat each other, and that's natural law,
So remember the old man in the middle of the forest.

[He turns suddenly. Then hobbles after them]

Eat and eat one another! It's another day. Ha, ha! Wah! Wah!

[They flee. He goes out.]

GROS JEAN.

[In another part of the wood] I have an arm of iron, and that's true, but I here since the last two days working for this damn white man, and I don't give a damn if he watching me. You know what I doing here with this bag and this piece of stick? Well, I go tell you. While I smoke a pipe. Let me just sit down, and I won't lose my patience. [He sits on a log] Well, you remember how I leave home, and then bounce up this old man who put me on to a work? Remember what the old son of a leaf-gathering beggar said? He said that working for the Devil was the shortest way to success. Well, I walked up through the bush then I come onto a large field. Estate-like, you know. Sugar, tobacco, and a hell of a big white house where they say the Devil lives. Ay-ay.

So two next black fellers bring me up to him. Big white man, his hand cold as an axe blade and his mind twice as sharp. So he say, "Gros Jean, we has a deal to make, right?" So I say, "Sure, boss!" He say the one that get the other one vex, the one who show the first sign of anger will be eaten rrruuunnnhhh, just like that, right? You think I stupid? I strong, I have some sense and my name not Gros Jean for nothing. That was two days ago. Well, Jesus, a man ain't rest since then! The first job I had, I had was to stand up in a sugar-cane field and count all the leaves of the cane. That take me up till four o'clock. I count all the leaves and then divide by the number of stalks. I must tell you there had times when I was getting vex but the old iron arm fix me, because there is patience in strength. The Devil ain't say anything. About seven o'clock, he tell me to go and catch about seventy fireflies. Well, you must try and catch fireflies! Is no easy. Had a time when I do so once, one whap with the hand! thinking was a bunch but was nothing, only stars! So in the middle of all that, this man come up to me and say, what's the matter, Joe, he always like he don't know my name, but I is me, Gros Jean, the strongest! And if you ain't know my name, you best don't call me nothing. Say, "What's matter, Mac? You vex or sumpin?" So I say, "No, I ain't vex!" Well, is two days now, and I ain't get a cent. I so tired I giddy. But I giving the old iron arm a rest from cramp, and breaking a little smoke. After all! If was only sensible work, if a man could get the work that suit him, cotton or sugar or something important! Plus he getting eighty-five per cent of the profit? Shucks, man, that ain't fair. Besides I could just bust his face, you know. But me mother ain't bring me up so. After all, man, after all, a man have to rest man. Shime!

[Enter Devil masked as a Planter.]

PLANTER.
Well, how's it progressing, Joe, tired?
GROS JEAN.
From where you was and now you come you hear me say I fagged? *[Slowly]* And Gros Jean is the name, boss.
PLANTER.
Tobacco break? Whistle's blown past lunch, boy.
GROS JEAN.
I taking a five here, chief. Black people have to rest too, and once I rest, chief, I do more work than most, right?
PLANTER.
That's right, Mac.
GROS JEAN.
[Gritting his teeth] Gros Jean . . . Gros . . . Jean . . . chief . . . !
PLANTER.
You sound a bit annoyed to me.
GROS JEAN.
[With a painful, fixed grin from now on] Have your fun. I know I ain't nobody yet, chief, but an old man tell me to have patience. And I ain't let you down yet, chief, hasn't I?
PLANTER.
That's right, Gros Chien, Gros Jean, Gros Jean, sorry. Can't tell one face from the next out here. How's the work then? *[Pacing up and down]*
GROS JEAN.
Chief, why you don't take a rest too somewhat? You have all this land, all this big house and so forth, people working for you as if is ants self, but is only work, work, work in your mind, ent you has enough?
PLANTER.
[Looking at his watch] Other people want what I have, Charley, and other people have more. Can't help myself, Joe, it's some sort of disease, and it spreads right down to the common man.
GROS JEAN.
I not no common man, boss. People going hear about Gros Jean. Because I come from that mountain forest,

don't mean I can't come like you, or because I black. One day all this could be mine!
PLANTER.
Yes, yes. Well anyway, Horace, time is flying, and I want these leaves checked, counted, filed and classified by weight and texture and then stacked . . . What's the matter, Francis?
GROS JEAN.
[To audience] You see how he provoking me, you don't think I should curse his . . . *[Turns, bites hard on pipe, grinning]* Look, I haven't let you down yet, boss, have I? I mean to say I take two three hours to catch your goat you send me to catch. I mean not so? Wait, chief, wait, listen . . . I ain't vex, boss. Ha-ha!
PLANTER.
Sit down, Joe, relax, you can't take it with you, they say, only time is money, and the heights that great men reached etc., and genius is ninety per cent perspiration and so forth . . . So, sit down, waste time, but I thought you were in a hurry . . . Henry.
GROS JEAN.
Boss. *[Smiling]* You really impatianate, yes. Ha-ha-ha! I mean I don't follow you, chief. After I count and carry all the cane leaves for you, ain't I, and look—when the wind blow them wrong side I ain't say nothing, and I'm smiling ain't I? *[Relaxes his expression, then resumes]* I'm smiling because I got confidence in the old iron arm, ain't it? And if I do it and have time to spare is the work and pay that matter, and is all you worried about, *big shot!* Ain't it? Excuse me, I mean to say, I'm smiling ain't I?
PLANTER.
Sorry, sorry, Gros Jean, sometimes we people in charge of industry forget that you people aren't machines. I mean people like you, Hubert . . .

[Gros Jean is about to sit.]

GROS JEAN.
[Rising] Gros Jean, chief, Gros Jean . . . Ha-ha!
PLANTER.
Gros Jean, very well . . . *[Pause]* Have your smoke. *[Pause]* Plenty of time. It might rain, people may be stealing from me now. The market is unsteady this year. *[Pause]* But we're human. *[Pause]* You don't know what it means to work hard, to have to employ hundreds of people. *[Embracing him]* You're worth more to me, Benton, than fifty men. So you should smoke, after all. *[Pause]* And such a pleasant disposition, always smiling. *[Pause, steps back]* Just like a skull. *[Long pause]* But remember, Mervin, I'd like you to try and finish this, you see I have a contract and the harder you work the more I . . .
GROS JEAN.
[Exploding, smashing pipe in anger] Jesus Christ what this damn country coming to a man cyant even get a god-

damned smoke? [*He tries to grin*] I ent vex, I ent vex, chief. Joke, joke, boss . . .

Explosion

[*When the smoke clears, the Devil, his Planter's mask removed, is sitting on the log, calmly nibbling the flesh from a bone.*]

DEVILS' VOICES OFF.
Bai Diable-là manger un'ti mamaille
Un!
(Give the Devil a child for dinner
One! . . .)

Blackout

SCENE TWO

*Music. Dawn. The forest. A cross marked "Gros Jean."
The creatures foraging. Enter Mi-Jean walking fast and
reading, a net slung over his shoulder.*)

BIRD.

[*To flute*]

Mi-Jean, Mi-Jean, *bon jour*, M'sieu Mi-Jean.

[*The creatures dance.*]

MI-JEAN.

[*Closes the book*]

Bird, you disturbing me!
Too much whistling without sense,
Is animal you are, so please know your place.
CRICKET.
Where you going, Mi-Jean?
MI-JEAN.

[*To the audience*]

But see my cross, *oui*, ay-ay!
Since from what time cricket
Does ask big man their business?
FROG.
You going to join your brother?
You are a man's size now.
MI-JEAN.

[*Again to the audience*]

Well, confusion on earth, frog could talk!
Gros Jean was one man, I is a next. Frog,
You ever study your face in
The mirror of a pool?
BIRD.
Mi-Jean, Mi-Jean,

Your brother is a little heap
Of white under the bamboo leaves,
Every morning the black beetles
More serious than a hundred priests,
Frowning like fifty undertakers
Come and bear a piece away
To build a chapel from his bones. Look, look!

[*Bird shows the cross. Mi-Jean kneels and peers through
his spectacles.*]

CRICKET.
Every morning I sit here,
And see the relics of success,
An arm of iron turned to rust,
Not strong enough to stir the dirt.
FROG.
Gros Jean was strong, but had no sense.
MI-JEAN.

[*Rising and dusting his clothes*]

He had the sin called over-confidence!
Listen, I . . .
BIRD.
Run, run, Papa Bois, Papa Bois . . .

[*All run off*]

OLD MAN.
Bon jour, Mi-Jean, Mi-Jean, *le philosophe*.
MI-JEAN.

[*To the audience*]

When my mother told me goodbye in tears,
She said, no one can know what the Devil wears.

[*To the Old Man*]

Bon jour, Papa Bois, how come you know my name?
OLD MAN.
Who in the heights, in any small hut hidden in the ferns, where the trees are always weeping, or any two men are ploughing on a wet day, wrapped in old cloaks, or down in the villages among the smoke and rum, has not heard of Mi-Jean the jurist, and the gift of his tongue, his prowess in argument, Mi-Jean, the *avocat*, the fisherman, the litigant? Come, come sir, don't be modest! I've been sitting there on the cold, crusty log, rough as the armoured bark of a frog, waiting to exchange knowledge with you. Ah, your brother's grave! How simple he was! Well, I'm half-blind, but I see you have one virtue more than your brother, fear. Nothing lives longer than brute strength, sir, except it is human cowardice. Come nearer, come nearer, and tell us why you left home? Sit down, you're among equals.

Derek Walcott

MI-JEAN.

I good just where I am.
I on my way to the sea
To become a rich captain,
The land work too hard,
Then to become a lawyer.

OLD MAN.

[Softly singing]

On land on sea no man is free,
All meet death, the enemy. I see,
Hence the net, the net and the book.

MI-JEAN.

What?

OLD MAN.

I say hence the book,
Hence the net, and the book.

MI-JEAN.

Ça c'est hence? (What is "hence"?)

OLD MAN.

Same as whereas, and hereunto affixed.
These are terms used in tautology and law.

MI-JEAN.

[Nodding blankly. Pause. Then:]

I see you have a cow-foot. Ain't that so?

OLD MAN.

Yes, yes. A cow's foot. You have an eye for detail!
Born with it, actually. Source of embarrassment.
Would you like some tobacco? What are you reading?

MI-JEAN.

[Opens the book]

This book have every knowledge it have;
I checking up on man with cow-foot, boss,
In the section call religion, and tropical superstition.
Bos . . . Bovis . . . Cow . . . foot . . . foot, boss? Boss foot?
Bovis?

OLD MAN.

Outside in the world they are wiser, now, Mi-Jean;
They don't believe in evil or the prevalence of devils,
Believe me, philosopher, nobody listens to old men;
Sit down next to me and have a bit of tobacco.
And since you need knowledge, I'll give you advice . . .

MI-JEAN.

[Still reading]

I don't smoke and I don't drink,
I keep my head clear, and advice,
I don't need none, but will listen.

[Shuts the book]

This book is Latin mainly.
It have bos, meaning cow,

and pes, meaning foot,
Boss' foot, bospes, cow-heel perhaps,
It have plenty recipe
But it don't give the source! [Sighs loudly] So!
Yes, apart from wisdom, I have no vices.

OLD MAN.

Life without sin. How about women?

MI-JEAN.

The downfall of man! I don't care for women,
Women don't have no brain. Their foot just like yours.

OLD MAN.

You believe in the Devil?
Oh, why don't you sit nearer,
Haven't you ever seen a cow-heel before?

MI-JEAN.

Not under a skirt, no. [Sighs loudly] Yes!
I believe in the Devil, yes,
Or so my mother make me,
And is either that, papa,
Or not believe in God.
And when I meet this devil,
Whatever shape he taking,
And I know he is not you,
Since he would never expose
His identity so early,
I will do all that he commands,
But you know how I will beat him,

[Sits near the Old Man]

With silence, and a smile.

[He smiles]

Too besides when I meet him,
I will know if God exist,
We calling that in philosophy

[Checks in the book]

We calling that in big knowledge,
Ah, polarities of belief,
When the existence of one object
Compels that of the other,
Bon Dieu, what terms, what terms!

[Sighs loudly, rests the book down]

Yes. Silence shall be my defence.

[He sings "The Song of Silence."]

I

Within this book of wisdom
Hear what the wise man say:
The man who is wise is dumb
And lives another day,
You cannot beat the system
Debate is just a hook,

Open your mouth, de bait in!
And is you they going to juck
CHORUS.
So when things dark, go blind
When nothing left, go deaf
When the blows come, be dumb
And hum, hum.

II

In Chapter Five from para-
Graph three, page 79,
This book opines how Socra-
Tes would have been better off blind.
God gave him eyes like all of we,
But he, he had to look.
The next thing, friends, was jail, *oui!*
Hemlock and him lock up!
CHORUS.
So when things dark, go blind, etc.

III

The third set of instruction
This self-said book declares
Is that the wise man's function
Is how to shut his ears
Against riot and ruction
That try to climb upstairs.
If you can hear, don't listen!
If you can see, don't look!
If you must talk, be quiet!
Or your mouth will dig your grave.

[While he sings his song, the Old Man goes behind a grove of bamboo, leisurely removes his robe and his mask, under which is the mask of the Devil; then he changes into the mask and clothes of the Planter.]

PLANTER.
[He sits on the log, legs crossed, smiling throughout the scene]
Ah, finished all the work I gave you, Mi-Jean?

[Mi-Jean nods]

And menial work didn't bore you, a thinker?

[Mi-Jean nods]

You're not one for small-talk, are you?

[Mi-Jean nods]

Did you catch the wild goat?

[Mi-Jean nods yes]

Frisky little bugger, wasn't he? Yes, sir, that's one hell of a goat. Some kid, what? Clever, however. How many canes were there on the estate?

[Mi-Jean uses ten fingers repeatedly.]

Don't waste words, eh? All right, all right. Look, you

don't mind a little chat while we work, do you? A bit of a gaff lightens labour. God Lord, man, you've been here for over two days and haven't had the common decency to even pass the time of day. Where did you get your reputation as a bush lawyer, I mean it's only manners, blast it.

[Mi-Jean cocks his head at the Planter.]

Oh, don't flatter yourself, young man, I'm not annoyed. It takes two to make a quarrel. Shut up, by all means. *[Rises]* Now, before it gets dark, I want you to come up to the house, check and polish the silver, rearrange my library and . . .

[The goat bleats. Mi-Jean frowns.]

Aha, looks like the old goat's broken loose again, son. Better drop what you're not doing and catch it before it's dark.

[Mi-Jean rises rapidly, runs off, returns.]

Ah, now you're smiling again, fixed him this time, haven't you?

[The goat bleats.]

Not quite, cunning animal, that goat, couldn't have tied him.

[Mi-Jean dashes out, annoyed, returns.]

Fast worker!

[The goat bleats.]

Look, before you dash off, I'd like to say here and now . . .

[The goat bleating as Mi-Jean, mumbling, smiling, points off.]

that I do admire your cheery persistence, your resigned nonchalance, so let me demonstrate something. There's a special kind of knot, and there's an end to that. Hence you take the rope thus, and whereas the goat being hereto affixed to the . . .

[Goat bleating, Mi-Jean raging inside.]

but if that doesn't fix him, then my recommendation is . . .
MI-JEAN.
Look!
PLANTER.
Yes?
MI-JEAN.
I think I know what I'm doing . . . sir . . .
PLANTER.
[Above the sound of bleating] Oh, sure, sure. But I was simply trying to explain just to help you out, that . . . *[Goat bleats]* . . . You see? He's gone off again! Just a little more patience . . . *[Mi-Jean is about to run off]* It's simply a

question of how you tie this knot, don't you see? [*Mi-Jean, collecting himself, nods, then tiredly smiles*] I mean, I've seen dumber men, not you, fail at this knot you know, it's just a matter of know-how, not really knowledge, just plain skill . . . [*Mi-Jean nodding, nodding*] You look the kind of fellow who doesn't mind a bit of expert advice. [*Goat bleats furiously*] And you'd better hurry up before it gets dark. Wait, remember how to tie the knot.

MI-JEAN.
[*Under control, nods*] Yes, I remember. [*Runs off, crosses the stage several times in a chase*]

PLANTER.
[*Walks up and down in a rage*] Well, what the hell, I thought I had him there, he's no fool, that's certain, for the Devil comes in through apertures. He doesn't know right from wrong, and he's not interested. The only entrance I could have got through his mouth, I tried to leave ajar, but the fool bolted it completely. There he goes chasing the bloody goat like a simpleton, and not even shouting at it. Good old Master Speak No Evil. I hope he breaks his God-supported neck, the dummy! [*He sits*] Here comes the comedy again, an eloquent goat and a tongueless biped!

[*The goat cavorts across and around the stage to merry music, with Mi-Jean behind him waving a rope and the net. Mi-Jean collapses.*]

PLANTER.
Tough life, eh?

[*Mi-Jean groans, nodding.*]

Don't let it get you down.

[*Goat bleats.*]

MI-JEAN.
That goat certainly making a plethora of cacophony.

PLANTER.
It's only a poor animal, in its own rut.

MI-JEAN.
[*Smiling*] Men are lustiferous animals also, but at least they have souls.

PLANTER.
Ah, the philosopher! The contemplative! An opinion at last! A man is no better than an animal. The one with two legs makes more noise and that makes him believe he can think. It is talk that makes men think they have souls. There's no difference, only in degree. No animal, but man, dear boy, savours such a variety of vices. He knows no season for lust, he is a kneeling hypocrite who on four legs, like a penitent capriped, prays to his maker, but is calculating the next vice. That's my case!

MI-JEAN.
Nonsensical verbiage! *Bettise!*

PLANTER.
It's not, you know, and you're getting annoyed.

MI-JEAN.
[*Shakes his head*] You can't get me into no argument! I have brains, but won't talk. [*Long pause*] All I say is that man is divine!

PLANTER.
You're more intelligent than the goat, you think?

MI-JEAN.
I not arguing! Anything you want.

PLANTER.
[*Rises*] Honestly, I'd like to hear what you think. You're the kind of chap I like to talk to. Your brother was a sort of politician, but you're a thinker.

[*Mi-Jean, rising, is about to lecture. The goat bleats.*]

Steady-on. For all we know, that may be poetry. Which Greek scholar contends in his theory of metempsychosis that the souls of men may return into animals?

MI-JEAN.
I never study Greek, but I . . . [*Goat bleats. Mi-Jean pauses*] I was saying that I never study no Greek, but I'd . . . [*Goat bleats*] It getting on like to have sense, eh?

PLANTER.
Why not?

MI-JEAN.
Listen, I ent mind doing what you proposed, anything physical, because that's ostentatious, but when you start theorising that there's an equality of importance in the creatures of this earth, when you animadvertently imbue mere animals with an animus or soul, I have to call you a crooked-minded pantheist . . . [*Goat bleats, sounding like "Hear, hear!"*] Oh, shut up, you can't hear two people talking? No, I'm not vexed, you know, but . . . [*Goat bleats.*]

PLANTER.
[*Advancing towards him*] Your argument interests me. It's nice to see ideas getting you excited. But logically now. The goat, I contend, may be a genius in its own right. For all we know, this may be the supreme goat, the apogee of capripeds, the voice of human tragedy, the Greek . . .

MI-JEAN.
Exaggerated hypothesis! Unsubstantiated!

PLANTER.
Since the goat is mine, and if you allow me, for argument's sake, to pursue my premise, then if you get vexed at the goat, who represents my view, then you are vexed with me, and the contract must be fulfilled.

MI-JEAN.
I don't mind talking to you, but don't insult me, telling me a goat have more sense than I, than me. Than both of we!

PLANTER.
[*Embracing him*] Descendant of the ape, how eloquent you

have become! How assured in logic! How marvellous in invention! And yet, poor shaving monkey, the animal in you is still in evidence, that goat . . . [*Goat sustains its bleating.*]

MI-JEAN.

Oh, shut you damn mouth, both o'all you! I ain't care who right who wrong! I talking now! What you ever study? I ain't even finish making my points and all two of you interrupting, breach of legal practice! O God, I not vex, I not vex . . .

[*Planter removes his mask, and the Devil advances on Mi-Jean.*]

Explosion
Blackout

[*The goat bleats once*]

DEVILS' VOICES OFF.

Bai Diable-là manger un'ti mamaille
(Give the Devil a child for dinner)
Un!
(One!)
Deux!
(Two! . . .)

INTERVAL

SCENE THREE

*Dawn. The forest. Two crosses marked "Gros Jean,"
"Mi-Jean." The Old Man sits on the log, the creatures
huddle near him. Ti-Jean, Mother, in the hut.*

DEVILS' VOICES OFF.

Bai Diable-là manger un'ti mamaille,
Un, deux, trois'ti mamaille!
Bai Diable-là manger un'ti mamaille,
Un, deux, trois'ti mamaille.

OLD MAN.

Aie! Feed the Devil the third, feed the Devil the third. Power is knowledge, knowledge is power, and the Devil devours them on the hour!

DEVILS.

Bai Diable-là manger un'ti mamaille
Un, deux, trois'ti mamaille!

OLD MAN.

[*To audience*] Well, that's two good meals finished with a calm temper, and if all goes mortally, one more is to come. [*Shrieks, points to where Ti-Jean is consoling his Mother*] Aie, ya, yie, a chicken is to come, a calf, a veal-witted young man, tender in flesh, soft in the head and bones, tenderer than old muscle power, and simpler than that net-empty atheist. For the next dish is man-wit,

common sense. But I can wait, I can wait, gathering damp rotting faggots, aie!

MOTHER.

[*To flute*]

If you leave me, my son,
I have empty hands left,
Nothing to grieve for.
You are hardly a man,
A stalk, bending in wind
With no will of its own,
Never proven your self
In battle or in wisdom,
I have kept you to my breast,
As the last of my chickens,
Not to feed the blind jaws
Of the carnivorous grave.

TI-JEAN.

You have told me yourself
Our lives are not ours,
That no one's life is theirs
Husband or wife,
Father or son,
That our life is God's own.

MOTHER.

You are hard, hard, Ti-Jean,
O what can I tell you?
I have never learnt enough.

TI-JEAN.

You have taught me this strength,
To do whatever we will
And love God is enough.

MOTHER.

I feel I shall never see you again.

TI-JEAN.

To return what we love is our glory, our pain.

OLD MAN.

Oh, enough of these sentiments, I'm hungry, and I'm cold!

TI-JEAN.

Now pray for me, *maman*,
The sun is in the leaves.

MOTHER.

The first of my children
Never asked for my strength,
The second of my children
Thought little of my knowledge,
The last of my sons, now,
Kneels down at my feet,
Instinct be your shield,
It is wiser than reason,
Conscience be your cause
And plain sense your sword.

[*The Bolom rolls towards the hut. Drums.*]

BOLOM.
Old tree shaken of fruit,
This green one must die.
MOTHER.
Aie, I hear it, I hear it,
The cry of the unborn!
But then have I not given
Birth and death to the dead?

[*The Bolom dances off, shrieking. Ti-Jean rises.*]

Oh, Ti-Jean, you are so small,
So small. [*Exit*]
TI-JEAN.
Yes, I small, *maman*, I small,
And I never learn from book,
But, like the small boy, David.

[*Sings*]

I go bring down, bring down Goliath,
Bring down below.
Bring down, bring down Goliath,
Bring down below.

[*He enters the forest.*]

TI-JEAN.
Ah, *bon matin, compère Crapaud,*
Still in your dressing gown?
FROG.
Ti-Jean, like your brothers you're making fun of me.
TI-JEAN
Why should I laugh at the frog and his fine bass voice?
FROG
You wouldn't call me handsome, would you?
TI-JEAN.

[*Kneels among the Creatures*]

Oh, I don't know, you have your own beauty.
Like the castanet music of the cricket over there.
CRICKET.
Crak, crak. Now say something nice to the firefly.
FIREFLY.
How can he? I don't look so hot in the daytime.
TI-JEAN.
But I have often mistaken you at night for a star.

[*Rises*]

Now friends, which way is shortest to the Devil's estate?
FROG.
Beware of an old man whose name is wordly wisdom.
FIREFLY.
With a pile of sticks on his back.
CRICKET.
. . . and a foot cloven like a beast.

TI-JEAN.
If he is an old man, and mortal,
He will judge everything on earth
By his own sad experience.
God bless you, small things.
It's a hard life you have,
Living in the forest.
FIREFLY.
God preserve you for that.
Bird, take the tree and cry
If the old man comes through
That grove of dry bamboo.

[*Bird flies off.*]

CRICKET.
Crashing through the thicket
With the cleft hoof of a beast.
FIREFLY.
For though we eat each other,
I can't tempt that frog too close,
And we never see each other for dinner,
We do not do it from evil.
FROG.
True. Is a long time I never eat a firefly.
FIREFLY.
Watch it, watch it, brother,
You don't want heartburn, do you?
TI-JEAN.
No, it is not from evil.
What are these crosses?
CRICKET.
Nothing. Do not look, Ti-Jean.
Why must you fight the Devil?
TI-JEAN.
To know evil early, life will be simpler.
FROG.
Not so, Ti-Jean, not so. Go back.

[*Ti-Jean goes to the crosses, weeps.*]

BIRD.
Weep-weep-weep-weep-quick,
The old man is coming, quick.
FROG.
If you need us, call us, brother, but
You understand we must move.

[*Ti-Jean stands over the crosses.*]

OLD MAN.
Ah, good morning, youngster! It's a damp, mournful walk
through the forest, isn't it, and only the cheep of a bird to
warm one. Makes old bones creak. Now it's drizzling.
Damn it.
TI-JEAN.
Bon jou, vieux cor', I find the world pleasant in the early
light.

OLD MAN.

They say, the people of the forest, when the sun and rain contend for mastery, they say that the Devil is beating his wife. Know what I say? I say it brings rheumatism, I don't believe in the Devil. Eighty-eight years, and never seen his face.

TI-JEAN.

Could you, being behind it?

OLD MAN.

Eh? Eh? I'm deaf, come nearer. Come here and shelter. Good. Some people find me ugly, monstrous ugly. Even the small insects sometimes. The snake moves from me, and this makes me sad. I was a woodsman once, but look now, I burn wood into ashes. Let me sit on this log awhile. Tobacco?

TI-JEAN.

No, thanks, sir.

OLD MAN.

Tell me, boy, is your father living? Or your mother perhaps? You look frail as an orphan.

TI-JEAN.

I think nothing dies. My brothers are dead but they live in memory of my mother.

OLD MAN.

You're very young, boy, to be talking so subtly. So you lost two brothers?

TI-JEAN.

I said I had brothers, I never said how many. May I see that foot, father?

OLD MAN.

In a while, in a while. No, I saw you looking at the two graves, so I presumed there were two. There were two, weren't there? Ah well, none can escape that evil that men call death.

TI-JEAN.

Whatever God made, we must consider blessed. I'm going to look at your foot.

OLD MAN.

Hold on, son. Whatever God made, we must consider blessed? Like the death of your mother?

TI-JEAN.

Like the death of my mother.

OLD MAN.

Like the vileness of the frog?

TI-JEAN.

[Advancing] Like the vileness of the frog.

OLD MAN.

Like the froth of the constrictor?

TI-JEAN.

Like the froth of the constrictor. [He is above the Old Man.]

OLD MAN.

Like the cloven cow's foot under an old man's skirt?

[Ti-Jean sweeps up the skirt, then drops it.]

What did you hope to find, but an old man's weary feet?

You're a forward little fool! Now, do you want some advice? Tell me how you'll face the Devil, and I'll give you advice.

TI-JEAN.

O help me, my brothers, help me to win.

[He retreats to the crosses.]

OLD MAN.

Getting frightened, aren't you? Don't be a coward, son. I gather twigs all day, in the darkness of the forest. And never feared man nor beast these eighty-eight years. I think you owe me some sort of apology.

[The Bird runs out and begins to peck at the rope, untying the faggots with his beak. The Old Man jumps up, enraged.]

Leave that alone, you damned . . .

TI-JEAN.

I'll help you, father.

[Instead, he loosens the bundle.]

OLD MAN.

I'll kill that bird. Why did you loosen my sticks? Haven't you any respect for the weariness of the old? You've had your little prank, now help me collect them. If you had a father you'd know what hard work was, In the dark of the forest, lighting damp faggots . . .

[Ti-Jean pretends to be assisting the Old Man, but carefully he lifts his skirt and sees that below the sackcloth robe he has a forked tail.]

TI-JEAN.

My mother always told me, my spirits were too merry, Now, here we are, old father, all in one rotten bundle.

OLD MAN.

What's come over you, you were frightened a while back?

TI-JEAN.

Which way to the Devil? Oh, you've never seen him. Tell me, does the Devil wear a hard, stiff tail?

OLD MAN.

How would I know. [Feels his rear, realises] Mm. Well, you go through that track, and you'll find a short-cut through the bamboo. It's wet, leaf-rotting path, then you come to the springs of sulphur, where the damned souls are cooking . . .

TI-JEAN.

You sure you not lying?

OLD MAN.

It's too early in the morning to answer shallow questions, That's a fine hat you're wearing, so I'll bid you goodbye.

[Ti-Jean lifts up a stick]

TI-JEAN.

Not until I know who you are, papa! Look, I'm in a great hurry, or I'll brain you with this;

If evil exists, let it come forward.
Human, or beast, let me see it plain.

[*The stage darkens. Drums. The Old Man rises.*]

OLD MAN.
Very well then, look!

[*He unmasks; the Devil's face. Howls, cymbals clash*]

DEVIL.
Had you not gotten me, fool,
Just a trifle angry,
I might have played the Old Man
In fairness to our bargain,
But this is no play, son.
For here is the Devil,
You asked for him early,
Impatient as the young.
Now remember our bargain,
The one who wastes his temper,
Will be eaten! Remember that!
Now, you will work!

TI-JEAN.
Cover your face, the wrinkled face of wisdom,
Twisted with memory of human pain,
Is easier to bear; this is like looking
At the blinding gaze of God.

DEVIL.

[*Replacing Old Man's mask, and changing*]

It is hard to distinguish us,
Combat to fair combat, then I cover my face,
And the sun comes out of the rain, and the clouds.
Now these are the conditions, and the work you must do.

TI-JEAN.
Wait, old man, if is anything stupid,
I don't have your patience, so you wasting time.

OLD MAN.
Then you must pay the penalty.
These are your orders:
I have an ass of a goat
That will not stay tied.
I want you to catch it
Tonight before sundown.
Over hill and valley
Wherever it gallops.
Then tie it good and hard.
And if it escapes
You must catch it again
As often as it gets loose
You try as many times.
If you should lose your temper . . .

TI-JEAN.
Where the hell is this goat?

OLD MAN.
Over there by the . . . wait.

The fool has run off.
He won't last very long.

[*Exit Ti-Jean. The Old Man sits down, rocking back and forth with laughter. Ti-Jean runs back.*]

OLD MAN.
Finished already?

TI-JEAN.
That's right. Anything else?

OLD MAN.
Ahm. Yes, yes, yes. Best I've seen, though.
Now I want you to go down to the edge of the cane field

[*The goat bleats.*]

Looks like you didn't tie him?

TI-JEAN.
I tied the damned thing up.
Something is wrong here.
I tied the thing up properly.

[*The Old Man laughs. Ti-Jean runs off. The Old Man dances with joy. Goat bleats, then stops suddenly. Ti-Jean returns with something wrapped in a banana leaf and sits down quietly. The Old Man watches him. Pause. No bleat.*]

OLD MAN.
What's that in your hands?

TI-JEAN.

[*Proffers the leaf*]

Goat seed.

[*The goat bleats girlishly.*]

OLD MAN.
His voice is changing.
I don't get you. Goat-seed?

TI-JEAN.
I tied the damn thing.
Then made it a eunuch.

[*The goat bleats weakly.*]

Sounds much nicer.

OLD MAN.
You er . . . fixed my one goat?
Then you must have been angry.

TI-JEAN.
No, I just couldn't see myself
Chasing the damned thing all night.
And anyhow, where I tied it,
She'll never move again.

OLD MAN.

[*Walking around stage*]

You sit there calm as hell
And tell me you er . . . altered Emilia?

732

TI-JEAN.
Funny goat, with a girl's name,
It's there by the plantain tree,
Just by the stones.
OLD MAN.
Boy, you have a hell of a nerve.
TI-JEAN.
It look like you vex.
OLD MAN.
Angry? I'm not angry. I'm not vexed at all.
You see? Look! I'm smiling.
What's an old goat anyhow?
Just the only goat I had.
Gave sour milk anyway.
TI-JEAN.

[Rising. Rubbing his hands]

Fine. Now, what's next on the agenda?
OLD MAN.
What? Yes, yes . . . Fixed the goat . . .
TI-JEAN.
Now look here, life is . . .
OLD MAN.
Enough of your catechism!
TI-JEAN.
Temper, temper. Or you might lose something. Now what
next?
OLD MAN.
Now, listen to this, boy.
Go down to the cane-fields
And before the next cloud
Start checking every blade,
Count each leaf on the stalk,
File them away properly
As fast as you can
Before the night comes,
Then report back to me.
Well, what are you waiting for?
TI-JEAN.
I got a bit tired chasing the goat,
I'm human you know.
OLD MAN.
I'm going back to the house,
I'll be back at dawn to check on your progress.

[Exit]

TI-JEAN.

[Goes to the edge of the cane-field]

Count all the canes, what a waste of time!

[Cups his hands]

Hey, all you niggers sweating there in the canes!
Hey, all you people working hard in the fields!

VOICES.

[Far off]

'Ayti? What happen? What you calling us for?
TI-JEAN.
You are poor damned souls working for the Devil?
VOICES.
Yes! Yes! What you want?
TI-JEAN.
Listen, I'm the new foreman! Listen to this:
The Devil say you must burn everything, now.
Burn the cane, burn the cotton! Burn everything now!
VOICES.
Burn everything now? Okay, boss!

[Drums. Cries. Caneburners' chorus]

TI-JEAN.
The man say Burn, burn, burn de cane!
CHORUS.
Burn, burn, burn de cane!
TI-JEAN.
You tired work for de man in vain!
CHORUS.
Burn, burn, burn de cane!

[Exeunt]

[The Frog enters.]

FROG.

[Sings]

And all night the night burned
Turning on its spit,
Until in the valley, the grid
Of the canefield glowed like coals,
When the devil, as lit as the dawn returned,
Dead drunk, and singing his song of lost souls.

[Enter Devil, drunk, with a bottle, singing]

DEVIL.
Down deep in hell, where it black like ink,
Where the oil does boil and the sulphur stink,
It ain't have no ice, no refrigerator
If you want water, and you ask the waiter,
He go bring brimstone with a saltpetre chaser,
While de devils bawling.

[He is carrying the Old Man's mask. Now he puts it on.] Oh, if
only the little creatures of this world could understand, but
they have no evil in them . . . so how the hell can they?
[The Cricket passes.] Cricket, cricket, it's the old man.
CRICKET.
Crek, crek, boo!
CHORUS.
Fire one! Fire one
Till the place burn down,

733

Fire one! Fire one.

DEVIL.

[*Flings the mask away*]

I'll be what I am, so to hell with you. I'll be what I am. I drink, and I drink, and I feel nothing. Oh, I lack heart to enjoy the brevity of the world! [*The Firefly passes, dancing.*] Get out of my way, you burning backside, I'm the prince of obscurity and I won't brook interruption! Trying to mislead me, because I been drinking. Behave, behave. That youngster is having terrible effect on me. Since he came to the estate, I've felt like a fool. First time in me life too. Look, just a while ago I nearly got angry at an insect that's just a half-arsed imitation of a star. It's wonderful! An insect brushes my dragonish hand, and my scales tighten with fear. Delightful! So this is what it means! I'm drunk, and hungry. [*The Frog, his eyes gleaming, hops across his path*] O God, O God, a monster! Jesus, help! Now that for one second was the knowledge of death. O Christ, how weary it is to be immortal. [*Sits down on log*] Another drink for confidence.

[*Sings*]

> When I was the Son of the Morning,
> When I was the Prince of Light.

[*He picks up the mask.*]

Oh, to hell with that! You lose a job, you lose a job. Ambition. Yet we were one light once up there, the old man and I, till even today some can't tell us apart.

[*He holds the mask up. Sings.*]

> And so I fell for forty days,
> Passing the stars in the endless pit.

Come here, frog, I'll give you a blessing. [*The Frog hops back, hissing.*] Why do you spit at me? Oh, nobody loves me, nobody loves me. No children of my own, no worries of my own. To hell with . . . [*Stands*] To hell with every stinking one of you, fish, flesh, fowl . . . I had the only love of God once [*Sits*] but I lost that, I lost even that.

[*Sings*]

> Leaning, leaning,
> Leaning on the everlasting arms . . .

To hell with dependence and the second-lieutenancy! I had a host of burnished helmets once, and a forest of soldiery waited on my cough, on my very belch. Firefly, firefly, you have a bit of hell behind you, so light me home. [*Roars at the Creatures*] Get out, get out, all of you . . . Oh, and yet this is fine, this is what they must call despondency, weakness. It's strange, but suddenly the world has

got bright, I can see ahead of me and yet I hope to die. I can make out the leaves, and . . . wait, the boy's coming. Back into the Planter. [*Wears the Planter's mask*]

TI-JEAN.

[*Enters, also with a bottle*] Oh, it's you, you're back late. Had a good dinner?

DEVIL.

You nearly scared me. How long you been hiding there?

TI-JEAN.

Oh, I just came through. Drunk as a fish.

DEVIL.

Finished the work?

TI-JEAN.

Yes, sir. All you told me. Cleaned the silver, made up the fifty rooms, skinned and ate curried goat for supper, and I had quite a bit of the wine.

DEVIL.

Somehow I like you, little man. You have courage. Your brothers had it too, but you are somehow different. Curried goat? . . .

TI-JEAN.

They began by doing what you suggested. Dangerous. So naturally when the whole thing tired them, they got angry with themselves. The one way to annoy you is rank disobedience. Curried goat, yes.

DEVIL.

We'll discuss all that in the morning. I'm a little drunk, and I am particularly tired. A nice bathtub of coals, and a pair of cool sheets, and sleep. You win for tonight. Tomorrow I'll think of something. Show me the way to go home.

TI-JEAN.

[*His arms around the Devil*]

> Oh, show me the way to go home,
> I'm tired and I want to go to bed,
> I had a little drink half an hour ago . . .

DEVIL.

[*Removing his arm*] Wait a minute, wait a minute . . . I don't smell liquor on you. What were you drinking?

TI-JEAN.

Wine, wine. You know, suspicion will be the end of you. That's why you don't have friends.

DEVIL.

You have a fine brain to be drunk. Listen, I'll help you. You must have a vice, just whisper it in my ear and I won't tell the old fellow with the big notebook.

TI-JEAN.

[*Holds up bottle*] This is my weakness. Got another drink in there?

DEVIL.

[*Passing the bottle*] This is powerful stuff, friend, liquid brimstone. May I call you friend?

TI-JEAN.

You may, you may. I have pity for all power. That's why I

love the old man with the windy beard. He never wastes it. He could finish you off, like that . . .

DEVIL.

Let's not argue religion, son. Politics and religion . . . You know, I'll confess to you. You nearly had me vexed several times today.

TI-JEAN.

How did my two brothers taste?

DEVIL.

Oh, let's forget it! Tonight we're all friends. It gets dull in that big house. Sometimes I wish I couldn't have everything I wanted. He spoiled me, you know, when I was his bright, starry lieutenant. Gave me everything I desired. I was God's spoiled son. Result: ingratitude. But he had it coming to him. Drink deep, boy, and let's take a rest from argument. Sleep, that's what I want, a nice clean bed. Tired as hell. Tired as hell. And I'm getting what I suspect is a hell of a headache. [A blaze lightens the wood] I think I'll be going up to the house. Why don't you come in, it's damp and cold out here. It's got suddenly bright. Is that fire?

TI-JEAN.

Looks like fire, yes.

DEVIL.

What do you think it is, friend?

TI-JEAN.

I think it's your house.

DEVIL.

I don't quite understand . . .

TI-JEAN.

Sit down. Have a drink. In fact, I'm pretty certain it's your home. I left a few things on fire in it.

DEVIL.

It's the only house I had, boy.

TI-JEAN.

My mother had three sons, she didn't get vexed. Why not smile and take a drink like a man?

DEVIL.

[Removing the Planter's mask]

What the hell do you think I care about your mother? The poor withered fool who thinks it's holy to be poor, who scraped her knees to the knuckle praying to an old beard that's been deaf since noise began? Or your two damned fools of brothers, the man of strength and the rhetorician? Come! Filambo! Azaz! Cacarat! You've burnt property that belongs to me.

[Assistant Devils appear and surround Ti-Jean.]

TI-JEAN.

You're not smiling, friend.

DEVIL.

Smiling? You expect me to smile? Listen to him! [The

Devils laugh] You share my liquor, eat out my 'fridge, treat you like a guest, tell you my troubles. I invite you to my house and you burn it!

TI-JEAN.

[Sings]

Who with the Devil tries to play fair,
Weaves the net of his own despair.
    Oh, smile; what's a house between drunkards?

DEVIL.

I've been watching you, you little nowhere nigger! You little squirt, you hackneyed cough between two immortalities, who do you think you are? You're dirt, and that's where you'll be when I'm finished with you. Burn my house, my receipts, all my papers, all my bloody triumphs.

TI-JEAN.

[To the Devils]

Does your master sound vexed to you?

DEVIL.

Seize him!

[The Bolom enters and stands between Ti-Jean and the Devil.]

BOLOM.

Master, be fair!

DEVIL.

He who would with the devil play fair,
Weaves the net of his own despair.
This shall be a magnificent ending:
A supper cooked by lightning and thunder.

[Raises fork]

MOTHER.

[In a white light in the hut]

Have mercy on my son,
Protect him from fear,
Protect him from despair,
And if he must die,
Let him die as a man,
Even as your Own Son
Fought the Devil and died.

DEVIL.

I never keep bargains. Now, tell me, you little fool, if you aren't afraid.

TI-JEAN.

I'm as scared as Christ.

DEVIL.

Burnt my house, poisoned the devotion of my servants, small things all of them, dependent on me.

TI-JEAN.
You must now keep
Your part of the bargain.
You must restore
My brothers to life.

DEVIL.
What a waste, you know yourself
I can never be destroyed.
They are dead. Dead, look!

[*The Brothers pass.*]

There are your two brothers,
In the agony where I put them,
One moaning from weakness,
Turning a mill-wheel
For the rest of his life,
The other blind as a bat,
Shrieking in doubt.

[*The two Brothers pass behind a red curtain of flame.*]

TI-JEAN.
O God.

DEVIL.
[*Laughing*] Seize him! Throw him into the fire.

TI-JEAN.
[*With a child's cry*] Mama!

DEVIL.
She can't hear you, boy.

TI-JEAN.
Well, then, you pay her what you owe me!
I make you laugh, and I make you vex,
That was the bet. You have to play fair.

DEVIL.
Who with the devil tries to play fair . . .

TI-JEAN.
[*Angrily*] I say you vex and you lose, man! Gimme me money!

DEVIL.
Go back, Bolom!

BOLOM.
Yes, he seems vexed,
But he shrieked with delight
When a mother strangled me
Before the world light.

DEVIL.
Be grateful, you would have amounted to nothing, child, a man. You would have suffered and returned to dirt.

BOLOM.
No, I would have known life, rain on my skin, sunlight on my forehead. Master, you have lost. Pay him! Reward him!

DEVIL.
For cruelty's sake I could wish you were born. Very well then, Ti-Jean. Look there, towards the hut, what do you see?

TI-JEAN.
I see my mother sleeping.

DEVIL.
And look down at your feet,
Falling here, like leaves,
What do you see? Filling this vessel?

TI-JEAN.
The shower of sovereigns,
Just as you promised me.
But something is wrong.
Since when you play fair?

BOLOM.
Look, look, there in the hut,
Look there, Ti-Jean, the walls,
The walls are glowing with gold.
Ti-Jean, you can't see it?
You have won, you have won!

TI-JEAN.
It is only the golden
Light of the sun, on
My mother asleep.

[*Light comes up on the hut.*]

DEVIL.
Not asleep, but dying, Ti-Jean.
But don't blame me for that!

TI-JEAN.
Mama!

DEVIL.
She cannot hear you, child.
Now, can you still sing?

FROG.
Sing, Ti-Jean, sing!
Show him you could win!
Show him what a man is!
Sing Ti-Jean . . . Listen,
All around you, nature
Still singing. The frog's
Croak doesn't stop for the dead;
The cricket is still merry,
The bird still plays its flute,
Every dawn, little Ti-Jean . . .

TI-JEAN.

[*Sings, at first falteringly*]

To the door of breath you gave the key,
Thank you, Lord,
The door is open, and I step free,
Amen, Lord . . .
Cloud after cloud like a silver stair
My lost ones waiting to greet me there
With their silent faces, and starlit hair
Amen, Lord.

[*Weeps*]

DEVIL.

What is this cooling my face, washing it like a
Wind of morning. Tears! Tears! Then is this the
Magnificence I have heard of, of
Man, the chink in his armour, the destruction of the
Self? Is this the strange, strange wonder that is
Sorrow? You have earned your gift, Ti-Jean, ask!

BOLOM.

Ask him for my life!
O God, I want all this
To happen to me!

TI-JEAN.

Is life you want, child?
You don't see what it bring?

BOLOM.

Yes, yes, Ti-Jean, life!

TI-JEAN.

Don't blame me when you suffering,
When you lose everything,
And when the time come
To put two cold coins
On your eyes. Sir, can you give him life.

DEVIL.

Just look!

BOLOM.

[Being born]

I am born, I shall die! I am born, I shall die!
O the wonder, and pride of it! I shall be man!
Ti-Jean, my brother!

DEVIL.

Farewell, little fool! Come, then,
Stretch your wings and soar, pass over the fields
Like the last shadow of night, imps, devils, bats,
Eazaz, Beelzebub, Cacarat, soar! Quick, quick the sun!
We shall meet again, Ti-Jean. You, and your new brother!
The features will change, but the fight is still on.

[Exeunt]

TI-JEAN.

Come then, little brother. And you, little creatures.
Ti-Jean must go on. Here's a bundle of sticks that
Old wisdom has forgotten. Together they are strong,

Apart, they are all rotten.
God look after the wise, and look after the strong,
But the fool in his folly will always live long.

[Sings]

Sunday morning I went to the chapel
Ring down below!
I met the devil with the book and the Bible.
Ring down below!
Ask him what he will have for dinner.

CHORUS.

Ring down below!

TI-JEAN.

Cricket leg and a frog with water.

CHORUS.

Ring down below!

TI-JEAN.

I leaving home and I have one mission!

CHORUS.

Ring down below!

TI-JEAN.

You come to me by your own decision.

CHORUS.

Ring down below!

TI-JEAN.

Down in hell you await your vision.

CHORUS.

Ring down below!

TI-JEAN.

I go bring down, bring down Goliath.

CHORUS.

Bring down below!

[Exeunt. The Creatures gather as before.]

FROG.

And so it was that Ti-Jean, a fool like all heroes, passed
through the tangled opinions of this life, loosening the
rotting faggots of knowledge from old men to bear them
safely on his shoulder, brother met brother on his way,
that God made him the clarity of the moon to lighten the
doubt of all travellers through the shadowy wood of life.
And bird, the rain is over, the moon is rising through the
leaves. Messieurs, creek. Crack.

CENTER STAGE THE TRINIDAD CARNIVAL

You got the great big long wall in China,
And in India the Taj Mahal,
I know the greatest wonder of them all
Is my Trinidad Carnival.

Though perhaps not as famous as Mardi Gras in Rio de Janeiro or New Orleans, Carnival in Trinidad, extolled here in the Mighty Douglas's calypso song, has been called "undoubtedly the greatest annual theatrical spectacle of all time"

(Erroll Hill, *The Trinidad Carnival*, 1972). Annually over 100,000 people appear in striking masquerades, street dances, and stage shows during the week before Lent. Most Christian societies enjoy some form of pre-Lenten "carnival," most of which are derived from pagan rites such as the Roman Saturnalia. Carnival is a period of indulgent merrymaking in which costumed revelers take to the streets to sing, dance, mime, perform, eat, drink, and carouse

before entering into a somber period of abstinence for 40 days. *Carnival* comes from a Latin phrase—*carne vale*—which means "flesh farewell," a bittersweet reminder that both eating meat and indulging in the pleasures of the flesh are forbidden for six weeks.

The essence of Carnival is role reversal; that is, a celebration of chaos in which normality is suspended for a few days. Streets conveying people to the workplace are sealed off and overrun

Spectacular costumes, perhaps derived from African masquerades, are one of the hallmarks of Trinidad-Tobago's pre-Lenten Carnival. Here we see Peter Samuels as king of the band "Papillon" in a costume, designed by Peter Minshell, titled "The Sacred and the Profane."

with merrymakers whose thoughts are far from the workaday world. Men dress as animals or women; the poor caricature the wealthy. Rationality, conventionality, and restraint give way to indulgence, fantasy, and play. The comic spirit reigns, as evidenced by the cartoonlike costumes, headpieces, and masks, the frenetic dancing, the bawdy and sensual music, the satiric plays improvised on makeshift stages and under tents. Ash Wednesday is the time for solemnity and reflection, but on Mardi Gras ("Fat Tuesday") there is only time for giving oneself to the spirit of Carnival.

Carnival in Trinidad is a fascinating hybrid of many cultures and ideologies: pagan and Christian, European and African, Indian and Spanish, Western and Eastern, ancient and modern, poor and wealthy. Trinidad dates the beginnings of its Carnival to 1783 and the arrival of French planters with their African slaves. Early Carnivals had a racist tone as the plantation owners imitated the dress and manners of the slaves and danced traditional African dances such as the *bamboula* and the *ghouba*. This typifies the "role reversal" aspect so prominent in Carnival. Today, Carnival has a more salutary effect on the twin-island nation of Trinidad-Tobago: the ethnic and social divisions in this multiracial culture are united in a common will to make each new carnival the greatest ever.

Trinidad's slaves were emancipated on August 1, 1834, an event which forever made Carnival a symbol of freedom for the masses. It was never again a plaything for the elite as it became a celebration of deliverance. Not surprisingly, many popular costumes are comic reminders of the days of oppression: Moco Jumbie, a cult figure found throughout West Africa, dances atop 10-to-15-foot stilts, wearing an Eton coat and lord admiral's hat to parody the European oppressor. Each Carnival begins with a *canboulay*, a military march mocking the imperial guards that subjugated the slaves. There is clearly a political dimension to this great Carnival that transcends its roots. *Ti-Jean and His Brothers* contains a song taken from the old *canboulay* as it merges the spirit of Carnival with contemporary political issues.

Masquerades were once used to channel the dead into the souls of the living, but modern masquerades mirror societal concerns. A grand masquerade, dating back to 1866, dominates the final two days of the festival. The maskers are transformed into possessed spirits on "the glorious Monday morning" that begins the masquerade. At dawn, act 1 begins; it is the *jouvay* (from a Creole expression, "Is it daybreak?") in which characters from island folklore are brought to life. Many are demonic (the *diablesse*); others are satiric, such as the popular Dame Lorraine, a "fashionable lady" played by a man in gaudy female dress, an example of the cross-dressing phenomenon throughout world theater. The masqueraders typify the spirit of mockery and misrule permeating Carnival. Act 2 presents traditional masks such as the Wild Indian, the Clowns, Midnight Robbers, and others that are often portrayed for generations within a single family. The third act introduces the big bands for which the island is famous. Act 4 is devoted to historical pageantry, a blend of past events, fantasy, and imagination in which islanders imitate world leaders and conquering heroes. At dusk on Tuesday, the final act brings together the various performers and—very importantly—the spectators in an enormous, spontaneous street dance, songfest, and mimed combat.

Drum dance competitions are held in bamboo huts built especially for Carnival. A masquerade king and queen in extravagant regalia preside over the dance competitions. A coronation ceremony is among the first orders of business; a *borokit* (from the Spanish *borriquito*, "little donkey"), that is, a comic horse's costume, is placed on the king, who then dances around the room carrying a wooden sword. He is accompanied by his queen, always a male in drag, who begs money to finance the spectacle. Shortly before midnight on Fat Tuesday, the masquerade concludes with a mock execution of the king of Carnival. The execution is accompanied by a chant as old as time:

And every year we dance and sing,
And every year we kill the king,
Because the old king must be slain
For the new king to rise again.

A contemporary production of the Rabinal Achí, *performed at the Palace of Fine Arts in Mexico City, suggests the ritual nature of the sole surviving drama from pre-Columbian Mesoamerica.*

CHAPTER 9

THE THEATER OF LATIN AMERICA

The Development of Latin American Theater

As the discussion of Caribbean theater suggested, when Columbus and subsequent Spanish explorers came to the Americas at the end of the fifteenth century, they found the indigenous peoples of both the islands and the mainland of Central and South America performing religious rites (*areítos*) that were distinctly theatrical in their use of song, dance, costumes, and gesture. The Incas of Perú, the Central American Maya, whose rituals are described in the accompanying Center Stage essay, and the Aztecs of Mexico were especially noted for their spectacular rituals, which often included blood sacrifice, an issue in *The Divine Narcissus*. Bloodletting was not a barbarous act, as is often assumed; rather, it was a deeply religious rite in which blood—the life force of the Aztec world—was returned to the gods from whence it came. Even after the Spanish conquered the indigenous peoples, missionary priests transformed native rituals as a means of converting the people to Christianity. In 1509, for instance, María de Toledo used simple dialogues (*elogas*) to educate the people of Santo Domingo; such practices could be found throughout Latin America. In 1526 a series of liturgical plays were performed in Mexico City in conjunction with the Feast of Corpus Christi; the actors were Indians who no doubt drew on their preconquest experiences to color the Christian plays.

Professional acting companies and playwrights accompanied the Spanish explorers; Tirso de Molina, one of the patriarchs of the Spanish secular theater, was such an artist. By the 1520s temporary theaters had been established in Lima, Perú, although the first permanent theater was not built there for another 300 years. Mexico City actually enjoyed a permanent, roofed theater (the *Coloseo*) as early as 1627. Most of the early drama was, as might be expected, based on traditional Spanish models: the *autos sacramentales* (see the discussion of *Life's a Dream* in Chapter 4), *comedias* (a generic term for nonliturgical plays), and *entremeses* (short comedies). Among the early dramatists of note in Latin America were Juan Pérez Ramírez (1545? –?), a priest born in Mexico who wrote a play aptly entitled *The Spiritual Wedding Between the Shepherd Peter and the Mexican Church* (1574); Juan Ruiz de Alarcón (1580–1639), who was born in Mexico but made his reputation in Spain; and Juan de Espinosa Medrano (1639–1688), a Peruvian who wrote "realistic" dramas in Quechua, a native dialect.

The most significant "New World" playwright, however, was a Catholic nun, Sor Juana Inés de la Cruz, whose play *The Divine Narcissus* remains the first true conquest drama of Latin America. If there is a distinctive feature to the drama of Central and South America, both older and contemporary, it may be found in the tension between the Eurocentric (specifically Spanish) tradition and the quest for a national identity. Each of the plays included in this anthology exhibits this central preoccupation of Latin American drama.

Most Spanish-American drama in the eighteenth century was modeled after contemporary Spanish plays and particularly the Neoclassic plays of France, which had established itself as an international leader in the arts. Because Spain was embroiled in censorship issues, the French models gained popularity. Pedro de Peralta Barnuevo (1664–1743), a Peruvian, patterned his topical satires after Molière and his serious works after Pierre Corneille. Still, there was some attempt to establish a national identity: Another Peruvian, Fray Francisco del Castillo (1716–1770) wrote *El charro* (*The Cowboy*), a satire on country life in the foothills of the Andes. *Love and the Ranch Girl* (c. 1790), by Juan Batista Marciel, used regional dialects to depict the tensions among natives and immigrants; it is the antecedent of the *gaucho* dramas that would proliferate in Argentina throughout the nineteenth century. Indeed, Latin American theater was—and still is—marked by a fervent populist tradition (see Spotlight box: Popular Theater in Latin America).

Nineteenth-century drama largely reflected the influence of European Romantic drama, especially in its call for the overthrow of monarchies. On September 16, 1810, no less than eight Latin American countries declared their independence from Spain; Mexico was among these and still celebrates the day (*Fiesta Patrias*) with street celebrations marked by "*El Grito*"—the exuberant "shout" of liberation. Mexico's best-known Romantic dramatists were Ignacio Rodríguez Galván (1816–1842) and Fernando Calderón (1809–1845), whose sensational melodramas are in the tradition of Victor Hugo's *Hernani* (see Chapter 5). South American dramatists—Peru's Felipe Pardo y Aliaga (1806–1868) and Chile's Daniel Barros Grez (1834–1904)—also followed the European models but did attempt to incorporate regional customs and colloquial speech in their social comedies.

With the advent of social realism in Europe, Latin American dramatists turned to more socially relevant drama. Mexico's Jose Peon y Contreras (1843–1907), like Chekhov a physician, wrote often-violent dramas in a quasirealistic mode. As in Europe and the United States, the growth of the modern Latin American theater took place largely in small theaters that experimented with form and content, uninhibited by commercial concerns. Argentina and Uruguay, which share the Rio de Plata as a common border (hence the term "Plata drama"), were among the most important centers of experimental "independent" theaters (see the discussion of such theaters in the Spotlight box, South Africa's Market Theater and the Independent Theater Phenomenon, in Chapter 8). Uruguay's most noted playwright, Florencio Sánchez, became a dominant voice in the independent theater movement and did much to advance social realism in his dramas, as did the Argentines Martiniano Leguizamón (1858–1935) and Nicolás Granada (1840–1915). Their work is comparable in style and historical importance to that of Ibsen, Shaw, O'Neill, and other early realists in Europe and the United States.

Universities and training schools also played an integral role in the development of a vibrant, literary theater throughout Mexico and South America. In Mexico a group of seven young dramatists, led by Celestino Gorostiza (1904–1966), founded an experimental company, Ulysses, which became Orientation in 1932. It was financed by the Mexican government and housed in an actor-training academy. Its importance to the development of contemporary Mexican drama is comparable to that of the Provincetown Playhouse in New York in 1915. Out of this enterprise came Mexico's dominant playwrights of the early twentieth century: Xavier Villarrutia (1903–1950) and especially Rudolfo Usigli. Villarrutia's *Invitation to Death* (1940) is sometimes called "the Mexican *Hamlet*," and Usigli's best work, *Crown of Dreams* (1943), is a multilayered historical drama about the Emperor Maximilian and Carlota in the waning years of European colonialism.

In 1941 Chile saw the birth of Teatro Experimental at the University of Chile in Santiago, which blended the European avant-garde with Chilean social concerns. Other significant university theaters—all of which promoted the growth of a national drama within their respective countries—could be found in Argentina, Uruguay, and Mexico (especially at the Autonomous University of Mexico, the world's largest university, where Elena Garro saw some of the earliest productions of her plays; see *A Solid Home*).

The dramas that evolved from the experimental independent and university theaters mix exceptional theatricality and a variety of styles. A term often used to describe the theatrical work of Latin America is *magic realism*, a fantastical blend of realism, surrealism, and other styles to heighten daily reality. Elena Garro's *A Solid Home* uses magic realism to take us into the world of the dead. Baz Lurhman's 1996 film version of *Romeo and Juliet* uses magic realism in its rendering of the famous tomb scene. The current generation of stage directors throughout the West has become noticeably enamored with magic realism.

Not all of the most significant theatrical activity in Central and South America occurs in formal theaters (however experimental), nor does it rely on traditionally scripted plays. Some of the most compelling theater may be found in the open spaces, meeting halls, and churches of villages, where traveling social activist theater companies interview locals about topical issues and create a short play that illustrates a problem. Townspeople contribute to the development of the play and—more importantly—suggest possible solutions to the problems. The Brazilian Agusto Boal, who began his theatrical career by staging irreverent comedies in colloquial speech in the 1950s, has developed techniques that actively involve the poor and powerless throughout South America; "the theater of the oppressed" (as he has named his collective work) has been influential artistically and politically throughout the Americas. Columbia's Enrique Buenaventura heads a similar enterprise, in which he merges Brechtian dialectics with local folklore. Because he appeals to all classes in his search for a truly inclusive drama, Buenaventura, an actor, director, playwright, and collective creator, stands at the very core of the contemporary populist theatrical movement in Latin America. Jack Warner, a Jesuit priest in Guatemala, formed a touring company modeled after Luis Valdez's El Teatro Campesino (see *No saco nada de la escuela*) that brings theater to the workers on the banana plantations to educate them about their political rights as well as their Mayan heritage.

Much of Latin America has, unfortunately, been subjected to tumultuous political episodes marked by military dictatorships, abductions, human rights violations, and repression of free speech. This sad history has affected theatrical activity, both positively and negatively. For instance, in Argentina, among the most troubled countries, Osvaldo Dragún, an outstanding playwright and director, founded Teatro Abierto (Open Theater) in the 1980s to introduce original dramatic works emphasizing the themes of political decay and economic devastation. The government tried to silence the theater by torching it during a theater festival. Similar events occurred in Mexico and Chile. CLETA (the Free Center for Artistic and Theatrical Expression) was founded in the late 1970s in Mexico City (and moved into the provinces) to address social, political, and religious repression, especially among the indigenous peoples of Mexico. One of its founders, Luis Cisneros, was kidnapped by government agents and held hostage for several months. In Chile, which suffered under the Pinochet government (see the introduction to *Paper Flowers* below), many artists fled to Europe and America. When they returned after the overthrow of the dictator, they brought with them a strong sense of the new experimental theater in Central and Eastern Europe, which enriched Chile's already adventurous drama.

In the mid–twentieth century many fine playwrights emerged from Central and South America, and such acclaimed Western theaters as the Royal Shakespeare Company and the New York Public Theater often perform their works. Among the best of these, by country, are:

Mexico: Emilio Carballido (1925–) and Luisa Josefina Hernandez (1928–)
Argentina: Griselda Gambaro (1928–)
Uruguay: Carlos Maggi (1922–)
Chile: Egon Wolff (1926– ; see *Paper Flowers*) and Alejandro Sieveking (1934–)
Venezuela: Román Chalbaud (1924–) and Isaac Chocrón (1932–)

Unfortunately, Latin American theater is still a relatively unknown entity; most current theater history texts pay scant attention to the drama of this important region. As the region becomes more independent of its colonial past and its social, political, and economic problems, its rich theatrical history and imaginative drama will surely be investigated with the same enthusiasm now afforded the theaters of Asia and Africa.

LATIN AMERICA

Artistic and Cultural Events

1300:
Tlatzaque act in religious celebrations; *Popul Vuh; Rabinal Achí*

1492:
Spanish observe *areítos* (rites)

1509:
Maria de Toledo uses *elogas* to educate indigenous people in Santo Domingo

c. 1525:
Professional acting troupes in Lima, Peru

1598:
Spanish soldiers perform *comedias* near El Paso, Texas

1690:
Sor Juana Inés de la Cruz' *The Divine Narcissus*

1820:
First permanent theater in Chile

1840s:
Gaucho drama in Argentina

1854:
Center for Dramatic Authors, Colombia

1925:
Grupo de los Siete Autores, Mexico

1930s:
Independent theater movement in Argentina

1938:
The Comediens of Brazil

1941:
Teatro Experimental de la Universidad de Chile

1943:
Nelson Rodrigues' *Bridal Gown* begins modern theater in Brazil

1950s:
"Generation of 1950," Chile; Enrique Buenaventura's Teatro Experimental de Cali, Colombia

1960:
Augusto Boal's "Theatre of the Oppressed," Brazil

1973:
Free Center of Theatre Arts, Mexico; Grupo Tierra Negra, Costa Rica

Pre-1900 C.E.   1900 C.E.

Historical and Political Events

c.1250–1450:
Classic Maya Civilization

1521:
Cortéz conquers Mexico; begins Spanish conquest

1810:
Eight Latin American countries declare independence from Spain

1916:
Mexican Revolution

1951:
Order of American States

1955:
General Perón overthrown by coup in Argentina

1968:
Student riots and massacre in Mexico City

1973:
Military coup in Chile under General Pinochet

1983:
Democracy restored in Argentina

MEXICO

Mexico City

CUBA

GUATEMALA
EL SALVADOR
COSTA RICA
COLOMBIA

Bogota
Cali
Quito

ECUADOR

PERU

Lima

ATLANTIC
OCEAN

BRAZIL

São Paulo

Rio de Janeiro

PACIFIC
OCEAN

Santiago

C H I L E

ARGENTINA

Buenos Aires

Aztec territory

Mayan territory

Spanish colonialists brought theater to Central and South America. Therefore, it is not surprising that many Latin American theater forms, especially in the southernmost regions of South America, can be traced to Europe. Mexican playwright Octavio Paz calls such forms *mestizo* ("mixed-blood") theater, that is, one in which the rituals and theatrical ceremonies of indigenous peoples such as the Maya and Aztecs have been combined with Spanish drama to create a "mixed" theater with a singular identity. And particularly in Brazil and the Caribbean, the African influence in the theater is strong. However, each of these forms has assumed an identity of its own and reflects the political and cultural realities of the people who attended the theater.

Popular entertainments, of which there are numerous types, have thrived in Latin America, largely because much of the population has not been formally educated. Accordingly, entertainment has been aimed at a working class, much the way Pixérécourt's melodramas catered to the tastes of Parisian laborers. Consider but a few of the many and fascinating entertainments developed in Latin America.

The *Costumbrista*

Costumbrista is a generic term referring to popular entertainments that feature local manners and customs of the common people. Though they were disdained by the upper classes, they thrived among the workers because they portrayed situations and local conflicts of the commoners, and, importantly, because they used colloquial speech. Most *costumbristas* were short and comical, not unlike any number of contemporary sitcoms on television. Each country, indeed regions within a country, developed a unique version of the *costumbrista*, which formed the bases for national theaters throughout the Latin world. By 1915 *costumbristas* became anachronistic to the Latin American public, but collectively they established a foundation on which subsequent theater would be based.

The *Zarzuela*

The *zarzuela*, a type of musical much lighter in tone and spirit than the opera, evolved in Spain during the seventeenth century. Drawing on the older *entremeses* (interludes) and *sainetes* (short farces), both of which had musical passages, Pedro Calderón developed these short, mostly comic playlets based on classical myths. Calderón began writing *zarzuelas* about 1652 at the request of King Felipe IV, whose royal hunting lodge, La Zarzuela (for the *zarzas*, or brambles, that surrounded it), hosted the first of these musical entertainments. The earliest *zarzuelas* were quite elaborate, akin to the Italian *intermezzi* and English masques. In the 1760s the *zarzuelas* turned to popular culture for subject matter and often reflected the lives of families in the cosmopolitan world of Madrid. By 1787 *zarzuelas* disappeared from the Spanish stage, but were rediscovered in the mid–nineteenth century, when they enjoyed a golden age. Folk music and dance were incorporated into the *zarzuelas*, particularly by Francisco Asenjo Barbieri (1823–1894), who wrote some 60 musicals, including *Pan y toros* [Bread and Bulls (1864)] and *Jugar con fuego* [Playing with Fire (1851)].

The Spanish brought the *zarzuela* to their colonies in Latin America, where *zarzuelas bufas* (comic musicals) and *bailetes* (dance musicals) became popular among immigrants and indigenous peoples, particularly in Mexico. The most notable theatrical event in Mexico City in 1806 was a performance of a musical adaptation (by Paisiello) of the Beamarchais comedy *The Barber of Seville*. Billed as "a comic opera in four acts," the piece was clearly in the *zarzuela* tradition. This opera *con zarzuela* remained popular among the citizens of the capital, and it was repeated with Mexican songs (*sonecitos del pais*). Throughout the Caribbean and South America one can still find both the *zarzuela* proper (a three-act musical) and the *zarzuela chica* (the "little *zarzuela*," or one-act musical), which frequently relies on audience participation.

The *Revista*

Brazil, South America's largest country, has its own rich musical theater tradition that has been influenced by the song, dance, and storytelling of Africa. In 1861 Carlos Gómez (1836–1886) wrote Brazil's first opera, *A noite de castelo* (*A Night in the Castle*), which deals with Brazil's identity as an emerging nation in the Southern Hemisphere. The *revista*, a musical review adorned by expensive and sophisticated costumes and scenery, is Brazil's variant on the *zarzuela*. As Brazilian music has influenced much popular music (especially jazz), the *revista* has had an international impact.

Gaucho Drama

South America developed a dramatic version of the American western, especially in Argentina and Uruguay, where the gaucho ruled the pampas. Like the American cowboy, the gaucho was a romantic symbol of the rugged individual who tamed a harsh land. He also enjoyed an almost mythic status among city dwellers who envied his ability to fly with the wind on his horse. Predictably, a national drama evolved celebrating the gaucho, his love of the land, and his freedom. Whereas the American western glorified men who conquered the frontier, the gaucho drama challenged European conquests and argued for a national identity. Gaucho drama represents the first truly national (i.e., non-Eurocentric) drama in South America in its celebration of the common worker on the pampas.

Fittingly, a former president of Argentina, Domingo Faustino Sarmiento, best defines the mythic appeal of the *gauchesco* character. In 1845 this former miner and bartender wrote *Facundo,* the most eloquent treatise on Argentina's gaucho writing. Of the *gauchesco*, he says:

He is a type that belongs to certain localities, an outlaw, a squatter, a misanthrope. . . . He knows the reality of the desert. His morality is natural . . . justice pursues him always. . . . He is a mysterious character who often roams the Pampas. He partakes of vices, but points his horse in the direction of the desert, without a sense of rush. . . . Sometimes he appears at the door of a country-dance, with a young maiden he has whisked away. Other times, he appears in front of the offended and seduced maiden's parents. This man is divorced from society, a savage in white face. He is not a bandit, nor a highwayman; he's a horseman.

Although Sarmiento sings of his Argentine countrymen, his remarks could apply to the American cowboy, especially those antiheroes popularized in the films of Clint Eastwood.

Immigration Plays

Much of Latin America, like the United States, saw an influx of immigrants from Europe and elsewhere. Though they sought riches and political freedom, they often found hardship and alienation. Among the most poignant immigration plays were the *Cocoliche* dramas of Argentina. In the 1870s the Podestá brothers, who owned a popular circus, added review sketches and variety acts as part of their tent entertainments. Among their most popular skits were those that dealt with a character named Cocoliche, an Italian immigrant who sought a more profitable life in the Americas. Cocoliche was a hard-working, well-intentioned laborer who was also comic, largely because of his linguistic difficulties. The Podestá skits blossomed into full-length plays depicting the misadventures of Cocoliche, whose very name became synonymous with the genre. Though the impulse behind the *Cocoliches* was comedic and escapist, a serious—and political—current nonetheless reflected the unpleasant realities of a changing world.

Similarly, Cuba developed a peculiarly potent form of populist entertainment that reflected social and political realities. Much like the American minstrel show, the *bufo Cubano* (also known as the *bufos Habañeros* after the capital, Havana) featured white performers in blackface to depict the various races that composed Cuba's population. There was the *gallego* (the Spaniard), the *negrito* (the African), and *chinos* or *mulattos* (persons of mixed ethnicity). Although the *bufo Cubano* enjoyed its greatest popularity from about 1869 to 1878, it continued into the twentieth century. Fidel Castro's 1959 revolution was, in part, precipitated by the Cuban people's resentment of the Eurocentrism that created and sustained the *bufo Cubano*.

CENTER STAGE   THEATER IN MESOAMERICA

The complex glyph writings, calendars, and buildings in the Central American jungles of Yucatan, Chiapas, and Guatemala verify the exceptional artistry of the Mayans, among the most intellectual peoples of Mesoamerica. Curiously, however, the Mayans had no word for "art" in their vocabulary because "art" was not an entity separate from other religious or social activities. Mayan art—including theatrical activity—was a functional tool that maintained order and harmony between individuals, within society, and especially between the world and the cosmos. Though enjoyed for its craftsmanship, Mayan art was not merely an object of aesthetic pleasure but a spiritual and social necessity.

A drawing of Huitzilopotli, the god of storms and war, and his temple (with sacred maguey cacti at top right) illustrate a history of the Aztecs written by Spanish conquerors in the sixteenth century. Occident and America worship Huitzilopotli in The Divine Narcissus.

Archaeologists have traced the origins of the Mayan culture to about 2000 B.C.E.; by the first century C.E., the Mayans had developed a variety of rituals performed by the principal social classes: peasants, priests, and nobles. They were bound by a common mythology set forth in the *Popol Vuh* (People's Book), a sacred tome that has been called the Old Testament of the Maya because it details the cosmogony, traditions, and history of the race. It was refined and passed from generation to generation orally or through the sacred glyphs. A version was preserved in the Quiche dialect of the Mayan language in the mid–sixteenth century C.E. Though this text was lost, Francisco Ximenez, a seventeenth-century priest working in Guatemala, transcribed the material when he borrowed a worn copy from one of his parishioners. The *Popol Vuh* is too complex to summarize here, but it glorifies the solar deity worshipped by the people of this warm-weather climate.

The Mayans were an agricultural people who valued harmony between the material and spiritual worlds. The majority of peasants worked as farmers who often achieved a degree of prosperity. Indeed, a recognizable middle class emerged, infusing the Mayan culture with a love of artistry and leisure time. Many Mayan peasants became prolific craftsmen, particularly in the arts, as painters, potters, sculptors, musicians, and *tlaquetzque* (entertainers). The combination of artistry and religious ceremonies in honor of the sun deity—and other Mayan gods—spawned dances, popular entertainment, and rituals inspired by various intoxicants (recall that the Greeks drank wine in their homage to Dionysus). Through documents passed down by the Spanish conquistadors, we know the indigenous peoples had a repertoire of more than a thousand choreographed dances. Likewise, peasant-actors wore spectacular costumes and masks to perform mythical stories to the accompaniment of drums and musical instruments. Just as goats and deer

were imitated in other cultures, the *tlaquetzque* dressed themselves as creatures of this jungle kingdom: ocelots, sacred snakes, and colorful birds.

The principal Mayan dramatic rituals were performed in mid-June when the sun is at its zenith. A fragment from a sixteenth-century Nahuatl manuscript recounts the invention of music at the command of the Tezcatlipoca, the god of heaven and the four quarters of the sky:

Wind the earth is sick from silence.
Though we possess light and color and
*   fruit,*
Yet we have no music.
We must bestow music on all creation.
. . . life should be all music!

The wind dutifully carries out the god's bidding and

Thus music was born on the bosom of
*   the earth.*
Thus did all things learn to sing:
the awakening dawn,
the dreaming man,
the awaiting mother,
the passing water and the flying bird.
Life was all music from then on.

Thus intertwined through the arts, the material world and the spiritual world are rendered inseparable in this great myth.

As evidenced by the glyphs, these rituals—in which the priests were both celebrants and mediators between the people and the orderly, often harsh, universe—were highly theatrical. Notable were the formalized costumes, masks, and especially the stylized physicality of the performers. Furthermore, sacrifices of both animals and humans were central events in the rituals. The Mayan theater space was a pyramid, its stage a stone altar, its people the audience, and the sacrificial offering itself was the sacred performance. To the Mayans, sacrifice was not a barbaric act, but a sacred duty that induced harmony between man and nature, manifestation of the belief that life naturally extended into death and vice versa. "Life," according to the Mexican scholar and writer Octavio Paz, "had no higher function than to flow into death."

Like the dramas of classical Greece, Mayan rituals also assumed a social, as well as spiritual, dimension. The Mayans were a hierarchical society, and the nobles enjoyed privilege, depending upon familial lineage. Again, as evidenced by sculptural works of art, vases, and jade plaques, we see an elaborate pageantry among Mayan nobles who used art as a propagandistic vehicle to explain their social standing within the cosmos. Thus dance rituals, as well as storytelling performances, were common means of asserting one's status. In the fourteenth century a Mayan court, for instance, could easily comprise more than a hundred artists whose sole purpose was to provide music, storytelling, and dance to aggrandize the aristocrat who presided over it. There was spirited competition among the nobles to produce the best artistic work. The artifacts of the so-called Late Classic period (*Chichen Itza*, c. 1250–1400 C.E.) attest to the superiority of Mayan artistry. We may assume that performance also became as sophisticated as other artistry, but theater, alas, is temporal. Performance records are difficult to maintain, and we have virtually no "scripts" and little empirical evidence of Mayan drama. The *Rabinal Achí* remains the single drama from the ancient Mayans.

The Rabinal Achí

The *Rabinal Achí* is a pre-Spanish conquest drama-cum-dance of Aeschylean proportions; it was first transcribed in Guatemala in 1859 from a performance by Indians in a remote village. Like Aeschylus's *Prometheus Bound*, this pageant has to do with bondage, sacrifice, and transgressions by mythical characters chronicled in the *Popol Vuh*. Like so many tragedies, it dramatizes the conflict between fierce pride and the personal responsibility associated

with political power. In short, the unknown storyteller of the *Rabinal Achí* matches Aeschylus in intellectual scope, but he goes beyond Aristotelian dramaturgy to create a mythic, magical world of tragic ecstasy.

Structured like the earliest Greek plays, the *Rabinal Achí* is composed of a series of alternating monologues, which clarify the character's actions, and choric dance sequences, which comment on the action. Its episodic plot dramatizes the religious, philosophical, and idealistic reasons why the Warrior Chief of the Quiché must meet his doom at the sacrificial altar. He has made choices that have affected his people and his captors. For this he must die. Unlike our own Greco-Roman dramatic tradition, which attaches guilt to our "errors in judgment," the Mayan hero's misjudgment displaced a cosmic schema much too difficult to decipher. Thus sacrificial death—and not merely mutilation as in *Oedipus*—was the only way to restore tranquility to the world.

Lamentably, we know little about the performance of the *Rabinal Achí* in the preconquest era. We can only imagine that it was majestic, colorful, and epic in nature. Given the Mayan emphasis on communion with their environment, it could only be satisfactorily played in the outdoors against a backdrop of the universe itself. Its cast was large and splendidly dressed. In addition to the three great warriors (Quiché, Rabinal, and Fifth Rain), the cast consisted of twin choruses of twelve Yellow Eagles and twelve Yellow Jaguars, as well as assorted soldiers, peasants, barons, and priests. Only portions of the text remain, but a sample suggests its majesty. In the epic's final scene, the Quiché Warrior prepares for his sacrificial death by divesting himself of his worldly possessions:

O my gold and silver, my bow and shield, my Toltec mace, my Yaqui axe! You are all that will remain of me! Even my sandals will be left! For here is

what our lord and master will be saying by now: "It is far too long since my valor and courage went hunting the game we like to see upon our table." Our lord and master will be saying that, but he will never guess that I am only waiting my doom here between Heaven and Earth! Alas! . . . If I must die here, oh let me change places with that squirrel or with that bird! They die upon the branches or on the tender grass where they find all their needs.

Mesoamerican theatrical activity was subsumed by European dramaturgy. Spanish priests, for example, used liturgical dramas to convert native peoples, which is perhaps why the Yaqui Easter (see Center Stage box, The Yaqui Easter of the Southwest United States) contains both preconquest and European dramatic elements. Its spirit is kept alive, however, in the late twentieth century by a number of socially conscious, politically active Hispanic-American theater companies. Luis Valdez's El Teatro Campesino is particularly active in this tradition. In 1974 Valdez's company performed *El baile de los gigantes* (*The Dance of the Giants*) in Mexico City. Based on material taken from the *Popol Vuh*, it depicts the gods before the first dawn and the creation of humans. Valdez, who narrated the play, intoned a contemporary version of an Aztec hymn to begin the performance:

Dear god of the sky, we came to this place so that you can concentrate all your energy on this town. We came in the name of justice, in the name of love, in the name of unity, in homage to the Solar Deity.

It is a hymn—like the reenactment of creation that followed it—that would not seem strange to the Greek Thespis or to the Japanese Zeami. It, like the Dionysian dithyramb or Noh chant, speaks to those elemental human concerns that are often realized through acts of theater.

THE DIVINE NARCISSUS
(EL DIVINO NARCISSO)
SOR JUANA INÉS DE LA CRUZ

SOR JUANA INÉS DE LA CRUZ (1648–1695)

Although she has been called "the ornament of her century" and is now recognized as the first significant playwright of the Americas, little was known about Sor Juana Inés de la Cruz until 1947. Guillermo Ramírez España discovered an extraordinary document, a public testimony written by Isabel Ramírez, the mother of Sor Juana. In her testimony, Isabel confirmed that on November 12, 1648, in the village of San Miguel Nepantla, she gave birth to Juana de Asbaje y Ramírez de Santillana. According to Isabel, Juana was the youngest of three daughters born out of wedlock; thus Juana was registered as illegitimate, or as "a daughter of the church." The father was captain Pedro Manuel de Asbaje. Isabel's testament was extraordinary because she openly proclaimed "I am a single woman and I have given birth to my natural children . . . [including] the nun Juana de la Cruz." For a single woman to make such a proclamation in this fiercely Catholic world was a courageous act, but Isabel Ramírez was a courageous and extraordinary woman. When her father died in 1669 Isabel took over the family estate, no easy task on a frontier outpost. Sor Juana was truly her mother's daughter in that she, too, broke new ground in seventeenth-century Spanish America.

Juana was a precocious child who entered school at the age of three. A popular legend says that at the age of six she begged to be sent to the university dressed as a man (women were denied access to the university). She learned Latin at the home of a relative in Mexico City; she is reputed to have mastered the language in a mere 20 lessons. At the age of 17 she became a lady-in-waiting to the Marqueza de Mancera at the palace in Mexico City, but left two years later (1667) to enter the Convento of San José de Carmelitas Descalzas. The marqueza attended the ceremony at which Sor Juana took her sacred vows. Within three months, however, the young nun became gravely ill and left the Carmelites. She later joined the Convento de San Jerónimo, where, among other duties, she was the bookkeeper. At San Jerónimo she began amassing what would become one of the largest personal libraries in the New World; it contained over 4,000 volumes of prose, histories, and scientific works.

Sor Juana became a nun partly because of her devout religious beliefs and—in no small part—because the religious life permitted her to pursue a literary career. Women, especially in post-Inquisition Spain, were not encouraged to write or involve themselves in the arts, but nuns were afforded both the education and the opportunity to write. Though Sor Juana wrote in a variety of dramatic genres, including imitations of the popular *comedias* and *sainetes* (interludes), she always maintained that the writer had an obligation to "study divine knowledge" or risk becoming "a slave to human [i.e., secular] writing." Furthermore, she claimed that a woman had a sacred duty to write for "the greater honor and glory" of her husband, Jesus Christ.

And write she did. As poet and dramatist she produced over 45,000 lines of material. At the age of 15 she wrote a dozen *villancicos* (brief compositions based on sacred writings) which were performed in Puebla and Oaxaca. Combined, they totaled some 5,500 lines of verse, some written in Nahuatl, an indigenous language of Mexico. Her mature work, as typified by *The Divine Narcissus,* reflects this early love of poetry, music, and indigenous material.

Her first dramatic work was *Los empeños de una casa* (*The Zeal of a House,* 1683), which was performed in a private home for the benefit of visiting viceroys. The play was a variant of popular *capa y espada* plays from Spain. Originally "saints plays," the *capa y espada* ("cloak and dagger") evolved into comedies of intrigue. Sor Juana looked to the works of Pedro Calderón de la Barca. Several years later she wrote *Amor es más laberinto* (*Love Is a Great Labyrinth*), which fuses secular and mythological themes. Her interest in mythology can also be seen in *The Divine Narcissus.* While the performance of her plays was limited to gentry in private homes, that in itself is remarkable. Imagine the irony of Spanish noblemen, steeped in a chauvinistic tradition, being entertained by the works of a woman!

In addition to a prolific writing career, Sor Juana performed scientific experiments, yet another manifestation of her curious mind. Unfortunately, by 1691 Mexico was besieged by mutinies, pestilence, and hunger, and Sor Juana abandoned her literary career to care for the dying and the needy. She sold her entire library, a collection of musical instruments, and other personal possessions to buy food and supplies for the suffering. Malnourished and overworked in service of the poor, Sor Juana died in April 1695.

THE DIVINE NARCISSUS (1690)

Sor Juana's short play represents two literary types. Generically, it is composed as an *auto sacramental,* that is, an allegorical drama developed in medieval Spain. Originally *autos* concerned purely theological topics, but they were secularized by Calderón. Historically, the play is the first notable example of "conquest literature," that is, literary material about the conquest of the Americas by the Spanish and other European colonialists. The tension between these two impulses—to convert and to conquer—makes the play remarkable.

On its simplest level, *The Divine Narcissus* recounts the story of the conversion of the indigenous Mexican people, allegorically represented by Occident ("the West") and his wife, America. When we first meet them, Occident and America are worshipping Huitzilopoxtli (HWEE-tlo-POX-lee), the Aztec god of war. Their hymns contain references to human sacrifice to appease the god who "sustains our kingdom and our harvest," a reminder that the theater is linked to ancient rituals. Sor Juana, who apparently learned of these rites from the Spanish conquistadors, is ambivalent about the bloodletting. On one hand, she seems to respect the passion of the indigenous peoples; on the other, her Christian background causes her to recoil at "the cruel sacrifice of humanity."

Her ambivalence is no less pronounced when the "heroes" of the story enter. Religion immediately condemns Zealot, who conquers "with arrogant blindness" and thereby brings disgrace. Throughout the play, Zealot is portrayed as a ruthless, but necessary, accomplice in the forced conversion of America. To achieve his ends Zealot eagerly employs the very tactics he and Religion condemn in the Aztecs: killing. As Religion and Zealot attempt to convert America, Sor Juana skillfully injects fragments of ancient songs to suggest that there is a true zealotry about the indigenous rites that makes that of the Christians pale by comparison. Similar tensions and ironies permeate the play, elevating it above the level of mere polemic.

Though Occident and America ultimately succumb to Religion's arguments (which Sor Juana sanctions by incorporating the words from Paul's Epistles), we remain skeptical of the conversion. This may be due to the 400-year perspective we bring to the play. Disease, exploitation, poverty, and the loss of a people's essential identity were lamentable by-products of Spain's conquest of the indigenous peoples. Yet Sor Juana raised many of these issues even as Spain was entrenching itself on Mexican soil. America's accusation to Religion that "your blindness prevents you from understanding the tranquility which lives within us" becomes an unfortunate prophecy of subsequent events. Accordingly, *The Divine Narcissus* emerges as the first testament of Latin American identity. On one hand, Sor Juana accepts the reality of the conquest, but she also laments that the cultural roots of a great civilization were lost in the quest to "enlighten this hemisphere."

Such issues would be raised again 300 years later, largely in the work of Luis Valdez and his Teatro Campesino. As the Chicano theater movement evolved from purely political issues, it again brought the god Huitzilopoxtli and his brothers to the stage. Near Mexico City in 1974, the Teatro Campesino performed a ritual drama called *El baile de los gigantes* (*The Dance of the Giants*). It recalled the creation—and, sadly, the defeat—of the nation of the *Tenochcas* (i.e., Aztecs), the soul of *"la raza."* How fitting that the play was performed on the very land that prompted Sor Juana to write *The Divine Narcissus*. (See Center Stage box, The Yaqui Easter of the Southwest United States, following the text of *The Divine Narcissus*.)

A 1681 portrait of the poet and playwright Sor Juana Inés de la Cruz, the first notable dramatist of the New World.

THE DIVINE NARCISSUS
(EL DIVINO NARCISSO)

SOR JUANA INÉS DE LA CRUZ

Translated and Adapted by Roberto D. Pomo

PERSONAGES
OCCIDENT
AMERICA
ZEALOT
RELIGION
MUSICIAN
SOLDIERS/AZTEC INDIANS
CHORUS AND DANCERS

SCENE I

(Enter Occident, a stunning and gallant Indian wearing a type of Aztec headpiece with America by his side who is also dressed in splendorous garb. They stare into the audience for a few seconds, then slowly face one another. At the count of five, Occident and America break into a stylized dance. A chorus of male and female Indian dancers

753

Sor Juana Inés de la Cruz

*enter the stage. As the chorus joins in the frantic dance,
Occident and America sit on their stone-like thrones.
They observe as the chorus continues to dance. The character of Music enters. Slowly he crosses down stage,
singing to the audience. Note: the dance should continue
as Music sings to the audience.*

MUSIC.
  Noble Mexicans,
  whose ancient lineage
  created the bright rays
  of the sun,
5 today we are blessed and
  consecrate our lives
  with devotion as we
  celebrate the power of
  the God of Seeds, the mighty
10 Huitzilopoxtli, the God of War!
  To him we owe our abundance.
  He who has sowed our fertile
  provinces,
  we stand devout, we are thankful
15 for the offerings of our first fruits.
  To him we offer our pure blood,
  and through this sacrifice and during
  this great feast, we honor
  Huitzilopoxtli!

OCCIDENT.
20 But, in our fair city,
  amongst so many gods,
  who have witnessed the cruel
  sacrifices of humanity,
  more than two thousand of them;
25 the shedding of blood,
  the pulsated entrails,
  the throbbing heart touching the cold ground;
  I repeat again, among so many gods,
  my attention embodies
30 Huitzilopoxtli.

AMERICA.
  And with due reason,
  for he sustains our kingdom
  and our harvest.
  Our hopes
35 are due to him—
  he who preserves our lives.
  What matters if America is replete
  with gold, if our lands are sterile?
  His protection spreads beyond
40 our corporal sustenance and
  purifies our souls.
  Therefore, let us all
  repeat:
  (*accompanied by music and a choral interlude*)

In this splendorous feast, we praise
Huitzilopoxtli!   45

SCENE II

RELIGION.
  Zealot,
  you
  who suffer the wrath
  of Christianity
  with arrogant blindness,   5
  celebrating idolatry
  and superstitious cults.
  Why bring disgrace to our
  Christian Religion?

ZEALOT.
  Religion, do not   10
  be so swift
  in judging my neglect,
  nor lament my caresses!
  For I shall raise my arm
  and my sword will avenge you!   15
  Stand aside as I
  avenge your
  injuries!

MUSIC.
  In this splendorous feast, we praise
  Huitzilopoxtli!   2

ZEALOT.
  I have arrived!
  All of you may leave!

RELIGION.
  No!
  I wish to speak
  in the hope that my mercy
  will bring peace
  before your wrath   2
  is upon them.

ZEALOT.
  Their bawdy rituals
  becomes them!

MUSIC.
  In this splendorous feast we praise
  Huitzilopoxtli!

RELIGION.
  Mighty and all-powerful
  Occident,
  Rich and beautiful America,
  you who live in misery bathed
  in your own riches,
  leave your profane cults
  which the evil spirits have
  bestowed upon you!

Open your eyes to the
truth!
Feel the warmth of my
love!

OCCIDENT.

45 My eyes do not recognize
you.

AMERICA.

What nations would dare
oppose the laws of our
ancient dominion?

OCCIDENT.

50 You, most beautiful
foreigner . . .
most appealing traveling
maiden . . .
who are you to disrupt
55 our pleasures?

RELIGION.

I am the Christian Religion!
Your domain shall be ours!

OCCIDENT.

Your determination has
charm . . .

AMERICA.

60 And your feigned insanity as well.

OCCIDENT.

A most eloquent trick, indeed!

AMERICA.

Without a doubt, she is insane.
Leave us now! Let us proceed
with our daily affairs.

MUSIC.

65 In this splendorous feast, we praise
Huitzilopoxtli!

ZEALOT.

Barbarous Occident,
in your blind, idolatrous
path,
70 how dare you reject
Religion, My sweet spouse?
Look deep at your iniquities!
Our God can no longer permit your
transgressions!
75 Punishment is His! I am His sword!

OCCIDENT.

Do you think your
countenance intimidates me?

ZEALOT.

I am a Zealot!
And since your excesses
80 lead you to forswear
Religion,
I shall punish your audacity

as His Servant; having seen
the limits of your tyrannical ways
for so very long.
85 His punishment is at hand!
We are His army
amidst steel flashes of lightning!
We are the ministers of His wrath,
the instruments of His rage!
90

OCCIDENT.

What god?
What excesses?
What turpitude
are you hinting at?
95 I do not know who you are!
Nor do I understand your vague
reasoning,
or your bold
assumptions
in not allowing my people
100 to say:

MUSIC.

In this splendorous feast, we praise
Huitzilopoxtli!

AMERICA.

You are a barbarian—
insane!
105 Your blindness prevents
you
from understanding
the tranquillity which
lives
110 within us.
If you refuse
you will be reduced to ashes!
Not even the wind will know of
your
115 whereabouts!
And you, my husband,
together with
your
vassals,
120

(to Occident)

ignore his words
and fantasies.
Let us proceed!

MUSIC.

In this splendorous feast, we praise
Huitzilopoxtli!
125

ZEALOT.

Since our first proposal
was rejected in arrogance,
our second one—war—
you shall heed.

130 TAKE UP ARMS!
THIS IS WAR!!

(Loud electronic sounds denoting trumpets, the clashing of steel swords, distorted cries and shouts)

OCCIDENT.
Why is heaven against me?
What arms are these
that my eyes
135 have never witnessed?
GUARDS!
PREPARE YOUR ARROWS!
SHOOT!!

(The playing space dims to total darkness. The electronic sound becomes almost intolerable in its intensity. From behind the rear scrim, silhouettes in stylized movement denote physical combat. This stylized movement should be choreographed in a ritualistic dance pattern. After a few seconds, total darkness again, followed by a shower of lightning effects.)

AMERICA.
Why is this lightning persecuting me?
140 These leaded pellets?
These monstrous centaurs running against my people?
WAR! WAR!
LONG LIVE THE KING!
LONG LIVE SPAIN!
145 FOR EVER AND EVER!

(Low intensity lighting from behind the scrim. The Indians retreat followed by the Spanish army.)

SCENE III

RELIGION.
Yield! Give up!
OCCIDENT.
Your brute strength, not your reason
compels me to do so.
ZEALOT.
Die, insolent America!
RELIGION.
5 Wait! She's needed alive!
ZEALOT.
Why defend her now
when she was so offensive?
RELIGION.
Your valor defeated her,
but my mercy
10 will preserve her life.
You win in strength; I
with reason and gentle
persuasion.

ZEALOT.
But you abhor her
wantonness? 15
Is it not best that they
should perish?
RELIGION.
Halt your sense of
justice!
I do not wish for them 20
to die, but only to be reformed
in eternal life.
AMERICA.
If you do not wish
for me to perish—
in your compassionate 25
guise—
then
will you try to defeat me
corporally
as well as 30
intellectually?
No, you're mistaken!
Even though I lament
my
freedom, 35
my
free will,
I shall always
worship
my deities! 40
OCCIDENT.
I am obliged to render
to your brute force,
but,
even in captivity, you will
never prevent me from 45
expressing,
that in here, *(pointing to his heart)*
I will always
praise,
honor, and 50
adore
Huitzilopoxtli!

SCENE IV

RELIGION.
What is this god that you honor so?
OCCIDENT.
A god of abundance,
a god who enriches our soil,
a god who gives us nourishment and fruits.
Even mother wind obeys our god— 5

he who cleanses our souls of sin.
Our god is everything!
I have said enough.

RELIGION.

(*as an aside*)
Bless me, my dear God!
What is this description?
This imitation?
This figure
who is not Thee?
What are these lies?
Oh, you fowl serpent,
whose seven mouths spill
venom!
My dear God, allow me
to speak in Your
Truth!

AMERICA.

What is this uncertainty
you imagine?
Have you ever met a god
who can confirm his
so-called deeds?

RELIGION.

It is with the doctrine of
Paul that I will speak
the truth—
just as he spoke to the
Athenians when
he warned them
against the worship of new gods.
It was Paul who uttered:
"It is not a new deity you are
seeking, but rather a voice
you have not yet heard."
And this is my quest!
Occident, hear me,
and hear me well!
My message will lead you
to eternal happiness!
These miracles you speak of—
these marvels you indicate—
these pretenses clouded
by a shield of superstition—
they are nothing but illusion.
If the ground is fertile
and the earth fruitful,
if the fields are sown
and the rain plentiful,
it is God
who provides!
For it matters not
the arms that till—
or the drops of rain
that fertilize—

or the warmth that
livens vegetation.
Without God and
His providence,
we are alone.

AMERICA.

If this is the case,
tell me:
would my hands
be able to touch
this
Deity?

RELIGION.

Although
His Divine Being is
immense and invisible,
He remains near to
our human nature, and only through
the unworthy hands of a priest
may He be touched.

AMERICA.

I agree with
your words. For no one
but the priests that serve
him
may touch our God nor enter
His temple.

ZEALOT.

Oh, how
you pretend
to know the
truth!

OCCIDENT.

In your burst of eloquence,
tell me.
Will this God of
rare substance
keep you,
sustain you—as
Huitzilopoxtli?

RELIGION.

I have warned you
that His incorporeal and infinite Majesty,
His blessed Being,
is always present within us
in the offering of the mass.
In the altar of the cross,
His pure and innocent blood
redeems our world.

AMERICA.

If I were to believe these
marvelous things;
is this loving Deity
capable of nourishing
our needs?

SCENE V

RELIGION.
105   Yes.
    Infinite wisdom among men
    is His ultimate plan.

AMERICA.
    I wish to see this
    Deity! Then, I
110   will believe!

OCCIDENT.
    So that once and for all
    you may abandon your
    beliefs.

RELIGION.
    Yes. And
115   you will be
    cleansed by the pure
    waters of
    baptism.

OCCIDENT.
120   For I know
    that before I kneel at
    His communion table,
    I must cleanse myself.
    This has been our ancient custom.

ZEALOT.
    Your deeds
125   do not need to be cleansed in
    that manner!

OCCIDENT.
    How then?

RELIGION.
    Only the sacrament
    of baptism will
130   wash away your sins!

AMERICA.
    As I hear your words,
    I am still lost, but
    my spirit is moved by some
    divine inspiration.

OCCIDENT.
135   I am moved as well! For
    I know that through
    His life and death—
    can knowledge be gained.

RELIGION.
    Let us go then.
140   I know your beliefs
    are metaphorical, coated
    in colorful rhetoric.
    But knowing that you seek
    tangible evidence more than
145   faith, your eyes must believe.

OCCIDENT.
    Yes. More than words,
    I must see it before my eyes.

RELIGION.
    Let us go, then.

ZEALOT.
    Tell me, Religion,
    how will you prove
    all this?

RELIGION.
    Through an allegorical play,
    these things will be shown
    to America and Occident
    so that they may believe.

ZEALOT.
    And what is the title
    of this allegorical play?

RELIGION.
    The Divine Narcissus,
    because this unhappy being
    had an idol that he worshipped—
    who pretended to partake
    of the sacrament of the Holy
    Communion. A being who
    impressed the gentiles
    with false signs.

ZEALOT.
    And where will you stage this play?

RELIGION.
    In the great seat of Madrid—
    the center of faith.
    Where the Catholic Kings
    imparted light and truth
    to the Indians and the Occident.

ZEALOT.
    Do you not think it
    inappropriate that
    a play written in Mexico
    be staged in Madrid?

RELIGION.
    It must be done to
    accomplish what
    is needed.
    It does not matter if the
    play is coarse and without
    polish, as long as it
    serves the purpose.

ZEALOT.
    Then tell me, Religion,
    how may you
    overcome the beliefs
    of these Indians?
    How can you take them to
    Madrid?

RELIGION.
    They will see

personages in the abstract,
whose words will be
45   heard.
And they will not recant,
not even if they are taken
to Madrid!
No form of intelligence,
50   or the giant seas
will prevent the truth
from being heard!

ZEALOT.
Knowing now the meaning
of the truth, both worlds must
55   kneel and implore forgiveness!

RELIGION.
And His divine enlightenment—

AMERICA.
whose supreme ground
caresses the humble Indian—

ZEALOT.
whose final counsel—

RELIGION.
60   enlightens this hemisphere—

AMERICA.
In all humbleness

we ask to be forgiven
for wanting a sign to be the Truth.

OCCIDENT.
Let us depart!
In my own agony, I
65   wish to know the Lord
who will give me
nourishment!

(*America, Occident and Zealot sing the following lines*)

Now that our indigenous pasts
have acquired faith in
70   the God of Seeds—
with joy, soft tears,
and festive voices—
we proclaim:

(*All*)

Blessed be the day
75   when we found
our Lord!

(*All exit in song and dance.*)

CENTER STAGE   THE YAQUI EASTER OF THE SOUTHWEST UNITED STATES

The rites of Native Americans merge with those of European Christians in the southwestern United States each Easter, a religious feast day that marks the triumph of life over death in the commemoration of the Resurrection of Christ. This Easter rite of the Yaqui Indians of southern Arizona is nearer than most ceremonies of Native Americans to formal theater and drama, perhaps because it is akin to medieval Passion plays about Christ's death. Jesuit priests who came to the region in 1617 at the invitation of the Yaqui not only brought religion to the indigenous peoples, but evidence suggests they also brought their knowledge of popular theater such as the Italian *commedia dell'arte*. The clowning *Chapayekas*, wearing grotesque masks as they mock Christian rites, are central players in the Yaqui Easter drama; their antics are similar in spirit and technique to the *zannis* of the *commedia*. These are contrasted with the sacred *Matachinis* ("the little angels"), whose mimetic dances attempt to drive away the *Fariseos*, the hypocritical Pharisees of the Bible. Thus the Yaqui Easter ritual is both a cosmic and a religious battle between virtues and vices, not unlike the medieval morality plays or the dance dramas of Asia. It is also comparable to *The Divine Narcissus*, Sor Juana's play about the conflict between indigenous and European rituals and theology.

The most compelling figure in this drama is the ancient, pagan Deer, which is danced by the most privileged of the Yaqui men. His dance, a blend of Spanish and indigenous steps, heightens the aesthetic and spiritual nature of the ceremony, held in the plaza of the Pueblo Pasqua near Tucson. As the sacrilegious *Chapayekas* worship an effigy of Judas in front of the church, the Deer dancer mysteriously appears: he is a slender young man wearing only a painted blanket about his waist. He carries sacred rattles, and a white kerchief and a stuffed deer's head with black, shining eyes cover his head. (The Japanese also have a deer dance in which the dancer is similarly costumed.) His dance consists of foot movements that imitate those of a deer's forelegs; there is minimal arm motion. His head moves gracefully as he glances carefully over his shoulder looking for possible danger. Although these movements may seem real, there is nothing naturalistic in the dance, as each move is calculated for symbolic effect. The dancer is transformed as the dance takes possession of his body. Intimidated by his artistry, the *Chapayekas* disperse.

The dance is repeated with variations throughout Holy Week, and the climax of the drama occurs on Good Friday. Women reenacting the pilgrimage of Christ to Calvary carry a statue of the mourning Virgin at the head of a procession even as the *Chapayekas* perform the Way of the Cross in the wrong direction to mock the sacred dance of the *Matachinis*. A solitary figure removes a bouquet of flowers from the sacred bier of the dead Christ and carries it ceremoniously into the church, and thus the *Chapayekas* are robbed of their triumph. Their artifacts—masks, rattles, swords, and sandals—are burned on a pyre while the effigy of Judas is led from town on a burro. The Deer dancer repeats his hypnotic movements as the audience celebrates a communal triumph with food and drink. On Easter Sunday, the Deer dancer leads the priest and his congregation into the church, where he dances atop the Christian altar. The Yaqui Easter ends with a Friendship Circle in which all participants, actors and audience alike, acknowledge their contact with chaos and the triumph of good over treachery.

The Deer dancer and Yaqui Indians dressed as the Soldiers of Judas collecting money for Easter rituals.

NO SACO NADA DE LA ESCUELA
(I DON'T GET NOTHIN' FROM SCHOOL)

L U I S   V A L D E Z

LUIS VALDEZ (1940–)

No individual is more responsible for the development of Mexican-American drama than Luis Valdez, and no other Chicano in any art medium has had more written about him and his work. From simple beginnings in farm fields in California's Central Valley in the 1960s, Valdez's theatrical—and now film—work truly entered the mainstream. He was the first Mexican-American to have a play produced on Broadway (*Zoot Suit*, 1981), and his 1987 film *La Bamba* (about Chicano rock star Richie Valens) was admired by critics and the public.

Valdez was born in Delano, California in 1940, the son of campesinos, the migrant farmworkers who picked grapes and other crops from the citrus groves of Southern California to the apple orchards of Washington State. In part because of their transient lifestyle, the children of campesinos often perform poorly in school (an issue in *No saco nada*) and frequently drop out. Valdez, however, persevered and graduated from high school, even while working as a ventriloquist at a local television station. He earned a scholarship to San Jose State College, where he took theater classes and eventually wrote his first play, *The Shrunken Head of Pancho Villa*. A surrealistic work about a young Mexican-American without a head (who represents "faceless" Chicanos struggling for recognition in mainstream America), the play received a lengthy standing ovation at its premiere production at SJSC and in reworked form has assumed major status in Valdez's compiled works.

After college Valdez joined the San Francisco Mime Troupe, a politically committed band of artists in the Bay Area who fused a *commedia dell'arte* style with social activism. When he returned to his home in Delano in 1965, he met Cesar Chavez, who was organizing the United Farm Workers in an attempt to gain better working conditions, wages, health care, and education for the campesinos. Valdez worked as a UFW recruiter for two years. Applying what he learned in the Mime Troupe, Valdez began a theater company—El Teatro Campesino—which performed short plays (*actos*) in fields, at union halls, in churches, even on flatbed trucks. The *actos* were an inventive combination of satirical clowning, Brechtian theater, folk plays, and agitprop designed to educate farmworkers about their rights and provoke them to act (specifically, to strike against the growers). Valdez also refers to these early *actos* as *huelguistas* ("strike plays") because they were performed during the period known as *La Huelga*, the prolonged grape boycott that eventually led to a victory for the UFW. It was the beginning of the civil rights movement for Hispanic Americans, and El Teatro Campesino's plays were as instrumental in its success as Martin Luther King Jr.'s speeches were for the African American movement. Note that *No saco nada* ends with the actors getting the audience to rise and shout "*La raza*" ("the race"), "*La huelga*" ("strike"), and "Chicano power" in the best agitprop tradition.

Valdez himself defines the purpose of *actos*:

> Inspire the audience to social action. Illuminate specific points about social problems. Satirize the opposition. Show or hint at a solution. Express what people are feeling.

Like South African township theater or the work of many of the theater collectives in Latin America, the *actos* performed by El Teatro Campesino epitomize rough theater as defined by Sir Peter Brook: "The Rough Theater is close to the people . . . the theater that's not a theater, the theater on carts, on wagons, on trestles, audiences standing, drinking, sitting round tables, audiences joining in, answering back." To further the bond between actors and performers, the *actos* were frequently accompanied by *corridos* and *rancheras*, popular songs that served as a kind of "living newspaper" to keep audiences informed about current events. Valdez's actors, it must be noted, were not trained professionals (though many became professional actors), but emerged from the ranks of the farmworkers themselves. Their presence lent a compelling authenticity to the message of the plays.

Among Valdez's best-known *actos* is *Los Vendidos* (1967), a satirical portrait of Mexican-American "sellouts" who contribute to the stereotypical notions Anglos have about Hispanics or who try to "pass" as Anglos. *The Dark Root of a Scream* (1967) and *Soldado Razo* (1970) are *actos* about the victimization of Hispanics during the Vietnam War. After the success of *La Huelga*, Valdez turned to mythological themes extolling the virtues of Aztlán, the sacred kingdom of the Aztecs and the repository of the greatness of "la raza." *Bernabé* (1970) is an especially poignant portrait of a young Chicano with learning disabilities on a quest for La Tierra, the mythical goddess of the land. In 1980 Valdez combined social activism and myth in *Zoot Suit*, a drama with music. Based on the infamous "zoot suit" riots in Los Angeles in the 1940s, the play portrays the tragedy of a "pachuco" (a street-smart Chicano noted for extravagant dress) who gradually realizes his link to his Aztec heritage. The play was among the most popular works of the 1981 Los Angeles theater season and was subsequently produced on Broadway, but was largely ignored by New York audiences whose Hispanic referent was Puerto Rican–Americans.

El Teatro Campesino is still based in San Juan Bautista, California. In addition to its stage work, it has contributed films and several television shows to contemporary culture. Each Christmas season, PBS broadcasts *La Pastorella*, a Chicano version of the Nativity featuring well-known Mexican-American performers such as Linda Ronstadt, Paul Rodriguez, Cheech Marin, and the Tejano rock band the Texas Tornados.

NO SACO NADA DE LA ESCUELA (1969)

Though it is not the best known of Valdez's *actos*, *No saco nada de la escuela* articulates most of the principal themes of El Teatro Campesino. Furthermore, it is the only *acto* to address the problems of other minorities in America, and its issues are still central to the national debate about the education of minorities. Although it seems a simple satire about the futility minorities face in the educational system, it is more complex than a first reading indicates. As Valdez warns in a short essay about the nature of *actos*, "What to a non-Chicano audience may seem like oversimplification . . . is to the Chicano a true expression of his social state and therefore reality."

The play, first performed at the Mexican Cultural Center in Fresno, is divided into three sections: grammar school, high school, and college. The oppressors are broadly drawn caricatures meant to elicit laughter and scorn from its audience: the old schoolteacher who explodes into violence; the redneck whose only talent is for racist insults; the smug college professor whose ignorance is appalling. The play's ingenuity rests in the three-step progression from ignorance to knowledge by its youthful protagonists, each of whom represents an element in minority culture. Francisco is a potential *vendido*, or sellout; he is effectively contrasted with Esperanza (ironically, her name means "hope"), a true *vendido* whose father is a well-to-do landowner. Ultimately, Francisco, like his African American counterpart, Malcolm, gains an awareness of his racial identity and the militancy that will effect change for his people. Similarly, Florence, the *gabacha* (white girl), represents '60s liberalism in her movement from self-absorption to an openness to others; she cannot, however, quite shake her old prejudices. Though she is a parody of antiwar, profeminist activists, she emerges as a more sympathetic character than the other Anglos.

The central character is Moctezuma, who epitomizes Chicanismo, that is, a fierce pride in "la raza." His name embodies the glory of the Aztecs, who ruled central and northern Mexico in the preconquest era. Like the insensitive teacher who sings "From the halls of Montezuma . . ." when she hears his name, most Anglos—and, ironically, many in Valdez's late 1960's audience—assume Montezuma is the correct pronunciation and spelling of the name of the last emperor of the Aztecs (1466–1520). However, this is an Anglicized version, and Valdez's hero wants his name restored to its preconquest form—Moctezuma—as a means of recapturing his racial and spiritual identity. When Moctezuma corrects the teacher's ignorant and insensitive pronunciation, Valdez was actually educating his audience about their heritage. In many ways *No saco nada* is more a tool to instruct the audience in the values of Chicanismo than a satire on the insensitivity of the majority culture. Like his African American counterpart, Malcolm (whose chosen name honors civil rights leader Malcolm X), Moctezuma becomes increasingly aware of his heritage, a progress that is marked in both cases by the inventive use of the alphabet game as the structural centerpiece of the play.

As its title suggests, the play argues that the educational system is irrelevant to the needs of the minority community, particularly in regard to the awareness of one's culture. The message in 1967 was that people had to educate themselves about their ethnicity, as suggested by the lines of the play. Since the play was written, various perceived weaknesses of contemporary education have been addressed, with varying degrees of success. Today multicultural education, ethnic studies programs, and similar curricular changes have become commonplace in both lower and higher education. Valdez's *acto* is a reminder that this was not always the case.

The figure of Richard Nixon is also central to the play, which was written during the Vietnam War. Nixon, who was a figure of ridicule in many alternative theater movements of the era, became an effigy to those opposed to a war that, many argued, was being fought primarily by the poor and especially by minorities. Though El Teatro Campesino specifically addressed this issue in such plays as *The Root of a Scream*, it is instructive that Valdez includes the issue in this play. School was seen as a haven for many middle-class young men who received deferrals while attending college. Minorities had less access to education and were therefore more likely to be drafted. This is another reason why *No saco nada* is such a scathing attack on the educational system. While its performers claimed to have learned "nothing" in school, the play they used to vent their anger at a system that excluded them was enormously instructive to its audience.

Teatro Espejo, *which has performed for 25 years at California State University, Sacramento, contin-ues the tradition of Luis Valdez's El Teatro Campesino in its performance of* Chicano Acto.

NO SACO NADA DE LA ESCUELA
(I DON'T GET NOTHIN' FROM SCHOOL)

LUIS VALDEZ

CHARACTERS:
FRANCISCO
MOCTEZUMA (MONTY)
MALCOLM
FLORENCE
ABRAHAM
GRADE SCHOOL TEACHER
ESPERANZA
COLLEGE PROFESSOR
NIXON
VATO

Elementary School. School Yard sounds: children play-ing, shouting, laughing. Four kids come running out. Flo-rence, a white girl in pigtails and freckles; Malcolm, a black boy; then Francisco and Moctezuma, two chicanitos.

ALL. (*A cheer.*) Yeah! Ring around the rosey, pocket full of posies, ashes, ashes, all fall down! Yeah! Let's do it again!

(*Francisco has been watching from the side. He is grabbed by Florence and Monty, and pulled into circle, trying to get in step.*) Ring around the rosey, pocket full of posies, ashes, ashes, we all fall down! (*Bell rings off stage.*)

FLORENCE. Oh! The bell! (*They jump to their places, and sit in two rows facing each other. Two on each side.*)

MONTY. Heh, look! Florence has a boyfriend! Florence has a boyfriend, y es un negro!

FLORENCE. No I don't. I don't have no boyfriend. (*Teacher enters, short bowlegged, old, ugly. She wears a white mask and her feet stomp as she walks. She carries a huge pencil, two feet long, and a sign which she places on a stand at upstage center.*)

TEACHER. (*Mimicking writing on blackboard.*) Elementary A-B-C's. (*Students begin to throw paper wads across the room at one another. Teacher turns, commands with high pitched voice.*) Children! I want those papers picked off the floor immediately! (*Students run to pick up papers. Then sit down.*) There now, that's better. (*Her version of cheerful-*

ness.) Good morning, class. (*Class begins to sing except for Francisco, who looks at others, bewildered. Teacher leads singing with her pencil.*)

ALL. Good morning to you, good morning to you, good morning dear teacher, good morning to you.

TEACHER. That's fine. Now for roll call. Florence.

FLORENCE. Here teacher.

TEACHER. Malcolm.

MALCOLM. Yeow.

TEACHER. Moc . . . Moc . . . (*She can't pronounce "Moctezuma."*) Ramírez!

MONTY. Here.

TEACHER. Francisco.

FRANCISCO. Aquí. (*Monty raises Francisco's hand.*)

TEACHER. Abraham.

MONTY. Teacher, teacher. He's outside. He's a crybaby.

(*Abraham comes running out and runs across front stage, crying. He is dressed in cowboy boots, baseball cap on sideways, face is pale white with freckles.*)

TEACHER. (*Helps him.*) There, there now, dear, don't cry. I want you to sit right there. (*Points to Monty.*)

ABRAHAM. Wah! I can't sit there, he's brown.

MONTY. No, I'm not. (*Rubs forearm trying to remove color.*)

TEACHER. (*Turns him around.*) Well, then I want you to sit right over there. (*Points towards Malcolm.*)

ABRAHAM. Wah! I can't sit there, he's Black.

TEACHER. Well, then do you see that nice little white girl over there? (*Points to Florence.*) Would you like to sit there?

ABRAHAM. (*Man's voice.*) Uh-huh!

TEACHER. Boy! (*Points to Malcolm.*) You move. (*Abraham sits next to Florence, Malcolm moves over by Monty and Francisco. They pantomime playing marbles.*)

TEACHER. Now, all rise for the flag salute. (*Sweetly.*) Stand up, Florence. Stand up, Abraham, dear. (*Turns to others.*) I said stand up! (*Monty, Malcolm and Francisco jump up and begin flag salute.*)

ALL. I pledge allegiance to the flag . . . (*Abraham sneaks behind the Teacher's back and pokes Francisco in the behind. Francisco thinks it was Monty and hits him, pushing him into Malcolm. They stand up straight again to continue and Abraham sneaks over, again he pokes Francisco who again hits Monty, who again pushes into Malcolm. Malcolm points to Abraham. All three then attack Abraham and throw him to the ground.*)

TEACHER. (*Turns screaming.*) Class! For heaven's sake!

(*Abraham, Monty and Francisco run back to their seats.*) Did they hurt you Abraham, dear? (*Turns to Monty and Francisco.*) You should have more respect!

FRANCISCO. Pero, yo no hice nada.

TEACHER. Shut up! (*Francisco cries.*) Shut up! I said shut up! (*Francisco continues crying. Teacher kicks him and he shuts up. Teacher moves to center stage.*) And now for our elementary A, B, C's. Florence, you're first.

FLORENCE. Here's an apple, teacher. (*Hands Teacher an apple.*)

TEACHER. Thank you, dear.

FLORENCE. (*Moves down stage center.*) A is for apple. B is for baby. And C is for candy. (*Pantomimes licking sucker and skips back to her seat giggling.*)

TEACHER. Very good! Now let's see who's next. Willie? (*She means Malcolm, who sits daydreaming.*) Willie? (*Malcolm does not respond.*) Willie! I meant you boy! (*Points at him.*)

MALCOLM. Teacher, my name ain't Willie. It's Malcolm.

TEACHER. It doesn't matter. It doesn't matter. Do your ABC's!

MALCOLM. A is for Alabama. B is for banjo and C is for cotton! (*Stamps foot, walks back to his seat. All the students are giggling.*)

TEACHER. Not bad at all, boy, not bad at all. Let's see. Who's next? Abraham dear? Say your ABC's.

ABRAHAM. A is for animal and B is for . . . black and brown!

(*Points to Monty and Francisco and Malcolm.*)

TEACHER. Oh! He's able to distinguish his colors. Go on.

ABRAHAM. And C is for . . . for . . .

TEACHER. It has a "kuh," "kuh" sound. (*Meaning cat.*)

ABRAHAM. Kill! (*Brightens up. Points to Francisco, Monty and Malcolm.*)

TEACHER. Oh, no, we mustn't say those things in class.

ABRAHAM. (*Crying.*) I promise never to say it again. Teacher, look. (*Points upward. Teacher looks and Abraham spits on Francisco, Monty and Malcolm. They start to get up but are interrupted by Teacher.*)

TEACHER. Class! Did you all know that Abraham here was named after one of our most famous presidents? Mr. Abraham Lincoln—the man who freed the slaves!

ALL. (*Aghast.*) Gaw-leee!

TEACHER. After they were forced to pick cotton against their own free will.

ALL. Shame, shame, shame.

TEACHER. (*To Abraham.*) Now, aren't you proud of your heritage?

ABRAHAM. A-huh. (*Laughing.*)

TEACHER. Of course, you are. Who's next. Moc . . . Moc . . . (*She can't pronounce his name.*) Ramírez!

MONTY. Yes, teacher?

TEACHER. How do you pronounce your name?

MONTY. Moctezuma.

TEACHER. What?

MONTY. Moctezuma.

TEACHER. Oh! What a funny name! (*She laughs and class joins her. Teacher stomps foot and shuts them up.*) Class! (*To Moctezuma.*) And what ever does it mean?

MONTY. He was an emperor in the times of the Indians. He was a Mexican like me.

TEACHER. Oh! You mean Montezuma.

MONTY. No, Moctezuma.

TEACHER. Montezuma.

MONTY. Moctezuma.

TEACHER. Montezuma!

MONTY. Moctezuma!

TEACHER. Montezuma! (*Begins to march up and down stage singing "The Marines Hymn."*) "From the halls of Monte-zoo-ma to the shore of Tripoli." (*Using her oversized pencil as a bayonet, she stabs Monty, who falls forward with head and arms hanging.*) Now what's your name, boy? (*Lifts his head.*)

MONTY. Monty.

TEACHER. Do your ABC's.

MONTY. A is for airplane, B is for boat and C is for . . . ah, C is for . . . for cucaracha!

TEACHER. What!

MONTY. (*Crying.*) Cuca . . . caca qui qui.

TEACHER. (*Twisting his ear.*) What you meant to say was cock-a-roach, right?

MONTY. Sí.

TEACHER. What? (*Twists his ear even more.*)

MONTY. Yes!

TEACHER. Yes, what?

MONTY. Yes, teacher!

TEACHER. Sit down! (*He sits down crying.*) And shut up! Let's see who's next. Oh, yes, Francisco.

FRANCISCO. ¿Qué?

TEACHER. Oh! Another one that can't speak English! Why do they send these kids to me? You can't communicate with them. Is there anybody here that can speak Spanish?

MONTY. I can, teacher.

TEACHER. Tell him to do his ABC's.

MONTY. Dice que digas tu ABC's.

FRANCISCO. Dile que no las sabo en inglés, nomás en español.

MONTY. Teacher, he don't know how.

TEACHER. Oh, sit down! This has been a most trying day! Class dismissed . . . (*Students start to run out cheering.*) except (*They freeze.*) for Monty and Franky. (*Teacher points to them. The rest of the class runs out.*)

MALCOLM. (*Offstage.*) You better give me that swing.

ABRAHAM. (*Offstage.*) No!

MALCOLM. (*Offstage.*) I'm gonna hit you.

ABRAHAM. (*Offstage.*) No. (*Slap is heard and then Abraham wails.*)

TEACHER. (*Teacher, Monty and Francisco freeze until after the above, then they begin to move again.*) Now look, boy. Tell him his name is no longer Francisco, but Franky.

MONTY. Dice que tu nombre ya no es Francisco, es Franky.

FRANCISCO. No es Francisco . . . Panchito.

MONTY. Hey, teacher, he said his name is still Francisco.

(*Francisco punches him in the back.*)

TEACHER. Look boy, Francisco . . . no; Franky . . . yes.

FRANCISCO. No. Francisco.

TEACHER. Franky!

FRANCISCO. Francisco!

TEACHER. Franky!

FRANCISCO. Okay. (*As Teacher begins to walk away to audience.*) Francisco.

TEACHER. It's Franky!

FRANCISCO. (*Grabs sign and throws it on the ground.*) Es Francisco, ya estufas.

TEACHER. Oh! You nasty boy! (*Beats him over the head twice.*) Remember the Alamo! (*Hits him again.*) And just for that, you don't pass.

MONTY. Teacher, teacher, do I pass? (*Picks up sign, and hands it to her.*)

TEACHER. I suppose so. You are learning to speak English. (*To audience.*) They shouldn't place these culturally deprived kids with the normal children. No, no, no. (*She leaves. Stomps out. Monty begins to follow.*)

FRANCISCO. (*Getting up from floor.*) Oye, Moctezuma, ¿qué dijo esa vieja chaparra y panzona?

MONTY. Dijo que tú no pasaste. You don't pass.

FRANCISCO. ¿Y tú pasaste?

MONTY. Sure, I pass. I speak good English and, besides my name isn't Moctezuma anymore . . . it's Monty.

FRANCISCO. No, es Moctezuma.

MONTY. Monty.

FRANCISCO. Moctezuma.

MONTY. It's Monty. See, you stupid? You never learn. (*Sticks his tongue out at him and leaves.*)

FRANCISCO. (*Crying.*) Entonces dile a tu teacher que coma chet! (*Leaves crying.*)

High School. Scene begins with same stand at center stage. High school teacher, male, grey business suit, white mask. Walks across stage. Places high school sign on board.

STUDENTS. (*Backstage, singing.*) On hail to thee, our Alma Mater, we'll always hold you dear. (*Then a cheer.*) Rah, rah, sis boom bah! Sock it to them, sock it to them! (*Florence enters stage right. Abraham enters stage left. His neck has a reddish tinge. He tries to hug Florence and is pushed away. He tries again and is pushed away. Florence continues walking.*)

ABRAHAM. Where you going?

FLORENCE. To class.

ABRAHAM. What do you mean to class? I thought we were going steady.

FLORENCE. We were going steady.

ABRAHAM. (*Mimicking her.*) What do you mean "We were going steady?"

FLORENCE. That's right. I saw you walking with that new girl, Esperanza.

ABRAHAM. That Mexican chick? Aw, you know what I want from her. Besides, you're the only girl I love. I'll even get down on my knees for you. (*Falls on knees.*)

FLORENCE. Oh! Abe, don't be ridiculous, get up.

ABRAHAM. (*Getting up.*) Does that mean we're still going steady?

FLORENCE. I guess so.

ABRAHAM. Hot dog! (*From stage right Francisco enters wearing dark glasses and strutting like a vato loco. Abraham to Florence.) See that spic over there? Just to show you how much I love you, I'm gonna kick his butt!

FLORENCE. Oh, Abe, you can't be racist!

ABRAHAM. Get out of my way. (Does warm up exercises like a boxer. Francisco has been watching him all along and has a knife in his hand, hidden behind his back so that it is not visible.) Heh, greaser, spic!

FRANCISCO. (Calmly.) You talking to me, vato?

ABRAHAM. You want some beef? (Raises his fists.)

FRANCISCO. (To audience.) Este vato quiere pedo. ¿Cómo la ven? ¡Pos que le ponga! (Pulls out a knife and goes after Abraham.)

ABRAHAM. (Backing up.) Heh, wait a minute! I didn't mean it. I was only fooling. I . . . (Francisco thrusts knife toward Abraham. Florence steps in between and stops the knife by holding Francisco's arm. Action freezes. From stage right Malcolm jumps in and struts downstage. He wears a do rag on his head, and sunglasses. He bops around, snapping his fingers; walks up to Francisco and Abraham; looks at knife, feels the blade and walks away as if nothing is happening. From stage right, Monty enters with his arm around Esperanza "Hopi." He runs up to Malcolm.)

MONTY. Hey, man, what's going on here?

MALCOLM. Say, baby, I don't know. I just don't get into these things. (Moves away.)

MONTY. (Stops him.) Hey, man, I said what's going on here?

MALCOLM. And I said I don't get into these things! What's the matter with you? Don't you understand? Don't you speak English?

MONTY. (Angered.) You think you're better than me, huh? (Monty grabs Malcolm by the throat, and Malcolm grabs him back. They start choking each other. Teacher enters stage center and observes the fight.)

MONTY. Nigger!

MALCOLM. Greaser!

MONTY. Coon!

MALCOLM. Spic!

ESPERANZA. Oh, Monty, Monty!

TEACHER. Okay, that's enough. Cut it out, boys! We can settle this after school in the gym. We might even charge admission. Everyone to your seats. (Monty and Malcolm separate. Francisco puts his knife away and all move back to their seats.)

TEACHER. Now, before we begin, I want to know who started that fight.

ABRAHAM. (Innocently.) Mr. White? He did, Sir.

FRANCISCO. (Stands up.) I didn't start anything. He insulted me!

ABRAHAM. Who you going to believe, him or me? Besides, he pulled a knife.

TEACHER. (To Francisco.) You did what? Get to the Principal's office immediately!

FRANCISCO. Orale, but you know what? This is the last time I'm going to the Principal's office for something

like this. (Exits mumbling.) Me la vas a pagar, ese, qué te crees.

TEACHER. I don't understand that boy. And he's one of the school's best athletes. (Opens mouth, sudden realization. Runs to exit, shouts after Francisco.) Don't forget to show up for baseball practice. The school needs you.

FLORENCE. (Stands.) Mr. White? I refuse to sit next to Abraham. He's a liar!

TEACHER. (Stands next to Abraham.) Why, Florence, Abe here is the son of one of our best grower families.

FLORENCE. Well, I don't care if you believe me or not. But I refuse to sit next to a liar. (Gives Abraham his ring.) And here's your ring.

TEACHER. All right, sit over here. (Florence moves across stage and sits next to Esperanza. Francisco comes strutting in, whistling.) I thought I told you to go to the Principal's office.

FRANCISCO. I did, man.

TEACHER. What did he say?

FRANCISCO. He told me not to beat on anymore of his gabachitos. (Taps Abraham on the head.)

TEACHER. (Angered.) All right, sit over there. (Indicates a spot beside Florence.) And you . . . (To Esperanza.) over here.

ESPERANZA. (Stops beside Francisco at center stage.) You rotten pachuco. (She sits besides Abraham.)

FRANCISCO. Uh que la . . . esta ruca, man. (He sits besides Florence.)

TEACHER. Now, class, before we begin our high school reports, I'd like to introduce a new student. Her name is Esperanza Espinoza. (He gives the pronunciation of her name with an Italian inflection.) It sounds Italian, I know, but I think she's Mexican-American. Isn't that right, dear?

ESPERANZA. (Self-consciously rising.) No, my parents were, but I'm Hawaiian. And you can just call me Hopi.

TEACHER. That's fine, Hopi. Now for our high school reports. Florence, you're first.

FLORENCE. (Drumbeats. Florence walks to center stage, swaying hips like a stripper.) A is for achievement. B is for betterment. And C is for (Bump and grind.) college! (More drumbeats as she walks back to her seat.)

TEACHER. (Impressed.) Well! It's good to see that you're thinking of your future. Let's see who's next. Oh yes, Willie.

MALCOLM. (Hops to his feet.) I told you, man, my name ain't Willie. It's Malcolm!

TEACHER. All right, you perfectionist! Get up there and give your report.

MALCOLM. (Struts to center stage. He begins to snap his fingers, setting a rhythm. Everybody joins in.) A is for Africa. B is for black like me. And C is for community like black ghetto.

ALL. (Still snapping to rhythm.) My goodness, Willie, you sure got rhythm. But then after all, all you people do. (Three final snaps.)

TEACHER. Now then, Willie, about your report. The first

two pages were fine, but that last part about the ghetto . . . don't you think it needs some improvement?

MALCOLM. You're telling me! Don't you think we know it?

TEACHER. Okay, that's a good C minus. Back to your seat. (*Malcolm sits down.*) Abraham, up front!

ABRAHAM. Jabol mein fuehrer! (*Stomps to center stage.*) A is for America: Love or leave it! (*Francisco and Malcolm stand up to leave.*)

TEACHER. Heh, you two! (*Motions for them to sit down.*)

ABRAHAM. B is for better: Better dead than red. And C is for kill, kill, kill! As in the United States Marine Corps. (*Snaps to attention.*)

TEACHER. (*Marches up like a Marine.*) Very good, Abraham!

ABRAHAM. (*Saluting.*) Thank you, sir.

TEACHER. That's an A plus, Abraham!

ABRAHAM. What did you expect, sir?

TEACHER. Dismissed! (*Abraham marches back to seat.*) Monty, up front!

MONTY. Yes, sir! (*Marches sloppily to stage center. Salutes and freezes.*)

TEACHER. (*With contempt.*) Cut that out, and give your report.

MONTY. A is for American. B is for beautiful, like America the Beautiful. And C is for country, like God bless this beautiful American country! Ooooh, I love it. (*He falls to his knees, kisses the floor.*)

TEACHER. (*Grabs Monty by the collar like a dog.*) Here, have a dog biscuit. (*Monty scarfs up imaginary dog biscuit, then is led back to his seat on all fours by Teacher.*) Now, who's next? Oh yes, Hopi.

ESPERANZA. (*Rises prissily, goes to center stage.*) A is for Avon, as in "Ding dong, Avon calling." B is for burgers, which I love, and beans, which I hate! (*Sneers at Francisco.*) And C is for can't as in "I can't speak Spanish." And we have a new Buick Riviera, and my sister goes to the University of California, and we live in a tract home . . .

TEACHER. (*Leading her back to her seat.*) Yes, dear! Just fine!

ESPERANZA. Really, really we do!

TEACHER. I believe you. That deserves a bean . . . uh, I mean B plus. (*Pause.*) Now let's hear from . . . Franky?

FRANCISCO. Yeah, Teach?

TEACHER. What do you mean "yeah, Teach?" You know my name is Mr. White.

FRANCISCO. I know what you name is, ese. But you seem to forget that my name is Francisco, loco.

TEACHER. Get up and give your report, you hoodlum.

FRANCISCO. Orale, ese vato, llévatela suave. (*Moves to center stage.*) A is for amor, como amor de mi raza.

TEACHER. What!

FRANCISCO. B is for barrio como where the raza lives. (*Teacher growls.*) And C is carnalismo.

TEACHER. (*Heated.*) How many times have I told you about speaking Spanish in my classroom? Now what did you say?

FRANCISCO. Carnalismo.

TEACHER. (*At the limit of his patience.*) And what does that mean?

FRANCISCO. Brotherhood.

TEACHER. (*Blows up.*) Get out!!

FRANCISCO. Why? I was only speaking my language. I'm a Chicano, ¿que no?

TEACHER. Because I don't understand you, and the rest of the class doesn't understand you.

FRANCISCO. So what? When I was small, I didn't understand English, and you kept flunking me and flunking me instead of teaching me.

TEACHER. You are permanently expelled from this high school!

FRANCISCO. Big deal! You call yourself a teacher! I can communicate in two languages. You can only communicate in one. Who's the teacher, Teach? (*Starts to exit.*)

MONTY. We're not all like that, teacher.

FRANCISCO. ¡Tú te me callas! (*Pushes Monty aside and exits.*)

TEACHER. That's the last straw! A is for attention. B is for brats like that. And C is for cut out. High school dismissed! (*Teacher exits, taking high school sign with him. Malcolm exits also at opposite side of stage. Abraham, Florence, Esperanza and Monty rise, facing each other.*)

MONTY. (*Looking at Florence.*) Oh, Hopi?

ESPERANZA. (*Looking at Abraham.*) Yes?

ABRAHAM. (*Looking at Esperanza.*) Oh, Flo?

FLORENCE. (*Looking at Monty.*) Yeah?

ABRAHAM AND MONTY. (*Together.*) Do you wanna break up?

FLORENCE AND ESPERANZA. (*Together.*) Yeah! (*Monty takes Florence by the arm; Abraham takes Esperanza.*)

MONTY. Oh boy, let's go to a party.

ABRAHAM. Let's go to a fiesta. (*all exit.*)

State College. Backstage sounds: Police siren, shouts of "pigs off campus!" College Professor enters and places sign on stand. It reads, "State College." Francisco enters pushing a broom.

FRANCISCO. Oh, professor?

PROFESSOR. Yes?

FRANCISCO. I want to go to college.

PROFESSOR. Didn't you drop out of high school?

FRANCISCO. Simón, but I still want to go to college. I want to educate myself.

PROFESSOR. Well, that's tough. (*Exits.*)

FRANCISCO. Pos, mira, qué jijo . . . (*Swings broom. Florence enters followed by Monty. Francisco freezes.*)

FLORENCE. Guess what, folks? Monty and I are living together. Isn't that right, Monty?

MONTY. That's right, baby. Just me and you.

FLORENCE. Do you love me, Monty?

MONTY. Oh, you know I do.

FLORENCE. Then, come to momma!

MONTY. Ay mamasota, una gabacha! (*He runs over to her and begins to kiss her passionately.*)

FLORENCE. (*Swooning.*) Oh, you Latin lovers.

MONTY. (*Suddenly peeved.*) Latin lovers? Your people have been oppressing my people for 150 years!

FLORENCE. Yes, Monty!

MONTY. You gabachas are all alike!

FLORENCE. (*The guilty liberal.*) Oh yes, Monty!

MONTY. And that's why I'm going to give it to you! (*Rolls up his sleeve, clenches fist.*) Right between the you-know-what. (*Grabs her and begins to kiss her again passionately.*) ¡Viva Zapata! (*Makes out again.*) ¡Viva Villa! (*Raises fist.*) ¡Viva la Revolución! (*Wraps a leg around her. Kisses her. Then falls to the floor exhausted.*)

FLORENCE. (*Sitting on his back.*) Oh, Monty. You do that so well.

MONTY. (*Puffing underneath.*) Shut up. While my people are starving in the barrio, your people are sitting fat and reech.

FLORENCE. Reech?

MONTY. Rich! Rich, you beech. Oh, my accent sleeped . . . slopped, sloped! What am I saying?

FLORENCE. (*Noticing Francisco.*) Monty, look, a chicken-o.

MONTY. A what?

FLORENCE. A Mexican-American?

MONTY. A what?

FLORENCE. An American of Mexican descent?

MONTY. I'm going to give you one more chance. I'm going to spell it out for you. (*Spells out C-H-I-C-A-N-O in the air.*) What's this?

FLORENCE. (*Reading his movements.*) C!

MONTY. And this and this? (*H and I.*)

FLORENCE. C-H-I .. . Chic! Chica . . . oh, Chicano! Chicano! (*Jumps up and down.*)

MONTY. Good! Now get out. And don't come back until I call you. (*Florence exits.*) 'Cause this is a job for . . . Supermacho! (*Approaches Francisco. Anglo accent to his Spanish.*) ¿Qué-húbole, easy vato loco? Heh, don't I know you?

FRANCISCO. ¿Qué nuevas?

MONTY. Isn't your name Francisco?

FRANCISCO. Simón.

MONTY. You're wanted.

FRANCISCO. No, I'm not! (*Begins to run across stage.*)

MONTY. For our program. (*Stops Francisco.*)

FRANCISCO. What program?

FLORENCE. (*Sticking her hand out from backstage.*) Now Monty?

MONTY. No, not yet. (*Turns to Francisco.*) Hey, man, you know la raza is getting together! You know we have 300 years of Chicano culture? You know our women are beautiful?! Just look at them, mamasotas!

FRANCISCO. Simón, están a toda madre.

MONTY. Pero primero necesitamos unos cuantos gritos como los meros machos. Mira, fíjate, ¡Que viva la raza! (*Francisco repeats.*) ¡Que viva la huelga! (*Francisco repeats.*)

FLORENCE. (*Enters.*) Look, Monty, I'm getting tired of waiting, godamit!

MONTY. (*Turns to Florence.*) Okay, just a minute. Just one more. (*Turns to Francisco.*) Uno más pero éste con muchos tú sabes qué, ¿eh? ¡Que viva la revolución!

FRANCISCO. ¡La revolución . . . ? (*Looks at Florence.*) Pos que viva, y a comenzar con esa gabacha, jija de . . .

MONTY. Hey, wait a minute, man. That's not where it's at, vato. This is what you call "universal love." I don't think you're ready for college. (*Florence jumps on Monty's back.*) And when you are, come look for me up at the Mexican Opportunity Commission Organization: MOCO. And I'm the Head Moco. Chicano power, carnal! (*Exits.*)

FRANCISCO. (*To audience.*) No, hombre, está más mocoso que la . . . (*Hopi and Abraham enter stage left. Abraham is wearing a ten gallon hat.*)

ESPERANZA. Guess what, folks? Abraham and I are engaged. Isn't that right, Abraham?

ABRAHAM. That's right, baby. Just me and you. (*He leans her over to kiss her.*)

ESPERANZA. (*Snapping back up. To Francisco.*) What are you looking at?

FRANCISCO. Oh! Esperanza, ¿no te acuerdas de mí?

ESPERANZA. My name is Hopi.

FRANCISCO. Orale, esa, no te . . .

ABRAHAM. Is that Mexican bothering you?

ESPERANZA. Just ignore him, sugar plum, just ignore him. (*They move stage right.*)

ABRAHAM. Do you know that my dad owns 20,000 acres of lettuce in the Salinas Valley?

ESPERANZA. Really!

ABRAHAM. And he has 200 dumb Mexicans just like him working for him.

ESPERANZA. Really!

ABRAHAM. My daddy's a genius!

ESPERANZA. Oh! You're so smart! You're so intelligent! Oh, you white god, you! (*Bows falling on her knees in worship.*)

ABRAHAM. Shucks. You don't have to do that. Why, you remind me of a little brown squaw my grandpappy used to have.

ESPERANZA. Squaw! (*Getting up in anger.*)

ABRAHAM: Don't get mad, my little taco. My little tamale. My little frijol. (*Pronounced free hole.*)

FRANCISCO. Free hole?

ABRAHAM. Besides, I've got a surprise for you. Why, just the other day my pappy made me president.

ESPERANZA. President?

ABRAHAM. President!

ESPERANZA. Of the company?

ABRAHAM. Of the Future Farmers of America.

ESPERANZA. (*Disappointed.*) Oh, Abraham.

FRANCISCO. (*Laughing, moves up to Hopi.*) ¡Oyes, por eso venistes al colegio? ¿A toparte con un pendejo?

ESPERANZA. Well, at least he's not out on the corner pushing dope.

ABRAHAM. You Mexicans ought to be out in the fields.

ESPERANZA. (*To Abraham.*) You tell him, sugar.

FRANCISCO. That's all you think I can do, huh? Well I'm gonna go to college on the E.O.P. program!

ESPERANZA. Look. I made it through college without any assistance. I don't see why you can't.

FRANCISCO. (*Mimics her.*) I made it through college . . . (*Professor enters stage center, Monty and Florence enter stage right.*)

PROFESSOR. Ladies and gentlemen, can we prepare for our college seminar? (*Spots Francisco.*) Aren't you the custodian?

FRANCISCO. Yes, but, a . . . Monty wants to talk to you.

MONTY. Oh, sir, we thought we might be able to get him in under MOCO, you know, Mexican Opportunity Commission Organization?

PROFESSOR. Now look, Monty, we got you in here and unless you want to be out, get back into your place. (*To Francisco.*) No, I'm sorry, there's no room. No room! (*Pushes him out.*)

FRANCISCO. I want to go to college!

PROFESSOR. These students, they don't understand. (*To audience.*) They don't realize that there is no room in our college, no room at all. In this college there is not room for one more student. Not one more minority student. (*Malcolm enters stage right wearing a black shirt, black leather jacket and black beret. He is carrying a rifle. Abraham begins to shake and points at him.*)

PROFESSOR. (*To Abraham.*) I'll handle it. (*Moves over to Malcolm.*) Pardon me, boy, but are you registered? (*Malcolm cocks rifle, Professor looks at rifle chamber, looks at Malcolm, looks at audience.*) He's registered.

ALL. He's registered.

FRANCISCO. (*Peeking back in.*) ¡Vistes eso, Moctezuma?

PROFESSOR. No, no, out! Out! (*Moctezuma helps Professor push Francisco out.*)

MONTY. (*Pushes him out.*) I'll see that it doesn't happen again, sir.

PROFESSOR. Well, see that it doesn't. Now class, in order to qualify for graduation, you must deliver one final report. And it must be concise, logical and have conviction. Miss Florence, you're first.

FLORENCE. A is for anti as in anti-war. B is for Berkeley as in anti-war Berkeley. And C is for chick as in anti-war Berkeley chick.

PROFESSOR. Well, that was a very personal and revealing account, Miss Florence, and that should qualify for . . .

ABRAHAM. That stunk! And if you pass her, I'll have your job. Remember, you are working for my daddy!

MONTY. Oh, sir, please give her one more chance.

PROFESSOR. Yes, just get back to your seat, Monty. I was about to say that it lacked conviction. Try again, Miss Florence. (*Stands next to her.*)

FLORENCE. A is for adult.

PROFESSOR. A-huh.

FLORENCE. B is for become, as to become an adult.

PROFESSOR. It happens to the best of us.

FLORENCE. And C is for cop-out, as to become an adult and cop-out.

PROFESSOR. That is the American way, Miss Florence. You will graduate! Let's see who's next . . . Malcolm.

MALCOLM. (*Moves forward menacingly.*) A is for Afro, as in Afro-American. B is for Black, as in Afro-American Black Panther. And C is for Cleaver, Eldridge Cleaver, Afro-American Black Panther! (*Gives panther salute.*)

PROFESSOR. Well, I see the logic, but I don't like it.

MALCOLM. Good, that's the way we want it!

PROFESSOR. All right! All right! You'll graduate.

ABRAHAM. He graduates? (*He begins to pantomime different ways of killing Malcolm. Machine gun, grenades, airplane and finally builds a rocket.*) A is for anti. (*Puts first stage of missile.*) B is for ballistic. (*Builds second stage.*) And M is for missile. (*Puts final stage on missile. During the above, Malcolm has just been standing, cool and collected. Everybody but Malcolm begins the countdown.*)

ALL. 5–4–3–2–1 Fire! (*They make whistling noise of a rocket in the air. As the rocket lands with a loud noise, Malcolm turns around and points gun at Abraham.*)

ABRAHAM. (*Scared like a boy.*) A is for animal. B is for back off. And C is for coward, Mama! (*Exits.*)

PROFESSOR. Abraham, come back! (*Francisco enters stage left dressed as a brown beret with rifle in hand.*)

FRANCISCO. ¿Ya ves, Moctezuma? (*Monty tries to push him out, but is thrown back.*) ¡Un lado!

PROFESSOR. Just a minute! Just a minute! (*To Francisco.*) You want to go to college? What are your qualifications?

FRANCISCO. My qualifications? Pos, mira que jijo de . . . (*Pulls back rifle into position to hit Teacher from the front and Malcolm pokes his gun at his back. They freeze and Esperanza walks over and moves around Francisco, checking him out. She moves back to her place.*)

PROFESSOR. (*Jumps up and they unfreeze.*) All right, you're in!

FRANCISCO. Where do I sit?

PROFESSOR. Over there! (*Frantically.*) This is getting out of hand. Monty, Monty, my boy, your report.

MONTY. A is for American like a Mexican-American.

PROFESSOR. Wonderful!

MONTY. And B is for bright, like a bright Mexican-American.

PROFESSOR. Great! Great!

MONTY. And C is for comprado like a bright, Mexican-American comprado.

PROFESSOR. Bought and sold! Monty, my boy, you will graduate. Congratulations! And as you go forward into this great society, I want you to remember one thing. (*Points forward.*) I want you always to move forward, move forward in that great American tradition. (*Monty* has been looking to where the Professor *has been pointing, gets scared and sneaks off to his place, moving backward.*) Forever forward. (*Looks around when he realizes that Monty has left.*) Monty! Monty! (*Getting hysterical.*) Oh! This is getting out of hand! Out of hand! Let's see. Oh, yes, Hopi?

ESPERANZA. (*She has been talking to Francisco and now has her arms around his neck.*) Who?

PROFESSOR. (*Scared.*) Hopi?

ESPERANZA. My name is Esperanza, you marrano!

PROFESSOR. Your report, please.

ESPERANZA. Orale, llévatela suave. (*Walks pachuca fashion to center stage.*) A is for action, as in acción social. B is for batos, as in acción social de batos. And C is for Chicana as in Acción Social de Batos y Chicanas. (*Francisco lets out with a grito.*)

FRANCISCO. ¿Y ahora qué dices, Moctezuma?

PROFESSOR. All right, Francisco, your report.

FRANCISCO. Hey, wait a minute, man. I just got in here.

MONTY. What's the matter? Can't do it, huh?

PROFESSOR. (*Regaining a sense of authority.*) Is that your problem, boy, can't you do it?

FRANCISCO. Yes, I can! And don't call me boy!

PROFESSOR. (*Cringes in fear again.*) Fine, fine.

FRANCISCO. A is for advanced, as the advanced culture of Indigenous American Aztlán. B is for bronze as in the advanced culture of Indigenous American Aztlán, which brought bronze civilization to the Western Hemisphere. And C is for century, as the advanced culture of Indigenous American Aztlán, which brought bronze civilization to the Western Hemisphere and which, moreover, will create el nuevo hombre in the twenty-first century, El Chicano. Give me my diploma.

PROFESSOR. Just a minute, hold it right there! (*Goes to side and grabs book.*) I have here in my hand the book of American knowledge. There is nothing in here about Astalan, nothing in here about Chicken-o. In fact there is nothing in here about nothing and, as you can see, (*Turns book towards the audience, there is a dollar sign printed on page.*) this is the honest truth which is close to all of our American hearts. No, I'm sorry, but under the circumstances, I don't think that you will (*Francisco has gun in Professor's face and Malcolm puts his rifle to his back.*) be here next year, because you will graduate. (*Malcolm and Francisco move to their places.*) And now, students, line up for that golden moment, graduation! And here to present the awards on this fine day is none other than that great statesman, that golden-mouthed orator, that old grape sucker himself, the President of the United States, Mr. Richard Nixon. (*Nixon moves in from stage right, he is wearing cap and gown, giving peace symbol. Shakes hands with Professor.*) A few words, please, Mr. President.

NIXON. I'd like to say just three things today, only three. First, don't forget that great American dollar which put you through college. (*Applause.*) Second, always kiss ass; and third, eat plenty of Salinas scab lettuce!

PROFESSOR. Thank you, Mr. President. Now, if you'll just step this way, we shall begin the awards. First, we have Miss Florence, a fine girl. (*Florence moves to centerstage, receives diploma. Nixon places a graduation cap on her head. Cap comes with white hood, which covers her head completely. She moves back to her place.*) Next we have, Monty. Good boy. (*Monty walks up and kisses the President's hand. Then he places cap over his own head, goes back to his place.*) Next is Willie.

PRESIDENT. Here we are, Willie.

MALCOLM. (*Takes diploma.*) My name is Malcolm, you white mutha. (*President and Professor duck.*)

PRESIDENT. And here's your white bag.

MALCOLM. I don't need that.

PROFESSOR. But what are you going to do without it?

MALCOLM. You're going to find out. (*He walks to stage right and whistles.*) Come here, baby. (*Florence takes off her cap, moves to center stage, throws cap on floor, walks off stage with Malcolm.*)

PRESIDENT. A militant!

PROFESSOR. That's okay. There's a whole lot of them that aren't. Next we have Francisco. (*Francisco moves up, takes diploma, moves quickly back to his place. President tries to put cap on him, misses and almost falls on Esperanza. He backs off cautiously.*)

PRESIDENT. Speedy, these Mexicans. Fast!

PROFESSOR. Next, we have Esperanza. (*She moves to center stage, takes diploma.*)

PRESIDENT. And here's your white bag.

ESPERANZA. I don't need your white bag!

PRESIDENT. But you can't exist in our society without me.

PROFESSOR. What are you going to do without your white bag? (*From audience someone gets up and yells, "Hey, I want to go to college."*)

ESPERANZA. That's what I'm going to do. I'm going to help my carnales get into college.

VATO. ¡Ayúdenme! (*Runs toward stage.*)

PROFESSOR. No! (*Francisco and Esperanza try to help Vato from audience. There's a tug of war.*)

VATO. ¡Sí! (*With Francisco and Esperanza.*)

PROFESSOR. No!

VATO. ¡Sí!

PROFESSOR. No!

VATO. ¡Sí! (*Jumps up onstage, pushing Professor back. Vato waves to audience and yells.*) Orale, I made it into college. (*Gives Chicano handshake to Francisco and Esperanza.*)

PRESIDENT. Well, I can see that my job here is done. I shall now take my students, student . . . into the great white world. Right face! Forward march! (*Exits stage right followed by Monty.*)

FRANCISCO. ¡Moctezuma! ¡Quédate con tu raza!

ESPERANZA. Ah, let him go. There's more where he came from.

Luis Valdez

FRANCISCO. ¡Pos, que le pongan! (*Students start coming in from all sides of stage, everyone starts pointing at Professor yelling.*) Teach us! Teach us!

PROFESSOR. Just a minute. Just a minute. (*To audience.*) So many brown faces, brown minds, brown ideas, what is this? A chocolate factory? (*Everybody jumps at him.*) I'm going to a college where they understand. Where they appreciate good white professors, where there won't be any Chicanos . . . like Fresno State College. President Baxter, help!!!

(*Exits stage right. Everybody starts looking for change. Vato begins to take collection.*)

FRANCISCO. ¿Colecta, para qué?

FIRST NEW STUDENT. La birria.

SECOND NEW STUDENT. La mota.

THIRD NEW STUDENT. El wine.

FRANCISCO. Pos, ¿no están bien, calabazas? Estamos en colegio. Hay que aprender de nuestra cultura, nuestra raza, de Aztlán.

VATO. (*Turns to next student.*) But who's going to teach us? (*They move on down the line asking each other the same question.*)

ESPERANZA. (*Last in line, asks Francisco.*) Who's going to teach us?

FRANCISCO. Who's going to teach us?

ALL. Our own people! (*They point at audience.*)

FRANCISCO. ¡Entonces, qué se dice? ¡Viva . . . !

ALL. !La raza!

FRANCISCO. ¡Viva!

ALL. ¡La huelga!

FRANCISCO. ¡Chicano!

ALL. Power! (*Actors get audience to shout "Chicano power." Then all sing "Bella Ciao."*)

A SOLID HOME
(UN HOGAR SOLIDO)
E L E N A   G A R R O

Elena Garro (1920–1999)

Elena Garro's first love was the theater: reading the classics of Spain's golden age as a child, touring provincial cities with other student actors, and performing in Mexico City's Palace of Fine Arts and in the university theater productions of the National Autonomous University of Mexico (UNAM). In the preface of the one-act play *El Árbol* (*The Tree*, 1967), Garro asserted:

> My first contact with the theater was in my childhood when I read the Spanish classics. *Lady Simpleton* (by Lope de Vega), *The Star of Sevilla* (another play attributed to Lope de Vega), *The Walls Have Ears* (by Juan Ruiz de Alarcón), *The Dog in the Manger* (Lope de Vega), *The Man Condemned for Lack of Faith* (by Tirso de Molina), etc. introduced me to the shining world of Spanish fantasy from which I still have not escaped. The discovery of a world which exists locked up in books and which can be re-created at will, revealed to me the possibility of living within a reality infinitely richer than everyday reality.

In 1937, at the young age of 17, Garro married the Mexican Nobel Prize winner Octavio Paz, who was in the earliest stages of his prominent and influential career. The two spent the first months of their marriage in Spain as part of the International Brigades, fighting against the armies of Francisco Franco. When they returned to Mexico, she began to write for the journal *Asi*, but she left her career as a journalist to accompany Paz to the United States, first to Berkeley (1943) and later to San Francisco (1945). After a short residence in New York, she went to France as a member of the Mexican diplomatic corps. Paz and Garro came to know the Parisian and expatriate artists and writers living in the French capital. In 1951 she followed Paz to Tokyo, where he served as ambassador for three years. On her return to Mexico, she began to publish some of her plays and wrote several movie scripts, two of which were successfully produced.

Garro became involved with the cause of the peasants fighting for agrarian reform, using her skills as a writer and her contacts within the government to help the movement. However, the Mexican president, seeking to minimize her influence, sent her to New York to isolate her from Mexican politics. When Paz returned to Paris as ambassador (1959), Garro left New York to join him, only to find that he had been granted a divorce by mail. Although this dissolution was later declared illegal, the separation was final and led eventually to a legal divorce.

From abroad, Garro made infrequent visits to Mexico, where she continued to support agrarian reformers and opposition groups. In 1968 she was briefly jailed as an instigator of the student demonstrations that culminated in the slaughter in Tlatelolco Plaza, where police killed hundreds of students and spectators at an antigovernment protest. After an additional 20 years abroad, she returned to Mexico City, and subsequently died in Cuernavaca in September 1999.

Although she was born in Puebla, Mexico, and did not leave her country until 1937, the fact that her father was a Spaniard and that she did not declare herself a Mexican when she turned 21 complicated her citizenship. In 1943 she had to undergo the difficult process of naturalization, and again she had problems in 1963 when she returned from Paris. In addition to her many years abroad, Garro allied herself with political causes unacceptable to the conservative governmental administration. Perhaps these obstacles only served to strengthen her sense of identity as a Mexican.

Garro published more novels and short stories than plays, consistent with the difficulties Latin American playwrights face in producing or publishing their work. However, from 1956 to 1958, the University of Veracruz published *Un hogar sólido*, containing 12 plays. The title play was produced, along with two others from the collection—"Los pilares de Doña Blanca" (*The Pillars of Doña Blanca*) and *Andarse por las ramas* (*To Beat Around the Bushes*)—during the 1957 season at UNAM. In 1963 she won the important Villaurrutia Prize for the book *Los recuerdos del provenir* (*Recollections of Things to Come*) and her play *La señora en su balcon* (*The Lady on Her Balcony*) was produced by the Mexican Studio Theater (Teatro Estudios de México) with such great success that it toured several Latin American countries.

A SOLID HOME (1957)

In an interview with Patricia Rosas Lopategui and Rhina Toruño, Garro claimed that one night in a bar on the Paseo de la Reforma (a central boulevard in Mexico City) while talking with her cousin Amalia Herñandez, founder of the Ballet Folklórico de México, she remarked: "What I need is a solid home." She had the title for a play, and when Octavio Paz asked her to write something for his theater Poesía en Voz Alta (Poetry Aloud), she completed the play in half an hour. She confesses that she had not given any thought to a possible relationship to Sartre's play *No Exit*, nor to any relationship to the Surrealists. This story may be true, but it is also the kind of mask Mexicans often adopt to avoid self-revelation. At the time of this interview, Garro still suffered repercussions from the bloody incident in Tlatelolco. After her experiences in jail, harsh criticism, and outrageous rumors, she no longer maintained ties with other intellectuals in Paris and even stopped going to the theater.

In *A Solid Home* the typical Mexican fascination with death takes an unexpected form, for the characters are neither ghosts nor *almas en pensa* (suffering souls). With a characteristic Mexican sense of humor about death (see Center Stage box, Día de los Muertos in Mexico, following the text of the play), Don Clement, the family patriarch, is always misplacing parts of his skeleton, and his granddaughter parades around using his femur as a toy trumpet. Doña Gertrude, his wife, is so embarrassed by the inappropriateness of her shroud that she dare not rise to greet her family members.

The play opens within a family crypt as several generations of Don Clement's family await the Final Judgment. Family members pass the time with complaints, laments for family members buried apart from the rest, and reminiscences about life. Suddenly they detect the approach of still another person suspended in a circle of light. She is Lydia, a daughter now reunited with her parents and other family members she has known only through photographs and family stories. The audience hears part of the graveside eulogy portraying Lydia's life as one of "unbreakable faith, Christian forbearance, and piety" as befits a proper Mexican woman—the wife and mother who denies herself as a sacrifice to her husband and children. She leaves behind "a solid Christian home," but Lydia feels she has missed something.

Lydia (or Lili, her childhood name) chats with Muni, a cousin whose body she identified in the police station. Presumably, Muni succumbed to a vagrant lifestyle while searching for "a solid city, like the home which we had as children." Lydia sought a more personal level of happiness ("a solid home"), but what she found was a house into which she poured her energies, passing the time performing wifely duties.

Where was the *hilo mágico* ("magic thread") that ties the invisible world together? Muni and the other adult characters explain that she will find it now, and as the curtain falls, she exclaims, "A solid home! That's what I am! The stone slabs of my tomb!"

Garro's play illustrates a most intriguing feature of Mexican (and Latin American) literature, art, and theater: magic realism. Its imaginative blend of Surrealistic images and realistic issues serves a higher purpose than mere theatricality, although it is among the most truly theatrical styles in world drama. Rather, magic realism encourages both artists and audience to transcend the limitations of our day-to-day existence by undertaking a spiritual journey that allows us to see essential truths about human existence. Just as Lydia must transcend the bounds of the "real" world in which she lives to understand the truth of her "reality," so, too, does magic realism permit us to escape the mundane and the obvious to see—better yet, to experience—the world as if for the first time.

Bernardíne Banning
Radford University

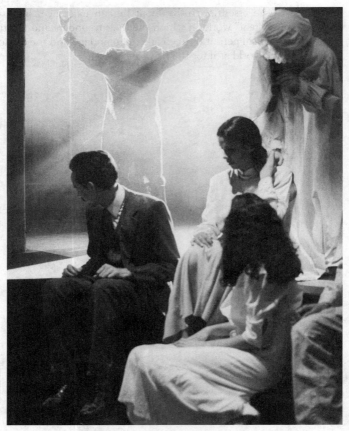

With the aid of magic realism, Vincente Mejía enters from the world of los muertos (the dead) in the Núcleo de Estudios Teatrales Drama School production of Elena Garro's A Solid Home, *directed by Sandra Félix.*

A SOLID HOME
(UN HOGAR SOLIDO)

E L E N A   G A R R O

C H A R A C T E R S
DON CLEMENT, *sixty years old*
DOÑA GERTRUDE, *forty years old*
MAMA JESSIE, *eighty years old*
KATIE, *five years old*

VINCENT MEJÍA, *twenty-three years old*
MUNI, *twenty-eight years old*
EVE, *a foreigner, twenty years old*
LYDIA, *thirty-two years old*

(Interior of a small room with stone walls and ceiling. There are neither windows nor doors. To the left, imbedded in the wall and of stone also, are some berths. In one of them, Mama Jessie in a nightgown and a lace sleep cap. The stage is very dark.)

VOICE OF DOÑA GERTRUDE. Clement! Clement! I hear footsteps!

VOICE OF DON CLEMENT. You're always hearing footsteps! Why must women be so impatient? Always anticipating what isn't going to happen, predicting calamities!

VOICE OF DOÑA GERTRUDE. Well, I hear them.

VOICE OF DON CLEMENT. No, woman, you're always mistaken. You're carried away by your nostalgia for catastrophes. . . .

VOICE OF DOÑA GERTRUDE. It's true . . . but this time I'm not mistaken.

VOICE OF KATIE. They're many feet, Gertrude! *(Katie comes out dressed in an ancient white dress, high black shoes, and a coral necklace. Her hair is tied at the nape of her neck with a red bow).* How nice! Now nice! Tra-la-la! Tra-la-la! *(She jumps and claps her hands.)*

DOÑA GERTRUDE *(appearing in a rose dress of the 1930s).* Children don't make mistakes. Aunt Katherine, isn't it true that someone is coming?

KATIE. Yes, I know it! I knew it from the first time that they came! I was so afraid here all alone. . . .

DON CLEMENT *(appearing in a black suit with white cuffs).* I believe that they're right. Gertrude! Gertrude! Help me find my metacarpuses. I always lose them and I can't shake hands without them.

VINCENT MEJÍA *(appearing in a uniform of an officer of Benito Juárez).* You read a lot, Don Clement, that's why you have the bad habit of forgetting things. Look at me, perfect in my uniform, always ready for any occasion!

MAMA JESSIE *(straightening up in her berth and poking out her head which is covered with the lace sleeping cap).* Katie's right! The steps are coming this way. *(She puts one hand behind her ear as though listening.)* The first ones have stopped . . . unless the Ramirezes have had a misfortune. . . . This neighborhood has already been very disappointing to us!

KATIE *(jumping).* You, go to sleep, Jessie! You only like to sleep:

Rock-a-bye Jessie.
on the tree top.
When the wind blows,
the cradle will rock.
When the bough bends,
the cradle will fall.
And down will come Jessie,
cradle and all.

MAMA JESSIE. And what do you want me to do? If they left me in my nightgown . . .

DON CLEMENT. Don't complain, Mama Jessie. We thought that out of respect . . .

DOÑA GERTRUDE. If it had been up to me, mama . . . , but what were the girls and Clement going to do?

(Many footsteps which stop and then start again are heard overhead.)

MAMA JESSIE. Katie! Come here and polish my forehead. I want it to shine like the North Star. Happy the day when I went through the house like lightning, sweeping, shaking the dust that would fall on the piano in deceptive gold mists. Then when everything shone like a comet. I'd break the ice on my bucket of water left out in the night air and bathe myself with water full of winter stars. Do you remember, Gertrude! That was living! Surrounded by my children straight and clean as lead pencils.

DOÑA GERTRUDE. Yes, mama. And I also remember the burnt cork you used to make circles under your eyes with, and the lemons you'd eat so that you'd look pale. And those nights when you would go with papa to the theater. How pretty you looked with your fan and your drop earrings!

MAMA JESSIE. You see, daughter, life is short. Each time that I would arrive at our box. . . .

DON CLEMENT *(interrupting).* For pity's sake, now I can't find my femur!

MAMA JESSIE. What a lack of courtesy! To interrupt a lady!

(Meanwhile, Katie has been helping Jessie arrange her nightcap.)

VINCENT MEJÍA. I saw Katie using it for a trumpet.

DOÑA GERTRUDE. Aunt Katie, where did you leave Clement's femur?

KATIE. Jessie, Jessie! They want to take my bugle away from me!

MAMA JESSIE. Gertrude, let this child alone! And as for you, let me tell you for a grown woman you're more spoiled than she is. . . .

DOÑA GERTRUDE. But, mama, don't be unjust. It's Clement's femur!

KATIE. Ugly! Bad! I'll hit you! It's not his femur, it's my little sugar bugle!

DON CLEMENT *(to Gertrude).* Could she have eaten it? Your aunt's unbearable.

DOÑA GERTRUDE. I don't know, Clement. My broken clavicle got lost. She liked the little streaks left along the scar a lot. And it was my favorite bone! It reminded me of the walls of my house, covered with heliotrope. I told you how I fell, didn't I? The day before, we'd gone to the circus. All of Chihuahua was in the stands to see the clown, Richard Bell. Suddenly a tightrope walker came out. She resembled a butterfly. I've never forgotten her. . . . *(A blow is heard above. Gertrude interrupts herself. Continuing:)* In the morning I climbed the fence to dance on one foot, because all night I'd dreamed that I was she. . . . *(Overhead a harder blow is heard.)* Of course, I didn't know that I had bones. As a little girl, one doesn't know anything. Because

I broke it, I always say that it was the first little bone that I had. It takes you by surprise!

(*The blows follow one another more rapidly.*)

VINCENT MEJÍA (*smoothing his mustache*). There's no doubt. Someone's coming. We have guests. (*He sings.*)
> When in darkness
> The moon glimmers
> And on the pool
> The swallow sings . . .

MAMA JESSIE. Be quiet, Vincent! This isn't the time to sing. Look at these unexpected guests! In my day people announced themselves before dropping in for a visit. There was more respect. Let's see now whom they're bringing us, probably one of these foreigners who married my girls! "God overwhelms the humble!" as my poor Raymond, may God have him in his Glory, used to say. . . .

VINCENT MEJÍA. You haven't improved at all, Jessie! You find defects in everything. Before, you were so agreeable. The only thing you liked was to dance polkas! (*He hums a tune and dances a few steps.*) Do you remember how we danced at that carnival? (*He continues dancing.*) Your pink dress spun around and around, and your neck was very close to my lips . . .

MAMA JESSIE. For heaven's sake, cousin Vincent! Don't remind me of those foolish things.

VINCENT MEJÍA (*laughing*). What would Raymond say now? He was so jealous. And you and I here together, while he rots there alone in that other cemetery.

DOÑA GERTRUDE. Uncle Vincent, be quiet. You're going to cause an argument.

DON CLEMENT (*alarmed*). I already explained to you, Mama Jessie, that at the time we didn't have the money to transfer him.

MAMA JESSIE. And the girls, why don't they bring him? Don't give me explanations. You always lacked tact.

(*A harder blow is heard.*)

KATIE. I saw a light! (*A ray of light enters.*) I saw a sword. St. Michael's coming to visit us again! Look at his sword!

VINCENT MEJÍA. Are we all here? Now then, easy does it!

DON CLEMENT. Muni and my sister-in-law are missing.

MAMA JESSIE. The foreigners, always keeping away!

DOÑA GERTRUDE. Muni, Muni! Someone's coming. Maybe it's one of your cousins. Aren't you happy, dear? You'll be able to play and laugh with them again. Let's see if that sadness leaves you.

(*Eve appears, blond, tall, sad, very young, in a traveling dress of the 1920s.*)

EVE. Muni was around here a moment ago. Muni, dear! Do you hear that blow? That's the way the sea beats against the rocks of my house. . . . None of you knew it. . . . It was a rock, high, like a wave, always beaten by the winds that lulled us to sleep at night. Swirls of salt covered its windows with sea stars. The walls in the kitchen had a golden glow which radiated from my father's hands, warm as the sun. . . . During the nights, creatures of wind, water, fire, and salt came in through the fireplace. They would huddle in the flames and sing in the water that dripped into the washstands. . . . Drip! Drop! Drip! Drop! Drip! Drop! . . . And iodine spread itself about the house like sleep. . . . The tail of a shining dolphin would announce day to us, with this light of fish scales and corals!

(*With the last sentence, Eve raises her arm and points to the torrent of light that enters the crypt when the first stone slab is moved above. The room is inundated with sunlight. All the luxurious clothes are dusty and all the faces pale. The child Katie jumps with pleasure.*)

KATIE. Look, Jessie! Someone's coming! Who's bringing him, Jessie? Lady Diptheria or Saint Michael?

MAMA JESSIE. Wait, child. We're going to see.

KATIE. Lady Diptheria brought me. Do you remember her? She had fingers of cotton and she wouldn't let me breathe. Did she frighten you, Jessie?

MAMA JESSIE. Yes, little sister. I remember that they took you away and the patio of the house remained strewn with purple petals. Mama cried a lot and we girls did too.

KATIE. Dummy! Didn't you know that you were going to come to play with me here? That day, St. Michael sat down beside me and wrote it with his sword of fire on the roof of my house. I didn't know how to read . . . and I read it. And was the school of the Misses Simson nice?

MAMA JESSIE. Very nice, Katie. Mama sent us with black ribbons. . . .

KATIE. And did you learn to spell? That's why mama was going to send me. . . .

MUNI (*comes in wearing pajamas, with a blue face and blond hair*). Who can it be?

(*Overhead, through the fragment of the vault open to the sky, a woman's feet are seen suspended in a circle of light.*)

DOÑA GERTRUDE. Clement, Clement! They're Lydia's feet. What a pleasure, daughter, what a pleasure that you've died so soon!

(*Everyone becomes silent. The descent of Lydia, suspended on ropes, begins. She is stiff, wearing a white dress, her arms crossed on her chest, her fingers in the form of a cross, and her head bowed. Her eyes are closed.*)

KATIE. Who's Lydia?

MUNI. Lydia's the daughter of my uncle Clement and my aunt Gertrude, Katie. (*He caresses the girl.*)

MAMA JESSIE. Now we have the whole bunch of grandchildren here. So many brats! Well, isn't the crematory oven more modern? As far as I'm concerned at least it seems more hygienic.

KATIE. Isn't it true, Jessie, that Lydia isn't for real?

MAMA JESSIE. I wish it were so, my dear. There's room here for everyone except my poor Raymond!

EVE. How she grew! When I came she was as little as Muni.

(*Lydia remains standing, in the midst of all of them, as they look at her. Then she opens her eyes and sees them.*)

LYDIA. Papa! (*She embraces him.*) Mama! Muni! (*She embraces them.*)

DOÑA GERTRUDE. You're looking very well, daughter.

LYDIA. And grandmother?

DON CLEMENT. She can't get up. Do you remember that we made the mistake of burying her in her nightgown?

MAMA JESSIE. Yes, Lili, here I am, lying down forever.

DOÑA GERTRUDE. My mother's notions! You already know, Lili, how well groomed she always was.

MAMA JESSIE. The worst thing will be, daughter, to present yourself this way before God, our Lord. Doesn't it seem a disgrace to you? Why didn't it occur to you to bring me a dress? That gray one with the brocade ruffles and the bouquet of violets at the neck. Do you remember it? I'd put it on for formal occasions . . . but no one remembers the old people. . . .

KATIE. When Saint Michael visits us, she hides.

LYDIA. And who are you, precious?

KATIE. Katie!

LYDIA. Of course! We had your picture on the piano! Now it's in Evie's house. How sad it was to look at you, so melancholy, painted in your white dress. I'd forgotten that you were here.

VINCENT MEJÍA. And aren't you pleased to meet me, niece?

LYDIA. Uncle Vincent! We also had your picture in the living room, with your uniform and your medal in a little red velvet box.

EVE. And don't you remember your Aunt Eve?

LYDIA. Aunt Eve! Yes, I just barely remember you, with your blond hair spread out in the sun . . . and I remember your purple parasol and your faded face under it, like that of a beautiful drowned woman . . . and your empty chair rocking to the rhythm of your song, after you had gone.

(*From the circle of light, a Voice comes forth.*)

VOICE. The general earth of our Mexico opens its arms to give you loving shelter. Virtuous woman, most exemplary mother, model wife, you leave an irreparable void . . .

MAMA JESSIE. Who's speaking to you with such familiarity?

LYDIA. It's Don Gregory de la Huerta Ramírez Puente, President of the Association of the Blind.

VINCENT MEJÍA. What madness! And what do so many blind people do together?

MAMA JESSIE. But why does he address you in such intimate terms?

DOÑA GERTRUDE. It's the style, mama, to address the dead familiarly.

VOICE. Most cruel loss, whose absence we shall feel in time. You leave us forever deprived of your boundless charm. You also leave a solid and Christian home in the most terrible neglect. The homes do tremble before inexorable Death. . . .

DON CLEMENT. Good God! But is that blustering fool still running around there?

MAMA JESSIE. What's useless abounds.

LYDIA. Yes, and now he's president of the bank, of the Knights of Columbus, of the Association for the Blind, the Flag Day and Mother's Day Committees.

VOICE. Only irrevocable faith, Christian resignation, and pity . . .

KATIE. Don Hilary always says the same thing.

MAMA JESSIE. It isn't Don Hilary, Katie. Don Hilary died trifling sixty-five years ago. . . .

KATIE (*not hearing her*). When they brought me, he said, "A little angel flew away!" And it wasn't true. I was here below, alone and very frightened. Isn't that so Vincent? Isn't it true that I don't tell lies?

VINCENT MEJÍA. You're telling me! Imagine, I arrived here, still stunned by the powder flashes, with my wounds open . . . and what do I see? Katie crying: "I want to see my mama! I want to see my mama!" What trouble she caused me! Believe me, I'd rather have fought the French. . . .

VOICE. Rest in peace!

(*They begin to replace the stone slabs. The scene becomes dark slowly.*)

KATIE. We were alone a long time, weren't we, Vincent? We didn't know what was happening, but no one came anymore.

MAMA JESSIE. I've already told you, Katie, we went to the capital, then the revolution came along. . . .

KATIE. Until one day Eve arrived. You said, Vincent, that she was a foreigner. . . .

VINCENT MEJÍA. The situation was a little tense and Eve didn't say a single word to us.

EVE. I too was restrained . . . and besides I was thinking of Muni . . . and of my home. . . . Everything was so quiet here.

(*Silence. They place the last slab.*)

LYDIA. And now, what'll we do?

DON CLEMENT. Wait.

LYDIA. Still wait?

DOÑA GERTRUDE. Yes, daughter. You'll see.

EVE. You'll see everything you want to see, except your home with your white pine table and the waves and the sails of the boats through your windows.

MUNI. Aren't you happy, Lili?

LYDIA. Yes, Muni, especially to see you. When I saw you that night lying in the courtyard of the police station, with that smell of urine that came from the broken flagstones, and you dead on the stretcher, between the feet of the policemen with your wrinkled pajamas and your blue face, I ask myself, "Why? Why?"

KATIE. Me too, Lili. I hadn't seen a blue dead person either. Then Jessie told me that cyanide has many artists' brushes, but only one tube of color, blue!

MAMA JESSIE. Don't bother that boy any longer! Blue looks very good on blonds.

MUNI. Why, cousin Lili? Haven't you seen stray dogs walk and walk along the sidewalks looking for bones in the butcher shops full of flies, and the butcher, with his fingers drenched in blood from cutting up the meat? Well, I no longer wanted to talk along atrocious sidewalks looking through the blood for a bone, nor look at those corners, shelters for drunks and urinals for dogs. I wanted a happy city, full of sunlight and moonlight. A solid city like the home we had as children, with sunshine in every door, moonlight for every window, and wandering stars in the rooms. Do you remember it, Lili? It had a labyrinth of laughs. Its kitchen was a crossroads; its garden, source of all the rivers; and all of it, the birthplace of Man. . . .

LYDIA. A solid home, Muni! That's just what I wanted . . . and you already know, they took me to a strange house. And in it I found only clocks and eyes without eyelids that looked at me for years. . . . I polished the floors so as not to see the thousands of dead words that the maids swept in the mornings. I shined the mirrors in order to drive away our hostile glances. I hoped that one morning the loving image would face me in the looking glass. I opened books in order to open avenues in that circular hell. I embroidered napkins with linked initials in order to find the magic, unbreakable thread that make two names into one. . . .

MUNI. I know, Lili.

LYDIA. But it was all useless. The furious eyes didn't stop looking at me ever. If I could find the spider that once lived in my house—with the invisible thread that unites the flower to light, the apple to fragrance, woman to man, I would sew loving eyelids to close the eyes that look at me and this house would enter into the solar order. Each balcony would be a different country. Its furniture would bloom. From its glasses jets of water would spurt. The sheets would turn into magic carpets in order to travel to sleep. From the hands of my children, castles, flags, and battles would come forth . . . but I didn't find the thread, Muni. . . .

MUNI. You told me that at the police station. In that strange courtyard, forever far from the other courtyard, in whose sky a belltower counted for us the hours that we had left to play.

LYDIA. Yes, Muni, and you I put away forever the last day

that we were children. Afterward, only a Lydia seated, facing the wall, waiting, remained.

MUNI. I couldn't grow, either, and live on the street corners. I wanted my home. . . .

EVE. Me too, Muni, my son, I wanted a solid home. A house that the sea would beat every night. Boom! Boom! A house that would laugh with my father's laugh full of fish and nets.

MUNI. Don't be sad, Lili. You'll find the thread, and you'll find the spider.

DON CLEMENT. Lili, aren't you happy? Now your house is the center of the sun, the heart of every star, the root of all the grasses, the most solid point of every stone.

MUNI. Yes, Lili, you still don't know it, but suddenly you won't need a house, nor a river. We'll not swim in the Mezcala River, we'll be the Mezcala.

DOÑA GERTRUDE. At times, daughter, you'll be very cold, and you'll be the snow falling on an unknown city or gray roofs and red caps.

KATIE. What I like most is being a piece of candy in a little girl's mouth. Or a sty, to make those who read near a window weep!

MUNI. Don't grieve when your eyes begin to disappear, because then you'll be all the eyes of the dogs looking at absurd feet.

MAMA JESSIE. Ah, child! May you never be the eyes of the blind, of a blind fish in the deepest abyss of the seas! You don't know the terrible feeling that I had. It was like seeing and not seeing things never thought of.

KATIE (*laughing and clapping*). You also were very frightened when you were the worm that came in and out of your mouth.

VINCENT MEJÍA. Well, for me, the worst thing was being a murderer's dagger!

MAMA JESSIE. Now the gophers will return. Don't shout when you yourself run along your face.

DON CLEMENT. Don't tell her that. You're going to frighten her. It's frightening to learn to be everything.

DOÑA GERTRUDE. Especially because in the world one scarcely learns to be a man.

LYDIA. And will I be able to be a pine tree with a nest of spiders and build a solid home?

DON CLEMENT. Of course! And you'll be the pine tree and the staircase and the fire.

LYDIA. And then?

MAMA JESSIE. Then God will call us to his bosom.

DON CLEMENT. After having learned to be all things, St. Michael's sword will appear, center of the universe, and by its light the divine armies of angels will come forth and we'll enter into the celestial order.

MUNI. I want to be the fold of an angel's tunic.

MAMA JESSIE. Your color will go very well. It'll give beautiful reflections. And I, what'll I do dressed in this nightgown?

KATIE. I want to be the index finger of God the Father!

ALL TOGETHER. Child!

EVE. And I, a wave sprinkled with salt, changed into a cloud!

LYDIA. And I the sewing fingers of the Virgin, embroidering . . . embroidering . . . !

DOÑA GERTRUDE. And I the music from the harp of St. Cecilia!

VINCENT MEJÍA. And I the rage of the sword of St. Gabriel!

DON CLEMENT. And I a particle of the stone of St. Peter!

KATIE. And I a window that looks at the world!

MAMA JESSIE. There'll no longer be a world, Katie, because we'll be all that after the Final Judgment.

KATIE (*weeping*). There'll no longer be a world. And when am I going to see it? I didn't see anything. I didn't even learn the spelling book. I want there to be a world.

VINCENT MEJÍA. Look at it now, Katie!

(*In the distance a trumpet is heard.*)

MAMA JESSIE. Jesus, Mary Most Pure! The trumpet of Final Judgment! And me in a nightgown! Pardon me, my Lord, this immodesty!

LYDIA. No, grandma, it's taps. There's a barracks near the cemetery.

MAMA JESSIE. Ah, yes, they had already told me! And I always forget it. Who had the bright idea of putting a barracks so close to us? What a government! It lends itself to so much confusion!

VINCENT MEJÍA. Taps! I'm going. I'm the wind that opens all the doors that I didn't open, that goes up the stairs that I never went up in a whirl, that runs along new streets in my officer's uniform and lifts the skirts of the pretty, unknown girls. . . . Ah, coolness! (*He disappears.*)

MAMA JESSIE. Rascal!

DON CLEMENT. Ah, rain on the water! (*He disappears.*)

DOÑA GERTRUDE. Wood in flames! (*She disappears.*)

MUNI. Do you hear? A dog howls. Ah, melancholy! (*She disappears.*)

KATIE. The table where nine children eat supper! I'm the game they play! (*She disappears.*)

MAMA JESSIE. The fresh heart of a head of lettuce! (*She disappears.*)

EVE. I'm the flash of fire that sinks into the black sea! (*She disappears.*)

LYDIA. A solid home! That's what I am! The stone slabs of my tomb! (*She disappears.*)

CURTAIN

CENTER STAGE   DÍA DE LOS MUERTOS IN MEXICO

Mexico's Día de los Muertos (Day of the Dead) is a traditional fiesta that celebrates life and death as a single entity in human experience. On November 1 and 2—which correspond to the Christian All Saints' and All Souls' Days, respectively (as well as Halloween)—even the tiniest Mexican villages are overrun by cavorting spirits, skeletons, and other impersonations of *los muertitos* ("the dead ones"). The celebration is simultaneously a sacred and satiric ritual, part street theater and part folk ceremony, that may be traced to ancient rites signaling the end of the growing season.

Mexico's fascination with death can be traced to the Aztec Empire. At the Grand Pyramid of Quetzalcoatl, near what is now Mexico City, Aztec worshippers could view thousands of human skulls on a rack adjacent to the sacred temple. Inside, dozens of clay jars held human remains. As recently as a hundred years ago, actual human skulls were exhumed for the Day of the Dead, after which they were carefully replaced under the supervision of village priests.

Today the Day of the Dead is observed over a two-day period, though preparations begin well in advance of November 1, when the souls of children (*los angelitos*) return to their families and loved ones. Special sweet breads (*panes de muertos*) are baked, and gifts (*ofertas*) are given to children, both living and deceased. Failing to give gifts for the dead is considered a serious offense; those who do not leave *ofertas* to their dead will see the spirits of weeping relatives visit their own graves. The souls of the children leave on the morning of November 2 as those of deceased adults arrive.

On November 2, a national holiday in Mexico, townspeople march en masse in a triumphant procession to the cemetery, where food is placed on the graves of loved ones. En route, young girls strew flower petals from the *Zempausuchitl* (the marigold) to attract the souls of the dead. A street band leads the procession, while drum-beating skeletons dance about the crowd, playing tricks on unsuspecting audience members to scare off anyone who might bring bad luck. After cleansing the graves, the living remain for a festive vigil in which the spirits of the departed are welcomed back. The merrymaking includes skits (*actos*) that make fun of death and dying. The clowning allows the survivors to laugh at death and to accept it as a natural part of life's process. They further comfort themselves with storytelling, music, and dancing. As night falls, a costume ball—the Dance of Death—commands the attention of revelers, many of whom wear costumes associated with death. Children amuse themselves by playing with puppets and other toys that bear images of death. They also eat sugar skeletons with their names written on the skulls.

Octavio Paz, Mexico's 1990 Nobel laureate, writes that Día de los Muertos is not only a national ritual but also a manifestation of the Mexican character. For the Mexican, "Death is not the natural end of life, but one phase of an infinite cycle. Life, death and resurrection are stages of a cosmic process that repeat itself continuously. . . . A civilization that denies death ends up denying life."

In *A Solid Home* Elena Garro reflects Mexico's unique celebration of death as she presents the ironic wit and theatricality that permeates Día de los Muertos.

José Guadalupe Posada revolutionized contemporary Mexican art with his pen-and-ink drawings of Día de los Muertos; well-dressed skeletons cavort in a graveyard in a sketch that epitomizes the spirited manner in which Mexicans confront death.

PAPER FLOWERS
(FLORES DE PAPEL)

A Play in Six Scenes

EGON WOLFF

EGON WOLFF (1926–)

Although a chemical engineer by training, Egon Wolff emerged as a leading voice in South American drama, particularly when *Paper Flowers* won the coveted *Casa de las Américas* Prize in 1970 as Latin America's best new play. The influential *Latin American Theatre Review* called the play "among the top three or four plays from all of Spanish America" in its Spring 1983 edition.

Wolff first wrote plays as an avocation, largely because he wished to address the social, political, and economic problems facing his native Chile. In 1963 he achieved national recognition for his play *The Invaders*, an Expressionistic work in which a rich industrialist dreams that his estate is invaded by the poor—a dream that becomes frighteningly true. Chileans considered the play prophetic when in 1970 Salvador Allende Gossens was elected president, the first Marxist to be elected democratically in the Western Hemisphere. Allende, who promised to turn Chile into a socialist state, was driven from office just three years later by a right-wing military coup led by Augusto Pinochet Ugarte.

As might be expected, Wolff's plays reflect the bitter and often violent struggles between Chile's wealthy and poor classes. He maintains his emphasis on class conflict because "people aren't listening." His plays are directed at the upper class, who—according to Wolff—have the responsibility and the power to change social circumstances in Chile (and elsewhere in Latin America). However, he does not write overt political dramas because "it doesn't interest me."

Wolff admits that his work has become increasingly darker, less hopeful. When he was younger he felt he had answers for the social problems he depicted. "I write for the present of Chile and that is enough. 'Future' is a word that sometimes terrifies me." He continues to write and to work as an engineer. His works have been produced throughout Latin America, the United States, and Great Britain, in both Spanish and English productions.

PAPER FLOWERS (1970)

Paper Flowers may remind North American audiences of Edward Albee's *The Zoo Story* (1958), a controversial one-act play about a New York drifter who accosts a middle-class man in Central Park, berates him for his indifference to the plight of the less fortunate, and finally forces the hapless bourgeois to commit a shocking act of violence that horribly joins the two men in the final moment. Europeans may align Wolff's drama with Harold Pinter's theater of menace because its ambiguous dialogue creates a tension that is simultaneously disturbing and darkly amusing. The plot is also Pinteresque: a seemingly "safe" room is invaded by a mysterious stranger whose presence becomes more menacing as the play progresses toward its frightening conclusion. That Wolff should invite comparisons with Albee and Pinter is not surprising, as the latter were among the West's most imitated playwrights during the 1960s.

Wolff may have absorbed both plot and stylistic elements from the likes of Albee and Pinter, but his work—particularly *Paper Flowers*—reflects the social and political realities that shaped Latin American drama in the 1970s. Wolff's native Chile was perhaps the most notorious example of a country run by an oppressive military dictatorship committed to the preservation of wealth by the few at the expense of the many. The Hake's debasement and eventual conquest of the middle-class Eva reflects the restless, revolutionary spirit among Latin America's poor. Wolff's antipathy toward middle-class complacency, which he believes contributes to anarchy and revolution among the oppressed, has been well documented. *Paper Flowers* is, in one respect, a dramatic working out of a manifesto issued by the Coordinating Committee of the Revolutionary Imagination in Buenos Aires in 1969:

> Art as produced by our society will always be absorbed and rendered useless by the bourgeois. . . . What is it we want to transform? The Latin American man—ourselves: victims of neocolonial exploitation, of our native oligarchy, of all the forms of degradation and humiliation, conscious and unconscious, which shape our human and cultural values, our very existence.

It was in this spirit that many theater companies and collectives were formed throughout Latin America. And it is in this spirit that the Hake tells Eva that "I only know what I am, what I seem and that I am what I don't seem. In other words, you have your fantasy and I have only reality, which is much poorer, much sadder, much more disillusioning." The destruction he wreaks on her well-ordered bourgeois home manifests Wolff's vision of the anarchy that awaits Chile—indeed much of South America—if the disparity between social classes is not addressed. The apocalyptic finale—a mock wedding between the warring classes—is Wolff's darkest resolution and suggests that the hope for reconciliation he expressed in a similar play (*The Invaders*, 1963) is impossible.

But *Paper Flowers* is a more intriguing play than so many of the political tracts that emerged throughout Latin America during this tumultuous period. On one hand, the play is a taut psychological thriller in which the Hake methodically destroys Eva's personality and absorbs it into his own, which is filled with self-loathing. Socioeconomics aside, the Hake's treacherous conquest of Eva recalls Iago's destruction of Othello, and—as in Shakespeare's play—we are simultaneously fascinated and repulsed by the audacity of his mischief. The skilled, yet destructive, tempter is among the oldest archetypes known to humanity. It is no accident that Wolff names his heroine Eva and makes a point of having the Hake discover her in the Botanical Garden painting picture-perfect flowers. The Hake—whose name in Spanish is El Merluza—is a predatory fish of the Chilean coastal waters noted for its sharp teeth and voracious appetite. He is a cousin of the infamous serpent in the Garden of Genesis, a seducer of the impressionable. Thus the playwright marries mythology with sociology, noting that because hake is a dietary staple of Chile's poor, it is an apt symbol of the socioeconomic conflict of the play.

On another level, *Paper Flowers* joins a rich treasury of literature devoted to "the battle of the sexes." The Hake's conquest is as much one of sexual domination as it is sociopolitical or psychological. He takes over not only Eva's habitat but her clothing as well (e.g., he wears her bathrobe in scene 3). And throughout the play his language (its ambiguity becomes a weapon by which he destroys Eva) is fraught with sexual innuendo that is simultaneously erotic and degrading. Such phrases as "anything you want to give me," "the way you cross your legs," and "you have to raise the chair skirt" abet the Hake's multilevel seduction of Eva. Again we are reminded of another play, *Miss Julie*. Although Wolff has said he did not know Strindberg's *Miss Julie* when he wrote *Paper Flowers*, there are nonetheless extraordinary similarities between the two works. The brutal killing of Eva's pet canary (compare Julie's green finch) is an obvious parallel. *Miss Julie* was a naturalistic drama that explored the hereditary forces that led to the countess's destruction, even as it reflected Strindberg's much-discussed misogyny. But Wolff is no misogynist, and the Hake's brutal degradation of Eva reflects the unfortunate reality of the subjugation of women throughout the world. In Latin America the problem is particularly exacerbated by the cult of *machismo* or "macho" by which one's manhood is validated by "owning" a woman. Note that the Hake refers (with his usual ambiguity) to the macho world of the streets, gangs, and violence. (Curiously, he is terrified by the ominous specter of Mario, who may or may not exist.) The converse of *machismo* is *mariannismo*, a term used by psychotherapists Rosa Maria Gil and Carmen Inoa Vazquez to describe a situation in which Latinas enable men by remaining faithful and submissive, regardless of how they are treated. Among the most frequently asked questions about the play and its meaning is, "Why does Eva allow the Hake to treat her so inhumanely?" It is the question, unfortunately, that we must ask ourselves about battered women. *Paper Flowers* may be read as a condemnation of both *machismo* and *mariannismo*, both of which contribute as much to the loss of human dignity as do socioeconomic circumstances.

Finally, Wolff's play explores one of literature's archetypal conflicts: the battle between rationality and raw passion. Our first impression of Eva's apartment (neat, orderly), her art (realistic, classical), and her language (lucid and in ordered paragraphs) suggests a rational mind. By contrast, the Hake lives in makeshift slums and speaks in halting, often incomplete sentences (marked by a disturbing lack of specificity) and creates art of trash (mostly old newspapers, the most transitory and disposable means of communication). We therefore think of him as raw, primitive, even uncivilized. As each scene progresses we note that his attempts at restraint give way to unbridled passion. Each outburst becomes more violent and destructive. Eventually, it is the Hake's modes of expression that triumphs. Eva's furniture, artwork, and ultimately her language are destroyed. In the end "she tries to speak, but can't. Once or twice she makes an effort that frustrates her, then she gives up." The Hake speaks, but in disjointed, often unintelligible gibberish ("Humba! Tekeke! Takumba!"), and when he does make sense, his message is terrifying ("many people, falling, have broken their necks"). His art—"dark, enormous, ragged paper flowers"—provides the play's final image, and the flowers dominate a landscape in which "total disorder reigns."

Wolff is not, of course, advocating the superiority of the Hake's "primitive" art. Hardly. Rather he seems to indict the old order, the Aristotelian imitation of the beautiful, because its indifference to the oppressed contributes to a world in which anarchy reigns. His ultimate message, in this play of many messages, seems to be that art has the responsibility to produce more than pretty pictures of pretty flowers, or it may be replaced by "paper flowers" and all that they imply.

The Hake (A. M. Garcia) continues his conquest of Eva (Marisa Saenz) in Egon Wolff's Paper Flowers, a play which deals with political as well as sexual conquests.

PAPER FLOWERS
(FLORES DE PAPEL)

A Play in Six Scenes

EGON WOLFF

Translated by Margaret Sayers Peden

The hake is a fish of the Chilean seacoast. It is long and thin-bodied, its large, acute-nosed mouth set with sharp teeth. It hunts the deep waters of the Pacific to feed its voracious appetite.

SCENE ONE

The living room of a small suburban apartment, carefully arranged, revealing a feminine hand. Comfortable. Intimate. Three doors in addition to the entrance. One, to the bedroom; one to the bathroom; the third to the kitchen.

One window.
A canary in a cage.
Somewhere, an easel with a half-finished painting. A box of oils.
Also, straw figures: fish, heads of animals, roosters, etc.

The stage is empty. Then Eva and The Hake enter. Eva, forty, is well dressed, with conscious elegance. The Hake, thirty, dirty, his hair uncombed, thin, pale. Eva, who opens the door, enters resolutely. She walks toward the kitchen. The Hake stands in the doorway. He carries two large paper bags. He is trembling visibly. He looks at the room with timid curiosity.

EVA (*returning from the kitchen*). Well, come in! Come in! Leave those in there, in the kitchen!

The Hake enters with respectful caution. Never taking his eyes from the objects in the room, he places the bags on the floor, in the middle of the room.

Not there! (*She points to the kitchen.*) In the kitchen. Next to the stove, please!

The Hake does as she says. He returns without the bags. Eva has gone into the bedroom. She comes out brushing her hair. She takes a bill from her wallet, which has been lying on a small table, and hands it to him.

EVA. Here you are, and . . . thanks very much.

The Hake refuses the bill she hands him. Take it! You're not going to tell me you carried my packages for nothing?

The Hake stares at her.

Well, then . . . thanks very much. You've been very kind.

The Hake continues to stare at her.

Very pleasant. There was no reason for you to do it. Thank you very much.

THE HAKE (*in an impersonal, painful voice*). I would rather you gave me a cup . . . of tea.

EVA (*a little surprised*). Tea?

THE HAKE. You do have some, don't you?

EVA. Yes, I do, but . . . I don't have time. (*She offers him the bill once more.*) You can buy yourself some tea anywhere with this. There's a drugstore on the corner.

THE HAKE. "Anywhere" wouldn't be the same.

EVA (*interested, amused*). Oh, no? Why?

THE HAKE. It wouldn't be the same.

He stares at her, continuously.

EVA. Well . . . but I don't have time, I already told you. Take this and go on. I have things to do.

THE HAKE. They're waiting for me down there.

EVA. Who's waiting for you?

THE HAKE. Miguel and "Birdy."

EVA. The two that were following us?

The Hake nods.

What do they want? Why are they waiting for you?

THE HAKE. To get me.

EVA. Well, what do you want me to do? (*Annoyed.*) Take this. I have things to do.

THE HAKE. They're going to kill me.

EVA. That's your affair. Don't bother me any more, I tell you. Go away!

THE HAKE. I didn't think you'd be so hard. You don't look it.

EVA. Well, then, you were mistaken.

THE HAKE. Since the first time I saw you, last year, painting those flowers in the Botanical Garden. I've thought you were different.

A pause.

EVA. The Botanical Garden? You saw me?

THE HAKE. You were behind the parrot's cage, painting some clumps of laurel. . . . (*He stares at her.*) You had on a light straw hat with a green ribbon. And a kerchief with some scenes of Venice.

EVA. You're a good observer, aren't you?

THE HAKE. I observe certain things.

EVA. So your offer today, to carry the packages for me. . . . (*Perturbed.*) What did you say you wanted.

THE HAKE. A cup of tea.

EVA. Wouldn't you rather have a bowl of soup? I'll bet you haven't eaten today.

THE HAKE. Anything you want to give me.

EVA. I have some soup from last night. Shall I warm it for you?

THE HAKE. If you want to.

EVA. Well, sit down while I fix it.

She goes into the kitchen. One hears the clatter of pots and pans. The Hake, meanwhile, stands fixed where he is, not moving a millimeter. Eva comes back after a while.

Sit down. Surely you're not going to stand there all day.

THE HAKE. Not in these clothes.

EVA (*from the kitchen*). I don't think the furniture will mind.

The Hake takes a newspaper from an inside pocket of his coat, doubles it carefully, scrupulously, and places it on one of the armchairs. He sits upon it. Eva watches his actions and smiles. She props open the kitchen door with a chair so she will be able to talk through the open door.

Do you go often to the Botanical Garden?

THE HAKE. Sometimes.

EVA. To look at the flowers?

THE HAKE. No, to give peanuts to the monkeys.

EVA. Do you like the monkeys?

The Hake shrugs his shoulders.

I think they're dirty . . . gross! I can't bear them. To watch them . . . there . . . picking their fleas in front of everybody. I can't stand them!

THE HAKE. They do what they can.

EVA. Do you have time for that?

THE HAKE. For what?

EVA. To go to the Garden?

THE HAKE. I arrange it.

EVA. I wish I had more!

At that moment The Hake is struck by uncontrollable spasms. They rack his entire body. They contort his face. He must hold on to the table to maintain his upright position. He turns his back to the door of the kitchen and clamps his arms between his legs. It concerns him that Eva not see him in this state. Nevertheless, Eva notices. Finally, he masters the spasms.

How do you do at the supermarket? Do you find many clients?

THE HAKE. There's always someone who finds his packages too heavy.

Eva comes out of the kitchen carrying soup and table service for them both. She places it all on the small table. As she does this, The Hake rises.

EVA. It isn't very warm, but I suppose you'd like it better that way. Sit down!

THE HAKE. I'm fine.

EVA. Sit down and help yourself.

The Hake takes the bowl and begins to take spoonfuls standing up.

But sit down, for Heaven's sake!

She returns to the kitchen and comes out again carrying a hard-boiled egg, a tomato, and a glass of milk. She places them on the table.

I'm not going to begin if you go on standing there like that.

THE HAKE. It's . . . considerate enough of you to invite me to have this. I wouldn't take advantage and sit down with you—where I don't belong.

EVA (*openly*). And if I tell you it doesn't matter to me?

THE HAKE. I thought you were saying it to make it seem . . . easy. (*He sits down.*) It isn't good to go too far. (*Indicating the soup.*) Is it because of your figure?

EVA (*laughing*). Yes. Because of my figure! If it weren't for this, I'd be big as a balloon! I have a terrible tendency to gain weight. I eat a piece of bread and I gain a pound.

THE HAKE. That's a shame.

EVA. Yes. And a nuisance.

THE HAKE. It's just the opposite with Mario.

EVA. Who's Mario?

THE HAKE. A friend. Every time he eats a piece of bread he loses half a pound. He's skin and bones. It comes from stubbornness. The doctors tell him he should eat more, but he's stubborn.

He looks in her eyes with an expressionless, concentrated look.

You shouldn't do that.

EVA. Do what?

THE HAKE. Eat so little. It might harm you. You might die.

EVA. Does it matter? Does it matter to anyone?

THE HAKE. It matters to me.

They eat a moment, in silence, each one concentrating on his soup. The Hake spoons his, but never takes his eyes off Eva. After a while, Eva rises nervously.

EVA (*half laughing*). So that's how you kill your time? Going

to the Botanical Garden to see how a lonely old woman kills *her* time painting the laurel in bloom?

She goes into the kitchen. She returns with salt and a napkin.

Because that's how I seem to you, isn't it? A lonely old woman? Killing time?

The Hake looks at her; he does not respond.

Let's see. Tell me! What do you think I am?

THE HAKE. A woman.

EVA. No, no! What I mean is: married or single?

THE HAKE. Married.

EVA (*with coquettish curiosity*). Why?

THE HAKE. From the way you cross your legs.

Eva laughs.

EVA. Oh, how amusing! And why? How do old maids cross their legs?

THE HAKE. (*expressionless*). They don't cross them.

Eva laughs nervously.

EVA. How amusing you are! (*Always half laughing.*) Tell me. Do you always stare at people?

The Hake immediately lowers his glance to his soup.

Well, you guessed (*touched; excited*). I'm married. Doesn't that worry you? What if my husband should enter suddenly and find me here with you?

THE HAKE (*low*). What *could* he think?

EVA (*still coquettish*). Why not?

THE HAKE. You shouldn't joke about being poor.

A moment of embarrassment. The Hake is struck by another attack, which he can scarcely suppress.

EVA (*doesn't know what to do*). Eat something, man. You haven't eaten a thing.

The Hake gestures that it doesn't matter.

A drink? Is that it? (*Pause.*) Do you need a drink to calm that trembling?

The Hake makes a vague gesture. Eva goes toward the kitchen and returns with a glass of wine, which The Hake grabs from her hands and drinks avidly. This finally calms him.

Almost, mmmm?

THE HAKE. Almost what?

EVA. Well . . . almost. I didn't mean to offend you. I wasn't amusing myself at your expense; it's just that it seems so . . . well, so strange, that you remember me. Among others. . . . There are other people who paint in the Garden. For instance, the old man in the blue corduroy hat. Have you seen him? The one who comes in the afternoons with his little cane stool. Sometimes with a dog, sometime without. (*Laughs.*) One day he got angry with me because of the way I use green tones. He practically yelled at me that it wasn't academic. I never knew what he meant by that. He walked around and around me, shaking his cane. I thought he was going to knock over my easel!

During this monologue, The Hake is almost doubled over.

Are you in pain?

THE HAKE. No.

EVA. Well, then, what's the matter?

THE HAKE. After my "dance," my stomach always knots up.

EVA. I have some tranquilizers. Do you want one?

THE HAKE. No, thank you.

EVA. Then, do you need a drink?

The Hake looks at her.

I mean, the trembling comes because of that, doesn't it?

There is no response. An embarrassing moment. Eva looks toward the kitchen.

Well, you'd better hurry because I have to leave soon. I open the store at two.

The Hake renews his slow spooning of soup. Eva returns with two peeled peaches. She places one in front of The Hake. She eats hers.

These peaches don't have the flavor they used to. I don't know what they do to them now. I remember when I was a child. We used to go with Mamma and Papa to a farm near the river where for practically nothing they let us go to the orchard and eat our fill of peaches and strawberries. What we could throw down! Those peaches really had flavor! Today they export the best ones and leave the leftovers for us. I remember that while Papa and Mamma sat down to eat at some tables that had been set under the trees, Alfredo and I—Alfredo is my brother—would go play in a barn that was close by. Climbing over the baler. . . . My brother Alfredo! He had a real obsession for doing the heroic thing. I remember he would hoist a handkerchief tied like a flag and we'd play "Take the Brigantine"! (*Laughs.*) He was the glorious captain, and I was the accursed corsair! Oh, what times! Silly, happy kids!

THE HAKE. If you throw me out, Miguel and "Birdy" will kill me.

EVA. And what do you want me to do? Leave you here?

THE HAKE. They're waiting for me around the corner, behind the pharmacy.

Eva goes to the window and looks out, barely raising the curtain.

EVA. There they are. They're looking up here.

She turns toward him.

Well. . . . What shall we do? I can't leave you here!

(*Hardening herself.*) I have to go to the store . . . soon. I've already told you.

The Hake suddenly explodes, a spurting, agitated, machine-gun rattle of words. The tone is monotonous, mournful, almost a litany. As he finishes, he has a new onslaught of trembling.

THE HAKE. "Birdy" has a meathook under his coat! He has a meathook and he's been waiting all morning for me to kill me! Because last night I won a few bucks from him shooting craps and he says I cheated on him! And it isn't true, because I won fair and square. Playing fair and square. He came to Julia's house this morning to look for me, but I saw him hide behind the oven and got past him and ran toward the river. All morning I hid in the bushes down by the tannery, until I went to the supermarket, and if you hadn't helped me, he'd have killed me! If you don't help me and hide me, he'll kill me! If you don't help me hide, I'll die, and I don't want to die! I don't want to die! I don't want to die!

EVA. There, it's all right. It's all right! Calm yourself. No one's going to do anything to you.

She doesn't know what to do.

I could notify the police. Do you want me to? So they'll arrest those men?

The Hake shakes his head.

Ah, yes. That's true. The code of honor, umm? You don't denounce each other.

The Hake is bent over. He shivers. Eva considers the situation a while.

I'll have to lock you up in here.

The Hake looks at her.

Because you understand, don't you? I don't know you. And besides, the lock and chain are on the outside. I'll have to lock you inside until I come back.

THE HAKE. I understand.

EVA. I'll lock the other rooms, too. You'll have to wait for me here.

THE HAKE. More than logical.

EVA. You have some magazines. Today's paper . . .

THE HAKE. Thank you. . . .

He smiles for the first time—a broad, open smile—that says nothing.

It's as if everything had been . . . well, prepared. . . . Ready. . . . The newspapers, I mean, and the magazines. I couldn't ask for anything more, to tell the truth. Anything else would be, well . . . ungrateful, I'd say.

EVA. Yes.

Eva removes the bowls. She goes into the bathroom and

then walks around combing her hair. The Hake eats a little of the peach. Then he gets up and walks toward the canary's cage.

THE HAKE. A pretty little bird. What's its name?
EVA. Goldie.
THE HAKE. Goldie, eh? (*He plays with it.*) Ps, ps, ps, ps! (*He gives it a piece of peach.*) You like that, eh? Ps, ps, ps, ps! You like to eat ripe fruit under the trees, eh, little glutton? (*Gives it another piece.*) Here, take it! That's it!

Eva closes the door to the bathroom. The Hake is alone.

You have quite a gullet, eh, you little queer? (*His voice takes on a tone of harshness.*) Did you know that I'm the cursed captain and you're the glorious corsair? Didn't you know that, you fuck-up? (*He shakes the cage.*) Didn't you know that? That I'm the cursed captain and you're the glorious corsair, you freaking bird? (*With a wounded voice.*) I don't know you! (*He shakes the cage again.*) I'll have to lock you up, because I don't know you, son-of-a-bitch bird. I'll have to chain you . . . !

Eva comes from the bathroom. She is ready to leave.

Ps, ps, ps, ps! Little canary . . . !

Eva turns on the radio.

EVA. I'll leave you this. Change it if you want.
THE HAKE. Thank you.

Eva walks toward the door.

Ma'am . . .
EVA (*turns.*). Yes?
THE HAKE. I knew. The thousand times I've seen you, I knew that you were what your eyes say you are. . . .
EVA. I'll be back at six. (*Points to the kitchen.*) If you want to help yourself to anything. . . .

She exits.
One hears the noise of the lock and the rattle of the chain.
The Hake shakes the cage.

THE HAKE. Eat your little peaches! Eat, you shit! Eat, you fruity corsair!

He is shaking the cage as the curtain falls.

SCENE TWO

The same evening, a little after six o'clock. The Hake is making a paper basket from doubled strips of newspaper. A paper bird hangs from the light fixture, a kind of gull, tied by a thread. The Hake is kneeling on the floor, surrounded by piles of scattered, disordered newspapers. The radio is playing a dance tune. Offstage, the sound of an automobile's brakes and the closing of its door. The Hake goes to

the window to look, peering out from behind the curtain. Then he returns to his work.

After the sound of the key in the lock and the rattle of the chain, Eva enters. She is carrying a paper bag from which the neck of a bottle protrudes.

EVA (*nervous; appearing to be casual*). You see? Three minutes after six. Not a minute before or a minute after!

She closes the door. She bumps into the bird.

And this? What is it? Did you make it?
THE HAKE. Nobody else has been here.
EVA. It's precious! You're quite an artist, you know? A gull?
THE HAKE. Do you think it is?
EVA. Yes, of course! A gull! Precious!
THE HAKE. Then it is.
EVA (*about the basket*). And that? A basket?

The Hake nods.

That's precious, too. Where did you learn the art?
THE HAKE. It's for you. . . .
EVA. What? The basket.
THE HAKE. Everything.
EVA. Oh, thank you!
THE HAKE. Providing it doesn't bother you. . . .
EVA. No. Why should it bother me?
THE HAKE. The newspapers, I mean. Because I have spread out all the papers this way. Everything messed up.

He begins hastily to pick up the papers. He folds them carefully.

EVA. No, it doesn't matter. . . .

She goes toward the kitchen.

But, where did you learn this?
THE HAKE. Around. I worked for a guy who worked with wicker. But he was a moron. He only knew how to make chairs. I know how to make flowers, too.
EVA. Flowers?
THE HAKE. Camellias.
EVA (*from the kitchen*). But . . . for Heaven's sake! The dishes! Who washed them?

The Hake does not respond. Eva enters from the kitchen.

You didn't have to do that.

The Hake shrugs his shoulders.

I'll bet you scrubbed the floor, too! It wasn't this shiny when I left.
THE HAKE. There was some wax here, and I thought a little polish wouldn't hurt it any.
EVA (*smiling*). I don't dare go into the bedroom. What might I find there?
THE HAKE. Nothing. How could I go in there without your permission?

Eva goes into the kitchen again and returns with a salami and some cheese and a few packages of cigarettes.

EVA. Speaking of surprises, don't think I forgot you. I thought, since the nights are cold and "a full stomach is one's best friend" . . . a few snacks. A little paté. And cheese. Gruyère. Very rich. It was especially recommended by the owner of the store, who's a friend of mine.

The Hake scarcely looks at what Eva is showing him. He has finished gathering up the newspapers in a carefully folded stack and is going to carry them to the kitchen. He runs into Eva, and this produces a brief business of getting into each other's way.

Where are you going?

THE HAKE (*referring to the papers*). I took them from the kitchen.

EVA. Leave them. It doesn't matter.

THE HAKE. Everything's going to be messy.

EVA (*a little impatient; nervous*). It doesn't matter, I tell you. (*Smiles.*) Put them down there. (*Always with a small, nervous smile that looks strange, almost as if she were laughing to herself.*) When I went into the store, I was so wild to get there, thinking about buying this, that I completely forgot to invent an . . . excuse, because the question was bound to come up, and it did. "Who are you buying all this for, dear? Don't tell me it's all for you?" At first, I didn't know what to say. I stammered out a couple of silly things, and then, when I was about out of breath, it occurred to me to say that it was for a picnic! (*Laughs.*) A picnic with some friends. Imagine! Me, on a picnic!

The Hake, kneeling on the floor again, folds and smooths the stack of newspapers with exaggerated care.

Because if I told her the truth. . . . Who do you think would have believed me?

THE HAKE. Nobody.

EVA. Yes. That's what I thought, too.

THE HAKE. In these cases you always offer a bowl of warm soup. (*Indicating the snacks.*) That would never occur to anyone. It's not necessary.

EVA (*laughs nervously*). Do you like it?

THE HAKE. What?

EVA. The salami? The cheese?

THE HAKE. You always ask two questions at once. I never know which to answer first.

EVA (*confused*). The salami?

THE HAKE. It turns my stomach.

EVA. You don't like it?

THE HAKE. It isn't that. It must be because my stomach isn't used to it. When you're only given rice soup and things like that, you develop a weak stomach. Once the sisters at the charity kitchen gave me roast meat with mushroom and I vomited for two days.

EVA. I should have thought of that. I shouldn't have bought it.

THE HAKE (*looks at her for the first time, with the look so typical of him—it says nothing*). Eat it with your friends on the picnic.

EVA. What friends? I don't have any friends.

THE HAKE. Tough luck for you.

Resumes his task.

EVA (*lively*). Well, I think I should start preparing dinner. That's my life. Eat, and then eat some more. A meal in the morning. A meal at noon. A meal at night! Sometimes I get to the point I think that's all life is: one big continuous meal, with an occasional pause for boredom, and then we begin eating again. And happiness too, naturally! Like a thin powdery dusting of sugar over the whole affair!

While speaking, she has gone from the kitchen to the bedroom, putting on and taking off a wool jacket, putting on and taking off some slippers, opening and closing closets, always with The Hake watching her imperturbably.

What foolish things one does. . . . Opening and closing closets. . . and putting clothes on and off . . . If you add up the days, the hours, you lose doing useless things . . .

She goes to the kitchen, where she can be heard working with the pans. She drops a glass. The noise of breaking glass.

Oh! How stupid I am! What's the matter with me today!

She comes out of the kitchen winding a handkerchief around her finger and walks toward the bedroom.

I cut myself! The day never passes that I don't have to go to my medicine chest!

The Hake rises.

THE HAKE. May I help you?

EVA (*from the bedroom*). No, let it be. I'm used to it. I told you. My fingers are covered with scars! The quarts of blood I've spilled! Not that I do it on purpose!

She comes out of the bedroom.

But a person wouldn't do a thing like that on purpose, do you think?

She hands him a pair of scissors and gauze.

Cut it here, will you, please?

The Hake cuts the gauze skillfully.

THE HAKE. Iodine, do you have any?

EVA. Yes.

She goes to the bedroom and returns with a little bottle of iodine that The Hake also uses with agility and skill. He paints the wound with iodine, places the gauze on it, and secures it with adhesive. Eva observes his movements. The Hake ostensively avoids all physical contact with her. He avoids her with prudent and delicate caution. Eva, on the other hand, doesn't show the same reticence; rather, curi-

ous sympathy, in contrast to his timidity. When The Hake finishes, he starts to tremble again. He sits down. He clasps his arms between his knees in his characteristic gesture. Eva goes to the kitchen and returns with a glass of wine. The Hake drinks avidly. The trembling subsides. He coughs.

Is that better?

The Hake nods.

It seems you have learned a little of everything around, haven't you? The only thing you don't seem to have learned is to talk. . . . Are you always so frugal with your words?

THE HAKE. Where I live there isn't much interest in listening.

EVA (*with irony*). I don't think where I live there is, either.

THE HAKE. Put on the jacket.

EVA. What did you say?

THE HAKE. The jacket and the slippers. . . .

EVA. Oh, that! No, I'm all right this way. . . .

THE HAKE. You were going to put them on.

EVA. Yes, but I'm fine. . . .

THE HAKE. Well, you were going to put them on. . . .

EVA. Yes, but . . . not now . . . and don't look at me like that! (*Laughs nervously.*) Don't look at me so much. Good Lord, what a starer you are! What a starer of a man! Do you always stare like that, tell me.

The Hake lowers his glance.

You're capable of making one completely . . .

She goes toward the kitchen.

Let's see, but I want to hear your story! Come on, tell me. Where did you learn to use your hands so well? In putting on gauze and adhesive, I mean?

From the kitchen.

You give the impression of being very familiar with them.

THE HAKE. I learned from an orderly, a sergeant.

EVA. Were you in the Army?

THE HAKE. In the hospital.

EVA. Ill?

THE HAKE. Something like that.

EVA. Like what? What was the matter?

THE HAKE. I can't talk like this. . . .

Eva comes out of the kitchen.

I can't talk like this . . . with you in the kitchen and me here, shouting. I can't talk if I don't see the other person's face. You'll forgive me, won't you? But I think you don't allow yourself sufficient . . . repose.

EVA (*her curiosity piqued*). Why do you say that?

THE HAKE. Because you're always going back and forth . . . up and down . . . moving things . . . changing things around . . . with no apparent reason. Since I came in here,

you haven't once stopped moving around. Have you looked, for example, at the basket I'm making?

EVA. I looked at it, yes . . .

THE HAKE. No, but really . . . looked at it?

EVA. Yes, I looked at it, I already told you.

THE HAKE. Thought about it?

EVA. Well . . .

THE HAKE. Do you like it?

EVA. Yes. I like it. I told you already.

THE HAKE. Why?

EVA (*anguished*). It's only a . . . basket.

THE HAKE. It's more than that.

Moment of embarrassment.

EVA. Yes, You're right. Forgive me. I told you, I'm a machine. I think it's because of the kind of life I have to lead.

THE HAKE. I could show you how I make the flowers, for example. Paper flowers.

EVA (*more than necessarily interested*). Yes. Let's see, show me!

She kneels down next to him.

THE HAKE (*taking a sheet of newspaper*). You take a sheet of newspaper, like this, and you double it from the corner, like this, you see? (*He does it.*) And it isn't an ordinary sheet of paper, as you will see. You take a piece of paper that has a lot of printing, or a large photograph, or a lot of photographs without any printing, you see? Like this. So that the flower has some meaning. Some continuity. Some beauty.

While he works and speaks, something is changing in him. Something that possesses and absorbs him.

For some people the paper of newspapers is just that. A strip of worthless paper that's only good to wrap meat, to plug holes, or to line suitcases. But it isn't that. Those who think so, it's clear, are marked, and you can recognize them by other superficial features. The paper from newspapers has a world of things to say. It takes whatever form you want to give it. It folds submissively. It allows itself to be handled without resistance. It occupies very little space in your pocket. And it is a faithful companion on winter nights. It keeps you company . . . tranquilly . . . silently . . . always ready, there it is, for any use whatever.

The flower is ready.

There it is! A camellia, you see?

He places it at Eva's brow.

To adorn the beautiful.

EVA. Who are you?

THE HAKE. I also make carnations and chrysanthemums, but that's a little more difficult, because you need scissors, and scissors aren't something they let you have, ordinarily. Even less on winter nights, down by the river.

His excitement continues to increase.

I also make fish and butterflies of paper! But that's much more difficult, because once you have them made, no one wants them. Because everyone wants fish in beautifully lighted fishbowls, and butterflies mounted on pins in little mahogany boxes. But made from dirty newspapers that are only good for lining suitcases, no! No one wants dirty paper butterflies, dirty from wrapping meat, mounted in lighted mahogany boxes! Nor does anyone want to dirty her brow with flowers of dirty paper!

As he finishes he is panting.

At least, that's what the bourgeois say . . . who are the arbiters of style . . . in everything . . . including the way you work . . . the paper . . . the newspapers.

He coughs. Brief pause.

EVA. Who are you?
THE HAKE. They call me "The Hake."
EVA. I mean . . . your name?
THE HAKE. I don't know. A name, one loses it around here in the streets, down a crack . . .
EVA. But you must have some name. I can't call you "The Hake."
THE HAKE (*with an expressionless face*). Why not?
EVA (*confused*). Well . . . because . . .
THE HAKE (*with the same lack of expression*). Because it's the name the gang uses.
EVA. It isn't a Christian name.
THE HAKE. And you're not part of the gang.
EVA (*with certain defiance*). No, no I'm not, if you want to put it like that. Among my friends we call each other by Christian names.
THE HAKE. I thought you told me you didn't have any friends.
EVA. It's a way of speaking.
THE HAKE. It must be, then, that between us—who aren't friends—we call each other by names that *aren't* Christian. (*Smiles, pacifying her.*) My mother calls me Robert.
EVA. That's better. I'll call you Robert, then.
THE HAKE. And Bobby.
EVA. Bobby?
THE HAKE. And pig. Pig before we ate. I had two mothers. She called me pig before we ate, Bobby, after.
EVA. Did she die?
THE HAKE. Something like that.

Eva rises, and with exaggerated vivacity goes to a piece of furniture and takes out some scissors and hands them to him.

EVA. Well! Here we're not on the shore of the river; we have scissors! Show me how you make the chrysanthemums!
THE HAKE (*rises*). I think it's time for me to go.
EVA (*hadn't thought about this*). Oh, yes! Of course! But, those men? Don't you think you're still in danger?

Eva rises and goes to the window.

There they are! They're still waiting for you!
THE HAKE. What do you think? That they're playing?
EVA. Well, what do they want? You haven't done anything except win a couple of dollars from them shooting dice! Isn't winning allowed among you?
THE HAKE. It's allowed. But you pay for it.
EVA. I don't understand! How can they be so vengeful?
THE HAKE. From watching how dogs fight over a piece of meat.
EVA. So, as soon as you leave the building they'll assault you?
THE HAKE. Their pulse won't miss a beat.
EVA. I can't allow them to do that.
THE HAKE. Shall I show you how I make paper chrysanthemums?
EVA. You stay here until those men go away.

The Hake begins to cut up pieces of paper. He is contained at first, but then goes about it with increasing fury.

THE HAKE. You take a piece of paper and you cut it from the corners, you see?

He does it.

You make some long cuts along the printed lines, you see? Until you make shreds of paper, the thinnest possible . . . with the finest points . . . until the whole sheet of paper, which originally was a newspaper, . . . looks like a big piece of shredded paper! As if a dog had made it his prey! Or a falcon! Or any rabid animal! Like when in the bus someone runs his razor along the seats and leaves his mark of stupor and rage there! Or when in the hospital the orderly pours iodine on a back shredded by the whip.
EVA. Bobby . . .

The Hake looks at her.

Do you mind if I call you Bobby?

The Hake continues to stare at her with eyes that express nothing.

Does it seem like a good idea . . . for you to sleep here? Tonight? In this big chair? I'll lend you some blankets. It doesn't matter to me.
THE HAKE. But you brought me salami and cheese so I'd leave.
EVA. Not now, Bobby. You can't go like this.
THE HAKE. If I stay I'll have to . . . take a bath, naturally?
EVA. Have I said that?

The Hake laughs and looks for laughter in Eva's face.

THE HAKE (*laughing*). No, no! Say it! "It would be better if you took a bath, Bobby!"
EVA. I already told you: it's just the same to me.
THE HAKE (*always laughing*). No, no! It isn't the same! Go on, say it! Confess! I want to hear how you say it! "It

would be better if you took a bath, Bobby, because like that, with those clothes and that filth . . . ," mmh? Come on!

EVA. All right, if you insist. "It would be better if you took a bath, Bobby."

THE HAKE (*suddenly serious*). But . . . I can't use your bathroom. How could such a thing ever occur to me?

EVA. Go ahead and use it! Did I say not to?

THE HAKE. No, naturally not. That's true, you didn't tell me! What ideas I have! How could you say such a thing to me?

Suddenly.

Shall I show you how I make paper chrysanthemums?

EVA. You already showed me.

THE HAKE (*never taking his eyes off her*). But you didn't look.

EVA (*protests*). Yes, I . . .

THE HAKE. No, you never looked.

EVA. Well, show me.

The Hake takes another sheet of paper and begins to cut it the same way he did the first.

THE HAKE. You take a sheet of paper and you cut it with the scissors from the corners, you see? You make some long cuts along the printed lines until you make shreds of paper, the thinnest possible . . . with the finest points . . . until the whole sheet of paper, which originally was a newspaper, . . . looks like a big piece of shredded paper! Or like a dog had made it his prey! Or a falcon! Or any rabid animal!

His voice has become tense. The words are squeezed from his mouth.

Or like in the bus when somebody runs a razor . . .

CURTAIN

SCENE THREE

The following day, early morning. The Hake is already up. It is obvious he has bathed and combed his hair. His clothing is folded on a chair. Next to it, his shoes. He has put on one of Eva's bathrobes, which is obviously short and tight on him. He is moving around the room, cleaning with a broom and a dustcloth. He opens the curtains. He runs the dustcloth over the furniture. From the kitchen, the noise of a teakettle. He hums a tune while he cleans. The sun floods in. The straw figures are no longer in view. In their place on the walls, and hanging from threads stretched from wall to wall, some paper flowers and a few butterflies. After a while.

EVA (*from the bedroom*). Good morning!

THE HAKE. Good morning.

EVA. How did you sleep?

THE HAKE. Couldn't be better!

EVA. Up so early?

THE HAKE. It's a beautiful morning!

EVA. What are you doing?

THE HAKE. A little cleaning!

EVA. But why?

She opens the bedroom door, which obviously has been locked. She enters, in a bathrobe, combing her hair.

You didn't have to . . .

She notices the appearance of The Hake. She cannot repress an expression of stupefied amusement.

THE HAKE (*gesturing to the bathrobe*). It was in the bathroom. It doesn't bother you, I suppose?

EVA. No, no. Why should it bother me?

THE HAKE. The soapsuds were so fragrant it must have gone to my head. I didn't know what I was doing. This morning I woke with this on.

EVA. That's fine.

THE HAKE. And then I said to myself: "Hake, you have to do something useful!" I looked around and I saw the blossoms of the mimosa and the beautiful swallows swooping after each other around the General's statue, and I said to myself: "Hake, you have to do something useful!" (*Laughs his characteristic laugh; a laugh that covers his whole face, but says nothing.*) On a day like this, even the river rats would like to come out dressed in lace! How do you like your eggs?

EVA. Eggs?

THE HAKE. Yes, eggs.

EVA. But, Bobby, I don't . . .

THE HAKE. Fried or boiled?

EVA (*resigned*). Boiled.

THE HAKE. I guessed! They're already boiling. That doesn't bother you, I suppose?

EVA. What?

THE HAKE. That I took the eggs like that, without permission?

EVA. Why should it bother me?

THE HAKE. You told me the same thing yesterday.

EVA. What?

THE HAKE. "Why should it bother me?" Curious how one always repeats himself, isn't it?

While he speaks, he has been straightening his improvised bed. He collects the blankets. He folds them carefully. Eva goes into the bathroom.

I used to have a friend, down south in a sawmill where I was working for a while, who had a little refrain too. "I'm innocent," he used to say all the time. When he got up, at breakfast, on the job . . . persistently. It was an obsession that made a martyr of him. "I'm innocent! I'm innocent!"

He drove us out of our minds! One day a few of us grabbed him and hung him up by his feet, so he wouldn't go on talking. No use! Even hanging upside down that way he kept on: "I'm innocent! . . . I'm innocent!" No one ever knew what he was innocent of! Simply, the poor man thought he was innocent of something, and that gave him strength to go on living! Curious things, refrains, aren't they? Sometimes they seem meaningless!

Eva comes out of the bathroom, tying a ribbon in her combed hair.

EVA. You woke up loquacious this morning, didn't you? You weren't, last night. I love to see you this way.

The Hake shrugs his shoulders, lifts the corner of the rug, sweeps.

THE HAKE. I already told you. The mimosa in bloom.

Eva looks at him.

EVA. Your face, too. You look different today.
THE HAKE (*smiles happily*). The bath . . .

Eva sees that the straw figures are not there.

EVA. And my figures?
THE HAKE. Mmh?
EVA. My straw figures? The burro's head? The rooster?
THE HAKE. I put them in the kitchen cabinet.
EVA (*surprised*). And why?
THE HAKE (*indicating the flowers*). I thought that these would look better.
EVA (*doesn't know what to say*). Oh, yes . . .
THE HAKE. It doesn't bother you, I suppose?
THE TWO IN CHORUS. No, why should it bother me?

The Hake laughs, then Eva.

EVA. Well, anyway, one of these days I was going to take them down. You just saved me the effort.
THE HAKE. Why? Didn't you like them?
EVA. Horrible.
THE HAKE. Why? I didn't think they were so bad.
EVA. Why did you take them down, then?
THE HAKE. Because I thought these would look better. That's all. Don't you agree?
EVA. Oh, yes.
THE HAKE. You shouldn't belittle your own work. Because . . . you made them yourself, didn't you?
EVA. In a weak moment.
THE HAKE. That's bad, that you expect so much of yourself.

He leaps toward the kitchen.

Those eggs must be well cooked by now!

From the kitchen.

By the way . . . the little bird . . . I gave him some seeds. Was that all right?
EVA (*goes to the cage; plays with the canary*). Yes, that's fine!
THE HAKE. I was going to give him some bread balls, but I remembered that he's a pet! That's a habit from feeding pigeons!
EVA. Bobby!
THE HAKE. Yes?
EVA. I heard voices last night.
THE HAKE. Voices?
EVA. Arguments! It seemed to me they were coming from the corridor! Did you hear anything?
THE HAKE. Arguments? No!
EVA. Like people arguing heatedly!
THE HAKE. I slept like a log! I couldn't hear a thing!
EVA. Strange! Then I heard something like a door being slammed! It must have been the neighbors. Some Italians who work in a cabaret. Sometimes they bring friends home with them in the middle of the night. They forget this is a building where people are . . .
THE HAKE. Quiet and unassuming.
EVA. What did you say?
THE HAKE. Quiet, unassuming people.
EVA. Well, yes . . . something like that! You always take the words out of my mouth!
THE HAKE. People who don't know how to act! I always say they should go live down by the river to learn how not to do it!

He comes out of the kitchen with a tray on which are two eggs in egg cups, two cups, a teapot, a creamer, a napkin, a butter dish, and biscuits, all very tastefully arranged in the clean, neat manner of an upper-class hotel. He has doubled the towel over his arm to serve as his napkin. He puts everything down with great skill and elegance.

EVA. Don't tell me you worked in a hotel, too?
THE HAKE (*very efficient; with a bow*). *Comment ditesvous, madame?*

Eva laughs.

The Hake is now serious.

Préférez-vous le beurre salé ou sans sel, madame?

Eva laughs good-naturedly.

EVA. Who are you, Bobby? Where did you learn to do that? You are diverse! Really diverse!
THE HAKE (*always serious*). One does what one can.

Both begin to eat their eggs.

EVA. Did you work in a hotel? Really?
THE HAKE. Mmh.
EVA. As a . . . waiter?
THE HAKE (*with his mouth full of egg*). As a thief.

Eva laughs.

It's true. It was a snobbish hotel; because of that I had to go in the back door so the public wouldn't see me, you understand?

Eva understands.

I had a contract as a washer. A dishwasher. It really wasn't a real contract. Just a slap on the back by the fat guy who ran the kitchen. A guy who liked to make himself important. (*He imitates.*) "All right, stupid, go stand over there by one of those sinks. Let's see if you can wash a plate!" He told me he'd give me a penny for every washed plate. He was tricky. He didn't tell me he'd deduct for all the ones I broke. In the evening when I went to pick up my money, I owed him two dollars.

EVA. You owed him?

THE HAKE. I owed him.

EVA. And the French?

THE HAKE. What about it?

EVA. Where did you learn it? There?

THE HAKE. I had to stay six days to pay my debt. Actually I never did pay it, because every day that passed, my debt was bigger. You understand, don't you?

EVA. Yes.

THE HAKE. After a week I realized that wasn't the way to get ahead. That's when I decided to steal a calculating machine, and I lifted . . .

EVA. That seems fair to me.

THE HAKE. Do you think so? They didn't.

EVA. But . . . the French? Where did you learn it? In another hotel?

THE HAKE. Painting some incubators for a guy in Saint Andrews.

EVA. Was he French?

THE HAKE. No, Yugoslavian. Do you know I can make silhouettes with my hands?

EVA. Silhouettes?

THE HAKE. Yes. (*He spoons the bottom of his cup.*) Dogs . . . foxes . . .

EVA. Let's see.

The Hake goes to close the curtains. He turns on the lamp that's on the table. He spreads the leaves of a magazine so it will stand on edge.

THE HAKE. Look! What do you see?

He throws the silhouette of a figure on the magazine.

EVA. A dog!

THE HAKE. And now?

EVA. A rabbit!

THE HAKE. And this?

EVA. A deer? Let's see, let me do it!

She tries.

No. It doesn't come out. How do you do it?

THE HAKE. The forefinger up. The thumb like this.

EVA (*holds out her hands to him*). You do it for me!

The Hake hesitates in taking her hands.

Come on!

THE HAKE (*taking her fingers with care*). Like this. No. This finger's stuck out.

EVA. A deer! (*Enthusiastic.*) Come on . . . another!

The Hake moves close to her. He holds her hands. This produces a brief, embarrassed paralysis of movement during which they look in each other's eyes. Then The Hake, confused, goes to the window and opens the curtains again. He turns off the lamp.

Bobby, there's no reason to be timid with me. (*Laughs.*) I'm not going to eat you, don't you know. (*Agitated.*) After all, having spent the night here together, gives us a right to . . . a certain familiarity, don't you think?

THE HAKE. Don't play with me, please.

EVA. But, Bobby, it's ridiculous. Just because you brushed my hand . . . it doesn't matter to me.

THE HAKE. One ought to keep his distance.

EVA. What distance?

THE HAKE (*indicating the bathrobe*). It's because you see me in this, and washed, that you forget.

EVA. What have I forgotten?

The Hake points to his clothes.

Don't be ridiculous. Have I shown in any way that it matters to me?

THE HAKE. It can't be.

EVA. If you insist.

THE HAKE. I'll have to go right now.

EVA. I'm not saying you should go.

The Hake rises and moves away from her. He turns his back.

THE HAKE (*suspiciously*). Why?

EVA. Why, what?

THE HAKE. Why do you want me to stay?

EVA. I haven't said you should stay. I've only said you don't have to go.

THE HAKE (*complaining*). Why is it my fault, I say?

EVA. But Bobby . . .

THE HAKE. Why is it my fault I was born as I was. I didn't ask my mother to be born where I was!

Eva rises.

EVA. But, Bobby, for Heaven's sake!

THE HAKE. I'm a simple man, but I have my pride!

EVA. Of course you have! Who says you don't?

She approaches him. To his back.

Bobby! I'm not the woman I seem to be. I'm just a woman

filled with a need for kindness! Perhaps it doesn't seem so, because I look so forceful, so . . . fulfilled. (*Smiles.*) But you see, I paint alone, laurel in bloom, Saturday afternoons in the Botanical Garden. Doesn't that seem . . . odd?

THE HAKE. I'll need new pants. If I stay here any longer, I'll need new pants. I can't put those back on.

Eva looks at him without speaking.

Because if I put those on, I can't stay here, isn't that right?

EVA. I hadn't thought about that.

THE HAKE (*never looking at her*). But now you think about it, isn't it true?

EVA. Well, perhaps . . .

THE HAKE (*his tone changes; he returns to his earlier manner of speaking, anxious, intense*). Because what if suddenly, someone came in here? Yes, suddenly, some friend of yours came in here, what explanation could we give them? If they see me here, with this on (*indicating the bathrobe*), or those (*indicating his pants*), sitting on one of your chairs like a king in his castle? Don't you see? They might think I'm a beggar from down by the river that you picked up out of pity to prevent the poor devil's turning up his paws before God meant him to, offering him something . . . some warm soup or salami. . . . It wouldn't be very correct, do you think? Sad, instead, don't you think? A sad, hopeless situation that neither you, nor I, could stand for very long, don't you agree? Because that would mean that you know as well as I . . . how could we avoid it? That you as well as I knew the sad reality. It would establish a situation of moral misery between us that would be very difficult . . . to disguise. Don't you think so?

EVA. And do you think a new pair of pants will change all that?

THE HAKE. We could play at it a little, deceive ourselves. Don't you think so?

EVA. You'll have to overcome that . . . that obsession, Bobby. I've noticed how it makes you suffer.

The Hake whirls around. A broad smile illuminates his face.

THE HAKE. Blue pants with a white stripe. A white stripe an inch wide, no more, no less. That's the kind I've always dreamed of.

EVA. We'll look for something you like.

THE HAKE (*like a happy child*). Will you do it? Really? Will you go yourself from store to store, looking for what I ask?

EVA. Why not?

The Hake takes her hands and pulls her up. He whirls her around.

THE HAKE. You're an angel. You're an angel! An angel!

EVA. Oh, for Heaven's sake, Bobby!

They stop. Eva is breathless.

What I meant is I find it meaningless! Really meaningless, Bobby! I don't notice things like that!

THE HAKE (*laughing in amusement; teasing slyly*). Yes, yes, you notice!

EVA. No, really, no.

THE HAKE (*reprimands her with a finger*). Yes, you notice! You notice!

EVA. Why do you say that to me? Why are you laughing?

The Hake laughs as if he were telling a funny and rather embarrassing story.

THE HAKE. Yesterday evening, when you arrived here, a friend brought you in her car and you didn't want to let her come up!

EVA (*denying effusively*). No . . .

THE HAKE. Yes, yes! I saw the gestures she was making. As if she wanted to come up with you, but you told her, with signs, too, that you were fine . . . that you didn't need anything, or something like that! It was amusing, extremely amusing, to see how you were trying to think of something . . . how you cast about, almost desperately, for some explanation!

Choked with laughter.

Waving your arms like this! Gasping for air!

EVA. No, no. That wasn't the reason . . .

THE HAKE. Yes, yes! But don't get mad. I understand! I understand! If you only knew how well I understand!

Suddenly becoming serious.

What did you tell your friend?

EVA. Well, I told her that . . .

THE HAKE. When I have new pants, we'll be free from embarrassment, you see. We can say I'm your cousin. A distant cousin who dropped in from the country, how does that seem? A cousin, or an uncle? Which seems better? More plausible?

A pause.

EVA. You're going to have to get that obsession out of your head, Bobby.

The Hake drops his arms, discouraged.

THE HAKE. Yes. Perhaps that comes from wandering around by the river so much, looking for things under the stones. From so much crawling around, looking for things, scratching for food. Finally, the world gets you right around the ankles. It's a little tiny world, the one you see, and in this tiny little world, we're the tiniest of all! Not even as high as a toad. You get a kind of subservient personality. Sub-something, anyway. (*He smiles again with an empty smile, radiant, meaningless.*) A "sub" personality . . . sub-normal . . . sub-ordinant . . . sub-jugated . . . sub-versive!

He stands before her, smiling happily.

A white stripe an inch wide. No more, no less. Will you buy them for me as I asked?

EVA (*worried*). I'll do what I can.

The Hake kisses her hands.

THE HAKE. You're an angel!

Eva pours herself some coffee.

EVA. If this means anything to you, Bobby, I should tell you that I've become very fond of you. In my opinion, you have a tremendous potential for becoming a . . . fulfilled man.

As she says "fulfilled," The Hake starts to tremble again. Eva wants to help him, but he waves her away. He calms down again.

I don't know what it is that torments you.

The Hake picks up the papers and begins to make flowers again.

Drink your coffee.

Eva walks to the kitchen.

This needs sugar.

Suddenly a scream from the kitchen.

What's this?

She enters. She is carrying the straw rooster and burro. One is hanging grotesquely from each hand; their necks are broken.

Why did you throw these into the trash can? And their necks . . . why did you break them?

THE HAKE. They didn't fit in the trash can.

EVA. But throw them away. You told me yourself you'd put them in the cabinet.

THE HAKE. But they didn't fit there either. (*Innocently protesting.*) But you told me yourself they were horrible!

EVA. Yes, but . . .

THE HAKE. I'll make you one of paper! I swear that when you come back this evening I'll have a rooster and a burro made of paper for you! Mmh? What do you say? With strong, red feet, and a great golden comb! A strong powerful rooster! Mmh? Is that all right?

EVA (*doesn't know what to say*). Well, I . . .

THE HAKE (*with his broad smile; playful, vacant*). It won't bother you if I do it, will it?

THE TWO IN CHORUS. No. why should it bother me!

The Hake laughs loudly. Eva enters in chorus. Both laugh with all their hearts. The Hake's, finally, with exaggeration, out of tune, drowning out Eva's laughter.

CURTAIN

SCENE FOUR

Evening of the same day. The arrangement of all the pieces of furniture has been changed. The canary cage, its door open, is empty. The shade of the floor lamp has been taken off. It serves now as a vase for three enormous paper flowers with wire stems. In addition, there are flowers hanging from the walls and from the lamp.

The Hake, his legs wrapped in a blanket of Scotch wool, a bottle of cognac at his side, is lounging in the big chair, watching television. One can see he has just washed his hair, because he has a towel wrapped around his head. He is apparently happy. The television entertains him enormously. The sound of shots from the screen, which cannot be seen. The shouting of Indians. Little by little The Hake becomes involved in the action. He imitates the movements he sees. He hides behind the chair. He shoots toward the set. He jumps on top of the chair. He shoots again. A bullet gets him. He "dies" ostentatiously in the middle of the living room floor.

He's lying there, sprawled on the floor, when the door opens and Eva enters. She is carrying several packages.

EVA. Bobby!

The Hake doesn't move.

Bobby! What's the matter?

She drops the packages on the floor. She kneels next to him.

What's the matter with you? (*She touches him.*) My God! (*She touches his face.*) Bobby. . . . (*She shakes him.*) Wake up! Bobby, for God's sake!

She looks around desperately. She goes into the kitchen. She runs back with a glass of water. She gives him a drink while she holds his head. The Hake opens one eye.

THE HAKE. Did you bring the pants?

EVA. Oh, God, Bobby! What did you do? You frightened me so!

THE HAKE. Blue? With white stripes?

Eva hands him a package, which The Hake opens eagerly, ripping the paper.

They're gray!

EVA. Yes. I couldn't find the ones you wanted.

THE HAKE (*injured*). But I asked you for blue ones!

EVA. I'm telling you. I couldn't find what you wanted.

THE HAKE (*screams*). Blue, with a white stripe! An inch wide! And you bring me gray! What do you want me to do with these?

EVA. I looked in all the stores, but . . .

THE HAKE. You didn't look enough.

EVA. Yes, I looked Bobby. I looked, but . . .

THE HAKE. You didn't look. Yesterday I saw three pairs in different stores.

He holds the pants up.

What am I going to look like in these? What will Mario say to me when he sees me dressed like this? That I'm one of those playboys from España Square, that's what he's going to say I look like. One of those playboys from the apartments in España Square, who aren't good for anything except to warm their women's beds! Playboys in skirts! Playboys with soft bellies! That's what he'll say I look like!

He throws them away.

I don't want them!

Eva picks them up dejectedly. She wraps them up again.

EVA. I didn't think it would matter so much.
THE HAKE. No, of course not. For a guy who goes around in rags, anything is good enough.
EVA. I wasn't thinking that when I did it.

A long embarrassing pause. The Hake turns off the television.

THE HAKE. Do you like the way I arranged the furniture?
EVA (*distraught*). Oh, yes . . . fine.
THE HAKE. Is it better this way?
EVA. Better, yes.
THE HAKE. And the flowers? Do you like them?
EVA. Pretty, yes.
THE HAKE. The canary got out.

Eva turns toward the cage.

EVA. Goldie! Oh, God! How did it happen?
THE HAKE (*in the middle of the room: the very picture of innocence*). I opened the door to give him some seeds, and zap! he got away!
EVA. And where is he?
THE HAKE. I don't know.

Eva goes to the window and looks outside.

It was when I opened the door to give him some seeds that he got away. He flew around the room a while; he went into the bedroom, into the kitchen, and then flew over my head again. I tried to catch him with a towel. I got a towel from the bathroom and tried to catch him. For a minute I thought I'd caught him. It was when he lighted on the frame of that picture. I stopped in front of him, waiting for the minute to throw the towel over him, but that's when I realized that he didn't *want* me to get him.

Eva turns toward him.

It was all up to me. I couldn't miss. It was a question of throwing the towel, zap! he would have been mine. But that's when I realized he didn't want me to catch him. Something in his attitude, you understand?
EVA. So you let him get away?
THE HAKE. I don't know. It was just that for a minute, I couldn't do anything. I think that's when he started to fly again; he flew around the whole apartment and, finally, went out that window . . . toward the mimosa blossoms. It must be my fault. I think that bird never liked me. From the first day, he always looked at me out of the corner of his eye, a little suspicious. It must be that he realized, before I did, that there wasn't room enough for both of us here.

His smile—that says nothing—returns.

Little creatures have tremendous insight in these matters. It's lucky that he left first, because if not, suddenly, it could have been me . . .

Eva disappears into the bedroom.

Did you know I'd given him a nickname? "Corsair." A strange name for a canary, I know, but it's just that that name reminds me of something! Maybe that it's necessary to be very brave to be able to bear a cage! "Corsair." Poor little thing.

He waits a while.

Do you want me to go?

Eva enters, putting on a robe over her dress. She can't help smiling at the appearance of The Hake standing in the middle of the room, his arms by his sides, wrapped up in the blanket, his head wrapped in the towel, his legs bare—guilty, abject, contrite.

EVA. And why should I want you to go?
THE HAKE. Because of the bird. Ever since I've come I haven't done anything but cause confusion.
EVA. You're just a spoiled child, Bobby.
THE HAKE. To be so unpleasant to you when I refused the beautiful pants you brought me.

Eva takes his hand.

EVA. Come on, you big baby. I've been thinking we need to talk about something. Clear something up.
THE HAKE. After all your affection . . .

Eva sits him beside her in the chair. She places a finger on his lips.

EVA. What were you doing in the Botanical Garden, the day I was painting the laurel, spoiled child?
THE HAKE. Well . . . wandering around.
EVA. Come on, tell me the truth.

The Hake maintains his distance from her.

THE HAKE. You talk to me as if you've known me for a long time.

EVA. You can treat me the same way if you want. I won't break because of it, you know.

THE HAKE. There you go again, laughing at me.

EVA (*impatient*). Oh, Bobby, come on! Why don't you drop it? We're not going to spend a lifetime this way, you so sensitive, and I not knowing how to take you. I know you're not what you seem or what you pretend to be. Some error, some slip "along life's road" (*She makes a gesture as if entertained at her own cliché.*) brought you where you find yourself now, but I know you aren't what you seem . . . or you don't seem to be what you *are* . . . None of that matters to me; you see I don't even ask you. Can you accuse me of that? Of having asked you?

The Hake shakes his head.

No, isn't that true? Then why don't you be yourself? Hmm? Shall we talk as equal to equal?

THE HAKE. As equal to what?

EVA. Well, as equal to equal, as I said.

THE HAKE. And if I weren't what I seem to be, or I didn't seem to be what I am, we wouldn't be speaking like this, isn't that right? As equal to equal . . .

EVA. Well, maybe not.

THE HAKE. Why?

EVA. Because your sensitivity would be in the way, preventing it. (*She moves a little closer to him.*) Come on, silly, tell me . . . what were you doing in the Garden?

THE HAKE. Looking at the parrots.

EVA. No, really? What were you doing?

THE HAKE. Mario had sent me to pick up cigarette butts in front of Orfeon kiosk, so we could grind up the tobacco and sell it at the Marquesa's brothel.

Pause.

EVA. So you don't want to confess, eh?

THE HAKE. Also Chancha, the deaf old woman who sells newspapers in front of the Congress, had asked me to pull some feathers out of the parrot's tail to make a decoration for her hat.

EVA. Yesterday, just after you arrived, you told me that you remembered me a year ago painting the blooming laurels in the Garden in my straw hat with a green ribbon. Unless you're terribly observant and have a very special memory, no one would believe that you'd remember those details so long, if it weren't for a very special reason.

THE HAKE. Special reason?

EVA. Special inclination.

THE HAKE. Special inclination?

He is standing far away from her, his back turned.

EVA. Oh, Bobby, don't be so . . . timid!

The Hake rises.

THE HAKE. It's just that it can't be!

EVA (*from her place*). Why?

THE HAKE. Where would all this lead?

EVA. Who cares? It's strange that you, with the life you lead, should worry about tomorrow. As if you had spent all your life looking ahead. I'll bet you've never worried about anything in your life. Why worry now? Am I worried, for example?

THE HAKE. It's different with you.

EVA. Why with me?

THE HAKE. Because you know what I don't know.

EVA. And what do I know?

THE HAKE. That I'm not what I seem or I don't seem to be what I am. On the other hand, I only know I am what I seem and not that I am not what I don't seem. In other words, you have your fantasy and I have only reality, which is much poorer, much sadder, much more disillusioning. . . . (*In a clipped voice.*) That's the advantage you have over me, although you tell me not to worry . . . what happens is that one worries so much about worrying that in the end he doesn't worry any more about worrying.

EVA. Bobby, Bobby, turn around!

The Hake turns. He doesn't look at her, however.

If you were only the poor vagabond you seem to be, we wouldn't even be able to have this conversation, don't you see? It would all have been over between us a long time ago. Yesterday perhaps. After I gave you your warm soup, I would have sent you away, because it's certain you would have ended up . . . boring me. There's nothing more boring than the conversation of the poor when they're complaining. Don't you agree?

The Hake thinks so. He nods his head, looking at the floor. Eva approaches him and takes his arm.

From the first moment I saw you, I knew who you were. I understand that your shyness must be a consequence of the bad treatment you've had from life. Things that have happened to you have made you pull into your shell. I want you to believe that I'm completely sincere when I tell you that doesn't matter to me. I place no false barriers between us, do you understand?

The Hake understands.

Do you believe I'm your friend, Bobby?

The Hake believes.

Then . . . ?

Eva waits.

THE HAKE. Then we'll have to change the furniture here.

EVA (*surprised*). The furniture? Why?

THE HAKE. I don't like it.

EVA. You don't like it?

THE HAKE. That's what I said.

EVA. Well . . . (*Doesn't know what to say.*) What do we . . . ?

THE HAKE. It has no class.

EVA. Class?

THE HAKE. Style. It has no style. (*With irritation.*) Trash you find by the thousands in any second-class junk store! Just looking at it makes me want to scream! It has no imagination, no fantasy, no dream of any kind!

Eva is stunned. The Hake whirls toward her.

Let's see! How much time did you spend choosing it?

EVA. Well, I . . .

THE HAKE. Not five minutes, I'll bet! You went in the store like someone going in to buy some aspirin and you pointed to the first piece of junk that met your eyes, I'll bet! Anything that would serve to throw your body on and fall asleep! Well, you're mistaken! You need to be a poet to choose furniture and give it the tone it deserves! All the nerve cells that decide taste must be aroused when the moment comes to decide! You're like that crazy old Fabian from the other side of the bay who'll set his ass down on anything he finds . . . an old paraffin tin . . . a rickety old suitcase . . . his shoes . . . on the chest of the old syphilitic Sandilla who bums around with him stealing railroad ties, anything at all. . . . As if one could resolve the problem that way! Choosing furniture is a liturgical act!

His excitement increases as he acts out what he has been describing. His concentration absorbs him completely. He concludes as if debating with another being that is within himself, as if arguing with someone whom he should convince.

You have to raise the chair skirt and see if the framework is made of poplar or of mahogany, because there is always some wretch who wants to trade you a cat for a hare and pass off poplar for mahogany, and that wouldn't be good, because your visitors might notice! Then, it's also important that all the nails be in place! All the nails, or rather all the glue, because it could be that it isn't satin fringe but only tufts of ordinary cloth some son-of-a-bitch wants to palm off! And it's also important, very important, of *primary* importance, to concern yourself with the form, the color, the design, whether it's brocade or velvet, whether the style today is an oblong silhouette or square design, whether the pegs are concave or convex, whether the sons-of-bitches have put in nails—nails, and not screws! Because when visitors sit down they shouldn't simply fall into a chair, but instead, when they bend their knees they should encounter . . . that's it, they should encounter the anatomy of a chair adjusted to their rumps.

All of that should be taken into account! All of that should be considered with the greatest care! Because all of it is of maximum importance! Of primary importance! Of the *most* primary importance. (*He concludes, exhausted.*) You must put life into it, life . . . if necessary . . . that's what that stupid Fabian can't understand! (*Pause.*) We have to change this furniture. We owe it to our visitors.

EVA. Well, we'll change it. You choose. Is that all right with you?

THE HAKE. When?

EVA. Tomorrow?

THE HAKE. I won't be here tomorrow.

EVA. Don't you understand, silly, that starting from today you'll be here tomorrow and all the days you want to?

THE HAKE. We'll have to go out.

EVA. For what?

THE HAKE. To choose the furniture.

EVA. Well, what about it? We'll go out, then.

THE HAKE. In what clothes?

EVA. I'll buy you a suit.

THE HAKE. Gray.

EVA. I thought you wanted blue with white stripes.

THE HAKE. That's for the pants. The suit I want gray. Gray with little white flecks, hardly visible. Better invisible than visible . . . better . . .

EVA. Whatever you say. Is that all right with you?

The Hake looks at her out of the corner of his eye. Distrustful. Icy.

THE HAKE. No, not unless you tell me what it will be like?

EVA. How *what* will be like?

THE HAKE. Walking through the streets.

EVA. I don't understand.

THE HAKE. Will I walk in front of you or behind you?

EVA. There you go again. Beside me, if you want to.

THE HAKE. How far away? A foot? Two? Have you thought about it? And what will we tell the store owner?

Eva looks at him. She does not answer.

Because there are suspicious types, tremendously suspicious. They see rags and they imagine a world of things. Just a simple glance at some rags awakens a whole mythological fantasy.

He turns toward Eve.

Do you understand what I mean? We have to be extremely careful. (*His face completely blank.*) Do you think it would be a good idea if we say I play . . . tennis?

EVA. Tennis? Why that?

THE HAKE. Doesn't your husband play tennis?

EVA. Yes. How did you know?

THE HAKE (*points toward the bedroom*). The pants and the racket there in the closet.

EVA. Curious, hmm?

THE HAKE. Do you think I could pass?

EVA. You could pass for anything at all!

The Hake's blank smile.

THE HAKE. Even for a gigolo, hmm?

EVA. Tonight you'll sleep here in the chair, but I won't lock my bedroom door. I no longer distrust you, you see?

The Hake takes her hands.

If you feel lonely, don't hesitate to call me. I sleep very lightly.

Very close to him.

Unless you're not attracted by ladies over forty who paint out of desperation, or for nostalgia's sake keep the clothes of a man who left his nest centuries ago. A woman alone who doesn't even know how to buy the right kind of furniture.

THE HAKE (*rigid again*). Will I have to . . . take a bath again?

Eva leans her head on his chest.

EVA. Oh, Bobby! Give up! Relax. (*After a while.*) Resting my head on your chest is like resting it on a rock. What has life done to you to make you like this?

THE HAKE. *Comment dîtes-vous, madame?*

EVA (*looks at him; kisses his cheek*). Oh, my love!

The Hake looks straight ahead. He is a rock. A sphinx.

THE HAKE. Yes. It is of the greatest importance, of absolutely primary importance, to choose appropriate words to say what one wishes to say. It involves a complete process of selection carefully prearranged by the spirit. A process that has nothing to do with one's own will. The fundamental thing is to believe in the beauty of one's own expression, since without the contribution of one's delivery, words, thrown out by pure whim, acquire a false dimension in which not even one's self, and certainly not others, can find anything that evokes even a lie. The important thing, then, is to say what one wants to say without saying it, so that others contribute the entire weight of their own . . . deception. Only this way may one be happy.

EVA. Oh, God!

The Hake begins to make little figures with his hands that he projects upon the front wall.

THE HAKE. A rabbit, see? An owl. A child. A frightened child. (*He looks at her.*) Do you have a hatchet?

EVA. Yes.

THE HAKE. And a saw? And a hammer?

EVA. Yes.

THE HAKE. Give them to me. Tonight I'll make the kind of furniture I like.

EVA. They're in the kitchen.

Eva goes into the kitchen. A scream.

What's this! What happened to Goldie!

She comes in with the dead canary hanging from her hand.

Who did this to him?

THE HAKE (*disconsolate; very rapidly, like a child caught doing something wrong*). I told you! I wanted to catch him, but he wouldn't let me. From the beginning he took a dislike to me! From the first glance, he looked at me out of the corner of his eye! I followed him all over the room! I begged him, I implored him to let me catch him, but he insisted on flying! He didn't want to hear my pleas. . . . (*Pause.*) When finally he couldn't fly any more, he was too worn out to understand the meaning of my pleas. He expired without giving me the opportunity to explain to him. (*Another pause.*) I could have loved that little bird. (*Sobs.*) I could have really loved him if he had only let me.

(*He looks at Eva.*)

Poor Goldie. Poor son-of-a-bitch.

CURTAIN

SCENE FIVE

The following morning. The radio is playing "The Waltz of the Dragon-Flies." The Hake, in tennis clothes, is kneeling in the middle of the living room, nailing together a rustic chair, or rather what seems to be a chair, from the remains of a torn-up chair. Of the original chair all that remains is a scattered pile of cotton and feathers, springs and ripped cloth. The wood frame, too, has been violently torn apart as if a bird of prey had seized upon it.

The pictures are no longer there. In their places hang pages from newspapers. There are more paper flowers scattered around. The flowers are larger now, more carelessly made. Simulacrums of flowers, as if made from whole pages of wadded newspapers, attached in the center to wire stems. The Hake hums happily to the music as he works.

After a while Eva appears, in her bathrobe, in the doorway. For a moment she watches The Hake working, then . . .

EVA. I heard you working all night long. It sounded as if a big rat had been trapped in my apartment.

She looks at the room.

You can't say you haven't been busy.

THE HAKE. Do you like it?

EVA. Good work.

THE HAKE. The fever got me. When I get the fever it's like

seeing double. I see one thing to do, and then another to be done. When I attack one, there's already another asking me to persist, and so on . . . Mario has never given me credit for being a carpenter.

EVA. He ought to come see now.

THE HAKE. He says I'm good for taking things apart . . . breaking them, but as for carpentry, real carpentry . . . doing it really right, you understand?

EVA. Yes.

THE HAKE. He says I'm no good. "You're a vandal," he tells me. He's continually telling me that. Perhaps because he's always seen me do just this: rebuilding scattered pieces, putting scraps together. Don't you think?

Eva has gone to sit down in the only remaining chair.

EVA. It must be because of that.

THE HAKE. That's the bad thing about Mario. He only has the imagination about a posteriori things. He doesn't have any imagination about a priori things. I think he ought to see me doing this now, don't you think?

EVA. That's what I told you.

THE HAKE. That would shut his big yap. Don't you think?

He doesn't wait for an answer. He holds on high, in triumph, the chair he has just finished.

Louis XV! What do you think? Or Louis XVI perhaps?

EVA. Restoration.

He finds the idea amusing. He laughs.

THE HAKE. Restoration, yes! That's funny, you know? Restoration. I hadn't thought about that. (*Still laughing.*) That's what I like about you, you know? You have a sense of humor. From the first moment I stuck my dirty paws into your kingdom. I come in here and I break all your furniture . . . I let your canary loose . . . I turn your closets inside out . . . I fill your room with horrible papers flowers and you're still . . . complacent! Always smiling!

EVA. So? What else is there for me to do?

THE HAKE. Yes. The force of circumstances?

EVA. Of destiny.

THE HAKE (*abruptly serious*). Destiny is cirrhosis of the liver or a lung punctured by a stupid life squandered in drunkenness. Don't confuse it with anything else. I'm here strictly because of some warm soup. Don't forget it.

He shows her again the chair on which he has been working.

Do you like it now?

Eva goes to the radio and turns it off.

EVA. Bobby . . . I left the door open last night. You didn't come in. (*The Hake concentrates on his work.*) I waited for you. (*Pause; uncertain smile.*) Since you didn't come in, you couldn't know that I even put on a special nightgown last night. The nightgown I wore my first night of . . .

love. (*She laughs.*) Afterwards, my husband made me wear it on our anniversaries. A long gown, celestial blue, with two rosettes here on the yoke. A gown that still has the odor of the pines at Saint Stephens. My husband thought so anyway. That it retained the odor of our first night under the pines at Saint Stephens . . . with the waves of the sea breaking nearby . . . almost at our feet . . . and the moon . . . the eternal moon. (*Smiles.*) An intrusive, friendly moon, witnessing our . . . passion.

She waits.

Would you believe it, Bobby? That I would be capable of that? Of a night of passion beneath the pines, with only the moon as witness, and the blue nightgown as a pillow?

She presses her hand to her forehead.

It doesn't seem possible to you, does it? That's what makes you so unjust, that you think that it isn't possible . . . or that it isn't possible any more. Because you *do* think that it isn't possible, don't you?

The Hake works.

Isn't that right? You think that it's no longer possible?

A vague evasive gesture; and an uncertain smile; brief dizziness.

That a woman like me, alone, oh God! . . . could strip herself of her prudery and open her arms to love, with only the aroma of the pines as witness . . . and the intrusive moon . . .

She looks at him.

Answer me. You don't even hear what I'm saying! Answer me! Do you think it's possible?

The Hake has finished his chair. He holds it in the air. He shakes it in triumph.

THE HAKE. I finished it! I finished it! Now I'd like to invite Mario to come see it! That would shut the old pessimist's trap! Firm structure, well assembled! Strong back, as ordered! Firmness in the line! Solid! Resistant! Do you like it?

EVA. Yes. I like it.

THE HAKE. A lie! You say it for some secret motive locked up in that head of yours. You say it out of compassion! I know the symptoms of the voice. I know each inflection of the voice when somebody speaks out of compassion. It's the voice of one who lowers his hand to give something, which is distinct from the voice of someone who raises his hand to receive something. Let's hear you say, "I like your chair."

EVA. I like your chair.

The Hake gives a cry of triumph.

THE HAKE. There, that's it! You see? That inflection in the

voice! That uncertain tremble! That painful quiver! YOU HAVE COMPASSION FOR ME!

The Hake shakes the chair. He looks at it with disgust.

This chair is horrible. Bad taste. Badly put together. Badly structured. Badly conceived. The risers don't fit. The back's coming apart.

He begins to tear it apart.

The pieces don't fit. You can see the hand that made it had no class.

With every word a piece of the chair is torn off.

No refinement, stubby, primitive, ordinary, shiftless, dumb, of a concept . . . made . . . by a man . . . of the . . . PEOPLE!

He shatters on the floor the few pieces that remain.

It was a chair that deserved to sit near a campfire of filthy trash by the shore of a river, not in a beautiful apartment on España Square.

He rests, finally.

The end of a dream. (*Looks at Eva.*) You should have told me, though.

EVA (*with the greatest naturalness possible*). Why should I tell you something I don't feel?

THE HAKE. Because this establishes an abyss between you and me, you understand? An abyss as wide as the distance around the world.

Declamatory, impersonal, once again sententious. Light.

Pity is the broken, hanging bridge that joins wrath to a full belly!

He smiles a vacant smile that covers his whole face.

Did you like that?

EVA. Oh, God, Bobby! How shall I take you?

The Hake looks at her, desolated.

I swear I don't know. As soon as you arrived I opened the door of my house to you; I received you in it with all my affection. I tried to give you everything I have, but you persist in . . . ignoring me.

The Hake stands in the middle of the room. As Eva speaks, everything in him takes on a desolate air, like a guilty child receiving a reprimand for something he's done, that he cannot now repair.

I speak to you with affection and you respond with irony. I want to be sincere with you and you reject me, saying that I'm lying. I do everything possible to erase between us any sign that recalls your . . . poverty, but you insist on recalling it.

The Hake begins to tremble. He is a child without shelter

who is cold, who is afraid. The smallest expression, diminished and sad, of the child of the ruins, hungry, abandoned, frozen.

I'm not the rich, cruel, and frivolous woman you think you see in me. I am a poor lonely woman, very lonely . . . hungry for friendship and affection. I offer you my love, Bobby.

She walks toward him and takes his face. His whole body shivers. A trembling that racks him, which he cannot control.

Oh, my love, be calm, be calm! I am here with you. Your woman is here with you and she's going to help you! Your woman is here with you and she's going to give you all the warmth you've been denied.

The Hake looks before him into the emptiness.

Bobby! Bobby! Look at me! I'm here! I love you! Do you hear me? I love you, Bobby, look at me! Bobby . . .

She shakes him.

Looks at me! For the love of God, look at me!

She shakes him violently.

I'm speaking to you! Listen to me!

Still shaking him.

Listen to me, you damned fool! Look at me!

Nothing. She falls at his feet. Slowly The Hake ceases trembling. A long pause. The "Waltz of the Dragon-Flies" sounds in the emptiness.

THE HAKE (*after the pause*). You still haven't told me how I look in the tennis outfit.

He says it without looking at her, his cold eyes staring into the emptiness straight ahead of him. Eva screams.

EVA. Oh! You don't want me to help you! Your arrogance, your pride, is so great you don't want me to help you!

She rises, wrathful.

So nobody can get near your precious body, huh? Well, I'm going to tell you what you look like in that outfit!

She moves away from him. She picks up the paper flowers and other paper objects and throws them at him as she screams.

Do you know what you look like? A puppet! A ridiculous, deformed puppet! You don't even have any chest! You don't have any shoulders. You don't have the carriage to wear an outfit like that! How dare you put it on!

She awaits his reaction, which doesn't come.

Do you know what you have to have to walk around in something like that? You have to have smooth muscles! Long, smooth, springy muscles! Sure and decisive movements! Not muscles like yours, twisted and starved, that are only fit for scarecrows!

She waits another moment. She moves closer to him. In his face.

You don't have shoulders! You have a hump!

She drops sobbing at his feet, her voice barely discernible.

You don't have muscles . . . you have . . . lumps!

THE HAKE (*distant; very lightly; as if reciting*). And then out of the thicket flew a little bird. He flew for an instant above the green foliage . . .

EVA. Oh . . .

THE HAKE. Over the scenery bathed in light! Fly, little Corsair, I told him . . .

Eva covers her ears.

Fly, little bird!

The Hake looks at her with smiling compassion. He sits down beside her. He is sententious.

Love is a truce between periods of exhaustion. Love is broken teeth in a hungry mouth. What do you say? Did you like it?

EVA (*looks at him through tearful eyes*). Go away.

The Hake looks at her, perplexed.

THE HAKE (*genuinely desolate*). Are your throwing me out?

EVA. Yes! Yes! Yes! Yes! Yes!

THE HAKE. And what am I going to do?

EVA. It doesn't matter to me! Get out!

THE HAKE. I told Mario . . . I told him: these rich people give up in a hurry. At the first opposition they throw the whole thing over. (*Laughs.*) They forget themselves in a good symphony or by giving up something for Lent.

He looks at her.

Do you know what I saw a monkey in a circus do once? That monkey was trying to reach his mate, but he couldn't because they had put them in two separate cages and there were bars between them. It must have been about one o'clock in the afternoon when I saw him try to reach her for the first time. That night he hadn't succeeded, but he was still trying. His chest was all bloody and his teeth were broken from the iron bars, but still he kept trying. It was the following day that he succeeded in getting close to her, when they carried the female monkey to his burial. Sad, isn't it?

He wants to talk. He sits down on the floor at Eva's feet, crossing his legs in the position of a Hindu.

That is, naturally, always considering that love still exists. Saint Simon, the fool of Constitution Bridge, says that it doesn't. Actually, he doesn't even say that any more. One can only deduce it, given his . . . peculiar attitude. Do you know what he does, or what he *doesn't* do? He sits there night and day, on the railing of the bridge, watching the water go by. If anyone speaks to him: nothing. If anyone pokes him: nothing. If anyone shouts at him: (*He shouts.*) Ahhhhhh! Nothing! It's just that nothing interests him any more. He's arrived at a state of complete renunciation of life, where not even struggle is possible any longer. They say that one day a dove made a nest in his hat and he wasn't even aware of it. It's a legend, naturally, but it illustrates the situation, don't you think? Don't you think it illustrates it?

EVA. Didn't you hear what I asked you?

THE HAKE. What?

EVA. That you leave?

THE HAKE. Do you believe that? That we've arrived at the point of spiritual starvation where not even struggle is possible?

Eva rises to her feet. She screams and flees toward the bedroom. She locks herself in. The Hake watches her flee, halfway between stupefaction and amusement.

Do you believe that, Corsair? That we've arrived at a point of lack of love where love is no longer possible?

He approaches the cage. He talks to it, as he hits it, amuses himself. The cage almost hits the ceiling. The blows grow more violent as he speaks as in an interview; making the clichés ridiculous.

"Do you believe that, Mr. Happy?" . . . "That the human soul, deprived of all consolation, finds itself in a lamentable stage of spiritual prostration, where not even mutual confidence is possible?" "Do you believe it, Miss Smile?"

A violent blow.

Do you believe it, you fruity bird? Umm? What do you say? Do you believe it, you son-of-a-bitching bird? Don't you think that flying around the room that way without even saying goodbye was really a fruity thing to do, you pig of a bird? Umm? What do you say? What do you say, you shit? (*Screams.*) Speak, you queer! SPEAK!

The cage shatters against the wall.

CURTAIN

SCENE SIX

The night of the same day.
Nothing of the original décor remains in the room.

Everything is turned upside down.
There are no longer any curtains. In their place hang men's pants.
From corner to corner are draped garlands made from men's shirts tied together by the sleeves, interwoven with others made of women's underwear.
Furniture has been constructed from pieces of the original furniture tied together with strips of wool jackets, torn blankets, and spreads.
The lamps that were hanging are now on the floor. Those that were on the floor are hanging.
The walls are covered with childish figures and drawings, made with burnt cork; "the cat," "the bad man," "the hand," etc. There are also sayings: "I am good" . . . "Christ is King" . . . "God is at my right hand" . . . "Long live me!"
In essence, nothing is in its rightful place. A cyclone has passed through the room. The only things that retain any appearance of premeditated arrangement are the paper flowers. Many new large paper flowers hang in profuse garlands from the walls and are distributed here and there on the floor.
Eva, standing in the midst of the disorder, is allowing herself to serve as model for a bridal gown, which The Hake is fitting to her body with careful solicitude.

THE HAKE (*pinning; making pleats*). Do you see? You see that with a little hope, a little good will, this was worth digging into the old trunk for? It's a little tight, it's true, . . . a little wrinkled, but we must concede that you never . . . suspected that sometime you would have "a second chance," umm?

He moves away, looking at his work.

Or was it for a first time that never was? Umm?

He adjusts a pleat.

There you are! That's it! A little tight through the hips, perhaps. The fault of too much starch, or the years . . . or carelessness, but it passes the test, doesn't it?

He adjusts another pleat. He is the tailor who speaks to his client, intimately, suggestively.

We oughtn't to have put it so far down in the trunk. I understand: because of a passing streetcar, a hand waving suggestively as it moves out of sight, or a word that was left unsaid, or all, all, all the imagination now passed under the bridge, we condemned it to the depths of the trunk, but what about the bells? The little bells? And the laughter at the entrance of the church? And the furtive kiss on the cheek? "Goodbye, Mary, I hope you'll be very happy!" "Good luck!" Doesn't that count, too? We shouldn't be so harsh with time. Objects, too, have a right to take revenge. We shouldn't expect that everything will take its just place, if we don't help it a little, don't you agree?

He moves away, he approaches again. Something about the total appearance displeases him. He rips one side of the dress.

Perhaps it's a question of ripping the cloth a little, in order to see the flesh.

He tears off a piece of the cretonne from the chair by his feet, and with it patches a piece of the torn dress. He smiles.

Sweet little brides! I've observed them! Crouched under the crepe myrtle in the park opposite the church; I've seen them, I've watched them. Not that I had any twisted feeling, like envy or anything like that! No! Why should I, when I had enough paper and scissors at hand?

He tears another piece of the dress and patches it with another strip of cretonne cloth.

They come walking through the high grass, their feet scarcely touching the ground, as if they were floating above the spikes of rye grass . . . they come shimmering over in the damp meadows . . . cadenced steps . . . radiant . . . in smooth white undulations, moving sinuously among the trunks of the oaks . . . straight toward the steps radiant in the sun . . . straight toward the gloved hand!

He speaks into her ear.

And there, at the same moment, before the lascivious glances of all the horrible dwarfs hidden behind the brick walls, hidden under the shadowy atrium, I have seen them . . . I have seen them!

He chokes. Trembles.

I have seen them! Open . . . ! The petals of their bodies! And offer . . . imagine! Offer! (*He shouts.*) Offer! (*He calms himself.*) . . . Their virgin corollas to the consummation of love.

A choked cry.

Oh, God!

He controls himself. He regains his festive tone. He rips a sleeve. He replaces it with another sleeve made from a scrap of paper.

There are some naturally who have a different version of the affair, Fabian, for example. One day I was with him under the crepe myrtle. He had lifted some tinned smoked oysters, and we were preparing to enjoy them . . .

He slashes the hem of the skirt with the scissors.

I should warn you that Fabian has an especially noisy way of moving his mouth when he eats, a manner like this, holding his food in his mouth . . . as if he were afraid it would get to his intestines too fast, or that he might finish too soon, or that it might end too soon the pleasure of his de-gus-ta-tion! The fact is that I don't know if it was his way of chewing, I mean, or my particular state of tension that day, or the stone under my elbow—because a stone had got under my elbow, a damned stone under my elbow! The fact is I don't know if it was that way of his of chewing, like I said, or the stone, or my particular state of tension . . . the fact is that Fabian irritates me! He drives me to madness, I must confess! I don't know if it were that, I say, or the other . . . the insolence of his type, you understand me? His brutal, his bestial insensitivity, or his way of chewing, or the stone, or my particular state of tension. The fact is that, looking toward the church, I suddenly say, "Look!" And he answers me, "Those bitches! Those bitches." Imagine. I looked at his puss and I saw the oil of the smoked oysters dribbling from the corners of his mouth . . . and his bloodshot eyes, you understand me? And his noisy, disagreeable, embarrassing, repugnant way of chewing! The fact is that *something* produced in me, you understand me, a particular state of uncontrollable tension . . . and I grabbed the other tin of oysters that was open, but not eaten, you understand me . . . ? And I pushed it . . . I ground it . . . I shoved it into his filthy puss!

The preceding in screams; he calms himself. Now angelical.

In that moment the church bells rang, and I felt that I had done something that had to be done, you understand? That I had fulfilled my duty! Because guys like Fabian don't know, can't imagine, can't conceive . . . the scope . . . the complete miracle signified by the sur-ren-der-of-one's-vir-gi-ni-ty!

Accentuating the words with false pronunciation, he completely vitiates the meaning.

THE . . . MOST . . . SPLEN-DID . . . OFFERING OF LOVE!

He is amused by his own idea.

Love is a broken bridge with a broken tooth with a broken crank that whirls beyond its four confines breaking heads! Love is a dog with three feet! A tramp with only one hand and two bananas.

He has torn most of the skirt and is replacing it with pieces of the curtain and pieces of his own shirt he has torn into strips. He looks at her.

What's the matter with you? Are you shivering?

Eva shivers, with the same trembling as The Hake.

Are you cold? Are you hot? What is it?

Pause. He waits.

Do you want to go for a stroll on the beach with the happy bridegroom? Gathering shells? Hand in hand, gathering sand dollars? Discussing the number, and the sex, and the number, and the names, and the number, and the sex, of the children that the splendid future will give you? Discussing the arrangement of the furniture . . . of the cretonne . . . of the colors . . . of the "No it's better here," "No it's better there," of the sizes . . . of the cretonne . . . of the furniture . . . (*His voice is growing louder, faster.*) of the positions of the cretonnes! Of the sizes! Of the numbers, of the children, of the furniture . . . of the sizes . . . of the children? Spea-king-of-love! Love with an L, an O, an E, an X, a U, a tongue, everything, with strength, without strength! The possibilities . . . of being! Of achieving! Of fleeing! Of love! Of solitude! Of death! With a tongue! Arriving! Arriving! Arriving!

He screams.

ARRIVING! ARRIVING! AR . . RI . . VING!

He pants.

Is that it? Is that the secret the refrigerator hides?

Of the original bride's dress, only the veil remains. The rest is a ragbag.

That's funny. Now we're two little brothers.

He rips off the rest of his shirt. He covers his head with a paper rosette in the manner of a crown from which hang long strips of paper that reach to his waist. He takes a board from a piece of furniture in the manner of a lance and brandishes it.

I am Ukelele, the Simba Warrior!

He circles around Eva, making grotesque contortions and amusing grimaces.

Uku! Azahanba! Humba! Tekeke! Takamba! Tumba!

He looks at her as a curious orangutan might regard his prey, with simian curiosity. He puts his face right up to hers.

Comment allez-vous, madame? Did you say something?
EVA (*with an effort*). I . . .
THE HAKE. Yes?
EVA. I . . .
THE HAKE. Yes?
EVA. I only . . .
THE HAKE. You only, yes . . . ? You already said that. You only . . .
EVA. I only . . .
THE HAKE. Yes?

Eva tries to speak, but can't. Once or twice she makes an effort that frustrates her, then gives up. A pause.

You only wanted to love me and for me to love you. Is that it?

Eva nods weakly.

Yes. But it's too late for that. Ukelele has his guts in his hands and now he doesn't know what to do with them.

He places one of the big paper flowers in the bodice of Eva's dress. It is so large it completely covers her face. He takes her arm in his.

Shall we go?

Someone is knocking at the door.

Yes! (*He yells.*) We're coming.

He looks at Eva with solicitude, like a very considerate sweetheart.

Are you ready?

His expression changes suddenly to the one we are accustomed to seeing. Sententious. Vacant.

As you see, it is of the greatest importance to have understood the game. To believe in each other. To confide mutually. To renounce your own identity, to the benefit of the identity of the other, until your own identity and the identity of the other, and your own identity . . . own . . . identity . . . of the other . . . identity . . . own . . . don't you think so?

Eva weakly agrees.

Mendelssohn's Wedding March. Their march begins. "Ukelele," very stiff, pathetic almost in his dignity, nude, covered only in rags; on his head is a crown of shredded paper. Eva by his side, her arm in his, absent, lost, beneath the immensity of her paper flower. The only real thing about her is the beautiful veil.

Before we arrive there, I think I should inform you about the geography of the river, of the dangers it offers. There are, out there, some dangerous depths, where on nights of the full moon—when the river flows swollen with broken furniture—many people, falling, have broken their necks.

They exit. In the room now, total disorder reigns. Everything is broken, undone. There remains in it only the new beauty. The dark, enormous, ragged paper flowers.

CURTAIN

APPENDIX A

THE STUDENT AS CRITIC

Now it is your turn to be a critic—to participate actively in the theater experience—by discussing your impressions of a play you read or see. You need not have written a play or acted, directed, or designed to be a thoughtful critic. Your qualifications? An idea sparked by a play or performance and the means to articulate that idea clearly and vividly.

Writing about the theater is an invaluable way to enhance your experience. First, it allows you to apply what you have learned about the theater to a specific play; second, it encourages you to consider what you have experienced and transform it into ideas of your own. Do not think of a critical essay as homework; rather, accept it as an opportunity to participate in the theater in a lively way.

You will likely be asked to write one of two kinds of critical papers, perhaps both:

- a production review of a live performance (or perhaps a film version) you have seen;
- an interpretive essay on an aspect or theme of a play you have read and/or seen.

Each has its own needs and style, yet both share common traits. They are specific in their judgment; they are supported by specific examples; and they offer a definite point of view.

The Production Review

Production reviews require a reasonably quick response to the play and its performance. Usually, the reviewer does not go back for a second look—though one of the advantages of a college production is that it is accessible and usually inexpensive. It may be possible (and useful) to see a show twice if circumstances permit.

The production review customarily assesses two things: the play itself and the production of the play (i.e., the acting, the direction, the designs, and the technical support). By the conclusion of your review, the reader ought to have a good idea of what the play is about, what it says, how well it says it, and the quality of its realization in live performance. It is quite possible you may admire the play, but have reservations about the performance—or vice versa. You may like elements of the plot or character, but have questions about other aspects of the scripted play, just as you may find some actors quite good, others less so. A good review is balanced: it does not uniformly praise a play and its production, nor does it unrelentingly castigate both. There are certainly times when a play gets a thoroughly glowing review, just as there are times when a thundering pan (i.e., negative review) is given. In most cases you will find that even the best plays and productions could be improved, while even the weakest at least show some potential. Good reviewers are sensitive to both possibilities.

If you can, try to read the play before you see it; a second reading may help jog your memory after you've seen it. Theater is meant to be enjoyed, so sit back and enjoy the show. It's best to jot down your ideas, key points, and memorable lines during intermission or after the play because actors hate to see audiences dutifully scribbling notes during performance. Please respect the actors and, if you must, take notes unobtrusively. Those lines or moments you remember most vividly are probably your best source of inspiration. Because of their unfamiliarity, at new plays it may indeed be necessary to jot down a significant line.

A well-written review begins with a "grabber," a vivid introduction that tells the reader something about the play, the production, and the reviewer's overall opinion of the event. It also prompts the reader to continue. In short, a good review opens much like a good play in production: it draws the audience into the play, raises questions about the experience to come, and establishes a dominant idea to be explored. Here's a good example taken from a review of August Wilson's *Ma Rainey's Black Bottom* written by Frank Rich of the *New York Times* (1984):

> Late in Act I of *Ma Rainey's Black Bottom*, a somber, aging band trombonist (Joe Seneca) tilts his head heavenward to sing the blues. The setting is a dilapidated Chicago recording studio of 1927, and the song sounds as old as time. "If I had my way," goes the lyric, "I would tear this building down." Once the play has ended that

lyric has almost become a prophecy. In *Ma Rainey's Black Bottom*, the writer August Wilson sends the entire history of black America crashing down upon our heads. The play is a searing inside account of what white racism does to its victims—and it floats on the same authentic artistry as the blues music it celebrates.

Note how this introduction captures some of the energy of the performance, as well as satisfying the reader's need to know what the play is about and whether it is a worthwhile experience.

Having secured the reader's interest, the reviewer then moves on to a summary of the play's plot and its thematic intentions. Plot summaries should be brief, usually no more than two to three sentences. Identify the principal characters and the conflicts in which they are engaged. It is not the reviewer's job to reveal how the conflicts are resolved—unless the playwright has contrived the resolution implausibly. While summarizing the plot the reviewer should also indicate something about the ambience of the work. This is especially important when environment is important to the play or when directors and designers have recontextualized a work by placing it in another milieu.

After identifying the play's issues (lovers flee to forest to escape tyrannical father, dejected salesman can no longer "cut it" on the road), the reviewer comments on its thematic values. Even the frothiest musical, such as *42nd Street*, offers a simple idea ("perseverance and a little bit of luck ultimately pays off"). Great plays, those that we call universal, usually suggest a number of themes. It is entirely possible, even probable, that a production will choose to explore one of those themes in a new or controversial manner, as when Arianne Mnouchkine staged *Tartuffe* in 1995 as a critique of the West's complicity in human rights violations in Bosnia-Herzegovina (see Chapter 4). Often the most interesting conflict in a production is that between the playwright and director, and the reviewer should address this issue. Reviewers ought to be confident enough to suggest an interpretation of the play (readers know it is not necessarily definitive). Such analyses are most credible when they are supported with specific evidence, such as lines from the text or the re-creation of a particular moment, that illustrate the theme. Comments about the originality or profundity of the play's themes are a useful way to conclude the discussion of the script.

A significant portion of the review must evaluate the performances of the principal actors, and perhaps of supporting ones whose work is especially noteworthy. While it is easy to toss around well-worn adjectives to describe actors—"scintillating," "memorable," "convincing," or "poor"—it is more useful (and challenging) to describe the actor at work. Rich's comments on Theresa Merritt's performance as Ma Rainey accomplish this:

[She] is Ma Rainey incarnate. A singing actress of both wit and power, she finds bitter humor in the character's

distorted sense of self: When she barks her outrageous demands to [the black musicians], we see a show business monster who's come a long way from her roots. Yet the roots can still be unearthed. In a rare reflective moment, she explains why she sings the blues. "You don't sing to feel better," Miss Merritt says tenderly. "You sing because that's a way of understanding life."

Here we get both a sense of the actor's emotional range and the reality of the character she creates. Never do we doubt that Miss Merritt was "scintillating" or "memorable," but here we understand why Rich judged her performance positively.

A note about negative criticism is in order because some reviewers often use it as an opportunity to show off their own wit rather than to remedy a weak performance. Even good reviewers succumb to this temptation, as when John Mason Brown dismissed Tallulah Bankhead's performance in Shakespeare's *Antony and Cleopatra:* " [She] barged down the Nile as Cleopatra last night—and sank." It is more constructive to discuss an actor's lack of emotional range or predictable vocal patterns than to summarize his or her work as poor or uninteresting. Though it is unlikely actors will read your reviews, discussing acting strengths and weaknesses in concrete terms is a constructive way to hone your critical thinking skills.

You may not have space or time to assess every actor's performance, but often you can single out a minor role and comment on the artistry an actor brings to it. And by all means, be sure to assess the ensemble effect of a production. A play dominated by a single actor may not, in the end, be as satisfying as one in which all actors—from stars to spear carriers—are contributing equally to the quality of the performance.

Designers do not want to read that their sets, costumes, and lighting were little more than "beautiful," "electric," or "marvelous." They want to know that their visual artistry contributed to the mood and ambience of the play, and perhaps even to its thematic intentions. Judge the design and technical work within the context of the whole production and not merely as a visual delight. Jo Mielziner's design for the 1949 Broadway production of *Death of a Salesman* was thoughtfully crystallized by T. C. Worsley in *The New Statesman* (August 6, 1949): "The stage design is skeletal; we see all three rooms at once, and we see, even more important, looming up behind, the great lowering claustrophobic cliff of concrete skyscrapers in which their living space is embedded." Writing like this elevates reviewing to an art form.

Your review ought to close with a brief statement that not only summarizes the impact of the production you saw, but that also beckons the reader to share in the experience. Rich's review of *Ma Rainey's Black Bottom* accomplishes this:

The lines [see comments on Merritt's acting above] might also apply to the play's author. Mr. Wilson can't mend the broken lives he unravels in *Ma Rainey's Black*

Bottom. But, like his heroine, he makes their suffering into art that forces us to understand and won't allow us to forget.

Finally, it might be useful to hear the words of a theater artist about the role of the critic-reviewer in the theater. Jack O'Brien is the artistic director of the Old Globe Theater in San Diego and a successful Broadway director:

Years ago I used to love the early reviews of Walter Kerr, and I used to hold them up to our critics today—and still do—because to write great criticism, to read criticism is not to hear something brilliantly torn apart and dissected and dismissed. It's to make you or somebody get off their dead asses and go out and buy a ticket. And if you can do that, I think you belong in some proximity to the theater. Not just to say, "This is what it means" and "This is where it's deficient," but to say, "If you care, see that performance. This actor is not delivering yet, but you're watching somebody beginning to achieve greatness." Or to create the idea that it *might* happen.

If you are not doing so already, make it part of your continuing theater education to read reviews regularly. Doing so will not only keep you abreast of what's new in the theater, but also sharpen your critical skills by learning from professional critics. Newspapers in major cities, mass-circulation magazines such as *Time, Newsweek,* and *Rolling Stone,* and theater periodicals such as *American Theater* or *Variety* regularly contain reviews. Soon you will find critics whose style and opinions you value. Also, each year since 1943 virtually every review of plays performed in New York has been collected and bound under the title, *New York Theatre Critics Reviews* (now *National Theatre Critics Reviews*); this series should be in your library. Spend an hour leafing through several volumes to get a feel for good critical writing. By no means should you take everything you read at face value. Learn to be as discriminating in your reading of reviews as you are in your theatergoing. It will not take you long to distinguish quality critical writing from inferior work, even if you have not seen the play in question.

Critical Essays

You have probably written a critical essay on a novel, poem, short story, or other literary work in which you analyzed a theme, character, or recurring image. Perhaps you have compared two authors' approaches to a given subject. Therefore, you already possess some skills and experience to write a critical essay about a play or several plays. This text and the course you are taking provide you with specific resources and the vocabulary to talk about the theater and playcraft.

The first step in writing a paper, of course, is to select a topic. Often your instructor will provide a topic or list of topics for you. A comment during class discussion or a lecture may suggest material for an essay. We have included some

commentary with each play to spark your imagination and critical thinking; also, a list of questions appended to the end of this essay may help you choose a topic. Perhaps the best sources, however, come from a gut feeling you have as you respond to a work or from a question you ask while reading or watching a play. Whatever its source, your topic ought to suggest some originality (does the world really need another essay on "Ambition in *Macbeth*"?). Topics that discuss the obvious are not going to challenge you or your reader.

Think of a topic as a problem that begs for a resolution—or, better yet, resolutions. Good art does not produce a single answer; rather, it opens the possibilities for a variety of answers. And what is important about your paper is that you devise a plausible solution to the problem you have defined—not necessarily *the* answer, because in the arts *the* answer does not exist.

Whether your paper is an *analysis* of plot structure, recurring images, or character development, a *comparison* (or *contrast*) of characters or themes, a *description* of a performance or design, an *interpretation* of a play's meaning, or simply a *response* to your reading or viewing of the play, write it from an *argumentative* or *persuasive* point of view. That is, make a claim and then argue your case. We have seen that many plays in ancient Greece contained an *agon* (debate) because it produced a well-defined conflict and its resolution. A good critical essay is also an *agon* in which you identify a problem and then persuade your audience that your ideas are reasonable. You do not have to convince your audience that your opinion is definitive; you should, however, make the case that it is plausible. As any good debater will tell you, the strength of your argument depends on the quality of the evidence.

A word of caution: do not try to address every aspect of a play in your paper. Sufficiently narrow your topic so that you can discuss it comfortably and in reasonable depth in the space you are allowed. Better to say a lot about a little than to say a little about a lot of things. Stanislavsky's observation that "less is more" applies to good writing as much as to good acting. Also, if you can cover a narrowly focused topic well (e.g., "Images of Disease in *Hamlet*"), your instructor may reasonably assume you could—time and space permitting—cover a much larger topic ("Imagery in *Hamlet*").

As you focus on your topic, it may prove useful to jot down key words, phrases, and ideas that relate to it; these will eventually pattern themselves into the key elements of your argument. Reread the play carefully, each time noting lines, speeches, and specific actions that relate to your topic. You may want to use colored markers to code dialogue, stage directions, or plot moments that provide evidence for your argument. Make notes on 3 x 5 cards so they can be readily organized as you create an outline for the paper. (By the way, directors and designers often work this way in preparation for a show.)

As you undertake this brainstorming session, your topic will more readily define itself. Once you have defined the problem and the evidence to support it, you are ready to construct a *thesis* or *proposition*—the major point you wish to argue in your paper. Like Stanislavsky's "superobjective," the thesis serves as a unifying agent that controls every element of the paper. A topic, by the way, is not itself a thesis. Topics are usually conveyed in nouns and phrases such as "imagery," "symbols," "irony," or "conflict." A thesis puts the noun into action: "Symbols of lightness and darkness convey the meaning of *Oedipus the King*," or "The conflict between Nora Helmer and Torvald reflects the conflict between old world patriarchy and a new social order in Europe in the late nineteenth century." Using action verbs—as opposed to "being" verbs—gives your paper energy; it is the same principle actors use as they frame objectives.

Your thesis needs testing to insure that you have sufficient support to sustain it. Usually a minimum of three major points or proofs are needed to substantiate your claim. Again, note that playwrights frequently observe this "rule of three" when devising their plots (see *Ti-Jean and His Brothers* and its accompanying essay) because three examples are usually sufficient to suggest a universal truth. Though you may think of a larger number, the length of your paper will probably dictate a maximum of five major points in your argument.

For each point you need evidence, usually drawn from the script of the play. Quotations, stage directions, major plot moments (e.g., reversal or recognition) are your best means of substantiating your case. You may also want to cite secondary sources, such as the comments of other critics and scholars. Your instructor will define the degree to which you should do this. Some want a paper based solely on your reading and/or viewing of the play; others expect something more along the lines of a traditional research paper.

Quotations are, of course, subject to interpretation, particularly in the modern theater, where dialogue can be intentionally ambiguous. A famous story describes Harold Pinter in attendance at a rehearsal of one of his plays. The actors and director Peter Wood were trying to interpret a particularly difficult line; frustrated, the director turned to Pinter and said, "What does this line mean?" Pinter wryly answered, "I don't know, Peter, I only heard it in my head as I was writing the play." However, as a critic you—like an actor—must assign a specific meaning to a line, unless, of course, your topic is about ambiguity, in which case you should suggest all potential meanings that occur to you. The bottom line is to be sure that you understand a given line thoroughly before using it as evidence. You therefore need some knowledge of the conditions that created the play: the historical backgrounds of the society and theater, the playwright's life and works, the prevailing philosophy of the age, and so on. The essays throughout this book have been written to inform you about the historical and theatrical milieus that inspired the plays.

Use quotations to support your claims because the text is primary evidence, but avoid stringing a number of quotes together. Your paper should emphasize your ideas about the play and its meaning to you; don't let your ideas become obscured by a barrage of quotes. Just as good actors use gestures sparingly and for emphasis, good critical writers similarly use quotes as emphatic support. Shakespeare's advice to "use all gently" is as applicable to writers as to actors.

OK; you have selected a topic about which you are enthused. You have read the play several times and dutifully taken notes. If necessary you have done some background reading about the play, its playwright, and the period in which it was written, and you have carefully framed a thesis statement. Are you ready to write? Not exactly. Just as actors need some rehearsal time before performance, you also need to do some preparation work. First, write an outline of your paper, which allows you to test your thesis by carefully lining up the major points you wish to make. Place the evidence you believe will support each argument under the appropriate section of your outline. List the evidentiary material by a key word and page/line number so you can quickly find it as you write the paper. In your outline you need not worry much about the razzle-dazzle attention-getter or the memorable conclusion; these are often best written last, when you have built your case. State your thesis in a single sentence at the top, then list the three-to-five major points you wish to make on its behalf. Under each major point list a couple of minor points, each with its own evidence. (We have included a sample outline of our own essay on *Ti-Jean and His Brothers* as a model; compare it with the finished essay in Chapter 8.) It's best to live with this outline for a couple of days (time permitting!) and adjust it as you get new insights. Again, this is very much the way an actor works in rehearsal: make some early choices, play with them, then adjust as new choices occur to you.

After your outline has been polished, you may want to preview your ideas by showing them to your instructor, who is a sort of "director" who gives you feedback about your choices. Then you can begin writing the paper in earnest. If you have done this groundwork, you will be surprised how easily the writing comes to you. Write quickly without much attention to the niceties of style and mechanics. These can be cleaned up later. For now, focus on discussing your ideas clearly and logically. Don't even worry about inserting full quotations at this time; that's easily done in the redraft. This stage is like an early run-through of a play in which the actors simply try to get from the first line to the last coherently. The "polish'n'perfect" stage comes later, much closer to opening.

After you have written the first draft, put it aside for a while. Come back to it fresh and with a critical eye toward polishing your writing style. Try reading your paper aloud, particularly to a friend or roommate; better yet, let the friend read your paper to you. Listen to the quality and clarity of the writing. It's often easier to hear a "clunker" of a sentence than it is to see it on the page. (This is why playwrights crave a reading of their play.) This technique is also quite useful for judging the appropriateness of support material; you will hear if a quotation sounds like a natural outgrowth of your argument.

Having written the main body of your paper and reworked its style and mechanics, you are now ready to write an attention-getting introduction and a memorable conclusion. Frankly, such elements have been the bane of writers since Aeschylus; we have no sure-fire formula to give you, as inspiration plays a pivotal role in composing introductions and conclusions. Just as a playwright tries to grab the audience's attention by raising questions about the subject matter, creating a tone, and providing a sense of direction for the remainder of the play (all in the first five minutes), so should you devise an introduction that will engage your reader. An opener such as "In this paper I am going to . . ." is a bit like opening a play with five pages of heavy-handed exposition. Skim the introductions to several essays in this text and see which opening paragraphs catch your interest. You should be able to formulate a few principles about attention-getters. As a general rule, limit your introduction to 10 to 15 percent of the length of your entire paper.

Conclusions should be about 5 percent of the length of the paper. A good conclusion should not only clinch your argument, but leave a lasting impression. You may want to summarize the main points of your argument, but present them freshly so that you are not merely rehashing what the reader knows. The one thing that should not appear in a conclusion is new evidentiary material; that belongs in the body of the argument.

A Few Technical Notes

Writing about drama raises particular problems, especially where quotations are concerned. Because you will be using a number of quotations, it is cumbersome and distracting to footnote each one. After an initial foot- or endnote, you can usually identify the quotation in parentheses, using one of several systems. In general, quotations of one-act verse dramas, such as Greek tragedies, are identified by line numbers, which are usually placed along the right-hand margin of the script (publishers' practices vary). Quotations from most classical dramas, such as those of Shakespeare and his contemporaries, are identified by act, scene, and line number(s). You might see Hamlet's "To be or not to be" soliloquoy identified as 3.1.55 ff., which means it is found in act 3, scene 1, lines 55 and following (or lines 55–89 if the full speech is cited). If you are dealing with several plays and have not specifically identified a quotation by play in your text, use a standard abbreviation for the play prior to the line numbers (e.g., *Hamlet* is H or Ham; *A Midsummer Night's Dream* is usually *MND*). Quotations from most modern plays are usually identified by the page number of the script from which they are taken. In all cases, however, cite the specific text from which you have quoted the lines; this is especially important for some classic plays because lines may actually be numbered differently from text to text (among other things, prose speeches often alter line numbers). There are two ways to cite the text in a footnote for the first quotation:

- provide all of the bibliographic information and add a phrase such as "all quotations are from this text and will hereafter be cited parenthetically";
- list the text in a Works Cited appendix at the end of the paper.

Your instructor will probably indicate which method is preferred.

Lengthy quotations from plays (that is, those over three lines long) should be set off from your text; this is usually done by indenting five spaces and single-spacing the extract. If the quotation is in verse, it should be reproduced as verse in your paper. You should make every effort to reproduce the verse as it is laid out in the original text by indenting appropriate lines. The shared line of Elizabethan playwriting would look like this:

QUEEN. Why, how now, Hamlet?
        HAMLET. What's the matter now?
QUEEN. Have you forgot me?
        HAMLET. No, by the rood, not so.
        (H., 3.4.13–14)

Note that extracts do not require quotation marks as they are clearly separated from your writing. Shorter quotations can be incorporated into the regular text by placing them in quotation marks. Any parenthetical line or page numbers are placed outside the quotation marks. If you are quoting a couple of lines of verse, indicate the break in the verse line by using a slash mark and capitalizing the second line. Thus, Hamlet's question "What is a man, / If his chief good and market of his time / Be but to sleep and feed?" (4.4.33–35) would be typed as you read it here. (*Note*: The "I" in "If" is capitalized because it is capitalized in the text; if it is not capitalized, do not capitalize it. If you wish to indicate it as a lowercase "i" because it is in the middle of your sentence, bracket your alteration from the original: "[I]f the chief good . . . .")

Titles of plays of any length are customarily identified by underlining or italicizing them (though newspapers generally put titles of plays in quotation marks). If your instructor has not indicated a specific format for annotations and bibliography (such as the *MLA* or *Chicago Manual of Style*), use one with which you are familiar or invest in a guidebook. The important thing is to be consistent in whichever format you use.

Throughout this book we have stressed the importance of the audience in the theater event. Ideally, plays set up a dialogue between artists and audience. In the theater, you cannot (in most cases) talk back to the playwright, actors, and technical artists, but you do send them signals of approval (laughter, applause, an "electric" silence) and disapproval (coughing, squirming in your seat, thumbing through the program). Critical writing allows you to participate in the dialogue more intensely than usual. You, too, become part of the process. It is both a responsibility and a creative act; perform it with enthusiasm and relish.

General Questions About a Play and Its Performance

As you read the plays in this text, keep the following questions and analytical principles in mind. You may wish to develop one of these into an essay.

The Four Dimensions of a Play

I. ACTION: *What happens?*
   A. Describe the basic action of the play in one sentence.
   B. Outline briefly, as a sequence of events, the plot.
   C. Identify the minor and the major crises, their climaxes, and the resolution to each crisis.
II. CHARACTER: *Who is the play about?*
   A. Who are the characters whose interaction creates the play?
   B. Describe the social/historical context in which the characters live. If relevant, define the hierarchy to which they belong.
   C. Which characters are:
      i. major (foreground)?
      ii. supporting (middleground)?
      iii. minor (background)?
   D. Name the principal interactions among these characters.
III. IDEA/THEME: *What is the play "about"?*
   A. Identify the principal conflict(s) of values the play represents.
   B. To what extent, and in what way, are these conflicts resolved?
IV. PERFORMANCE: *What aspects of live performance are implicit in the script?*
   A. Evidence of the circumstances of the original performance
      i. place (theater space) and occasion
      ii. actors (and style of acting) and the audience's relationship to actors
      iii. specific conventions (e.g., asides, soliloquies, direct address to audience, etc.)
   B. Audible qualities
      i. language (prose, poetry, elevated, "street")
      ii. music, song, sound effects
   C. Visual qualities
      i. *presentational* (nonrealistic) or *representational* (realistic)
      ii. scenery, costumes, props, visual effects
      iii. actors in motion: blocking, business, composition

Other Questions You Might Ask Include:

1. How is this play different from others you have read?
2. From what perspective do we see the events (psychological, political, ethical, moral, heroic, etc.)?

3. What is the conflict in terms of opposing principles (i.e., society vs. the individual, ideas vs. conformity, one right vs. another, etc.)?
4. Why is each character necessary to the play's argument or theme?
5. What general or universal experience does the play seem to be dramatizing? (I.e., if an old play is worth reading/seeing today, it should tell us something permanent about human nature and the problems of life.)
6. What is the playwright's attitude toward the material (skeptical, critical, pessimistic, sympathetic, neutral, objective, sentimental)? What features or elements of the play seem to be the source of this attitude (e.g., a character you can trust, the arrangement of the incidents)?
7. What special formal characteristics of the play make it different from earlier plays of its kind?

A Sample Outline for a Critical Essay on *Ti-Jean and His Brothers* (see Chapter 8)

THESIS: Derek Walcott combines traditional storytelling and theater techniques and a contemporary political sensibility to create a modern parable in *Ti-Jean and His Brothers*.

I. INTRODUCTION (*establishes background for essay and states the thesis*)
   A. "Dancing with the devil" is a popular subject in dramatic literature.
      1. *Ancient:* Theatrical rituals and ceremonies described in Chapter 1 of this text provide numerous examples of diabolic figures.
      2. *Classical Drama:* Medieval morality plays and classical tragedies, such as *Othello*, used either real or symbolic devils to tell their stories.
      3. *Modern Drama:* We have invented new names, such as neuroses and obsessions, for our demons in modern plays.
   B. *Ti-Jean and His Brothers* combines ancient and modern sensibilities to create a contemporary parable.

II. BODY (*presents the proofs for the thesis*)
   A. *Ti-Jean and His Brothers* uses traditional elements of the folktale; these are governed by "the rule of three."
      1. Plot structure and the rule of three
         a. Twin prologues
            i. the fantasy world
            ii. the "real" world
         b. Three scenes in which a brother confronts the devil
      2. Archetypal characters

    a. The Suffering Mother

    b. The Three Brothers

       i. "Big brother": physical prowess

      ii. "Middle brother": intellectual prowess

     iii. "Little brother": wit and common sense

B. *Ti-Jean and His Brothers* offers a universal folk theme and a contemporary political theme to instruct its audience.

    1. Folk theme

      a. "Rite of passage" play in which brothers journey into the forest.

      b. Natural wit is superior to raw strength or learned intelligence.

    2. Political theme

      a. A critique of old colonial system that exploits island workers.

      b. Aligned with traditional *canboulay*, the nineteenth-century rebellion that ultimately freed the slaves, in Trinidad.

    c. Play traces evolution of Africans in the Caribbean from exploited manual laborers to resourceful "Anglo-Africans."

C. The superb theatricality of the play engages audience and promotes Walcott's message.

    1. Audible qualities: music, poetry, language

    2. Visual elements: colorful costuming, fantasy elements, masks, strong moments of physical conflict

III. CONCLUSION (*reaffirms thesis and links play to world drama*)

    A. Walcott has not invented new subject matter or theater techniques.

    B. Yet the play retains its appeal because of its combination of universal themes and contemporary issues.

APPENDIX B

GLOSSARY OF TERMS

act: the primary division of the action of a play. A play can consist of a single act or comprise two, three, four, or five acts; ten-act plays are not uncommon in India. *Also*, to represent or perform an action onstage.

action: what happens in the story line of a play; a **plot** consists of events that create the play's action.

acto: Spanish term for an act of a play; in contemporary American theater, it is usually a short satiric play on social issues important to Chicanos.

afterpiece: a short entertainment, usually a song or dance, performed at the conclusion of a play.

agitprop: short for "agitation-propaganda," a form of drama that incites the emotions ("agitation") and then teaches social and political lessons to encourage the audience to engage in a particular political action. Clifford Odets's play *Waiting for Lefty* and the *actos* of Luis Valdez are agitprop.

agon: Greek term for "debate" or "contest"; both tragedies and comedies had formal *agons* in which the central idea of the drama was debated.

alienation effect: from the German term *Verfremdungseffekt* (from the verb *verfremden*, "to make strange"); this was Brecht's technique for making the audience stand back and objectively observe the action of a play so that it might judge its social issues. Elements such as songs, political speeches, signboards, storytellers, and direct address "alienate" the audience from the action of the play.

allegory: a play in which symbolic fictional characters portray truths or generalizations about human existence; medieval **morality plays** were allegories, as is Dickens's famous story *A Christmas Carol.*

alternative theater: generic term for theater practice and theory that is outside the traditional commercial theater; usually avant-garde and experimental, it depends on collective creation by its practitioners, most of whom are bound by a common ideology.

anankē: Greek term for "necessity" or "that which has to be"; *anankē* was the force in the universe that kept "the natural order of things."

antagonist: the character who opposes the **protagonist,** or central character of a play; for example, Claudius in *Hamlet.*

antimasque: grotesque parodies of **masques,** usually involving monstrous figures.

antistrophe: one of the three principal divisions of a Greek ode; it means "counterturn" (see **strophe**).

Aoi-no-ue play: the "ghost play" in **Noh** drama in which a vengeful spirit returns to torment a wrongdoer.

apron: the part of the stage closest to the audience and in front of the proscenium. In theaters without a proscenium (such as the Elizabethan theater), virtually the entire stage becomes an **apron stage** (sometimes called a **thrust stage**). In some historical periods, such as the Restoration, all acting took place on the apron.

aragoto: the "rough" or masculine style of **Kabuki** performance, usually adopted in samurai and other military roles.

archetypal character: a recurring figure who transcends the particulars of time and place to take on a symbolic value with universal appeal; a primary example. For example, Prometheus is the archetype of the human who takes on suffering for the greater good.

archon: a wealthy Greek citizen who provided the financial backing for the drama festivals; the forerunner of the contemporary producer.

arena theater: theater configuration in which the audience sits on all sides of the stage; sometimes referred to as "theater in the round."

areítos: pre-Columbian ritual dramas using song, dance, mime, and the spoken word that were performed in Cuba, Puerto Rico, and other parts of the Caribbean; they represent some of the first performances recorded by Europeans in the New World.

aside: a performance convention in which a character speaks directly to the audience while the other characters do not hear him or her.

atmosphere: the mood of a play created by scenery, lighting, sound, movement, and other effects.

Atsu-mori play: "warrior play" in **Noh** drama in which a military man disguises himself as a priest to repent a life of violence.

autos sacramentales: religious dramas performed in Spain during the Middle Ages; in the Renaissance they became secularized, but retained their allegorical nature. Also known simply as *autos*.

avant-garde: an intelligentsia that develops new or experimental forms, especially in the arts.

bailetes: dance musicals in the Spanish-language theater.

ballad opera: genre in which popular songs and ballads are inserted into the action to advance plot, character, or theme. John Gay's *The Beggar's Opera* (1727) is the prototype of the genre, which gradually evolved into **musical theater.**

beat: the smallest motivational unit of a playscript; it may be only a phrase or sentence in which a character manifests a particular need that must be fulfilled (see also **unit**).

benevolence: a philosophic belief in the innate goodness of humanity and the corresponding belief that humans have an obligation to use their natural instincts of love and charity; benevolence (or "sensibility") is particularly prominent in sentimental comedies, domestic tragedies, and many melodramas.

bill: the list and order of acts in a vaudeville show; also, the order of acts in a theatrical presentation.

blank verse: poetic speech that does not rhyme; it is customarily written in **iambic pentameter** in English.

blocking: the movement and positioning of actors on the stage.

bourgeois tragedy (also **domestic tragedy** and *le Drame*): serious dramas devoted to common people faced with everyday problems.

braggart warrior: stock character of the Roman theater (and subsequent ages); he was portrayed as a boastful soldier who, in reality, was a coward. The most common Roman name was **Miles Gloriosis;** Shakespeare's Sir John Falstaff is the best-known braggart warrior.

bufo Cubano: Cuban versions of the **minstrel show.**

burlesque: 1. a comic parody of a serious work; 2. a theatrical entertainment comprising broadly humorous skits and short turns ("blackouts"), songs, dances, and frequently striptease acts.

business: actions performed by actors, such as drinking, smoking, comic beatings, and the like.

cabaret: variety show, associated with the German theater, in which political skits and songs are performed in a restaurant and/or barroom.

canziones: Italian word for "song," particularly those placed between acts of Renaissance comedies.

carros: Spanish pageant wagons.

catharsis: the emotional cleansing initiated by the tragic experience; for the character it is the recognition and acceptance of his or her error; for the audience, it is the sum total of the pity and fear created by the play.

ceremony: an action performed formally and meant to sanction a political, social, or religious concept; it usually lacks the deeper significance of a **ritual.** Examples of a ceremony include a graduation or swearing-in.

character: 1. a person in a play; 2. the personality of such a person; 3. one of the six elements of drama as defined by

Aristotle. (See also **stock character** and **archetypal character.**)

Children of the Pear Garden: traditional term for actors in Chinese theater, so named because the Tang emperor Ming Huan established a school for actors in the pear garden of his estate.

ching: a character role in Chinese opera, usually distinguished by a painted face.

ching hsi: the Peking Opera or, more broadly, Chinese opera.

choreography: the arrangement and movement of performers onstage; though the term customarily applies to dancers, it is also used to denote the orchestrated movement of actors, especially in stage combat.

choric speech: a speech spoken by a group; also, a speech which describes offstage action.

chorus: a group (usually 12–15) of singer-dancers in Greek drama participating in or commenting on the action of the play; in other ages (e.g., the Elizabethan theater) the chorus was a single figure who speaks the prologue and epilogue and comments on the action.

ch'ou: a stock character of the Chinese theater; the clown or trickster.

ch'uan-ch'i: form of classical Chinese drama derived from the southern provinces; forerunner of the Peking Opera.

chūnori: ("riding the sky") flying effects in the **Kabuki** theater.

City Dionysia: spring festivals held in honor of **Dionysus** in Greek city-states; one of the highlights of these annual events was the presentation of a series of tragic and comic plays.

Classicism: dramatic style that emphasizes order, harmony, balance, and the unities of time, place, and action. Characteristically, classical plays use few characters and follow a single line of action. *Oedipus the King* typifies the classical play.

climax: the resolution of the protagonist's principal conflict; the climax usually grows out of the **crisis** and brings about a play's **denouement,** or falling action.

closet drama: a play not intended for performance; such plays are usually read within a circle of acquaintances. Some historians believe Seneca's tragedies were closet dramas.

cocoliche: comic dramas from Argentina dealing with the problems of immigrants.

comedia: generic Spanish term for a play, both comic and serious.

comedy: a primary dramatic genre that usually ends happily and treats its subject matter lightly.

comedy of humors: comic genre that focuses on a single personality flaw of a character; it was based on the medieval belief that human behavior was influenced by bodily fluids (or "humors") and that an imbalance of these fluids led to erratic behavior.

Comedy of Manners: comic genre that satirizes the behaviors, fashions, and mores of a given social class or set.

Restoration comedies and Molière's *Tartuffe* typify the Comedy of Manners. Such plays demand a sophisticated and knowledgeable audience.

comic relief: humorous scenes inserted in tragic or serious dramas that provide emotional relief from the play's weighty issues; comic relief can, however, also provide an alternate perspective to the serious issues of the play. The gravedigger in *Hamlet* provides both comic relief and a commentary on death.

commedia dell'arte: popular improvised comedy performed by street entertainers during the Italian Renaissance; it featured such characters as Harlequin and Pantalone, and relied on physical or "slapstick" comedy (beatings, pratfalls, etc.).

commedia erudita: "learned" comedy written for court academies in the Italian Renaissance; based on Latin models and observing the classical unities.

concetti: set comic speeches by actors in the *commedia dell'arte*; for example, the Capitano's *concetti* might include boastful descriptions of his military prowess.

conflict: the opposition of forces. In drama, there are two types of conflict: **external conflict** occurs when an individual is at odds with another person, society, or nature; **internal conflict** refers to an individual at odds with himself or herself.

context: the "given circumstances" of a text, including the historical, social, and interpersonal backgrounds of the characters.

convention: an established technique or device which the audience agrees to accept as "real" in a performance; the "ground rules" under which a particular play will be performed. Examples include asides, soliloquies, the use of mime, and shifting scenery in view of the audience. Conventions change from age to age, from production to production.

corrales: Spanish term for theaters.

costumbristas: popular entertainments in Latin America that reflect the manners, dress, music, and dance of the common people.

coup de théâtre: French for "stroke of theater"; either a sudden sensational turn in a play (e.g., when the screen falls in *The School for Scandal*) or a spectacular moment that stops the show (e.g., the ascension of Mephistopholes and Grizabella in *Cats*).

crisis: that moment in a play at which the protagonist faces the greatest conflict; it is the turning point of the play and precipitates the **climax**.

curtain line: 1. the point where the curtain falls and meets the stage floor; it usually marks the line between the auditorium and the playing space in realistic theater; 2. a contrived line spoken as the curtain falls to end an act, usually to heighten the dramatic impact of a scene (especially in melodrama).

cyclic plot: form of plotting especially popular in the modern theater in which the end of a play repeats the opening action, usually to show that there are no resolutions to life's problems and that humans are trapped in their existence.

dama: Spanish for "lady," the virtuous heroine of romance dramas.

deconstructionism: postmodern critical approach that "constructs" new meanings of old texts by subverting (or "deconstructing") them; based on the premise that language is an imprecise instrument that has been manipulated by the traditional Eurocentric worldview. Theater productions, as well as written criticism, can be deconstructionist.

decorum: Neoclassic belief that characters were required to behave according to expectations based on their social status, sex, age, etc.; sometimes referred to as *bienseance* ("good sense").

denouement (falling action): the final outcome of the dramatic action in which the fate of the characters is determined, harmony is restored, and destinies are settled; it follows the climax.

desengaño: Spanish term meaning "disillusionment," that is, the act of removing all illusions about the world; theater and drama was a means of achieving *desengaño*.

deus ex machina: literally, "the god from the machine," a reference to the practice of lowering a god onto the stage in the ancient Greek and Roman theaters; as a literary term it refers to a character that is introduced late in the play to provide a contrived solution to an apparently insolvable problem. See the ending of *Tartuffe* for an example.

deuteragonist(s): secondary character(s) in a play.

dialogue: the exchange of speeches by two or more characters in a play. Also, a generic term referring to the words in a script.

diction: one of the six Aristotelian elements of the drama; it deals with the language of a play and the manner in which characters speak; as an acting term it refers to the clarity with which an actor speaks.

didactic theater: propagandist theater whose primary aim is to instruct or teach. Most medieval religious plays were didactic in that they instructed audiences about the Bible or morality. Most modern didactic theater, such as Brecht's, is political.

didaskolos: in the Greek theater, the "teacher" of the chorus; the forerunner of the modern choreographer and choral director.

Diderot's paradox: the ability of an actor to exhibit extreme emotion while maintaining an inner control that allows for the successful artistic creation of the emotion; named for the eighteenth-century French philosopher and playwright Denis Diderot.

dikē: Greek term for "the natural order of things."

Dionysia: communal celebrations in ancient Greece held in honor of the god Dionysus; a three-day theatrical competition was a central event in the Dionysia.

Dionysus (Roman, Bacchus): Greek god of wine and—by extension—creativity, passion, and irrational behavior.

diorama: a scenic representation in which sculptured figures and miniatures are displayed against a painted background; the effect suggests a realistic panorama.

director: the theatrical artist most responsible for coordinating the work of the actors, designers, and technicians as they interpret the work of the playwright.

directorial concept: the director's interpretation of the play and the means by which he or she achieves it.

dithyramb: hymns sung in honor of Dionysus in ancient Greece; according to Aristotle, these hymns gradually developed into plays.

downstage line: performance mode in which the actors stand in a semicircle on the forestage and deliver their lines; the style was popular in France in the seventeenth and eighteenth centuries.

drama: a composition in verse or prose that portrays the actions of characters in conflict; the literary form of a play; a series of events involving intense conflict.

dramatis personae: a list of characters appearing in a play; the Latin term for "persons of the drama." Characters may be listed by order of importance to the play, order of appearance, or (as in the Renaissance) in hierarchical order.

dramaturgy: the art of writing and crafting plays.

drao: a Greek word meaning "to act" or "to do"; **drama** derives from this term.

duke's seat: the ideal seat in a court theater from which the ranking official could view the action (and especially the scenic perspective) from a perfect vantage point.

ekkyklema: a wheeled platform used to display dead bodies or suggest an interior scene in the Greek theater.

emotion memory: acting technique in which the performer summons up the memory of a particular emotional experience and transfers it to the emotional life of the character he or she portrays.

Enlightenment: eighteenth-century philosophic movement characterized by an emphasis on rationalism and a rejection of traditional religious, political, and social beliefs in favor of empiricism and the new science.

ensemble pathos: term coined by Francis Ferguson to describe playwriting style that focuses not on the plight of a single individual but on a group of people; the audience's emotional response is therefore dispersed among the group. The plays of Chekhov epitomize ensemble pathos.

entr'acte: short entertainment (such as a song or dance) inserted between the acts of a play; also, the musical overture preceding the second act of a musical theater piece.

entremeses: Spanish term for "interludes," that is, short plays performed between courses of a banquet or other affair; forerunner of classical Spanish drama.

environmental theater: performance mode in which the action is not confined to a traditional stage but uses the entire "environment" for the presentation of the play; the action frequently takes place in and around the spectators (who are often encouraged to participate in the play).

epic theater: non-Aristotelian theater espoused by Bertolt Brecht aimed at the audience's intellect rather than its emotions; it seeks to instruct audiences so that they may deal with contemporary moral problems and social realities, via nonrealistic modes of performance.

epilogue: a formal speech, usually in verse, addressed to the audience by an actor after a play; epilogues were especially popular in the seventeenth and eighteenth centuries. Often called a "curtain speech."

episode: the equivalent of an act in a Greek play; episodes advance the story line (see *stasimon*).

episodic plot: a story with a series of events, often unrelated, which can take place over great periods of time and in many locales; the events of an episodic plot are not necessarily causally related. Epic dramas, the history plays of Shakespeare, and the works of Brecht are episodic in structure.

epode: a lyric poem sung by the chorus in a Greek tragedy; one of the three parts of the **stasimon**.

Erinyes: the Furies, who in Greek theology were charged with the duty of keeping order, usually through revenge or torment.

Eumenides: "the Kindly Ones," who supplanted the Erinyes and kept order through justice.

existentialism: predominantly twentieth-century philosophy that argues that humans define themselves (i.e., their "existence" rather than their "essence") by the choices and actions they freely and consciously make. Existentialism has influenced much mid-twentieth-century drama, especially that of the absurdists.

exodos: the formal song of exit for the chorus in a Greek play; customarily it sums up the meaning of the play. See the last choric speech in *Oedipus the King* for an example.

exposition: essential information that an audience needs to know about a character or events (particularly those that happen prior to the first scene). Usually exposition is found in the first act or scene, but **distributed exposition** may be found throughout the play.

Expressionism: Early-twentieth-century literary and performance style that attempted to create the inner workings of the human mind by showing subjective states of reality through distortion, nightmarish images, and similar devices.

external actor: an actor whose primary emphasis and training are on such things as voice, physicality, and gesture.

extravaganza: lavish and spectacular stage show, often re-creating famous military battles or stories from the Wild West.

fabliau: bawdy tales popular in the Late Middle Ages; they may have inspired early secular comedies.

familienstücke: form of German domestic drama that focuses on the plight of families in crisis (e.g., losing the family homestead); influenced the melodrama.

farce: comic genre that depends on an elaborately contrived, usually improbable plot, broadly drawn stock characters, and physical humor. Most farces are amoral and exist to entertain.

feminist theater: theater practice, theory, and criticism devoted to drama by women and/or about the problems of women in society.

floorplan: a set designer's drawing of the layout of the stage to show the spatial relationships between set pieces, placement of platforms, entrances, exits, and so on. The rehearsal room floor is usually taped to designate the various elements of the floorplan.

foil: a character who serves as a contrast to another (and usually central) character; Laertes and Fortinbras are foils to Hamlet.

follies: theatrical variety show using song and dance, and (frequently) scantily clad female performers.

foreshadowing: hints of events or actions to come in a play; usually foreshadowing helps create suspense.

formalism: late-twentieth-century performance style that emphasizes external and visual elements. The works of Robert Wilson typify formalism.

fourth wall: convention of the realistic theater in which the audience assumes it is looking through an invisible wall into an actual room; this wall is determined by the opening in the proscenium arch.

gagaku: ancient Japanese folk dance from which **Noh** drama may have evolved.

galán: Spanish for "gallant," the handsome and virtuous male character in romantic dramas.

gamos: in Greek Old Comedy, the formal union of the sexes at the conclusion of the play. The *gamos* is a particular form of the *komos*.

gauchescos: Argentine plays about "gauchos" (cowboys), comparable to westerns of the United States.

genero chico: Spanish-American variety shows similar to the vaudeville or music hall. Also known as a *puchero* ("stew").

genre: a category of play characterized by a particular style, form, and content; for example, tragedy, comedy, tragicomedy, melodrama, farce.

genzai **play:** one of the five types of **Noh** drama; a "living person piece" usually dealing with madness, obsessions, and passion.

gestus: the most important term in Brecht's vocabulary for actors; it refers to the social reality the character is asked to play (as opposed to the psychological reality of Stanislavskian acting).

gracioso: stock character in Spanish dramas, usually the "fool" or "wise fool" who stands outside the action and comments on the folly of his betters.

Great Chain of Being: Medieval worldview that used the metaphor of a chain to show that all of creation was linked: God was at the superior end of the chain, nonliving matter at the other. The concept influenced both the ideas of medieval and Renaissance dramas and the structure of the plays (e.g., the highest-ranking person onstage invariably was given the final speech of the play).

griot: African term for storyteller.

groundlings: generic term for the members of an audience at an Elizabethan public theater who stood in the "pit" (i.e., on the ground) in such theaters as the Globe.

habit à la Romaine: classical French costuming meant to suggest the clothing of Roman antiquity.

hamartia: Greek term (which means "missing the mark") usually applied to the flaw or error in judgment that leads to the downfall of the tragic hero.

hana: Japanese term meaning "flower" applied to the aesthetics of acting in the **Noh** theater; it is achieved through rigorous training and sacrificing oneself to the art.

hanimichi ("flowery way"): the runway from the back of the auditorium to the **Kabuki** stage which actors use for entrances and exits.

happy idea: the problem to be tested in Greek Old Comedy, usually established in the prologue. In *Lysistrata* the happy idea is that the women should refrain from sex with their husbands until the war is ended.

hashigakari: a bridgeway in the Japanese **Noh** theater over which actors enter the stage; traditionally, it is decorated with three small pine trees.

hayagawari: quick-change and physical transformation effects in the **Kabuki** theater (e.g., a woman is changed into a spider).

heavens: in the Elizabethan public theater (such as the Globe), the area beneath the roof that covered the stage. It was painted with astrological signs and heavenly bodies to suggest the firmament. Often deities would descend to the stage from the heavens.

hero (fem, **heroine**): the central character of a play, usually the character who undergoes the most pronounced change; in Romantic drama and melodrama the hero is usually the person who embodies "good." The twentieth century has seen the emergence of the **antihero**, a character who may not be "good" but who is still the central figure in the drama. Willy Loman is an antihero.

high comedy: sophisticated comedy that depends on witty dialogue, social satire, and sophisticated characters for impact. The plays of George Bernard Shaw typify high comedy.

historification: setting the action of a play in the historic past to draw parallels with contemporary events; among Brecht's favorite devices for creating an **alienation effect** for his audience.

histriones: Latin word for "actors"; **histrionic** refers to deliberately theatrical displays of emotion.

honmizu: water effects in the **Kabuki** theater (e.g., creating a waterfall or a running brook).

hsieh-tzu: the "wedge" in classical Chinese drama; it was inserted between acts or, occasionally, as the prologue to a play.

hua lien: the "painted face" roles in Chinese drama.

hua pu: folk dramas in the Chinese theater.

hubris: the most common term for tragic flaw, usually ascribed to excessive pride or arrogance. Prometheus is a victim of hubris when he steals the fire of the gods.

hypokrites: the original Greek term for "actor"; originally it meant "answerer."

iambic pentameter: the metrical pattern in a line of verse (especially **blank verse**) in which five unaccented syllables alternate with five accented syllables: puh-POM puh-POM puh-POM puh-POM puh-POM. The pattern is most compatible with the normal rhythms of English speech, and was a fixture of Elizabethan verse.

imitation: the act of representing (or re-creating) another person through voice and gesture; see *mimesis*. Imitation is one of the founding principles of the theatrical arts.

independent theater(s): generic term for (mostly) small theaters at the end of the nineteenth century whose aim was not commercial success but artistic and social drama. The Théâtre-Libre in Paris, the Abbey Theatre in Ireland, and the Provincetown Playhouse in America typify the independent theater movement.

integrated actor: an actor who combines both internal and external techniques as the basis of his or her work.

interlude: short play or entertainment performed between courses of a banquet or other function in the early Renaissance; in England, interludes evolved into allegorical dramas and paved the way for secular plays.

intermezzi: Italian term for "interludes"; in Renaissance Italy they evolved into spectacular entertainments held at court (see **masques**).

internal actor: an actor who relies on inner technique as the source of his or her performance; emotion memory, subtext, and psychological motivations are central to the internal approach.

irony: 1. an unexpected reversal of fortune (or *peripitea*) in a drama in which characters expect exactly the opposite of what occurs; 2. dramatic irony occurs when a character is deprived of knowledge that other characters and the audience share.

Jacobean tragedy: cynical, often violent, drama written during the early seventeenth century in England; stems from a pessimistic worldview and contends that all people, innocent and evildoers, ultimately die violent deaths.

jeu des paumes: early French theater spaces derived from tennis courts.

jidaimono: historical plays in the **Kabuki** theater which glorify the samurai code.

Kabuki: traditional Japanese popular drama that uses song and dance and is performed in a highly stylized manner in elaborate costumes and fanciful makeup; the Kabuki dates from the early seventeenth century.

Kabuki-za: the most prestigious **Kabuki** theater in Japan.

Kadensho: Zeami's seven-book treatise on **Noh** playwriting and performance.

kagami no ma: the "mirror room" in which Japanese **Noh** actors dress and prepare for performance through meditation.

kami (waki) **play:** one of the five types of **Noh** drama; a "god play" which celebrates an auspicious religious event.

kata: basic movement and vocal patterns used by **Kabuki** actors to create atmosphere and psychological states; they are antirealistic and employ exaggeration and rhythm.

kazura **play:** one of the five types of **Noh** drama; a "woman play" about an illustrious woman; these are sometimes referred to as "wig plays" because they are acted by men dressed as women.

keren: tricks and other scenic effects in the **Kabuki** theater (e.g., disappearances, transformations, etc.).

kiri **plays:** one of the five types of **Noh** drama; a "demon play" in which the protagonist is a demon, devil, or other supernatural figure.

kojo: an announcement made to the audience during a **Kabuki** play, usually to praise an actor for his accomplishments.

kokata: a child character in Japanese **Noh** drama, usually symbolizing a new order.

komos: literally "a joyful union"; it is the denouement in classical comedy and is usually marked by a wedding, a dance, or a banquet.

koryphaios: the leader of the chorus in Greek drama.

kothornoi: elevated boots (or buskins) worn by actors in the Greek theater.

K'un-chü: populist plays from the south of China which influenced the development of the Peking Opera.

k'ung-meng: stock character—the heroic king—in classical Chinese drama.

kyōgen: 1. short farces in the Japanese theater; usually accompanying the **Noh** drama; 2. a clown character in a **Noh** drama.

lazzi: Italian term for comic stage business (e.g., a beating, a pratfall).

laughing comedy: term coined by Oliver Goldsmith in 1772 to describe conventional comedy of wit and humor, as opposed to the sentimental comedy.

linear plot: the most traditional form of plotting, beginning with exposition and building through a series of minor crises to a major crisis and climax. Linear plots are usually based on causality, that is, one event "causes" another to happen.

liturgical drama: dramas enacted as part of a church service (or liturgy). In the Middle Ages such plays told stories from the Bible and Christian lore and eventually moved outside the churches.

logeion: in the Greek theater, a raised platform on which the principal characters are thought to have stood while performing; the forerunner of the modern raised stage.

low comedy: comedy that usually relies on physical humor or crude wordplay, as opposed to the more sophisticated **high comedy**.

ludi: Latin term for "play" or "games."

machiavel: stock character, usually villainous, who uses cunning, duplicity, and other amoral behaviors to achieve his ends; named for Niccoló Machiavelli, who suggested that "the end justifies the means" in his political treatise, *The Prince*. Iago is a well-known stage machiavel.

"magic if": Stanislavsky's term for the trigger that allows the actor to enter into the emotional life of a character: "Under these circumstances, what would I do *if* I were this character?"

magic realism: theatrical style, especially popular in Mexico and Latin America, which fuses realism, Surrealism, and other modes that transcend the limitations of day-to-day existence; Elena Garro's play *A Solid Home* typifies the use of magic realism.

mai: solemn dances of the **Noh** theater of Japan.

maschere: Italian word for "masked performers"; collective term for actors in the *commedia dell'arte*.

mask: 1. a device that hides the face to conceal an identity; 2. a pose or false front, especially true of a "psychological mask."

masque: Renaissance entertainments in which courtiers and royalty dressed in elaborate costumes and performed brief plays against majestic scenery; poetry, song, and dance were integral to the masque, which usually culminated spectacularly, often with the reigning official elevated into the heavens. Ben Jonson was the foremost composer of masques in Europe.

masquerade: theatrical activity characterized by the use of elaborate masks, oversized costumes, and vigorous physical dancing and other mimetic actions; the Carnival in Trinidad, the New Orleans Mardi Gras, and the Yoruban Festival are examples of masquerades.

mēchanē: the "machine" used to lower the gods from the heavens in the Greek theater (see also *deus ex machina*).

melodrama: the dramatic genre characterized by an emphasis on plot over characterization; typically, characters are defined as heroes or villains, conflicts are defined along moral lines, and the resolution rewards the good and punishes the wicked. Spectacle and action are important to the melodramatic effect.

mestizo: Spanish for "of mixed blood"; refers to plays that are a mixture of the drama of Spain and indigenous dramas of Latin America.

metanarrative: postmodern term for the "new myths" created by a synthesis of traditional stories and modern sensibilities. Stoppard's *Rosencrantz and Guildenstern Are Dead* is a metanarrative on *Hamlet*.

metatheater: dramatic genre that purposefully blurs the distinction between a play-as-a-work-of-art and life itself to establish a link between the artificial world of the stage and the real world of the audience.

method acting: strongly internalized acting that emphasizes emotion memory and personal experience in creating a character. The term is closely associated with Lee Strasberg's teaching at New York's Actors Studio.

michiyuki: circular movement about the stage meant to imply a long journey in both the **Noh** and **Kabuki** theaters.

mie: formal pose adopted by a **Kabuki** actor on his entrance; it allows the audience time to reflect on his costume and his psychological state (see *kata*).

Miles Gloriosis: see **braggart warrior**.

mimesis: Greek term referring to the art of imitation through physical and vocal means.

minstrel show: popular American theatrical entertainments in the nineteenth century comprising a variety of comic skits, songs, and dances performed by actors in blackface.

miracle play: medieval play depicting the lives of the saints and church figures.

mise en scène: the arrangement of actors and scenery on the stage for a theatrical production; the physical setting for the action; sometimes used to denote the sixth of Aristotle's elements of the theater: spectacle.

mizumono: **Kabuki** plays whose setting includes water (e.g., lakes, the ocean, etc.); noted for their spectacular water effects (*honmizu*).

moira: Greek term for "fate" or "the sharer out." Customarily, fate was depicted as three sisters who spun out the thread of one's life. One spun the thread, the second determined its length, and the third (representing death) cut the thread.

monologue: a lengthy speech spoken by a single character, usually to other characters (see **soliloquy**).

moral interlude: early Renaissance play that was didactic and dealt with proper and improper conduct in secular matters; the secular equivalent of the religious **morality play**.

morality play: medieval drama that portrayed moral dilemmas through allegorical figures such as Everyman and various virtues (Strength, Beauty) and vices (Gluttony, Rumor). Most moralities (such as *Everyman*) dealt with the way in which the Christian meets death.

mudras: mime and dance gestures used by actors in the theater of India.

multiculturalism: the incorporation into an artwork of the values and modes of expression of those other than traditional Eurocentricism. Soyinka's *Death and the King's Horseman* is a multicultural work.

music: one of the six Aristotelian elements of the drama; it refers to song, melody, and rhythm.

musical theater: genre that uses song, music, and dance as an integral part of the play's action; it is not usually as elevated as **opera** or even **operetta**. **Musical theater** can be further divided into musical drama (e.g., *West Side Story*) or musical comedy (e.g., *Guys and Dolls*).

mystery play: in the medieval theater, a short play depicting events from the Bible. A number of mysteries were strung together to form a cycle, which attempted to tell the story of humanity from the Creation to the Day of Judgment. The term is derived from a medieval word which referred to the "masters" or skilled workmen to whom the performance of the plays was assigned. *Abraham and Isaac* is a typical mystery play.

mythos: the story (see *praxis* and **plot**).

naguata: the ensemble of orchestra and singing chorus in the **Kabuki** theater.

nātaka **play:** Sanskrit play based on traditional mythology or history, usually five to seven acts in length. *Śakuntalā* is a *nātaka* play (see *prakarana* **play**).

naturalism: a particular form of realism that emphasizes environment; naturalism was also a philosophical movement that saw humans as products of their heredity and environment.

natyamandapa: the playhouse of classical theater in India.

Nātyaśātra (*Treatise on Drama*): the so-called Fifth Veda, a sacred text devoted to dramatic theory and stage practice in the theater of India.

Neoclassicism: Renaissance movement that consciously imitated the classical style of the Greeks and Romans; noted for its strict adherence to the rules of dramatic writing and its emphasis on morality and decorum. The plays of Jean Racine epitomize Neoclassicism.

New Comedy: post-Aristophanic comedy dealing with the lives and actions of common people; usually New Comedy is apolitical and focuses on the follies of ordinary people. Menander is said to have originated New Comedy, and the Roman playwrights Plautus and Terence perfected it. Most television sitcoms are derived from New Comedy.

new stagecraft: early-twentieth-century movement that moved away from pictorial realism to more abstract settings designed to evoke mood and emphasize the language of a play.

Noh (Nō) theater: the classical dance-drama of Japan, distinguished by a fusion of dance, poetry, music, mime, and meditation.

obligatory scene (also *scène à faire*): climactic scene which the audience comes to expect; usually, the ultimate confrontation between the protagonist and antagonist which leads to the resolution of the play's conflict; in the well-made play, the obligatory scene is often marked by the revelation of a secret.

ode: a song sung by the chorus in a Greek play, usually between episodes of the plot. Odes, divided into sections called **strophes**, **antistrophes**, and **epodes**, were used to comment on the action.

odori: temple dancers of Japan; the forerunners of **Kabuki** performers.

Old Comedy: Ancient Greek comedy, most associated with the plays of Aristophanes, which was satirical in its depiction of civic affairs. (See Spotlight box, Greek Old Comedy, Chapter 3.)

onkos: a large headpiece, containing a mask, worn by actors in the Greek theater.

onnagata: traditional **Kabuki** role in which a male plays a woman; it also refers to the acting style used to play feminine beauty.

onno: the original women's **Kabuki** of seventeenth-century Japan.

opera: a drama almost exclusively sung to orchestral accompaniment; operas usually deal with tragic and heroic themes (e.g., *Madame Butterfly* or the *Ring* cycle).

opéra bouffe: satirical comic opera (e.g., *Orpheus in Hades*).

operetta: "little opera," a romantic and comic play that incorporates considerable music, song, and dance (e.g., *The Merry Widow* or *The Mikado*).

orchestra: the large (c. 70-foot-diameter) circle in a Greek theater in which the chorus sang, danced, and stood during a play. It was located between the audience and the *logeion.*

overture: an orchestral piece played before the beginning of an opera, operetta, or musical play; overtures were also often played before nonmusical plays in the eighteenth and nineteenth centuries.

pageant wagon (or **pageant**): medieval stage built on wagons or carts that could be transported through towns; often, two wagons were used, one for scenery, a second for an acting platform.

pantomime: dumb shows that emphasize spectacle.

parabisis: the "harangue" in Greek Old Comedy in which the playwright addresses topical issues of personal concern.

parados: 1. the song of entry for the chorus in a Greek play; 2. the path or aisles on which the chorus entered or exited, located on either side of the playing space.

pastiche: postmodern playwriting technique that fuses a variety of styles, genres, and story lines to create a new form. Stoppard's *Rosencrantz and Guildenstern Are Dead* is a pastiche of Shakespeare's *Hamlet*, Beckett's *Waiting for Godot*, absurdist theater, vaudeville, and existentialist tract.

pastoral drama: play dealing with rustic life; it extols the virtues of simple living by contrasting it with the corrupt life of the city; evolved in Italy during the Renaissance and may have been patterned after the **satyr play** of ancient Greece. The **romance** is an outgrowth of the pastoral drama.

Peking Opera: generic term for populist Chinese theater, originating in the eighteenth century, which uses song, dance, and nonrealistic means to tell melodramatic stories; the national theater of China.

periaktoi: prisms that served as the principal scenic effect in the Greek theater; locales such as a forest, a palace, or a seacoast were painted on each side of the triangle, which could be turned to reveal a new location.

peripeteia: Aristotelian term for "reversal" in a play, that is, the moment when the fortunes of the protagonist are drastically changed.

perspective: technique, used by scenic designers, of representing on a flat surface (such as a canvas drop) the spatial relation of objects as they might appear to the eye.

pictorial realism: the attempt to suggest "real life" on the stage through painterly devices.

pit: in Restoration and eighteenth-century theaters, the seating (occasionally standing) area immediately in front of the stage, customarily inhabited by fops and rakes. Today the pit usually refers to the orchestra pit, a recessed area in front of (or often beneath) the stage where an orchestra sits during a performance.

plaudite: a formal speech at the end of classical comedies in which the speaker asks the audience's forgiveness for any transgressions and requests applause.

play: literary genre in which a story (plot) is presented by actors imitating characters before an audience. One might say that a play is a script "on its feet."

play-within-the-play: a usually brief play inserted into the action of a larger play, often to comment on or illuminate the primary play. The "mousetrap scene" (act 3, scene 2) in *Hamlet* is probably the best-known play-within-the-play in the theater.

plot: the first of Aristotle's six elements of theater; the structure of a play's story line (see *praxis*).

pluralism: the inclusion of many cultures, races, and lifestyles into an enterprise; in the theater, this includes multicultural/racial drama, feminist drama, gay and lesbian drama; in general, pluralism is an alternative to traditional male-dominated, Eurocentric art.

poetic justice: moral doctrine that requires that the good be rewarded for their benevolent deeds and that the wicked be punished for their transgressions; the doctrine is particularly influential on the resolution of melodramas and sentimental comedies.

Poetics: Aristotle's treatise on dramatic theory and stage practice; in particular, it defines and discusses tragedy. Written in the mid–fourth century B.C.E., it is the germinal work on dramatic theory in Western theater.

point of attack: that moment nearest the beginning of the play in which the major conflict to be resolved occurs; sometimes called the inciting moment.

poor theater: Jerzy Grotowski's term for a theater which seeks (by choice or necessity) to eliminate everything not entirely essential to the performance (e.g., scenery, elaborate costumes, makeup, high-tech lighting); "found" objects and costumes are used and the actors themselves create effects to support the production (see also *via negativa*).

postmodernism: late-twentieth-century critical, literary, and performance movement that reacts to modern art and literature; postmodernists suggest that truth is no longer verifiable, and that new art forms are best created by freely mixing previous styles and themes.

prakarana **play:** Sanskrit play invented by the playwright, usually ten acts in length. *The Little Clay Cart* is a *prakarana* play (see also *nātaka* play).

praxis: the action of a story; that is, the arrangement of the events of the story calculated to bring about a desired response from the audience.

presentational style: performance mode in which the actors openly acknowledge the presence of the audience and play to it.

problem plays: usually refers to a series of plays written by Shakespeare in the first decade of the seventeenth century that do not neatly fit into the traditional generic categories

of comedy and tragedy; they include *Measure for Measure* and *Troilus and Cressida*.

prologue: the opening action of a Greek play; it usually is a dialogue between two or three characters and establishes the problem of the play. It now refers to an opening section of a play that is not part of the first scene or act.

proscenium: in modern theaters, the wall that separates the stage from the auditorium and provides the **arch** that frames it; often referred to as the "picture frame" stage.

protagonist: literally, "the first debater," but the term applies to the central character in a drama.

punto de honor: Spanish for "point of honor," applied to a form of drama in which the hero must defend the honor of his family, his lady, or himself.

queer theater/theory: drama, theory, and criticism concerned with the problems confronting gays and lesbians in society.

quid pro quo: Latin for "something for something"; a playwriting term applied to a situation in which one, two, or more characters unknowingly misunderstand a situation, which further enmeshes them in the play's action.

raisonneur: common term applied to a character who speaks for society or the playwright; customarily, the *raisonneur* gives advice to the **protagonist**. Tiresias in *Oedipus the King* and Cléante in *Tartuffe* are *raisonneurs*.

rake (or rakehell): comic hero who lives by the code of love and uses deceit, cunning, and seduction to attain his conquests; such characters were especially popular in late-seventeenth- and eighteenth-century comedies.

ran-i: Japanese term for "the sublime," referring to the ecstasy and exaltation produced by advanced artistry.

rasa: the ultimate goal of performance in the theater of India; roughly translated as "flavor," rasa refers to the emotional state or mood that the playwright hopes to engender in the audience. A given play has a dominant rasa and each component act has its own rasa.

realism: an attempt to re-create actual life onstage in a manner that employs the details and routines of daily dress, speech, environment, and situations. Ibsen's social dramas typify realism (see also **naturalism**).

recognition (*anagnōrisis*): a character discovers a truth previously unknown; in tragedy it is the awareness of the error in judgment that leads to the character's downfall; originally, it referred to the recognition of one character by another (e.g., Electra recognizes her long-lost brother, Orestes) but the term now applies to the discovery of an error or a truth about oneself.

régisseur: Continental term for the stage director.

renderings: a scenery or costume designer's drawings of the set or costumes; these are usually colored or painted to suggest what the finished product will look like.

repartée: witty verbal exchanges between characters, especially in high comedy.

representational style: performance mode in which the actors seem to ignore the presence of the audience.

revenge tragedy: Elizabethan-Jacobean drama that depended on sensational events, murders, and revenge for plot; the Roman tragedies of Seneca were the models for revenge tragedies.

reversal (*peripitea*): a drastic change in fortune, usually for the protagonist of a play. In tragedy the reversal is calamitous and leads to the downfall of the principal character; in comedy, the reversal usually brings about good fortune and a happy resolution to the play.

reviewer: a theater critic who attends a play in performance and assesses the quality of the script, the performances and designs, and the overall experience.

revistas: Brazilian popular entertainments, usually musicals.

revue: theatrical presentation usually composed of loosely related skits, songs, and dances (see **vaudeville**).

rhapsode: Greek term for poet, storyteller, and myth maker; Homer is the best known of the rhapsodes.

rising action: the series of minor crises in a plot that build toward the major crisis and climax.

ritual: a formal and customarily repeated act, usually according to religious or social customs; a ritual generally has greater significance than a **ceremony** (e.g., a baptism or wedding). Early rituals often were intended to control the outcome of events.

ritualized enactment: symbolic actions performed in a pattern and progression that eventually become highly controlled and precise in their execution.

romance: drama about imaginary characters involved in events from a remote place and time, usually involving heroic deeds in a mysterious setting; *Śakuntalā* and Shakespeare's *The Tempest* are romances.

Romanticism: late-eighteenth and early-nineteenth-century philosophical and artistic movement marked by an emotional appeal to the heroic, adventurous, remote, mysterious, or idealized. Romanticism celebrated the common people and is aligned with the democratic revolution.

roppō: a stylized walk—part dance, part martial art—used by a **Kabuki** actor as he enters the stage on the *hanimichi*; literally, it means "six directions" and refers to the vigorous turns he executes during the walk. A *tobiroppō* is an exit walk and often occurs after the curtain is closed.

sainetes: short farces in the Spanish-language theater.

Sanskrit drama: the classical court theater of India that thrived until c. 1000 C.E.

satire: species of comic drama that holds human follies and institutions up to ridicule and scorn; the use of wit, irony, or sarcasm to expose vice and folly. *The Importance of Being Earnest* is a satire.

satyr plays: early Greek comedy in which actors dressed in animal skins (particularly goats) and performed often bawdy parodies of serious dramas; the **satyrs** were the mythological creatures (half-man, half-goat) who served and protected Dionysus.

scenario: an outline of a play that denotes the principal actions of the plot; actors in the *commedia dell'arte* improvised plays from their **scenarii**.

scene: the secondary division of a play; acts may be divided into scenes. Also, the locale of a play's action.

scenery: the backdrops, furniture, and other visual accessories that help define the locale and mood of a play.

Senecan tragedy: Renaissance tragedy modeled after the Roman plays of Seneca; noted for the use of the supernatural and violent resolutions to the plot (e.g., Shakespeare's *Titus Andronicus*).

sentimental comedy (also **weeping comedy**, *comédie larmoyant*): popular eighteenth-century comedies marked by emotional idealism and excessive feeling.

sermons joyeaux: medieval French burlesques of church sermons.

set: the scenery constructed for a particular play; usually, it is three dimensional (as opposed to painted drops).

setting: the locale of a play's action and the scenic elements that help define it.

sewamono: domestic dramas in the **Kabuki** theater, usually portraying the world of the merchant class.

shaman: a holy person who uses magic and ritual for the purpose of curing the sick, divining hidden mysteries, or controlling events. Shamans are often storytellers who preserve a community's myths.

shared line: two or more speeches in verse combined to form a line of iambic pentameter. This is usually a cue for the actors to pick up the pace.

sheng: male roles in Chinese opera (usually non-"character" roles).

shibai: common term for **Kabuki** theaters, derived from Japanese term for "grass sitting" (a reference to the grassy slope on which audiences sat in one of the earliest Kabuki theaters).

Shingeki: the new or alternative (to the **Kabuki** and **Noh**) theater of contemporary Japan.

shite: the protagonist or principal character in a Japanese **Noh** drama; literally, the term means "doer."

shura-mono play: one of the five types of **Noh** drama; a "warrior play" in which the protagonist, usually a slain warrior, returns as a ghost to relieve human suffering.

siglo d'oro drama: Spanish drama from the seventeenth-century golden age, particularly the plays of Lope De Vega and Pedro Calderón.

skene: the "hut" or building that served as the scenic background for the Greek theater. It provided an area for actors to change, masked their entrances, and denoted locale. Traditionally, the *skene* had three to five doors.

slapstick: a form of comedy that depends exclusively on physical humor such as beatings, chases, and pratfalls. The term is derived from a prop devised by actors in the *commedia dell'arte* that was used to administer beatings. The films of the Three Stooges epitomize slapstick comedy.

soliloquy: a theater convention in which a character speaks his or her thoughts aloud to the audience; it is particularly associated with Elizabethan drama.

sotties: short French farces that portray religious and/or political leaders as fools.

spectacle: one of the six Aristotelian elements of the drama; it refers to the visual elements of a play—scenery, costume, movement, gesture, and so on (see also **mise-en-scène**).

spine: see **superobjective**.

spirit cult performance: theatricalized ritual in which a medium, thought to be possessed by spirits of the dead, assumes a character while in a trance state.

sporagmos: a scapegoat or sacrificial victim who takes on suffering for the greater good of a tribe or community. A tragic hero, such as Oedipus, may be considered a sporagmos.

stage direction: the playwright's instructions to the actors, designers, and directors concerning setting, motivations, and characterization.

Stage Yankee: popular American comic figure noted for his ingenuity, honesty, and patriotism; he usually outwits his "betters" and triumphs because he adheres to American virtues.

stasimon: the choral odes in a Greek play; they alternate with **episodes** and are used to comment on the action, project the play's message, and create the emotional atmosphere.

stichomythia: stage dialogue in which characters alternate single lines to increase dramatic tension. Though the term is Greek in origin, it is found in many eras of theater.

stock character: instantly recognizable type of figure that reoccurs in many works (e.g., the young lover, the grouchy old man, the sassy servant, the braggart soldier).

storytelling performance: preliterate form of drama, especially common in Africa, in which a narrator tells a story while enacting the central roles; others may play roles as well as provide song and dance to accompany the tale.

strophe: one of the three principal divisions of a choral ode in a Greek play; it means "turn" and suggests something about the dance nature of the odes.

Sturm und Drang: German for "storm and stress," a philosophical and artistic movement in the late eighteenth century characterized by high emotion and rousing action that often dealt with an individual's revolt against society; the forerunner of **Romanticism**.

style: the manner in which a play is performed. The two principal styles are **presentational**, in which the actors openly acknowledge the presence of the audience and play to it, and **representational**, in which the actors seem to ignore the presence of the audience. Style implies the degree of "reality" or artificiality of a performance.

subplot: a secondary plot in a play which often parallels the major plot; e.g., in *Hamlet* the story of the Norwegian prince Fortinbras constitutes a subplot.

subtext: literally, "the text beneath the text"; it refers to the implied or underlying meaning of a line. Sometimes also called "the intentional meaning."

superobjective: Stanislavsky's term for the primary motivation of a character (e.g., Oedipus's superobjective is "to find the truth").

suspension of disbelief: Coleridge's term for an audience's willingness to accept events onstage as true or plausible during the course of a play.

sūtradhara: a storyteller in India, often a Brahmin priest.

symbolism: a literary or theatrical device in which an object or action suggests another meaning beyond its literal meaning. Willy's worn suitcases in *Death of a Salesman* symbolize his life and failures. Also, a theatrical style popular in the early twentieth century that relied almost exclusively on symbols for its impact; such plays as Garciá Lorca's *Blood Wedding* typify symbolist drama.

sympathetic (homeopathic) magic: when humans imitate an act of nature in the hope that nature, in turn, will imitate humans and thereby produce a desired result (e.g., a Native American rain dance).

the System: term applied to Stanislavsky's approach to actor training at the Moscow Art Theater; a blend of external technique with strong psychological analysis of the character.

tableaux vivants: French for "living pictures," spectacular scenes which often re-created historical events or violent situations (such as guillotinings). Today a tableau refers to a "freeze" in which the actors do not move.

tan: female roles in Chinese opera.

tetralogy: a grouping of four plays by theme and content; in the ancient Greek theater the tetralogy customarily comprised three tragedies (a **trilogy**) and a **satyr play**. Shakespeare wrote two tetralogies (the four plays dealing with King Henry V, and the four plays dealing with King Henry VI and the rise and fall of Richard III).

text: the printed version of a play; a script (see also **context** and **subtext**).

theater: the art form by which drama is realized; also, the formal space in which a drama is performed.

theater collectives: alternative theater companies, usually bound by a common ideology, who create works collectively; often they live in communes. The Living Theater (USA), the Théâtre du Soleil (France), Committed Artists (South Africa), and Grupo Teatro Escambray (Cuba) are examples of collectives.

theater of cruelty: movement associated with the theories of Antonin Artaud, who forced audiences to purge their inhumanity ("the Plague") by stripping away their defense mechanisms through an assault on the senses.

theater of the absurd: dramatic movement of the mid–twentieth century concerned with the metaphysical anguish of the human condition in a world that defies rational sense; it relies on plotless dramas, discursive dialogue, motiveless behavior, and ambiguity. The plays of Samuel Beckett exemplify absurdist drama.

theatrical (theatricality): the formal and stylized use of costumes, makeup, scenery, properties, lighting, and sound as a means of performance; with theatricality there is no pretense of realism.

theatron: Greek term for "the seeing place;" the area of a Greek theater where the audience sat.

thesis play (also, *pièce à thèse* and "discussion drama"): social drama in which contemporary problems are illustrated and discussed; typified by the early works of Ibsen, Shaw, and Odets. Most thesis plays are presented in a realistic or naturalistic style.

thought: one of the six Aristotelean elements of the drama; it deals with the idea or thematic values of a play.

thrust stage: a stage or acting area that is projected into the audience and is usually surrounded by the audience on three sides. The classical Greek theater and the Elizabethan public theaters used thrust stages.

thymele: the sacred altar in a Greek theater; it was customarily placed in the center of the **orchestra** and is a reminder of the religious roots of Greek drama.

tirade: a lengthy, highly emotional speech most often associated with the French Neoclassic theater; a strong outpouring of emotion.

tiring house: in the Elizabethan public theater, the area behind the stage where the actors dressed (or attired) themselves; the term also applies to the entire architectural structure (customarily four stories) that backed the playing space.

tlatquetzque: professional entertainers or actors in the Mayan culture, often dressed as ocelots, sacred snakes, or colorful birds.

total theater: twentieth-century performance mode that employs multisensory, multimedia techniques to assault the audience's senses. Traditional performance techniques are often combined with film, video, slide shows, electronic soundtracks, light shows, etc.

township theater: performances derived from the townships of South Africa in which actors often improvise dialogue and stories and use "found" materials for costumes and props.

tragedy: one of the principal dramatic genres, in which a central character is in conflict with an external, as well as internal, force; the conflict ends disastrously for the character and provokes pity and fear in the audience.

tragicomedy: one of the principal dramatic genres, which blends serious and comic elements; frequently the serious is treated comically, while the comic is given a more somber treatment. The plays of Anton Chekhov and Samuel Beckett typify tragicomedy.

trap(door): a hole cut in the stage floor (covered by a hinged door) that allows for entrances and exits below the stage; often used for special effects (e.g., the apparition of ghosts).

trilogy: a collection of three plays usually related by theme or characters. Aeschylus's *Oresteia* is a trilogy dealing with the fall of the house of Atreus. Neil Simon's *Brighton Beach* trilogy portrays the playwright's early life.

trope: antiphonal biblical passage set to music and sung in Christian ceremonies in the Middle Ages; eventually tropes—such as the *Quem Queritas* trope—grew into dramas in which events from Scripture were acted before the congregation.

tsa chu: Chinese term for classical Yuan drama.

ts'ao-ts'ao: stock villain in classical Chinese drama; usually a counselor to the emperor.

tsure: a secondary character in Japanese **Noh** drama who accompanies the **shite**.

unities: refer to the time, place, and action of a drama. The Neoclassicists believed that a play ought to be confined to a single action that takes place in a single location and occurs within a short time span.

vaudeville: stage entertainment comprising a variety of unrelated acts such as songs, dances, magic, comedy, etc. Originally, a vaudeville was a French entertainment that combined pantomime, dance, and music to tell a simple story.

Vedas: sacred Hindu scriptures; the Fifth Veda is a sacred text on dramatic theory written by Brahma to illustrate how the gods invented drama as a means of enlightenment for humans (see **Nātyasātra**).

Verfremdungseffekt: Brecht's term for the **alienation effect**.

verisimilitude: "likeness to truth," the attempt to put a truthful picture of life onstage. Although it purported to "realism," verisimilitude, especially in the Renaissance, offered an idealized view of "real life."

via negativa: Grotowski's motto for the **poor theater**, which means to refrain from doing. It encourages actors to rely solely on their resources, and not externals, for the creation of the theater act.

wagoto: the refined, delicate acting style of the **Kabuki** theater, most often used to portray handsome young men, lovers, and princes.

waki: an objective third party in Japanese **Noh** drama; he is usually a holy person who watches from the side and comments on the actions of the **shite**.

wakushu: the young men's (boy's) **Kabuki** of seventeenth-century Japan.

well-made play: also, *pièce bien faite*; a drama in which a carefully constructed plot is designed to create suspense and forward movement, often at the expense of characterization. Such plays frequently employ a withheld secret, confrontations between heroes and villains, a series of minor crises building to a climax and resolution in which all the conflicts are neatly worked out. Although *Oedipus the King* is the prototype of the well-made play, it is a genre that flourished in the nineteenth century, especially in the works of Eúgene Scribe.

wen hsi: domestic, usually romantic, stories in the Peking, or Chinese, Opera.

Wild West shows: popular American **extravaganzas** of the late nineteenth century which re-created frontier life, battles with Native Americans, and so on; associated with Buffalo Bill Cody.

wu: Chinese term for story and also for storyteller.

wu-hsi: military plays in the Chinese or Peking Opera.

ya pu: traditional classical drama of the Chinese theater, usually associated with the court and scholars (as opposed to the *hua pu,* or folk drama).

yarō: mature male **Kabuki** performers.

yūgen: Japanese term for "mysterious beauty"; it is the goal of Noh drama and seeks to achieve a mood of quietness, meditation, and aesthetic gratification.

zanni: collective term for comedians in the Italian *commedia dell'arte*; usually, these were unnamed characters who played a variety of roles and added bits of clowning to the action.

zarzuela: Spanish term applied to musical comedy; begun by Calderón in seventeenth-century Spain and brought to the New World by Spanish colonists. ***Zarzuelas bufas*** are "comical musicals," while ***bailetes*** are "dance musicals."

Chapter 1: Stories, Rituals, and Theater

Blau, Herbert. *The Audience*. Baltimore: John Hopkins University Press, 1990.

Carlson, Marvin. *Theories of the Theatre: A Historical and Critical Survey from the Greeks to the Present*. Ithaca: Cornell University Press, 1985.

Covarrubias, Miguel. *Island of Bali*. New York: Alfred A. Knopf, 1950.

Kirby, E. T. *Ur-Drama*. New York: New York University Press, 1975.

Lommel, Andreas. *Shamanism: The Beginnings of Art*. New York: McGraw-Hill, 1967.

Schechner, Richard and Willa Appel. *By Means of Performance: Intercultural Studies of Theater and Ritual*. Cambridge: Cambridge University Press, 1990.

Turner, Victor. *From Ritual to Theatre*. New York: Performing Arts Journal Publications, 1982.

Chapter 2: From Theater to Drama

DRAMATIC THEORY

Dukore, Bernard F. *Dramatic Theory and Criticism: Greeks to Grotowski*. New York: Holt, Rinehart and Winston, 1974.

Frye, Northrop. *The Anatomy of Criticism*. Princeton: Princeton University Press, 1957.

Hoy, Cyrus. *The Hyacinth Room: An Investigation into the Nature of Comedy, Tragedy, and Tragicomedy*. New York: Chatto and Windus, 1984.

Langer, Suzanne. *Feeling and Form: A Theory of Art*. New York: Scribner and Sons, 1953.

Pavis, Patrice. *Languages of the Stage: Essays in the Semiology of the Theatre*. New York: Performing Arts Journal Publications, 1982.

States, Bert O. *Great Reckonings in Little Rooms: On the Phenomenology of Theater*. Berkeley: University of California Press, 1985.

TRAGEDY AND MELODRAMA

Butcher, S. H. *Aristotle's Theory of Poetry and Fine Art*. London: Macmillan, 1895.

Else, Gerald. *Aristotle's Poetics: The Argument*. Cambridge, MA: Harvard University Press, 1957.

Smith, James L. *Melodrama*. London: Methuen, 1973.

COMEDY AND FARCE

Bergson, Henri. *Laughter*. Trans. Cloudesley Brereton and Frank Rothwell. London: Macmillan and Company, 1917.

Bermel, Albert. *Farce: A History from Aristophanes to Woody Allen*. New York: Simon and Schuster, 1982.

Hirst, David L. *Tragicomedy*. London: Methuen, 1984.

Kerr, Walter. *Tragedy and Comedy*. New York: 1967.

Lauter, Paul, ed. *Theories of Comedy*. Garden City: Anchor Books, 1964.

Olson, Elder. *The Theory of Comedy*. Bloomington: Indiana University Press, 1968.

STYLES AND CONVENTIONS

Russell, Douglas. *Period Style for the Theater*. 2nd ed. Boston: Allyn and Bacon, 1987.

St. Denis, Michel. *The Rediscovery of Style*. New York: Theater Arts Books, 1960.

THEATER ARCHITECTURE, SPACES

Carlson, Marvin. *Places of Performance: The Semiotics of Theatre Architecture*. Ithaca: Cornell University Press, 1989.

Leacroft, Helen and Richard. *The Theatre*. New York: Roy Publishers, 1961.

McNamara, Brooks. *Theatres, Spaces, Environments*. New York: Drama Book Specialists, 1975.

Mullin, Donald C. *The Development of the Playhouse: A Survey of Theater Architecture from the Renaissance to the Present*. Berkeley: University of California Press, 1970.

Chapter 3: The Theater of Greece and Rome

GREECE

Arnott, Peter. *The Ancient Greek and Roman Theater*. New York: Random House, 1971.

Bieber, Margarete. *The History of the Greek and Roman Theater*. Princeton: Princeton University Press, 1939.

Bowra, C. M. *Sophoclean Tragedy*. Oxford: The Clarendon Press, 1947.

Deardon, C. W. *The Stage of Aristophanes*. London: Athlone Press, 1976.

Des Bouvrie, Synnove. *Women in Greek Tragedy: An Anthopological Approach*. Oslo: Symbolue Osloenses, 1991.

Harriott, Rosemary M. *Aristophanes: Poet and Dramatist*. Baltimore: Croom Helm, 1986.

Kitto, H. D. F. *Greek Tragedy: A Literary Study*. London: Methuen, 1939.

Kott, Jan. *The Eating of the Gods: An Interpretation of Greek Tragedy.* Trans. Boleslaw Taborski and Edward J. Czerwinski. New York: Random House, 1970.

Lloyd-Jones, Hugh. *Greek Comedy. Hellenistic Literature, Greek Religion, and Miscellanea.* Oxford: Oxford University Press, 1990.

Murray, Gilbert. *Aeschylus: The Creator of Tragedy.* Oxford: The Clarendon Press, 1940.

O'Brien, M. J., ed. *Twentieth-Century Interpretations of Oedipus Rex.* Englewood Cliffs: Prentice-Hall, 1968.

Pickard-Cambridge, Arthur W. *The Dramatic Festivals of Athens.* Oxford: The Clarendon Press, 1953.

Reckford, Kenneth. *Aristophanes' Old and New Comedy.* Chapel Hill: University of North Carolina Press, 1987.

Taplin, Oliver. *Greek Tragedy in Action.* Berkeley: University of California Press, 1978.

Walcot, Peter. *Greek Drama in Its Theatrical and Social Context.* Cardiff: University of Wales Press, 1976.

Winkler, John J. and Froma I. Zeitlin, eds. *Nothing to Do with Dionysus? Athenian Drama in Its Social Context.* Princeton: Princeton University Press, 1990.

ROME

Beare, William. *The Roman Stage.* London: Methuen, 1964.

Duckworth, George E. *The Nature of Roman Comedy: A Study in Popular Entertainment.* Princeton: Princeton University Press, 1952.

Lucas, Frank L. *Seneca and Elizabethan Tragedy.* Cambridge: Cambridge University Press, 1922.

Segal, Eric. *Roman Laughter: The Comedy of Plautus.* Cambridge, MA: Harvard University Press, 1968.

Chapter 4: The Early Modern Theater

THE MIDDLE AGES

Axton, Richard. *European Drama of the Early Middle Ages.* Pittsburgh: University of Pittsburgh Press, 1973.

Case, Sue-Ellen. "Reviewing Hrotsvita," *Theater Journal* 35, no. 4 (1983), 533–42.

Craig, Hardin. *English Religious Drama of the Middle Ages.* Oxford: The Clarendon Press, 1960.

Holme, Bryan. *Medieval Pageant.* London: Thames and Hudson, 1987.

Potter, Robert A. *The English Morality Play: Origins, History, and Influence of a Dramatic Tradition.* London: Routledge & Kegan Paul, 1975.

Southern, Richard. *The Medieval Theater in the Round.* London: Faber and Faber, 1957.

Woolf, Rosemary. *The English Mystery Plays.* Berkeley: University of California Press, 1972.

THE EUROPEAN RENAISSANCE

England

Adams, John Cranford. *The Globe Playhouse: Its Design and Equipment.* New York: Barnes and Noble, 1961.

Bradbrook, Muriel C. *Themes and Conventions of Elizabethan Tragedy.* Cambridge: Cambridge University Press, 1935.

Cohen, Walter. *Drama of a Nation: Public Theater in Renaissance England and Spain.* Ithaca: Cornell University Press, 1985.

Dessen, Alan C. *Elizabethan Stage Conventions and Modern Interpreters.* Cambridge: Harvard University Press, 1978.

Gurr, Andrew. *The Shakespearean Stage: 1574–1642.* New York: Cambridge University Press, 1984.

Hotson, Leslie. *Shakespeare's Wooden O.* New York: Macmillan, 1960.

Leacroft, Richard. *The Development of the Elizabethan Playhouse.* Ithaca: Cornell University Press, 1973.

Orgel, Stephen. *The Illusion of Power: Political Theater in the English Renaissance.* Berkeley: University of California Press, 1975.

Schoenbaum, Sam. *William Shakespeare: A Documentary Life.* New York: Oxford University Press, 1975.

Smith, Irwin. *Shakespeare's Blackfriars Playhouse: Its History and Design.* New York: New York University Press, 1964.

Tillyard, E. M. W. *The Elizabethan World Picture.* New York: Vintage Books, n.d.

Spain

Allen, John J. *The Reconstruction of a Spanish Golden Age Playhouse.* Gainesville: University of Florida Press, 1983.

Arias, Ricardo. *The Spanish Sacramental Plays.* Boston: Twayne, 1980.

Crawford, J. P. W. *Spanish Drama Before Lope de Vega.* Philadelphia: University of Pennsylvania Press, 1967.

Kamen, Henry. *Golden Age Spain.* Houndmills, UK: Macmillan Education, 1988.

Kelly, James F. *Lope de Vega and the Spanish Drama.* New York: Haskell House, 1971.

McKendrick, Melveena. *Theater in Spain: 1400–1700.* Cambridge: Cambridge University Press, 1989.

Parker, Alexander. *The Mind and Art of Calderón.* Cambridge: Harvard University Press, 1988.

Wardropper, Bruce W., ed. *Critical Essays on the Theater of Calderón.* New York: New York University Press, 1965.

Wilson, Margaret. *Spanish Drama of the Golden Age.* Oxford: The Clarendon Press, 1969.

France and Italy

Arnott, Peter. *An Introduction to French Theater.* Totowa: Roman and Littlefield, 1977.

Burkhardt, Jacob. *The Civilization of the Renaissance in Italy.* Oxford: Oxford University Press, 1981.

Cook, Albert. *French Tragedy.* Chicago: Swallow Press, 1964.

Duchartre, Pierre Louis. *The Italian Comedy, the Improvisation, Scenarios, Lives, Attitudes, Portraits, and Masks of the Illustrious Characters of the Commedia dell'Arte.* Trans. Randolph T. Weaver. London: Dover, 1966.

Hewitt, Bernard, ed. *The Renaissance Stage: Documents of Serlio, Sabbattini, and Furtenbach.* Coral Gables: University of Miami Press, 1958.

Howarth, W. D. *Molière: A Playwright and His Audience.* New York: Cambridge University Press, 1982.

Lea, K. M. *Italian Popular Comedy, a Study of the Commedia dell'Arte, 1560–1620.* 2 vols. Oxford: The Clarendon Press, 1934.

Nagler, K. M. *Theater Festivals of the Medici, 1539–1637.* New Haven: Yale University Press, 1964.

White, John. *The Birth and Rebirth of Pictorial Space.* London: Faber and Faber, 1957.

Wiley, William Leon. *The Hotel du Bourgogne: Another Look at France's First Public Theater.* Chapel Hill: University of North Carolina Press, 1969.

THE LATE SEVENTEENTH AND EIGHTEENTH CENTURIES

Gilder, Rosamond. *Enter the Actress: The First Women in the Theatre*. Boston: Houghton Mifflin Co., 1931.

Holland, Peter. *The Ornament of Action: Text and Performance in Restoration Comedy*. Cambridge: Cambridge University Press, 1979.

Loftis, John. ed. *Sheridan and the Drama of Georgian England*. Cambridge: Harvard University Press, 1986.

Lynch, James J. *Box, Pit, and Gallery: Stage and Society in Johnson's London*. Berkeley: University of California Press, 1953.

Muir, Kenneth. *The Comedy of Manners*. London: Hutchinson, 1970.

Price, Cecil. *Theatre in the Age of Garrick*. Oxford: The Clarendon Press, 1973.

Styan, J. L. *Restoration Comedy in Performance*. Cambridge: Harvard University Press, 1986.

Wilcox, John. *The Relation of Molière to Restoration Comedy*. New York: B. Blom, 1964.

Chapter 5: The Modern Theater

ROMANTICISM

Bowra, C. M. *The Romantic Imagination*. New York: Oxford University Press, 1961.

Carlson, Marvin. *The French Stage in the Nineteenth Century*. Metuchen: Scarecrow Press, 1972.

Grimsted, David. *Melodrama Unveiled: American Theater and Culture, 1800–1850*. Chicago: University of Chicago Press, 1968.

Lacey, Alexander, *Pixérécourt and the French Romantic Drama*. Toronto: University of Toronto Press, 1928.

Lewis, Philip C. *Trouping: How the Show Came to Town*. New York: Harper and Row, 1973.

Moody, Richard. *America Takes the Stage: Romanticism in American Drama and Theater, 1750–1900*. Bloomington: Indiana University Press, 1955.

Peyre, Henri. *What Is Romanticism?* Trans. Roda Roberts. Tuscaloosa: University of Alabama Press, 1977.

UNCLE TOM'S CABIN AND THE MINSTREL SHOW

Birdoff, Harry. *The World's Greatest Hit*. New York: Vanni, 1947.

Gosset, Thomas F. *Uncle Tom's Cabin and American Culture*. Dallas: Southern Methodist University Press, 1985.

Wittke, Carl. *Tambo and Bones: A History of the American Minstrel Stage*. Durham: Duke University Press, 1930.

REALISM AND NATURALISM

General

Bentley, Eric. ed. *The Theory of the Modern Stage: An Introduction to Modern Theatre and Drama*. Baltimore: Penguin, 1976.

Brockett, Oscar G. and Robert Findlay. *Century of Innovation: A History of European and American Theatre and Drama Since 1870*. Englewood Cliffs: Prentice-Hall, 1973.

Gassner, John. *Directions in Modern Drama and Theater*. New York: Rinehart and Winston, 1967.

Gilman, Richard. *The Making of Modern Drama: A Study of Buchner, Ibsen, Strindberg, Chekhov, Pirandello, Brecht, Beckett, Handke*. New York: Farrar, Straus, and Giroux, 1987.

Miller, Anna Irene. *The Independent Theatre in Europe, 1887 to the Present*. New York: B. Blom, 1966.

Roken, Freddie. *Theatrical Space in Ibsen, Chekhov, and Strindberg: Public Forms of Privacy*. Ann Arbor: University of Michigan Press, 1986.

Styan, John. *Modern Drama in Theory and Practice: Realism and Naturalism*. New York: Cambridge University Press, 1983.

Taylor, John Russel. *The Rise and Fall of the Well-Made Play*. New York: Methuen, 1967.

Valency, Maurice. *The Flower and the Castle: An Introduction to Modern Drama*. New York: Macmillan, 1963.

England

Brown, John Russell, ed. *Modern British Dramatists: A Collection of Critical Essays*. Englewood Cliffs: Prentice Hall, 1968.

Crompton, Louis. *Shaw the Dramatist*. Lincoln: University of Nebraska Press, 1969.

Elsom, John. *Post-War British Theatre Criticism*. London: Routledge & Kegan Paul, 1971.

Findlater, Richard. *At the Royal Court: 25 Years of the English Stage Company*. London: Random House, 1974.

Marowitz, Charles and Simon Trussler. *Theater at Work: Playwrights and Productions in the Modern British Theater*. New York: Methuen, 1968.

Taylor, John Russell. *Anger and After: A Guide to the New British Drama*. London: Penguin, 1962.

France

Antoine, Andre. *Memoirs of the Theatre-libre*. Trans. Marvin Carlson. Coral Gables: University of Miami Press, 1964.

Carter, Lawson. *Zola and the Theater*. New Haven: Yale University Press, 1963.

Fowlie, Wallace. *Dionysus in Paris: A Guide to French Contemporary Theater*. New York: Meridion Books, 1959.

Guicharnaud, Jacques. *Modern French Theater from Giradoux to Beckett*. New Haven: Yale University Press, 1961.

Waxman, S. M. *Antoine and the Theatre-Libre*. Cambridge: Harvard University Press, 1926.

Germany

Grube, Max. *The Story of the Meiningen*. Trans. Ann Marie Koller. Coral Gables: University of Miami Press, 1963.

Piscator, Erwin. *The Political Theater*. Trans. Hugh Rorrison. New York: Avon Books, 1978.

Shaw, Leroy R. *The German Theater Today*. Austin: University of Texas Press, 1963.

Ireland

Hunt, Hugh. *The Abbey: Ireland's National Theatre, 1904–1979*. New York: Columbia University Press, 1979.

Simpson, Alan. *Beckett, Behan, and the Theatre in Dublin*. London: Routledge & Kegan Paul, 1962.

Russia

Gorchakov, Nikolai. *Stanislavsky Directs*. Trans. Miriam Goldina. New York: Funk and Wagnalls, 1955.

Houghton, Norris. *Moscow Rehearsals*. New York: Harcourt Brace Jovanovich, 1936.

Magarshack, David. *Chekhov*. London: Faber and Faber, 1952.

Stanislavsky, Konstantin. *My Life in Art*. Trans. J. J. Robbins. New York: Theatre Arts Books, 1924.

Styan, Joseph. *Chekhov in Performance: A Commentary on the Major Plays*. Cambridge: Harvard University Press, 1971.

Valency, Maurice. *The Breaking String: The Plays of Anton Chekhov*. New York: Oxford University Press, 1966.

Scandanavia

Bradbrook, Muriel C. *Ibsen the Norwegian*. Hamden: Archon Books, 1966.

Klaf, Franklin S. *Strindberg: Origins of Psychology in Modern Drama.* New York: Citadel Press, 1963.

Shaw, George Bernard. *The Quintessence of Ibsenism.* London: Brentano's, 1913.

Spain

Ilie, Paul. *The Surrealist Mode in Spanish Literature.* Ann Arbor: University of Michigan Press, 1968.

Lima, Robert. *The Theatre of García Lorca.* New York: Las Americas Pub. Co., 1963.

United States

Beckerman, Bernard and Howard Siegman, eds. *On Stage: Selected Theater Reviews from the New York Times, 1920–1970.* New York: Quadrangle, 1973.

Bigsby, C. W. E. *A Critical Introduction to Twentieth Century American Drama,* 3 vols. Cambridge: Harvard University Press, 1982–85.

Chinoy, Helen Krich and Linda Walsh Jenkins. *Women in the American Theatre.* New York: Theatre Communications Group, 1987.

Clurman, Harold. *The Fervent Years: The Story of the Group Theatre and the Thirties.* New York: Hill and Wang, 1945.

Demastes, William W. *Beyond Naturalism: A New Realism in the American Theatre.* Westport: Greenwood Press, 1988.

France, Rachel. *A Century of Plays by American Women.* New York: Richards Rosen Press, 1979.

Goldstein, Malcolm. *The Political Stage: American Drama and Theater of the Great Depression.* New York: Oxford University Press, 1974.

Jacobs, Susan. *On Stage: The Making of a Broadway Play.* New York: Alfred A.Knopf, 1967.

Lahr, John. *Up Against the Fourth Wall.* New York: Grove Press, 1970.

Lynes, Russell. *The Lively Audience: A Social History of the Visual and Performing Arts in America, 1890–1950.* New York: Harper and Row, 1985.

Murphy, Brenda. *American Realism and American Drama, 1880–1940.* Cambridge and New York: Cambridge University Press, 1987.

Parker, Dorothy. ed. *Essays on Modern American Drama: Williams, Miller, Albee, and Shepard.* Toronto: University of Toronto Press, 1987.

Reynolds, R. C. *Stage Left, The Development of American Social Drama in the Thirties.* Troy: Whitson, 1986.

Scharine, Richard G. *From Class to Caste in American Drama: Political and Social Themes Since the 1930s.* Westport: Greenwood Press, 1991.

EXPRESSIONISM AND THE EPIC THEATER

Benjamin, Walter. *Understanding Brecht.* London: New Left Books, 1977.

Brecht, Bertolt. *Brecht on Theatre.* Trans. John Willet. New York: Methuen, 1964.

Esslin, Martin. *Brecht: The Man and His Work.* New York: Doubleday, 1960.

Miller, Arthur. *Timebends: A Life.* New York: Grove Press, 1987.

Ritchie, J. M. *German Expressionist Drama.* Boston: Twayne, 1976.

Valgemae, Mardi. *Accelerted Grimace: Expressionism in the American Drama of the 1920s.* Carbondale: Southern Illinois University Press, 1972.

Willet, John, ed. *Brecht on Theatre: The Development of an Aesthetic.* New York: Hill and Wang, 1964.

ABSURDISM

Esslin, Martin. *The Theatre of the Absurd.* New York: Doubleday, 1961.

Chapter 6: The Contemporary Theater

Artaud, Antonin. *The Theatre and Its Double.* Trans. M. C. Richards. New York: Grove Press, 1958.

Birringer, Johannes. *Theatre, Theory, Postmodernism.* Bloomington: Indiana University Press, 1991.

Blau, Herbert. *The Eye of the Prey: Subversions of the Postmodern.* Bloomington: Indiana University Press, 1987.

Case, Sue-Ellen. *Feminism and the Theatre.* New York: Macmillan, 1987.

Dolan, Jill. *The Feminist Spectator as Critic.* Ann Arbor: University of Michigan Press, 1988.

Grotowski, Jerzy. *Towards a Poor Theatre.* New York: Simon and Schuster, 1968.

Hart, Lynda, ed. *Making a Spectacle: Feminist Essays on Contemporary Women's Theatre.* Ann Arbor: University of Michigan Press, 1989.

Jencks, Charles. *What Is Post-modernism?* London: Academy Editions, 1996.

Malpede, Karen, ed. *Women in Theatre: Compassion and Hope.* New York: Drama Book Specialists, 1983.

Marranca, Bonnie. *Theatre of Images.* New York: Drama Book Specialists, 1985.

Pavis, Patrice. *Theatre at the Crossroads of Culture.* Trans. Loren Kruger. London and New York: Routledge, 1992.

Rostagno, Aldo. *We, the Living Theatre.* New York: Ballantine Books, 1970.

Schechner, Richard. *The End of Humanism: Writing on Performance.* New York: Theatre Arts Books, 1982.

Schecter, Joel. *Durov's Pig: Clowns, Politics, and Theatre.* New York: Theater Arts Books, 1985.

Wandor, Michelene. *Carry On, Understudies: Theatre and Sexual Politics.* London: Routledge & Kegan Paul, 1986.

Weales, Gerald. *The Jumping-Off Place: American Drama in the 1960s, from Broadway to Off-Off Broadway to Happenings.* New York: Macmillan, 1969.

Wellwarth, George E. *The Theater of Protest and Paradox: Developments in the Avant-Garde Drama.* Rev. ed. New York: New York University Press, 1971.

Chapter 7: The Theater of Asia

INDIA

Bowers, Faubion. *Dance in India.* New York: AMS Press, 1953.

Garagi, Balwant. *Folk Theater of India.* Seattle: University of Washington Press, 1966.

Iyer, K. B. *Kathakali: The Sacred Dance-Drama of Malabar.* London: Luzac, 1955.

Nemichandra, Jain. *The Indian Theater: Tradition, Continuity, Change.* New Delhi: Vikas Publishing House, 1992.

Richmond, Farley, et al., eds. *Indian Theater:Traditions of Performance.* Honolulu: University of Hawaii Press, 1990.

Shekhar, Indu. *Sanskrit Drama: Its Origins and Decline.* New Delhi: Munshiram Mancharal, 1977.

Srampickal, Jacob. *Voice of the Voiceless: The Power of People's Theater in India.* London and New York: St. Martin's Press, 1994.

Wells, Henry H. *The Classical Drama of India*. Bombay and New York: Asia Publishing House, 1963.

CHINA

Chang, Pe-Chin. *Chinese Opera and the Painted Face*. Taipei: Mei Ya Publications, 1979.

Dolby, William. *A History of Chinese Drama*. London: P. Elek, 1976.

Halson, Elizabeth. *Peking Opera: A Short Guide*. London: Oxford University Press, 1966.

Hung, Josephine Huang. *Children of the Pear Garden*. Taipei: Mei Ya Publications, 1961.

Hsu, Tao-Ching. *The Chinese Conception of Theatre*. Seattle and London: University of Washington Press, 1985.

Mackerras, Colin. *The Performing Arts in Contemporary China*. London and Boston: Routledge & Kegan Paul, 1981.

Scott, A. C. *Traditional Chinese Plays*. 3 vols. Madison: University of Wisconsin Press, 1970, 1975.

Wu, Zuguang, Zuolin Huang, and Shaowu Mei. *Peking Opera and Mei Lan-fang*. Beijing: New World Press, 1981.

Zung, Cecelia S. C. *Secrets of the Chinese Drama*. New York: B. Blom, 1964.

JAPAN

Arnott, Peter. *The Theaters of Japan*. New York: Macmillan, 1969.

Goodman, David G., *Japanese Drama and Culture in the 1960s: The Return of the Gods*. Armonk: M. E. Sharpe, 1988.

Keene, Donald. *Nō: The Classical Drama of Japan*. Tokyo and Palo Alto: Kodansha International, 1966.

Kirby, E. T. "The Origins of Nō Drama," *Educational Theatre Journal* 25, no. 3 (1973), 269–84.

Motokiyo, Zeami. *On the Art of the No Drama*. Trans. J. Thomas Rimer and Kamazaki Masakazu. Princeton: Princeton University Press, 1980.

Ortolani, Benito. *The Japanese Theatre: From Shamanistic Ritual to Contemporary Pluralism*. Princeton: Princeton University Press, 1994.

Rimer, J. Thomas. *Toward a Modern Japanese Theater*. Princeton: Princeton University Press, 1974.

Senda, Akihiko. *The Voyage of Contemporary Japanese Theater*. Trans. J. Thomas Rimer. Honolulu: University of Hawaii Press, 1997.

Suzuki, Tadashi. *The Way of Acting*. Trans. J. Thomas Rimer. New York: Theatre Communications Group, 1986.

Yoshinobu Inoura and Toshio Kawatake. *The Traditional Theater of Japan*. Tokyo: Weatherhill, 1981.

Zeami. *Kadensho*. Trans. Chuichi Sakurai et al. Kyoto: Sumiya-Shinobe Publications International, 1971.

Chapter 8: The Theater of Africa and the African Diaspora

AFRICA

Banham, Martin with C. Wake. *African Theater Today*. London: Pitman's, 1976.

Banham, Martin et al. *The Cambridge Guide to African and Caribbean Theatre*. Cambridge: Cambridge University Press, 1994.

Ekwueme, Victoria C. "Story Theatre in Africa: An Essay in Description," *Yale/Theatre* 3, no. 2 (1971), 79–83.

Gotrick, Karl. *Apidan Theatre and Modern Drama*. Göteborg: Almquist and Wisken International, 1984.

Graham-White, Anthony. *The Drama of Black Africa*. London and New York: Samuel French, 1974.

Kirby, E. T. "Indigenous African Theatre," *Drama Review* 18, no. 4 (1974), 22–33.

Soyinka, Wole. *Myth, Literature, and the African World*. Cambridge: Cambridge University Press, 1976.

AFRICAN AMERICAN THEATER

Fabre, Genevieve. *Drumbeats and Metaphor: Contemporary Afro-American Theatre*. Cambridge: Harvard University Press, 1983.

Haskin, James. *Black Theatre in America*. New York: Thomas Y. Crowell, 1982.

Hatch, James V. *The Black Image on the American Stage*. New York: Drama Book Specialists, 1970.

Hill, Errol. *The Theater of Black Americans*. 2 vols. Englewood Cliffs: Applause Theatre Books, 1980.

Hughes, Langston and Milton Meltzer. *Black Magic: A Pictorial History of Black Entertainers in America*. New York: Prentice-Hall, 1967.

Sanders, L. C. *The Development of Black Theater in America: From Shadows to Selves*. Baton Rouge: Louisiana State University Press, 1988.

Williams, Mance. *Black Theatre in the 1960s and 1970s: A Historical-Critical Analysis of the Movement*. Westport: Greenwood Press, 1985.

Woll, Albert. *Black Musical Theatre from Coontown to Dreamgirls*. Baton Rouge: Louisiana State University Press, 1989.

THE CARIBBEAN

Collins, J. A. *Contemporary Theater in Puerto Rico*. Rio Piedras: Editorial Universitaria-Universidad de Puerto Rico, 1979.

Corsbie, K. *Theatre in the Caribbean*. London: Faber and Faber, 1984.

Leal, R. *A Brief History of Cuban Theatre*. Havana: Editorial Letras Cubanas, 1980.

Omotoso, K. *The Theatrical into Theatre: A Study of Drama and Theatre in the English-Speaking Caribbean*. London: New Beacon Books, 1982.

Perereira, J. R. "The Black Presence in Cuban Theatre," *Afro-Hispanic Review* 2, no. 1 (January 1983), 23–35.

Phillips, J. B. *Contemporary Puerto Rican Drama*. New York: Plaza Mayor Ediciones, 1972.

Rohlehr, G. *Calypso and Society in Pre-Independence Trinidad*. Port of Spain, Trinidad: G. Rohlehr, 1990.

Chapter 9: The Theater of Latin America

MESOAMERICA

Coe, Michael D. *The Maya*. Rev. ed. New York: Prager, 1980.

Edmundson, Munro S. *The Book of Counsel: The Popol Vuh of the Quiche Maya of Guatemala*. New Orleans: Tulane University Middle America Research Institute, 1971.

Irving, Thomas Ballantine, ed. *The Maya's Own Words*. Culver City: Labyrinthos, 1985.

Shank, Theodore. "A Return to Mayan and Aztec Roots," *Drama Review* 18, no. 4 (1974), 58–70.

Tedlock, Dennis, ed., and trans. *Popol Vuh: The Definitive Edition of the Mayan Book of the Dawn of Life and the Glories of Gods and Kings*. New York: Simon and Schuster, 1985.

MEXICO AND MEXICAN-AMERICAN

Bagby, Beth. "El teatro campesino: Interview with Luis Valdez." *The Drama Review: Thirty Years of Commentary on the Avant-Garde*. Eds. Brooks McNamara and Jill Dolan. Ann Arbor: University Microfilms International, 1986.

Huerta, Jorge. *Chicano Theater: Themes and Forms*. Ypsilanti, MI: Bilingual Press, 1982.

Leonard, Irving A. *Baroque Times in Old Mexico*. Ann Arbor: University of Michigan Press, 1959.

SOUTH AMERICA

Albuquerque, Severino João. *Violent Acts: A Study of Contemporary Latin American Theatre*. Detroit: Wayne State University Press, 1991.

Arrizon, Alicia. *Latina Performance: Traversing the Stage*. Bloomington: Indiana University Press, 1999.

Boal, Augusto. *Theatre of the Oppressed*. Trans. Charles McBride and Maria-Odilia Leal. New York: Theatre Communications Group, 1985.

Cajiao Salas, Teresa and Margarita Vargas, eds. *Women Writing Women: An Anthology of Spanish-American Theater of the 1980s*. Albany: State University of New York Press, 1997.

Cortes, Eladio and Mirta Barrea, eds. *Dictionary of Latin American Theater*. Westport: Greenwood Press, 2000.

Dauster, Frank, ed. *Perspectives on Contemporary Spanish American Theatre*. Lewisburg, PA: Bucknell University Press, 1996.

Larson, Catherine and Margarita Vargas, eds. *Latin American Women Dramatists: Theater, Texts, and Theories*. Bloomington: Indiana University Press, 1998.

Luzuriaga, Gerardo, ed. *Popular Theater for Social Change in Latin America: Essays in Spanish and English*. Los Angeles: UCLA Latin American Center Publications, 1978.

Lyday, Leon F. and George W. Woodyard, eds. *Dramatists in Revolt: The New Latin American Theater*. Austin: University of Texas Press, 1976.

Oliver, William I., ed. *Voices of Change in Spanish American Theatre: An Anthology*. Austin: University of Texas Press, 1971.

Pianca, Marina. "The Latin American Theatre of Exile." *Theatre Research International* 14 (1989): 174–85.

Taylor, Diana. *Theatre of Crisis: Drama and Politics in Latin America*. Lexington, KY: University Press of Kentucky, 1991.

Weiss, Judith A. and Leslie Damasceno et al. *Latin American Popular Theatre: The First Five Centuries*. Albuquerque: University of New Mexico Press, 1993.

Woodyard, George, ed. *The Modern Stage in Latin America: Six Plays*. New York: E. P. Dutton, 1971.

ACKNOWLEDGMENTS

Anonymous. *Everyman.* Footnotes accompanying *Everyman* by Sylvan Barnet, from *Types of Drama: Plays and Contexts*, Seventh Edition by Sylvan Barnet, Morton Berman, William Burto, and Ken Draya. Copyright © 1997 by Sylvan Barnet, Morton Berman, William Burto, and Ken Draya.

Anonymous. *The Qing Ding Pearl.* Reprinted with the permission of Scribner, a Division of Simon & Schuster from *Famous Chinese Plays,* translated and edited by L.C. Arlington and Harold Acton (Russell & Russell, NY, 1963).

Edward Albee. *The American Dream.* Copyright © 1961, Renewed 1988 by Edward Albee. Reprinted by permission of William Morris Agency, Inc. on behalf of the Author. CAUTION: Professionals and amateurs are hereby warned that *The American Dream* is subject to royalty. It is fully protected under the copyright laws of the United States of America and all countries covered by the International Copyright Union (including the Dominion of Canada and the rest of the British Commonwealth), the Berne Convention, the Pan-American Copyright Convention and the Universal Copyright Convention as well as all countries with which the United States has reciprocal copyright relations. All rights, including professional/amateur stage rights, motion picture, recitation, lecturing, public reading, radio broadcasting, television, video or sound recording, all other forms of mechanical or electronic reproduction, such as CD-ROM, CD-I, information storage and retrieval systems and photocopying, and the rights of translation into foreign languages, are strictly reserved. Particular emphasis is laid upon the matter of readings, permission for which must be secured from the Author's agent in writing. Inquiries concerning rights should be addressed to: William Morris Agency, Inc., 1325 Avenue of the Americas, New York, New York 10019, Attn: Owen Laster.

Bertolt Brecht. *The Good Woman of Setzuan* by Bertolt Brecht. Copyright by Eric Bentley, 1947, as an unpublished MS, Registration No. D-12239. © Copyright 1956, 1961 by Eric Bentley. Epilogue © Copyright by Eric Bentley. From *Parables for the Theatre, Two plays by Bertolt Brecht*, translated by Eric Bentley. Reprinted by permission of the University of Minnesota Press.

Anton Chekhov. *The Cherry Orchard* by Anton Chekhov. From *Chekhov: The Major Plays* by Anton Chekhov, translated by Ann Dunnigan. Copyright © 1964 by Ann Dunnigan. Used by permission of Dutton Signet, a division of Penguin Putnam Inc.

Caryl Churchill. *Top Girls* by Caryl Churchill. Reprinted by permission of Methuen Publishing Ltd.

Athol Fugard. *"MASTER HAROLD". . . and the boys.* From *"MASTER HAROLD". . . and the boys* by Athol Fugard. Copyright © 1982 by Athol Fugard. Reprinted by permission of Alfred A. Knopf, a Division of Random House, Inc. CAUTION: Professionals and amateurs are hereby warned that *"MASTER HAROLD". . . and the boys* is subject to a royalty. It is fully protected under the copyright laws of the United States of America, the British Commonwealth, including Canada, and all other countries of the copyright Union. All rights, including professional, amateur, motion pictures, recitation, lecture, public reading, radio broadcasting, television, and the rights of translation into foreign languages are strictly reserved. In its present form the play is dedicated to the reading public only. The amateur live stage performance rights to *"MASTER HAROLD". . . and the boys* are controlled exclusively by Samuel French, Inc., and royalty arrangements and licenses must be secured well in advance of presentation. PLEASE NOTE that amateur royalty fees are set upon application in accordance with your producing circumstances. When applying for a royalty quotation for a license please give us the number of performances, intended dates of production, your seating capacity and admission fee. Royalties are payable one week before the opening performance of the play to Samuel French, Inc., at 45 W. 25th Street, New York, NY 10010; or at 7623 Sunset Blvd., Hollywood, CA 90046, or to Samuel French (Canada), Ltd., 80 Richmond Street East, Toronto, Ontario, Canada M5C 1Pl. For all other rights than those stipulated above, apply to William Morris Agency, Inc., 1350 Ave. of the Americas, New York, NY 10019.

Elena Garro. *A Solid Home* by Elena Garro, from *Selected Latin American One-Act Plays*, Francesca Colecchia and Julio Matas, eds. and trans. Published in 1973 by the University of Pittsburgh Press. Reprinted by permission of the publisher.

Namiki Gohei III. *Kanjinchō, A Kabuki Play*, by Namiki Gohei. English Adaptation by James R. Brandon and Tamako Niwa. Copyright © 1966 by Samuel French, Inc. CAUTION: Professionals and amateurs are hereby warned that *Kanjinchō* being fully protected under the copyright laws of the United States of America, the British Commonwealth countries, including Canada and the other countries of the Copyright Union, is subject to a royalty. All rights, including professional, amateur, motion picture, recitation, public reading, radio, television, and cable broadcasting, and the rights of

PHOTO CREDITS

INDEX

Abbey Theatre (Dublin), 290, 557
Abe, Kobo, 592
Abraham and Isaac, 105
    commentary on, 109–110
    play text, 111–115
Absurd comedy/theater. *See* Theater,
    absurdism in
Abydos Passion Play, 11, 12, 608
Actor(s)/ acting, 5, 9–10
    Brechtian, 352
    in Chinese theater, 569–571
      alienation effect, 351–352
    in commedia dell'arte, 136
    in contemporary theater, 469–471
    definitions, 9
    in French theater, 258
    in Greek theater, 61, 62
    in Middle Ages, 105
    in Renaissance Europe, 136, 141–142
Actors Studio (New York), 290
Actos, 761, 762
A-effect. *See* Alienation effect
Aeschylus, 9, 50, 52, 56, 57, 59, 61, 62, 88,
    472, 563, 749
Affected Ladies, The, 226
African theater. *See* Theater
African Theater (New York), 672
After the Fall, 388
Agamemnon, 61, 148
Age of humanism, 134
Agitprop theater, 612
Agon, 59, 69
    Old Comedy, 93
Aiken, George, 278–280
Ain't Misbehavin', 673
Ajagemo, 668
Ajax, 60
Akalaitis, Joanne, 470, 504
Akropolis, 468
Albee, Edward, 30, 44, 290, 439, 441–443,
    504, 783
Aldridge, Ira, 672
Alexander, Bill, 263
Alford, Allen, 639–641
Al-Hakim, Tewfik, 54
Alienation effect, 351–352, 354
Alison's House, 21
Alleyn, Edward, 141
Alley Theater (Houston), 442

All My Sons, 388, 389, 432, 434
All's Well That Ends Well, 147
Alternative theater, 468–469
Altman, Robert, 504
American Buffalo, 32
American Clock, 388
American Dream, The, 30
    commentary on, 442–443
    play text, 444–458
American Negro Theater, 672
American Repertory Theater, 358
Amlothi, 149
*Amor es mas laberinto (Love Is a Great
    Labyrinth)*, 621
Amphitryon, 97, 259
Anachronisms, 110
Anamu Theater Collective (Puerto Rico),
    712
Ananke, 59, 65
Anatomy of Drama, The, 8
Andarse por las Ramas, 774
Anderson, Dame Judith, 147
Anderson, Robert, 504
Anderson, Sherwood, 33
Angels in America, 23, 350
    Part One: *Millennium Approaches*, 30
      commentary on, 504–506, 541–543
      play text, 507–539
      review of, 540–541
    Part Two: *Perestroika*, 504, 505
Anna Lucasta, 672
Antagonist, 23–24, 49
Anticharacter, 30
Antigone, 63
Antimasque, 139
Antistrophes, 60
Antoine, André, 290, 592
Antony and Cleopatra, 147
Aposentos, 223
Appolonian, 640, 668
Aragoto, 589
Archetypes, 29
    star-crossed lovers, 590–591
Archetypes, Imprecators and Victims of Fate,
    668
Archon, 88
Arden, John, 291
Areítos, 710, 741
Aristophanes, 8, 61, 62, 93

Aristotle, 4, 8, 9, 24–34, 38, 40–41, 45, 56,
    59, 91, 96, 142, 323, 351–352, 469, 641
    and six elements of drama, 24–35
    The Poetics excerpt, 26–27
Arlecchino, 107, 136, 566
Arnaux, J. A., 672
Arouet, François-Marie. *See* Voltaire
Ars Poetica, 96
Artaud, Antonin, 467–468, 548
Art of Poetry, The. *See Ars Poetica*
Artiles, Freddy, 711
Arts Guild of St. Lucia, 714
Arts Theatre (London), 440
Asides, 49, 266, 268–269
Asinimali, 613
As Is, 505
Astor Place Company of Colored Tragedians
    (New York), 672
As You Like It, 147
Ataka, 593
At the End of Blood's Journey, 711
At the Foot of the Mountain (Minneapolis),
    469
At the Hawk's Well, 585
Audience, 7, 35, 46
Augustine, 221–222
Auleum, 97
Auteur, 469
Autos. *See* Autos sacramentales
Autos sacramentales, 134, 221, 223
Autumn in the Palace of Han, 570
Awake and Sing, 291
Aware, 588
Ayame, Yoshizaw, 589
Ayckbourne, Allen, 266
Aztecs, 748, 751

Baal, 355
Bacchae, The, 56, 588
Bailetes, 746
Bald Soprano, The, 439, 442
Bannard, Walter D., 467
Banning, Bernardín, 774–775
Baraka, Amiri (Everett LeRoi Jones), 30, 607,
    672, 676
Barbierei, Niccolo, 136
Barbieri, Francisco Asenjo, 746
Barong trance dance (Bali), 4–6, 467, 548
Barrier, The, 672

Barros Grez, Daniel, 742
Barton, John, 48
Basement Theater, 714
Batista Marciel, Juan, 742
Beattie, John, 610
Beck, Julian, 468
Beckett, Samuel, 25, 30, 44, 288, 324, 438,
    439–440, 585
Becque, Henri, 287
Beggar's Opera, The, 354
Behn, Mrs. Aphra, 267, 268
Benign comedy, 42
Benitez-Rojo, Antonio, 710
Benkei, 24, 29, 586, 588, 593–594
Bentley, Eric, 45, 284
Berger, Peter, 465
Bergson, Henri, 55
Berliner Ensemble, 355
Bernabe, 762
Bernhardt, Sarah, 147
Bernstein, Leonard, 287
Betsy, the, 104
Bharata, 9, 547, 552
Bhuta, 553
Biomechanics, 353
Birdoff, Harry, 279
Birth of Tragedy, The, 604
Bjornson, Maria, 470
Blackfriars Theatre, 150, 210–211
Black Horizon on the Hill (Pittsburgh), 676
Blake, Eubie, 673
Blin, Roger, 440
Blood Knot, 616
Blood Wedding, 468
Blue Blood and Black, 713
Boal, Agusto, 38, 469, 743
Boar's Head (Theater), 210
Bogart, Anne, 470
Bogosian, Eric, 33
Bond, Edward, 291
Booger Dance (Cherokee), 137
Boor, The, 324
Boorstin, Daniel, 11
Booth, Edwin, 214–215
Booth stages, 106, 108
Bosman and Lena, 616
Boston Playwright's Theater, 714
Boulevard theaters, 277
Boulton, Marjorie, 10
Bourgeois tragedy, 270
Boys in the Band, The, 505
Bradley, A. C., 140
Braggart warrior, 29, 136
Brahm, Otto, 290
Brahma, 547, 552, 553
Branagh, Kenneth, 93, 147
Brand, 292, 293
Bread and Puppet Theater, 712
Breaking String, The, 325
Brecht, Bertolt, 25, 30, 38, 49, 50, 110,
    350–352, 353–357, 468–470, 473, 474,
    504, 571, 585
Breeze, Binta, 712
B'rer Rabbit, 136
Brighella, 136
Brighton Pavillion (England), 47
Britten, Sir Benjamin, 585

Brockett, Oscar, 294
Broken Glass, 388, 389
Brome Manor (England), 109
Brook, Peter, 35, 135, 467, 470, 557
Brothers (Adelphoi), 93, 97
Brown, John Mason, 429, 431–433
Brown, Lenox, 713
Brown, William Henry, 672
Brustein, Robert, 41, 472
Bubblin' Brown Sugar, 673
Buddhist thought, 582, 594
Bufo Cubano, 747
Bufos Habañeros, 747
Bulgakov, Mikail, 262–263
Bullins, Ed, 672, 677
Bunraku puppetry, 591
Buontalenti, Bernardo, 138
Burbage, Richard, 141, 146, 211, 212–213
Burton, Richard 214–216
Butchers, The, 290

Cabaret, 350
Cabinet of Doctor Caligari, The, 350
Café Cino, 638
Calderón, Fernando, 742
Calderón, Pedro (Pedro Calderón de la
    Barca), 140, 143, 220–222, 746, 751
Calypso music, 716, 738
Calypso plays, 713
Camille, 286
Campbell, Douglas, 66, 92
Camus, Albert, 438
Canboulay, 716, 739
Cao Yu, 562
Capa y espada plays, 751
Capeman, The, 472
Capitano, 136
Carballido, Emilio, 743
Caribbean theater. See Theater
Carnival (Trinidad), 7–8, 713, 716, 738–739
Case, Sue Ellen, 59
Castillo, del, Francìsco Fray, 742
Cataline, 292
Catharsis, 41, 323, 352
Cats, 11, 139
Caucasian Chalk Circle, The, 355
Causality, 38
    in climactic plotting, 25
Cavea, 97
Cazuela, 223
Ceremonial performances, 611
Ceremony(ies)
    defined, 7
    theatricality of, 3, 4, 7
    versus drama, 24
    versus ritual, 7
Cessaire, Aime, 614
Chalbaud, Roman, 743
Chapayepkas, 760
Chaplin, Charlie, 43, 135, 352
Character(s), 27, 28–30, 105
Characterization, 76. See also Actor(s)/acting
Charro, el, 742
Chavez, Cesar, 761
Chekhov, Anton, 29, 30, 48, 273, 288–289,
    324–326, 438, 592

Cherry Orchard, The, 31, 34, 48
    commentary on, 325–326
    play text, 327–347
Chhau, 556
Chicanismo, 763
Chikamatsu Monzaemon, 586–587
Chikwakwa Travelling Theater Company, 614
Children of the Pear Garden, 560
Chinese theater. See Theater
Ch'ing dynasty, 561
Ching hsi, 561
Chip Woman's Fortune, The, 670, 672
Chocrón, Issac, 743
Chorus, 49
    Aristotle's definition, 27
Ch'ou, 136, 562, 567
Chronegk, Ludwig, 268
Chunori, 588
Churchill, Caryl, 291, 470, 473–474
Churning of the Ocean, The, 552
Cino, Joe, 638
Circus Maximus, 97
Cisneros, Luis, 749
City Dionysia. See Dionysia (City)
Clark-Bekederemo, John Pepper, 614
Classicism, 49, 60
Climactic plot, 25, See also Plot
Climax, 28, 60
Close, Glenn, 149
Cloud Nine, 473
Clouds, The, 93
Clurman, Harold, 468
Cobb, Lee J. 431, 433
Cockettes, The, 469
Cocoleche plays, 747
Cohn, Roy, 506, 540
Coleridge, Samuel Taylor, 13, 49, 151
Colored Museum, The, 675
Coloseo (Mexico City), 741
Columbina, 136
Come Blow Your Horn, 93
Comedias (Spanish), 134, 220, 223
Comedie Française, 277–278, 742
Comedy, 26, 42–43
    in African theater, 611
    bawdry, 42
    cross-dressing in, 43
    Greek Old Comedy, 93
    Middle Comedy, 93
    New Comedy, 93
    versus tragedy, 38, 42,
Comedy of Errors, The, 97, 146
Comedy of Manners, 42, 266, 267
Comic characters/heroes, 42
Commedia a mascera, 136
Commedia dell'arte, 13, 96, 100, 136–137,
    226, 438, 567, 760
Commedia dell'arte all'improviso, 136
Commedia erudita, 97
Commedia improvisa, 136
Commedia non scrita, 136
Committed Artists, 613
Compañías, 223
Complication, 28, 60
Comte, Auguste, 285
Concetti, 135
Concise History of Theater, The, 9

Conflict
  defined, 23–24
  importance of, 24
Confradías, 223
Confucianism, 565, 594
Congo Square (New Orleans), 672
Congreve, William, 266, 267
Connection, The, 468
Conniving servant, 62
Connor, Edric, 713
Conscious Lovers, The, 269–270
Constant Prince, The, 220, 468
Context, 33
Conventions (theatrical), 49–50
  of African theater, 615
  of Chinese theater, 564–570
  of Greek theater, 60–61
  of Kabuki theater, 587–591
  of Noh theater, 361, 583–584
  of Restoration theater, 266–268
  of theater in India, 553–557
Cook, George Cram, 21, 290
Coplan, David, 612
Coriolanus, 147
Corneille, Pierre, 140, 141–142, 266, 742
Corpus Christi cycles, 105, 107, 221
Corral de la Cruz, 223
Corral del Principe, 223
Corrales, 143, 221, 223
Corridos, 762
Corriere, Sergio, 469, 711
Costumbristas, 746
Costumes, 34
Country bumpkin, 97
Country Wife, The, 267, 268, 269
Covent Garden (London), 278
Coward, Noel, 266
Coyote stories, 4, 136
Crawford, Cheryl, 468
Creation of the World and Other Business, The, 388
Creators, The, 11
Cromwell, 278
Cromwell, Oliver, 266
Cross-dressing, 43
  in comedy, 43
  in contemporary theater, 471
Crowley, Mart, 505
Crown of Dreams, 742
Croyden, Margaret, 467
Crucible, The, 388, 434, 470
Crucifixion, The, 110
Cubists, 13, 464
cummings, e. e., 33
Curlew River, 585
Curtain Theatre, 210
Cyclic plot, 25. *See also* Plot
Cymbeline, 147

Dadaism, 438
Dalang, 547
Dance and the Railroad, The, 31, 607
Dance in the Forest, A, 639
Dance of death, 323
Dance of the Giants, The, 752
Danjūrō, Ichikawa, 586, 588
Darby, William, 134
Dark Root of Scream, The, 762

Darwin, Charles, 285, 287
Davies, Henrietta Vinto, 672
Davis, Ossie, 672
Death, (character) 117–118, 119
Death and the King's Horseman, 7, 29, 30–31, 40, 610, 668
  commentary on, 640–641
  play text, 642–668
Death of a Salesman, 48, 50, 388, 389, 563, 677
  commentary on, 389–391
  play text, 392–428
  reviews of, 429–434
Death of the Last Black Man in the Whole Entire World, The, 32
De Beaumarchais, Pierre Caron, 276
De Beauvoir, Simone, 465
Deconstructionism, 471–472
Decorum, 142
Deer dancer, 136, 221
De Ghelderode, Michel, 45
Deipkloof Hall (South Africa), 612–613
De la Cruz, Sor Juana Inés, 7, 741, 750–751, 752
Delaney, Sheilah, 291
De La Taille, Jean, 142
Delicate Balance, A, 441, 442
De los Gobos, Farfan, 134
De Marivaux, Pierre, 267
De Molina Tirso, 741
Dengaku (field dance), 9, 582
Denouement, 28
De Onis, Federico, 465
De Peralta Barnuevo, Pedro, 742
De Pixérécourt, Guilbert, 277, 746
Derrida, Jacques, 465, 471
Desengaño, 220, 221–220
Deus ex machina, 61, 227, 285
Devil character/figures, 107, 136, 714–716
Devine, George, 638
DeWitt, Johannes, 210
Dholmo, Herbert, 614
Diá de los Muertos, 7, 136, 782
Dialogue, 33
Diaspora
  African, 607
  Chinese, 607
  Jewish, 607
Diction, 31–34
Diderot, Denis, 276
Dike, 59, 60
Dionysia (City), 56–57, 58, 61, 88–89, 547
Dionysus, 8, 56–58, 88, 640, 749
Dioramas, 277
Direct address, 46
Director
  rise of, 286
Discussion dramas/plays, 469, 616
Dithyramb, 7, 56, 57, 60, 552, 748
Divine Narcissus, The, 7, 741
  commentary on, 748
  play text, 750–752
Doctor character, 136
Doctor Faustus, 118
Doll's House, A, 7, 14, 48, 284, 285, 286, 297, 326
  commentary on, 293–294
  play text, 295–323

Domestic tragedy, 270
Dominus gregis, 98
Donkey Market, The, 45
Dorset Garden Theater, 268
Dragún, Osvaldo, 712, 743
Drama
  versus ceremony and ritual, 7
  defined, 23
  elements of, 23, 24–34
  genres of, 35–46
  speech in. *See* Diction; Dramatic speech
  versus theater, 23
Drama of King Shotaway, The, 672
Dramatic criticism, 471–472
Dramatic Imagination, The, 5
Dramatic speech, 31–34
Dramatists, versus storytellers, 23
Dream on Monkey Mountain, 714
Dream Play, A, 350
Dromenon, 56
Drury Lane Theater, 270
Dryden, John, 258, 266, 267
Duchess of Malfi, The, 139
Duerrenmatt, Friedreich, 45
Duke Georg II, 286
Dumas *fils,* Alexander, 286, 468
Dunlap, William, 277
Dunnock, Mildred, 431, 433
Durang, Christopher, 266
Dybbuk, The, 504
Dyskalos (The Grouch), 62

Edward II, 504
Einstein, Albert, 464
Ekkyklema, 61
El arbol (The Tree), 773
El baile de los gigantes (The Dance of the Giants), 749
Elckerlyc, 117
Eliot, T. S., 12, 464
Elogas, 741
Else, Gerald, 41, 56, 57
El Teatro Campesino (San Juan Batista, CA), 469, 743, 761, 762, 763
El Teatro Espejo (Sacramento, CA), 764
Emperor Jones, The, 672
Enactments
  ritualized, 610
  simple, 610
Enemy of the People, An, 292
English Stage Company (London), 638
English theater. *See* Theater
Enlightenment, Age of, 276
Entertainment, need for, 13–14
Entrements, 138
Entreméses, 138, 220, 746
Epic theater, 49, 350–352
  versus dramatic theater, 351
Episodes, 60, 89, 93
Episodic plot, 25. *See also* Plot
Epstein, Lisa Jo, 262–263
Erinyes, 59
España, Guillermo Ramírez, 750
Espinosa Medrano de, Juan, 741
Ethel Barrymore Theater, 674
Etherege, George, 267
Euba, Femi, 668
Eubie, 673

Eugene O'Neill Center, 676
Eumenides, The, 59
Euripides, 56, 57, 59, 60, 61, 62, 276, 592
Everyman, 105
    commentary on, 117–119
    play text, 119–131
Existentialism, 438
Exodos, 60
Exposition, 26–27
Expressionism, 49, 350
    German, 350, 471

Facundo, 747
Faithful Shepardess, The, 139
Falling action, 28
False Confessions, The, 267
Familienstücke, 277
Farándulas, 223
Farce, 44–45
Farcir, 44
Fate, 43
Fate of a Cockroach, 45
Federal Theater Project, 21
Félix, Sandra, 776
Feminine Mystique, 465
Feminism, 465, 469, 471
Feminist criticism, 471
Fen, 473
Fences, 676
    commentary on, 677–678
    play text, 679–706
Ferber, Edna, 21
Ferguson, Francis, 289
Festival of Arts and Culture (FESTAC)
    (Africa), 614
Fierstein, Harvey, 443, 505, 541
First Folio, 146
First World Festival of Negro Arts, 614
Fiske, Minnie Maddern, 288
Flower Drum opera. *See* Hua-gu Opera
    Company
Fo, Dario, 45
Folk rituals and festivals, 3–8
Fop, 268–269
Forced Marriage, The, 226
Foreman, Richard, 504
Formalism, 350
Fornes, Maria Irene, 31
Forrest, Edwin, 98
Fortune, 43
Foster, Stephen, 281
Fragmentation, 471
Free Southern Theater (New Orleans),
    672
Free Theater movement (Japan), 592
Frei Buhne (Germany), 290
French theater. *See* Theater
Freud, Sigmund, 285
Friedan, Betty, 465
Frons scaenae, 97
Frye, Northrop, 11
Fugard, Athol (Harold Athol Lanning
    Fugard), 607, 610, 616–617, 638
Fuller, Charles, 672
*Funny Thing Happened on the Way to the
    Forum, A*, 97
Furies, 52, 59
Futurism, 350

Galiano 108 Theatre, 711
Galileo, 355
Gambaro, Griselda, 743
Gamos, in Old Comedy, 93
García Lorca, Federico, 468
Garnachas, 223
Garro, Elena, 7, 742, 773
Garza, Armando, 620
Gaucho plays, 746
Gay, John, 354
Gay and lesbian
    criticism, 472
    issues, 469, 504–506
Gay plays, 504–505
Gender criticism, 472
Generality, 142
Genres (dramatic), 35–46
    subgenres, 35
Genre seriaux, 270
Genrouku period, 586
Genzai, 582
German expressionism, 350
Gestus, 352, 355
Ghosts, 290. 292
Ghost Sonata, The, 350
Gibbs, Patrick, 92
Gibson, Mel, 147, 149, 440
Gielgud, Sir John, 214, 215–216
Gil, Rosa Maria, 785
Gilpin, Charles, 672
Glasgow Citizens' Theater, 48
Glaspell, Susan, 14, 15, 21, 33, 34, 288, 290
Globe Theatre (London), 108, 146, 150,
    210–211, 212–213
Goa Hindu Association (Bombay), 555
God plays, 582, 583
Gohei, Namiki, III, 593
Gohei, Namiki, IV, 593
Goldoni, Carlo, 136
Goldsmith, Oliver, 266, 270, 272
Gómez, Carlos, 747
Good Woman of Setzuan, The, 25, 30, 31, 352,
    354
    commentary on, 355–357
    play text, 358–387
Gordone, Charles, 672
Gorostiza, Celestina, 742
Gozzi, Carlo, 136
Granada, Nicolás, 742
Grand Kabuki Theater (Japan), 595
Gran Siecle, 134
Great Celestial Cow, The, 467
Great Chain of Being, 134, 137–140
Great Theater of the World, The, 221
Greek Old Comedy, 92, 93
Greek theater. *See* Theater
Greek Tragedy in Action, 43
Gregory, Lady Augusta, 290
Grex, 98
Grien, J. T., 290
Griot, 3, 610, 615
Gropius, Walter, 353
Grotesque comedy, 42
Grotowski, Jerzy, 7, 612, 714
Grouch, The, 29, 62
Groundlings, 212, 213
Group Theater, 290, 468
Grupo Teatro Escambray (Cuba), 469

Guangdong Guild Hall (Tianjin), 565
Guerin, Mona, 712
Guthrie, Sir Tyrone, 91–92
"Guthrie Directs 'Ritual' Performance of *Oedipus Rex* at Edinburgh Fête," 92–93
Guthrie Theater (Minneapolis), 37, 94
Gwynn, Nell, 267

Habit a la romaine, 258
Hair, 467
Hairy Ape, The, 286
Hall, Edward, 138, 139
Hall, Sir Peter, 52, 440
Hamartia, 40
Hamlet, Prince of Denmark, 6, 25, 29, 32, 41,
    43, 46, 96, 137, 141, 554
    commentary on, 147–151
    at the Globe Theater, 212–213
    Oedipal implications in, 149, 216
    play text, 152–210
    reviews of, 214–217
Hanimichi, 49, 587, 588
Hansberry, Lorraine, 290, 291, 607, 672, 674,
    675
Hanswurst, 136
Happy Days, 44
Happy idea, 93
Harlem Renaissance, 672
Harlequin. *See* Arlecchino
Harmony of the Spheres, The, 138
Harrison, Jane, 57
Hartnoll, Phyllis, 7
Hasegawa, Shigure, 291
Hashigakari, 584, 585
Hauptmann, Gerhardt, 285, 288, 290
Havergill, Giles, 48
Hawkins, William, 429, 430–431
Hayagawari, 590
Hebbels, Friedrich, 28–29
Hedda Gabler, 292
Hegel, Georg W. F., 40
Hellman, Lillian, 290
Hellmouth, 106–107
Hemvi, Jacob, 614
Henri Christophe, 714
Henry V, 48, 212
Hephaisteion (Theseion), 47
Hernandez, Luisa Josefina, 743
Hernani, 142, 277–278, 440, 467, 742
Herne, James A., 288
Hilarodi, 135
Hill, Errol, 713, 738
Hilo magico, 774
Historification, 105, 352, 356
History of the Danish People, 149, 150
Histriones, 104
Hobbes, Thomas, 267
Hobbler, 43, 569
Hoffman, Dustin, 49
Hoffman, William, 505
Homeopathic magic, 610
Honmizu, 588
Hooks, Robert, 672
Horace, 31, 96
Hosay, 713
Hôtel de Bourgogne, 259
Howard, G. C., 279
Hsaio sheng, 569

Hsieh-tzu, 560
Hsu, Tao-ching, 12, 49
Hua-gu, 561
Hua-gu Opera Company (Hunan Province), 561, 566–568
Hua lien, 561
Huang Shang, 572
Hua pu, 561
Hua tan, 567, 569
Hubris, 40–41
Hughes, Langston, 672
Hugo, Victor, 142, 278–279, 290, 467, 742
Huitzilopotli, 748
Humanism, 134
Hume, David, 464, 607
Hu qin, 570
Hybris. See Hubris
Hypokrites, 3, 57

Iambic pentameter, 148–149
Ibadan University, 614
Ibsen, Henrik, 7, 44, 273, 284, 286, 288, 290, 291, 292–294, 323, 324, 351, 468, 616
Ichikawa (All-Girl) Kabuki-za, 588
Icres, Fernand, 290
Idea, 30, 35
Iffland, Agust, 277
Ikernofret, 10
Il guido maestro, 136
Iliad, The, 25
Illuminations, 105–106
Illusion, The, 504
Imaginary Invalid, The, 226, 227
Imagination, drama and, 3, 5
Imitation, 9
Immigration plays, 747
Imposter, The, 258
Inamorati, 136
Incident at Vichy, 388
Inciting incident, 27
Independent theater movement, 289–290, 614, 638
Independent Theater, The, 290
Indian theater. See Theater
Inge, William, 324
Interlude, 138
Intermezzi, 138
International School of Theater of Latin America and the Caribbean, 712
In the Township Tonight!, 612
Intimate Theatre (Stockholm), 290
Invaders, The, 783
Invitation to Death, 742
Ionesco, Eugene, 25, 45, 438, 439
Island, The, 616

Japanese theater. See Theater; Kabuki theater; Noh theater
Jelly's Last Jam, 673
Jessner, Leopold, 353
Jessner-steps, 353
Jesus Christ, Superstar, 467
Jidaimono, 586–589
Jim Crow, 280
Joculatores, 104
Joe Turner's Come and Gone, 676
Johnson, Samuel, 42

Joint Stock Theater Group, 473
Jones, Ernest, 149
Jones, Errol, 713
Jones, Inigo, 134, 139
Jones, LeRoi. See Amiri Baraka
Jones, Robert Edmund, 5
Jongleurs, 104
Jonson, Ben, 139, 146
Joseph, E. J., 713
Jugar con fuego, 746
Juhachiban, 593
Julius Caesar, 147, 286
Jung, Carl, 29, 285

Kabuki Reform Movement, 592
Kabuki theater, 34, 42, 46, 49, 135, 548, 582
architecture, 588
conventions of, 587–589
evolution of, 272, 585–586
types of drama in, 586–587
See also Theater
Kabuki-za, 587, 588
Kadensho, The, 24, 582, 584
Kagama no ma, 584, 585
Kaiser, Georg, 350
Kálidása, 33, 43, 472, 554–556
Kami plays, 582
Kan'ami, 9, 582
Kani, John, 272, 616, 638
Kanjinchō. See Subscription List, The
Kaoru, Morimoto, 592
Kaoru, Osani, 592
Kata, 589–590
Kathakali dance theater, 557
Kazama, Ayumi, 547
Kazura play, 582
Kempe, Will, 146
Kennedy, Adrienne, 672
Kennedy, Arthur, 431, 433
Keren, 588
Kernan, Alvin, 118
Kerr, Walter, 811
Khan, Kublai, 560
Khon, 547
Ki, 591
King, Jr., Martin Luther, 674
King Charles I, 139, 266
King Charles II, 141, 266
King Edward II, 504
King Felipe IV, 134
King Henry VI, 146
King Henry VIII, 138–139
King Jab Jab, 713
King James I, 139, 146
King Lear, 137, 147, 438, 467
King Louis XIV, 140, 142, 226, 227, 228, 258–260
King's Men, the, 134, 146, 211
Kinji, Shinodo (Namiki Gohei III), 593
Kirby, E. T., 57, 610
Kiri plays, 582
Kita Sadayo, 583
Kitto, H. D. F., 61
Klinger, Friedrich, 277
Knight's Tale, The, 554
Kofukuji Temple, 582
Kokata, 583
Komachi at Sekidera, 7, 25

Komos, 42, 60, 563
in Lysistrata, 93
in Old Comedy, 93
Korean Drama Center, 152
Kornfeld, Paul, 350
Koryphaeus, 61, 88
Kothornoi, 61, 62, 88
Kott, Jan, 147, 438
Kotzebue, August, 277
Kramer, Larry, 505
Krapp's Last Tape, 441
Krasnaya Presnya (Moscow), 36
Kumadori, 589
Kushner, Tony, 30, 44, 504–506, 540–543
Kyd, Thomas, 150, 212
Kyōgen, 582, 583, 584

L.S.D., 470
La Bamba, 762
La Cage Aux Folles, 505
La Dame aux Camilias (Camille), 286
Lady from Dubuque, The, 443
Lady on Her Balcony, The, 774
Lafayette Players (New York), 672
Lahr, Bert, 440
La Mama Experimental Theater Club (New York), 638
Langer, Suzanne, 11
Lantern festival, 563
Lao-sheng, 569
La Pastorella, 762
La señora en su balcon, 774
"Last-Mama-on-the-Couch Play, The," 675
La tranche a vie, 287
Laughing comedy, 270
Lazzi, 136
Learned Ladies, The, 226
Le Cid, 142, 278
LeCompte, Elizabeth, 470
Le drame, 270
Lee, Ming Cho, 470
Legree, Simon, 278–280, 572
Leguizamo, John, 33
Leguizamo Leguizamón, Martiniano, 742
Lenones, 135
Les Misérables, 278
Lesson from Aloes, A, 616
Leviathan, The, 267
Levi–Strauss, Claude, 466
Life's a Dream, 29, 137, 140
commentary on, 221–222
Lillo, George, 270
Lincoln Center (New York), 327, 642
Lion and the Jewel, The, 639
Lion King, The, 6, 7, 11, 30
Literary Arts Society (Japan), 591
Little Carib Theater (Trinidad–Tobago), 713, 714, 716
Little Clay Cart, The, 553
Little theater movement, 290
Little Theater Movement (Jamaica), 710
Liu, Wu-chi, 565
Living person pieces, 582
Living Theater, The, 468
Li Yu, 561
Logeion, 58, 61
London Merchant, The, 270
Long Day's Journey into Night, A, 288

Long Wharf Theater, 272
Look Back in Anger, 45, 291, 438
Lope de Vega, 135, 220, 223, 276
Lorca, Federico García, 468
Lord Chamberlain's Men, 146, 212–213
Lord of the Dance, 9, 48, 552, 553
Los empeños de una casa (The Zeal of a House), 751
Los pilares de Doña Blanca, 774
Los recuerdos del prevenir, 774
Los Vendidos, 762
Love and the Ranch Girls, 742
Love is a Great Labyrinth, 751
Love's Labor's Lost, 147, 266
Luckmann, Thomas, 465
Lucky Pearl, The. See *Qing Ding Pearl, The*
Ludi Romani, 96
Ludlam, Charles, 504
L'Umorismo, 45
Lurhman, Baz, 742
Lyotard, Jean François, 466, 469
Lysistrata, 42, 93

Macbeth, 96, 147, 148–149
McBurnie, Beryl, 713
McClendon, Rose, 672
Machine plays, 226
Machismo, 784–785
McLuhan, Marshall, 60, 461
McNally, Terrence, 443, 505
Maestery guilds, 105
Maggi, Carlos, 743
Magic realism, 48, 742, 774
Mahābhārāta, The, 25, 467, 554
Makerere Travelling Theater Company, 608
Makerere University, 614
Make your own meaning syndrome (MYOM), 470
Malina, Judith, 468
Mallory, Sir Thomas, 554
Mamet, David, 46, 288, 290
Manaka, Matsamela, 612
Man and Superman, 32
Manin, Manny, 638
Mann, Thomas, 43
Man of Mode, The, 267
Mansions, 106
Man Who Had All the Luck, The, 388
Man Who Turned into A Stick, The, 592
Ma Rainey's Black Bottom, 676, 677, 809–811
Maraj, Ralph, 713
Maraniss, James, 221
Marat/Sade, 467
Mariannismo, 784–785
Marin, Cheech, 762
Marivaudage, 266
Market Theatre (Johannesburg, South Africa), 290, 614, 638
Mark Taper Forum (Los Angeles), 714
Marlowe, Christopher, 505
Marqués, Rene, 712
Marquez, Rosa Luisa, 712
Marriage a la Mode, 267
Marriage Proposal, The, 324
Martial Law in Trinidad, 713
Martin, Jane, 33
Martin, Steve, 440
Marx, Karl, 285

Maschere, 136
Mask(s)
   cultural significance of, 11–13
   Greek, 61
   Japanese, 40
   of medieval devil character, 107
   in Noh theater, 583–584
   in ritual, 12
   in Roman theater, 98
   as spectacle element, 35
Masque of Queens Celebrated from the House of Fame, The, 139
Masquerades, 739
   in African theater, 611
Masques, 138–139
Master Builder, The, 292
"MASTER HAROLD". . . and the boys, 614, 616, 638
   commentary on, 617–619
   play text, 620–637
Matachinis, 760
Mat-shed theaters, 331
Matsuri, 251
Matura, Mustapha, 607, 713
Mayan theater, 11, 617–619
Mbaquanga music (South Africa), 34, 613
Measure for Measure, 147
Mechané, 61
Medea, 142
Medicis, 134
Mei Lan-fang, 35, 571, 573
Meiningen Company (Berlin), 286–287
Meiring, Sheila, 616
Mellerdramer, 44
Melodrama, 44–45, 276–277, 565, 571
   mellerdramer, 44
   versus tragedy, 44
Melo drame, 44
Memphite Drama, 10
Menaechmi, The, 97, 146
Menander, 62, 92, 96, 266
Men's Kabuki, 586
Mephisto, 460
Merchant of Venice, The, 48, 147
Merritt, Theresa, 810
Merry Wives of Windsor, The, 147
Mestizo drama, 746
Metacommentary, 9, 10
Metanarratives, 469
Metropolis, 350
Mexican Cultural Center (Fresno, CA), 762
Mexican Studio Theater, 773
Meyer, Michael, 294
Meyerhold, Vesold, 352
Michiyuki, 590
Middle Ages, theater in. See Theater
Middle Comedy, 93
Middle Temple, 210
Midsummer festivals, 8, 11
Midsummer Night's Dream, A, 8, 93, 104, 147
Mie, 49, 589
Mielziner, Jo, 392
Miller, Arthur, 22, 40, 50, 57, 290, 350, 388–391, 429, 430–434, 441, 470, 563, 676, 677
Mimesis, 4
Mimi, 104
Ming drama, 561

Ming Huang, 560
Minstrel shows, 280–281
Miracle plays, 117
"Mirror Images," 10
Misanthrope, The, 226
Miser, The, 226, 227
Miss Julie, 784
Mitchell, Cameron, 431, 433
Mitra, Dinabandhu, 557
Mizumonon, 588
Mnouchkine, Arianne, 260–263, 460, 467, 557
Moira, 65
Mojin Shoka, 546
Mokae, Zakes, 617
Molière (Jean-Baptiste Poquelin), 33, 134, 135, 136, 143, 226–227, 258, 263, 266, 742
Molina, Tirso de, 741
Monkey King, 136
Monologue, 33
Monstrous Regiment, 473
Montdory, 258
Morality, 142
Morality plays, 105, 117–118
Mors, (Death) 118
Morton, Jelly Roll, 673
Moscow Art Theater, 289, 324, 325, 638
Moses, Gilbert, 672
Mother Courage and Her Children, 352, 355
Mountebank stage, 136
Mrozek, Slawomir, 45
MTV, 31, 467
Mtwa, Percy, 607
Much Ado About Nothing, 93, 147
Mudras, 49, 553, 556
Mulatto, 672
Müller, Heiner, 465
Multicultural criticism, 472
Mummery, 104
Murray, Gilbert, 57
Music (as dramatic element), 34, 641
My Children! My Africa!, 616, 617
MYOM syndrome, 470
Mystery plays, 105, 109–110
Mythos, 23, 38

Naharro, Bartolome de Torres, 220
Naguata, 588, 590–591
Nataka plays, 35, 553
National Council for Culture (Cuba), 711
National Noh Theater (Japan), 584
National Theatre (Great Britain), 52,
National Theater of the Deaf, 469
Naturalism, 287
Natyamandapa, 556
Nātyaśāstra The (Treatise on Drama), 4, 24, 29, 552, 553, 582
Naumachiae, 97
Neel Darpana, 557
Negro Ensemble Company (New York), 672
Nemiroff, Bob, 674
Neoclassicism, 142–143
   in Renaissance Europe, 142
   versus Romanticism, 142–143
New Comedy (Greek), 62, 93,
New York Free Shakespeare Festival, 47, 714
New York Theater Critics Reviews, 811

Index

Ngema, Mbongeni, 469, 638
Nicostratus, 88
Nietzsche, Friedrich, 62, 285, 464
Night of the Assassins, 711
'Night Mother, 288
Nixon, Richard M., 563
Nixon in China, 351
Noah, 110
No Exit, 438, 774
Noh (Nō) theater, 7, 9, 25, 34, 42, 48, 548, 592, 593,
    architecture of, 583–584
    characteristics of, 582–585
    conventions of, 583–584
    evolution of, 9, 547, 582
    influence on Western theater, 585
    types of drama in, 582–583, 749
No Place to Be Somebody, 672
Normal Heart, The, 505
Norman, Marsha, 46, 288
No saco nada de la escuela, 761
    commentary on, 761–762
    play text, 763–772
Ntshona, Winston, 272, 616, 754
Núcleo de Estudios Teatrales Drama School, 776

O! Babylon!, 714
O'Brien, Jack, 811
Obatala Festival, 7, 23, 668
Obligatory scene, 28, 284,
Odes, 60
"Ode to Oedipus," 91–92
Odets, Clifford, 290, 291
Odori, 585, 586
Oedipus at Colonus, 63
Oedipus Rex. See *Oedipus the King*
Oedipus the King, 14, 23, 25, 26–27, 60, 62, 284, 544
    background for plot, 64
    commentary, 63–65
    first performance of, 88–89
    "Guthrie Directs 'Ritual' Performance of Oedipus Rex at Edinburgh Fête," 92
    "Ode to Oedipus," 191–192
    play text, 66–87
    at the Teatro Olympico, 90
Off-Broadway, 638
Off-off-Broadway, 638
Ogun, 9, 472, 640, 641, 668
Ogunde, Hubert, 614
Oklahoma!, 674
Okuni, 586
Old Comedy (Greek), 92
Olivier, Sir Laurence, 149, 216
O'Neill, Eugene, 21, 285, 288, 350, 388, 504
O'Neill, Frederick, 672
Onkos, 61, 62, 88
Onnagata style, 586, 589
Onna no issho, 592
Onno, 586
"On the Art of Tragedy," 142
"On the Spectacles," 98
Onuora, Oku, 712
Orchestra, 58, 61, 88,
   in Roman theaters, 97
Oresteia, The, 50, 52, 59, 563, 621,
Orestes, 148

Orton, Joe, 45
Osborne, John, 45, 291, 616
Oshogbo Center for the Arts (Nigeria), 48
Osiris myth, 12
Othello, 147, 471
Our Town, 42, 50
Ox Cart, The, 712

Pachuco, 762
Pageant wagons, 106, 107
Palacio Buen Retiro, 134
Palais Royale, 226, 259, 260
Palladio, Andrea, 90
Pan, 570
Panoramas, 277
Pantalone, 135, 136
Pantomimes, 277
Pan y toros, 746
Paper Flowers, 48, 711
    commentary on, 783–785
    play text, 786–808
Papp, Joseph, 714
Parabisis, 93
Parados, 60, 61, 89, 93
Pardo y Aliaga, Felipe, 742
Parks, Suzan Lori, 32, 672
Parterre, 258, 259
Passion plays, 9
    Abydos, 9, 10
    Valenciennes, 106,
Patronage system, 134, 137
Pause (stage direction), 33–34
Paz, Octavio, 746, 748, 773, 782
Peer Gynt, 291, 292
Peisthetairos, 56, 88
Peking Opera, 34, 561–562, 571
Pelopennesian War, 62, 93
Peon y Contreras, Jose, 742
Peréz Ramiréz, Juan, 741
Performer, 35
Perfumed Handkerchief, The, 266
Periaktoi, 61
Pericles, 147
Peripeteia, 39, 63
Peter Pickleherring, 136
Petit Bourbon Theatre, 226
Phallus, in Old Comedy, 92
Piano Lesson, The, 676
Picking Turnips, 136, 566–567
Pièce a these, 286
Pièce bien faite, 284
Pigafetta, Filippo, 90
Pillars of Doña Blanca, The, 774
Pillars of Society, The, 286, 291
Pinter, Harold, 44, 440, 442, 464, 470, 783
Pirandello, Luigi, 45, 464, 470
Piscator, Erwin, 353
Plata drama, 742
Platea, 106
Plato, 4, 24
Plautus, 43, 93, 136, 146, 266
Playboy of the Western World, The, 607
Playland, 616
Play of Giants, A, 639
Play(s)
    defined, 23
    versus stories, 23
    structure of, Greek, 60

Plays for Dancers, 585
Playwright, 23, 62
Playwright's Theater, 290
Plotless plays, 25
Plot(s)
    Aristotle's definition, 26
    defined, 25
    elements of, 26–27
    types of, 25, 470
Podesta Brothers Circus, 747
Poesía en Voz Alta Theatre, 774
Poetic justice, 44, 142, 565, 572
Poetics, The, 24, 26–27, 38, 56, 59, 63, 96
Point of attack, 27–28
Poitier, Sidney, 674
Polish Laboratory Theater, 468
Polus of Aegina, 61
Poor theater, 468–469, 612
"Poor Theatre," 7, 612, 714
Pope Urban VI, 105
Popol Vuh, The, 9, 747
Poquelin, Jean-Baptiste. See Molière
Posada, José Guadalupe, 782
Post-Modern Condition, The: A Report on Knowledge, 466
Postmodernism, 465–467
Post-Modernism in the Social Sciences, 466
Prakarana plays, 553
Praxis, 23, 38
Prefiguration, 110
Presentational style, 46
Pretenders, The, 291
Price, The, 388, 389
Pride, 40–41
Prologue, 60, 93
Prometheus, 29, 41, 640
Prometheus Bound, 749
Propoledia, 220
Proscenium, 36
Protagonist, 23, 59
Proteus and the Adamantine Rock, 139
Provincetown Players, 290, 638, 639
Provincetown Playhouse (New York), 21, 290
Publius Terentius Afer. See Terence
Pulpitum, 97
Punch, 136
Pygmalion, 44, 276
Pyramid texts, 10

Qian Lung, Emperor, 561
Qing Ding Pearl, The, 104, 547, 564, 565, 569
    commentary on, 571–572
    play text, 573–578
Qing dynasty, 561, 562
Queen Elzabeth I, 139, 213
Queen Henrietta Maria, 139
Quem Quaeritis trope, 104–105
"Quintessence of Ibsenism, The," 288

Rabinal Achí, The, 9, 749
Racine, Jean, 140, 143
Raisin in the Sun, A, 44, 270, 290, 679
    commentary on, 674–675
Rake (Rakehell), 267, 268
Ramírzez, Isabel, 750
Rancheras, 762
Ran-i, 582
Rasas, 553

Realism, 46, 285–291. *See also* Theater
Recognition, 30, 37, 39, 60
   in comedy, 43
Recognition of Śakuntalā, The, 23, 25, 39, 42,
   547, 553
   commentary on, 554–556
Red Bull Theatre, 210
Redemption, The, 611
Rees, Roger, 152
Renaissance theater. *See* Theater
Repartee, 267
Repeating Island, The, 710
Representational style, 46
Restoration comedy, 266, 268, 269
Restoration (England), 266
Restricted theaters, 277
Retribution plays, 565
Reversal, 30, 39, 60, 284
   in comedy, 42
Reversal of fortune, 30
Reviewers, 809–811
Revista, 746
Revolutionary theater, 612
Rhapsodes, 4
Rhinoceros, 469
Rice, Thomas D., 280
Rich, Frank, 540–541, 809, 810–811
Richard III, 147
Richards, Lloyd, 676
Richardson, Willis, 670, 672
Ride Down Mount Morgan, The, 388
Ridgeway, William, 57
Right You Are, If You Think You Are, 464
Rising action, 28, 60
Ritual Expectancy, 8
Ritual(s)
   versus ceremony, 7
   in contemporary theater, 467–468
   defined, 6–7
   versus drama, 24
   enactments, 610
   feminist works based on, 469
   modern, 8–10
   satisfying need for entertainment, 13–14
   versus theater, 6–8
   theatricality of, 3, 4
Road to Mecca, The, 616
Road, The, 639
Robbers, The, 277
Roberts, Arthur, 713
Robin Hood plays, 104, 276, 560
Rockaby, 33, 44
Rodrigues, Damaso, 620
Rodriguez, Paul, 762
Rodríques, Galván Ignacio, 742
Rogers, De Wilton, 712
Romance, 544
Roman theater. *See* Theater
Romanticism, 49, 142, 143, 273, 276–278, 467
   melodrama and, 276–277
   timeline, 274
Romeo and Juliet, 147, 212, 742
Ronstadt, Linda, 762
Roppo, 588
Rorty, Richard, 466
Roscius, 98
Rosencrantz and Guildenstern Are Dead, 2, 440,
   471

Rose Theater, 210
Rosmersholm, 292
Rounds, 106, 108
Rousseau, Jean-Jacques, 44, 276
Rover, The, 267, 268
Royal Court Theatre (London), 473
Royal Opera House, 36
Royal Shakespeare Company (RSC), 48, 222,
   259, 262–263, 351, 355, 440, 467,
   743
Ruiz de Alarcén, Juan, 741

Sabi, 584, 590
Sadhyas, 552
Sainetes, 746
Saint Cecilia, 711
St. George Play, 105
Saints plays, 105
Śakuntalā. See Recognition of Śakuntalā, The
Salmacida Spolia, 139
Sanchéz, Florencio, 742
Sandbox, The, 441, 442
San Francisco Mime Troupe, 761
Sanskrit drama, 553. *See also* Theater, Indian
Sarafina!, 612
Sarmiento, Domingo Faustino, 746
Saro-Wiwa, Ken, 639
Sartre, Jean Paul, 774
Satire, 42
Saturnalia, 738
Satyrs, 56
Savran, David, 541–543
Scaenae, 97
Scaliger, Julius Caesar, 142
Scapin, 226
Scarmozzi, Vincenzo, 90
Scenario, 135
Scene a faire, 284
Scenery, 34–35
Schiller, Friedrich, 276, 277
Schneider, Alan, 440
School for Scandal, The, 270
Schultz, Roger, 620
Schumann, Peter, 712
Scott, George C., 440
Scribe, Eugene, 284, 288, 469
Scurrae, 104
Seagull, The, 324, 325, 638
Seascape, 441
Second Blackfriars Theatre, 210–211
Second Sex, The, 465
Second Shepherd's Play, The, 105
Secrets, 106
Sedes, 106
Seiphemo, Rapulana, 620
Sellars, Peter, 466
Seneca, 96, 146, 150
Senex (Old Man) character, 96
Sen Gupta, Rudra Prasad, 295
Sen Gupta, Swatilekha, 295
Sentimental comedy, 42, 268–270
Serban, Andrei, 358
Serious Money, 473, 474
Serlio, Sebastiano, 134, 140
Sermons joyeaux, 104
Serpent Players, 616
"Seven Books of the Poetics," 142
7:84 Theatre Company, 473

Seven Guitars, 676, 677
Sewamono, 586–587
Shadow puppets, 547
Shakespeare, William, 8, 25, 32, 33, 43, 48,
   134, 135, 137, 143, 146–147, 212–213,
   222, 266, 276, 470, 471, 504, 672
   understanding language of plays of,
   148–149
"Shakespeare á la Russe: Kozintsev's *Hamlet*,"
   216–217
Shakespearean Tragedy, 140
Shaman, 4
Shange, Ntozaki, 672
Shankar, Uday, 557
Shave, 610–611
Shaw, [George] Bernard, 32, 44, 266, 285, 288,
   290, 291, 292, 324, 325, 351, 468, 586
Sheng, 562
Shengeki, 470
Sher, Antony, 259, 262–263
Sheridan, Richard Brinsley, 266, 270, 272
She Stoops to Conquer, 270
Shibai, 586
Shite role, 583, 584
Shoyo, Tsubouchi, 591–592
Shrunken Head of Pancho Villa, The, 761
Shui hsui, 569
Shu pan, 570
Shura-mono plays, 582
Sieveking, Alejandro, 943
Siglo d'Oro, 134, 220–222
Silence (stage direction), 33–34
Silk Cotton Grove, 713
Simon, Barney, 607, 638
Simon, Francesca, 670–671
Simon, Neil, 92, 266, 290
Simon, Paul, 472
Simultaneous stage, 106
Sitahal, Errol, 713
Śīva, 9, 48, 552, 553
Six Characters in Search of an Author, 470
Sizwe Bansi Is Dead, 616
Skene, 58, 61, 88, 89
Slapstick comedy, 42, 45, 135
   versus farce, 45
Slave Ship, 611
Slavs!, 504
Slice of life, 287
Smeraldina, 136
Smith, Anna Deavere, 33, 471
Smith, Michael, 712
Social Construction of Reality, The, 465
Social realists, 290–291
Softcops, 473
Soldado Razo, 762
Soldier's Play, A, 672
Solid Home, A, 7, 773
   commentary on, 742
   play text, 776–781
Soliloquy(ies), 33
Sondheim, Stephen, 287
Sophocles, 9, 14, 57, 61, 62, 63, 64, 65, 88,
   89, 90, 91, 284
Soruki, Shindo. *See* Namiki Gohei III
Sotties, 104
South African Township Theater, 614
Soyinka, Wole (Akinwande Oluwole
   Soyinka) 7, 38, 607, 614, 639

Index

Space, 35
Spanish Tragedy, The, 150, 212
Spartacus, 276
Spectacle, 34–35
Spirit cult performances, 610–611
Spiritual Wedding Between the Shepherd Peter and the Mexican Church, The, 741
Split Britches, 469
Springer, Pearl, 713
Spring Festival (China), 560, 562–563
Stage direction, 33
Stanislavsky, Constantin, 135, 286, 288, 289, 325
    system of acting, 352
Star Theater (Bombay), 557
Star-crossed lovers archetype, 547
Stasimon, 60, 89, 93
Statements After an Arrest Under the Immorality Act, 616
Steele, Richard, 269
Stein, Peter, 470, 471
Sternheim, Karl, 350
Stevens, Martin, 118
Stevens Theatre Company, 444
Stewart, Ellen, 638
Stock characters, 29, 96–97
    in Chinese drama, 561–562
Stoicism, 96
Stoppard, Tom, 25, 45, 266, 440, 470
Storyteller(s), versus dramatists, 23
Storytelling, 3–6,
    in African theater, 610
Stowe, Harriet Beecher, 278–280
Street theater
    African, 615
    in Trinidad-Tobago, 713
Strindberg, August, 287, 288, 290, 324, 350, 468
Strophes, 60, 89, 93
Study of History, A, 465
Sturm und Drang, 279
Sturm und Drang movement, 279
Styles, of drama, 46–48
Subplots, 26
Subscription List, The (*Kanjinchō*), 24, 29, 42, 548, 586, 587, 588, 589, 591
    commentary on, 593–594
    play text, 595–604
Subtext, 33
Sudo, Sayaka, 547
Sung dynasty, 560
Super objective, 352
Suppressed Desires, 21
Surrealism, 350
Surugaku (monkey dance), 9, 582
sūtradhara, 3
Suzuki, Tadashi, 11, 470, 585, 589, 592
Svoboda, Joseph, 470
Swados, Elizabeth, 358
Swan Theatre, 210, 211
Symbols, theatricality of, 3
Sympathetic magic, 610
Synge, John Millington, 7, 290
System (of Stanislavsky), 352

Tableau vivants, 277
Tagore, Rabindranath, 557
Ta hiera, 56

Talquetzque, 9, 747
Taming of the Shrew, The, 93, 212
Tan, 562, 569
Tanabata Festival, 7, 547
Taplin, Oliver, 43
Tarantella, 7, 323
Tartuffe, 42, 43, 61, 140, 226
    commentary on, 227–228, 262–263
    controversy over, 258–260
    play text, 229–257
    production at Théâtre du Soleil, 260–262
Taubman, Howard, 215–216
Taymor, Julie, 6, 470
Teatro Campesino. *See* El Teatro Campesino
Teatro de Arena (Brazil), 469
Teatro de Arte La Cueva (Cuba), 638
Teatro Ehierto, 743
Teatro Estudios de Mexico, 774
Teatro Experimental, University of Chile, 742
Teatro Farnese (Parma, Italy), 97
Teatro Olympico, (Vicenza, Italy), 90–91, 97
Tempest, The, 139, 147, 221, 554
Terence, 93, 97, 146, 266
Terese Raquin, 288
Tertulian, 98
Texas Tornados, 762
Text, 33
Tezcatlipoca, 748
Theater
    absurdism in, 438–439
        time line, 436
    African
        and the diaspora, 607
        conventions of, 615
        postcolonial (in Africa), 611–615
        roots of, 610–611
        time line, 608
        typical performance modes, 610–611
    African American, 672–673
        time line, 670
    architecture
        in England, 210–211
        in France, 258
        in India, 556
        proscenium arch, 36
        rise of intimate theaters, 290
        in-the-round, 36
        Spanish corrales, 143, 221, 223
        thrust, 37
    Asian countries, 547–549
        characteristics common to, 548
        versus Western, 548
    Brazilian, 638
    Caribbean, 708–739
        time line, 708
    Chilean, 783
    Chinese, 266
        acting technique in, 569–570
        contemporary, 562–563
        conventions of, 564–570
        history of, 273, 560–563
        Maoist, 563
        music and sound in, 570
        origins, 9, 560
        playwriting, 564–564
        stage in, 565–566
        staging devices in, 568–569
        time line, 558

as communication, 3
contemporary
    acting in, 469–471
    alternative theater, 468–469
    dramatic criticism in, 471–472
    feminism in, 469, 472
    gay and lesbian issues in, 469, 504–506
    influences on, 464–465
    playwriting in, 469–470
    postmodernism and, 465–467
    theater collectives, 468–469
    theater of cruelty, 467–468
    time line, 462
creative impulses prefiguring, 3–13
Cuban, 638, 711
as cultural common ground, 9, 11–13
    derivation of term, 23
    versus drama, 23
    during Puritanism, 266–267
    elements necessary to create, 35
Elizabethan, 108, 556
    architecture of, 210–211
English
    time lines, 144, 264
    epic theater, 49, 350–352
    expressionism and, 350–352
    expressionism in, 350
French
    acting in, 142–143
    architecture of, 258
    time line, 224
Greek, 53–62
    architecture and scenery, 58, 60–61
    classical, 48–49, 469
    cultural influences on 59–60,
    development of theatrical space, 58, 60–61
    origins of, 8, 9, 56–57
    time line, 54
Haitian, 712
Indian
    architecture of, 556
    conventions of, 553–557
    dance theater, 553, 557
    folk drama, 557
    modern, 557
    origins of, 9, 552–558
    time line, 550
    types of drama in, 553, 557
in the industrial age, 353
Jamaican, 712
Japanese, 547, 580–604. *See also* Kabuki theater; Noh theater
    contemporary (Shingeki), 591–592
    conventions of Kabuki theater, 587–591
    conventions of Noh theater, 583–584
    Tanabata Festival, 590–591
    time line, 580
late seventeenth and eighteenth century
    bourgeois tragedy, 270
    laughing comedy, 270
    sentimental comedy, 269, 270
Latin American 741–808
    independent theaters, 638
    playwriting, 743
    popular theater, 746–747
    time line, 744
in Mesoamerica, 747–749

as metacommentary, 9, 10
in Middle Ages, 9, 104–131
    conventions of, 105–107
    cultural meaning of plays, 107
    performance conventions in, 105–107
    religious drama, 11, 104–105, 109–110,
        117–118
    rites and folk drama, 104
    stage types, 106–108
    time line, 102
modern
    defined, 101
origins of, 9
Puerto Rican, 711–712
realism, 284–347
    fathers of, 285–286
    influences on, 284–285
    intimate theaters, 289–290
    naturalism and, 287
    problem play, 286
    rise of director in, 286–287
    second generation of playwrights,
        290–291
    time line, 282
Renaissance Europe
    acting in, 136, 141–142
    commedia dell'arte, 136–137
    commedia erudita, 97
    cultural and intellectual influences on,
        97, 134, 137, 140
    Great Chain of Being and, 134, 137–140
    hierarchic structure, 138–140
    masques, 138–139
    need for order and, 137–138
    playhouses in, 140, 210–211, 223, 258
    playwriting in, 142–143
    scenery in, 134, 138–139, 141
    time line, 132
    tragedy in, 140–141
Restoration, 267–268
    comedies of, 268–269
    conventions of, 268–269
Roman, 96–98
    acting in, 97–98
    architecture of, 97
    development of, 96
    fall of Rome and, 98
    plays of, 97–98
    playwrights of, 96–97
    popular entertainments of, 96
    stock characters of, 96–97
    time line, 94
Romanticism in, 273, 276–281
    time line, 274
Spain, 220–223
    architecture of, 223
    time line, 218
Trinidad-Tobago, 712–713
"Theater as It Was and Is," 5
Théâtre de Babylon (Paris), 440
Théâtre du Marais (Paris), 258
Théâtre du Soleil (Paris), 50, 260–262, 467
Theatre Escambray (Cuba), 711
Théâtre-Libre (Paris), 290
Theater of cruelty, 441, 467–468
Theater of menace, 783
Theater of the fabulous, 504, 541
Theatre of the ridiculous, 504, 541

"Theatre Set Free, A," 290
Theatricalism, 64
Theatrical style, 48
Theatron, 23, 58, 61, 88, 97
Theme, 30–31
Theodoric the Great, 104
Theory of illumination, 222
Thesis play, 286
Thespians, 56
Thespis, 56, 57, 59
Thiong'o, Ngugiwa, 614
Thomaso, 684
Thought, 41–42
Threepenny Opera, The, 354
Three Sisters, The, 324, 432
Three Tall Women, 442
Thymele, 56, 58, 88
Ti–Jean and His Brothers, 7, 352, 713, 739
    commentary on, 714–716
    play text, 717–737
Timon of Athens, 147
Tiny Alice, 441
Tirades, 258
Titanic, 40
Titus Andronicus, 147
Tlaquetzque, 618
Tobacco Road, 674
To Beat Around the Bushes, 774
Tobiroppo, 588
Toledo, María de, 741
Tolstoy, Count Leo, 290, 325
Tomaselli, Keyan, 612
Tonight We Improvise, 638
Tooth of Crime, 32
Top Girls, 42, 352, 470, 471, 473
    commentary on, 474–475
    play text, 476–503
Torelli, Giacomo, 134
Townsend, Sue, 42
Township Fever!, 613
Township theater, 25, 34, 608, 612–613
Toynbee, Arnold, 465
Tractatus Coislinianus, 42
Tragedy, 9, 35, 38–42
    Aristotle's definition, 25, 38–42
    versus comedy, 38
    defined, 38
    Greek, 62
    versus melodrama, 44
    origin of term, 56
"Tragedy and the Common Man," 40,
    429–430
Tragedy of Miriam, The, 682
Tragic action, 40
Tragic characters/heroes, 40–42
Tragic flaw, 40, 429–430
Tragicomedy, 43–46
Trance dance, 4–6, 468
Trap doors, 277
Treadmills, 277
Treatise on Drama (Nātyaśāstra), 4, 24, 29,
    552, 553, 582
Trial of Zawngendaba, The, 606
Triana, José, 711
Tricks of Scapin, The, 226
Trickster character, 93, 136
    in African theater, 611
    in Chinese theater, 566

Trickster of Seville, The, 221
Trifles, 14, 21
    commentary on, 14, 25–34
    play text, 15–20
Trinidad Carnival, 713, 716, 738–739
Trinidad Carnival, The, 738
Trinidad Drama Club, 713
Trinidad Tent Theater, 713
Trinidad Theater Workshop, 714, 716
Troilus and Cressida, 137, 147, 504
Trojan Women, The, 592
Tropes, 104–105
Troupe de Monsieur, 226
Tsá chu, 560
Tsure, 583
Turkey, The, 45
Twelfth Night, 42, 104, 147
Twilight: Los Angeles, 1992, 33, 471
Two Gentlemen of Verona, 147

Ubu Roi, 438
Ulysses Theatre, 742
Uncle Tom's Cabin, 44, 270, 277, 281, 563,
    571
    commentary on, 278–280
Uncle Vanya, 324
Under Milkwood, 469
Under the Dragonstick, 567–568
Unfortunate Bride, The, 682
Unfortunate Happy Lady, The, 682
Un Hogar Solido. See Solid Home, A
University of the West Indies, 713
University of Zimbabwe, 614
Ur–Hamlet, 150
Usigli, Rudolfo, 742

Valdez, Luis, 469, 743, 749, 752, 761
Valenciennes Passion Play, 106
Valency, Maurice, 325
Valley Song, 616
Vazquez, Carmen Inoa, 785
Vedas, 9, 552
Venationes, 97
Venice Preserv'd, 267
Ventriloquism, 472
Venturi, Robert, 465
Verfremdungseffeckt, 351–352, 354
Verge, The, 21
Verse, plays in, 33, 148–149
Vestuario, 223
Via negativa, 468
Victor, the Child of the Forest, 277
Vietnam War, 93, 762
View from the Bridge, A, 388
Villancicos, 750
Villarrutia, Xavier, 742
Vinegar Tom, 473
Virginia Minstrels, 280
Vishnu, 553
Vocabulary, theatrical, 3
Vogel, Paula, 541
Volpone, 469
Voltaire (François-Marie Arouet), 276
Vraisemblance, 142, 258

Wagato style, 589
Wagner, Robin, 541
Waiting for Godot, 25, 46, 272, 438, 439–440

Wakashu, 586
Waki plays, 582, 583, 584
Walcott, Derek, 7–8, 607, 713, 714
Waller, Fats, 673
Walpole, Horace, 42
Ward, Douglas Turner, 672
Warner, Jack, 743
Warrior plays, 582
Wasserstein, Wendy, 266, 324
Water sleeves, 569
Way of the World, The, 267
Weavers, The, 285
Wedekind, Frank, 350
Weeping comedy. See Sentimental comedy
Weigel, Helene, 355
Weill, Kurt, 354
Welcoming of the Drum, The, 547
Well-made play, 284, 288, 469
Wen-hsi, 561
West Side Story, 287
When We Dead Awaken, 292
White Haired Girl, The, 563
Whitehall (Court Theater), 134, 139
Who's Afraid of Virginia Woolf?, 441, 442
Wig plays, 582
Wild Duck, The, 292
Wilde, Oscar, 266, 504, 614, 674
Wilder, Thornton, 23, 42, 50

Williams, Robin, 440
Williams, Tennessee, 30, 56, 92, 288, 290, 324, 350, 388, 441, 504
William Tell, 276, 286
"Willing suspension of disbelief," 13, 35, 49
Wilson, August, 291, 472, 585, 607, 673, 676–677
Wilson, Lanford, 505
Wilson, Robert, 465, 470
Wine dance, 42
Winkler, John, 56
Winter's Tale, The, 139, 147
Wittgenstein, Ludwig, 464
Wolfe, George C., 607
Wolff, Egon, 48, 743, 783–785
Woman plays, 582
Woman's Life, A, 586
Women's Interart, 469
Women's Kabuki, 586, 588
Women's Playwright Project, 469
Wooster Group (New York), 470
World Festival of Negro Arts, 614
World's Greatest Hit, The, 278
Woyzeck, 438
Woza Albert!, 350, 469, 638
Wren, Christopher S., 429, 433–434
Wu-hsi, 561
Wycherly, William, 266, 268–269

Yale School of Drama, 673, 676
Ya pu, 561
Yaqui Easter, 7, 136, 221, 749, 752, 760
Yaro, 586
Yeats, William Butler, 92, 290, 557, 585
Ye Bare and Ye Cubbe, 134
Yin tzu, 355, 570
Yong-go, 547
Yoruban people
culture of, 640
festivals of, 668
Yoruba Traveling Theater, 614
Yuan drama, 560–561
Yuan Dynasty, 560
Yugen, 582

Zanni, 136
Zarzeula, 746
bufas, 746
chico, 746
Zeal of a House, The, 751
Zeami, Kanze Motokiyo, 7, 9, 33, 472, 582, 584, 749
Zeitlin, Froma, 56
Zibbaldoni, 135
Zola, Emile, 287–288, 290
Zoo Story, The, 440
Zoot Suit, 761